EDUCATIONAL PSYCHOLOGY:
Interdisciplinary Connections

Jeffery Neal Swartwood
State University of New York, Cortland

Project Development Manager: Terri Beaudette

Managing Editor: Joyce Bianchini

Production Manager: Della Brackett

Sales Manager: Robert Rappeport

Director of Business Development: Richard Schofield

Typesetting: Rhonda Minnema

Permissions Coordinator: Janai Bryand

Acquisitions: Coordinator: Jenefier Winchell

Cover and Interior Design: Esther Scannell

Photo Researcher: Michelle Hipkins and Rhonda Minnema

Text and Cover Printing: R.R. Donnelley

For information address BVT Publishing, LLC, P.O. Box 492831, Redding, CA 96049-2831

Some ancillaries, including electronic and print components, may not be available to customers outside the United States.

Hardcover ISBN: 978-1-60229-882-8
Softcover ISBN: 978-1-61882-316-8
Loose-leaf ISBN: 978-1-59602-929-3
eBook: 978-1-61882-1614

The publisher of affordable textbooks

About the Author

Jeffery Neal Swartwood earned his PhD at the University of Tennessee, Knoxville, in 1994. He completed his graduate training in the Brain Research and Neuropsychology Laboratory, specializing in developmental neuroscience. There, he conducted basic and applied research involving children with disabilities, as well as typically developing children. He then completed a two-year clinical post-doctoral training program at the Johns Hopkins University School of Medicine, Department of Pediatrics. His primary responsibilities involved conducting comprehensive assessments of children with developmental and learning differences, with a focus on the formulation of appropriate educational placement recommendations.

Dr. Swartwood is currently an Associate Professor of Psychology at the State University of New York, Cortland. He teaches courses in Educational Psychology, Motivation, Learning and Memory, and Abnormal Psychology, as well as basic research and experimental courses. His scholarly research focuses on executive function and attention in children and young adults. Currently, he is working on extending his research program to incorporate a Positive Psychology perspective, exploring mindfulness based approaches to education. He has published scholarly works in *Pediatric Neurology, the Journal of Psychoeducational Assessment, Physiology and Behavior,* and *the Creativity Research Journal.* In addition, he actively shares his work with colleagues, teachers, and pre-service teachers through workshops and conference presentations.

Brief Contents

Table of Contents

Chapter 4

Chapter 5

Chapter 6

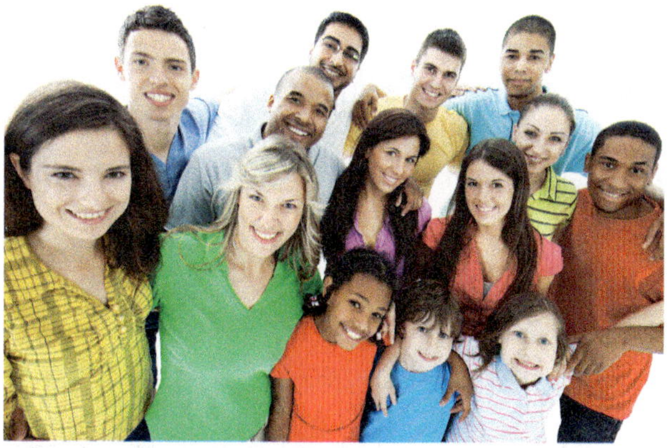

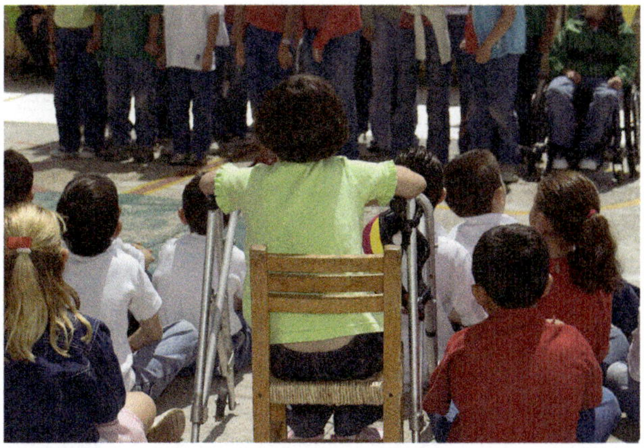

Chapter 15

Preface

My path to authoring this textbook evolved from a fundamental love of working with children and young adults, combined with a respect and passion for science. In addition, I believe I have a unique perspective on education and psychology that I could not find in other textbooks currently on the market: I wanted to provide a resource for others interested in how this point of view furthers the educational mission of our country and informs educational best practice. My journey into educational psychology, however, did not begin with a typical graduate program in that field. Like many of us, my education and professional career seemed to take on a life of its own, moving in many directions. In this preface, I would like to detail some of that history to help you understand my perspective.

I began my doctoral education in the Brain Research and Neuropsychology Laboratory at the University of Tennessee, Knoxville. This position was a natural fit, building on my long-standing strengths in the sciences. Additionally, I pursued work in this lab because the primary focus of the work was on children with disabilities and how they compared to more typically developing peers. I found this fascinating and wanted to learn more. Specifically, my laboratory work centered on understanding the electroencephalographic differences between children with and those without a primary diagnosis of AD/HD. Through this work, I began to develop a more general interest in learning and how it is realized through formal education. Because of this interest, I completed a pre-doctoral internship at the Southeastern Biofeedback and Neurobehavioral Institute. There, I helped children with a variety of developmental disabilities learn to gain control over their attentional resources through EEG biofeedback. In a supplemental role, I also became involved in cognitive remediation, helping children directly address academic issues through remedial techniques grounded in cognitive psychological theory. This compilation of work moved my professional focus toward the field of educational psychology. In short, building upon my neuroscience background, I broadened my focus to the general intersection of psychology and education.

After I received my doctorate, I was accepted as a clinical post-doctoral fellow at The Johns Hopkins University School of Medicine, Department of Pediatrics, Kennedy Krieger Institute. I was told it was my unique background in neuroscience and education that was pivotal in securing this highly competitive position. Once on the job, I found that I was able to use my skills to bring a fresh perspective to the assessment of children with learning differences. I assessed hundreds of children with difficulties spanning all of the DSM classifications applied to children. With each case, I learned more about the breadth of individual differences and how to help children and young adults learn and grow in a formal educational setting.

It was also in this role that I was introduced to phenomenal power of interdisciplinary collaboration. At the Kennedy Krieger Institute, a team of specialists trained in the child's unique presenting needs sees each child. Disciplines can include speech language pathology, behavioral psychology, education, clinical psychology, medicine, nursing, and occasionally other disciplines unique to the case. Each week, the entire team meets to review their findings for a particular child. Interdisciplinary conferences begin with professionals from each discipline formally presenting their findings and recommendations, followed by an in-depth dialogue on the child's needs, and culminate in summary recommendations evolving from the exchange. This experience had a significant and lasting impact on my views of professional applied work and how it can be dramatically enhanced through the shared perspectives of different disciplines. It changed, forever, my views on education and how to generate best practic es for positive learning outcomes.

After my post-doctoral experience, I accepted an academic position at the State University of New York, Cortland that was primarily focused on educational psychology. It was here that I developed a passion for teaching pre-service teachers and other emerging professionals. Over the years, I used several educational psychology textbooks. However, I found that, as a group, they lacked what I believe to be the most current and forward thinking ideas in the field. Namely, they were written without an eye toward how traditional educational psychology topics can be presented through the lens of strong interdisciplinary collaboration. Additionally, I found that existing textbooks were weak in their coverage of learning differences.

Now, a few years later, I have finally produced a textbook addressing these issues. I have maintained much of the traditional layout of educational psychology textbooks, but with updated content to better mirror current best practices and interdisciplinary perspectives. I have also significantly strengthened the coverage on learning differences. I felt this was particularly important since many pre-service regular education teachers receive limited exposure to this material. Throughout the book, I tried to maintain a straightforward, easy to read writing style. I hope you will be able to use this book in your college course and keep it as a resource in your professional life.

My sincere best wishes in all your learning endeavors.

Jeffery N. Swartwood, PhD
Associate Professor of Psychology
State University of New York, Cortland
Jeff.Swartwood@cortland.edu

Instructor Supplements

A complete teaching package is available to instructors who adopt this book. This package includes an **instructor's manual**, **test bank**, **course management software**, and **PowerPoint slides**.

Instructor's Manual

A comprehensive manual provides a wealth of teaching suggestions, objectives and resources, class activities, and discussion questions.

Test Bank

An extensive test bank of over one thousand questions is available to instructors in both hard copy and electronic form. Each chapter consists of fifty multiple choice, twenty true/false, and five essay questions. Each question is referenced to the appropriate text section/topic to make test creation quick and easy.

Course Management Software

BVT's Course Management Software (Respondus) allows for the creation of randomly generated tests and quizzes that can be downloaded directly into a wide variety of course management environments such as Blackboard, Web CT, Desire 2 Learn, Angel, E Learning, and others.

PowerPoint™ Slides

A set of PowerPoint slides includes charts, tables, and graphs from the text, as well as overview slides and bullet-pointed lists designed to guide lectures and discussions.

Student Resources

Student resources are available for this textbook at www.BVT*Lab*.com. These resources are geared towards students needing additional assistance as well as those seeking complete mastery of the content. The following resources are available:

Practice Questions

Students can work through hundreds of practice questions online. Questions are multiple choice or true/false format and are graded instantly for immediate feedback.

Flashcards

BVT*Lab* includes sets of flashcards for each chapter that reinforce the key terms and concepts from the textbook.

Chapter Summaries

A convenient and concise chapter summary is available as a study aid for each chapter.

Study Guide

A thorough and practical student study guide includes learning objectives, chapter outlines, questions, and ideas that help the student review the material presented in this text. The study guide is available in both physical and online formats.

BVT*Lab*

BVT*Lab* is a simple, robust, online lab for college instructors and their students. It is an affordable option for students, with student lab fees costing only $19.99 for a full-semester course. Even if you do not use the lab as your online classroom, your students can still take advantage of the many student resources available In the lab.

BVT*Lab* for Instructors

Course Setup

BVT*Lab* has an easy-to-use, intuitive interface that allows instructors to quickly set up their courses and grade books, and replicate them from section to section and semester to semester. Multiple choice and true/false questions can be delivered online as practice questions, homework assignments, quizzes, and tests—each of which draws from a separate bank of questions. Homework, quizzes, and tests have assigned start and end times; tests can be proctored in the computer lab or self-proctored for distance learners. Instructors can preview and manually select questions assigned to students, or they can use the "quick-pick" feature in BVT*Lab* to generate sets of questions.

Grade Book

Using an assigned passcode, students register into the grade book. All homework, quizzes, and tests are automatically graded and recorded in the grade book. In addition, instructors can manually enter or modify scores, with provisions for extra credit, attendance, and participation grades. Grade books can be printed, or downloaded for transfer to various school course management systems.

Communications Tools

Instructors can post discussion threads to a class forum and then monitor and moderate student replies. Important notifications can also be sent directly to each student via email

BVT*Lab* for Students BVT*Lab*

BVT*Lab* is a comprehensive online learning environment designed to help students succeed. It provides a complete online classroom, as well as the practice questions, learning aids, and communication tools that students need for success. For classes taught within the lab, students can view their grades for all completed work and also review prior homework and quizzes to identify areas that require additional study.

An online discussion forum allows students to interact with each other and the instructor to explore challenging concepts and share other resources, while providing an online community for distance learning.

Even if a class is not taught in the lab, students are always welcome to login as a guest and explore the many student resources described above.

BVT Online Student Bookstore

For convenience and savings, students have the added option of purchasing this textbook and associated resources in the following formats at www.BVTLab.com:

- Full-color, hardcover textbook
- Full-color, softcover textbook
- Loose-leaf black & white textbook
- eBook subscription (six months)
- BVT*Lab*
- Online student resource package
- Study guide—hard copy or eBook subscription

Customization

BVT's Custom Publishing Division can help you modify this book's content to satisfy your specific instructional needs. The following are examples of customization:

- Rearrangement of chapters to follow the order of your syllabus
- Deletion of chapters not covered in your course
- Addition of paragraphs, sections or chapters you or your colleagues have written for this course
- Editing of the existing content, down to the word level
- Addition of handouts, lecture notes, syllabus, etc.
- Incorporation of student worksheets into the textbook

All of these customizations will be professionally typeset to produce a seamless textbook of the highest quality, with an updated table of contents to reflect the customized content.

Acknowledgements

This book would not be possible without the tireless support of my colleague and the mother of my children, Dr. Michie Odle. Her feedback on all parts of the manuscript was invaluable. I would also like to thank the members of my immediate family for their encouragement during the development of this book: Projects of this magnitude can consume one's everyday life, yet my family never failed to affirm my commitment to the project and provide their loving support.

Schuyler, Lexington, and India

Finally, I dedicate this book to my parents, Judith and David Swartwood. I have enjoyed many gifts in my life, but the greatest of these is the good fortune of being their son. They are the definition of unconditional love.

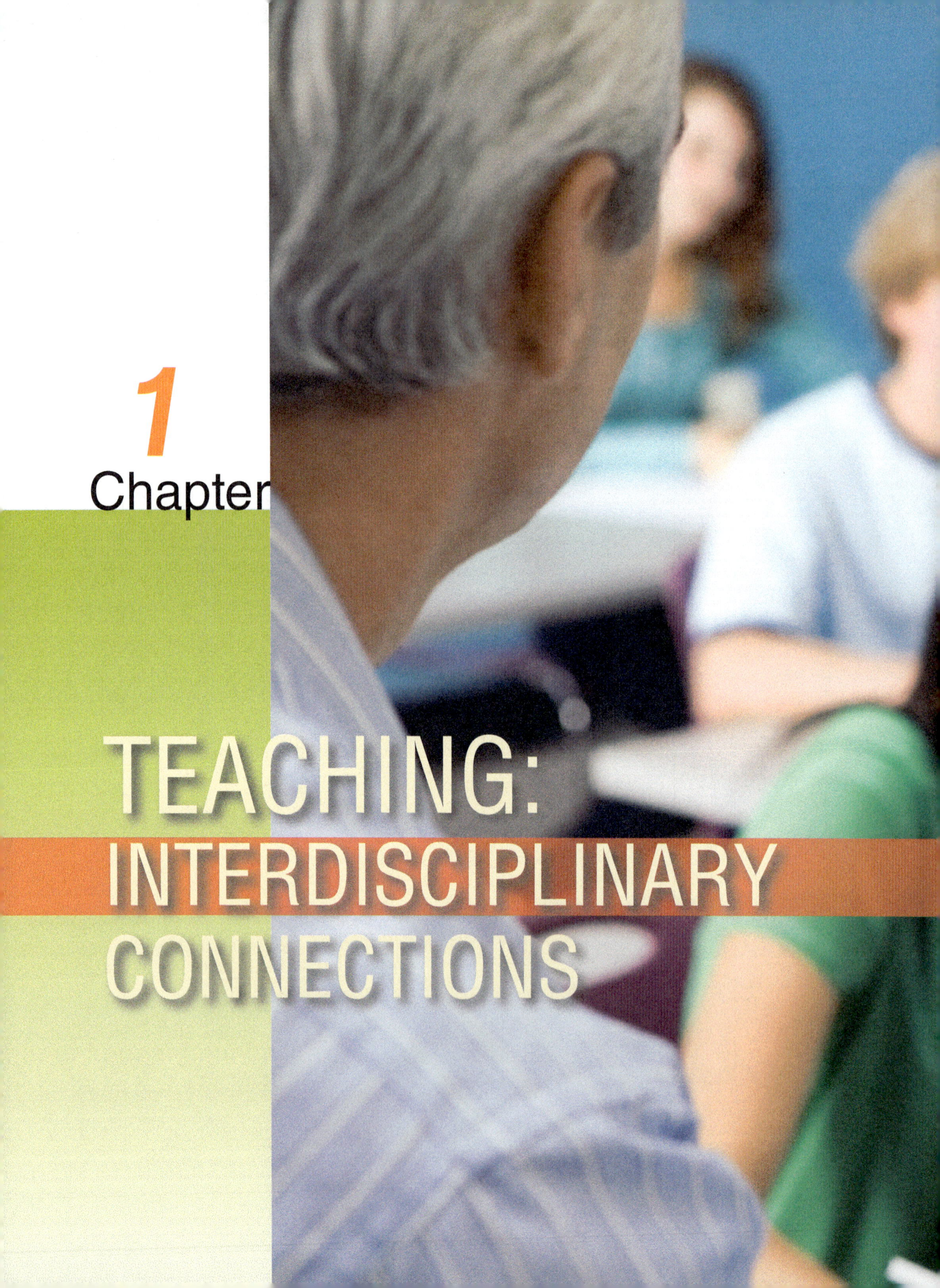

1 Chapter

TEACHING: INTERDISCIPLINARY CONNECTIONS

What's It All About ...

What is the field of educational psychology?

How do teachers develop expertise?

In what way(s) can collaboration help teachers educate effectively?

Chapter Objectives

- Define the field of educational psychology.
- Explain how educational psychology is important to teachers.
- Describe how educational psychology is building a science-based practice.
- Define action research.

- Understand the role of professional knowledge in instructional excellence.
- Describe the expert teacher prototype.

- Understand the importance of an interdisciplinary collaboration model.
- Learn how to effectively use interdisciplinary and collaborative tools in the classroom.

EXTENDED OUTLINE

Teaching: Interdisciplinary Connections

I. What's It All About ...
II. From Today's Headlines
III. Educational Psychology
  A. What is educational psychology?
  B. Why is educational psychology important to teachers?
  C. Educational psychology: Building a science-based practice
    1. Experimental research
    2. Single subject experimental research
    3. Descriptive research
    4. Correlational research
  D. Discovering action research
  E. Summarize and reflect
IV. Becoming an Effective Teacher
  A. Professional knowledge
    1. Subject knowledge
    2. General teaching strategies
    3. Decision making and knowledge application
  B. The expert teacher prototype
  C. Summarize and reflect
V. Interdisciplinary and Collaborative Education
  A. Teaching today: The importance of an interdisciplinary foundation
    1. The changing American classroom
    2. Individualizing education
  B. Using interdisciplinary and collaborative tools in the classroom
    1. What is educational collaboration?
    2. Individual assistance models
  C. Summarize and reflect
VI. The Chapter in Review
VIII. Interdisciplinary Case Focus

From Today's Headlines

Vol. I No. I Teaching World, 2012

WHAT IS TEACHER EXCELLENCE?

You are a new science teacher and this is your first day of instruction. Everyone has arrived, and you are ready to begin your first lesson. You decide to start with a basic question to get the students thinking—What makes objects fall to the earth? Everyone looks at you with an expression of quiet tolerance and responds—GRAVITY! You respond with an expression of awe and wonderment, but suddenly you develop a questioning look and ask—What IS gravity? This time their self-assured looks change as they think about how to describe something so … obvious.

This situation is even more interesting because it is not really a story about a teacher lecturing to a fifth grade science class—this is author Bill Robertson giving a workshop

to teachers. Bill has published several books including *Stop Faking It! Finally Understanding Science so You Can Teach It* (2004). He frequently gives seminars to help teachers develop a deeper and more comprehensive understanding of scientific concepts. In other words, he helps them enhance their subject-matter competence.

It seems almost everyone is becoming more concerned about teacher quality. From federal and state governments, to administrators and parents, everyone wants exceptional teachers.

In an effort to raise teacher quality, the most recent legislation for public schools mandates increased standards for teachers. The No Child Left Behind (NCLB) Act requires that new teachers have a bachelor's degree and full state certification.

Additionally, teachers of core academic subjects must meet state requirements for competency in those subject areas.

MAKE THE CONNECTION

Bill Robertson's quest for excellence in teaching science parallels our nation's concerns regarding high quality teachers. Everyone wants teachers that inspire us to learn. We also want knowledgeable teachers who are responsive to our individual learning needs.

In this chapter, we explore these important issues. We will look at teacher expertise, examining research on the nature of teaching excellence. We will also look at the impact of changing societal factors and federal laws on the role of the teacher. Today's classroom is different from the classroom in which we grew up, often resulting in more demanding teaching expectations. Finally, we will discuss interdisciplinary collaboration and how it can help our teachers achieve instructional excellence.

EDUCATIONAL PSYCHOLOGY

Teaching is an exciting and rewarding profession. In almost no other field do you have the opportunity to make such a dramatic impact on others. Think for a minute about all the teachers you have had. Do you have a favorite teacher? What qualities did this teacher possess? How can you develop these skills? The ultimate goal of this book is to assist you on your road to becoming a great teacher by exposing you to the science of teaching and learning. Additionally, it will focus on how today's teachers work collaboratively to produce the best educational experience. Let's begin by taking a look at educational psychology and why it is important to teachers and other professionals associated with education.

What Is Educational Psychology?

Educational psychology

Discipline concerned with the development, evaluation, and application of our understanding of human learning and behavior in an educational setting

Educational psychology is a unique discipline with roots in traditional psychology and education. It is not, however, two separate disciplines working in parallel. Today, educational psychology is a unified discipline that has developed a unique area of inquiry distinct from either psychology or education. **Educational psychology** is defined as a discipline concerned with the development, evaluation, and application of our understanding of human learning and behavior in an educational setting (Wittrock & Farley, 1989). It emphasizes how an understanding of these areas translates into effective learning and instruction. This is an important definition because it emphasizes a concern with best practices in teaching and a focus on student learning. This may be easiest to understand by visualizing a traditional classroom, with students on one side of the teacher's desk and the teacher on the other. Although we will discuss the merits of using this type of classroom arrangement in a later chapter, it is a good analogy to help remember two key factors impacting a successful learning environment. First, from the teacher's side of the desk, we can think about all the techniques and tools teachers use to promote learning. Teachers need to be concerned with their lesson plans and how they are going to convey concepts. They need to consider what instructional levels are appropriate for the students in the class. They also need to make decisions about what supports (e.g., technology, activities, materials, etc.) could be used to further the educational objectives for the day. All of these things are important and will have a dramatic impact on the way learning occurs.

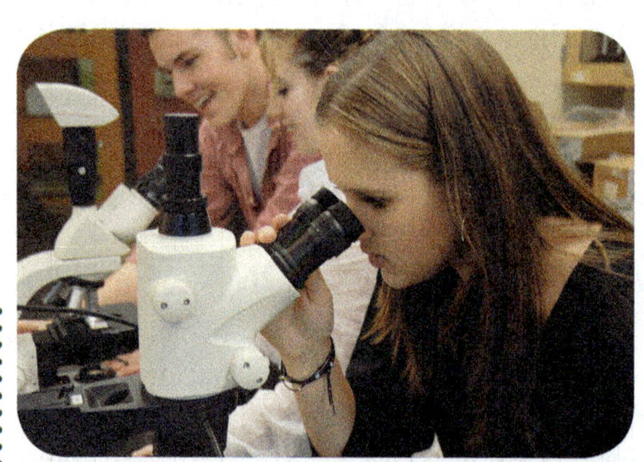

From the teacher's side of the desk, we can think about all the techniques and tools teachers use to promote learning.

Second, it is also just as important to consider the students' side of the desk. From their perspective, what factors impact learning? Things like motivation, organization, intellectual ability, and individual background influence educational progress. Teachers who are knowledgeable about how both "sides of the desk" factor into the educational equation will create successful educational environments.

Educational psychology encompasses both of these perspectives. It centers on how we teach *and* how we learn. This focus is realized through two mutually dependent channels: research and practice. That is, success in the classroom depends on scientific research into educational best practices and how this research translates into everyday teaching. Ideally, researchers conduct scientific investigations into teaching practices and learning issues resulting in a sound knowledge base. Teachers then use this knowledge to practice meaningful and effective education. In reality, the process is far more complex. Education is happening today in classrooms all over the world. Are teachers in these classrooms creating the best learning environment possible? The answer is really yes and no. Today is a particular place in history, and teachers are using available tools to do the best possible job. However, that does not mean future research will not give us insights into new and innovative educational techniques.

The interplay between research and actual practice is an important part of how we educate, and the field of educational psychology provides critical information on how to create productive exchanges. Students first encountering educational psychology often get a better sense of what it encompasses by looking at some common questions educational psychologists strive to answer (see Table 1.1). As you can see, educational psychologists are interested in a wide variety of questions related to the areas of teaching and learning. Answers to these questions are continuously changing as we learn about how to create stimulating and productive learning environments.

Table 1.1 What Is Educational Psychology?

Common Questions Educational Psychologists Investigate

- What motivates students?
- Why are some people better students than others?
- How should reading, writing, or arithmetic be taught?
- Is it better to study alone or in a group?
- What makes a good teacher?
- How can technology be used to support learning?
- Are tests really fair?
- What are good ways to study?

SOURCE: Modified from Educational Psychology Q&A prepared by the Division of Educational Psychology of the American Psychological Association, 1993.

Why Is Educational Psychology Important to Teachers?

One way to think about why educational psychology is important to teachers is to consider the products from both the research and practice sides of the field. As research informs and the practice of teaching and practice raises new questions to research, the educational psychologists generate a body of knowledge or tools to help teachers produce better learning outcomes. Many factors impact effective teaching—such as knowing basic learning principles and developmental processes, understanding the characteristics of individual learners, and having knowledge of a variety of teaching methods. In this book, we will cover research and theory regarding each of these factors, providing you with the foundation necessary to develop into an effective teacher.

Educational Psychology: Building a Science-Based Practice

As mentioned in the preceding section, the interaction between educational research and actual educational practice is critical. Important research discoveries are of little use if they do not make their way into classroom practice. Similarly, if classroom practitioners do not communicate effectively with researchers, scientific investigations may move in directions having little relevance to real life educational settings. This issue is becoming increasingly important in today's political and social climate as parents and teachers across the nation demand higher standards and greater accountability in education. The hope is that by using scientific research to develop best teaching practices, we will foster greater academic achievement. The need to move toward a science-based educational practice is supported by evidence indicating little academic progress over the last few decades (Figures 1.1 and 1.2).

Federal and state offices have committed significant resources to raise academic achievement over the years. Despite these efforts, achievement has not dramatically increased over the last thirty-five years (Rampey, Dion, & Donahue, 2009). As these graphs show, reading and math scores have failed to positively respond to our nation's attempts to increase overall achievement. Current research from the Department of Education (2002) indicates that part of the issue may be a lack of studies using appropriate research methodologies. In particular,

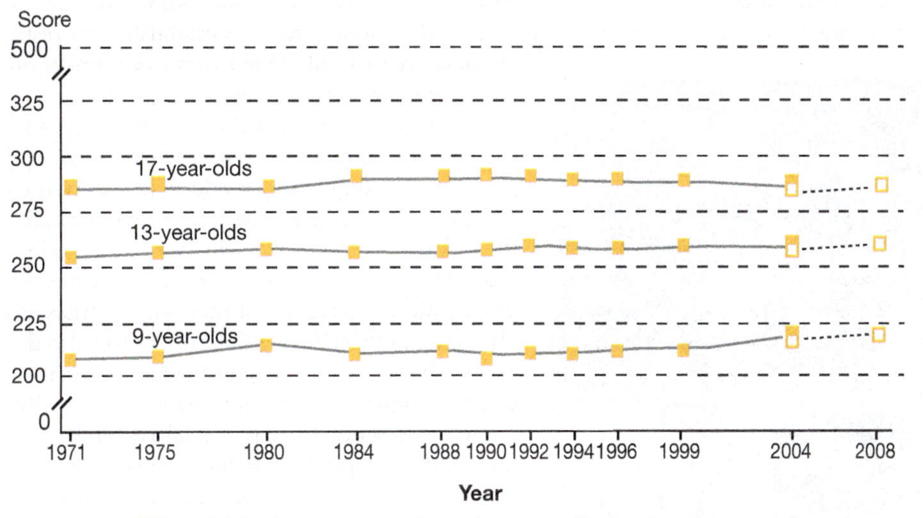

Figure 1.1 Average Reading Scale Scores on the Long-Term Trend National Assessment of Educational Progress (NAEP), by Age: Various Years, 1971 through 2008

Figure 1.2

Average Mathematics Scale Scores on the Long-Term Trend National Assessment of Educational Progress (NAEP), by Age: Various Years, 1973 through 2009

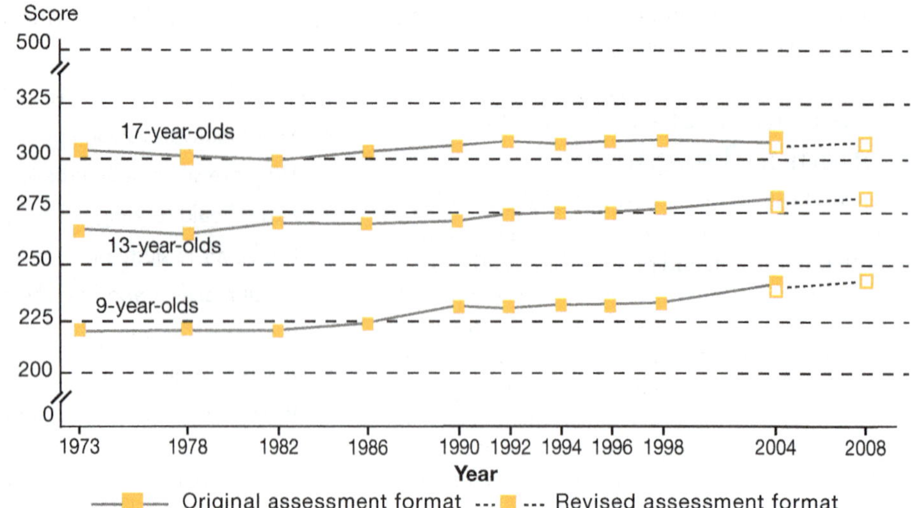

NOTE: Includes public and private schools. NAEP scores range from 0 to 500. Scores for the revised assessment format reflect the inclusion of and accommodations for students with disabilities and English language learners. For more information on NAEP, see supplemental note 4.

SOURCE: Rampey, B. D., Dion, G. S., and Donahue, P. L. (2009). NAEP 2008 *Trends in Academic Progress in Reading and Mathematics* (NCES 2009-479). National Center for Education Statistics, Institute of Education Sciences, U.S. Department of Education, Washington, DC.

studies using randomized trial designs are infrequently used in educational research. Randomized trial designs are important because they directly link a particular educational practice with the resulting educational outcome. Not all research designs are used in this way. We will review randomized trial designs, along with other research approaches, in the next section. Steps are currently being taken at the national level to encourage more randomized study designs and, hopefully, more academic progress.

No Child Left Behind

Act signed into law on January 8, 2002, not only reauthorizing public funding for primary and secondary education, but also introducing a number of research-focused educational reforms

Empirical

Based on observation or experience

The most significant driving force for educational change comes from the **No Child Left Behind** (NCLB) Act, which was signed into law on January 8, 2002. This legislation not only reauthorized public funding for primary and secondary education but also introduced a number of research-focused educational reforms. One of the most important of these was the specification that education reforms be evidence-based. This means that educational practices must meet more rigorous validation standards for effectiveness—before they are implemented as reform efforts. Up until now, educational practices have not been held to any methodological standard. In fact, many educational practices have extremely limited **empirical** (based on observation or experience) research support. To address this issue, NCLB encourages rigorous methodological standards for educational research. This not only establishes standards for educational researchers, it also creates a need for all teachers to become knowledgeable about research methods. As the ultimate users of the educational practices established by research, teachers are in a unique position to comment on the reality of their usefulness and effectiveness.

To help teachers develop the skills necessary to use and understand research, teacher education programs are making stronger efforts to ensure teachers are trained to read and interpret scientific studies. In the following sections, we will examine experimental research methods. As you will see, experimental designs typically make use of randomized trials as emphasized in the NCLB legislation. We will also discuss descriptive, correlational, and single-participant research designs. These designs have traditionally had a strong presence in educational research. We will highlight appropriate uses for each type of research. We will also explore the application of research in the classroom—discussing the importance of critically evaluating research, being able to conduct one's own research in the classroom, and using science to guide teaching practice. Before we begin our discussion of research, however, consider one real-life example of science-based education. Started in the 1970s, the Sesame Workshop sought to develop ways to integrate the vast amount of information coming from researchers with actual teaching practices. They brought together individuals from many disciplines including research, teaching, psychology, medicine, artists, musicians, actors, and others. What they came up with is the remarkably successful public television program *Sesame Street*. This program continues to achieve what we all hope for in our everyday teaching. That is, creation of engaging and meaningful learning experiences firmly grounded in scientific practice. Their approach has broadened over the last thirty years with programming targeted to science, literacy, math, and basic preschool preparation. They continue to create these programs with the close collaboration of scientists and educators. In addition, they actively monitor their effectiveness and remain strong advocates for accountability. Their success story is an example of how educational professionals can partner with researchers to produce positive and effective learning environments.

Experimental Research

Experimental research describes a set of procedures used in science to infer that one event leads to or causes another. This means an experimental research study can support the assertion that a particular intervention is the cause of a particular outcome. For this reason, experimental procedures are extremely valuable when evaluating educational practices. The following section reviews basic experimental methodology and identifies key methodological features emphasized by the U.S. Department of Education as important in the scientific evaluation of educational practices.

Experimental research

Set of procedures used in science to infer that one event leads to or causes another

The basic approach in experimental research simply involves changing some aspect of the environment and recording the resulting changes. Using this method, a researcher establishes whether there is a causal relation between the change made by the researcher and the subsequent outcome. **Manipulation** refers to changes the researcher makes to the environment. At the most basic level, an experiment consists of manipulating a variable in one group of people compared to another group not receiving the manipulation. For example, your educational psychology professor might want to investigate the effects of using a study guide on test performance. To investigate this effect, the professor obtains a small grant to buy several study guides. She intends to give the study guides to some students and compare their test performance to students who do not receive the study guide. The study guide is referred to as the treatment or **independent variable**, and this is the variable being manipulated by the experimenter. The **experimental group** of students will receive the study guide, and the students who do not will serve as a comparison, or **control group**. The researcher is interested in whether student test performance depends on their access to the study guide. This is why student test performance is considered a *dependent* variable in this study. The value or score of the **dependent variable** depends on the treatment manipulation (e.g., study guide). It is what is measured in the study.

Manipulation

Change the researcher makes to the environment

Independent variable

Variable being manipulated by the experimenter

Experimental group

Group that receives the experimental manipulation

Control group

Group that serves as a comparison group

Dependent variable

What is measured in the study, depending on the treatment manipulation

Although the purpose of the experiment may seem simple, the application of the treatment must be carefully arranged. One important aspect of applying the treatment is **random assignment**. Random assignment is the process of assigning study participants to groups (e.g., study guide group vs. no study guide group) in a random fashion. A simple way to conceptualize this process is to put twenty names in a hat and then blindly pull out names, alternating the placement of the individuals into the two groups. Researchers actually use more sophisticated methods for random assignment, but the same basic idea applies. The importance of conducting a study trial using random assignment of participants cannot be overemphasized. Consider the study guide example. What if the researcher assigned students to the study guide group by selecting students on the left side of the room? It is entirely possible these students are sitting together because they have certain traits in common. Perhaps they are all members of the honor society in education and sit together because of that common experience. This would effectively load the treatment group (e.g., study guide) with the most academically talented students. Differences between experimental and control groups at the end of the study would be difficult to interpret because higher grades in the study guide group could be attributed to *either* the study guide

Random assignment

Process of assigning study participants to groups in a random fashion

Random assignment is the process of assigning study participants to groups in a random fashion.

or the greater academic skill inherent in the group. Random assignment increases the probability of starting the experiment with **comparable groups**. That is, the group receiving the treatment (study guide) and the comparison group (no study guide) are likely to be equal on any given characteristic. Using random assignment, rather than seating arrangements, to establish groups would make it highly unlikely that all the academically talented students were placed in one group.

Randomized trials (research designs using random assignment) are one of the primary research components emphasized by the U.S. Department of Education Rigorous Evidence Checklist. (see Table 1.2). Randomized trials provide a *quality* baseline for experimental research because causal inferences can only be made using a properly designed experimental study.

Comparable groups

Groups that are typically formed using random assignment to conditions

Randomized trials

Experimental studies that employ random assignment to groups

Generalization

Referring to the appropriateness of applying research results to settings that differ from the research setting

The U.S. Department of Education also emphasizes that educational practices should demonstrate effectiveness in more than one study. This means a single study is typically not sufficient to support the use of a given intervention. U.S. Department of Education guidelines indicate that research on educational practices should be conducted in more than one implementation site, implemented in typical school or community *environments*, and implemented in settings similar to the setting in which it is to be used (U.S. Department of Education, 2003). The purpose of these guidelines is to ensure a *quantity* of evidence is present before a particular practice is considered appropriate for general use. This focus on the quantity of evidence necessary to establish effectiveness also addresses the problem of whether the results of a study can be generalized. **Generalization** refers to the appropriateness of applying research results to settings that differ from the research setting. For example, can research conducted in urban public schools in Pennsylvania be applied to students in rural California? A similar issue also plagues laboratory based research since the artificial environment of the experimental lab does not always capture the complexity of a natural school environment. Only when an educational practice is validated in many experimental studies, across many settings, can results be generalized to a larger school population.

To help educators identify research studies meeting rigorous evidence standards, the Department of Education supported the development of the *What Works Clearinghouse* (WWC). This organization assesses the strength of research support for educational interventions. Using research experts from many disciplines—including educators, psychologists, economists, sociologists, and experts in communication—they produce easily accessible information on educational research. The clearinghouse provides a variety of reports including study, intervention, and topic reports. *Study reports* contain information on a specific scientific study. The report gives information on experimental factors such as type of participants, experimental setting, intervention description, type of comparison group, primary outcomes and measurements, and teacher training. *Intervention reports* provide an assessment of the research support for a given educational intervention. For example, an intervention report would detail the research support for the Cognitive Tutor® program to help students learn algebra. *Topic reports* provide information on the availability of strong research support for interventions in a particular topic area (e.g., dropout prevention or middle school math).

Single Subject Experimental Research

Single-participant research

Research that uses an experimental design to investigate the effect of a treatment on a single person

The large group randomized trial designs discussed in the preceding section are only one type of research using an experimental approach. **Single-participant research** uses an experimental design to investigate the effect of a treatment on a single person. Often, it is difficult to implement a given treatment to a large group of participants, so researchers elect to use single-participant methodology. The main difference between the experimental approach and a single-participant research study is the focus on an individual rather than the average performance of a group of people. For example, imagine you are a researcher who is interested in how a particular type of reading approach works with children who have different learning needs. Your goal is not only to determine whether the reading approach will produce positive results but also to assess the interaction between the approach and the individual. In this case, you

TABLE 1.2 U.S. Department of Education Rigorous Evidence Checklist

Step	Criteria
Step 1—Is the intervention supported by "strong" evidence of effectiveness?	**A. The quality of evidence needed by "strong" evidence, randomized controlled trials that are well-designed and implemented:** • The study should clearly describe the intervention. • Be alert to any indication that the random assignment process may have been compromised. • The study should provide data showing that there are no systematic differences between the intervention and control groups prior to the intervention. • The study should use outcome measures that are "valid." • The percent of study participants that the study has lost track of when collecting outcome data should be small, and should not differ between the intervention and control groups. • The study should collect and report outcome data even for those members of the intervention group who do not participate in or complete the intervention. • The study should preferably obtain data on long-term outcomes of the intervention. • If the study makes a claim that the intervention is effective, it should report (i) the size of the effect and (ii) statistical tests showing the effect is unlikely to be the result of chance. • A study's claim that the intervention's effect on a subgroup (e.g., Hispanic students) is different than its effect on the overall population in the study should be treated with caution. • The study should report the intervention's effects on all the outcomes that the study measures, not just those for which there is a positive effect. **B. Quantity of evidence needed to establish "strong" evidence of effectiveness:** • The intervention should be demonstrated effective through well-designed randomized controlled trials in more than one site of implementation. • These sites should be typical school or community settings. • The trials should demonstrate the intervention's effectiveness in school settings similar to yours.
Step 2—If the intervention is not supported by "strong" evidence, is it nevertheless supported by "possible" evidence of effectiveness?	**A. Circumstances in which a comparison-group study can constitute "possible" evidence:** • The study's intervention and comparison groups should be very closely matched. • The comparison group should not be comprised of individuals who had the option to participate in the intervention but declined. • The study should preferably choose the intervention/comparison groups and outcome measure "prospectively." • The study should meet the checklist items listed above for a well-designed, randomized controlled trial. **B. Studies that do *not* meet the threshold for "possible" evidence of effectiveness include:** • Pre-post studies • Comparison-group studies in which the intervention and comparison groups are not well-matched • "Meta-analyses" that combine the results of individual studies which do not themselves meet the threshold for "possible" evidence

SOURCE: U.S. Department of Education, Institute of Education Sciences, National Center for Education Evaluation and Regional Assistance: December 2003.

A single participant research study focuses on an individual rather that the average performance of a group of people.

might want to use a single-participant design. Focusing on one person's response to the treatment clarifies how the treatment affects a particular person. A single person's response might be overlooked when focusing on the average response of a large group of research participants. This does not mean that single-participant research is always better (or worse) than studies employing large numbers of participants; it really depends on the nature of the variables and the question the research is striving to answer.

A single-participant research design can take many forms, but there is a basic idea inherent in the approach. The goal is to alternate recording behavior while a participant is receiving a treatment with a recording of the same behavior at a separate time when the treatment is not present. **Baseline** refers to the time when participant responses are recorded in the absence of a treatment. One typical approach is shown in Figure 1.3.

As Figure 1.3 indicates, the **A-B-A-B single-participant design** begins with recording a baseline. This baseline is a record of the behavior of interest in the natural ongoing environment. After recording the baseline, the researcher introduces the treatment and again records the behavior of interest. The goal is to see if the treatment changes the behavior of interest. Does the behavior increase, decrease, or remain the same after the introduction of the treatment? After recording behavior during the treatment phase, the process repeats. The researcher removes the treatment and records a second baseline, followed by the reintroduction of the treatment.

A study conducted in 2003 by Scott Methe and John Hintze is a good example of an A-B-A-B design. They were interested in examining the effect of teacher modeling of sustained silent reading (SSR). SSR is a reading technique designed to enhance a student's independent reading. Students participating in SSR are required to stop everything at predetermine points during the day, choose a book, and begin reading silently. This study was conducted to determine if the teacher's modeling of this behavior would increase the amount of student on-task behavior. To investigate the potential for teacher modeling to facilitate SSR, they used an A-B-A-B single-participant design. Each study participant was first observed and the amount of on-task reading behavior recorded. Then the treatment was introduced (teacher modeling of the desired behavior). Student behavior was also recorded during the treatment. This was followed by a withdrawal of the treatment and a second baseline recording. The final step was the reintroduction of the teacher modeling. The results of the study are presented in Figure 1.4.

Baseline

Participant responses that are recorded during the absence of a treatment

A-B-A-B single-participant design

Using an alternating presentation of the intervention with the recording of a baseline

Looking at Figure 1.4 it is clear that the percentage of on-task behavior increased during the treatment phases of the study. This provides evidence that the treatment, the teacher modeling, was the critical variable responsible for increases in on-task reading behavior.

The A-B-A-B design is sometimes abbreviated to a single reversal phase know as an A-B-A design. Similarly, additional reversal phases can be added to further support the effectiveness of a treatment (e.g., A-B-A-B-A-B). The goal is to alternate the introduction of the treatment with baseline recordings to show how changes in behavior relate to the treatment.

Figure 1.3
A-B-A-B Single-Participant Experimental Design

A	B	A	B
Baseline Measure	Treatment Condition	Baseline Measure	Treatment Condition

Descriptive Research

Experimental research regarding effective educational practice is clearly needed, yet it is often difficult to apply in educational settings. For example, classrooms are not created using random assignment, and treatments are often difficult to implement for only some of the students within a classroom. Additionally, single-participant reversal designs are not always possible. Once a task is learned, it may be impossible to return to a pre-learning state in order to record a second baseline. These limitations often lead educational researchers to turn to descrip-

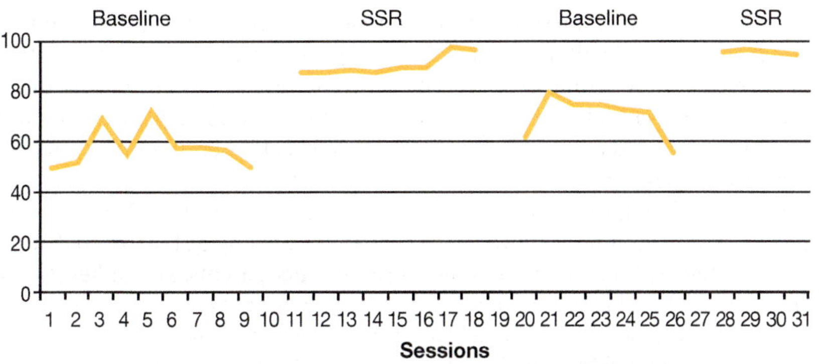

Figure 1.4

Results of A-B-A-B Single-Participant Design Study

SOURCE: Methe, S. A. and Hintze, J. M. (2003). Evaluating teacher modeling as a strategy to increase student reading behavior. *School Psychology Review, 32*(4), 617–623.

tive methods. **Descriptive research methods** accurately describe a behavior or environmental condition of interest. An important distinction between experimental and descriptive research is that descriptive research does not support the formation of causal inferences. It does, however, provide detailed information about students, teaching, and learning within a given context. To demonstrate a descriptive approach, let's go back to the study guide example presented above. Instead of attempting to control the assignment of study guides, a researcher or teacher using a descriptive research method would simply examine the natural use of the study guides among students. For example, the researcher might ask her educational psychology students to keep a "study diary" for the semester. She provides students guidelines for documenting their study efforts and makes the study guide available to all students if they wish to use it. She clarifies that the goal in collecting this information is to only document how students study, not to dictate a particular approach. This way she is more likely to capture naturally occurring behavior. After test one, she examines the diaries, recording the amount of time students used their study guides and comparing it to their scores on the test. She finds that students who use the study guide generally do better on the test. This conclusion does not necessarily mean that study guide use is causing better grades, just that the two appear related. Again, to determine if a causal relation exists, an experimental methodology must be used. Since our researcher did not randomly assign students to groups, the students' grades may be higher due to another naturally occurring phenomenon, which she did not measure. What if, for example, the more conscientious students used their study guides more frequently? These students also came to class more consistently, took better notes, and studied for more hours than the less conscientious students. These students might have done better on the test regardless of whether or not they used the study guide. While we can't make causal inferences with descriptive research, it does allow us to see trends and natural associations between variables. Descriptive studies help define the inter-workings of the behavior of interest and often serve as a source of information for later experimental research.

Descriptive research method

Research method that accurately describes a behavior or environmental condition of interest

One additional note to make regarding descriptive research: often the purpose of a descriptive study is to focus on describing the behavior of a single individual. This type of descriptive study is called a case study. A **case study** is the intensive description of a single individual. Case studies are important sources of information and often raise questions that are further investigated using experimental methodologies. For example, a case study of a successful teacher with major depression might uncover an extremely difficult childhood. The teacher was able to move past his difficult childhood to reach professional success but still struggles with interpersonal problems, which lead to his ongoing difficulties with depression. A closer examination of his childhood reveals that despite difficulties at home, he was fortunate to have ongoing support from an aunt who lived nearby. The teacher attributed much of his professional success to his aunt's support. This hypothetical case

Case study

The intensive description of a single individual or unified cohort

Conscientious students use their study guides more frequently. These students also attend classes more consistently, take better notes, and study more than the less conscientious students.

study raises some interesting questions. Does consistent support during childhood help children with exceptionally difficult upbringings achieve greater professional success? The answer to this question cannot be found with the data from the case study, but raising the question gives researchers important ideas for experimental studies. Like descriptive studies in general, case studies often serve this purpose—providing needed background information and raising important research questions.

One often cited descriptive case study involved a girl named *Genie.* (This was not her real name, but the name used in research reports.) Genie was a young girl discovered at the age of thirteen. She was the victim of long standing abuse from her parents. Her father suffered from mental and emotional problems, and her mother (twenty years younger than her father) was partially blind from cataracts and a detached retina. Believing Genie was retarded, her father decided to keep her confined in a small room with very little human contact. She was physically abused whenever she would speak and typically was restrained to prevent even the most basic movements. Her mother was also the victim of her husband's abuse and did little to oppose him.

The story of Genie made national headlines when she was discovered in 1970. After receiving treatment for malnutrition, Genie became the subject of intense scientific scrutiny. History has documented few children who were raised with little human intervention. Scientists call these children *feral children.* After stabilizing Genie's health, scientists began an in-depth case study of her life and abilities. One question scientists raised was whether Genie could learn language (Curtiss, 1977). At the time of her discovery, she did little more than make unintelligible sounds. Scientists have theorized that language must be acquired during a specific time of our lives—a *critical period*—if language is to develop normally. Immediately, scientists and therapists began to work with Genie to see if she could learn the fundamentals of language after the age of thirteen. Ultimately, Genie was unable master a full understanding of linguistic structure. Scientists speculated on whether there was indeed a critical period for language development or whether Genie was intellectually limited or permanently damaged from her abuse. Scientists never agreed on the nature of her language difficulties. Establishing the *cause* of her difficulties proved elusive. In fact, the scientific community began to raise serious questions about the scientific conduct of the Genie research. The incredible story of this exceptional girl, however, and the questions she raises about the fundamental acquisition of language continue to educate and inspire scientists and students alike. This captivating look at a whole person is one of the advantages of the case study approach. Genie currently lives in an adult foster home in southern California.

Correlational Research

Correlational studies

Studies that not only describe events but also establish how events relate to each other.

Correlation

Statistical technique used to establish the nature of the relation between variables

Correlational coefficient

The numerical product resulting from the correlation formula

Strength

The tendency for values of one variable to co-occur with values of another variable

The goal of a **correlational study** is not only to describe events but also to establish how events relate to each other. For example, a purely descriptive study might document how many times a teacher smiles and how many questions the students ask. The answers to these questions help describe classroom dynamics. A correlational study goes beyond description, however, actually specifying how events relate. In the above example, it may be that more frequent smiling by the teacher is associated with more questions from the student. Alternatively, the two may have no relation to each other. The teacher smiling is not related to any particular amount of questioning from the students. Correlational studies use a statistical technique called correlation to help make sense of the data collected. In the study guide example from the previous section, the researcher probably used a **correlation** to help understand the relation between study guide use and test performance. The **correlation coefficient** is a single number derived from a statistical formula that quantifies the nature of the relation between two variables. The number can range between a negative one and a positive one, including the endpoints. Let's say that the correlation coefficient in our study guide example (between test grades and amount of study guide use) was a positive .89. This single value tells us two important things about the relation between our variables. First, it tells us about the strength of the relation. **Strength** is the tendency for values of one variable to co-occur with values of another variable. The closer to 1 the correlation coefficient is, the greater the strength between the study variables. Our correlation of .89 in the study guide example indicates that the relation between study guide use and test grades is strong. Higher scores on the test corresponded with increased study guide use for many, but not all, of the students. If higher scores corresponded with study guide use for *all* students, we would have a perfect relation. Perfect relations are represented with a value of one. Thus, strength is represented numerically by how far the correlation value is from zero. A weak relation between variables will yield a correlation close to zero, moderate relations about .5, and strong correlations closer to 1.0. For the purposes of determining strength, the sign (positive or negative) of the number is irrelevant. For example, a correlation of a negative .98 is actually stronger than a positive correlation of .90.

Whether the correlation coefficient is positive or negative is, however, an important piece of information. **Direction** provides an indication of how two variables change in relation to each other. For example, do high scores on one variable tend to associate with low scores on the other variable? The sign of the number, positive or negative, represents the direction of the correlation value. A positive sign indicates the variables tend to rise or fall together (as the value of one goes up so does the other *or* if the value of one goes down, so does the other). A negative sign indicates the variables tend to change opposite each other (as one variable goes up in value, the other goes down). The fact that the correlation coefficient .89 in our study guide example is positive indicates that frequent use of the study guide corresponded with high grades on the test. If the number were negative, high study guide use would have corresponded with lower test grades. Figure 1.5 provides a graphical depiction of both strength and direction of a correlation.

Direction

Provides an indication of how *two* variables change in relation to each other

Correlations help us describe relations between variables in a correlational study. It is tempting, however, to infer, incorrectly, causation from a correlational study. What if the researcher in the study guide example told her class that she conducted a research study that showed frequent use of the study guide was associated with higher grades? While this statement was true in the example and clearly designed to encourage more study guide use, should you rush out and buy the study guide? A critical evaluation of the research allows us to consider the possibility that the study guide might or might not increase performance. In fact, other variables, such as total study time or student conscientiousness, might have caused the increased test scores.

Even though cause and effect cannot be determined using descriptive methods, their contribution to science is no less than other methodologies. Descriptive methods are, in fact, critical for highlighting important relations. If we fail to describe our variables of interest in a rich and comprehensive way, we may miss important factors influencing student learning. In the final analysis, it is clear that both descriptive and experimental methodologies positively affect the practice of science within the field of education.

Discovering Action Research

While there is clearly a trend toward focusing on the science-based practice of education, our schools are not simply on hold, waiting for a scientifically validated and comprehensive body of knowledge regarding effective teaching practices to evolve. Teachers are in the classroom every day, using our current tools and knowledge to guide their practice. A wealth of research data exists regarding effective teaching, and the literature can be quite overwhelming. Different studies sometimes show different results, even though they cover the same topic. How, then, can teachers determine the validity of a given research study or make informed judgments

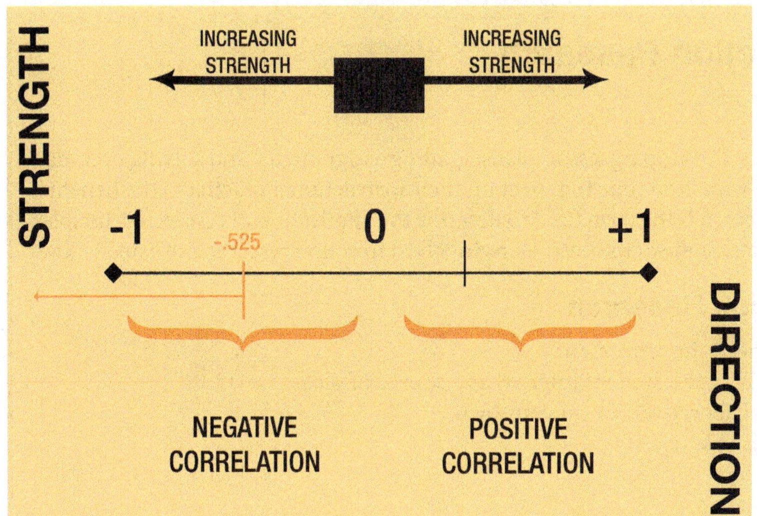

Figure 1.5

Graphical Depiction of Both Strength and Direction of a Correlation

FOR EXAMPLE: A negative correlation (–.525) was found between college students who missed four or more educational methods classes and their semester grade.

Strength—The size of the correlation indicates moderate strength.

Direction—The sign of the correlation (negative) indicates that the more classes a student missed the lower their overall grade in the course (high values corresponding to low values).

In general, the process of critically evaluating one's own teaching is known as reflective teaching.

about what information to apply in their classrooms? A first step is to evaluate the study according to the Rigorous Evidence Checklist developed by the U.S. Office of Education and presented earlier in Table 1.2. While these standards are a good place to start, and they are indeed rigorous, relatively few studies will make the grade. For this reason, teachers must be able to think critically about research and how to use scientific information to inform their teaching.

Teachers who have a solid understanding of research methods are not only able to critically evaluate research—they are also able to use action research in their classrooms. **Action research** involves a teacher applying both descriptive and experimental research methods to assess the effectiveness of certain educational approaches or to solve certain problems (Arhar, Holly, & Kasten, 2001; Hansen & Brady, 2011). As action researchers, teachers conduct investigations in their own classrooms, systematically observing outcomes, collecting and analyzing data, and drawing conclusions. By using action research, teachers can better evaluate the effectiveness of their own teaching while still benefiting from information derived from the scientific community. Additionally, action research deepens a sense of professional community among faculty, increases teacher perceptions regarding accountability, and nurtures a sustainable desire for professional growth (Gilles, Wilson, & Elias, 2010).

Action research

Research that involves a teacher applying both descriptive and experimental research methods to assess the effectiveness of certain educational approaches or to solve everyday problems

Reflective teaching

The process in which a teacher critically evaluates his/her own teaching

In general, the process of critically evaluating your own teaching is known as **reflective teaching** (Schon, 1983; Cruickshank, 1987; Minott, 2011). Many teachers spend a great deal of time not only planning and carrying out instructional activities but also evaluating their success. In other words, they are constantly analyzing their own teaching and using their reflections to improve learning. Some researchers suggest that excellence in teaching is based in this insightful, reflective quality (Schon, 1983; Wolfensberger, Piniel, Canella, & Kyburz-Graber, 2010) and that teachers can benefit from purposeful instruction in reflective techniques (Kennedy, Long, & Camins, 2009). Additionally, others believe teachers need to be able to think artistically and creatively when evaluating research results (Gage & Berliner, 1989). In fact, some researchers argue that teaching is more of an art form than it is a science (Dawe, 1984; Flinders, 1989). As the field of education moves toward establishing more science-based standards, it is important to remember that these scientifically derived standards are important guidelines; however, they do not negate the importance of reflective judgment, creativity, and skilled decision making on the part of our nation's teachers.

In The Classroom

APPLYING THEORY

Action Research

THEORY BASICS

Using *action research* is often difficult for teachers. Developing lesson plans, grading assignments, and solving everyday problems takes time and effort, leaving teachers with little time to reflect on their instructional practices. The benefits, however, are usually worth the effort. Action research is the term used to describe the application of research principles by teachers in their everyday instructional practice. Some of the basic steps involved in action research are listed below.

Basic Steps to Successful Action Research

- Analyze what aspect of your teaching needs improvement.
- Use the observations of others (e.g., colleagues, student interns) as a source of ideas.
- Decide whether you will be working collaboratively or on your own.
- Determine how you want to assess your progress.

(continues)

- Think about how you will interpret your results.
- Reflect upon your success and make plans for future action research projects.

CLASSROOM EXAMPLE

Ms. Carolyn Neilson is a fifth grade teacher. Every year she sponsors a student intern and enjoys working collaboratively to develop educational goals. One day during a planning meeting, the intern mentioned he was concerned about transitions between classes. He felt students were disruptive and often agitated at the beginning of the next lesson. Ms. Neilson decided to conduct an action research project to test alternative transitioning approaches. Initially, with the help of her intern, she recorded student behavior in a daily log prior to making any changes. After two weeks of observation, she introduced a new transition protocol to the students. She informed the students they would be using transition leaders to help students move from one lesson to the next. Every day a team of five students would be selected at random to be the transition leaders. They would have a morning meeting with Ms. Neilson, during which she would give instructions on how to handle the day's transitions. When a given lesson ended, the team went to the front of the room and handled the transition. Ms. Neilson and her intern recorded student behavior for a period of two weeks during these transitional times. An additional two-week period followed, where the traditional teacher mediated transition was re-implemented.

After the entire six-week period, Ms. Neilson qualitatively examined the behavior logs. She noted that during the transition leader phase of the research project, the students were noticeably more positive. She also noticed the professional behavior exhibited by the transition leaders. The only negative observation made during this period was that students were typically louder during the student-mediated transitions. Encouraged by the results, Ms. Neilson made plans for another project. She planned to use the transition leader model with modifications to address the loudness of the students. She also decided to use the students of a colleague in the same grade as a control group.

Teachers should realize that success with teaching is usually equal to the time devoted to its improvement. Great teachers are not born, but are created through hard work. Action research is an excellent tool to help your teaching improve.

Action research can be an important tool to help you develop your teaching expertise. Teachers who regularly use action research report they like the approach because it is practical, inexpensive, and often requires little additional time. It empowers teachers to take action and solve problems. Even if you do little more than systematically observe your own teaching, you will find that you move closer to the reflective teaching style characteristic of expert teachers.

SUMMARIZE AND REFLECT

1. Educational psychology brings together the fields of psychology and education to understand thinking and behavior as it applies to instruction and learning.
2. One reason educational psychology is important for teachers is that it provides teachers with research-based tools for improving teaching and learning.
3. Scientific researchers work in tandem with classroom teachers to build an effective and useful body of instructional and learning knowledge.
4. Basic research methodology includes experimental research methodologies and more descriptive procedures.
5. Some research designs focus on a single participant and still maintain the qualities of an experiment. These single-participant designs are typically called ABA designs.
6. Teachers can act as researchers themselves, applying research methodologies to everyday educational problems. This is called action research.

INFORMED APPLICATION

1. Develop a list of what an educational psychologist might be able to tell you regarding a student that is failing to pick up basic reading skills.
2. Imagine you want to try a new mathematics instruction program for a student struggling with long division. What would be an appropriate research methodology to help you determine if the program is successful?
3. Explain how an emphasis on action research can help teachers provide instruction that is more effective.

BECOMING AN EFFECTIVE TEACHER

The second part of this chapter is about becoming an effective teacher. As we just learned in the proceeding section, today's teachers are striving to become more science-based. This is an important step toward more effective education, but we must also pay close attention to a teacher's professional development. Productive learning environments will not work, even if we have proven instructional strategies, if we do not have high quality teachers to implement those strategies. In an attempt to determine critical teacher qualities, educational psychology researchers investigate commonalities among teaching experts. The next section looks at this research, emphasizing its relevance to a teacher's professional growth.

Psychologists have long studied the differences between experts and novices in a variety of domains such as playing chess or solving physics problems.

Professional Knowledge

Psychologists have long studied the differences between experts and novices in a variety of domains such as playing chess or solving physics problems (Anderson, 1995). We know that expert chess players, for example, seem to choose their moves with little effort, basing their choices on memories of previous games. Novice chess players, on the other hand, must think about each move, requiring more cognitive resources to play the game. In the same way, expert teachers can effortlessly handle daily situations requiring more thought on the part of novice teachers. Research shows that effective teachers are able to more quickly access both subject matter and classroom management information than novice teachers (Berliner, 1986). This allows them to plan instruction more efficiently and implement instructional plans more effectively. It also allows them to improvise in situations requiring a deviation from the planned lesson when necessary and to adapt instruction to meet the needs of individual learners

Subject Knowledge

So, how does one learn to be an expert teacher? This is a difficult question since research indicates effective teachers possess a set of often hard-to-define skills. Likely, you can think of more than one great teacher you have had over the course of your educational career. Were they great in the same way? Some may have been great mentors with a dynamic personality. Others may have demonstrated their expertise through an exceptional ability to present new material and make it engaging. Often, expert teachers vary considerably from subject to subject and use very different methods. Shulman (1987) proposed that expert teachers need a combination of different factors to achieve expertise. One of these factors is subject knowledge. This may seem obvious, but teachers vary considerably in their experience and comfort level with the subject they teach. Perhaps you are a math teacher at a high school, and you primarily teach algebra. Certainly, high school algebra teachers should know the math they are teaching, but experts go beyond a basic understanding of the facts (Rongjin, Yeping, & Xiaoya, 2010). Their knowledge of the subject includes a well-developed understanding of how learning the subject progresses. They also have a good sense of the difficulties students are likely to encounter and how to provide appropriate guidance. This more complete understanding of the subject allows expert teachers to guide learning in a way that is unavailable to the novice teacher.

General Teaching Strategies

Another characteristic expert teachers have in common is an awareness of general teaching strategies (Hardré, Nanny, Refai, Chen, & Slater, 2010). This is sometimes referred to as pedagogical knowledge. This typically includes things like basic classroom organization, behavioral management techniques, motivational approaches, and techniques for evaluation. Expert teachers are proficient with these strategies and have the experience and judgment to use them appropriately. These topics are covered in detail later in the book.

Decision Making and Knowledge Application

Expert teachers have an extensive knowledge of how to apply particular techniques in the teaching of their subject matter (Ghasemi, Momeni, Jafarzadehpur, Rezaee, & Taheri, 2011). This includes knowing specific characteristics of their students that require unique tailoring of instruction, such as their cultural background, family situation, emotional development, or intellectual ability level. This kind of pedagogical content knowledge also allows them to meet the learning needs of a wider range of students. In other words, it is not enough for teachers to simply know their subject, nor can they simply be knowledgeable about different methods of instruction or learning settings; expert teachers must know how to effectively *use* different lessons to teach their subject to a *specific* type of student. The hands-on, small-group-based methods that the science teacher uses in class, for example, may not be appropriate for use by an English teacher. Expert teachers must be able to problem solve learning issues and make appropriate decisions about how to adjust the learning path to bring about the most effective learning environment for each student. As you can see, the professional knowledge necessary for expertise in teaching is quite complicated. For this reason, expert teachers may use very different teaching methods and still show expertise in teaching.

The Expert Teacher Prototype

Sternberg and Horvath (1995) further developed the idea that there are multiple qualities potentially leading to an expertise in teaching. They propose that instead of teaching expertise being reached through a definitive set of criteria, expert teaching is a "fuzzy," or difficult to define, category. They conceptualize expert teaching using a prototype model, where similarities between expert teachers fall into three general categories: knowledge, efficiency, and insight (Figure 1.6). The prototype model defines expert teaching as a set of broad areas, which may be developed to a different degree in different teachers. This differs from the preceding section suggesting expert teachers have the same knowledge and skills. According to the prototype expert teacher model, one teacher might be considered expert because of her unrivaled content knowledge in her field, while another might be considered expert because of his insightful and creative problem-solving abilities. These teachers both show similarity to the overall expert prototype, yet both reveal very different strengths. Of course, other elements of the prototype must also be met to a sufficient degree for the person with unrivaled knowledge to be considered an expert teacher. Consider, for example, a history professor who has written several successful books on the development of civil rights, yet has no knowledge of pedagogy (teaching techniques). He would not be considered an expert teacher. Throughout this book, we will explore expert teaching from a number of perspectives, focusing on the ways in which these prototypical qualities of expert teachers may manifest in the classroom. The next section will elaborate on this topic by exploring the collaborative role teachers have with other professionals and how this enables teachers to expand their educational tools to help children learn and grow.

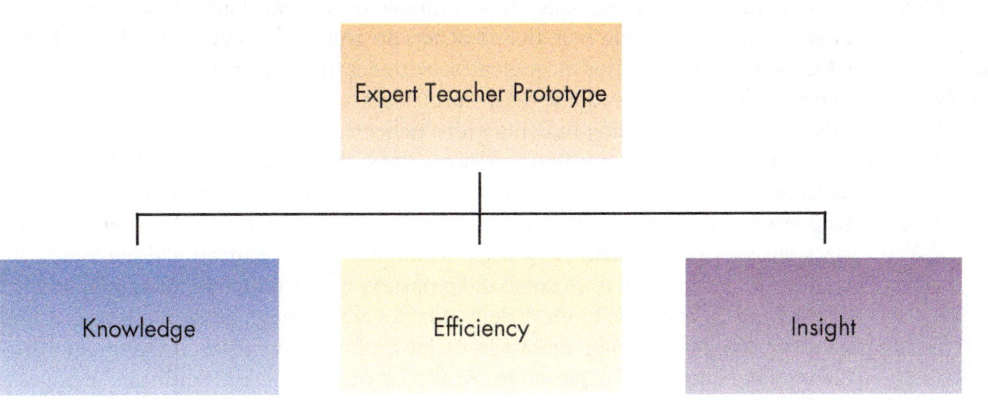

Figure 1.6
Prototype Expert Teacher Model

SUMMARIZE AND REFLECT

1. Expert teachers contribute to our understanding of instructional excellence by providing real-life role models.
2. Expert teachers have many traits in common including a thorough knowledge of the subject matter, general teaching strategies, and excellent decision-making skills.
3. Expert teachers also demonstrate remarkable judgment in applying their knowledge.
4. The expert teaching prototype model moves away from detailing specific expert teacher characteristics, in favor of general categories of knowledge and behavior experts possess. These "fuzzy" or less specific categories include knowledge, efficiency, and insight.

INFORMED APPLICATION

1. Consider all the teachers you have had over your lifetime. Which teachers stand out as the best? What qualities characterize their teaching?
2. Research has shown that expert teachers have certain qualities in common. Imagine yourself as a teacher. What are your teaching strengths? What qualities may require further development?
3. Research has also suggested that expertise in teaching may be less about developing specific qualities and more about the unique combination of skills the teacher possesses. Consider your own teaching skills. How can you develop a combination of skills that is unique and effective?

INTERDISCIPLINARY AND COLLABORATIVE EDUCATION

So far, we have looked at the field of educational psychology and its importance to teachers. We have also reviewed important teacher qualities established through research on expert teachers. This final section integrates this foundation with the educational climate and practice in today's classrooms.

Teaching Today: The Importance of an Interdisciplinary Foundation

To achieve a truly productive learning environment, educators must bring together an understanding of proven, science-based, educational practices and an appreciation of important teacher qualities. This process, however, takes place in a real-life context; and this context is rapidly changing. Historically, education has taken place in a very circumscribed environment consisting primarily of a single instructor and a relatively fixed number of students. Over time, though, we have seen dramatic changes to this framework. One of these changes includes the way teachers work collaboratively with each other. Students often have multiple instructors, particularly in the higher grades. Today, more than ever, these teachers are truly collaborating to achieve positive educational outcomes. This movement also extends to colleges where students may participate in learning communities where professors collaborate to integrate material from different courses providing students with a richer learning experience.

> **GET THE FACTS**
>
> **2020**
>
> The year researchers believe that there will no longer be a majority culture in the American student population.
>
> Pallas, Natriello, and McDill (1989)

The most obvious question is why are these changes taking place? The answer is complex, but it is based on two criteria: 1) the need to teach in more efficient and effective ways coupled with 2) changing student demographics. The first point emphasizes our society's demand for greater accountability for educational outcomes. We want to see evidence that we are making positive and productive changes in the lives of students. In response to these demands, we are making changes in how we think about traditional teaching, embracing a far more collaborative environment. These changes in educational perspective are also co-occurring with significant changes in the broad range of diversity students bring to today's classroom. This leads to an ever-increasing body of knowledge necessary to provide effective and sensitive instruction. There are limits to what individual teachers can learn, and those limits push teachers to specialize in their training. This, however, has the potential for decentralizing our educational focus, as teachers possess greater depth of knowledge in certain areas but lack sufficient breadth. This means that our specialized instructors need to learn to work collaboratively to produce the holistic and individualized educational system that society demands. These interrelated factors are indeed complicated, but we will address them in detail throughout the text. Let's begin our look at these issues by examining exactly how the students we teach are changing the fundamental structure of our classrooms. We will then review how instructor collaboration can help address needs resulting from these changes.

The U.S. population is becoming progressively more diverse in terms of race/ethnicity, socioeconomic background, and disability status and these demographic changes are mirrored in the nation's schools.

The Changing American Classroom

The U.S. population is becoming progressively more diverse in terms of race/ethnicity, socioeconomic background, and disability status; and these demographic changes are mirrored in the nation's schools (Safran & Safran, 1996). For example, the percentage of non-white students increased from approximately 35.8% in 1996 to 43.5% in 2006 (Figure 1.7, NCES, 2008); and researchers estimate that this number will increase to over 50% by the year 2020 (Pallas, Natriello, & McDill, 1989). This increase is even more pronounced in urban districts. In 1994, non-white students comprised about 72% of the total school enrollment in the twenty-five largest school districts in the U.S., and this percentage is expected to continue to grow (National Center for Education Statistics, 1997).

Not only are classrooms becoming more diverse in terms of race, ethnicity, socioeconomic status, and language, but increasing numbers of students with disabilities are also being included in the regular education classroom. Research from the U.S. Department of Education (2006) shows, for example, between 1995 and 2004, the percentage of students with disabilities educated in regular classes for most of the day increased from 45.3% to 52.1% (see Figure 1.8).

These statistics demonstrate how our nation's classrooms are changing. On a positive note, these changes provide a culturally rich educational environment, which enables educators to better prepare students to be a part of the global community. It also means, however, that today's teachers must be prepared to meet a variety of individual learning needs.

Individualizing Education

Today's teachers are being increasingly challenged to meet the needs of students who show a wide range of individual differences in learning, behavior, and cultural experience (Whitten & Dieker, 1995; Gay, 2006). The traditional educational model of one teacher successfully teaching twenty to thirty students is being challenged more frequently as general education teachers are faced with a greater variety of student learning needs (Safran & Safran, 1996). As noted above, a general education classroom may be comprised of students who have very different backgrounds. Additionally, regular education teachers are spending more time with students with disabilities. While students

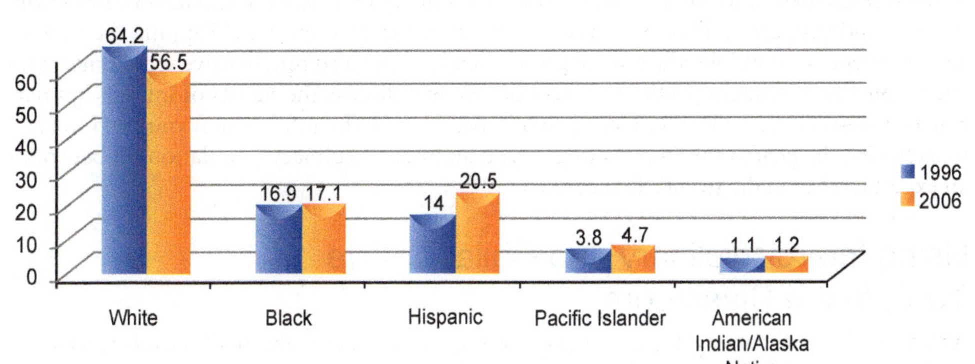

Figure 1.7

The Increase of Diversity in the American Classroom

SOURCE: U.S. Department of Education, National Center for Education Statistics, Current Population Survey, *Digest of Educational Statistics,* 2008.

Figure 1.8

Percentage of Students Ages 6 Through 21 with Disabilities Receiving Special Education and Related Services Under IDEA, Part B, by Educational Environment: Fall 1995 Through 2004

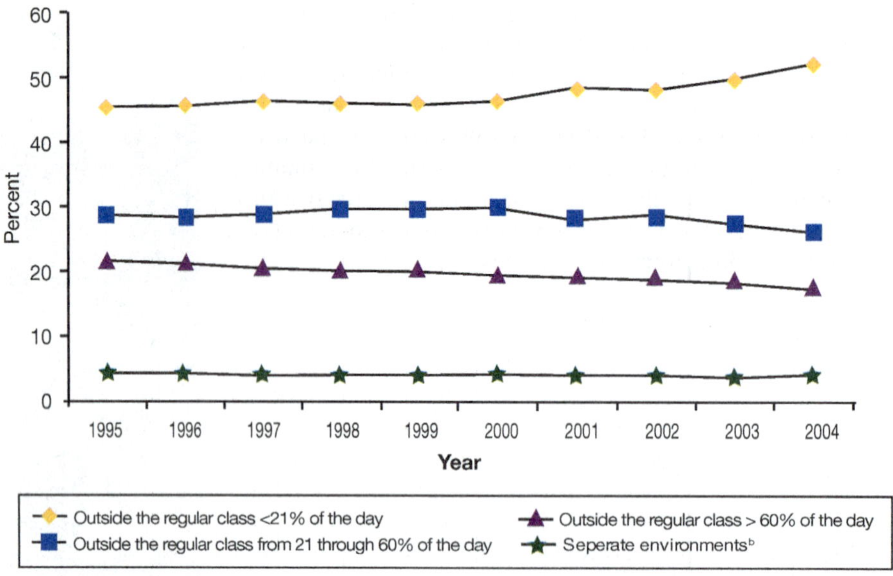

SOURCE: U.S. Department of Education, Office of Special Education Programs, Data Analysis System (DANS), OMB #1820–0517: "Part B, *Individuals with Disabilities Education Act*, Implementation of FAPE Requirements," 1995–2004. Data updated as of July 30, 2005. Also table 2–5 in vol. 2 of this report. These data are for the 50 states, District of Columbia, BIA schools, Puerto Rico, and the four outlying areas.

[a] Percentage was calculated by dividing the number of students ages 6 through 21 with disabilities in the educational environment by the number of students ages 6 through 21 with disabilities in all environments. The result was multiplied by 100 to produce a percentage.

[b] The category of separate environments includes public and private *residential facilities, public* and *private separate schools* and *homebound/hospital environments*.

with disabilities receive special education support according to federal special education law, the amount of support depends on the learning needs of the individual (IDEIA, 2004). Further, many students who do not meet the criteria for special education may also have significant learning and behavioral needs (Wang, Reynolds, & Walberg, 1994/1995). These students do not qualify for formalized special education support, yet they have specific individual learning needs and are often difficult to teach (Safran & Safran, 1996). These challenges make speaking of the "typical" student increasingly difficult. There are likely to be large individual differences—and wide-ranging learning needs—among students in any given classroom. This led many researchers to focus on how our nation's teacher training programs are preparing teachers for this new American classroom.

Banks (1991) proposes that teacher education programs embrace a multicultural education focus, so they can "receive the knowledge, skills, and attitudes needed to work effectively with students from diverse racial, ethnic, and social class groups." Safran and Safran (1996) assert that in order to effectively meet the needs of all students, teachers must receive knowledgeable training which includes "(a) the atypical student, (b) ways to manage and actually teach a classroom with a vast range of individual differences, (c) changing attitudes and skills about professional collaboration, and (d) resources beyond the public schools." In short, today's teachers are faced with the challenge of teaching students who may need more than standard programming, and these teachers need an avenue for developing the professional knowledge necessary to effectively teach these students. As a result, interdisciplinary knowledge and collaboration among teachers and supporting personnel has become increasingly important. Tapping the training and experience of multiple educational professionals brings a comprehensive set of skills to the educational environment. In the next section, we will discuss the merits of interdisciplinary collaboration. While no textbook can provide you with all the information you need to teach successfully, the goal of this book is to give you an interdisciplinary foundation for becoming an expert teacher in the twenty-first century.

Using Interdisciplinary and Collaborative Tools in the Classroom

As we have been discussing, the long-held view that one teacher is able to effectively teach every student in his or her classroom does not match the reality of education today. In many ways, developing expertise in teaching in the twenty-first century requires more extensive professional knowledge than ever before. Recall our discussion of expert teaching. Expert teachers show knowledge of subject matter, knowledge of teaching methods, and knowledge of how to use these methods when teaching a particular subject. They also show knowledge about how to *adapt* their teaching for students with different learning needs. In this era of increasing individual difference in the classroom, this aspect of expertise may be the most difficult to achieve. Professional collaboration can help teachers move beyond their own knowledge to produce creative solutions for meeting individualized learning needs. **Interdisciplinary collaboration** involves the collaboration of educational professionals from a variety of disciplines (e.g., education, psychology, social work, medicine, behavior management, etc.) to produce learning environments sensitive to individual learning needs. Through collaborative and interdisciplinary interactions, teachers increase the professional knowledge they bring to the education of students. Additionally, through ongoing collaboration, teachers continue to learn and develop professionally. This increase in the scope of professional skill will better enable teachers to serve future students (Brown, Gable, Hendrickson, & Algozzine, 1991; Nelson, Houston, Hoffman, & Bradham, 2011; Bloodworth & Peterson, 2011).

Research indicates that general education teachers are better able to meet the individual learning needs of students when supported by colleagues with specialized knowledge.

Interdisciplinary collaboration

The collaboration of educational professionals from a variety of disciplines to produce learning environments sensitive to individual learning needs

What Is Educational Collaboration?

Research indicates that general education teachers are better able to meet the individual learning needs of students when supported by colleagues with specialized knowledge (Graden, 1989; Pugach & Johnson, 1989; Sulkowski, Wingfield, Jones, & Coulter, 2011). As mentioned in the previous section, student body diversification in terms of race/ethnicity, language, socioeconomic status, and other factors makes it difficult for a single teacher to meet the needs of all students.

In addition to these cultural factors, addressing the unique needs of students with disabilities requires specialized knowledge and training. In fact, some researchers assert that part of the reason for the continuing increases in the number of students referred for special education may be based in the inadequacies of support systems available for teachers (Reschly, 1988; Nelson, Smith, Taylor, Dodd, & Reavis, 1991; Ajayi, 2011). In other words, when general education teachers are faced with these students, they may not have the knowledge necessary to intervene effectively. This may result in some children being referred for special education who could have their learning needs met by the general education teacher—if appropriate supports were available. For this reason, many schools have adopted pre-referral intervention or collaborative assistance models to support general education teachers in meeting the needs of a diverse student body (Whitten & Dieker, 1995; Safran & Safran, 1996).

Pre-referral means that students, who would normally be referred for special education services, receive intervention prior to the referral. The hope is that effective intervention can take place in the regular education classroom through a collaborative relationship between the general education teacher and other professionals. This eases the burden on special education by making better use of existing educational expertise. Federal legislation actually encourages states to use 15% of special education funds for pre-referral approaches (IDEIA, 2004). Pre-referral (or individual assistance models) provides teachers with guidelines and support for using collaborative relationships.

F.A.Q.

Bev Reynolds—"The idea of interdisciplinary collaboration is a little confusing. Is this like when we talked about Educational Psychology having roots in the disciplines of Education and Psychology?"

Professor Walberg—"Actually there is an important distinction here. Educational Psychology isn't really interdisciplinary because it isn't a field that involves the collaboration of two distinct fields. It is its own field. Here we are talking about interdisciplinary in the sense that schools are increasingly using collaboration between educational professionals from different disciplines to help support student learning."

Individual Assistance Models

Fuchs, Fuchs, and Bahr (1990) describe pre-referral intervention as accommodating the learning needs of students with more specialized needs through modified instruction or classroom management. The general education teacher undertakes these interventions, with assistance via consultation or collaboration with other professionals who contribute their knowledge and problem solving skills (Fuchs, Fuchs, Bahr, Fernstrom, & Stecker, 1990). While many teachers informally seek support from colleagues (Whitten & Dieker, 1995), some schools have initiated a formal approach for this type of collaboration. These support programs have many different names, such as individual assistance, pre-referral intervention, or mainstream assistance teams (Safran & Safran, 1996). These approaches provide teachers with a formalized avenue for interacting with other education professionals when trying to meet the individualized learning needs of students; they can reduce the stress teachers face when dealing with learning issues (Lhospital & Gregory, 2009). Through these interdisciplinary collaborations, effective interventions take advantage of the multiple perspectives and levels of expertise of the team members (Bay & O'Connor, 1994). There are, however, team needs that must be met for successful collaboration to occur—such as sufficient staff training in team procedures, adequate number of staff members, and sufficient time for collaboration to occur (Yetter & Doll, 2007). For example, consider Mr. Armani who is a fourth grade teacher. He has been working with his students on subtracting multiple digit numbers involving regrouping. The class is doing well, but three students are significantly behind. Two of these students are in special education and have a history of difficulty with mathematics. The third student, Sarah, has typically done well in math and has no difficulty with her other subjects. Mr. Armani is concerned about her progress and would like to implement an intervention before Sarah falls so far behind that she needs a referral for a special education assessment. Mr. Armani begins by speaking with his schools pre-referral intervention team. The team suggests an initial interview with her parents to determine if there are any issues at home contributing to her difficulties. It turns out that her parents are in the process of separating, and Sarah is having difficulty adjusting to that news. Her normally neat room is disorganized, and she fails to clean it properly when asked. She does not return home from the neighbor's house at a pre-agreed upon time. She also appears distracted during homework. All of these issues began when her parents told her about the impending separation. Mr. Armani begins to reexamine Sarah's classroom work in light of this new information. He noticed that her problem is not with mechanics but with her ability to follow a step-by-step process required to solve the problems. She appears to skip steps, rushing to get to a solution.

Mr. Armani discusses the situation with her parents and the pre-referral intervention team at the school. They decide to ask for assistance from the school social worker. The social worker is at Sarah's school on Thursdays and has time to see her for thirty minutes at the end of her regularly scheduled appointments. The social worker's goal is to assess Sarah's perception of her parent's separation and to work on her adjustment to the situation. The intervention team also arranges for Sarah to spend time with a sixth grade student twice a week to help her work on problems in a careful step-by-step manner. Finally, Mr. Armani sets up a meeting with Mr. Krauss who teaches Sarah's brother. He hopes to determine if her brother is experiencing similar difficulties.

This example illustrates the benefit of using a pre-referral team to help provide programming for at-risk students. Often schools are able to use existing resources to help support students who are experiencing difficulty. The team model also helps school professionals and parents use the broader range of services available to an intervention team, compared to the services of any single team member. The collaborative work of professionals does not always circumvent a student's need for special education; it does, however, provide a framework for educational professionals to work as a team to provide all students with the best learning environment.

Research on pre-referral interventions suggests a positive influence on student learning and behavior. Most studies have not focused on student outcomes (Rock & Zigmond, 2001) but on reduction in special education placements. University led collaborative programs clearly show that this approach results in decreases in the number of students identified for special education (Chalfant & Pysh, 1989; Graden, Casey, & Bronstrom, 1985; Fuchs, Fuchs, & Bahr, 1990; Hoover, 2010). A number of different intervention approaches are being implemented in the field, however; and some research suggests that intervention quality may have a significant impact on whether numbers of students identified for special education actually decrease (Flugum & Reschly, 1994). For example, quality programs specifically address such issues as keeping the lines of communication open among professionals, making time for appropriate and consistent consultation, and providing needed educational materials. Another line of research on intervention assistance models has focused on the attitudes and beliefs of teachers. While studies show mixed results regarding teachers' belief in intervention assistance programs (Rock & Zigmond, 2001), they do report decreased feelings of helplessness and frustration (Ingalls & Hammond, 1996).

SUMMARIZE AND REFLECT

1. Changes in today's classrooms have led to a greater emphasis on how collaborative teaching models can help address evolving student needs.
2. The American student population is changing with respect to socioeconomic status, ethnicity, and ability level. Such changes have underscored the need to tailor education to the individual needs of students.
3. Teachers do not need to work in isolation to educate. Instead they can work in collaboration with others, building on the strengths of colleagues.
4. Working in an interdisciplinary environment allows students to benefit from multiple educators with unique talents and skills. This greater pool of resources makes it more likely that each student will receive instruction appropriate to their individual needs.

INFORMED APPLICATION

1. You have a new student in your class this year. The student was formally educated in a self-contained classroom for students with intellectual limitations. The school district decided that these students would be better served in the regular classroom. You assume you will be working closely with the special educator, but what other collaborative relations could help you meet the needs of your new student?
2. Your school has developed a system for helping teachers address students who are failing to learn at a typical rate. This pre-referral system is intended to serve as an intervention approach prior to any special education referral. Your principal has asked you to serve on the pre-referral team. What unique skills and knowledge could you bring to the team to help enhance their intervention efforts?

THE CHAPTER IN REVIEW

Check out our website ▶ www.BVTLab.com for chapter-by-chapter flashcards, practice quizzes, summaries, and more.

In this chapter, we began by reviewing the field of educational psychology. Educational psychology is a relatively new field of scientific inquiry. It merges research from psychology on thinking, reasoning, and human behavior with research on educational best practices. We then explored the importance of this field for educators, emphasizing the importance for communication between practicing teachers and researchers. This communication helps focus research in directions that are more relevant to real-life teaching environments. We also discussed how education is under constant scrutiny and how society is making increased demands for science-based educational practices. Educational psychologists engage in research designed to address this need. Also, educators are practicing science every day in their classrooms as they investigate what works and what needs improvement. They constantly engage in what is known as action research.

The second part of the chapter examined the qualities typical of expert teachers. A researcher often focuses on expert teachers as a source of information regarding important teacher characteristics. Early research in this area has shown expert teachers have several common characteristics. Expert teachers are well versed in their subject matter, possess an extensive knowledge of general teaching practices, and have a sound base of knowledge for making educational decisions. We also looked at current research into expert teaching that moves away from detailing specific characteristics and instead focuses on "fuzzy" or more general characteristics. General areas that have surfaced as important indicators of expertise include knowledge, efficiency, and insight.

The final section of the chapter examines how today's classrooms are becoming increasingly diverse. This leads to a greater need to tailor education so the unique needs of each student are met. At times, this is difficult for a single teacher, necessitating the collaboration of multiple educational professionals. Most schools recognize this need for increased collaboration among educators. Schools have already had similar collaborative models in place for students in special education. More progressive schools realize that implementing a similar model for all students helps insure education is meeting the unique needs of each student. Some of these schools have informal mechanisms for collaboration, while others have well-developed systems to promote interdisciplinary collaboration.

Interdisciplinary Case Focus

principal special educator
teacher parents psychologist
social worker physical educator
nurse peers doctor

Meet the Team An Interdisciplinary Case Focus is presented at the end of each chapter. This feature gives the reader examples of how interdisciplinary cooperation helps create effective learning environments. There are many ways to put together a team of dedicated individuals to help support student learning. Sometimes the regular education teacher simply coordinates with the parent to address isolated issues. Other situations necessitate a broader team, drawing on the skills of a variety of professionals.

This first Interdisciplinary Case Focus introduces you to the professions typically involved in collaborative education.

Regular Educator The regular educator (primary, secondary, physical, health, etc.) is the central person involved in interdisciplinary education. As the primary instructor of students in the general education program, the regular education teacher is often responsible for intervention implementation and overall coordination of the process. Preparation of regular education teachers varies by state, but generally includes a bachelor's or master's degree in education and additional preparation to teach specific subject areas.

Parent The parent or guardian is a crucial member of any educational team. Without close collaboration with the parent, interventions tend to be inconsistent. The parent is the best source of information about the student's history and provides the group with information on the student's life outside school. Additionally, parents frequently bring their own professional expertise.

Special Educator The special educator works with a student's individual learning needs. He/she specifically coordinates the education of students in the special education program and also plays a role in the education of students in the regular education program. Training of special educators usually consists of a bachelor's or master's degree. Preparation programs may be specifically in special education or a dual program of both regular and special education. Often special educators have expertise with specific populations (i.e., learning disabilities, autism, hearing impaired, etc.).

Social Worker Social work is an extremely versatile field. Social workers address a wide variety of issues related to personal improvement. Social workers who specialize in education work with family life issues, interpersonal problems, traumatic events, etc. Typically, the focus of their work is to establish a sense of well-being and to promote academic achievement. Training in social work can be at the bachelor's level, but most states require a master's degree for certification.

Psychologist The psychologist usually plays one of two roles in an educational situation. The first role is to provide assessment of cognitive and behavioral functioning, which leads to appropriate recommendations. The psychologist may also play a role similar to the social worker and may also provide direct clinical treatment, helping students through a particular life issue. Training for the psychologist involved in school systems is at the master's or doctoral level.

Speech Language Pathologist The speech language pathologist handles problems with speech sounds or the ability to communicate effectively and addresses problems with fluency, articulation, and abnormalities of voice quality. He/she also helps students who have difficulty understanding what people say to them or with how they express themselves. Training for the speech language pathologist is typically at the bachelor's or master's degree level.

Behavior Specialist Individuals with specific training in helping behavioral issues is increasing in popularity. These individuals assess and treat behavioral problems. They work closely with the regular educator to develop interventions that continue once the behavior specialist is no longer involved. The training of the behavior specialist is becoming more consistent with national organizations providing standards for professional certification. Behavioral specialists often work with a bachelor's degree, but many have master's and doctoral degrees in the field.

This preview provides you with a brief overview of the individuals involved in education today. Depending on the nature of the situation, other professionals may participate on an intervention team (e.g., medical, administration, etc.). The Interdisciplinary Case Focus presented at the end of each chapter provides you with situations illustrating how these individuals work together to produce effective education that is sensitive to the unique needs of the student.

Key Terms

TERM	*Page*	*TERM*	*Page*
A-B-A-B single-participant design	10	Empirical	6
Action research	14	Experimental group	7
Baseline	10	Experimental research	7
Case study	11	Generalization	8
Comparable groups	8	Independent variable	7
Control group	7	Interdisciplinary collaboration	21
Correlation	12	Manipulation	7
Correlational coefficient	12	No Child Left Behind	6
Correlational studies	12	Random assignment	7
Dependent variable	7	Randomized trials	8
Descriptive research method	11	Reflective teaching	14
Direction	13	Single-participant research	8
Educational psychology	4	Strength	12

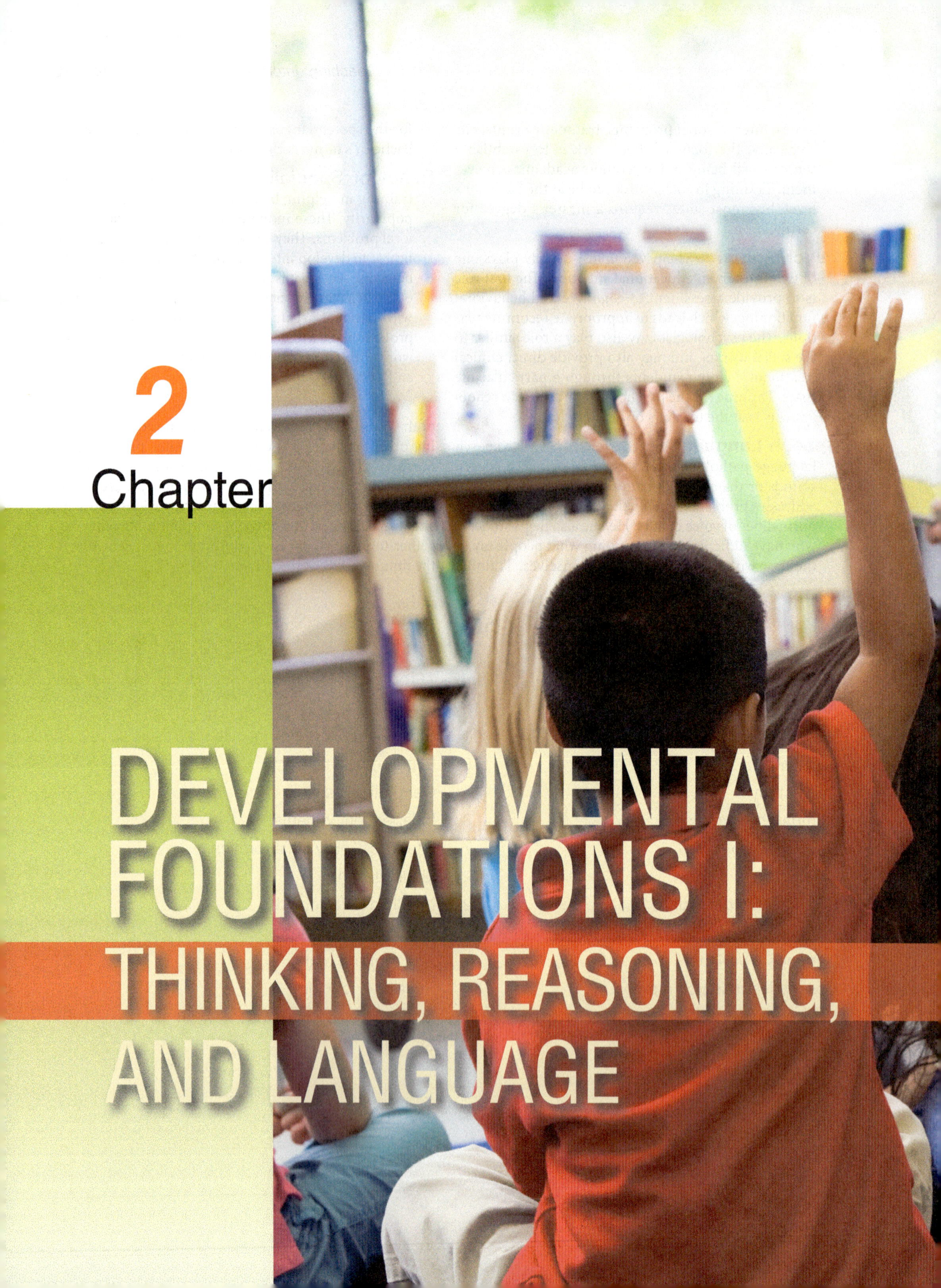

2

Chapter

DEVELOPMENTAL FOUNDATIONS I: THINKING, REASONING, AND LANGUAGE

What's It All About ...

What is development? How do we develop over time?

What do we know about the brain and development?

How do social interactions affect the development of our thinking and impact our teaching?

When do we achieve specific developmental skills and how does this relate to instruction?

How do we acquire language? What exactly is acquired?

Chapter Objectives

- Understand basic theories related to the developmental perspective.
- Appreciate the developmental path and its implications for understanding the whole person.

- Understand basic brain processes.
- Review the basics of the developmental neuroscience perspective.
- Learn different ways that an appreciation of developmental neuroscience can help promote effective education.

- Appreciate the difference between *what* cognitive skills develop over time versus *how* they develop.
- Understand the importance of Vygotsky's views on social interactions and language.
- Review the concepts of zone of proximal development and scaffolding.

- Learn the general principles guiding the work of Piaget.
- Understand the stages of Piaget's developmental theory.
- Evaluate Piaget's theory.
- Apply Piagetian theory to developmentally appropriate instruction.
- Compare Piaget's and Vygotsky's theories

- Learn the different components of language.
- Understand different language acquisition theories.

EXTENDED OUTLINE

Developmental Foundations I: Thinking, Reasoning, and Language

I. What's It All About …

II. From Today's Headlines

III. Typical Development and Developmental Differences
   - A. The developmental process
     1. Defining development
     2. Principles of development
        - a. Principle #1—development proceeds at different rates
        - b. Principle #2—development is an orderly and gradual process
        - c. Principle #3—development occurs in a sociocultural context
   - B. Developmental differences: relative perspective
     1. Interindividual comparisons
     2. Intraindividual comparisons
   - C. Summarize and reflect

IV. Cognition and Developmental Neuroscience
   - A. Basic brain processes
   - B. Developmental neuroscience
   - C. Implications for teaching and learning
   - D. Summarize and reflect

V. Vygotsky and the Interactive Nature of Thinking
   - A. Perspectives on development: which skills develop versus how skills develop
   - B. The importance of social interaction and language
   - C. Instruction: the zone of proximal development and scaffolding
   - D. Summarize and reflect

VI. Piaget and the Inquisitive Child
   - A. Basic principles
   - B. Stages of development
     1. Sensorimotor
     2. Preoperational
     3. Concrete operations
     4. Formal operations
   - C. Evaluating Piaget's theory
     1. Underestimating the abilities of children
     2. Overestimating the abilities of adolescents
     3. Cognitive development and culture
     4. Limited explanations for cognitive changes
     5. Extending Piaget's theory: neo-Piagetian theory and brain research

- D. Piaget and developmentally appropriate instruction
  1. Use disequilibrium to motivate
  2. Appreciate the construction of knowledge
  3. Build understanding
- E. Piaget and Vygotsky: important comparisons
- F. Summarize and reflect

VII. Language Development
- A. Components of language
- B. Language acquisition theories
  1. Reinforcement versus maturation
  2. Interactionist perspective
- C. Language and linguistic diversity in the classroom
  1. Phonology
  2. Morphology
  3. Semantics
  4. Syntax
  5. Pragmatics
- D. Summarize and reflect

VIII. The Chapter in Review

IX. Interdisciplinary Case Focus

From Today's Headlines

Vol. I No. 2 Teaching World, 2012

HOW DO SOCIAL INTERACTIONS IMPACT DEVELOPMENT?

For eight years, Ground Hog Day has been about more than weather predictions. February 2 is also the observance of *Job Shadowing Day.* This is a nationwide event bringing over a million young people into the work place. Students begin the process by shadowing a mentor at a place of employment. Students are matched with mentors from all facets of the workplace—including marketing, retail, finance, communications, advertising, the sciences, and education. Students get a firsthand look at possible job sites and interact one-on-one with a mentor. Although the mentoring experience begins in February, programming is scheduled throughout the year.

Students report many positive outcomes from such an experience. For example, they learn about the realities of being a manager at a local retail store or a newscaster on the evening news. They learn this through a structured mentoring relationship with someone working in the field. This relationship teaches them how to think about the workplace.

It also helps them learn about the structure of a particular work environment, and how to operate and problem solve within that context.

This approach to learning has many advantages. The close connection between the learner and the teacher makes education very personable and sensitive to the unique needs of the individual. The mentor provides valuable modeling of real-life, work-related behaviors and also gives the learner tools for thinking about the career.

MAKE THE CONNECTION

Job shadowing is an excellent example of the power of social relationships to help guide the learning process. Social relations can influence the development of what we do and the way in which we think. In this chapter, we will first take a look at the general concept of development. Then we will specifically look at the development of our thinking and reasoning ability. Like the Job Shadowing Program, educators are becoming increasingly sensitive to the social environment of students and how to use that environment to support the process of learning. We will also examine specific skills developing over our lives, including our incredible capacity for communication.

TYPICAL DEVELOPMENT AND DEVELOPMENTAL DIFFERENCES

Next time you're in class, look around you. We are all unique, special, and different; yet, most of us took our first steps within six months of each other and said our first word when we were about a year old. We all learned to hold a pencil, went to our first day of school, dealt with fractions in third or fourth grade, and handled the social and academic complexities of high school. Within this similarity, however, is uniqueness. A few of us had trouble learning to hold a pencil, some of us loved fractions, and some of us excelled academically in high school. If you are one of the few students who did not struggle at all with fractions, you are not considered abnormal—yet you did develop differently. Your love of fractions may have developed for a variety of reasons, such as your analytical ability, brain organization, parental involvement, or motivating teacher. Likely, however, a combination of developmental, psychosocial, and educational factors interacted to influence your success with this form of math. Further, your success with fractions probably influenced your success in mastering more advanced math concepts. Thus, the interaction among many domains of development has important implications for teaching and learning.

This chapter addresses the similarities in our development, as well as the differences we demonstrate along the way. We will introduce you to the new field of cognitive neuroscience and outline the ways in which research on brain development may update our understanding of developmental similarities and differences. We will also explore the ideas of the influential theorists Lev Vygotsky and Jean Piaget, applying their theories to children's thinking and learning development. Finally, we focus in on a very special developmental process—the development of language. We will explore theories of language development and outline the basic components of language. We will also outline how language differences affect teaching and learning.

The Developmental Process

People are constantly changing throughout their lifespans. Children's bodies undergo enormous changes as they progress from helpless newborn to coordinated toddler. Children also go through changes in their ability to think about their world. They learn to communicate using sophisticated language tools. They also learn to interact with others in socially complex ways. These changes represent our unique human experiences, and researchers have gathered an impressive body of knowledge regarding this process. Let's turn now to a look at some of the concepts that lay the groundwork for a study of development.

Development

Systematic continuities and changes in the individual over the course of life

Adaptations

Environmentally dependent changes that allow us to better function in the world

Defining Development

Development refers to systematic continuities and changes in the individual over the course of life (Shaffer & Kipp, 2010). Developmental changes are not transitory, like changes in mood, but follow a specific order and are relatively permanent. Some developmental changes are the result of adaptation. **Adaptations** are environmentally dependent changes that allow us to better function in the world. For example, when a child who has had no experience in a structured pre-K program enters school, she may have difficulty sitting during circle time, being quiet while her teacher is talking, and raising her hand to speak during class time. As she gains experience in her new environment, however, she is likely to adapt, changing her behavior to better meet the demands of the classroom.

As students gain experience in a class environment they will generally adapt to meet the demands of their classroom.

There are many ways that we might change to become better suited to our environment. We might change the way we think about ourselves (personal development), the way we interact with others (social development), or as the example above indicates, the way we regulate our own behavior (self-regulation development). We may also make adaptive changes in the way we think or remember (cognitive development), depending on our experiences. A third grader who has had great difficulty memorizing his multiplication tables might be taught to use physical movement and rhythm while rehearsing the multiplication facts—a memory strategy designed to engage both verbal and nonverbal areas of the brain. As he adapts or changes his memorization strategies, he greatly improves his recall of the multiplication facts, effectively meeting the environmental demands of third grade math. This type of developmental change is very different from maturation. **Maturation** refers to changes occurring naturally, irrespective of environmental demands. Maturational changes are largely genetically driven. For example, we are all genetically programmed to reach a certain height; and this is likely to be unaffected by the environment, unless we experience severe malnutrition or physical injury.

Maturation

Changes occurring naturally, irrespective of environmental demands

Often, we must reach a certain maturational level before we can acquire a particular skill. Take for example an eight-month-old infant who is just learning to crawl. Walking would clearly allow her to move about the world more easily; yet until her musculature develops enough to support walking, this adaptive skill cannot be achieved. Clearly, maturation is important in the development of walking. It is, however, much more difficult to determine the role of maturation in more complex human behaviors such as cognition, language, and socialization. Maturation and adaptation interact in complex ways, making it difficult to tease apart the specific role of either process as development becomes more complex. This leads us to the first of three important developmental principles.

Principles of Development

Principle #1—Development proceeds at different rates Although there are similarities in our development, we each progress at a unique developmental pace. This individual pacing occurs for both maturation and adaptation based development. Take puberty, for example. Some of us began to show pubertal changes at ten or eleven years of age, while others showed no signs of puberty until the age of thirteen or fourteen. We all went through similar physical changes, yet the process began at varying times, impacting other aspects of our functioning. When we reached puberty, we learned to adapt and incorporated these new feelings and physical characteristics into our lives. For some of us, adapting to change is easy; for others, the experience is more difficult. There are likely many factors playing a role in whether the experience is positive or negative for a given individual. Research shows that the way we adapt to the changes of puberty is strongly related to maturational timing, or how early we enter puberty. Males who enter puberty at younger ages are likely to be more popular and to be given more responsibilities from adults (Simmons & Blyth, 1987), while females who enter puberty early are more likely to experience social difficulties and lack self-confidence (Peterson, 1985; Blumenthal et al., 2011). Thus, individual variation in rate of development may interact with rate of social adaptation, which may in turn influence other areas of development.

Principle #2—Development is an orderly and gradual process Most of us crawled before we walked and walked before we ran. This example of the progressive development of motor skills illustrates the orderly progression of skill acquisition that occurs in children. Further, we did not learn to walk in an hour or a day but learned gradually, over the course of many years. The developmental progression of motor skills is less complicated, and easier to quantify, than determining the sequence of cognitive development. However, most theorists agree that cognitive development also proceeds in a systematic, orderly, and gradual manner. Theorists, however, disagree about particular cognitive milestones and their sequence in cognitive development.

Principle #3—Development occurs in a sociocultural context Different cultures, subcultures, social classes, racial or ethnic groups, and disability groups have unique socialization experiences, which exert strong influences on the values, beliefs, and competencies of individuals who are members of the group (Rogoff & Chavajay, 1995; Martin, 2007; Cole & Packer,

2011). By viewing development as occurring within social, cultural, and historical contexts, we lay the foundation for developing an understanding and appreciation of diversity and multiculturalism. This requires a more encompassing conceptualization of *difference*, which leads us to the next section on developmental differences.

Developmental Differences: Relative Perspective

In this section, we will explore the concept of developmental differences, an observable phenomenon in every classroom. Whenever we talk about difference, we are automatically making a comparison. Take Charlie, for example, who is able to read fluidly. Although we know something important about his academic level, we don't know if his skill in this area differs from those of other children. If we learn that Charlie is only four years old, however, we can compare him to other four-year-olds and see that his reading skills are clearly above average. This determination of difference was made based on an **interindividual comparison**, or a comparison between children. We may also be interested in making **intraindividual comparisons**, or comparisons within an individual. In Charlie's case, we might wish to know if he is advanced in other areas of development, as well as in reading, before we can determine an appropriate educational placement. We could compare his functioning in many different areas to determine areas of strength and weakness, outlining an academic plan to best suit his individual needs. Thus, the concept of difference is always relative, involving comparisons between or within individuals.

Interindividual comparison

A comparison between individuals

Intraindividual comparison

A comparison within an individual

Interindividual Comparisons

As our classrooms become increasingly diverse with regard to student culture, social class, race, ethnicity, and disability status, we are faced with the important task of providing educational experiences that support student differences. While the needs of students with significant developmental delays are usually addressed through Special Education, many students have developmental differences that do not meet criteria for inclusion in this program. This means today's regular education teachers are expected, more than ever, to work with students who have a variety of educational needs. This makes an understanding of developmental difference central to the field of education.

Developmental theorists have long debated the nature of developmental difference. Some argue that individuals with an atypical developmental progression are simply delayed in their development, acquiring the usual set of skills but at a slower rate. Others argue that individuals with atypical development are acquiring a different set of skills and are qualitatively different from those following a typical developmental path. Yet, how different does a child have to be from what is considered typical before that difference is seen as a problem rather than a manifestation of individual variation? We can answer this question by quantifying the difference, as we will discuss at length in Chapter 10; however, the answer almost always involves some measure of subjective judgment. Recall the important developmental principle discussed earlier in the chapter that development proceeds at different rates. This, in fact, dictates that we should *expect* variations in development between individuals, both within and between groups. A study of the behavior of children with autism illustrates this concept. The researchers explored whether the daily living skills of children with autism were qualitatively different (different in type) or simply delayed when compared to children with mental retardation or a group of typically developing children (VanMeter, Fein, Morris, Waterhouse & Allen, 1997). Results indicated that the pattern of daily living skills of children with autism *as a group* was indeed different, not just delayed, when compared to the other groups. They also noted, however, that the patterns of daily living skills were highly variable within the group of children with autism. This study illustrates the importance of considering individual

Today's regular education teachers are expected, more than ever, to work with students who have a variety of educational needs, such as autism.

differences, even among individuals who are grouped based on certain atypical traits. Thus, it is important to look closely at patterns of behavior *within* an individual, intraindividual, in addition to making comparisons *between* individuals, interindividual, (Weinert & Helmke, 1998; Molenaar, Huizenga, & Nesselroade, 2003). This leads us to the next section, which emphasizes the importance of understanding intraindividual strengths and weaknesses.

Intraindividual Comparisons

In searching for an understanding of why discrepancies or differences in human development exist, it is easy to narrowly focus on differences between individuals (interindividual). By focusing on the way a child differs from others, we often lose sight of interacting strengths and weaknesses within the child. For example, if Samantha develops a problem with aggression, parents and teachers typically direct their attention to normalizing her behavior relative to other children. They want her to act more like other children. This approach may bring about change in Samantha's behavior, but Samantha does not experience her occasional acts of aggression as isolated events in an otherwise peaceful day. In fact, her aggressive actions are only one manifestation of her complex experience of the world. Attempts to understand the aggression by looking only at Samantha's overt (observable) actions is like trying to understand how to drive a car by looking only at the steering wheel. Although focusing on specific issues may produce results, effective intervention is best achieved by understanding the complexities of the whole person.

One way to think about the whole person is to imagine an individual as a composite of many dimensions. For example, on the passivity-aggression dimension, Samantha might tend toward aggressive behaviors and prefer to be physically confrontational, as opposed to reserved and accepting of frustrating situations.

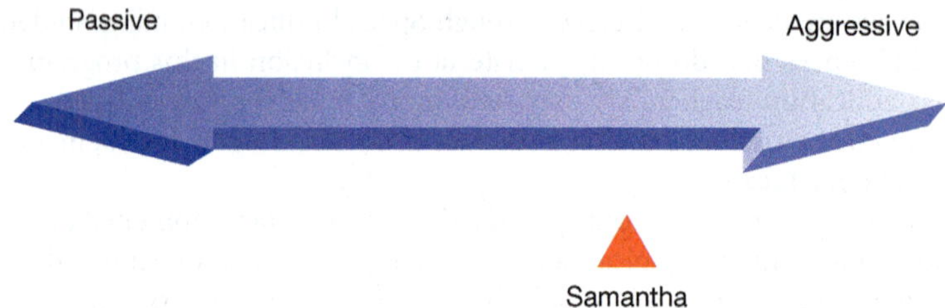

This is, however, only one of Samantha's many personal dimensions. We could also look at an infinite number of other dimensions, such as emotionality, communications skills, intellectual ability, or sociability. If you think of all of these dimensions as lines extending from a single point in all directions, the resulting shape would be a spherical (Figure 2.1). Unlike a typical sphere, this one would have an irregular surface. There would be depressions representing dimensional categories that are less developed. There would also be peaks representing areas of strength. This dimensional model helps us appreciate how an issue in a specific developmental dimension is best understood in the context of the whole person. For example, Figure 2.1 shows such a dimensional model for Samantha, who has problems with aggression. The multi-colored sphere represents a composite of all Samantha's behavioral and cognitive dimensions. Sample dimensions are labeled as lines extending from the center of the sphere. Black lines represent areas where Samantha has limitations. Orange lines represent dimensions of functioning that are typical. Gray lines represent areas that are in excess of what is typical. This example shows that not only does Samantha have an excessive number of aggressive behaviors but also that she is highly emotional and easily frustrated. Further, and most importantly, she has significant deficits in communication skills, a component which likely impacts her frustration level, emotionality, and aggression. Given this additional information regarding other dimensions of Samantha's functioning, it is clear that her behavior problem would be addressed most effectively by focusing on her communication skills, as well as her aggressive behavior.

This dimensional model of intraindividual difference is particularly important in educational settings since all students have a unique learning style made up of different strengths and weaknesses (Kolb, 1984; Gardner, 1996). Considerable research has been undertaken to better

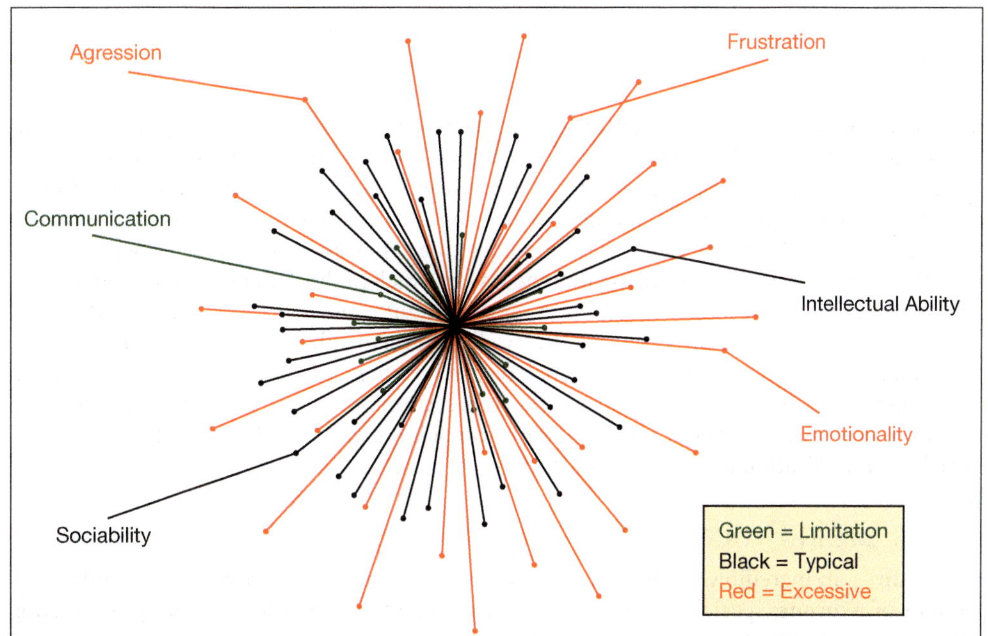

Figure 2.1
Dimensional Model for Samantha

understand the impact of different learning styles in the classroom, and research shows that effective learning is enhanced when teachers consider individual strengths and weakness when planning instruction (Reif, 1993; Dunn & Dunn, 1999; Mayer, 2011). Tailoring instruction to meet the needs of increasingly diverse learners is a central challenge for today's educators (NASBE, 2001), requiring knowledge of research and theory across many disciplines (Tate & Debroux, 2001).

SUMMARIZE AND REFLECT

1. Development refers to the ways we change over the course of a lifetime.
2. It is important to consider the interaction between adaptation and maturational types of development.
3. The following are the three major principles of development: a) Development proceeds at different rates. b) Development is an orderly and gradual process. c) Development occurs in a sociocultural context.
4. Discussion of interindividual differences underscores the importance of viewing typical and atypical development as existing on a continuum of functioning.
5. Intraindividual differences illustrate that a narrow focus on a specific problem area may result in a failure to appreciate more complex interactions among an individual's strengths and weaknesses.
6. Consideration of intraindividual differences is becoming more important as our classrooms become increasingly diverse with regard to student culture, social class, race, ethnicity, and disability status.
7. It is important to acquire interdisciplinary knowledge of research and theory in order to better meet the needs of all learners.

INFORMED APPLICATION

1. The second principle of development is that development is orderly and gradual. How would this principle affect a teacher's standard tenth-grade math curriculum for a student who demonstrates exceptional learning ability?
2. How could a teacher use the concept of interindividual and intraindividual differences to help a student who is reluctant to participate in science experiments?
3. Consider what fields of study you would investigate to help you deal with an increasingly hostile classroom divided along ethnic lines. How would you go about identifying knowledgeable educational professionals from these fields within your own school district?

COGNITION AND DEVELOPMENTAL NEUROSCIENCE

Cognitive neuroscience

The study of relations between the brain and thinking

Neurons

Specialized brain cells that send and receive information by conducting electrochemical impulses

Synapses

Tiny spaces across which neurons communicate with each other

Neurotransmitter

A chemical that is released from one neuron and received by another to facilitate communication between them

Synaptogenesis

A process in which neurons form synapses as a function of experience

Cerebral cortex

The area of the brain most directly implicated in thinking and learning

Cognitive neuroscience is the study of relations between the brain and thinking. We are learning about the brain and cognition at an exponential rate, and this research has many implications for educational practice. Neuroscience research complements our understanding of individual and developmental differences in learning and has been used as support for a variety of instructional styles. Some researchers argue that the application of neuroscience research to the classroom is premature, asserting that the way in which findings in neuroscience map onto what we know of development, cognition, and learning is unclear (Stanovich, 1998; Bruer, 1999; Dommett, Devonshire, Plateau, Westwell, & Greenfield, 2011). In order to critically evaluate generalizations from neuroscience research to the classroom, we need a functional understanding of the brain and its processes. This section provides a broad overview of brain function, as well as an introduction to major research findings in developmental neuroscience, which have application to teaching and learning.

Basic Brain Processes

The brain is an incredibly complex structure of the human body composed of hundreds of billions of **neurons**, specialized brain cells that send and receive information by conducting electrochemical impulses. Neurons communicate with each other across tiny spaces called **synapses** (Figure 2.2). Communication across the synapse is made possible by the transmission of chemical **neurotransmitters** that are released from one neuron and received by another. Neurons in the brain form synapses as a function of experience, a process known as **synaptogenesis**. As more and more synapses form among neurons, they begin to develop into organized circuits, or networks, allowing distant neurons in the brain to communicate with one another. The nature of neuronal communication is at least partially dependent on its physical location in the brain. Certain areas and structures in the brain are designed to carry out specialized functions.

The **cerebral cortex**, which is the area of the brain most directly implicated in thinking and learning, is one of the most highly specialized brain areas. The cerebral cortex can be divided into four different lobes: *frontal, temporal, parietal,* and *occipital* (Figure 2.3). Each of these brain areas is specialized for certain functions, although most human activities require many brain areas working together. For example, the **temporal lobe** is the part of the brain primarily involved in processing auditory information; yet in order to hear and interpret language, many different areas of the brain must work together. The temporal lobes are also important in memory and selective attention, with people who have temporal injuries exhibiting a wide range of problems related to auditory processing, verbal learning, and sensory integration (Kolb & Wishaw, 1990; Flinker, Chang, Barbaro, Berger, & Knight, 2011).

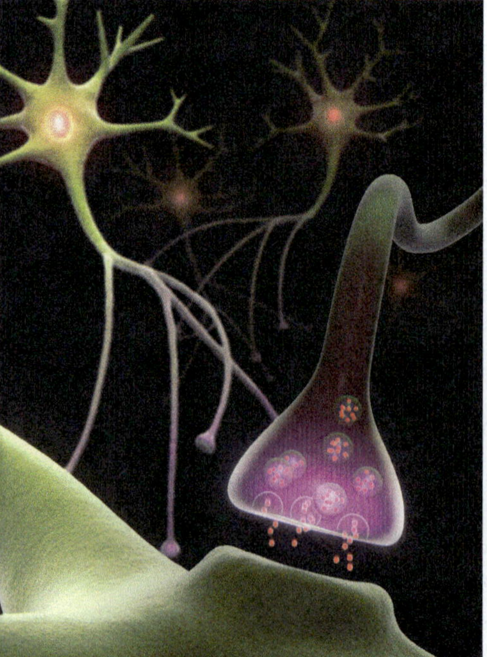

Figure 2.2

Synapses

The **frontal lobes** play a role in many human behaviors, including planning, anticipating consequences, and inhibiting behavior—behaviors, which are known collectively as *executive functions.* The frontal lobes also play a role in language, problem solving, and movement. People who have damage to this important brain area often have a wide variety of deficits

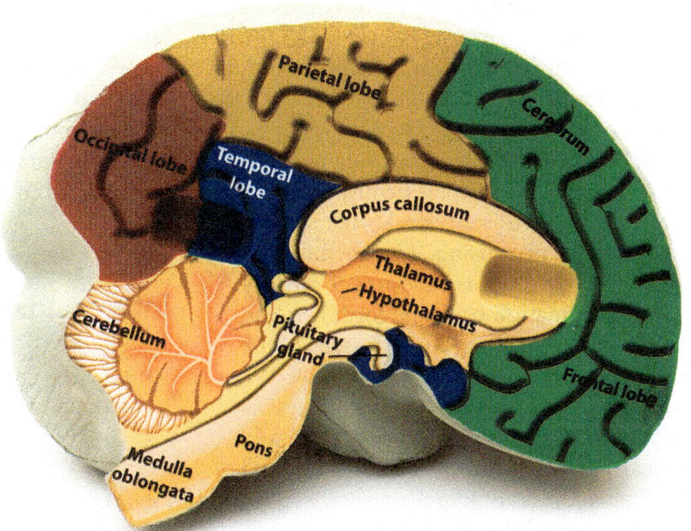

Figure 2.3

The Four Lobes of the Cerebral Cortex

(Kolb & Wishaw, 1990; Reilly, Rodriguez, Peele, & Grossman, 2011), including impulsive behavior, poor judgment, and difficulty planning for the future. This cognitive and behavioral profile is similar to the problems seen in children with attention deficit/hyperactivity disorder, or (AD/HD) (see Chapter 11), leading many researchers to believe this disorder may have origins in frontal lobes deficits (Barkley, 1998).

The **parietal lobes** are responsible for integrating somatosensory information, such as touch, temperature, and pain. The parietal lobes are also involved in spatial activities such as being able to visualize the way an object will look from different angles and understanding the relationship among objects in space. These skills strongly correlate with math performance (Friedman, 1995; Desco et al., 2011). Damage to the parietal lobes can result in problems with spatial relations, abnormalities in body image, and impaired body senses (Kandel, Schwartz, & Jessel, 1991).

The **occipital lobes** are primarily responsible for visual processing. Damage to this region can result in visual perceptual problems; and if the damage is extensive enough, blindness. Near the area of the juncture between the occipital, temporal, and parietal lobes lies an area of the brain called the angular gyrus, which is important in reading and writing activities (Shaywitz & Shaywitz, 1998). People who have damage to the area of the angular gyrus lose the ability to read and write, while language function is maintained.

Another important aspect of the cerebral cortex is that it is divided down the midline into left and right hemispheres, each of which contains all four lobes discussed above. The two cerebral hemispheres are connected by a band of axons called the corpus callosum. The **corpus callosum** allows information to travel back and forth between the left and the right sides of the brain. Each side of the brain has specialized functions similar to the specialization seen in the four lobes of the brain. First, the right side of the brain controls the motor functions of the left side of the body, and the left side of the brain controls the motor functions of the right side of the body. For example, moving your right arm results from a brain signal originating in the left hemisphere. We consider specialized brain functions lateralized when they are primarily controlled by one hemisphere. Like motor function, language ability is another **lateralized brain function**. In most right- and left-handed people, language is lateralized to the left hemisphere. The right hemisphere is more dominant for non-verbal, visuospatial, creativity, and emotional processing (Mihov, Denzler, & Forster, 2010). A few left-handed people show the opposite pattern, and some individuals show a mixed laterality, or a lack of hemispheric dominance. This mixed laterality

Interconnections

See Chapter 11 for a complete discussion of the identification and education of students with Attention Deficit/Hyperactivity Disorder.

Temporal lobe

The part of the brain primarily involved in processing auditory information

Frontal lobes

Portion of the brain that plays a role in many human behaviors, including planning, anticipating consequences, and inhibiting behavior

Parietal lobes

Portion of the brain that is responsible for integrating somatosensory information, such as touch, temperature, and pain

Occipital lobes

Portion of the brain that is primarily responsible for visual processing

Corpus callosum

Section of the brain that allows information to travel back and forth between the left and the right sides of the brain

Lateralized brain function

A specialized brain function primarily controlled by one hemisphere has been correlated with learning disabilities in reading; however, a causal relationship has not been established.

Left-brain/right-brain research is quite popular, and attempts have been made to develop teaching strategies designed to better engage one hemisphere or the other. The usefulness of left-brain/right-brain distinction in the classroom, however, is relatively limited. Although much of teaching and learning involves language, it is inaccurate to assume that the left hemisphere is in complete control in the classroom. While the left hemisphere may be more involved in the processing of verbal information, an intact corpus callosum constantly sends information back and forth between hemispheres resulting in both sides of the brain operating in all learning activities. We do have evidence, however, that when teaching a primarily left-hemisphere language task, such as learning the initial sounds of the letters of the alphabet, addition of a multisensory component to instruction (a practice which activates all of the brain's lobes in both hemispheres) can be highly effective (Wagmeister, 2000). While multisensory appro aches to instruction have often been cited as effective in the scientific literature (Moustafa, 1999), the neuroscience perspective offers us the ability to better explain *why* it's effective.

Interconnections

See Chapter 1 for a discussion of how to interpret a statistical correlation.

Developmental Neuroscience

Developmental neuroscience

The study of the orderly progression of changes in the brain that occur across the lifespan

Developmental neuroscience is the study of the orderly progression of changes in the brain that occur across the lifespan. Research from developmental neuroscience confirms much of what we already know and are already implementing in the classroom. What follows is a brief summary of some of the most exciting findings in this area and a discussion about generalizing findings to classroom practices.

First, research tells us that brain development is dependent on experience, or environmental input. Animals deprived of experiences during development do not develop connecting circuits in the brain, which are as complex and organized as animals that receive stimulation (Rakic, Bourgeois, & Goldman-Rakic, 1994). Further, raising animals in enriched environments leads to an increase in the number of connections in the brain (Comery, Stamoudis, Irwin, & Greenough, 1996; Diamond, 1978). These findings indicate that brain development increases in complexity and organization as a function of experience. Research also shows that the brain is most receptive to environmental input in childhood. Synaptogenesis peaks in early childhood, remains high through middle childhood, and begins to decline after about age fourteen (Greenough, 1997). Although the brain continues to form new connections as a function of experience throughout life, it forms connections more intensely during childhood.

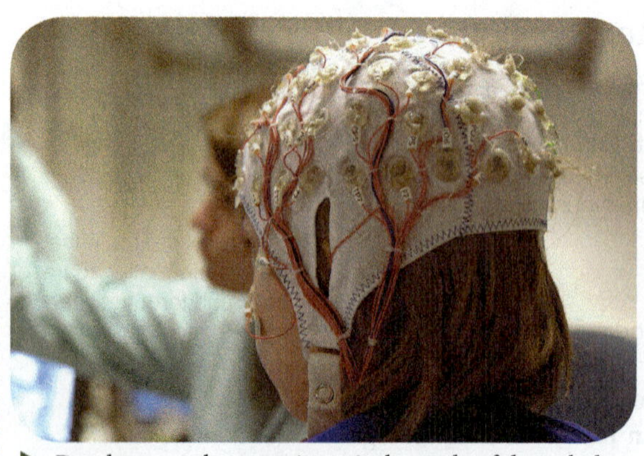

Developmental neuroscience is the study of the orderly progression of changes in the brain that occur across the lifespan.

Implications for Teaching and Learning

Since the brain develops as a function of experience, it follows that teachers, by providing learning experiences, are helping increase the complexity and organization of their students' brains (James, 2010; Rushton, Juola-Rushton, & Larkin, 2010). While we know that effective teaching increases learning, neuroscience research gives us a physiological basis for this phenomenon. Research indicates that using meaningful contexts for teaching new information enhances learning (Billingsley, 1993). If we reflect on research findings from a variety of disciplines—including education, cognitive science, and developmental neuroscience—we may better understand why the use of meaningful context enhances learning. As discussed previously, neuroscience research tells us that when learning occurs, new connections are made between neurons; and these connections in the brain are organized into networks, or circuits (Elman et al., 1997). Examining learning at the level of the neuron is looking at the **microstructure**. This is important when documenting the foundation of learning, but it is difficult to translate this information into functionally relevant learning strategies. That is, knowing that specific neurons are communicating more does not usually lead to an instructional strategy that teachers can use in the classroom. More typically, brain-based educators are interested in the **macrostructure** of learning. This approach focuses on whole brain structures (rather than specific neurons) and how they operate during learning.

Microstructure

The level of learning involving the neuron

Macrostructure

The level of learning involving the operation of whole brain structures

When a student is attempting to learn something new, putting the new information in a meaningful context causes already existing circuits of neurons to activate, enabling the student to link the new information to existing knowledge. Cognitive psychologists call this linking of new information to information already known as **elaboration**, and it has been shown to be a very powerful memory technique (Anderson, 1995; Holland, Addis, & Kensinger, 2011). (See Chapter 6.) Now, let's think about how these research findings might apply in a classroom example. Joy, who is trying to learn the addition fact 2 + 2 = 4, can already count and identify numbers and has one-to-one correspondence. This means she already has neural networks with regard to numbers; and when she repeats the math fact, she activates these networks. If we give Joy a context for understanding the math fact, however, she will activate much larger areas of already existing neurons in her brain, making it easier for her to link the new information to the information she already knows. We might, for example, ask her how many apples she would have if she were already holding two and her friend gave her two more. This might result in her activating networks regarding numbers, quantity, apples, and friends, among others. If we actually give her apples to manipulate as we work on the math fact, she will activate already existing networks in her motor and somatosensory cortex. Thus another effective teaching practice, multisensory instruction, can be understood more fully with the addition of a neuroscience perspective. While this research may only give us limited information with which we can develop curricula or programs, it does expand our understanding of how the brain is working during teaching and learning. Further, neuroscience is a rapidly developing field of study, and the future may yield more specific information that can be applied to educational practice and policy.

Elaboration

The linking of new information to information already known

Interconnections

Elaboration is further defined and discussed in Chapter 6.

While neuroscience research indicates that experiences are important for brain development and may help us better understand the learning process, the question of exactly which experiences are necessary for optimal human brain development is unanswered. Clearly, animals raised in enriched environments develop more synapses than those raised in impoverished environments, but how does this research relate to the development of human brains? We know that students from culturally impoverished backgrounds are more likely to have academic difficulty (Hirsch, 2001), and studies have shown that global, long-term neglect of human babies can severely stunt brain development (Perry, 2002). However, we do not yet have a good definition of the construct "enriched environment" in humans. In fact, it has been pointed out that the term 'enriched environment,' when applied to humans, has the potential to become value-laden and biased toward environments, which are culturally preferred and middle-class (Bruer, 1998). This does not mean that we should not pursue the notion of enriched environments, but it is necessary to carefully approach the idea from a culture and class sensitive perspective.

Elaboration is the linking of new information to information already known. The student already knows how to count; now she is learning to add.

SUMMARIZE AND REFLECT

1. Cognitive neuroscience is a field of study that focuses on the relationship between the brain and cognition.
2. Neural communication is important in development. Of particular importance is the role of experience in synaptogenesis, or the formation of new connections in the brain.
3. The brain develops areas specialized for carrying out certain functions, including the basic specializations of the four lobes of the cerebral cortex and the left and right hemispheres.
4. Brain areas may be specialized for specific functions, but most human activities require the use of many areas of the brain working together through circuits, or networks of neurons.
5. Neuroscience research demonstrates the dynamic interaction between the functioning of an individual's brain physiology, experiences, and development.
6. There are many educational implications of these findings for helping us better understand the complexities of both typical and atypical development.
7. Neuroscience research is growing at an exponential rate and may have implications for classroom practice, but we must be careful how we make connections between brain functioning and education.

INFORMED APPLICATION

1. How could an understanding of synaptogenesis shape the way a teacher perceives his/her daily role in the classroom?
2. In what way could teachers use knowledge of the specialized function of the brain to assist a student struggling with comprehension while taking notes?
3. Neural network theory provides a framework for understanding and improving some aspects of learning. Using this theoretical approach, how can a teacher help design an instructional plan for teaching the poetry of William Shakespeare?

VYGOTSKY AND THE INTERACTIVE NATURE OF THINKING

Sociocultural theorist

A theorist interested in the nature of social interactions and the ways in which social processes shape an individual's thinking

During the early part of the twentieth century, the Russian theorist Lev Semenovich Vygotsky (1896–1934) developed a theory of development, which received relatively little attention in the United States until the 1970s and 1980s, when his ideas became widely circulated among educators. Vygotsky is considered a **sociocultural theorist** because of his interest in the nature of social interactions and the ways in which social processes shape an individual's thinking. Educators came to realize that Vygotsky's sociocultural theory had direct bearing on the process of formal schooling and the pivotal role of the teacher since formal education is inherently a dynamic social process. Vygotsky's basic theoretical premise is a departure from many developmental theorists, focusing on the *process* of development rather than the *product*.

Perspectives on Development: Which Skills Develop versus How Skills Develop

Education is a complex process ultimately resulting in a variety of learning products. Here the term *products* refers to any outcome resulting from a learning process, such as reading, understanding the function of cells, or riding a bicycle, etc. While both learning products and the process by which they are learned are important, theorists place varying levels of emphasis on each. In other words, some theorists emphasize what is learned or acquired during the developmental years (product), whereas others emphasize the nature of the path making these changes possible (process). Vygotsky chose to focus on the process behind development changes. This is a departure from popular stage theorists, who favor a theoretical approach that clearly outlines specific skills acquired during development. Stage theory takes a particular developmental continuum and divides it into unique stages. Characteristics or products acquired during each stage are then explicitly outlined. For example, a stage theorist might document that children typically begin to develop the ability to assign unique words to objects around twelve- to fifteen-months of age. Describing when a child starts to develop language is important in that it gives us a sense of *what* to expect from a child at a given age, yet it fails to give us a comprehensive account of *how* these skills develop. That is, how did the child begin to learn verbal labels? Vygotsky's theory adds to our understanding of cognitive development by providing a mechanism for understanding *how* an individual's thinking and reasoning changes over time. Given this focus, Vygotsky's theory can be viewed as a process theory. A **process theorist** deemphasizes the development of specific skills, like verbal labeling, and instead focuses on what made the development of the skill possible. As you will see in the next section, Vygotsky considers the relationship between a student and a teacher—or, more generally, between a learner and a knower,—as the fundamental process for making possible the changes in cognitive development.

Process theorist

A theorist who deemphasizes the development of specific skills, such as verbal labeling, and focuses instead on what made the development of the skill possible

The Importance of Social Interaction and Language

As we grow and develop, it is clear that we undergo many striking changes in our ability to function in the world. We learn to talk and communicate our wants, our bodies become more coordinated and better able to operate within our environment, and our unique sense of ourselves begins to take shape. The fact that we all change over the course of our lives is quite clear, but equally clear is the fact that these changes are influenced by the environment in which we live. Children reared in different environments develop different ways to communicate, different physical capabilities, and different personalities. Most developmental theorists place such individual change at the center of their theory, trying to understand how individual changes lead to different ways of functioning in the world. For example, consider a young child who learns to read. How does the development of reading ability affect the child's functioning in the world? This is a very traditional question asked by developmental psychologists. Vygotsky's approach differed from traditional ways of looking at development in that his primary focus was on the effect of social interactions. He proposed that it is the interactions we have with others that are of primary importance in the process of development. First, we learn to more effectively interact with others by using tools such as speech, and then later use these social processes to understand and influence our own thinking and behavior (see Figure 2.4).

To get a better understanding of Vygotsky's unique perspective, consider a young child named Mora who is learning to talk. As she is busily playing one day, she becomes hungry and wants a cookie. She goes into the kitchen and ineffectively tries to reach the cookie jar. Her father notices her effort and asks if she wants a cookie. Since Mora has a very limited vocabulary, the father takes a cookie and holds it up in front of her and says clearly, "Cookie." Later in the week the child again wants a cookie, but this time approaches the father directly and says, "Coopie." Despite her articulation error, Mora is clearly using speech in a social context to get something she wants. This type of situation repeats itself across countless situations over several years until the child is able to interact with others in a very sophisticated manner.

Intermental changes

Modifications in thinking resulting from our social interactions

Intramental changes

The process of adapting socially derived mental processes to govern our own thinking and behavior

Vygotsky called this type of socially mediated change an intermental change, as illustrated in Figure 2.5 (Wertsch & Tulviste, 1992). **Intermental changes** are modifications in thinking resulting from our social interactions. "Mental" in this sense is not an activity exclusively within the mind of an individual. Vygotsky actually saw mental actions occurring in the socially mediated space between individuals. For him, this is the primary place for developmental changes in thinking. The difficulty you are probably experiencing right now in trying to understand a "social mental process" is a testament to how differently our society has thought of this activity. Simply put, Vygotsky believed that social processes are the fundamental basis for thinking. A secondary process called **intramental changes** refers to how individuals adapt socially derived mental processes to govern their own thinking and behavior.

Egocentric speech

The use of overt speaking by an individual to modify his or her own actions

Private speech

The use of subvocal speaking addressed to oneself for the purpose of self-regulation

For example, as Mora increases her level of linguistic proficiency, she begins to use "speech" to modify her individual actions. This **egocentric speech** begins as overt talking while carrying out an activity (Piaget, 1959; Vygotsky, 1986; Gredler, 2009). As Mora becomes more adept at guiding her own performance through speech, she will begin to use **private speech**,

Figure 2.4

Traditional Developmental Theories versus Vygotsky's Developmental Theory

Traditional Developmental Theories → Individuals change their thinking and behavior → results in changes in how the individual operates in their world.

Vygotsky's Developmental Theory → Changes in how the individual operates in their world (specifically how they internalize aspects of the world through social interaction) → results in the individual changing their thinking and behavior.

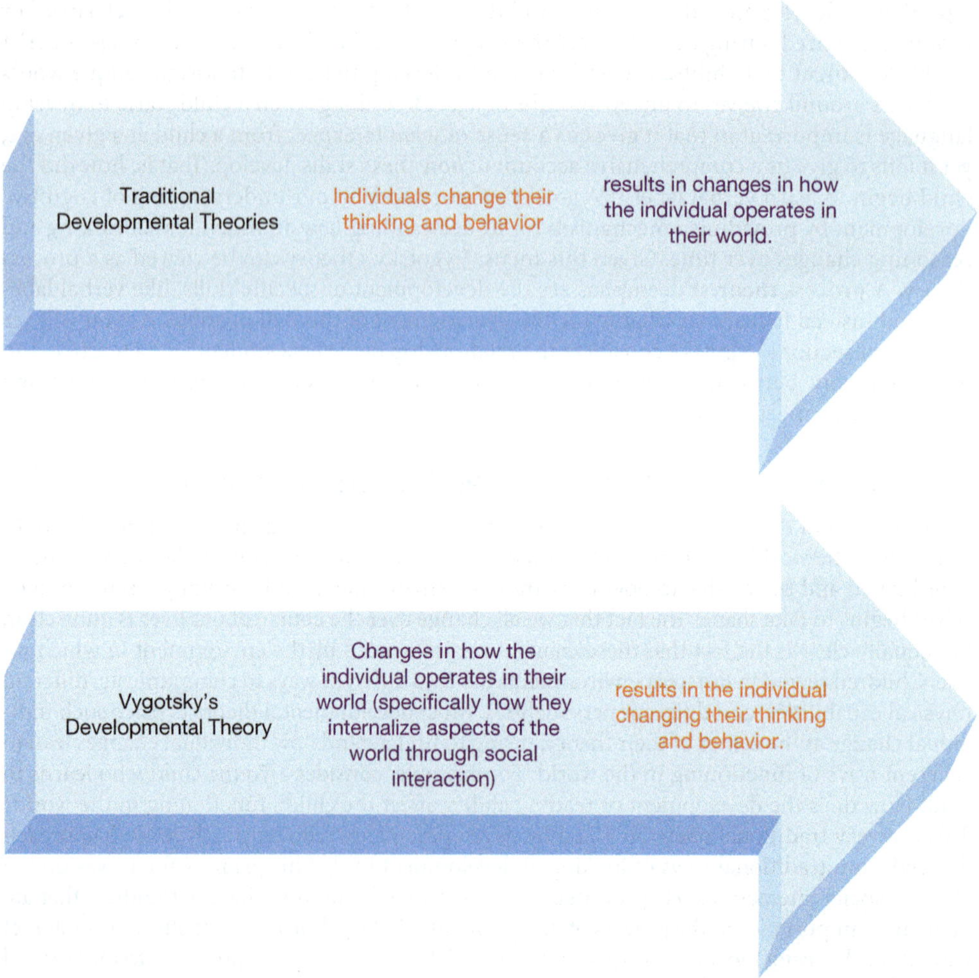

which eliminates overt talking, but will continue to use subvocal speech to guide her actions. This type of speech is addressed to the self, as opposed to others, and is used for the purpose of self-regulation (Fox & Riconscente, 2008), rather than communication (Diaz & Berk, 1992; Bivens & Berk, 1990). According to Vygotsky, this inner form of speech is thinking, which is developed via social mental processes. Thus, Vygotsky's theory focuses on the process by which our thinking develops, with language and sociocultural interactions as fundamentals of this process.

Vygotsky recognized the importance of his theory for formal education since many of society's fundamental mental tools are relayed to the individual during the formal educational process. Examples of these fundamental tools are not only verbal words and language but also written language, counting systems, works of art, maps, diagrams, etc. (Cole & Wertsch, 1996). It is in the school environment, through intermental processes or social interactions with others, that we learn to use these social and cultural tools in our thinking; that is, the processes become intramental. It is important at this point to emphasize that since our mental products are directly derived from our interactions at a social level, society and culture dictate how we perceive ourselves and the world around us. According to Vygotsky, we are able to direct our mental tools to whatever attracts our interest; however, the tools we have available for this work are simply those derived from the larger social context. This places educators in a very sensitive position because they significantly impact how students experience the social world and, therefore, how they come to think for themselves (Smagorinsky, 2007).

Figure 2.5

Dimensional Model for Samantha

The way that Jan reflects upon her own behavior is a product of the way she learned to think and reason from her social interactions with others. According to Vygotsky, it is this learning from others that is the primary or fundamental process in development, with individual thinking developing as a secondary process.

In The Classroom

APPLYING THEORY

Vygotsky

THEORY BASICS

The idea that there is a form of thinking and reasoning present in our interactions with others, rather than in our own minds, is difficult for most individuals growing up in western societies. In our culture, we typically think of reasoning as a quality of the individual or a skill that an individual possesses. According to Vygotsky, however, these individual abilities are actually byproducts of a primary "mental" process present in the interactions *between* individuals. In general, societies communicate to the individual ways to think and reason instead of using skills inherent in the individual. Vygotsky suggested that the only mental abilities we have are taught to us through our interactions with others. Social interactions not only teach us fundamental communication tools like language but also other general approaches to mental processing like problem solving and perception. The reasoning skills present in the social world are called intermental processes, and the skills that are adopted and used by an individual are called intramental processes.

(continues)

CLASSROOM APPLICATION

Teachers often have difficulty figuring out how to take this theory and apply it to instruction. One approach to making this application successful is to remember that the key point—how we think as individuals—comes from our exposure to the "thinking" of people around us. Teachers should take this into consideration whenever they are teaching their students new material.

Teachers: Make a strong attempt to interact with each student providing guiding information to aid the student in his/her understanding of the material.

Through social interactions with the teacher, students are able to clarify how the teacher is working through the problem, and they are then more competent in solving the problem on their own. Vygotsky referred to this guiding approach as scaffolding. It is the way the teacher communicates the new mental skill. It is then the responsibility of the student to use that skill appropriately.

Teachers: Provide the general framework for understanding a new lesson in a way that is personal and meets the need of each student.

For example, if a math teacher shows her students how to reduce fractions, she would likely show the students several sample items. She might also provide examples for the student to solve with her guidance. Both of these methods help communicate how to think about the problem. Teachers who follow Vygotsky's work would likely extend these traditional approaches with other ways to think about the topic. The teacher could demonstrate the application of reducing fractions by baking a cake, modifying the distance run by the track team, or cutting wood to make a tree house. Have the students engage in these activities in a small group with an advanced student or a student from a higher grade. The social interaction will help to communicate the new skill more effectively.

Teachers: Consider that in our current information age, Internet sources of information are readily available, which can greatly expand the student's world from which they learn.

Although we may have a typical approach to the instruction of fractions, the Internet can be a gateway to other societies and their approach to education. This helps students benefit from the ever-growing world culture and the problem solving tools present in other societies. Encourage students to conduct research on the Internet while maintaining a critical perspective.

Instruction: The Zone of Proximal Development and Scaffolding

Zone of proximal development

The distance between the skills a child has already internalized and the skills he or she could learn with appropriate assistance

Vygotsky's ideas provide a theoretical foundation for teaching, whereby the social environment of the classroom is used to optimize cognitive development. The benefit of a Vygotskian approach to instruction is that much of the natural social interactions that occur between a teacher and student can be purposefully directed to enhance the educational process. For example, during the beginning of a new school year, teachers spend considerable time getting to know the students and helping them become familiar with the classroom. Although this is typically viewed as somewhat peripheral to actual instruction time, Vygotsky's theory holds that this social interaction has the potential for dramatic impact on education. If we apply Vygotsky's ideas to the classroom, the earliest part of the educational process consists of a preliminary dynamic between student and teacher. During this time, the teacher begins to learn three types of information. First, the teacher acquires an understanding of what skills a student has already acquired and can perform independently. These skills are likely to benefit from continued reinforcement, but are not as likely to need the active guidance of the instructor. The teacher must then develop a sense of what skills are realistically beyond the child's current ability, even if help is given. This leaves a third piece of information that the teacher needs to acquire; that is, discovering what the student has not already acquired but is capable of learning with assistance. Vygotsky referred to this area of potential development as the **zone of proximal development** (see Figure 2.6), or the distance between the skills the child has already internalized and the skills the child could learn with appropriate assistance (Vygotsky, 1978; Tharp & Gallimore, 1988; Wass, Harland, & Mercer, 2011).

Kara loves to paint and is ready to learn more. Her current skill level is fairly basic.

Figure 2.6

Zone of Proximal Development

With instruction, Kara is able to extend her current skill level, painting with more complexity and detail.

The additional skills Kara is able to master with the assistance of a teacher are considered skills within her Zone of Proximal Development.

If the teacher uses interactions with students as a tool to understand the child's particular zone of proximal development, then sensitive and effective instruction becomes a reality. It is important to remember that much of the teacher's assessment of a child's zone of proximal development can be imbedded in everyday interactions. It is also important to realize that each child's zone of proximal development is likely to vary, not only in terms of absolute level, but also in relative distance between known skills and skills the child could learn with assistance. That is, some students will only be able to learn a few skills beyond their current level of development, whereas other students will have a greater range of skills that they could potentially learn with appropriate assistance.

After a teacher has successfully determined the zone of proximal development for each child, instruction can be tailored to the student, or to groups of students who have similar zones of proximal development for a given skill. Jerome Bruner first used the term *scaffolding* in the 1970s to refer to instruction that is based on Vygotsky's notion of supporting the development of new skills within a student's zone of proximal development (Bruner, 1978; Wood, Bruner, & Ross, 1976). **Scaffolding** does not use explicit step-by-step instructions—it supports learning by helping the student engage in purposeful and meaningful usage of psychological tools (Doolittle, 1997). The scaffolding process requires being receptive to a student's current skill level, providing support, and then fading the support so the student can become self-reliant. For example, a teacher may model a particular learning product, but also provide critical foundations necessary to reach the desired outcome. The student then attempts the skill on her own, with the teacher monitoring student performance and providing sensitive feedback. Over time, the teacher minimizes assistance, and the intermental dynamic becomes intramental, with the student moving toward independent practice (Jonassen, 1998; Rosenshine & Meister, 1992).

Scaffolding

A method of instruction that supports learning by helping the student engage in purposeful and meaningful use of psychological tools

Vygotsky's ideas provide us with valuable insights into the process of effective education. Yet, if a teacher must begin each new school year with a systematic assessment of each child's individual developmental level, followed by individualized instruction for each

child based on that assessment, then a classroom of twenty-five children becomes difficult, if not impossible, to teach. While every teacher is indeed confronted with as many unique zones of proximal development as they have children in class, development is an orderly and gradual process, one that proceeds similarly for most children. Teachers should, and are expected, to factor this into their educational programming. This helps teachers educate a group of students, while still providing the support each student needs. We are now going to turn our attention to another developmental theorist, whose theory of cognitive development was fundamental in shaping our expectations regarding what children learn or are capable of learning at particular ages. As you will see, his theory is quite different from the work of Vygotsky, but still pivotal in shaping education.

SUMMARIZE AND REFLECT

1. Lev Vygotsky's sociocultural theory of development provides an emphasis on process, focusing on social interactions and language as mediators of cognitive change.
2. Cognitive development is driven by the primary process of *inter*mental change and then adapted as an *intra*mental process.
3. Vygotskian theory includes the concept of the zone of proximal development and its role in the educational process.
4. Scaffolding, instructions which supports the development of new skills within a student's zone of proximal development, allows students to accomplish what they are not sufficiently expert to do independently.

INFORMED APPLICATION

1. Considering Vygotsky's theories regarding intermental and intramental cognitive changes, what should a teacher consider during a lesson on the role of women in Middle Eastern societies?
2. To help teachers provide instruction within the zone of proximal development, what suggestions would you provide regarding teacher/student interactions early in the school year?

PIAGET AND THE INQUISITIVE CHILD

Jean Piaget was born the same year as Lev Vygotsky; however, unlike Vygotsky, he lived a long life (1896–1980). During his extraordinary career, he became one of the most prolific and influential scientists of the twentieth century, contributing much to our understanding of the developing child and greatly impacting education practice. Like Vygotsky, Piaget was interested in understanding the development of mental abilities (Piaget, 1952, 1954, 1959, 1963, 1970). Piaget's focus was children's active, inquisitive exploration of the world, and he used a descriptive observational method. His observations resulted in a detailed theory regarding *what* children and adolescents are able to accomplish cognitively at different ages, viewing cognitive development as an orderly sequence of stages. As mentioned previously, theorists using a stage approach divide the developmental process into discrete sections to help categorize and understand changes. Piaget divided the development of cognitive processes into four stages, each identified by qualitative changes in a child's thinking. Piaget believed that these qualitative changes in thinking were facilitated by the child's active exploration and attempts to understand the world.

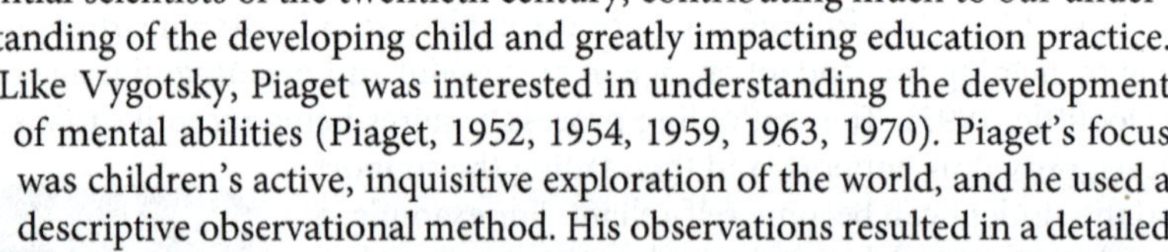

Basic Principles

Piaget's quest to understand the developing mind resulted in a vast amount of research and observation. From this work, it became clear to Piaget that a child's cognitive development was far from haphazard; rather, key developmental processes systematically drove it. He believed cognitive changes result from three basic processes: *equilibration, assimilation,* and *accommodation* (Piaget, 1952). When our understanding of the world is adequate for making sense of the situations we encounter, Piaget theorized a state of **cognitive equilibrium** existed. Throughout our lifetimes, however, we are faced with the difficult task of changing our views in order to understand a new situation. For example, we may feel we are quite capable of explaining basic addition to a five-year-old child until we meet a child with significant learning problems. The child's inability to benefit from our explanation or demonstration may necessitate the development of new ways to view additive concepts. **Disequilibrium** is the state where our current understanding is insufficient to make sense of a new experience. In other words, no longer does our understanding of addition meet the demands of this new situation. In order to restore equilibrium, we must adapt to this new situation—a process that Piaget called **equilibration**. Piaget argued that individuals are inherently driven to correct a state of disequilibrium in order to adapt to new situations (Wadsworth, 1996).

Cognitive equilibrium

The state in which our understanding of the world is adequate for making sense of the situations we encounter

Disequilibrium

The state in which our current understanding of the world is insufficient to make sense of a new situation

Equilibration

The restoration of equilibrium by adapting to the situation that had caused disequilibrium

How does this adaptation take place? Consider a young boy who is studying magnets in his science class. During the course of the lesson, he plays with the magnet and the accompanying metal shapes. By the end of the lesson, he tells his teacher, "Magnets stick to metal." At this point, we would say the boy has organized certain experiences into an understanding of magnetism. This is what Piaget called a **schema,** or an organized understanding of related elements. The next day the young boy finds his magnet and proceeds to "stick" the magnet to other types of metal around the classroom. He sees that the magnet is attracted to the teacher's filing cabinet and the metal door in much the same way it was to the items in the magnet kit. This illustrates the process of **assimilation**, or when an existing schema is satisfactorily used to explain a new experience. Here, the boy's observation that the magnet sticks to different metal items around the class affirms his understanding of magnetism developed the previous day. His understanding of the world and his experiences are in equilibrium. When he tries to put the magnet on the chrome chair, however, his schema regarding magnetism no longer works. This time the magnet falls to the floor. He tries to place the magnet on the chair a second time with the same result. He runs to his teacher and tells her, "Magnets don't stick to chair metal." This experience exemplifies the process of **accommodation**, whereby an existing schema is altered to better account for a new experience.

Schema

Organized ways of understanding related elements

Assimilation

A process in which an existing schema is satisfactorily used to explain a new experience

Accommodation

A process in which an existing schema is altered to better account for a new experience

In The Classroom

APPLYING THEORY

Piaget

THEORY BASICS

Piaget's theory provides a mechanism for how students come to an understanding of new information. As new information is encountered, the student actively tries to make sense of the information. They compare the new information with information already known. Essentially, they ask themselves, "Can I understand this new information with the knowledge I currently have?" If their existing knowledge were sufficient to understand the new information, Piaget would say the student *assimilated* the information. If the student needed to make modifications to what they already knew, then Piaget would say that the student accommodated the information.

(continues)

CLASSROOM APPLICATION

Jennifer, a third grader who is learning about predators in the marine life section of her science book, has started reading about the great white shark. Her teacher explains that sharks are really just another type of fish, having gills and laying eggs like other fish. The next day, Jennifer learns about another type of marine predator, the killer whale. Her teacher explains that although killer whales live in the ocean, they are not actually fish but mammals. Like other mammals, they have lungs and breathe air and also give birth to live young.

In this example, Jennifer is able to assimilate the information about great white sharks because the information is similar to her existing knowledge about marine life. The information about killer whales, however, must be accommodated because Jennifer's current understanding of marine life does not allow for the presence of aquatic mammals.

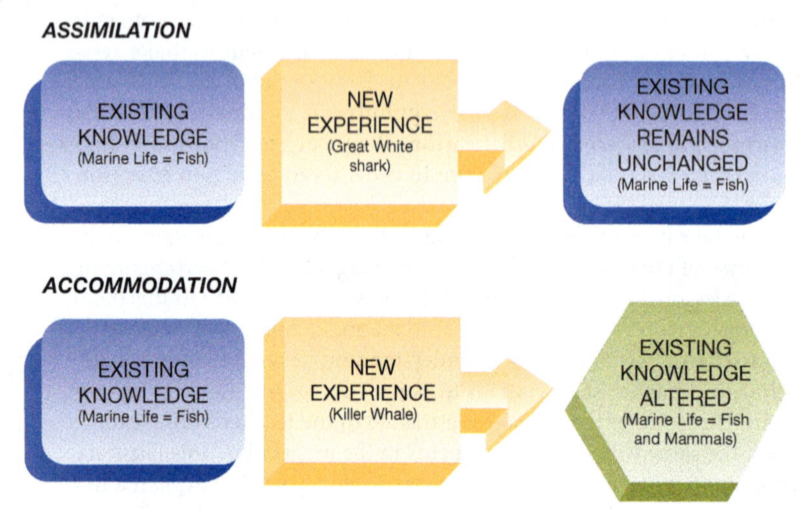

Teachers: Consider the existing knowledge base of a student when teaching new information.

The nature of a student's knowledge has a direct impact on what they do when new information is presented. By thinking ahead, teachers can watch for those times when new information is qualitatively different from what the students already know. This can help the teacher present the information in a way that helps the students make the necessary adjustments (accommodations) to their thinking. Similarly, if new information is just an extension of existing knowledge, teachers can help students recognize the utility of using what they already know to understand the new information.

Using the processes of assimilation and accommodation, the developing child learns to adapt their thinking to their experiences. This allows enormous flexibility in how children establish their unique way of being in the world and also creates a constantly changing understanding of the world. According to Piaget, these cognitive changes are not stored randomly; rather, he saw humans as incredible organizers, who inherit a basic tendency to organize experiences and knowledge into meaningful associations.

Each new experience a child encounters results in new information. Sometimes experiences merely underscore the child's current understanding of the world (assimilation). Other experiences require the child to modify his current understanding in order to make sense of the new experience (accommodation). Either way, the child becomes more knowledgeable. Piaget believed that as we acquire new information and knowledge, we naturally look for connections to existing information. We look for similarities and differences between the old and new information, and consequently we move toward an understanding of the world that is a closer approximation of the complex world in which we live. For example, a preschool teacher might begin a lesson on shapes by identifying a yellow triangular-shaped block. The teacher points to the block and says, "Triangle." After a brief period of time the child can readily pick out the yellow triangle from a basket of other blocks. Several weeks later the teacher presents the basket of blocks to the child. The teacher has removed all the yellow blocks, but has included several green and blue triangles. The teacher asks the child to pick out the triangle. The child indicates that there are no "triangles" in the basket. Having carefully planned this instructional moment, the teacher readily explains that it is the shape of the block that makes it a triangle, not the color. The teacher continues the lesson, providing multiple opportunities for the student to practice the concept. The second part of this lesson presents the student with additional information about how to understand a certain aspect of his world. This new information is not retained by the child as a completely new and unrelated fact but as a piece of information related to other information already learned. As children acquire new knowledge, their relatively simple view of the world is gradually replaced with an organizational structure more closely corresponding to the richness and complexity present in the world around them.

In sum, using the fundamental processes of equilibration, assimilation, and accommodation, children build an organized understanding of the world. According to Piaget's research, children develop this organized understanding of the world, similarly, in a defined pattern of cognitive development. Piaget's account of this pattern, or his Stage Theory of Development, is discussed in the next section.

Stages of Development

Piaget based his theory of cognitive development on observations of children. The basis for his theory is simply that children change noticeably in the way they see the world as they get older. Piaget observed that younger children think, not just fewer thoughts, but also think *differently* than older children. Thus, a seven-year-old can solve problems that a four-year-old cannot, and a four-year-old makes errors in reasoning that a seven-year-old will not. Piaget theorized that these changes are based both in maturation and adaptation, with children becoming able to adapt in new ways as they mature. Piaget believed that all humans develop cognitively in the same sequence of qualitatively different stages—an idea termed **invariant sequencing**. While Piaget outlined typical ages at which children reach each of these stages, he also noted that individual children develop at different rates; and it is possible that some individuals may not move into the highest stages of cognitive development. We now turn to Piaget's four stages of cognitive development: sensorimotor, preoperational, concrete operational, and formal operations. Table 2.1 provides an overview of the stages followed by an in-depth look at each stage.

Invariant sequencing
The idea that all humans develop cognitively in the same sequence of qualitatively different stages

Table 2.1 Piaget's Four Stages of Cognitive Development

Piagetian Stage	Approximate Age Range	General Characteristics
Sensorimotor	0–2 years	Object Permanence Intentional Behavior
Preoperational	2–7 years	Symbolic Representation (Semiotic Function) Egocentrism Centration
Concrete Operations	7–11 years	Conservation (Decentration/Transformation) Reversibility Classification Seriation
Formal Operations	11 years–adult	Hypothetico-Deductive Reasoning Adolescent Egocentrism

Sensorimotor

Object permanence

A child's ability to mentally represent or think about an object after it has been removed from his or her field of vision or other senses

Intentional behavior

Refers to the purposeful manipulation of the environment to achieve an outcome

The sensorimotor stage is so named because in this stage, the child's primary mechanisms for exploring the world are sensory and motor. Infants and toddlers think about their world through their ability to see and touch; therefore, much of early learning is directly dependent on a child's ability to actively interact with people and objects. During this early period of cognitive development, children achieve one of the first of Piaget's cognitive milestones, object permanence. **Object permanence** is the child's ability to mentally represent, or think about, an object after it has been removed from her field of vision or other senses. As an adult, it may be difficult to imagine a time when you did not appreciate that an object's permanence is independent of sight or touch, but this is a unique mental ability you acquired early in life. For most children, the beginning of an understanding of object permanence occurs during the first year (Marcovitch & Zelazo, 1999). The presence or lack of object permanence can be observed by watching a child's behavior after an object has been removed from her field of vision. Children who have not yet acquired object permanence will typically treat the removal of an interesting object with indifference, not even looking for the object when it is gone. Quite simply, if it is out of sight, it no longer exists. Once a child has begun to achieve object permanence, she will look for the object, moving in a deliberate manner to reacquire it.

Once a child has begun to achieve object permanence, most often during the first year, he will look for an object, moving in a deliberate manner to reacquire it.

The development of object permanence is directly related to a more general tendency toward intentional behavior. **Intentional behavior** refers to the purposeful manipulation of the environment to achieve an outcome. Early in the sensorimotor period, children fail to differentiate between the outside world and their own bodies, with self and the environment seen as roughly equivalent. As children develop, they become aware that they are able to control some aspects of the world and that there is a difference between self-control and manipulation of the environment. Through trial and error, children begin to develop better control over their bodies in the process of manipulating the environment, consequentially becoming better able to interact with the world and meet their needs. Their behavior has moved from being almost random to being purposeful and goal-directed. These new mental abilities lay the foundation for the more sophisticated cognitive challenges acquired in the next stage of cognitive development, the preoperational period.

Preoperational

Operations

Our application of mental resources

Symbolic representation

The ability to represent an object or experience with a symbol

Semiotic function

The use of symbolic representation

Egocentric

The inability to view the world from someone else's perspective

When children enter the preoperational stage, they are not so dependent on actual experiences; instead they develop better ways of representing things mentally (see Figure 2.7). Piaget referred to our application of mental resources as **operations**; thus children in the preoperational period are laying the groundwork necessary for the concrete operations developed in the next stage.

One of the necessary steps toward the development of operations is **symbolic representation**, or the ability to represent an object or experience with a symbol. For example, when a boy uses his pencil to play "airplanes" with a classmate, he is using symbolic representation. Piaget referred to this use of symbolic representation as a **semiotic function**. A child's ability to use symbolic representation develops rapidly during the preoperational period (Gleason, Sebanc, & Hartup, 2000). This is especially true for language development, which is perhaps the most sophisticated use of symbolic representation.

Despite the dramatic development of symbolic thinking in the preoperational period, mental activity of children in this stage is still far from abstract. The thinking of the child in the preoperational period is still tied to symbols of actual objects (rather than abstract concepts) or immediate experiences, and problems are solved based only on what is actually perceived. Piaget referred to children's thinking in this stage as **egocentric**, or the inability to view the world from someone else's perspective. This is commonly seen in children's play behavior (Ruffman & Olson, 1989). Imagine a young boy playing hide-and-seek with his father. The child diligently tries to find the ideal hiding place and exclaims loudly, "This table is a great hiding place." He then places himself behind the table, taking care to move his head so that

Figure 2.7

Preoperational Stage of Reasoning

Jimmy, a seven-year-old child, is in Piaget's preoperational stage of reasoning. He can easily use a concrete object like a pencil to play an imaginary game of "airplanes." Both the pencil and the airplane are within his direct experiences. He is not yet ready, however, to think about abstract concepts like "freedom." When presented with the word freedom, he thinks about its meaning in terms of concrete objects like the Statue of Liberty. He is not able to think about its relation to the general state of being free. This is because children in the preoperational stage still need to think about these concepts in terms of something they can see and touch.

he cannot see his father. What the boy fails to appreciate is that from his father's perspective, the father not only heard the child's comment regarding the hiding place, he could also see the child's legs under the table. This reliance on actual perception also leads to other errors in reasoning such as **centration**, or the inability to think of more than one aspect of a problem at a time. Like egocentric thinking, centration is a problem with being bound by one's perceptions. For adults and children alike, every situation has certain elements that capture our attention more so than others. When several adolescents enter the school cafeteria, for example, one person may immediately notice how many boys are in the room. Another member of the group may exclaim that it is pizza day, and yet another's attention may be drawn to the presence of the principal in the corner of the room. Each person in this example can be said to have found different prominent factors (or salient factors) in the cafeteria environment. As individuals grow, they develop greater facility in directing their attention and thoughts to factors other than those that may be more salient for the individual. The child in the preoperational period, however, is quite limited in this ability. Typically, they are drawn to the most salient aspect of a situation and have difficulty attending to other aspects of their environment (Flavell, Green, & Flavell, 1989). This causes children in the preoperational period to center their thoughts and general mental ability on a single aspect of a situation, which is problematic if the situation requires a flexible perspective. Consider one of Piaget's classic problems used in his study of children's thinking, the conservation task (Flavell, 1963). The **conservation task** requires the child to consider two environmental factors at the same time to generate a correct answer.

Centration

The inability to think of more than one aspect of a problem at a time

Conservation task

A problem that requires a child to consider two environmental factors at the same time to generate a correct answer

One version of the conservation task presents the child with two rows of five buttons (see Figure 2.8). Initially, the buttons are laid out evenly with the buttons in one row directly above the buttons in the other row. The experimenter then asks the child which row has the most buttons. Children typically respond with the obvious fact, that the rows have the same number of buttons. The experimenter then moves one of the rows of buttons, spacing them further apart and again asking the child to identify which row has more buttons. Children in the preoperational period are likely to respond that the row with the buttons spread out has *more* buttons. What is immediately salient for the child is the length of the row; and the child is bound by this perception, showing little facility to adjust his perceptions to account for both the number of buttons and the length of the row. To successfully reason through a conservation task, the child must *decenter*, or focus on more than one aspect of the problem at the same time. To answer the problem correctly, the child must attend to the fact that one row of buttons is longer *and* attend to the fact that there are still five buttons in the row. Without attending to both features, the child is unable to answer the question correctly.

In the above example, the child attended to the beginning and end states of the problem, deemphasizing the intermediate steps. In other words, the child attended to the row of buttons before and after they were moved, but failed to fully appreciate that these two states were achieved by moving the buttons, not adding any buttons. Piaget called this a problem with **transformation**, or having knowledge of the sequence of changes when a situation is transformed. For example, if a preoperational child's watches a teacher using play dough, first

Transformation

The sequence of changes when a situation is transformed

Figure 2.8

Conservation Task

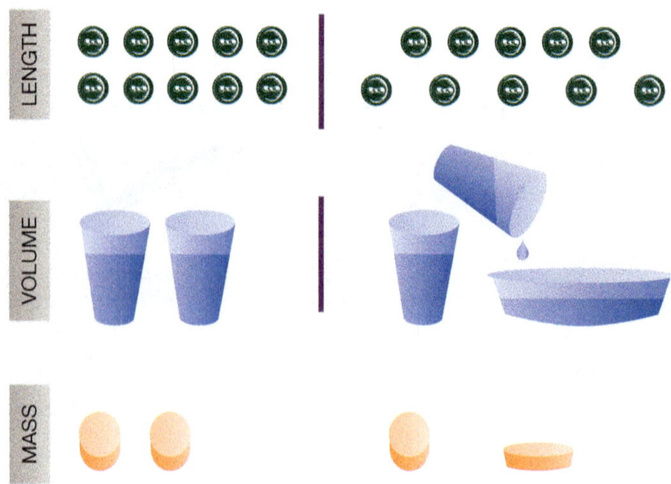

forming a ball of dough and then rolling it out on the desk, the child is likely to tell her, "Wow, we have a lot more dough now!" The child attends to the initial ball of dough and the perceptually larger rolled out dough, but has difficulty appreciating the intermediate steps that would help her realize it is still the same amount of dough. Nothing was added or removed. In fact, if the child's teacher tells her to mentally reverse the sequence of events involved in the dough rolling, she is unlikely to be able to do so. That is, she has not yet achieved **reversibility**, or the ability to mentally represent and "undo" events in a logical sequence. These errors in reasoning experienced by children in the preoperational period are, however, temporary. Over time, children adapt their thinking to enable them to better operate within their world, and many reasoning errors characteristic of the preoperational period are resolved as the child moves into the concrete operational stage.

Reversibility

The ability to mentally represent and "undo" events in a logical sequence

Concrete Operations

During the concrete operational stage, children move beyond strict ties to perception in favor of logical reasoning. As children gain a greater appreciation of the workings of the world, they are able to recognize perceptual irregularities and reason through situations where things are not as they appear to be by using logic. This is a significant step forward in mental ability and is made possible by the resolution of several issues prominent during the preoperational period. The child in the concrete operational period is now able to accurately solve problems of conservation. They are able to **decenter** their thinking from the most salient features of the problem to a consideration of other relevant factors. For example, when a child in the concrete operational stage is asked how many buttons are in the row with the buttons spread out, she recognizes that spreading out the buttons does not change the quantity and answers, "the number of buttons is the same, so both rows are equal."

Decenter

Change in thinking from focusing on the most salient features of the problem to a consideration of other relevant factors

This stage is also characterized by an ability to follow transformations from beginning to end. When a ball is dropped onto a table, for example, the concrete operational child is not only able to draw a picture of the ball at the starting and ending positions but at intermediate positions as well (see Figure 2.9).

Concrete operational children are also able to mentally reverse a transformation. Recall that a child in the preoperational period has difficulty holding a sequence of events in memory and logically reversing the sequence from end to beginning. Children in the concrete operational stage are able to make such two-way logical deductions. If given index cards with pictures of the beginning, ending, and intermediate stages of the ball illustration above, a concrete operational child can place them in order from the end state, through the intermediate steps, to the beginning state.

Children in the concrete operational stage also develop a far more elaborate structure for the classification of objects (Kyhl, 1995). **Classification** is the ability to mentally organize observed similarities and differences in the environment. Instead of only having knowledge of simple categories, children are able to understand the complex relations between

Classification

The ability to mentally organize observed similarities and differences in the environment

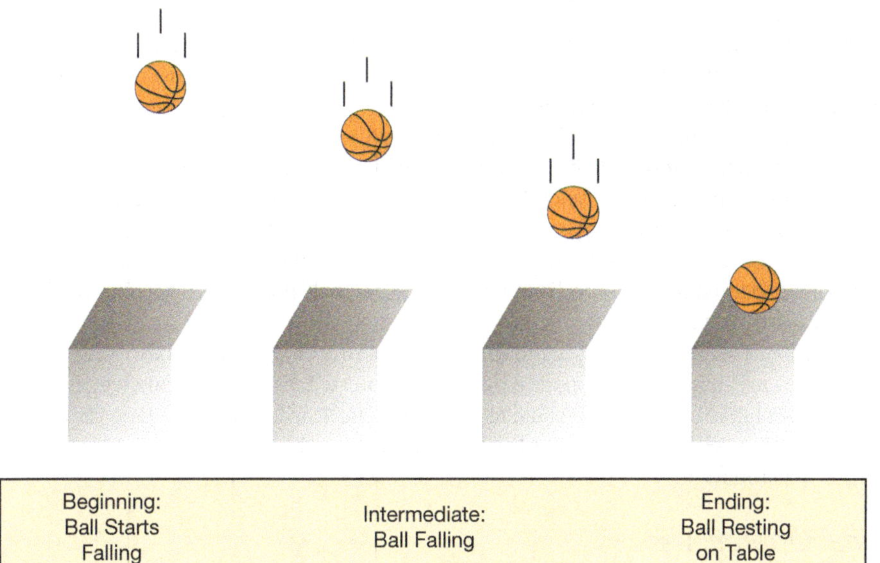

Figure 2.9

Concrete Operational Stage Illustration

memberships in multiple categories. For example, a concrete operational child who is presented with a container full of buttons of different shapes, sizes, and colors can easily sort them by category. Additionally, they also understand that one category may include another; that is, some blue buttons may also fit within the large button category. This type of complex classification requires decentered thinking, as children must think about more than one aspect of the problem at a time. As children move through the concrete operational stage, they begin to develop more intricate category relations, allowing them to think about the world in new ways.

Seriation

The ability to arrange objects into an orderly sequence

Another concept mastered during the concrete operational period is **seriation**, or the ability to arrange objects into an orderly sequence. Seriation applies to a variety of object dimensions, including length, mass, and volume. One of Piaget's classic seriation tasks involves presenting a child with a set of sticks of varying lengths (see Figure 2.10). The child is then asked to put the sticks in order from smallest to largest. Preoperational children have difficulty with this task, even when the solution is demonstrated for them. They either place the sticks randomly or are only able to order a pair of sticks at a time, creating pairs of small and large sticks. Children moving into the concrete operational stage begin to recognize that there should be an orderly progression in the heights of the sticks, ordering the tops of the sticks to create a continuous upward slope; however, they frequently ignore the bottoms of the sticks, which are not lined up on a straight horizontal. Finally, the child who has fully mastered concrete operations

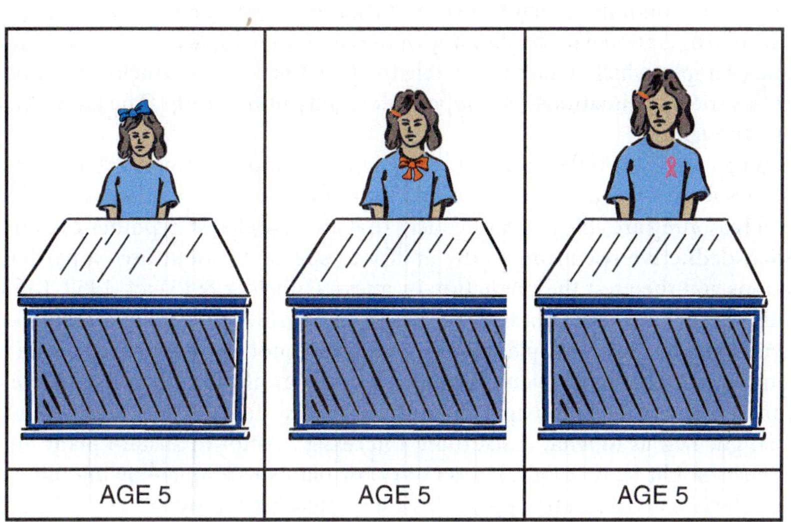

Figure 2.10

One of Piaget's Classic Seriation Tasks

is able to complete the task accurately, recognizing that any one stick in the sequence has two important relations; that is, it is larger than the sticks before it in the sequence and yet, at the same time, smaller than the sticks coming after it in the sequence. This realization allows them to appropriately place the sticks in order.

The new collection of mental abilities achieved in the concrete operational stage gives children the ability to more effectively operate in their world; however, the concrete operational period is so named because children can conduct operations only with things that they have had concrete, or actual, experience. For example, a student may be able to understand the dynamic and complex interactions between fish and plants in their classroom fish tank. They have learned which fish can live well together, which plants play specific roles in maintaining a healthy aquatic environment, and which fish and plants will survive in this habitat. When asked questions regarding general principles of ecology and aquatic animal behavior, however, they are unable to extrapolate from their experiences, having knowledge only of their classroom fish tank. In order to be able to speculate about what might be true for as yet unexplored areas, they will need to master formal operations, which occur in Piaget's final stage of cognitive development.

Formal Operations

The formal operational stage is in many ways similar to the concrete operational stage. Individuals at this stage develop sophisticated classifications systems. They are also able to logically reason in forward and reversed directions. The fundamental difference in reasoning at the formal operational stage is that individuals are now able to use their reasoning abilities for situations with which they have had no direct experience. For this reason, formal operational reasoning is frequently referred to as "might be" reasoning, whereby individuals are able to apply their reasoning and problem solving to completely abstract issues. To help make the distinction between concrete operations and formal operations, consider the following example of a social studies teacher trying to explain the economic principles of import and export to a child in the concrete operational stage. The teacher explains that the history of the child's home state indicated economic prosperity depended on the state's development of trade agreements with neighboring states. States that failed to successfully develop import and export routes were economically unstable, given the limited resources available locally. When the child clearly understands the example, the teacher asks the child to explain how this situation might apply to the countries of Europe. European countries were studied the previous term. The child attempts a solution, but is unable to generalize his learning to the European context, as his understanding of the process of importing/exporting was dependent on the example related to his home state. Now let's consider the same situation, but this time the student is an older adolescent in the formal operations stage. This student is likely to successfully generalize to the concept of importing and exporting to the European countries, not only because they understood the specific example, but also because they understood the essential *form* of this basic economic principle; hence, the name *formal operations.* In other words, the student's formal operational understanding of the economic impact of trade is independent of any specific example, which makes it possible to apply the general principle of importing and exporting in variety of situations. This type of flexibility in thinking is the hallmark of formal operational thought.

The ability to think independently of specific examples or context is important because it allows for general principles and methods of thinking. Individuals capable of formal operational reasoning are able to explore ideas that are completely hypothetical. For example, **hypothetico-deductive reasoning** is the ability to speculate about how a particular situation functions and then test the prediction or guess. (Inhelder & Piaget, 1958; Kuhn, Amsel, O'Loughlin, 1988). Let's say that a student is assigned a project involving discovering the necessary environmental factors for plant life. The student is not allowed to use outside references but is required to solve the problem through observation. If the student is capable of formal thought, then they are likely to begin the project by first developing a series of **hypotheses**, or educated guesses, as to what constitutes a necessary factor to sustain plant life. Perhaps one hypothesis might be that light is necessary for plants to live. Following this prediction, the student devises a systematic approach to investigating the hypothesis. The student decides to put one plant outdoors in direct sunlight, an identical plant in partial shade, and a

Hypothetico-deductive reasoning
The ability to speculate about how a particular situation functions and then test the prediction or guess

Hypothesis
An educated guess

third plant under a cardboard box in complete darkness. Based on the results of this investigation, the student *deduces* whether light is necessary for plant growth. She then turns her attention to her next hypothesis regarding plant life. Her systematic approach to the problem indicates she has internalized the basic hypothetico-deductive process, enabling her to speculate about possible outcomes and test ideas accordingly.

Individuals capable of formal operational reasoning are able to explore ideas that are completely hypothetical so they can speculate about how a particular situation functions and then test the prediction or guess.

While it is beneficial to be able to reason about the possible outcomes of a particular situation without having to wait for the situation to actually resolve, individuals in the early stages of formal operations often use this newfound ability in a more universal way than is actually productive. Adolescents moving into the formal operations stage are likely to vigorously argue points of politics, religion, or morality based on ideas they have been able to deduce through logic. These logical deductions appear to them to be flawless and as immutable as actual reality; however, they often fail to recognize potential validity of other perspectives. Piaget referred to an adolescent's focus on their own thoughts and the inability to see the perspective of others as **adolescent egocentrism**. It is important to recognize that this is not the egocentrism observed in preoperational children. In the preoperational period, children simply fail to understand that there is any difference between another's perspective and their own. Adolescents recognize that others have a different perspective. The difference in the two types of egocentrism is that adolescents are often so convinced by their own logic that they assume anyone who challenges their reasoning is demonstrating flawed judgment. They fail to recognize that there may be factors of which others are aware that they (the adolescents) have not considered or assumptions, which they have made, that are not valid. If an adolescent recognizes that others have a different perspective but they invalidate that perspective, it makes it difficult to benefit from that perspective. In a functional sense, they are also being egocentric since they are not benefiting from the perspective of others. Research indicates that this type of reasoning may extend into early adulthood (Frankenberger, 2000). However, as individuals progress in their mastery of formal operations, they become better able to understand that multiple perspectives exist with regard to abstract problems, and their thinking becomes less egocentric. Piaget's notion of adolescent egocentrism helps explain the idealism and questioning of authority that may occur during adolescence; and while this may not make it easier to relate to adolescents, it does help to inform our understanding of adolescent behavior and its relation to cognitive development.

Adolescent egocentrism

An adolescent's focus on his or her own thoughts and the inability to see the perspective of others

Evaluating Piaget's Theory

Piaget's theory is unquestionably one of the most influential developmental theories, and his ideas have strongly impacted our educational methods (Beilin, 1992a; Voyat, 1998); however, this does not mean that Piaget's ideas and research go unchallenged. There is a growing body of research that qualifies, and at times contradicts, some of Piaget's tenets. The most commonly cited of these criticisms is that Piaget's theory underestimates the competence of children (Gelman & Baillargeon, 1983; Siegal, 1991; Baillargeon, 1997; Gelman & Ebeling, 1989).

Underestimating the Abilities of Children

Recall that Piaget based his theory on observations of children as they engaged in a variety of cognitive tasks, which he believed tested certain cognitive abilities. Newer studies—which have modified Piaget's instructions, simplified questions, or otherwise made tests more available to children—suggest that younger children are more capable than Piaget thought. For example, Baillargeon (1987) developed a different object permanence task that used the child's indication of surprise, rather than an active search for an object, as the indicator of the child's understanding of object permanence. This approach produced evidence that children as young as three- to four-months of age have an appreciation of the permanence of objects. It is important to note, however, that newer studies that alter Piaget's tasks may not necessarily be measuring the same things Piaget was assessing; and the information obtained, therefore, might not contradict, as much as expand or refine, Piaget's ideas (Lourenco & Machado, 1996).

Overestimating the Abilities of Adolescents

Piaget's theory has also been criticized for failing to capture the distribution of skills present in adolescents and young adults. Based on Piaget's theory, individuals begin moving into the formal operations stage around the age of eleven. His theory, however, is somewhat misleading because additional studies indicate that few individuals may ever actually show formal operational thinking. Studies have shown that only 3% of ten- to twelve-year-olds (Flieller, 1999), 9% of fifteen-year-olds (Epstein, 1980), and 20 to 25% of college freshman (Kamii, 1984) were adept formal reasoners. Thus, Piaget's ideas regarding the typical age at which formal operational thinking is reached may have overestimated the abilities of adolescents and adults. Research also provides some evidence for an upward trend in the percentage of thirteen- to fifteen-year-olds proficient with formal reasoning, with a 1967 study finding that 5% were mature formal operators and a 1996 study finding that 15% were consistently able to reason at a formal level (Flieller, 1999). This increase in the percentage of formal thinkers was attributed to a greater tendency for teachers to instruct with tables and structural diagrams that require more formal types of thinking, suggesting that formal operational thinking may be influenced by education more than initially proposed by Piaget.

Cognitive Development and Culture

Another often cited criticism of Piaget's work is his tendency to ignore the impact of social interactions and culture (Winegar & Valsiner, 1992; Buck-Morss, 1982; Broughton, 1981). Although a careful review of Piaget's work indicates an ongoing concern with the impact of social interactions (Devries, 1997), he did not articulate a clear mechanism for how social interactions and culture affect cognitive development. Studies specifically examining Piaget's theory across cultures have generally supported the order of Piaget's stages, but have found cultural differences in the rate of progression through the stages (Rogoff & Chavajay, 1995; Hughes & Noppe, 1991; Leadbeater, 1991). Studies also indicate that there may be differences in rate of progression through stages between socioeconomic groups within a particular culture (Case, 1975). These findings suggest that culture may play a more central role in development than Piaget's theory assumes.

Early social interactions and culture affect cognitive development.

Limited Explanations for Cognitive Changes

Piaget has also been criticized for developing a theory that is predominantly descriptive and providing little explanation for how changes in cognitive development occur (Boden, 1979; Flanagan, 1992; Campbell & Bickard, 1986). He argued, however, that before we can engage in a productive search for an *explanation* for cognitive development, we first need an account of *what* those changes are (Piaget, 1947). Piaget did, however, attempt to develop a complete theory of cognitive development, including how the process occurs. Recall his thoughts on mechanisms of change (equilibration, assimilation, and accommodation) outlined earlier in this section.

Neo-Piagetian theorists

A group of researchers attempting to retain much of Piaget's original insights and to extend those insights to better account for the latest research findings

Extending Piaget's Theory: Neo-Piagetian Theory and Brain Research

Many of today's theorists continue to find Piaget's basic tenets a useful framework for understanding development. A growing group of researchers, generally referred to as **neo-Piagetian theorists**, attempt to retain much of Piaget's original insights and to extend those insights to better account for the latest research findings. Most neo-Piagetian theorists maintain the stage-like approach proposed by Piaget, but they have refined what defines a stage. Rather than viewing development as a stage, which generally corresponds to years of age, newer research (Case, 1998, 1992) has supported the idea that stages exist within a specific domain, such as motor development, math ability, or social ability. Development within one domain does not necessarily indicate development in other domains, and there is much variability in individual strengths and weaknesses. Using chronological age as a benchmark for development is therefore problematic because it may or may not apply to all domain areas.

Current theorists also add to Piaget's conceptualization of maturation, equilibration, and assimilation/accommodation as driving forces behind developmental changes. One information-processing theorist, for example, proposes that as children learn from their interactions with the world, they develop rules for understanding. These rules are later challenged by new experiences that do not completely conform to the rule. This requires the individual to engage in rule assessment to develop rules more consistent with current experiences (Siegler, 1998). Not unlike assimilation and accommodation, this approach encourages teachers to provide educational experiences that challenge children and provide them with a vehicle for change. Other researchers in the area of cognitive psychology are also beginning to provide a more specific account of how cognitive development progresses in such areas as memory, problem solving, and attention, allowing us to expand on Piaget's seminal ideas and better understand the way cognitive development influences teaching and learning.

Recall from the developmental neuroscience section (see earlier section of this chapter) that brains change as a function of experience, a finding that is consistent with Piaget's idea: children develop cognitively as a function of experiences, which challenge their cognitive equilibrium. Also consistent with Piaget's theory is the research indicating that brain development is most prolific during childhood. In fact, some neuroscience studies have shown correspondence between periods of brain growth and changes in cognitive development, providing support for Piaget's stage theory of cognitive development. For example, research indicates that brain growth peaks can be seen between the ages of two to four, six to eight, ten to twelve, and fourteen to seventeen (Epstein, 1974, 1977); these ranges are quite similar to those proposed by Piaget. Developmental changes in the electrical activity of the brain (Hudspeth & Pribram, 1990), as well as changes in cortical organization (Thatcher, Giudice, & Walker, 1987), have also been shown to correspond with Piaget's stages of cognitive development. Some researchers have measured brain functioning during children's completion of conservation and categorization tasks, which indicate developmental changes in brain activity between conservers and non-conservers (Strauder, 1993), and concrete and formal operational thinkers (Van der Molen & Ridderinkhof, 1998). While this research does not prove that Piaget's theory is without flaws, it does provide a physiological basis for understanding the cognitive changes that occur during development. Additionally, some research has helped to clarify aspects of Piaget's theory, such as one study which demonstrated that adult brains still show certain activity patterns indicating they have not fully overcome earlier cognitive limitations (Leroux, Spiess, & Zago, 2009).

See the earlier section of this chapter for a discussion of developmental neuoscience.

Piaget's theory, while not without problems, is eminent, and his ideas continue to exert influence in both psychology and education. Now that we have explored Piaget's theory at length, let's consider the application of his theory to educational practice.

Piaget and Developmentally Appropriate Instruction

Piaget's theory has greatly influenced education over the last fifty years, inspiring curriculum reform and greatly changing education practice (Case, 1985b). His descriptions of cognitive skills attained at different ages are often used as a foundation for deciding developmentally appropriate methods and curricula (Ojose, 2008; Hinde & Perry, 2007). His theory also provides instructors with a general approach to motivating students to learn.

Use Disequilibrium to Motivate

Recall that according to Piaget's theory, a child becomes motivated to learn when his representations of the world are challenged by new, conflicting information. Piaget referred to this as a state of disequilibrium and argued that children have a natural tendency to find ways to alter their existing schemas so they can incorporate the new information. This returns them to a state of equilibrium. This is an important point to consider when providing "developmentally appropriate" instruction; that is, instruction should be tailored to challenge a child's existing schema by producing disequilibrium (Walsh, 1991). In order to optimize the construction of knowledge, teachers must challenge children to go beyond existing mental structures, so that the equilibration process begins. The following example illustrates instruction that challenges a student's existing classification schemes. The teacher gives May, a five-year-old child in the preoperational stage, a yellow car and asks her to choose another similar toy from the toy box. May is able to do so with ease, choosing a yellow yo-yo. When asked to pick another similar toy, she chooses a round wooden block because it is similar in shape to the yo-yo. The particular feature May pays attention to changes based on whatever feature is most salient for her at the moment. She pays little attention to maintaining a grouping based on a common feature (e.g., picking only cars). In order to challenge her toward disequilibrium, the teacher might plan a lesson whereby the goal is to group several objects into a set based on function. This requires May to focus on a particular similarity across a group of objects, rather than whatever happens to be most salient for her at the time. This challenges her existing cognitive structures regarding classification of objects and motivates her to learn.

Appreciate the Construction of Knowledge

Piaget's theory is also notable for his view that children actively construct knowledge of the world through active exploration (see Chapter 12). Since the publication of his theory, this idea of knowledge construction has developed steadily and is becoming a primary area of focus in education. While all teachers should strive to develop appropriate instructional methods, Piaget has taught us that it is equally important to pay attention to the learning process from the perspective of the student. Learners are not merely passive recipients of the knowledge taught by the instructor but are actively constructing their understanding. For example, in his high school health class, Michael completed a lesson designed to help him understand the importance of fats in his diet. Michael reflected upon this information and decided that he did not consume enough fat. Over the course of the next few weeks, Michael began to shift a greater portion of his total calories to fats. In fact, he reasoned that if he really ate a significant amount of fats, his health would improve proportionately. About a month later, Michael began to notice that his weight had increased substantially, and he had less energy. This example demonstrates that what is taught and what is learned are not necessarily the same thing. Although the health teacher provided accurate information on nutrition and dietary fat, instruction is only part of the learning equation. Michael's knowledge construction is another important factor. Rather than passively learning the facts being taught, he attempted to integrate the information into his own life, applying the information in a way that seemed appropriate. Besides providing facts and information, developing meaningful contexts, which are learner focused, better allows students to construct their own knowledge.

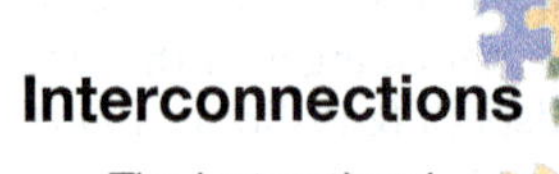

Interconnections

The instructional implications of knowledge construction are discussed in Chapter 12.

Build Understanding

In addition to his providing us with a student-centered perspective on learning, Piaget also stressed the importance of understanding learning as a building process. An art teacher may want her students to paint their interpretation of Van Gogh's *Sunflowers*, but she will have to start by teaching some basic painting principles. The novice begins the learning process by developing an appreciation of the basic learning elements in that domain. In the art class, the teacher will likely need to begin with basics such as lighting, perspective, and brush

techniques. Each one of these will require a complex dynamic between teaching and learning. They will also require the student to build meaningful relationships between each element to become an effective painter. Teachers must facilitate learning by providing a solid foundation of information, as well as providing support for more advanced content integration. Piaget's theory clearly indicates that it is impractical for the teacher to begin at the highest level of skill; rather, building and integrating skills is the key to effective learning.

Piaget and Vygotsky: Important Comparisons

Despite considerable attention in the scientific literature on the differences between Piaget and Vygotsky, there are actually many similarities between their theories (Shayer, 2003). Fundamentally, both theorists are constructivists (Walsh, 1991; Fowler, 1994; Siegler & Ellis, 1996). Both theories have, as central tenets, the idea that knowledge and learning are active processes and that each child constructs his own understanding of the world. Further, they both discuss the role of social interaction in development, including interpersonal interactions, cultural interactions, and historical influences (Devries, 1997; Piaget, 1965; Piaget & Inhelder, 1966; Vygotsky, 1981). They differed, however, in how central the social processes were in cognitive development. While Vygotsky placed social interactions at the center of his theory, Piaget was less specific about how social interactions influence development. Valsiner and Winegar (1992) suggest that Piaget and Vygotsky differ in *contextualizing* development in a social world versus developing a *contextual* approach. Piaget's theory follows a contextualizing approach, which means that development is influenced by social interactions but is, nevertheless, a distinct process that is driven by the child's exploration of the world. Piaget saw the importance of considering the context in which a child develops, but he emphasized that development is still primarily occurring within, and because of, the child. Vygotsky's contextual approach, on the other hand, places no such boundary between the social world and an individual's development within that context. He saw individuals as deriving their thinking from larger societal patterns of thinking, and, therefore, saw distinguishing between the two as unnecessary and inappropriate.

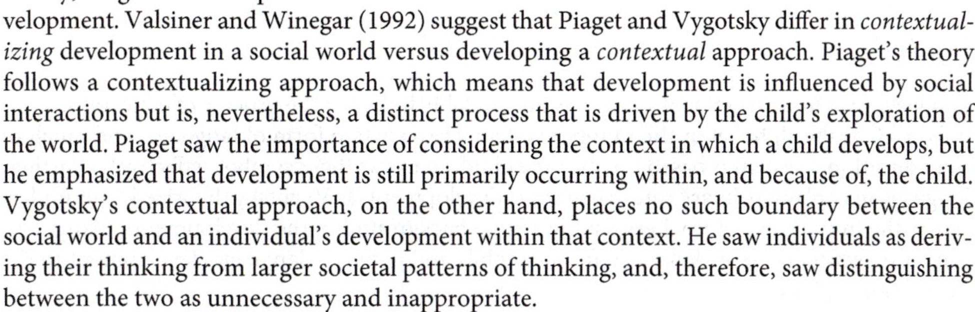

Piaget and Vygotsky also emphasized different types of social interactions. Piaget believed that interactions between peers produced the strongest influence on development. He theorized that conceptual differences between peers are likely to lead to disequilibrium and subsequently to adaptations in thinking. He believed interactions with adults were problematic because children would be less likely to engage in adaptive behaviors, preferring to simply accept the adult's point of view, given their superior status in the social dynamic. Vygotsky had a very different perspective on interpersonal interactions. He believed that an individual's way of thinking is derived from social interactions with someone that is more knowledgeable. Adults, by virtue of their greater experience, are likely to have mental skills the child has yet to internalize; therefore, the adult is in a unique position to facilitate the child's cognitive development. Another child, according to Vygotsky, is likely to have similar cognitive structures and can therefore offer little in terms of furthering development (Tudge & Winterhoff, 1993).

While the theories of Vygotsky and Piaget have fundamental differences, they can be used in a complimentary manner (Fuson, 2009), as can be seen in the constructivist approach to teaching and learning. In contrast to the behaviorist view that was pervasive in education in the early and middle 1900s, the constructivist perspective views the role of the learner as dynamic and active in cognitive development. The theories of both Piaget and Vygotsky embody this perspective, without minimizing the importance of a learner's interactions in the environment. For Piaget, these interactions involve active exploration of the environment and symbolic representations of the world. For Vygotsky, the interactions with the environment that shape thinking are social and language based. In the next section we will further explore language, arguably the most complex symbolic representation system we use, and the foundation it plays in complex social interactions.

SUMMARIZE AND REFLECT

1. Jean Piaget developed one of the most influential theories of cognitive development.
2. According to Piaget, children seek to maintain equilibrium between their schema and their experiences through the processes of assimilation, accommodation, and equilibration.
3. Piaget's theory has four cognitive stages of development: sensorimotor, preoperational, concrete operational, and formal operational. These stages highlight characteristic patterns of thinking exhibited within each stage.
4. Piaget's theory has implications for developmentally appropriate instruction.
5. Comparison of the theories of Piaget and Vygotsky emphasizes the importance of both theorists in the development of the constructivist teaching approach.

INFORMED APPLICATION

1. How could the processes of accommodation and assimilation affect student learning during a physical education lesson on Rugby?
2. Adolescent egocentrism is a potential barrier to effective interactions with teenagers. What steps can a teacher take to support student learning while being sensitive to the problems associated with this issue in cognitive development?

LANGUAGE DEVELOPMENT

Language, as our instructional vehicle, is unavoidably linked to the process of education. Symbols, such as the alphabet or the number system, are a written form of language; and much of our educational system is based on teaching children to use these symbols effectively. Further, language may play a primary role in cognitive development, as Vygotsky theorized. This underscores the importance of teachers having a solid background in the development of language. The next section presents language fundamentals and connects language development to the instructional process.

Components of Language

Semantics

The meaning of words

Syntax

The order of words to create meaning

Language is communication of ideas through the use of symbols. These symbols may be spoken, written, or expressed in a manual form of communication such as sign language. For example, the word *cat* symbolizes a specific small, furry animal. Understanding the meaning of words is referred to as **semantics**—the first of the five components of language we will cover (see Table 2.2). When we speak the word *cat*, we are semantically representing the idea of this animal through *expressive* language, or language production. To understand or comprehend the word *cat* when it is spoken, one uses *receptive* language.

Words are not the only way we can represent ideas. **Syntax**, our second component of language, is our ability to put words together in a certain order to represent more complicated

Table 2.2 The Five Components of Language

Language Component	*Definition*
1) Semantics	Word meaning
2) Syntax	Word order
3) Phonology	Speech sounds
4) Morphemes	Smallest unit of language that is meaningful
5) Pragmatics	Communicating appropriately within a context

ideas. For example, "The cat ran from the dog" has a very different meaning from "The dog ran from the cat." Changing single words in minor ways can dramatically affect meaning. In spoken languages, letters represent certain sounds, or phonemes. **Phonology** is our third component of language and refers to speech sounds. Phonemes have no meaning when standing alone; for example, the letter *c* in the word *cat* is meaningless by itself. Change the *c* to an *r*, however, and the meaning of the word, and the sentence, changes. The fourth component of language is **morphemes,** or the smallest unit of meaning in a language, such as the affixes placed at the beginning or ending of word stems (e.g., *ed, ing,* and *un*). Morphemes can be single letters or combinations of letters. Adding the letter s to the word dog, for example, changes the number of animals represented because in English, adding s to the end of a noun usually makes the noun plural. The fifth component of language involves the social aspects of communication, or pragmatics. **Pragmatic language** allows us to communicate appropriately within a given context, such as taking turns in a conversation, standing an appropriate distance away from the person to whom we are speaking, and providing feedback to indicate that we are listening. Before we review these components in more detail, let's first look at two general theories about the acquisition of language.

Phonology

The sounds in speech

Morpheme

The smallest unit of meaning in a language

Pragmatic language

Language used to communicate appropriately within a given context

Language Acquisition Theories

The question of how we acquire our incredibly complex language ability is frequently debated. We know learning plays a role in the development of language, because we are not born with the ability to produce or understand it. Yet, while learning clearly plays a role, maturation also appears to be important. Children worldwide acquire language in the much the same way and at about the same time, regardless of culture or language structure, suggesting a biological influence.

Reinforcement versus Maturation

The idea that we learn language exclusively via the behavioral learning principles of imitation and reinforcement, as proposed by B. F. Skinner in the 1950s, is difficult to support (Skinner, 1957). Skinner's idea was that language or verbal behavior was no different than any other aspect of our behavior. It is controlled by the same reinforcement and punishment principles (see Chapter 4). This view, however, has been challenged as providing an incomplete view of language learning (Chomsky, 1967). While the average two-year-old has about two hundred words in her expressive vocabulary (words that she has clearly been exposed to), there are an infinite number of ways in which these words can be put together. Even very young children produce original sentences—saying things that they have never heard before or been rewarded for, such as "Truck fast" or "Here, Mommy, cake." This indicates that more than imitation and reinforcement are operating in the development of this generative aspect of human language (Chomsky, 1965). The linguist Noam Chomsky became world famous in the 1960s by proposing that humans come into the world prewired to acquire language, possessing what he called a language-acquisition device (LAD). His theory that humans are born preprogrammed to acquire language, or the Nativists' perspective, emphasizes the role of biology and maturation—the nature side of the nature-nurture debate.

Interconnections

Skinner's behavioral theories are reviewed and discussed in Chapter 4.

According to his original ideas, humans are born with an innate understanding of the basic functions of language. He referred to this as the deep structure of language. Deep language structure was then translated into our overt language (the surface structure) based on the language used in our particular cultural environment. This process was called transformational grammar (Chomsky, *Syntactic Structures,* 1957). This theory directly contrasts the behaviorist notion that the environment, or nurture, is responsible for the acquisition of language.

Another developmental phenomenon, which points to maturation as an important process in language acquisition, is the fact that children develop language at a phenomenal rate. At around eighteen to twenty-four months, children experience a tremendous increase in vocabulary, learning up to twenty new words per week (Reznick & Goldfield, 1992). The average

Children develop language at a phenomenal rate.

two-year-old, with her two hundred word vocabulary, will have learned to recognize around ten thousand new words by the time she enters first grade, and thirty thousand more by the time she reaches fifth grade (Anglin, 1993). This rapid and exponential growth in language in the first few years of life differs from second language learning later in life, a point to which anyone taking a foreign language in college can attest. Eric Lenneberg, in the 1960s, tried to explain this later difficulty with learning language, proposing that we have a window of opportunity for acquiring language easily. He proposed a critical period in language development, a window of opportunity that is strongest initially early in early childhood and ends around adolescence. Lenneberg based his ideas on research findings with individuals who had brain injuries in the language areas of the brain, causing loss of language skills, a clinical condition known as **aphasia**. Adults with aphasia, Lenneberg noted, require intensive therapy in order to reestablish even rudimentary language skills, while children with aphasia often recover in a manner that appears effortless. Since the development of the critical-period hypothesis, many studies have been completed that support the idea of a window of opportunity in language development, at least for acquiring syntax (Hoff, 2001; Patkowski, 1980). Many contemporary theorists, however, prefer to refer to this window as a sensitive, rather than critical, period in development. The fact that we are able to learn second languages in adulthood, for example, even if it is effortful, indicates the window of opportunity never really closes.

Aphasia

A clinical condition in which language skills are lost due to injury in the language areas of the brain

Interactionist Perspective

Many contemporary theorists believe that maturation and learning interact significantly in language development (Bohannon & Bonvillian, 1997; Tomasello, 1995; Rice, 1989). They argue that humans, as a species, are indeed biologically predisposed to learn language easily early in life and in relatively the same way. We learn language easily, not because of a language acquisition device, but rather for the same reason that we all develop cognitively in much the same way, because we all have brains that develop, or mature, in a similar manner. What we learned of brain development in the developmental neuroscience section of this chapter supports this integrationist view of language development. Recall that research indicates infants come into the world biologically primed to make synaptic connections in their brains as a function of experience, in this case exposure to language. Also supporting this biological predisposition is the finding that most people use the left hemisphere for processing language (Pujol, Deus, Losilla, & Capdevila, 1999). Thus, most people have highly organized areas of neuronal connection existing in the same location in the brain, suggesting that, as a species, we may have specific neurons that are genetically preprogrammed to make connections when exposed to language.

Finally, a number of other processes also interact with maturation and learning in the development of language, including cognitive, motivational, and social factors. For example, research shows that language development and cognitive development are strongly linked with children's use of language, adapting along with their changing understanding of the world (Shaeffer, 2002). Language also serves a social, communicative function. We are motivated to use language not only because we want to express our ideas and understanding of the world but also so that others can understand our ideas. We may learn to use grammatically correct sentences, for example, because it is necessary for us to interact with others socially (Bates, 1999). In line with Vygotsky's ideas regarding cognitive development, many integrationists believe that the process of a child's interacting with others who are linguistically more sophisticated initiates the development of the brain's language centers, which in turn allows the child to interact in new ways (Bloom, Margulis, Tinker, & Fujita, 1996). In the next section, we will explore language in the classroom, where the complex interaction of biological, environmental, cognitive, and social factors in the development of language is easily seen.

F.A.Q.

Max Palen—"The reinforcement theory seems reasonable, but I don't understand the maturation view. According to this view, is reinforcement meaningless?

Professor Campbell—"Many contemporary linguists recognize the importance of both processes. Imagine putting your clothes away in a closet without any shelves. This would be a fairly disorganized process. Now imagine putting clothes in a closet with built-in shelves. The process would be much more organized and efficient. Maturationists simply proposed we have built-in shelves for language. We can still be reinforced for what goes onto the shelves."

Language and Linguistic Diversity in the Classroom

Language develops in much the same way and at about the same time for most people. Like Piaget's cognitive stages, language learning proceeds through a series of developmental milestones (e.g., first words, joining words, etc.). Language milestones are based on normative data, however, and should be used cautiously when charting an individual child's progress regarding language development. Teachers should, however, have a basic understanding of linguistic trends. Moats and Lyon (1996) assert that "a new approach to teacher education is needed that emphasizes the importance of language knowledge for literacy instruction, as well as its skilled application to instructional planning" (p. 73). In this section, we will focus on language development in the preschool and school-age period, exploring the classroom significance of each of the five components of language outlined earlier.

F.A.Q.

Anne Rome—"That makes sense, but explain how this perspective is supported by neuroscience research?"

Professor Campbell—"One of the best sources of research evidence supporting that we are at least somewhat pre-wired for language comes from the simple fact that the vast majority of people have language functioning specialized on the left side of the brain. This is well over what would be expected by chance. It seems the brain is designed to place control of language on this side of the brain."

Phonology

The songs and rhymes preschool children love serve an important purpose; that is, they are exercises in receptive phonology. When we try to think of a word that rhymes with *cat*, we might exchange the *c* for an *r*, manipulating the speech sounds so that the word we choose, in this case *rat*, "sounds" the same except for the beginning. In kindergarten, much of the curriculum centers on the development of sound-symbol correspondence, or learning that each letter has a particular sound. In first grade, most children begin to understand that words are made up of these speech sounds blended together in left to right order, whether this is taught implicitly or explicitly. Some children, however, do not have good phonological awareness skills, and research shows that these children may have difficulty learning to read (Lyon & Chhabra, 1996). **Phonological awareness** refers to the ability to recognize different units of sound within words. Research also suggests that children who show problems with phonological awareness may require instruction that is tailored to their individual learning needs in order to avoid reading failure and later diagnosis of learning disability (Lyon, 1997).

The songs and rhymes preschool children love serve an important purpose; that is, they are exercises in receptive phonology.

Expressive phonology involves the production of speech sounds. During the preschool years, it is not atypical for children to have difficulty producing some of the sounds in their native language, especially the following letters: *s*, *th*, *z*, and *v* (Bowen, 1998). These problems may persist in early elementary school, resolving without intervention; however, pronunciation problems, which are very severe or which hinder communication, may require specific intervention. Children with expressive phonology problems respond well to speech/language intervention, and many collaborative techniques have been developed as alternatives to the traditional articulation interventions.

Phonological awareness

The ability to recognize different units of sound within words

Morphology

A morpheme is the smallest unit of meaning in a language. Morphemes may be single words, grammatical modifiers such as prefixes and suffixes, or the inflection used to convey a specific meaning in a sentence. Children begin to understand the rules for using grammatical morphemes, such as the plural and possessive forms of nouns, the complicated conjugation of the verb *to be*, and the appropriate use of prepositions in the preschool years. Many preschoolers, in fact, *overextend* these rules, making errors in their use of grammatical morphemes. A three-year-old who says, "I goed to the store" or "I brush my tooths" is actually showing a beginning understanding of the morphological rules of English; he is simply applying the rules in cases which are exceptions to the rule. The majority of children start school with sophisticated implicit knowledge of morphology rules, and this knowledge is further developed via explicit teaching. When we teach the formation of plurals, possessives, or verb tenses, for example, we are actually teaching the morphological rules of Standard English. Many students find verb tenses and plural forms easy to learn since they naturally use these when speaking. Not all children, however, have equal degrees of experience with the Standard English morphology. Children who have limited English proficiency may be accustomed to using a language that has different morphology rules. Cultural differences in English language use may also influence knowledge of Standard English morphology. Ebonics, or the speech form used in some communities of African Americans, has morphological rules, which differ from those of Standard English, particularly with regard to verb tenses and pluralization (Rickford, 1997). Since a child's sophistication with regard to morphology rules can influence reading and spelling skills, this places many students at a distinct disadvantage when learning to read, spell, and express their thoughts in written form. Furthermore, moving to a second language can have disruptive effects on morphological structure that persist into adulthood (Clahsen, Felser, Neubauer, Sato, & Silva, 2010). This issue lies at the heart of the controversy regarding whether teaching should be accomplished using Standard English or a student's primary language or dialect, a debate that we will explore from both sides in Chapter 8.

Semantics

Recall that semantics refers to the meaningful basis of language, both of individual words and combinations of words. Children understand far more than they can produce, or their receptive language is more advanced than their expressive language, at all ages (Oviatt, 1980). Preschoolers show not only exponential growth in their vocabularies, they also begin to understand and use relational words, such as high/low, in/on, and here/there. According to research, vocabulary knowledge increases from around ten thousand words in first grade to around forty thousand words in fifth grade (Anglin, 1993). There is much individual variability, however, in vocabulary knowledge. Some research indicates that children from low-income backgrounds may have heard only 50% of the words and can understand only 50% of the meanings of words understood by children from high-income backgrounds, putting them at a distinct disadvantage in the classroom (Hirsch, 2001; Walker, 1994). In addition, there are increasing numbers of students in the U.S. with limited English proficiency (LEP). These students may have typical, or even advanced, vocabularies in their native languages, but they are at a significant disadvantage at an English only school (DelCampo & DelCampo, 2000). We will discuss these and other issues related to linguistic diversity in more detail in Chapter 8.

Metalinguistic awareness

The ability to think about language and language rules by reflecting on language itself

Syntax

All languages have syntax or rules for word order. Most of us speak in syntactically correct sentences; that is, the order in which we place our words follows the rules of English. Even preschool children follow these rules although they have never been explicitly taught to do so. In fact, trying to learn the syntactical rules of English explicitly is often quite difficult, even for a native English speaker. For example, many of us remember the difficulty we had in high school identifying the *direct object* or *past participle* in a sentence. When we are able to think about language and language rules by reflecting on language itself, instead of using it to communicate, we are showing **metalinguistic awareness**. Metalinguistic awareness increases significantly with age, allowing us to understand and use sentences that are increasingly complex (Whitehurst & Lonigan, 1998). Additionally, research shows that students benefit from instructional approaches that support metalinguistic awareness (Zipke, 2008). Interestingly, when learning a second language in adulthood, we generally start from a metalinguistic perspective, developing an awareness of the rules first and then constructing our sentences accordingly. Speaking or writing can be a tedious process when having to think about syntactical rules, as many of us well know from taking foreign language classes in high school and college. Students who have native languages other than English may experience problems in the classroom related to the unfamiliar syntax. Other students that have English as their native language may have less experience with complicated syntax because of language impover-

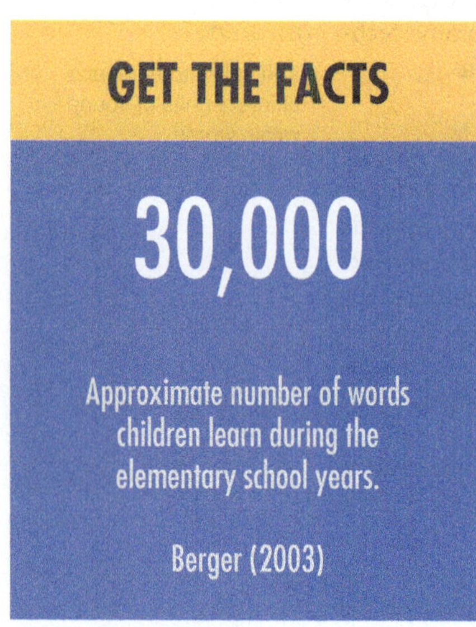

ishment or limitation in the exposure to rich language usage. In fact, some researchers believe that the reading achievement gap which exists between low-income and middle class students may in actuality be a language gap, with low income students showing a lack of familiarity with complex syntactical structures, as well as the decreased vocabulary knowledge discussed earlier (Hirsch, 2001). Thus, instruction that is language sensitive may help us to build not only functional reading skills but also literacy for challenging and diverse texts.

Pragmatics

Pragmatic language, or communicating appropriately in a given context, makes a significant impact on a student's social functioning (Schumaker & Deschler, 1984; Coplan & Weeks, 2009). Students with pragmatic language problems may have difficulty using language in a socially acceptable manner; they may speak too loudly, stand too closely, enter conversations inappropriately, or interrupt because they have trouble taking turns in a conversation. They may also have trouble understanding the verbal and nonverbal communication cues of others, including understanding facial expressions, body language, or other nonverbal "hints." One particular area of difficulty for children with pragmatic language problems involves understanding the true meaning of an indirect request. For example, your roommate asks you, "Could you turn the music down?" You know she really is not asking but rather telling you to turn it down. A child with pragmatic language problems may not understand a request that is phrased as a question and answer "Yes" to the question, "Must you tap your pencil?" Frequently, this type of response causes others to think the child is being oppositional, when in fact the child simply missed the point of the indirect request. This is an important aspect of language functioning to consider in the classroom. Research shows that teachers "ask politely" quite frequently, with some studies showing rates as high as 27% of the utterances of K–8 teachers consisting of indirect requests (Lazar, Warr-Leeper, Nicholson, & Johnson, 1989). Most pragmatic rules are implicit; that is, no one ever really teaches us out loud that we should stand a distance of around two feet away from a stranger with whom we are conversing. Yet, we feel very uncomfortable when someone violates this rule. We learn pragmatic language skills through our interactions with others over time; therefore, many pragmatic rules are culturally mediated, including loudness of voice, amount of eye contact, and use of gestures (Hurley, 1992). Additionally, non-native English speakers have been shown to have difficulty understanding appropriate responses for initiating and maintaining conversations, as well as for adjusting request strategies to meet classroom norms (Wolfson, 1989; Ellis, 1992). It is frequently very difficult to identify exactly where a student is having difficulty in a conversation or interaction, much less to explicitly teach the subtle language skills that will help him better navigate socially in the classroom.

SUMMARIZE AND REFLECT

1. Language has the following components: semantics, syntax, morphology, phonology, and pragmatics.
2. Maturation and learning play a role in the acquisition of language. Research evidence indicates that not only are both processes important but also the complexity of language development is best explained by an interaction between the two.
3. Language and linguistic diversity are important aspects of the classroom environment. The impact of language and linguistic diversity on academic and social functioning is affected by the developmental progression of the five components of language.

INFORMED APPLICATION

1. Teachers often experience a situation where a student appears to be learning effectively, understanding directions, and engaged in learning, but when questioned demonstrates limited learning. Assuming the student did indeed learn the material effectively, what aspect of language function likely explains the student's difficulty when questioned?
2. One of the most under appreciated aspects of linguistic functioning is pragmatic language facility. How can a teacher enhance lesson plan development to improve this aspect of communication?

THE CHAPTER IN REVIEW

In this chapter, we explored the developmental foundations of thinking, reasoning, and language from a variety of perspectives. Since human development is one of the most complex phenomena we study, there are an infinite number of places on which to focus in our quest to understand the development of cognition and language. We started our exploration by viewing development from a broad perspective, with a focus on the basic developmental processes of maturation and adaptation and an emphasis on the inextricable interaction between the two in human development. We discussed similarities and differences in development between individuals; and we highlighted the importance of being aware of the interaction between intraindividual strengths and weaknesses, as well as interindividual differences. We then explored the ways in which our understanding of development may be both validated and furthered by research in cognitive neuroscience, highlighting basic brain processes and function and major research findings which may have implications for teaching and learning. We reviewed in detail the influential theories of Lev Vygotsky and Jean Piaget, outlining each of their perspectives on developmental change and discussing implications of their theories for the classroom. We compared their theories, emphasizing that while they essentially viewed development through different lenses, both of their theories have strongly influenced the field of education and the constructivist view of teaching and learning. Finally, we focused our attention on the uniquely human phenomenon of language, exploring theories of language acquisition from both maturational and learning perspectives, again providing evidence that the interaction of the two is paramount in development. We outlined the five components of language and explored language and linguistic diversity in the classroom, illustrating the complex interaction among biological, environmental, cognitive, and social factors in the development of each component of language and the impact of language and linguistic diversity in the classroom.

Interdisciplinary Case Focus

principal special educator
teacher parents psychologist
social worker physical educator
nurse peers doctor

Meet Drew, a six-year-old boy who is having great difficulty adjusting to the increased structure of Ms. Craig's first grade classroom. Drew has trouble staying in his seat, keeping his hands to himself, and being quiet when Ms. Craig is talking. He also has difficulty with task persistence, seldom completing assignments. If he does finish, he often forgets to turn in his work. He has lost his home/school folder three times since school began, and twice he accidentally threw his lunch box away. He has yet to learn to raise his hand, interrupting other children or blurting out answers impulsively when his teacher has called on another child. So far, Ms. Craig has been able to accommodate many of Drew's behaviors by allowing him to sit outside the circle during circle time so that he can move around, by moving the desks of the other children so that they are outside his reach, and by providing multiple verbal prompts to help him stay on task and turn in his work. While these efforts have been somewhat effective, Ms. Craig is aware of the possibility that Drew may have attention deficit/hyperactivity disorder (AD/HD); and with his parents' consent she refers him for testing.

Assessment

Educator Ms. Craig shared information with the school psychologist regarding Drew's behavior in class, as well as her attempts at intervention. She indicated that she was unsure if Drew's behavior is significantly different from average for his age since he is the youngest child in her class, and she expressed the hope that he would improve as the year progressed.

Psychologist Jackie Robes, PhD, the school psychologist, first conferred with Drew's teacher since Ms. Craig was most familiar with his behavioral issues in the classroom. She then conducted a detailed interview with Drew's parents, asking questions regarding his early development and his behavior in other situations—as well as questions related to his inattention, impulsivity, and hyperactivity. She had Drew's parents complete standardized behavior rating scales, so that she could compare Drew's behavior to the behavior of other children his age across a variety of settings. Results indicated that while Drew may be more active and inattentive than other children his age, he is not significantly so. Dr. Robes also had Drew's teacher complete a standardized rating scale, with similar results. Consulting with Drew's family physician, Drew was not diagnosed with AD/HD.

Parents Drew's parents reported concern regarding his problems in class, and they expressed interest in doing whatever they could to help. They said that Drew has always been an active child who is somewhat easily distracted; however, he did not seem to have significant problems in his preschool or kindergarten classes. They also indicated that they have recently divorced and are sharing custody of Drew. Drew's father reported that he had just moved into a new house and was still unpacking boxes, and he wondered if the divorce and moving between houses could be affecting Drew in school.

Social Worker Michael Young, LCSW, met with Drew's parents to discuss their concerns regarding Drew's adjustment to their divorce, as well as to discuss various aspects of their shared custody arrangement.

Collaborative Intervention Plan

While Drew's behaviors did not meet the criteria necessary for a diagnosis of AD/HD, they will likely continue to interfere with his functioning in the classroom; and each member of the interdisciplinary assessment team had something to offer regarding intervention.

Educator Ms. Craig, after consulting with the school psychologist, developed some simple strategies that helped Drew dramatically. One of the most successful strategies involved a brief home/school collaborative reward program that she and Drew's parents implemented together. Initially, Drew received three extra minutes of playtime whenever he raised his hand before speaking. He was easily able to succeed with this plan, and Ms. Craig added new criteria each week. She used this home/school reward system and other ideas that the psychologist offered not only with Drew but also with several other students. She found that her classroom quickly became more manageable.

Psychologist Dr. Robes provided Drew's teacher with several possible ideas for helping to decrease his problem behavior. She explained that while Drew did not have AD/HD, many of his problems were on the same spectrum. Clearly Drew's problem behaviors resulted from a complicated set of factors, including changes in his family and home situation, as well as possible mild attention and activity problems. She made several suggestions, including giving Drew formalized time to move around, a structured verbal prompt schedule, a "buddy" to sit next to who would be a good role model, and a positive, home/school collaborative behavior program to be implemented with both parents.

Parents Drew's parents agreed to implement a consistent home/school collaborative program to reward improvements in Drew's classroom behavior. They discussed and implemented some of the scheduling and organization techniques for minimizing the disruption involved in Drew's movement between two houses. They also helped Drew become involved in a local support group for children of families in transition.

Social Worker Michael provided Drew's parents with strategies for maximizing the logistics of shared custody, including organization and scheduling ideas. He told them about a local, community family services support program called "Children with Two Houses" and gave them the director's contact information. He also offered his support in the future and expressed that he was impressed with their willingness to work with the team to help Drew.

Key Terms

TERM	*Page*
Accommodation	47
Adaptations	31
Adolescent egocentrism	55
Aphasia	62
Assimilation	47
Centration	51
Cerebral cortex	36
Classification	52
Cognitive equilibrium	47
Cognitive neuroscience	36
Conservation task	51
Corpus callosum	37
Decenter	52
Development	31
Developmental neuroscience	38
Disequilibrium	47
Egocentric	50
Egocentric speech	41
Elaboration	39
Equilibration	47
Frontal lobes	37
Hypothesis	54
Hypothetico-deductive reasoning	54
Intentional behavior	50
Interindividual comparison	33
Intermental changes	41
Intraindividual comparison	33
Intramental changes	41
Invariant sequencing	49
Lateralized brain function	37
Macrostructure	39

TERM	*Page*
Maturation	32
Metalinguistic awareness	64
Microstructure	39
Morpheme	61
Neo-Piagetian theorists	56
Neurons	36
Neurotransmitter	36
Object permanence	50
Occipital lobes	37
Operations	50
Parietal lobes	37
Phonological awareness	63
Phonology	61
Pragmatic language	61
Private speech	41
Process theorist	41
Reversibility	52
Scaffolding	45
Schema	47
Semantics	60
Semiotic function	50
Seriation	53
Sociocultural theorist	40
Symbolic representation	50
Synapses	36
Synaptogenesis	36
Syntax	60
Temporal lobe	37
Transformation	51
Zone of proximal development	44

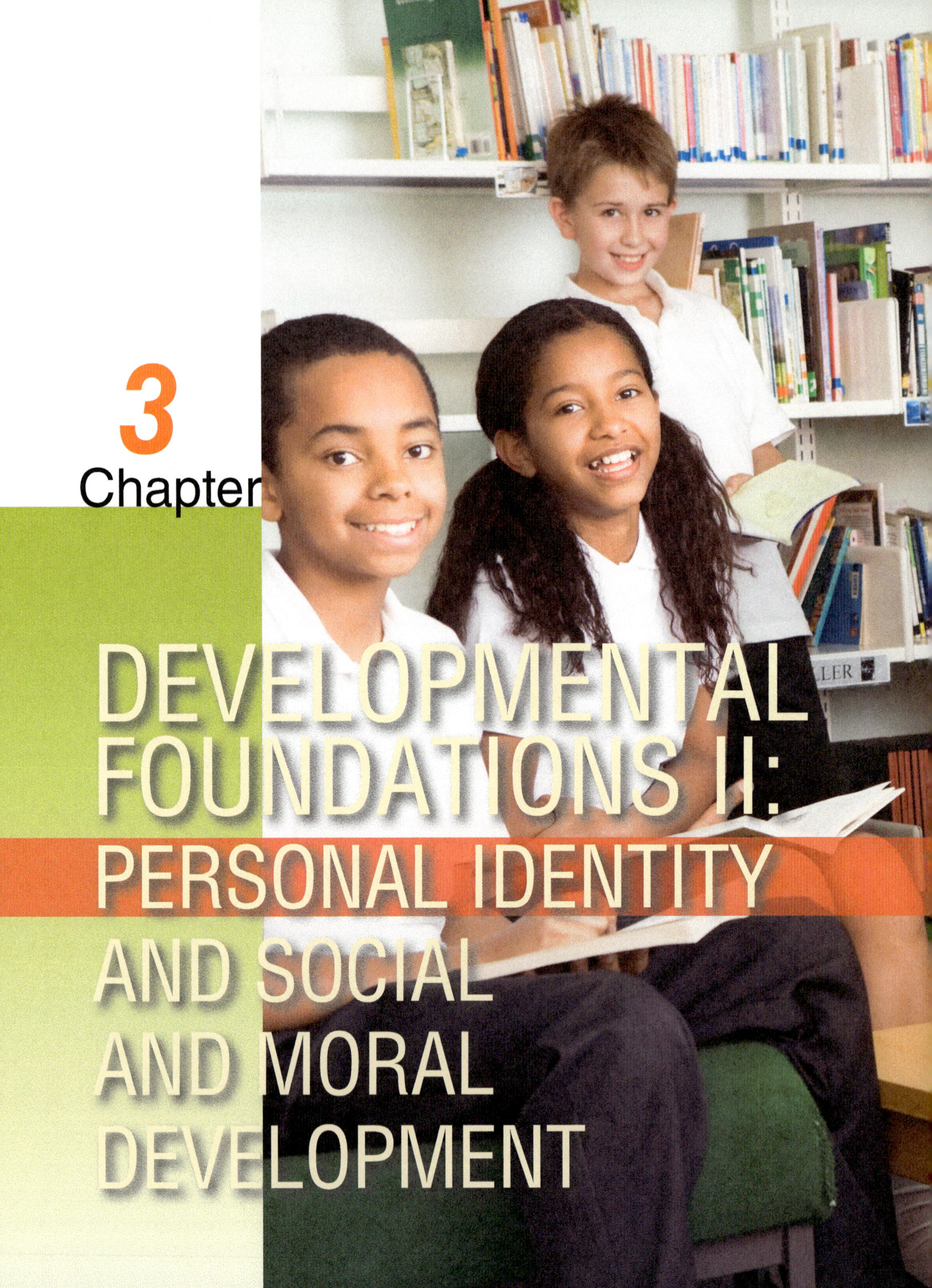

Chapter 3

DEVELOPMENTAL FOUNDATIONS II: PERSONAL IDENTITY AND SOCIAL AND MORAL DEVELOPMENT

What's It All About ...

How do we develop an understanding of ourselves?

What social factors influence the development of our identity?

How is our behavior and thinking influenced by social interactions?

What is morality? How do we develop social responsibility?

Chapter Objectives

- Understand the difference between self-concept and self-esteem.
- Describe factors influencing the development of self-perceptions.
- Explain how self-perceptions relate to academic success.
- Explain how to promote accurate and positive self-perceptions in the classroom.

- Review basic principles of social development.
- Understand the importance of Erikson's stage theory of psychosocial development.
- Explain how to promote the development of personal identity in the classroom.

- Understand agents of socialization.
- Describe the relation between the development of social behavior and social thinking.
- Explain how to promote social development in the classroom.

- Describe Piaget's theory of morality.
- Describe Kohlberg's theory of moral development.
- Explain criticisms of Kohlberg's theory and alternative points of view.
- Understand how to address problematic moral and social behaviors in school.
- Explain how to promote moral and socially responsible behaviors in the classroom.

EXTENDED OUTLINE

Developmental Foundations II: Personal Identity and Social and Moral Development

I. What's It All About ...
II. From Today's Headlines
III. The Development of Self-Perceptions
  A. Self-concept
  B. Self-esteem
    1. Self-esteem and gender
    2. Self-esteem and ethnicity
  C. Self-efficacy
  D. Influences on the development of self-perceptions
    1. Social experiences
    2. Social comparisons
    3. Success and failure experiences
  E. Self-perceptions and academic success
  F. Promoting accurate and positive self-perceptions in the classroom
    1. Using the zone of proximal development
    2. Teaching students to respect differences
  G. Summarize and reflect
IV. Erikson's Theory of Psychosocial Development
  A. Basic principles: psychosocial crises and lifespan development
  B. Erikson's Stage Theory of Psychosocial Development
    1. Preschool development
      a. Trust versus mistrust (birth to twelve–eighteen months)
      b. Autonomy versus shame and doubt (eighteen months to three years)
      c. Initiative versus guilt (three to six years)
    2. School age development
      a. Industry versus inferiority (six to twelve years)
      b. Identity versus role confusion (twelve to eighteen years)
    3. Adult development
      a. Intimacy versus isolation (Young adulthood)
      b. Generativity versus stagnation (middle adulthood)
      c. Integrity versus despair (late adulthood)
  C. Promoting the development of personal identity in the classroom
    1. Preschool development
    2. School age development
    3. Adolescent development
  D. Summarize and reflect
V. Personal Development and Socialization
  A. Agents of socialization
    1. Parents
    2. Teachers
    3. Peers
  B. The development of social behavior and social thinking
    1. Social skills
    2. Social competence
    3. Social cognition
  C. Promoting social development in the classroom
  D. Summarize and reflect

VI. The Development of Morality and Social Responsibility
   A. Piaget's Theory of Morality
   B. Kohlberg's Theory of Moral Development
      1. Preconventional
      2. Conventional
      3. Postconventional
   C. Criticisms of Kohlberg's theory and alternatives
      1. The stages
      2. Hypothetical moral dilemmas
      3. Male biased
   D. Problematic moral and social behaviors in school
      1. Aggression and bullying
      2. Victimization
      3. Cheating
   E. Promoting moral and socially responsible behaviors in the classroom
      1. Moral and character education programs
      2. Moral processing
   F. Summarize and reflect
VII. The Chapter in Review
VIII. Interdisciplinary Case Focus

From Today's Headlines

Vol. I No. 3 Teaching World, 2012

HOW DO WE DEVELOP GOOD CHARACTER?

Students and parents have noticed a renewed emphasis in the development of good character. Alarming statistics showing our youth engaged in a wide variety of negative behaviors fuels this interest. The Josephson Institute of Ethics has conducted a nationwide survey on the attitudes, values, and behaviors of high school students for several years. Although the 2008 report shows improvement in some areas, responses to many questions indicate problems.

Survey Highlights

(Responses based on behaviors over the previous twelve months)

- 82% admit they lied to parent
- 65% admit they lied to teacher
- 31% copied an Internet document
- 64% cheated during a test at school
- 82% copied another's homework
- 30% stole something from a store
- 23% cheated or bent the rules to win in sports

These data indicate a substantial number of youth are resorting to behaviors indicating a lack of good character. This is striking given that virtually all of the survey respondents (98%) indicated it was important for them to be a person of good character. The obvious question: Why the discrepancy between self-perception and actual behavior?

Many believe the answer lies in a failure to teach our children the basics of good moral character. To address this issue, many programs have been developed to help schools provide explicit instruction in what they believe to be fundamental facets of good character. These programs typically focus on qualities such as respect, fairness, and good citizenship among others.

These programs are not without critics; however, what constitutes good character is frequently debated. This debate raises some important questions. What is character? What factors influence its development? Is character related to other personal qualities?

MAKE THE CONNECTION

This chapter will cover a variety of topics related to personal development. We will examine how we come to understand ourselves and how we develop a sense of personal identity. Understanding how students develop their self-perceptions is important, but does not always help us predict how they will behave, as this survey indicates. We will also look at how social factors interact with self-perceptions to direct behavior. Finally, we will discuss morality and character and the issues raised by the Josephson Institute study.

THE DEVELOPMENT OF SELF-PERCEPTIONS

Take a minute and think about the last person you met. What were your initial impressions? What kind of attitude did he/she have? Would you describe the person as kind or mean, outspoken or quiet, popular or someone who keeps to him/herself? You could probably answer each of these questions without much difficulty. This is because making judgments about others seems relatively straightforward. Of course, we may not always be accurate, but the assessment seems almost automatic. Now, consider the same series of questions, but this time consider yourself. What kind of attitude do you have? Are you kind, but quiet and reserved? Are you outspoken, or sometimes overbearing? Most of us find an examination of ourselves far more difficult than an examination of someone else. In fact, we often spend little time getting to know the most important person in our lives, our self.

In this section, we will explore factors influencing the development of a sense of self. We will also examine how a student's conception of self influences success in the classroom. How might self-perception influence classroom functioning? Students have beliefs about their overall academic ability or intelligence and their ability in specific academic areas (Marsh, 1994). Research shows that if students perceive themselves as competent in these abilities, they are more likely to be academically motivated (Phillips, 1984). This can then translate into academic success (Marsh, 1992; Gage & Berliner, 1992; Shavelson & Bolus, 1982; Tsereteli, Martskvishvili, Aptarashvili, Darsavelidze, & Sadzaglishvili, 2010). Yet, which comes first, positive self-perceptions or academic success? In this section, we will outline factors influencing the development of the self and explore the effects of self-views on classroom performance. We will also outline strategies to help students develop accurate and positive reflections of their strengths and weaknesses.

Self-Concept

Self-concept

Typically, one's perceptions about oneself

Defining self-concept may seem relatively straightforward; however, a close examination of the research reveals an intricately, complex part of ourselves. **Self-concept** is typically defined as a person's perceptions about who he/she is (Shavelson, 1982). The vast number of areas to which it can be applied complicates this seemingly simple definition. For example, we can have ideas about our physical capabilities, our ability to socialize at a party, or our ability to do well in this class (Pintrich & Schunk, 2002; Gore & Cross, 2011). Self-concept is further complicated by the fact that an idea about our self can be very broad, such as "I am smart." This implies that your intellectual ability makes it possible to succeed in most classes. It might also be very specific, such as "I am only good at language arts." Most researchers agree that self-concept cannot be adequately understood without looking at both the general and the specific ideas we have about ourselves (Marsh, 1994).

Self-concept is, therefore, best depicted in a hierarchical model, like the one depicted in Figure 3.1. According to this model, an individual's general self-concept is made up of ideas about oneself across many situational-specific areas (Shavelson & Bolus, 1976, 1982; Byrne &

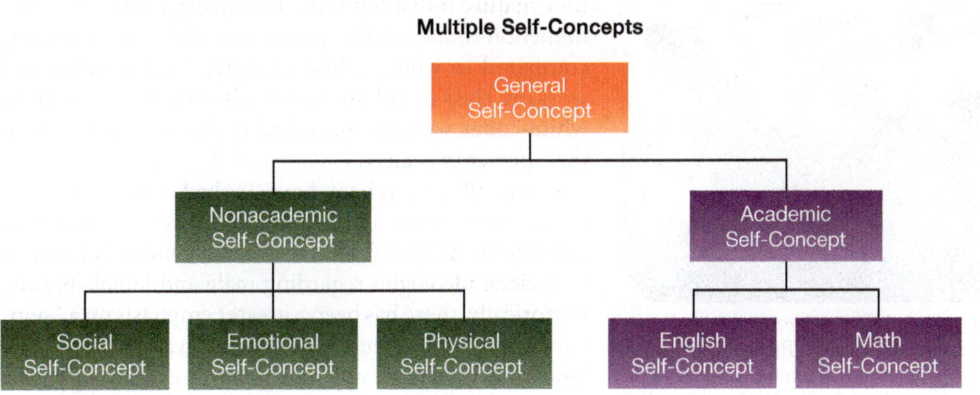

Figure 3.1
Multiple Self-Concepts

Gavin, 1996). Although it is unrealistic to represent all of the potential components of an individual's self-concept, research suggests that specific self-perceptions in the areas of physical, social, emotional, and academic functioning play an important role in determining general self-concept (Shavelson & Bolus, 1982). Of particular interest to educators is the academic self-concept, which can also be hierarchically divided into specific areas, such as a self-concept in math and English (Byrne & Gavin, 1996). For example, if someone were to ask you if you like math, how long would it take you to respond? For most of us, we have a clearly defined sense of our math ability. Our self-concept with respect to math, English, and other academic subjects is usually a well-defined part of our overall self-concept. Later in the chapter we will discuss how we come to these perceptions and how educators can influence their development.

Self-Esteem

Self-esteem

Generally, the level of regard we have for ourselves

Reflective appraisal

The interplay between how we view ourselves and how others view us

Another factor related to self-concept is self-esteem. **Self-esteem** is generally defined as the level of regard we have for ourselves (Harter, 1993). That is, self-esteem is how positive or negative, superior or inferior, valuable or worthless we feel about ourselves (Thorits, 1999). We develop our self-esteem through a complex interaction between beliefs about our identity and social interactions with others (McMullin & Cairney, 2004). These self-opinions are particularly impacted by the views held by important people in our lives (Rosenberg & Perlin, 1978). There is a constant interplay between how we view ourselves and how others view us. This interaction has been termed **reflective appraisal**.

Another interesting finding regarding self-esteem is its strong relation to physical attractiveness (Harter, 2000). Harter's research has shown that even children as young as four show a strong relation between perceptions of attractiveness and self-esteem. The stronger a person's beliefs are about his/her attractiveness, the higher that individual's self-esteem. Additionally, Harter's research examined the possibility that other factors might better predict self-esteem. For example, Harter examined whether academic success would be a better predictor of self-esteem for gifted and learning disabled students. She hypothesized that academic success might be a better predictor of self-esteem for these students because of its high personal relevance. Contrary to her predictions, perceived physical attractiveness remained the best predictor of self-esteem. Harter proposed that these findings relate to the fact that one's attractiveness is always on display and, therefore, ever present in an individual's daily life. Other factors, like academic success or athletic ability, only become significant at certain times.

Self-Esteem and Gender

The findings regarding attractiveness and self-esteem also lead to some interesting gender differences. The most widely reported finding regarding gender differences and self-esteem is that as adults, women have lower levels of self-esteem compared to men (Josephs, Markus, & Tafarodi, 1992; Rosenfield, 1999). Further indication is that boys and girls are similar on measures of self-esteem through early adolescence, and then they begin to show differences as they mature into adulthood. Rosenberg relates this phenomenon to the relative power men have in our society compared to women. Interestingly, she also finds that working class men have lower self-esteem compared to white-collar workers, presumably due to differences in their power in society.

Some researchers attribute gender differences to the societal ideologies regarding male and female beauty. Throughout history there has been greater emphasis placed on female beauty.

Not all researchers have looked toward societal power as an explanation for adult gender differences in self-esteem. Harter (1999) attributes gender differences to societal ideologies regarding male and female beauty. Historically, there has been a greater emphasis on a "standard" for female beauty. Therefore, deviations from this "standard" are more apparent for women. Susan Faludi

(1999), however, has speculated that the existing gender differences in self-esteem may decrease in the future as our society begins to develop more defined standards for male beauty.

A final point to consider regarding self-esteem and gender is that self-esteem is not necessarily a single unified belief. This is an important consideration when reviewing research in this area. Many researchers conceptualize self-esteem as a global evaluative judgment, applied in the broadest sense (Brodbar, 1980). Studies using this type of definition have produced varied findings, but overall have found small differences in self-esteem favoring males compared to females (Kling, Hyde, Showers, & Buswell, 1999). We may also, however, have self-judgments within specific areas (e.g., academics, athletics, creative arts, etc.) that might vary considerably. These domain specific types of self-judgments are most typically researched under the heading self-concept (discussed above), rather than self-esteem. For example, Marsh (1989) reported higher ratings for math self-concept in males and higher language arts self-concept ratings in females. Marsh noted that these findings are generally consistent with gender stereotypes present in our society. A recent review study on a domain specific framework for self-esteem found some interesting differences (Gentile et al., 2009). Men scored higher on self-esteem associated with physical appearance, athleticism, personal self, and self-satisfaction. Women scored higher on self-esteem related to behavioral conduct and morality. No differences were found on self-esteem measures related to academics, social acceptance, family, and emotional self-esteem. These findings underscore the importance to consider research in an area collectively. As you can see, it is difficult to determine the answer to the question, "Are there gender differences in self-esteem?"

Self-Esteem and Ethnicity

In addition to research on gender differences in self-esteem, many studies have sought to determine if self-esteem is influenced by racial or ethnic identification. Chapman and Mullis (2000) conducted a study on coping mechanisms and self-esteem between individuals who identify as either African Americans or Caucasian Americans. Results from this study found no self-esteem differences between these groups. These results are similar to other studies finding no significant differences between African Americans and Caucasians in reported self-esteem (Wade, 1991; Zimmerman, Copeland, Shope, & Dielman, 1997). It is important to note that other studies have found differences with African Americans reporting higher levels of self-esteem compared to Caucasians (Maton et al., 1996; Smith, 1995; Wilson, 1989). As with the self-esteem research, answers are illusive.

Many studies have sought to determine if self-esteem is influenced by racial or ethnic identification.

Another issue frequently addressed in this area is the difference between group self-esteem and personal self-esteem. **Group self-esteem** refers to an individual's judgment about a group of people to which they belong. **Personal self-esteem** refers to judgments about one's own personal abilities or competencies (Porter & Washington, 1993). The distinction is important in that individuals' beliefs about their own worth may differ substantially from their judgments about a larger group to which they belong (Phelps, Taylor, & Gerard, 2001; Aboud & Skerry, 1984). As we will see later in the chapter, educators often need to clarify the nature of a student's self-esteem issues in order to implement effective interventions. At times, it may be that the student is experiencing difficulty with self-perceptions due to personal failures. Other students may experience self-esteem loss due to their ideas about a larger racial or ethnic group with which they identify.

Group self-esteem

An individual's judgment about a group of people to which he or she belongs

Personal self-esteem

An individual's judgments about his/her personal abilities or competencies

Self-Efficacy

Also related to self-concept is the construct self-efficacy. **Self-efficacy** refers to beliefs about one's abilities to produce effects in the world (Bandura, 1994). Individuals who have high levels of self-efficacy believe they can work hard to master difficult tasks. In other words, they believe they are capable of achieving their goals (e.g., "This math problem is difficult; but if I work hard, I can solve it."). Research shows that individuals with high self-efficacy are more

Self-efficacy

Beliefs about one's abilities to produce effects in the worlds likely to view difficult tasks as challenges, rather than threats or insurmountable obstacles. On the other hand, people who have low levels of self-efficacy are likely to dwell on the potential for failure, their own inadequacies, or the obstacles they will encounter as they attempt the task (Bandura, 1994). A student's level of self-efficacy may influence the manner in which he or she approaches academic challenges, thereby affecting classroom functioning (Brady-Amoon & Fuertes, 2011).

Influences on the Development of Self-Perceptions

Now that we have outlined some of the most commonly studied ways we look at ourselves, we turn to the question of how these self-perceptions develop. What makes a child have a positive self-concept, high self-esteem, and a belief in his or her personal self-efficacy? Research indicates that several factors influence the development of self-views, including social experiences, social comparisons, and success or failure experiences across a variety of domains (Harter, 1998; Marsh, 1994; Diller, 1954).

Social Experiences

Much of what we think about ourselves depends on our social experiences with others. Cooley's looking-glass self-theory holds that we develop our sense of self according to how others regard us. This theory asserts that a student thinks she is smart or athletic because that is how others view her. She gains this knowledge of what others think through verbal and nonverbal social experiences with parents, friends, classmates, and teachers (Harter, 1998). According to this model, self-concept represents a child's internalization of the views of others.

Social Comparisons

While the way others see us may influence our self-perceptions, research also shows that we also make our own evaluations about ourselves via social comparisons. Not only does a student listen to others tell him he is good in math, he also compares his performance with the person sitting next to him—his brothers or sisters, or anyone else who he sees as comparable. Social comparisons such as these allow children to measure their performance against the performance of their peers, thereby assisting in the development of their self-concepts (Marsh, 1994).

Success and Failure Experiences

Self-perceptions also develop as a result of the success or failure a child experiences over time (Diller, 1954). Research shows, for example, that children begin to develop reading self-concepts within the first few months of starting school, and these self-views relate to the ease or difficulty with which they learn to read (Chapman, Tunmer, & Prochnow, 2000). Those who learn to read more easily develop more positive reading self-concepts. They also show a higher level of reading performance over time than those with low reading self-concepts. Does the more positive reading self-concept cause the higher performance in reading, or do the students who were better readers continue to improve in reading, regardless of reading self-concept? This question has been heavily debated among researchers, and we will explore both sides of the argument in the following section.

Self-Perceptions and Academic Success

Our beliefs about ourselves significantly influence our success in school. As we learned in the previous section, self-concept is multidimensional. This means that we have multiple perceptions about ourselves, including our physical and academic ability, as well as a general sense of our ability to function socially. Each of these parts of our self-concept may influence performance in the classroom. Additionally, these perceptions may interact with each other, making global recommendations for academic success difficult (Shavelson & Bolus, 1982). For example, children who see themselves as physically competent may fare better socially with their peers. This social success may then lead to more positive perceptions of their own emotional functioning. These mutually dependent perceptions make the understanding and modifications of students' perceptions difficult. Changes in one aspect of our functioning often lead to other changes. Additionally, there is the question of exactly what aspects of our self-concept have a direct bearing on academic success.

It seems that physical, social, and emotional self-perceptions would influence academic functioning, yet research shows that non-academic aspects of self-concept are not significantly related to academic work (Marsh, 1992). General academic self-concept, however, is moderately correlated with academic achievement; and area specific academic self-concepts (e.g., math and English) are strongly correlated with achievement in that area (Marsh, 1992; Gage & Berliner, 1992; Areepattamannil, Freeman, & Klinger, 2011). That is, as academic self-concept goes up, so does achievement. The relation between self-esteem and academic achievement is also positive with higher self-esteem scores related to higher achievement. In general, students with higher self-esteem are more likely to have favorable attitudes toward school (Marsh, 1990; Cauley & Tyler, 1989). However, it is important to remember that a strong relation does not mean that one thing is *causing* the other. The nature of the relation between self-concepts and academic achievement is still being clarified through research.

Students' academic self-concept is correlated with their academic achievements.

Self-esteem has also been shown to predict how people respond to negative feedback when completing a task. Those with higher self-esteem perform better following negative feedback compared to those with lower self-esteem (Brockner, Derr, & Laing, 1987). For example, Margaret is working in a small group on a new type of algebra problem. All of the students in the group ask Margaret to solve the problem because she is the class "brain." Flattered by the other student's comments, Margaret attempts a solution to the problem. After she finishes, the teacher inspects the "group's" work. She informs the group that their answer is wrong and asks them to try again. Everyone but Margaret immediately begins to exclaim that the problem is impossible. Margaret, however, thinks carefully about the teacher's comments and immediately takes another approach to solving the problem. This example demonstrates how positive self-esteem (Margaret perceived herself as smart and capable at math) can promote task engagement even after receiving negative feedback.

The picture is quite similar with regard to self-efficacy. Students who score higher on measures of self-efficacy show higher academic achievement (Bandura, 1997; Bong, 1999; Areepattamannil, Freeman, & Klinger, 2011). This means if you view yourself as academically capable, you tend to have higher academic scores. In fact, the goals students set appear to be affected by perceived self-efficacy, with those having stronger self-efficacy setting higher goals and exhibiting stronger goal commitment (Bandura, 1997).

In summary, having a more positive self-concept, self-esteem, and self-efficacy relates to greater academic achievement. The question is, however, which comes first, positive self-perceptions or academic success? Should we work to increase positive self-perceptions so that academic achievement will increase, or should we

Having a more positive self-concept, self-esteem, and self-efficacy relates to great achievement.

work toward increasing academic achievement so that self-perceptions will become more positive? Likely, the relationship between self-perceptions and academic success is interrelated (Hoge, Smit, & Hanson, 1990). For example, Mark learned his multiplication facts easily and more quickly than the other students in class. His teacher and parents, through verbal and nonverbal communication, relayed reinforcing messages to Mark regarding his academic success. In this example, Mark experienced genuine success in math. He was able to make social comparisons to his peers regarding his math skills, recognizing his mastery of multiplication was more complete than other students. He also benefited from the positive views from his teacher and parents regarding his facility with multiplication, internalizing their views as his own. Mark's positive self-perceptions developed as a function of these influences and affected his math development. As he worked on math, he naturally received some corrective remarks from his teacher. His positive self-perceptions allowed him to view such feedback as constructive, rather than critical, and to make changes in his work without feeling demoralized. He started attempting more challenging math problems and worked on them with more commitment than his fellow students who had negative self-views with regard to math. This level of engagement in math significantly influenced his performance, resulting in further academic success in math. This example illustrates the complexity and multidimensional nature of the relation between self-perception and student performance. It may be difficult to separate the roles of academic success and positive self-perceptions in student achievement, but the contribution of each is quite clear.

Promoting Accurate and Positive Self-Perceptions in the Classroom

Educators certainly strive to develop academic skill in their students, but they are also in a unique position to promote positive self-views. As the preceding sections demonstrated, the relation between positive self-views and achievement is complicated, but clearly present. As a teacher, it is important to recognize the complex interplay between self-views and achievement, taking care to promote positive self-perceptions. We now turn to some specific techniques teachers can use to help students achieve academically and personally.

Using the Zone of Proximal Development

Vygotsky's notion of teaching within the zone of proximal development (see Chapter 2) fits well with what we know about the development of positive self-perceptions. That is, if we teach at a level within a child's reach, while providing sufficient challenge for the child, then genuine success is possible. Genuine success occurs when children's growth is encouraged and their performance is realistically and positively assessed (Clifford, 1999). Promoting positive self-perceptions, however, has met with criticism. Some researchers assert that teachers, in the name of promoting positive self-perceptions, give students easy tasks, overlook errors, de-emphasize failed attempts, and ignore faulty performances (Slater, 2002). Without challenge, these researchers argue, these self-esteem enhancing efforts are in fact self-defeating since students cannot develop feelings of competence, determination, and personal control (Clifford, 1999). Thus, students need positive, yet accurate, information regarding their performance, so that they can succeed and feel empowered by their improvement.

Teachers should strive to teach at a level within a child's reach and still provide sufficient challenge for the child. This helps make genuine success possible.

In The Classroom

APPLYING THEORY

Self-Concepts

THEORY BASICS

Research has shown that positive self-concepts relate to stronger academic performance (Marsh, 1992; Gage & Berliner, 1992; Bandura, 1997; Bong, 1999). It has also been suggested that attempting to preserve self-concepts at the expense of accurate feedback can lead to problems with perceptions of competence, determination, and personal control (Slater, 2002; Clifford, 1999). The question then: How do we give students realistic and accurate feedback, while helping students to feel academically capable?

CLASSROOM EXAMPLE

Max, a new student in Mr. Lopez's fourth grade classroom, was having difficulty completing his math assignments in the allotted time. Max's records from third grade indicated he had done well in math, and he was clearly an invested student. The work he finished was always neat and accurate, but his grade in math was suffering due to work that was incomplete. Mr. Lopez conducted a brief, informal assessment of Max's math skills and noticed Max worked quickly through addition and subtraction problems, but spent an inordinate amount of time on simple multiplication. He sat down with Max and discussed the concept of multiplication, which Max quite obviously grasped. Max was, however, unable to answer quickly queries regarding even the simplest multiplication facts, clearly adding silently to solve each problem. Mr. Lopez commented positively on Max's understanding of multiplication and his mastery of addition facts. He explained to Max that his success was dependent on his excellent grasp of the concept of multiplication and the fact he could add so quickly. He told Max his ability to add quickly showed he knew his addition facts, and he could do the same with multiplication. This would take practice and some assistance, but he would ultimately be able to finish his assignments more easily.

Teachers: Give positive, accurate, and constructive feedback where possible. Such feedback is geared toward a climate of improvement, particularly when students have difficulty meeting task demands.

Mr. Lopez approached Max's problem with memorizing his multiplication facts from several different avenues, including flash cards and a multi-modal approach using music and a computer program. He also involved Max's parents through daily progress notes, and he set up a peer-based multiplication practice group. Mr. Lopez focused on Max's strengths and how he could improve, instead of on what Max was doing wrong and had failed to learn. This resulted in Max not only learning his multiplication facts but also helped preserve his positive self-perceptions regarding his math skills and his ability to improve through effort.

Teaching Students to Respect Differences

Another factor to consider when promoting positive self-views is that every classroom will have students with a range of abilities. Differing abilities can lead to a source of esteem for some but may, also, result in feelings of inadequacy in others. How can teachers assist students in developing positive self-perceptions, when many of the social comparisons students make are implicit and outside their control? While it is impossible to eradicate social comparisons, teachers *can* help students develop a respect for and an understanding of individual differences, a goal that we will discuss at length in Chapter 8. For example, Ms. Janke, a fifth grade teacher, specifically designs collaborative learning activities that allow children with differing abilities to contribute to the completion of a project. She chooses group members thoughtfully, reflecting on the strengths and weaknesses of individual students and designing exercises to call on specific areas of competence. The task might involve reading, writing, role-playing, drawing, computing, and/or building models. If students can view themselves and their classmates as unique individuals, each with strengths and weaknesses, and each a part of a supportive community for learning, then the negative effects of social comparisons on self-views may be greatly reduced.

SUMMARIZE AND REFLECT

1. Differentiate between the concepts of self, including self-concept, self-esteem, and self-efficacy.
2. Self-concepts are hierarchical and multidimensional, with general self-concept being made up of ideas about oneself across many specific areas.
3. There are a variety of influences on the development of self-perceptions, including socialization experiences, social comparisons, and success and failure experiences across a variety of domains.
4. There is a complex and likely reciprocal relationship between self-views and academic functioning.
5. There are a variety of strategies for promoting accurate and positive self-perceptions in the classroom, with a focus on providing both challenge and support to facilitate the development of feelings of competence, determination, and personal control.

INFORMED APPLICATION

1. Rhonda's physical education teacher has just demonstrated how to do a front handspring during their gymnastic unit. Her teacher asks for a volunteer to try. Rhonda quickly raises her hand. What concepts of self seem relevant in this example and why?
2. As a teacher, you are aware of the relation between positive self-concepts and higher academic achievement. You are considering taking steps to teach directly positive self-perceptions. What factors should you consider when making your decision?

ERIKSON'S THEORY OF PSYCHOSOCIAL DEVELOPMENT

The developmental theory of Erik Erikson is one of the most often-cited theories of how we grow and change over the lifespan. The popularity of this theory is often attributed to the clear ties made between changes experienced by an individual and how the environment shapes these changes. His theory is also notable for its coverage of the entire lifespan. Unlike the many theories of his contemporaries, Erikson noted distinct changes in the individual from birth through old age.

Basic Principles: Psychosocial Crises and Lifespan Development

Psychosocial theory

A theory that emphasizes integration of psychological changes and the social world

Developmental crisis

A particular life event important in the development of individual identity

Erikson's theory is called a **psychosocial theory** of development because of its integration of psychological changes and the social world. He asserted that an individual's unique psychological make-up evolved over time, as key events are encountered and resolved. His theory outlines *eight* important life events that form the building blocks of individual identity. For example, one of the most prominent of these life events is the crucial period when a person begins to negotiate the difficult question, "Who am I?" Erikson referred to these important events as developmental crises. A **developmental crisis** is a particular life event important in the development of individual identity. The individual strives to resolve each crisis, incorporating elements of what he called healthy and unhealthy social influences. For example, a teenage girl may receive encouragement from her art teacher, believing she has exceptional talent in sculpting. She, therefore, decides she would like to pursue a career in art. She tells her parents of her decision, only to receive limited support and several remarks about the benefits of being a doctor. Thus, she has experienced different responses from important people in

Erik Erikson

her life. Her teacher's support gave her feelings of direction, and her parent's response left her somewhat confused. She will likely incorporate both types of feedback in her attempts to establish a meaningful identity. Although supportive remarks such as those made by her teacher are important and lead to a positive or healthy resolution of this crisis, the comments from her parents are also important. They give her a more critical perspective on her decision to pursue a career in art. Erikson believed that both types of feedback were important in the development of the individual. He felt that only when the types of comments that lead to confusion begin to outweigh supportive and nurturing comments does the individual begin to experience a negative outcome to the developmental crisis. The following section provides a brief account of each of Erikson's eight stages.

Erikson's Stage Theory of Psychosocial Development

As with many developmental theories, Erikson describes the stages to illustrate changes (see Table 3.1) we experience across the lifespan. The following section provides a brief description of Erikson's eight stages. The stages are grouped around educationally relevant times: preschool development, school-aged development, and adult development. As was discussed in Chapter 2, keep in mind that stage theories give the appearance that development occurs during specific times; however, this is not always accurate. Erikson's theory is presented in stages for ease of understanding. True development is a continuous process, slowly evolving as the individual ages. The age ranges and periods below which are used to describe his theory are only guidelines, used primarily to help the reader organize the material.

Preschool Development

Trust versus mistrust (birth to twelve–eighteen months) Erikson believed the first important developmental crisis encountered involved the issue of trust. The newborn child is essentially helpless and relies on others for basic survival. Most infants receive reliable and relatively consistent care, but even this varies over time. If basic care becomes too variable and challenges the comfort level of the infant, the infant may begin to develop a sense that the world is an unreliable place and become mistrustful. We all experience some feelings of trust and mistrust during this important developmental period. It is only those children who experience more mistrustful situations than trusting and reliable situations that will ultimately achieve an unhealthy resolution of the crisis.

Table 3.1 Psychosocial Development: Erikson's Stage Theory

Stage	Approximate Age	Relevant Life Event
1. Trust vs. Mistrust	Birth to 12–18 months	Feeding
2. Autonomy vs. Shame/Doubt	18 months to 3 years	Toilet Training
3. Initiative vs. Guilt	3 to 6 years	Personal Direction
4. Industry vs. Inferiority	6 to 12 years	Primary Grades
5. Identity vs. Role Confusion	Adolescence	Secondary Grades
6. Intimacy vs. Isolation	Young Adulthood	Pair Bonding
7. Generativity vs. Stagnation	Middle Adulthood	Nurturing
8. Ego Integrity vs. Despair	Late Adulthood	Life Reflection

Learning to button clothing is another example of how children learn to be independent.

Autonomy versus shame and doubt (eighteen months to three years) Children begin to rely less on others after a period of time and begin to enjoy doing things for themselves. This sense of autonomy develops gradually with appropriate and patient guidance from caregivers. Caregivers, however, often have busy lives and have difficulty giving children the necessary time and space to develop these self-help skills. Often children are rushed or discouraged because they take too long or they do not perform adequately. Toilet training is a frequently cited example of one of these important skills. Children are initially reliant on parents for basic toileting needs; however, during this developmental crisis, they begin to take control of this aspect of their lives, developing an overall sense of self-sufficiency. Toilet training is just one example of the many situations that children are faced with that influence the resolution of the autonomy versus shame and doubt crisis.

Initiative versus guilt (three to six years) Erikson theorized that the next major issue children work through involves the desire to become an increasingly active participant in life. Children at this stage love to initiate activities and are constantly moving from one task to another. This can present problems for parents and caregivers who typically have more limited energy and time to devote to these tasks. This results in some requests being denied or discouraged and others supported. Parents who discourage child-initiated activities need to be careful how the situation is perceived. Children may feel they have unduly burdened their parents and develop feelings of guilt. Parents who are sensitive to a child's need to initiate activities help them understand the practical limitations of daily life.

School Age Development

Industry versus inferiority (six to twelve years) At some point in a child's life, activity initiation becomes secondary to task success. This co-occurs with the beginning of formal education. Students quickly learn to make comparative judgments regarding their work and the work of others. Success becomes more important as students attempt to receive favorable grades, and they often use the performance of other students to assess their own. When teachers and parents help students select a range of activities that results in a satisfactory amount of overall success, feelings of inferiority are minimized. Students who do not receive such guidance are at risk for attempting too many tasks beyond their current level and coping with a sense of failure.

Identity versus role confusion (twelve to eighteen years) As mentioned in the opening section, one of Erikson's developmental crises surrounds the establishment of identity. He held that it is important for young adults to establish an identity in occupation, gender roles, politics, and religion. Without successful identity formation in these areas, the adolescent is likely to experience role confusion. James Marcia has expanded on Erikson's early work. Marcia's theory provides additional insights into the process of developing a sense of identity. He identified four identity statuses to explain unique differences in how young adults search for an answer to the question, "Who am I?" (Marcia, 1966). Each of these four identity statuses involves the concepts of exploration and commitment (see Table 3.2). **Exploration** is the idea that the individual is actively experimenting with different lifestyles and ways of being in the world. **Commitment** is when an individual has decided on a particular identity.

Exploration

An individual's active experimentation with different lifestyles and ways of being in the world

Commitment

The individual's decision on a particular identity

Identity achievement

Achievement characterized by both exploration and commitment

Marcia's first identity status is **identity achievement**. This status is characterized by both exploration and commitment. Individuals have investigated relevant options and have committed to a particular way of life. Take, for example, a student who participates in a variety of organizations and clubs he finds interesting. The student begins to learn that he enjoys some clubs more than others and begins to devote more of his time to one or two organizations. This process helps the student affirm certain values he already has and offers additional views that are new and exciting. Ultimately, the student experiencing identity achievement selects a particular way of life and sets out to pursue this lifestyle in an active way. Research indicates that

Table 3.2 Identity Statuses: Marcia

Identity Status	Exploration	Commitment
Achievement	Active exploration	Strong commitment
Foreclosure	Limited exploration	Strong commitment
Moratorium	Active exploration	Delayed commitment
Diffusion	Limited exploration	No commitment

only about 20% of eighteen-year-olds achieve stable identity, although this number increases to around 60% by the age of twenty-four (Meilman, 1979).

Identity foreclosure is characterized by commitment, but not active exploration. Individuals taking this approach to establishing an identity readily commit to a particular way of life without exploring other options. Frequently this is seen when a young adult simply adopts the lifestyle of their parents. They attend school for the same career, hold similar political and religious views, and recreate familiar gender roles in their own home. A less typical pattern involves the individuals making a strong and immediate identification with a persuasive group, or a group that effectively advocates for the individual to join. Rather than seeking out a group affiliation through exploration, the individual simply assumes the qualities of a group who strongly solicited their membership. Either of these foreclosure patterns is potentially problematic. Individuals who have not experienced different ways of living tend to be less tolerant of alternative lifestyles.

Identity diffusion is an approach to identity formation that involves neither exploration nor a strong commitment. Individuals experiencing diffusion make few attempts to engage in activities that help to establish a strong sense of identity. They are not committed to any particular ideology, nor do they maintain stable group affiliations. This identity status is also problematic and may result in disillusion, withdrawal, or apathy.

Identity moratorium is a process in which the individual focuses on exploration, delaying making any commitment. This approach is becoming more common, as young adults postpone early commitments in favor of a more protracted exploration during the college years.

F.A.Q.

Sam Keen—"I'm not sure I'm clear on the difference between the initiation stage and the industry stage. How do you tell the difference?"

Professor Lorenzo— "They probably seem similar because they are both about doing and initiating activities. The earlier stage of initiative versus guilt is just about the desire to engage in a variety of activities. The child's focus is on DOING. The industry versus inferiority stage is also about doing, but the child now focuses on the SUCCESSFUL completion of the activity. To distinguish the two, pay attention to what the child is focusing on: doing or success."

Adult Development

Intimacy versus isolation (young adulthood) Erikson's work is particularly notable for its coverage of developmental issues beyond the adolescent years. Building on our sense of identity, we move toward life experiences involving the development of a deeper connection, or intimacy, with another person. In order to develop a successful intimate relation with another, a person must first successfully resolve the identity stage. In other words, to develop a mutually satisfying intimate relationship, we need to have a sense of our own individuality. Sharing ourselves with others in an intimate way involves the potential loss of personal independence. Individuals who are trying to move toward relations that are more intimate may resist this loss of independence, resulting in frequent break-ups and a failure to maintain a mutually loving bond with another. Thus, the inability to obtain successful intimacy leads to isolation and loss in life quality.

Generativity versus stagnation (middle adulthood) The journey into middle adulthood is met with a growing sense of our obligation to others and to the next generation. Individuals who successfully negotiate this stage develop ways to nurture their sense of pro-

Identity foreclosure

Achievement characterized by commitment, but not active exploration

Identity diffusion

An approach to identity formation that involves neither exploration nor a strong commitment

Identity moratorium

A process where the individual focuses on exploration, but delays making any commitment

It is important for older adults to reflect back on their lives and see a life lived with purpose, which leads to a sense of integrity.

ductivity and creativity. Having and raising children is an approach many individuals take toward a successful resolution of this stage. Erikson did, however, intend a broader interpretation of nurturing and productivity. He believed that in addition to the raising of children, individuals also begin to develop a sense of responsibility to their communities and to the world at large. To foster these additional avenues of productivity, individuals begin to take a more active interest in community projects, social causes, and world issues. Individuals who fail to develop such endeavors may feel a sense of stagnation and an approach to life characterized by fruitless, repetitive daily activities.

Integrity versus despair (late adulthood) One of the last personal crises with which we struggle is the acceptance of impending death and the fact that our lives are primarily historical, rather than in the future. It is important that older adults reflect back on their lives and see a life lived with purpose. This leads the individual to a sense of integrity and that life was well lived. Individuals who fail to experience this perspective on life have difficulty resolving this crisis in a positive way, often falling into despair.

Promoting the Development of Personal Identity in the Classroom

The lifelong search for who we are is profoundly influenced by the events, people, and experiences we have during our school years. From that one all-important teacher to the school nurse or that favorite physical education teacher, people from our school years play a pivotal role in our personal growth. One of the most interesting changes we are seeing is the increasing amount of time children are spending in structured educational settings at younger and younger ages. This trend furthers the significant impact of others, outside the family, on a child's development. Let's take a look at how educators can implement some of Erikson's theories during a child's preschool years.

Preschool Development

Erikson's theories give the preschool instructor/caregiver an effective framework for providing a stimulating and nurturing environment. Recall, from Erikson's first stage, the importance of providing a consistent approach to early care services. Service providers for infant care need to be sensitive to the need to develop a sense of trust. This is challenging when infant to caregiver ratios often exceed four-to-one (staff ratios are typically governed by state law). Imagine how many infants you could care for at one time. Appropriate staffing makes it possible to provide young children with responsive care in a structured setting. Careful scheduling of infant care is important, but caregivers should also maintain a certain amount of flexibility to meet the dynamic needs of individual children. This will lead to the child developing a trusting view of the world and will provide a solid foundation for the next developmental crisis.

As children develop and become more capable of self-mediated activities, the preschool teacher becomes an important support for autonomous behavior. Most daily activities at the preschool level are fairly regulated given the need to supervise numerous students with limited staffing. This may lead teachers to favor more direct assistance for tasks rather than allowing students the time needed to complete tasks more autonomously. More direct assistance, however, creates an environment where children may doubt their ability to complete tasks. To avoid this difficulty, preschool teachers can create flexible instruction plans that focus more on process, as opposed to completion. Teachers should also minimize attention to total task time and instead focus on the child's need for new experiences to guide transition times. For example, instead of developing a lesson plan for a fifteen-minute sensory table activity, teachers should simply begin the sensory table activity while concurrently setting up a second activity. As the students begin to tire of the sensory table activity, they are redirected to the second activity. Total time spent at the sensory table will vary for each child. This not only gives each child the necessary time to develop a sense of mastery over the first task but also allows each child to feel more autonomy with regard to the task. When children take control over their activities, they are less likely to feel a sense of doubt. When they have many mastery experiences over time, successful resolution of the autonomy versus doubt crisis is the results.

The preschool age is an important time for children to learn to work together as well as autonomously.

Any visit to a local preschool will immediately demonstrate that children love to initiate activities. Preschoolers will constantly ask to start one task after another, usually oblivious to the time needed to set-up the activity, or the energy needed to clean up after they move on to another task. This may lead to frustration on the part of the preschool teacher. With multiple students for each teacher, being able to meet the demands for rapid task turnover is incredibly difficult. Teachers compensate with structured lesson plans, but children still make multiple requests for new activities, often becoming upset if told they have to wait. Part of this waiting process is educational as it teaches the child the realities of operating in a social world; however, teachers may inadvertently communicate another message if they are not careful. Subtle cues of voice or body language may communicate to a student that their request is unreasonable and lead to the student feeling guilty for asking. Although students need to develop a realistic sense of what is possible in a structured care setting, feelings of guilt are counterproductive. Teachers who reinforce and validate student efforts to begin new activities, while providing guidance and limits, are less likely to undermine the development of a sense of initiative in children. Students that are applauded for their desire to try new things *and* taught appropriate avenues for making these tasks possible are more likely to resolve the initiative versus guilt crisis in a positive way. There are multiple ways to organize activities so that this occurs. A "centers" approach, for example, makes it possible to offer multiple activity areas for exploration. While the teacher controls which activity centers are open and the number of students at each center, the students have choice in their activities and when they would like transitions to occur. One way to organize this is to label each activity center with a numbered envelope that represents the number of students who can participate at that activity at one time. Students have a popsicle stick with their name on it. As they move from one center to the next, they move their popsicle stick into the envelop at that new station. The number written on the envelope is the number of popsicle sticks allowed and therefore designates the number of children to work at that activity. This gives children the flexibility to initiate different activities, while giving the teacher the ability to manage the flow of activity at each center.

School Age Development

Even children who have an extensive history of structured care experience traditional school from a different perspective. Schools are charged with creating learning environments, but issues surrounding learning progress and accountability keep assessment an integral part of the process. Assessment can take many forms and will be covered more extensively in Chapter 15; in general, however, assessment refers to any activity or experience that gives the teacher a sense of a child's progress. Assessment has many advantages, but it also is one of the chief mechanisms fostering peer comparisons. Peer comparison leads to greater importance being placed on success during the formal school years.

All children will confront both success and failure, but it is important to monitor task development to facilitate as many successes as possible. This is particularly important during the elementary school years. Children build their academic sense of self during this important time, and teachers are significant mediators of their perceptions of academic success.

Teachers provide students with choices, encouraging specific activities or providing needed structure to help promote a successful outcome. Children will show individual variation in their need for such guidance, so an accommodating classroom is necessary. For example, if a fourth-grade math teacher is planning a lesson on basic division, she will likely find that students will vary in their progression through the material. She may begin with an overall lecture to the entire class, providing the basic information needed to begin independent or small-group work. During follow-up sessions on the materials, she can place children in groups of varying size and composition to help ensure the success of each child. She might choose to group students according to a common skill level, minimizing the perception that some students are too far ahead or behind. She might also group more advanced students with those students struggling with the material. This would help the advanced students develop an understanding of the material from the perspective of the teacher, while providing the necessary supports for the students needing more assistance. She might also choose to allow students to work independently at the beginning, while she works with students individually and focuses on basic skill mastery. Once a foundation is achieved, the teacher can move on to other learning tasks.

The reality of classroom teaching is that all of these approaches may be necessary to accommodate the varying learning needs of students. What is important is that the teacher maintains an underlying goal of student success and implements the necessary environmental variables to make learning rewarding. When this occurs, students are able to develop a sense of industry, minimizing feelings of inferiority and successfully resolving Erikson's fourth psychosocial crisis.

Adolescent Development

Building on the foundation laid during the earlier grades, the secondary grade student begins to seriously navigate the complex factors impacting a sense of self. This often presents unique problems for teachers as students begin to demand a wider range of personal and academic freedoms to engage in their search for self. Teachers often learn to accept a greater range of appropriate dress and manners as students attempt to find an accepting and personally meaningful peer group. Teachers who provide a supportive interaction style, while setting clear limits regarding appropriate behavior, are likely to have less difficulty dealing with identity related issues in the classroom. Teachers are in a unique position to provide objective and constructive support for choices. Those who take a narrower stance during this time may find themselves in an antagonistic environment where little education or growth is possible.

SUMMARIZE AND REFLECT

1. Erik Erikson provided a stage theory of psychosocial development. His theory is based on our progression through eight developmental stages.
2. Erikson's stages have both positive and negative resolutions, each outcome forming the building blocks for identity.
3. James Marcia's research expanded on Erikson's work on identity and provided examples of four identity statuses.
4. Classroom situations were presented relevant to each of the developmental stages Erikson proposed in children, with a focus on strategies promoting psychosocial development in the classroom.

INFORMED APPLICATION

1. Each student develops a unique identity. Consider what developmental factors would move a student toward a sense of identity that supports academic achievement.
2. According to Erikson's theory, identity is shaped by the social world around us. What do you think the teacher's role is in influencing a student's social world?

PERSONAL DEVELOPMENT AND SOCIALIZATION

Think about your classroom experiences, either as a child or as a prospective teacher. The ways students relate to one another and to the teacher make for complicated dynamics influencing the entire classroom experience. Some students relate to peers easily, while others have more difficulty. The same student who gets along well with his friends may have problems interacting with the teacher. Some students, unfortunately, have difficulty interacting with peers and teachers, a pattern related to a host of other problems. What influences our ability to develop and maintain relationships with others? Why are some children more liked than others? Why do some children exhibit a reactive, aggressive pattern of behaviors, while others are more passive and withdrawn?

In this section, we will explore personal development, or the way we develop unique personality characteristics, behavior patterns, and ways of relating with others. We will start by looking at factors influencing the tremendous individual variability seen in personal development. We will then focus on ways personal development relates to socialization and interpersonal functioning. Finally, we will direct our attention toward strategies for promoting healthy personal, social, and emotional development in the classroom.

Agents of Socialization

Think about the words you used to describe yourself at the beginning of this chapter. You likely described not only your physical appearance but also dimensions of your personality. Personality traits are consistent ways of behaving in the world that make a person unique. For example, some of us are more extroverted, or more social than others, frequently seeking out experiences with other people. Whether we are extroverted or more of the "loner" type depends on a complex interaction between our inherited predispositions and our socialization experiences. **Socialization** refers to the way in which other members of our society influence our behaviors. While our earliest socialization experiences are usually provided in the context of the family, once children reach school age, teachers and peers become important agents of socialization.

Socialization

The way in which other members of our society influence our behaviors

Parents

Socialization and biology interact in an extremely complicated manner in personal development. For example, research indicates some of us may have an inherited tendency to move toward new, highly interactive situations, while others are more likely to withdraw from new situations (Kagan, Snidman, Kahn, & Towsley, 2007). The way a parent helps the child with a "wait and see" attitude to handle new situations may have long-term influences on personality and adjustment, including the degree to which they seek out relationships and interactions with other people. In fact, research shows that early parenting styles that are sensitive and responsive to an infant's individual temperamental characteristics are related to positive, long-term outcomes (Martin & Fox, 2006). Parenting continues to be a major socialization influence in later childhood and adolescence, with responsive parent/child interaction patterns leading to healthier personal development.

Teachers

When a child enters school, teachers become important agents of socialization, influencing relationship formation, social competence, and the development of prosocial behaviors. Teachers that are responsive to the individual variability in student social behavior are more likely to foster the development of social competence in the classroom for all students.

Peers

Studies also show peer relationships are an important component of socialization and personal development, playing a role in the development of self-perceptions and predicting social competence (Bukowski & Hoza, 1989; Studsrod & Bru, 2011). Peer acceptance, or the degree to which a child is liked or disliked by peers, is an important element in a child's

When children enter school their teachers become important agents in their socialization, influencing relationship formation, social competence, and the development of prosocial behaviors.

socialization experience. In fact, research shows that a child's ability to get along with other children predicts adjustment in adulthood. Children with social deficits are likely to experience continued interpersonal difficulties as adults (Sheridan, Hungelmann, & Poppenga Maughan, 1999). A child's peer-acceptance category refers to the degree to which he/she is actively liked or disliked by his/her peers. This status within a classroom exists on a continuum, and characteristics associated with lower peer status include social class, race, ethnicity, and disability status (Cohen, 1998; Kavale & Forness, 1995). A significant body of research has been conducted to examine the characteristics of children who are actively disliked or rejected by peers (Gifford-Smith & Brownell, 2003; Bierman, Smoot, & Aumiller, 1993; Nesdale et al., 2009). Classmates generally identify these children as the "least liked" in the class and they are often socially isolated or actively excluded from peer activities (Gifford-Smith & Brownell, 2003). Studies show that peer-rejected children differ from non-rejected children in many ways, including their behavior, social problem solving, aggressive behavior, activity level, and cognitive and academic functioning (Newcomb, Bukowski, & Pattee, 1993). Research suggests that the link between rejection and aggression may be mediated by how peers think about the rejected child's behavior, such as interpreting ambiguous actions as hostile (Feldman & Dodge, 1987). Not all rejected children, however, are aggressive. Non-normative, or unusual behavior, has been linked to rejected status in non-aggressive children, with non-aggressive rejected children being described by peers as strange or socially awkward (Gifford-Smith, 1998; Kingery, Erdley, Marshall, Whitaker, & Reuter, 2010). Peer rejection has been linked to a number of negative developmental outcomes, including dropping out of school, engaging in delinquent behavior, and experiencing emotional and psychological problems (Kupersmidt & Coie, 1990).

Peer-neglected students

Onlookers who are not excluded from the group, but do not actively participate

Some children are not actively disliked or excluded, but neither do their peers actively like them. These children are often referred to as **peer-neglected**; they are frequently onlookers who are not excluded from the group, but do not actively participate. Peer-neglected children are often quiet and have few friends, either by choice or because of problems interacting socially (Rubin & Krasnor, 1986). While teachers often easily identify peer-rejected children, the neglected status of a child often goes unnoticed by teachers (Wentzel & Asher, 1995). In fact, teachers may view these children positively in terms of motivation, independence, and classroom behavior. Neglected children do not appear to be at an increased risk for negative developmental outcomes, and research shows that children may move in and out of neglected status over time.

Children who are well liked in a classroom have been shown to exhibit such characteristics as concern for others, helpfulness, cooperation, and empathy (Caprara, Barbaranelli, Pastorelli, Bandura, & Zimbardo, 2000). These characteristics appear to be related to social cognition and perspective taking. Studies show that children with high peer acceptance are more likely to engage in associative play, social conversation, and acceptance of peer overtures (Coie & Kupersmidt, 1983); and they also show a social cognitive pattern that prioritizes the maintenance of harmonious relationships with peers (Dodge & Price, 1994). In fact, the peer-rejected children often behave in ways directly opposite to the behaviors of peer-accepted children. Peer-rejected children are likely to interpret ambiguous overtures as hostile; whereas peer-accepted children are more likely to perceive benign intent (Dodge & Price, 1994). Thus, children who show high peer acceptance are likely to exhibit prosocial behaviors and have more positive social cognitions. This knowledge of the characteristics associated with peer acceptance provides us with a foundation for developing interventions to facilitate social competence and peer acceptance. We turn now to the promotion of social development and social competence for all children in a classroom.

The Development of Social Behavior and Social Thinking

Many of our socialization experiences are explicit, or clearly articulated, in the form of rules and spoken expectations. Saying "please," "thank you," and "excuse me" are generally taught, for example, using verbal prompts, in addition to observing others using these terms. Some social skills, however, are not taught explicitly. Rather, they are learned in a manner that is implicit, or unspoken. How, for example, do we learn how close to stand to other people when we talk to them? Seldom do we receive explicit lessons in "personal space," yet we clearly know when someone is standing too close to us in conversation because we feel uncomfortable. The development of social skills, social competence, and even our thoughts about social behavior play a role in our successful navigation of the all too complex world of interpersonal interactions.

Social Skills

Early in life, we begin our journey toward successful socializations. As mentioned in the introduction, some of this early learning involves verbal customs observed in society. For example, when a neighbor's mother offers us something to eat, we typically respond with "thank you." Our language is filled with these socially relevant terms. In addition to a verbal means to socialize, we also learn non-verbal techniques for socializing with others. Most of us learn these non-verbal social skills, often called **pragmatic language** skills, through our socialization experiences with family members, teachers, and peers. Research shows some children pick up these skills more easily than others do. For example, one notable exception is children with attention deficit/hyperactivity disorder (AD/HD). They often have problems such as standing too close to other children, speaking too loudly during conversation, and taking turns during conversation. These behaviors can cause a child with AD/HD to have problems with peer interactions, which are an important part of healthy personal and social development. Non-native English speakers or those from culturally diverse backgrounds may also learn different pragmatic language skills such as amount of eye contact, use of gestures when speaking, or loudness of voice (Hurley, 1992). These differences may contribute to perceptions of "difference" on the part of other students and may result in peer acceptance issues. Other social skills are more overt, consisting of learned behaviors allowing students to function in social contexts (Sheridan & Walker, 1999). For example, the skill of "joining in" a group of other children might involve many combinations of behaviors that may be verbal, non-verbal, or both. Some of these may be more accepted by peers than other behaviors. A child may choose to ask to join the group, to stand close by and wait to make eye contact with one of the task leaders, to wait to be asked to join in, or to wait for the right moment and physically join the activity.

Pragmatic language
Non-verbal social skills used to promote socialization

Early in life we begin our journey toward successful socializations.

Social Competence

Social skills are observable and measurable, and they can be conceptualized in terms of overt behaviors. The ability to use social skills appropriately within a given context in order to function effectively represents a child's social competence. **Social competence** is based not only on the social skills a child has learned but also on how they are used and received by other children in a given context. Social competence exists on a continuum, rather than being an all-or-none phenomenon. That is, we would not say a child either has social competence or not; we would consider, instead, how much competence the child exhibits. We will explore strategies for helping all children develop social competence in the next section.

Social competence
Behavior based not only on the social skills a child has learned but also on how those are used and received by other children in a given context

Social Cognition

Social cognitions, or the ways in which we perceive or think about social situations, also influence our social relationships. Like social skills, social cognitions develop through our socialization experiences. One of these social cognitions is the ability to take the perspective of

Social cognition
The ways in which an individual perceives or thinks about social situations

Egocentric

Thinking that is characterized by one's own perspective

another. The perspective-taking ability increases as children develop cognitively and become better able to view an issue from another's perspective. While perspective-taking begins to develop in very early childhood, young children continue to be **egocentric,** or dominated by their own perspective. As they become more effective perspective-takers, children are better able to handle conflict more successfully, are more likely to display empathy and compassion, and are more likely to be accepting of difference. Children who are poor perspective-takers are less likely to accept those who are different and are more likely to resolve conflicts in an aggressive or negative manner, often misinterpreting the actions or intentions of other people as hostile (Feldman & Dodge, 1987).

Promoting Social Development in the Classroom

While many social skills are based in non-verbal, pragmatic language based behaviors, these implicit rules for interacting with others can be made explicit (Sheridan et al., 2011). Speaking directly about rules of personal space, for example, can be an enlightening experience for children with social skills problems. In fact, when provided with explicit social skills instruction, many children ask questions such as, "Why didn't anyone ever tell me this before?"

Of central importance in any social skills intervention effort is the actual social validity of the skills being taught. That is, the skills should be meaningful and functional in the specific social context where they are to be used (Carey & Stoner, 1994). Think for a moment about an eleven-year-old attempting to use appropriate "joining in" behaviors. While it might seem that verbally asking to join an activity on the playground is a desired use of social skills, in some eleven-year-old contexts this behavior might actually be counterproductive. The "Hi guys, can I play?" approach might not meet the "cool" criteria. For this reason, contextualized approaches to teaching social skills are necessary, whereby members of the peer group provide input regarding functional skills and serve as a relevant training group (Sheridan et al., 1999). The classroom provides an optimal environment for promoting positive social interactions, and the classroom teacher can play a key role in helping students develop both social skills and social competence. In order to do this, teachers must be able to identify children who are having social difficulties in the classroom. They must then identify the target situations where the breakdown in social competence occurs. This could be on the playground, in group activities, or in the classroom. Finally, the teacher must identify the behaviors peers deem as important and set up an environment for teaching these behaviors. This may involve any number of activities—such as explicit role-playing exercises among members of the classroom, modeling on the part of a socially accepted peer, group problem solving, or direct verbal instruction and practice within the peer groups. Once the behaviors are learned and implemented appropriately, they should be naturally reinforced within the peer group context.

As we discussed earlier, research clearly implicates prosocial behaviors in peer acceptance. This includes behaviors such as empathy, cooperation, and helpfulness. These behaviors hinge on the ability to take the perspective of another and to accurately assess the thoughts and intent of others. In order to promote the development of these behaviors, teachers may use a variety of strategies aimed at explicitly pointing out multiple perspectives or multiple interpretations of ambiguous situations. Teachers with a diverse classroom are in a unique position to promote perspective-taking since multiple perspectives can be explicitly examined and validated, promoting a diverse array of friendships and peer-interaction patterns (Howes & Wu, 1990).

Researchers who study perspective-taking often use a scenario-based approach where a situation is presented which can be interpreted from a number of different perspectives. Using these scenarios, Robert Selman and colleagues have explored the developmental progression of perspective-taking ability, describing five levels of ability, as summarized in Table 3.3 (Selman & Schultz, 1990). While the age ranges for each level are quite broad, and there is much individual variability in the development of perspective-taking, Selman's model can help a teacher broadly determine where to start with students of a particular age range. For example, for early elementary school students, whose thoughts about the feelings of others are often one-dimensional, a teacher might explicitly explore scenarios where mixed or contradictory feelings exist. These could be hypothetical scenarios, or a teacher could use his or her understanding of Selman's research as a foundation to develop scenarios based on students' real-life contexts. These meaningful scenarios could be verbally presented to a group of students, with each

Table 3.3 Social Perspective Taking: Selman's Stages

Stage of Role Taking	Age Range	Description
0. Egocentric or Undifferentiated Perspective	3 to 6 years	Children fail to demonstrate any awareness of the perspective of others
1. Social-informational Role Taking	6 to 8 years	Children recognize that others can have different perspectives, but only if they received different information.
2. Self-Reflective Role Taking	8 to 10 years	Children now recognize that others can have a different perspective, regardless of information received. They recognize they can take the perspective of others and others can take their perspective.
3. Mutual Role Taking	10 to 12 years	Children can now consider their own perspective while evaluating the perspective of another. They can also consider the point of view of a third party outside their own experience.
4. Societal Role Taking	12 to 15 years and older	Adolescents attempt to understand their own perspective and that of others with respect to the larger societal context.

member of the group presenting his/her own perspective and the teacher explicitly addressing the differences. The more diverse the group is, the more likely that multiple perspectives will emerge—and the better the opportunity for bridging barriers among diverse groups.

Assisting students in developing accurate assessments of the behaviors and intentions of others is particularly important for students who frequently misinterpret social cues (Graham, 1997). Recall that students with low peer acceptance tend to perceive hostile intent in an ambiguous situation, whereas students with high peer acceptance tend to see benevolence (Dodge & Price, 1994). Like perspective-taking, accurate and positive social cognition patterns can be promoted using a variety of strategies (Hudley & Graham, 1993). For example, a teacher can set up a situation where a student carrying books is "bumped" into by another student (Dodge & Price, 1994). Each of the students in the group watching the event can then share his/her perspective on what the "bumper's" intent was. The teacher can explicitly address the alternative perspectives, encouraging students to see that there are multiple possibilities. Students can also bring up their own examples of personal experiences or discuss contextually based (and therefore meaningful) interactions described by the teacher. These exercises, when implemented with a group of students, also encourage an understanding of multiple perspectives.

SUMMARIZE AND REFLECT

1. Personal development and socialization are important parts of the growth process. It is important to understand the relative influences of parents, teachers, and peers as agents of socialization.
2. The development of appropriate social skills is important. Understanding how social skills are used and received by other children and the ways that children perceive social situations are important socialization factors.
3. Social competence is the ability to use social skills appropriately in a given context to function effectively. Effective socialization highlights the relationship between social competence and peer acceptance.
4. Another important aspect of social development is peer acceptance. There are several different peer acceptance statuses.
5. There are strategies for enhancing social skills and social competence that promote peer acceptance in the classroom.

(continues)

INFORMED APPLICATION

1. As a classroom teacher, what situations or activities do you think an understanding of social skill development would be needed to educate effectively?
2. How important is peer acceptance? Do you think there are qualitative differences in the importance of peer acceptance as children get older? Is peer acceptance more of an issue for situations outside the classroom?

THE DEVELOPMENT OF MORALITY AND SOCIAL RESPONSIBILITY

Imagine you are a teacher walking down the school hall. You overhear a student comment that she pretended to be sick last Sunday, so she would not have to go to her family reunion. For a moment, you consider giving the student a lecture on honesty. You then decide that this situation is really outside your area of responsibility, and you keep walking. Was it your responsibility to talk with the student about her choice to pretend she was sick? Does the degree or importance of her dishonesty matter in your decision to keep walking? We are constantly making decisions about our behavior for which there is not a clear right or wrong answer. **Morality** generally refers to an established standard for human conduct. When we make decisions regarding right or wrong in ill-defined situations, such as the one presented above, we must make moral judgments that are quite subjective. In order to make these judgments, we can consider situational factors, as well as our internalized standards of moral conduct. If you knew, for example, that the student who avoided the reunion did so because of distress over her parents' recent divorce, would you still consider her act of dishonesty as wrong? Likely, your judgments regarding the morality of her actions are somewhat flexible, depending on situational factors. Young children, on the other hand, are likely to disregard situational information entirely. Researchers have discovered developmental trends in moral decision-making, contrasting the ways young children reason about moral issues with the practices of older children and adults. We turn now to an exploration of these research findings and their implications for the classroom.

Morality

Generally refers to an established standard for human conduct

Piaget's Theory of Morality

Jean Piaget

One of the first researchers to investigate moral reasoning was Jean Piaget. Throughout his work on cognitive development, Piaget was fascinated by how individuals of varying ages interpreted the same moral situation. His original research generally showed that children around the age of six reason qualitatively differently than twelve-year-old children (Piaget, 1965). When presented with a situation involving a moral transgression, a six-year-old child is likely to make decisions about an appropriate consequence based on the magnitude of the transgression. For example, Sarah was playing with a ball in the living room when she accidentally bounced the ball against her mother's china cabinet, breaking eight of her antique dishes. On the same day, Sarah's neighbor Mike was caught breaking his sister's porcelain doll because she made fun of his new haircut. When a six-year-old child is asked whether Sarah or Mike should receive the greater consequence, most would indicate Sarah. This is because six-year-olds typically ignore information about intent (e.g., Mike intentionally breaking the doll) and center on amount of damage (e.g., Sarah broke eight dishes). Piaget referred to this type of reasoning as **moral realism.** His studies indicated that as children get older they begin to appreciate the importance of intent in making moral decisions. This more encompassing view was termed morality of cooperation. In addition to the importance of recognizing intent, children moving from moral realism to the morality of cooperation begin to change their views of rules. Initially, children view rules as absolute and independent of the situation. Later, children come to realize that rules are made by people, and as such, can be modified by people. This is why Piaget labeled the later approach to moral reasoning as the **morality of cooperation**, because rules are essentially mutually agreed upon standards. Rules only have meaning by the cooperation of the individuals following them.

Moral realism

Refers to thinking that centers on the magnitude of a transgression

Morality of cooperation

Refers to thinking that centers on the intent behind the transgression

Kohlberg's Theory of Moral Development

At about the same time that Piaget's publications on moral development were receiving increasing attention, Lawrence Kohlberg was beginning to publish what was to become one of the most well-known and controversial theories of moral development (Kohlberg, 1963). Kohlberg's theory of moral development was a stage theory similar to Piaget's theory of cognitive development. Kohlberg's approach to investigating moral development involved presenting research participants with brief scenarios called **moral dilemmas**. These dilemmas presented the research participant with a morally difficult situation and asked that the participant provide an answer and an explanation. A classic example of a moral dilemma used in Kohlberg's research is as follows:

Moral dilemmas

Research tools pioneered by Lawrence Kohlberg that presented the research participant with a morally difficult situation and asked that the participant provide an answer and an explanation for his/her choice

> In Europe, a woman was near death from a rare form of cancer. There was one drug that the doctors thought might save her, a form of radium that a druggist in the same town had recently discovered. The druggist was charging $2,000, ten times what the drug cost him to make. The sick woman's husband, Heinz, went to everyone he knew to borrow the money, but he could only get together about half of what the drug cost. He told the druggist that his wife was dying and asked him to sell it cheaper or let him pay later. But the druggist said no. So, Heinz got desperate and broke into the man's store to steal the drug for his wife, (Kohlberg, 1984, 186)

Kohlberg was interested in how individuals of different ages would address scenarios like the one above. After extensive investigation over a significant period of time, his data indicated that there are qualitative differences in moral reasoning as we grow and develop. This led to his formation of his stage theory of moral development. He divided moral reasoning into three broad levels, with each main level further subdivided into two stages (see Table 3.4).

Preconventional

At the **preconventional** level of moral reasoning, moral decisions are typically based on consequences that have personal impact. That is, children reason through a situation by assessing its impact on their own functioning. For example, Jane is taking a spelling quiz when the teacher is suddenly called from the room. Staring down at her test, she begins to realize that she is not doing very well and considers looking on another student's paper. If this situation is occurring in a first grade classroom, the girl is likely to base her decision regarding whether or not to cheat on either the likelihood of being caught and punished, or on the likelihood of improving her grade. Decisions made at stage 1 of the preconventional level revolve around avoiding punishment, while the focus of stage 2 reasoning is on reward. Both of these orientations involve an outcome that has direct bearing on the individual. Consistent with a stage approach to development, Kohlberg held that children first reason at stage 1 of the preconventional level, moving toward a stage 2 orientation as they develop.

Preconventional

Levels of moral reasoning that are typically based on consequences that have personal impact

Will I get into trouble if I don't return the dollar?

Table 3.4 Moral Development: Kohlberg

Level	Stage	General Reasoning Approach
Preconventional	1. Punishment—Obedience 2. Personal Reward	Judgments based on personal impact
Conventional	3. Good boy—Nice girl 4. Law and Order	Judgment based on the expectations of others
Postconventional	5. Social Contract 6. Universal Ethical Principle	Judgment based on personal value system

Conventional

Conventional

Level of moral reasoning that is based on the expectations of individuals other than the self

The second level of moral reasoning outlined by Kohlberg is the **conventional** level of moral reasoning. At the conventional level, moral reasoning is based on the expectations of individuals other than the self. The child begins to look beyond their own interests and consider the cost of failing to conform to the expectations of others or of society. In the cheating example above, if the child were in the conventional level of moral reasoning, she would think beyond reward and punishment and consider how the cheating would affect the perceptions of her teacher or parents, as well. When a child makes moral decisions based on the expectations of significant others, they are reasoning at stage 3 of the conventional level. When they begin to make moral decisions in terms of larger societal laws and norms, they move into stage 4 of the conventional level. If the child in the cheating example thinks, "I'm not going to look on Frank's paper because cheating is against the school rules," then she is reasoning at a stage 4 level. She has generalized the concept of the "other" to societal laws, in addition to specific people. At stage 4 of the conventional level, children develop a "member of society" perspective. Thus, individuals who reason at the conventional level make decisions based on the expectations of others; they likely believe that rules must be upheld consistently, regardless of the situation.

Postconventional

Postconventional

Level of moral reasoning that goes beyond specific laws or personal expectations and is based on the underlying principles for such laws

At the **postconventional** level of moral reasoning, reasoning goes beyond specific laws or personal expectations and is based on the underlying principles for such laws. If the girl in the cheating example were a college student in a Spanish class, she would be more likely to consider *why* we have rules against cheating. She might reflect on the value of a college degree if everyone simply cheated on tests. She might consider the importance of personal integrity and justice in making her decision not to cheat on the test. When individuals base their moral reasoning on the underlying principle behind the rule or fundamental concepts—like justice, integrity, or personal philosophy—they are reasoning beyond the conventional level. Individuals reasoning at stage 5 view laws as important, but they see that laws must be questioned if they do not uphold individual rights. At stage 6, morality is based on universal ethical principles of right and wrong on which laws are based—such as justice and respect for human rights and dignity—which may conflict with and transcend social laws and rules. While Kohlberg's theory differentiates between stage 5 and stage 6 postconventional reasoning, it appears that stage 6 morality may rarely be reached. Stages 1–5, however, have received substantial empirical support (Power, Higgins, & Kohlberg, 1989).

Criticisms of Kohlberg's Theory and Alternatives

Kohlberg's theory of moral development is one of the most often-cited theories of moral development; however, it is also one of the most criticized. Since Kohlberg's original publication in 1963, numerous researchers have published studies that further assess the application of Kohlberg's theories. Results confirm much of his work, but also point to other aspects of moral development important to consider. We will first examine issues common to all stage theories, followed by other common criticisms leveled against Kohlberg's theory.

The Stages

Stage theories, such as Kohlberg's, are usually criticized for their oversimplification of development. They make it appear that development is a linear process, traveling in a forward direction and never back. This, however, almost never adequately describes real-life development. Consistent with this perspective, studies have shown that although the stage order proposed by Kohlberg is generally true, it is too simple to capture the unique path an individual takes toward higher levels of moral reasoning. Individuals may move in a three-step forward/two-step back modality. In other words, we often make significant gains in our moral reasoning ability, only to fall back to more immature reasoning. We also seem to be able to have exceptional insights into some issues, while remaining rather simplistic with others. For example, a student walking down the hall may find a dollar on the ground and simply put it in his pocket, reasoning that "It is just a dollar," and therefore not worthy of any effort to find the owner. As he continues down the hall, he notices an elderly teacher, arms full of books, trying to get her classroom door open. He quickly makes his way down the hall and helps the teacher with her books. This example demonstrates how quickly our moral reasoning can change. Kohlberg would probably classify the student's earlier reasoning as preconventional; however, a few seconds later that same student was selflessly helping another and probably reasoning at a postconventional level. That is, he probably went to help the elderly teacher because he thought helping elders was the right thing to do, rather than concentrating on whether there was some sort of school rule governing the situation. What is important to remember about Kohlberg's stages is that although we may move back and forth between moral stages, it is likely that our reasoning overall is primarily consistent with one particular level (Colby & Kohlberg, 1984). It is this general reasoning ability that Kohlberg captured in his groundbreaking research.

Hypothetical Moral Dilemmas

Another often-cited criticism of Kohlberg is that he focused too heavily on hypothetical moral decisions, rather than actual moral behaviors people exhibit in everyday life (Blasi, 1980). Kohlberg investigated moral reasoning using fictional narratives, where respondents reported what they would do in a similar situation. One of his actual moral decision scenarios, The Heinz Dilemma, was presented earlier in this section. These scenarios are potentially problematic because what people say they would do in response to a written scenario and what kind of behavior they would actually engage in if placed in the situation, may not be the same. There is evidence that moral reasoning does, indeed, relate to moral behavior. Kohlberg (1975) himself found that as children demonstrate higher levels of moral reasoning based on his narratives, they are less likely to cheat when given the opportunity. This provides support that what we say we would do is at least somewhat related to our actual behavior. Additional support comes from a study of adolescents indicating that those reasoning at lower levels on Kohlberg's tasks are more likely to be involved in delinquent behaviors and drug use compared to those reasoning at higher levels (Greeg, Gibbs, & Basinger, 1994). Again, this ties reports of moral behavior to actual behavior. Keep in mind that this relation between reported behavior and actual behavior is far from perfect. There are trends, but this does not mean we always act in accord with what we say we are going to do.

Male Biased

Perhaps the most significant criticism of Kohlberg's theory is that his research was initially based on a study of males. Kohlberg's original theory, published in 1963, was based on a core group of boys ages ten, thirteen, and sixteen. Later studies extended his findings to other ages and to girls, but the basic theory remained the same. This has led some researchers to question the appropriateness of extending these findings to all individuals.

Carol Gilligan provides another perspective on moral reasoning (Gilligan, 1982). She believes that although Kohlberg's characterization of morality may indeed apply to all individuals, there is another dimension to morality that may be more important to women. She views Kohlberg's theory of morality as a theory of justice, whereby moral reasoning seeks to establish a position with respect to equality or oppression. Gilligan does not negate that this is an important quality of moral reasoning, but she argues that there is another morality—a *morality of caring*. From this perspective, morality is not driven by the just treatment of others but by the appropriate care of those in need. For example, let us say you and a friend are

Carol Gilligan

leaving a restaurant and someone jumps out from behind a car and grabs your friend. Are you going to help your friend? Why or why not? Kohlberg's theory would emphasize aspects of your decision making process surrounding the unjustness of such an unprovoked attack. According to Gilligan's theory, however, you would emphasize that your decision is based on your valuing or caring for your friend. Who is right? In reality, probably both are. In her research, Gilligan has found that both men and women express concern for both perspectives of morality, but women tend to be more concerned with a morality based on the care ideal. Men, on the other hand, are typically more concerned with the justice perspective exemplified by Kohlberg's theory.

Problematic Moral and Social Behaviors in School

The recent push toward formalized instruction in morality in schools is largely due to concerns regarding increases in negative youth behavior. Specifically, increases in aggressive behaviors on the part of students have led many schools to adopt instruction in morality. There are many structured programs available, each focusing on a somewhat different method of implementation or behaviors addressed. The next section looks at several common problematic moral or social behaviors seen in our schools. The final section examines ways to address these behaviors.

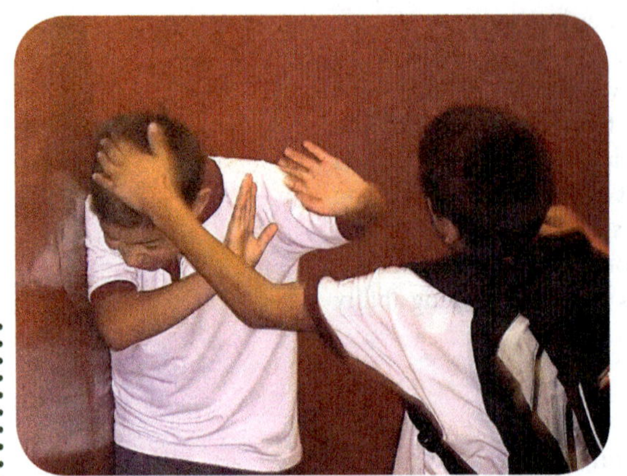

Aggression is a longstanding problem in our schools. The classic manifestation of aggression at school is the bully.

Aggression and Bullying

Aggression is a longstanding problem in our schools (Smith, 2011). Some researchers differentiate between direct and indirect aggressive behaviors. Direct or overt aggression includes behaviors such as teasing, taunting, or hitting; indirect or relational aggression includes intentional exclusion or rumor spreading. Research indicates that gender differences exist in the use of overt versus relational aggression, with girls being more likely to take a relational aggression approach (Ahmad & Smith, 1994; Crick, Bigbee, & Howes, 1996). Aggressive behavior can take many forms, but generally involves the immediate intent to harm another (Anderson & Bushman, 2002). The classic manifestation of aggression in schools is the bully.

Bullying is typically seen as a specialized sub-set of aggressive behavior. Green (2000) defines bullying according to five main elements:

1. The bully intends to inflict harm or fear upon the victim.
2. Aggression toward the victim occurs repeatedly.
3. The victim does not provoke bullying behavior by using verbal or physical aggression.
4. Bullying occurs in a familiar social group.
5. The bully is more powerful (either real or perceived power) than the victim.

Bullying, whether overt or relational, is a pervasive phenomenon. There have been several large-scale studies in a variety of countries, including the U.S., and prevalence rates appear comparable cross-culturally (Carney & Merrell, 2001). One recent study found that a total of 29% of their national U.S. sample reported moderate or frequent involvement in bullying, either as the bully, the victim, or both (Nansel et al., 2001). This is particularly problematic in that there appears to be considerable personal cost to both the bully and the victims of the aggression. Bullying is associated with a host of negative factors—including poor social and emotional adjustment, infrequent close peer relationships, higher incidence of drug and alcohol use, poor academic achievement, and increased likelihood of criminal behavior (Nansel et al., 2001; Olweus, 1993). Victimization is also associated with negative outcomes, including anxiety, depression, and low self-esteem (Craig, 1998; Carney & Merrell, 2001).

Victimization

The phenomenon of bullying behavior inherently involves two people: the bully and the victim. The particular characteristic a bully exhibits is likely to vary from person to person; however, research has shown some common qualities. Bernstein and Watson (1997) found that bullies show a limited ability to relate to the emotional experiences of others. Although bullies may lack empathy for others, they do not seem to differ from their peers in terms of their self-esteem (Carney & Merrell, 2001). Thus, it appears that bullies are not necessarily engaging in aggressive behavior to compensate for inadequate self-views. They do appear to have a need to feel in control and powerful, and they are generally more defiant and oppositional with adults (Batsche & Knoff, 1994).

GET THE FACTS

75%

Number of high school students reporting being involved in some form of serious cheating.

Rutger's Management Education Center

Like their bullying counterparts, victim characteristics also vary from individual to individual, but some commonalities have been reported. Craig (1998) found that victims of bullying behavior experienced a heightened sense of anxiety that frequently led to feelings of depression. Carney and Merrell (2001) indicated that victims were more likely to have a limited social support network and low self-esteem. Research also indicates that being in the role of the victim is a stable phenomenon, with some victims continuing to experience victimization for several years (Olweus, 1977) Research has also shown academic declines in victims of bullying (Juvonen, Wang, & Espinoza, 2011). The question of why victims are chosen by bullies is difficult to answer. Research shows that some victimization may occur because the victim responds passively to the aggressive intents of others. This type of victim tends to be insecure and withdraws when attacked (Carney & Merrell, 2001). Other victims may alternate between the role of the victim and the bully. These victims typically appear anxious, hyperactive, or aggressive and are perceived as having poor social skills by classmates (Green, 2000). This behavioral pattern is not viewed positively by classmates and is typically interpreted as irritating or offensive.

Educators and researchers have developed a wide range of services and programs to address the problem of bullying. There are measurement instruments that can help educators identify bullying and victims (Bully Victimization Scale—BVS—by Reynolds: Pearson Publisher). Other resources include information on preventing bullying by increasing supervision, developing appropriate classroom rules, providing consequences for bullying behavior, and developing conversations with bullies and with their victims. The fundamental premise is that it is necessary to develop a school environment where students feel safe from physical and emotional harm so that learning can take place. Such programs have been found to reduce bullying by as much as 50% (Olweus & Limber, 1999).

Cheating

Another important aspect of academic life that is directly impacted by students' morality is cheating. Students cheat for a variety of reasons: desire for better grades, peer pressure, assignments perceived as overly difficult, parental expectations, and the perception of the task as meaningless. As a result of these factors, many students willingly put themselves in a compromised position by copying another student's work, allowing others to copy their work, giving question answers to students in another class, or gaining access to exam questions before test administration. The prevalence rates for cheating vary across cultures and across grades within a culture. A 2001 national survey conducted by Rutgers' Management Education Center of forty-five hundred high school students found that 75% of the respondents reported being involved in some form of serious cheating at least once. Other researchers have found similar results. Johnson and Farkas (1997) found that 68% of thirteen hundred high school students reported the cheating problem as "somewhat serious" or "very serious." Evans and Craig (1990) found similar results with 64% of middle school stu-

Many students are willing to compromise their standards by cheating on tests and homework.

dents reporting that cheating is a "serious problem." Overall, research confirms that cheating across all students and grades has been increasing over the last few decades (Jensen, Arnett, Feldman, & Cauffman, 2002; Jones, 2011).

One important question to ask is whether students perceive cheating behavior as dishonest. McLaughlin and Ross (1989) demonstrated that although there was general agreement about what constitutes cheating between students and teachers, students did not consider it cheating when they obtained old copies of tests. While there is some discontinuity between the ideas of students and teachers regarding what constitute cheating, there is also a great deal of similarity. Research has also shown that students largely view the same types of behaviors as cheating as do teachers (Davis, Grover, Becker, & McGregor, 1992). The general similarity between teachers and students in their perception of cheating means that actual cheating is not due to a misunderstanding about what constitutes cheating; rather, students appear to knowingly engage in acts of cheating. The obvious question is, "Why?"

As mentioned above, students justify cheating along many dimensions. There does, however, appear to be a similar theme expressed by both students and teachers that societal expectations are dramatically changing with respect to education. We are placing ever-increasing demands on our educators for higher academic success of students. Subsequently, students are feeling increasing pressure from teachers to perform well. Parents also have higher academic expectations, given their belief that much of their child's future revolves around their academic record. These pressures give rise to the problem of learning for the recognition that success brings, rather than learning for the sake of gaining knowledge. In fact, students who show a strong orientation toward learning instead of grades are significantly less likely to cheat (Huss et al., 1993). In order to address the serious cheating situation in this country, we need to adopt an approach to education where learning is not viewed as secondary to achievement.

Promoting Moral and Socially Responsible Behaviors in the Classroom

Public health studies show that youth violence is a pervasive and ongoing issue (Hamburg, 1998; Snyder & Sickmund, 1999), and instruction in moral and socially responsible behavior has become an increasingly popular topic in education (Wynne 1997; Milson & Mehlig, 2001; DeVitis & Yu, 2011). While there is much debate regarding causal factors in youth crime, many researchers propose a failure of the primary socialization process (Lickona, 1991; Wynne & Ryan, 1997), that is, a failure in the lessons learned from the early social experiences encountered by children. To combat this failure, researchers and educators have developed a host of educational approaches aimed at influencing morality. These approaches are based on the idea that the behavioral disturbances we are seeing nationwide are attributable to inappropriate moral development during the early socialization period. We now turn our attention to some of the morality based educational programs currently being used in the field.

Moral and Character Education Programs

Moral education programs

Programs that usually provide instruction using moral dilemmas, which encourage children to construct their own sense of morality

Character education programs

Programs that focus on the transmission of certain core values with instruction taking place through activities that allow for the practice of moral behavior

Moral education programs focus on developing appropriate moral reasoning (Wynne, 1997). Instruction typically takes place using moral dilemmas, encouraging children to construct their own sense of morality. **Character education programs**, on the other hand, focus more on the transmission of certain core values (Milson & Mehlig, 2001). Instruction takes place through activities allowing practice of moral behavior (see Table 3.5). Moral education has been criticized because it fails to provide right or wrong answers and is usually taught using examples, rather than real-life situations. Character education has been criticized because it focuses too heavily on behavior and adoption of another's moral code, rather than thinking and self-creation of morality.

Both of these approaches, however, may have a similar issue in that they focus heavily on *components of morality*—such as thinking, feeling, and behavior—that is, how we think about a moral issue, how we feel about the issue, and what we actually do about the issue. The components of morality are extremely complex (thoughts, feelings, behaviors), with each component being made up of a multitude of sub-components (e.g., feelings—fear, doubt, anger, joy). Studying how all these interact to generate morality is exceedingly complex, and some

Table 3.5 Moral and Character Education Programs

Morality and Character	Moral Education Programs	Character Education Programs
	Program Focus Individual Morality	**Program Focus** Transmission of core values
	Method Individuals work on Moral Dilemma Scenarios	**Method** Activities involving the actual practicing of core values
	Benefit Encourages individual reasoning	**Benefit** Emphasizes actual changes in behavior
	Problems Provides no right or wrong answers	**Problems** Question regarding which core values are taught

researchers suggest that this research may be beyond our current methodological and instructional capabilities.

Moral Processing

Bebeau (1999) suggests an alternative process approach to the conceptualization of morality, rather than the component approach. Essentially, this approach moves away from the question of what a moral decision is made of, and instead, it focuses on the processes an individual engages in to come to a moral decision. Focusing on how one makes a moral decision, instead of what constitutes a moral decision, allows for progression toward a positive moral product, without discovering the potentially unsolvable question of the basic composition of morality. The processes Bebeau defines are moral sensitivity, moral judgment, moral motivation, and moral character. This process approach does not imply a linear or a systematic process; rather, all processes may proceed together, ultimately resulting in a particular action or lack of action. One of the benefits of this approach is that it allows for the identification of the reason behind a *failure* to make an appropriate moral decision or action. Once the faulty process is identified, instructional support based on this aspect of the process can take place. Thus, the process approach allows an individualized approach to moral instruction. Which instructional support is most appropriate in a given circumstance will depend on the nature of the problem. Not all moral or character based programs address all moral processes, and some programs focus on only one of these processes.

All of these approaches have research to support effectiveness, yet gains in moral behavior are at best moderate. In part, this may be due to overly broad estimation about what these programs are able to accomplish. Muriel Bebeau (1999) compares the public's response to moral education programs to the public's response to the introduction of the Head Start Program. Both programs suffered from an initial expectation that they were going to solve society's larger problems, such as violence and criminal behavior. We have learned from the Head Start Program, however, that such lofty outcome measures are extremely difficult to document. Outcome measurements from the Head Start Program have moved to more proximate or immediate effects, such as parental need for social services, school attendance, and appropriate grade for age placement. The moral education is poised to suffer from the same societal issues if care is not taken to develop systematic, specific, and realistic outcome measures. This is not to say that the programs are ineffective. Quite the contrary, moral education programs show great promise. However, educators and researchers must be mindful that global theories about human nature usually make for poor dependent measures for childhood interventions.

SUMMARIZE AND REFLECT

1. Lawrence Kohlberg developed a stage theory of moral development, outlining three levels of moral reasoning, each with two sub stages. He provides examples of reasoning consistent with each substage of the preconventional, conventional, and postconventional levels of moral reasoning.
2. There are, however, critics of Kohlberg's theory; it is often contrasted with the work of Carol Gilligan on the morality of caring.
3. Other moral and behavioral problems are important to consider, such as the prevalent problems of bullying and cheating. Bullies and victims have observable characteristics that often lead to a variety of negative outcomes.
4. Cheating is another serious educational issue, but there are strategies for the prevention of both bullying and cheating.
5. Moral education and character education are educational approaches aimed at influencing morality.

INFORMED APPLICATION

1. What is considered moral behavior is often different for different people. Develop an example where the teacher's definition of moral behavior is in conflict with a student's parents. How can the conflict be resolved?
2. What sort of practical difference would you expect in your students if your school administration adopted a moral education or a character education program?

THE CHAPTER IN REVIEW

In this chapter, we explored the developmental foundations of personal identity and social and moral development. We started our exploration with a focus on the development of self-perceptions, including self-concept, self-esteem, and self-efficacy. We discussed the way in which general self-conceptions are composed of ideas about ourselves regarding areas that are more specific. We then outlined the relative influences of socialization experiences, social comparisons, and success and failure experiences in the development of self-view. We discussed the complex relationship between self-perceptions and academic success, and we outlined strategies for promoting self-views that are both accurate and positive.

We then turned to a discussion of psychosocial development, outlining Erik Erikson's renowned theory of psychosocial development. We explored the psychosocial crises that define each of his eight developmental stages, highlighting both positive and negative outcome possibilities. We reviewed James Marcia's research that expanded Erikson's research and outlined the four identity statuses that comprise his theory. We then focused on strategies for promoting psychosocial development in the classroom, relating our examples to Erikson's theory.

Next, we explored personal development and socialization, focusing on the influences of parents, teachers, and peers in the socialization process. We highlighted the importance of social skills and how these are used in the development of social competence. We then related social competence to peer acceptance and sociometric status in the classroom. We also outlined strategies for enhancing social functioning and peer acceptance among all children in a classroom.

Finally, we turned to a discussion of the development of morality and social responsibility. We outlined Kohlberg's justice based stage theory of moral development, contrasting his ideas with Carol Gilligan's theory of a morality of caring. We next explored morality in the schools, focusing on bullying and cheating, outlining strategies for their prevention. Lastly, we discussed educational approaches designed to promote moral and socially responsibility in the classroom.

Interdisciplinary Case Focus

principal *special educator*
teacher *parents* *psychologist*
social worker *physical educator*
nurse *peers* *doctor*

Gage is an eight-year-old child who is having significant difficulty interacting with peers in Mrs. DePaull's third grade class. He is frequently disruptive in class, often speaking out of turn or without raising his hand. His classmates seem to avoid him, and he does not appear to have any friends in the class. Mrs. DePaull has actively encouraged other students to include Gage in activities since it does not happen naturally, but this strategy did not seem to help. Mrs. DePaull even asked individual students why they do not include Gage in activities. She received responses such as, "He's weird," "He gets on people's nerves," and "He is so annoying." She has intervened several times when the other children actively exclude him, but this just seems to make things worse. Mrs. DePaull has noticed that Gage's disruptive behaviors are escalating. She knows that she has an opportunity to intervene and assist Gage in developing peer relationships, but she first has to understand where the breakdown is in his interpersonal functioning. She also knows that Gage's problems can be viewed from a number of different perspectives, and that interventions can be planned on multiple levels, so she consults with several colleagues to help her plan a more intensive intervention effort.

Interdisciplinary Perspectives and Interventions

Psychologist Dr. Gail Lin, the school psychologist, offers the following advice to Mrs. DePaull:

"Gage appears to be on the path toward a rejected status in the classroom, if he is not already there. Your concern regarding Gage's disruptive behavior is important, but even more important are the negative developmental outcomes that he will likely experience due to peer acceptance problems. From a social information processing perspective, Gage likely perceives social situations differently than do the other children. To address this, you could bring up, either verbally or via role-playing, classroom examples of social interactions and encourage students to describe the intent of each person in the interaction. You can then explicitly address the alternative perspectives, encouraging Gage and the other students to see that there are multiple possibilities. These exercises not only encourage the development of perspective taking but also give Gage the opportunity to observe the social perceptions of others."

Speech Language Pathologist Brad Stevens, S.L.P., the school's speech pathologist, offers the following advice:

"Gage's problems might be related to his language development, particularly with regard to pragmatics. His speaking out of turn may result from his lack of understanding of conversational space and subtle cues for turn-taking, as opposed to impulsivity. If this is the case, you can create an environment where turn-taking is required and explicitly outline the rules in use. You can verbally identify the generally implicit cues for turn-taking and provide opportunities for practice among members of a group. Other children in the class likely have some difficulty with this, as well. Although their problems may be mild compared to Gage's, this intervention could be helpful to multiple children in you class."

Social Worker Jay Hirsh, L.C.S.W., the school's clinical social worker, offers the following:

Gage also appears to have trouble with social skills, particularly with joining-in behaviors. He also has difficulty becoming an active participant with group activities. While this may relate to his turn-taking problems, it might also be related to the unspoken classroom norms for appropriate joining-in behavior. Mrs. DePaull might set up a group activity and explicitly address the way each of the children become participants. She might also ask the students to reflect on and describe their own behaviors. She could have one of the students role-play an unsuccessful joining-in attempt and have the other students comment on why it was unsuccessful. In any of these exercises, Gage could be either a participant or an observer. Again, many children in the class would likely benefit from explicit instruction with regard to these social skills.

In summary, appropriate interventions for helping Gage develop interpersonal relationships are dependent on his teacher's understanding of the intricacies of social development from a variety of perspectives. Using knowledge of classroom social statuses, language, social skills, and cognition, Mrs. Depaull can create effective learning environments for helping Gage become an active, included member of the class. In fact, her ability to integrate this interdisciplinary information and apply it in her skillful teaching likely has far-reaching developmental implications for Gage.

Key Terms

TERM	*Page*	*TERM*	*Page*
Character education programs	100	Moral realism	94
Commitment	84	Peer-neglected students	90
Conventional	96	Personal self-esteem	77
Developmental crisis	82	Postconventional	96
Egocentric	92	Pragmatic language	91
Exploration	84	Preconventional	95
Group self-esteem	77	Psychosocial theory	82
Identity achievement	84	Reflective appraisal	76
Identity diffusion	85	Self-concept	75
Identity foreclosure	85	Self-efficacy	77
Identity moratorium	85	Self-esteem	76
Moral dilemmas	95	Social cognition	91
Moral education programs	100	Social competence	91
Morality	94	Socialization	89
Morality of cooperation	94		

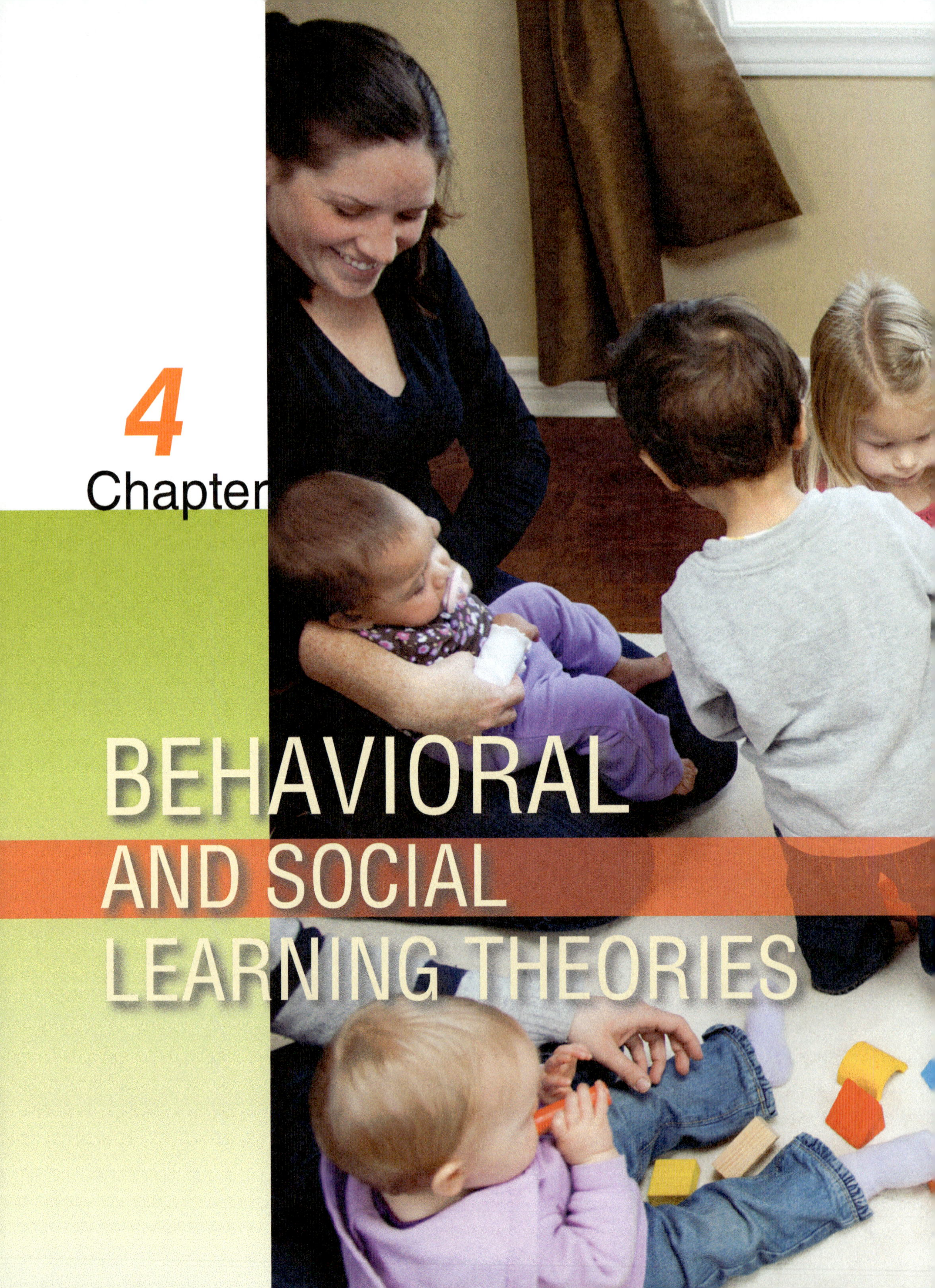

4 Chapter

BEHAVIORAL AND SOCIAL LEARNING THEORIES

What's It All About ...

What is behaviorism?

How do we learn by associating events that occur together?

How do consequences shape the way we learn?

In what ways do social relationships affect our learning?

Chapter Objectives

- Define general learning.
- Describe learning from the behavioral perspective.

- Understand the theories of Pavlov and Watson and the importance of contiguity.
- Define the basic components of classical conditioning.
- Distinguish between generalization and discrimination.
- Explain extinction.
- Describe the limitations of classical conditioning.

- Understand the similarities and difference between the theories of Thorndike and Skinner.
- Define reinforcement.
- Describe the schedules of reinforcement.
- Define punishment.
- Distinguish between shaping and extinction.
- Describe how to modify antecedent conditions.
- Explain applied behavior analysis.
- Review the limitations of operant conditioning.

- Describe Bandura's theory of modeling and observational learning.
- Define social cognitive theory.
- Explain self-regulation.

EXTENDED OUTLINE

Behavioral and Social Learning Theories

I. What's It All About …
II. From Today's Headlines
III. Behaviorism—A Focus on What We Do
  A. Learning
    1. Learning defined
    2. Learning orientations
  B. Behavioral perspective
    1. Founding of behaviorism
    2. Behavioral terminology
  C. Summarize and reflect
IV. Classical Conditioning: Learning by Association
  A. Pavlov and Watson: importance of contiguity
  B. Basic components of classical conditioning
  C. Generalization versus discrimination
  D. Extinction
  E. Limitations of classical conditioning
  F. Summarize and reflect
V. Operant Conditioning: Learning by Consequence
  A. Thorndike and Skinner
  B. Reinforcement
    1. Positive reinforcement
    2. Negative reinforcement
  C. Schedules of reinforcement
    1. Continuous versus intermittent
    2. Intermittent: ratio versus interval schedules
    3. Intermittent: fixed versus variable schedules
    4. Using schedules of reinforcement to modify behavior
  D. Punishment
    1. Presentation punishment
    2. Removal punishment
  E. Shaping and extinction
  F. Cueing and prompting
  G. Applied behavior analysis
  H. Limitations of operant conditioning
  I. Summarize and reflect
VI. Social Theories: Learning by Observation
  A. Bandura—modeling and observational learning
  B. Social cognitive theory
  C. Self-regulation
    1. Self-management
    2. Cognitive behavior modification
  D. Summarize and reflect
VII. The Chapter in Review
VIII. Interdisciplinary Case Focus

From Today's Headlines

Vol. I No. 4 Teaching World, 2012

Paying Students for Better Grades Is Partially Effective, Study Says ...

The Examiner, Baltimore, MD,
by Mike Silvesteri

It is one of the most controversial educational practices—paying students for grades. Many object to the idea, but some schools are convinced that paying students for increases in academic performance is both effective and ethical.

Baltimore City schools are using a financial incentive program to help encourage students to perform academically.

Their decision is based in part on research that shows financial incentives are associated with higher academic scores. The article cites a research study from the Center for Research on Education Outcomes at Stanford University, which shows that incentives can improve academic performance. This study of one hundred charter schools across the nation showed that providing students with incentives increased some aspects of academic performance. They also indicated that incentives do not necessarily have to involve money. For example, some incentive programs involved allowing students to pelt their principal with water balloons.

The Baltimore city schools use shoes as well as money (up to $110) as incentives.

Proponents of the Baltimore plan believe that incentives help energize students and facilitate engagement in the learning process. Opponents believe that paying for grades sends the wrong message, believing that learning should be its own reward.

MAKE THE CONNECTION

Paying students for grades is an excellent example of the often controversial world of behavior management. In this chapter, we will closely examine theories behind such practices. We will begin by reviewing how students learn by associating events that occur together. We will then move on to learning that is shaped by consequences like receiving money for grades. There is no question that behavioral principles are effective tools of change in certain circumstances, but it is important for teachers to understand how to use them effectively and appropriately.

BEHAVIORISM—A FOCUS ON WHAT WE DO

The next time you are in a crowded room, look around at what the other people are doing. Perhaps some are walking purposefully to the nearest exit. Some people may be reading the newspaper or talking with a friend. The world is filled with people engaging in a wide range of behaviors every minute of every day. Looking at people's behavior often leads to questions. "Why are they doing that?" "What are they talking about?" The answers are actually quite complicated. Answering the question, "Why do people behave as they do?" depends upon your individual perspective. For each of us, certain aspects of a situation are more important than others. For example, in an attempt to figure out why one student is yelling at another, some of us would wonder, "What is he thinking about?" Others would want to know, "What could possibly motivate him to behave like that?" This chapter strives to help you understand the behavior you see people engaged in, a focus on what people *do*. Other important questions, such as what people *think* about, will be covered in the next chapter.

Learning

Sophie, an eight-year-old in Mr. Prine's third grade class, is working on learning her multiplication facts. Last week, when her teacher asked what four times three was, she replied "Sixteen." Today, she not only knows the correct answer to four times three, but she also knows all of the three and four multiplication facts. What accounts for this change in behavior? Did she study hard after school with her older sister? Did she merely mature physically, leading to a natural expansion in her multiplication skills. Perhaps, she knew her three and four multiplication tables six months ago but was not feeling well last week and could only remember the answer to three times four, instead of four times three. All of these situations relate to learning. Defining learning is relatively straightforward; however, explaining and changing behavior often requires considerable expertise.

A student's outside factors, such as studying hard or not feeling well, can contribute to what is remembered while learning.

Learning Defined

In the broadest sense, **learning** refers to a lasting change in an individual resulting from experience (Gredler, 2001; Mazur, 1990). So, exactly what happened when Sophie learned her multiplication facts? What is it about Sophie that changed because of her learning experience? Did she increase her knowledge, change her behavior, or change structures within her brain? Depending on the theoretical perspective we use to view Sophie's learning, the answer will be very different. As was mentioned in the opening remarks to the chapter, learning means different things to different people. Let's take a look at some of those different points of view.

Learning

A lasting change in an individual resulting from experience

Learning Orientations

One could probably list many different perspectives on behavior, but this text will focus on only a few of the most prominent. For example, a *cognitive* psychologist might say Sophie increased her knowledge through memorization. Cognitive psychology focuses on an individual's ability to think and reason. A *neuroscientist* might say that she formed new connections between cells of the brain. Neuroscience is just beginning to make meaningful contributions to the advancement of education. We might also focus on Sophie's *motivation* to study or the benefit of *social* relationships to support academic success. Motivation and social learning are covered later in the text. A *behaviorist* would say that Sophie exhibited a change in her overt behavior, or her ability to say her multiplication facts. Focusing on behavior, we can see, is the hallmark of the behavioral perspective and is the primary focus of this chapter.

Behavioral Perspective

Like all historical events, the behavioral perspective emerged in a historical context. When behaviorism first emerged, our society was undergoing widespread changes, which made it possible for this perspective on learning to flourish in psychological and educational circles. Although this text focuses on psychology as it relates to education, the behavioral movement extended well beyond the classroom. The next section describes the historical events surrounding the widespread endorsement of the behavioral point of view. We will also introduce some basic terminology behaviorists use to describe behavior.

Founding of Behaviorism

Sigmund Freud

In the late 1800s, the predominant school of thought in psychology was psychoanalytic theory, founded by Sigmund Freud. His theory placed an emphasis on internal events and subconscious thoughts. For example, Zack may display an almost obsessive desire to achieve. Subconsciously, he feels that if he does not succeed, he will not be loved. If asked about his strong desire to achieve, he might show little insight, reporting he "likes to get A's." Additionally, Freud believed much of our mental life was influenced by events occurring in childhood. Perhaps Zack received conditional care and support from his parents during childhood, which led to his unknowing search for love and acceptance. This perspective thrived across the world for many years, but ultimately people became dissatisfied with the ability of this approach to account for behavior. For example, if you have a high school student experiencing depression and, therefore, lacks engagement in school, what is the cause? The Freudian point of view would focus on thoughts and feelings, particularly those impacted by childhood events the student may not even remember. This focus on unconscious thoughts lacked specificity and made it difficult to investigate and apply Freudian theory in a consistent way.

John Watson

The behavioral perspective emerged partly in reaction to Sigmund Freud's theoretical orientation (Freud & Strachey, 1964), as well as to other theories of the mind prominent at that time. In the early 1900s, John Watson asserted that psychology should be objective and scientific, as opposed to the subjective and theoretical work of Freud and his followers (Watson, 1913, 1928, & 1931). Watson proposed a new psychology that focused on observable events and behavior (called overt behavior). He asserted that inferring the existence of phenomena that occur inside a person, like thinking or feeling, was unnecessary and unscientific. Watson's ideas were appealing to many scientists, and research in the behavioral tradition spread rapidly. Behavioral researchers have uncovered a number of basic principles of learning; and there are many direct applications of this research, from education and parenting to marketing and business. In short, our understanding of learning is influenced in a significant way by the contribution of behavioral research. Additionally, the behavioral perspective has much to offer in the way of direct applications in the classroom. We turn now to a more detailed exploration of the behavioral perspective and its basic terminology.

Behavioral Terminology

Behaviorists view environmental experience as the central force in learning. This means we behave based upon the experiences we have during our life. This leads to a focus on observable behaviors or things that we can actually observe people do. Recall that from a behaviorist's perspective, internal mental events are theoretical and not appropriate for scientific study. Using this behaviorally based definition of learning, researchers have studied behavior for over one hundred years, contributing much to our understanding of leaning.

Students of behavioral theory must first begin to view the world as an endless stream of interconnected behaviors. That is, any given behavior is impacted by preceding events and will influence, in turn, future behaviors. Think about your own behaviors since you woke up today. What led you to that first action after you opened your eyes? What happened next? What events early in the day affected later events? Again, behavior is ongoing, without a specific beginning or end.

Figure 4.1
Key Terms Used in Behavioral Theory

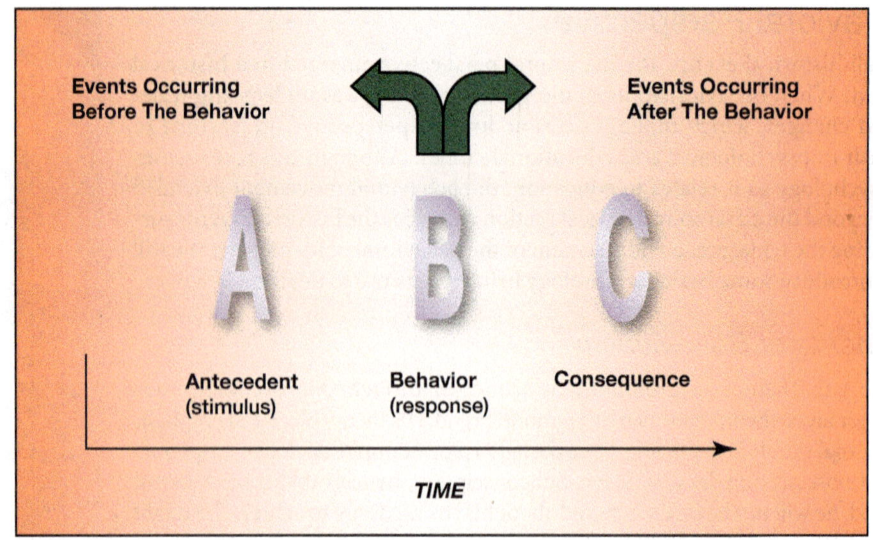

So, how then do we examine behavior occurring in such an endless stream of events? Typically, the behaviorist begins by picking out some *behavior of interest.* Perhaps you are interested in why a student hit another student, or why one student cheated by looking at another student's exam. What is important is that the behavior of interest is clearly defined. Next, the behaviorist may attempt to figure out what events led up to the behavior of interest, as well as what happened immediately after the behavior.

Stimulus
Event leading to a response

Antecedent
An event occurring before the behavior of interest, having an effect on its expression

Consequence
Event occurring after the behavior of interest

The key terms used in behavioral theory involve a specific environmental stimulus, the response that follows, and the potential association between the stimulus and the response (Burton, Moore, & Magliar, 1996; Carr & Briggs, 2011). For example, being called on to answer a question (a stimulus) might make your heart race (a response). Behaviorists are concerned with how such associations are made, how they are strengthened or weakened, and how they are maintained. Events leading to a response are referred to as the **stimulus**. Some stimuli play a role in the expression of behavior and are, therefore, called **antecedents**, which simply refer to an event occurring before the behavior of interest and having an effect on its expression. Behaviorists also study how responses are changed by the events that come after the stimulus. Events occurring after a behavior of interest are called **consequences**. For example, the teacher notices the student's panic when she calls on him and gently guides him to the correct answer. This consequence will probably lead to a different response the next time. Reviewing this basic approach to naming the important factors in the ongoing stream of behavior, we first have the behavior of interest, which is called the response. Again, it is often a good idea to begin applying behavioral theory by clearly defining the behavior of interest. Events preceding the response are called antecedents, and events coming after the response are called consequences. Figure 4.1 provides a graphical depiction of this typical naming convention. Using the first letter of each of the important terms makes the acronym A B C, which students usually find easy to remember.

SUMMARIZE AND REFLECT

1. Learning is defined as a lasting change in an individual resulting from experience.
2. Researchers study learning from many perspectives. Some scientists view learning as a change in knowledge resulting from experience, while others focus on experience related changes in the brain. Behaviorists view learning as a change in behavior occurring because of experience.
3. Behavioral theory is based on the fundamental assumption that the focus of psychology is on observable behavior only.
4. Early behaviorists, such as John Watson, asserted that the existence of phenomena that occur inside a person, such as thinking or feeling, couldn't be proven scientifically. He strongly proposed that psychology should be limited to the objective and scientific study of observable behavior.

(continues)

5. Behaviorists use a common approach to defining and understanding behavior. Behaviorists focus on a given behavior (response), relevant antecedent events (stimuli), and events occurring after the behavior (consequences).

INFORMED APPLICATION

1. As a ninth grade teacher, you consistently have a problem with students becoming restless five minutes before the end of each period. Based on behavioral principles, what aspects of this problem are relevant when trying to design a behavior modification program?
2. Teachers often struggle with getting students to internalize basic math facts like multiplication tables. This issue can be approached from different perspectives. If the teacher operates from a behavioral perspective, what is she going to emphasize to help the students learn more effectively?

CLASSICAL CONDITIONING—LEARNING BY ASSOCIATION

Now that we have reviewed the basic idea behind behavioral theory, we will begin with the first of the three behavioral theories covered in this chapter. This section covers a type of behavioral theory called classical conditioning. **Classical conditioning** is a behavioral theory based on our ability to learn by associating events that co-occur in the environment. Using the terms from the previous section, the theory is based on the association made between a stimulus and response in our environment. For example, you experience a sense of excitement at the sight of your biology teacher because you associate her with fun classroom experiments. This type of learning emphasizes the importance of learning through events occurring together in time. This co-occurrence of events (e.g., a stimulus and a response) is called **contiguity**. Before we turn to a more detailed account of the processes involved in classical conditioning, let us first look at the individuals whose research brought us this important theory and the historical events surrounding its discoveries.

Classical conditioning

A behavioral theory based on our ability to learn by associating events that co-occur in the environment

Contiguity

The co-occurrence of events

Pavlov and Watson: Importance of Contiguity

The story of classical conditioning begins with a Russian physiologist named Ivan Pavlov (1849–1936). Pavlov was one of world's most renowned scientists. His work on the physiology of digestion led to the Nobel Prize in 1904 and was followed by additional outstanding achievements while he served as Director of Russia's Institute of Experimental Medicine. His primary research focus was the investigation of digestion using an experimental method that allowed for continuous monitoring of organ systems in live animals. Related to this research, he began to investigate the causes of salivation in dogs. A colleague proposed that a "mental" reflex, or an automatic response, caused salivation to food. Through a series of experiments, Pavlov was able to show that sometimes salivation is learned, rather than an automatic process. Based on this research, he believed he discovered a fundamental building block of learning. His theory indicated we are born with certain behavioral responses to the environment; however, we can *learn* to extend this foundation, responding in new ways that are sensitive to the world around us. For example, we may be born with a tendency to exhibit fear when we encounter an unexpected loud noise—a startle response. We can, however, learn to startle to other environmental stimuli, such as of sight of a large dog. Pavlov called this type of learning *classical conditioning*, and he believed it explained the behavioral capabilities of lower animals and humans (Pavlov, 1928).

Ivan Pavlov

In 1903, as Pavlov was first presenting his findings at the International Medical Congress in Madrid, a young American psychologist named John B. Watson was receiving his doctoral degree. Watson was strongly influenced by the work of Pavlov and studied many of his principles as they applied to the physiology and behavior of animals. As a professor of psychology at The Johns Hopkins University, Watson also began to study Pavlovian conditioning in human infants. He believed humans were indeed more complicated than lower animals but generally operated on the same principles. In 1913, he published a paper detailing his ideas, essentially founding what would become the *Behavioral School of Psychology*. This "school" was essentially a group of researchers who embraced Watson's perspectives on learning. This was an important event because this school of thought would dominate psychology for the next fifty years, dramatically influencing society through educational and child-rearing practices.

Basic Components of Classical Conditioning

The process of classical conditioning begins with instinctive behaviors we do not have to learn, such as salivating at the sight of food or being startled by the sound of a loud noise (Abramson, Brown, & Langley, 2011). Consider the behavior of the following children: Jane touches a hot stove and immediately withdraws her hand. Bill hears a loud noise and startles. Michael hits his head and begins to cry. A behavior occurred in each of these examples. The question is, did any of these children learn their reactions? Are they examples of behaviors we come into this world prepared to exhibit? Pavlov believed they were unlearned behaviors and referred to them **unconditioned responses (UCR)**. Pavlov used the term *conditioned* to refer to learning; therefore, something that is unconditioned is something that does not have to be learned. Table 4.1 presents a few examples of potential unconditioned responses. In addition to proposing a term for behaviors that are unlearned, Pavlov also proposed a term for the environmental events that trigger the unlearned response. For example, the loud noise that triggered Bill's unconditioned startle response is called the **unconditioned stimulus (UCS)**. The unconditioned stimulus is defined as the environmental event that brings about the unconditioned response. The unconditioned stimulus and the resulting unconditioned response are the basic elements of classical conditioning. The idea is that through our life experiences we build upon these basic stimulus/response pairs to create the complex behaviors typical of our species. Let's consider the following example from a fourth grade, language arts class:

Table 4.1 Unconditioned Responses

Unconditioned responses typically include basic reflexes and certain emotional responses.

Examples

- Salivation
- Fear
- Startle
- Withdrawal
- Eye blink

Unconditioned responses (UCR)

The behavioral response to the unconditioned stimulus without previous learning

Unconditioned stimulus (UCS)

The environmental event that brings about the unconditioned response without previous learning

> Mr. Goodsell is the language arts teacher for a fourth grade class at St. Michael's School. He has assigned a new project this semester involving the writing of a report on the topic of "social justice." The project includes a ten-minute presentation. Terrell, a student in the class, was excited about writing the report. He had recently read a chapter in geography about a country where women were not allowed to show their faces in public and thought that it would make an interesting report. In the week before the assignment was due, Terrell worked hard on his report and the presentation. On the day he was to present, he confidently went to the front of the class and gave his report from the podium. His teacher congratulated him on his thoroughness and the class applauded. As he was walking back to his seat, another student leaned over and told him he couldn't believe he did his report on such a "sissy" topic. Several of the students overheard and laughed quietly. Terrell immediately felt his face flush and his heart beat faster. He tried to say something, but only managed a few halting words. He continued on to his seat and put his head down.
>
> It wasn't until the following year that Terrell had to make another presentation, this time for his math class. He had to do a report on a prominent mathematician. As before, he dutifully prepared and began to look forward to the presentation. On the day of the presentation, he began to walk to the front of the class, but slowed down as he approached the podium. Although his previous public speaking experience was met with excitement, the excitement was now replaced with a peculiar feeling. His heart was racing, his face felt hot, and he couldn't remember the first word of his presentation.

Let's try to interpret Terrell's situation in terms of classical conditioning. The first step is to identify an unconditioned stimulus/response pair. Terrell's response following the student's remark about his social justice report can be viewed as an unlearned response. Terrell experienced several physiological symptoms, including a racing heart rate and blushing. This is a typical human response to situations that are unexpected or take us off-guard and does not require direct learning. In terms of classical conditioning, the physiological response experienced by Terrell would be the unconditioned response, and the unexpected student remarks would be the unconditioned stimulus.

The next part of the classical conditioning involves the **neutral stimulus (NS)**. The neutral stimulus is something in the environment, which initially has nothing to do with the unconditioned response. In this example, the experience of making a presentation at the podium was initially unrelated to the behavioral response of heart racing or blushing. In other words, the experience of making a presentation from a podium does not naturally elicit a racing heart or blushing.

Neutral stimulus (NS)

Something in the environment that initially fails to elicit the unconditioned response

The neutral stimulus in Terrell's situation is the experience of giving a presentation from the podium and the unconditioned stimulus is the rude remark made by the student. In classical conditioning, the timing of the neutral stimulus (presentation from podium) and unconditioned stimulus (rude remark) are extremely important. In general, for classical conditioning to be effective, the neutral stimulus is introduced prior to the unconditioned stimulus. In Terrell's case, the presentation (neutral stimulus) immediately precedes the unkind remark (unconditioned stimulus). This *pairing* of the neutral stimulus and the unconditioned stimulus is the basis for learning through association and is crucial for the classical conditioning process. Without this pairing, classical conditioning would not occur. For some stimuli, a single pairing of the neutral and unconditioned stimuli can produce learning; for others, multiple pairings are required for learning. In our example, the single pairing of the presentation from the podium and the student's remark and the laughter following were powerful enough to produce learning. We know this because Terrell's next experience with giving a presentation resulted in a new response.

When Terrell went to make his presentation in math, it was clear that he had learned to fear public speaking; whereas, just a year before he looked forward to it. This learned behavioral response, fear of public speaking, is called the **conditioned response (CR)**. Pavlov called this the *conditioned* response because it is the product of learning. The learning occurs through the pairing or association between the neutral stimulus (the first presentation Terrell gave from the podium) and the unconditioned stimulus (the unkind remarks). Their pairing caused an association, whereby the neutral stimulus did not remain neutral. When Terrell began his second presentation, the formally neutral stimulus (giving a presentation from the podium) became a **conditioned stimulus (CS)**, eliciting a new response (racing heart and blushing). The conditioned stimulus is an environmental stimulus that brings about a response through the process of learning, and in this case it is the podium in the math class. Figure 4.2 provides a graphical depiction of Terrell's learning process.

Conditioned response (CR)

The behavioral response to the conditioned stimulus brought about through a learned association

Conditioned stimulus (CS)

The environmental event that brings about the conditioned stimulus through a learned association

Generalization versus Discrimination

Following the initial discovery of classical conditioning, behavioral scientists turned to the question of how we are able to learn something in one situation and then apply that learning to another similar situation. This transfer of learning came to be known as generalization. **Generalization** is defined as emitting a conditioned response to a stimulus that is similar to, but not exactly the same as, the conditioned stimulus. Through generalization, we extend our learning to situations beyond the context in which they were originally learned. Consider Janelle, a pre-K student at a local childcare center. One day, she was out on the school playground and was about to slide down the slide when a bee stung her leg. Janelle became very upset when this occurred and developed a fear of the slide through classical conditioning. Interestingly, Janelle also refused to go down the slide at her neighbor's house, at the fast-food restaurant down the street, and at the local water park. She even began to display anxiety about using the ladder to go up and down her brother's bunk bed. In this example, Janelle's fear of the slide extended to a number of similar situations. From a classical conditioning perspective, her fear of slides and ladders developed as follows: Initially, the playground slide became a conditioned stimulus, eliciting a conditioned response of fear after being paired with the bee sting (unconditioned stimulus) and the resulting pain (unconditioned response). This learning occurred on the school's playground, and it would seem that it should be limited to

Generalization

A conditioned response to a stimulus that is similar to, but not exactly the same as, the conditioned stimulus

Figure 4.2
Terrell's Learning Process

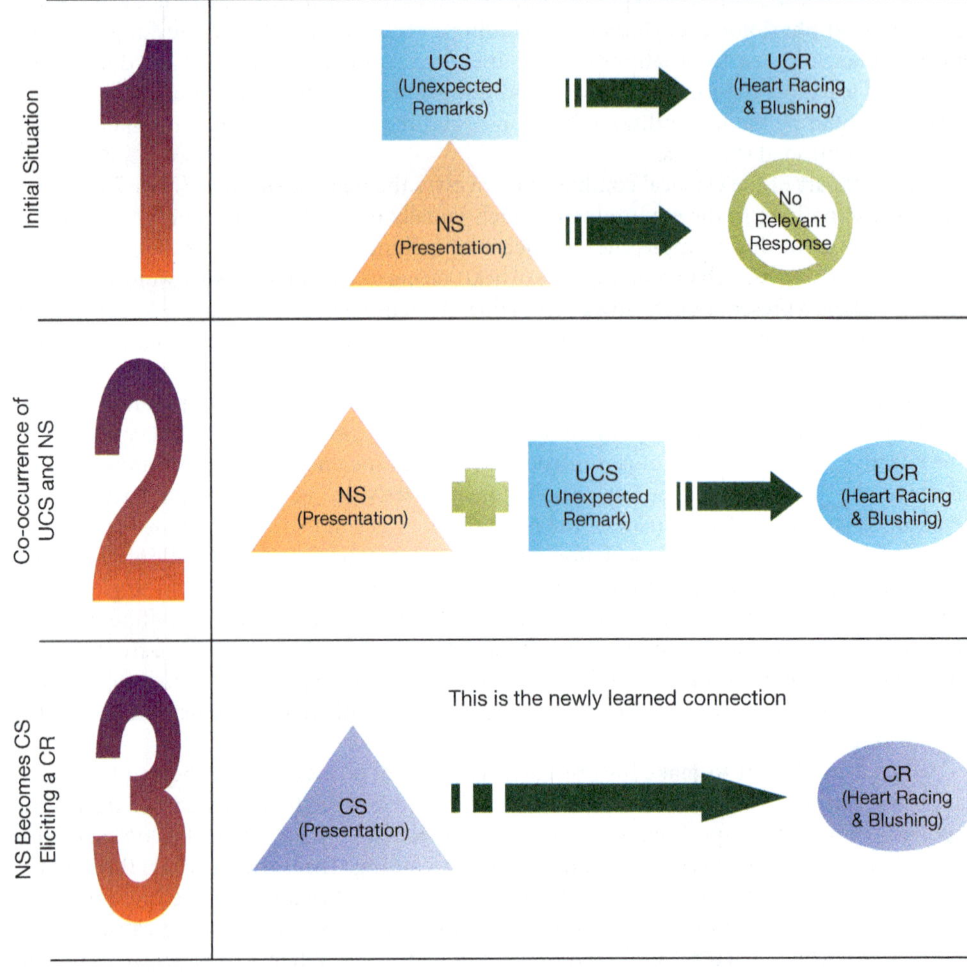

LEGEND:

UCS - Unconditioned Stimulus
NS - Neutral Stimulus
CS - Conditioned Stimulus
UCR - Unconditioned Response
CR - Conditioned Respose

Discrimination

Ability to tell the difference between stimuli, allowing someone to limit a conditioned response to the original conditioned stimulus

that particular slide. After all, it is unlikely that all slides and ladders harbor bees. Learning, however, is remarkably flexible.

Janelle learned from her experience at the playground slide and began to *generalize*, or extend, her fear response to other situations. She even went so far as to generalize her newfound fear of the playground slide to any situation where she had to climb a ladder, as demonstrated by her response to her brother's bunk bed. Generalization becomes more likely when there is a high degree of similarity between the learning context and the context in which the learning extends. That is, different looking slides should evoke less fear. Janelle's fear of all slides and ladders indicates a high degree of generalization. Helping her overcome her newfound fear of slides, ladders, and high places will take time and patience. She will need to learn to distinguish between different situations where she is likely to be hurt.

Discrimination involves being able to tell the difference between stimuli, allowing someone to limit a conditioned response to the original conditioned stimulus (Vervliet, Iberico, Vervoort, & Baeyens, 2011). Janelle will need to discriminate, or see the difference between the original playground situation and other similar situations that she encounters. For example, if Janelle only showed a fear response around the slide at school and not around other slides, we would say she is using discrimination. Generalization and discrimination are not necessarily bad or good. Oftentimes, we want students to generalize, applying something they learned to

F.A.Q.

Valerie Schmitt—"Both the UCR and the CR are heart racing and blushing. Are they really the same?"

Professor Rainwater—"The UCR and the CR may look the same, but they differ in that they are preceded by different events. The UCS elicited the UCR (rude remark); however, the CS elicited the CR (presentation). So, you can always tell the difference between the UCR and the CR by looking at what came immediately *before* the response."

other similar situations. For instance, when we teach students to associate learning with enjoyment, we might pair a new learning task with events students naturally enjoy (e.g., games involving physical activity like running, jumping, etc.). We may begin with pairing one learning activity with physical activity (by making it a sort of game) but hope their enjoyment with the current activity generalizes to other learning situations. At other times, we want students to appreciate the differences between situations and behave accordingly. Perhaps we have a student who has developed a fear of math. We would want to intervene and address his fear, but we also want to make sure his fear does not generalize to other classes. Having a basic knowledge of the principles of classical conditioning allows us to examine student learning from a unique perspective, facilitating our ability to create responsive learning environments. By being able to identify the basic elements of classical conditioning in a learning situation, we can examine learning goals and explicitly encourage generalization or discrimination of stimuli accordingly.

F.A.Q.

John Forsythe—"The NS and the CS also appear to be the same thing. Are they?"

Professor Rainwater—"The NS and the CS both involve the presentation, but at different points in time. The NS is the presentation prior to being paired with the UCS (rude remark). The CS is the presentation after pairing. The CS is distinguished by the fact that it can now do something new, namely, it can elicit heart racing and blushing. It could not elicit this response prior to pairing with the UCS."

Extinction

Once a student has become classically conditioned, is it possible to alter his behavior, so that it returns to pre-conditioning levels? The answer is yes, and it involves the process of **extinction**. Extinction is the elimination of a classically conditioned response. This is accomplished by presenting the *conditioned* stimulus alone, making sure that the *unconditioned* stimulus is not present. Each presentation of a conditioned stimulus without the accompanying unconditioned stimulus weakens the association between the two, resulting in eventual extinction of the classically conditioned response. In the example of Janelle's classically conditioned fear of slides, repeatedly exposing her to slides (conditioned stimulus) while ensuring that she did not come into contact with any stinging insects (unconditioned stimulus) would result in the eventual extinction of her fear response. Similarly, Terrell's classically conditioned fear of public speaking could be extinguished by having him make repeated public presentations, making sure the presentation was not associated with any rude remarks.

Extinction (classical conditioning)
Elimination of a classically conditioned response, typically accomplished by presenting the conditioned stimulus alone

Classical conditioning theory was groundbreaking research at the time it was developed. It was quickly heralded as a fundamental building block of learning. Researchers, however, soon learned that it failed to take into account a critical learning factor, consequences. The next section reviews this important issue and how it limits classical conditioning as a complete explanation for learning.

Elimination of a classically conditioned response (such as a fear of slides) is possible through the process of extinction.

Limitation of Classical Conditioning

Classical conditioning is primarily about a behavior and the earlier event that caused its occurrence. The theory, however, fails to take into account the influence of events occurring *after* the behavior of interest. For example, a third grade teacher was introducing a new math concept. When the teacher called on each of the children to participate in the lesson, she praised those who answered her questions correctly. Could the events occurring *after* the student's response, in this case the teacher's verbal praise, influence learning?

Classical conditioning focuses on the antecedents of behavior and the behavior or response itself. What classical conditioning fails to account for is the influence of consequences, or events occurring *after* the behavior of interest, on future expression of the behavior. Recall Terrell's classically conditioned fear of public speaking. What happened after the students made the rude remarks and Terrell took his seat? Did the teacher notice the situation? Did the teacher give Terrell help interpreting the remarks? Did other students, perhaps a good friend, help Terrell interpret the remark? Any of these possible situations could have had a dramatic effect on Terrell's **acquisition**, or initial learning, of a fear response. Also, remember that all of these possible situations would have occurred *after* Terrell's negative behavioral response (heart racing and blushing).

Acquisition
The initial learning of a response

Research in the behavioral tradition indicates that, in addition to the associative type of learning exemplified in Pavlov's and Watson's classical conditioning, consequences have a strong influence on learning. The next section focuses on learning by consequences and the remarkable work of E. L. Thorndike and B. F. Skinner.

SUMMARIZE AND REFLECT

1. Classical conditioning theory began with the work of the Russian physiologist Ivan Pavlov. His initial work on the physiology of digestion led to his discovery of a type of learning, which he called classical conditioning.
2. John B. Watson expanded conditioning theory, further outlining the basic processes involved in classical conditioning.
3. The basic elements of classical conditioning are the unconditioned stimulus, the unconditioned response, the conditioned stimulus, the conditioned response, and the neutral stimulus.
4. In order to produce classical conditioning it is important to pair the unconditioned stimulus and the neutral stimulus.
5. This type of learning can be transferred from one situation to another similar situation, a process known as generalization.
6. Discrimination is when an individual is able to discriminate between stimuli, recognizing that a new stimulus differs from the conditioned stimulus.
7. Extinction is the process of returning a behavior to a level before classical conditioning took place.

INFORMED APPLICATION

1. Physical education teachers often go to considerable effort to help students enjoy participating in athletic activities. How can you use classical conditioning to help students learn to associate physical education with positive behavioral responses? Identify each of the components of classical conditioning.
2. Students often learn a desirable classically conditioned response in a specific environment (perhaps in traditional classroom environments). How can teachers help students generalize such desirable responses to other situations (art room, study hall, auditorium)?

OPERANT CONDITIONING—LEARNING BY CONSEQUENCE

The second of the three behavioral theories we are covering in this chapter is called operant conditioning. Operant conditioning differs from classical conditioning presented earlier in that it focuses on a different part of the behavioral stream. Recall from the beginning of the chapter that behavior can be viewed as an ongoing stream with earlier events affecting current behavior and current behavior affecting later behaviors. Operant conditioning theorists recognize the importance of this behavioral stream. Their early research, however, was particularly notable for their departure from the stimulus and response focus of classical conditioning. Operant conditioning is a learning theory focusing on how consequences shape the expression of behavior. We will begin with an overview of the earliest work in this area and then review important terminology and applications of the theory.

Law of effect

Principle of behavior stating that a behavior resulting in satisfying events increase the likelihood of that behavior in the future

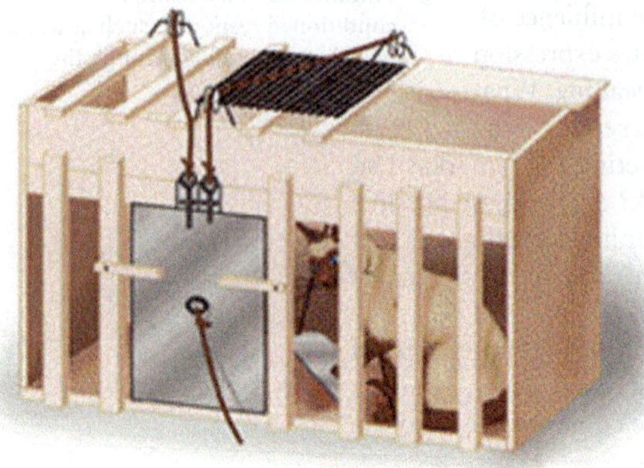

Thorndike and Skinner

E. L. Thorndike pioneered the formal investigation of the effects of consequences on learning (Hilgard & Bower, 1966; Milson, Bohan, Glanzer, & Null, 2010). Through unique studies with cats placed in a "puzzle box," Thorndike established the power of a satisfying result on the frequency of behavior. In these experiments, the cats had to negotiate a trap door using a string on a pulley. When the cats successfully opened the door, they were able to escape and eat. Cats who successfully completed the task were quicker to solve the "puzzle box" when returned to the box at a later time. The satisfying nature of getting to eat facilitated the cat's performance on the second trial. Thorndike's puzzle box research led to the **law of effect**.

This law states that behaviors resulting in satisfying events increase the likelihood of the behavior in the future. The law of effect became the first major principle of consequential learning and laid the foundation for another researcher who would forever change the face of psychology, B. F. Skinner.

B. F. Skinner

B. F. Skinner is one of the most recognized names in psychology primarily because of his groundbreaking research in the 1940s and 1950s. The focus of his research was to extend the learning by association principles established by Pavlov and Watson to include principles related to learning by consequences. He believed that unlike learning by association, which is limited by the number of our innate responses, learning by consequences occurs by an individual operating on the environment in an infinite number of ways. Further, he believed that the consequences of these operations produce changes in our future behavior. This focus on how we operate on the environment and the consequences of these operations led Skinner to define a new theory of learning, which he called **operant conditioning**. Operant conditioning is learning based on how operants (behaviors) are influenced by the consequences that follow (Catania, 1997). For example, Tanya raises her hand frequently in class. From an operant conditioning perspective, she has learned to operate in her environment in this way because of the consequences she receives. Her teacher likely rewards her students by calling on them when they have their hands appropriately raised. While this is a classroom example, Skinner's initial research was far more controlled than the average classroom. He initially investigated the effects of consequences on behavior through the use of a specialized mechanical device called a **Skinner box**. Most of these Skinner boxes were small enclosures, suitable for a rat or pigeon, which included a device that allowed the animal to make a response (lever pressing or key pecking) and a device to deliver a consequence such as a food tray or mild shock (see Figure 4.3). This extremely controlled environment allowed him to specifically examine the effects of environmental consequences on behavior. Largely through his research with animals, Skinner outlined a number of basic behavioral learning principles that went far beyond Thorndike's Law of Effect. Subsequent research by Skinner and others has extended his learning principles to humans in an almost limitless number of situations. We turn now to an in-depth exploration of the basic principles of learning by consequences outlined by Skinner.

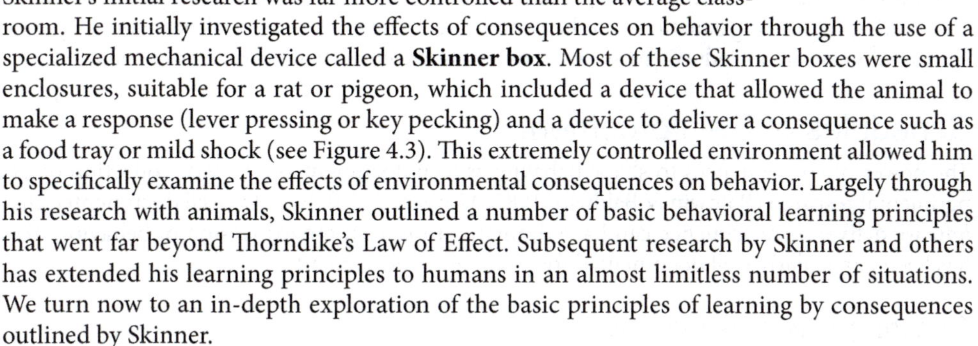

Operant conditioning

A learning theory focusing on how consequences shape the expression of behavior

Skinner Box

Research tool used to investigate the effects of consequences on behavior through the use of a specialized mechanical device

Reinforcer

A favorable outcome occurring after a behavior of interest

Reinforcement

Skinner's research further specified the relation between behavior and consequence. Similar to Thorndike's Law of Effect, Skinner demonstrated that when favorable circumstances follow a given behavior, the behavior would likely continue in the future. He called this process reinforcement. The favorable outcome occurring after the behavior is called a **reinforcer**. For example, Meghan seemed especially well prepared for social studies, so her teacher let her help set up a class group exercise. Assisting the teacher with the group activity (reinforcer) was a pleasant activity for Meghan, reinforcing her excellent class preparation. Skinner's research demonstrated that there are two types of reinforcement.

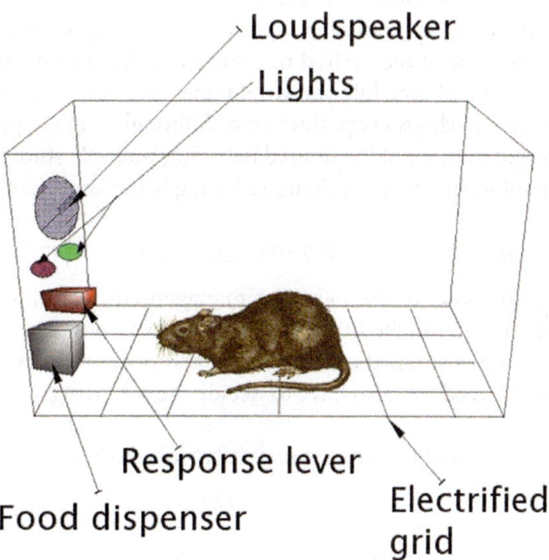

Figure 4.3

Skinner Box

Positive Reinforcement

Positive reinforcement

Something positive that is added to the environment in order to increase the frequency of a desired behavior

This type of reinforcement is called **positive reinforcement** because something positive is added to the environment in order to increase the frequency of a desired behavior. Giving someone something they want as a consequence for behaving in a certain way is a common practice and is easily understood. For example, Rena was presented with a coupon for a free ice cream at a local restaurant because she had perfect attendance during the current marking period. Rena's behavior of attending class was *reinforced* by the coupon, the *reinforcer*—teachers, parents, and employers use this type of consequence with great regularity. Its focus on positive events also serves to make this a particularly favored behavioral management technique. Positive reinforcement, however, is not the only way to *reinforce* someone.

Negative Reinforcement

Negative reinforcement

The removal of something negative from the environment in order to increase the frequency of a desired response

Skinner demonstrated another type of reinforcement he called **negative reinforcement.** Negative reinforcement is when you remove something negative from the environment in order to increase the frequency of a desired response. Like positive reinforcement, negative reinforcement is accomplished by creating a favorable circumstance. In this case, *removing something negative* or aversive creates the favorable circumstance. Removing something negative from the environment can be very reinforcing. For example, taking away tonight's homework because of excellent classroom behavior is viewed favorably by the students and encourages their good behavior. In this example of negative reinforcement, the reinforcer is the *removal* of the negatively perceived homework. Just as with positive reinforcement, negative reinforcement increases the likelihood of behavior being repeated in the future. Both positive and negative reinforcement encourage behavior. That is, they increase the frequency of behavior in the future. Reinforcement is an important part of behavior, but creating reinforcing situations can be complicated. The next section takes a look at specific ways reinforcers are introduced to an environment to create particular patterns of behavior.

Schedules of Reinforcement

The power of consequences to shape behavior is well documented by a vast collection of experimental research (Baldwin & Baldwin, 1988; Morgan, 2010). It is also well documented that *how* we deliver a consequence can have dramatic impact on the expression of behavior. This has been particularly well documented for positive reinforcement.

Continuous versus Intermittent

Schedule of reinforcement

The timing and delivery of reinforcement

Continuous reinforcement

Reinforcement that is provided at every instance of a desired behavior

Intermittent schedule of reinforcement

Reinforcement for only some of the desired responses

The timing and delivery of reinforcement is referred to as **schedule of reinforcement.** For example, reinforcers may be given after every instance of a desired behavior, or they may be given for only some of the desired responses. Reinforcing every instance of a desired behavior is called **continuous reinforcement.** For example, if you gave out extra minutes of recess *every* time a student raised their hand appropriately, you would be using a continuous reinforcement schedule. Reinforcing only *some* of the desired responses is called an **intermittent schedule of reinforcement.** To use this type of schedule you would only give out extra minutes of recess for some appropriate hand raises, perhaps every third one. Although it may appear that continuous reinforcement would result in more of the desired behavior, multiple studies indicate using an intermittent schedule of reinforcement results in more lasting behavioral change (Baldwin & Baldwin, 1988; Grant, 2011).

Intermittent: Ratio versus Interval Schedules

If you wish to use behavior management techniques to achieve lasting behavior change, an intermittent schedule is the appropriate choice. Deciding to reinforce on an intermittent schedule, however, is the easy part. In addition to determining exactly what behavior is going to be reinforced, we also have to decide the following:

- *Will we simply count behaviors to determine which ones will be reinforced?*

OR

- *Will we deliver reinforcement after a certain period of time?*

- *Will the pattern of reinforcement remain constant?*

OR

- *Will we vary the pattern we use to reinforce?*

First, let's address whether we will reinforce based on *number* of responses or on behavior produced at a particular point in *time*. **Ratio schedules of reinforcement** require reinforcing a certain number of responses. For example, Ms. Belmont is interested in reinforcing students for raising their hands before speaking. She is planning on reinforcing on a ratio schedule and will use a simple verbal reinforcer, "Thank you for raising your hand, [student name], what is your question?" Since she is reinforcing on a ratio schedule, she will be counting each appropriate instance of behavior and providing the verbal reinforcer for a predetermined number of behaviors. She has decided that on the third instance of appropriate hand raising, she will deliver the verbal reinforcer. On non-reinforced instances of appropriate hand raising, she will simply say the student's name. The important point to remember about ratio schedules is that it is based on reinforcement of a certain *number* of responses.

Ratio schedule of reinforcement

The schedule requiring the reinforcement of a certain number of responses

Compare the above ratio schedule to a schedule based on time. **Interval schedules of reinforcement** provides reinforcement for the first instance of a desired behavior following a period of time. This schedule of reinforcement establishes a period of "wait time" during which no reinforcement is possible. After the time period has elapsed, the student is reinforced for the first instance of the desired response. Using the hand raising example, the instructor would first start a timer for a prescribed wait period —let's say three minutes. During the three minutes, the student will not receive any reinforcements for appropriate hand raises. After the timer indicates the three minutes are up, however, the student is reinforced for the first appropriate hand raise they make. Following the reinforcement, the timer is reset and the wait period begins again. The important point to remember here is that interval schedules of reinforcement are based on a predetermined period of *time*.

Interval schedule of reinforcement

A schedule that provides reinforcement for the first instance of a desired behavior after a certain period of time

Intermittent: Fixed versus Variable Schedules

Next, let's answer the question whether the reinforcement schedule will stay the same or will it be periodically changed. Reinforcement schedules that remain constant are called **fixed schedules of reinforcement**. If a teacher were using a ratio schedule and wished to fix the schedule, he would simply set the number of required behaviors and keep this number for the duration of the reinforcement period. Using the hand raising example, he would reinforce only after a predetermined number of hand raises, perhaps three, and always reinforce the third hand raise.

Fixed schedule of reinforcement

Reinforcement that is provided at a constant rate

Compare this to a **variable schedule of reinforcement** where the number of hand raises required for reinforcement varies. Using a variable schedule would require the instructor to reinforce an initial number of hand raises, perhaps three, and then to vary the next number of hand raises necessary for reinforcement, perhaps giving the reinforcer after five appropriate hand raises. The number of required hand raises would change after each reinforced hand raise. This variation typically occurs around a predetermined average. If the instructor wanted to variably reinforce around a predetermined average of three, she might initially reinforce for three hand raises, followed by one hand raise, followed by five hand raises. The average of these three variations, (3 + 1 + 5)/3, would equal the predetermined average of three.

Variable schedule of reinforcement

Reinforcement that varies over time

Fixed and variable schedules of reinforcement also apply to interval schedules of reinforcement. A fixed interval schedule assigns a constant wait period, perhaps three minutes, before reinforcing behavior. A variable interval schedule requires the instructor vary the wait period, perhaps three minutes, followed by one minute, followed by five minutes. Combining the qualities of the ratio and interval schedules with the qualities of fixed versus variable schedules results in four schedules of reinforcement: fixed ratio—FR; variable ratio—VR; fixed interval—FI; and variable interval—VI (see Table 4.2). By convention, we typically denote the intermittent value by placing a number after the above abbreviations. For example, a schedule involving reinforcement after every third response would be called a FR3 schedule. A schedule involving reinforcement after a time period that varies around an average of five minutes would be called a VI5 schedule. Also, keep in mind that these intermittent schedules of reinforcement are simply ways to determine how reinforcers are delivered. The ultimate goal is to promote or encourage some desirable behavior.

Table 4.2 Schedules of Reinforcement

Type of Schedule	Description	Characteristic	Overall Category
1) Fixed Ratio	Stable Reinforcement	Reinforcement based on Number	Intermittent
2) Variable Ratio	Changing Reinforcement		
3) Fixed Interval	Stable Reinforcement	Reinforcement based on Time	
4) Variable Interval	Changing Reinforcement		
Reinforce every instance of a desired behavior			Continuous

Using Schedules of Reinforcement to Modify Behavior

When deciding which schedule of reinforcement to use, it is important to realize that different schedules result in different behavior patterns. First, variable reinforcement, either ratio or interval, makes it difficult for students to predict when a reinforcer is going to follow a behavior. At times, it takes relatively few behaviors to get a reinforcer. At other times, numerous behaviors are required before a reinforcer is delivered. The pattern is unpredictable, leading students to engage in desirable behaviors at a fairly steady pace as they try to gain reinforcement. If a steady stream of behavior is desirable, then a variable schedule of reinforcement is the best choice (Parry-Cruwys et al., 2011).

Second, fixed schedules produce a very different behavioral pattern. Under a fixed schedule of reinforcement, students begin to appreciate the regularity of the reinforcement schedule. That is, students are able to predict when they are going to receive reinforcement. A fixed schedule of reinforcement leads to faster initial learning and to an unstable pattern of responses. On a fixed reinforcement schedule, students quickly become aware that they simply have to produce a certain number of responses (fixed ratio) or have to wait a fixed amount of time (fixed interval) before reinforcement is possible. Either schedule will eventually produce a pause after reinforcement. Once students desire another reinforcer in a Fixed Ratio Schedule, or sense that the wait period is about to end in a Fixed Interval Schedule, they will rapidly emit the necessary behavior until a reinforcer is delivered. Students then pause to enjoy the reinforcement, secure in the knowledge of what is needed to get another reinforcer. Teachers who wish to produce rapid student responses often use fixed ratio schedules of reinforcement. Fixed ratio schedules produce rapid learning, but can be problematic because it also results in rapid extinction (elimination of the behavior) when the reinforcers are removed. This problem can be alleviated by carefully changing schedules of reinforcement—starting with a fixed schedule and moving to a variable one.

Punishment

An unpleasant consequence for a behavior, which decreases the likelihood of the behavior recurring

Scheduling reinforcements is an important part of encouraging desirable behavior. Knowing what types of reinforcement schedules are available and how to implement them effectively gives teachers a valuable set of tools to help them establish an appropriate behavioral climate. Reinforcement, however, is not the only approach to managing behavior. The next section reviews an equally important type of consequential learning.

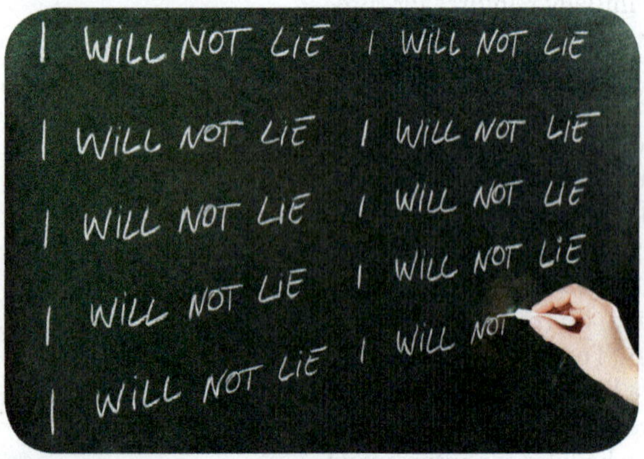

Punishment is an unpleasant consequence for bad behavior, which helps decrease the likelihood of the behavior being repeated.

Punishment

Skinner was interested in how to increase the frequency of a desired behavior *and* how to decrease undesirable behaviors. **Punishment** is an unpleasant consequence for a behavior, which decreases the likelihood of the behavior recurring. For example,

Mary realized that her students were having difficulty working together during a science lesson. After speaking with the class, it became clear the class had become sharply divided over a single comment someone supposedly made the week before. Mary discussed appropriate ways to resolve conflicts between students. She also underscored the importance of not letting such things stand in the way of their education. She set up a reinforcement schedule to address the problem, hoping to encourage cooperative work. After only marginal results, Mary decided to introduce a new consequence, in addition to modifying her reinforcement plan. She decided that any student failing to work in a civil and cooperative manner would have to write a lengthy report on the lesson that day. Mary felt the addition of this punishment was warranted because the student's learning was adversely affected by the disagreements. She also believed the situation had persisted long enough. She carefully chose the nature of her punishment, such that it might also serve as a learning tool. This example shows how educators can use punishment to help guide behavior. Skinner's research actually provided evidence for two types of punishment.

Presentation Punishment

Presentation punishment involves adding something negative to the environment in order to decrease the frequency of an undesirable behavior. For example, Ms. Schilpert has strict rules regarding aggression in her classroom. If any student is caught hitting another student, they are required to write a letter of apology to both the student and the class. All of the students are very uncomfortable about having to write such a letter. The introduction of the letter as a consequence to aggressive behavior is an example of presentation punishment. It adds something to the misbehaving child's environment that would otherwise not be there, and the student views it as an unpleasant consequence.

Presentation punishment
The addition of something negative to the environment in order to decrease the frequency of an undesirable behavior

Removal Punishment

Another type of unpleasant consequence involves the loss of something desirable. This type of punishment is called **removal punishment.** Removal punishment involves removing something from the environment in order to decrease the frequency of an undesirable behavior. This is a fairly common practice in educational settings and includes any removal of privileges as a consequence for unacceptable behavior. Some examples of removal punishment might include losing recess time or the freedom to sit anywhere in the classroom. Both types of punishment, presentation and removal, are summarized in Table 4.3 along with both types of reinforcement, positive and negative.

Removal punishment
The removal of something desirable

Table 4.3 Consequential Learning

Important Components	**Environment**—Adding or removing something from the individual's environment
	Consequence—viewed as positive or negative by the individual behaving
	Behavioral Change—Behavior is expected to increase or decrease in frequency in the future

Type of Consequence	Definition
Positive Reinforcement	You **add** something *positive* to the environment in order to ***increase*** the frequency of a desirable behavior
Negative Reinforcement	You **remove** something *negative* from the environment in order to ***increase*** the frequency of a desirable behavior
Presentation Punishment	You **add** something *negative* to the environment in order to ***decrease*** the frequency of an undesirable behavior
Removal Punishment	You **remove** something *positive* from the environment in order to ***decrease*** the frequency of an undesirable behavior

In The Classroom

APPLYING THEORY

Applying Consequences

Students frequently have difficulty identifying operant conditioning processes in complicated, real-life situations. Although the definitions of reinforcement and punishment may seem relatively clear, when one is faced with the actual complexity of real-life behavior, application of the terms is sometimes difficult. Students new to operant theory may find it helpful to follow step-by-step guidelines for identifying operant principles in action. Consider the following scenario:

CLASSROOM EXAMPLE

Mr. Martin is the teacher of a seventh grade math class. While teaching a new concept one day, he notices the students becoming restless and talking among themselves. Unhappy with this behavior, Mr. Martin says to the students that he interprets their restlessness and talkativeness as indication that they already understand the lesson and are becoming bored. He says that since they are bored, they will just move ahead to the test on the material. He moves toward his desk to retrieve the test, and sounds of protest are heard from the students. They begin to complain about the test, claiming that they will fail because they don't know what they are doing. They beg Mr. Martin to reconsider and promise to be more attentive. Mr. Martin looks at them thoughtfully and then agrees to let them out of the exam, smiling to himself at his clever behavior management style. While the students are indeed more attentive during the rest of the math lesson, they exhibit similar inattentive behavior the next day. Mr. Martin again threatens a test, and the previous day's situation is repeated. Later in the week, Mr. Martin makes an appointment with his principal to discuss the behavior of his students. Even after his careful behavior management, his students have become progressively whiny and belligerent, complaining loudly and showing an inappropriate level of distress every time he asks them to do anything.

THEORY APPLICATION

The first step is to identify the behavior of interest. While there are many behaviors depicted in the above scenario, the student's misbehavior is the one of interest. In the passage above, underline the behavior and place a "B" over the relevant words. Next, underline the consequence, which follows the behavior, and place a "C" over the words. The following excerpts illustrate this process.

B
"... complain about the test ..."
C
"... let them out of the exam ..."

Now, the next step is to examine the phrase marked "C" and ask the following questions:

1. **Was the consequence added to the environment or removed from the environment?**

2. **Was the consequence viewed as favorable or unfavorable by the person behaving in "B"?**

The answer to the first question is that something was *removed* from the environment—in this case, the test. Mr. Martin had previously introduced the exam and was now removing the exam from their day. The answer to the second question is that the consequence was viewed as pleasant. The scenario clearly indicates that the student's viewed the test as aversive. Thus canceling the test was a pleasant consequence. Be careful to answer this second question from the perspective of the person behaving in "B" and not others mentioned in the passage.

(continues)

The final step is to look at the behavior in "B" and ask the question, "Do you expect the frequency of the behavior to increase or decrease in the future?" The answer to this question will depend on whether the consequence was perceived as favorable or unfavorable. Since the students did not want to take the test, its removal was a favorable event. This would lead us to expect the behavior resulting in this favorable event to increase in the future. You now have enough information to determine what type of consequence is represented in the passage. We have a consequence involving the removing of something negative resulting in an increase in the frequency of the behavior, which is the definition of *negative reinforcement* (see Table 4.3).

Teachers should be reflective about how their actions serve as consequences for student actions. How teachers behave potentially shapes the expression of student behavior. Developing a thoughtful, engaged interaction style helps teachers recognize how their actions influence student behavior. This, combined with a thorough understanding of behavioral principles, puts teachers in a more informed position.

Mr. Martin inadvertently reinforced the complaining behavior of his students when he said he would not require them to take the test. He proceeded to engage in this threaten-then-give-in pattern frequently, which explains the progressive increase in his students' complaining behavior. This behavior management pattern is actually quite common and usually results in the behavioral problems experienced by Mr. Martin.

Shaping and Extinction

Now that you are familiar with the basic processes involved with learning by consequences, let's take a look at other aspects of this approach to learning. The basic consequences reviewed in the previous section are only the beginning of the whole story of learning by consequences. Everyday learning is grounded in these basic processes, but a more complete understanding necessitates an appreciation of how the basic operant processes interact with other facets of everyday life. In this section, we will take a closer look at the processes of shaping and extinction to illustrate this point.

Teachers often find themselves in the position of wanting to encourage a particular type of behavior. This is difficult, however, if the student never engages in the desired behavior. To encourage the development of a desired behavior that a student never produces, the teacher can use a modified reinforcement approach called shaping. **Shaping** is the reinforcement of progressively closer approximations of a desired response. Using shaping, a teacher would need to catch the student engaging in behaviors resembling the desired response and begin reinforcing those behaviors. If you want a restless student to sit with a learning group, for example, but he never voluntarily sits down, shaping can help. The student will produce a range of behaviors during the learning group, some of which are more related to sitting still than other behaviors. He may not ever sit down and quietly work with his group, yet if his behavior is examined closely, he does engage in some behaviors that are closer to sitting than others. For example, let's observe the behavior of Matt who will not sit in his chair during group work. Observation indicates that the closest he comes to his group is two feet away, a distance from which he impulsively makes comments to the group. At other times, he is on the other side of the room, about fifteen feet away, and unable to participate at all. From this range of behaviors (two feet to fifteen feet away from the group), his teacher would select the behavior that is most similar to the desired behavior. In this case, his teacher would reinforce his being two feet away from the group. The type of reinforcer would depend on the child, but often simple verbal praise is all that is needed. This will increase the frequency of his being two feet away. In an attempt to be two feet away and achieve reinforcement, Matt will alter his behavioral range, introducing some new behaviors. These new behaviors include moving from about four feet away to standing with the group. The teacher then reinforces a different behavior from this new range that is even more similar to the desired response. As the criteria needed for reinforcement change and closer and closer approximations of actual sitting behavior are reinforced, the range of behaviors Matt produces will eventually include sitting. At this point, his teacher simply reinforces him each time he sits

Shaping

The reinforcement of progressively closer approximations of a desired response

with the group. As you can see, shaping involves the application of operant learning principles in a complicated natural environment.

Extinction (operant conditioning)
The process of no longer reinforcing a given behavior

Another real-life issue involves the modification of behaviors already in existence. **Extinction** is the process of no longer reinforcing a given behavior. This is particularly relevant when the instructor wishes to completely remove the expression of a given behavior, such as issues surrounding student safety. Mr. Scerba is an eleventh grade chemistry teacher and is having trouble with a student following directions. The student frequently begins using laboratory chemicals before he completely explains the assignment. Once, this caused an unexpected chemical reaction, starting a small fire on the student's lab table. Mr. Scerba temporarily suspended the student's laboratory privileges, but he wanted to find another solution. This is an excellent situation in which to apply an extinction paradigm. According to the definition of extinction, Mr. Scerba simply needs to identify the specific reinforcer supporting the student's premature task initiation and then remove the reinforcer. In order to determine the reinforcer, Mr. Scerba reinstates the student's laboratory privileges under strict observation by a teacher's aide. During the observation, the aide notices the student looking about nervously and appearing to repeatedly scan the work area as the instructions were given. A subsequent interview with the student reveals that he experiences severe anxiety regarding the possibility that he will not be able to finish the lab within the forty-five minute time limit. He further indicates that he feels he is not as smart as the other students and needs to begin before they do, just to keep up. The additional time the student allocated himself by starting early had been reinforcing, in that it had allowed him to finish on time more often than not. Mr. Scerba decided to remove this self-administered reinforcer by allowing the class two periods to complete the lab assignments. Under these new circumstances, the student never started the lab assignment early and appeared to pay more attention during the lab introduction by Mr. Scerba. His increased understanding of the assignment allowed him to handle the laboratory chemicals appropriately. The removal of the reinforcing situation—starting early so that he could finish on time—reduced his unsafe lab behavior to zero. Thus his undesired behavior, starting early, was eliminated without the use of punishment, as Mr. Scerba had hoped.

F.A.Q.

Michael Richmond—"This is the second time in this chapter we have discussed extinction—exactly what are the two types?

Professor Maxwell—"The first time we encountered extinction was during our discussion of classical conditioning. To extinguish a classically conditioned response you repeatedly present the conditioned stimulus without the unconditioned stimulus. Our current discussion concerns extinction of an operant conditioned response. To extinct an operant conditioned response, you remove the reinforcement supporting the behavior."

Extinction is a simple process based on a fundamental principle of operant conditioning: people will not engage in behaviors without reinforcement. When the reinforcement that maintains a behavior is removed, the behavior will eventually extinguish. "Eventually" is an important word here because research shows that use of extinction may initially cause the undesired behavior to increase, rather than decrease. Any increase in behavior following the removal of a reinforcer is temporary. Without reinforcement, the behavior will ultimately cease. Consider the case of Amy, who has just started school. Amy's mother indicates on the first day of school that Amy has a tantrum problem, sometimes lying on the floor and crying for two or three minutes at a time. Amy's teacher knows enough about operant conditioning to know that at home the tantrums likely result in both positive and negative reinforcement for Amy. She is determined to provide no reinforcement at all for tantrum behavior, starting an extinction plan from day one in the classroom. When Amy starts to scream loudly as task demands increase, her teacher continues to work with the other students, telling Amy that when she is ready to participate, she should come right over and join them. Amy proceeds to fall to the floor, kicking her feet and crying. Her teacher continues to work with the other students, ignoring Amy's behavior as best she can. When her behavior does not provide the consequences that it always has in the past, Amy screams and kicks louder than she ever has before. The tantrum continues for a total of eight minutes, far longer than any previous episode. This initial increase in the undesired behavior is characteristic of the initial stages of an extinction plan. After her eight-minute tantrum, Amy settles down, looking curiously at the activity in which her teacher and the other students are engaging. Soon, she stands up, brushes herself off, and joins the group. Amy has several

F.A.Q.

Regina Griswald—"It seems like shaping takes an enormous amount of time and effort. Is it really that difficult?"

Professor Maxwell—"Shaping does indeed take significant time and planning. Remember, only use shaping when the student fails to produce the desired behavior. If they already engage in the desired behavior, even infrequently, use reinforcement to encourage the behavior."

more tantrums in the classroom during the first week of school, but they are progressively much more quiet and of shorter duration. By the second week, the tantrums are successfully extinguished in the classroom, although Amy continues to engage in tantrum behavior frequently at home. This indicates that Amy is able to discriminate between the two different contexts of home and school, tailoring her behavior according to the different reinforcement contingencies present in each environment.

When reinforcement that maintains tantrum behavior is removed, the behavior will eventually extinguish.

Cueing and Prompting

Learning by consequences emphasizes events occurring after a behavior of interest; however, for maximal learning, it is often productive to consider events occurring *before* the behavior (Mackiewicz, Wood, Cooke, & Mazzotti, 2011). **Cueing** is a manipulation of the environment before the behavior of interest. It typically involves changing some part of the classroom environment, such as flashing the overhead lights or ringing a bell. The purpose of providing a cue is to let the students know that you are expecting them to start engaging in a specific behavior, like settling down in their seats to begin a lesson. Another way you can help students know that you want them to behave a certain way is to provide a verbal command, reminding them what the "cue" means. **Prompting** is providing a verbal reminder that a specific behavior is expected. A teacher may say, "I just rang the bell, it is time for you to return to your seats." It is typical to introduce both a cue and a prompt. Later, a teacher may wish to remove the prompt, using only the cue as the signal for the desired behavior. Consider Kara who is having trouble settling down after morning free time. The teacher has scheduled social studies during this time, and Kara has difficulty finding her seat and getting her work out without explicit instructions from the teacher. The teacher has decided to change the classroom environment just prior to the time when the students are expected to get ready for social studies. First, she takes out a xylophone and puts it on her desk. At the end of free time, she plays the song frequently heard at the beginning of a horse race. She also provides a verbal prompt as an additional measure to help Kara learn to manage her behavior. An appropriate prompt might be, "Free time has ended, please follow the classroom procedures for the next activity." In this case, the behavior of interest is getting ready for class and the cue was the song on the xylophone. The purpose of cueing and prompting is to give the child a unique stimulus (antecedent) to increase the probability of appropriate behavior. The teacher is likely to continue to administer both the cue and the prompt until the Kara reliably gets ready for social studies. At that time, she should first remove the verbal prompt and just play the song on the xylophone (Alberto & Troutman, 2006). Kara's behavior may initially become unstable; but with consistent cueing and appropriate consequence, she should again develop a stable and productive pattern of behavior. Over time, the teacher will likely be able to remove the cue and have Kara behave appropriately using only the natural classroom environment to facilitate her behavior.

Cueing

A manipulation of the environment before the behavior of interest

Prompting

Providing a verbal reminder that a specific behavior is expected

Applied Behavior Analysis

The behavioral principles reviewed in this section have enjoyed great success in research, educational, and parenting circles. Terms once confined to the research laboratory are now commonly used in the classroom and at home. Before you began reading this section, you probably could have described an example of someone being punished. Similarly, you probably could have described how to reinforce someone for doing well on a test. You are now, however, more knowledgeable about how to provide reinforcement to achieve a particular pattern of behavior. These are all examples of applying behavioral principles. Application of behavioral principles in this way is somewhat informal, but leads us to a discussion of more formal approaches to applying behaviorism.

Applied behavior analysis (ABA) is a professional field that has emerged to address the need for more formal and accountable application of behavioral principles (Alberto & Troutman, 2006). ABA practitioners follow the basic behavioral perspective outlined in this chapter.

Applied behavior analysis (ABA)

A professional field which has emerged to address the need for more formal and accountable application of behavioral principles

That is, they view behavior as occurring in a specific context, with relevant events occurring before and after a behavior of interest. Behavior analysts typically follow a basic procedure for isolating and modifying a behavior of interest:

1. Record baseline information.

2. Identify a target behavior.

3. Implement treatment.

4. Record and review outcome.

Baseline

Record of a behavior of interest prior to any intervention

Treatment

Modifications to the environment in order to produce behavioral change

This approach begins with recording **baseline information**. This means all relevant information surrounding the behavior of interest is recorded prior to any intervention. Typically, the behavior analyst records events occurring before and after the behavior of interest. This makes it possible for them to determine which antecedents and consequences are contributing to the problem behavior. Once an adequate baseline is recorded, the behaviorist targets a specific behavior for change and develops a working plan or **treatment** for how to modify the behavior. Next, the treatment is implemented. Implementation of the treatment is accomplished through a specific set of steps complete with requirements for recording results. Recording results is an integral and important part of the ABA approach. Proper record keeping allows the behavior analyst to assess the effectiveness of her treatment approach. It also allows for greater accountability, an important topic in today's political climate. The accountability issue will be covered in detail in Chapter 9.

Issues surrounding educational accountability are covered in Chapter 9.

Performance based

Idea that a treatment professional is concerned with actual behavior and the situational events impacting its expression

The fundamental approach taken by the behavior analyst described above is supported by several key factors implicit in behavioral work. Sulzer-Azaroff and Mayer (1977) outline four important attributes of ABA. First, the work of the behavior analyst is **performance based**. This means that the behavior analyst is concerned with actual behavior and the situational events impacting its expression. ABA is not concerned with vague or theoretical concepts like "Michael is lazy," or "Sierra is impulsive." Concepts like "lazy" or "impulsive" are too ill defined to be useful to the behavior analyst. What might be lazy to one instructor might be called daydreaming by another. This is why ABA is concerned with the student's actual performance or overt behaviors. For example, Michael failed to complete assignments one, five and seven on February 13 *not* Michael was lazy on these days.

Second, ABA is grounded in the principles of behaviorism. Behavioral principles provide the working tools behavior analysts use to conduct their work. Behavioral principles are effectively applied to a wide range of settings and conditions (Kazdin, 2001; Soorya, Carpenter, & Romanczyk, 2011). Reinforcement and punishment have both been used effectively regardless of gender, age or culture (Wielkiewicz, 1995; Maag, 2001).

Third, ABA is considered "analytic" because it analyzes a given situation and demonstrates how a given behavior is related to events in the environment. Rather than guess about the relation between different behaviors, behavior analysts actually demonstrate the presence of a relation by using the four-step process outlined previously. By systematically applying a well-developed treatment and charting behavioral change, the behavior analyst is able to demonstrate a particular behavioral relation.

Fourth, ABA is an applied field. It is an applied extension of decades of controlled research. It certainly continues to change and evolve from continued research in the area, but it is primarily concerned with the application of behavioral principles in real situations (Bloh & Axelrod, 2008). This, of course, carries with it all the challenges and ethical considerations encountered whenever researched based theories are applied. Behavior analysts are well trained in behavioral principles, but also in ethics, constantly questioning whether their interventions are appropriate.

In conclusion, ABA is a relatively new field, making use of well-established principles of learning. Historically, ABA has been prominent in the treatment of individuals with disabilities, but it is now more widely used. Despite this increase in use and application, the use of behavioral principles has met with criticism. The next section reviews some of the more common criticisms.

Limitations of Operant Conditioning

As the proceeding section demonstrates, operant conditioning helps educators create productive learning environments. Some researchers and educators, however, believe using behavioral principles to manage behavior results in significant problems. Criticisms of behavioral theory take many forms, but are generally about the following issues:

- *Focusing on external control of behavior*
- *Decreasing a student's self-motivated learning*
- *Ignoring the impact of a student's thinking on behavior*
- *Emphasizing good conduct over academic learning*

As any first-year teacher quickly learns, there are far too many students in a typical class to develop a behavior management plan for each one. We rely on most students appropriately managing their own behavior. The question is, do behavior management techniques move a student toward more self-managed behavior? Do students develop a greater need for external control of behavior? The issue here is the ultimate goal of education. Do we want to develop students who rely heavily on external controls to behave appropriately, or do we want to move our students toward self-management of behavior? Most would agree we want to encourage students to manage their own behavior, including their academic behaviors like studying. There are occasions when manipulation of the environment by the teacher is needed to help a particular student in a particular situation, but education is moving toward limiting this type of external control. We are likely to see this trend increase in the future, as teachers are required to implement more individual lesson experiences to our increasingly diverse population.

Learning because it is an enjoyable activity (as opposed to learning for a reward) is something most teachers would like to see in their students. Does external reinforcement, however, decrease one's desire to learn? There has been some debate about this issue. Some studies have shown that although reinforcers can increase the frequency of a behavior, the behavior often drops below pre-reinforcement levels once reinforcement is stopped (Lepper & Hodell, 1989). Other researchers have found reinforcement has little effect on one's natural desire to learn (Cameron & Pierce, 1994, 1996). What does this mean? Researchers have speculated that students learn to behave for the reinforcer under a behavior management protocol. Once the reinforcer is removed, the behavior drops dramatically. This is particularly important because the drop in behavior is to levels lower than existed before the reinforcer was introduced. This means the students used to engage in the behavior for the sake of the behavior itself, but then learned that without being reinforced, they were no longer willing to perform the behavior. The extent to which such findings can be generalized to typical classroom behaviors is not clear; however, teachers are encouraged to be mindful of the potential for this effect.

A third concern regarding the use of behavioral principles is that the approach ignores the potential for a student's thinking to impact their behavior. Consider your own behavior for a moment. Why are you reading this text? Are you being rewarded for your reading behavior? Is someone taking you out to dinner if you finish reading this chapter? What about your thoughts and feelings? Are you reading because you want to learn, you enjoy the material, or you are scared about getting behind in class? Some have criticized behavioral theory because it ignores such internal factors as thinking and emotions. This is particularly striking given education's apparent goal to develop the way to think. Thinking and reasoning will be explored in more detail in the next chapter.

A final point to consider is the tendency for behavioral techniques to emphasize good behavior, rather than learning. Although some behavior programs are designed to achieve an academic goal, often they are designed to modify a specific overt behavior, like aggression. As this chapter demonstrated, behaviorists focus on behaviors we can see rather than internal events, like thinking. It is true that educating in a behaviorally disruptive classroom is not productive; however, do we want to focus education on behaving well? Obviously, we need good behavior *and* good learning to create productive educational environments. The point here is that teachers need to be aware of the possibility of focusing too heavily on overt behavior when using behavior management techniques.

SUMMARIZE AND REFLECT

1. E. L. Thorndike developed the **law of effect**, a principle which holds that behaviors resulting in satisfying results are more likely to reoccur in the future.
2. B. F. Skinner expanded Thorndike's ideas clarifying the effects of both favorable and unfavorable consequences on future behavior.
3. Skinner called learning by consequences **operant conditioning**. Investigation of operant conditioning led to four different types of consequences.
4. These consequences include reinforcement, which increases the likelihood of a behavior, and punishment, which decreases the likelihood of a behavior. These consequences can be further differentiated between positive and negative reinforcement and presentation and removal punishment.
5. There are different schedules for reinforcement delivery, including fixed/intermittent and ratio/interval schedules. Behavioral effects vary depending on which combination of these reinforcement schedules are used.
6. Like classical conditioning, operant conditioning includes the concepts of generalization and extinction. It is also important to be able to recognize the impact of antecedent events in operant learning.
7. **Applied behavior analysis** is an applied field that is based on the principles of behavioral learning theory.

INFORMED APPLICATION

1. Operant learning principles are often discussed in terms of their ability to modify observable behavior. How can the same principles be used to help a student increase their reading comprehension?
2. You want to encourage students to study in a more consistent manner, rather than waiting until the last minute. What kind of reinforcer could you use, and what kind of schedule for delivery would help you achieve your goals?

SOCIAL THEORIES: LEARNING BY OBSERVATION

Social interactions play an important role in most of our everyday lives. This section explores whether these social interactions influence learning. As you will see, theorists have proposed that learning by observation of others contributes significantly to the way we behave.

Bandura—Modeling and Observational Learning

Social theories of learning were developed to explain how our social interactions change learning. For example, social learning theorists study how observation of others impacts our behavior. They also investigate how we use other people as models for appropriate behavior. One of the most prominent of these social learning theorists, Albert Bandura, was particularly interested in the phenomenon of observational learning, which he believed played a central role in human behavior. Observational learning is simply learning by observing others. For example, if you see the teacher tell a friend to stop passing notes in class, you might stop writing notes yourself. Your behavior was changed by observing another student. Bandura developed a program of research designed to outline the principles of learning through observation. In fact, one of his experiments has become one of the best-known research studies in psychology. In this experiment, children observed someone else (a model) showing either aggressive or non-aggressive behavior toward an inflated doll which bounces back when knocked down—the well-

Albert Bandura's "Bobo doll" experiment.

known Bobo doll. Later, the children were allowed to play with the doll. Those exposed to the aggressive model behaved aggressively toward the doll. Those exposed to the non-aggressive model failed to demonstrate an equal level of aggressiveness (Bandura, Ross, & Ross, 1961). This research suggested people learn not only through direct reinforcement and punishment but also by observing others behave. The idea that observational learning does not require direct action or behavior on the part of the learner was a break from prominent behavioral theories at the time. In effect, Bandura differentiated between acquisition of a behavior (learning) and performance (behaving) for the first time. This contradicted the behaviorist notion that learning is understood only through observable events and behaviors. His new conceptualization of learning required exploration of cognitions or thinking (Bandura, 1963) and led to a new area of social theory.

Social Cognitive Theory

Bandura began to redefine behaviorally oriented theories, calling his new approach social cognitive theory (Bandura, 1985). He used this title because of his emphasis on cognitions, or how we think and reason. Many research studies have supported and helped to expand **social cognitive theory**, and a number of basic principles have emerged.

Social cognitive theory

Theory emphasizing how social process and thinking impact behavior

One of the basic principles of social cognitive theory is learning can occur when we observe another's behavior being reinforced or punished. Learning can also occur in the absence of any apparent reinforcement of a model's behavior. If we observe someone's behavior being reinforced, for example, we are more likely to engage in that behavior ourselves, either immediately or in the future. The behavior might be exactly the same or slightly altered. Eight-year-old CJ, for example, watches Erin as she presents an oral report. Erin uses a cardboard box as a pretend television set, while she acts like an imaginary newscaster. Their teacher, Mr. Hines, is very impressed with Erin's presentation and openly praises her creativity and originality. The class claps loudly as Erin sits down. CJ, who is scheduled to give his presentation the following day, had been planning to read from note cards. He goes home that afternoon and tells his mother he needs something different and creative, and they look up presentation techniques together on the Internet. The next day CJ's presentation includes a charades component and several physical props. He, too, sits down to praise and applause. Clearly, CJ observed Erin's behavior and changed his own accordingly. In this case, he observed Erin being positively reinforced for her creativity and originality, and tried to capture these qualities in his presentation. This type of learning is easily understood as a form of **vicarious learning**, with the learner being vicariously influenced by the consequences another person received. When you increase a behavior from watching someone else receive reinforcement, we call this a **vicarious reinforcement**. Similarly, when you decrease a behavior because you saw someone receive punishment, we call it **vicarious punishment**.

Interconnections

Cognitive theories and their application to education are covered in Chapter 5.

Vicarious learning

Learning that is vicariously influenced by the consequences another person receives

Vicarious reinforcement

Increasing a behavior in one participant by watching another receive reinforcement

Vicarious punishment

Decreasing a behavior in one participant by seeing another receive punishment

Bandura believed learning from models involved four key processes (Bandura, 1986):

- *Attention*
- *Retention*
- *Reproduction*
- *Motivation*

The role of attention is quite simple. In order for learning to occur, we have to first notice or *attend* to the behavior of a model. Behaviors and consequences, whether they pertain to ourselves or others, occur around us all the time. Most of these behaviors go unnoticed because we do not direct our attention toward them. We also have to *retain*, or remember, the behaviors we observe in others. Bandura holds that we remember modeled behaviors by mentally representing them. *Reproduction* of modeled behaviors occurs when we call the mentally represented behaviors into action, resulting in imitation of what we observed. Finally, *motivation* determines which behaviors will or will not be reproduced. We not only remember a modeled behavior, we also develop expectations regarding the consequences of that behavior.

This final point regarding expectations leads to another basic principle of social cognitive theory. This theory holds that we develop *expectations* about the reinforcement and punishment we might receive for certain behaviors. These expectations are based on our observations of what happens to others, in addition to our own experiences. CJ, for example, changed his report style after seeing Erin receive positive reinforcement for being creative and original. Did he simply reproduce a behavior he saw reinforced, or did he change his behavior because he *expected* to obtain similar reinforcement? Bandura (1986) proposed we learn from reinforcement and punishment when we understand there is a relation between the modeled behavior and the consequence. Thus, learning involves not just behavior and consequence but also a cognitive link between the two, resulting in an expectation regarding future consequences. These expectations impact the choices we make about our behavior. This differs significantly from the behavioral perspective described earlier in this chapter. The behaviorists saw behavioral predispositions as being driven by a person's history of reward and punishment, factors which are outside one's personal control. What this means is that social cognitive theory goes beyond the basic views of the behaviorists and considers internal thoughts as important factors in determining behavior. We will go into more detail about the importance of thinking in the next chapter, but let's look at one additional topic that has evolved out of the work of the social theorist, self-regulation.

Self-Regulation

Self-regulation

The potential capacity to direct one's own behavior

Social cognitive theories regarding the impact of thinking on behavior ushered in a renewed interest in how thinking influences the management of our own behavior. This potential capacity to direct our own behavior is called **self-regulation** (Bandura, 1977; Pressley, 1995; Winne, 1995) and has close ties to the observational research of the social theorists. Bandura proposed we observe and reflect on our own behavior. We are constantly evaluating our behavior based on personal standards. These standards derive from our interactions with the world, beginning in the early years of life through our interactions with care givers (Bernier, Carlson, & Whipple, 2010). As we grow and develop, these interactions become internally mediated as we engage in self-reinforcement and punishment, such as "I did a great job and feel proud of myself" or "I failed at this task and feel bad about it." Such internal performance feedback serves to motivate and support behavior, but can also produce negative emotions like anxiety, worry, thought suppression, and fear of negative evaluation. These negative emotions are counterproductive and serve to decrease our sense of self-regulation (Magno, 2010). It is important for students to remember to operate from a positive framework, directing behavior toward relevant goals. Some goals may relate to social activities; others may relate to academics. Achieving goals requires successful management of our behavior.

As we grow and develop we engage in self-reinforcement and punishment such as "I did a great job" or "I failed at this and I feel bad."

Self-management

Observational learning has also been shown to play a role in the development of goal states. For example, in one self-reward/modeling study, Bandura (1964) showed that children would evaluate their own behavior and manage their own consequences based on modeled behavior. In this study, children participated in a bowling activity where they could reward themselves with candy. Half the children were exposed to models whose self-rewards were based on a high performance standard, while the other half of the children were exposed to a low performance standard. Those children exposed to the high performance standard model rewarded themselves on a similar high standard criterion; whereas, those exposed to the low performance standard model set lower self-reward criteria for themselves. This shows that we often manage our own behavior by giving ourselves rewards we feel are appropriate. Our standards for what is appropriate are shaped by people we observe.

Cognitive Behavior Modification

Another approach to modifying our behavior is to use self-management of consequences presented above and add an additional component, a cognitive process. Researchers have found that self-management can be enhanced by altering our thinking about our behavior in addition to managing external factors (Greimel & Kroner-Herwig, 2011). For example, if you are trying to get a student to work on being more consistent with their studying, you might want to establish a self-delivered reward system. You can also look at what the student is thinking about when they attempt to study. What are their goals, expectations, and conceptualization of the task? Teachers might wish to implement the reward program, but adding in a procedure for addressing inappropriate expectations or misconceptions could help produce better results. For example, sometimes students have unrealistic expectations for how long they can reasonably concentrate on homework without a break. Depending on their age, the student who believes they can work productively for ninety minutes straight might be better off studying in thirty-minute sessions. Similarly, students often have an ineffective conceptualization of what studying is supposed to produce. They tend to focus on the upcoming test, rather than simply learning and appreciating the material. Sometimes, helping a student work toward mastery of the material, while minimizing fear of the test, can help the student think about the task in a more productive way.

Students need to set their goals and estimate how long they can spend on a certain assignment at a reasonable and attainable time.

SUMMARIZE AND REFLECT

1. Social cognitive theory builds on the basic principles of learning outlined by the behaviorists, adding the role of thinking into the learning equation.
2. Albert Bandura is one of the most prominent theorists in the field of social cognitive theory.
3. According to social cognitive theory, people learn by observation and direct experience. What a person learns may not be evident in the individual's actual behavior, indicating learning is represented cognitively.
4. The cognitions people have regarding the relation between behaviors and consequences drive expectations regarding the effects of future behavior.
5. Social cognitive theorists contend that we all think or reflect on the behavioral principles of reinforcement and punishment, implicitly deciding whether a behavior is likely to lead to a good or bad outcome and changing our actions accordingly.
6. The fact that we can choose whether or not to behave in certain ways involves reflection on potential behaviors and consequences. Through self-regulation, we set standards for ourselves and our behavior, work toward these goals, and reinforce or punish ourselves accordingly.
7. This view is a departure from traditional behavioral theory, which holds that we are directed externally by our environments.

INFORMED APPLICATION

1. In between periods, a student comes up to you and asks if he can turn in his research paper that is two days late. The assignment is clearly done and in his hands. What do you do? How will your decision affect the student's future performance? How will your decision affect the other students in the class?
2. Considering observation learning theory, what are some of the advantages of teaching in a group format versus individually? How might group size affect advantages of teaching in a group format?

THE CHAPTER IN REVIEW

Check out our website ▶ www.BVTLab.com for chapter-by-chapter flashcards, practice quizzes, summaries, and more.

In this chapter, we explored the behavioral perspective on learning, which began with Ivan Pavlov's discovery of classical conditioning. We traced the development of behavioral theory first through the work of John Watson, discussing in detail the basic processes in classical conditioning. We outlined the relative roles of the unconditioned stimulus, the unconditioned response, the conditioned stimulus, and the conditioned response in this form of learning. We also discussed generalization and discrimination in classical conditioning, focusing on the application of these processes in education. Next, we turned to the work of B. F. Skinner, who further developed the behavioral perspective of learning with his extensive research regarding the role of consequences in learning. We outlined a number of basic principles of learning discovered by Skinner, defining consequences which increase the likelihood of a behavior recurring (positive and negative reinforcement) and consequences which decrease the likelihood of a behavior recurring (presentation and removal punishment). We then explored Skinner's research on the timing and presentation of consequences, outlining the characteristic behavioral responses produced by different reinforcement schedules (intermittent/fixed, ratio/interval). Finally, we turned to the social theorists, most notably Albert Bandura, who eventually brought internal mental events in the form of cognitions, or thinking, back into the learning equation. We highlighted Bandura's proposal that we can learn from models, as well as how he used words such as expectations and self-reflection in combination with behavioral principles. We also discussed how Bandura's work suggests we have a choice regarding whether or not to behave in certain ways, in that we can think about, or reflect on, potential behaviors and consequences. In summary, while we may or may not purposely choose to use the principles of learning presented in this chapter in our teaching, having this knowledge allows us to examine the learning context from a unique perspective, potentially increasing our ability to create effective learning environments.

Interdisciplinary Case Focus

principal *special educator*
teacher *parents* *psychologist*
social worker *physical educator*
nurse *peers* *doctor*

It's Kathy Coolidge's first year teaching third grade, and it is the third week of school. She had been so excited about finally having her own class, and everything started out beautifully. While it took a week to establish her authority, most of the students responded well to her classroom structure and discipline. Brent, however, continues to disrupt the class all too frequently. In fact, his behavior is getting worse, despite her attempts to consistently let him know that his disruptions will not be tolerated. Initially, he made noises, spoke without raising his hand, and randomly bothered the other students. Kathy calmly explained the rules to him each time, outlining the consequences for continued disruption. Brent had to be separated from the other children a few times during the second week, when he was so obnoxious during small group work that the other children could not benefit from instruction. This week he has started disrupting the class almost every time Kathy tries to have them engage in a focused activity, such as reading group. It is only Tuesday, and Brent has been sent to the office three times. The thing that is so difficult to understand is that during unstructured times or independent seatwork, Brent is relatively quiet. He also seems to pay attention and participate appropriately during math time. Kathy doesn't want the principal to think that she can't control her class, so she doesn't want to continue to send Brent to the office. She is also concerned about his learning—he misses much of what she tries to teach. When she works with him one-on-one, he responds well, but he needs frequent repetition of directions and cueing regarding what to do next on a given assignment. Records from Brent's previous school indicate slightly below average academic skills. Recognizing that she needs more information than the sketchy records Brent's previous school provided, she sets up an afternoon meeting with his parents. She also seeks advice from another more experienced teacher at her school regarding her problems with Brent. Finally, she sends an e-mail to her classroom discipline teacher from college, asking for any insight she might have regarding the situation.

Parents Brent's parents are astounded that Brent is causing trouble in class. His mother says that she never once had even a note come home from school regarding his behavior. In fact, she says that during his second grade parent/teacher conferences, his teacher usually remarked how quiet he was in class. The only problem ever mentioned regarding Brent's behavior was that he would not speak in front of the rest of the class. His second grade teacher said she understood he was shy, so she had not pushed him; however, his lack of participation was a constant factor. Brent's parents were also astounded that his teacher saw him as shy. They said he is not shy at all at home or in other structured activities, such as sports; they see these school reports of shyness or behavior problems as totally out of character for him.

Jack Kline, fourth grade teacher Jack Kline is a fellow teacher and has years of experience teaching elementary school children. After listening to Kathy's situation, he tells her she should consider the possibility Brent might have some language based learning problems that are just beginning to show up. Jack said since Brent's behavior during math is not consistent with his behavior in other subjects, it could be a red flag that something might be going on related to reading or language. He said he has taught several children who have significant reading problems, but actually excel at math. He also said the fact that Brent only disrupts during group work, together with his previous teacher's reports of his difficulty speaking in front of others, suggests he is trying to avoid an interactive type of learning environment. This could be because he is embarrassed about not really knowing what's going on or not being able meet task demands. Jack suggests Kathy conduct an informal assessment regarding Brent's language skills and reading comprehension and consider referring him for testing if the results indicate significant weaknesses.

Professor Paul Hopkins, Classroom Discipline Instructor, South State University Professor Hopkins' e-mail reply to Kathy's explanation of her situation was as follows:

> Hi Kathy,
>
> I can probably sum this situation up for you in two words: avoidance learning. Remember negative reinforcement involves having something that you don't like removed from the environment as a function of a behavior. It sounds like when Brent misbehaves, the consequence is that he gets out of an unpleasant situation. In other words, removal from the group may not be a punishment for Brent but rather negative reinforcement. Now, I can't tell you why working in a group would be unpleasant for this child, but I can speak with some certainty as to the power of avoidance learning. Let me know if I can be of further assistance—I am confident that you will be successful in figuring this out.
>
> Good luck,
>
> Dr. Hopkins

Wrapping It Up

Kathy reflected on Brent's behavior in new ways after her interactions with his parents, Mr. Kline, and Dr. Hopkins. The e-mail from Dr. Hopkins was quite enlightening. She remembered avoidance learning, and she knew all about reinforcement and punishment. She had not, however, been looking at Brent's behavior from a behavioral learning principles perspective. As soon as she read the e-mail, she thought, "Of course!" She immediately stopped using removal from the group as a consequence. She sat down with Brent and talked with him about his behavior in group activities. She told him she really wanted him in the group and was going to stop removing him from the group or sending him to the office when he became disruptive. She then started an extinction based strategy, whereby she gave no response when he made disruptive noises. Initially, Brent got even louder, but he quickly began to show decreases in his disruptive behavior. Kathy also made sure she only directed simply stated questions toward Brent during group work, in case Mr. Kline was right about his language functioning. She did conduct an informal assessment of Brent's language and reading skills and found he had significant difficulty following multi-step directions, making sense of complex sentences, and comprehending what he read. His decoding skills were pretty good, so she thought that his reading problems might be related to a larger language processing problem. She referred him for testing, and her assessment of his problems were right on target. He had significant receptive language problems, which the speech language pathologist said were most significant under conditions of complex language interchange, such as group work. Brent began receiving speech/language therapy twice a week, and Kathy consulted with his therapist regarding ways of accommodating his problems in the classroom. She began providing him with bulleted, step-by-step instructions when directions were complex. Kathy's classroom quickly became exactly what she had been hoping for as a first year teacher—an exciting and supportive community for learning.

Key Terms

TERM	*Page*
Acquisition	117
Antecedent	112
Applied behavior analysis (ABA)	127
Baseline	128
Classical conditioning	113
Conditioned response (CR)	115
Conditioned stimulus (CS)	115
Consequence	112
Contiguity	113
Continuous reinforcement	120
Cueing	127
Discrimination	116
Extinction (classical conditioning)	117
Extinction (operant conditioning)	126
Fixed schedule of reinforcement	121
Generalization	115
Intermittent schedule of reinforcement	120
Interval schedule of reinforcement	121
Law of effect	118
Learning	110
Negative reinforcement	120
Neutral stimulus (NS)	115
Operant conditioning	119
Performance based	128
Positive reinforcement	120
Presentation punishment	123
Prompting	127
Punishment	122
Ratio schedule of reinforcement	121
Reinforcer	119
Removal punishment	123
Schedule of reinforcement	120
Self-regulation	132
Shaping	125
Skinner Box	119
Social cognitive theory	131
Stimulus	112
Treatment	128
Unconditioned responses (UCR)	114
Unconditioned stimulus (UCS)	114
Variable schedule of reinforcement	121
Vicarious learning	131
Vicarious punishment	131
Vicarious reinforcement	131

5 Chapter

COGNITIVE LEARNING THEORIES

What's It All About ...

What is cognitive psychology?

How do we process and store memories?

How do we build an efficient and accessible knowledge database?

How does reflection on our own thinking impact learning?

Chapter Objectives

- Understand the cognitive perspective.
- Describe memory as a foundation for knowledge.

- Review the information processing model of memory.
- Describe characteristics of sensory memory.
- Describe characteristics of working memory.
- Describe characteristics of long-term memory.

- Describe the organization of knowledge and memory.
- List and explain multiple types of memory.
- Describe how to effectively build knowledge.

- Describe metacognitive knowledge.
- Describe metacognitive regulation.
- Describe metacognitive instruction.

EXTENDED OUTLINE

Cognitive Learning Theory

I. What's It All About ...
II. From Today's Headlines
III. Cognition: A Focus on What We Think
  A. Cognitive perspective
  B. Memory as a foundation for knowledge
  C. Summarize and reflect
IV. The Information Processing Model of Memory
  A. Sensory memory
    1. Attention
    2. Perception
  B. Working memory
    1. Capacity and duration
    2. Chunking and rehearsal
    3. Components of working memory
    4. Phonological loop
    5. Visuospatial sketchpad
    6. Central executive
    7. Forgetting
  C. Long-term memory
    1. Capacity and duration
    2. Elaboration, organization, and context
    3. Forgetting
    4. Proactive and retroactive interference
    5. Retrieval cues
  D. Summarize and reflect
V. The Organization of Knowledge and Memory
  A. Multiple types of knowledge
    1. Declarative knowledge
    2. Procedural knowledge
    3. Conditional knowledge
  B. Building knowledge and improving memory
    1. Mnemonics
    2. Automating knowledge
    3. When and where to apply knowledge
  C. Summarize and reflect
VI. Metacognition
  A. Metacognitive knowledge
  B. Metacognitive regulation
  C. Metacognitive instruction
  D. Summarize and reflect
VII. The Chapter in Review
VIII. Interdisciplinary Case Focus

From Today's Headlines

Vol. I No. 5 Teaching World, 2012

AMAZING MEMORY

What would you do if you needed someone's phone number? Chances are you would look it up in the phone book or maybe on the Internet. If you lived in Raipur, India, however, you would have another option. Just ask Rampal Thukral. Mr. Thukral has managed to memorize an astonishing twenty-seven thousand telephone numbers. This is even more remarkable in that ten years ago at the age of forty-six, he was only able to remember six-thousand numbers. This means he was able to memorize twenty-one thousand phone numbers during his late forties and early fifties—not bad given the conventional wisdom that memory becomes more difficult with age.

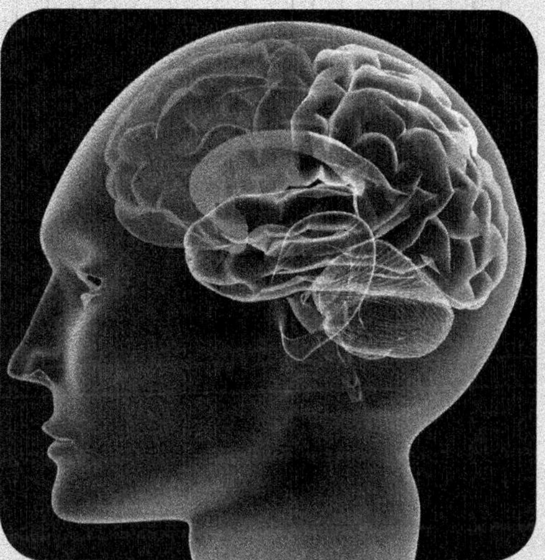

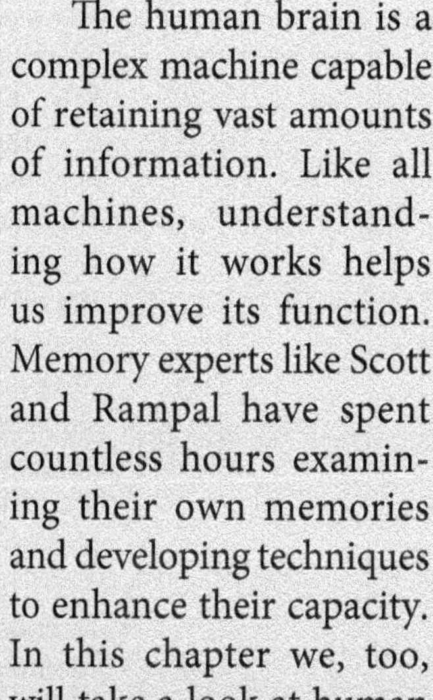

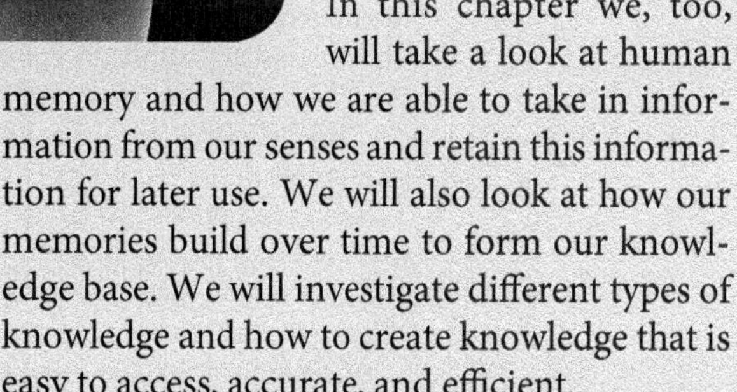

Another incredible memorizer is Scott Hagwood, a former engineer from Fayetteville, North Carolina. Scott has been the winner of the U.S. Memory Championship. To win this competition, he had to memorize lengthy unpublished and non-rhyming poems, memorize a list of four hundred random words in order, and memorize hundreds of ones and zeros in random order.

Scott does not believe he was born with an amazing memory. He says he purposefully developed his memory using memory improvement techniques. In fact, he now gives seminars on how anyone can become a super memorizer.

MAKE THE CONNECTION

Rampal Thukral and Scott Hagwood are remarkable examples of our amazing memory capabilities. This chapter will look at some of the fundamental aspects of human thinking that make such feats possible.

The human brain is a complex machine capable of retaining vast amounts of information. Like all machines, understanding how it works helps us improve its function. Memory experts like Scott and Rampal have spent countless hours examining their own memories and developing techniques to enhance their capacity. In this chapter we, too, will take a look at human memory and how we are able to take in information from our senses and retain this information for later use. We will also look at how our memories build over time to form our knowledge base. We will investigate different types of knowledge and how to create knowledge that is easy to access, accurate, and efficient.

Let's begin our exploration of these concepts with a general overview of the cognitive perspective and its focus on topics like memory and knowledge.

COGNITION—A FOCUS ON WHAT WE THINK

In the last chapter, we introduced the concept of learning, defining it as a lasting change in an individual resulting from experience. One of the most debated questions in learning theory, however, is a lasting change in *what*? The behavioral perspective of learning is focused on observable behavior. That is, what is changed during learning is our actual behavior—the things that we *do*. This chapter will continue our look at learning, focusing on cognitive views. Cognitive theorists differ from behaviorists in that they emphasize the way we *think*. For example, if we were to look at your performance on a test of this material, we could examine how certain rewards (good grades or positive comments from friends or instructor) work to alter your behavior (study time and techniques). This would be a typical behavioral approach. Distinguish this type of approach from one attempting to understand your test performance by looking at your thoughts. Perhaps you love the material or see it as vital information to your future success as a teacher. Perhaps you are in the class with a friend and you have a strong desire to perform better. Looking at these factors and their impact on your performance is typical of a cognitive approach to learning. Again, the focus is on what we *think*. In this chapter, we will examine this theoretical perspective in detail.

Interconnections

The behavioral perspective is covered in detail in Chapter 4.

Cognitive Perspective

Cognitive perspective

Theories and research related to an understanding of thinking and reasoning

The **cognitive perspective** includes theories and research related to an understanding of thinking and reasoning. This perspective includes research on a wide range of cognitive processes, or mental activities: memory, knowledge, problem solving, attention, comprehension, as well as many others. One of the best ways to develop an understanding of the cognitive perspective is to compare it to the behavioral perspective covered in the last chapter.

The primary difference between the cognitive and behavioral perspectives in terms of learning is in the interpretation of mental activities (thinking and reasoning). Both perspectives acknowledge that people have an elaborate mental life; however, where the perspectives differ is in the ability of these mental activities to alter our behavior. For example, Markus is an eleven-year-old boy interested in using meditation to improve his basketball skills. His physical education instructor had some tapes of professional basketball players demonstrating various shots that Markus studied diligently. After his review of the tapes, he began daily meditation where he visualized the professional athletes correctly making various shots. By the end of the week, he began working with his physical education teacher on perfecting his technique. The question here is whether meditation is able to improve his basketball performance. Can we improve our performance by thinking about the activity? Do we need actual instruction with a teacher providing appropriate feedback to improve?

The answer to these questions is quite complicated, but it emphasizes a fundamental difference between the cognitive and behavioral perspectives. Cognitive theorists believe that mental activities (such as Markus' meditation) play a direct role in the expression of behavior. This means that although environmental events are important in determining behavior, our *thoughts* can intervene and redirect behavior. Graphically, this idea is represented in Figure 5.1.

The belief that mental activities influence the expression of behavior makes vastly different interpretations of learning possible. Unlike the traditional behaviorist view of the individual as a passive respondent to environmental changes, cognitive theorists hold that people actively think about their environments and behavior. They engage in mental processes, like planning and goal setting, which have direct bearing on behavior. This leads to another important point of comparison between behavioral and cognitive perspectives.

Consequences (reinforcement and punishment) under the cognitive perspective do not exclusively determine behavior. Instead, they provide us with feedback about the possible results of our behavior. We are able to consider this feedback and use it to help us decide which type of behavior is best. Again, consequences themselves do not determine behavior according to the cognitive perspective.

When comparing the behavioral and cognitive perspectives, it is important to underscore that both behavioral and cognitive perspectives are theoretical. This means that each perspective

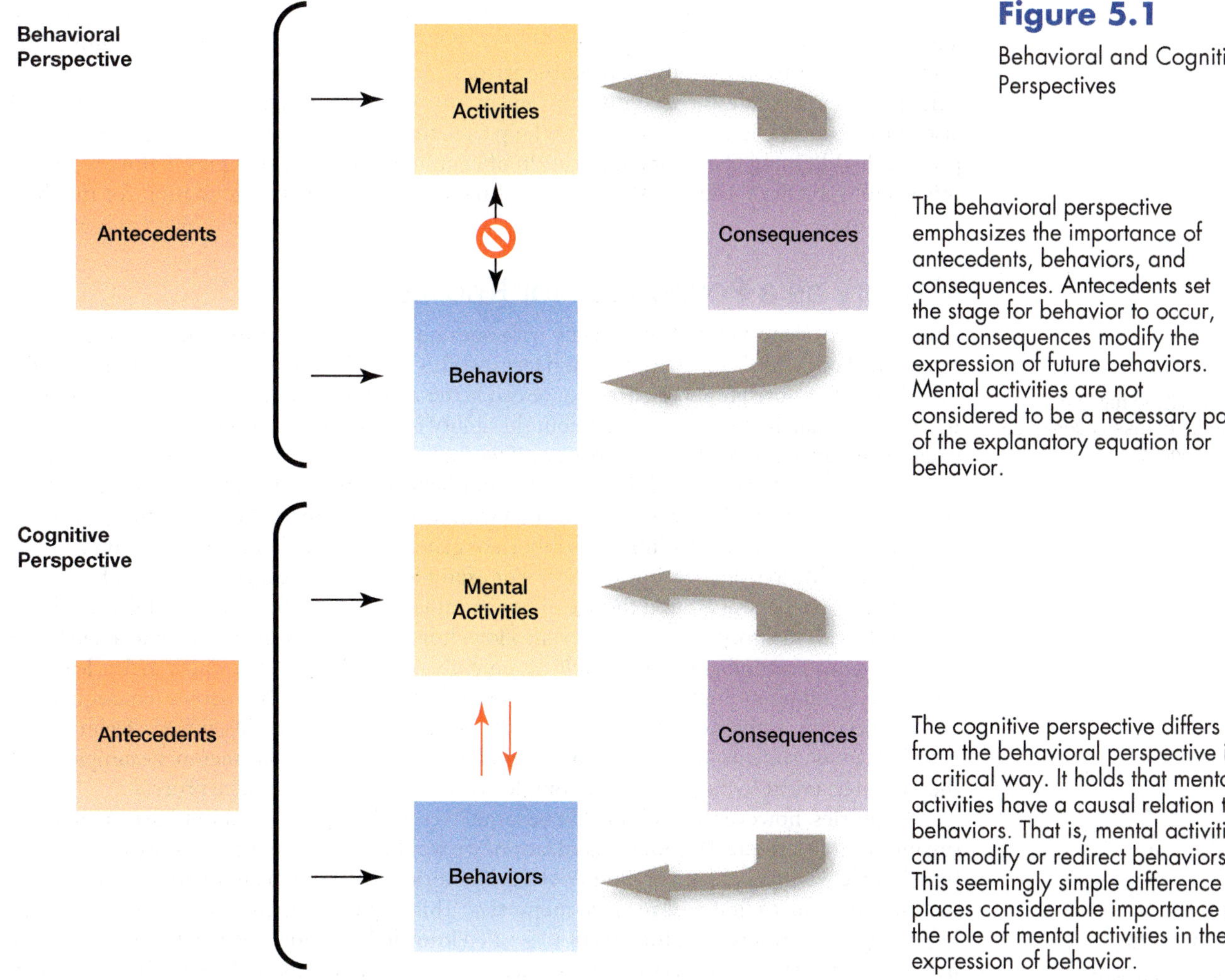

Figure 5.1

Behavioral and Cognitive Perspectives

The behavioral perspective emphasizes the importance of antecedents, behaviors, and consequences. Antecedents set the stage for behavior to occur, and consequences modify the expression of future behaviors. Mental activities are not considered to be a necessary part of the explanatory equation for behavior.

The cognitive perspective differs from the behavioral perspective in a critical way. It holds that mental activities have a causal relation to behaviors. That is, mental activities can modify or redirect behaviors. This seemingly simple difference places considerable importance on the role of mental activities in the expression of behavior.

is an attempt to explain human behavior. Sometimes students will ask, "Which theory is right?" Both theories have research support that demonstrates their usefulness in certain contexts. At this point, it is not so much whether one perspective is right or wrong but under what circumstances does a particular point of view become useful.

The cognitive perspective began to gain prominence during the latter half of the twentieth century. Feeling like the behaviorists failed to capture the complexity of the human experience, cognitive theorists began to study how thinking impacted behavior. The movement toward a cognitive perspective was also promoted by the advent of the computer. Being able to design machines capable of mirroring some of the complexity of human thinking enabled cognitive theorists to develop specific models for how we accomplish thought processes like knowledge acquisition and memorization.

Early cognitive researchers frequently employed a computer metaphor in the study of human thinking, comparing the way humans think with the way computers operate (Barutta, Cornejo, & Ibanez, 2011). This "mind as computer" perspective allowed cognition to be conceptualized as an information processing system. This view is based on the many similarities between human thinking and computers. For example, computers and humans both take in information, store this information, process it in some way, retrieve it from memory, and produce an output. In fact, humans build computers and humans write computer programs. It follows that the way computers "think" mirrors the way we think.

Researchers using a computer model to study human cognition learned much about the workings of the human mind, paving the way for the cognitive perspective to become a dominant force in psychology. In this chapter, we'll explore this research and the resulting theories regarding the multifaceted nature of human cognition, and we'll discuss topics such as memory, knowledge, and metacognition. We will outline the discoveries of information processing theorists regarding multiple memory stores, and we will also discuss different conceptualizations of knowledge. Throughout the chapter, we will also consider how cognitive research can help us better understand the teaching and learning process, highlighting classroom application of cognitive learning principles. Before we begin this exploration, let's examine the concept of memory, which is the foundation for much of our thinking.

Memory as a Foundation for Knowledge

Memory

The ability to retain a mental representation of our experiences

Human beings share a remarkable quality with one another: we are able to retain a mental representation of our experiences. The common term for this mental representation is **memory**. Memory allows us to store life experiences, so we can better adapt to the ever-changing world around us. Imagine what life would be like without the ability to remember events or experiences. Every situation we encountered would be new, as if we had never experienced anything like it before. This would make it very difficult for us to alter our behavior to best suit a particular life circumstance. In fact, our only behavior would be that with which we were born through our genetic endowment. Humans are hardly limited to inborn or genetically driven behaviors. We have a highly developed ability to store new information. For example, an infant recognizes her mother's face, preferring it to others, at around the age of two months (Slater, 2000). When a toddler touches a hot radiator, his memory of the painful event allows him to alter his future behavior to avoid being burned again. A second grader is capable of remembering basic addition, which makes learning and understanding multiplication possible. Not only can we remember people, consequences, and information, as these examples illustrate, we can also remember events, images, feelings, and coordinated movements. In fact, there are a limitless number of everyday memory examples, and they are a testament to the remarkable complexity of memory as a cognitive process.

Memories, however, would quickly become overwhelming if we did not have an efficient organization technique. Without organization, we would have an enormous store of information, but we would be unable to find relevant memories. The human ability to organize information allows us to find and retrieve memories. This storage of memories in a complex but highly organized reservoir of information is called **knowledge**. Knowledge makes it possible for us to match the face of the person walking across the street to the name "Brent," so that we can call him by name when we say hello. Knowledge allows a physical education teacher to temper her expectations regarding a second grade basketball game. She knows that young children have a different capacity for motor skills and educates accordingly. Knowledge is far from random or haphazard. Quite the contrary, as you will see in this chapter, the development of knowledge follows a highly organized, yet flexible course.

Knowledge

The accumulation of memories over time into a complex, but highly organized body of information

The next section will look more closely at how we form memories. We will explore in detail a popular framework for understanding how we form memories. Afterward, we will return to the concept of knowledge and look at different types of knowledge and varying techniques for building a sound knowledge base.

SUMMARIZE AND REFLECT

1. There are a variety of differences between cognitive and behavioral interpretations of learning. The behaviorist views the individual as a relatively passive respondent to environmental changes. The cognitive theorist views people as actively thinking about their environments and purposefully altering their behavior.
2. Cognitive and behavioral scientists focus on similar scientific methods.
3. Cognitive psychologists began scientifically exploring topics such as memory and specific kinds of knowledge using a computer metaphor to guide their research.
4. Memory is the foundation for knowledge. It is defined as mental representations of experiences.
5. Knowledge is defined as organized sets of accumulated memories.

(continues)

INFORMED APPLICATION

1. A common problem teachers face is a student who seems to lack investment in academic success. Consider this issue from both the behavioral and cognitive perspective. How might each theory direct intervention efforts?
2. In addition to critical thinking skills, one of the primary goals of education is to help students build a solid foundation of knowledge. Develop a lesson plan using some aspect of cognitive theory to improve knowledge construction.

THE INFORMATION-PROCESSING MODEL OF MEMORY

The information-processing model views memory as a process (Halford & Andrews, 2011). This means memorization is not a specific event, but the product of several step-like processes. It is the combination of these steps that results in our ability to retain and recall information. Information-processing models are based on a model proposed by Atkinson and Shiffrin in 1968. The basic steps of the information-processing model are presented graphically in Figure 5.2.

The information-processing model consists of three core components: sensory memory, working memory, and long-term memory. According to this model, information flows in from the environment and is processed by one, two, or all of the components. The outcome of this process will determine the nature of our memories. In addition to the core components, there are also important cognitive processes serving to link the individual components into a single functioning system. These processes are generally referred to as **executive control processes**. These components direct the flow of information through the memory system and impact effectiveness. Let's turn now to a detailed account of each of the information-processing model's main components.

Executive control processes

Memory components that direct the flow of information through the memory system and impact effectiveness

Sensory Memory

Take a moment to sit very still, and concentrate on each of your senses. Starting with vision, begin to notice all the colors, shapes and objects within your visual field. Continue with each of your other senses. What can you hear, feel, taste, and smell? Did you notice these sensory experiences before you focused your attention on them? Likely, you did not really think about the smell in the room before you were directed to do so. We typically under-appreciate the vast amount of sensory information coming in through our senses every second of the day; yet, it is through this sensory information that we come to construct our understanding of the world. What happens to all the sights, smells, and sounds that enter through our senses? Obviously, it would be highly inefficient to try to process all incoming sensory information. The next time

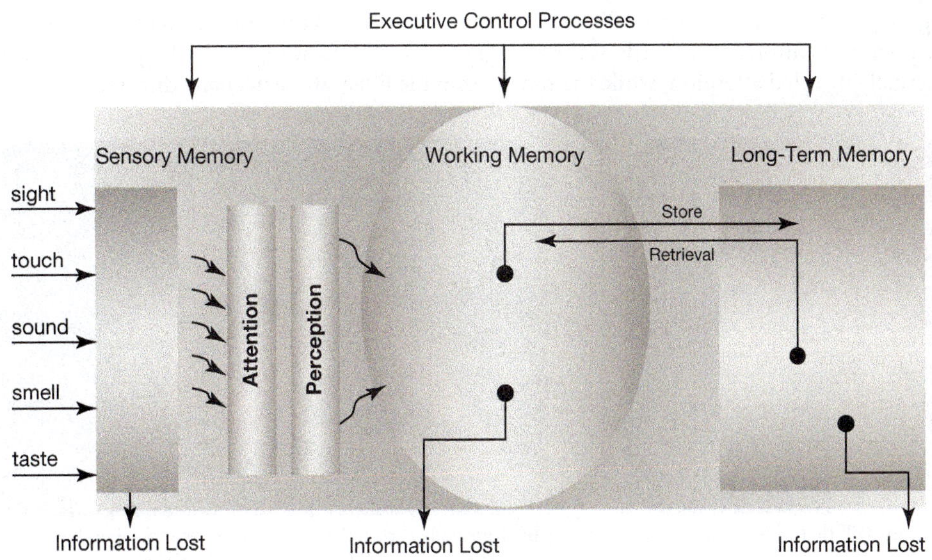

Figure 5.2
Information Processing Model

you are with a friend, take a quick look around the room and then close your eyes. Have your friend ask you a question about anything in the room. Did you know the answer? Chances are, even though you were just looking at the room, you were unable to answer correctly. The reason lies in the way our sensory memories function. **Sensory memory** acts as a temporary holding system for incoming sensory information. The memory store appears to have unlimited storage *capacity*, taking in countless sights, sounds, tastes, smells, and physical sensations. Holding this vast amount of sensory information in our memory allows us enough time to select certain information for additional processing. For example, a student listening to a lecture on this chapter is actually taking in other sensory information at the same time. They are sensing the sounds coming from the other students, the feel of their clothing, the image of someone walking by the classroom, etc. It is the sound of the teacher's voice, however, that is most critical; and the sensory memory store allows us to hold all these sensations and pick the voice of the teacher for further processing.

Sensory memory

Memory that acts as a temporary holding system for incoming sensory information

What about all the information in which we are not interested? What would life be like if we retained *all* information coming in through our senses? Likely, things would quickly get very confusing. We really don't need to remember what color shirt a student from another class was wearing as they passed by the door or the sound of a wet shoe on the hallway floor. Most of our incoming sensory information is not needed and, therefore, is quickly lost from the sensory memory store, a process known as **sensory decay**. Research shows that the amount of time it takes for a particular sensory memory to decay depends on the particular sense, but sensory memory is always very brief (Cheour et al., 2002). For example, visual memories typically last for about one second and auditory memories for about two to four seconds (Leahey & Harris, 1977; Pashler & Carrier, 1996). The important point to remember is that while sensory memory may have an unlimited *capacity*, it also has a very short *duration*, lasting only a few seconds. Not all sensory memories decay, however. Some of these memories are selected for further processing (like the sound of the teacher's voice in the preceding example) through two mechanisms: attention and perception.

Sensory decay

Refers to the majority of our incoming sensory information that is not needed and therefore is quickly lost from the sensory memory

Attention

Attention is a cognitive resource fundamental to storing memories. **Attention** directs sensory memories toward the next component in the process, working memory. When you attend to the sound of your teacher's voice, for example, you select that memory for additional processing. If you had not paid attention to the sound of the voice, that particular sensory memory would have decayed. Sometimes, directing our attention is easier than others. For example, think about how much effort it takes to pay attention to a really good action/adventure movie. It probably does not take much effort at all since the movie is very engaging and easily captures our attention. Now, consider how difficult it is to carefully read one hundred pages of your biology textbook in one evening. In this situation, the textbook material is less likely to naturally engage your attention resources. To read the material, you will probably need to constantly refocus your attention to the words as the evening progresses. Reading the biology book requires internally directed attention, while the movie example illustrates externally directed attention.

Attention

That which directs sensory memories toward the next component in the information processing model of memory, working memory

Externally directed attention is all that is required when watching an good movie

Internally directed attention is necessary when having to read one hundred pages of a textbook in one evening.

Allocation of attention resources is extremely important in the classroom. While purposefully directing attention requires effort for all of us, some individuals appear to have better control than others. Classroom environments can also vary substantially in how much they externally mediate a student's attention resources. Even in the most engaging classroom environment, all students will be required to attend to tasks that may not be inherently engaging. If the student is able to internally direct his attention, he has a better chance of meeting with task success. If he experiences difficulty directing his attention toward less engaging tasks, then important information coming in through his senses will decay, and he will not benefit from the educationally relevant information available to him. Teachers face this situation almost every day. They stand in front of the class, provide directions, and ask the class to begin the task. Almost invariably, at least one student will miss the instructions and not know what to do. What happened? Did the student not hear the teacher's instructions? While this is one possible explanation, another possibility lies in a breakdown in the direction of attention resources.

In all likelihood, the student did "hear" the instructions. At least, the sounds registered in the student's sensory memory. The student was, however, paying attention to an interesting crack on his desk at the time, thus focusing his attention elsewhere. Again, without attention, sensory memories simply decay. This has obvious implications for creating educationally productive environments. Students vary significantly in their ability to purposefully direct attention. In fact, the ability to direct attention can be viewed as a continuum, with some students having excellent control and others having poor control. Teachers who are sensitive to individual differences among students are in a better position to provide appropriate supports. These supports require the teacher to make important classroom information the most engaging aspect of the instructional environment. The supports may be simple, such as repeating instructions one-on-one. They may also require more effort, such as setting up a cueing system or posting written instructions. It should be noted that students who require more substantial support in directing their attention might be at-risk for attention deficit hyperactivity disorder (AD/HD). AD/HD is a behaviorally defined diagnosis used to describe children who have a unique set of problems, one of which involves significant difficulty with directed attention. Our focus in this chapter is to help you develop a basic understanding of cognitive processes. We will outline strategies for providing more substantial external supports for children with ADHD in Chapter 11.

Interconnections

Teaching students with attentional deficits is challenging. Instructional strategies are covered in detail in Chapter 11.

Perception

Perception is the cognitive process of assigning meaning to incoming sensory information. Take a look at the symbol below. What letter do you see? Is it an A or an H? Actually, it is neither. The symbol is not a perfect representation of either an A or an H. You may have *perceived* the lines as either an A or an H because you tried to assign meaning to the incoming sensory information.

Perception

The cognitive process of assigning meaning to incoming sensory information

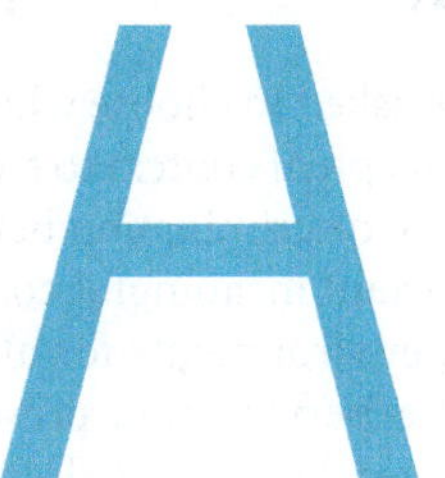

In the early part of the twentieth century, a group of psychologists became interested in the role that perception plays in shaping our understanding of the world. Collectively, these psychologists were called the **Gestalt psychologists**. *Gestalt* is a German word meaning "configuration," and these scientists were so named because they believed that our perception of sensory information depends on the form or configuration of the information. Research conducted by the Gestalt psychologists led to their outlining four basic perceptual processes, presented in Figure 5.3.

Gestalt psychologists

The group of psychologists interested in the role that perception plays in shaping our understanding of the world

Figure 5.3

Four Basic Perceptual Processes

Similarity

Proximity

Continuity

Closure

Gestalt principles are important to consider because they help us appreciate the degree to which we actively try to make sense of the world (Gallace & Spence, 2011). Instead of always perceiving the world as made up of individual items, we actively seek patterns, forms, or meaningful configurations.

Along with attention, perception helps sensory memories move into working memory. Attention and perception often work together to determine which information moves into working memory since it is not always enough to just pay attention to something. We may attend to a particular sensory item, but fail to make any sense of it, resulting in the memory being lost through decay. To actively process information we not only need to pay attention to it, we must also perceive it as meaningful. Recall the symbol presented earlier. We will now alter the context in which this symbol is presented, making it more meaningful and causing you to perceive the lines as both an A and an H. As you can see below, the additional context provided by neighboring letters of the alphabet causes you to *perceive* the same symbol differently in the two words.

TAE CAT

The symbol now has meaning, and the information it provides can move on to the working memory store for additional processing. In the classroom, providing a meaningful context for *to-be-learned* information is an important avenue for facilitating learning. Consider the situation of a child in kindergarten presented with the words BAT and HAT. While the child may not be able to read the words when they are presented on flashcards, providing a context by adding pictures above the words allows them to perceive the letter configurations as meaningful so they can "read" the words.

BAT **HAT**

In first grade, the child might be asked to choose which picture is represented by the word *HAT*. This provides a meaningful perceptual context to facilitate the processing of the information in working memory, encouraging discrimination between the *B* and *H* sounds.

While it is easy to see how important meaningful context is in perception, it is often quite challenging to create such learning environments for all students. A student's cognitive development, level of knowledge, past experiences, or present skill level may not allow them to benefit from a lesson in the way the teacher intended. By asking questions regarding student perceptions and carefully listening to the responses, teachers can develop responsive learning environments that maximize movement of sensory memories into working memory. The important point to remember is that students are actively trying to make sense of the world, and teachers can use this to help students master curricular goals.

Bottom-up processing

Process by which an individual attempts to arrive at a meaningful perception using sensory items to build an appropriate understanding

Another factor to consider when trying to understand students' perceptions is whether they are building meaning from incoming sensory information or from prior knowledge retrieved from memory. **Bottom-up processing** occurs when an individual attempts to arrive at a meaningful perception by using sensory items to build an appropriate understanding. For example, a child in kindergarten might read a new word, *CAT*, by matching a sound to each letter, blending the sounds together in order, and ultimately recognizing the word, conjuring up an image of her own pet. Meaningful perceptions can also be reached using **top-down processing,** or using existing knowledge, to guide our understanding of new information (Liu et al., 2011). Again, using the kindergarten example of reading the word *CAT*, we might show a picture of a cat with the word printed underneath. In this way, the child can start with something they already know (prior knowledge) and then interpret the incoming visual information (C-A-T) in light of that idea. It is important to remember that meaningful interpretations of sensory information may use either bottom-up or top-down processing, and both types of processing have implications for classroom instruction.

Top-down processing

Process of using existing knowledge to guide our understanding of new information

Attention and perception are both important components of human information processing, yet most of this work takes place outside our awareness. For example, you didn't have to think about whether you were going to attend or how to interpret the symbols below; you simply looked at the words while you were reading, and your perceptual set allowed you to read them as THE CAT. As soon as you directed your attention to the words and derived meaning from them, the information was immediately transferred to the next phase in the information processing system, working memory.

THE CAT

Working Memory

What we now call working memory was originally conceived as just another temporary memory store on the way to permanent memory, so it was given the name short-term memory. Later research, however, revealed that both temporary storage and active processing occur in this intermediate store. In fact, our conscious thinking and reasoning occur here. **Working memory** is a term that better describes a memory store where information can be both temporarily stored and consciously processed. The information processed in working memory may come from the sensory store or, as we will see in the next section, from long-term memory. Recall, this information can be understood graphically using the figure at the beginning of this section.

Working memory

A term that better describes a memory store where information can be both temporarily stored and consciously processed

Consider the following example. First, recall your own phone number, including the area code. You weren't thinking about your phone number at all before reading the previous sentence. In fact, it was outside your conscious awareness, housed in the long-term memory store. In order to remember your phone number, you brought the information from long-term memory into your working memory store, and it became *conscious*. Our ability to selectively move information into working memory allows us to maintain a vast unconscious long-term store of information.

Remember that working memory also allows us to process incoming information from sensory memory, to which we assign meaning based on information from long-term memory. In this way, working memory allows us to integrate our sensory experiences with information we have already learned. Extensive research has been conducted to better understand the information processing, which occurs in working memory. Cognitive scientists have explored the duration and capacity of working memory, as well as information transfer from working to long-term memory. We turn now to an exploration of this groundbreaking research regarding human thinking.

Capacity and Duration

In 1956, George Miller, a psychologist at Princeton University, claimed to have been "persecuted by an integer." He was haunted, in fact, by the number seven. In the 1950s, researchers studying human mental function had repeatedly found evidence of limits on human processing of sensory information (Pollack, 1952; Garner, 1953), and Miller couldn't help but notice these limits all hovered around the number seven. In his seminal paper, *The Magical Number 7 Plus or Minus 2,* Miller outlined for the first time what has now become standard knowledge

in cognitive psychology—the capacity of working memory is around 7 ± 2 items. This limited capacity is easily demonstrated with a simple example. Have a friend write down twenty 2-digit numbers and then read them aloud to you, one per second. After she finishes, quickly write down as many of the numbers as you can. If you were only able to recall seven or so numbers, you are not alone. In fact, research shows that any person who attempts this task will probably be able to recall somewhere between five to nine numbers. Practically, this means we have significant limitations on how many things we can think about at once.

Not only do we have limitations on the number of items we can consider at once, but also on the amount of time items stay in working memory (Gabales & Birney, 2011). In other words, working memory has both a limited capacity and limited duration. The duration of working memory is around thirty seconds. An effective way to demonstrate the duration of working memory is to have a friend tell you his or her parents' phone number, without area code. Repeat it back to ensure it is in working memory. Then immediately start counting backwards by threes from one hundred. Keep counting backwards until you reach zero. After you reach zero, see if you can recall the phone number. Most people will be unable to fully recall the number, particularly if the number is unlike other phone numbers with which they are familiar. The phone number was quickly lost because of the limited duration of working memory.

GET THE FACTS

7

Items

Capacity of working memory is about 7 items.

Miller (1956)

The limited duration and capacity of working memory, however, can be altered. If the 30-second duration and 7 ± 2 capacities were absolute, our thinking would be limited and inflexible. To achieve the incredible flexibility characteristic of human thinking, we need to have a mechanism for maintaining memories in working memory for longer periods of time. We also need a tool to enable us to think about more information at one time. The cognitive mechanisms of chunking and rehearsal help address these issues.

Chunking and Rehearsal

We can increase the amount of information we process in working memory, without increasing its capacity, by changing the way we think. In order to do this, we combine several individual pieces of information into a single meaningful unit, or chunk of information. **Chunking** essentially allows us to expand the amount of information available in working memory without increasing its capacity. For example, if you try to remember the following series of letters, you will exceed the capacity of working memory.

Chunking

Process that essentially allows us to expand the amount of information available in working memory, without increasing its capacity

H P S U C E D T C Y O A G O N O I Y L A L

The twenty-one letters in this sequence will overwhelm your working memory store, causing earlier items to leave the store to make room for the newer items. The trick to easily remembering all of these letters is to take certain letters and group them together into smaller chunks of information. Although it may not be obvious, these letters combine to form two words.

E D U C A T I O N A L P S Y C H O L O G Y

Thinking of these letters as two simple words reduces the load on working memory from a virtually impossible twenty-one items, down to a very manageable two. While the capacity is still limited to 7 ± 2 items, the "items" contain more information. Now that the words "Educational Psychology" are in your working memory, how can you keep them there for more than a few seconds?

The cognitive strategy of **rehearsal**, or repetitively thinking about the information, increases the length of time information stays in working memory without changing the 30-second duration. Essentially, each time you think about a piece of information, the 30-second clock begins. If you think about the information again after twenty-five seconds, the clock

Rehearsal

Refers to the general process of actively thinking about information starts over. There are two primary types of rehearsal, maintenance and elaborative.

Maintenance rehearsal is the process of mentally repeating information currently held in working memory. For example, try to commit the following number sequence to memory: 4-3-2-7-9-6-1. In order to complete this task, you are likely to mentally repeat the number sequence to yourself several times. Similarly, when a physical education teacher asks his students to get a soccer ball out of the storage closet, dribble it the length of the gym, and line up on the west wall of the gym, the students are likely to continue to repeat these instructions to themselves until they are in position along the wall. This repeating of information can maintain information in working memory for an indefinite period of time; however, it requires constant effort. It is also rather inefficient at getting the information into the long-term store. For example, without looking back, what was that number sequence you just tried to remember? While it might not be difficult to keep the list of numbers in memory for a few minutes by using maintenance rehearsal, it is unlikely you were able to commit this meaningless information to long-term memory. It would require much effort and many, many repetitions of the information before it would move into the long-term store. Remember the amount of practice required to commit multiplication facts to long-term memory? While this type of rehearsal will eventually result in information moving into long-term memory, it requires a great deal of practice.

Maintenance rehearsal

The specific process of mentally repeating information currently held in working memory

A more efficient strategy for moving information from working memory to long-term memory is to use elaborative rehearsal. **Elaborative rehearsal** is the process of taking something you are trying to learn and connecting it to something you already know. If students can create a meaningful association between a new piece of information and something they already know, the new item will be much easier to recall. This is why it is easier to learn about the national deficit in social studies when you realize it is similar to asking your parents for an advance on your allowance. While this example of elaboration is student driven, teachers can also provide elaborative associations to assist students in learning new information, such as using the acronym ROY-G-BIV for learning the color spectrum (red, orange, yellow, green, blue, indigo, violet). Many of us were taught the elaborative association, "spring forward–fall back," to help us remember whether to move the clock forward or backward as a function of daylight savings time. These types of elaborative associations dramatically increase retention of information, moving the storage demand from working memory to the long-term store. Before we turn to a discussion of long-term memory, however, let's take a closer look at the way different types of information are processed in working memory.

Elaborative rehearsal

The specific process of taking something you are trying to learn and connecting it to something you already know

Components of Working Memory

In 1974, Baddeley and Hitch proposed that working memory is not a single entity but actually consists of three different components: a phonological loop for auditory or verbal information, a visuospatial sketchpad for visual information, and a central executive for the management of attentional resources. Newer research has provided considerable support for this interpretation of working memory. Figure 5.4 provides a graphical representation of these concepts.

Phonological Loop

One of the most extensively studied of these components is the phonological loop. Recall from Chapter 2 that phonology refers to speech sounds. Essentially, the **phonological loop** is the part of working memory that allows us to repeat auditory and verbal information. When we use the maintenance rehearsal strategy of holding information in working memory by silently repeating the information, the phonological loop is in operation. While the phonological loop is a fairly reliable system, it is susceptible to competition from new information that

Phonological loop

The part of working memory which allows us to repeat auditory and verbal information

Figure 5.4
Components of Working Memory

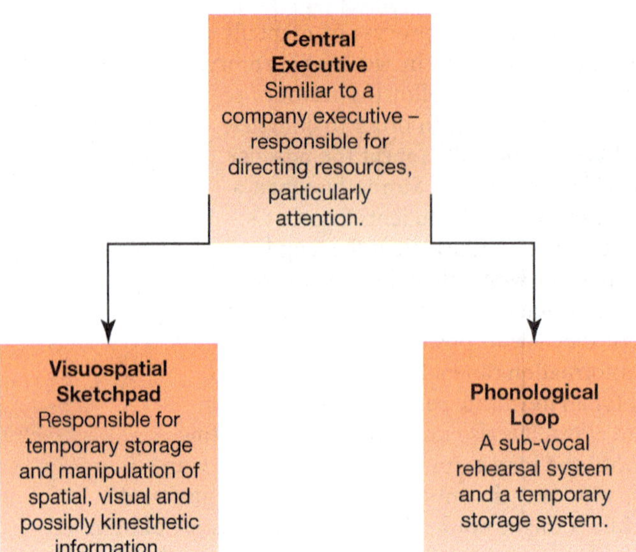

is phonologically similar. For example, you will have little difficulty remembering a series of words such as *pit, day, cow, soak, pen;* but you are likely to have more difficulty with words such as *man, cat, map, cab, can* (Baddeley, 1966a). Research suggests that the reason the second list is more difficult is due to the phonetic similarity of the words. Each word contains the short *a* sound, and each word has at least one other sound present in another word. In effect, we say the words to ourselves in the phonological loop, and we get confused when the sounds of the words are too similar.

The phonological loop also appears to have some important time constraints which are based on the length of time it takes us to say a chunk of verbal information. Research shows we can only hold as much information in the phonological loop as we can say to ourselves within a 1.5- to 2-second time period. Thus, the processing of information in the phonological loop requires a new constraint on the classically cited five to nine items for working memory. While the capacity of the phonological loop is also five to nine items, these items must take less than about two seconds to say. For example, if you are asked to memorize five to nine digits, you can easily repeat these to yourself within a 2-second timeframe. What if you were asked to memorize five to nine multi-syllable words? Repeating a list where each unit of information takes a larger amount of time to say is problematic because the total time exceeds the 1.5- to 2-second limit of the phonological loop (Gray, 2002).

The phonological loop represents our verbal working memory, and it is likely influential in learning a spoken language, since sound patterns linked to meaning are required for language learning. It also appears to be important for classroom achievement and is sensitive to memory enhancing instruction (St. Clair-Thompson, Stevens, Hunt, & Bolder, 2010). Children who experience problems with the functioning of the phonological loop may show speech and language delays (Baddeley, Gathercole, & Papagno, 1998). Further, the efficient operation of the phonological loop is often used as an indicator of intellectual potential. The Wechsler intelligence tests, for example, includes a digit span subtest, which measures short-term auditory memory (Wechsler

The phonological loop represents our verbal working memory, and is likely influential in learning a spoken language.

et al., 1981). Additionally, research on the phonological loop and intellectual ability show that phonological loop performance becomes more impaired as intellectual ability decreases (Schuchardt, Gebhardt, & Maehler, 2010).

While research shows that children as young as three years old store phonological information in working memory, active and efficient rehearsal within the phonological loop does not develop until later in childhood. It appears this happens around the time children begin to learn to read (Gathercole & Adams, 1993; Adams & Hitch, 1994). In fact, some research suggests that problems with the phonological loop may be related to difficulty with reading acquisition (Gathercole & Baddeley, 1990, 1993). Interestingly, research on the function of the phonological loop and mathematics shows that the phonological loop is more important in mediating performance at earlier ages (Meyer, Salimpoor, Wu, Geary, & Menon, 2010). The visual-spatial sketchpad becomes increasing important as children develop. The next section reviews this important component of working memory.

The Visuospatial Sketchpad

The visuospatial sketchpad is the component of working memory responsible for spatial, visual, and possibly kinesthetic (movement) information. Just like the phonological loop system, the visuospatial system has a limited duration and is sensitive to interference from other visual information. For example, if you were to ask students to engage in a visual task such as mentally rotating a figure presented on the board, they would be particularly compromised by other visually oriented information, but not necessarily by incoming auditory information. This is not to say that the visuospatial and phonological systems are completely independent, as both systems are constrained by the overall limited capacity and duration of working memory.

Research regarding the visuospatial sketchpad indicates it also has educational implications. Studies show that the functioning of the visuospatial system is important for maintaining an accurate line track when reading. It is also important for keeping the reader oriented to the text layout on a page (Baddeley, 2003). Further, it has been proposed that the visuospatial sketchpad may help us maintain a representation of the grammatical elements of a sentence from beginning to end so that accurate comprehension is possible (Phillips, Jarrold, Baddeley, Grant, & Karmiloff-Smith, 2004). Recent research on visuospatial processing indicates, however, that maintaining even a simple visual representation for more than a few seconds is very effortful. Successful representation of the item requires constant refocusing of attention (Baddeley, Cocchini, Della Sala, Logie, & Spinnler, 1999). The purposeful direction of attention places strong demands on the last of our three components of working memory, the central executive.

The Central Executive

Central executive

The supervisory system of working memory that manages the allocation of resources

The **central executive** is the supervisory system of working memory, managing the allocation of resources. Depending on the nature of the task, the central executive may tap the phonological loop, the visuospatial sketchpad, or both. It also controls the use of information from sensory memory, the retrieval of information from long-term memory, and the integration of such information with reasoning or planning tasks. Its responsibilities are similar to those of a company executive, taking little part in the actual work of the system but providing much needed direction and overall vision (Baddeley, 1986). The functions of the central executive system are the least understood of the components of working memory, largely because these functions are complex and many. The central executive is responsible not only for directing attention and integrating information from other memory systems but also for planning and directing future thinking and behavior. If we go back to the "mind as computer" metaphor presented earlier, the central executive is like the central processing unit of a computer (CPU). The CPU is responsible for retrieving appropriate information from the hard drive, running the appropriate programs, and producing a usable output.

Researchers have looked extensively for a specific region in the brain where this CPU-like system might be located, and much evidence points toward the frontal lobes as important in central executive processes (Baddeley, 1986; Wilkins, Shallice, & McCarthy, 1987; Cohen et al., 1994). In fact, people who have damage to the frontal lobes show significant problems across a wide range of cognitive and behavioral processes, outlined in Table 5.1.

Collectively, these processes are known as executive functions. As you can see in the table, problems with any or all of these functions could negatively influence classroom performance. We'll return to the topic of executive function deficits in Chapter 12, when we discuss AD/HD in detail. Now, we'll turn our attention to one of the problems with working memory, the ease with which we forget information.

Forgetting

Information in working memory is not intended to last for a significant period of time. How then, does information leave working memory, and where does it go? Sometimes, information is moved to the long-term store (which we will discuss in the next section). At other times, information is simply lost or replaced. Multiple theories have been proposed to explain this phenomenon, but the two most investigated are decay theory and interference theory. **Decay theory** asserts that, over time, information not actively rehearsed or transferred to long-term memory will gradually weaken and fade away. Another popular theory about why we easily lose information from working memory is called **interference theory**. This theory maintains that memories do not simply decay over time; instead, the information becomes interfered with by older memories or incoming information (Szmalec, Verbruggen, Vandierendonck, & Kemps, 2011). Both processes are likely important determinants of everyday information loss in working memory (Waugh & Norman, 1965). In short, working memory is easily overloaded by our attempts to write and rewrite information in the same mental space and time limited system. Next, we'll turn our attention to the memory store that is virtually impossible to overload, long-term memory.

Decay theory

Belief that, over time, information not actively rehearsed or transferred to long-term memory will gradually weaken and fade away

Interference theory

Belief that memories do not simply decay over time; instead, the information becomes interfered with by older memories or incoming information

Interconnections

See Chapter 12 for a discussion of executive functions as they relate to Attention Deficit/Hyperactivity Disorder.

Long-Term Memory

Long-term memory is an important part of the information processing system, as it is responsible for the *relatively* permanent storage of information. This type of storage system allows us to retain memories of our past experiences, which can be brought back into working memory for additional processing. It is because of our long-term store that we can learn from our experiences. The formation of long-term memories (knowledge) has traditionally been the goal of education; yet, moving information into the long-term store and retrieving it on demand is

Table 5.1 Executive Functioning

	Skill
Executive Functioning	Directing long-term memory storage and retrieval
	Inhibition of reflexive behavioral responses
	Directing attention and filtering extraneous information
	Interrupting and returning to an ongoing activity
	Regulating social behavior, including empathetic responses
	Modifying motor behavior based on feedback
	Shifting cognitive resources based on task demands

Adapted from McCloskey, 2001.

often quite difficult. In the following sections, we'll examine the factors important in storing and retrieving information from long-term memory.

Capacity and Duration

The capacity of long-term memory is similar to sensory memory in that it appears to be virtually unlimited. Investigations of some of the oldest people alive indicate they are still capable of storing new information in the long-term store. This is an impressive feat, given the wealth of information collected over an individual's lifespan. The duration of long-term memory also appears to be unlimited. Again, as we grow old, most of us maintain vivid memories of life experiences across many years. The problems we experience recalling specific information are not based in the capacity or duration of long-term memory. Instead, problems are usually associated with organizational and relational issues. Without sophisticated storage procedures, the vast warehouse of long-term memory would be inaccessible. For example, imagine all the books in the Library of Congress randomly stored throughout the building. Finding a particular book would be nearly impossible.

Elaboration

Refers to the idea of making connections between material you are trying to learn and information already known

Elaboration, Organization, and Context

In order to keep information from getting lost in long-term memory, we use a variety tagging and filing techniques. The first strategy we will consider involves attaching new information to something we have already learned, a process called elaboration. Recall that we have already encountered the process of elaboration in our discussion of elaborative rehearsal in working memory. Again, **elaboration** refers to the idea of making connections between material you are trying to learn and information already known. These "known" memories located within the long-term store basically provide an anchor for the new information you are trying to learn. Making direct attempts to elaborate information you are learning can have dramatic effects on your ability to recall the information. Using elaboration, however, is not always an easy process. In fact, elaboration is a skill; and like all skills, the more time and effort spent practicing, the more expert one becomes. Teachers can help students learn to elaborate through examples, but ultimately it is the student who is in the best position to make connections between new material and the wealth of information they already know.

F.A.Q.

Nelson Krackauer—"Should I constantly be trying to make these elaboration connections in all my classes?"

Professor Rainwater—"Yes and no. Elaboration is definitely a powerful tool to help you learn information, but not all information is created equal. When learning some information, like motor skills, you may benefit more from practice and appropriate modeling."

Teachers who incorporate elaborative techniques into their teaching can greatly assist students in learning specific content. For example, Mr. Ouellette, in his chemistry class, decided to have his students use elaboration to better remember the noble gasses. In the past, he typically introduced the topic by reviewing the structure of the periodic table of elements, reminding the students that different chemical groups have a similar configuration of atomic elements. He explained that the noble gases are organized together in a group because each has eight electrons in their outer shell. Mr. Ouellette found that students had significant difficulty at quiz time without requiring the students to think about the noble gasses by linking the new information to already known information. Therefore, this year he decided to try a different approach—he required them to use elaboration. In order to help them take the new information on the noble gases and connect it to something known, he formed groups and had each research an every-day use for their assigned noble gas. He then had the students present their findings. The most common uses found were as follows: Krypton—computer monitors, Helium—party balloons, Neon—lights, Argon—incandescent light bulbs, and Xenon—Pyrex glass. This elaborative exercise had very effective results. Every student not only remembered the entire list of noble gases, they also even showed a remarkable improvement in being able to describe the atomic properties they have in common.

F.A.Q.

John Forsythe—"As a future teacher, I'm a little intimidated by the thought of having to create these elaborative connections for my students. Any advice?"

Professor Rainwater—"Remember that these elaborations are inherently about the student's own experiences and knowledge base. As a teacher, you don't have to create elaborations for them, as much as provide appropriate activities and guidance for them to develop the connections on their own."

By linking new information to knowledge we already have in long-term memory, we create tags or handles by which we can easily grasp the information at a later date. These memory tags are essentially a method of organizing our experiences according to what we already know. Luckily, as we learned back in Chapter 2 in

Teachers who incorporate elaborative techniques into their teaching can greatly assist students in learning specific content.

our discussion of Piaget, human beings are incredible organizers. Each new learning situation is almost immediately compared to existing memories for similarities and differences. In other words, much of how we organize information into the long-term store depends on elaborative thinking. We learn about a civil war in another country and recognize similarities to our own civil war. We learn new vocabulary in language arts and immediately notice similar root words. We learn a new sport and realize the necessary skills are very different from any other sport we have played. In this way, we naturally organize our world, creating an integrated body of knowledge.

Sometimes, however, our memory tags get lost in a sea of other information, and we cannot retrieve a memory we know we once had. The ease with which we can access information stored in long-term memory depends on how organized we were learning the information. Remember using the card catalog at the library in elementary school? If you were given a new card to file and you placed it in the correct drawer and in perfect alphabetical order, the odds that you could find the card again would be 100%. What would happen if you didn't bother with alphabetical order? What if you saw the author's name began with a B, you pulled the B drawer open, and you haphazardly placed the card in the drawer. What are the odds you could find it again? Well, in the short-term, the task is not too difficult. With the drawer still open, it is relatively easy to remember about where you placed the card. What would happen, though, after you file hundreds of other cards over several days or weeks? Would you remember where you put any particular card? This card catalog example is a good metaphor for what happens when you cram for an exam. Often we are able to retain enough information to pass the test, but the next week you find you have forgotten most of what you learned. This example is useful in illustrating the distinction between permanent duration and functional access (Howe, 1970; Broadbent, 1958). While long-term memories may be permanent, the information must be organized in such a way that we can find it again. This makes information functional.

A second strategy to consider makes use of our extraordinary potential for organization. As stated earlier, humans are incredible organizers. If we are presented with information in random order, we will spontaneously organize the information into related groups (Bousfield, 1953). We can also take advantage of pre-organized information, learning new material more efficiently when it is presented in an organized manner. Unfortunately, students often disregard the organization of material presented in textbooks and in class when they study. Take, for example, the common study technique of making note cards. Students frequently take information, particularly definition/term information, and create note cards with the term on one side and the definition on the other. Typically, students will study the cards in order and then shuffle the deck to better test their knowledge. What does shuffling the cards mean in terms of organization? Essentially, studying the cards in random order completely divorces the study experience from any type of organization. Most textbooks are highly organized, with much thought going into the progression of ideas. Students who study their note cards in the order the material appears in the chapter take advantage of the organization already present in the textbook. In the same way, briefly previewing the structural elements of a reading (headings, sub-headings, etc.) can be used to identify the organization of the material (Robinson, 1970). This

The way with which we store our long term memories is important for our retrieval of them at a later date. We want to keep them organized like a library catalog.

can be accomplished by conducting a scan of the bolded heading material, or by reviewing the chapter outline presented at the beginning of the chapter. By explicitly teaching this strategy for promoting organization, teachers can assist students in developing effective study skills (Wong, 1994; McWhorter, 1996).

A final strategy to consider regarding the movement of information into the long term store is the role of environmental context. When presenting a student with new information, the presentation does not happen in isolation. In fact, the information to be learned is just one of many pieces of information running through working memory at a given point in time. For example, as a teacher presents information on a new topic, other information is also present in the classroom. Perhaps someone makes a quiet joke, passes a note, drops a pencil, or makes a funny noise. All of these incidental events have the potential to be learned, or associated, with the teacher's information because they occur in the same context. A wide variety of environmental cues may become unintentionally associated with the new material. This may make it difficult to access the information if the learning environment differs substantially from the testing environment. In the classroom, for example, teachers frequently create learning environments that are relaxed and more closely match the natural behavior of children. When it comes time to take a test, however, teachers often have students sit in an unusually quiet room, with no interactions or movement allowed. Ideally, the learning environment and the testing environment should be similar to optimize the effects of context. As educators move toward more collaborative and natural learning environments, it should be noted that assessments are still largely conducted in traditional formats. Teachers can facilitate student learning by trying to be more sensitive to how well the learning environment corresponds to the testing environment.

Small behaviors have the potential to be associated with a teacher's lesson when they occur at the same time.

Forgetting

Carefully elaborating and organizing learning material makes it easier to later recall, but there are still times when we are unable to recall something we have learned. Some theorists have proposed that memories can be lost from long-term memory in the same way they are lost from working memory—through the processes of interference or decay (Anderson, 1983). Others hold that information is not displaced or gone; rather, forgetting occurs due to insufficient retrieval cues to prompt recall (Tulving, 1968). Recall that decay occurs when the memory trace weakens and is lost over time. According to this theory, once a memory has decayed, it is gone from the permanent store and is no longer available for recall. The idea that memories might decay in long-term memory just as they do in short-term memory is supported by the fact that we are more likely to forget with the passage of time. Studies show, however, that once we have learned something such as a list of words, and then forget the list, it is much easier to relearn the same list than it is to learn a new list of words. There is more research support for the idea that interference plays a role in forgetting information in long-term memory (Bahrick & Phelps, 1987; Keppel & Underwood, 1962; Altmann & Schunn, 2002).

Proactive and Retroactive Interference

Recall that interference occurs when a memory is displaced by other information. In the long-term store, either older memories or newly learned information can interfere with recall. For example, let's say you were taking a test on educational psychology and were having difficulty remembering one of Piaget's cognitive stages. In an attempt to recall the first of Piaget's stages (the sensorimotor stage), you inadvertently keep remembering a similar example from another theorist you learned about the semester before in child psychology (Freud's oral stage). In this case, the earlier memory is interfering with your attempts to recall the information from your

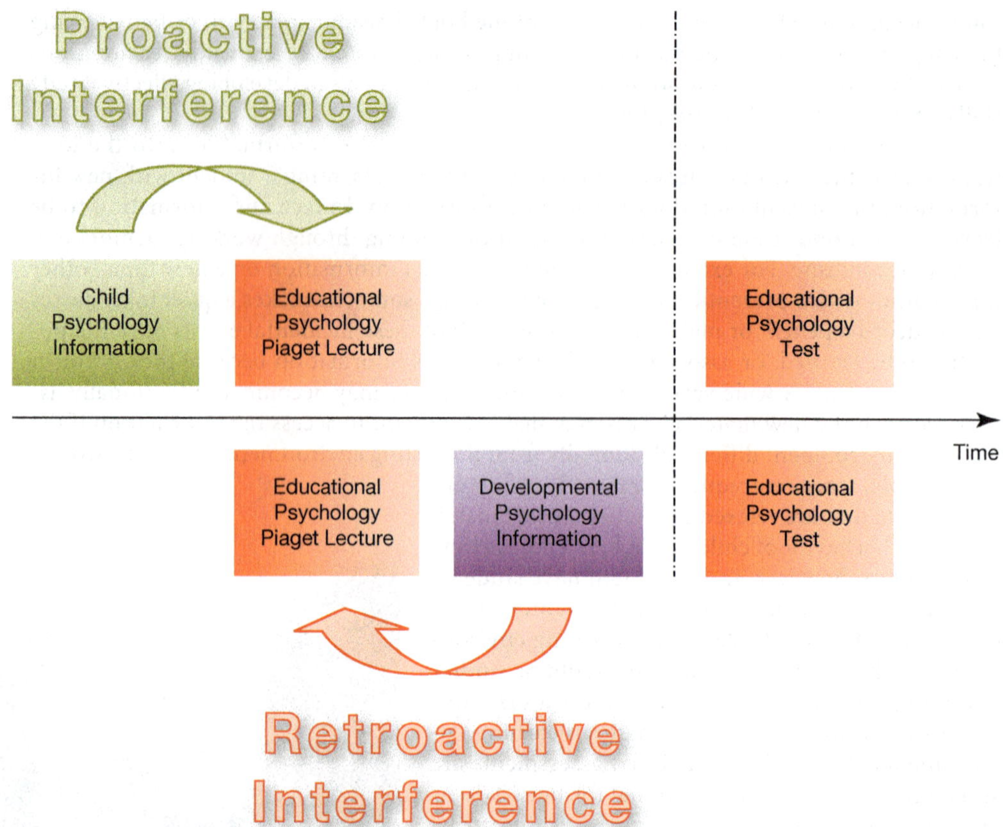

Figure 5.5

Proactive Interference and Retroactive Interference

Proactive interference

Older memories interfering with your attempts to recall information

Retroactive interference

Newer memories interfering with your attempts to recall information

current class. This type of interference is called **proactive interference** and is illustrated in Figure 5.5. Alternatively, a newly learned piece of information may interfere with the recall of an older memory. Using the same example above, let's say you just learned about Piaget's stages today in your educational psychology class, and later in the week you learn about Freud's stage theory of development in a developmental class. If, when you sit down to take your educational psychology test, you have trouble with questions related to Piaget because you keep remembering the material related to Freud, you are experiencing retroactive interference. **Retroactive interference** occurs when new information interferes with recall of previously learned information and is also illustrated in Figure 5.5. Thus, proactive interference occurs when past learning affects future learning, and retroactive interference occurs when newer learning affects past learning. Both types of interference have been shown to play a significant role in forgetting from the long-term store (Wahlheim & Jacoby, 2011).

Retrieval Cues

Retrieval cue

Information or some aspect of the environment that helps you recall a memory

While interference clearly plays a role in some cases of forgetting, a lack of retrieval cues may also influence whether or not we are able to recall a specific piece of information (Nairne, 2000). A **retrieval cue** is simply information or some aspect of the environment that helps you recall a memory. Have you ever walked down the hall to get something and then drawn a complete blank about what you are supposed to be looking for? In order to remember, you have to walk back to wherever you were, and maybe even reengage in whatever task you had been working on, before you can remember the item. This is an example of what happens when we don't have the appropriate retrieval cues to access specific information. The issue of retrieval cues underscores the importance of developing effective encoding skills. That is, remembering information is strongly related to how we learned the information in the first place. Have you ever had the experience of studying hard for an exam, knowing that you have learned the information, and then being unable to answer the questions on the test? Sometimes, this is due to **encoding specificity**, or memorizing the information in a specific way. For example, what if you memorized the fact that the capacity of short term memory is around seven items, and then were presented with a multiple choice question which did not include the number seven anywhere in the answer. In your studying for the test, you used the number seven as your memory tag. In a sense, you filed the memory with the expectation that the retrieval cue of the number seven would prompt your memory, and without it, you are unable to answer the question correctly. Perhaps the answer choices included "five to nine items" instead of 7 ± 2 and you failed to recognize the similarity.

Encoding specificity

Storing memories in a specific way which may limit recall to certain situations

Multiple-choice exams provide retrieval cues, which may allow you to recognize the learned information, as long as the memory tags you used match the cues provided in the question. Essay-based tests, on the other hand, require you to recall information in long-term memory with fewer retrieval cues. Many students, therefore, perceive recall based exams as more difficult. This is, in fact, supported by research, which shows performance is often better on recognition tests that provide retrieval cues (Lockhart, 2000). While this may be true in general, some recognition based test items may be more difficult than others, due to the similarity or degree of correctness of alternative responses. In this way, problems with retrieval cues and interference can work together to make learned information difficult to recall. For example, some alternatives on multiple-choice tests contain correct information, but it just doesn't apply to the particular question. In this case, several of the alternative answers may be recognized as correct, causing recall of information that does not pertain to that particular question to interfere with your memory for the correct response. In the next section, we'll explore the concept of knowledge formation in more detail.

SUMMARIZE AND REFLECT

1. One of the most cited models of memory is the information-processing model of memory. This model conceptualizes memory as a process, with information moving from sensory memory to working memory and finally to long-term memory.
2. According to this model, the roles of attention and perception in moving information from sensory memory to working memory are highlighted.
3. One of the components of this memory model is working memory. Working memory has a very limited capacity and duration.
4. Rehearsal and chunking are important working memory processes for holding information. There are important differences between maintenance and elaborative types of rehearsal.
5. Working memory can be divided into three sub-components: the phonological loop, the visuospatial sketchpad, and the central executive.
6. Long-term memory potentially has an unlimited capacity and duration. The cognitive processes of elaboration, organization, and context form the basis for strategies to keep information from getting lost in the vast expanse of long-term memory.
7. Forgetting is an issue for memories held in the long-term store. There are theories based on decay, interference, and retrieval cue failure.

INFORMED APPLICATION

1. The concept of chunking is important for teachers. Teaching students to develop sound associations between related sources of information helps students conceptualize broader amounts of information. Using the information from the text, develop an instructional plan where the teacher uses an understanding of chunking to teach more effectively.
2. Consider a science teacher giving a lecture on gravity. How can students use the concept of elaboration to more effectively retain the information?

THE ORGANIZATION OF KNOWLEDGE AND MEMORY

As we've seen, humans have a remarkable ability to retain information, but the formation of accessible long-term memories is a complicated process requiring the efficient use of a number of cognitive activities. Successful retention of life experiences leads to an accumulation of information over time. This accumulation of information results in **knowledge**.

Knowledge

The accumulation of memories over time into a complex, but highly organized body of information

Multiple Types of Knowledge

Knowledge is formed in a systematic and organized fashion. If all our memories were stored in a simplistic organizational structure, perhaps in the order they were learned, recall would be difficult and extremely time consuming. Think about the memory storage of a typical computer. Most computers simply record information in a sequential fashion, starting at the center of the hard disk and working out toward the edge. Searching such an organizational system is inefficient and usually takes a considerable amount of time. To test this idea, try closing out of a word processing document and then using the search feature to find it on the hard drive. Although you were just using the file, the search is not likely to be instantaneous although computers are improving at a remarkable rate, becoming more "human-like" every year.

In human terms, conducting a search for information across the entire long-term memory store would be inefficient. Imagine always needing to pause before you are able to answer a friend's question or to recall the necessary steps to take when your car begins to slide in the snow or rain. Luckily, we don't have to search the entire long-term memory store for a specific piece of information; instead, we have the ability to store and retrieve memories in a highly organized manner. This section will examine this organization of information, emphasizing the presence of at least three distinct knowledge stores—declarative, procedural, and conditional.

Declarative Knowledge

Declarative knowledge

Information that can be stated or declared

Declarative knowledge is information that can be stated or declared. For example, if you were asked to define the word *lion*, you would need to access declarative knowledge. Perhaps you would recall that lions are mammals, have large manes, are carnivores, and live in Africa. Think about the information you are learning in this class, the lecture you might someday give in your social studies class on the civil war, or even the conversation you had with your roommate about your date the previous night. All of these situations involve the use of declarative knowledge, things you know and can easily state. Declarative knowledge can be sub-divided into two types: episodic and semantic (Tulving, 1993).

Episodic knowledge

Personal information that is tied to a specific time and place

Episodic knowledge is personal information that is tied to a specific time and place (Conway, 2009; Eichenbaum, Sauvage, Fortin, Komorowski, & Lipton, 2011). For example, your relaying the events of last night's date to your roommate involves an episodic memory. It is a personal memory, grounded in events, which took place at a specific time and place. Compare this type of information to your definition of the word *lion*. The meaning of the word lion is unlikely to involve episodic memories. For example, let's say you answered the question with the fact that lions were mammals. Where were you when you learned this information—in class, at home, visiting the zoo? Most of us are unable to remember the exact time and place we learned that lions were mammals. The knowledge appears to be disconnected from the episode in which it was learned; therefore, we would not consider the knowledge episodic. This is quite different from the knowledge you have of your daily life events. These episodic memories are a rich documentary of your life and are clearly tied to locations and specific times in your life.

The concept of schema was first encountered in Chapter 2 during a discussion of Piaget's developmental theory.

Semantic knowledge

Information made up of memories for specific facts, regardless of the time and place the facts were learned

Schema

The way we appear to organize related semantic memories together

Semantic knowledge is made up of memories for specific facts, regardless of the time and place the facts were learned. For most of us, the knowledge that lions are mammals is a semantic memory. Semantic knowledge allows us to apply meaning to the word *lion*, without basing that meaning on a location or specific time in our lives. Much of our knowledge appears to operate in this manner, and we appear to organize related semantic memories into **schema**.

Recall, we first encountered the term *schema* in our discussion of Piaget in Chapter 2. Piaget used the term *schema* to refer to a body of related information, and semantic memories, which are organized together because they are related in some way, are called schemas. For example, you probably have a schema for what a college class is like, containing information on lectures, note taking, group work, etc. Research shows that our schemas may actually influence what we think, see, or hear as we go about our lives. For example, one study had students learn a list of words, which were all related to bedtime (e.g., nightstand, bed, alarm, moon, etc.). The list consisted of more than twenty words, so students found it difficult to remember all the words due to the limitations of working memory. The words they did recall proved to be quite interesting. In addition to the recall of words presented, participants in the study frequently recalled different words associated with bedtime, such as *pillow*, which were not mentioned in the list. These responses were explained in terms of schemas. The participants appeared to have a schema for bedtime that included some of the stated words, as well as some words not stated. While the students in this experiment made errors in their recall of the list, there is usually practical value to using one's schema in daily life.

By using existing schema, we can respond to incomplete information in appropriate ways. For example, when a teacher says to his class, "Complete items three to fifteen on page 74," he does not include in his directions some important steps for completing the task. Although the teacher did not explicitly state it, students are expected to locate a piece of paper and a pencil and record their answers to the questions on the paper. They do this without being told because they have a *schema* for answering workbook items. The schema allows them to behave as expected, despite incomplete information. In fact, if asked whether the teacher told them to take out a piece of paper and pencil, many students would probably answer, "Yes."

Building upon schema-based research, knowledge experts and neuroscientists have begun to develop an even more elaborate framework for understanding semantic knowledge called semantic networks. **Semantic networks** are representational structures designed to explain the relation between items within a schema (Goni et al., 2011). Figure 5.6 shows a simple semantic network. A simple model is easier to understand, but complex models better capture the incredible interconnectedness of our semantic knowledge.

Semantic networks

Representational structures designed to explain the relation between items within a schema

The semantic network model assumes that our knowledge is highly interconnected and that recall of any particular item causes a more general activation of all related concepts. Graphically, this activation is represented by a series of interconnected nodes. The **nodes** are specific elements within the semantic network representing concepts like *people* or *world*. The connections represent the activation trends occurring after a particular node is activated. A longer line means it takes a longer period of time to activate the next node. In general, the graphical model is created such that longer connectors mean a weaker connection between the two nodes. To help clarify this process, consider the following studies.

Nodes

Specific elements within the semantic network representing concepts

Research examining how long it takes to recall a word following the activation of another word supports semantic network theory. For example, if you were asked the question, "What is a monkey's favorite fruit?" you might respond "banana." This causes the node for banana to become activated, which in turn causes a *spreading activation* to all nodes connected to bananas. Research shows that if you have previously activated the node for banana, you will respond more quickly to any question to which the answer is semantically related. For example, you would respond faster to the question, "What is the traditional gift given from student to teacher?" than the question, "What is the capitol of the United States?" This is because the connector between banana and apple is much shorter (stronger) than the connector between banana and Washington, DC (weaker).

Over time, the conceptual basis for semantic networks has been broadened to incorporate newer research on brain anatomy and physiology. These newer theories have gone beyond theoretical networks and have based knowledge storage and retrieval on our understanding of how the brain actually works. This led to the development of Connectionist Networks and

Figure 5.6

A Simple Semantic Network

Connectionist network theorists

Theorists that have related knowledge storage and retrieval to the actual functioning of the neuron

Parallel Distributed Processing theories. **Connectionist network theorists** have related knowledge storage and retrieval to the actual functioning of the *neuron*. As we reviewed in Chapter 2, neurons are the basic building blocks of the brain and function by sending signals to other neurons. There are literally billions of neurons in the brain, and communication across neurons appear to function in a parallel fashion with millions and millions of neurons communicating with each other at the same time. This parallel activity gives rise to our remarkable ability to respond to even extremely complicated environmental stimuli with great speed and flexibility. Consider for example, the simple semantic network presented in Figure 5.6. How is the node for *people* represented at the level of the brain? The theoretical concept of the "people node" is probably a vast collection of interconnected neurons firing in a particular configuration. It is unlikely that a node for *people* actually exists in a particular location in the brain. Instead, it exists as collection of many brain cells communicating in a unique way. According to this theory, the interconnectedness of the neuronal cells *is* the node for the concept of people. This neural circuit is then connected to other interconnected sets of neurons related to people. As you can see, viewing semantic memories in terms of the way neurons operate is significantly more complicated than even the complex visual depiction of a semantic network illustrates. This model does, however, begin to conceptualize memory in a way that better represents the complexity of human cognition, leaving the computer metaphor far behind.

As you can see, declarative knowledge represents an important part of our knowledge base, but it is only one part. When you first started reading about declarative knowledge, you probably thought all memories were declarative. After all, if you can't say what you know, then you must not really know it. Actually, research supports at least two other knowledge stores that do not lend themselves to verbal declaration: procedural and conditional knowledge.

Procedural Knowledge

Procedural knowledge is typically referred to as *how to* knowledge because it involves knowledge of how to perform certain actions. Sometimes, we are able to perform an activity that we cannot describe in words. Consider, for example, something as simple as riding a bicycle. If you were asked to write down a step-by-step guide to riding a bicycle, you would quickly find that verbalizing the procedure is quite difficult. Imagine the complexity of such a guide. You would have to describe how to mount the bicycle, which way to face, how to put your feet on the pedals, and how to balance while you move your feet in an alternating pattern—all the while steering effectively using the handlebars. While these steps are each important for riding a bicycle, do they adequately describe what you have to do to ride one? Could someone who has never ridden a bicycle read our description and ride away happily? Obviously, that would not be likely. This difficulty in verbally describing how to ride a bicycle is typical of procedural knowledge because this type of knowledge is not coded verbally. Instead, it is coded as an automated sequence of actions that have to change as a function of environmental demands, such as having a tree in your biking path. To demonstrate your knowledge of bike riding, you would simply need to get on a bicycle and start riding. In the classroom, many tasks require procedural knowledge, including such activities as cutting, writing, and typing. Procedural knowledge may also be of particular concern for physical education teachers, since the coordination of motor skills is required for most activities.

Procedural knowledge
"How to" knowledge that involves knowledge of how to perform certain actions

Conditional Knowledge

A final type of knowledge to consider is **conditional knowledge**, or knowledge about the appropriate application of procedural and declarative information. For example, think about how you speak to children versus how you speak to your peers. In all likelihood, you make substantial changes to both the content and structure of your speech, depending on the audience. How do you know to do this? Similarly, when you have to figure out how to put a set of fifty chairs into five rows, how do you know whether to multiply or divide? Conditional knowledge allows you to know which conditions necessitate the use of specific actions.

Conditional knowledge
Knowledge about the appropriate application of procedural and declarative information

A teacher's conditional knowledge is highly important for effective teaching. When students experience difficultly with a particular lesson, for example, how does the teacher know how to help them? Perhaps the students simply misunderstood the lesson, and all the teacher needs to do is repeat the original explanation. Perhaps they need a few minutes of independent practice, to watch a model solve the problem, or to work with a more knowledgeable peer. Teachers often need to consider a multitude of different educational approaches to find the one appropriate for the given student. Finding the correct approach accomplishes two important things. First, it helps the students' progress and supports their learning. Second, it also helps to facilitate the teacher's conditional knowledge base. The teacher now knows how to provide appropriate instructional support for this particular problem or misunderstanding. Over time, successful teachers build a conditional knowledge base of teaching techniques that work for children with very different individual learning needs over a variety of situations. Advancement of this type of knowledge helps novice teachers move toward becoming expert teachers.

Procedural knowledge is knowledge of how to perform certain tasks. Sometimes, we are able to perform a task but cannot describe what we did.

As we have seen in this section, our declarative, procedural, and conditional knowledge stores are comprised of different types of information and are important for different cognitive and behavioral tasks. We have not yet explored, however, how these different types of knowledge develop. In the next section, we will discuss the development of each type of knowledge, as well as techniques for improving students' ability to use these knowledge stores effectively.

Building Knowledge and Improving Memory

Earlier in the chapter, we outlined the important roles of elaboration, organization, and context in learning new information, describing how this information accumulates over time forming our knowledge base. In this section, we will further explore the development of knowledge, focusing on techniques for increasing and optimizing declarative, procedural, and conditional knowledge.

Mnemonics

Mnemonics

Term generally applied to a wide variety of techniques used to improve memory

Mnemonics (ni-'mä-niks) is an unusual word generally applied to a wide variety of techniques used to improve memory. Mnemonics are used to enhance recall of memories from our declarative knowledge base. As we discussed earlier, we naturally organize our memories when we transfer them to long-term memory. This organization, however, varies widely in quality and effectiveness. Like most skills, we can learn to organize information in such a way as to make it more accessible later. Mnemonics are techniques that organize information via specific forms of elaboration. Recall elaboration is the process of connecting new information to information already well learned. The particular type of elaboration varies according to the mnemonic used. For example, the most common mnemonic is the **acronym approach**. This approach works well with simple lists. To help memorize the information, the first letter of each item on the list is taken and rearranged to form a familiar word. In keeping with the notion of elaboration, the idea is that the word you form is very familiar to you and difficult to forget. If you can create a strong association between the acronym and the list, the familiarity with the word will help you recall the list. For example, when memorizing the sequence of operations to perform in an algebra problem, the acronym FOIL (First, Outer, Inner, Last) can be very useful and is difficult to forget.

Acronym approach

A mnemonic where the first letter of each item on the list is taken and rearranged to form a familiar word

The difficulty with the acronym approach is that this type of elaboration does not require a very meaningful association between the material to be learned and the information in long-term memory. In the FOIL example, the word is completely unrelated to algebra. This may make the approach less effective for learning conceptual types of information. Similarly, anatomy students are familiar with learning the names of the cranial nerves by using the acronym *On Old Olympus' Towering Tops, A Finn And German Viewed Some Hops* (olfactory, optic, oculomotor, trochlear, trigeminal, abducens, facial, acoustic, glossopharyngeal, vagus, spinal accessory, hypoglossal). While this is effective for memorizing the names of the cranial nerves, it is not really helpful in learning the function or position of each of the nerves.

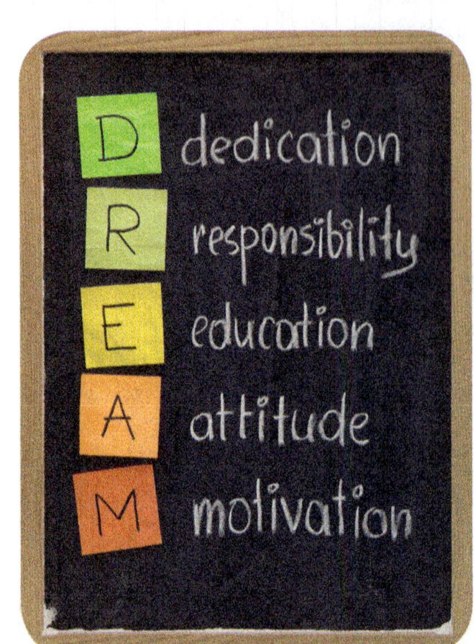

Mnemonics that use visual imagery are also very effective in facilitating recall (Paivio, 1986). Visual mnemonics create a visual code for the information being learned, in addition to the more common auditory code. This dual code approach enhances elaboration and facilitates recall. One common type of visual mnemonic is the **method of loci**. This is a memorization approach that is excellent for learning items that can be visualized (Cornoldi & DeBeni, 1996). The process begins with the individual imagining a familiar location, such as a path from home to work or a specific room. Once a clear image of the location is created, the individual then proceeds to create visual images of the new information and imbeds these images along the well-known path. For example, if you wanted to remember the colors of the rainbow you might create a mental image of your bedroom and then systematically "paint" the room the appropriate colors. Begin the process at a specific location, perhaps to the right of the door, and proceed to imbed the colors in some way along the edges of the room until you are back at the left side of the door. Perhaps you begin by painting the dresser to the right of the door a bright red. With the method of loci, it helps if you make the image unusual, so imagine the paint can as being ten times larger than normal and sitting in the center of the dresser dripping with paint. Continue to imbed the images around the room, one-after-the-other, until you reach the left side of the door. Once this is accomplished, all you need to do is take a mental walk around your room. To recall the information, start with the desk to the right of the door and simply "see" the first item you are trying to recall in the imbedded image. As with the acronym method, this technique typically works well for concrete nouns, which are easy to imagine, and need to be recalled in a specific order.

Method of loci

A memorization approach that is excellent for learning items that can be visualized

Another popular visual technique is the **keyword method**. This mnemonic is particularly useful if you are trying to use a visualization technique for remembering more abstract words. To use this approach you first think of an easily visualized word that sounds like the abstract word you are trying to remember. This easily visualized word becomes the *keyword*, acting as the key or gateway to the phonetically similar abstract word. Next, you relate the definition of

Keyword method

A mnemonic that is particularly useful if you are trying to use a visualization technique for remembering more abstract words the abstract word to the keyword. At this point, recall of the keyword should lead to the associated definition. For example, let's say you are trying to remember the definition for the word *exigent* (which means demanding). An appropriate keyword would be *exit*, because it is similar to the first part of the word. Now, imagine a door with a large exit sign and standing at the door is your professor *demanding* your research paper. The next time you see the word exigent, you will probably remember the keyword exit, the exit sign and door, and the professor demanding the paper. This process led you to the definition, "demanding." This mnemonic has been shown to be particularly effective for learning foreign language words (Bellezza, 1996). Other mnemonics involving imbedding to-be-learned information in a familiar visual image have also shown promise in learning foreign language alphabet letters (Shmidman & Ehri, 2010).

Automating Knowledge

Another way to improve memory and build a solid knowledge base is to create automated sources of knowledge. This is particularly true for procedural memories. Recall that procedural knowledge consists of how-to memories, like *how to* ride a bicycle. The development of procedural knowledge, however, takes practice before it becomes automatic. Often, we need to break complex activities into smaller parts so that students can practice individual steps before being able to perform a complex activity (Ericcson & Chalmers, 1994). Consider writing in cursive, for example. We can't just tell students how to write neatly and legibly in cursive. Instead, we teach them how to write each individual cursive letter, and they need a significant amount of practice before they can reliably form the letters correctly. As is often the case with procedural learning, observing a model actually performing the desired behavior and then having time to practice is an important component in teaching handwriting (Wright & Wright, 1980).

While cursive writing is at first slow and laborious, with practice it becomes an automatic process that requires little thought. The same is true for other types of procedural knowledge, from dribbling a basketball to typing on a word processor. Thus, accessing procedural knowledge becomes automatic over time, leaving more of our limited cognitive resources available for other tasks. Think about how often you engage in a procedural activity, like driving a car, while simultaneously engaging in another task, like carrying on a conversation or reading a map for navigation. It is relatively easy for most individuals to think about a wide range of things while riding a bike or driving a car because these activities do not require active cognitive resources. In other words, you are able to use your procedural knowledge without having to actively think about it.

The path to automation of procedural memories begins with the *cognitive stage* (see Figure 5.7). At this point in the process, each step of the procedure still requires active cognitive resources. That is, we still have to think about each step in the procedure. Let's go back to the example of learning to write. When a child first begins to write, he has to really think about how to hold the pencil correctly, requiring a significant portion of his cognitive resources. These thoughts directly compete with other thoughts, making it difficult to think about other aspects of the writing process. Over time and with repeated practice, holding the pencil correctly begins to become more automatic. Then, the child can pick up the pencil and write whole words correctly, without even thinking about how the pencil feels in his hand or having to look at model letters. He does, however, have to pay close attention to the spaces he puts between words. This is the *associative stage* of automating his procedural knowledge of writing. At this point, parts of the overall process have become automatic; however, he still has to actively think about the next step at certain key points, like when he finishes or begins a new word.

For most people it is relatively easy to perform multiple tasks at the same time, such as driving a car and reading a navigation system.

The final step in this process is the *autonomous stage*. This stage is the final integration of the whole process into one cohesive unit. When a child is able to write fluidly—without having to think about holding the pencil, forming the letters, or spacing the words—his procedural knowledge of writing has reached the autonomous stage. Now that writing is an automated script, he can think about the development of the ideas he wants to express more freely.

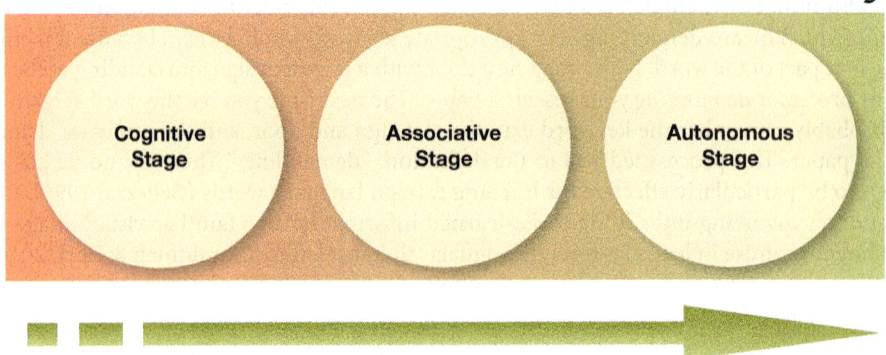

Figure 5.7
Procedural Memory

These automated scripts occur quite frequently as we go about our daily lives. Think about the last time you drove a car. What exactly were you doing while driving? How many traffic lights did you pass? Did you use your turn signal every time you changed direction? Chances are you have very little recollection of these specifics because your driving behavior is automated. In the same way, we develop automated knowledge of our daily routines. Have you ever noticed that at the beginning of the semester you have to check your schedule several times a day? Soon, you really won't have to look to see when or where you have class, as the routine becomes automated. In the same way, many students in a classroom may feel overwhelmed at the beginning of the school year, finding it difficult to manage a new, complicated daily routine. Teachers can assist students in developing automated knowledge regarding the daily routine by breaking the day into steps or component parts and making sure they deviate as little as possible from the set routine during the initial stages of learning. Automatization allows students to divert more cognitive resources toward their studies and daily activities, instead of having to focus on what is supposed to be happening next.

In The Classroom

APPLYING THEORY

Procedural Knowledge

THEORY BASICS

As discussed in the textbook, procedural knowledge is *how-to* knowledge. It is that aspect of knowledge that allows us to ride a bike or drive a car. The development of procedural knowledge is difficult, typically requiring significant mental effort as you begin to learn the skill. This necessity to actively think about each step in the overall process starts to fade as parts of the skill are learned and performed more automatically. Ultimately, the individual can participate in the activity with little conscious effort, freeing them to think about other things.

CLASSROOM APPLICATION

Educators typically overlook research on the development of procedural knowledge. Often it is difficult to recognize situations where well-developed procedural knowledge can help curricular goals. One type of educational environment, however, is a natural place to emphasize this important aspect of knowledge. Physical education has enjoyed increased attention as our nation realizes the importance of maintaining a healthy and active lifestyle. Physical fitness goals, however, are often difficult to maintain over time. Part of the problem stems from a failure to learn exercises properly. This leads to a struggle with the mechanics of the exercise program in addition to other barriers to success, like allocating time, establishing consistency, and avoiding injury.

(continues)

Teachers Help students develop procedural automaticity, which in turn helps students engage in more productive physical activities.

To apply theories on the development of procedural knowledge, it is important for the educator to recognize the overall process. Students are likely to become frustrated at the beginning of a learning task because they have to think about each step. This is often magnified when teachers demonstrate a skill. They see how the teacher performs the skill with relative ease, which serves to highlight their difficulty. The demonstration is important, but it is also important for the teacher to help the student understand the overall process. Emphasize that everyone has to "think" about the skill in the beginning. It is a necessary step toward the overall goal. Next, try to break the skill down into to smaller parts that are more manageable and help the student to appreciate when these smaller steps become more fluid and automatic. This helps motivate students as they realize they are indeed making progress. Continue to provide many opportunities for practice, and eventually you will have your students enjoying their new skills. They will be able to complete them with less cognitive effort, which allows them to fully enjoy the benefits of being active.

When and Where to Apply Knowledge

The third type of knowledge we introduced above was conditional knowledge, or knowledge about when and how to use declarative and procedural knowledge. Like declarative and procedural knowledge, conditional knowledge develops over time. Specifically, conditional knowledge builds as a series of condition-to-action rules (Anderson, 1995). In other words, we develop rules for ourselves regarding how to respond to specific situations or events, and we form these rules based upon our experience with the world. We try different behaviors and are met with differing levels of success. These experiences help us develop a pool of knowledge regarding the appropriateness of various actions across a wide range of conditions.

Teachers can help students develop this knowledge base by providing consistent feedback regarding behavior. Students need appropriate feedback across many situations to begin to appreciate the situational specificity of their actions. Knowing when to add or subtract when given a word problem, for example, depends on conditional knowledge. Without feedback regarding correct and incorrect performance on word problems, students have great difficulty learning to execute the appropriate manipulations. Classroom behavior also depends on conditional knowledge. Most students develop an understanding of what actions are appropriate in the classroom in the early grades. Even first graders know, for example, that bringing out a soccer ball during class and starting a game is inappropriate. Teaching students how to raise their hand to speak, wait in line, or ask for assistance can be more challenging, as these require a conditional knowledge store regarding a number of more ambiguous conditions.

SUMMARIZE AND REFLECT

1. Knowledge is the organized accumulation of information in memory.
2. There are three distinct knowledge stores: declarative, procedural, and conditional knowledge.
3. The declarative store consists of verbal memories, which can be stated or declared, differentiating between episodic and semantic memories.

(continues)

4. The semantic network model of memory includes the connectionist and parallel distributed processing theories of memory, which use the way neurons are organized and operate in the brain as a model for memory.
5. Procedural knowledge is knowledge of how to perform actions. This type of knowledge is nonverbal and automated, which makes it difficult to verbalize.
6. Conditional knowledge is knowledge about the situationally appropriate application of procedural and declarative knowledge.
7. Mnemonics are used for enhancing declarative memory. The acronym, method of loci, and keyword approaches were highlighted, giving classroom examples.
8. Improving procedural learning emphasizes the importance of breaking complex procedural activities into individual steps and providing opportunities for practice. The path to automatization of procedural memories starts with the cognitive stage, moves through the associative stage, and finally reaches the autonomous stage.
9. Conditional knowledge is a series of rules about how to respond to specific situations or events. These rules are based on experiences with the world. It is important for teachers to give appropriate feedback regarding correct and incorrect student performance to encourage the development of conditional knowledge.

INFORMED APPLICATION

1. You are teaching the states and their capitals. What can you do to help your students retain the information?
2. Consider how a well-developed knowledge base can help a graduating student perform in the work place.

METACOGNITION

Metacognition

A mental process everyone uses in their daily lives—thinking about our own thinking

Metacognition refers to a mental process everyone uses in their daily life—thinking about one's own thinking. What exactly does *thinking about thinking* mean? Consider the following example. Jared is a tenth grade student studying for his geometry test. Since he is having difficulty with the material, he stays after school to work with his teacher. His teacher decides that Jared understands the problems conceptually, but he does not check his work for accuracy. This leads him to get off track mid-way through a problem, and he ends up correctly solving the wrong problem. To address this issue, his teacher instructs Jared to ask himself the following question when he is halfway through a problem: *"How can I check to make sure I am on track?"* Upon the completion of each geometry problem, Jared is instructed to ask himself, *"What can I do to check the accuracy of my answer?"* These questions require Jared to think about his own thinking with regard to solving geometry problems. He might, for example, reflect on techniques such as working the problem backward or rechecking his math, in order to confirm his answer.

By asking himself these questions, Jared is using metacognitive knowledge, which helps him think and reflect on his own thought processes. This is similar to an individual observing a conversation between two friends. In a sense, he is putting himself in the position of being an outside observer of his own thinking and critically examining his thinking about geometry problems for appropriateness and effectiveness. Metacognition has traditionally been sub-divided into at least two distinct processes: metacognitive knowledge and metacognitive regulation, which often work together.

Metacognitive Knowledge

Metacognitive knowledge

Information we acquire about how thinking occurs

Flavell, in 1979, proposed that metacognitive knowledge was a distinct component of metacognition. **Metacognitive knowledge** is information that we acquire about how thinking occurs. Perhaps you have learned that studying in a lunchroom or common area is distracting, making it difficult for you to focus. When you study, you use this knowledge about your own cognitive processes to choose a specifically appropriate environment for studying. This knowledge about your own thinking is only one type of metacognitive knowledge. In fact, metacognitive knowledge can be further sub-divided into three areas: knowledge about how we think, knowledge about the nature of a given task, and knowledge about what strategy to use for a given task (Flavell, 1979, 1987).

The *first* sub-component of metacognitive knowledge is knowledge about how we think. Perhaps you know that you learn best visually, for example. This knowledge is metacognitive, allowing us to think about our own thinking and set up the environmental conditions that we know are effective. This aspect of metacognitive knowledge can be important for increasing learning, allowing us to recognize our own cognitive strengths and act accordingly. Usually, this occurs naturally, and we begin to structure our environments to maximize learning. For example, you may know that your approach to math tends to be haphazard, resulting in multiple errors, so you make sure that you always check your work. Similarly, you may recognize that writing seems to come naturally to you, so you choose a paper over an oral report.

Metacognition refers to our contemplation of our own thinking. It allows us to keep ourselves on track with specific tasks.

Sometimes, however, students do not easily develop metacognitive knowledge regarding their own learning, requiring direction in evaluating and building on cognitive strengths. Eight-year-old Steven, for example, has excellent verbal skills, but he has significant difficulty with math. He becomes frustrated when working only with numbers and symbols; yet, he does very well with word problems. Given this cognitive profile, Steven's teacher helps him interpret numbers as real-life representations. Later, as his math skills become automated, Steven's verbal interpretation of the numbers will no longer be required

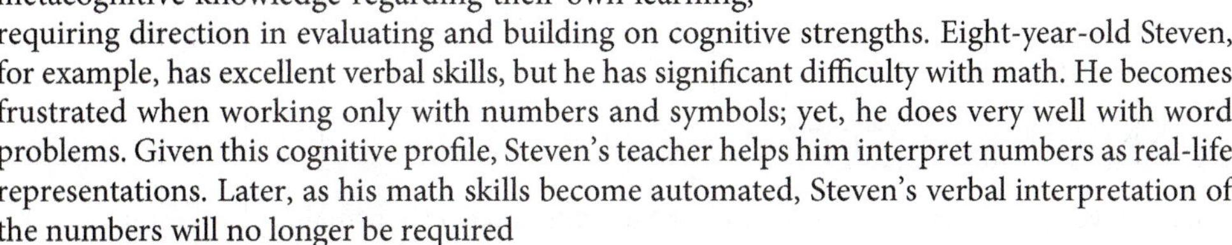

The *second* sub-component of metacognitive knowledge is knowledge about specific task variables, such as having the knowledge that spelling sentences will take much longer to complete than a reading worksheet. This type of metacognitive knowledge allows students to allocate their time more effectively. In the same way, we know that we can read a popular magazine cover to cover in less time than it takes to read a chapter of a textbook. Without this knowledge regarding the specific task demands, we would have considerable difficulty managing our daily assignments.

The *third* component of metacognitive knowledge relates to strategy use. Metacognitive strategies involve our awareness of available strategies for completing a task or solving a problem. Consider, for example, a student who frequently becomes confused regarding the appropriate sequence of steps in solving an algebra equation. By using the mnemonic "Please Excuse My Dear Aunt Sally," (Parentheses, Exponents, Multiplication/Division, Addition/Subtraction) when solving equations, she employs a metacognitive strategy to direct the process. Essentially, this strategy is a predetermined plan for helping solve the problem.

By using the mnemonic "Please Excuse My Dear Aunt Sally," (Parentheses, Exponents, Multiplication/Division, Addition/Subtraction) when solving equations, the student employs a metacognitive strategy to direct the process.

Metacognitive Regulation

Metacognitive regulation involves evaluating the outcome of our efforts to use metacognitive strategies (Livingston, 1997). This aspect of metacognition is essential for overseeing these processes and ensuring that a particular goal has been achieved. For example, the questions used by Jared in the beginning of this section represent his attempts to govern his geometry problem solving. The questions help him govern his thinking and move him closer to achieving his goal. Metacognitive regulation is an important part of the learning process. Without regulation, learning would be inefficient, with individuals having little control over the effectiveness of their learning. Metacognitive regulation typically involves planning a learning strategy, monitoring progress, and evaluating the effectiveness of the process (Brown, 1987; Nelson, 1996). Research has docu-

Metacognitive regulation
Evaluating the outcome of our efforts to use metacognitive strategies

mented that our ability to plan, monitor, and evaluate our learning develops over time as we become better able to direct our own learning (Cotterall & Murray, 2009).

Metacognitive Instruction

Like most skills, there is variation in the degree to which individuals naturally engage in metacognition. Most individuals engage in metacognition without explicit awareness of the process (Perner, 2000); however, providing explicit instruction in metacognition may prove effective (Sheid, 1993; Schneider, 2008). Typically, programs to enhance metacognitive abilities center on developing the ability to think in new and unique ways, to develop different strategies for approaching a task, and to better reflect on one's thinking. In addition to providing knowledge about how to use metacognitive thinking, it is also important to provide ample practice. Providing strategies without a structured program requiring practice typically results in less efficient cognitive control (Livingston, 1996). It is important to remember that metacognition is a natural process, which can be facilitated by explicit instruction, helping less successful students to become more aware of, and thereby better able to regulate, their own learning processes.

SUMMARIZE AND REFLECT

1. Metacognition is the higher-level process of thinking about our thoughts and decision-making processes.
2. This important aspect of human thinking can be divided into two distinct processes: metacognitive knowledge and metacognitive regulation.
3. Metacognitive knowledge consists of three important areas: knowledge of how we think, knowledge about the nature of a given task, and knowledge about what strategy to use for a given task.
4. Metacognitive regulation involves evaluating the outcomes of efforts to use cognitive and metacognitive strategies.
5. Metacognition is an important part of learning. Most individuals engage in metacognition without explicit awareness of the process.
6. Research on effective instruction in metacognitive strategies in the classroom illustrates that teaching metacognitive skills can help students to become more aware of, and better regulate, their own learning.

INFORMED APPLICATION

1. Consider a student that is having difficulty with writing essays on tests. What strategies can you develop to help his performance? Include strategies to improve his metacognitive knowledge, as well as his metacognitive regulation.

THE CHAPTER IN REVIEW

In this chapter, we explored cognitive views of learning. We started out by comparing the cognitive and behavioral perspectives on learning, emphasizing that both use scientific methods to explore answers to different questions. We discussed memory and knowledge as the foundation for cognitive research, and we reviewed research and theory regarding the basic processes involved in human memory and thinking. We outlined the information-processing model of human memory, which conceptualizes human memory as involving multiple stores. We took an in-depth look at sensory, working, and long-term memory stores, outlining cognitive processes involved in moving information from one store to another. We discussed research on getting information into long-term memory, as well as retrieval. We discussed the importance of organization of memories into specialized knowledge stores, exploring declarative, procedural, and conditional knowledge in detail. We also described the importance of each of these types of knowledge in the classroom and discussed strategies for increasing and optimizing declarative, procedural, and conditional memory. Finally, we discussed metacognition and the importance of students' thinking about their own thinking in the learning process, highlighting research on the teaching of metacognitive strategies to increase learning.

Interdisciplinary Case Focus

principal *special educator*
teacher *parents* *psychologist*
social worker *physical educator*
nurse *peers* *doctor*

Jack Johnson, a third grader in Mrs. Klein's classroom, is a creative and curious child, who has always excelled academically. At the beginning of the year, he showed a significant strength in his conceptual understanding of multiplication. In fact, Mrs. Klein often had Jack work collaboratively using manipulatives with other children who were having more difficulty. Manipulatives is a general term referring to any object the student can manipulate or handle (e.g., blocks) that helps them conceptualize a task. Recently, however, Jack has begun having trouble finishing his math assignments on time. Instead of looking forward to math time, as he did at the beginning of the year, Jack appears to try to avoid it. Mrs. Klein sits down with Jack as he works a set of simple multiplication practice sets, trying to figure out the nature of his problem. It quickly becomes apparent that Jack has not memorized his multiplication facts, working each problem by adding the numbers quietly. In fact, she notices that he actually counts on his fingers. Obviously, he never memorized his addition facts either. She initially thinks he must not have spent any time working to memorize the math facts since he easily commits information to memory in other subjects, such as social studies. She asks Jack if he has practiced at home with the flash cards they made in class earlier in the year. Jack becomes very upset, saying that he "hates those dumb cards" and starts to cry. Mrs. Klein decides to talk to Jack's parents regarding his attempts to memorize the multiplication facts, recognizing that this task has been quite difficult for him. She also seeks advice from several colleagues regarding ideas for helping to reduce Jack's newfound frustration with math.

Parent Jack's mother, Rita Johnson, tells Mrs. Klein that Jack has spent hours practicing with the flash cards. While he always came up with the right answer, it was never automatic. She could tell that he was "doing the math" in his head each time, so she tried using a time limit for each fact, moving on to the next card after ten seconds. This was very frustrating for Jack; and since he didn't seem to be having any problems finishing his math homework, they stopped working with the flashcards. She figured that he would just memorize the multiplication facts on his own after having to use them over and over again in class.

Teacher Dena Schefler, Mrs. Klein's colleague, who has been a third grade teacher for fifteen years, tells her that this problem is not uncommon. Many children, in her opinion, never memorize math facts completely, resulting in slower problem solving. She says that depending on the degree of memorization failure, this can become a much larger problem as students move on toward more complicated math problems. She recently attended a workshop on alternative strategies for teaching information traditionally learned via rote memorization, and suggested using mnemonics, visual imagery, music, and/or movement for increasing memorization success. She refers Mrs. Klein to the website, www.multiplication.com, for ideas regarding these strategies.

Psychologist Charles Farrell, the school psychologist, helps explain why Jack has trouble committing math facts to memory. He explains that when children try to memorize multiplication facts they usually have to do so without any elaborative cues. In other words, it's difficult to relate $8 \times 4 = 32$ to other memories they already have, since the math fact doesn't really have meaning except as a numerical operation. In contrast, information in social studies or reading is inherently more meaningful since the ideas are easy to imagine, sequence, and relate to a child's own experiences. He says that it is not impossible to strategically attach meaning to multiplication facts, however, and that there are many commercial packages for purchase. He knows of one, for example, which sets the multiplication tables to music. He encourages Mrs. Klein to read about strategies such as these on the website recommended by Ms. Schefler since many of them can be implemented without having to purchase a commercial product.

Mrs. Klein takes the advice of her colleagues and seeks out alternative strategies for helping Jack (and quite a few of the other children) to more easily memorize the multiplication tables. She finds a number of easy "tricks" to help students relate the facts to other meaningful information, including a number of simple rhymes, such as:

$2 \times 2 = 4$

Two shoes kicked the door, two times two equals four.

$3 \times 4 = 12$

One–two–three–four, One–two is three times four.

$3 \times 8 = 24$

A tree on skates fell on the floor, three times eight is twenty-four.

$5 \times 5 = 25$

Two fives jump off the high dive, five times five is twenty-five.

$6 \times 8 = 48$

Six asked eight for a date, six times eight is forty-eight.

$7 \times 7 = 49$

7×7 is 49, you are cool; you are fine!

$7 \times 8 = 56$

Five–six–seven-eight, Fifty-six is seven times eight.

She also finds a number of games to play with the students that are easy and fun, and they really seemed to help Jack. One of the most successful of these activities involved pinning a multiplication fact to each child's shirt and pretending their name for the day was the answer to the problem. Jack's shirt said $8 \times 4 =$, so he was 32 for the day. By calling each of the children by their "answer name" for a whole day, the entire class participated in the exercise and reinforced everyone's learning.

Finally, the website that Ms. Schefler recommended not only had information regarding alternative memorization strategies but also games and techniques for helping children visualize and understand the concept behind multiplication. She began to use these activities in class, and she sent home a newsletter for parents, suggesting specific activities to try at home.

Key Terms

TERM	Page	TERM	Page
Acronym approach	164	Memory	144
Attention	146	Metacognition	168
Bottom-up processing	149	Metacognitive knowledge	168
Central executive	153	Metacognitive regulation	169
Chunking	150	Method of loci	164
Cognitive perspective	142	Mnemonics	164
Conditional knowledge	163	Nodes	161
Connectionist network theorists	162	Perception	147
Decay theory	154	Phonological loop	151
Declarative knowledge	160	Proactive interference	158
Elaboration	155	Procedural knowledge	163
Elaborative rehearsal	151	Rehearsal	150
Encoding specificity	159	Retrieval cue	158
Episodic knowledge	160	Retroactive interference	158
Executive control processes	145	Schema	160
Gestalt psychologists	147	Semantic knowledge	160
Interference theory	154	Semantic networks	161
Keyword method	164	Sensory decay	146
Knowledge	144	Sensory memory	146
Knowledge	160	Top-down processing	149
Maintenance rehearsal	151	Working memory	149

6 Chapter

HIGHER-ORDER COGNITIVE LEARNING

What's It All About ...

How do students approach problem solving and critical thinking?

What is metacognition?
How does it affect studying?

What is transfer?
How does it contribute to meaningful learning?

Chapter Objectives

- Define a problem.
- Use problem-solving strategies.
- Understand the factors affecting problem solving.
- Understand problem-solving differences between experts and novices.
- Learn how to think critically.

- Understand metacognition and the impact on learning.
- Review effective study strategies.

- Describe the difference between general versus specific transfer.
- Describe a positive versus negative transfer.
- Understand factors affecting transfer.

EXTENDED OUTLINE

Higher-Order Cognitive Learning

I. What's It All About ...

II. From Today's Headlines

III. Problem Solving and Critical Thinking
   - A. Defining a problem
   - B. Problem-solving strategies
   - C. Factors affecting problem solving
     1. Surface versus deep structure
     2. Fixation versus flexibility
   - D. Differences between experts and novices
     1. Development of expertise
     2. Impact on education
   - E. Critical thinking
     1. Elements of thought
     2. Encouraging critical thinking through questioning
   - F. Summarize and reflect

IV. Metacognition and Study Strategies
   - A. Metacognition and learning
   - B. Study strategies
     1. Note taking and summarizing
     2. Scheduling and time management
     3. Teaching study strategies
   - C. Summarize and reflect

V. Transfer
   - A. General versus specific transfer
   - B. Positive, negative transfer
   - C. Strategies affecting transfer
     1. Learning context
     2. Similarity between learning and application
   - D. Summarize and reflect

VI. The Chapter in Review

VII. Interdisciplinary Case Focus

From Today's Headlines

Vol. I No. 6 Teaching World, 2012

HIGH QUALITY STANDARDS

A curriculum based on critical thinking can enlighten our students.
San Francisco Chronicle, October 14, 2007

Linda Darling-Hammond (Stanford University) believes we have a significant problem in America that is leading our nation to fall further behind other countries in educational achievement. Writing for the *San Francisco Chronicle,* Darling-Hammond contends that America's educational challenges stem from our focus on broad state standards that encourage little educational depth. For example, she compares questions on America's National Assessment of Educational Progress (NAEP) to questions asked on similar instruments in other countries. One of the NAEP biology questions asks students to identify two elements present in Earth's atmosphere from a list. A typical question on a similar test in Australia presents students with a narrative on how a virus works and then asks them to design a drug to kill the virus, explain how it works, and then design an experiment to test the drug.

Her comparison underscores a lack of emphasis on critical thinking skills, problem solving, and connecting content to real-world situations. She comments, "We need to encourage our schools to teach and evaluate the higher-order thinking and performance skills that leading nations emphasize in their systems ...."

MAKE THE CONNECTION

Dr. Darling-Hammond's article stresses the importance of fostering educational outcomes that go beyond memorization of facts. In this chapter, you will gain an appreciation for what it means to educate at this deeper level. In addition, you will learn about how students approach problems and how to enhance problem solving through effective strategies and critical thinking skills. You will also learn how to help students monitor their own thinking. Finally, we will look at the importance of transferring what we learn in one context to another. As you will see, learning to transfer knowledge creates active learners.

PROBLEM SOLVING AND CRITICAL THINKING

This chapter continues our look at cognitive psychology and its application to school settings. Specifically, we will examine cognitive abilities that lead to higher levels of learning. That is, learning that goes beyond basic factual learning. Higher-level learning involves complex processes, which allow us to solve novel problems and think critically about information. Higher-level cognitions also make it possible for us to take our understanding of an existing problem and transfer it to a new problem. The term higher-order cognitive learning evolved out of a need for a general term to capture the range of thinking skills that transcend a particular subject. Every discipline (e.g., science, English, math, art, etc.) has a collection of knowledge, and it is vital that our schools continue to impart this information to our students. It is also exceedingly important to recognize that we have thinking skills, which go beyond these facts, that allow us to use this information in creative and dynamic ways. These skills include problem solving, critical thinking, creative thinking, and decision making among others. To capture this range of thinking skills, researchers began to use the collective term higher-order cognitive learning. Again, these are skills not rooted in a particular set of facts but are tools generally applied to produce desired outcomes (Underbakkee, Borg, & Peterson, 1993; Halpern, 1993; Struck & Little, 2011).

Defining a Problem

We will begin our look at higher-order thinking by examining how we solve problems. The first step in solving a problem is recognizing its presence and having the desire or need to seek a solution. In schools, this is typically a structured process guided by the teacher, but can also arise in any number of informal situations. Teachers can present problems as examples during a lesson, while students work in small groups, or during assessment. Consider a few typical problems students encounter in school.

SCIENCE CLASS—*Explain how a cruise ship is able to float on water.*

ENGLISH CLASS—*Write a persuasive argument supporting home schooling.*

PHYSICAL EDUCATION—*Describe the effects of Title IX on women's sports.*

MATH CLASS—*Mike is on a bike going 16 miles an hour. Sam is one mile ahead of Mike, traveling at 15 miles an hour. How long will it take Mike to catch up with Sam?*

What does a student think about when trying to come up with a solution to these problems? What went through your mind as you read the questions? Solving problems is not a set skill or approach. It is dependent on your prior knowledge of the topic, what you were just thinking about before you encountered the problem, and your ability to connect key elements of the current problem to similar problems you have solved in the past. For example, consider the science question presented above. In your attempt to solve the problem, you are likely to pay attention to the specific type of boat mentioned and your prior experience with such ships. You may also have recently read a book or article about cruise ships, which may influence your thinking about the problem. Additionally, you may recognize that the problem is similar to any problem involving one object displacing another. As you can see, all of these factors combine in unique and complicated ways to support your problem solving ability. Sometimes your unique perspective helps you move toward an appropriate solution. At other times, we seem to be prisoners of our experiences making it difficult to find solutions.

Ill-defined

Having many appropriate responses and multiple paths to achieving a solution

In trying to understand these complicated factors, first consider the overall nature of the problem. Some problems are **ill-defined**, which means there are many appropriate responses and multiple paths to achieving a solution (Jonassen, 1997; Shin, Jonassen, & MaGee, 2003;

Choi & Lee, 2008). The English and physical education problems presented above are examples of ill-defined problems. You could approach an essay on home schooling from multiple perspectives: academic, social, family, etc. Either of these approaches would be appropriate given the general nature of the stated problem. Other problems are more specific. **Well-defined problems** have a clear methodology designed to achieve a single correct answer. The math problem is the best example of a well-defined problem. There is a clear mathematical approach to achieve the correct answer. The science problem is somewhere in between an ill-defined and well-defined problem. The problem is stated with few facts, which leaves the students with some discretion when solving the problem. Still, there is one general conclusion that is the most appropriate answer, regardless of what ship is considered.

Well-defined

When problems have a clear methodology designed to achieve a single correct answer

Identifying whether a problem is well-defined or ill-defined is a good place to begin solving a problem. It gives you a sense of the quality of answer most appropriate to the situation. Often problems presented in an academic context are well-defined, particularly early in the learning process. The presence of a single correct answer gives students a clearly defined learning path. Teachers, however, need to exercise caution when giving *only* well-defined problems. Well-defined problems are well received by students because of their clear structure, but many (if not most) problems encountered in everyday life are not well-defined. Simple everyday problems, like the following, are often ill-defined: How do you get your cat out of the tree? How do you get to work when you car does not start? These are real issues, and students need exposure to solving these types of ill-defined problems.

Problem-Solving Strategies

Defining the problem at hand is an important first step. It creates boundaries around possible solutions and provides needed direction for effective problem solving. What follows is a search for an effective strategy to solving the problem. Researchers often divide general problem solving strategies into two areas: algorithms and heuristics. An **algorithm** is a specific series of steps leading from an initial problem to a predetermined end state. Algorithms are entirely domain or subject specific. This means that every subject will have algorithms specific to its subject matter. For example, you may have an algorithm in chemistry that provides instructions for taking certain ingredients and combining them to form a new substance. In mathematics, you may have an algorithm for solving a cross multiplication problem (Handa, 2009). Algorithms are advantageous because they always work; that is, they always lead to a solution. They can be complicated at times, and yet accurately following the algorithmic steps will lead to a correct solution.

Algorithm

A specific series of steps leading from an initial problem to a predetermined end state

Educational algorithms are beneficial because they give students clear steps to reach academic success (Lopez Fernandez & Velazquez Estrella, 2011). This potentially decreases anxiety and relieves performance pressures. It also helps teachers identify specific issues when students fail to accurately solve problems. They can guide students through a self-reflective process, identifying which steps were inappropriately applied. As you will see later in the chapter, this ability to reflect on one's own thought processes is important part of academic success.

Algorithms are powerful learning tools, but unfortunately most academic and real-life problems do not have such clear solutions. Everyday types of problems rarely have neat, clean solutions. To help students deal with these ill-defined problems, teachers use heuristic problem solving strategies. **Heuristics** are problem solving strategies that increase the probability of finding a solution, but do not guarantee a solution. For example, an English teacher may ask

Heuristics

Problem-solving strategies that increase the probability of finding a solution, but do not guarantee a solution

Teachers use problem solving strategies called heuristics to help students deal with ill-defined problems.

students to write a five-page paper on a controversial topic. He wants the students to write two pages on one side of the topic, two pages on the opposing side, and one page of personal opinion. This presents a *problem* for students. How do you gather information to support the two sides of the issue? What sources do you use? How do you integrate the information on the two sides of the issue with your personal opinion? These issues present students with multiple challenges. One popular heuristic approach in language arts courses involves the use of rubrics. **Rubrics** are traditionally thought of as scoring tools for subjective assessments (e.g., essays, short answers). For example, with the assignment above a teacher would set consistent criteria by which the paper would be graded. Rubrics, however, are also powerful instructional tools (De La Paz, 2009). Used in this way, rubrics serve as a general map to create informed strategies for approaching the paper. As mentioned above, this heuristic type of approach does not guarantee an outcome, but it can greatly increase assignment clarity and student comfort with the task. Another heuristic approach is called **subgoaling** (Altmann & Trafton, 2002; Anderson, Kushmerick, & Lebiere, 1993; Reed, 2000; Abrahamson, Trninic, Gutierrez, Huth, & Lee, 2011). This approach involves taking a larger task and breaking it down into smaller, more manageable steps. Using the research paper example, students could begin by listing each of the steps needed to complete the whole process: locating source materials for the first side, writing summaries of the sources, locating source materials for the opposing view, summarizing these sources, developing a personal opinion, and finally integrating the preceding steps into a cohesive paper. Once you have divided the overall task into specific sub-goals, you can focus more effectively on only the next step in the process. Students find this less overwhelming than trying to figure out how to write the whole paper as a single process.

Rubrics

Traditionally thought of as scoring tools for subjective assessments

Subgoaling

Taking a larger task and breaking it down into smaller, more manageable steps

Means-end analysis

A comparison between the final goal state and the current state

Another effective problem solving heuristic is **means-ends analysis**. Using this problem solving heuristic involves a comparison between the final-goal state and the current state. For example, in your Spanish class you are assigned a problem where you have to act out an everyday experience with a fellow student completely in Spanish. Initially this may seem intimidating, but you can use a means-ends analysis to achieve the final performance. Envision you and your partner in front of the class performing your skit. Ask yourself, what do we need to achieve the end product? You will likely think about deciding on a topic, writing a script, translating it into Spanish, and practicing your lines. Perhaps you will work on these things with your partner, or you may decide to divide the tasks and work independently. Regardless, completing any of these tasks will move you and your partner closer to the end goal of the actual performance. Focusing on decreasing the "distance" between where you are and where you want to be helps you work toward a problem solution.

Factors Affecting Problem Solving

There are several factors influencing a student's ability to solve problems. For example, the student may feel intimidated by a problem because it is novel and not within his current life experience. He might actually possess the necessary skill to solve the problem, but fails to do so, fearing the problem is beyond his ability. At other times, problems seem similar to past events, but the apparent similarity blocks the student's ability to develop creative solutions. Students not only need to learn problem-solving skills, they also need to become sensitive to these additional elements affecting their ultimate success.

Surface versus Deep Structure

Surface structure

The superficial structure of a problem

Surface structure refers to the superficial structure of a problem. It is the structure presented by the description of the problem. To illustrate surface structure, consider the following problems:

PROBLEM 1—*Why are diamonds so expensive?*

PROBLEM 2—*Why do countries regulate how many fish are caught in the ocean?*

On the surface, these two problems appear quite different. The first one is about money and diamonds. The second involves fishing regulations. Students are likely to look at these two problems very differently because their content is different. The first problem is likely to start students thinking about money, rich people, expensive cars, etc. The second problem is likely to start the students thinking of animals, humane treatment, global protection, etc. There is, however, a common element underlying the answer to each problem. This common element is both problems' deep structure. **Deep structure** refers to an underlying principle behind the solution to a problem. In both of these problems, there is an issue of supply and demand. An understanding of how supply affects demand explains both situations. Diamonds are rare and in great demand. Their scarcity combined with high demand enables diamond sellers to charge high prices. Similarly, as the seas are over-fished, fish become scarce. This combined with great worldwide demand for seafood causes prices to increase. To prevent fish from becoming too expensive, governments closely regulate the amount of fish caught over a given period. Again, the reason for the regulation of fish catching is the same as the reason for expensive diamonds: they are both situations involving the principle of supply and demand.

Deep structure

An underlying principle behind the solution to a problem

It is important for students to develop an ability to recognize the deep structure of a problem. It is not that the surface structure is unimportant; however, a failure to recognize the deep structure of a problem makes it difficult for students to learn a particular problem solving approach and apply it to new situations. The surface structure brings up related memories and directs students to think in a certain way. In addition, students need awareness that the surface structure may not efficiently lead to a correct solution. Recognition of this fact encourages students to reevaluate problems, looking for deep structure meaning. In fact, it is the underlying premise of education that learning in the school context will transfer to situations outside of school—despite apparent surface structure differences.

Fixation versus Flexibility

Another potential problem with solving problems is functional fixedness. **Functional fixedness** refers to an inability to move beyond the established understanding of an object, which is necessary to solve a problem. The term originated more than fifty years ago from a group of German psychologists interested in problem solving (Dunker, 1945). What they found is that people often have perceptions or ways of thinking about objects (e.g., thumb tack, candle, box, etc.) when solving a problem, but they have difficulty modifying their thoughts beyond the object's *intended* use. For example, imagine you are standing on a ladder mounting a new lighting fixture to the outside of your house. You are trying to read the instructions while you work, but the wind keeps blowing the paper off the ladder. In this case, you might not immediately think to use the hammer in your tool belt to weigh the paper down because that is not how you typically use a hammer. Similarly, students have difficulty finding solutions to problems because their prior knowledge limits their ability to look at the problem from a novel perspective. Interestingly, this phenomenon does not appear to be unique to industrialized nations, as studies have shown that functional fixedness is evident in indigenous people from Ecuador with little exposure to modern life (German & Barrett, 2005).

Functional fixedness

An inability to move beyond the established understanding of an object, which is necessary to solve a problem

Overcoming functional fixedness requires students to maintain mental flexibility. They need to move beyond the intended or standard use of an object. They also need to recognize that the typical approach to a problem is not necessarily the *correct* approach. Problems often require novel solutions, particularly as you move beyond basic classroom learning and apply learning to real life problems. This means it is important to find ways to move beyond typical solutions to problems to avoid functional fixedness (Isaksen, Dorval, & Treffinger, 2011). One technique is to analyze problem solving strategies into components (Carnevale, 1998). For example, a teacher may have a typical approach to dealing with a student who is failing. This approach, however, may not be working for a particular student, necessitating a different strategy. The teacher should reorganize the problem by looking at her current approach and breaking it down to individual components (e.g., notes home to parent, homework assignment book, study guides, etc.). The teacher should ask herself "What is the function of each component? Can that particular function be modified or used in a different way?" Thinking of each step in isolation may help her develop other tools to accomplish the same function. Developing alternative solutions helps teachers move away from fixating on a single correct solution to a problem.

Differences Between Experts and Novices

Learning to avoid fixation by maintaining a flexible mindset is part of a larger process of moving from novice to expert. Investigating differences between novices and experts is an exciting and vibrant area of research. An expert is an individual that has reached a high level of performance in a particular area through experience (Foley & Hart, 1992). There are two important elements to this definition. First, experts are typically only "experts" in a particular domain. That is, they are not experts in everything, only experts in a particular area, skill, or academic subject. Second, their expertise is the result of years of experience in the field. Experts are not born; they are created through extensive deliberate practice (Ericsson & Lehmann, 1996; Harre, Bossomaier, & Snyder, 2011). Through experiences within their area, experts learn to set clear goals, engage in repeated practice, and pay close attention to feedback regarding quality of learning attempts (Ericsson, Krampe, & Tresh-Romer, 1993). There are many studies comparing experts to novices in an effort to understand the nature of an exceptional learning outcome. To begin our examination of this research, we will detail key principles that characterize the functioning of experts (see Table 6.1). These key principles draw from two widely cited reviews of expertise (Feltovich, Prietula, & Ericsson, 2006; National Research Council, 1999).

Experts are typically only "experts" in one area; for example, you wouldn't visit the doctor to get your car fixed.

As indicated in the table, there are several principles that define expertise. First, experts are able to identify meaningful patterns that are unavailable to their novice counterparts. Their expertise gives them a more productive lens with which to view the situation. For example, Table 6.2 shows what experts and novices notice while watching a classroom video. As you can see, experts have a far more developed sense of what is really going on in the video. Experts also better organize their knowledge. They center knowledge of their domain of expertise on big ideas or theories. This provides a far better framework for interpreting problems. Figure 6.1

Table 6.1 Key Principles of Expertise

	Key Word(s)	Associated Principle	
1	Notice	EXPERTS…	… notice different things compared to novices.
2	Deep Understanding		… organize their knowledge more meaningfully.
3	Conditionalized		… are better at retrieving relevant knowledge.
4	Effort		… retrieve relevant knowledge with less attentional effort.
5	Expertise ≠ Expert Teacher		… do not necessarily have an ability to teach effectively.
6	Flexibility		… have varying levels of flexibility in their approach to new situations.

Table 6.2 What Expert and Novice Teachers Saw When Watching the Same Classroom Video

Video Tape of Classroom	Information *Experts* Derived from Watching the Video	Information *Novices* Derived from Watching the Video
Scene 1	On the left monitor, the students' note taking indicates that they have seen sheets like this and have had presentations like this before. It's fairly efficient at this point because they're used to the format they are using.	I can't tell what they are doing. They're getting ready for class, but I can't tell what they're doing.
Scene 2	I don't understand why the students can't be finding out this information on their own rather than listening to someone tell them because if you watch the faces of most of them, they start out for about the first 2 or 3 minutes sort of paying attention to what's going on and then just drift off.	She's trying to communicate with them here about something, but I sure couldn't tell what it was.
Scene 3	I haven't heard a bell, but the students are already at their desks and seem to be doing purposeful activity and this is about the time that I decide they must be an accelerated group because they came into the room and started something, rather than just sitting down and socializing.	It is a lot to watch.

SOURCE: Sabers, Cushing, & Berliner (1991)

demonstrates cognitive maps generated by expert versus novice individuals after exposure to information on human motivation (Coco, 1999). The greater depth of the cognitive map from the expert allows them to extrapolate better ideas about human behavior.

Because of the qualities described above, experts are able to retrieve relevant (conditionalized) information more efficiently and with less attentional effort. This results in additional cognitive resources available to the expert. Greater cognitive resources translate into the potential for a more flexible approach to problem solving. There are challenges, however, to the realization of an expert's skill. For example, one study found that when expert *teachers* were taken out of their classrooms and placed in a laboratory where they had to provide a thirty-minute lesson on probability, they experienced extreme distress, anger, and other negative emotional states (Berliner et al., 1988). One teacher even quit the study. In general, they expressed the need for more time to prepare and that they did not know these students. Therefore, they could not provide the sensitive instruction they felt was appropriate. In other words, the teachers were able to express their expertise in their typical educational environments, but this ability did not necessarily translate to other situations. Similarly, *expertise* does not mean the expert (e.g., expert engineers, doctors, managers, etc.) can teach. There is a difference between knowing content (expertise) and possessing the teaching tools (pedagogy) to convey content effectively to students.

A final point to note is that expertise is difficult to develop (Klein & Hoffman, 1993). Expertise typically develops over a significant period of time through extensive practice. It is a long-term developmental process and cannot be given to a novice. Teachers, however, can help students appreciate the characteristics of experts, as well as the time and commitment necessary to develop expertise (Hardre & Chen, 2005). We next explore the idea of developing expertise in more detail.

Development of Expertise

When considering the development of expertise, one of the first questions typically asked is, how long does it take? At first, it may seem the answer is illusive, but researchers have found some creative ways to provide an estimate. Turner (1995) conducted a survey study where he asked teachers how long it took before they were no longer surprised by what they experienced in the classroom. Their intention was to get a sense for when teachers develop enough experience so that most classroom challenges fall within their wealth of experience. This point could be considered a marker for the development of expertise. On average, his survey re-

Figure 6.1
Cognitive Maps

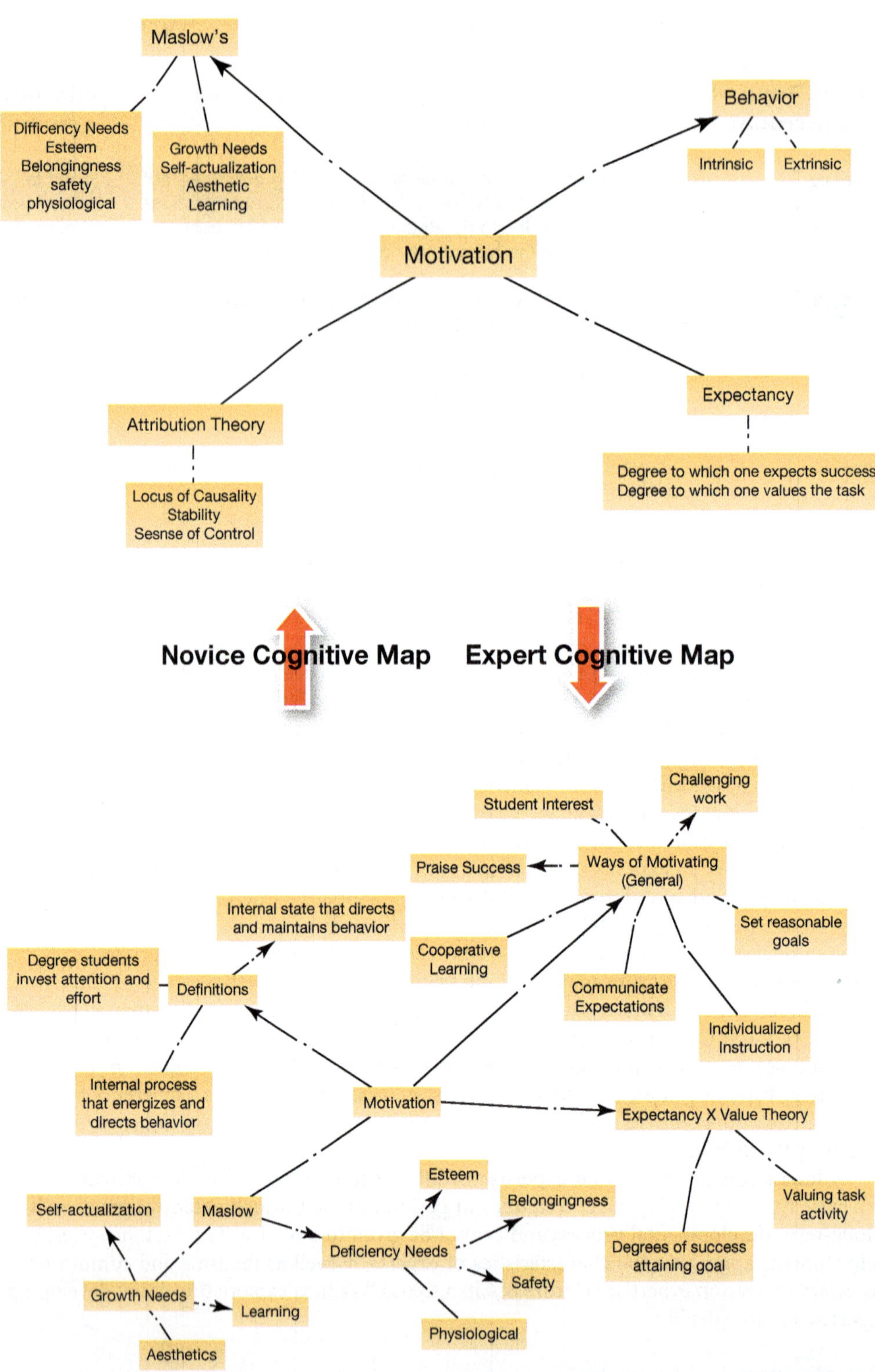

spondents who were currently identified as exemplary teachers reported they were no longer surprised after approximately 4.5 years. Another study took a different approach to identifying the point where teachers develop expertise. Lopez (1995) examined teacher achievement data on a standardized test over many years. He noted that teachers continued to score higher each year following their initial year, and this trend continued through year seven when scores leveled out. Again, this is another potential marker for how long it takes teachers to develop some measure of expertise. Reflecting on our initial question, an informed answer would be that

expertise potentially develops between four to seven years after teaching begins. This is still a substantial range based on limited findings, but it does present a framework for beginning to look at the timeline for developing expertise.

A second important question to consider is what do teachers need to develop expertise? Research from the development of expertise in sports indicates three primary elements are needed to achieve expertise: the desire to be excellent, good coaching, and intense practice (Starkes, Deakin, Allard, Hodges, & Hayes, 1996; Drake, 2011). Applying these findings to teachers, it is likely that many educators come to the profession with a strong desire for excellence. One of the most reported reasons why undergraduate pre-service teachers went into teaching is a love of children and a desire to help, which likely indicates a natural motivation to excel (Reif & Warring, 2002). However, what about adequate coaching and opportunities for practice? These elements are more difficult to substantiate as consistent and sufficient components of a teacher's career. Beyond their pre-service education, teachers seldom have the structured guidance of an experienced mentor, nor do they have regular opportunities for supportive practice. They are typically put directly into real educational settings and expected to perform. This is analogous to putting a runner into a race without the necessary practice to encourage success. One could claim that the teacher's higher education curriculum provides all the necessary coaching and practice; however, as any teacher knows, no amount of preparation can adequately address all the myriad of questions arising on the job. It is critically important that teachers have access to appropriate coaching and practice during their early careers.

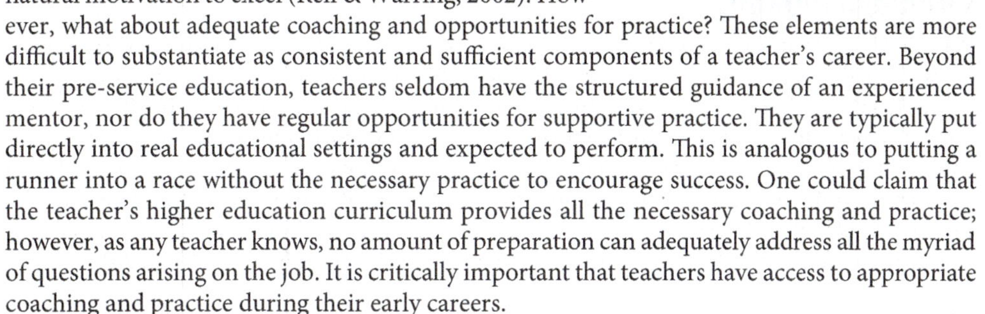

A final question to consider regarding the development of expertise is whether there is only *one* type of expertise teachers can develop. Research suggests that experts are not created equally. Some experts are extraordinary content experts with a vast array of domain specific knowledge (e.g., an in-depth understanding of earth science). Other experts, however, go beyond the boundaries of a particular domain and are able to express their expertise dynamically and creatively. Researchers have made an analogy between experts and artisans and virtuosos (Bransford, Brown, & Cocking, 1999; Miller, 1978). Using this analogy, an artisan is like a content expert. They are adept at a particular craft and can produce beautiful products within a relatively narrow range (e.g., a maker of fine oil landscape paintings). They seek to use their existing knowledge to complete a known task with greater efficiency. Artisan experts, however, do not necessarily produce creative or novel products. A virtuoso is analogous to our broader, more encompassing type of expert capable of going beyond a specified domain, demonstrating a range of mastery (e.g., a renowned painter that transcends artistic schools, creating works in oil and charcoal in both impressionistic and abstract styles). They seek opportunities for growth and exploration beyond the given task. Other researchers have made similar distinctions using the psychological constructs of fluid and crystallized knowledge (Bereiter & Scardamalia, 1993; Ackerman, 2011). **Crystallized expertise** represents a thorough understanding of an area gained by experience and expressed through a well-rehearsed framework. On the other hand, **fluid (also called adaptive) expertise** represents skills expressed through an unfamiliar problem, often generating novel and creative solutions. Both types of expertise are valuable and have a positive impact on the process of education.

Crystallized expertise

A thorough understanding of an area gained by experience and expressed through a well-rehearsed framework

Fluid (also called adaptive) expertise

Skills expressed through an unfamiliar problem, often generating novel and creative solutions

Impact on Education

Berliner (2004) details how research on the development of expertise potentially influences education. First, educational programs failing to integrate classroom observation are at risk for negative learning outcomes. This may result in a deficient profes-

Teaching is one of the most complex professions.

sional growth and a decrease in the likelihood of developing expertise. Second, "coaching" matters when teachers are trying to learn complex activities. Teaching is certainly one of the most complex professions, and adequate access to supported learning activities can decrease the teacher dropout rate by 50%, in addition to increasing job satisfaction (Berliner, 2004). Similarly, consistent opportunities for deliberate practice have been associated with positive instruction in Eastern societies (Lewis & Tsuchida, 1998). Third, the contextualized nature of at least some expertise (see Key Principles of Experts above) means that general K–12 state licensure is of questionable utility. Teachers with expertise at a particular grade may be ineffective after switching grade levels. Likewise, success in an urban school district does not mean teachers will achieve productive learning from students in a rural-based school. Finally, traditional paper and pencil measures of teacher development may underestimate expertise. These tests are administered in an environment that varies considerably from the actual teaching environment and may not capture a teacher's best performance. Using scoring of actual video footage of teachers in their classrooms may have greater validity.

Critical Thinking

Critical thinking

The process by which the thinker improves the quality of his or her thinking by skillfully taking charge of the structures inherent in thinking and imposing intellectual standards

A topic often discussed in conjunction with expertise is critical thinking. **Critical thinking** has been defined as a process by which the thinker improves the quality of his or her thinking by skillfully taking charge of the structures inherent in thinking and imposing intellectual standards (Paul & Elder, 2004). Essentially, critical thinking improves the quality and functionality of thinking. It would seem we are naturally inclined to think critically, but without deliberate instruction, guidance, and practice, thinking is often biased, distorted, partial, and uninformed (Elder & Paul, 2010). To develop our thinking ability and use it critically, we need to understand the basic elements of thought and the role they play in critical analysis (Golding, 2011).

Elements of Thought

Researchers have theorized that critical thinking involves eight elements of thought as depicted in Figure 6.2 (Paul & Elder, 2004; Elder & Paul, 2010) and that successful processing in these areas promotes learning and academic success. According to the research literature, it is important to be able to think about what we are learning (beyond basic memorization), while interpreting and identifying important relations (Paul, 2005; Kurfiss, 1988). Learning to think critically involves an explicit analysis of thought and how we use thinking to solve problems.

When examining Figure 6.2, thinking about your purpose or what you are trying to accomplish is a primary element of thought. In any learning objective, your purpose should be clear and justifiable. Next, your purpose leads to the development of questions. Questions provide the framework for a problem and influences thought progression. Once a sufficiently clear question is devised, the student moves forward with information collection. Information sources become the objects of thought used in an effort to understand and solve a problem. Thinking about information relative to the problem leads to inferences or conclusions. Inferences should logically follow from the information. Collecting information and making inferences will ultimately lead to the development of concepts, ideas, theories, and principles. This is our way of making sense of the world we experience. When developing concepts, students need to exhibit caution about making unjustified assumptions. Assumptions are beliefs that do not necessarily derive from experience. These are potentially detrimental to successful and critical thinking.

Any attempt to think critically is likely to lead to other lines of thought. These are called logical implications. This is a natural and often intelligent extension of critical thinking, but we need to be careful and thoughtful about how our thinking results in behavior or actions. It is beneficial to consider the implications of our thinking and possible actions before they translate into actual behaviors. Finally, it is always important to consider our individual perspective or point of view. We are susceptible to our own perspective on the world, but need to be mindful that others have potentially different and valid ways of looking at the same issue.

These eight elements of thought give structure to our critical processing of information. The narrative above (Figure 6.2) describes one way the elements interact to help us think in ways that are productive and lead to positive learning experiences. Keep in mind that the nature

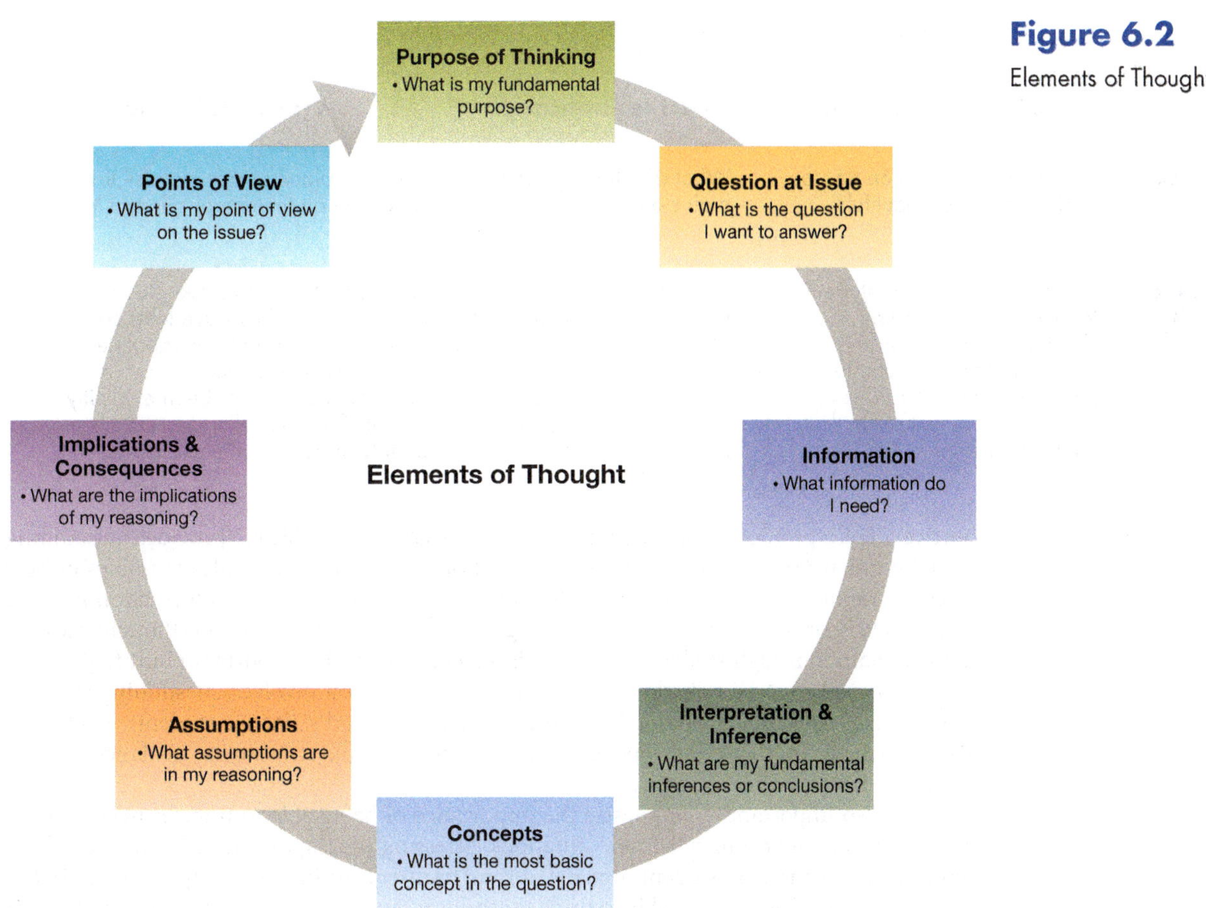

Figure 6.2
Elements of Thought

of how these elements interact will depend on the question at hand. Some questions stress the impact of how our point of view affects our assumptions. Other issues focus on the insight we have regarding the basic concepts present in our question or basic purpose. The essential point is to be aware of all the elements of thought and how they influence our critical thinking ability. Being able to think critically helps students effectively learn and use course content (Ennis, 1990). It also is invaluable to students when dealing with learning situations that are less well defined (Tsui, 2000, 2002)—a quality that defines much of our everyday experiences.

In addition to understanding what positive steps can be taken to enhance our ability to think critically, it is also important to be mindful of potential barriers to critical thinking (Snyder & Snyder, 2008). First, training of pre-service and in-service teachers in the mechanisms of critical thinking is limited. Despite consistent evidence regarding the merits of learning to think critically, curriculum still focuses heavily on content knowledge. Second, although there are some notable exceptions, there are few substantive supports for developing learning experiences that promote critical thinking. Third, it is difficult for an individual to look beyond his or her own preconceptions regarding an issue. Students and teachers alike adhere to what is known and move reluctantly to a position of critical analysis. Finally, learning tasks and assessments supporting critical thinking often take more time to accomplish than their content-based counterparts. Awareness of these barriers, however, can contribute to a reduction of their effects on the development of critical thinking skills.

Encouraging Critical Thinking Through Questioning

Instructional practices can have a dramatic effect on a student's ability to think critically. One important way teachers can promote critical thinking is through frequent and probing questioning (Paul & Elder, 2004; Browne & Freeman, 2000). Teachers should use direct questioning that is clear, relevant, and as concrete as possible. Questions should be asked in a civil and sup-

Table 6.3 Questioning Guidelines that Promote Critical Thinking

	Make it Personal	Fact Identification	Critical Thinking
Question	Which cloud formation do you think is the most beautiful?	What are three types of high clouds?	Do other planets have clouds? If so, speculate on the composition of Venus' clouds.
Outcome Benefit	This question asks the student to take material learned in science class regarding clouds and to connect it to prior life experience. This is an elaborative technique that improves memory.	Fact-based questions reinforce content learning. Content learning is an important educational process providing a foundation for higher forms of learning.	This type of question asks student to consider what they have learned about Earth's clouds and to extrapolate beyond those facts to consider a question that has not been explicitly taught. These ill-defined questions more closely mirror real-life challenges.

portive tone to promote motivation and student engagement. Table 6.3 provides questioning guidelines that promote critical thinking. Additionally, Table 6.4 provides examples of how teachers use questioning to promote different cognitive outcomes. The information in these tables underscores the importance of creating a learning environment that is thought provoking and maintains high student interest. It is also reinforces the important point that not all questions need to serve a single purpose. Effective instruction involves questioning at many levels, which helps develop knowledgeable, independent, and reflective students. Instead of always trying to ask the "right" type of question, teachers should strive to use a balance of questions that meet their lesson goals.

It is also important to emphasize the importance of being able to transfer new learning in a classroom environment to new situations. Stressing the importance of critical thinking across subject areas helps students understand and transfer learning effectively (Halpern, 1998). Ultimately, the value of being able to think critically accentuates the ability to solve real-world problems, consequently developing valued and contributing members of society. Transfer of learning is the topic of the next section.

Table 6.4 Effective Teacher-Initiated Questioning

1	Create a classroom culture open to dialogue.
2	Use both preplanned and emerging questions.
3	Select an appropriate level of questions based on learners' needs.
4	Avoid trick questions and those that require only a Yes or No response.
5	Phrase questions carefully, concisely, and clearly.
6	Address questions to the group or to the individuals randomly.
7	Use sufficient wait time.
8	Respond to answers given by students.
9	Deliberately frame questions to promote student interest.
10	Use questions to identify learning objectives for follow-up self-study.

SUMMARIZE AND REFLECT

1. This section introduced the idea of problem solving. Problem solving begins with a recognition that a problem exists and defining the nature of the problem. Some problems are clear and well-defined, but many real-life problems lack structure and a clear solution.
2. Solving problems often takes one of two general approaches. Algorithms are specific, step-by-step solutions to a well-defined problem. Most problems, however, do not have algorithmic solutions, necessitating the use of heuristics. Heuristics are general approaches to solving ill-defined problems. They do not guarantee a solution but can be used in a wider array of situations.
3. Heuristic problem solving is often supported by breaking tasks down into smaller, more manageable steps (subgoaling) or by trying to decrease the distance between your current situation and the place you want to be at the end of solving the problem (means-end analysis).
4. There are a variety of factors affecting problem solving. One factor is the degree to which students recognize the difference between superficial or surface aspects of the problem and deeper, more principle-based aspects of the problem.
5. Students must also learn to avoid fixating on a single approach to solving a problem and consider novel solutions. Maintaining a flexible mindset supports effective problem solving.
6. Experts in an area typically demonstrate effective problem solving strategies, recognizing deep structure elements of a problem and maintaining cognitive flexibility.
7. Critical thinking is the process of developing more effective thinking skills. Problem solving relies on developing an ability to examine one's thinking and to make changes to produce more effective problem solving. Teachers can promote the development of critical thinking skills by using appropriate questioning.

INFORMED APPLICATION

1. Imagine a recent problem you encountered in real life. Relative to this event, first describe the event in terms of its surface structure. Next, consider the deep structure of the problem, elaborating on possible underlying reasons for the problem.
2. Consider an area in which you consider yourself an expert. Provide a cognitive map representing your understanding in this area.
3. Which element of thought do you think is most crucial to the development of critical thinking? Why?

METACOGNITION AND STUDY STRATEGIES

Helping students develop tools to govern their own thinking is as important as the content they learn. Some students naturally focus on their study skills, while others focus on test taking strategies. Some students feel that sitting near the front of the classroom helps them focus and learn; others use active engagement and frequent questioning to stay attentive and on task. These are attempts to manage cognitive resources and learn effectively. All too often, the development of such skills is unstructured and unguided. In this section, instructional techniques that purposefully direct students to expand such skills are reviewed.

Metacognition and Learning

Metacognition refers to awareness of our thought processes and our ability to exert control over our thinking (Brown, 1987). Specifying the exact nature of metacognition has proven difficult. In a simple sense, metacognition is thinking about thoughts, knowing about knowledge, or reflecting on one's actions. It is challenging, however, to identifying actual instances of metacognition (Weinert, 1987). When applying general definitions of metacognition several questions arise: Do students actually have to make use of metacognitive knowledge? Does metacognition have to be conscious and verbalized? Does metacognition have to generalize across domains? Essentially, the answers to these questions separate cognitions from metacognitions.

Metacognition

The awareness of our thought processes and our ability to exert control over our thinking

Table 6.5 Student Questions Promoting Metacognition

1	What have I learned in the past that will help me with the current task?
2	How will reading this section translate into academic success?
3	What information is important to remember and why?
4	Is my current learning progress sufficient to ensure I am well prepared for the test?
5	How can I alter my learning plan to meet the challenges of the task?
6	Did my learning outcome match my expectations?
7	How does learning in one task relate to a learning experience during another task?

Research suggests that metacognition needs to be more than a simple description of one's thoughts or actions (Georghiades, 2004; Tarricone, 2011). Students who successfully use metacognition are able to recognize the important elements of a procedure, acknowledge mistakes and potential causes, identify critical relations, and monitor the connection between learning and academic outcome (Georghiades, 2004). Table 6.5 identifies questions students can ask to help promote their own metacognitive awareness. These questions help students select, monitor, and use study strategies. This metacognitive ability promotes academic competence (Mastropieri & Scruggs, 1997). The ability also helps students modify their study approach to meet the unique demands of the learning task. Students who fail to develop these skills have greater difficulty with organization, study skill selection, and ultimately academic success (Case, Mamlin, Harris, & Graham, 1995).

Understanding the nature of metacognition is important if teachers and students are to improve learning. Researchers have investigated how metacognition affects performance (Chmiliar, 1997), and have centered on three broad areas of research:

1. Knowledge about when, where, and why to use strategies
2. Utilization of strategies by students without assistance, and monitoring cognition through evaluation and strategy modification
3. Assessment of the limits of knowledge

In general, studies find that it takes a significant amount of time to develop skill with metacognition, that monitoring our cognitions is inconsistent, and that some metacognitive strategies are particularly difficult to learn and apply. Research, however, has shown that instruction can improve these challenges (Deshler, Ellis, & Lenz, 1996). Interestingly, much of the research on metacognition is conducted on student beliefs about metacognition and not on actual academic success. There are, however, some notable exceptions. For example, one study implemented lesson plans in science classes designed to foster metacognition. The intervention lasted for two years and included students eleven and twelve years of age. Findings clearly showed improved academic functioning following training in metacognition. Also of great importance: the study documented that increases in academic functioning were not limited to science. Students also showed improvements in math and English, even though the intervention was limited to science classes. This shows that students naturally generalized what they were learning in science class to other academic areas (Adey & Shayer, 1994; Adey, Robertson, & Venville, 2002; Adey, Shayer, & Yates, 1989).

Study Strategies

Our discussion of metacognition naturally leads into a discussion of study strategies. The techniques students use to study are often forms of metacognition. They enable students to become familiar with their own thinking and to exert greater control of their thoughts.

Study skills/strategies are unique competencies and are distinguished by the following characteristics (Gettinger & Seibert, 2002; Novak & Gowin, 1984; Rohwer, 1984):

1. **Studying is a skill.** It helps students organize, retain, and use information.
2. **Studying is intentional.** Studying is not passive and haphazard; it is deliberate and requires purposeful effort.
3. **Studying is highly individualistic.** Initial instruction in study skills may be a social dynamic between student and teacher, but ultimately studying is a deeply personal process, unique to each student.
4. **Studying is a form of self-regulation.** Learning to study sets the stage for larger progress in personal re'gulation throughout life.

These points emphasize the importance of recognizing that studying is a developmental process. Students move from a novice position, with few skills at their disposal, to highly efficient learners with the ability to guide their academic progress. Students move beyond the limited use of *study tactics* and actually become adept users of study strategies. That is, they are able to take the range of tactics at their disposal and think, plan, and monitor the implementation of those tactics to manage their learning path (Paris & Winograd, 1990).

Comparison of high-achieving and low-achieving students highlights additional study related differences. In terms of reading, high-achieving students demonstrate the following (Pressley & Afflerbach, 1995):

GET THE FACTS

25%

The number of 12th-graders reporting they never studied.

National Center for Educational Statistics (1990)

1. Complete an overview of the material before reading.
2. Identify successfully the most important information, which often requires the students read ahead or backward.
3. Recognize important relations in the material.
4. Connect the present material to already learned material.
5. Modify their learning approach when it does not produce sufficient learning.
6. Monitor level of comprehension, adjusting reading approach as needed to produce adequate learning.

In contrast, low-achieving students often feel overwhelmed by the nature of the learning task and are simply unlikely to continue to put forth the necessary effort to master the material. Part of their difficulty involves inadequate time management and studying for long periods at one sitting (Jones, Slate, Blake, & Holifield, 1992). They are also more sensitive to interruptions from everyday factors like cell phones, television, music, or general inability to concentrate effectively (Nicaise & Gettinger, 1995). In the final analysis, good students have a wealth of study tactics at their disposal. Additionally, they have a well-developed sense of when and where to use them. Let's take a look at some of these important related study skills.

Note Taking and Summarizing

Notes are condensed written accounts generated while simultaneously listening to a lecture, while studying a text, or through observation (Piolat, Olive, & Kellogg, 2005). Although note taking occurs in a variety of life contexts, academic note taking is critically important for students and often governs the extent of their academic success (Piolat & Boch, 2004; Bohay, Blakely, Tamplin, & Radvansky, 2011). It is also important to note that taking their own notes, rather than using notes provided by the instructor, appears to be an important mediator of academic success (Russell, Caris, Harris, & Hendricson, 1983). Taking your own notes promotes two cognitive events (DiVesta & Gray, 1972; Kiewra, 1989; Mayer, 1989). First, personal note taking helps the student *encode* the information in a more permanent fashion. Using

Notes

Condensed written accounts generated while simultaneously listening to a lecture, while studying a text, or through observation

Figure 6.3

Ways a Teacher Can Help Students with Note Taking

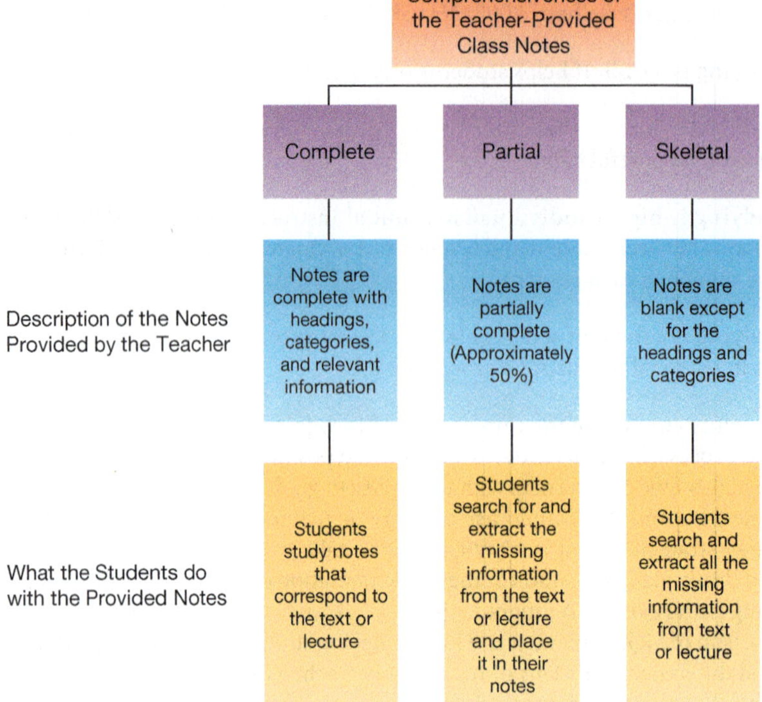

SOURCE: Katayma, A. D. (1997). *Getting students involved in note taking: Why partial notes benefit learners more than complete notes*. Annual meeting of the Mid-South Educational Research Association. Memphis, TN.

instructor-provided notes puts students in a passive learning role and decreases the probability of deep processing. Second, taking notes also creates an external memory store. Students are unable to recall all information presented in a lecture, and notes provide documentation of what was said and can be referred to as often as needed to learn the material.

The instructor can provide different levels of support for the student in terms of providing lecture notes. Figure 6.3 shows three different ways a teacher can help students with note taking.

As demonstrated in the figure, there are different ways teachers can provide support for note taking. The more effective techniques appear to be those that scaffold the material (see Chapter 2 for a detailed discussion of Scaffolding) for the student, rather than providing a complete set of ready-made notes (Katayma, 1997; Russell, Caris, Harris, & Hendricson, 1983). The reason for the greater success of partial notes is that they force the student to generate the majority of the details for themselves. This generative approach helps students make connections from the learning material to events already known to the students (Wittrock, 1990). Such elaborative connections make the material more memorable and easier to retrieve later.

This generative approach is also important when students create summaries of learning material. They need to go beyond mere replication of the material presented and connect the material to real events in their own lives. They can approach this task by relying on internal insights, or they can take proactive steps and ask their teacher direct questions that promote connections to real-life events. This kind of *intentional elaboration* helps students master and retain information. Research shows that such generative questions, as opposed to questions that only serve to reiterate the material, do a better job of helping students learn the material and retain it for later use (Wittrock, 1990). When students consistently ground new information in events and situations already familiar to them, they automatically create long-lasting connections to the new material. This integrates the new material into their long-term memory stores in a more effective and permanent way. It is also important to realize that merely providing students with structured partial outlines, without encouraging students to take a generative approach to understanding the material, is only helpful in learning the main ideas of the text. Outlines with headings and broad summaries can indeed help students retain the broad ideas of a chapter, but fail to help them attend to the deep structure of the reading (Lorch, Lorch, & Inman, 1993). To understand the deep structure of the material, students need to take an active role in learning—asking questions and connecting information to their own lives in meaningful ways.

Scheduling and Time Management

Students who have difficulty with academic success often have poor organization and time management skills (Gersten, 1998; Langberg et al., 2011). It is, therefore, important for students to appreciate factors influencing their ability to manage time effectively. Research shows that there are several general guidelines for making the most of our time (Archambeault, 1992):

1. Tackle your most difficult work at times when you are awake and refreshed and least likely to be distracted.

2. Breakdown longer assignments into smaller more manageable tasks that can be completed in a short time frame.

3. Avoid spending too much time on one type of task—read for a short time, switch to outlining, and then switch to note cards or working with a partner.

4. Create a flexible study schedule, but be flexible when situations arise requiring your attention. This will reduce overall frustration while keeping you moving forward.

The key point in scheduling and time management is consistency. Remain flexible, but always move back to your regular schedule as soon as possible. Also, remember that an effective study schedule is a *personal* schedule. What works for your friend might not work for you. Experiment with different schedules to see what works best for you. The best time managers have discovered the unique mix of flexibility and scheduling that works for their learning situation (Archambeault, 1992).

Effective time-management skills can help students deal with stress and improve their grades (Gortner-Lahmers & Sulauf, 2000; Poser, 2003). Time management and scheduling attempts often fail because students strive to follow a schedule perfectly. They also start a schedule at a point in the grading period where they are already behind. The schedule is an attempt to correct an existing problem. Schedules work best when created at the beginning of a marking period and when they establish a realistic view of what the student can accomplish based on historical precedent. To begin time management it is helpful to think of scheduling as a cyclical process (see Figure 6.4).

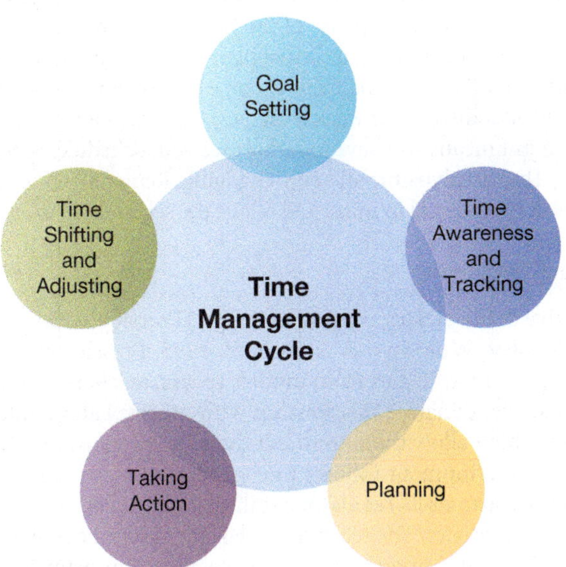

Figure 6.4
Time Management Cycle

Following this time management cycle, begin the academic year by formulating goals. Set goals for grades, study hours per week, class attendance, note taking, etc. You should also divide goals into short-term projects, medium range tasks, and those projects that are long-term. Keep each goal broken down into small manageable units of time. Again, the earlier you begin this process, the better your probability of success. The next step is crucial and involves getting a sense of where you spend your time: To document where you spend your time, it is helpful to follow a journaling technique. This is relatively easy using a cell phone with a timer application (or buying a watch with an hourly chime) and a small journal you can easily carry in your pocket. For a week (or more if possible), wear your watch and carry your journal everywhere. Set your cell phone or watch to vibrate or chime at the top of the hour (having a vibration or chime go off on the half-hour as well is even more informative). Whenever the cell phone vibrates or chimes, open your journal and simply write down exactly what you are doing. Do this for at least a week. This may seem difficult and time consuming, but it can be an invaluable tool to help you realize where you spend your time.

At the end of your observation period, set aside some time to analyze your journal entries. Develop general categories for your activities (eating, socializing, studying, playing, sleeping, etc.) and then start recording how many hours/minutes you spend on each activity. What most students realize is that they spend relatively few hours studying during the week. Most are usually surprised to find out just how much time they spend *eating*.

Armed with information about where you are currently spending your time, you are in a better position to make changes to your schedule. Start planning a daily schedule that will move you closer to your goals. *Remember to be realistic*. The most rigorous schedule in the world is not helpful if you cannot follow it. Make a realistic assessment of how you are currently operating and then make subtle changes to move you closer to your goals. You can make further adjustments later. Some students find external aids helpful in managing their newly developed schedule. Some will use traditional calendars and day planners; others will use a pocket computer, a Palm, a Smartphone, or an iPhone. In the end, the "tool" you use to maintain your schedule is only good if it is used consistently.

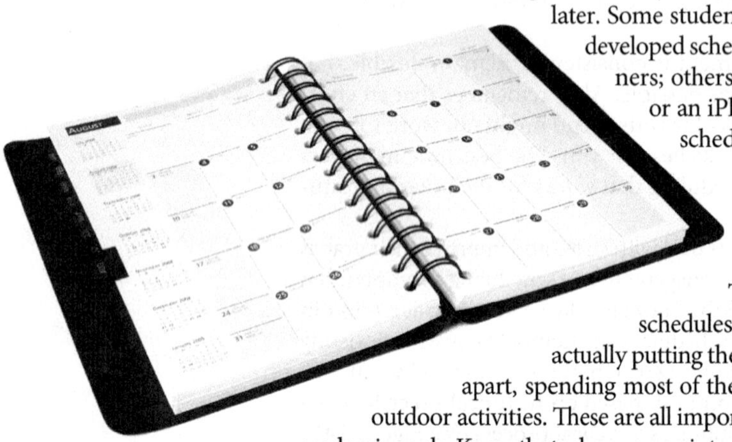

The next step is to be *active*. This means you will need to implement the plan you set out for yourself. Many students love to plan at the beginning of the semester. They eagerly buy books and planners. They spend hours creating elaborate color-coded daily schedules for every conceivable activity. When it comes down to actually putting their plan into action, however, they often fall completely apart, spending most of their time socializing with friends, eating, and enjoying outdoor activities. These are all important activities, but they do not help them achieve their academic goals. Know that when you go into the semester, things will not go exactly as planned. This does not mean the plan was bad or poorly executed, but it simply needs adjustment to better meet your lifestyle and needs. This is the next phase of the time management cycle—time shifting and adjusting. It is normal and expected that your initial plan will need updating to handle unexpected difficulties. Some weeks you will procrastinate more than expected. Sometimes there will be an activity we feel strongly about attending; other weeks will have more tests and assignments than initially anticipated. *This is ok*. It just means you have to re-balance your schedule. Schedules are not meant to be static documents. They are dynamic and ever changing. Remember, they are just tools to help you achieve your goals. Keep the goal in mind and adjust the schedule to meet that goal.

Teaching Study Strategies

Over the years, effective study strategies have emerged (Pressley, 1994; Pressley, Borkowski, & Schneider, 1989; Pressley, Woloshyn & Associates, 1995; Pressley et al., 1990). In general, students begin learning study strategies from models (peers, teachers, parents). This is a social process, involving an active, dynamic relationship with others. Later students begin to internalize study strategies, which allow them to direct their own cognitions. This social-cognitive model of study strategy development follows four general phases (Zimmerman & Kitsantas, 1997). Initially, students learn a self-regulatory task through *social modeling*, often using the classroom instructor as the model. The teacher models the desired behavior, breaking it down into manageable steps. Students are rewarded for successful demonstration of the skill and are given supportive, corrective feedback as needed. Teachers also typically make use of **cognitive modeling** (Prognow, 1992; Yilmaz, 2011). This is an aspect of modeling where the teachers model their own thoughts by talking aloud as they go about a reasoning task. Through cognitive modeling, the students not only get instruction on the study strategy, but they observe how the strategy operates. Some students can stop at this phase of the social modeling process. Their own internal abilities allow them to take teacher modeling of the skill and subsequently apply the strategy themselves in a variety of contexts. Many students, however, require additional support to achieve self-regulated behavior.

Cognitive modeling

The teacher models his/her own thoughts for the student, by talking aloud as that same teacher reasons through a task

The second phase is the *imitative level.* During this phase, students use practice exercises where they demonstrate their newly formed skills in a structured supportive environment. Teachers provide each student with the particular degree of scaffolding needed to continue their development (see Chapter 2 for more on Scaffolding). Scaffolding in this way is called cognitive coaching (Prognow, 1992). **Cognitive coaching** helps students move from a teacher supported level of performance, to a level of performance relying exclusively on the student's abilities (Pressley, Hogan, Warton-McDonald, Missretta, & Ettenberger, 1996).

Cognitive coaching

Process that helps students move from a teacher supported level of performance, to a level of performance relying exclusively on the student's abilities

The next two phases involve a gradual moving away from teacher support and an increased reliance on the self. During the third phase, students work with novel situations and further develop using their skills independently. These *transfer* exercises help students recognize the broader applicability of their learning and prepare them for using their knowledge in the real world. The fourth and final phase of learning a study strategy occurs when the student is able to independently apply their study skills to novel situations in the real world. That is, they have become fully independent users of their knowledge, no longer relying on the teacher or artificial learning situations. At this point, the student is autonomous, functioning independently and effectively to achieve desired learning outcomes.

One final note on teaching study strategies concerns the recognition of the practical challenges teachers face when attempting to provide students with instruction in this area. The often rigid curricular calendar makes it difficult for teachers to spend quality time on teaching these skills. Even teachers who manage to allocate time to teaching study skills usually provide instruction to whole groups, making it difficult to give each student the necessary personal attention needed to develop study skills that meet his/her unique learning needs. Teachers also find it challenging to coordinate instruction with other teachers. Such co-instruction in study skills is desirable because it helps students recognize the broader application of the skill and ultimately increases transfer to new situations.

SUMMARIZE AND REFLECT

1. The second part of this chapter examined metacognition. Metacognition is essentially thinking about our thinking. It is a self-reflective process that examines how we apply our cognitive resources.
2. Teachers can support metacognition in a variety of ways, particularly through using appropriate student questioning. Research has demonstrated that instruction in metacognition produces greater achievement.
3. Study strategies are one area of metacognitive research. Study techniques are more effective if they support metacognitive awareness.
4. Note taking is a typical educational practice, but can be adapted to promote greater reflection. Providing less structure for notes and encouraging students to extract important elements for themselves appears to be an important mediator of metacognition.
5. Scheduling and time management are potential barriers to academic achievement. Often students lack awareness of where they spend their time, leading to ineffective study planning. Students can learn to better plan for academic studying, promoting higher levels of achievement.
6. Metacognitive research has supported the idea of a time management cycle. Greater awareness of the factors involved in this cycle is crucial to effective time management.
7. The chapter covered techniques for direct teaching of study strategies. Techniques like cognitive modeling and cognitive coaching helps students learn and implement study techniques.

(continues)

INFORMED APPLICATION

1. Imagine you are the parent of a tenth grader. You read an article on metacognition and want to help your child develop this skill. Pick one aspect of metacognition and describe how you would coordinate with your child's classroom teacher to produce greater metacognitive skill.
2. How do you manage your study time? Identify an area of time management that you could improve to better prepare for your courses.

TRANSFER

In this final section, we will focus on how we apply what we learn outside the original learning context. This refers to issues of transfer. Transfer is our ability to apply learning in one context or situation to a novel or unexplored situation (Gentile, 2000). For example, if we learn to mix colors in art class to achieve certain results, do we transfer that knowledge to science class when we learn about the absorption and reflection of light waves to produce our perception of color? Ultimately, transfer is the goal of education. We want students to learn effectively in school and achieve, but academic achievement is not very useful if we cannot transfer that success to real-life situations. In this section, we will look at issues of transfer and learn the how to promote successful learning transfer.

General versus Specific Transfer

Parents are commonly asked, "Why do I have to learn long division, or French, or ancient history?" A logical response is that learning such subjects contributes to your growth as a well-rounded productive citizen. Such subjects help you learn to think and reason. These important life skills will help you navigate more difficult paths as an adult. However, is this really true? Does learning math help you to "think" better, in general, or to be more logical in our actions? Does learning a foreign language help us learn how to communicate in a general sense? Teachers and parents would like for the answer to be "yes." It seems reasonable that there are general benefits to the standard or typical curriculum, beyond the basic skills and their direct application. **General transfer** is the idea that learning skills or reasoning approaches in one content area leads to a general ability that applies to *different* situations. Current research, however, tends to argue against such general transfer of learning (Driscoll, 2005; Pugh, Bergin, & Rocks, 2003; Helsdingen, 2011). For example, the logic needed to navigate many math problems does not necessarily translate into better logical ability when solving chemical equations.

General transfer

The idea that learning skills or reasoning approaches in one content area lead to a general ability that applies to different situations

Specific transfer refers to our ability to take learning in one situation and apply it to a *similar* situation. For example, learning the basics of representing form in painting class is likely to transfer to a sculpting class. The learning is within the same general domain. The more closely the two domains are related the higher the rate of transfer (Fuchs et al., 2003; Phye, 2001).

Specific transfer

The act of taking learning in one situation and applying it to a similar situation

Positive, Negative Transfer

Another way to look at the issue of transfer is whether learning in one situation transfers to another situation in a way that supports learning or makes it more difficult. **Positive transfer** is when learning in a previous situation promotes learning in a future situation (Perkins & Salomon, 1992). For example, consider the situation in Figure 6.5. In this example, Mary demonstrates positive transfer of the ability to use the "ed" suffix to form a verb in the past tense.

Positive transfer

The act of taking learning in a previous situation to promote learning in a future situation

Figure 6.5
Positive Transfer

Mary learned in her language arts class that putting "ed" on the end of a verb makes it past tense. She easily translates the present tense sentence "I was the first to *finish* today," to the past tense, "I was the first *finished* yesterday."

At home the next week, Mary's mother asked her to correct her math assignment. She easily replies, "I *corrected* my assignment two hours ago."

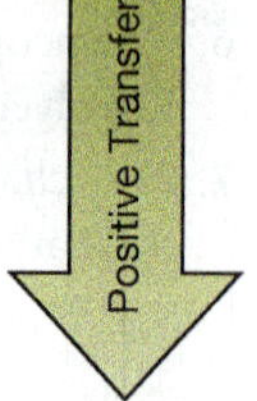

In math class, Mark learned how to add two fractions to make a whole. For example, he learned that when you add 1/3 to 2/3 you get 3/3 or a whole object. He practiced this concept with wooden blocks in the shape of pie pieces.

Later in the week, Mark's mother brought out a cake for dinner. She started to cut one piece for each member of the family of six. Mark quickly interjected that he could do it because he learned how in math class. His mother said okay, reminding him that he would need one piece for each person. Mark immediately cut the cake into three equal pieces.

Figure 6.6
Negative Transfer

She learned the rule in school, but learning in that context extended successfully to another situation. This is an instance of positive transfer.

Negative transfer is when learning in one situation fails to generalize to other settings. Consider the example in Figure 6.6. In this example, Mark clearly has some basic understanding of part/whole relationships, but it is very limited. He is not yet able to appreciate the broader implications of dividing wholes into multiple pieces. In fact, his previous learning with dividing a whole into thirds prevented him from appropriately solving the problem with the cake. Here we have an instance of negative transfer. That is, Mark's earlier learning in class caused him to solve the cake problem incorrectly. This is likely to occur when the students fail to appreciate critical differences between earlier learned material and the current problem. They may also mistakenly see value in a prior experience and its ability to help solve the problem at hand.

Negative transfer
The act of learning in one situation fails to generalize to other settings

Positive transfer is more likely when the learner connects concepts, principles, or skills between the two learning situations. This connection is not always conscious; it is best, however, when the learner makes a conscious link between information already in memory and the characteristics of the current learning situation. Finally, in most learning situations, motivation plays a role in success. Positive transfer is more likely if the learner sees value in using prior knowledge to solve a problem (Shunk, 1996). Benefiting from positive transfer is affected by the way information is encoded. Learning information through limited concrete examples can help simplify a concept, but exposure to the concept in a variety of situations helps promote positive transfer.

Strategies Affecting Transfer

Formal education supports students in their cognitive, social, and physical development. Educators hope to create knowledge that is useful in the school context and knowledge that will help students grow and develop into thoughtful, productive citizens. To achieve this aim, teachers need to help students create knowledge that positively transfers to life beyond the school years. How does this occur? What are the factors that promote positive transfer and help students grow and learn throughout life?

Learning Context

Imagine a young girl learning to count at her day care program. She absentmindedly wanders around her home reciting, "One, two, three, four," etc. She seems quite proud of herself and fascinated with the idea of counting. Wanting to help, her father decided to go one step further and see if she could count with true one-to-one correspondence. That is, an understanding that a specific number of objects has one correct verbal label (two blocks are labeled "two"). The father had given his daughter a set of wooden blocks some years back and takes from this collection all the blue squares. He sits down with his daughter and explains, "We are going to play a counting game." Clearly thrilled, the young girl is paying close attention. The father begins by showing her a single blue square and asks her to "count." She absolutely beams as she sings out "One, two, three, four," at which point her father stopped her. He gives her the "daddy look" and clearly pointed to the block and said "one." This elicited a negligible frown from her, the one often reserved for those we find unenlightened. Undaunted, the father continues. This time he puts out two blocks and again asks her to count. This time she was more cautious and simply said "one." The father gave her a slight smile and then

demonstrated counting the two blocks, "one, two." She began to wrinkle her brow in deepest concentration, surely the same face Einstein made when he figured out the theory of relativity. Next, the father put out five blocks and counted them aloud. He continues the process, varying the number of blocks until she began to see the pattern. Being a somewhat obsessive child, she is able to continue the game for well over an hour. By the time the second hour ends, she could reliably count any of the blocks placed before her up to a total of ten. She was quite pleased, and so was her father. Father and daughter played the game multiple times in the weeks to come. Sometimes it would take her a few minutes to recall the lesson, but the learning savings was evident. Now, this would be a nice father/daughter story if that was the end, but it really would not have much to do with transfer and the learning context. So, here is what happens next.

A short time after the beginning of these games, the whole family was sitting down to dinner and the father asked his slightly older son to bring in enough chairs to the family room table for dinner. The father observed while his son verbally mediates the task by counting aloud, "One for Daddy, one for Mommy ...." The father watched his daughter's face go from bright and alert to deeply troubled. As soon as the boy began counting chairs, the father heard a loud little girl voice scream, "NO!" She flew out of the room in a clear panic. Not knowing what to make of the outburst, the father stood for a moment. A few seconds later, the young girl ran back into the room with her blue squares in hand. She laid out the first one and said, "One," while unceremoniously pushing one of the chairs away from the table. Controlling his humorous delight at his clever child, the father put on his most serious "daddy face" and pointed to the single blue block and said, "One blue block." Next he looked at the chair and said, "One chair." He then proceeded around the room to find anything that had multiple objects and began counting them. The look on the young girl's face was one of sheer horror. It was as if her mind was screaming, "You've got to be kidding me. When does this end?"

The young girl's initial learning experience was circumscribed around a specific set of manipulatives, the blue blocks. The father was so intent on having her master that limited task that he failed to consider a basic principle of transfer.

When learning is tied too specifically to a particular learning context (e.g., counting the blue blocks), then it may be difficult for the individual to transfer learning to a new context. Similarly, learning that occurs in an artificial context, far removed from real-life, is also unlikely to transfer effectively. The initial learning context is crucial for setting the stage for efficient and natural transfer. Learning is not an isolated event contained within the school environment. Students need to take their education and apply it to authentic environments.

Transferring out

Transferring of what we learn in school to another setting

Inert knowledge

The results from our failure to recognize how to apply learning beyond the original learning context

Similarity Between Learning and Application

The issue of the learning context is crucial for appreciating and promoting transfer. First, let's clarify that there are really two broad factors affecting transfer. The first involves transfer of what we learn in school to another setting (e.g., social interaction, sports, clubs, home-life, or even other academic learning settings). We will refer to this as **transferring out**. What we learn in school, however, does not automatically transfer to other situations. Real-life situations may rely on similar knowledge or skill, but lack key elements that cue the student to apply previously learned information. Learning information in school but failing to apply it outside of the school creates inert knowledge. **Inert knowledge** results from our failure to recognize how to apply learning beyond the original learning context. For example, a student may learn a unit on percentages in math class. The student clearly demonstrates an understanding of the concept and can find percentages of whole numbers and fractional quantities. The same student, however, may struggle with calculating the final price of a new shirt that is on the 30% off sale rack at a department store. Transferring out can also refer to the application of learning from one subject to another. For example, it is difficult for some students to apply what they learn in a calculus class to a physics class despite both classes using similar mathematical skill.

Even though a student may clearly understand the concept of percentages of whole numbers, he may have a difficult time at the department store calculating the cost of an item that is 30% off.

Students also struggle with **transferring in** prior knowledge to a given learning situation. When teachers begin a new lesson, they are teaching students who bring to the learning situation a wide variety of preconceptions, ideas, and unique life experiences. All of these unique qualities affect how well the student is able to transfer existing knowledge into the teacher's lesson. Consider, for example, a physical education lesson where students have to navigate a series of obstacles in a limited amount of time. Students work in teams, with each team member's score contributing to the overall team score. The team with the lowest score (fastest time) wins the competition. The teacher chooses team captains, but then each captain alternates choosing team members. Both team captains clearly adopt a strategy of choosing the biggest and strongest classmates for their team. Their prior experience with athletic challenges leads them to believe that choosing a team based on physical size and strength would be effective. This prior knowledge transfers into their actions during the lesson. What the captains fail to realize is that the larger and stronger students are not necessarily the fastest—and speed is a critical variable in successfully completing the challenge. They also failed to examine the obstacle course, which consists of several tubes that students must crawl through to reach the finish line. Again, size and strength are actually disadvantages in these situations. To help promote effective transfer, consider the Principles of Transfer presented in Table 6.6.

Transferring in

Bringing to the learning situation a wide variety of preconceptions, ideas, and unique life experiences

Both transferring in and transferring out affect the quality of learning. Teachers need to appreciate the impact of both transfer issues and design lessons that help students transfer knowledge more effectively. A critical variable in helping students achieve appropriate levels of transfer is identifying common elements across situations. Often teachers make connections to knowledge application outside the classroom (transferring out), but they only focus on the superficial similarities between situations. As we discussed earlier in this chapter, there is typically a surface structure and a deep structure to a given problem. Asking students to recognize surface similarities between situations is likely to have a limited effect on their ability to transfer out knowledge. Teachers need to develop a critical eye for how to recognize deep structure commonalities between situations. For example, an understanding of the efforts of Great Britain to colonize new worlds would seem to help students understand the colonies established by Spain. This is likely to be true on some level, but a closer look at both countries may reveal that their economic situations, religious beliefs, and ruling monarchs lead each country to explore and expand their empires for very different reasons. Failure to recognize the true nature of their colonialization efforts makes it difficult for students to transfer this knowledge appropriately to other academic pursuits.

Table 6.6 Principles of Transfer

Principle	Description
Transfer needs to be well grounded.	The initial learning context needs to move beyond basic memorization of facts. Students need a deep appreciation of the principles behind the facts they are learning. Understanding underlying principles increases the likelihood of transferring understanding to a novel situation.
Transfer is improved when students are given sufficient time to explore ideas.	Students only process so much information from a one-time presentation of concepts. They need time to process information and repeatedly practice their fragile understanding of concepts. This promotes connections to other aspects of their lives and understanding of the world.
Transfer is increased when teachers present organized learning experiences.	Teachers can help students learn to transfer their understanding to novel situations by providing experiences that promote generalization. Presenting contrasting cases and situating new learning experiences in multiple settings helps students learn to transfer knowledge more effectively.
Transfer is strongly affected by student motivation.	Transfer is more likely when student are engaged in their work and attentive during lessons. Teachers can help support motivation by presenting assignments appropriate to each student's unique learning level. This encourages success and fosters engagement in the material.

Table 6.7 Recognizing Similarities in Deep Structure Across Situations

Visual representations often help students appreciate the structural similarities between two situations. Tables, figures, flow charts, and Venn diagrams help students appreciate important connections.

Providing students with problem solving activities across subject domains (English, math, science, etc.) and across social situations (school, home, sports, etc.) creates the potential for students to recognize common deep structure elements. Teachers, however, will often need to provide explicit instruction in these elements to realize this potential.

It is also important to encourage students to develop their own skill with recognizing important or significant similarities between situations. Teachers can provide low risk (not graded or with limited impact on overall grade) challenges for students to develop this ability. This can be further supported with small group activities where students share their ideas with peers.

The same is true for transferring in issues. If teachers are able to help students determine what is relevant in their personal experiences to a given lesson, they will be in a better position to help students use their prior knowledge in a positive way. They will support the student's ability to learn and benefit from the lesson. This, of course, necessitates that teachers develop a richer and more extensive relationship with their students, which can be challenging given the extensive demands placed on our teachers today. Table 6.7 list several techniques teachers can use to help students recognize key features across situations, thereby promoting successful knowledge transfer. Following these guidelines and the basic principles of transfer presented earlier promotes **meaningful learning**. This is when learning is not separate or isolated from one's life experiences but is deeply integrated into their development and understanding of the world. Achieving successful transfer makes learning meaningful and helps students build a deeper level of knowledge.

Meaningful learning

Learning that is not separate or isolated from a person's life experiences but deeply integrated into his/her development and understanding of the world

SUMMARIZE AND REFLECT

1. The final part of this chapter looked at the importance of transfer. Transfer is the process of applying learning in one context to another.
2. Two broad types of transfer were discussed. General transfer is the idea that learning in one context (e.g., school) produces general principles that the learner can then apply in a wide variety of situations. Specific transfer is the selective application of learning in one context to situations that are similar.
3. When students are able to transfer learning, we call this positive transfer. That is, learning in a previous situation promotes learning in a later situation. Negative transfer is when earlier learning impedes learning at a later time.
4. There are many factors affecting transfer. One of the most important is the nature of the original learning context.
5. Creating successful positive transfer depends on how we teach. Providing students with new information in a way that helps them appreciate deep structural elements and gives them opportunities to practice transfer in multiple settings helps students transfer learning.
6. With appropriate learning experiences, students are more likely to take classroom-based learning and apply it to real-life situations (transfer out) and use personal experiences to solve academic problems effectively (transfer in). These factors are important in making learning experiences meaningful.

INFORMED APPLICATION

1. Describe a situation from your own college experience that exemplifies negative transfer.
2. How can you use current events to promote "transferring in" with high school English students studying Shakespeare? Provide an example.

THE CHAPTER IN REVIEW

Check out our website ▶ www.BVTLab.com for chapter-by-chapter flashcards, practice quizzes, summaries, and more.

This chapter examined higher-order learning processes. These processes go beyond basic memorization of information and promote deeper learning that is more useful. There were three broad areas reviewed: problem solving, metacognition, and transfer. The concept of problem solving provides a foundation for understanding higher-order learning. Problem solving refers to the set of processes through which an individual progresses during learning. Problems are sometimes well-defined, having a clear learning path and solution. At other times, problems are ill-defined, lacking a single correct set of steps to achieve a solution. Many real-life issues are ill-defined problems. Problem solving techniques, like algorithms (typically applied in well-defined situations) and heuristics (more useful in ill-defined learning tasks), can help students learn to problem solve effectively. Additionally, students need to learn to appreciate the surface and deep structure of a problem. Often education focuses too heavily on surface elements of a problem, failing to emphasize the principles underlying a problem. Being able to appreciate the deep structure of a problem is indicative of the type of thinking experienced by experts. Experts are more likely to think critically about their own thinking, leading to better problem solving strategies. Critical thinking is characterized by eight elements of thought. Appreciation of how these elements influence our problem solving helps build critical thinking skills.

Problem solving techniques often require metacognition. Metacognition is defined as thinking about our thought processes. Many study strategies use metacognitive processes to support learning. Note taking is a common educational technique to improve learning. Teachers can help a student's metacognitive awareness of the material by providing limited notes for students and requiring that the students extract important principles for themselves. Similarly, structuring activities that encourage students to summarize important aspects of a learning task helps promote metacognition. Another study technique to consider is simply time management. Effective studying requires students to make the most of their study time. Like note taking, time-management ability can be improved with assignments designed to increase awareness of how students spend their time.

Teaching these types of study strategies is important. Research has shown that increasing metacognitive awareness increases achievement. Teachers can use cognitive modeling and cognitive coaching to help students learn to be aware of their own thinking and to make changes to their thought process that improve learning.

The final section of this chapter examined educational transfer. Transfer refers to how students use learning to affect changes in other aspects of their lives. Positive transfer is when students successfully use prior learning to enhance their ability to solve a problem. Negative transfer is when prior learning actually makes it more difficult to solve a problem. Factors affecting transfer include the nature of the original learning context. Teachers can help students transfer learning to other situations by providing learning experiences that identify the deep structure of a lesson and gives the student multiple opportunities to practice applying the information. Applying the information learned in school to other situations is called transferring out. Using prior learning to support a lesson is transferring in. Both are important aspects of creating a meaningful learning experience.

Interdisciplinary Case Focus

principal *special educator*
teacher *parents* *psychologist*
social worker *physical educator*
nurse *peers* *doctor*

Instructional Methods Promoting a Higher Level of Learning

Collaborative Lesson

English Classroom Mary Drain is a tenth grade English teacher at Marrow High School. Her school district has approved a standard reading list for high school students, and tenth graders are required to read *Lord of the Flies* by William Golding. She has always found the story interesting and never has difficulty getting the students to discuss the story. The story can clearly be read at two different levels. On one level, it is the story of a group of boys stranded on an island and their attempts to create a manageable society in which to live. The story takes several violent turns as the boys struggle for dominance in the challenging island environment. The story is also widely recognized as allegorical, representing the disturbing and often violent nature of mankind. Ms. Drain feels that she is basically successful in getting her students to appreciate both levels of analysis, but she is always left with the feeling that there is a deeper lesson the students fail to understand fully. It is like they can appreciate the surface structure of the story of the stranded boys, but they only achieve a limited understanding of the deep structure of the story representing the nature of man. Over the years, she has developed a sense that they need to conceptualize the deeper meaning of the story in other situations. She doubts her ability to create such situations in her own class, but believes that working collaboratively with another teacher could produce the level of learning she has been striving to achieve. At a recent school-wide staff meeting, she found herself looking around the room for a teacher that might be able to work with her on this assignment. She notices Ms. Caldwell, the psychology teacher, and decides that this could make an excellent ally in her quest for deeper student learning.

Psychology Classroom Regina Caldwell is the psychology teacher at Marrow High School. She has been teaching part-time at the school for several years. She thoroughly enjoys psychology and looks forward to helping students appreciate the complexities of human behavior and thinking. At the beginning of the school year, she was approached by one of the English teachers, Ms. Drain, to see if she was interested in developing a collaborative lesson on the book *Lord of the Flies*. At first, she is reluctant to agree because she only has limited familiarity with the book. Ms. Drain assures her the book is short and that she will be covering the content. Ms. Drain is interested in having her look more closely at the sociological and psychological aspects of the story. After a brief discussion of the book, Ms. Caldwell agrees to help with the lesson.

Collaboration After Ms. Caldwell agrees to help with Ms. Drain's lesson, they set up a meeting to discuss how to approach the collaborative assignment. Ms. Drain begins the meeting with another brief summary of the book and the two levels of analysis she covers in her class. As she is presenting her summary, Ms. Caldwell immediately begins to see many connections to her psychology course. After Ms. Drain finishes her summary, Ms. Caldwell details some of her thoughts on how to integrate the story content into her class. After some discussion, the teachers decide that Ms. Drain will begin her coverage of the story at the same time Ms. Caldwell begins her section on social psychology. Both teachers agree that this is the most natural place to make connections between the two courses. They also note that it is unfortunate that they do not have a philosophy course at their school because there are so many philosophical issues raised by the book.

Both teachers decide to approach their respective courses in the way they usually do, but to follow-up with an assignment that will be coordinated. In both classes, the teachers will create a follow-up lesson on appreciating surface versus deep structure in class material. Ms. Drain will describe how these concepts relate to the book, and Ms. Caldwell will expand the concepts to the social psychology section of her course. Ms. Drain will follow this discussion with a written assignment designed to get the students to identify both surface and deep structure elements of the lesson. Ms. Drain will give her class an out-of-class observational assignment. Her students will have to do a one-hour observation of the local elementary school kids on the playground during recess. Specifically, they will be asked to identify social behaviors they discussed in class, including aggression. After their observation, they will dedicate a specific class day to discuss what they observed (surface structure) and possible reasons for the observed behavior (deeper structure). She will specifically make a point to bring up issues of learned behaviors versus more innate characteristics of people.

The final part of their lesson is a joint class assignment in the school cafeteria including the students from both courses. The students will be divided up into groups of four, two students from English and two students from psychology. Each group is presented with a single question to discuss—"Is mankind inherently aggressive?" Both teachers notice that the students in each group readily begin to share their recent educational experiences. They share their own ideas on the question based on their educational and personal experience, and they ask questions about their group member's experiences. At the end of the class, the teachers provide some final remarks on how the lesson evolved and what they hoped to achieve. Finally, they assign a reflection paper on the group discussion.

Conclusion After the students turn in their reflection papers, Ms. Drain and Ms. Caldwell set up a meeting to discuss the pros and cons of their experience with the collaborative lesson. Both teachers were impressed with the level of discussion during the joint class. They were also impressed with the level of discussion present in most of the reflection papers. The students appeared to gain a much deeper appreciation of the content in both classes. Many of the students not only discussed the content of the two classes but also made direct connections to other areas of their lives (situations with friends, family, work, etc.). The teachers were pleased with the outcome of the collaborative lesson and were surprised how little extra effort it took to work together on this assignment compared to past years. They also felt that the students were left with a memorable educational experience that they were likely to take with them to other learning situations. On the downside, they noted that in their school there was little support for this type of work. They decided to approach the school principle and ask her to start a task force to begin looking at more systematic school-wide approaches to working collaboratively.

Key Terms

TERM	*Page*
Algorithm	179
Cognitive coaching	195
Cognitive modeling	195
Critical thinking	186
Crystallized expertise	185
Deep structure	181
Fluid (also called adaptive) expertise	185
Functional fixedness	181
General transfer	196
Heuristics	179
Ill-defined	178
Inert knowledge	198
Meaningful learning	200
Means-end analysis	180
Metacognition	189
Negative transfer	197
Notes	191
Positive transfer	196
Rubrics	180
Specific transfer	196
Subgoaling	180
Surface structure	180
Transferring in	199
Transferring out	198
Well-defined	179

7
Chapter
MOTIVATION

What's It All About ...

What is motivation?

How do the different psychological perspectives explain motivated behavior?

What impact do goals have on motivation?

Chapter Objectives

- Define motivation.
- Describe fundamental motivational concepts.

- Describe the behavioral view of motivation.
- Describe the humanistic view of motivation.
- Describe the cognitive view of motivation.
- Describe sociological view of motivation.

- Explain the difference between two types of achievement goals: mastery and performance.
- Describe work avoidance goals.
- Review the importance of social goals.
- Explain how to set goals effectively.

EXTENDED OUTLINE

Motivation

I. What's It All About ...

II. From Today's Headlines

III. Motivation—A Focus on Why We Act
   - A. Defining motivation
   - B. Motivation concepts
     1. Intrinsic and extrinsic motivation
     2. State and trait views of motivation
     3. Summarize and reflect

IV. Perspectives on Motivation
   - A. Behavioral views of motivation
     1. Internal constructs
     2. Consequences
   - B. Humanistic views of motivation
     1. Maslow's hierarchy of needs
     2. Optimal human experience and positive psychology
   - C. Cognitive views of motivation
     1. Attribution theory
     2. Expectancy and value theory
   - D. Sociological views of motivation
   - E. Summarize and reflect

V. Goals and Motivation
   - A. Achievement goals: mastery and performance
   - B. Work avoidance goals
   - C. Social goals
   - D. Goal setting
   - E. Summarize and reflect

VI. The Chapter in Review

VII. Interdisciplinary Case Focus

From Today's Headlines

Vol. I No. 7 Teaching World, 2012

THE BEST TEACHER I'VE EVER SEEN

That was the headline from a 2005 *Washington Post* article by staff writer Nic Anderson. The article was about an amazing teacher named Hortense Adams. Ms. Adams won the Agnes Meyer Outstanding Teacher Award, in large part for her gift to motivate students. Her principal wrote, in a letter to the nominating committee:

"To be a master teacher, you have to reach into people's heart and soul," he said. "When they can't do math, you see a mathematician. When they can't write, you see an author. She has this way of demanding so much from her students. Other teachers couldn't get away with it. But she does because her students know she cares about them so much."

Ms. Adams is a veteran teacher. In fact, she declines to answer questions about just how long she has been teaching. For her, it is not about the time spent teaching. She sees teaching as a profession providing countless opportunities to keep yourself renewed. She believes you need to keep your students motivated to learn and you need to keep yourself motivated. She remarks that flexibility is the key. She constantly seeks fresh projects and makes a concerted effort to shake up her lessons every year.

MAKE THE CONNECTION

As Ms. Adams illustrates, teachers need to engage their students and motivate them to invest in the learning process. At times, it seems that Ms. Adams accomplishes this daunting task by simply being a supportive and positive force in the lives of her students.

These qualities are indeed important, but scientific research has provided us with additional information on what factors contribute to motivation. In this chapter, we will begin our look at the concept of motivation. We will look at environmental factors, such as reinforcement, and their role in producing motivated behavior. We will also examine cognitive factors influencing motivation, such as a student's wants and needs. A third factor we will explore is social motivators—looking at how social relationships influence the development and direction of motivation.

MOTIVATION—A FOCUS ON WHY WE ACT

To begin our exploration of *motivation*, think about the following question: "How well are you going to do in educational psychology?" Some of you immediately thought, "I'm going to do great!" Others thought, "Well, it depends on how hard the tests are." Still others thought, "I'm just doing what I have to do to get a *C*." How well you do may actually depend on a variety of factors other than academic capability. For example, research shows some students make *A*'s because they want good grades. Some simply want to learn all they can about the subject and the *A*'s come naturally. Others put forth little effort because grades aren't important to them or they think they can't do it. Some students believe that it's better to fail without trying, rather than try and fail. Even when a student does make an *A*, some will say it was because they worked hard, others will say the tests were easy, and still others will say it was just luck. Each of these responses reflects a different facet of motivation. In this chapter, we'll explore these different sources of motivation, looking at what directs people to initiate behavior, participate in activities, and sustain their efforts.

Defining Motivation

Motivation refers to the reasons why we behave. Our motives fuel, direct, and sustain our behavior. For example, when we are motivated to complete a task, we begin the task, sustain our work on the task, and ultimately complete the task. Thus, motivation typically involves intention to reach a desired goal. The idea of intending to reach a goal, or directing one's behavior toward a desired outcome, can be found in most current theories of motivation (Deci, Vallerand, Pelletier, & Ryan, 1991). Some researchers focus on what is involved in directing and sustaining behaviors. Others are more concerned with why we are motivated toward goals, focusing on what fuels or energizes our desire for certain outcomes (Franken, 2007). Teachers typically focus on motivation to learn and succeed in school (Stipek, 2002). Studies based on teacher perception find that motivation to learn is exemplified by students who are able to find value, meaning, and reward in learning (Marshall, 1987). Students who demonstrate a strong motivation to learn appear to have a long-term commitment to the quality of the learning process (Ames, 1990). While it seems obvious to say that students learn because they are motivated, actually uncovering the reasons we choose, work toward, and reach certain academic outcomes is complicated. For example, when you study for a test, is it for the grade or because you want to learn the material? Is your studying a relatively consistent trait, or does it depend on the situation? In the next section, we will explore some basic concepts in contemporary motivation research that address these questions.

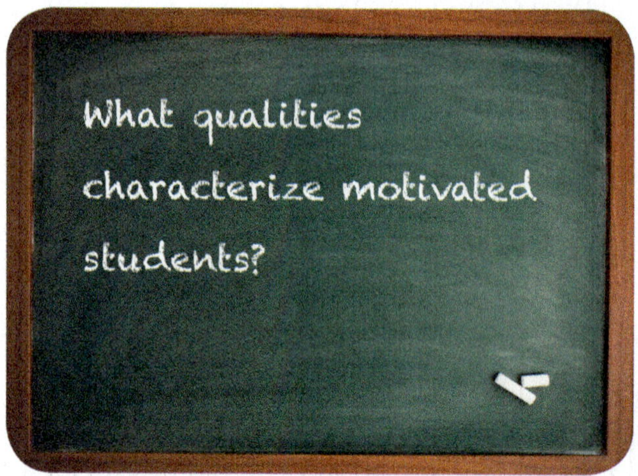

Incentive

Essentially, the promise of a reward

Incentives are essentially rewards for finishing something. The child who finishes his dinner gets to pick dessert from the dessert tray.

Motivational Concepts

Motivation is a complicated topic and integrates many aspects of our lives. Take the biological motive of hunger, for example. Hunger can be viewed as an internally driven state. That is, hunger produces an uncomfortable physical state, and we are motivated to eat in order to decrease this feeling. This doesn't explain all of our eating behavior, however, because we also eat when we are not hungry. Sometimes, there are incentives to eat that are not linked to hunger. **Incentives** are essentially the promise of a reward. The dessert tray at the end of dinner is a good example. The sight of wonderful deserts holds the promise of great tasting food. Depending on the situation, eating occurs in response to internal states, incentives, or a combination of both. The reasons we learn are even more complicated. Certainly society provides many rewards for academically successfully students (scholarships, good jobs, higher levels of financial compensation, etc.). Grades also provide students with ongoing incentives for academic success. Human learning is so complex, however, that a whole host of theories have been developed to address our motivation to learn and succeed. Let's look at a few of the most enduring concepts in the field of motivation.

Intrinsic and Extrinsic Motivation

A basic concept in the study of the motivation to learn involves the question of whether learning is determined by internal or external factors. For example, you studied hard for your last test in biology. If you studied because you were interested in the material, your behavior was motivated by an internal factor—your interest. In other words, your studying was **intrinsically motivated**, or initiated and directed by internal processes. People engage in intrinsically motivated behaviors without the necessity of external rewards. The activity is inherently interesting or enjoyable (Deci & Ryan, 1985). Some behavior, however, is motivated by factors outside of the individual. **Extrinsically motivated behavior** involves actions that produce an externally mediated outcome. If, for example, you studied for your test because you wanted a good grade, external factors motivated your behavior. You engaged in studying because getting an *A* is rewarding. Recall from Chapter 4 that behavioral learning theory holds that organisms behave as a function of consequences. According to this perspective, all behavior is motivated by external factors in the form of reinforcement and punishment (see Table 7.1).

Intrinsically motivated behavior

The internal process that initiates and directs one's behavior

Extrinsically motivated behavior

Actions that are produced by an externally mediated outcome

Interconnections

The behavioral perspective is covered in detail in Chapter 4.

Since not all classroom activities are inherently interesting (think of learning your multiplication tables), extrinsic reinforcement is frequently used in the classroom. A considerable body of research demonstrating how external rewards increase the frequency of behavior (Skinner, 1974; Akin-Little, Eckert, Lovett, Little, 2004) supports the use of extrinsic motivation in education. Consider, for example, the common practice of using a performance based grading system as extrinsic motivators. Rewarding a student who has studied hard with a good grade is positively reinforcing the studying behavior. What if the student studies hard and does not make a good grade? In this case, the consequence for studying is punishing. According to operant theory, this would lead to a decrease in future studying behavior. As you can see, providing extrinsic reinforcement is complicated, leading to both desirable and problematic outcomes.

Research in the behavioral tradition also indicates that if reinforcement stops, behavior will decrease and eventually become extinct (Leahey & Harris, 2001). In the studying example, if we want the student to maintain studying behavior, good grades need to reliably follow studying. What would happen if we removed grading systems completely, for all students? Would you study as hard? Some schools are actually putting that philosophy to the test. *Big Picture Schools* are high schools based on a different educational philosophy (Hendrie, 2004). Established in 1995 by Dennis Littky and Elliot Washor, these schools diverged from traditional instructional models. Students do not attend traditional classes or take typical tests. Instead, students are encouraged to engage in real world problems. Students work closely with a mentor (fifteen students to one mentor) throughout their entire high school career.

Table 7.1 Examples of Extrinsic Reinforcers

Teacher praise
Grades
Participation in a preferred activity for completing an assignment
Desirable things to eat (e.g., pizza party)
Extra credit
Free time

They develop extensive portfolios of their work, learning, and experiences. They give oral presentations on their experiences. The focus is on developing the motivation, skills, and personal qualities to achieve success in higher education. The hope is that these non-traditional schools will be better able to develop mindful learners.

The idea is that by focusing on the bigger learning picture, the students are able to transfer learning more effectively. Instead of learning calculus in a classroom, students can learn with an engineer as they actually use math in authentic situations. The connection between learning and application is more natural. Students in these schools typically maintain high levels of motivation and readily participate in the educational process (Adler, 2005). Students still participate in some standardized achievement tests and often outscore comparable area schools. They also report very high percentages of students attending college—some as high as 90% (Wolk, 2010). They also report attendance rates above 90% in school districts where attendance often falls below 50%. These statistics have generated notoriety for Big Picture schools on the national level. They have received large grants from the Bill and Melinda Gates Education Foundation. With additional resources, they have been able to expand into sixteen states and the District of Columbia, as well as other countries, including the Netherlands, Australia, Canada, and Israel. The success of these schools demonstrates that placing students at the center of the instructional equation can bring about positive outcomes.

As you can see, while extrinsic reinforcement can be an effective tool in the classroom, there are other motivational factors impacting student success. In fact, there is much controversy today regarding the positive and negative effects of extrinsic reinforcement on the motivation to learn. Some researchers assert that if behaviors in which we engage because we naturally enjoy them are suddenly extrinsically reinforced, we may become dependent on the extrinsic reinforcer. In other words, extrinsic reinforcement may undermine intrinsic motivation (Deci & Ryan, 1985; Deci, Koestner, & Ryan, 1999). For example, a teacher may be impressed with a student who has made dramatic improvements in mathematics since the beginning of the school year. To encourage development, the teacher begins to allow the student to take on organizational tasks in the classroom (like taking lunch count, organizing the daily board, acting as leader in line). The student is thrilled with these rewards and begins to work even harder to improve. As the term progresses, the teacher realizes that other students are also improving and begins to distribute rewards for excellent work more equally among class members. Realizing that he is no longer getting preferred treatment in class, the student begins to work with less diligence and his work suffers accordingly. This was obviously not the intention of the teacher but is a possible outcome of reinforcing existing intrinsically motivated activities. The relation between extrinsic and intrinsic reinforcement is, however, complicated. Some research shows that extrinsic motivation may undermine intrinsic motivation to learn while other research shows extrinsic motivation may enhance it (Akin-Little, Eckert, Lovett, & Little, 2004). For example, a greater sense of autonomy appears protective against some of the potential negative effects of rewards on intrinsic motivation (Hagger & Chatzisarantis, 2011). We will return to the issue of intrinsic versus extrinsic motivation in Chapter 14 when we discuss self-regulation theory, a perspective that focuses on intrinsic motivation and the use of active and volitional forms of extrinsic motivation to enhance learning (Ryan & Deci, 2000).

How does extrinsic reinforcement affect intrinsically motivated behavior?

State and Trait Views of Motivation

Another aspect of motivation theory is whether behavior is determined by an individual's inherent traits or by the situations in which they find themselves. Some theorists

Interconnections

Self-regulation and goal setting will be covered in Chapter 14.

(Pintrich, 2000; Murphy & Alexander, 2000) argue that people possess motivational traits, which cause them to behave in similar ways, regardless of the situation. **Traits** are relatively enduring characteristics of the individual. In this context, we are referring to psychological traits, but the idea is consistent with physical traits like having green eyes. For example, researchers have conducted studies on individual differences in need for achievement (McClelland, 1954; Accordino, Accordino, & Slaney, 2000), indicating that some individuals exhibit a consistent need to achieve over time and across situations.

Traits

Relatively enduring characteristics of the individual (In this context, we are referring to psychological traits; however, the idea is consistent with physical traits like having green eyes.)

In contrast, **state theories** show how our motivation depends on the situation (Hirschfeld, Lawson, & Mossholder, 2004). Probably the most extreme example of this perspective comes from behavioral theory where all behavior is determined by environmental consequences. In other words, the environment in which you live determines everything you do. Behavioral theorists do not rely on any internal constructs like traits to explain behavior. Your behavior is entirely state dependent—dependent on environmental circumstances. If a student studies for a test, then he or she is being rewarded for that behavior. Behaviorists would not say that the student studies because he or she has a general trait characterized by consistent study behavior. Contemporary motivational research on learning continues to focus on the importance of different reinforcers, as well as on other environmental variables, such as the contexts in which people learn (Weiner, 1990).

State theories

Theories that show how our motivation depends on the situation

Researchers continue to disagree about whether behavior results from individual characteristics (trait theory) or qualities of the situation (state theory). Each of these lines of research has contributed to our understanding of the motivation to learn, and it may be that the state/trait dimension in motivation is more of a continuum than a dichotomy. That is, trait and state influences on behavior likely interact to produce behavior; further, cognitive researchers believe this interaction between the person and the situation is mediated by our thoughts, expectations, and problem-solving ability. As you can see, what motivates behavior is studied using a variety of psychological constructs. Depending on the theoretical perspective, different aspects of the individual and the environment are highlighted in an attempt to explain behavior. To help clarify how an understanding of motivation is influenced by a person's psychological perspective, we turn now to a closer look at the most prominent theoretical perspectives in the field of motivation.

SUMMARIZE AND REFLECT

1. Motivation is defined as something that arouses, directs and maintains behavior.
2. Motivation typically involves some sort of goal or desired outcome.
3. There are two traditional views of motivation. The first looks at sources of motivation coming from within the individual. Such motivators are referred to as intrinsic motivators. Qualities like personal fulfillment and task enjoyment are representative of this type of motivation.
4. Intrinsic motivation is contrasted with sources of motivation that lie outside of the person. These extrinsic motivators take many forms including grades, praise, or financial compensation.
5. The second traditional view of motivation examines whether our motivation is stable across situations or varies depending on the situation. The trait view holds that motivation is a relatively stable characteristic. This is contrasted with state views, which hold that motivation is variable, depending on the situation.

INFORMED APPLICATION

1. Describe a lesson plan for any subject or topic that interests you. Now, consider how to modify your plan to enhance the student's motivation. What factors regarding motivation are important to consider?
2. A student demonstrates an extreme disengagement in the learning process. His life situation is clearly complex, but as the teacher you are invested in improving his motivation. How can you use the concept of state versus trait motivation to frame your understanding of the student's motivation? How could this lead to practical changes in how you approach motivating the student?

PERSPECTIVES ON MOTIVATION

Motivational theory encompasses a wide range of behaviors, thoughts, and situations and is influenced by one's psychological perspective. That is, what you view as important determinants of motivation will be highly dependent on your particular perspective on psychology. Psychology as a field of study has established several schools of thought or perspectives on the nature of behavior. These perspectives include the more dominant schools of behavioral and cognitive theory, but also humanistic theory and its more current manifestation, positive psychology. Each of these perspectives views motivation in a unique way, investigating a unique subset of topics relevant to their theoretical perspective. The next section examines each of these schools of thought, its unique perspective, and its view on the exciting topic of motivation.

Behavioral Views of Motivation

As discussed in Chapter 4, behavioral scientists are interested in observable behavior, emphasizing the effects of prior events and behavioral consequences. For example, to understand why a third-grade girl suddenly developed a fear of going to art class, a behaviorist would carefully describe the child's environment before (prior events) and after (consequences) the expression of fear. They would attempt to identify key factors present in the child's world that set the stage for the fear reaction and consequences supporting the behavior. What the behaviorist is unlikely to do is to ask the question, "What is motivating the child's fear?" Let's take a look at why the behaviorist has difficulty with this question.

The behavioral view of psychology is discussed in detail in Chapter 4.

Internal Constructs

The behaviorist typically does not attribute causes of behavior to internal constructs such as motivation. Behavioral theorists view internal events or constructs as personally relevant, but unnecessary to explain the cause of behavior. That is, we all have a sense that our mental lives are vibrant and important to our daily lives, but behaviorists believe these events fail to contribute to an understanding of why we behave as we do. Understanding of behavior comes from a close examination of the individual's environment. According to the behaviorist, behavior is supported by certain environmental factors, and behavior modification occurs by systematic alteration of these factors. For example, the behaviorist would help the girl with the fear of going to art class, presented earlier, by making changes to her environment. Perhaps the fear developed because of a critical remark made by the teacher regarding a new project. The behaviorist would likely counter the effects of this event by arranging several additional art projects for which the child was given the necessary supports to ensure success. The reinforcing nature of achieving success would counter the feelings of fear as the student learned to enjoy art. Behaviorists abandoned introspective analysis of feelings and thoughts because they felt such constructs were ambiguous and ill defined, and did not contribute to an understanding of the causes of behavior. The hallmark of their perspective is that behavior can be successfully managed by manipulation of appropriate environmental events.

Reinforcements

Positive environmental events following a behavior of interest resulting in an increase in the frequency of the behavior

Punishments

Aversive environmental situations that result in a decrease in the frequency of behavior

Consequences

The behaviorist sees the determinants of behavior as residing in the individual's environment. Of primary importance are the consequences that follow behavior, such as reinforcements and punishments. **Reinforcements** are positive environmental events following a behavior of interest resulting in an increase in the frequency of the behavior. **Punishments** are similar, but involve aversive situations that result in a decrease in the frequency of behavior. Behavioral theory holds that consequences, such a reinforcements and punishments, shape the expression of behavior, thus providing an explanation for why we act.

F.A.Q.

Porsha Vance—"What is the basic difference between reinforcement and punishment?"

Professor Holbert—"Reinforcement produces an increase in the frequency of the behavior. That is, following reinforcement of a behavior, the student is likely to increase the amount of behavior produced. Punishment decreases the frequency of a behavior."

Humanistic Views of Motivation

Another perspective on human motivation comes from a field of study historically called humanistic theory. Humanistic theory rose to prominence during the 1960s, in part as a reaction to the overly mechanistic behavioral approach. Consistent with the social and cultural movement at the time, humanistic theorists emphasized the unique needs and wants of every individual. They sought to move away from the focus on managing behavior by manipulating environmental variables, choosing instead to look inward toward more personal explanations for why we act. The movement, however, was relatively short lived and quickly eclipsed by yet another movement during the 1970s, cognitive theory. Cognitive theory, in conjunction with a steady interest in behavioral theory, dominated psychology until recently. Currently, a resurgence of interest in personal variables, such as fulfillment and optimal growth, has seen a return to some of the basic tenets of humanistic theory, a movement known as positive psychology. Before we look at positive psychology, however, let's look at one of the prominent theorists of the original humanistic movement.

F.A.Q.

Tim Akroyd—"I remember from an earlier chapter that there were actually two types of reinforcement and two types of punishment. What were they?"

Professor Holbert—"Good question! Basically you can reinforce behavior by giving a student something desirable (e.g., verbal praise, free time, etc.) or removing something they don't like. Either situation is viewed as reinforcing by the student. Similarly, punishment works by introducing something undesirable or removing something they like (e.g., when a parent takes away driving privileges because of a speeding ticket.)"

Maslow's Hierarchy of Needs

Abraham Maslow was one of the most prominent researchers in the humanistic movement. Although his initial training was in behavioral theory, he gradually moved toward the investigation of internal factors like individual needs and personal growth. In 1954, he published a chapter detailing his revolutionary theory of human motivation. Essentially, his theory maintained that what motivated people was a desire to satisfy individual needs. The theory met with criticism at the time, but ultimately gained widespread acclaim during the social and civil rights movement of the 1960s. Maslow's work emphasized how the typical individual attempts to achieve optimal mental health. This was a radical departure from other theories of psychology primarily focusing on mental illness and atypical behaviors. The central premise in Maslow's theory is that people spend their lives striving to satisfy an ever-changing series of needs. These motivational needs can be represented graphically as a pyramid (see Figure 7.1) and are referred to as a **hierarchy of needs**.

Hierarchy of needs

Graphical representation of Abraham Maslow's motivational theory regarding needs

Maslow's theory holds that from the time we are born, we have a perception that we are deficient in something and therefore strive to acquire it. For example, we initially attempt to satisfy our basic physiological needs like eating. Young children uses their limited repertoire of skills, such as crying, to elicit appropriate care from others. This need, however, lessens over

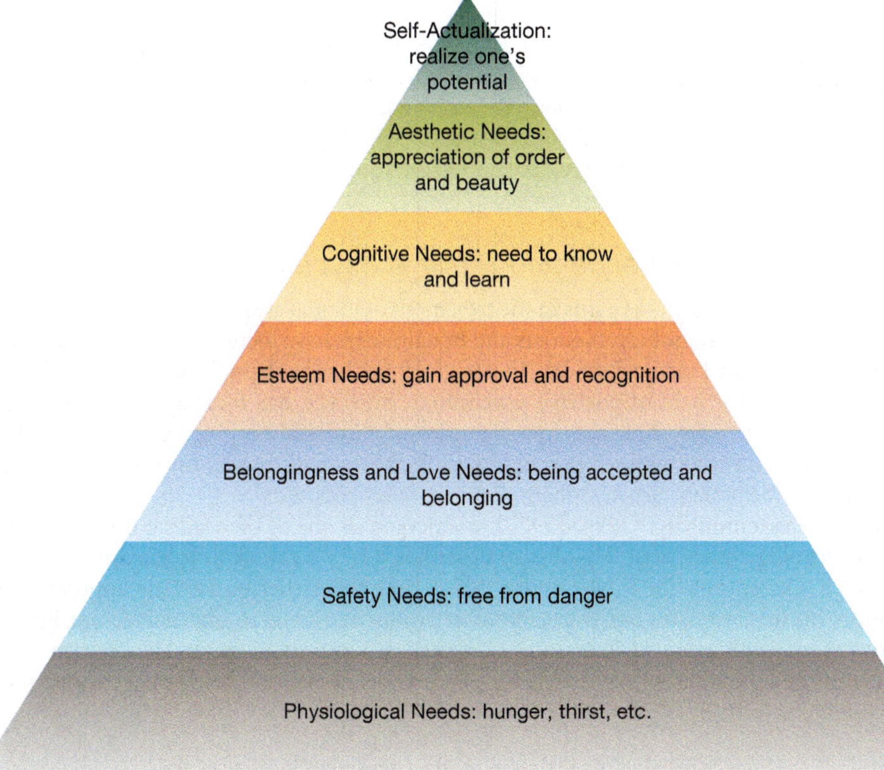

Figure 7.1

Maslow's Hierarchy of Needs

time as individual's become adept at gaining food and shelter. In a sense, we worry less about our physiological needs as we become more competent in meeting those needs. Next, our focus shifts to another perceived deficit, the need for safety, represented as a shift up the pyramid to the next level. As with our physiological needs, we initially spend considerable time and energy meeting our need for safety, moving on to other needs as we learn to satisfy the current need. We continue in this way, moving up the hierarchy of needs, trying to meet needs we perceive are in deficit.

According to Maslow's theory, our attempt to meet our *deficit needs* ends with an attempt to satisfy a very different kind of need, the need to grow and develop. *Growth needs* surround things like learning, appreciation of the arts, and ultimately, self-actualization. The need to self-actualize is at the top of Maslow's hierarchy and represents the final growth need. **Self-actualization** is the need to reach our fullest potential. Think about this for a moment. What are you ultimately going to achieve? What are your capabilities? How are you going to realize your potential? Your motivation to answer questions such as these relates to the process of self-actualization. Unlike the deficit needs, growth needs such as self-actualization do not lessen as we strive to meet the need. In fact, as we begin the journey to toward self-actualization, we typically develop a stronger motivation state. This increases our drive to become the most we can be and furthers the self-actualization process.

Self-actualization

The need to reach our fullest potential

Maslow's theory has been criticized as showing an overly simplistic view of the human condition. Rather than dealing with needs in the step-by-step fashion exemplified by Maslow's hierarchy, people often address needs from multiple levels at the same time (Freitas & Leonard, 2011). For instance, students often wrestle with issues of belongingness, while at the same time trying to develop, through their friends, a sense of positive regard or esteem. Maslow has also been criticized for his methodology. Maslow chose to develop his theory based on individuals he felt were self-actualized. He did not study individuals at random, leaving open the possibility that his theory is an accurate description of only those individuals studied. Maslow recognized the limitations of his approach, noting that he interpreted his work as merely a starting point for other investigators using more rigorous methodologies. Despite these criticisms, Maslow's theory was critically important in ushering in a renewed interest in internal constructs. He also directed psychological research toward the investigation of *mental health*, rather than mental disabilities so prominent in behavioral and Freudian theory. This focus on the typical individual and his/her journey toward personal fulfillment is currently enjoying a resurgence of interests.

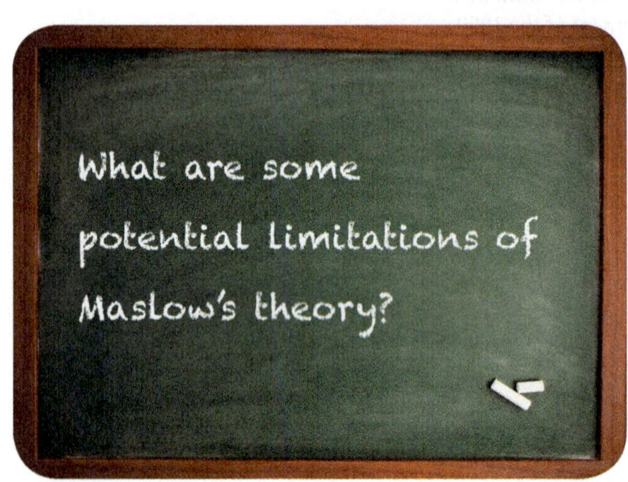

Optimal Human Experience and Positive Psychology

Psychology has made enormous gains in the treatment of mental and behavioral problems. For most of the history of psychology, theorists and practitioners have focused on treating disorders following the traditional medical model. That is, the focus has been on the diagnosis and treatment of disorders. The field of **positive psychology**, however, has recently picked up where Maslow left off. Positive psychologists investigate how *typically* developing individuals can lead better lives. The shift is away from psychological problems and toward nurturing personally relevant success (Seligman, Ernst, Gilham, Reivich, & Linkins, 2009).

Positive psychology

Psychology that investigates how typically developing individuals can lead better lives

Mihaly Csikszentmihalyi (1990, 1997) has emerged as one of the leading theorists in the positive psychology movement. His theory describes how we can achieve maximal personal fulfillment (Csikszentmihalhi & Nakamura, 2011). Like the earlier humanistic approaches to motivation, his theory relates our engagement in productive living to internal factors. Specifically, his theory emphasizes the interactions between two important factors: our perception of task difficulty and the skills we have available to meet task demands. The degree to which these factors interact effectively is called **flow** (see Figure 7.2).

Flow

A state where there is a maximal sense of fulfillment derived from a well-developed skill meeting a challenging task

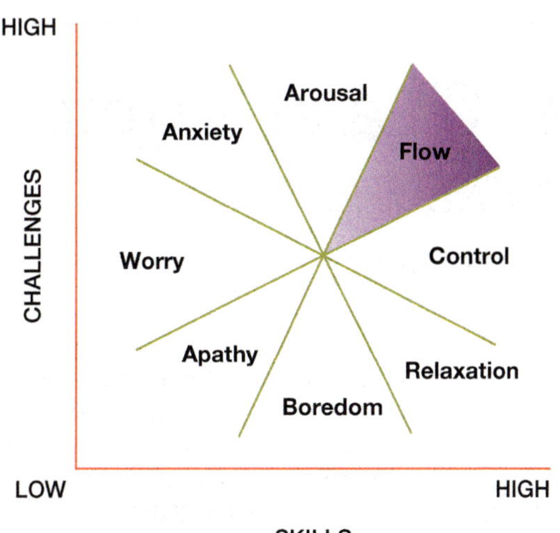

Figure 7.2
Flow

The idea of creating flow is to create that feeling we most notably associate with certain athletic experiences or games. At times, we feel so completely engrossed in a sport or game that we have a sense of oneness with the activity. There is a match between the challenge presented by the activity and our ability to meet that challenge. There is a level of satisfaction so complete that we feel we are functioning at an optimal level. Csikszentmihalyi has investigated this maximal sense of fulfillment and described it as achieving flow. Flow is dependent on the level of challenge presented by the activity. Activities that present too little challenge are unworthy of our investment and lead to apathy or boredom. Flow is also dependent on our perception of our own skills. Engagement in tasks for which we have a high skill level can lead to relaxation or a sense of control. Flow, however, is only created when we feel we are engaging in a challenging activity for which we have sufficient skill.

Flow theory has obvious implications for education. In fact, Csikszentmihalyi, a professor of psychology and education, acknowledges the importance of youth finding flow in their work and leisure activities. As an experience, flow evolves from an interaction between the individual and the situation. Teachers can help manage environmental variables and encourage personal development so that flow is more likely. Table 7.2 provides a list of flow elements relevant to education and a brief description of their application.

Table 7.2 Elements of Flow

Flow Element	Description
Task we can complete	Flow is achieved when there is a clear point defining completion of the activity. Break larger tasks into smaller ones to help students maintain a sense of completion.
Ability to concentrate	Flow is characterized by being free from distraction. Experiencing flow channels one's focus to the present task or activity. Teachers can help this process by providing appropriately supportive environments.
Task that has clear goals	Students will more fully engage in tasks for which there are clear goals. Goals help structure the activity and direct appropriate use of resources.
Task that provides immediate feedback	Teachers should make sure students have a firm sense of when they reach activity milestones. Finishing a task may be intrinsically rewarding, or the teacher may provide external rewards.
Deep, but effortless involvement	Flow requires that there is a suspension of fear and anxiety about the outcome. The individual is completely absorbed in doing the task. Teachers need to create a "safe" environment, one where students feel they are able to lose themselves in a task.

In The Classroom

APPLYING THEORY

Flow Theory

THEORY BASICS

As you have just learned, flow theory is concerned with optimal environments for learning and performance. This had direct application to educational learning environments and instructional planning. Some have defined the overriding principle of instruction as the creation of environments where students gain knowledge under optimal conditions (Chan & Ahern, 1999). Similarly, researchers have argued that learning should be inherently interesting, in addition to resulting in a learning product (Rieber, Smith, & Noah, 1998; Rieber & Matzko, 2001).

CLASSROOM APPLICATION

In general, assignments that are open are more likely to lead to a sense of flow. These are assignments that do not have a prescribed learning path but are open to the ideas and directions generated by the learners. Activities where the students are *active* in participating in learning are also more likely to create a sense of flow. Additionally, activities based on a project help students focus and increase immersion in the task. (Rieber, Smith, & Noah, 1998). Maintaining a sense of curiosity is also important. Help students develop goals while keeping them curious about the outcome. Students should perceive they have considerable control over the direction of the project, increasing their sense of ownership over the learning process. Providing clear and immediate feedback is also crucial if students are to learn effectively. Finally, try to maintain a close watch on individual student progress. Learning should be rewarding, not frustrating, resulting in an increase in self-esteem.

Teachers: Constantly strive to design lessons where students are presented with activities that challenge them, while ensuring they have the necessary skills and an easily accessible source of immediate feedback. These situations are more likely to create a strong sense of flow.

Cognitive Views of Motivation

The humanistic movement of the 1960s provided an alternative view of human behavior. It stood in striking opposition to the pervasive behavioral theories at the time. The humanists, however, were not to be the strongest voice to challenge behavioral theories. That voice came from the cognitive theorists who rose to prominence in the 1970s and have continued to be a powerful force in psychology. Cognitive theory holds that our thoughts, feelings, plans, and expectations have a direct impact on the expression of our behavior. Similarly, cognitive research supports that our thinking can have a direct impact on our motivation to act. Cognitive theorists view people as active and curious; we actively evaluate the world around us and look for meaning in how the world works. Through this process we develop beliefs and expectations about people and their behavior. This, in turn, impacts our behavior and ultimately the choices we make in life. An understanding of how students establish such patterns of thinking can help teachers educate more effectively.

Attribution Theory

The basic assumption behind attribution theory is that we actively search for the causes of events happening in our lives. Consider your attempts to explain why you did not score well on a particular test. Perhaps you felt the test was too difficult. Maybe you thought the test was fair, but you did not study as much as needed; or maybe you decided that the subject matter was not your specialty and you just couldn't do any better. All of these possibilities represent your attempts to determine *cause*. **Attribution theory** describes our attempts to determine causes for events happening in our lives and that, subsequently, impact our level of motivation (Weiner, 2011).

Attribution theory

Theory that describes our attempts to determine causes for events happening in our lives and subsequently impacts our level of motivation

Table 7.3 Weiner's Attribution Theory

Attribution Source	Description
Locus	Perception that an outcome results from internal or external factors: *Internal*—I earned an *A* because I tried hard. *External*—I earned an *A* because the test was easy.
Stability	Perception of how likely an outcome is to occur again: *Stable*—I always get *A*'s because I'm smart. *Unstable*—I was lucky I got an *A* this time.
Controllability	Perception of whether an outcome was under someone's control: *Controllable*—I could get an *A* if he would write a reasonable test. *Uncontrollable*—I'll never make an *A* because I was born stupid.

Attribution theory has received considerable attention from educators. This is because educators are particularly interested in how students attribute success or failure during the learning process. Bernard Weiner (1985, 1986, 2000) has published several studies on attribution and learning. His theory describes how we make attributions along three dimensions (see Table 7.3).

For example, let's say a student gets her first test back and smiles with delight at her grade of 98 out of 100. She says to her friend, "I told you I was good at math!" According to Weiner's theory, the student is attributing the cause of her good grade to an internal factor—her natural facility with mathematics. This type of attribution represents one end of an *internal/external dimension*. Sometimes we look at the events occurring in our lives and attribute cause to our own abilities, like the student in the above example. At other times, we attribute cause to external events. Students who attribute a good grade to the ease of the test are making an external attribution for their success.

Another attributional dimension is based on the perceived stability of the outcome. When we attribute cause to a temporary source, like an unusual amount of effort, we believe the outcome is unstable and unlikely to occur again in the future. This type of attribution falls along the *stable/unstable dimension*. The above student's attribution to her natural ability with math appears to indicate a relatively stable cause. That is, she is likely to continue to do well in math because she is a good math student.

Weiner's third attributional dimension is *controllable/uncontrollable*. This dimension reflects the degree to which we believe an outcome is under someone's control. For example, let's say you failed to make the school's volleyball team. You comment, "That coach didn't pick me because he only wants seniors on the team." This indicates a perception that team selection was under the control of the coach and that the outcome was undesirable. Another way to look at the situation is to say, "The coach didn't pick me because he was under orders from the principal to only pick seniors." This statement indicates that team selection was not under the control of the coach. Perceptions of controllability lead to particular emotional outcomes. If you believe the coach deliberately did not choose you for the team, then you might be inclined to think negatively about him. Alternatively, if you believe your failure to make the team was not under the coach's control, you are much less likely to have hostile feelings toward the coach. Our attributional style has a direct bearing on our emotional experiences.

When students meet with success or failure, teachers should take the time to explore their attributions. Teachers can help students understand the nature of their views on success and failure. Some students may have realistic attributions regarding the events and behaviors leading to certain outcomes. Others may inappropriately make attributions to unrealistic causes. Help students see these issues and encourage more effective attributions. For example, a student may consistently attribute academic failure to stable causes (e.g., I fail every test because I just can't learn). Helping the student to see that success is directly related to effective preparation will encourage them to focus on applying effort to studying, rather than giving up. Of course, the teacher will need to provide concrete solutions to help the student develop the necessary study skills, encouraging a view that failure is temporary and something that can be avoided in the future through better test preparation.

Expectancy and Value Theory

Expectancy and value theorists

Theorists that believe motivation results from the interaction between our expectancy for success and the value we place on the outcome

Expectancy and value theorists believe motivation results from the interaction between our expectancy for success and the value we place on the outcome (Wigfield & Eccles, 1992, 2000; Pintrich & Schunk, 2002; Nagengast et al., 2011). For example, you might have a history of doing well in psychology classes and therefore expect to do well in your new educational psychology course. Taking the course might also satisfy graduation requirements, so you value a successful completion of the course. The combination of your positive expectation and your desire for a good grade results in a high level of motivation.

Expectancy for success

Our perception regarding the potential outcome of a situation

Self-schema

Term used to refer to the collection of ways we view ourselves

Expectancy for success is our perception regarding the potential outcome of a situation. It is our guess about the probability of success. Research has shown that expectancy derives from two factors: task difficulty and self-schemas. Our perceptions about the difficulty of a task clearly affect our expectancy for success. If we believe a task is extremely difficult, we lower our expectations for success accordingly. Similarly, we have high expectations for success when we feel a task is easy. Another important factor is how we view our capability. For some things, we see ourselves as being highly competent. Perhaps we feel we are good at athletics, so we have a high expectation for success when learning a new sport. How do you view yourself? Do you see yourself as smart, funny, social, or reliable? **Self-schema** is a term used to refer to the collection of ways we view ourselves. Depending on our self-schemas, we may be more or less motivated to anticipate success. If we see ourselves as being bad at math, then we may demonstrate little motivation to do our math homework, even though the assignment is easy. As you can see, our self-schemas and our perception of task difficulty interact to determine our expectations regarding success.

Task value

The value or priority that we place on situational outcomes

Task value refers to the value or priority we place on situational outcomes. For example, Marsha wants to play soccer with her team after school, but she is more interested in seeing the latest movie. Seeing the movie and playing soccer are both valued, but the movie has a higher value for Marsha. Establishing whether we value a given task results from many competing factors. Table 7.4 reviews typical questions on which we reflect when determining the value of a task.

Task value refers to the value of priority we place on tasks. The girl who is thinking of joining the school choir will practice hard and determine how much she likes singing before she makes her decision.

To illustrate the factors contributing to how much we value a task, consider a young girl who wants to join the school chorus. In trying to make her decision, she will probably consider just how much she likes singing. She thinks about how much time she spends learning the words to songs on the radio and how she really tries to improve the sound of her voice. She determines that she really likes singing—it is *(1) intrinsically interesting*. She also considers how happy she will be if she does well. Performing well in the chorus affirms her perception of herself as a good singer and, therefore, is *(2) important* to her. As she continues to reflect on whether joining the chorus is a good idea, she begins to consider if the experience will help her with a future career in music. She remembers a famous pop singer who said in an interview that she started in her school chorus. The young girl decides that being in the chorus would indeed be *(3) useful* to her future. Finally, she begins to consider the downsides to participating in the chorus, such as the number of hours per week and how participating will make it difficult to do other activities. Participation in chorus will only be possible at the *(4) cost* of participation in other activities

We may not be as systematic in our value assessment as this example implies, but we are still likely to consider these factors in some way. It is also important to remember that how someone feels about one of these factors influences the others. For example, the student in the above example may not want to spend the required number of

Table 7.4 Typical Questions Reflected on When Determining the Value of a Task

Things We VALUE about a Task	Questions We Ask Ourselves
1. Intrinsic Interest	"Is there something interesting about the task?"
2. Importance	"Will participating in the task tell me something important about myself?"
3. Utility Value	"In what way is participating in the task useful to me?"
4. Cost	"What is the downside to participating in the task?"

hours in chorus but thinks it might really help her future. Everyone achieves a balance among such conflicting issues resulting in more or less motivation.

Sociological Views of Motivation

Another important perspective to consider is the impact of one's social group on motivation. Think about your own educational experience. How did your friends, family, or cultural group affect your motivation to do well in school? As we reviewed earlier in the chapter, we all have a need to affiliate with others (Murray, 1938). This need to affiliate may vary from person to person (O'Connor & Rosenblood, 1996), but all students are affected by their social relationships. Educators are beginning to consider these influences more carefully, trying to better understand the effect of social relationships on the learning process.

Community of learners
A collection of individuals gathered for the purpose of meeting a learning objective

Legitimate peripheral participation
Emphasis on the initial participation of new learners typically along the periphery of the learning community

An interesting theory of how social relations and learning interact comes from the work of Lave and Wenger (1991). Their work focuses on how learning takes place within a social context. They emphasize that each individual within that context is constantly evolving in terms of their perceptions of themselves as they are learning. Consider a fifth grade math class where they are introducing algebraic concepts. Most students will consider themselves reasonably uninformed at the beginning of the lesson. This stage, however, is critical to the overall growth the student will ultimately experience within this community of learners. **Community of learners** is simply a collection of individuals gathered for the purpose of meeting a learning objective. This initial phase of the learning process within a community of learners has been termed **legitimate peripheral participation**, emphasizing that initial participation of new learners is typically along the periphery of the learning community (Lave & Wenger, 1991). This is viewed as a necessary and beneficial stage in the overall learning process (Coll & Paku, 2011). It is a time of observation and a way for the beginner to learn the necessary rules governing the interactions of the group. As students learn the material, however, they will be less distinguishable from the teacher in terms of their vocabulary, skill, and performance. This movement from novice to proficient learner is entirely dependent on the particular class of learners. In classes where learning is valued, students will be encouraged by social relationships to grow and develop. The quality of their learning will be a product of their unique community. If students place themselves in a social group that devalues academic success, the quality of the learning product will be compromised. This makes it important for teachers to encourage students to identify with a community of learners that values excellence and mastery.

A community of learners is simply a group of individuals gathered together for the purpose of meeting a learning objective.

SUMMARIZE AND REFLECT

1. Understanding motivation will depend on one's psychological perspective. Having a tendency to look at a student's thoughts when explaining performance will naturally lead to an understanding of motivation as internal. Focusing on how the environment impacts behavior leads to an understanding of motivation as external. It is important to realize that an understanding of motivation depends on these types of perspective.
2. One perspective on motivation is behaviorism. Behaviorists generally avoid internal concepts like motivation, instead focusing on environmental consequences like reinforcement to explain why we behave.
3. Another perspective is the humanistic perspective. This perspective emphasizes the importance of looking at an individual's wants and needs to understand why he/she behaves. The humanistic perspective relates to the newer field of positive psychology. Researchers in this field discuss how strong motivation comes from being challenged and feeling like you have the skills to meet that challenge.
4. The cognitive perspective focuses on how our thinking about a situation influences behavior. Our search for the causes of outcomes impacts our thinking and feeling about a situation and often alters the direction of future behavior.
5. Expectations are an important cognitive element to consider when explaining behavior. Expectations are determined by the probability of success and the value of a particular outcome.
6. It is also important to understand the impact of social and cultural factors motivating students.

INFORMED APPLICATION

1. A student has been doing well in your seventh grade social studies class. Her work is thorough, thoughtful, and organized. Lately, however she has been having trouble with another student who acts out frequently. She is clearly distressed by the other student's outbursts, and her grades are slipping. How can you use expectancy theory to understand the situation? How would you approach improving the situation?
2. Present arguments for and against teachers taking an active role in helping students negotiate social relationships. Is it a part of the teachers job? How could socialization patterns impact motivation to achieve?

GOALS AND MOTIVATION

The various perspectives on motivation discussed in the previous section help teachers understand what makes for a successful and personally fulfilling academic experience. The different emphasis of each perspective can be confusing at times, but they help teachers develop insight into what motivates student's behavior, thinking, and interpersonal interactions. In this section we will focus in on how these perspectives help teachers understand how students set and pursue goals. When we pursue or work toward a certain outcome, or goal, we are engaging in goal directed behavior. **Goal directed behavior** involves striving to accomplish a desired outcome. When it comes to achievement in the classroom, two types of goals have been extensively studied: performance goals and mastery goals (Dweck, 1986; Ames & Archer, 1988; Tollefson, 2000; Ames, 1992).

Goal directed behavior

Behavior that involves striving to accomplish a desired outcome

Achievement Goals: Mastery and Performance

When trying to achieve a goal, students often take a mastery or performance approach. **Mastery oriented students** focus on learning the material. **Performance oriented students** are more concerned about how they will be judged (see Table 7.5).

Mastery oriented students

A student focused on learning the material

Performance oriented students

One more concerned about how his/her performance will be judged

Students who set mastery and performance goals have different concepts of success (Nicholls, Patashnick, Cheung, Thorkildsen, & Lauer, 1989). Students with performance goals are focusing on social comparisons. A student may make a comparison to normative standards or to the performance of others they know (Ames, 1984). In contrast, mastery goals are based in the intrinsic value of learning (Butler, 1987), and the belief that one's efforts will lead to new knowledge or skill (Ames, 1992). In the case of mastery goals, standards are self-referenced,

Table 7.5 Mastery Oriented Students versus Performance Oriented Students

PERFORMANCE GOALS

Individuals who set performance goals are invested in successful outcomes. They want to win and also to avoid being embarrassed.

MASTERY GOALS

Individuals who set mastery goals are interested in self-improvement. They focus on learning and want to avoid failure to master the task.

rather than looking to some outside norm to define their success. Mastery oriented learners are motivated to engage in the process of learning as they work to understand and master content, even if failures occur along the way (Ames, 1992; Tollefson, 2000).

If you're thinking that the concepts of performance and mastery goals seem to be somewhat similar to the concepts of intrinsic and extrinsic reinforcement discussed at the beginning of the chapter, you're right. Performance goals are largely based on extrinsic motivation. A student with a performance orientation would likely work hard on assignments that were graded. Mastery goals, on the other hand, are based in intrinsic motivation. Regardless of whether an assignment is graded, a student with a mastery goal orientation would put in the same amount of work. Research suggests that a mastery orientation is more likely to produce positive attitudes toward learning (Patrick, Kaplan, & Ryan, 2011). Further, a mastery orientation is more likely to produce achievement behavior, which continues over time (Ames, 1992). In contrast, performance goal orientations relate to the use of superficial learning strategies, a desire to seek positive evaluations and to avoid negative ones, and an avoidance of challenge (Dweck, 1986; Nolen, 1988). They have also been shown to relate to student beliefs that it is ability, rather than effort, which drives success (Hidi & Harackiewicz, 2000). While studies which contrast mastery and performance goal orientations clearly illustrate the benefits of a mastery goal orientation over a performance one, performance goals have not always been found to have negative effects. Some researchers find positive effects of performance goals on a variety of learning related constructs, such as cognitive engagement and academic performance (Hidi & Harackiewicz, 2000). Further, the two types of goal orientations do not always operate in isolation. Both mastery and performance goals may be in operation at the same time. In fact, some research indicates that students who have both mastery and performance goals show increases in self-regulation and higher grades than those who have only mastery goals (Ainley, 1993; Pintrich 2000; Roebken, 2007).

How do performance and mastery goals relate to intrinsic and extrinsic reinforcement?

Work Avoidance Goals

Work-avoidant goals

Goals set to get work done with as little exertion or effort as possible

Both mastery and performance goals relate to a student's motivation to achieve. Not all students, however, have a desire to achieve. In fact, the goal for some students is to do as little work as possible. A student with a **work-avoidant goal** orientation gets work done with as little exertion or effort as possible (Nichols et al., 1990; Pintrich & Schunk, 2002). Work avoidant learners do not want to learn or look smart—they simply want to avoid work. It appears that work-avoidant goals may also combine with other types of goals to influence cognitive engagement and academic achievement (Ainley, 1993). For example, a student with a performance goal orientation may also show work-avoidant goals, striving to "beat" his classmates with as little effort as possible. These traits ultimately undermine student learning and lead to academic difficulties. Identifying what aspect of a student's behavior supports work avoidance is difficult. Some teachers have students keep daily journals to help identify what behaviors negatively impact academic success. It is also important for teachers to help students develop an appreciation for the positive outcomes associated with active engagement in the learning process.

Social Goals

When considering social goals, it is important for teachers to remember that we have an inherent need to affiliate with others (see section on Maslow earlier in this chapter). Social relationships can be a great source of support for a student. A student's pursuit of social goals may positively influence the pursuit of academic goals by promoting positive classroom behaviors and enhancing teacher and peer relations (Wentzel, 1989, 1991; Cecchini Estrada, Gonzalez-Mesa, Mendez-Gimenez, & Fernandez-Rio, 2011). At times, students may gravitate toward each other because of their mutual success in school. Their social relationships formed around a perception of themselves as being good at school. In this situation, students may expend considerable effort to maintain their academic success so they maintain their social bonds.

Of course, social relations can work in the opposite direction. Some friendships form because students see themselves as struggling in school. This can exert a negative influence on learning as students prioritize other activities. For example, students may be distracted from learning tasks in order to attend to conflicting social concerns (Entwistle & Kozeki, 1985). Even if students see themselves as academically capable, they may still develop social relationships that pull them away from the activities supporting academic success. Research shows that when a student's peer group does not value (or actively discourages) academic achievement, negative effects on school performance result (Kinderman, McCollam, & Gibson, 1996).

Research also indicates that students may have multiple social and academic goals that interact in complicated ways to affect engagement in learning and academic achievement (Meece, 1991). Educational success requires students to negotiate a difficult balance between powerful socialization needs and the demanding work required for academic success. If teachers find that hanging out with friends is competing with school (Urdan & Maehr, 1995), they should explore ways to help the students meet their social needs in academically productive ways. A conversation with a student might help to identify preferred peer relationships. The teacher can then pair these friends for group activities in school. The teacher can also give outside class assignments to help bring academic focus to activities outside of school. This approach uses desirable social relationships to encourage spending time on beneficial academic tasks. Students are already socializing after school, and this approach simply builds upon this existing relationship to help a student produce academically. Working with a student's existing social goals helps the student learn to participate in social activities in ways that do not detract from, but support, his/her academic progress.

Goal Setting

Research on goal setting indicates that goals serve four primary functions (Lock & Latham, 2002). These include the following:

- *Directs behavior toward goal-relevant behaviors* Goals help us engage in behaviors that support our goals and away from behaviors that are irrelevant to achieving our goals.
- *Provides an energizing effect that helps people move toward their goals* Goals lead to more energetic efforts to succeed.

- *Helps with persistence* Goals lead to long-lasting efforts to achieve a desired outcome.
- *Encourages effective use of new or existing knowledge and strategies* Goals promote the development of new and inventive solutions to any barriers to goal achievement.

As these factors indicate, setting goals leads to a variety of positive outcomes. Research has also shown that goals are more effective if they are specific and challenging and are realized in the near future (Zimmerman & Schunk, 2001). When we set goals that are too vague and ill-defined, it makes it difficult for us to recognize when we are failing to make satisfactory progress. Goals such as "I want better grades" are typically too vague to be helpful. Also, goals that are perceived as too easy are unlikely to motivate us to adequately pursue the goal. Goals should be challenging enough to engage us in the task, but not too difficult. Lastly, we are more likely to try to achieve something if the results of that activity are realized in the near future. Goals surrounding events too far in the future are typically overlooked in favor of goals with immediate results.

Goals provide much needed guidance and structure and can have lasting positive effects into adulthood (Hill, Jackson, Roberts, Lapsley, & Brandenberger, 2011). Teachers can provide enormous support by educating students on appropriate goal setting strategies. They are also in a good position to encourage students to consider the benefits of academic achievement in realizing life goals. Teachers can make goal setting a part of their curricular plan. Teachers and students should share in the development of overall classroom goals. Teachers can also work with students individually to develop appropriate personal goals. This provides students and teachers with focus and direction, both of which enhance motivation. Co-development of goals also helps students fully engage in meeting goals.

SUMMARIZE AND REFLECT

1. Goals are essentially desired outcomes and can be categorized in a variety of ways. Goals impact the quality of our motivational state.
2. Achievement goals can be directed toward mastery or performance. Mastery goals emphasize the need to learn the material. Performance goals relate to obtaining a positive appraisal from someone.
3. Work avoidance goals are also common. Often what is important for a student is simply to make it through the day with as little effort as possible.
4. Social goals are important for students as they learn to negotiate the difficult task of relating to others. Students may have difficulty balancing these goals with academic goals and benefit from structure and guidance from the teacher.
5. Goal setting has been shown to provide a variety of positive effects on motivation, such as helping students arouse, direct, and maintain behavior.
6. Goals also help to encourage problem solving when goals are blocked. In general, goals should be specific and challenging and realized in the near future.

INFORMED APPLICATION

1. Mastery goals are often challenging to encourage, especially given the extensive societal pressure on performance. Educators trying to teach more in less time complicate this effort. What are some practical suggestions for meeting basic performance standards while supporting the development of mastery goals?
2. Create an assignment to help students realize the extent of their work avoidance behaviors. The assignment should be able to be completed within one week and provide each student with personal information regarding his/her own behaviors. Also, create discussion questions for the class to consider following the assignment.

THE CHAPTER IN REVIEW

Check out our website
▶ www.BVTLab.com
for chapter-by-chapter flashcards, practice quizzes, summaries, and more.

This chapter begins our exploration of what motivates people to act. As educators look to find ways to encourage academic excellence, they quickly learn that motivating students is complicated. To begin our discussion of this exciting, but difficult topic, we began by looking at how motivation is defined and some basic conceptualizations of motivation common in the field. We looked at how behavior is motivated by internal factors such as wants and need. These motivators are called intrinsic. We also looked at extrinsic motivators that reside in the environment and include things like grades, money, and praise.

The next section reviewed how an understanding of motivation depends on your perspective. Behaviorists look to the environment to explain why we act. They are primarily interested in how consequences, like reinforcement, shape the expression of behavior. Another perspective on motivation emphasizes cognitions, or how we think about a situation. This perspective has gained considerable prominence in recent years as we strive to better understand how our thoughts are tied to our actions. We looked at how motivation is influenced by our search for the causes of events happening in our lives. We also looked at how our expectations for success interact with how much we value a particular outcome. Finally, we discussed the importance of looking at how social and cultural factors impact our motivation.

Another factor influencing our behavior comes from the goals we set. Goals to achieve often surround learning the material (mastery) or obtaining a positive judgment (performance). In educational settings, academically related goals are not the only relevant goals, however. Another important goal we need to consider is work avoidant goals. Students often spend time trying to get through their school day with as little work as possible. Obviously, these goals compete with achievement-oriented goals. Social goals are also important for students. We discussed why these goals are meaningful to students and how teachers can incorporate these goals into their educational plan to help students learn. The final part of this section covered goal setting. We looked at the positive influence of goals on behavior. We also reviewed how goals should be specific and challenging and realized in the near future.

Interdisciplinary Case Focus

principal special educator
teacher parents psychologist
social worker physical educator
nurse peers doctor

Mr. Max Wertheimer is a ninth grade social studies teacher working on an American history unit. He just gave a test on prominent figures from this time period only to have half of the class fail. Mr. Wertheimer is not only disappointed in the results but also confused about how to fix the problem. He had known from past experience that this section was difficult for the students, so he had taken steps to make the material more available for the student. He found engaging documentary and fictional films on the topic. He gave what he thought were fun and exciting in-class assignments. He even tried to make sure that he projected an excited tone when he lectured. Clearly his plan did not work, but he was not sure what else to do.

He thought about the student's attitude and behavior as they were learning the material. He determined it was generally polite, but not exactly glowing with excitement. Even after he returned the tests, the students seemed to have little investment in doing better. He began to wonder if the problem was just in his class, or perhaps it was a phase and would eventually pass. He decided not to wait, however, and immediately made appointments to talk to the school psychologist about ways to motivate the students. He also made an appointment with the ninth grade science teacher to see if the students were having similar difficulties in her class.

School Psychologist Mary Smith, the school psychologist, was not surprised by Mr. Wertheimer's story. She told him that students at this age often have difficulty focusing on academic material because so many other issues are surfacing for the students. She explained that students at this age are particularly interested in finding ways to look good in the eyes of their peers. This leads many students to prioritize social obligations, which sometimes leaves little time for studying. She suggested that instead of trying to engage the students through watching films, he should try to do things that allow students to interact. Watching films is a solitary activity and does not meet their need to socialize and to be held in high regard by their peers. Perhaps he could have the students work collaboratively to reenact certain historical events. Students could research the material with his providing some structure. They could design the "play" and even make costumes. This certainly would help with the student's need to socialize and to learn the material; however, he would also need to ensure their success given their sensitivity to how they are perceived by others. He could have all groups provide at least one positive comment and one constructive suggestion about their projects. This would guide possible negativity in a more positive direction and give the students useful information before they did their reenactment before the group. Mr. Wertheimer was very excited about the suggestion and left to make appropriate preparations.

Ninth Grade Science Teacher After his meeting with the school psychologist, Mr. Wertheimer went to talk with his colleague who teaches science. He began the meeting with a review of his problems. He also reviewed the suggestions made by the school psychologists. Ms. Rocquemore was surprised by the student's failure on the test. At the same time Mr. Wertheimer was teaching his section on historical figures, she was teaching a new lesson on basic physical concepts, and the students appeared to love it. In fact, their grade on the material was the highest this year.

Mr. Wertheimer and Ms. Rocquemore decide to use the student's natural enjoyment of her science lesson to reinforce Mr. Wertheimer's lesson. The students were still going to reenact historical events surrounding great figures in American history, but each group of students had to pick a figure that also made some contribution to science. Many early American figures made significant contributions to agriculture, architecture, and technology. They had little difficulty coming up with a list for the students. They also planned for Ms. Rocquemore to go into to more detail in her class about the nature of the scientific contribution made by these individuals.

Parents After more reflection, Mr. Wertheimer decided to follow through on one additional idea. He went to the next meeting of the PTA and asked if the parents of his students could stay for a few minutes after the meeting to help him with a class project. He described his plan for presenting the lesson and indicated that the students would likely do a better job if each group had a parent sponsor. The parent would help each group acquire the materials for its reenactment, as well as provide an after school location for the students to practice. He quickly found enough volunteers for each group.

Conclusion This interdisciplinary case study emphasizes the importance of using resources to help support appropriate and engaging learning environments. Mr. Wertheimer's first positive step following the students' failure on the test was to realize he needed help to solve the problem. Today's teachers need to learn how to efficiently use available resources to achieve maximal learning. Recognizing the possible psychological nature of the problem, Mr. Wertheimer wisely sought out the advice of his school psychologist. It was also a good idea to discuss the issue with a colleague, especially one that shares the same students. Finally, recognizing the importance of parents in student learning is critical. Parents can provide enormous support to teachers, often needing only a little structure and guidance.

Key Terms

TERM	*Page*	*TERM*	*Page*
Attribution theory	216	Mastery oriented students	220
Community of learners	219	Performance oriented students	220
Expectancy and value theorists	218	Positive psychology	214
Expectancy for success	218	Punishments	212
Extrinsically motivated behavior	209	Reinforcements	212
Flow	214	Self-actualization	214
Goal directed behavior	220	Self-schema	218
Hierarchy of needs	213	State theories	211
Incentive	208	Task value	218
Intrinsically motivated behavior	209	Traits	211
Legitimate peripheral participation	219	Work-avoidant goals	222

8
Chapter
INDIVIDUALS,
GROUPS, AND
SOCIETY

What's It All About ...

How do individual differences influence education?

In what ways do groups differ from each other?

How do societal and cultural factors affect education?

Chapter Objectives

- Understand the diverging educational landscape.
- Review how to create an authentic integration of individuality.

- Describe differences between girls and boys.
- Review linguistic differences.
- Understand variations in family structure.

- Understand the impact of socioeconomic status (SES).
- Define ethnicity.
- Explain culturally sensitive instruction.

EXTENDED OUTLINE

Individuals, Groups, and Society

I. What's It All About ...
II. From Today's Headlines
III. Individual Variation and Shared Education
    A. The diverging educational landscape
    B. Diversity, individuals, and instruction
        1. Differentiated instruction as a foundation for appreciating diversity
            a. Basic principles of differentiated instruction
            b. Differentiated instruction and diversity
        2. Equity and equality
        3. Mutual respect
    C. Summarize and reflect
IV. We're Not All the Same
    A. Girls and boys
        1. Gender role and identity
            a. Biology of gender development
            b. The impact of learning on gender development
            c. Cognitive influences on gender development
        2. Gender stereotypes
        3. Behavioral and cognitive differences
        4. Gender bias
    B. Linguistic differences
        1. Regional dialects
        2. English as a Second Language and Bilingual Education
    C. Families
        1. Traditional homes and the nuclear family
        2. Intergenerational child rearing
        3. Same-sex parents
        4. Single-parent and blended families
    D. Summarize and reflect
V. Culture and Society
    A. Socioeconomic status (SES)
        1. Educational experience and SES
        2. Family and SES
    B. Ethnicity
        1. Race versus ethnicity
        2. Ethnic trends
    C. Culturally sensitive instruction
        1. Cultural identification
        2. Multicultural education
    D. Summarize and reflect
VI. The Chapter in Review
VII. Interdisciplinary Case Focus

From Today's Headlines

Vol. I No. 8 Teaching World, 2012

DO YOU SPEAK AMERICAN?

The idea of an *American language* is as complex as it is controversial. The controversy is often about what exactly is taught in our schools. However, saying we should simply teach "English" doesn't really simplify the situation. This is because English is not a single entity. Do we teach the brand of English spoken in the Deep South or maybe the English of the typical New Yorker? Some might argue that both regions speak the same English but with a different accent. Closer examination, however, reveals that regional language differences are more than just differences in pronunciation. They are different dialects, complete with unique vocabulary and rules of grammar.

The type of English we actually teach in schools more closely resembles the language spoken by newscasters on the evening news. Educators refer to this form of English as *Standard English*. Like regional dialects, Standard English is rule governed with a common vocabulary. Is it, however, "correct" English? This is a difficult question. Correct is ultimately what our society mutually agrees upon, and it doesn't look like agreement is coming in the near future. The United States hasn't even reached agreement as to whether English should be the official language in our country. Individual states (twenty-five) have adopted English as their only official language—but not our country. Addressing regional or even cultural variations of English is even more difficult. States like California have tried to deal with cultural dialects like African American English with enormous controversy and little success.

The debate over what form of English should be taught in our schools is highly interconnected with attempts to embrace a broader range of diversity. Schools often work hard to help students gain exposure to different cultures and different ways of being in the world, but with greater cultural diversity comes greater linguistic diversity. How do we validate a student's individual heritage, while devaluing the language that is inherent in that culture? Is it different if the student represents a cultural group outside the United States (e.g., Mexican) or a cultural group within our own boarders (e.g., Southerners)? These are difficult questions, and we are still looking for answers.

The title of this *From Today's Headlines* feature is also the title of a PBS documentary on the fascinating complexities of the English language. The three-hour series and accompanying website (www.pbs.org/speak) explore why it is easy to tell the difference between students in Long Island, New York, from students in Montgomery, Alabama. Language is a powerful tool. It can be used to enhance our ability to work together. It can also be used as a tool to socially isolate segments of our population. *Do You Speak American*? is an engaging resource,

(continues)

helping educators explore learning approaches, which uses our differences to create a richer understanding of our living language.

MAKE THE CONNECTION

Ask people around the country if they speak "American" and you will probably get a confident "Yes." As a whole, people are proud of the way they speak, seeing their language as an outward sign of who they are. In this chapter, we will take a closer look at how students differ in their use of language. We will also examine the underlying culture language represents. Our focus in this chapter is not only to better understand linguistic and cultural diversity but also to develop a broader appreciation for individual differences. We will look at how boys differ from girls and how children from traditional and non-traditional families differ. We will also look at educational approaches that affirm individuality and help students use their unique characteristics to achieve success. Let's begin with a closer examination of demographic changes in our country and how schools can adapt to those changes to achieve academic excellence.

INDIVIDUAL VARIATION AND SHARED EDUCATION

Schools today are facing many changes. Our traditional curriculum is changing to accommodate our rapidly growing knowledge base. Instructional strategies are changing to make better use of student-centered approaches. In fact, our entire educational outlook is beginning to change in response to our growing sense of the world as an integrated community. The globalization of our culture is influenced by our increased interactions with other countries and also because of greater diversification of the American population.

In today's schools, a diverse student body shares classrooms, gyms, and art and music rooms. We are integrating to an extent that is unprecedented in American culture. Experts predict that sometime between 2040 and 2050 our demographic changes will result in the absence of a majority culture for the first time in the history of the United States (Banks, 2002; Meece & Kurtz-Costes, 2001; Nasser, 2000). How are we going to prepare our students to learn, work, and play in this diverse environment? At a fundamental level, the answer lies in our appreciation, understanding, and respect for individuality. In this chapter, we are going to look at how educators increasingly emphasize individuality in their instruction. Helping student's value individual variation allows teachers to build upon the unique characteristics students bring to the educational environment. This results in a much richer and comprehensive educational experience.

We will begin our look at individual variation with our educational lens focused on the individual. We are going to look at an instructional model specifically designed to tailor education to individual needs. We will also examine the concepts of equity and mutual respect, which form the cornerstone of individual instruction. The second section of the chapter pulls back from individuals and looks at groups of people that we often perceive to have common traits. We will look at how boys and girls are thought to differ and how to critically evaluate our resulting biases. We will also look at how regional and cultural speech patterns affect some of our commonly held educational beliefs. Similarly, we will explore how family groups are changing and the new challenges this presents for educators. The last section of the chapter will pull back even further from specific individuals, looking at trends present across our entire society. We will review the influence of social and economic factors on education. We will also examine how educational practices can be more sensitive to multicultural environments.

The Diverging Educational Landscape

American society is a vibrant, dynamic collection of cultures and peoples. Since the beginning of our country, we have seen continuous changes in our population composition, distribution, and cultural make-up. The second half of the twentieth century was especially notable, as we saw dramatic changes in immigration trends, family structure, poverty, and cultural representation. Many of these trends are expected to continue throughout the twenty-first century. This necessitates corresponding changes in education, as schools constantly work to meet our diverse societal needs. **Diversity** is often difficult to define, but at a fundamental level, it is about individuality or difference. People vary in countless ways; often, however, diversity means differences in ethnicity and race, gender, sexual orientation, intellectual ability, income level, and religious affiliation. This list, however, is far from inclusive. Different situations emphasize different diversity dimensions, such as athleticism, attractiveness, health, age, and educational level. School systems deal with all of these factors as they attempt to provide instruction that is sensitive to every student's needs. As educational institutions strive to deal with greater diversity, they often focus on the concepts of acceptance and mutual respect. This means we need a clear understanding of how people differ and what this means to the educational environment. A close examination of recent demographic trends reveals many societal differences and how they are changing over time as shown in Table 8.1 (Olson, 2000; Bianchi & Casper, 2000).

Diversity

Often difficult to define, but at a fundamental level, is about individuality or difference

As these data show, our educational system is facing a number of societal changes. Schools are constantly struggling with the increasing number of students in our educational system. They are also dealing with a rapidly changing immigration population and high rates of marital disruption. These societal factors present many challenges to our nation's schools, but some schools are impacted to a greater extent. For example, U.S. census data indicates that only eighteen states will see increases in their school-aged population. Other states will actually see decreases. Even in states facing significant changes, much of the growth is in metropolitan areas. Large metropolitan areas have higher rates of immigration and struggle with high poverty rates.

Poverty affects many children in the United States. Approximately 1 in 6 children live in a home where the annual income is below the poverty line.

Poverty affects many children in the U.S. Approximately one in every five to six children lives in a home where the annual household income is below the poverty line. The poverty line varies, depending on the size of the family; but for a family of three poverty is defined as an after tax income of $14,128. Although the total number of children living in poverty decreased steadily in the late 1990s, the number of these children is still large and places unique demands

Table 8.1 National Trends Shaping Education in the Twenty-First Century

The school-age population will grow by 3.7 million to 55.2 million in 2020.
About three out of every four U.S. citizens live in greater metropolitan areas.
By 2040, there will no longer be a single racial/ethnic demographic that accounts for greater than 50% of the population.
In 1960, the top five foreign-born populations in the U.S. were: Italy (1.2 million), Germany (.9 million), Canada (.9 million), Poland (.7 million), and Soviet Union (.6 million).
In 1999, the top five foreign-born populations in the U.S. were from Mexico (7.1 million), Philippines (1.5 million), Vietnam (.9 million), Cuba (.9 million), and China (.8 million).
Two-parent family households with children dropped from 44% to 24% of all households between 1960 and 2000.
About 19% of U.S. children (13.3 million) live in poverty.
Children growing up in poverty are more likely to drop out of school, repeat a grade, or experience a violent crime.

on our school system. Children who live in poverty are at-risk for a variety of negative outcomes, and school systems are becoming increasingly creative in their attempts to meet the unique educational needs of these students.

So how are we addressing these complicated societal issues? Part of the answer lies in our schools making efficient use of their available resources. Teachers, psychologists, special educators, medical professionals, speech and language experts, and families are realizing that working collaboratively is a more efficient use of professional talent. Their collective talent far exceeds any individual training and therefore provides an educational team that is in the best position to address a wide range of issues. This is consistent with the overriding theme of this book—emphasizing interdisciplinary collaboration. One way to conceptualize this collaborative approach is to think of a simple puzzle. The whole puzzle represents the best educational approach for a given child. The individual pieces represent the expertise brought to the educational puzzle by teachers, supporting professionals, and family members. To assemble the entire puzzle, we need each of the pieces to fit together. In educational terms, this means we need everyone communicating and working together to educate each child. Imagine if a parent had to learn to do the job of the school nurse or the classroom teacher had to learn to administer the school. Stepping too far out of our expertise is inefficient. Appropriately collaborating with other educational professionals efficiently uses resources, creates sensitive instruction, and allows students to benefit from different perspectives and expertise.

The benefits of collaborative educational approaches, however, can only emerge when educators remain sensitive to the needs of the students they teach. The best educational team can only be effective if the team members continually strive to better understand the students they teach. The demographic changes reviewed above make this difficult. Despite our reputation as a "melting pot" of individuals from different racial, ethnic, and religious backgrounds, our country has always had a clear majority population. This makes education easier in one sense as teachers historically geared educational efforts to this majority. The majority population is Caucasian, Christian, and of European descent. Even immigration trends through the middle part of the twentieth century did little to change the make-up of our country, as the majority of immigrants came from European countries whose cultural heritage mirrored the American cultural majority. Today, immigration trends are different. The highest rates of immigration are from Mexico, Cuba and Asian countries. This immigration shift is quickly bringing about a change in the cultural, racial, and ethnic makeup of the country. These changes are necessitating corresponding changes in education. Let's begin with a look at how schools can provide education in a way that embraces and affirms our diverse range of students.

Diversity, Individuals, and Instruction

Historically, education has focused on teaching the typical or average student. Differences between students were often overlooked as teachers sought to produce a single, best instructional approach. Today, this approach is increasingly problematic because of our diverse American population. The changes detailed in the previous section challenge the idea of a typical student and make it difficult to envision a single best educational approach. Schools are now moving toward more sensitive and individualized instruction, an approach that varies depending on the unique needs of each student. This approach enhances education in two important ways. First, at an individual level, it encourages our students to recognize and value their unique qualities. It also helps students to think about their individual characteristics as strengths and to use them to build a successful educational outlook. Second, it helps our students develop a sensitivity and appreciation of individual differences observed in others. This is becoming increasingly important as world cultures come together into a global community.

Recognizing the importance of supporting individuality, however, is only the beginning of a larger process. We need to develop an educational plan to integrate individual differences into our schools in a meaningful way. Our approach should be authentic in the sense that it mirrors real life and the way in which we interact and learn in our homes, communities, and work place. Diversity initiatives have been around for years, but often these initiatives address diversity in a superficial way. As Robert Chase, President of the National Education Association (NEA), noted in a 2000 *NEA Today* article, "Celebrating Diversity" must be more than a slogan. It needs to be a way of life. He went on to say that when schools address diversity in a truly meaningful way and recognize it as a strength, schools transform into "superior real world" learning environments.

How do we infuse our schools and educational planning with an appreciation of diversity? One approach is to broaden our *existing* educational plans to better include diversity initiatives. This is advantageous because existing plans are likely to account for specific school needs and are already familiar to teachers. For example, most schools have instructional plans designed to address the education of students with different *learning* needs. Teachers have a variety of learning tools to help students with reading difficulty, language problems, or attention issues. Learning needs, however, are usually defined as cognitive, or about thinking and reasoning. In reality, learning is much more. Learning is influenced by our culture, friendships, and activities, in addition to cognitive factors. To support learning in this broader and more realistic sense, we need to modify our perception of what it means to learn. At first glance, this may seem like an enormous task, but it is possible to build from existing educational programs designed to meet unique cognitive needs. This saves time and energy and makes integrating other aspects of diversity into instruction more natural for teachers. Let's take a look at a learning approach known as differentiated instruction and how its basic tenets can help support the broader aspects of diversity initiatives.

Differentiated Instruction as a Foundation for Appreciating Diversity

The differentiated instruction approach traditionally helps teachers educate in mixed-ability classrooms. In other words, it helps teachers provide instruction depending on the unique abilities each student brings to the educational environment (e.g., strengths in math or weakness in writing). Although this approach focuses on academic ability, it encompasses valuable methods applicable to a broader conceptualization of individuality. We will begin with a basic discussion of differentiated instruction and then return to the idea of tailoring its basic tenets to diversity in the broadest sense.

Basic principles of differentiated instruction One of the foremost scholars in this field is Carol Ann Tomlinson of the University of Virginia. Through her research and experience, she has developed and defined an approach to instruction called differentiated instruction (Tomlinson, 2001). This approach provides an educational model recognizing individuality and actively addressing it through the teacher's instructional plan. According to this approach, teachers provide multiple instructional opportunities and pathways. Individual student strengths then progress through the instructional path most appropriate to their needs. Perhaps one of the most concise ways of understanding differentiated instruction is to compare what it is, to what it *is not* (see Table 8.2).

As you can see from Table 8.2, differentiated instruction encompasses a variety of elements. At the forefront is the idea that teaching should be proactive. This means teachers should prepare multiple approaches to a lesson knowing students will have unique learning needs. The teacher delivers the lessons depending on the needs of each student; and because the teacher is proactively prepared to meet these needs, instruction is more productive and effective. In other words, the teacher does not wait to see if students need multiple learning paths. The teacher begins with this assumption and prepares accordingly.

Other important constructs within the differentiated instruction framework include maintaining a student focus, as well as a focus on quality, not quantity. Some teachers attempt to provide differentiated instruction through adjusting the *amount* of work to the ability level of the learner. More advanced learners get more work, and students who struggle get less work. Differentiated instruction does not take this quantitative approach. Teachers providing differentiated instruction make available multiple instructional avenues that actually differ in the quality of the instruction. For example, instead of limiting the amount of work assigned to a struggling student, a teacher providing true differentiated instruction would use alternative educational approaches. Perhaps a student having trouble with fractions would benefit from an experiential approach where part/whole concepts were explored in an athletic context like baseball.

Table 8.2 Differentiated Instruction

What it is ...	What it is NOT ...
PROACTIVE	The "individualized instruction" of the 1970s.
Type of instruction, not amount.	Chaotic
Assessment at all points in the learning process, not just at the end.	Just another way to provide lessons for groups of similar students.
Provides multiple approaches to content, process, and product.	Tailoring the same lesson to individual learners.
Student-centered	
A blend of whole-class, group, and individual instruction.	
A dynamic, ongoing process.	

Adapted from Tomlinson, *How to Differentiate Instruction in Mixed-Ability Classrooms,* 2001.

Differentiated instruction is an ongoing process using frequent assessments to guide education. The focus is on the student and the learning approach best suited to their learning needs. Teachers providing differentiated instruction often use multiple instructional approaches delivered in whole-group, small group, and individual formats. The needs of the student determine the most appropriate format.

It is also important to realize that differentiated instruction does not assume each student has a different learning need. Individualized instruction approaches developed during the 1970s operated under this assumption. Ultimately, this necessitated that teachers develop a unique lesson plan for each student. Differentiated instruction more closely resembles the old-fashioned, one-room schoolhouse. Confronted with a diverse group of students, the one-room-schoolhouse teacher interacted with the students, developing a sense of each student's learning needs. This necessitated the development of multiple learning approaches. Students were commonly grouped (frequently across different ages) for lessons, while the teacher provided instructional assistance as needed. Managing this environment may look chaotic, but these teachers became skilled at managing multiple learning environments occurring at the same time.

Differentiated instruction and diversity Now that we have a better idea about what differentiated instruction is and what it is not, let's take a look at how characteristics of differentiated instructions can be used to address diversity in a broader sense. As was discussed at the beginning of this section, differentiated instruction is typically discussed in terms of academic ability. The fundamental characteristics of this approach, however, can be used to address other educationally relevant factors. For example, one of the fundamental concepts of differentiated instruction is to be proactive, preparing multiple instructional plans for a given lesson. Teachers typically create these instructional plans to address learning needs based on ability; however, as was discussed above, learning is also influenced by ethnic background, social ability, and primary language. Just like a teacher may create an alternative poetry assignment for students unable to appreciate the typical lesson, she may also create an alternative learning experience for individuals whose ethnic background does not lend itself to an appreciation of the literature content. For example, a teacher may be covering the work of a famous European poet. The poem is structured around a social situation familiar to individuals living at that time. Present-day students from European descent may better relate to the material, given that they share a common heritage. Students from different cultural backgrounds may have difficulty with the material, not because of a difference in ability, but because they lack the cultural framework exemplified in the poem. Perhaps the student was raised in a non-European country or maybe even a specific cultural environment in our country that is dramatically different from mainstream culture. Either situation may require the teacher go beyond a single instructional approach to reach each student.

Even if the historical context of the poem is so far removed from current living situations that it is similarly difficult for all students, instruction may still benefit from modifications based on each student's current life situation. The fundamental idea here is that teachers should be mindful of all the potential factors impacting learning and plan accordingly. Many of the issues limiting learning are not ability related but related to other dynamics or personal characteristics. Teachers need to acknowledge this diverse environment and provide differentiated instruction accordingly. Differentiated instruction provides a concrete structure for authentically integrating each individual into the overall educational plan. A variety of researchers and teachers have examined the differentiated instructional approach and have found it successfully supports students with a diverse range of needs (McTighe & Brown, 2005; Benjamin, 2002; Moll, 2005; Smutny, 2003).

Equity and Equality

As we begin to move closer to instructional models acknowledging, valuing, and incorporating individuality into teaching, issues of equity and respect begin to surface. When teachers differentiate instruction, they necessarily provide different educational experiences to students. This is one of the primary goals of differentiated instruction. This difference in instruction, however, also introduces the questions of whether all students are getting *equal* instruction. **Equality** means maintaining similarity or being impartial. Educationally, this has traditionally meant teachers strive to provide similar instruction to all students. This is different from **equity**, which means freedom from bias. Providing equitable educational services means students have the right to instructional techniques appropriate for their individual learning needs. In other words, teachers should not provide biased instruction against students with unique learning needs. It is critical for teachers to consider this difference between *equity* and *equality* (Marshall, 2002).

Equality

Maintaining similarity or being impartial

Equity

Freedom from bias

Equality is a concept that runs deep in American culture. It is the foundation for our justice system, and many would argue that it is also a guiding principle behind education. Educational services have grown tremendously in this country. It has moved from its initial conceptualization as a service for relatively affluent males of European descent, to a system open to boys and girls of all demographic backgrounds. This contributes to our view that education needs to be *equal*. That is, it needs to be provided equally to all members of society. Disregard for interpersonal differences, however, is often detrimental to the learning outcomes for students falling outside mainstream society (Kozol, 1991; Slavin, 1997/1998).

At times, providing equal education seems at odds with current trends encouraging instructional approaches that are sensitive to the student being taught. If we teach John differently than Jane, are we providing equal instruction? This issue of differential instruction addresses issues of equity. Equitable educational practices provide instruction based on individual need. This necessitates that educators broaden their understanding of what it means to provide equal services. Equal does not have to refer to a particular instructional approach. For example, it is possible to provide John with instruction that is different from Jane (thereby addressing equity) while still providing an equal educational experience. Concepts of *equality* are changing to mean that each student has the same right to an instructional approach that is sensitive to their unique learning needs. Thinking of equality in this way actually leads to the use a variety of instructional approaches. The approach is dependent on the student. This results in an educational system that values the *equal* rights of all students to *equitable* instructional practices. Recall from the previous section that differentiated instruction is not about giving some students less work and others more work based on their ability. Differentiated instruction is about providing multiple avenues of learning so that each student achieves maximal learning. It is an attempt to give teachers multiple tools to reach each student's unique learning capabilities (Goodwin & Macdonald, 1997). All students are expected and held accountable for striving to achieve their learning potential. The path differs for each student, but the teacher has the same goal for all students. When conceptualized in this

Equality is a concept that runs deep in American cultures. Many would argue it is a guiding principle behind education.

way, differentiated instruction is not only equitable but also provides an equivalent framework for helping students succeed. If we want to see positive learning outcomes for all children, we need to address instructional equity (Slavin, 1997/1998; Darling-Hammond & Falk, 1997).

Mutual Respect

Mutual respect

A quality whereby students and teachers have a fundamental belief that everyone in the learning situation is participating fully

There are many practical issues with which to deal when tailoring learning experiences to the unique needs of the individual. Unlike traditional classrooms, there is going to be considerable activity and movement as students access learning tools specific to their needs. Multiple small groups and individual projects are likely to co-occur, interspersed with whole group instruction. Children are naturally curious and will quickly notice that peers are not all completing the same assignments. This may foster negative emotions like envy or anger because students feel that other students are doing the "fun" lesson or are "getting off easy." To be successful, teaching to individual needs requires that educators develop a sense of **mutual respect** in their classrooms. Students need to develop an educational focus that is not exclusively performance driven, and teachers need to emphasize that every student had a unique learning path. The development of mutual respect is a reciprocal process (Smyth, 2005) with students and teachers learning from each other. Students need to view school as a place to achieve genuine learning. They need to focus on using the available learning tools to master the material. They also need to develop a respect for the teacher and the other students—that they too are invested in his or her learning. Without respecting that everyone in the class is committed to the same end, differentiated instruction becomes competitive. When teachers emphasize a climate of mutual respect, students are more likely to engage in learning and succeed (Cothran & Ennis, 2000). Mutual respect should be considered one of the founding pillars of educational success.

Of course, respect extends beyond learning tasks. Students need to develop a sense of their classmates as human beings with the capacity for pain, guilt, and embarrassment—also with joy, pride, and acceptance. Working with others in challenging environments requires a deep respect for all people. We may be working on different tasks. We may live in different homes or wear different clothes. We may look different and have different skin color. We may practice different religions. We are all, however, human beings with a fundamental right to respect. Our differences are often striking and hard to understand; yet if we can teach our students to start with a premise of acceptance, respect, and compassion, we can build an understanding and even an appreciation of our differences.

SUMMARIZE AND REFLECT

1. America is experiencing demographic changes such as changes in immigration, population, and poverty rates. These changes are having a substantial impact on our school system. Addressing these changes is proving to be challenging, but schools are making strides to support our individual qualities in real and meaningful ways.
2. Existing educational approaches like differentiated instruction can help give teachers concrete guidelines for authentically integrating individuality into the classroom.
3. It is important to establish a sense of equity among students. The concept of equity differs from equality, and both are important to successful education.
4. To establish an effective classroom environment, teachers and students need to develop a deep mutual respect for each other.

INFORMED APPLICATION

1. Consider a classroom where the students are mostly from the same socioeconomic background, race, religion, and basic family structure. Then, consider a student body where the students vary along these dimensions. What sort of instructional challenges are you likely to encounter when teaching these two very different types of classes?
2. Imagine you are a regular education teacher, but you have three students from the special education program in your classroom for most of the day. What is more important to encourage, a sense of equity across students or a sense of equality?

WE'RE NOT ALL THE SAME.

The second section of this chapter will further explore the ways in which we differ. As we saw in the first section, everyone is unique and differs from others in some way. The goal of this section is to add to our understanding of *individual* differences by examining differences between *groups* of similar people. Again, we are all unique, but there are some interesting differences that emerge when we look at trends across groups of people. Specifically, we will look at what things girls have in common and how they are different as a group from boys. We will also look at regional dialects, exploring how the Cajuns of Louisiana speak differently from many African Americans living in urban centers. We will also explore changes in the structure of families and the unique challenges facing children from traditional versus non-traditional homes.

Girls and Boys

From the time we are born, our gender has been an important mediator of our interactions with the world. Even if we try to avoid treating boys and girls differently at home, expectations regarding gender are so pervasive in our society it is difficult to avoid doing so. In this section, we are going to examine individual differences based on gender. We will begin with a look at how we come to an understanding of our own gender. We will examine the role we portray based upon our gender and how this role relates to actual ideas we have about our gender identity. Next, we will focus on the development of our understanding of someone else's gender. We will also look at common stereotypes regarding gender and discuss how they are learned. Finally, we will look at differences in the actual behavior and thinking of boys and girls.

Gender Role and Identity

One of the most enduring and controversial topics in education is gender. **Gender** refers to the psychological, behavioral, and cultural factors related to being male or female. It is typically distinguished from **sex**, which refers to biological aspects of being male or female. Our sense of being male or female is a complicated interaction between sex and gender and has deep roots in our developmental history. As we learn and grow, we are constantly shaped by events telling us about what it means to be a boy or girl. Such events influence two related, but separate, processes. **Gender identity** is that part of you related to the experience of being male or female. It is a personal understanding of your gender. The public expression of your gender is your **gender role**. For example, you may have a well-developed sense of yourself as being female. You identify with other women and feel that you relate well with women. The role you play in society, however, is different. You have chosen to take on more traditionally masculine roles in terms of home-life, work, and leisure activities. In this case, we would say your gender identity is female and your gender role is masculine (Lefrancois, 2001). For most of us, there is general consistency between our identity and the role we play in society.

Gender
The psychological, behavioral, and cultural factors related to being male or female

Sex
Biological aspects of being male or female

Gender identity
That part of a person related to the experience of being male or female

Gender role
The public expression of one's gender

It is important to think of masculinity and femininity as points on a continuum rather than either/or concepts. Few of us take our gender roles to such an extreme that we embrace none of the characteristics typical of the other gender. Men who work in traditional male jobs and enjoy recreational activities typical of men can also enjoying nurturing and caring for their children, a trait more commonly ascribed to women. So how then do we acquire these roles? Are they biological or learned? Do we simply mimic behaviors we observe in others? Like most answers to questions of human behavior, these are complicated.

Biology of gender development There is some support for biological interpretations for the development of gender identity and gender roles. Much of the difference we see between men and women is the product of differences in a substance known as testosterone. Both men and women produce chemicals, which convert into testosterone from the adrenal gland (located above the kidneys); however, men also produce large quantities of testosterone from the testes. Testosterone has been shown to have dramatic effects on behavior. In humans, girls who have exposure to high levels of testosterone while in utero will demonstrate a birth defect of the adrenal glands, which show interesting changes in behavior (Collaer & Hines, 1995). Girls affected with this condition have been shown to take on more masculine gender roles. They engage in more rough-and-tumble play, choose toys more consistent with boys, and show little interest is feminine clothing, jewelry, and doll play. Studies like this provide some evidence that gender related behaviors are mediated by biological factors. Biological explanations for the gender roles we adopt, however, are limited (Ruble, 1988; Berenbaum, Blakemore, & Beltz, 2011). Therefore, if gender roles are not exclusively determined by our biology, what other factors drive the development of our gender role and identity?

The impact of learning on gender development Learning theorists suggest that much of our sense of being male or female is learned through reinforcing and punishing socialization experiences. Although we are seeing greater tolerances for behaviors that fail to conform to societal norms, there is still ample evidence that boys and girls are rewarded for exhibiting gender consistent behaviors and discouraged from displaying gender inconsistent behavior (Lott & Maluso, 2001). Consider the question you are likely to ask upon hearing that a friend has given birth—is it a boy or a girl? From the very beginning we identify individuals as being male and female. As parents, we are more likely to wrestle with our son and play dolls with our daughter. Similarly, peers typically have fairly clear boundaries for gender appropriate behaviors. Chief among these is that boys play with boys and girls play with girls. In fact, children generally demonstrate a preference for playmates of the same sex by age four. This preference continues to grow through adolescence where young adults spend about 90% of their time with same sex friends (Maccoby, 2002). This close affiliation with same sex friends further reinforces the learning of gender specific behaviors and potentially magnifies gender differences.

Cognitive influences on gender development The gender roles we adopt evolve out of an understanding of ourselves as male or female. Lawrence Kohlberg (1966), whose work on morality we encountered in Chapter 3, also developed a theory regarding how we acquire a gender identity. According to his theory, we begin to think of ourselves as male or female around two to three years of age. This is an important milestone because it sets the stage for later gender role development. Although we begin to think of ourselves as belonging to one gender at a fairly young age, we do not consistently identify an individual as male or female until the age of six or seven. Young children often confuse actual gender with gender specific behaviors. For example, if you put a male doll in a dress and ask a child if the doll is a boy or girl, he is likely to say a girl because the doll is wearing a dress. It is not until later that children establish **gender constancy,** or the idea that one's sex is constant regardless of the behaviors exhibited. Even after children exhibit gender constancy, there may still be discrepancies between our gender identity and the roles we adopt.

Interconnections

How we develop our sense of morality is covered in Chapter 3.

Gender constancy

The idea that one's sex is constant regardless of the behaviors exhibited

Gender schemas

Our ideas about gender appropriate behaviors

Our gender roles are also influenced by our ideas about gender appropriate behaviors, or what we call **gender schemas** (Martin & Halverson, 1981). As children develop, they begin to notice which friends are of the same gender. Distinguishing between male and female typically leads to all-girl or all-boy groups. It is within these single gender groups that children begin developing a sense of gender specific behaviors. Their understanding of what behaviors are appropriate for a boy or a girl then leads to a change in their actual behavior. For example, if a girl perceives that a toy is a "girl's" toy, she will be more likely to play with it and remember more details about it than if the same toy were perceived as a "boy's" toy (Martin, Eisenbud, & Rose, 1995; Martin & Dinella, 2001; Liben & Signorella, 1993). What is important to remember is that our gender schemas lead to a differential exposure to the world and ultimately shapes the gender roles we adopt as adults.

Gender Stereotypes

Much of what we learn during our early years regarding gender specific behaviors is stereotyped. A **stereotype** is an oversimplified opinion, attitude, or judgment held by members of a group. **Gender stereotypes** are vague conceptualizations regarding issues related to one's gender. Ask almost anyone what girls or boys are like, and they will probably give you an opinion. Ideas regarding what it means to be male and female vary from person to person, but some trends are apparent. Table 8.3 lists common traits adults express regarding girls and boys. As you can see, there are common themes in our perceptions of being male and female. Girls are seen as being more sensitive to interpersonal issues and more emotional. Boys are seen as more active in their play and more independent. So the question is, are these generalizations true? The answer—it depends on the person.

Stereotype

An oversimplified opinion, attitude, or judgment held by members of a group

Gender stereotype

Vague conceptualizations regarding issues related to one's gender

Teachers need to keep in mind that personal traits like those in Table 8.3 are really broad continuums and everyone expresses some aspect of a given trait at some point in their life. On some days girls are more likely to engage in rough-and-tumble play than other days. Boys may demonstrate care and compassion for a friend today and then move toward fierce independence the next. The traits presented in the table represent gender difference when you consider the average behavior of large groups of children. We are all individuals, so the extent to which these gender trends apply to us will vary. Interestingly, there are also some cultural differences (Williams & Best, 1982). For example, Italians view *endurance* as a female characteristic, but most other countries see this as masculine. Nigerians see *affiliation* as neutral, but most countries see it as feminine. This shows that there is a lack of uniformity in gender stereotypes across cultures. It should be noted, however, that there are far more similarities than differences.

The extent to which we hold gender stereotypes varies over our lifetime. In the early elementary school years, gender stereotypes begin to form. These stereotypes come from a variety of information sources. Parents often have different expectations regarding sons and daughters (Shaffer, 2000; Ruble & Martin, 1998; Fagot, 1995; Block, 1983, 1984). Parents often expect and provide opportunities for sons to be independent and explore their environment. Conversely, parents often restrict their daughter's ability to interact and explore the environment. There are also differences in toy selection (Ruble & Martin, 1998; O'Brien & Huston, 1985; Campbell, 1986). Almost any commercial toy store has clearly defined toy areas based on gender. The "boy aisle" is usually filled with action figures, trucks, war toys, and sports equipment. The "girl aisle" is stocked with Barbie® dolls, kitchen tools, and items fostering the more nurturing behaviors. It is remarkable how little these aisles change over the years and are a testament to our continued use of gender-based stereotypes.

Behavioral and Cognitive Difference

It appears that early in our lives we learn to identify ourselves as a boy or a girl. Our understanding of our own gender changes over time, becoming a more constant or fixed perception. We also learn early on what "girl" activities or "boy" activities are. These perceptions are usually reinforced by the child's social relationships. Society also shapes our understanding of gender roles by providing commercial products clearly tailored to commonly held gender stereotypes.

There are many aspects of behavior showing differences between boys and girls, but the two most common are motor performance and aggression. Motor performance refers to the way in which we use our bodies during activities. Research on gender differences in motor

Table 8.3 Common Gender Stereotypes Adults Hold Regarding Children

Females		**Males**	
Gentle	Sympathetic	Self-reliant	Dominant
Neat and clean	Well-mannered	Competitive	Independent
Eager to soothe hurt feelings	Cries and get upset easily	Enjoys mechanical things	Enjoys rough play

performance usually demonstrates more highly developed skills in boys (Eisenberg, Martin, & Fabes, 1996). Differences begin to show up in elementary school, but are not very large. These differences, however, broaden during the middle school years with boys outperforming girls in skill areas like jumping, climbing, throwing, and kicking (Smoll & Schutz, 1990). It is important to remember that these reports are referring to group averages and may not apply to individual students. For example, the boys on average may run faster in Mr. Cosby's seventh grade physical education class, but the fastest runner might be a girl. Always exercise caution when applying group data to individuals.

Boys typically show more of an aggressive physical response compared to girls.

Another behavior dimension showing gender differences is aggression. When boys are provoked, they typically show a more aggressive physical response compared to girls (Ostrov, Keating, & Ostrov, 2004). Physical aggression differences are found early in the developmental period and persist into adulthood. Differences are also reported across many cultures. Physical aggression is not, however, the only form of aggression. Another type of aggression is verbal aggression. When verbal aggression is examined for gender differences, results either fail to find any difference or show that girls are more aggressive than boys (Eagly & Steffen, 1986). Similarly, studies looking at relational aggression show differences favoring girls. **Relational aggression** refers to aggressive acts that manipulate relationships between people. For example, a teenager may convince her friends to ignore or make fun of another classmate (Underwood, 2003, 2004). This kind of aggressive act is more common among girls than boys.

Relational aggression

Aggressive acts that manipulate relationships between people

Another way boys can differ from girls is in how they think, or what we call cognitions. To begin our look at cognitive gender differences, let's first look at global cognitive measure like intelligence. Researchers have consistently failed to find any differences in overall intelligence (Halpern, 2000). That is, on measures of general cognitive ability, we do not see differences in the performance of boys and girls. We do, however, see gender differences when we look at cognitive performance within a specific academic area.

A variety of studies have found boys outperform girls in the area of science. In a 2001 National Assessment of Educational Progress study, researchers found boys performed better on science questions in grades four, eight, and twelve (years that were assessed in the study). Similar results were found in a 1997 study of academic ability, especially for average and high ability students (Burkham, Lee, & Smerdon, 1997). These differences may have something to do with the number of male role models available in science. More science teachers are male, particularly in the higher grades. This may help male students identify with science teachers, encouraging excellence in this area. Additionally, girls do not appear to have as much interest in science compared to boys and experience lower self-concept (Ackerman, Bowen, Beier, & Kanfer, 2001). It should also be noted that gender differences might be culturally dependent. Research on Asian Americans has not found gender differences in science performance (Yee, 1992).

Differences in math performance favoring boys have also been found (Eisenberg et al., 1996). Differences, however, may be changing. Newer studies have not found such differences (Coley, 2001). Still, such stereotypes appear culturally pervasive (Cvencek, Meltzoff, & Greenwald, 2011) Math differences have been explained by differences in parental expectations. Parents often believe their sons have greater math talent and are better suited to a career in mathematics (Eccles et al., 1991). Cultural factors, however, also appear to influence gender differences in math. For example, research shows that African American girls out score African American boys on math tests (Grossman & Grossman, 1994).

Verbal ability

Ability to use and express oneself in words

A final cognitive difference we will consider is verbal skills. Generally, **verbal ability** relates to our ability to use and express ourselves in words. Gender differences in verbal ability gained widespread exposure following the publication of the now classic book *The Psychology of Sex Differences* by Eleanor Maccoby and Carol Jacklin (1974). Their book provided the first truly synthesized collection of research based on sex differences. One difference highlighted in the text was a difference in verbal ability favoring girls. Current research continues to provide support for this difference. In 1998 and 2001, studies conducted by the National Assessment and Educational

Practice organization showed girls outperform boys on reading and writing tests in grades four, eight and twelve. Not all evidence, however, paints the same picture. As students graduate from high school and prepare for college, many take the Scholastic Assessment Test (SAT). Data from the makers of this test (Educational Testing Service–ETS) show that there is no difference on the verbal section of the test (ETS, 2002) between young men and women.

Gender Bias

As we saw in the preceding section, research indicates there are a variety of differences between boys and girls. The exact explanation for these difficulties may stem from inherent biological differences like hormones, but there is evidence that environmental factors play a significant role. One important environmental factor is a child's teacher. Teachers can positively influence students' gender perceptions of themselves and others. With supportive encouragement, a student can recognize and understand biases based on gender and learn to overcome negative biases.

Early research pointed to nurturing both male and female qualities in all students. This is an androgynous approach to gender equity. **Androgyny** refers to someone who has both masculine and feminine qualities. This approach to gender proved to be difficult. Gender concepts are so deeply entrenched in our society that it was difficult to get students to embrace qualities of the other gender. One study tried to implement an androgynous curriculum for a year with ninth graders and actually found that boys had even stronger traditional gender role attitudes after the year was complete (Guttentag & Bray, 1976). Today, some researchers are advocating for gender transcendence (Pleck, 1983). **Gender-role transcendence** is when we shift our educational focus beyond gender. According to this approach, we do not discount the importance of gender related issues, but teachers strive to focus on the whole person, not just on being male or female (Eccles, 1987).

Androgyny

Having both masculine and feminine qualities

Gender-role transcendence

Shifting of educational focus beyond gender

Other gender related issues encountered by teachers and their students include biases in print materials. Gender bias in textbooks is improving, but some books still present stereotypical gender information. It is helpful to discuss these perceptions with students and challenge students to think of alternative presentations of the information. Similarly, there are also gender issues related to spoken language. Again, teachers need to consider their own language use. Words are powerful and convey direct and indirect information to the student. Attempt to use either gender-neutral terminology (e.g., "they" or "them") or gender inclusive phrases ("him or her" or "his or hers"). Also, try to use gender-neutral job descriptors such as "Flight Attendant" instead of "Stewardess."

Teachers should also think about how they address gender in their classroom activities. Consider what type of information you convey to your students during activities. Do you call on girls more than boys? Do you group students according to gender for small group work? Do boys and girls only sit next to students of the same gender? Do you provide boys with more help than girls? These actions are typically noticed by students and affect their perceptions of gender equity. It is also important to try to focus on the accomplishments of the students. Focusing too heavily on gender equity may inadvertently model for students an inappropriate preoccupation with gender. Make sure all students have equal access to all educational opportunities.

Linguistic Differences

Our next topic is about how different groups of people communicate. Linguistic differences, or difference in language use, are increasingly highlighted in American culture. In part due to the growing world sensitivity to different cultures, teachers are moving toward educational approaches that embrace the increasingly diverse array of student cultural backgrounds. What and where are these cultures? You can travel almost anywhere in the country and clearly recognize different ways of speaking. People across the country use different vocabulary and have different accents. They speak at a different pace or use different gestures while speaking. Linguistic differences are everywhere. We are also seeing an increase in the number of languages spoken in our country. Some American regions like Louisiana have been using multiple languages since our country's beginning. Other regions like south Florida have recently seen increases in other languages due to changing immigration trends. These linguistic differences bring with them educational challenges. The focus of this section is to better understand these issues.

Regional Dialects

Dialects

Regional or socially distinct forms of a language having their own characteristic pronunciation, grammar, and vocabulary

Standard English

Form of English taught in schools and typically used in professional circles

Since the founding of our country, the English language has undergone rapid and constant change. Today, Americans invent more new words and phrases in a single month than most countries do in a year. Often changes are bounded by geography, giving us the metropolitan efficiency of the New Yorker, the genteel softness of the southeast, and the expressive and dynamic rhythms of the inner city urban dwellers. We call these different ways of speaking dialects. **Dialects** are regional or socially distinct forms of a language having their own characteristic pronunciation, grammar, and vocabulary. Consistent with the inventive nature of Americans, our language style and technique is constantly changing and evolving. This ever-changing nature of language often creates controversy in schools where teachers are charged with teaching "English." The obvious question is *which* English do we teach? The form of English taught in schools and typically used in professional circles is referred to as **Standard English**. This form of English, however, is not clearly defined. In fact, some would argue that this standard form is not really spoken by anyone, but is a merger of the regional dialects. So, what are these dialects and what should be taught in the schools? This question has been the center of considerable educational controversy for a long time. Let's first take a look at a few of our regional dialects and then consider instruction in "English."

The number of distinct American dialects is debatable, but most agree that there are at least three: New England, Southern, and Western/General. Some experts, however, list as many as twenty-four separate and distinct dialects. Table 8.4 list additional dialects found in the United States. What distinguishes these dialects are their heritage, pronunciation, and grammar, as well as their use in everyday communication.

One of the most prominent of the American dialects is spoken by Americans of African descent. This dialect is known by many names: Black English, Black English vernacular, African American Vernacular English (AAVE), Ebonics, and African American English. Although most dialects engender some degree of controversy, our country's race relation history makes the dialect(s) of African Americans a unique case (Yancy, 2011).

What is African American English? Like all dialects it has a unique vocabulary and grammatical rules. Some "Black" vocabulary words have moved out of ethnically isolated African American groups into the mainstream culture: *phat* (meaning excellent) and *bling-bling* (meaning glittery and expensive jewelry). Other vocabulary terms are still predominantly used within this micro-culture, like *ashy* (meaning the whitish appearance of dark skin when dry). African American English also has distinct pronunciation rules. Often final consonants are omitted from words such as *frien* (friend) or *wha* (what), the th sound (math) is pronounced like an f, and some vowels sounds (ride) are pronounced with a long ah (rahd). Grammatical

Table 8.4 American Dialects

A-Prefixing	African American
Californian	Cajun
Chicano English	Lumbee
Midwest	New York City
Pacific Northwest	Pittsburghese
R-ful Southern	Smoky Mountains
Spanglish	Texan

differences include the omission of certain verbs like *is* and *are* ("Marc playing" instead of "Marc is playing"). These omissions, however, follow unique rules and do not always take place. For example, it is "ungrammatical" in African American English to omit the verb *is* at the end of a sentence ("Where Marc is?" instead of "Where Marc"). As you can see, African American English is not a willful disregard for the rules of language. It is a way of communicating complete with all the major linguistic components including vocabulary, pronunciation, and grammar. The controversy over African American English is not, however, over its legitimacy or validity as a true language but over how schools address its use in formal schooling. Before we look at these instructional issues, let's look at another linguistic dialect found in the United States.

Cajun English is a regional dialect spoken in parts of southern Louisiana. It is a mixture of influences including French, certain Caribbean islands, and English. Essentially, Cajun English is the English spoken by these Americans who are often bilingual in French. Neither their English nor French, however, conform to a standard form of either language as both languages evolved along unique paths. Grammatically, Cajun English is different in the use of definite and indefinite articles ("Will you have *a* coffee?" instead of "Will you have some coffee?"), but it is the pronunciation that gives Cajun English is most recognizable qualities. Cajuns routinely change diphthongs (like "high" which uses the combined sounds of /ai/) to monophthongs ("high" would be pronounced as "ha"). Cajuns also typically alter the /th/ phoneme, using a /t/ or /d/ instead ("dat" instead of "that"). As with African American English, Cajun English is a unique, rule governed, and systematic deviation from Standard English forms.

It is interesting to compare the two dialects in today's society. Our larger American society often views African American English as a failure to accommodate to mainstream American society. Cajun English, however, is often *perceived* more favorably and has resulted in dramatic increases in tourism to small Louisiana towns. The *reality* of Cajun English in Louisiana, however, more closely resembles the treatment of African American English. For most of the history of Louisiana, the Cajun dialect has been used to isolate and socially stigmatize certain social classes. It is only in recent history that it has gained popularity as a culturally interesting segment of the population.

This leads us to the topic of instruction and the educational treatment of different dialects. Teaching English in a way that is sensitive to dialects is a controversial issue. Part of the reason is that the United States has no official language. This is often misunderstood, as many Americans confuse English as a *recognized* language in this country for an *official* language. This lack of an official language makes it difficult to mandate instruction in Standard English only. In other words, without an official language, the door is open to consider instruction in various English dialects or in another language entirely. Some individual states have independently addressed this issue by adopting an official language of the state. The legislative influences on instruction in a standard form of English are only part of the issue. For centuries, dialects have been used socially to support prejudice, discrimination, and social elitism. Some argue that not to instruct all students in Standard English is to leave students open to these negative social outcomes. On the other side is the argument that dialects are a rich and important part of our American history. Dialects are a living commentary on the great inventiveness of the American spirit. We should celebrate and embrace our dialectical differences in our educational system. Some teachers have tried to resolve these two sides by highlighting the positive aspect of each (Delpit, 1995).

There is a certain reality to the climate of professional environments and the language rules that are supported, and it is important that students have the linguistic tools to be successful in these venues. Moving back and forth from a dialect to the more standard form of the language has been termed **code-switching** (White, 2011). Code-switching also refers to a change from a formal language you might use in business and the informal language you use with friends. In addition to giving students the tools to code-switch effectively, teachers can also help students appreciate the incredible history and linguistic complexity behind a dialect. Appreciation of the history of a dialect gives students another vehicle with which to view history, and a close examination of dialectical structure helps students understand language in general. Teachers can also help students appreciate dialectical difference by dispelling common myths regarding dialects (see Table 8.5).

Code-switching

Moving back and forth from a dialect to the more standard form of the language

Table 8.5 Dialect Myths and Reality

Myth	Reality
A dialect is something someone else speaks.	Everyone who speaks a language speaks some dialect of the language; it is not possible to speak a language without speaking a dialect of the language.
Dialects always have highly noticeable features that set them apart.	Some dialects get much more attention than others; the status of a dialect, however, is unrelated to public commentary about its special characteristics.
Only varieties of a language spoken by socially disfavored groups are dialects.	The notion of dialect exists apart from the social status of the language variety; there are socially favored as well as socially disfavored dialects.
Dialects result from unsuccessful attempts to speak the "correct" form of a language.	Dialect speakers acquire their language by adopting the speech feature of those around them, not by failing in their attempts to adopt standard language features.
Dialects have no linguistic patterning in their own right; they are derivations from standard speech.	Dialects, like all language systems, are systematic and regular; furthermore, socially disfavored dialects can be described with the same kind of precision as standard language varieties.
Dialects inherently carry negative connotations.	Dialects are not necessarily positively or negatively valued; their social values are derived strictly from the social position of their community of speakers.

SOURCE: Wolfram, W. & Schilling-Estes, N. (1998). *American English: Dialects and variation,* Oxford: Basil Blackwell.

English as a Second Language and Bilingual Education

The education of students who speak languages other than English also presents unique challenges. To begin our discussion of this issue, it is important to recognize that over the years, federal legislation has influenced the education of students for whom English is a second language. Civil Rights legislation during the 1960s coupled with the Supreme Court case of *Lau v. Nichols* basically left school systems with two options for educating children with limited or no English-speaking ability. The first is to provide a special form of English instruction, which is sensitive to their limited English experience. This has become known as **English as a second language (ESL)** instruction. The other option is to teach these students in their native language while progressively building instruction in English. The goal of these programs is to develop English proficiency, but to use native language instruction to support educational progress while English skills are developing (Adamson, 2004; Diaz-Rico, 2004). This is called **bilingual education.**

English as a second language (ESL)

A special form of English instruction, which is sensitive to a learner's limited English experience

Bilingual education

Educational practice that teaches students in their native language, while progressively building instruction in English

The specific approach a school takes depends on the nature of their student population. ESL instruction is favored in school districts where there are large numbers of students speaking a variety of languages. In these schools districts, the sheer number of languages (twenty to thirty different languages in some districts) makes it impossible to use the bilingual educational model. It is simply not practical to locate and hire a teacher to educate every student in his or her native language. Bilingual education is more typically used when you have a significant population of students who have a common non-English native language. In this country, bilingual education is most typically used with Spanish speaking students in Florida and in southern states bordering Mexico. In both ESL and bilingual programs, the goal is to help students achieve proficiency in oral communication used in everyday conversations (contextualized language skills) and in academic skills used in completing course material (decontextualized language skills) (Snow, 1987). Educators recognize the importance of both skills. In fact, parents and families eager to assimilate into American culture often value these English skills to the exclusion of their native language and the culture it represents.

Teaching students for whom English is a second language is not just about instruction in academic skills. Language is invariably tied to a specific culture, so when you teach a new language, you are also teaching a different culture. This presents unique challenges to students adapting to American life. Some students and their families struggle to maintain their identity while learning American culture. Both are clearly important for these students. Students need to feel that their unique qualities are valued. They also need to appreciate the culture of their new country and how to effectively operate within an American cultural framework.

Families

A final group difference we will consider in this chapter is family structure. Home life in today's society varies substantially from student to student. Some students live in homes with their biological mother and father. Others live with adoptive parents. Still others live with only one parent, with a grandparent, or even with two parents of the same sex. If there is any common rule for families, it is that there are no rules. Families have become almost as unique as individuals, and each family has its own set of strengths and weaknesses.

Traditional Homes and the Nuclear Family

We will begin our look at families with an examination of the traditional nuclear family. These traditional family environments have enjoyed a long history. They also, however, have been the source of many rigid perceptions regarding the roles each family member plays. It wasn't too far in the past that fathers were expected to work outside the home, mothers stayed at home and nurtured the children, and the children focused on their development so they could become productive citizens. This type of traditional family structure is becoming increasingly difficult to find. The boundaries between parental roles are changing. Children are exploring the world around them with greater ease and frequency, thanks to technological innovations like the Internet. We are seeing significant changes to family structure in a relatively brief amount of time.

The nuclear family is only one of the different types of families that we see today.

The common term used to refer to a traditional family structure is a nuclear family. A **nuclear family** is a family unit consisting of a mother, father, and their children. A distinction is typically made between a **family of orientation**, which is the family unit we were in as children, and the **family of procreation**, which is the family we participate in as parents. Figure 8.1 diagrams this distinction. In the nuclear family, the husband and wife share in the creation of the home. Together they earn money, keep the house, and raise and nurture the children. Historically, the division of these tasks has been rigidly divided along gender lines. This promoted the gender roles we discussed earlier in the chapter. These roles are becoming more flexible but still support gender based perceptions regarding typical home life.

Nuclear family

A family unit consisting of a mother, father, and their children

Family of orientation

The family unit we were in as children

Family of procreation

The family we participate in as parents

All family units have their share of problems and successes, and traditional nuclear families are no exception. There is, however, evidence that children from this type of home environment are not as likely to develop behavioral and educational trouble. According to a 2002 study on family structure, children who live with both of their biological parents have the lowest risk for childhood problems (Moore, Jekielek, & Emig, 2002). This finding is a fairly robust and consistent developmental finding. At first glance, one might conclude that a student in your class whose parents are divorced is destined for trouble. This is one of the most common problems with the application of research findings. The student whose parents are divorced might be at greater risk, but that does not mean that he will have trouble. The data cited above is about general trends present in our society. Whether individuals will actually experience trouble for which they are at risk depends on a variety of factors. It is also important to appreciate that a significant percentage of children from traditional two parent homes

Figure 8.1

Distinction Between Families of Orientation and Families of Procreation

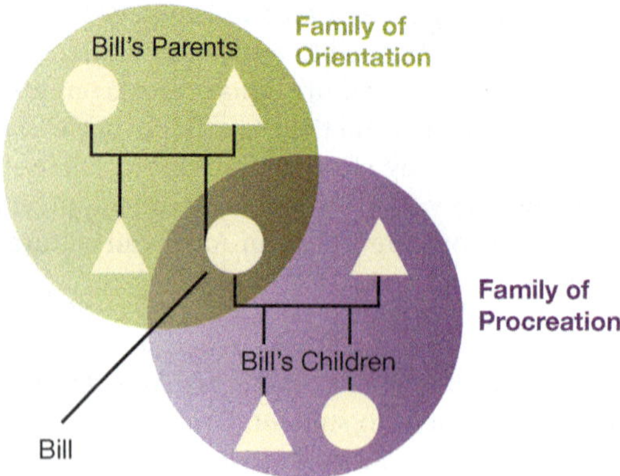

also experience behavioral and academic difficulties. Teachers should be aware of trends, but cautious in their application to individuals.

Extended family

Relatives of the nuclear family that share the emotional and often financial functions of the family

Matriarchal families

Families in which managerial roles for distribution of financial assets, socialization of the children, and general family dynamics run on the mother's side of the family

Patriarchal families

Families in which managerial roles for distribution of financial assets, socialization of the children, and general family dynamics run on the father's side of the family

Egalitarian families

Families in which managerial roles for distribution of financial assets, socialization of the children, and general family dynamics are shared on both sides of the family

A network of relatives often supports the nuclear family. **Extended family** members are relatives of the nuclear family that share the emotional and often financial functions of the family. The involvement of the extended family is highly variable. Involvement is frequently supported by cultural traditions within the family. This is especially prominent in American families from Italian, Asian, and Native American descent. In these families, members are often socialized to consider the needs of the family before their own.

Given the number of people involved in an extended family, certain members of the family are often given managerial roles for distribution of financial assets, socialization of the children, and general family dynamics. Families where this role runs on the mother's side of the family are called **matriarchal** families. Families where the father's side of the family plays this role are **patriarchal** families. Families where everyone shares family roles equally are called **egalitarian** families. Worldwide, patriarchal families are more common. In America, egalitarian families are more common.

Having a well-integrated extended family can have enormous benefits. There are more hands to help with the children. This gives parents more time to devote to their relationship. Parents who have a healthy, low-conflict, relationship better support happy well-adjusted children. Extended families can also provide a larger financial support structure; thus, when families experience financial hardship, family assistance is spread across multiple people. This eases the burden on any one family member.

Of course, not everything is positive for extended families. With more people, there are usually more opinions and the resulting potential for more conflict. Developing clear lines of authority (discussed above) is one approach to managing a larger family. It is interesting to note, the extended family model was the most common model in early American history. As our society became more industrialized, we also became more mobile and extended families were not able to maintain close integrated contact over great distances. Another important factor in the reduction of involvement of extended family members is the significant divorce rate in our country. We will examine divorce in detail later in this section, but divorce can complicate a child's involvement with extended family members. The decrease in the number of traditional nuclear families has led to an increase in the number of non-traditional families. Let's turn to a brief review of two of these increasingly common family units.

Intergenerational Child Rearing

Over the last ten to fifteen years, there has been a 30% increase in the number of children raised by their grandparents. The 2000 U.S. Census indicates 4.5 million children are living in grandparent-headed households. This totals 6.3% of all children under the age of eighteen. Additionally, there are approximately 1.5 million children (2.1% of children under the age of eighteen) living with relatives other than grandparents. **Intergenerational childrearing** is the practice of rearing children by grandparents. **Kinship rearing** is

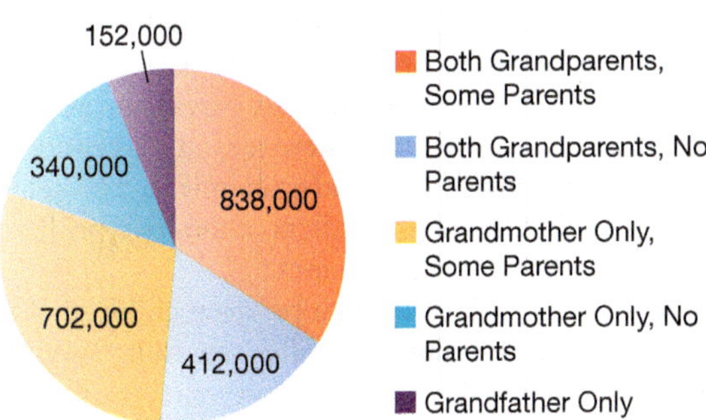

Figure 8.2

Types of Grandparent-Headed Families

the more general term used to refer to children reared by family members other than the child's parents. Analysis of the 1997 U.S. Census data indicates some interesting trends regarding the composition of intergenerational families. Figure 8.2 shows the percentage of intergenerational families headed by grandparents with or without parental involvement.

Intergenerational child rearing

The practice of grandparents rearing children

Kinship rearing

The more general term used to refer to children reared by family members other than the child's parents

As you can see from the figure, the largest sub-group of intergenerational families is grandparents raising their grandchildren with some parental involvement. The smallest subgroup was grandfathers living with their grandchildren only. Degree of parental involvement for households headed by grandfathers only was not analyzed because of the low overall numbers for this subgroup. More current data from the 2010 American Community Survey indicates the total number of grandparent headed households has grown to a total of 2,882,224. The survey also indicates that 1,963,771 of these households had some parental presence and 918,453 had no parental involvement.

The structural distinctions between intergenerational families shown in Figure 8.2 correspond to unique challenges for children. For example, children in households with grandmother only and no parental involvement are most likely to be poor and to receive public assistance. Children in households with both grandparents and no parental involvement are the most likely to be uninsured. These qualities are usually driven by the reasons behind the intergenerational rearing situation. The most common explanation for why these children are in the care of their grandparents include increased drug abuse among parents, teen pregnancy, divorce, increases in single parent homes, mental and physical illnesses, AIDS, and child abuse (Minkler, 1998).

National attention to the issues surrounding intergenerational families has led to the development of a variety of resources. Some of the national-based resources include the following: American Association of Retired People (AARP) Grandparent Information Center, Generations United, Grand Parent Again, and GrandsPlace. These resources provide assistance with family life issues, healthcare, public policy, educational issues, and financial planning. In addition to programs assisting grandparents, there are a variety of programs and social services designed to help parents address issues commonly resulting in their children being raised by their parents. Teachers are also a positive force in the lives of these families. They can bring understanding and support to the unique challenges of these families. They can also be an important referral source that helps families access much needed services.

Same-Sex Parents

Another non-traditional family structure involves parents of the same gender. The union of individuals of the same gender has been the subject of many articles in the popular press as states wrestle with the legal issues surrounding these unions. We are also seeing greater attention given to the children living in these unique families. Considerable research has been conducted on the effects of same-sex parents on the development of the child (Stacey & Biblarz, 2001; Perrin, 1998). In general, the research supports that these families have much in common with more traditional fam-

ily structures. Studies of early childhood psychosocial development find few if any differences between families with same-sex parents compared to opposite-sex parents (Patterson, 2000). This also appears to be the case as children of same-sex parents grow into adolescence (Wainright, Russell, & Patterson, 2004). Adolescent differences in perceptions of parental warmth, autonomy, integration into the neighborhood, and academic success seldom vary according to whether one has same-sex parents. In fact, regardless of family type, it was the closeness with their parents that predicted positive school outcomes.

Despite the relative similarity in development between children of same-sex parents and opposite-sex parents, there are still substantial hurdles regarding support, acknowledgement, and acceptance through the school system. Few schools systems offer specialized support for families with same-sex parents. Societal comfort levels regarding non-traditional families is growing, but there are still significant political and religious belief systems which discourage open and direct support for the unique needs of these families (Caspar, Schultz, & Wickens, 1992). Despite the often charged sociopolitical climate surrounding same-sex parents, teachers need to place the educational needs of the child first. This means teachers need to gather relevant information regarding the unique needs of these children and their families and support the child's educational progress (Martino & Cumming-Potvin, 2011). What are these unique needs? Let's look at a few.

Families with same-sex parents are often complicated by multiple biological and non-biological caregivers. Sometimes the child has the involvement of same-sex parents (one of which is a biological parent), as well as a heterosexual biological parent from a previous relationship. Sometimes the child's primary caregiver has no biological or legal involvement with the child, but is the same-sex partner of one of the child's biological parents. The sheer number of variation of family members involved in the life of a child with same-sex parents often makes for unique demands from the child's teacher. Teachers need to develop an on-going relationship with the family member most involved in their academic life. They also need to be sensitive to the legal realities of the child's custody arrangement. Other issues involved in the schooling of a child with same-sex parents include the following (Ryan & Martin, 2000):

- Prejudice and discriminatory behavior
- Efforts to appear "liberal-minded" may actually lead to a suppression of relevant questions as individuals avoid discussions they mistakenly feel are not necessary.
- Mistaken belief that the level of discussion regarding romantic relations involves more explicit detail with children with same-sex parents.
- Fear of accidentally saying something offensive
- Lack of faculty's knowledge about homosexuality

Addressing these issues can be challenging, but there are steps school systems and teachers can take to improve the situation for families with same-sex parents. One important step is to provide a structured setting for school faculty and staff to examine their belief structure regarding same-sex partnerships. Teachers need a safe environment to explore their perceptions and tools for ensuring the best education for the child, regardless of their belief system. Additionally, teachers need accurate and up-to-date information regarding custody and relevant legal issues. Teachers need to know how to meet their legal responsibility with respect to parents, while showing sensitivity to the child's entire family. Schools should also develop policy materials clearly specifying the school's position on diverse family constellations. Ultimately, educating children from families with same-sex parents is no different than any other child. The goal is simply to do what it takes to construct the best learning environment.

Single-Parent and Blended Families

Another group of students teachers will encounter are children from divorced homes. The actual number of marriages ending in divorce is commonly reported as 50% based on statistics from the National Center for Health Statistics. This estimate is usually based on the total

In The Classroom

APPLYING THEORY

Public Schools and Sexual Orientation

CLASSROOM APPLICATION

Addressing issues involving sexual orientation and education is potentially challenging. Some argue that schools should not address issues of sexuality, believing these are under the purview of parents and families. Other groups believe this to be primarily a private and religious matter, highlighting the role of religious and spiritual groups as appropriate venues for discussion. Still, public schools have to deal with the constitutional rights of all individuals, and an individual's free speech is one of many protected constitutional rights. This leaves schools in the position where they often need to address issues of sexuality in some form. Sometimes it is because same-sex parents demand equal voice in the education of their child. Other times it is because of the establishment of a student support group for individuals with a gay, lesbian, bisexual, or transgendered sexual orientation. It is extremely difficult for school systems to manage the often deeply divided opinions over sexual orientation and come to an effective solution.

For the classroom teacher, the issues are similar but also more personal. Teachers will struggle with their own personal beliefs and how they act on those beliefs given their professional obligation. The following guidelines will help teachers negotiate these sensitive issues and protect a student's free speech rights (Public Schools and Sexual Orientation: A first amendment for finding common ground, First Amendment Center and Bridge Builders, 2006):

Teachers should take seriously any complaints of name-calling, harassment, and/or discrimination regardless of the reason. Make clear the range of acceptable and unacceptable behaviors, taking the time to properly investigate the nature of the incident.

Teachers should assure parents and students that the school district will listen carefully, be fair to all parties, and try hard to avoid choosing sides in the broader national conflict.

Teachers should not be afraid to talk openly about these issues. It is seldom effective to try to avoid these issues in the hopes that they will just go away. These are sensitive issues and need the full attention of teachers.

Teachers should strive to keep community discussion a local one. Solving the larger societal issue is rarely practical.

Teachers should respond fairly and equitably to the variety of home environments of students; teachers do not, however, have to define "family" in the broader culture to do so.

Teachers should be careful to not discriminate against student clubs or student expression simply because the political or religious message is unpopular or potentially offensive to some. Teachers need to support the fair and equitable expression of all viewpoints.

number of marriages per one thousand people divided by the total number of divorces per one thousand people. In 2003, there were 7.5 marriages/1000 and 3.8 divorces/1000. This approach may lead to an inflated divorce rate because the people getting married are not necessarily the same people getting divorced. Other approaches to calculating the divorce rate lead to a more conservative estimate of 41% (Hurley, 2005). Regardless, divorce still affects millions of American families and potentially has a variety of negative educational outcomes.

Child adjustment following divorce depends on a number of factors. Children appear to handle divorce better when parents maintain a positive relationship, quality schooling is present, and parents are able to meet their financial obligations (Cox & Harter, 2001). Children also appear to fare better when parents and the school encourage independence, while still providing limits and control of their actions (Hetherington, 1995, 2000; Hetherington & Kelly, 2002; Baumrind, 1996). In general, boys have higher rates of behavior problems, and girls have increased difficulty in their interactions with boys following divorce. Adjustment, however, is highly individual; some children and adolescents respond to divorce with greater maturity and an increased ability to cope with issues. As one would expect, the first two years are particularly problematic for children, but three out of four children adapt and become well adjusted.

In addition to the general trends in child development following divorce, there are significant environmental and family structure changes. Children find themselves moving from a two-parent home to a home where only one parent is available. A 2003 census report indicated that approximately 27% of families are single-parent homes. Single-parent homes present many challenges to both parent and child. There is often a substantial decrease in the amount of time the parent has available to spend with the child as he/she try to run the household, work, establish new adult relationships, and deal with child issues like homework, birthday parties, play-dates, etc. Another issue these families often face is remarriage. Approximately two out of three single parents will remarry following divorce, and about half of these marriages will again result in divorce (Furstenburg & Cherlin, 1991). **Blended families** refers to families where single parents that remarry create step-relations and potentially half-sibling relationships. These families bring new adjustment issues as children accommodate to yet another living situation.

Blended family

Families in which single-parents who re-marry create step-relations and potentially half-sibling relationships

There is no easy formula for helping children adjust to a divorce, but there are some general guidelines. One of the most consistent findings is that open and frequent communication between parents and between parent and child greatly increases the probability of successfully resolving divorce related issues. Families should also ensure that everyone remains invested and engaged in the family. Family time should be prioritized, as this provides opportunities for bonding and shared growth and provides a structured time for communication. Extended family members and teachers can also become important resources as these children adapt to their new circumstances. Finally, parents and teachers should strive to maintain a quality educational experience. Quality education is an important predictor for later adjustment of the child.

SUMMARIZE AND REFLECT

1. As we grow up, a variety of differences emerge between boys and girls. There are differences in our sense of being male or female resulting in specific differences in behavior and cognitions.
2. It is important for educators to be aware of gender biases and ways to avoid them in an educational setting.
3. There are a variety of regional differences in dialect across the country. Each one differs in how it compares to the perception of a *Standard English.*
4. Students who speak more than one language often present unique challenges for schools.
5. The nature of family is also changing. The traditional family model is broadening to include a variety of other family structures. There are families where grandparents are raising their grandchildren and families with parents of the same sex.
6. Divorce also affects families and results in a complex array of potential difficulties for single parents.

INFORMED APPLICATION

1. Consider some of the subtle ways a teacher can communicate a gender bias to their students.
2. What are the pros and cons of providing active support for regional or cultural dialects?
3. As a teacher of a student with same-sex parents, what can you do to insure fair and legally appropriate treatment of both parents?

CULTURE AND SOCIETY

The final section of this chapter examines individual differences according to larger, societal dimensions. For example, consider the following students. Maria lives in a middle-class single parent family. Her mother died in a car accident when she was very young. Her grandparents were born in Mexico and immigrated to the United States as adults. Her family maintains many of her grandparent's traditions, and she is bilingual in Spanish and English. Compare Maria's situation to Ryan's family background. Ryan's family lives in an affluent section of a major metropolitan area. His family is of African descent, but his family has lived in the United States as far back as anyone can remember. His parents are both lawyers and earn a comfortable living. He identifies with his African ancestry on many levels and actively tries to incorporate his history into his family life.

Both Maria and Ryan have many unique qualities. As we discussed earlier in the chapter, their gender difference is likely to impact their behavior and their thinking. Maria's bilingual ability also distinguishes her and may impact her education. Ryan and Maria also differ according to their family group. Maria lives in a single-parent home, whereas Ryan enjoys the support of both his parents.

The stories of Ryan and Maria highlight many of the ways individuals differ. For example, Maria and Ryan differ in their family's social and economic situation. Maria lives in a middle income home common in our country. Ryan enjoys the resources and lifestyle common to a much smaller, affluent segment of our society. Maria and Ryan also differ in their ethnic background, which in turn results in cultural differences in the home. Both appear to connect with their cultural heritage, but they are likely to experience their cultural background in different ways. The goal of this section is to help you develop an appreciation of individual differences at this level.

Socioeconomic Status (SES)

Socioeconomic status (SES) relates to economic differences between individuals and families; it also relates to prestige, power, and political influence. Reported divisions in social class vary depending on the source, but typically include some grouping of upper class, middle class, and lower class. Frequently these broad categories are further subdivided to provide a more accurate representation of the individuals within these classes (see Figure 8.3, adapted from Charon, 1986).

Socioeconomic status has long been viewed as a strong predictor of academic success (Coleman, 1966). In general, the trend is that as SES decreases, academic issues increase. Much of the research on SES and achievement has focused on economically disadvantaged families. As discussed at the beginning of this chapter, there are many children living in poverty. This brings about environmental challenges like crime, drug abuse, and sub-standard living conditions (Tobler, Komro, Dabroski, & Aveyard, 2011). It also frequently means children are being educated in less than ideal schooling environments.

Upper Class	Upper Middle Class	Lower Middle Class	Working Class	Lower Class
Income Over $145,000	Income Over $85,000	Income Over $35,000	Income Over $20,000	Income Less than $20,000
Employment High Prestige Jobs	Employment White-Collar Professional	Employment Blue-Collar Skilled Workers	Employment Blue-Collar	Employment Minimum Wage or None
Power National, Regional, and Local Political Influence	Power Regional, and Local Political Influence	Power Local Political Influence	Power Limited	Power Very little or None
Percentage of Population 1–3%	Percentage of the Population 10%	Percentage of the Population 30–40%	Percentage of the Population 30–40%	Percentage of the Population 20–25%

Figure 8.3
Social Class Structure

Educational Experience and SES

The quality of a student's educational experience is influenced by their socioeconomic status. Children from a higher SES achieve more regardless of racial or ethnic background (Conger, Conger, & Elder, 1997; McLoyd, 1998). Achievement is also likely to be influenced by the expectations of the teacher. Teachers tend to expect less of students from lower SES levels (Bowles & Gintis, 1976). They wait longer for high SES students to answer a question (Spring, 2005). They also are more likely to give high SES students a second try to answer a question and to provide more praise. This differs from how teachers often address students from lower SES backgrounds. Lower expectations for students from low SES backgrounds may lead students to develop a negative self-perception (Caldas & Bankston, 1997; Spring, 2005).

Students from lower SES backgrounds are also likely to have their educational experience compromised by inadequate school facilities and high student-to-teacher ratios. Public schools typically rely on property taxes for funding. This leads to generous funding for wealthier areas and leaves poorer areas struggling to meet student needs (Kozol, 1991; Education Trust, 2005). Students in poorer areas typically do not have adequate facilities including lab equipment, projectors, books, etc. (Leacock, 1971; Powers, 1996). The lack of necessary funding also leads to lower teacher salaries. This, in turn, leads to higher teacher turn over and the subsequent employment of newer, less experienced teachers. It also leads to the liberal use of substitutes (Ehrenberg, Brewer, Gamoran, & Williams, 2001). The teacher problem is compounded by larger class sizes. Larger classes and less experienced teachers often lead to noisy and disruptive classroom environments.

Family and SES

There are a variety of family factors influenced by SES. Families from different SES levels appear to have different educational values and expectations. Families from high SES levels help their children to be achievement oriented. They actively teach their children qualities like restraint, self-discipline, and responsibility. This leads to children who are more academically successful (Wilson, 1987). Parents in lower SES levels typically focus on the behavior of the child, rather than the child's attitudes and ideas about academic success. This gives the child knowledge about what behaviors are expected (e.g., do your homework), but fails to give them an appreciation of how these behaviors are linked to success through qualities like self-discipline.

Families from lower SES levels often have difficulty meeting the demands of daily life. To help them cope, parents encourage children to help maintain the home, take care of younger siblings, and provide for themselves. Compare this situation to middle class families. Having greater freedom from worries about daily life, children from middle-class homes are taught to focus on the future. They are encouraged to think about their life plan and the consequences of their actions. Consequences for inappropriate behavior are typically non-physical, which encourages thoughtfulness instead of fear (Maccoby, 1980; Parke & Buriel, 1998). All of this leads to greater skills supporting academic success for students from higher SES backgrounds. Students who are thoughtful, feel safe, and focus on the results of their behavior are more likely to do well in school.

Ethnicity

Ethnicity is a frequent topic of discussion in schools. This is in part due to the inherent qualities of a public system of education. Since schools are open to all, students are likely to encounter students from differing cultural backgrounds. Bringing together individuals from different cultures is potentially an excellent opportunity to learn about human difference, but only if teachers help students understand the differences they observe. All too often, students use differences in negative ways. Differences can lead to inappropriate groups, resulting in some students feeling included and others feeling disliked. Encouraging students to view differences in a positive way helps students learn and grow as human beings. They are also in a better position to become active participants in our remarkable global community. This section looks at ethnicity, discusses its relation to race, and reviews what we know about ethnic trends.

Race versus Ethnicity

Before we begin to look at specific educational issues surrounding cultural background, we are going to examine the terms *race* and *ethnicity*. These terms are occasionally used interchangeably, occasionally used together, or sometimes avoided altogether.

Let's look at typical definitions for each term. **Race** refers to a group of people with biologically inherited traits viewed as socially significant. These biological traits commonly refer to skin color, nose and lip shape, and hair texture and color. **Ethnicity** refers to any distinguishable group of people who have a common culture. The distinguishing qualities vary from group to group and may include geographical location, physical attributes, or cultural traditions (Diller & Moule, 2005). Race and ethnicity, according to these definitions, are separate constructs. In reality, they are interrelated. A group of individuals may have biological traits in common and also share a unique cultural heritage (i.e., sharing race and ethnicity). Other groups may have a common cultural heritage, but come from different racial backgrounds. Additionally, some have avoided the term *race* altogether because humans have been racially mixing for thousands of years—resulting in no pure races (Betancourt & Lopez, 1993). Given these difficulties, it is often unclear how to refer to educational factors related to race and/or ethnicity. In general, referring exclusively to race is uncommon in an educational context. The lack of agreement regarding the exact nature of race makes it difficult to use. More common is the use of both terms (i.e., race/ethnicity). This use highlights the interrelated nature of these two factors. It is also common to use just the term *ethnicity*. This use focuses on the social and political aspects of culture. It does not negate that there are certain physical traits associated with certain groups, but focuses on important situational factors. To illustrate this point consider the following example. You are working on creating strong and productive work groups in your science class. You recognize that a large percentage of your students are of Asian descent, recently relocating to the United States. Your experience with these students has taught you they have unique ways of operating within a small group. They appear to be highly interdependent, relying on one another to finish an assignment. This strikes you as different from students born and raised in the U.S. You see these students as more independent and in need of more explicit instruction in effective group interactions. You conduct some research on the topic and discover that this is a common cultural difference. You decide to incorporate this information into your lesson. Your hope is that the students will learn about how different cultures interact in groups and that this will lead them to be more productive during your science lesson. This situation is particularly relevant to the overall discussion of race and ethnicity because of the unique situation of one of your students. Jin was born and raised in China and has recently immigrated to the U.S. Her father is Chinese, but her mother is French. Her facial features are more like her mother's; in fact, people are often surprised when she speaks with a heavy Chinese accent. Culturally, Jin is like other students from China. She shares the same cultural heritage and has many similar ways of operating in the world. Her racial makeup, however, is different, resulting in a cosmetic appearance that is similar to the students born and raised in her new home in the U.S. In this situation, using both race and ethnicity is not the best term to use when thinking about Jin and her performance in small groups. It would be better to refer to her ethnic background, as it is this quality that has the most direct impact on her performance in this situation.

Race

A group of people with biologically inherited traits viewed as socially significant

Ethnicity

Any distinguishable group of people who have a common culture, ethnic background, or cultural affiliation

F.A.Q.

Ryan Lafleur—"So I'm still confused. What term is most appropriate to use, race or ethnicity?"

Professor Booher—"Your confusion is understandable. Unfortunately, there isn't a clear answer. The best you can do is really assess what you are trying to convey and then select the term with the most similar definition. It is also, however, fairly common to use the term '*race/ethnicity*,' which is less specific but avoids some of the potential difficulties in choosing a single term."

As you can see from the example, terminology can often be confusing in this area. It is important, however, to remember that these terms raise sensitive issues, and care should be taken to reflect and think about the meaning you want to convey. Not everyone who uses these terms may be operating with the same definitions, making assessment of someone's intent important. Ask questions so you understand what someone intends to say, and then you can negotiate what specific terms are appropriate to represent that meaning.

Ethnic Trends

Before we begin an examination of ethnic cultures and education, let's look at some educational trends in the U.S. related to ethnicity. As we review this material, it is important to maintain a critical perspective. The data below represent large national survey data. As was discussed earlier in the chapter, the extent to which a national trend applies to an individual varies. Teachers

Figure 8.4
Percentage of Public Elementary and Secondary Students, by Race/Ethnicity: School Year 2000–01

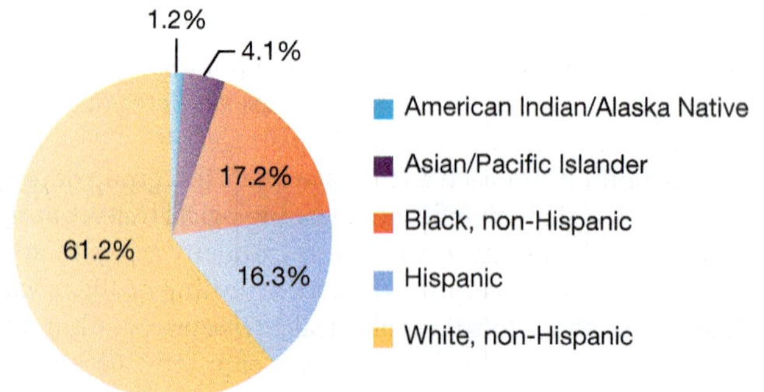

NOTE: Percentages for categories shown may not sum to total because of rounding.
SOURCE: U.S. Department of Education, National Center for Education Statistics, Common Core of Data (CDD), "State Non-fiscal Survey of Public Elementary/Secondary Education," 2000–01.

should be informed regarding national trends, as this gives the teacher information necessary to develop a sensitive perspective. Teachers, however, always should be mindful of the difference between general tends and an individual's reality. Bearing that in mind, here are some overall trends in our school systems today.

First, let's look at overall demographic trends (Figure 8.4). As you can see from the figure, the largest percentage of students comes from White, non-Hispanic backgrounds. This, however, is across the entire U.S. In some states, there is no clear majority demographic (e.g., California and Hawaii). This is also true for some urban areas (e.g., Houston and New York City).

It is also important to consider demographic changes over time. As shown in Figure 8.5, the percentage of Black, non-Hispanic students has increased slightly since 1972, but we have seen large increases in the number of students from Hispanic backgrounds. We have also seen increases in students from other minority backgrounds.

Academic trends vary across subject area and by ethnic background. We see higher levels of performance in mathematics and reading from students with a White, non-Hispanic background (see Figures 8.6A and 8.6B). This is in comparison to students classified as Black or Hispanic. It should be noted that these classification systems are often criticized for being too general. New U.S. census data has broken down some of these categories to better represent the

Figure 8.5
Percent of Public School Students Enrolled in Grades K–12 Who Were Minorities, by Race/Ethnicity: 1972–2000

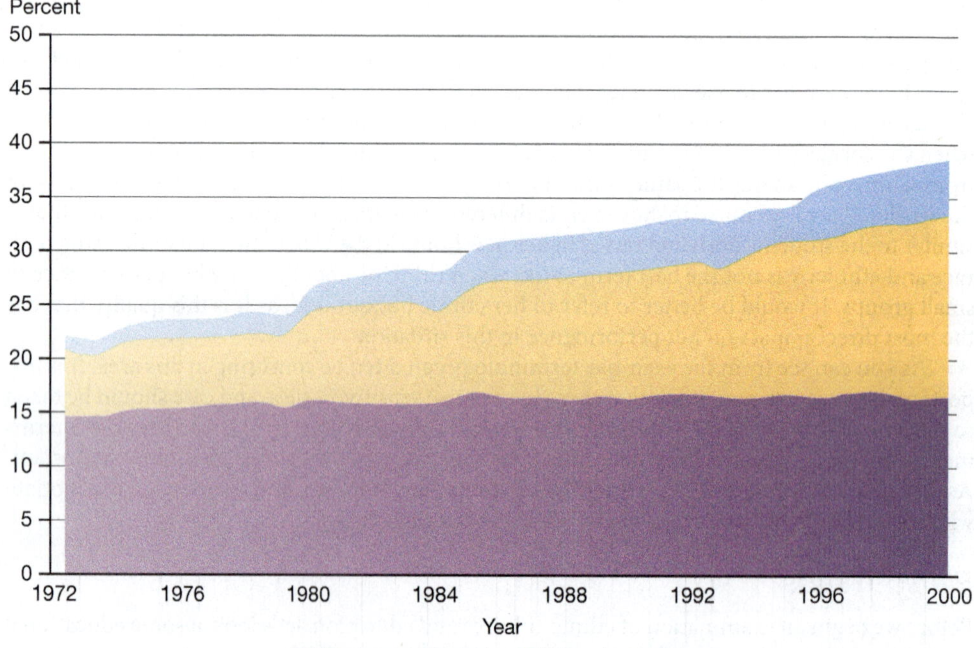

SOURCE: U.S. Department of Education, National Center for Education Statistics, *The Condition of Education, 2002*, based on U.S. Department of Commerce, Bureau of the Census, October, Current Population Surveys, 1972–2000.

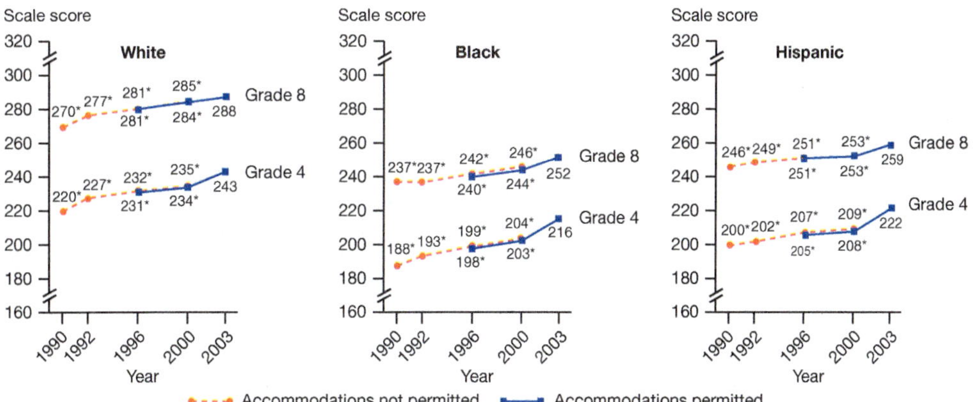

Figure 8.6A

Academic Trends in Mathematics by Ethnic Background

SOURCE: U.S. Department of Education, National Center for Education Statistics, National Assessment of Educational Progress (NAEP), 1990, 1992, 1996, 2000, and 2003 Mathematics Assessments. (Adapted from the first figure on p. 13 of the publication from which this article is excerpted.)

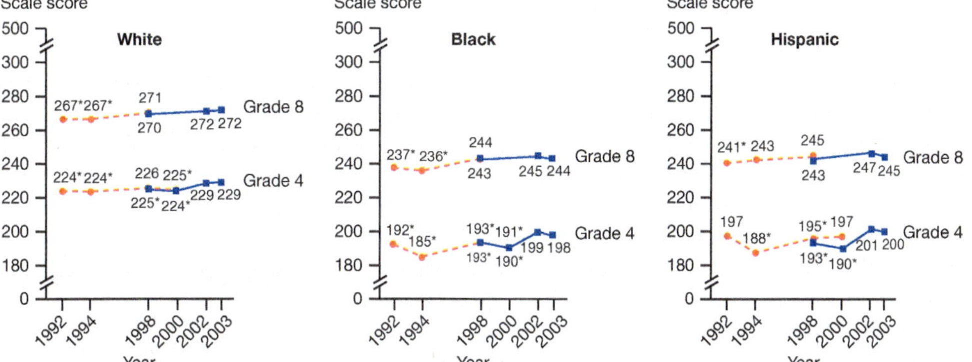

Figure 8.6B

Academic Trends in Reading by Ethnic Background

*Significantly different from 2003

NOTE: Data were not collected at grade 8 in 2000. In addition to allowing for accommodations, the accommodations-permitted results at grade 4 (1998–2003) differ slightly from the previous years' results, and from previously reported results for 1998 and 2000, due to changes in sample weighting procedures. Significance tests were performed using unrounded numbers.

SOURCE: U.S. Department of Education, National Center for Education Statistics, National Assessment of Educational Progress (NAEP), 1992, 1994, 1998, 2000, 2002, and 2003 Reading Assessments. (Adapted from the first figure on p. 13 of the publication from which this article is excerpted.)

population. They have also allowed for respondents to endorse more than one demographic category to better reflect the qualities and attributes of individuals with clear mixed-racial backgrounds (recall that we all have a mixed-racial background to some extent); however, it remains difficult to capture the unique qualities of individuals in the national surveys.

The academic trends reflected in Figures 8.6A and 8.6B appear to extend to other behavioral and social dimensions. One logical outcome of academic difficulties is that students are more likely to repeat grades and to drop out of school. Figure 8.7 shows that students from Black, Hispanic, and American Indian/Alaska Native backgrounds are more likely than students from White backgrounds to repeat a grade or suffer a suspension or expulsion. Interestingly, students from Asian/Pacific Islander background are less likely than all other ethnic backgrounds to experience these difficulties.

Data on dropout rates indicates a similar trend. As shown in Figure 8.8, students from Black or Hispanic backgrounds are more likely to drop out of school compared to students from a White background. The highest dropout rates are for students from Hispanic backgrounds. It is important to note, however, that overall dropout rates are decreasing for all ethnic groups.

So why are students from some ethnic groups having greater academic difficulty? The answer lies in the larger social, economic, and political situation for individuals from these backgrounds. The financial status of a student's family has far reaching impact on their lives.

Figure 8.7
Percent of Elementary and Secondary Students Who Had Ever Repeated a Grade or Been Suspended/Expelled, by Race/Ethnicity: 199

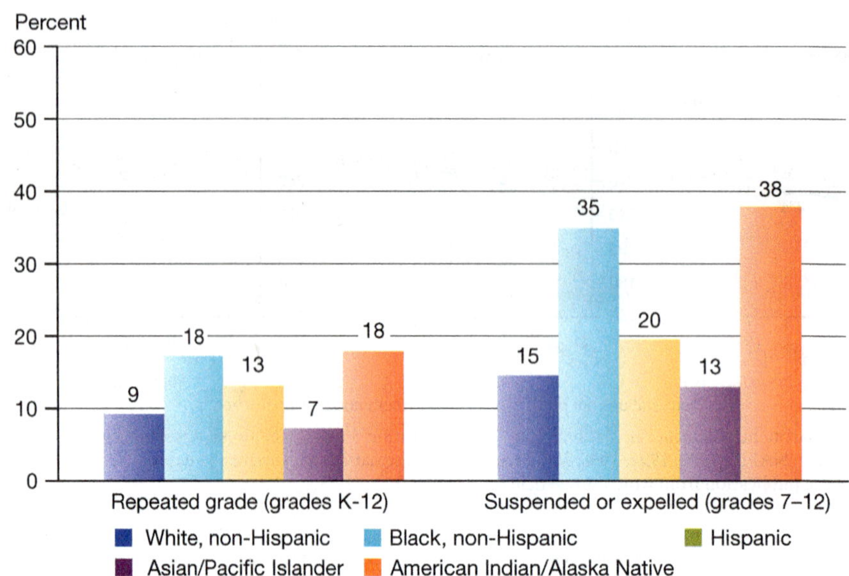

Students whose families have limited financial resources are more likely to live in areas with high crime rates. They are more likely to be exposed to drug use. Their parents are more likely to experience high levels of stress. Their schools typically mirror their financial difficulties, having difficulty providing ideal educational experiences. Looking at the ethnic breakdown of individuals from the poorest segments of our society, we find that about 40% of families from an African background and 40% of families from a Hispanic background live below the poverty. The disproportionately higher number of children from these backgrounds and the difficulties they experience in daily living leads to a disproportionately high number of academic problems. For example, the lack of security experienced by students in high crime areas translates into greater fear and anxiety at school. Again, because a larger number of students from minority backgrounds experience these challenging living environments they tend to experience more safety issues and subsequently greater fear at school (see Figure 8.9).

Interconnections

The human need for safety is covered in Chapter 7.

Figure 8.8
Status Dropouts: Dropout Rates of 16- to 24-Year-Olds, by Race/Ethnicity: October 1972–2001

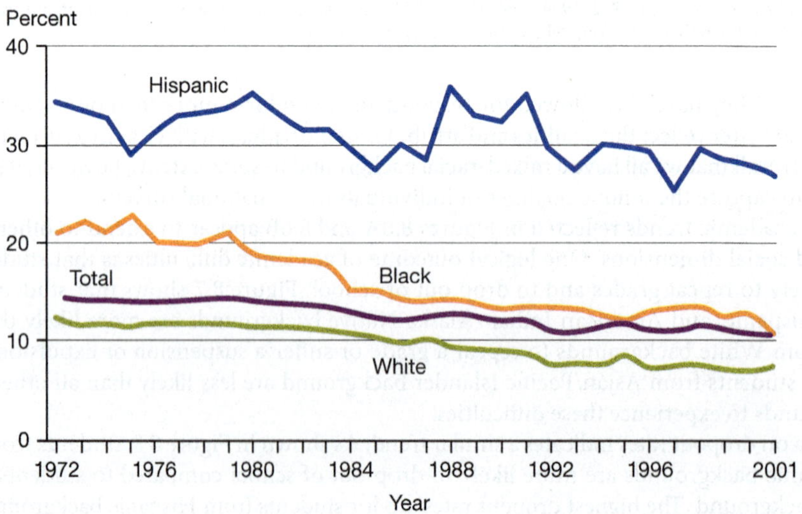

NOTE: Due to relatively small sample sizes, American Indians or Alaska Natives and Asians or Pacific Islanders are included in the total but are not shown separately. The erratic nature of the Hispanic status rates reflects, in part, the historically small sample size of Hispanics. Black includes African American, and Hispanic includes Latino. Race categories exclude Hispanic origin unless specified.

SOURCE: U.S. Department of Commerce, Bureau of the Census, Current Population Survey (CPS), October 1972–2001

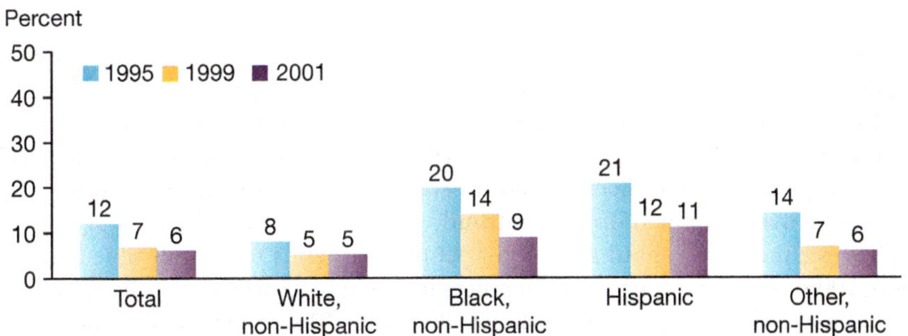

Figure 8.9

Percentage of Students Ages Twelve Through Eighteen Who Reported Fear at School or on the Way to and from School During the Previous Six Months, by Race/Ethnicity; 1995, 1999, and 2001

NOTE: In 1995 and 1999, students reported fear of "attack or harm" at school during the previous 6 months. In 2001, students reported fear of "attack or threat of attack" at school during the previous 6 months. Includes students who reported that they sometime or most of the time feared being victimized in this way. See Appendix B for details.
SOURCE: U.S. Department of Justice, Bureau of Justice Statistics, School Crime Supplement to the National Crime Victimization Survey, January–June 1995, 1999, and 2001

Lack of feeling safe at school is likely to have a negative influence as students focus on their need for safety, rather than their academic studies. This relates to the need for safety discussed in Chapter 7 with the work of Abraham Maslow. Fear and related stresses are only a small part of the overall picture. Academic success of students from ethnic minorities may be negatively impacted by a variety of other factors. For example, students from ethnic minorities are more likely to experience teen pregnancy (Moore, Simms, & Betsey, 1986), come from single parent homes (Rector, Johnson, & Fagan, 2001), have less qualified teachers (Darling-Hammond, 1999), and have parents with less than a high school education (Vernez & Krop, 1999). All of these factors impact the potential for academic success.

In conclusion, results from national educational surveys indicate some alarming trends. In general, it appears that on average students from ethnic minority backgrounds are experiencing greater academic challenges. There are notable exceptions, however, as in the lower percentage of students from an Asian/Pacific Islander background repeating a grade or getting expelled from school compared to all other racial/ethnic backgrounds. Being informed about these overall trends can help teachers develop a sensitive framework for understanding ethnic trends. Again, teachers should also exercise caution when applying this information to specific individuals.

Culturally Sensitive Instruction

Our final section examines how teachers can bring the diverse array of cultural backgrounds into the classroom in sensitive and informative ways. As you will see, it is important for teachers to inspire a sense of curiosity and wonder regarding the world's cultures. They also need to be mindful of the tendency for some students to use cultural information to socially isolate or distance themselves from other students. With careful planning, however, students can gain an appreciation of culture, both the culture of others and their own.

Cultural Identification

Before we look at cultural aspects of education, it is important to first examine how the individual experiences their own ethnic or cultural identity. Coming to a sense of one's own cultural or ethnic background is difficult. It also appears to differ depending on whether your ethnic background is consistent with that of the majority culture. For individuals from ethnic *minority* backgrounds, their identification process begins with an immersion into a particular culture, grounded in the family unit. That is, they live, work, and play in a particular setting with unique rules, values, traditions, and often religious beliefs. This process is generally supportive and builds confidence in the individual. Individuals from these minority backgrounds, however, ultimately need to resolve their unique cultural qualities with that of the majority culture. This is frequently a negative process as they receive less than positive messages from movies, television, and print media (Chavez & Guido-DiBrito, 1999; Taylor, Walker, Austin, Thoth, & Welch, 2011). It is interesting that there really is not a comparable process for individuals from the majority culture. In the U.S., children from European backgrounds grow up in a society where general ideas about what it means to be an American are consistent with their ethnic background. This makes the process of ethnic identification different for majority and minority populations. Let's review some models that try to describe this process in more detail.

Identity development for individuals from minority cultural backgrounds involves the resolution of two important issues (Phinney, 1990). *First*, they need to come to terms with various stereotypes and prejudices present in society. As discussed earlier in the chapter, a stereotype is an oversimplified opinion, attitude, or judgment held by members of a group. A **prejudice** is a judgment about a group of people that tends to be inflexible and irrational (Macionis, 2005). The stereotypes and prejudices inherent in a society typically raise substantial conflicts in the people to whom they are directed (Gaunt, 2011). They threaten their self-esteem and must be resolved in order to establish a healthy identification with their cultural group. *Second*, the people affected need to contend with differences in their value system compared to the value system of the majority culture. Successful resolution of these systems typically results in individuals from ethnic minority backgrounds developing a bicultural value system. That is, they use one value system when interacting with people they identify as belonging to their cultural group and another value system when dealing with the majority culture.

Prejudice

A judgment about a group of people that tends to be inflexible and irrational rather than based on adequate knowledge

This process of cultural identification is quite different for individuals from the majority culture. White Americans place high value on competition. Also, they view time as linear and a commodity, much like goods and services. They value independence and support the development of autonomy. Again, the development of these ideologies is often transparent. Members of the white ethnic group are inherently the same as the general view of what it means to be American. This means that white Americans do not have to deal with stereotypes and prejudices in the same way as Americans from minority backgrounds. This is not to say that there are no stereotypes regarding white Americans or that people do not hold prejudices against white Americans. They certainly do. It is just that the path to resolution of these issues is different. White Americans enjoy the perception that their values and way of being in the world are normal or typical. A large part of education regarding cultures is to move away from ideas of placing culture in a hierarchy (i.e., my family's culture is "right") and to move toward being knowledgeable and respectful of all cultures.

Multicultural Education

Multicultural education

An educational ideal that students from all racial/ ethnic and social class groups will have an equitable educational experience

Multicultural education is an educational ideal that students from all racial/ethnic and social class groups will have an equitable educational experience. One of the leading researchers in this field is James Banks. He has been a tireless advocate for multicultural education. His five-dimension approach to understanding multicultural education is one of the most cited (Banks, 1995). According to this approach, five interrelated dimensions drive multicultural

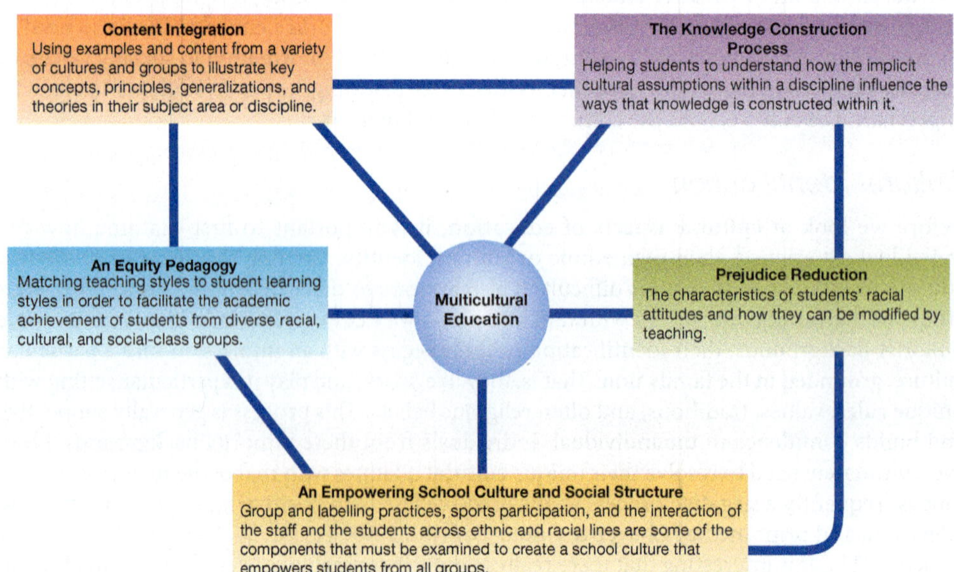

Figure 8.10
The Five Dimensions of Multicultural Education

education (see Figure 8.10). Let's take a brief look at each and consider how they interact to bring about effective educational practice.

The first of his dimensions is *content integration*. This refers to how teachers infuse different cultural views into the curriculum being taught (Irby, Tong, & Lara-Alecio, 2011). Often teachers learning about multicultural education focus entirely on this single dimension. They make concerted efforts to discover different cultural factors relevant to a particular discussion and mistakenly believe this will bring about multicultural understanding. The process of multicultural education is actually much broader and includes four other dimensions. Additionally, teachers need to be careful not to infuse their curriculum in trivial ways. Changes in curriculum to highlight culture need to be truly integrated; otherwise, teachers marginalize the content, and it is far less effective.

The second dimension is *knowledge construction*. This dimension underscores the need to not only teach particular content but also to help students gain an appreciation of the information source. What we often teach in this area is knowledge *facts*, but this is really just a body of information we all agree is relevant. It is constructed by people and is reflective of the biases and political climate in which it is developed. Students need to be aware of this knowledge construction process. Of course, to help students evaluate the knowledge construction process, it is important that some knowledge has been integrated into their curriculum (the first dimension). This is one reason these dimensions should always be viewed as highly interdependent.

The third dimension is *prejudice reduction*. As we discussed in the last section, the presence of different cultures leads to a variety of stereotypes and prejudices. Teachers need to recognize this process and help students address the issue. Often teachers can reduce prejudicial thinking by providing an example of someone engaging in prejudicial behavior. They can also use direct modeling of such behavior. Children may even engage more readily in such experiential activities. Children look to adults for how to understand group differences. Teachers who present cultural information in an objective and non-prejudicial manner facilitate this type of understanding in their students. Additionally, teachers can provide direct instruction in the democratic ideals of justice and equality.

The fourth dimension is *equity pedagogy*. The term pedagogy alone refers to the tools the teacher brings to his or her professional endeavors. *Equity pedagogy* essentially means that a teacher's tools are valuable in helping each and every student learn and achieve (Yang & Montgomery, 2011). Teachers following equity pedagogy have an underlying philosophy that all students can learn with the right support. Pedagogical tools are not viewed hierarchically with some tools being seen as better than others. Rather, all educational tools are considered useful depending on the needs of the student. Often this approach necessitates that teachers reevaluate the standard curriculum. Teaching to a diverse array of students requires teachers to be inventive if they are going to find the appropriate tools needed to provide an equitable education. It also necessitates that teachers really get to know their students. They need to talk to them, learning about their daily lives and family backgrounds. The more thoroughly a teacher knows the students, the better able he/she will be in providing sensitive instruction.

The fifth and final dimension is *empowering the school culture and social structure*. Unlike the other dimensions, this one extends beyond the classroom. Essentially, this dimension refers to school changes that remove any barriers that have traditionally disadvantaged certain students. This is an important part of the overall process. Individual teachers may make significant strides in the implementation of the other four dimensions; however, if the overall climate of the school does not fully support those efforts, it will be difficult to maintain.

SUMMARIZE AND REFLECT

1. The final section of this chapter examined socioeconomic status (SES). It covered generally reported SES trends.
2. Of particular importance are families in the lower socioeconomic levels and the educational challenges they encounter.
3. Race and ethnicity are important constructs for educators to understand. They are interconnected terms, but distinct with unique applications.

(continues)

4. There are many complexities behind cultural identification, including differences in identification between members of the cultural majority and minority.
5. Multicultural education is increasingly highlighted in today's schools. Research has identified several key characteristics that promote successful multicultural education.

INFORMED APPLICATION

1. Teachers often believe they are immune from prejudice, assuming they will provide all students with an equal educational experience. Research, however, has shown this is not always the case. In addition to the examples provided in the book, what are some additional ways teachers might inadvertently demonstrate prejudicial actions?
2. Describe a brief lesson on any aspect of the American Civil War. Consider how learning such a lesson could be impacted by a student's cultural identification.

THE CHAPTER IN REVIEW

Check out our website ▶ www.BVTLab.com for chapter-by-chapter flashcards, practice quizzes, summaries, and more.

This chapter focused on education as it relates to individuals, groups, and society. The first section began with a review of changes in the composition of students in our schools. We covered increases in the total student population, changing immigration trends, and children living in poverty. Next, we looked at differential instruction as an educational model designed to help meet the needs of such a diverse population. We also discussed the need for equity and mutual respect in schools with a diverse student population. Overall, this section maintained a focus on the individual and their unique school experience.

The second section of the chapter moved away from a focus on the individual and turned to an examination of group differences. We started with an examination of how boys differ from girls. We looked at how children identify with being male or female. We also looked at common stereotypes related to gender. Next, we reviewed differences in the behavior and cognitive patterns of girls and boys. Critical evaluation and application of these gender differences was highlighted. The next part of the chapter focused on language related differences. We examined regional differences in speech patterns or dialect. We also looked at bilingual education and English as a second language (ESL) as typical approaches schools take to educate children who speak more than one language. The last part of this section covered family issues. Family structure is becoming more complex as divorce rates climb and new family models are explored, such as intergenerational families and families with same-sex parents.

The last section of the chapter focused on broader social and political factors impacting the lives of children. We first explored the concept of socioeconomic status or SES. In particular, we looked at families in the lower end of the SES spectrum and their educational challenges. Next, we addressed the frequently misunderstood terms of race and ethnicity. We defined the terms and discussed guidelines for appropriate use. We also outlined general educational trends based on ethnicity. The final part of the chapter looked at the exciting area of multicultural education. We discussed strategies for successfully integrating education about different cultures in the school system. We also talked about the general process of identifying with a particular culture.

Interdisciplinary Case Focus

principal special educator teacher parents psychologist social worker physical educator nurse peers doctor

Ms. Kyra Blankner is a seventh grade English teacher in small city in the northwest. She has been teaching for twenty-five years and thoroughly enjoys helping her students gain a better command of the English language. Recently, however, she feels her efforts are being poorly received because her students are "changing." At times, she has difficulty in understanding students as they talk in the halls. Their vocabulary is evolving, using words that have one meaning for her, but clearly have another meaning for each other. She was also distressed over their use of grammar in casual conversations until she began to notice regularities in their "incorrect" usage. She began to realize the students were not being lazy or careless with their use of the English language but were changing the language. They were using existing vocabulary in new ways and inventing new words. They were changing the rules of grammar, but using these "new" rules carefully and consistently. She began to ask herself questions: "What language do I teach these students? Do I teach them the standard form of English and somehow make allowances for their new way of communicating? Do I discourage their deviation from traditional English?" Before she did anything, she decided to collect some information.

Parents The first group of people with whom she wanted to speak was the student's parents. If she was going to make any sort of shift in her teaching, she needed to better understand the extent of this new way of communicating. Working with her school principal, she sent a letter home to the parents of her students asking them to attend a focus group after school. She indicated they would be discussing communication, and the pros and cons of using non-traditional forms of English. To her surprise, a large number of parents expressed an interest in attending.

Ms. Blankner felt the focus group was a big success. The parents were very open and honest in their responses and sympathetic to her dilemma. Some parents knew exactly what she was experiencing and clearly made every effort to stop these "wrong" ways of speaking. One parent said, "What kind of job is Bobby going to get if this is how he speaks?" Some of the other parents were in agreement, but some approached the issue differently. Many parents openly acknowledged that the way their children spoke was consistent with how they spoke in the home and in their community. One parent said, "This is just the way it is where we live. Kids need to fit in." Another parent followed up by saying, "I don't think it is just about fitting in; this is the language of our community."

After considerable discussion, it became clear that parents wanted their children to learn the standard form of English that Ms. Blankner was well prepared to teach. There was acknowledgement that this form of English was the English of the business world, and they wanted their children to be able to function in that world. They did, however, want their children's typical form of communication to be supported in some way. They didn't want their children to feel badly about the way they spoke. They worried about their self-perceptions. Toward the end of the session, they asked Ms. Blankner if there was some way she could use their existing way of speaking to actually help them learn Standard English. One parent noted that when she took Spanish in high school, she felt like she learned English for the first time. The comparison helped her appreciate both languages. This struck Ms. Blankner as a great idea, and she told the parents she would work on it and get back to them with her plan.

Spanish and French Instructors After considerable reflection, Ms. Blankner decided to consult with the school's foreign language teachers. In a meeting with the Spanish and French teachers, she explained the situation and the ideas, which came from the meeting with the parents. Ms. Speight, the Spanish teacher, indicated that she often used a student's knowledge of English to help her students understand Spanish. She indicated this was particularly true for grammar. Mr. Vick, the French teacher agreed. He suggested that Ms. Blankner develop exercises where students have to use code-switching. He explained that this was a term from bilingual education, which meant that students had to change from using the codes of one language to the codes, or rules, of another language. This not only teaches them the codes of the new language (i.e., French) but also actually reinforces their appreciation and understanding of their existing language (i.e., English). Ms. Blankner really liked this idea, but realized that she did not have enough information regarding the "language" the students were using. She decided to call a professor of language at the local university to see if she could help.

Professor Salma Portez Dr. Portez is a language professor specializing in American dialects. She readily accepts an appointment with Ms. Blankner to discuss her ideas. During their meeting, Dr. Portez explains that the type of speech being used by Ms. Blankner's students sounds like the dialect used in urban, inner city environments. It is particularly common among African American youth in this setting. Ms. Blankner initially expresses concern because their city is fairly small and doesn't match her ideas about "urban" environments. She also notes that most of her students are of Caucasian descent. Dr. Portez explains that she was referring to general trends. The language examples that Ms. Blankner mentioned were consistent with the urban dialect, but she had an idea how they could specifically document the language used by her students and develop an educational tool to help her meet her goals.

They decide that one of Dr. Portez's research assistants would work in Ms. Blankner's school for the next month. His job would be to observe student language in casual settings and document vocabulary and grammar use. He would also make arrangements with parents to observe the students during extracurricular activities. After the month of observation Dr. Portez would review the data and with the help of Ms. Blankner devise an educational approach to use with her students.

Conclusion After the observation month, Dr. Portez calls Ms. Blankner to arrange a meeting to discuss the results. It turns out that the students were indeed using a grammatical structure consistent with African American English. Dr. Portez gave Ms. Blankner several articles and charts detailing the "rules" of this language and also provided information on Southern English, Californian English, and Spanglish. She suggested Ms. Blankner begin with specialized lessons on each of these different dialects. Then she could give the students an exercise where she would begin with the presentation of a linguistic sample. The sample would be randomly selected from any of the regional dialects. The students' task would be to identify which dialect the language sample represents. They would then have to identify the specific language rule in use. Finally, they would code-switch the sample into Standard English. This approach had several advantages. It would help the students better appreciate the complexities of verbal communication. They would be able to appreciate how their expressions were governed by rules and that all languages had this in common. The approach would validate that different dialects were indeed rule-governed language, while also giving the students the skills to move into standard forms of English to communicate. This seemed to meet everyone's needs, and she excitedly left the meeting to begin preparations for her new "English" lessons.

Key Terms

TERM	Page	TERM	Page
Androgyny	243	Gender-role transcendence	243
Bilingual education	246	Gender schemas	240
Blended family	252	Gender stereotype	241
Code-switching	245	Intergenerational child rearing	249
Dialects	244	Kinship rearing	249
Diversity	233	Matriarchal families	248
Egalitarian families	248	Multicultural education	260
English as a second language (ESL)	246	Mutual respect	238
Equality	237	Nuclear family	247
Equity	237	Patriarchal families	248
Ethnicity	255	Prejudice	260
Extended family	248	Race	255
Family of orientation	247	Relational aggression	242
Family of procreation	247	Sex	239
Gender	239	Standard English	244
Gender constancy	240	Stereotype	241
Gender identity	239	Verbal ability	242
Gender role	239		

9

Chapter

STANDARDIZED TESTING AND UNDERSTANDING LEARNER DIFFERENCES

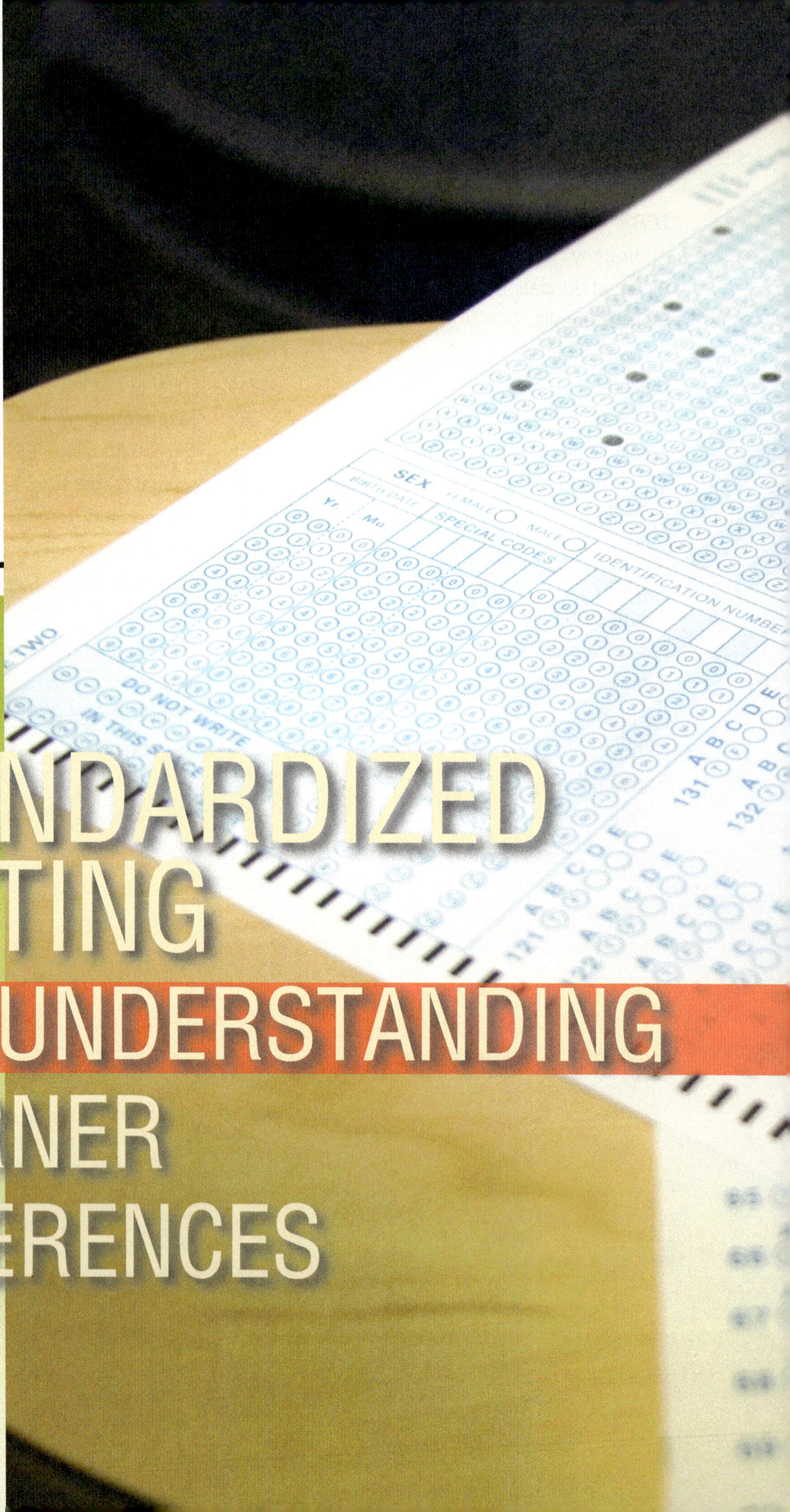

What's It All About ...

What is testing?

Issues with standardized tests

Types of testing

Types of standardized tests

Interpreting standardized tests

Chapter Objectives

- Describe the difference between testing and assessment.
- Describe the difference between measurement and evaluation.
- Understand how standardized assessment differs from classroom assessment.
- Explain how standardized testing is used for identification and providing services.
- Describe how standardized testing is used for accountability.

- How is high-stakes testing affecting students?
- Understand testing biases and issues of diversity.
- Describe issues with "Teaching the Test."

- Describe norm-referenced tests.
- Describe criterion-referenced tests.
- Explain the difference between placement, formative, diagnostic, and summative tests.

- Review aptitude tests.
- Review achievement tests.
- Review intelligence tests.
- Review standardized assessment for teachers.

- Understand basic testing concepts.
- Understand reliability and validity.
- Explain how to share test results with the student and family.

EXTENDED OUTLINE

Standardized Testing and Understanding Learner Differences

I. What's It All About ...
II. From Today's Headlines
III. What Is Testing?
  A. Testing versus assessment
  B. Measurement versus evaluation
  C. Standardized versus classroom assessment
  D. Uses of standardized testing in education
    1. Identification and services
    2. Accountability
  E. Summarize and reflect
IV. Issues in Standardized Testing
  A. High-stakes testing
  B. Testing biases and issues of diversity
  C. Teaching the test
  D. Summarize and reflect
V. Types of Testing
  A. Norm versus criterion-referenced tests
  B. Assessment categories
    1. Placement assessments
    2. Formative assessments
    3. Diagnostic assessments
    4. Summative assessments
  C. Summarize and reflect
VI. Types of Standardized Tests
  A. Aptitude tests
  B. Achievement tests
  C. Behavioral tests
  D. Intelligence tests: a special case
    1. Brief history of the Binet Intelligence Scale
    2. Theories of intelligence
      a. General intelligence
      b. Multiple intelligences
    3. Just what do intelligence tests measure?
  E. Standardized assessments for teachers
  F. Summarize and reflect
VII. Interpreting Standardized Test Scores
  A. Basic testing concepts
    1. Central tendency
    2. Standard deviation and normal deviation
    3. Types of scores
  B. Reliability and validity
  C. Sharing tests' results with the student and family
  D. Summarize and reflect
VIII. The Chapter in Review
IX. Interdisciplinary Case Focus

From Today's Headlines

Vol. I No. 9 Teaching World, 2012

State to Revisit Tests as Graduation Requirement

Associated Press, Baltimore, MD
September 24, 2008

The *Associated Press* published an article on the ongoing debate in the State of Maryland over requiring standardized tests for graduation. The *High School Assessments* are being required for the first time for Maryland seniors. Students must pass tests in English, algebra, biology, and government. Alternatively, they can graduate if their combined score on all four exams equals the sum of four passing scores. As of June 2009, 88% of students have met the requirement.

The assistant state superintendent for accountability and assessment stated that the tests would not adversely affect graduation rates, but some school board members claimed this "simply couldn't be true." Additionally, concerns were raised about the potential for the test to disproportionally affect students from minority backgrounds and those students for whom English is a second language. State School Superintendent Nancy supports the test, indicating the requirement has resulted in substantial improvements in instruction.

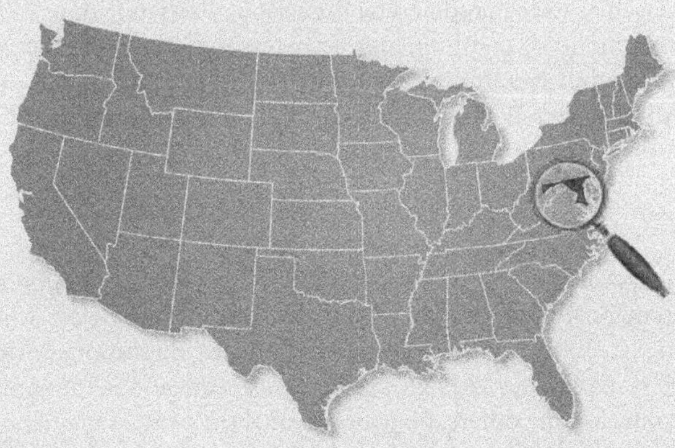

MAKE THE CONNECTION

There is often considerable controversy over the appropriate use of standardized tests. In this chapter, we will take a close look at how these test are used. As reported in this article, some standardized tests are used to determine the end result of a learning process, but there are other important uses to consider. It is also important to consider the potential negative impact these tests have on the overall learning environment. The consequences of not passing a test can be so great as to create undue pressure on the student. Such *high stakes testing* is coming under greater scrutiny as educators try to balance the need to document learning with creating a fair and positive learning environment.

In this chapter, we will learn about a wide variety of standardized tests including behavioral, aptitude, achievement, and intelligence tests. We will discuss how to interpret standardized test results and how to convey results to students and their families. A thorough understanding of standardized tests puts educators in the best position to use them in a fair and effective way.

WHAT IS TESTING?

This chapter covers the many issues surrounding educational testing. Testing has proven to be an enduring part of the educational landscape, but it is not without its critics. Some view testing as counterproductive, creating high pressure learning environments. Others contend testing is a necessary part of education because it helps guide teachers' instructional practice and determines the effectiveness of our educational institutions. Whether you support current testing practices or hope for change, testing is likely to be a part of schooling for years to come. The purpose of this chapter is to give you a better understanding of the testing process and its use in schools. The first part of this chapter will look at what we consider testing and how it differs from other related educational practices. We will also look at the difference between the types of testing that routinely take place in classrooms, as well as standardized types of tests typically administered by school systems according to state mandates. The rest of the chapter will primarily focus on standardized tests.

GET THE FACTS

20–30%

Amount of time many teachers spend using some form of assessment

Stiggins (2001)

Standardized tests can be useful tools to chart the overall progress of large groups of students. They do, however, have significant limitations. The second part of the chapter will look at these limitations and the extent to which such tests serve a useful function in education. The third part of the chapter will look at the different types of testing approaches available to schools. We will review appropriate uses for different test types and highlight concerns regarding their use. A section will follow on specific types of tests (achievement, behavioral, intelligence, etc.). The final section will look closely at how to interpret test scores. We will look at several practical aspects regarding the use of test scores, as well as issues involved in sharing test scores with parents and family.

Testing versus Assessment

Assessment is an integral part of education. Some studies report that teachers spend as much as 20% to 30% of their time engaged in some form of assessment activity (Stiggins, 2001). This means it is important for teachers to understand the nature of assessment and how it affects students. It is also important for teachers to make a distinction between assessment and testing.

Assessment

Process of collecting relevant data and information on student performance

Testing

A measurement or sample of behavior

Assessment is the process of collecting relevant data and information on student performance (Linn & Miller, 2005). It includes information on the student's classroom performance, extracurricular activities, and personal history, often supported by various testing results. **Testing** is a measurement or sample of behavior (Anastasi, 1990). Testing includes tests made and administered by the teacher, as well as tests mandated by the school district or state. What is important to remember is that assessment is a comprehensive process that often incorporates testing. Testing plays a supportive role but has limited utility by itself. Assessments involve actual inferences based on information gathered about the student. Assessments help teachers come to conclusions about student progress and their educational needs.

Measurement versus Evaluation

Evaluation

The systematic investigation of the worth or merit of an object

Measurement

Process of quantifying performance, effectiveness, or characteristics of some area of interest

Another important distinction teachers should be aware of is the difference between evaluation and measurement. **Evaluation** is the systematic investigation of the worth or merit of an object, where an object is virtually any area of interest (Joint Committee on Standards for Educational Evaluation, 1981). In schools, evaluations take place for student performance, educational programs, school effectiveness, and teacher quality, among others. **Measurement** is the process of quantifying performance, effectiveness, or characteristics of some area of interest. This involves taking something of interest and assigning a numeric value. We can measure a student's understanding of fractions, a school's graduation rate, or a teacher's time spent involved in small group discussions.

Evaluations are process oriented. They typically have a series of defined steps that lead to a conclusion regarding the effectiveness of the area being assessed (Gall, Borg, & Gall, 1996). For example, the evaluation of the effectiveness of an educational program is likely to include the following steps:

- Specify project goals and evaluation objectives.
- Establish appropriate standards.

- Plan an evaluation design.
- Select data gathering methods.
- Collect data.
- Process, summarize, and analyze data.
- Contrast data with evaluation standards.
- Report results and provide feedback.

Adapted from Payne, D. A. (1994). *Designing educational project and program evaluations: A practical overview based on research and experience. Boston: Kluwer Academic Publishers.*

As you can see, evaluations are a defined series of steps designed to answer questions regarding effectiveness. The evaluation process is likely to incorporate many *measurements* as evaluators seek to represent behaviors or events as numbers. Representing events as numbers allows for easy comparisons. There are problems with this process, however, as not all educational areas of interest are easily represented with numerical data (Caffarella, 2002).

Classroom test

Usually self-developed by the teacher or a commercially available assessment for the express purpose of helping teachers evaluate the performance of a particular student

Standardized test

Commercially available tests that assess a wide range of academic and personal skills

Standardization

Means that the test has uniform or "standard" content, administration procedure, scoring protocol, and format for presenting results

Standardized versus Classroom Assessment

The classroom teacher uses a type of testing that differs from the mandated tests required in most states. Put simply, a classroom teacher uses **classroom tests**. These tests are usually self-developed or are commercially available for the express purpose of helping the teacher assess the performance of a particular student. The goal of classroom testing is not to compare the performance of one student to another but to document individual learning. Classroom tests take many forms: homework, quizzes, informal class discussions, chapter tests, experiments, and presentations. Each of these testing approaches is likely to vary substantially from one teacher to another.

Standardized tests are quite different. **Standardization** means the test has uniform or "standard" content, administration procedure, scoring protocol, and format for presenting results. Individuals do not construct these tests; instead, large companies who can handle the significant resources needed for test development produce these documents. As you will see in the next part of this section, standardized tests are commercially available and assess a wide range of academic and personal skills. School administrators often purchase these tests to document learning progress for a particular grade level in one school compared to other schools.

As you can see from Figure 9.1, *classroom tests* and *standardized tests* differ in their development and use. Understanding their impact on education and learning involves a careful review of their unique applications. It is difficult to cover all these factors in a single chapter, so the remainder of this chapter will focus only on standardized tests. We focus on standardized tests at this point because an understanding of their use is critical to the material presented in the next two chapters on unique learning needs and the special education system. We will return to issues involved with classroom testing in Chapter 15.

F.A.Q.

Matt Martindale—"How does assessment compare to evaluation?"

Carrasquillo—"These terms are similar, but have a different focus." Assessments are a collection of data regarding a student's performance. They may include a variety of tests, but are more comprehensive than any one test. Assessments are used to create a comprehensive picture of a student's performance over a particular time period. Evaluations go beyond assessment. They are not just a summary of performance but a process whereby someone is making a **judgment** about the effectiveness or worthiness of something, typically a program or service, but sometimes a student who is perhaps applying for a scholarship."

Uses of Standardized Testing in Education

Ideally, standardized testing should help promote learning and guide teachers in their creation of sensitive learning environments. Testing can help promote understanding if used carefully and teachers take a comprehensive approach to the testing process. There are, however, many issues surrounding current educational testing. Let's take a look at some of the specific uses of educational testing.

Identification and Service

In 1975, a landmark piece of legislation passed causing major changes in teaching. The Education for All Handicapped Children Act [Public Law (PL) 94–142] mandates a free and appropriate public education for all children with disabilities.

Figure 9.1

Classroom Tests versus Standardized Tests

CLASSROOM TESTS	STANDARDIZED TESTS

Example The teacher presents a lesson on movement of tectonic plates during a geology lecture in science class. The next week, the teacher gives the students a classroom test on their understanding of the geological concepts presented the previous week. The test has multiple-choice items, short answers, matching, and an essay question.	**Example** The state requires Smith Elementary School to assess all fourth grade students in reading and math. To meet this obligation, individual schools administer the TerraNova® test. Students are administered the test as a group using uniform instructions and administration procedures provided by the test publisher. The results help schools establish student progress in these areas.
Typical Uses: Documenting student progress on specific curricular goals with a focus on charting individual learning.	**Typical Uses:** Establishing whether schools produce adequate learning progress with a focus on comparing the learning outcome of one group of students to another.

This was groundbreaking legislation and brought significant reform to the education of children with special learning needs. It also highlighted the need for tools to identify children with special needs. The law has undergone several revisions, most recently in 2004, and is now referred to as the Individuals with Disabilities Education Improvement Act (IDEIA). If educators are going to make a commitment to educating children with special needs, how do we identify those students in need of services? Standardized testing is one of the primary tools used in the identification process. These tests are designed to assess everything from intelligence, memory, and language, to a whole host of behavioral (e.g., aggression) and emotional (e.g., depression) factors. The specific tests used in an assessment would ideally be based on the unique qualities of the student, but all too frequently tests are based on a general referral question. The **referral question** defines the suspected problem or issue (i.e., "Does the student have a learning disability in math?"). This question provides direction for assessment but often fails to capture the unique issues experienced by the student. For example, a student having trouble in math might receive a standard battery of tests designed to assess a learning disability. This is a logical response to the student's problems; however, it may be incomplete for students with complex or unique problems. The student may not have a learning disability in math but, rather, a problem with understanding language. It may be that the language challenge surfaced first in math because of the linguistic complexity involved in teaching math. Comprehensive testing gives us a holistic view of the student and makes diagnosis and treatment more effective.

Referral question

Question that defines the suspected problem or issue

Testing to identify unique student needs is another area where collaboration among professionals helps to produce quality education. Using a variety of experts (psychologists, doctors, social workers, teachers, parents) to conduct an assessment produces a more comprehensive understanding of the individual. Not only do different professionals rely on different tools for assessment, they also bring to the situation a unique perspective. Such collaborative approaches are becoming more common as schools strive to develop precise and effective interventions. For more information on testing and identification of needed services, turn to Chapter 10 (Special Education) and Chapter 11 (Exceptional Learning).

Accountability

Another educational use for testing is accountability. As a public institution, schools are accountable to the American people. This means that the public has the right to assurances that schools are educating in an effective manner. This accountability has been around since the beginning of public schooling, but it has taken a different direction in recent years (Levinson, 2011). In particular, the No Child Left Behind Act of 2001 (NCLB) has established more stringent methods for determining accountability.

There are many issues involved in determining educational accountability. One important factor is responsibility. The responsibility for performance of our schools is a shared responsibility. Teachers, administrators, parents, and lawmakers all share in the responsibility for appropriate education. The next accountability issue is how to determine education success. This is where schools have traditionally relied heavily on testing. As with testing to determine learning outcomes, testing to assess accountability has typically focused on single tests. This has the advantage of being relatively inexpensive and consistent. This information, however, is limited and needs to be viewed in context of other types of information. In addition to tests measuring learning outcomes, schools should include other sources of information when judging student progress. This could include graduation rates, classroom assignments, and other teacher-developed assessments. Schools should also consider including parental feedback. Parents can provide valuable information to help schools understand test results. It is also important to remember that not all schools are created equal. Funding, extracurricular resources, and teacher quality vary across schools. All of these factors affect student success.

SUMMARIZE AND REFLECT

1. The practice of testing in educational settings has a long, well-established history.
2. There is an important distinction between testing and assessment. Assessment is a larger decision making process which often includes testing.
3. There is also a distinction between measurement and evaluation. Measurement is a process of quantifying a behavior or aspect of performance. Evaluation is a specific process educators go through to determine the effectiveness or worth of a school program or classroom instructional technique. Evaluation may incorporate some quantification of behavior (measurement), but is also likely to use other sources of information when determining effectiveness.
4. Additionally, standardized tests differ from classroom tests. Standardized tests are usually commercially available tests used by schools to track learning progress. They compare the performance of one group of students to another. Classroom tests are more individualistic. Created by the teacher, they chart the academic progress of an individual student.
5. Testing is used frequently in education, and the reasons we test are many. One of the reasons for testing is to understand more completely the students we teach. There are many types of tests; used carefully and comprehensively, they help us build a thorough understanding of each student's needs.
6. Tests are often used to help identify students with special needs and to design intervention services. Testing can also assess educational quality and effectiveness

INFORMED APPLICATION

1. Create a three-step process for assessing a student's understanding of how to multiply double-digit numbers. Keep in mind the distinction between testing and assessment.
2. How would you evaluate the readiness of a student to graduate from high school? Consider traditional approaches as well as alternative approaches to making this important decision.
3. Imagine you are a member of your local school board. You want an answer to the very simple question, "Are students learning?" What can you recommend to school principals to answer the question?

ISSUES IN STANDARDIZED TESTING

Testing can be a valuable process in education. It helps us learn something about a particular student's academic progress. It can determine if a student requires special assistance to learn effectively. It can also help schools communicate to the public the extent to which they are succeeding in educating our children. Testing, however, can also have some unwanted side effects. Testing can produce unusual amounts of anxiety and pressure. Tests do not always equally reflect the learning of all populations. Tests can also pull teachers away from their regular curriculum in an attempt to "train" students to perform better on a particular test. This section will look at these issues and review some ways to minimize these potentially negative effects.

High-Stakes Testing

High-stakes testing

Testing practices that result in excessively important consequences

The ever-increasing focus on testing in education has led some students to experience excessive testing pressure. **High-stakes testing** refers to testing practices that result in excessively important consequences (Bovaird, Geisnger, & Buckendahl, 2011). The nature of the consequence varies (failure to graduate from high school, not getting into the school's gifted program, losing a financial scholarship, etc.); however, the idea that significant personal and educational cost result from performance on a test has led to some concern. Everyone has trouble on tests from time to time. What if the next test you took determined whether you would receive a scholarship or grant for your education? The stress created by undue consequences being placed on a single measure of performance has gained attention in recent years. Often this affects individual students, but high-stakes testing also affects entire schools as new legislation establishes procedures for sanctioning schools who fail to perform up to state standards.

High-stakes testing refers to testing practices that result in overly important consequences. This has led to some students experiencing excessive testing pressure.

Testing has always been a part of education. Yet, as our understanding of the educational process changes, so does our testing needs. Educational testing serves the needs of the individual teacher and also the needs of our society to understand the progress and effectiveness of education. For these reasons, testing has become more central to the educational process than ever before. The No Child Left Behind (NCLB) legislation of 2001 reauthorized spending for public schools. It also introduced stringent mandates for annual student testing. The law requires states to test students in reading and math in grades three through eight and again in high school. The law also requires states to develop standards for performance in these areas and to ensure tests are actually testing whether students meet these standards. It should be noted that not all states support the NCLB legislation. Some states have even chosen to opt-out of NCLB, forgoing significant federal funding.

NCLB has led to substantial increases in academic testing in schools. School administrators are paying closer attention to their curriculum and how it relates to state standards. Teachers are increasingly concerned with how to give students the necessary information to meet these standards. This has led to an educational climate that is increasingly sensitive to testing. Some have argued that this focus on testing is inappropriate. They believe teachers are so busy teaching students how to perform on state tests that they are pulled away from teaching the curriculum. Others contend state tests are too narrow and only provide a limited view of how our students are performing. These criticisms are important to consider and represent real concerns. It is important for teachers to remember testing is just a tool. It can be used well, or it can be used inappropriately. Ideally, it is a tool to help us gather necessary information to educate effectively. The purpose of this chapter is to help teachers develop their understanding of testing, placing them in a better position to use tests well.

The impact of high-stakes testing on different levels of the educational system is detailed in Table 9.1. Making sure tests have reasonable and appropriate consequences actually begins with the test's development. Educational professionals need to be mindful of what the test was developed to measure and to use it according to its intended purpose. Tests are not appropriate for all situations. It takes careful research and planning to choose the best test for a

Table 9.1 Impact of High-Stakes Testing

LEVEL	RELEVANT CONSEQUENCES
At the School Level	The results of high-stakes testing: • Distribute financial rewards to high-performing or improving schools • Close or restructure low-performing schools
At the Educator Level	The results of high-stakes testing: • Give teachers or principals bonuses for high classroom or school test scores • Replace/remove teachers or principals from schools with low classroom or school test scores
At the Student Level	The results of high-stakes testing: • Promote students to the next grade based on test results • Grant students a high school diploma based on tests results • Provide special diplomas or scholarships for college tuition to high-performing students • Give students from failing schools the option to enroll elsewhere

Adapted from *Balanced View: High-Stakes Testing,* Westchester Institute for Human Services Research, Volume 7(1), 2003.

given purpose. Following test selection, there are a number of things that can be done to help ensure the consequences for test performance are reasonable and contextualized in the overall educational environment. The Standards for Educational and Psychological Testing group (collaboratively created by the American Psychological Association, the American Educational Research Association, and the National Council on Measurement in Education) has published basic guidelines for using tests in a meaningful and appropriate way. In general, guidelines emphasize standardized types of tests, but the guidelines are important when using any test type.

- *Any decision about a student's continued education—such as retention, tracking, or graduation—should not be based on the results of a single test, but should include other relevant and valid information.*

- *When test results substantially contribute to decisions made about student promotion or graduation, there should be evidence that the test addresses only the specific or generalized content and skills that the student has had an opportunity to learn. For tests that will determine a student's eligibility for promotion to the next grade or for high school graduation, students should be granted, if needed, multiple opportunities to demonstrate mastery of materials through equivalent testing procedures.*

- *When a school district, state, or some other authority mandates a test, the ways in which the test results are intended to be used should be clearly described. It is also the responsibility of those who mandate the test to monitor its impact, particularly on racial and ethnic-minority students of lower socioeconomic status, and to identify and minimize potential negative consequences of such testing.*

- *In some cases, special accommodations for students with limited English proficiency may be necessary to obtain valid test scores.*

- *Likewise, special accommodation may be needed to ensure that test scores are valid for students with disabilities.*

Following these guidelines does not eliminate the consequences of testing, but it does make testing more reasonable and fair. In fact, completely removing the real and significant consequences from the educational system may adversely affect overall school performance. Research on the effectiveness of high-stakes testing is limited, but some general findings are beginning to emerge. Research conducted on the educational performance of students in states relying on high-stakes tests finds increased academic performance (Carnoy & Loeb, 2003; Raymond & Hanushek, 2003). This is particularly true for ethnic-minority students.

Other research shows high-stakes testing has positive effects on the classroom environment. For example, case study data (see Chapter 1 for a review of this type of research) shows that implementation of a high-stakes test encourages teachers to develop more effective instructional techniques (Stecher, 2002; Borko & Elliott, 1999). High-stakes tests can also lead teachers to advocate effectively for needed resources (Wolf, Borko, McIver, Elliott, 1999). Some schools respond to the pressures of high-stakes testing by reaffirming their commitment to success and finding the necessary resources to make success a reality. This creates a "no excuses" environment in the classroom, and teachers and students jointly share in the commitment to learning. Similarly, studies from New York state's "all-Regents" (rigorous standardized test in a variety of subject areas) high schools show that the pressure to succeed in five core areas actually results in greater teacher commitment to work hard to achieve student success (Bishop & Mane, 1999).

Interconnections

Case study research methodology is covered in Chapter 1.

The outcomes from states adopting high-stakes testing are not all positive. There is no clear evidence that high-stakes testing increases high school graduation rates (Marchant & Paulson, 2005). This means that although there appears to be real learning gains, these gains are not translating into increases in long-term academic success. There is also evidence that high-stakes testing leads to greater focus on the areas tested (reading, math) rather than those not included in the assessment such as the arts, physical education, and music (Corbett & Wilson, 1991; Koretz, Mitchell, Barron, Keith, 1996; Stecher, Barron, Chun, Ross, 2000; Berliner, 2011). Some of the most difficult evidence to find relates to the cost of implementing high-stakes testing. One comprehensive book on school accountability, however, indicates that such testing generally costs between $5 to $25 dollars per pupil (Hoxby, 2002). The difference in cost depends on the number of subject areas tested. It also depends on whether states use ready-made tests or tests customized to state curriculum standards. Either way, the cost compared to the $3,500 per student cost incurred by the State of Tennessee to reduce class size appears relatively inexpensive.

Testing Biases and Issues of Diversity

Cultural bias

An unfair penalty on a test that results due to a student's gender, ethnicity, socioeconomic status, religion, or other such group-defining characteristic

Another potential issue with standardized tests is the possibility that the tests are biased against some students. **Cultural bias** refers to an unfair penalty on a test due to a student's gender, ethnicity, socioeconomic status, religion, or other such group-defining characteristic (Popham, 2005). Consider the following example (Mohan, 1992):

1. Bill ran out on his front porch to watch the fire truck. He lives in ______.

   a. a big apartment b. a city house c. a trailer

2. Pam went to a party with a tall pointed hat, long black cape, and a broom. She was dressed as a ______.

   a. witch b. ghost c. Cowgirl d. pumpkin

3. In the story, the French regarded potatoes like most Canadians regard:

   a. spinach b. tomatoes c. horse meat d. margarine

4. In the first colonies in America, making clothing took time. The women first had to spin the yarn. Clothes for the colonial family were then usually made in _____.

   a. factories b. homes c. luxury d. China

The issue with these examples is that they require culturally specific knowledge. If you have limited experience with different living environments, you might be at a distinct disadvantage on the first question. Similarly, a limited exposure to Canadian culture would make it difficult to answer the third question. Questions become culturally biased when these types of disadvantages uniquely affect a particular group. In other words, a test is culturally biased when it produces different scores for groups of students, when differences in learning do not exist. For example, a test that indicates a math difference between Latin Americans and Caucasian Americans when differences do not exist would be considered culturally biased.

Major test makers go to elaborate means to make certain their tests are not biased (Sattler, 2001). They actively recruit individuals from all lifestyles when standardizing their test. Additionally, they screen questions for bias against a particular cultural group (Linn & Miller, 2005). Despite these measures to develop culturally fair tests, individual schools who use standardized tests should take steps to review the appropriateness of the test for their particular student population. It is also important to use a variety of assessment tools to guard against the negative impact of a single, biased test.

Teaching the Test

The widespread implementation of standardized testing and relative importance of their outcomes brings up the question whether teachers should specifically teach material they know is on the test. There are several things teachers can do to help students effectively demonstrate their learning on a test, but directly teaching to the test is inappropriate (McMillan, 2000; Steeves, Hodgson, & Peterson, 2002). Teachers should also avoid the following when preparing students for standardized tests:

- Don't describe the test as difficult in an effort to get the students to take it more seriously.
- Don't use old versions of the test to teach the students unless specifically recommended to do so by the test maker.
- Don't try to encourage performance by telling students that their performance on this single test will drastically affect their academic lives.
- Don't modify existing well-planned curriculum simply to support higher test performance.

[Adapted from McMillan, 2000]

Avoiding these practices helps minimize student anxiety regarding testing, allowing them to successfully focus on the test. Teachers can also help students prepare for standardized tests by directly teaching creative problem solving, how to analyze the meaning of a question, weighing answer alternatives, and how to resist impulsive answers (Popham, 2005). These skills will help students remove some of the practical difficulties with taking standardized tests, allowing them to express their knowledge more effectively.

SUMMARIZE AND REFLECT

1. Our extensive use of testing is a potential source of problems. High-stakes testing refers to tests that promote negative learning environments.
2. Additionally, a test may differentially measure learning depending on a student's particular population demographic.
3. Another potential problem with high-stakes testing is that teachers might sacrifice their typical instruction in favor of teaching specific content so that students can do well on a test.
4. There are many techniques that minimize the potentially damaging effects of testing.

INFORMED APPLICATION

1. Imagine you are a fourth grade teacher and your class has to take the mandated state tests in math and language arts. The test is only a month away. Consider the advantages and disadvantages of changing your typical instruction to better prepare the students for the test.

TYPES OF TESTING

There are many ways to test in schools. Sometimes tests compare the performance of students in a particular grade with similar students across the state or even the nation. Some tests examine if students have mastered a particular standard of performance. Still others are used to design instruction that is sensitive to the needs of a student. The next section will review the nature of each of these approaches to testing and how to use them appropriately.

Norm versus Criterion Referenced Testing

Norm-based testing

Assessment that compares the performance of a given student against other students the same age

Standards-based testing (criterion-based)

Assessment that compares the performance of a given student against some predetermined criteria or standard

Test bias

Testing situations failing to measure accurately a skill or type of knowledge for a particular segment of the student population

Objective scoring

When the answer to a question does not depend on the opinion/judgment of the individual grading the test

Another issue surfacing in the accountability testing movement is the benefit of **norm-based testing** over **standards-based testing** (also known as **criterion-based testing**). Norm-based tests compare the performance of a given student against other students the same age. For example, a student tested in mathematics has his test performance compared to other students (locally or nationally) on the same test. Norm-based tests partially satisfy needs for accountability and have for a long time. They are inexpensive to administer, easy to score and provide a consistent measure of performance. Despite these advantages, there are limitations. The consistent nature of the test translates into less flexibility, possibly making the test less appropriate for some students. For example, the wording of a question may be beyond the life experience of a student, causing him to miss the question. Another student with equal skills who is familiar with the context of the question is able to get the correct answer. This would mean the test is able to document the skills of one student but not another, despite equal ability. In other words, it creates an unequal opportunity for students to exhibit their knowledge. As discussed earlier in the chapter, **test bias** refers to testing situations failing to measure accurately a skill or type of knowledge for a particular segment of the student population.

Consider the two questions shown in Figure 9.2. Both questions ask students to demonstrate the same mathematical skill. The first question, however, is biased in favor of students with better vocabularies or more extensive medical knowledge. The issue is not necessarily whether either of these questions is "bad"; the issue is that the first question is simply assessing more than math. If assessment of knowledge beyond math is the goal of the assessment instrument, then the first question is fine. If the assessment is intended to exclusively assess math, then the second question is better suited to the task.

Another issue with norm-referenced tests is how they are scored. To enhance the tests consistency and reliability, scoring is extremely objective. **Objective scoring** means the answer to a question does not depend on the individual grading the test. A simple multiple-choice

Figure 9.2

Biased Question Example

What percentage of offices in the Medical Mall shown at right specializes in service for children?

What percentage of the blocks shown at right are green?

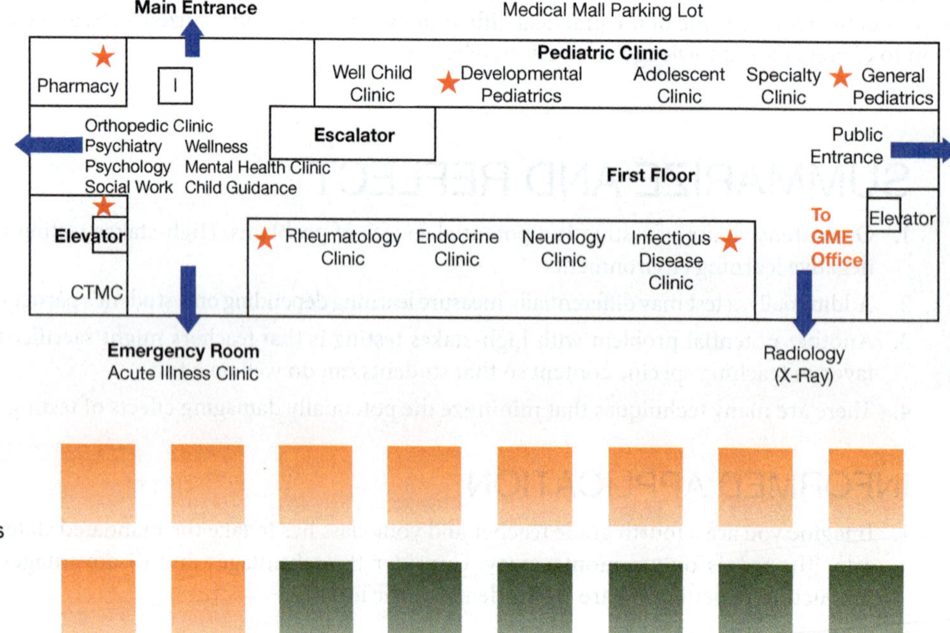

question is a good example of an objective question. The answer to a given multiple-choice question remains the same no matter who grades the test. Compare this to **subjective scoring** where the evaluator has to make a judgment about the "correctness" of a given response. An essay question is usually more subjective. The teacher grading an essay question may have certain criteria for grading the essay, but there is likely to be some judgment involved in assigning a grade. Again, objective scoring makes grading a test easy, consistent, and inexpensive. It does, however, limit the types of questions that can be asked.

Subjective scoring
Where the evaluator has to make a judgment about the "correctness" of a given response

Norm-referenced tests have been criticized because they do not usually allow students to create an answer. Instead, norm-referenced tests focus on recognizing the correct answer from a set of printed choices to maintain *objectivity*. This means that norm-referenced tests are better suited to measuring factual knowledge (e.g., terms, names, dates) and less able to assess the critical thinking involved in creating a solution to a less structured question. For example, providing a response to an essay question like "How did the economic specialization of the North and South affect the outcome of the Civil War?" requires more critical thinking than a factual question like "Did the North or the South have more industrial factories?"

A multiple choice test is a good example of an objective question.

A final point to consider with norm-referenced tests doesn't actually involve the test itself, but how it is used. Norm-referenced tests usually are not well suited to help us understand how learning progresses, just the result. The other potential issue is that norm-referenced tests fundamentally answer the same question, "How does a student's performance compare to others?" If we are trying to address accountability issues (e.g., school performance or teacher quality), is this type of comparative question the one we want to ask? Over the past few years, educators have become increasingly interested in answering two alternative questions:

> *What level of learning do we want to see our students achieve?*
>
> AND
>
> *Have our students reached this level of achievement?*

Notice that neither of these questions asks about the performance of one student compared to another. Instead, both questions relate to establishing and reaching a predetermined standard. Let's consider standards-based assessment in more detail.

The "standards movement" is currently being driven by the NCLB legislation mentioned earlier. According to the law, states must establish standards for student learning. They must also use assessments aligned to those standards to establish learning effectiveness. States can either elect to do this by creating their own assessments, or they can choose to modify commercially available tests. What is important is that school assessments are refocusing on meeting pre-established "standards," rather than relying exclusively on normative (student-to-student) comparisons. This has created a different educational climate. Teacher and administrators have mixed responses to this educational perspective on achievement. Critics contend that standards will negatively affect some students, particularly more advanced students. This is because standards are developed at levels states feel are appropriate for most students. This means the absolute learning level specified in the state standard is going to be too advanced for a few students, too limited for some, but about right for most. Where does this leave instruction for advanced students or students struggling with learning? If most instruction is geared to meet the standard, then students requiring instruction that is more individual will not be well served (Harrington, 1982). This is a real concern, and teachers and schools need to consider this carefully as standards-based instruction, curriculum, and assessment gains momentum.

Some teachers are also concerned that teaching to particular standards will take away from their creative freedom and make instruction less exciting and engaging. Also, they are concerned that they will spend most of their instructional time teaching students how to take a

Table 9.2 Teacher Perceptions of the Benefits of Standards-Based Education

QUALITY	DESCRIPTION
Fosters More Teacher Collaboration	Because grade-level teachers teach the same content at the same time, there are more opportunities for collaboration. In this environment, teachers actively seek out one another to share ideas and improve lesson plans. Teaching is no longer a lonely profession.
Encourages Use of "Benchmark Tests" as a Diagnostic Tool	To complement state testing (which usually occurs annually), some school districts have developed benchmark tests to assess student progress. This gives teachers ongoing feedback about the effectiveness of their teaching. This provides opportunities for brainstorming, which can lead to instructional improvements.
Creates Clear Job Expectations for Teachers	By looking at state standards, a teacher can understand what his or her students are expected to learn. This takes guesswork and fear out of the process of teacher evaluation.
Provides Inspiration When Student Achievement Improves	When test scores come back and teachers see improvement in student learning, it reinforces they are making a difference. Their morale improves, and they are willing to work even harder to improve student achievement

Adapted from DeRoche, 2004.

test. They contend teaching to take a test artificially constrains the learning environment (Lewis, 2003). They believe leaning needs flexibility so teachers can pursue learning objectives that evolve as instruction progresses. Teaching too strictly to a standard may compromise this flexibility and actually interfere with optimal learning (Haladyna, Nolen, & Hass, 1991; Johnson & Johnson, 2002).

On the positive side, some teachers are thoroughly embracing the standards movement. They feel that moving toward instruction based on detailed standards is helping to make their job clearer. Clear professional objectives are, in turn, helping teachers have a clearer plan for meeting the needs of their job. Some feel this is giving teachers a stronger sense of purpose and accomplishment. Qualitative information from teachers indicates that at least some teachers are benefiting professionally from a strong standards-based approach to education (see Table 9.2).

Another consideration in the standards-based movement is the impact on student achievement. Recent research from the Educational Projects in Education Research Center (Swanson, 2006) reports there is substantial evidence demonstrating a consistent positive relation between adoption of state standards and student achievement. Specifically, they analyzed data from the National Assessment of Educational Progress (NAEP) from 1997–2006. NAEP has tracked reading and math performance in grades four and eight. Results indicate that states adopting clear and specific standards were likely to have greater levels of achievement. The effect was stronger for math than reading. These findings further support a standards approach to education, indicating student learning is actually improving when states use clear standards.

As you can see, standards-based assessments have the potential for both a positive and negative impact. Most assessments produce a mixture of support and concerns. What is important is to recognize issues that are raised and to work collaboratively toward innovative solutions.

Assessment Categories

Testing's rise in prominence has been hotly debated. On one side of the debate, testing supporters argue that testing helps us better understand the state of the educational system and ensure its continued improvement. Critics argue testing is actually interfering with education, taking away from valuable instructional time. The issue may not be testing in general but the *type* of testing. There are many types of tests, and each test is designed to meet a particular need.

Human learning is complex and assessing that learning with a single test is unrealistic. Ideally, educators need to use a variety of tests to capture the learning needs of each student.

Table 9.3 Testing Categories

TEST TYPE	TESTING QUESTION
Placement Assessment	What information is needed before we begin to teach a given student?
Formative Assessment	How do we measure learning progress?
Diagnostic Assessment	What is the nature of a significant learning issue?
Summative Assessment	Was the educational goal achieved?

Failure to take a comprehensive approach to testing leads to problems capturing the whole student. So how can we use testing to demonstrate student learning and knowledge?

One way to look at tests is to group them according to their purpose. Educational researchers have identified four main testing categories as shown in Table 9.3 (Aiken, 2000). The first question we will consider is, *What information is needed before we begin to teach a given student?* It is important for teachers to have information on students' learning abilities and potential problems before teaching begins. Such information is valuable to the teacher when making necessary placement decisions. For example, does the second grade teacher begin the year expecting her students to read, or should she begin with supporting reading foundations? Some students will probably be reading quite well, while others continue to struggle. Without knowing the reading ability of each student, the teacher is unable to teach effectively. Failure to determine learning needs early in the school year increases the probability that advanced students will find the class boring and struggling students will be overwhelmed. Neither situation is positive, and both can be avoided by using placement assessments.

Placement Assessments

Placement assessments help teachers plan effective and rewarding learning experiences for individual students. Placement assessments come in many forms including previous report cards, self-reports from the students, and academic pre-tests (Linn & Miller, 2005). Actually asking the students about their learning interests provides the teacher with excellent information. For example, teachers can approach self-reports *informally*, asking students early in the year to reflect on their academic strengths and weaknesses. The teacher may also use *formal* instruments to assess self-perceptions such as the Academic Motivation Scale by the Childhood Development Project (1993) or the Academic Motivation Scale by Vallerand et al., (1992). Both of these instruments survey various aspects of the student's self-perceptions affecting academic success. The student may not have an accurate understanding of their abilities, but perception of their potential for success is an important mediator of learning. **Pre-tests** also help teachers determine a student's existing knowledge (Petscher, 2011). Along with self-report information, teachers can use a variety of informal and formal approaches to gathering information on what students already know, what skills are developing, and what learning objectives are beyond their current abilities. Both self-report and pre-test information give the teacher an idea of where to begin. The beginning, however, is only the start of a larger educational journey. Once started, how do we determine if learning is progressing appropriately?

Placement assessment

Assessment that helps teachers plan effective and rewarding learning experiences for individual students

Pre-test

Test that helps teachers determine a student's existing knowledge

Formative Assessments

Formative assessment provides information regarding how learning is progressing. It is not usually a single test, but a series of tests designed to give ongoing information about a student's learning. There are a variety of formal and informal formative assessments including classroom question and answering, interim quizzes, and homework. The exact format of these

Formative assessment

Assessment providing information regarding how learning is progressing

There are several ways to gain ongoing information about a student's learning. One of them is homework.

assessments is likely to vary with the style and training of the teacher, but all serve a common purpose. That is, formative assessments help the teacher determine if the student is making satisfactory progress. Perhaps the teacher notices a particular student is having difficulty completing homework. This might mean the student is having difficulty with the material, but it might also mean the student is having trouble at home. The teacher could compare the student's homework with classroom quizzes to see if performance is uniformly low. If the student is able to do well with classroom quizzes, but fails to accurately complete homework, this might indicate the need to address a home situation. Notice that formative assessments give the teacher the opportunity to intervene before the child encounters excessive failure. This is an important aspect of formative assessments. They give the teacher ongoing information, which allows for intervention before issues become more serious.

Diagnostic Assessments

Diagnostic assessment

Assessment used to give teachers very precise information on how to address a student's learning difficulty

Despite excellent use of formative assessments, some students still experience significant learning issues. This is when educators turn to diagnostic assessments. **Diagnostic assessments** are used to give teachers very precise information on how to address a student's learning difficulty (Llosa, Beck, & Zhao, 2011). It is unlikely that the daily, ongoing formative types of assessments used by teachers will serve this purpose. Diagnostic tests are conducted by school professionals with specialized training and are likely to consist of several individual tests covering a variety of areas. The results of these diagnostic assessments usually lead to a written intervention plan. It *may* also lead to a specific diagnostic label and participation in the schools special education program. It is important to underscore that participation in special education this is not always the outcome of diagnostic testing. It entirely depends on the unique needs of the student. As we have been discussing throughout this book, many special learning needs are addressed effectively in the regular classroom with appropriate supports. Addressing more significant learning and behavioral issues is covered in Chapters 10 and 11.

Interconnections

Chapter 10 covers the Special Education System and Chapter 11 looks at attention, giftedness, and creativity.

Summative Assessments

Summative assessment

Assessment designed to determine if the student achieved the educational goal

The fourth type of assessment is also the most controversial. **Summative assessment** is designed to answer the question, "Did the student achieve the educational goal?" Unlike formative assessments, summative assessments reveal the result of the learning process (Harrison & Howard, 2011). Examples of summative assessments include overall or comprehensive tests and state tests. The controversial nature of these tests is not whether they provide useful information but that they are often used to the exclusion of the other types of tests. Use of summative tests without formative tests leads to information on whether students succeeded, but little information on how to make achievement a reality. In order to reach a goal, educators need information on *how* to reach it. This is unlikely to come from summative assessments but could come from formative, diagnostic, and placement assessments. These assessments typically occur before summative types of assessment.

This leads us back to the initial question regarding how to understand the needs of the whole student. The answer lies in the use of a variety of assessments. Each test is a single puzzle piece in a larger educational puzzle. If we are to meet the learning needs of each student, we must identify tests that give us information regarding the whole learning process (see Figure 9.3). Used together, a comprehensive assessment plan can lead to effective and productive teaching.

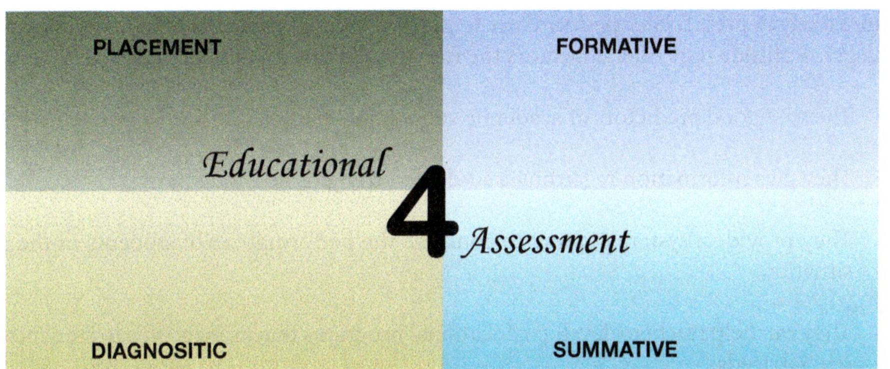

Figure 9.3
Comprehensive Assessment Plan

SUMMARIZE AND REFLECT

1. Testing can take many forms. Some tests compare student performance to others in the same grade or age group. Other tests establish benchmarks or standards and measure to see if students have achieved specified criteria.
2. Still other tests are used to guide instruction. These tests help determine a student's current skill level and dynamically guide a student through their unique learning path.
3. There are also traditional types of tests, which simply measure whether students acquired the information being taught.
4. All of these tests have benefits and potential drawbacks. This section reviewed issues involved with using each type of testing.

INFORMED APPLICATION

1. You are a tenth grade English teacher interested in developing an assessment protocol that will allow you to successfully evaluate the readiness of each student to move on to grade eleven at the end of the year. Devise an assessment procedure that is sensitive to the four types of assessment.

TYPES OF STANDARDIZED TESTS

There are varieties of tests teachers and school professionals can use to obtain information on student performance. Some of these tests focus on the learning potential of the student. Other tests look at the actual achievement of the student in different subject areas. Additionally, the intelligence test has gained prominence in education. It is a commonly administered test and has many uses. It has become a particularly popular in assessments to determine eligibility for special education services. In this section, we will explore each of these types of tests. We will begin with a group of tests designed to *predict* how well a student will learn.

Aptitude Tests

Aptitude tests predict how well a student will perform when placed in a new learning situation. They are a measure of student learning capability. Examples of aptitude tests have historically included intelligence tests, but theorists are beginning to consider these tests a separate category given unique issues surrounding our understanding and measurement of intelligence (Linn & Miller, 2005). Other aptitude tests include college entrance exams, such as the Scholastic Assessment Test (SAT). Most test users distinguish between aptitude tests and achievement tests, but in reality they are quite similar. Both tests consist of items that assess knowledge. There is some difference in that achievement tests typically focus on recent learning, whereas aptitude tests examine learning over the lifespan. Both tests, however, are dependent on knowledge acquisition and prior learning. What really distinguishes the tests is how they are used. As we saw in the last section, achievement tests assess recent learning in a specific area. Aptitude tests

Aptitude test
Test that predicts how well a student will perform when placed in a new learning situation

are more likely to predict later performance (e.g., a high school student's potential performance in college). Aptitude tests offer educators the following qualities (Macklem, 1990):

- They are good predictors of academic success (Stevens & Clauser, 1996; Sax, 1989).
- They give information regarding a student's strengths and weaknesses.
- They provide a systematic way to compare the performances of students in the same situation.
- They can help teachers develop educational programs that are sensitive to students with special needs.

Despite their many advantages, teachers should exercise caution when interpreting aptitude test results. Teachers need to consider whether the questions on the test are truly assessing skills and abilities important to the student's situation. Also, it is critical to reflect on the meaning of a student's performance on a single test in the context of the whole student. That is, testing only provides a brief glimpse into the skills and capabilities of a student. No single test completely reflects a student's academic progress—it is one piece of the student's academic experience. Considering these cautions helps teachers use aptitude tests appropriately and in the best interest of the student.

Achievement Tests

Achievement test

Test that assesses a student's current learning level in a specific academic area

Achievement tests assess a student's current learning level in a specific academic area—such as reading, writing, or mathematics (Andrews, Saklofske, & Janzen, 2001). These tests provide a snapshot of the student's achievement in the content area. Table 9.4 provides an overview of the major content areas and specific skills commonly assessed. The specific skills covered on a given test vary, but most cover these broad areas. Additionally, some tests cover other academic areas like science and social studies.

Administration of a standardized achievement tests is in either a group or individual format. In the group format, the test is administered to several students at the same time. Each student works independently during the course of the test. Often group-administered tests involve independent reading and students record their responses on "bubble" or scan sheets. These tests are easy and relatively inexpensive to use and provide a quick glimpse of student's current

Table 9.4 Achievement Tests: Content Areas Commonly Assessed

CONTENT AREA	SPECIFIC SKILL
Reading	• Vocabulary • Comprehension • Word analysis • Word recognition • Reading fluency
Writing	• Spelling • Writing fluency • Dictation • Editing
Mathematics	• Problem solving • Concepts • Computation • Procedures

current learning levels. The group format, however, has some drawbacks. Students with reading difficulty may experience greater problems given the independent nature of the testing environment. In addition, students who suffer from test anxiety may have difficulty given the impersonal setting and limited support. Group achievement tests are most commonly used to screen for potential learning problems. Given the potential drawbacks of group achievement tests, teachers typically avoid using them to change or alter a student's educational program. If a special learning need is suspected based on the results of a group administered achievement test, the student is referred for an individual assessment, which offers the evaluator more control over testing.

During an individual assessment, a single administrator gives an achievement test to a *single* student (Vaughan-Jensen, Adame, McLean, & Gamez, 2011). The personal setting helps assure the test results are representative of the student's best performance. Administrating a test one-on-one makes it possible for the examiner to monitor closely the student's engagement, anxiety, and compliance with test instructions. Additionally, the personal testing situation allows the examiner to better contextualize test performance when communicating exam results. Was the student engaged in the test? Was the student excessively anxious? This additional information is often invaluable when trying to understand the student's performance and how to make changes to the student's educational plan. Table 9.5 provides a list of common individual and group administered achievement tests.

Behavioral Tests

As educators become more sensitive to assessing the whole student, it is more common to see evaluators use behavioral measures. **Behavioral assessments** provide a standardized tool for assessing a student's behavior, emotionality, and social interactions. The range of attributes assessed depends on the instrument used, but generally include attention, aggression, depression, anxiety, social skills, and conduct problems. As with other standardized tests, behavioral assessments provide a convenient way to compare the behavioral functioning of one student to others of similar age. Table 9.6 provides a list of commonly used behavioral assessments and the areas covered by the test.

Behavioral assessment

Assessment that provides a standardized tool for assessing a student's behavior, emotionality, and social interactions

The increased use of behavioral testing is in part due to increased sensitivity to educating the whole child, but it is also due to changing federal legislation governing special education. Beginning in 1997, educational legislation (Individuals with Disabilities Education Act—IDEA) included direct mandates for behavioral assessment. The law requires educators to assess relevant *behavioral factors,* in addition to cognitive issues, when evaluating students for possible placement within special education. Additionally, the team responsible for special education programming must include appropriate *positive behavioral interventions and strategies.* For students in special education, IDEA also stipulates that a *functional behavioral assessment* must be conducted before a change in educational placement occurs, if that change is based on inappropriate behavior. This naturally leads to the question, "What exactly is a Functional Behavioral Assessment?" A **functional behavioral assessment (FBA)** is an evaluation to determine

Functional behavioral assessment (FBA)

An evaluation to determine the cause of a student's behavior

Table 9.5 Common Group and Individually Administered Achievement Tests

GROUP	INDIVIDUAL
Iowa Test of Basic Skills	The Kaufman Test of Educational Achievement
Stanford Achievement Tests	The Peabody Individual Achievement Test
Metropolitan Achievement Tests	The Woodstock-Johnson Tests of Achievement
California Test of Basic Skills	The Diagnostic Achievement Battery
Comprehensive Tests of Basic Skills	Wechsler Individual Achievement Tests

Table 9.6 Commonly Used Behavioral Assessments

INSTRUMENT	AREAS ASSESSED
Child Behavior Checklist (CBCL)	Withdrawn, somatic complaints, anxious/depressed, delinquent behavior, aggressive behavior, social problems, thought problems, attention problems
Conner's Rating Scales	Inattention, impulsivity, hyperactivity, conduct problems, oppositional behavior, anxiety, somatization, self-esteem, mood, family functions
Revised Children's Manifest Anxiety Scale (RCMAS)	Anxiety
Behavior Assessment System for Children (BASC)	Aggression, hyperactivity, conduct problems, anxiety, depression, somatization, attention problems, learning problems, atypical behaviors, withdrawal, adaptability, leadership, social skills, study skills
Children's Depression Inventory (CDI)	Thought, emotional, and behavioral signs of depression
Social Skills Rating System (SSRS)	Behaviors relating to teacher-student relations, peer acceptance, academic performance

the cause of a student's behavior. The term "functional" refers to the function a behavior plays in the student's daily life. For example, does the behavior help the student get attention, avoid work, or make friends? Evaluation of any student with special needs may include a FBA, but is it an educational "best practice" for all students experiencing behavioral problems?

The process of conducting a FBA includes the elements shown in Table 9.7. As you can see, a FBA is not a casual attempt at behavioral intervention, but a sophisticated process with a well-documented history of effectiveness (Gable, Hendrickson, & Sasso, 1995). Given the technicalities involved in conducting a thorough and effective FBA, it is important to make sure that the individual conducting the assessment has appropriate training (Fallon, Zhang, & Kim, 2011). Until recently, obtaining an appropriately trained individual to conduct these assessments was difficult. There was no national certification, so individual qualifications were based on educational history and relevant experience. The Behavior Analysis Certification Board established a process for certifying behavior specialists. The availability of these certified professionals provides schools and related professionals a standard for behavioral care. We shall return to the importance of quality behavioral assessments in the next chapter.

Table 9.7 Components of a Functional Behavioral Analysis

COMPONENT	DESCRIPTION
Baseline	A functional behavioral analysis begins with a thorough recording of the natural, on-going behavior of the student. This is called taking a **baseline**.
Identification	From the baseline, a specific behavior will be identified or targeted for change.
Definition/Context	The targeted behavior is given a specific definition.
Hypothesis	A hypothesis is an educated guess as to the cause of the targeted behavior. The hypothesis carefully predicts how the behavior functions in the student's daily life.
Intervention	Interventions necessarily vary from situation to situation, but are always conducted in a well-planned and systematically implemented intervention plan.
Data Collection/ Reflection	As the intervention takes place, all relevant behaviors are recorded. This allows for reflection on the effectiveness of the intervention and plans for continued improvement.

Intelligence Tests: A Special Case

Perhaps no other test in the history of assessment has been both heralded and criticized as has the intelligence test. Educationally, it remains one of the most frequently used assessment instruments. Teachers, parents, administrators, and even the individual student place enormous importance on the outcome of these tests. How did intelligence tests rise to such prominence? What special information can we obtain from these tests? Why is there still so much controversy over their use? This section will look at the answers to these questions. We will begin with a look at the historical development of the intelligence test. We will then compare them to the intelligence tests in use today. We will explore the theoretical underpinnings of the test and see how different test developers approach intelligence from varying perspectives. Finally, we will look specifically at what intelligence tests measure and how to use them appropriately.

Brief History of the Binet Intelligence Scale

Alfred Binet (1857–1911) was born in Nice, France, to a father who was a physician and a mother who was an artist. His parents separated when he was young, and he moved to Paris with his mother. He was initially educated as a lawyer, but quickly moved into a series of medically and later psychologically related fields. In 1891, Binet accepted a position at the Laboratory of Psychology at Paris' famed Sorbonne University. He remained at the laboratory until his death in 1911. During his parenting years, Binet became increasingly interested in the development of his two children. Like Piaget (see Chapter 2) a few years later, his personal life provided an informal laboratory for his developing theories. Also important at this time was his appointment to the *Commission for the Retarded.* His role on the commission was to answer the following question: What sort of test should be given to students suspected of learning problems, which might place them in a special classroom? His investigation of this question ultimately led to his world famous test of intelligence.

His initial exploration into the construct of intelligence led to the publication of the book *L'Etude Experimentale de l'Intelligence* (Experimental Studies of Intelligence) in 1903. This book detailed a basic methodology for investigating intelligence and laid the groundwork for his intelligence test. In 1905, a paper written by Binet and his colleague, Theodore Simon, announced the development of an objective measure of intellectual ability. The purpose of the test was to distinguish students with mental retardation from their peers. The actual test was then published a couple of months later and known as the Binet-Simon Scale. The scale underwent many revisions, including important revisions by Lewis Terman at Stanford University in California. It was at this point that the test took on its current name, the Stanford-Binet. The **Stanford-Binet Test** is currently in its fifth major revision and is one of the most frequently used tests of intelligence.

Interconnections

Piaget's theory of cognitive development is covered in Chapter 2.

Stanford-Binet Intelligence Test

One of the most frequently used tests of intelligence, currently in its fifth major revision

The theory and methodology behind the Binet scales are important because they influenced the conceptualization of intelligence in effect today. Theoretically, Binet envisioned intelligence as a single construct. That is, he believed we each function in the world driven by a single intellectual ability. He referred to this as a person's *mental ability.* His work on students with intellectual limitations strongly influenced this conceptualization. He believed that students with mental retardation had a mental age that was inconsistent with their chronological age. A student with mental retardation might have a chronological age (based on his/her birth date) of ten, but a mental age of five. Before his intellectual test, the idea of "mental age" was just a theoretical construct. His test operationalized mental age by giving professionals a means to quantify this concept.

Binet thought it important for his test to provide a numerical product he could use in determining the need for special services. He wanted to assign students a number based on his assessment, and then that number could be used to determine the necessity for services. To generate this number, he developed a very simple formula based on the division of mental age and chronological age (see Figure 9.4). This *quotient* became the first intelligence score and was

Figure 9.4

Binet's Intelligence Quotient Formula

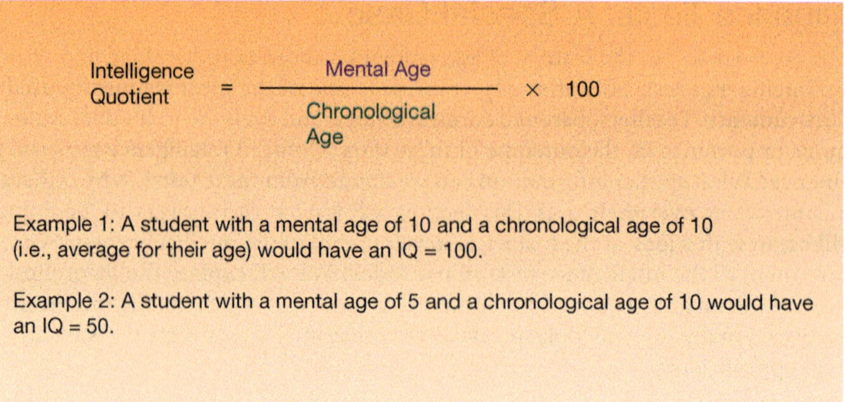

Intelligence quotient

Original term used by Alfred Binet to refer to the quantitative measure of an individual's intelligence

known as the **intelligence quotient**. This was quickly abbreviated to IQ, and the terminology is still in use today.

As you can see from the formula, individuals with a mental age equal to their chronological age would have an IQ score of 100. This means that if your IQ score is 100, you function intellectually as expected for someone your age. IQ scores still use 100 to represent average intellectual performance, but we now approach the calculation of IQ very differently.

Theories of Intelligence

Binet's work was indeed groundbreaking in that it brought intelligence out of the purely theoretical and put it into an actual measurable product. Teachers no longer had to speculate how "smart" a student was; the student could simply be "tested." There were many positive outcomes of this process, but there are also some serious cautions to consider. One of the most important is the lack of association between the measurement of intelligence and the theory of intelligence. Intellectual tests approach measurement from a particular way of understanding intelligence. Essentially, IQ tests are "answering" a question. As every parent knows, ask a five-year-old, "How did the cookie jar get broken?" and you will get a very different answer from the question, "Did you break the cookie jar?" IQ test are no different. Educators need to know what *question* an intellectual assessment answers and whether the answer is really addressing their needs. Let's look at two popular conceptualizations of intelligence and then how these theories impact our measurement of intelligence.

General intelligence

General intelligence

Idea that there is one broad cognitive ability governing intelligent behavior

General intelligence is the idea that there is one broad cognitive ability governing intelligent behavior. It is usually abbreviated by a lower case *g*. To demonstrate the popularity of this perspective, over the next week ask several of your friends if they are intelligent and record their responses. You will likely get some variation, but most will probably refer to something similar to general intelligence. Figure 9.5 outlines popular ways of thinking about general intelligence.

What is important to recognize about each of the "answers" depicted in Figure 9.5 is that they come from a general intelligence perspective. Again, this means that intelligence is viewed as a singular entity. The work of Binet contributed significantly to our thinking about intelligence. His test took intelligent behavior and reduced it to a single score, furthering the idea of intelligence as "one."

Charles Spearman (1927) also produced significant scientific works from this perspective. He proposed that intelligence was a single mental attribute, which he abbreviated as *g* for *general intelligence*. He believed general intelligence was a pervasive attribute governing the performance of most tasks. He also proposed that general intelligence interacted with specific abilities in a given area (e.g., music, math, etc.). He abbreviated this as *s*. Although he theorized both *g* and *s* were important in understanding intelligent behavior, he placed greater emphasis on *g*. He believes that since *g* was the more enduring quality and less sensitive to task variations, it was the most important characteristic.

Over the years since Spearman's initial work, many theorists have supported the *g* perspective (Carroll, 1993; Neisser et al., 1996). Most notably, *g* is used as the foundation

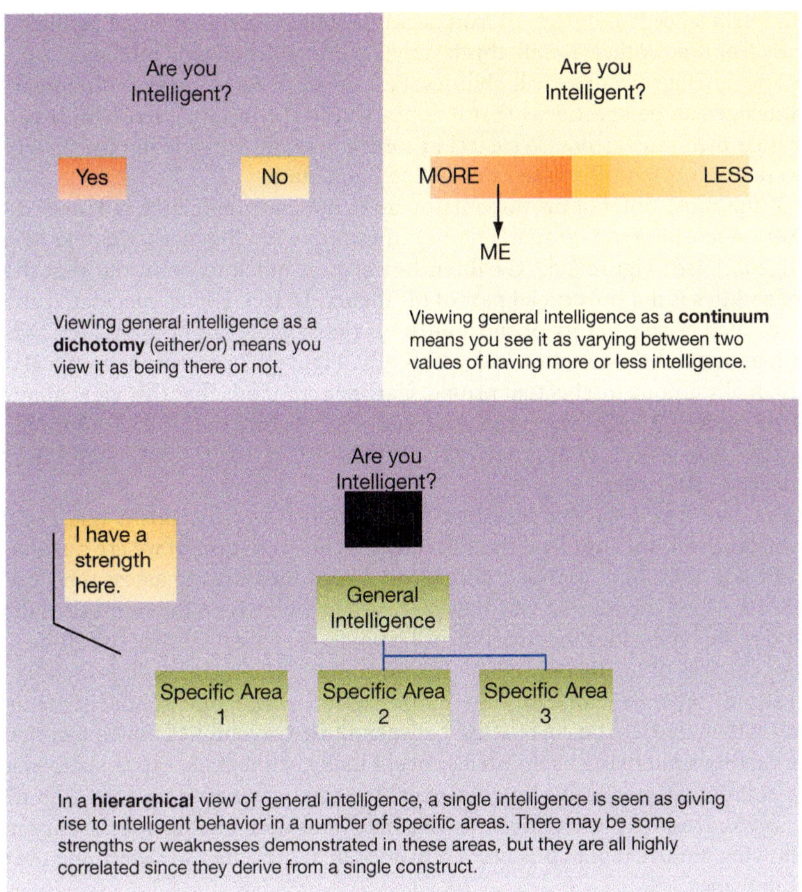

Figure 9.5
Popular Ways of Thinking about General Intelligence

for most of the standardized intellectual assessments we have today. These include the Stanford-Binet discussed previously and the Wechsler series of tests produced by David Wechsler (1991). Both of these instruments produce a single full-scale intelligence quotient and numerous sub-scores based on different portions of the test. These sub-scores give additional information regarding performance in specific areas. These scores are subsets of the individual's overall intellectual performance. This is similar to the hierarchical perspective presented in Figure 9.5.

The general intelligence perspective is a controversial topic within the field of education. On the positive side, popular IQ tests (such as the Wechsler) have been repeatedly found to do a good job at predicting academic success as determined by school grades (Sattler, 2001). IQ scores also correlate well with achievement tests. Additionally, there is growing evidence that IQ tests correlate positively with real-life outcomes such as job success and earning potential (Bouchard, 2004; Wagner, 1997; Ceci, 1991; (Danner, Hagemann, Schankin, Hager, & Funke, 2011)). This supporting evidence also brings up some significant reservations. Although IQ does a good job at predicting certain real-world outcomes, it does not do a *perfect* job. This means there are still other relevant factors in determining life outcomes. Factors such as motivation, education, and the ability to interact well with others (interpersonal skills) also appear to play an important role in our success (Wagner & Sternberg, 1986; Goleman, 1995; Sternberg & Wagner, 1993). It may be that our tools (the typical IQ test) used to measure intellectual performance fail to capture all of the important aspects of intelligence. Let's turn our attention to another theory of intelligence that is gaining considerable popularity, especially in educational circles.

Multiple intelligences
Idea that intelligence is not a single construct, but rather a collection of distinct abilities

Multiple intelligences

Multiple intelligences is the idea that intelligence is not a single construct but a collection of distinct abilities. Each "intelligence" in this view is relatively independent of the others. If it is true that intelligence is not derived from a single ability, then individual abilities may vary substantially from each other. Recall, this is unlikely under the general intelligence perspective since only one intelligence drives all abilities. Part of the attractiveness and popularity of the multiple intelligences perspective is that it appears to fit the intuitive sense most people have regarding their own intelligence. We excel in some areas and struggle in others. Our sense of our intellectual ability typically varies depending on the task.

One of the most notable proponents of this view of intelligence is Howard Gardner (1983, 1999). According to Gardner's theory of multiple intelligences, there are eight separate intelligences (see Figure 9.6). Gardner, however, is quick to point out that the specific number of abilities is not the crucial part of his theory. In fact, he has speculated about other intelligences such as spirituality or the ability to contemplate larger life issues. What is important is that our abilities function independently. Figure 9.7 presents a graphical depiction of an individual's unique intellectual profile. Gardner contends that this view of intelligence is important because it encourages researchers and educators to think about intelligence in different ways. It provides an alternative framework for trying to understand the complex learning needs of students.

Gardner's work is not without critics. Chief among the criticisms is that the theory of multiple intelligences does not lend itself to scientific investigation. If we are not able to identify each of these abilities, it makes it difficult to design measures to assess their presence or absence (Klein, 1998). Recall that Gardner places less emphasis on the number of intellectual abilities and more on the idea that intelligence consists of separate distinct abilities. This leads to another criticism of his theory, which is that some of the abilities described by Gardner are not really so separate. For example, mathematical ability and spatial sense are highly correlated (Sattler, 2001). The correlation between these two abilities may mean that there is a common ability underlying each intelligence. Finally, some have expressed concerns that Gardner's abilities are not really "intelligences" but are personality traits or cognitive styles (Morgan, 1996). Despite these criticisms, Gardner's multiple intelligences theory maintains a wide following. Future research is needed to address criticisms and determine the future of this exciting theory.

Triarchic theory of intelligence

Intelligence theory proposed by Robert Sternberg seeing intelligence as the compilation of three separate abilities

There are other theories of intelligence that draw from the multiple intelligence perspective. Robert Sternberg (1985, 1990) has developed a **triarchic theory of intelligence** (see Figure 9.8). Like Gardner, Sternberg's theory looks at intelligence as a compilation of distinct

Figure 9.6

Gardner's Multiple Intelligences

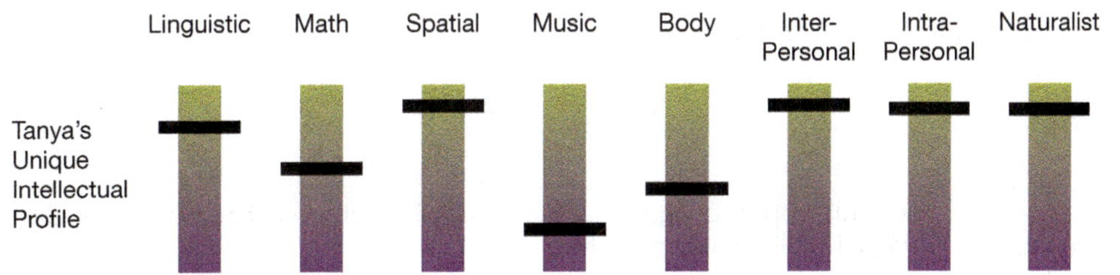

Figure 9.7

Graphical Depiction of an Individual's Unique Intellectual Profile

abilities. Instead of the eight intelligences proposed by Gardner, Sternberg details three areas of intellectual functioning. *Analytic/componential intelligence* is similar to the type of intelligence assessed by traditional tests of intellectual functioning. It emphasizes problem solving commonly used in academic settings. *Creative/experiential intelligence* is that part of intelligent behavior that allows for creative and effective responses to novel situations. It involves insight into problems and the ability to connect relevant aspects of novel situations. *Practical/contextual intelligence* is the way an individual interacts and understands their world. This component of intelligence is probably one of the most important of Sternberg's contributions to intelligence theory. Sternberg notes that intelligent behavior happens in real life and leads to real outcomes, not just classroom performance. His practical intelligence component gives his theory a real-life focus that is important as theorists attempt to translate intelligence theory into practical applications. It also helps to broaden the often narrow focus seen in intelligence theoretical work.

Multiple intelligence theories such as those of Gardner and Sternberg are already finding their way into classroom instruction. Some applications have research support (Hajhashemi, Ghombavani, & Amirkhiz, 2011), but teachers need to exercise caution when trying to apply the theory before adequate research investigations are conducted. For example, some teachers are taking Gardner's eight intelligences and directly teaching along these dimensions. That is, they take a given lesson and teach in such a way as to emphasize each ability dimension. Often this creates a forced and mechanical feel to the instructional environment. Some research has failed to find support for the effectiveness of such teaching. In one study (Callahan, Tomlinson, & Plucker, 1997), students at risk for failing were taught using an instructional approach based on multiple intelligences. Results indicated no apparent increases in achievement or self-concept. It is clear that more research will help us determine the ability of multiple intelligences theory to account for intelligent human behavior. Future research also needs to examine why the theory appeals to so many educators and what instructional applications produce positive effects. In an attempt to address some of the misconceptions of multiple intelligences, Gardner published an article (1995) detailing his opinions regarding important educational implications (see Table 9.8).

Dr. Robert Sternberg

Just What Do Intelligence Tests Measure?

Given the prominence of intelligence testing in education, it is important for teachers to have a strong sense of what IQ tests measure. It is easy to assume that a high score on an intelligence test means a student will do well in your class, will do well on today's assignment, and/or will have the answer to the question you just asked. This may or may not be true. As was discussed earlier, IQ tests are good predictors of academic success, not a guarantee. Similarly, lower intelligence scores do not necessarily mean a student will have trouble academically. People are

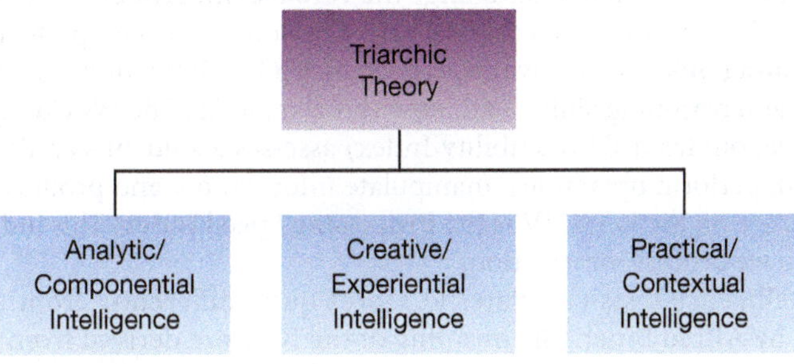

Figure 9.8

Robert Sternberg's Theory of Triarchic Intelligence

Table 9.8 Multiple Intelligences in the Classroom

DO	DON'T
Cultivate desired characteristics. Help students identify and develop intellectual characteristics that are valued by the community and society.	Teach all subjects using all "intelligences." Subjects do not need to be taught using all intellectual approaches.
	Go simply through the motions of "exercising" a particular intelligence. Supporting intellectual development involves appropriate, integrated instruction, not just superficial exposure.
Approach a concept, subject matter, or discipline in a variety of ways. Support learning using more than one appropriate instructional approach.	Use materials associated with an intelligence as a background activity. Supporting intellectual involves active education rather than passive exposure to an activity.
Personalize education. Educate based on the individual strengths and weakness of each student.	Use an intelligence as a simple memory technique. Intellectual development is more than just developing multiple techniques to aid memory.
	Evaluate or grade intelligences without regard of context or content. What is important about the "intelligences" is how they are used, not how much we have.

Adapted from Gardner (1995), *Phi Delta Kappan*, 77, 200–209

Full scale intelligence quotient score

The global measure of intellectual functioning

Index scores

Additional information on specific aspects of intellectual functioning

Verbal comprehension index

A measure of verbal reasoning and comprehension ability

Perceptual reasoning index

Measure that requires visual organization, comprehension, and reasoning ability with non-verbal material

Working Memory Index

Assesses a student's abilities to temporarily hold information, perform operations, manipulate information, and produce correct results

complex, and there are many factors determining academic success or failure. To make good and appropriate use of intellectual testing, teachers need not only to be aware of the theoretical underpinnings of the test but also the nature of the test items.

To illustrate a typical problem with intelligence testing, consider the questions: Is it reasonable to expect a student a student with a superior IQ score to make the next jump shot on the basketball court? Shouldn't the test cover basketball playing if you are going to apply the results to that situation? Teachers are sometimes so unfamiliar with the test that it is difficult to make sound inferences from IQ scores to actual student performance. The next section will provide a detailed overview of one of the most commonly used IQ tests. We will then discuss test scoring, as well as how to interpret and apply scores appropriately.

David Wechsler produced a series of intellectual measures covering all school-age children and adults. His intellectual assessment series includes the Wechsler Primary and Preschool Scale of Intelligence III (WPPSI), Wechsler Intelligence Scale for Children IV (WISC), and the Wechsler Adult Intelligence Scale IV (WAIS). This overview will focus on the WISC since it is the test most encountered by teachers. Each of the Wechsler tests, however, is similar with test items appropriate for the age range.

The WISC IV has a total of ten core tests and five supplemental tests. The ten core tests are required to calculate a **full scale intelligence quotient score** (FSIQ). The FSIQ is the global measure of intellectual functioning. Administration of the supplemental tests enables the calculation of additional scores called **index scores.** Index scores provide additional information on specific aspects of intellectual functioning. The **verbal comprehension index** (formally the Verbal IQ score—VIQ) provides a measure of verbal reasoning and comprehension ability. The **perceptual reasoning index** (formally the performance IQ—PIQ) requires visual organization, comprehension, and reasoning ability with non-verbal material. The **Working Memory Index** (formally the Freedom from Distractibility Index) assesses a student's ability to temporarily hold information, perform operations, manipulate information, and produce correct results. The final index score on the WISC IV is the **Processing Speed Index.** This index measures the speed with which we process information.

Today's intelligence tests calculate IQ scores quite differently from the score originally developed by Alfred Binet. The meaning of the IQ score derived from Binet's original formula actually changes as the individual ages. This means that IQ would appear to vary over time, even if actual intelligence was stable. This presented a number of application problems, so researches looked for alternative approaches to generate an intelligence score. The result was the **Deviation IQ**, which is still in use today. Calculating IQ using a deviation approach involves two separate processes. First, researchers collect performance data on the intellectual test from thousands of individuals. The researchers attempt to draw participants from all segments of the population, so the resulting database of scores accurately reflects American society. The second process occurs after the original database is collected and involves administering the test to an individual for clinical reasons, such as, for example, testing a student to answer a specific question regarding their performance at school. Comparing this single student's score on the IQ test to the existing database of scores provides a comparative or relative interpretation. The specific nature of how the "comparison" is formulated is complicated, but, essentially, we look to see how far the individual's score deviates from scores in the database.

Processing Speed Index

Measures the speed with which we process information

Deviation IQ

Intelligence scores calculated by using a current method for greater reliability and validity

Once the deviation IQ is calculated, assigning meaning to a numerical IQ score begins. Usually this starts with the verbal descriptor suggested by the specific IQ test. Table 9.9 provides a list of typical labels. You will notice that a label is provided for a range of scores rather than a specific number. You should also notice that the "average, intellectually limited, and very superior" ranges are larger than the others. This translates into specific diagnostic issues covered in the next chapter.

Although assigning meaning to a student's performance on an IQ test begins with a simple verbal label, it should not end there. What an IQ score means is entirely dependent on the life of student. Intellectual ability is manifested in the life of the individual in a variety of ways. The same IQ score may lead to great academic and personal success for one student and failure and emotional trouble for another. All professionals need to be extremely cautious when considering the meaning of an IQ score. This is true regardless of IQ range.

The previous section provided some details regarding the content of a typical IQ test. The nature of this content is important to consider when determining what a score means for a particular student. When a teacher thinks a student can or cannot do some classroom activity based on the knowledge of the student's IQ score, that teacher should remember what is actually on an IQ test. How directly related to the classroom activity are the individual subtests of the IQ test? Often the skill a teacher is attempting to teach in a class goes way beyond the skills and abilities measured on an intellectual assessment. Classroom performance taps other abilities such a motivation, social skills, and self-perceptions. These are not emphasized on an IQ test, yet are important mediators of academic success. It is important to remember the meaning of an IQ score is "applied" by the people involved. It is not that IQ scores have inherent meaning and determine outcomes; rather, they provide information that needs to be contextualized in the life of the person being assessed. Table 9.10 provides additional cautions when using IQ scores.

Table 9.9 Typical IQ Verbal Descriptors and Ranges

DESCRIPTORS	IQ RANGE
Very Superior	130–Highest score on the test
Superior	120–129
High Average	110–119
Average	90–109
Low Average	80–89
Borderline	70–79
Intellectually Limited	Lowest score on the test–69

Table 9.10 Cautions When Using IQ SCORES

IQ scores are a measurement and susceptible to error like any other measurement. They provide an estimate of intellectual ability. Many support using an IQ range rather than a specific number given the problem associated with measurement error.
IQ scores should always be interpreted in the context of the whole individual.
IQ scores do not guarantee outcomes.
IQ scores do not determine the "value" or "worth" of an individual.
The construct of IQ is still widely debated. This should mean caution when assigning meaning to a particular score.
IQ scores are best used by individuals who remain up-to-date on current research on the meaning and application of intellectual assessments.

Standardized Assessments for Teachers

Becoming a teacher is one of the most regulated professions in history. All fifty states have rigorous licensing and education standards for becoming a teacher. How do states determine if all this education is producing quality teachers? The answer lies in the controversial area of teacher assessments.

The idea of turning the tables on teachers and asking them to take a test has been around for some time. As a nation, we have been developing a growing appreciation for the importance of high-quality teachers. This has led to stringent standards for licensure. Individual states license teachers, so standards for professional development vary according to state guidelines. Despite this variation, there is growing cohesion in the process of testing teacher preparedness. Currently, about forty states and territorial jurisdictions use the **Praxis**™ series for assessing teacher preparation and performance. The Praxis is actually a series of three different tests (see Table 9.11). Individual states can adopt any one of the individual tests or all three. States not electing to use the Praxis have similar instruments for assessing teachers.

Praxis™

A series of tests for assessing teacher preparation and performance

The process of assessing teacher preparation does not begin with these tests. It actually begins with each state defining the qualities they feel are important in a well-prepared

Table 9.11 The Praxis Series: Professional Assessments for Beginning Teachers®

TEST	DESCRIPTION
PRAXIS I™: Pre-Professional Skills Tests	Praxis I is taken by preservice* teachers early in their undergraduate careers. It assesses their basic reading, writing, and math skills. *Preservice simply refers to teaching majors prior to their actual service as teachers
PRAXIS II™: Subject Assessments	Praxis II is taken by preservice teachers toward the end of their undergraduate education. It tests their understanding of the principles of teaching and learning. It also assesses subject matter competency.
PRAXIS III™: Teacher Performance Assessments	Praxis III is taken by teachers after they graduate and are actively teaching. Assessment is conducted primarily by classroom observation. Depending on the state, it may also include portfolio assessment.

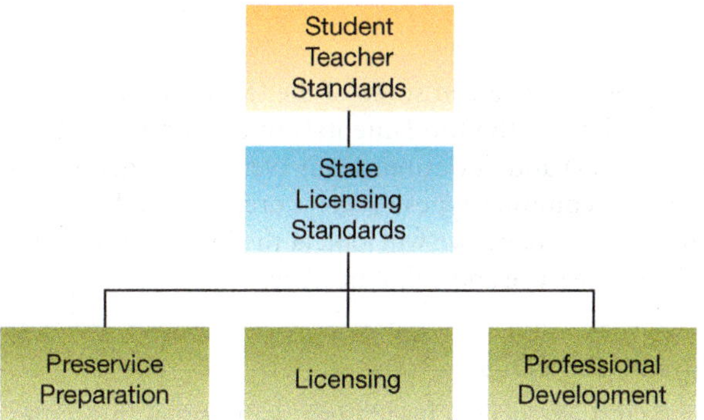

Figure 9.9

State Teacher Policy Framework

teacher. This is the process of developing standards. **Teaching standards** are clearly defined goals states have for the development of high-quality teachers. Most state standards follow the "core" standards developed by the **Interstate New Teacher Assessment and Support Consortium (INTASC)**. This consortium consists of state education associations and national educational organizations. It is important to appreciate that the development of standards necessarily precedes the development of assessments. Even states using the Praxis series can tailor the test to meet their unique state standards. Figure 9.9 provides a visual representation of state policy formation.

Teaching standards

Clearly defined goals that states employ for the development of high-quality teachers

Interstate New Teacher Assessment and Support Consortium (INTASC)

A consortium that consists of state education associations and national educational organizations

In addition to providing a "core" set of standards, INTASC also has started the development of a teacher assessment instrument. The *Test for Teaching Knowledge* measures beginning teacher knowledge and skill. The test specifically addresses INTASC core model standards.

We are likely to see more teacher assessments in the future as the nation's spotlight continues to shine on the quality of teacher education. It is critical to remember in this assessment sensitive environment that tests are not a means unto themselves. Tests are one tool to measure key aspects of the teacher preparation process. They need to be firmly grounded in a well-developed set of standards. Failing to focus considerable energy into developing clearly articulated standards ultimately leads to assessments that fail to measure anything meaningful.

SUMMARIZE AND REFLECT

1. The first part of the section focused on how we test by looking at specific tests.
2. There are a variety of test types including aptitude tests, achievement tests, and behavioral tests.
3. Intelligence testing, which has achieved a unique place in education, is a frequently used form of test. Modern intelligence testing began with the work of Alfred Binet.
4. There is a conceptual theory behind the testing of intellectual ability. One theory views intelligence as a single ability. Other theorists view intelligence as a compilation of several distinct abilities.
5. Using intelligence tests appropriately requires an understanding of intelligence test scores. It is important to know how educational professionals assign meaning to intelligence test scores.
6. There are many important cautions when using information on intellectual performance.
7. The area of teacher testing is becoming increasingly important. Teachers are being subjected to increasing testing as part of an on-going effort to improve teacher quality.

INFORMED APPLICATION

1. Your school district is implementing a new program for gifted students. They want to use a single cut off score on an IQ test to determine eligibility for the program. What are the pros and cons of using such a system?

INTERPRETING STANDARDIZED TEST SCORES

This section of the chapter will give you some of the technical information needed to understand tests scores. We will cover the fundamentals of descriptive statistics such as measures of central tendency (averages) and deviations from average (range, standard deviation). Next, we will review some of the common types of test scores reported on standardized tests, such as grade and age equivalents. Finally, we will look at the importance of determining whether a particular test is a reliable measure and valid measure.

Basic Testing Concepts

To understand how we test, we need a basic understanding of the scores generated by tests. A fundamental concept in testing is that we need tools to *describe* a group of scores. For example, we need to know if the scores were generally high or low. We also need to know if most students achieved a similar score. Imagine you are the teacher of a tenth grade math class. You have twenty-five students in your class. You just administered their first chapter test and are looking over the distribution of their scores. A common approach to examining score distributions is to generate a **frequency distribution**. This is a graphical depiction of how many students earned each of the possible scores on the test. For example, seven students scored an 80, seven scored a 75, two scored a 90, etc. To graph this information, you would create a bar chart with one bar for each possible score. The number of students earning each score is represented by the height of the bar. For example, the height of the bar for a score of 80 would be higher than the bar for the score of 90 because more students earned a score of 80. See Figure 9.10 to see a sample frequency distribution. As you can see from this example, the frequency distribution is an excellent way to represent visually how a group of students performed on a test. It also illustrates the concept of central tendency.

Frequency distribution

Graphical depiction of how many students obtained a given score

Central Tendency

Central tendency is the tendency for scores to cluster around the center of a distribution of scores. Not all scores will cluster toward the center of a distribution, but central tendency is a fairly robust phenomenon across a wide range of areas. In general, when large groups of people are measured, most people will score somewhere close to the middle, with fewer people scoring very high or very low.

Central tendency

The tendency for scores to cluster around the center of a distribution of scores

To describe how much scores cluster in the center of a distribution, we have developed several measures of central tendency. The **mean** is calculated by adding all the scores and then dividing the sum by the total number of scores. For example, using the example above, when you add each of the twenty-five test scores you get 1,920. Dividing this score by the total number of scores (25), you get 80. The mean for this set of scores is 80 and provides a measure of where the scores are clustering in this particular distribution.

Mean

The measure of central tendency calculated by adding all the scores and then dividing the sum by the total number of scores

There are, however, other ways to measure central tendency of a group of scores. The **median** is the score occurring in the middle of a ranked distribution. To compute the median in this example, you would first rank the scores from highest to lowest. Simply write down all twenty-five scores in a column, starting with the highest score, followed by the second highest score, all the way down to the lowest score. The median is the score in the middle of the column of scores. So, for twenty-five scores the middle score would be the thirteenth score (twelve scores above it and twelve scores below it). The only difficulty with determining the

Median

The score that occurs in the middle of a ranked distribution

Figure 9.10

Frequency Distribution

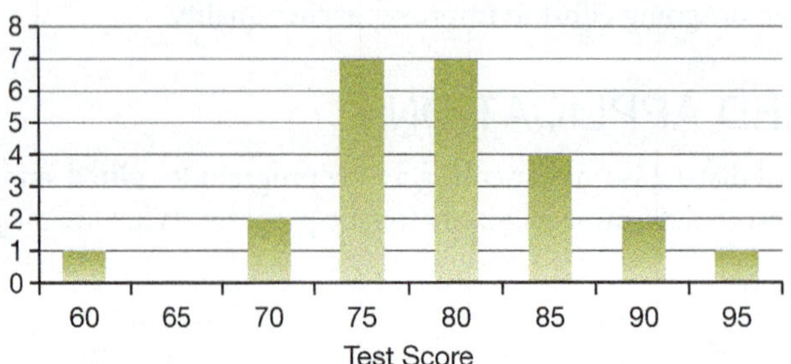

median is when you have an even number of scores. If you have an even number of scores (e.g., twenty-four scores), then there is no exact middle score. With twenty-four scores, the middle is between the twelfth and thirteenth scores. To determine the median in this case, you take the two scores that surround the middle of the distribution and calculate a simple average (add the two scores and divide by 2). This average is the median for an even number of scores.

A final measure of central tendency that we will consider is the mode. The **mode** is the score in a distribution occurring most frequently. The easiest way to determine the mode is to use a frequency distribution. Visually inspect the frequency distribution and see what "bar" is the highest. Since height of individual bars represents how frequently a given score was earned, the score with the highest bar is the mode. Notice that distributions frequently have more than one mode, or most frequent score. This happens when more than one score occurs most frequently. The above example has two modes, 75 and 80, each score occurs seven times. Figure 9.11 further illustrates the concepts of mean, median, and mode for an alternative set of scores. Test scores for a sample civics test are presented down the right side of the figure. The mean, median, and mode are highlighted on a frequency distribution of the test scores. Notice, all three of these measurements of central tendency are near the center of the distribution; however, the actual score varies. This is because of the different way in which the scores are calculated.

Mode

The score that occurs most frequently in a distribution

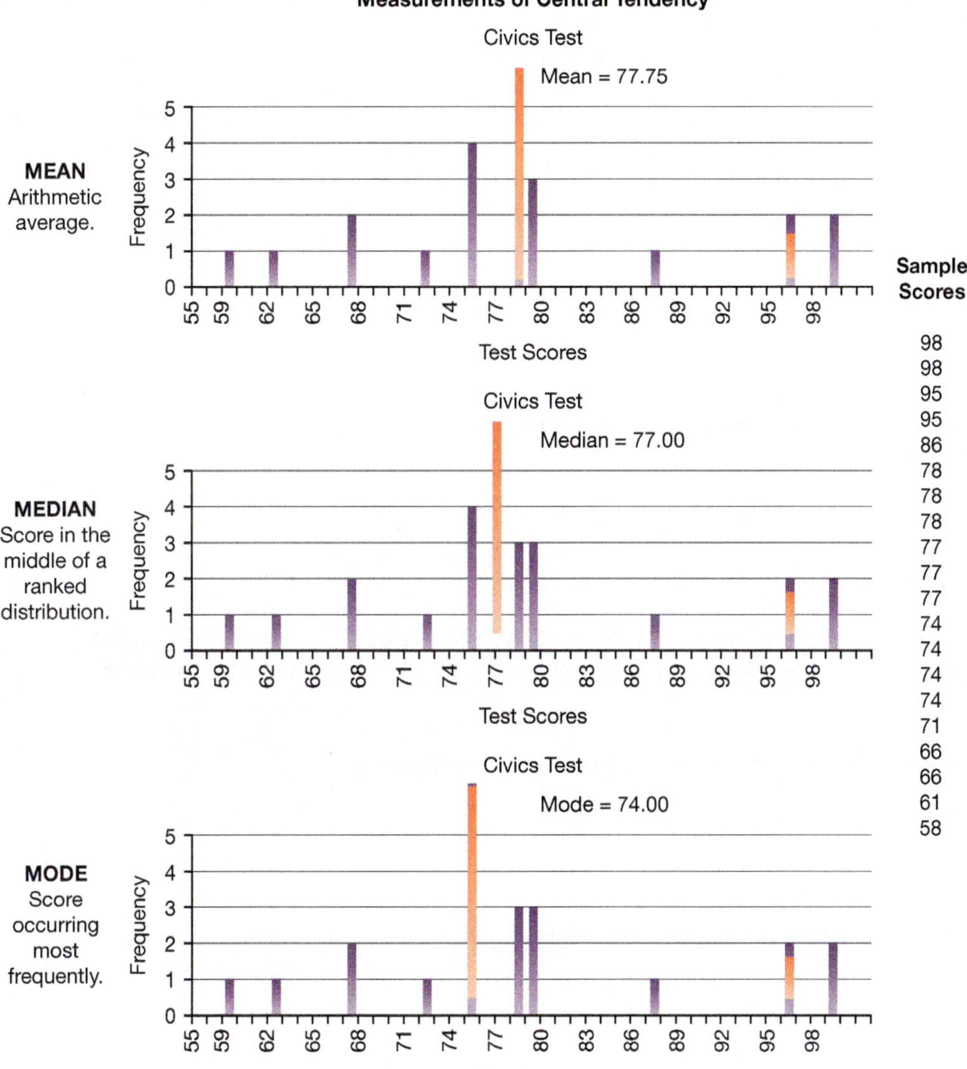

Figure 9.11

Measurements of Central Tendency

Figure 9.12

Science Test Distribution Scores

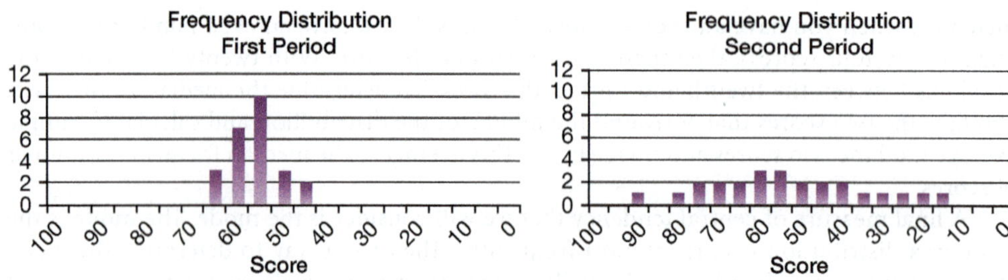

Standard Deviation and the Normal Deviation

Another important quality to explore when looking at scores from a group is how far apart they occur or deviate from each other. As we saw in the last section, often scores cluster around a mean score with fewer scores occurring as you move away from the mean. This deviation from the mean has important implications for interpretation. Imagine you are a second grade teacher and your students just took a science test. The mean (or average) score was a 57. Since the mean was so low, you are going to spend some additional time reviewing the basic concepts on the test. Figure 9.12 represents two different scenarios regarding the distribution of scores on the science test. The frequency distribution from the "first period" indicates a case in which most scores are tightly clustered around the mean score of 57. The graph for the second period indicates scores varied widely from the mean. Will your remedial efforts differ depending on the nature of how the scores deviate from the mean?

The teacher from the first period would likely approach instruction from a different perspective. Students appear to have a similar knowledge of the subject matter as represented by the similarity in scores. Contrast this to the frequency distribution for the second period class. Based on this distribution, the teacher would have to make an effort to create learning environments tailored to individual students since the students vary significantly in their understanding of the material.

Table 9.12 Cautions When Using IQ SCORES

Step 1	Add each of the scores to get a sum.	
Step 2	Divide the sum in Step 1 by the total number of scores, creating an average. This is abbreviated $\bar{X}$.	
Step 3	Now, go back to the first score and subtract it from the average. Then square this difference. Repeat this procedure for each score. $(X-\bar{X})^2$ You will end up with a squared difference for each of your original scores.	
Step 4	After you complete Step 3, add up all the squared differences you calculated. Summing the squared differences is abbreviated $\sum(X-\bar{X})^2$.	Formula for calculating a standard deviation: $\sqrt{\frac{\sum(X-\bar{X})^2}{N}}$
Step 5	Take the sum of the squared differences created in Step 4 and divide it by the total number of scores. $\frac{\sum(X-\bar{X})^2}{N}$.	
Step 6	Finally, take the square root of the number generated in Step 5. $\sqrt{\frac{\sum(X-\bar{X})^2}{N}}$.	

As you can see, deviation from the mean on assessments can affect instructional efforts. The **standard deviation** is a measure of variability. It tells us how much the scores are varying from the mean. For example, in the frequency distributions presented above, the first period has a smaller standard deviation compared to second period. The first period scores *deviate* less, or are less spread out across the range of possible scores. To calculate the standard deviation, follow the steps in Table 9.12.

Standard deviation
Measure of variability

The formula above creates a single number called the standard deviation. This number can be used to help us understand the variability of scores. The first period scores would result in a smaller standard deviation compared to the second period. The smaller number for the first period indicates scores for this group are more similar and deviate less from each other. This is important information and helps teachers develop educational programming that is more sensitive to the specific students they instruct.

To make use of the standard deviation, teachers typically calculate the standard deviation value and then add and subtract it from the mathematical average to create a range of scores. For example, if a teacher has a group of scores that has an average of 75 and standard deviation of 5, then the teacher can get a sense of how variable the scores are by adding 5 to 75 (80) and subtracting 5 from 75 (70). This means that one standard deviation away from the mean creates a range from 70–80. Two standard deviations away from the mean would create the range 65–85. These ranges are important because standard deviation ranges follow a consistent rule.

The standard deviation follows the **68/95/99.7 Rule**. This rule is summarized in Table 9.13. According to the rule, 68% of the scores in a given group will fall within 1 standard deviation above and below the mean. For example, if the mean score was 75 and the standard deviation was 5, then 68% of the scores would fall between 70 (75 – 5) and 80 (75 + 5). Similarly, this rule holds that 95% of the scores will fall between 2 standard deviations above and below the mean. Finally, 99.7% of the scores will fall between 3 standard deviations above and below the mean. Again, the smaller the standard deviation, the tighter the scores cluster around the average score. Larger standard deviations mean the scores are more spread out across the distribution.

68/95/99.7 Rule
General rule describing the variation typically observed in a group of scores

Standard deviations help teachers and parents understand performance on a variety of tests. For example, Sammy is a fourth grade student referred for possible inclusion in the gifted program. In addition to assessing several classroom performance factors, Sammy was given an individually administered IQ test. His score on the test was 3.2 standard deviations above the mean (see Figure 9.13). Knowing the 68/95/99.7 rule, his teacher easily recognizes his score as highly unusual. Since 99.7% of students score within 3 standard deviations above and below the mean, his score is only achieved by a fraction of 1% of students. As you can see, understanding score variability and the standard deviation helps to put a student's score on a test into perspective.

It is also important to realize that score variability can be expressed more simply by giving the range of scores. The **range** of a set of scores is the highest and lowest score. For example,

Range
Set of scores including the highest to lowest scores

Table 9.13 The 68/95/99.7 Rule

68% of the scores fall within 1 standard deviation of the mean
95% of the scores fall within 2 standard deviations of the mean
99.7% of the scores fall within 3 standard deviations of the mean

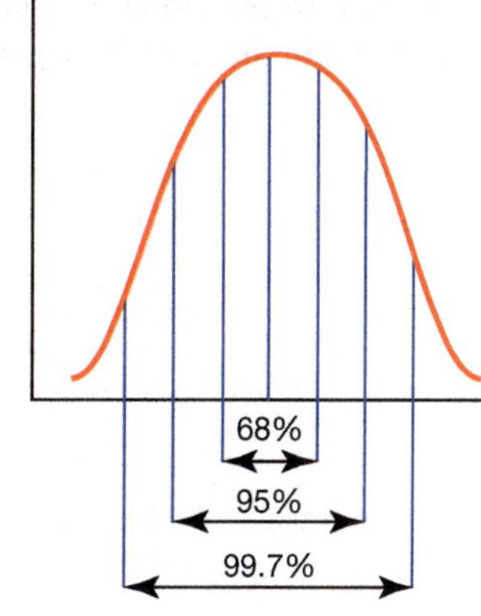

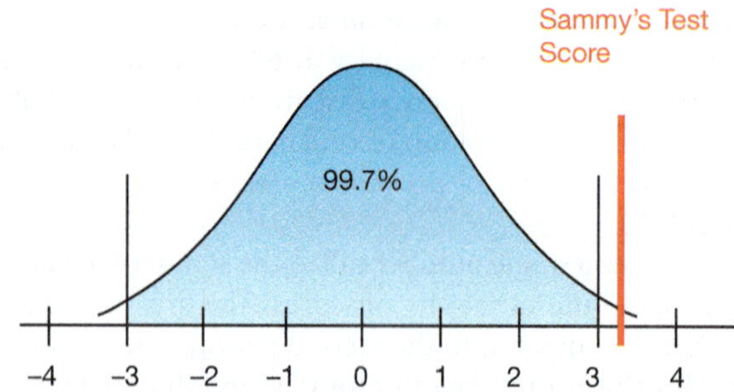

Figure 9.13
Sammy's Test Score

the range of scores on a spelling pretest might be 95–32 (out of 100). The range on the actual spelling test a week later might be 100–84. From the ranges, the teacher can see that scores have generally improved and shifted to the higher end of possible scores. The range can be useful to capture variability in scores, but range should be used with caution. If there is a single score in a distribution that is unusual compared to the others, the range may be deceptive. For example, the ranges cited above for the spelling pretest might be misleading if only one student scored a 32. Perhaps all the other students scored an 84 or better. The apparent improvement on the actual spelling test may be attributable to single student. This is unclear looking only at the range. Standard deviations are similarly affected by unusually high or low scores, but not as significantly as the range.

Normal distribution

Distribution of scores characterized by most scores clustering close to the average

When a distribution of scores is characterized by most scores clustering close to the average, we call this a **normal distribution**. The normal distribution is known by a number of names including the "bell curve" because of its distinctive shape. In addition to following the 68/95/99.7 rule, normal distributions are also characterized by half of the scores falling above the mean and half the scores falling below the mean. Most standardized tests produce a normal distribution of scores when administered to a large group of individuals. Figure 9.14 shows a normal distribution for an IQ test.

Type of Scores

Standardized tests produce many different types of scores. Most of these scores, however, are based on the average score and the standard deviation. The exact values for average and standard deviation vary depending on the test. On some tests, a score of 50 represents average. Other tests might define average as a score of 500. The numbering system used to represent average is somewhat arbitrary. Note that this is very different from the way we use the average score on a typical classroom test. Rarely do teachers establish grades based on standard deviations away from the mean. Teachers typically assign a particular point range with a letter grade. These point ranges usually have nothing to do with the standard deviation. Standard tests are different. Their scoring system is typically based on the standard deviation.

Figure 9.15 shows a typical normal distribution with the mean in the center of the distribution. Under this distribution are several rows of standard scores. As you can see, an IQ is scored so that the average score is a 100 with a standard deviation of about 15. What is important to remember is that although the scoring system used for a given test differs, they are similar in that they have a mean and standard deviation. Interpreting these scores requires

Figure 9.14
Normal Distribution

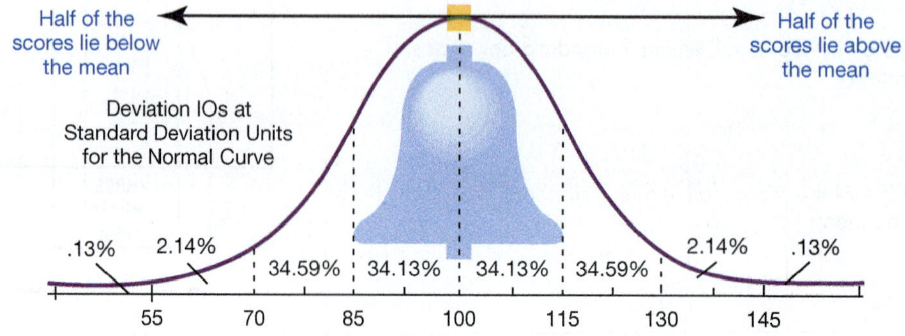

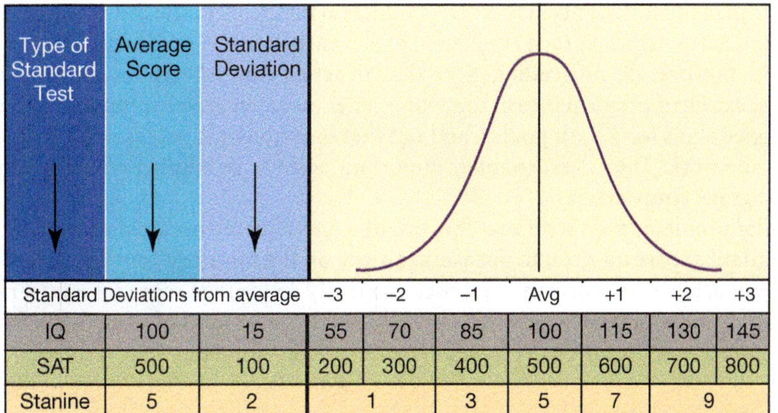

Figure 9.15
A Typical Normal Distribution

knowledge of these values. For example, two students who vary by fifty points on an IQ test are performing very differently compared to two students differing by fifty points on a SAT test. The standard deviation for the IQ test is 15, so the two students vary by more than *3 standard deviations.* The standard deviation for the SAT is 100, so these two students only differ by half of one standard deviation. As you can see, different test makers use different scoring systems; however, a fundamental understanding of means, standard deviations, and the normal distribution allows us to interpret any scoring system. It is also important to realize that since standard scores are based on the normal distribution, it is possible to convert from one scoring system to another system. For example, if you wish to convert a 700 on the SAT to a stanine, you would assign a stanine corresponding to 2 standard deviations above the mean. This would equal a stanine of 9. Stanines are a common measurement scale used on many standardized tests of achievement.

In addition to the scoring systems used by standardized tests, test results are often expressed in terms of grade level. **Grade equivalents** express performance in terms of an approximate grade level. This is accomplished by giving a particular test to many students at each grade level. The test makers obtain a mean performance for each grade level. Then when a student is given the test, his score can be compared to the previously determined grade averages. For example, Frankie is in his third month of the sixth grade. He is given a reading test and obtains a score of 36. Previous testing indicated that sixth graders in their third month of school obtained an average score of 36, the exact score Frankie received. This means that Frankie is right on target for his grade and would be given an equivalent score of sixth grade, third month. The grade equivalent score helps contextualize the score in terms of the familiar concept of academic grades. Although parents and teachers find this information helpful, there are some cautions to consider. It would seem reasonable to assume that a student who is in the sixth grade who scored at the eleventh grade level on a math test would be capable of eleventh grade math. Often this is not the case because the actual test items an eleventh grader would be administered would probably not be given to the sixth grader (see Figure 9.16).

Grade equivalents
Performance results expressed in terms of an approximate grade level

As you can see from the figure, sixth grade students are typically started at test item 25. They are not started at test item 1, because previous testing indicates that most all of sixth grade students correctly answer the lower items. The figure also indicates that this student continued to answer questions correctly until question 49. The average sixth grader, however, is usually only able to answer questions through 36. This means the student with a score of 49 is doing

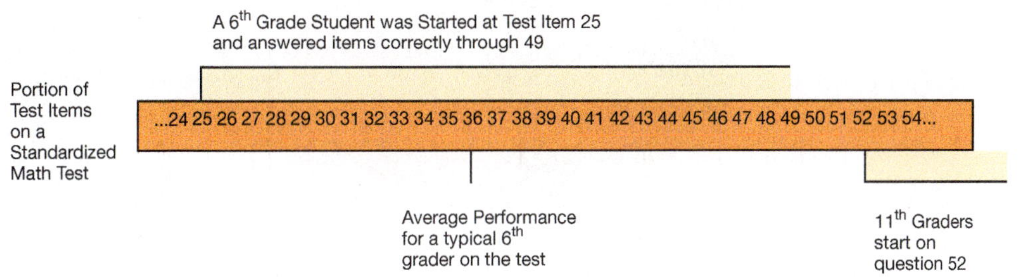

Figure 9.16
Grade Equivalents

much better than most students his age. Depending on the shape of the distribution, a raw score of 49 may indeed generate a grade equivalent of eleventh grade. A grade equivalent of eleventh grade would, however, be misleading given that an actual eleventh grader starts the test at test item 52. The excellent performance of the sixth grader more accurately represents exceptionally well-developed skills for a sixth grader, and not that the student is necessarily capable of doing eleventh grade work. This is an *extremely* important point to remember when helping parents understand grade equivalents.

Age-equivalents

Results usually based on comparing a student's score on a test to the average score on the same test for various ages

A similar problem exists with **age-equivalents**. Age-equivalents are usually based on comparing a student's score on a test to the average score on the same test for various ages. Perhaps a ten-year-old achieved a score on a test that is actually an average score for a fifteen-year-old. This does not mean that the ten-year-old is capable of the same kind of work as the fifteen-year-old. The ten-year-old simply has very well-developed skills for a ten-year-old.

Reliability and Validity

Reliability

Consistency of test results where giving a test to the same person on multiple occasions, would produce comparable results each time

Two additional concepts are fundamental to understanding the testing process. **Reliability** is when a test produces consistent results. In other words, if you give a test to the same person on multiple occasions, you would obtain comparable results each time. This does not mean *identical* results, just similar results. The idea behind reliability is that the test is able to measure consistently and vary substantially due to error. If you were to try to measure how fast a child could run by counting aloud, you would likely make errors because counting is not particularly reliable. You could accidentally introduce error into your measurement by counting slightly faster or slower. This concept of testing error and reliability can be thought of as an equation. The measured test score is equal to the true test score plus error (see Figure 9.17). For example, you attempt to guess the correct height of a woman who walked by you this morning. Your guess was 5 feet 8 inches, but the woman was actually 5 feet 6 inches. Your actual guess included her true height and two inches of "error." Your guess is like a score on a test. The actual height of the woman is a part of your guess, but there is also a certain amount of error because judging height by sight is difficult. In assessment, the same principle applies. Let's say you give a social studies test on World War I. Randy, an eighth-grade student, makes an 85 on the test. This test score is comprised of Randy's actual knowledge plus any error in measuring that knowledge. Most tests do an imperfect job of capturing what they are measuring. Students may know more than they can show because the type of test question (e.g., multiple choice) is difficult for them. They may also suffer anxiety over being tested, which masks their true knowledge. Students may also get credit for knowing more than they do through lucky guesses or cheating. Makers of standardized tests typically give you the actual test score plus a **confidence interval**. The confidence interval is a range of scores believed to contain the student's true score. The inherent error involved in measuring makes it difficult to represent performance with a single score, but we are able to

Confidence interval

Range of scores believed to contain the student's true score

Figure 9.17
Reliability

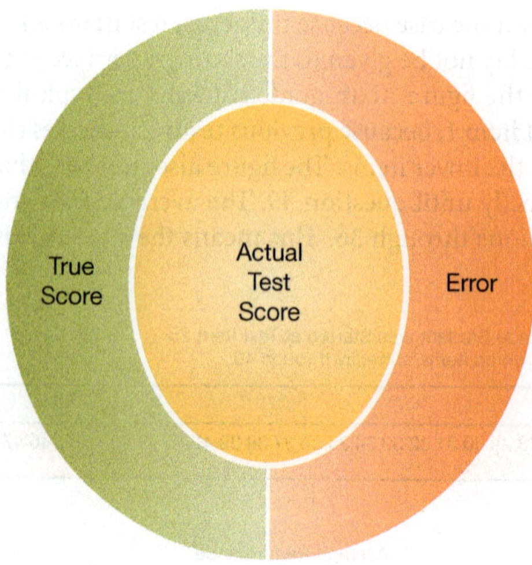

state that a particular range of scores contains the true score. For example, a student may earn a score of 107 on a standardized test of reading with a corresponding confidence interval of 103–111. This means that the students true score is likely to be somewhere between 103 and 111. When making educational decisions, teachers should always consider the confidence interval in addition to the test score.

You could imagine that if your test had considerable error, retesting Randy on the same knowledge is likely to vary because the test is not doing such a great job of assessing his actual knowledge. If the test has little error (and Randy's knowledge remains constant), then a similar score would be obtained on repeated tests. This is why it is best to use reliable tests. There are several approaches to determine test reliability. **Test-retest reliability** uses two administrations of the test. The test is given once and then given again later. Reliability is determined by assessing the similarity in scores across the two administrations. **Alternate form reliability** is established by giving comparable forms of the same test to the same students. Again, reliability is determined by looking at similarity in scores. **Split-half reliability** divides the test items of a single test into two groups (e.g., odd numbered items and even numbered items). Then the two groups are compared to see if respondents perform similarly. There are cautions to consider when using these techniques to determine reliability (see Table 9.13).

Test-retest reliability

Consistency based on two administrations of a test

Alternate form reliability

Consistency established by giving comparable forms of the same test to the same students

Split-half reliability

Consistency based on dividing the test items of a single test into two groups

Even though a test reliably measures a particular skill or knowledge, the test might not measure the skill intended. A classic example is head circumference as a measure of intellectual ability. The size of someone's head is not related to how smart they are, but the example is helpful when trying to understand reliability. Using a tape to measure head circumference is likely to produce very reliable measurements. That is, each time we measure the size of someone's head, the measurements are likely to be identical because head size is stable (at least for adults). The problem, however, is if you intend to use head circumference as a measurement of intelligence. **Validity** refers to whether a test measures what it intends it measures. If a test says it measures intelligence, does it indeed measure intellectual ability? Using a tape measure is not a valid measure of intelligence.

Validity

Whether a test measures what it intends to measure

Often we have an idea of something we would like to measure. In education, this could be motivation, intelligence, attention, aggression, participation, etc. To measure these things we essentially have to take the idea and construct and translate it into a test. The degree to which this translation successfully embodies the original construct gets at the idea of validity. In addition to matching your test to a particular construct, current research on validity indicates it is also important to examine the decisions resulting from the test results (Linn & Gronlund, 2000; Popham, 2002; McMillian, 2002). This means we need to examine the inferences people make based on the results. For example, it would be important to ask what is inferred from a test result indicating an unusually limited ability to pay attention? Answer to such a question are just as important as questions about how accurately the test actually measures attention.

Table 9.13 Potential Problems When Determining Reliability

TYPE OF RELIABILITY	CAUTIONS
Test-Retest	Caution: Students may do better on the second testing because • they are familiar with the test, or • they learned the answers to the questions after the first administration of the test.
Alternate Form	Caution: Students may still increase their performance on the second test because they are familiar and more comfortable with the testing process even though the items are different.
Split Half	Caution: Reliability usually increases with increasing numbers of test items. Since determining split-half reliability necessitates dividing the test in half, the reliability obtained by this method is often less than other approaches using the whole test.

Table 9.14 Types of Validity

DESCRIPTION	EXAMPLE
Content Related	A middle school has developed a comprehensive end-of-the-year science test for their sixth graders. The test's content related validity would be based on the inclusion of test items directly related to the content taught to the students.
Criterion Related	The same middle school in the above example also gives a standardized test of science ability to the sixth graders. A comparison of the school developed test with the standardized test explores the criterion related validity of the new test.
Construct Related	Using the example above, the middle school is satisfied with the new science test's content and criterion related validity. The school continues to use the new test over a period of ten years. Additional information from the students' performance in science, career choices, student self-interest reports, other newly developed tests all indicate that this test provides a valid measurement of the construct of science ability.

Content-related validity

Strength of a test established by examining whether relevant content domains are included in the test

Criterion-related validity

Prediction about the strength of the performance on a test against some other related criterion

Construct-related validity

A judgment as to whether the test accurately measures the intended construct

Like reliability, validity can be assessed using a variety of approaches. **Content-related validity** is established by examining whether relevant content domains are included in the test (see Table 9.14 for examples of different types of validity). A potential issue with this form of validity is that it presumes that relevant domains are actually known. **Criterion-related validity** is a prediction about the performance on a test against some other related criterion. A potential drawback to this approach to validity is that the comparison test may have its own validity problems. **Construct-related validity** is a judgment as to whether the test accurately measures the intended construct. This is the broadest form of validity and is established over a period of years through cumulated evidence. Keep in mind, for a test to be considered valid, it must also be reliable. A test could not be considered valid if it provided one measurement on an initial testing and something entirely different on a second testing. Imagine an intelligence test indicating a student is performing in the superior range one month and in the intellectually limited range the next month.

Sharing Testing Results with the Student and Family

An important piece of the testing puzzle is how to communicate the results of a test to parents or guardians. This is often a difficult process because parents have very different levels of expertise in testing. Some parents will have an extensive background in testing and likely know more than the teacher about how to appropriately interpret the results. Other parents have never seen a standardized test score and need basic information about what each score means. Remember, parents generally want to know if their student is achieving and how they can help the student do better in areas of weakness. The level of detail you choose to provide needs to be sensitive to the specific needs of the parents and yet attempt to meet the same goal. Linn and Miller (2005) present some basic guidelines to help teachers prepare for a parent conference where test scores will be discussed.

To prepare for the conference, review the following:

1. Be prepared to describe what the test measures.
2. Explain the meaning of the test scores.
3. Clarify the accuracy of the test scores.
4. Discuss the use of the test results.

When speaking to parents, teachers want to be careful not to present a picture that any given test score means that their child is destined for a particular outcome.

When trying to describe what a test measures, teachers should be careful not to present a picture that any given test score means that the child is destined for a particular outcome. There are no tests that have such predictive validity. Some tests are indeed *associated* with certain outcomes, but they are probabilities and may or may not apply in a particular situation. It is best to present tests as a measure of progress to date while emphasizing that future success depends on many factors.

Explaining the meaning of test results can also be challenging, depending on the level of experience of the parents. In general, standardized tests use scores that compare the performance of the student to their peers. Help parents understand how their child is doing compared to others, but also underscore what specific skills their child has mastered and what areas need additional work. This gives parents something concrete on which to focus and makes future improvements seem possible. Teachers should also strongly emphasize that tests are imperfect instruments—they provide a best guess of the student's current functioning. Parents often find it helpful to look at confidence intervals for a test score.

A final point to consider: Teachers need to explain how the test scores are used. Parents often have considerable anxiety regarding what the scores mean in terms of the daily life of their child. Many tests are used as measures of global progress of the entire grade or school and have little direct bearing on the actual educational programming of the child. Other tests are specifically conducted to determine how to best meet the needs of the student. As always, teachers should view parents as important collaborators in the education of the student. Parents feel empowered when their interpretations of test scores are genuinely heard and play a meaningful role in the actual education of their child.

SUMMARIZE AND REFLECT

1. A comprehensive understanding of assessment and evaluation of individual differences is grounded in an understanding of basic testing concepts.
2. Key testing concepts include central tendency, standard deviation, frequency distribution, and grade equivalents.
3. Reliability refers to how consistently a test generates a test score over time.
4. Validity refers to how accurately a test measures what it is supposed to be measuring.
5. Testing of future teachers and of teachers currently working in schools is increasing as we strive to increase teacher quality.

INFORMED APPLICATION

1. How would a pre-school teacher develop a reliable and valid measure of whether a student can accurately identify the correct sound associated with each letter of the alphabet?

THE CHAPTER IN REVIEW

Testing is an integral part of the educational process, and developing a thorough understanding of testing is essential for teachers. This chapter focused on several themes: what exactly is testing, how we use testing in education, issues with the testing process, types of testing, types of actual tests, and how to interpret and communicate test results.

There are many reasons why we conduct testing in schools. Tests are used to assess student learning, but testing is also conducted for a variety of other reasons. We began the chapter with a basic discussion of what testing is and how it compares to the larger process of assessment and evaluation. In the next section of the chapter, we began looking at testing as a tool to help us understand students. If used with planning and care, testing can help teachers develop more comprehensive profiles of the students, their lives, and their potential to succeed. We also use testing to identify students in need of special assistance. Every student is unique with specific educational needs, but some needs are so significant that they require additional resources. Testing can help teachers identify those needs. Testing is also used to insure students are receiving a quality education. Tests help us monitor student progress and identify schools needing improvements.

The next part of the chapter reviews various issues with using tests. We examined the phenomenon of high-stakes testing. Despite the benefits of testing, attaching too many consequences to a student's performance on a test creates a negative educational environment. We also look at how some tests may be biased against certain groups of students, making it difficult to accurately measure their knowledge and abilities. Taking time out of the educational day to teach students how to take these tests was also discussed.

The next two sections examined different approaches to testing and their appropriate uses. We looked at the difference between norm-referenced tests and criterion-referenced tests. We also looked at how tests can be used to plan effective instruction. Next, we turned to a discussion of different types of tests available to teachers. First, we looked at the frequently used achievement tests. These tests assess achievement in academic domains such as reading, writing, and mathematics. We compared group versus individual test administration and also appropriate uses of test results. Next, we discussed aptitude tests. We compared these tests to achievement tests, noting their similarities. We also distinguished the aptitude test based on its focus on predicting future success. Behavioral assessments are growing in frequency with increased mandates for testing in recent federal legislation. We discussed changes to the laws, highlighting the functional behavioral assessment. The final type of test we reviewed was teacher testing. With growing concern regarding teacher quality, states are paying closer attention to the preparation of teachers and the assessment of their skills.

The final part of the section covered intelligence testing as a special type of educational test. Perhaps no other test in the history of education has been so frequently used and also so misunderstood. We began our look at intelligence testing by reviewing the history of the development of the modern IQ test. Next, we looked at two major theories of intelligence. General intelligence assumes there is only one single intellectual ability from which all other specific abilities derive, while multiple intelligence views intellectual functioning as several distinct abilities. The last part of the section explored the meaning behind IQ test scores. Interpretation is usually a series of steps beginning with an interpretive label provided by the test manufacturers. From this, testing professionals build an understanding of the scores, what they mean to the individual, and their unique circumstance. We also reviewed several cautions educators should consider when using intelligence test scores.

The last section of the chapter focused on understanding how to interpret test scores. The first part of this section reviewed basic testing concepts: central tendency, standard deviation, reliability, and validity. Each of these concepts plays a role in a teacher's ability to use and understand test scores. We also reviewed steps educators can take to communicate effectively with parents and guardians about test results.

Interdisciplinary Case Focus

principal *special educator*
teacher *parents* *psychologist*
social worker *physical educator*
nurse *peers* *doctor*

Two years ago, Simon Memorial High School established a pre-referral intervention team. The purpose of the team is to provide necessary assessment and intervention for students at-risk for academic failure. The program targets students not in the school's special education program. The hope is that with early intervention, students can use well-planned supports to improve their academic situation and reduce the need for special education services. The team consists of several classroom teachers from a variety of subject areas, the school's physical education teacher, the president of the local PTA, the school psychologist, and the school nurse. Students are typically referred by teachers, but occasionally referrals come from parents with the assistance and support of the school principal.

Today's Case

Donnie is a sixteen-year-old young man in regular education classes. He was referred to the pre-referral intervention team by the school principal, Mr. Thomas. He had been in close contact with Donnie's parents over the course of the previous year, trying to help Donnie with organizational issues. The extent of Donnie's problems were significant enough that Mr. Thomas felt a referral to the team might generate some additional tools to help Donnie succeed.

Assessment Phase The team convened after school to review Donnie's records from the previous year. Academic records indicated strong grades, with some variability. It was noted that math grades were somewhat lower compared to other subject areas. It was also noted that Donnie excelled in athletics. He played baseball throughout his school years and recently joined the football team. There was also a period in sixth grade where Donnie's grades dropped substantially.

It was determined that the first step was to interview Donnie's language arts teacher, math teacher, and parents (his parents are divorced). The interviews were divided between the team members. They agreed to reconvene in one week to compare notes.

Interview Results

Parents Donnie's mother and father were interviewed together. The parents seemed amicable and related well. It was also clear they were invested in Donnie's success. They described Donnie as a bright and capable young man. They both noted that they have had to make strong efforts all of his life to help him stay organized. They said it takes him twice as long as their other children to do his homework. He often is just staring out in space and needs a verbal reminder to get to work. Donnie is aware of this tendency and is easily embarrassed when it is brought to his attention. He is eager to please and tries hard to do well. They note that Donnie is extremely well spoken with an enormous vocabulary. He is very social and has many friends.

English Teacher His English teacher's story was similar to his parents. Ms. Michaels said she thoroughly enjoys Donnie. She said he is extremely popular. She noted that much of his popularity is due to his comedic talents. She has noticed that when Donnie does not have the "stage" and is just a regular participant in a group, he has some trouble keeping track of the conversation, occasionally asking questions that were already answered earlier in the conversation. Academically, she feels that Donnie is at the top of the class but that he requires help with some of the mechanics of the classroom, such as turning things in on time. She also noted that the problem seems to be getting worse, particularly during group work when his distractibility is noticed by the other students.

Math Teacher Donnie's math teacher, Mr. Botsworth, also gave positive comments regarding Donnie's interpersonal skills. He did, however, express greater concern regarding his classroom performance. He feels Donnie is quite bright, but he seems to have considerable difficulty staying on track. He also feels that Donnie is becoming increasingly moody and is reacting negatively to redirections. He clearly noted that he thought Donnie might have trouble with language use, but his problems were not consistent. For example, he appeared to do well when verbally interacting with other students. He did suggest that his math class is run primarily with verbal direction and instruction. Very little of the class is directed through readings.

Academic and Behavioral Assessments

Based on the evidence from the interviews, the team decided to conduct a standardized academic assessment. The psychologist also contacted the district's speech/language pathologist to do a brief language screening. The psychologist conducted a behavioral survey with Donnie's parents and Donnie. The academic assessments showed above average skills in all areas assessed by the test including reading, writing, math, science, and humanities. Math reasoning was actually the highest score. The speech language screen was positive with Donnie scoring above average on both receptive and expressive language skills. The behavioral assessment was interesting. Reports from the parents demonstrated below average attentional skills. It also showed a tendency toward emotional sensitivity. It was noted that neither of these sub-scores were in the clinically significant range, just lower compared to his other profile scores. Donnie's self-report was similar, but his perceptions of his emotional sensitivity were much lower, scoring lower than 87% of students his age.

Conclusions and Intervention Plan

The team met and reviewed all the interview and assessment information. First, they all agreed that Donnie was an academically talented young man. There was no evidence that Donnie's difficulties were related to a general intellectual issue. They also concluded that there wasn't any substantial information that his greater difficulty in math was related to a specific learning issue in that subject area. The language screen did not support their initial discussion that Donnie's difficulty in math was language related. Given these favorable academic and language reports, the team began to focus on the behavioral data. The team noted a clear and consistent weakness in Donnie's ability to pay attention. It was noted, however, that current reports do not support that his problems are a clinically significant weakness. The emotional sensitivity also showed up as a weakness and a significant weakness from Donnie's perspective. During the team's discussion, it came out that Donnie's parents divorced during his sixth grade year—the same year his grades were so poor. This was interpreted as additional evidence of Donnie's sensitivity to the emotional climate of his world. The physical education teacher also noted that the football coach was extremely strict and at time verbally harsh. He wondered if Donnie's emotional sensitivity was making his football experience overly negative. He also wondered if Donnie's attentional weakness was leading to more difficulties and perhaps more negative attention from the coach, especially since it was a new sport for Donnie. One of the teachers followed-up on this line of reasoning and suggested the same thing may be happening in math class. Without consistently available written directions in math, Donnie's wandering attention would put him at a unique disadvantage. He may be getting lost because of his attentional issues and then becoming overly sensitive when his teacher provides redirection. It appears this is particularly problematic when provided in a public way.

The team decided on the following intervention suggestions. The recommendations were made to Donnie's parents and his teachers. All supported the recommendations.

1. The team decided that the first step was to review the team's recommendations with Donnie. He is a mature and invested young man, and the team felt a greater appreciation of his own strengths and weaknesses would be an excellent asset to his success. The psychologist agreed to present the results to Donnie.
2. With Donnie's permission, the team agreed that a conversation with Donnie's football coach would help to sensitize him to the situation. It was agreed that football was very important to Donnie, and the best approach was to try to make the team experience more positive rather than leave the team.
3. It was determined that with Mr. Botsworth's help math class could be supported with written directives regarding class assignments. Mr. Botsworth's student intern was interested in the situation and agreed to take his lesson plans and provide posted overviews of the day's lessons at the beginning of class. She also agreed to meet with Donnie twice a week to make sure he was understanding the lessons and staying on track.
4. It was recommended to all of Donnie's teachers that they make every effort to make comments and suggestions to Donnie in a private way. This would help avoid Donnie's heightened negative reaction to receiving directions.
5. It was recommended that Donnie's parents continue their careful management of his home assignments.
6. It was also recommended that Donnie meet every other week with the school psychologist to develop strategies to deal effectively with his reactive emotionality.

[STUDENT NOTE] There are a variety of positive outcomes for schools using a pre-referral system (described in detail in Chapter 1). First, the teams typically use little direct funding. Donnie's assessment did not cost the school in terms of direct funding. It did cost in terms of time and energy of school professionals. Often this cost is realized by the principal giving team members release time from their classroom duties. This generates a real cost to the school, but careful management and planning can help minimize this cost. Second, the savings associated with avoiding an unnecessary assessment through the special education system can be substantial. In many ways, this approach is really just a systematic approach to managing existing resources. Third, the interdisciplinary nature of these teams helps bring a variety of perspectives to the issue under discussion. This tends to produce a more comprehensive look at the student's life and more effective recommendations.

Key Terms

TERM	*Page*
68/95/99.7 Rule	299
Achievement test	284
Age-equivalents	302
Alternate form reliability	303
Aptitude test	283
Assessment	270
Behavioral assessment	285
Central tendency	296
Classroom test	271
Confidence interval	302
Construct-related validity	304
Content-related validity	304
Criterion-related validity	304
Cultural bias	276
Deviation IQ	293
Diagnostic assessment	282
Evaluation	270
Formative assessment	281
Frequency distribution	296
Full scale intelligence quotient score	292
Functional behavioral assessment (FBA)	285
General intelligence	288
Grade equivalents	301
High-stakes testing	274
Index scores	292
Intelligence quotient	288
Interstate New Teacher Assessment and Support Consortium (INTASC)	295
Mean	296
Measurement	270
Median	296
Mode	297
Multiple intelligences	289
Normal distribution	300
Norm-based testing	278
Objective scoring	278
Perceptual reasoning index	292
Placement assessment	281
Praxis™	294
Pre-test	281
Processing Speed Index	293
Range	299
Referral question	272
Reliability	302
Split-half reliability	303
Standard deviation	299
Standardization	271
Standardized test	271
Standards-based testing (criterion-based)	278
Stanford-Binet Intelligence Test	287
Subjective scoring	279
Summative assessment	282
Teaching standards	295
Test bias	278
Testing	270
Test-retest reliability	303
Triarchic theory of intelligence	290
Validity	303
Verbal comprehension index	292
Working Memory Index	292

10 Chapter

SPECIAL EDUCATION: STUDENT IDENTIFICATION AND LEARNING NEEDS

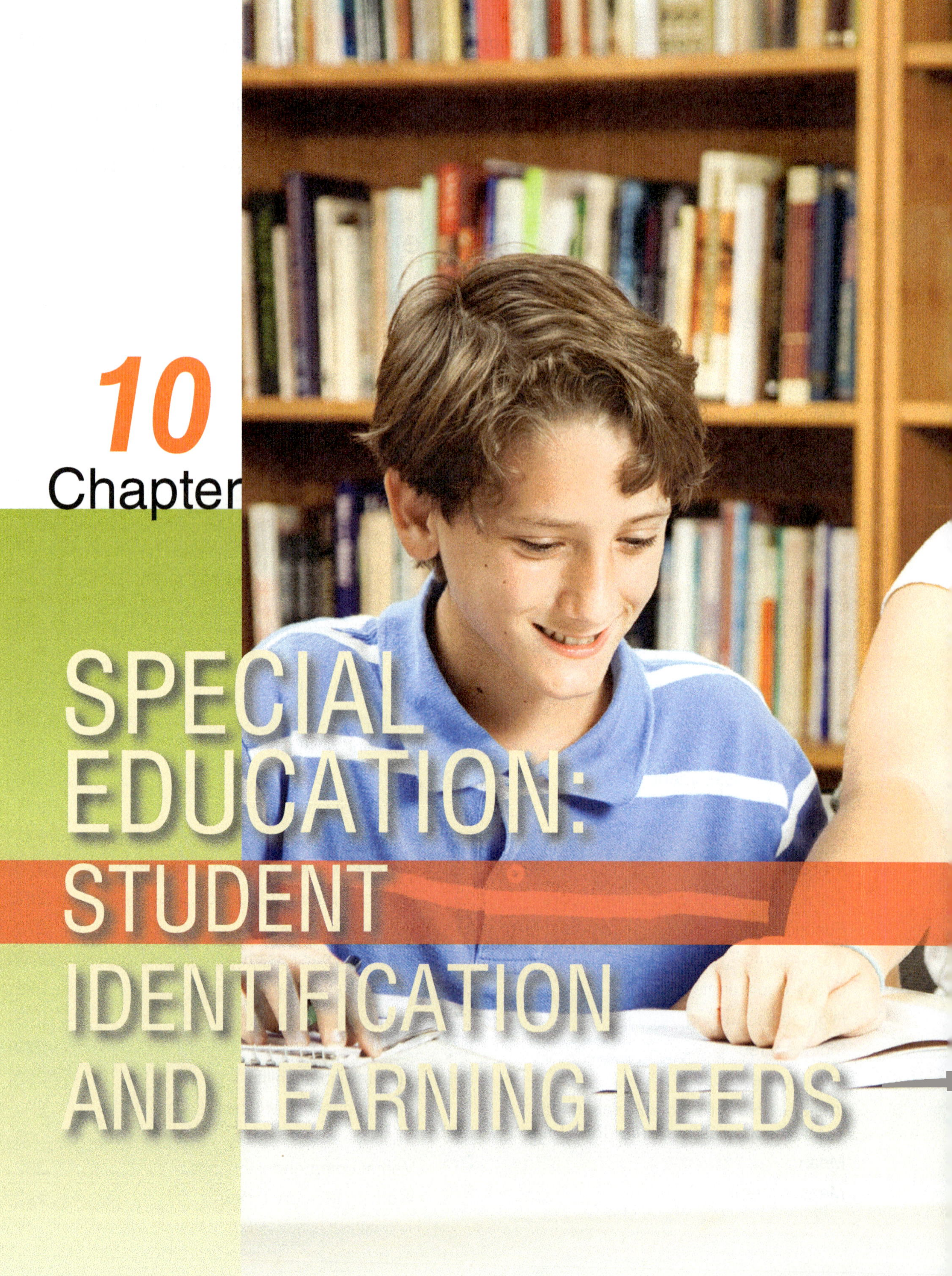

What's It All About ...

Why do we have special education?

How does special education work?

What are special education disability categories?

Chapter Objectives

- Understand the importance of person-first language.
- Understand the benefits and drawbacks to the labeling process.
- Review special education legislation.
- Evaluate the process of inclusion.

- Review the special education process.
- Understand how the special education team is formed.
- Learn how an Individualized Education Plan (IEP) is written.

- Review disability classifications involving cognitive and learning issues.
- Review disability classifications involving social and behavioral issues.
- Review disability classifications involving sensory, physical, and health challenges.
- Understand the unique impact of multiple impairments.

EXTENDED OUTLINE

Special Education: Student Identification and Learning Needs

- I. What's It All About ...
- II. From Today's Headlines
- III. Special Education: Legislation and Practice
  - A. Person-first language
  - B. Labeling
    - 1. Benefits
    - 2. Limitations
  - C. Legislation
  - D. Inclusion
  - E. Summarize and reflect
- IV. Special Education: Collaborative Evaluation and Intervention
  - A. Process overview
  - B. Special education evaluation team
  - C. Individualized Education Program (IEP)
  - D. Summarize and reflect
- V. Special Education Disability Classifications
  - A. Cognitive and academic challenges
    - 1. Specific learning disability
    - 2. Speech or language impairment
    - 3. Mental retardation
  - B. Social and behavioral problems
    - 1. Autism
    - 2. Emotional disturbance
  - C. Sensory, physical, and health challenges
    - 1. Hearing impairment and deafness
    - 2. Visual impairment
    - 3. Deaf-blindness
    - 4. Orthopedic impairment
    - 5. Other health impaired
  - D. Multiple impairments
    - 1. Multiple disabilities
    - 2. Traumatic brain injury
  - E. Summarize and reflect
- VI. The Chapter in Review
- VII. Interdisciplinary Case Focus

From Today's Headlines

Vol. I No. 10 Teaching World, 2012

To Include or Not to Include

Our schools are undergoing significant changes, including how we prepare teachers and the demands we place on our students. In many ways, we are changing the very nature of the student/teacher relationship. One of the most talked about of these changes is the recent trend to include more students with disabilities in the regular education environment.

The inclusion movement changes the way students with disabilities interface with the regular educational system. Historically, students with disabilities were pulled out of the regular classroom in favor of a more specialized educational setting. All that is changing, however, and changing fast.

Today, many believe that our primary responsibility is to keep students with disabilities in the regular educational environment. Some would even contend it is never appropriate to remove a student with disabilities from the same classroom as their nondisabled peers. The idea is that every student has an inherent right to a typical educational experience. It is argued that if the student cannot be brought to needed special services, then the special services can be brought to the student.

However, to what extent do schools include students with disabilities in the regular classroom? The answer is far from simple. Consider the case of nine-year-old Taylor Shine. As reported in an October 9, 2005, article in the *Pittsburgh Post-Gazette*, Taylor is a boy with autism. He is currently attending Cornell Middle School in a regular education environment. Despite special services provided in the classroom and daily attendance by his mother, Taylor still has difficulty with school activities. Taylor's mother has requested that Taylor move to a more specialized school setting; but according to the article, the school reports it is confident that Taylor's needs can be met in the regular education setting. Educators in favor of fully including all students with disabilities see Taylor's case as a success story. Taylor's mother views things differently. Ms. Shine is quoted as seriously questioning the appropriateness of inclusion in her son's case.

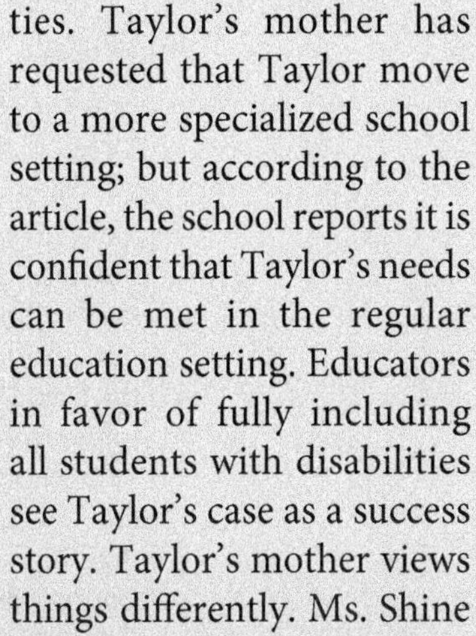

"So many people only hear about inclusion," Ms. Shine said. "But I'm trying to get him into a more restrictive environment. I'm not against inclusion, but in my case, I want him where he can learn and come to his maximum potential. In the situation he's in now, he screams, throws tantrums and injures himself and isn't learning anything."

Ms. Shine's case is not unique, as schools move to address rising pressure to include students in the regular education setting. Courts have become involved, and verdicts generally support greater inclusion of students with disabilities.

(continues)

MAKE THE CONNECTION

A seemingly simple question about the Shine case is, "Who is right?" Is the school system right to want to keep Taylor with his peers? Is his mother right to want to remove Taylor from his regular classroom in an effort to give him a more specialized learning environment? As you can imagine, the answer is far from simple.

The educational system governing Taylor's instruction is the special education system. This is a system established by law in the 1970s. It has changed over time in an effort to keep pace with our understanding of educational best practice. Currently, there is specific language in the law requiring schools to document the need to remove any student with an established disability from their regular classroom. In this chapter we will learn more about the specifics of special education. We will learn what the system is and how it operates. We will also learn about students like Taylor and how they are identified as needing special services. After you finish this chapter, you will have a better understanding of the factors affecting cases like the Shines'.

SPECIAL EDUCATION: LEGISLATION AND PRACTICE

One of our greatest skills is simply to notice differences. Walk into your house at the end of the day, and you easily notice a moved chair or a tilted lampshade. This may not seem remarkable, but consider the hundreds of objects in your home. Having the ability to recognize relatively small differences in such a rich environment is truly amazing. The same is true for our ability to notice differences in people. Ever try to describe someone you just met to a friend? It is doubtful the friend would be able to recognize the person from your description. You, however, are able to recognize the person at the mall among hundreds of other people.

Schools are places where we are constantly using our ability to notice differences. Teachers need to recognize differences in learning potential, social skills, and motivation because of their impact on academic success. The best teachers spend their time developing skills to notice subtle individual differences. Recognizing differences in your students, however, is only half the battle. Once a teacher recognizes differences, it is important to evaluate those differences to establish if a student requires special attention. **Evaluation** requires judgment. It is a reflective process and one that necessarily depends on the available information. Do you help the young man falling behind in math, or do you see this as a normal cycle in academic performance? Do you send the student to a teacher with special training in teaching math, or try to help yourself? Are there possible negative outcomes resulting from intervening? These are all important questions, and the answers have real impact on the lives of students. Essentially, we are discussing two fundamental aspects of the instructional process:

Evaluation

The reflective process of determining the worth or merit of an object, depending on the available information

- In what ways do students perform differently?
- Can we use our knowledge of student differences to educate more appropriately?

In education, we have established formal and informal systems for guiding our perception of *differences*. The most recognized of these is the special education system. As you read this chapter, you will begin to appreciate how special education is simply a system for documenting how a particular student differs and what is needed to provide appropriate education given that difference. It is a system that guides our perceptual process and encourages equality and consistency in how we recognize student differences. In this chapter and the next, we will closely examine how we determine student differences and their impact on educational performance. We will cover the special education system, and we will examine how this system provides a framework for identifying students with different learning needs. We will look at the important process of labeling those differences and the benefits and potential drawbacks. We will also look at the relevant laws governing the special education system. In the next chapter, we will look at special needs not typically served under the special education system.

Person-First Language

Language is a powerful educational tool. In many ways, it is the heart of the teacher/student relationship. As such, it is critical that teachers use language in positive, clear, and socially appropriate ways. When dealing with unique student needs, language use becomes a sensitive issue. Historically, little thought was given to how we refer to individuals who learned, spoke, walked, or behaved differently. It was commonplace to hear teachers talking about their new "mentally retarded student." Today, education has moved away from language that defines a person by a single characteristic. Using the term *mentally retarded child* places the characteristic of mental retardation before the child. Linguistically, this makes mental retardation a powerful descriptor of the person. Using language that makes the person primary and any particular characteristic secondary has the advantage of maintaining the importance of the whole person. Many organizations have adopted this person-first approach, including the American Psychological Association and the Federal Office of Civil Rights. Table 10.1 provides examples of person-first language.

As you can see from the table, modifying language can emphasize the person. Advocates for person-first language remind us that individuals with exceptionalities are, indeed, people first. They are not defined by a disability. They are complicated individuals with many strengths and weakness. Their strengths are just as important to recognize as their weaknesses. Failure to use person-first language focuses more on a single difference, rather than individual strengths. We need to be able to discuss learning differences, but we can use language in ways that preserve a focus on the whole person.

Labeling

Before discussing special education, let's discuss in more detail what it means to be different. Being different is an interesting phenomenon. First, different is really a perception or a judgment. It is not an absolute condition. Actually, we are all *different* or *special*. If we conceptualize differences as positive, differences become an asset or something desirable. All too often, being different is not viewed positively. This is particularly noticeable in our schools. Some differences are social; others are academic or behavioral. So, how does recognition of differences turn into a judgment of being positive or negative? The answer is complicated. Our society values some characteristics and devalues others. This influences our thinking and focuses our perceptions in one direction or another.

Often this process is informal, relying on judgment and perception. Academic performance, however, is different. In schools, we document student progress through assessments. This results in our positive and negative perceptions building on a specific assessment scale. Teachers label certain scores as "passing" and others as "failing." Naturally, students value

Table 10.1 Person-First Language

Person-First Language	Non-Person-First Language
He has a learning disability	The learning disabled child
A student who is blind	A blind student
Students with special needs	Special needs students
Students without disabilities	Normal students

passing grades and hope to avoid failing grades. Similarly, standardized tests scores (discussed in Chapter 9) have acceptable scores and scores judged as atypical.

Interconnections

Standardized testing and application of standard scores is covered in Chapter 9.

Another factor influencing the valuation process is the language we use to *label* the difference. Non-specific labels (e.g., she is acting "weird") are not likely to generate consistent perceptions or judgment. For students, "weird" may mean one thing today and something entirely different another day. It is also a student assigned label, rather than a label from an authority figure. This produces less rigid perceptions. Labels perceived to be medical, psychological, or educational from an authority figure are different. Students often perceive these labels as permanent and negative. Let's consider some of the broader *labels* used in education.

Disability

Usually a reduced capacity to perform in some domain

Handicap

A situational disadvantage

One approach to looking at differences and providing a value judgment is to label something as a **disability**. Disability usually refers to a reduced capacity to perform in some domain. Using this definition, a student has a disability if they experience diminished capacity leading to a limitation. Perhaps the student has a diminished ability to use his/her legs, leading to a limitation in mobility. Disability is often confused with **handicap**. This term is actually quite different. Handicap refers to a situational disadvantage. This means that the person has a disability affecting their performance in that particular situation. For example, having limited mobility is likely to affect your performance in physical education class, but not in an academic class. A movement related disability is a *handicap* in the physical education class only. This is an important distinction. It reminds us that a specific inability does not affect every aspect of a person's life. A disability may always be a part of a person, but it does not limit their performance in all situations. In fact, there are probably many more situations where a person with a disability is not handicapped than situations where that person is.

A movement-related disability may only be a handicap in the physical education class.

In addition to general labels like disability and handicap, there are many labels specific to a student's type of disability. We will get into specifics regarding definitions, identification, and educational programming in the final section of this chapter. First, let's discuss the overall benefits and liabilities of using such labels. As we have been discussing, labeling is a natural outgrowth of our inherent tendency to notice differences. Assigning a label, however, carries consequences. Some of those consequences are positive; others negatively affect the person. Table 10.2 lists some of the benefits and concerns of using labels with students who have special educational needs.

Benefits

As you can see from the table, labeling students provides a number of benefits. Labeling enables students to qualify for needed special education services. We will learn in this chapter that participation in special education requires a student meet certain eligibility criteria. These criteria are grouped around thirteen diagnostic labels. Without qualifying for one of these labels, students are ineligible for services. Labels also help professionals communicate more effectively when programming for students with special needs. When the special educator says to the physical education teacher, "Michele has autism," the teacher has a general sense of Michele's special needs. This is because most professionals are familiar with the criteria that diagnostically label autism. These criteria are not all inclusive, but they do create a general framework for understanding the special needs of an individual. Labels also help parents and professionals access information on students with similar differences because research, treatment, and educational information are often cataloged using diagnostic labels. For example, a parent may have a sense that his/her child's behavior is unusual. If testing reveals mild autistic symptoms, then the parent has a very specific label from which to gather information and support. Not all of the information on autism will be

Table 10.2 Benefits and Concerns of Using Labels with Special Needs Populations

Benefits	Concerns
Labels serve as a means for accessing funding and administering education programs.	Labels can be stigmatizing and may lead to inappropriate and negative stereotyping.
Labels allow professionals to communicate efficiently and in a meaningful fashion.	Labeling has the potential of focusing attention on limitations and what a person cannot do instead of on an individual's capabilities and strengths.
Research efforts frequently focus on specific diagnostic categories or labels.	Labels can sometimes be used as an excuse or reason for delivering ineffective instructions: e.g., "Marvin can't learn his multiplication facts because he is mentally retarded."
Labels establish an individual's eligibility for service.	Labels can contribute to diminished self-concept, lower self-expectations, and poor self-esteem.
Treatments, instructions, and support services are differentially provided based on a label—e.g., sign language for a student who is deaf, or an accelerated or enriched curriculum for pupils who are gifted and talented.	Labels are typically inadequate for instructional purposes; they do not accurately reflect the educational or therapeutic needs of the individual student.
Labels heighten the visibility of the unique needs of persons with disabilities.	Labeling can lead to reduced opportunities for normalized experiences in school and community life.
Advocacy and special groups, such as the Autism Society of America or the National Federation for the Blind, typically have an interest in assisting particular groups of citizens with disabling conditions.	A label can give the impression of permanence; the need for some labels evaporates upon leaving the school environment.

Adapted from Gargiulo, special education in *Contemporary Society*, 2006.

applicable to their child, but the label helps narrow what can seem like an overwhelming amount of information on development. Overall, many believe that the benefits of labeling outweigh the limitations (Macmillian & Meyers, 1979; Mesibov, Adams, & Klinger, 1997).

Limitations

Despite these benefits, labeling has some unwanted effects (Lauchlan & Boyle, 2007). We hope that peers will handle the knowledge that a student has a particular diagnostic label with respect; however, it is often used as a source of ridicule. Labeling can also inappropriately focus a teacher's attention on a student's difficulty rather than strengths. For example, research with learning disabilities has shown that it can lead to problems with self-concept and self-esteem (Durrant, Cunningham, & Voelker, 1990; Jodrell, 2010), negative perceptions by teachers and peers (Gresham & MacMillan, 1997), and difficulties with social interactions (Sabornie, 1994). It should be noted that not all research on labeling indicate negative outcomes. Some research has actually found an increase in self-esteem of students with learning disabilities following diagnosis (Heyman, 1990; MacMaster, Donovan, & MacIntyre, 2002). Teachers need to evaluate research for its applicability to a particular situation.

At times, it can seem like a label is a prescription for treatment. If a student has a learning disability, then the teacher provides a particular educational program. Although this is true in a general sense, such one-to-one correspondence between diagnosis and educational programming is rarely seen. As we have repeatedly underscored in this text, students are individuals—their learning needs are specific and unique. This makes it difficult to develop uniform educational prescriptions for a given need. The label, however, does help the teacher get a general picture of the student's difficulties. A final point to consider is that labels convey a sense of permanence. Sometimes this is true, but not always. Special education is a system of support, and this support is provided as long as it is needed. For many, the hope is that the extra support is temporary and will help students transition back into the regular education curriculum. Although many share this hope, the reality is often different. For example, in 2002 the

Department of Education looked at special education students fourteen years of age and older to determine whether they continued with services. They found that only 3.5% returned to the regular education classroom. Findings such as this lead some to propose other service delivery models that make it less likely students will enter and remain in special education (Gallagher, 2006; Deno, 1970; Simonsen et al., 2010).

Legislation

Teachers are involved in one of the most important service professions. They carry the primary responsibility for the academic development of our children. They also play a significant role in the development of our children's behavior, social skills, and even their value system and morality. Teachers also play an important civic and societal role as they bring to reality our national commitment to educate all children. The educational role and the public role that teachers play constantly evolve with changes in our society. Changes to special education have been particularly visible in recent history, as our country makes relatively rapid and far-reaching changes to the education of children with special needs. Court decisions and legislative acts have mandated schools make sweeping reforms in how they educate students with exceptional learning needs (Yell & Drasgow, 2010). A comprehensive coverage of court decisions is beyond the scope of this book, but there are key pieces of legislation teachers should know. These laws affect all teachers as they progress through their professional careers. It is, therefore, critical that teachers understand the basic protections provided by these laws and how they affect education. In this chapter, we will focus on special education law. In the next chapter, we will examine laws governing students outside special education.

To ensure that adequate services reach every student in need, a critical piece of legislation was passed in 1975. The **Education for All Handicapped Children Act** (Public Law 94–142) provided for "free and appropriate" educational services for all children with handicaps. This law formally established special education and a new era in how schools addressed unique educational needs. Specifically, the law provided students with special needs specific educational rights, including the following:

Education for All Handicapped Children Act (Public Law 94–142)

Law that provides "free and appropriate" educational services for all children with handicaps

- First, it provided needed funding for schools providing services to students with disabilities. Special education service delivery is costly, and a national funding source was needed to support local school efforts.
- Second, the law specified that each specific needs student must have an Individualized Education Program (IEP). This is a formal document detailing the nature of the special education services for each child. The process of writing an IEP is reviewed in the next section.
- Third, special education services must be provided in the least restrictive environment (LRE). This means students need to receive appropriate services, but these services need to interfere as little as possible with the typical educational experience of the child.
- Additionally, the law provided specific rights to parents of students with disabilities. The process for determining need for services and basic procedures for service delivery are clearly specified in the law. In addition, the law necessitates that parents participate in a meaningful way in the educational process.

The Education for All Handicapped Children Act provided a foundation for special education services. It has also undergone several revisions as the law adapts to changing societal needs and is now referred to as the Individuals with Disabilities Education Act (IDEA). The most recent change actually modified the name slightly, renaming the law the Individuals with Disabilities Education Improvement Act (IDEIA). Although the acronym IDEIA is technically the most accurate and current, most articles and researchers still use the term IDEA. In general, in this text we will continue to use IDEA to refer to all the legislative revisions through 2004. Table 10.3 details the changes to the original legislation. As you can see from the table, there have been substantial changes to the law governing special education. In general, efforts have been made to increase the availability of services. Services are now provided to preschool

Table 10.3 Changes to the Education for All Handicapped Children Act of 1975

YEAR	NAME OF THE LAW	PRIMARY CHANGES
1986	PL99–457 Amendments to the Education for all Handicapped Children Act	This revision primarily extended the availability of special education services to children aged three to five inclusive. The original legislation provided funding for preschool programs, but it was voluntary. The 1986 revision made it mandatory.
1990	PL101–476 (IDEA) amendments to the Education for all Handicap Children Act—was renamed to Individuals with Disabilities Education Act (IDEA)	The 1990 revision involved many changes. One of the most noticeable was the change in name. This was made to more accurately reflect the terminology used in schools. Other changes included specific mandates for transition planning for students after they graduate, specific categories for autism and traumatic brain injury, and provisions that make it possible for families to sue schools in federal courts for IEP violations.
1997	PL105–17 amendments to IDEA	This was a comprehensive revision of IDEA. There were numerous changes including the following: • Disciplinary guidelines for students with disabilities • Inclusion of regular educators on the IEP team • Availability of mediation services to resolve disputes • Students ages three to nine can now be classified as "developmentally delayed" rather than a specific category. • Greater flexibility in the tools used to assess the need for special education services • New formulation for allocating funding based on census data • Performance goals were required for students receiving special education services.
2004	PL108–446 Individuals with Disabilities Education Improvement Act (IDEIA) and reauthorization of IDEA	Revisions in IDEA include changes to align the law with the No Child Left Behind Act (2001). Other changes include the following: • How schools establish parental consent for evaluation • Time line for completing evaluations • Evaluation of suspected learning disabilities • Use of functional behavioral assessments when dealing with misbehavior

students. They are also provided to children with autism and traumatic brain injury as separate disability categories. There has also been numerous procedural improvements which insure parental involvement, integration with regular education, family rights, comprehensive and sensitive identification, and equitable funding distribution. These changes attempt to address known issues with special education and also to meet changing perspectives on students with disabilities. One of the most significant changes affecting education is the push toward greater inclusion of students with disabilities in the general classroom.

Inclusion

Inclusion is the practice of grouping children for education based on traditional factors like age and location of the student's home. According to Inclusion practices, students *are not excluded* from their typical classroom placement for reasons like disability status, learning ability, behavior, health, or social ability. As a student reading this text, you may be having difficulty writing down a definition for inclusion or find this confusing. You are not alone. Inclusion has emerged as one of the most debated educational issues of the twenty-first century. It is heralded as a moral imperative by some (Association for Persons with Severe Handicaps—TASH), and considered educationally misguided by others. Even the definition of inclusion is hotly debated. Most definitions incorporate the idea that students with special needs are *included* in the general classroom. That is, they are not excluded from participating in instruction in their

Inclusion

The practice of grouping children for education based on traditional factors like age and location of the student's home

home school setting. **Home school** is usually defined as the school they would attend if they did not have a disability. For example, let's say a school district wanted to include a fourteen-year-old student with mental retardation. They would first determine her home school. This would be the same school that she would normally attend based on the location of her parent's home and the local school zoning. She would attend the same school and the same classroom as her fourteen-year-old neighbor who was not diagnosed with mental retardation. The next question is whether she stays in that classroom all day or only part of the day. This is another controversial topic within the world of inclusion.

Home school

Usually defined as the school that a student would attend if he/she did not have a disability

When implementing inclusion, the question is often how much do we include students with disabilities? **Full inclusion** is when *all* students are maintained in their home school classroom setting *all* the time. Sometimes, however, students with special needs receive services using other approaches. **Pull-out services** provide educational services outside the regular classroom. A specially trained teacher, often in another specifically dedicated classroom, provides services. The number of hours a day a student is pulled-out of the regular classroom will vary. This means the degree to which the student is *included* will also vary.

Full inclusion

Educational practice where ALL students are maintained in their home school classroom setting ALL the time

Pull-out services

Educational services that are provided outside the regular classroom

It is important to realize that not all students receiving special education services are included in the regular classroom. Some students receive *all* their educational services in specialized classrooms within the regular school. Others receive all their services in separate specialized educational schools. These varying approaches to providing special education services represent a continuum of service. Figure 10.1 graphically depicts the inclusion continuum.

As you can see from the figure, full inclusion represents a limited part of the inclusion spectrum. Some, however, view full inclusion as the most appropriate way of meeting the legislatively mandated least restrictive environment (LRE) discussed earlier (Bennett, DeLuca, & Burns, 1997; Fox & Ysseldyke, 1997). Still, most schools consider many options when making decisions about how to educate in the least restrictive environment. Often a combination of

Figure 10.1

Inclusion Continuum

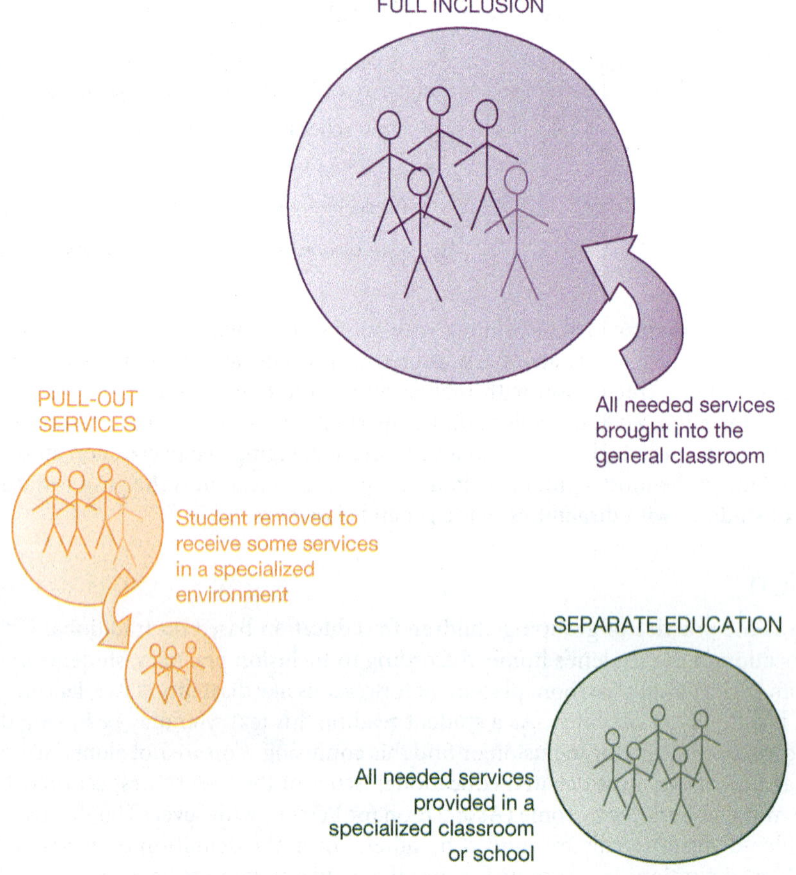

Interconnections

See the chapter opening feature ***From Today's Headlines*** for an example of issues with service delivery.

service delivery options is viewed as the most appropriate educational approach. (See this chapter's opening feature, *From Today's Headlines,* for a real-life example of this issue.) For example, a student has specific remedial needs after a brain related injury. It is not possible for the school to recreate the rehabilitation facilities in the regular education classroom. The student needs the rehabilitation, but also needs an appropriate education. In this case, balancing the appropriate education mandate and the LRE mandate may necessitate the student spending some of their day at a rehabilitation facility—particularly if the rehabilitation requires extensive hours and continues for an extended period. Helping a child with a disability may require a very specialized environment, an environment that cannot be effectively or practically recreated in the regular classroom and still maintain instructional effectiveness for all students. At this point, there is no clear resolution to the debate over full inclusion. The courts tend to favor an inclusion practice over self-contained classrooms for student with disabilities (Osborne & DiMattia, 1994), but not necessarily full inclusion.

SUMMARIZE AND REFLECT

1. Special education is essentially a system for guiding our perception of differences. It is also a system responsible for guiding how we change educational programming based on observed differences.
2. A natural outcome of the system is that we use labels to help organize and deliver services. Labeling has both positive and negative effects on students, and we outlined several of these issues. We also reviewed how our laws governing special education further support the use of labels.
3. Special education began in the 1970s with the passing of new education legislation. Laws that govern special education have changed over the years, changing the nature of the system.
4. Inclusion is becoming an increasingly prominent feature of special education, changing the way educators think about placement decisions.

INFORMED APPLICATION

1. Placement in the special education system is fundamentally based on a perception that a student has unique learning needs that cannot be met in the regular education system. Consider how it might be possible to have two students with the same learning problem, but only one is determined to qualify for special education services.
2. Examine your thoughts on providing educational labels. As a teacher, what are some ways you can maximize the positive aspects of labeling and minimize the drawbacks?

SPECIAL EDUCATION: COLLABORATIVE EVALUATION AND INTERVENTION

Qualifying a student for special education services is a comprehensive process. *Before* assessment even begins, students go through a variety of less formal interventions to determine if a referral for special education services is warranted. This process is called **pre-referral**. Pre-referral interventions are efforts to address specialized student needs without formal participation in special education. For example, after a collaborative meeting of teachers and parents, a student with attention problems may receive classroom accommodations for testing. The student's primary problem is with needing extended time on tests, and the modification results in successful test performance. Making such accommodations maximizes existing classroom supports and minimizes unwarranted referrals for special education evaluation. Such pre-referral efforts are described in detail in Chapter 1.

Pre-referral interventions

Efforts to address specialized student needs without formal participation in special education

Interconnections

The pre-referral process is introduced in Chapter 1.

If difficulties are not appropriately addressed using pre-referral techniques, then a referral for a special education evaluation may be necessary. This section provides an overview of the procedure used to determine eligibility for special education services. We will cover the time line for completing a special education evaluation. We will also cover the formation and composition of the team conducting the evaluation. Finally, we will look at the document generated by the evaluation team. This document is called the Individualized Education Program (IEP) and provides a road map for the implementation of services. We will begin with an overview of the process and the mandated time line.

Process Overview

There are several steps students go through when referred for possible inclusion in the special education program. To some extent, the nature of these steps depends on the age of the child, the nature of the disability, and the state in which they live. There are, however, steps that are common in most referrals. Figure 10.2 provides a graphical depiction of these steps. In addition to this typical chain of events, the IDEA (2004) legislation specifically mandates a maximum of sixty days from the time parents sign the informed consent form until the completion of the evaluation. The sixty-day maximum is superseded if the state has established an alternative time line. For example, some states start the sixty-day process from the time the student is referred for evaluation. Since referral precedes signing the informed consent, these states actually have less time to complete the evaluation.

Two critical elements in this evaluation process are the formation of the evaluation team and the generation of the Individualized Education Program (IEP). The evaluation team is actually charged with the development of the IEP, so its composition and collaborative effectiveness are important. We will first look at how the team is formed and then review relevant factors influencing its success.

Figure 10.2

Common Steps in a Referral

Special Education Evaluation Team

The team assembled to review a student's eligibility for special education services is known by different names. Since federal law gives individual states considerable flexibility when implementing services, states have developed unique team models. Some qualities of these teams, however, are mandated by law and consistent across states. The mandated composition of the team is listed in Figure 10.3.

The special education team builds on the strengths of the interdisciplinary model. According to this model, team members work in highly collaborative ways to achieve a desired outcome. When meeting special educational needs, the team consists of professionals and family as dictated by the learning needs of the student. The idea is to build on the expertise of each team member to create a uniquely tailored educational experience. As you have seen throughout this text, interdisciplinary teams have several advantages. They are often an efficient use of resources and individual training strengths and help professionals feel connected and engaged in their professional duties. In addition, they create an environment where team members can learn from other professionals. They are also excellent tools for generating novel and creative solutions to complex issues. Each team member brings a unique perception of the student's needs given their background and experience. This is particularly true for the student's parent or guardian who plays a significant and meaningful role on the team. Parents are in a position

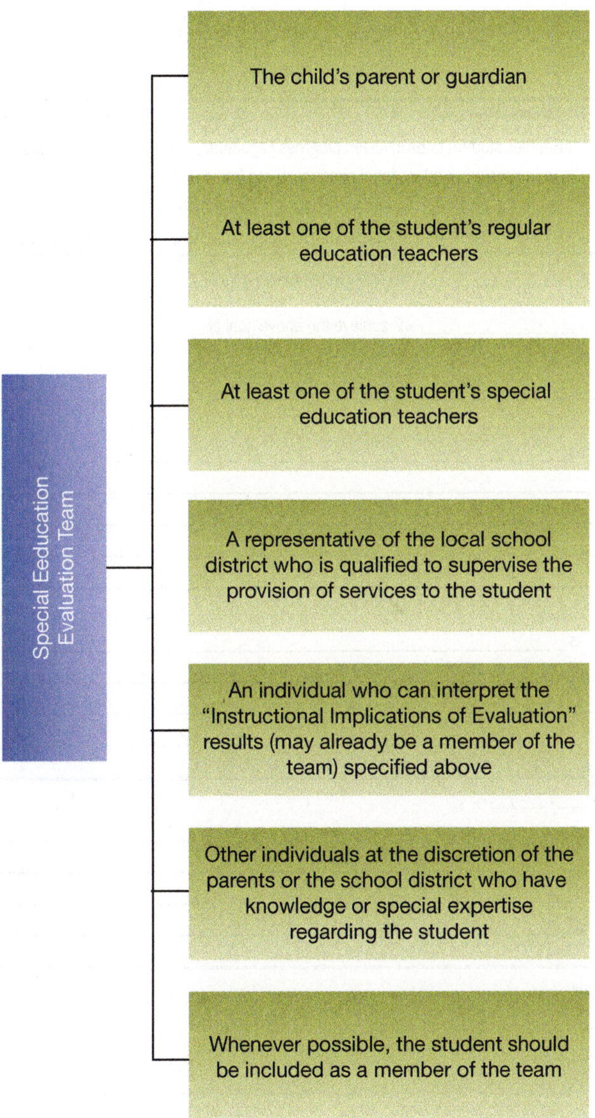

Figure 10.3
Evaluation Team Composition

to help the team understand evaluation results in terms of the student's day-to-day functioning. This is also true of the students themselves when their age and level of maturity allows them to fully participate in the team evaluation process. Probably one of the most important points to remember about the evaluation process is that the group shares decisions. It is a collaborative decision process; the effectiveness and accuracy of the outcome depends on the level of participation of the team members (Zigmond, Kloo, & Lemons, 2011).

Individualized Education Program (IEP)

Individualized Education Program (IEP)

A legal document specifying how the school is going to meet its obligation to provide Free and Appropriate Public Education (FAPE) to a student with special needs

The special education evaluation team is responsible for determining eligibility for services. They are also charged with developing an intervention plan if services are needed. The plan for implementing services is detailed in a document called the **Individualized Education Program (IEP)**. The IEP is a legal document specifying how the school is going to meet its obligation to provide free and appropriate public education (FAPE) to a student with special needs (see Figure 10.4). The specific format of the document depends on individual state regulations and even particular school preferences. Some are generated with the help of specialized computer software. Others are written by hand on state forms. Regardless of the specific format used, federal law specifies certain components that must be present in the IEP. These components are listed in Table 10.4.

Figure 10.4

Individualized Education Program (IEP)

ANNUAL GOALS AND BENCHMARKS Page ____ of ____

Name ______________________ IEP Date ____/____/____

Area of Need Baseline	Measurable Annual Goal #_____ ☐ Enables student to be involved/progress in general curriculum/state standard ______________ ☐ Addresses other educational needs resulting from the disability ☐ Linguistically appropriate ☐ Transition Goal: ☐ Education/Training ☐ Employment ☐ Independent Living Person(s) Responsible ______________________

Benchmark 1 Within _______ _______, will achieve the above goal at _________

Benchmark 2 Within _______ _______, will achieve the above goal at _________

Benchmark 3 Within _______ _______, will achieve the above goal at _________

Progress Report 1 ___/___/___
Summary of Progress ______________________
Comments ______________________

Progress Report 2 ___/___/___
Summary of Progress ______________________
Comments ______________________

Progress Report 3 ___/___/___
Summary of Progress ______________________
Comments ______________________

Goal: Annual Review
Date ___/___/___
Goal Met ☐ Yes ☐ No
Comments ______________________

Table 10.4 Mandatory Components of an Individualized Education Program (IEP)

COMPONENT	DESCRIPTION
1	A statement of the student's present level of educational performance
2	Documentation of consideration of general and special factors
3	A statement of measurable annual goals
4	A statement of special education and related services and supplementary aids and services to be provided to the student
5	A statement of the program's modifications or supports for school personnel that will be provided for the student
6	An explanation of the extent to which the student will not participate with non-disabled children in regular school activities
7	A statement of any individual modifications in the administration of statewide or district wide assessment of student achievement
8	The projected date for initiation, anticipated frequency, location, and duration of the services and modifications
9	A statement about transition services needed to focus the student's courses of study beginning the year the student turns fourteen
10	A statement about transition services needed by the student beginning at age sixteen including needed interagency responsibility and linkages
11	A statement (to be included at least one year before the student reaches the age of majority , e.g., eighteen) informing the student of his/her rights that will transfer when he/she reach the age of majority
12	A statement of how progress toward annual goals will be measured and how parents will be notified regarding progress

As you can see from the table, an IEP is a complex document. The depth of information is designed to address three primary objectives. First, the information documents the student's current level of functioning. The second objective of the IEP is to establish goals and objectives to guide the student toward a successful educational experience. The team is responsible for determining appropriate and reasonable goals sensitive to the student's unique circumstances. Finally, the team is responsible for determining what services and supports will help the child reach the documented educational goals. Again, the uniqueness of each student's needs necessitates creative solutions. Every student presents an individual profile of strengths and weakness and will need an individualized combination of supports to achieve educational and personal success.

SUMMARIZE AND REFLECT

1. Students must qualify for special education services by meeting guidelines for disability categories.
2. Federal legislation governs special education, specifically the Individuals with Disabilities Education Act (IDEA) that mandates the formation of an interdisciplinary team to govern the evaluation process.
3. The effectiveness of the interdisciplinary team is impacted by the team's ability to engage in effective collaboration.
4. The Individualized Education Program (IEP) is a required component of the special education process and governs how services translate into appropriate educational goals.

(continues)

INFORMED APPLICATION

1. What are some different situations that might lead to a special education referral?
2. What aspects of a student's learning problems would lead to a different composition of the special education evaluation team?

SPECIAL EDUCATION DISABILITY CLASSIFICATIONS

Educational programming varies for each disability category.

As discussed earlier, the Individuals with Disabilities Education Act (IDEA) defines thirteen disability categories. These categories provide the basis for tracking and managing the special education system. They also help coordinate services to students. This section will introduce you to each disability category. We will review the federal eligibility criteria and, where relevant, medical or psychological diagnostic criteria. We will then look at educational programming for each disability category. We will cover educational accommodations, as well as curricular modifications. **Accommodations** maintain existing educational procedures but make allowances for special needs (i.e., extra time on tests, preferential seating). **Modifications** are changes in the typical educational process (i.e., use of different tests, curricular changes, changes to classroom environment).

Special education disability categories will be reviewed according to four areas of concern: cognitive and academic difficulties; social and behavioral problems; sensory, physical, and health challenges; and multiple impairments. We will learn how we define each disability, the tools we use to assess student need, and important educational programming options. As you read and learn about these disabilities, keep in mind that effective educational programming and intervention considers the whole student, not just their primary difficulty or category label. It is unrealistic to develop educational supports without a full understanding of the student and that student's unique life circumstances.

Cognitive and Academic Challenges

There are several disability categories related to cognitive functioning and academic learning. Some students have difficulty with learning in a particular subject area. Others have more generalized problems. Still others have developmental delays in their ability to think and reason. This section will look at how we define, identify, and teach these students. (See Table 10.5 for a description of specific learning disabilities.)

Accommodation

Service that maintains existing educational procedures for students, while making allowances for special needs

Modification

Change in the typical educational process

Table 10.5 Description of Specific Learning Disability Under IDEA

Under IDEA, **specific learning disability** means a disorder in one or more of the basic psychological processes involved in understanding or in using language, spoken or written, that may manifest itself in an imperfect ability to listen, think, speak, read, write, spell, or to do mathematical calculations. The term includes such conditions as perceptual disabilities, brain injury, minimal brain dysfunction, dyslexia, and developmental aphasia. The term does not include learning problems that are primarily the result of visual, hearing, or motor disabilities; of mental retardation; of emotional disturbance; or of environmental, cultural, or economic disadvantage.

SOURCE: National Dissemination Center for Children with Disabilities (NICHCY), 2005.

Specific Learning Disability

What are learning disabilities? Students classified as learning disabled constitute the largest special education population. Records published by the Department of Education indicate that about half (49.9%) of all student receiving special education services are served under this category.

Since the late 1970s, the number of students identified as having a learning disability has risen 260%. Some attribute this increase to continued vagueness in the diagnostic criteria for the disability (Hallahan, Lloyd, Kauffman, Weiss, & Martinez, 2005). Others assert that the increase is due to better diagnostic tools, greater public awareness of these disabilities, and greater acceptance (Lerner, 2003). Let's first look at how we define this rapidly expanding disability category.

The federal definition of learning disability indicates it can affect multiple domain areas, including traditional academic areas such as reading, writing, and mathematics. It can also affect other areas, such as listening, thinking, speaking, or spelling. As you can see, the definition is quite broad, covering many different academic skills.

Part of the reason for such a broad definition is that there is still considerable debate over how learning disabilities should be defined. In 1990, Hammill documented eleven "official" definitions from widely recognized associations. Attempting to capture the essential elements of such definitions has proven difficult. Ultimately, each field or discipline—including medicine, psychology, science, and education—develops a definition in keeping with its own perspective. Gargiulo (2006) summarizes the basic elements in common with definitions of learning disabilities (see Table 10.6).

How do we identify learning disabilities? The process of determining eligibility for special education services begins with a thorough evaluation. Documenting learning potential and learning achievement are common components of an assessment for learning disabilities. **Learning potential** is intended to be a measure of a student's general ability to learn. This is distinguished from actual achievement. **Learning achievement** is a measure of what a student has achieved in academic work. The idea is that if a student has an adequate level of learning potential, but is not achieving academically, then the student has a specific learning issue in that area (Kavale, Fuchs, & Scruggs, 1994; Fuchs, Fuchs, Mathes, & Lipsey, 2000). Learning potential is typically assessed using an individualized intelligence test, and learning achievement is measured using a standardized achievement test (see Chapter 9). Practically, the student only needs to be assessed in the academic area under consideration; however, the entire test battery is typically administered. This helps strengthen the evidence that the learning problem is indeed specific. For example, if a student scores in the average range on an IQ test, average on a test of reading, sub-average on a test of math, and average on a test of writing, it is clearer that the learning challenge is limited to the area of mathematics.

Interconnections

Chapter 9 examined the role of intelligence and achievement testing in assessment.

Learning potential

The measure of a student's general ability to learn

Learning achievement

The measure of what a student has achieved through academic work

Table 10.6 Common Components of Definitions of Learning Disabilities

1	Intellectual functioning within the normal range
2	Significant gap or discrepancy between a student's assumed potential and the student's actual achievement
3	Inference that learning disabilities are not primarily caused by other disabilities or extrinsic factors
4	Difficulty in learning in one or more academic areas
5	Presumption of central nervous system dysfunction

Although standardized intellectual and achievement tests are commonly used in the assessment of learning disabilities, they are not without critics. Some believe that such tests are far too limited to yield a true picture of the student's abilities. An alternative approach to standardized testing is to use **authentic assessments,** which use assessment procedures resembling the actual work the student completes at school, home, or in daily life work. An example of an authentic test gaining attention is the **portfolio**. Portfolios are a collection of work sample and products used to determine student progress (Taylor, 1997). Portfolios provide a real-life approach to assessment, meaningfully derived from the student's actual work. The problem leveled against using portfolios for assessment purposes is that they are often difficult to objectively grade and interpret. Prior to collecting student work, users of the portfolio system have to determine how they are going to assess progress. Grading such a diverse array of work is often difficult given the variety of materials. It is also challenging to maintain objectivity. At present, it is unclear if portfolios will become a regular part of a learning disability assessment protocol. Few school systems use portfolios for eligibility decisions at this point.

Authentic assessment

Assessment that resembles the actual work the student completes at school, home, or in daily life work

Portfolio

A collection of work samples and products used to determine student progress

Some assessment approaches attempt to combine the qualities of the standardized test and the authentic testing process. **Curriculum-based assessment (CBA)** assesses student progress using a standard assessment tool, but the test is derived from actual schoolwork detailed in the school's curriculum. This helps ensure the test is directly related to what the students are doing in the classroom. It is "standardized" in the sense that it is an actual test that the students take in a systematic fashion. Unlike traditional standardized tests, however, the focus is on comparing the student's own performance over time (not to the performance of other students). This enables the teachers to chart progress and devise appropriate interventions.

Curriculum-based assessment (CBA)

Measurement of student progress using a standard assessment tool, with the test being derived from actual schoolwork detailed in the school's curriculum

One of the newest identification approaches for learning disabilities is **Response to Intervention (RTI)**. RTI is a multistep process to provide quality instruction to students with learning difficulties and to determine the need for special education services (Wixson, 2011). RTI is not a model for learning disability identification; rather it is a process for adapting instruction based on the unique needs of the student. The process typically begins with some form of formal or informal assessments that reveals a student is at-risk for developing a learning issue. The teacher then designs an intervention appropriate for the student's struggles. Depending on the student's response to the intervention, the teacher may need to adapt instruction, providing a more intensive intervention. Finally, if the difficulty persists, then educators from different disciplines typically convene an intervention team to determine the degree of supports necessary for success and whether the student would benefit from inclusion in the special education program. This approach maintains a positive focus and concentrates efforts on developing intervention strategies, depending on how the student responds to increasingly intense intervention efforts.

Response to Intervention (RTI)

A multistep process to provide quality instruction to students with learning difficulties and to determine need for special education services

How do we teach students with learning disabilities? Students with learning disabilities are educated primarily in the regular classroom (45.3%) or a resource room (37.8%). It is important to note, however, that the growth of the number of students served in the regular classroom is a recent trend. Due to the inclusion movement discussed earlier, more students with exceptional learning needs are receiving instruction in the regular classroom. The type of instruction these students receive in this environment varies. The nature of the domain (reading, math, listening, etc.) of disability combined with personal as well as institutional factors will determine the type of educational programming.

Regardless of the type of learning disability, one general educational approach to learning issues is **cognitive training**. This is a term used to describe educational approaches focused on the modification of a student's thought processes. Instructional efforts concentrate on changing the student's thinking about the material in order to produce changes in academic performance. Teachers use this approach in a variety of formal and informal ways. If teachers help a student reflect on thinking that resulted at an incorrect answer, they are encouraging the student to develop an awareness of his/her cognitions. This relates to the idea of **metacognition,** or thinking about our thought processes, discussed in Chapter 5. Using this approach, the teacher can help the student recognize errors in thinking and develop effective solutions for modifying thoughts regarding the subject matter. For example, the teacher may help the

Cognitive training

Term used to describe educational approaches that attempt to modify a student's thought processes

Metacognition

Broadly defined as thinking about one's own thought processes

Interconnections

The concept of metacognition and its importance in the educational process is covered in Chapter 5.

student approach a social studies test by taking information on the U.S. Civil War and helping the student connect it to modern-day events. The student learns to recognize similarities and differences between historical information and events in the news today. Perhaps the teacher compares the U.S. Civil War to the 1991 Chechnya declaration of independence from Russia in order to help the student appreciate common themes in the sociopolitical development of nations. This approach differs from typical approaches to learning material involving memorization of facts. The greater depth of understanding required to make such comparisons encourages a deeper level of understanding. Teachers further enhance this process by letting students come up with their own comparisons. Having students create their own comparisons is an excellent technique to maintain student engagement.

Direct Instruction (DI) is often used to teach the basic phonetic decoding skills involved in reading.

Another approach frequently used when teaching students with learning disabilities is **Direct Instruction (DI)**. This is a systematic approach for teaching a defined academic skill. For example, DI is often used to teach the basic phonetic and decoding skills involved in reading (Stockard, 2010). The philosophy is that students will learn more efficiently when instruction is clear and consistent. Under Direct Instruction, a learning task is divided into clearly defined steps. Each step is then taught until the student reaches mastery. Other steps then build upon preceding steps. Learning is detailed and specific and students are taught under a controlled and prescribed situation. Table 10.7 provides six basic steps for providing DI (Gersten & Keating, 1987). During a DI lesson, the teacher is not free to respond in spontaneous and creative ways but instead has a set script of responses to encourage a specific type of learning. DI models help students develop specific skills and a solid foundation. The rigid implementation procedures, however, do not allow teachers to create novel responses to the unique ongoing needs of the student.

Direct Instruction (DI)
A systematic approach for teaching a defined academic skill

Speech or Language Impairment

What are speech and language impairments? Most animals use some form of language to communicate with each other, but humans have taken language development to extraordinary levels. What is also remarkable is that for the vast majority of the population, this ability develops with relative ease. For some individuals, however, the process is marked by unique challenges. IDEA defines speech or language impairment as a disorder of either the mechanics of speech or the actual use of language to communicate (see Table 10.8).

There are three primary disorders of speech: phonological disorder, fluency disorder, and voicing problems. **Phonological disorders** are characterized by articulation errors during speech production. Perhaps the student omits certain consonant sounds, or substitutes one speech sound for another, or even distorts certain speech sounds. For example, a student who says "I wike ice cream," is substituting the *w* sound for the *l* sound. Often this begins in the developmental period

Phonological disorder
Disorder characterized by articulation errors occurring during speech production

Table 10.7 Six Key Components of Direct Instruction

1	An explicitly step-by-step strategy
2	Development of mastery at each step in the process
3	Strategy (or process) corrections for student errors
4	Gradual fading from teacher-directed activities toward independent work
5	Use of adequate, systematic practice with range of examples
6	Cumulative review of newly learned concepts

Table 10.8 Description of Speech or Language Impairment under IDEA

Under IDEA, **speech** or **language impairment** means a communication disorder such as stuttering, impaired articulation, language impairment, or a voice impairment that adversely affects a child's educational performance.

SOURCE: National Dissemination Center for Children with Disabilities (NICHCY), 2005.

Fluency disorder

More commonly referred to as stuttering

Voice disorders

An abnormality of one or more of the three characteristics of voice: pitch, intensity (loudness), and quality, but often unrecognized as a speech problem

Language disorder

Problems associated with understanding and expressing language

Expressive language disorder

A disorder where the individual has difficulty using language to express intent or meaning

Mixed receptive-expressive language disorder

Characterized by difficulties understanding the language of others, as well as difficulties with language expression

because the child has difficulty making certain speech sounds. **Fluency disorders** are more commonly referred to as stuttering. The nature of a fluency problem, however, often goes beyond popular perceptions of stuttering. Students may repeat initial consonant sounds like *wh*, but may also repeat sounds in the middle of the word or even whole words. Fluency disorders also cover problems with a student's pace of speech. Some students speak in a rapid-fire way that makes their speech unintelligible. This is called clustering and may be related to poor speech planning. **Voicing disorders** are often unrecognized as a speech problem. They are characterized by unusual vocal qualities like excessive hoarseness, pitch, loudness, etc. This can make it difficult to understand the child. It can also cause social difficulties if peers perceive the abnormality as odd or atypical. It may even cause damage to the vocal apparatus if left untreated.

Language disorders refer to problems associated with understanding and expressing language (Grela, Collisson, & Arthur, 2011). We often divide language disorders into two broad categories. **Expressive language disorder** is a disorder where the individual has difficulty using language to express intent or meaning. Individuals having trouble with language expression may have trouble producing sentences of age appropriate length or complexity. They may have a limited vocabulary and make frequent tense errors. The other broad classification for language disorders is **mixed receptive-expressive language disorder.** This disorder is characterized by difficulties understanding the language of others, as well as difficulties with language expression. The child may experience difficulty understanding directions, following lectures, understanding the intent of others, as well as the expressive language difficulties discussed above. Typically, we do not diagnose pure receptive language disorders since disorders in language reception are likely to involve an expressive component. For example, if a student has difficulty understanding verbal directions provided by the teacher, his difficulty is likely to be evidenced in his communication following the instructions.

How do we identify speech and language impairments? A speech and language evaluation is likely to vary depending on the referral question. Questions regarding the student's ability to communicate effectively usually result in an assessment of both expressive and receptive language ability. Often students are too young at the time of referral to produce a significant amount of verbal language. There are tests designed for this situation that stress prelinguistic skill. These tests often consist of direct observation and parental interview. They document communication attempts and compare them to other children of the same age.

Like most suspected disabilities, children suspected of having language or speech problems often receive an initial screening. If a screening shows that the child is having significant trouble, a referral is made to a speech/language pathologist who is specially trained to conduct a thorough language evaluation. An interdisciplinary special education team described earlier in this chapter then determines eligibility for special education services and program planning

How do we teach students with speech and language impairments? Interestingly, the vast majority of students with speech and language difficulties (87.4%) receive services in the regular education classroom (Department of Education, 2002). This is very different from most other special education categories and is an excellent example of effective inclusion. Much of the success of including speech and language assistance is due to the nature of the interventions. Many of the intervention techniques used with these students involve changes to the linguistic style of the teacher. Speech language pathologists often work closely with classroom teachers to modify how they verbally interact with students. Teachers are encouraged to use simple and brief instructions. They are also instructed to make generous use of visual aids, gestures, and other non-verbal cues. Teachers should avoid repeating instructions; rather, they should rephrase directions using simplified language. They should also recognize when students become tired. Students are likely to have greater problems with language and communication when fatigued.

Speech problems often require some one-on-one therapy. Therapy sessions may be on a pull-out basis, but reinforcement of the skills is needed in the classroom and home environments. Therapy sessions focus on helping the child understand the nature of their difficulty and techniques to resolve the issue. Therapists show students how to manipulate tongue movements, airflow, and mouth position to correctly make sounds. Similarly, therapy for voicing problems helps students use their voices in appropriate and safe ways. Treatment for fluency problems is often more complex. What may begin as a mild fluency irregularity may quickly become complicated by the defensive behaviors and ineffective coping strategies used by the individual. The social and educational ramifications of the problem further complicate treatment. In general, students benefit from early interventions and intensive treatments (Prins, 1970).

Mental Retardation

What is mental retardation? The nature of intellectual limitations and the public perception of individuals who experience these difficulties have a long and problematic history. Even today, the general population is still dealing with what it means to have mental retardation. (See Table 10.9 for a description of mental retardation under IDEA.) What can someone do who is intellectually limited? Can they hold a job? Are *all* individuals with mental retardation like our neighbor's child? Answers to these questions are important. They are important to the individuals wrestling with the experience of having mental retardation—and also for society as our world deals with how to integrate these individuals into our lives, homes, schools, and work place. Let's first begin our look at mental retardation with its definition.

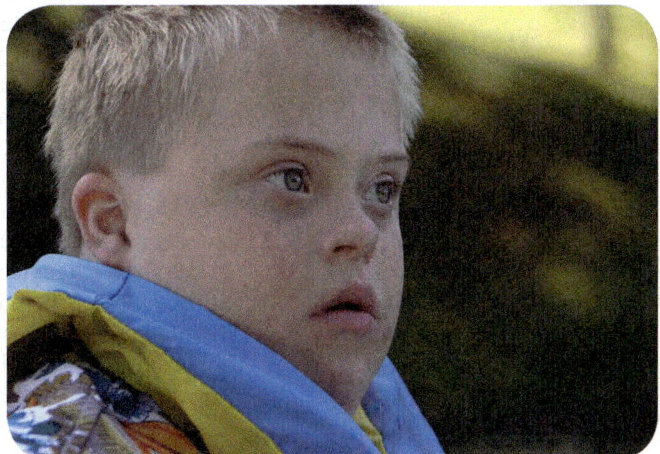

Mental retardation is defined as documented intellectual limitations, impaired adaptive functioning, and that the impairment is apparent in the individual's developmental period.

Unlike other special education classifications, there is a consistent approach used to define mental retardation. *First,* intellectual limitations need to be documented. These limitations are considered significant for someone their age. The exact word used to describe these significant intellectual impairments varies. Some use the term *subaverage* (as in the federal definition) others use the term *limited* or the phrase *below normal.* All of these refer to the same concept. The *second* characteristic of mental retardation involves impaired adaptive functioning. **Adaptive functions** refer to how the individual adapts to the world in which they live. Can they dress and feed themselves? Can they get around the neighborhood? It encompasses conceptual, social, and practical skills people need to meet the demands of everyday life (Luckasson et al., 2002). The rationale for including adaptive measurements is that if individuals have significant intellectual impairments, there should be some manifestation of this limitation in their daily life. The *third* part of the definition for mental retardation is that the impairment is apparent or is manifested during the developmental period. This qualification is intended to distinguish intellectual limitations present in the natural course of the individual's development from limitations acquired through trauma. Often individuals involved in head injuries have substantial intellectual impairments, but these impairments are

Adaptive functions
How the individual adapts to the world in which they live

Table 10.9 Description of Mental Retardation under IDEA

Under IDEA, **Mental Retardation** means significantly subaverage general intellectual functioning, existing concurrently [at the same time] with deficits in adaptive behavior and manifested during the developmental period, which adversely affects a child's educational performance.

SOURCE: National Dissemination Center for Children with Disabilities (NICHCY), 2005.

unique and require a different treatment approach. Intellectual impairments stemming from injury are addressed under a different special education category discussed later in the chapter. It should also be noted that a diagnosis of mental retardation is frequently diagnosed in conjunction with other disabilities. For example, children with autism or Down's syndrome often have a concurrent diagnosis of mental retardation. This, however, is not *always* the case. Some students with autism actually have high intellectual functioning.

How do we identify students with mental retardation? Almost all assessment protocols for mental retardation use an individually administered IQ test. IQ tests were discussed in detail in Chapter 9. The generally accepted medical diagnostic manual, *the Diagnostic and Statistical Manual of Mental Disorders-IV,* indicates that an IQ of about 70 or below is required for a diagnosis of mental retardation. Assessment for adaptive behavior is usually completed by interview with the child's parent or guardian. Survey instruments have many questions related to daily living, and the parent is asked if the child is capable of completing each skill. The results are scored using a standard scoring system similar to an IQ test. A similar standard of about 70 or below is used for diagnostic purposes. The third part of the diagnostic definition for mental retardation is also established by interview. Parents are asked about the point when the child's exceptionality was recognized. Again, limitations need to be documented during the student's developmental period.

Interconnections

Interpretation of intelligence scores is covered in Chapter 9.

F.A.Q.

Dana Johnson—"I'm confused. You mean if you have an IQ in the retarded range, you still might not be diagnosed as *'mentally retarded?'*"

Professor Stortz—"First, we don't refer to the lower end of the IQ range as *'retarded.'* It can be viewed as being insensitive. The range of lower IQ scores is more appropriately referred to as *'intellectually limited.'* The answer to your question, however, is YES. A low IQ is only one of three criteria you must meet to qualify for a Mental Retardation diagnosis."

How do we teach students with mental retardation? Students with mental retardation are frequently educated in separate educational environments. Only 14% of these students receive their education in the regular classroom. When deciding on appropriate instruction, educators need to keep in mind the extremely wide range of abilities possessed by individuals diagnosed with mental retardation. Some of these individuals lead a relatively independent life, with intermittent supports. On the other end of the continuum are students who need full-time, constant supervision and support. With such a wide range of ability, it becomes extremely important to create educational programming on an individual basis.

The range of educational services for students with mental retardation includes academic skills, self-help and domestic skills, social skills, and transitional programming. The specific child dictates the depth of programming in each area. Individuals with milder impairments may spend most of their academic day engaged in traditional academic work. This is supplemented with instruction in the other areas as needed. Students with more significant impairment may receive less academic work and the work they receive may be directly related to a particular life function, like cooking or buying something at the store. Students with the most significant impairments may spend little time on academic subjects, but educators need to be careful when making such decisions. Often students are capable of more than initially thought with appropriate supports. It is also important to realize most students can make improvements in their overall life function with appropriate supports. For some students, this may mean improvements in a socially appropriate smile or facial gesture. For others, this may include accurately balancing their checkbook. Keeping an open mind and maintaining a curricular plan based on careful assessments is the best approach to helping students with mental retardation achieve their potential.

F.A.Q.

Michael Wyatt—"The other criteria are low adaptive skills and it has to show up early—right? Why are these extra things necessary?"

Professor Stortz—"Good question, Mike. The adaptive skill criteria are to make sure that low intellectual skills has a functional impact on the student's everyday life. If lower intellectual skills do not affect the student's life, then we are likely dealing with a different issue. Similarly, if you have typical intellectual and adaptive functioning through childhood and then develop issues later on, it is likely we are dealing with a medical problem or perhaps a traumatic injury."

Social and Behavioral Problems

Social development is one of the most striking and observable ways students change over time. Students learn to take turns, play games, work in groups, and relate to each other in increasingly complex ways. Not all students, however, develop the necessary social skills to effectively participate in educational programs. Similarly, some students have behavioral or emotional issues preventing them from achieving educational success. This section will look at special education disability categories related to social and behavioral problems.

Autism

What is autism? **Autistic disorder** is characterized by impairments in social relatedness and communication, as well as issues with repetitive (or stereotyped) behaviors. Table 10.10 presents the Federal description (IDEA) of this disability. As you can see from the description, children with autism have multiple issues, which potentially impair their ability to benefit from regular instruction.

Autistic disorder
Characterized by impairments in social relatedness and communication, as well as issues with repetitive (or stereotyped) behaviors

Impairment in communication ability means students are likely to have difficulty expressing ideas verbally. They are also likely to have difficulty understanding or processing the language of someone else. Non-verbal communication may also be impaired. These students may not appreciate common gestures and body language. Their own non-verbal expressions may not accurately reflect their intent. This difficulty with communication translates into a general problem relating to others. Individuals with autism have difficulty interacting in social situations. With some individuals, this may be so serious that the individual appears to ignore the outside world. Also evident in their behavior is repetitive or stereotyped behaviors. These behaviors are repeated over and over in the same way (e.g., hand flapping, rocking, biting, etc.). The term *stereotyped* highlights the consistent nature of these repeated behaviors.

Autism occurs in approximately 1 to 1.5 million people in the U.S. (Autism Society of America, 2003). Autism is also four times more common in boys than girls. The exact cause of the disorder remains elusive. Some researchers have linked it to neurobiological abnormalities or damage (Volkmar & E. J. Nelson, 1990; Volkmar & Pauls, 2003; Trottier, Srivastava, & Walker, 1999; Volkmar, 2011) or learned behaviors (LaVigna, 1985; Lovaas, 1993).

Despite the difficulties understanding the cause of autism, the reality of the educational difficulties is abundantly clear. The problems of autistic individuals with social relatedness are completely opposed to the teacher/student educational model used in most classrooms. Imagine the difficulty teaching a student who barely reacts to your presence, let alone your instructional efforts. Even in milder forms of the disorder where the student clearly interacts with others, the quality of the interaction often leads to negative reactions from peers and frustration. Similarly, communication is a foundation for effective education. Producing lesson plans for students with autism that minimize direct communication and maximize experiential learning are difficult to develop. Children with autism can often communicate, but it is situationally dependent and inconsistent in quality. This also places unusual demands on the creative ability of the teacher to work with such limitations. From the perspective of the other students, the repetitive and stereotypical nature of autistic behavior is a source of confusion and often frustration.

How do we identify students with autism? In addition to the primary characteristics described above, evaluations for autism often include intellectual assessments. Approximately 50 to 70% of individuals with autism have intellectual limitations (Freeman, 2000). Some individuals with autism, however, have normal to above-normal intellectual ability, underscoring the importance of a thorough assessment. Like their non-disabled peers, IQ score is a good predictor of later academic success (Rutter, 1980).

Table 10.10 Description of Autism Under IDEA

Under IDEA, **Autism** means a developmental disability significantly affecting verbal and nonverbal communication and social interaction, generally evident before age three that adversely affects educational performance. Characteristics often associated with autism are engaging in repetitive activities and stereotyped movements, resistance to changes in daily routines or the environment, and unusual responses to sensory experiences. The term *autism* does not apply if the child's educational performance is adversely affected primarily because the child has emotional disturbance as defined under emotional disturbance disability classification.

SOURCE: National Dissemination Center for Children with Disabilities (NICHCY), 2005.

Other assessment instruments used in the diagnosis of autism include behavior-rating scales. Popular scales include the Childhood Autism Rating Scale, CARS (Schopler, Reichler, & Renner, 1986); the Autism Behavior Checklist, ABC (Krug, Arick, & Almond, 1980); and the Gilliam Autism Rating Scale, GARS (Gilliam, 1995). These instruments specifically address the diagnostic criteria for the disorder, providing documentation of the child's relevant behavioral limitations.

Other frequently used tests are the Autism Diagnostic Observation Scale, ADOS (Lord et al., 1989) and the Autism Diagnostic Interview/Revised, ADI-R (Lord, Rutter, & LeCouteur, 1994). These two instruments provide information from direct interactions with the child and parent. Like most instruments in this area, information is specifically gathered along the diagnostic criteria for autism. One last type of assessment to consider is the **functional assessment**. This approach to testing assesses whether the child has the necessary skills to perform in a certain area (i.e., living independently at home or in a sheltered setting). The Psychoeducational Profile–Revised, PEP-R (Shopler, Reichler, Bashford, Lansing, & Marcus, 1990) is a typical instrument in this area. This test provides relevant diagnostic information regarding a student's social functioning, language capabilities, and stereotypical behaviors; however, it can also provide information on skill acquisition that translate into curricular goals.

Functional assessment

Comprehensive set of assessment procedures used to determine the function that problematic behaviors serve in the life of the student

How do we teach students with autism? Children with autism are educated in a wide variety of settings. Figure 10.5 provides information on the settings where children with autism are educated. Almost half of children with autism are educated in a separate classroom in the regular school setting. About a quarter of these students are educated in the regular classroom. Other lesser-used settings are a separate school, a resource room, a residential facility, or a hospital/homebound environment.

The educational setting used with any given student with autism is influenced by the severity of the symptoms and also by the values embraced by the school system. Some school districts have a strong commitment to maintaining students in the regular classroom. In these school districts, it is more likely that even students with significant impairments will receive education within the regular classroom with appropriate supports.

There are several instructional systems available to teach students with autism. Many of these systems lack sufficient research support to warrant use in schools systems. Most schools choose to address the fundamental symptoms of the disorder, rather than adopt a comprehensive intervention system. That is, approaches focus on increasing communication, social skills, and decreasing repetitive and stereotypical behaviors (Grey & Garand, 1993). There are many communication alternatives used to help students with autism. Technology provides excellent options for alternative communication approaches. Computers can be programmed to accept different input modalities (e.g., movements, keystrokes, etc.), which are then translated in to speech. Similarly, communication cards can be used. These are cards the child uses by pointing to a picture which express his/her needs. Figure 10.6 is a communication card for toileting. Cards can be adapted to meet the specific needs of the student and the situation. These options are helpful for students who have difficulty with oral speech.

Figure 10.5

Settings Where Children with Autism Are Educated

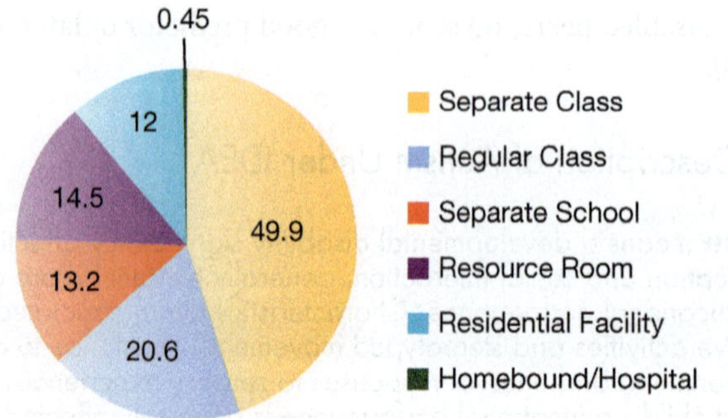

SOURCE: U.S. Department of Education, Twenty-Fourth Annual Report to Congress on the Implementation of the Individuals with Disabilities Education Act, 2002.

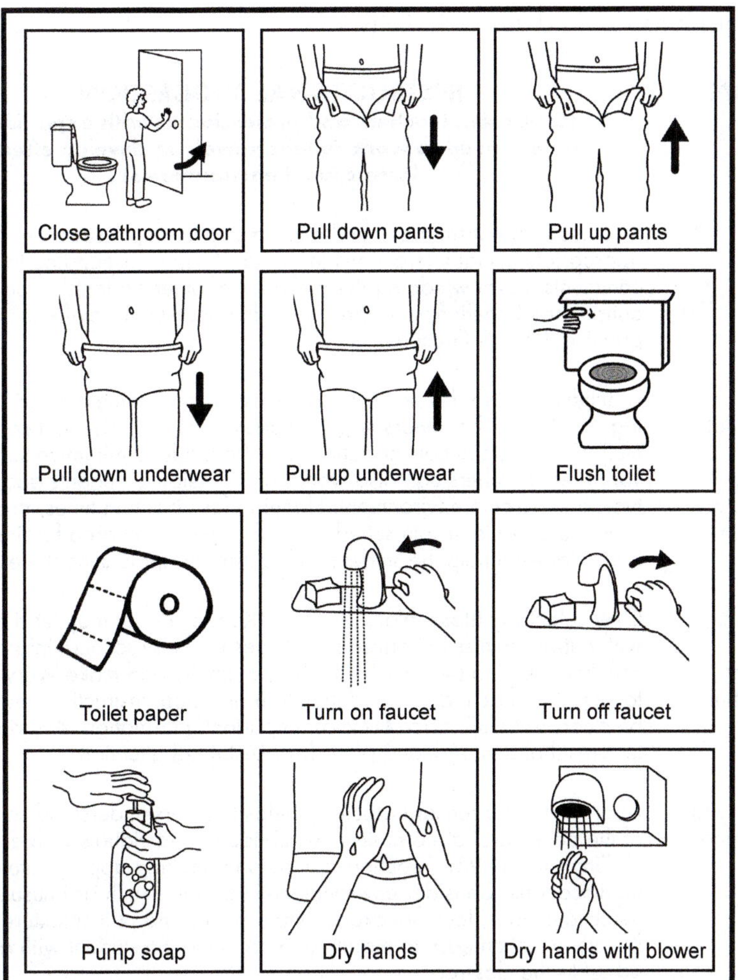

Figure 10.6
Communication Card for Toileting

Source: Published with permission of www.Do2Learn.com.

Social skills are challenging to remediate. The specific skills needed to interact effectively with others are complicated. Educational efforts to help children with autism develop better interaction skills often break down a typical social situation and reinforce each separate skill. With consistent feedback and multiple opportunities to practice a given skill, these children can often develop a successful skill set, enabling them to interact more effectively.

The student with autism can present a challenge to teachers. Classroom teachers typically work in close collaboration with other professionals experienced in the field. Table 10.11 provides a summary of some of the issues involved in educating students with autism. It is important to remember that education is a collaborative effort. Many educational professionals and family members share the education of students with autism. Together, this educational team can provide the student with a supportive instructional experience.

Emotional Disturbance

What are emotional disturbances? Emotional disturbance is a broad special education classification covering many problems. It includes things like aggressive acting out, conduct problems, anxiety, and depression. It is difficult to generally define students who receive special education assistance under this category because their problems manifest in different ways. Table 10.12 provides the definition for classification purposes. You will notice that the amount of language devoted to defining this category is more extensive than for many of the other special education definitions. The complexity of the definition is a product of the complexity of the issues served under this category.

Table 10.11 Instructional Suggestions for Students with Autism

AREA	DESCRIPTION	INSTRUCTIONAL SUGGESTION (Classroom teachers and professionals with expertise in autism need to work collaboratively to develop effective instructional environments)
Social Interactions	Difficulty with establishing social relationships	Students with autism may need explicit step-by-step instructions in appropriate social interactions (e.g., turn taking, responding to comments, acknowledging the presence of other students). Students with autism may benefit from appropriate demonstration, reinforcement and practice (Elliot & Gresham, 1991).
Atypical Behaviors	Student may demonstrate unusual behaviors such as hand flapping, rocking, spinning, or preoccupation with one specific interest.	Teachers need to develop an awareness of environmental variables that trigger atypical behaviors (e.g., schedule changes, physical contact, etc.). Classroom accommodations can be made to minimize such variables. Teachers can also work toward helping students adapt to the typical classroom environment. Planning for transition times, providing a predictable classroom schedule, and a relaxation area for times of frustration—all help the student with autism adapt to school life.
Attention	Student may be overly selective when attending to environmental stimuli.	Over selectivity (Rosenblatt, Bloom, & Koegel,1995) may lead the student with autism to miss important social cues and instructional information. Teachers need to be sensitive to this possibility and make every effort to help the student direct and maintain attention. Instruction needs to be clear and emphasize the most important information. Avoid lengthy lectures that demand long periods of sustained attention.
Sensory Reactivity	Excessive sensitivity to light, touch, or sound	Appreciation of sensory reactivity helps teachers understand some of the behavioral abnormalities exhibited by individuals with autism (Gillingham, 1995). Teachers can help by making appropriate classroom modifications. Consider environmental variables such as unusual reflections, fans, loud speakers, temperature, and object texture. These factors are often easy to modify and can help the student with autism adjust to the classroom.
Communication	Impairment of expressive and receptive language skills	Most students with autism will need some structured assistance to achieve effective communication skills (Koegel & Koegel, 1995). General suggestions for improving communication skills include: use social stories to demonstrate appropriate communication, teach new vocabulary, reinforce any communication attempts with appropriate reinforcers, teach listening skills, and use structured play settings to demonstrate communication.

Adapted from *Teaching Students with Autism: A Guide for Educators*, Saskatchewan Education, Special Education Unit, 1999.

To operationalize the federal definition, practitioners often use a dimensional approach to identifying educationally relevant problems (Coleman & Webber, 2002; Wicks-Nelson & Israel, 2003). This approach defines four important dimensions to consider when determining whether a problem warrants special assistance. The four dimensions include the frequency or rate of the behavior, the intensity of the behavior, the behavior's duration, and the expression of the behavior relative to other children of the same age. This approach examines if the frequency, intensity, and duration of the behavior is unusual for the child's age. For example, let's say we have a student displaying aggressive behavior. Using the four dimensions approach, we would look to see if the behavior was more frequent than in other children. We would also want to know if the expression of the aggression was more intense than usual. Finally, does the aggressiveness last longer than we would expect for a child of this age. Following this approach helps to contextualize the behavior according to what is typical for children.

When defining an emotional disturbance, it is equally important to clarify what is *not* considered a part of this disability category. The federal definition specifically mentions that a

Table 10.12 Description of Emotional Disturbance Under IDEA

Under IDEA, **Emotional Disturbance means** a condition exhibiting one or more of the following characteristics over a long period of time and to a marked degree that adversely affects a child's educational performance:

(a) An inability to learn that cannot be explained by intellectual, sensory, or health factors

(b) An inability to build or maintain satisfactory interpersonal relationships with peers and teachers

(c) Inappropriate types of behavior or feelings under normal circumstances

(d) A general pervasive mood of unhappiness or depression

(e) A tendency to develop physical symptoms or fears associated with personal or school problems

The term includes schizophrenia. The term does not apply to children who are socially maladjusted, unless it is determined that they have an emotional disturbance.

SOURCE: National Dissemination Center for Children with Disabilities (NICHCY), 2005.

social maladjustment is not covered under this category. What constitutes social maladjustment is debated but Raiser and Van Nagel (1980) provided an often-cited definition:

> [Students who are socially maladjusted] are those whose social, not emotional, behaviors inhibit meaningful normative growth and development. Specifically, they disregard or defy authority, refuse to meet minimal standards of conduct required in regular schools relating to society's normative expectations ... They are chronic social offenders.

Distinguishing between social maladjustment and emotional disturbance is difficult. Many researches contend that making this distinction is not only difficult, but also unfounded (Cullinan, 2002; Stein & Merrell, 1992). Students with social maladjustments are still difficult to manage in the classroom. Their problems often interfere with their academic performance and require special attention. Some researches argue that the exclusionary clause in the federal definition too narrowly focuses services, leaving many children without needed help (Duncan, Forness, & Hartsough, 1995).

How do we identify an emotional disturbance? The U.S. Department of Education reports that 8.2% of students in special education are receiving services under this category. This amounts to 473,663 students (U.S. Department of Education, 2002) and makes it the fourth largest special education category. Identification of students requiring services under the emotional disturbance classification is difficult. The broad range of issues covered by the definition makes it hard to establish a proven identification process. Some approaches are, however, more common than other approaches.

Functional Behavioral Assessment is one such approach. In fact, federal law mandates it in certain circumstances. This type of assessment is covered in detail in Chapter 9. In general, this approach starts with the position that behaviors are supported by their consequences. That is, they do not occur unless something is gained or rewarded. The goal of the assessment is to determine what consequences are supporting the behavior. It is also important to examine elements in the child's environment prior to the behavior in question to see what is "setting the stage" for the occurrence of the behavior. Based on this information, a plan is made to modify the expression of the behavior. Results are systematically recorded and analyzed for success.

Other assessment approaches emphasize different aspects of the diagnostic process. For example, the **person-centered planning** approach stresses the importance of developing a long-term plan for the student prior to any changes in educational programming (Gage & Falvey, 1995). Treatment then follows the "vision" for the student. **Strength-based assessment** emphasizes the importance of using a student's strengths during intervention (Epstein, Rudolf, &

Functional Behavioral Assessment (FBA)

An evaluation to determine the cause of a student's behavior

Person-centered planning

The approach that stresses the importance of developing a long-term plan for the student prior to any changes in educational programming

Strength-based assessment

An assessment that emphasizes the importance of using a student's strengths during intervention

Epstein, 2000). All too often, treatment focuses on a student's deficits and fails to document and effectively use an area of strength to support a deficit.

Positive behavioral support

An approach that is designed to apply behavioral supports in a proactive way to help prevent behavior problems

Life space intervention

An approach that is an insight based approach designed to give students a better perspective on how they function in the world

Conflict resolution

A set of approaches that attempt to improve social interactions through successful mediation of conflict

How do we teach students with emotional disturbances? There are a variety of teaching approaches schools can use to help children served under the emotional disturbance IDEA category. Each program takes a different approach to intervention, but there are some common themes. Many programs aim to help students achieve some insight into their problems, while trying to give them necessary skills to make changes. They focus on self-control, self-esteem, social skills, and academic achievement. Career planning should also be a part of the educational plan for secondary education students.

Behavior modification is probably the most used program for the treatment of children with emotional disturbances. Like the functional behavior assessment discussed previously, it is based on the principles of behaviorism. Students working under a behavior modification program learn in highly structured environments. Teachers provide consistent and well-planned feedback for everything from behavior to academics. The approach is time-consuming and often requires professional assistance. Given this level of support, smaller self-contained classrooms and separate schools may benefit more from this approach; however, successful behavioral interventions are possible in the regular classroom with appropriate supports and planning. Some schools are also taking a proactive approach, attempting to encourage appropriate behavior before problems surface. The **positive behavioral support** approach is designed to apply behavioral supports in a proactive way to help prevent behavior problems. The approach also provides behavioral supports, contextualized in a positive way, to stop problem behaviors from escalating (Sugai et al., 1999).

Emotional disturbances can include aggressive acting out, conduct problems, anxiety, and depression.

Even with a good behavioral program in place, many educators are turning to additional systems to help provide students with an awareness of their behavior. The **Life Space Intervention** approach is an insight based approach designed to give students a better perspective on how they function in the world. The approach promotes building positive relationships, resolving crises effectively, and fostering responsible behavior. Another approach focuses more exclusively on resolving conflicts. **Conflict resolution** actually refers to a group of approaches that attempt to improve social interactions through successful mediation of conflict. Conflicts often produce negative behaviors such as fighting, insulting, and threatening. They also produce passive behaviors such as ignoring the conflict or person, giving in, and refusing to listen. Conflict resolution provides a system to avoid these potentially ineffectual behaviors, increasing the potential for positive social interactions. Table 10.13 provides a summary of the basic steps in successful conflict resolutions.

Time management

Techniques that help students structure daily tasks, manage study time to produce maximal results, and transition effectively between tasks

In addition to direct assistance with socially related conflicts, teachers can institute environmental modifications to decrease the likelihood of behavior problems. Often students get into trouble because of frustration with schoolwork. For example, helping students better manage their time can lead to more productive and effective work, which in turn supports feelings of success rather than frustration. **Time management** involves helping student's structure daily tasks, manage study time to produce maximal results, and transition effectively between tasks. Students often have little awareness of how they spend their day. Time management skills help to create awareness of how they spend their time and how to modify their current schedule to be more academically successful. This eases stress and frustration and helps students avoid acting-out behaviors.

Table 10.13 Four Steps Involved in Conflict Resolution

1	Individuals agree to follow basic ground rules, such as no name-calling or interrupting.
2	Each person gets a chance to tell his or her side of the story. A mediator is often used to help the individual accurately convey their meaning and to help the other person understand the meaning of the message.
3	Next, the participants develop possible solutions to the problem.
4	Finally, a solution is agreed upon. It is important that the solution is specific and viewed as possible by all parties.

Teachers can also help avoid behavior problems by paying careful attention to the arrangement of the classroom and how close the students are to each other. Research shows that students are much more likely to exhibit problematic behavior the further they are from the teacher (Weinstein, 1979; Gunter, Shores, Jack, Rasmussen, & Flowers, 1995). Teachers can increase their proximity to students who have emotional and behavioral difficulties. They can also create the perception of closeness by asking frequent questions and interacting briefly with students. Teachers should also ensure the classroom is free of overly congested areas and that procedures for using classroom facilities are clear.

Sensory, Physical, and Health Challenges

Human beings are highly complex organisms. Hundreds of biological systems work together to give us our ability to think, move, see, hear, and interact with the world. These systems, however, do not always function appropriately, presenting the individual with unique challenges. This section will look at sensory, physical and health challenges. We will review how such challenges are identified and what educators can do to provide an appropriate educational environment.

Hearing Impairment

What are hearing impairments? Hearing is one of our most prominent senses. All through the day, we use our hearing ability to mediate almost all of our activities. Despite this reliance on hearing, individuals with hearing loss are able to lead full and independent lives with appropriate supports and accommodations. Hearing impairments as a special education category actually encompass many different levels of impairment. Some students have mild hearing loss with minimal impact on their educational lives. Others students have significant losses and require sophisticated supports.

One of the first problems encountered when learning about hearing is what terminology is appropriate. The term hearing impairment is the preferred term for special education purposes, but it is rejected by many experiencing hearing abnormalities. Some believe framing their life circumstance in terms of *impairment* is negative. For the purposes of this section, we will use terminology consistent with IDEA, while acknowledging the difficulty in discussing this area in a sensitive manner. Another definitional issue with hearing impairments concerns the word *deaf*. We will cover the special education definition in the next section, but typically individuals classified as *deaf* are unable to process linguistic information through hearing (Kuder, 2003). This is different for the type of hearing impairments covered under the hearing impairment disability classification.

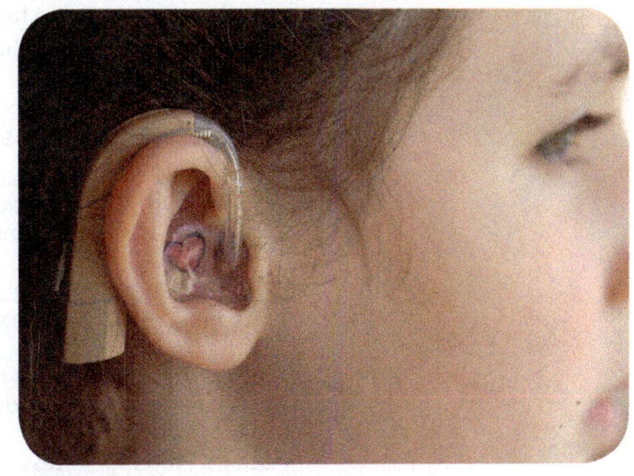

Table 10.14 presents the IDEA definition for hearing loss. The definition is broad, including any hearing problem having a negative impact on a child's educational performance. The issue may be permanent or may vary over time.

Table 10.14 Description of Hearing Impairment Under IDEA

Under IDEA, **Hearing Impairment** means impairment in hearing, whether permanent or fluctuating, that adversely affects a child's educational performance but is not included under the definition of "deafness."

SOURCE: National Dissemination Center for Children with Disabilities (NICHCY), 2005.

How do we identify a hearing impairment? Hearing problems are classified according to the nature of the hearing impairment. Table 10.15 describes the most commonly diagnosed hearing problems. An audiologist uses a variety of instruments to identify the exact nature of the hearing loss. Correct identification of the problem is crucial to providing appropriate supports. Students who are candidates for amplification devices will need a different support structure from students with profound hearing loss. An air-conduction audiometry test can indicate a conductive hearing loss, but it needs to be compared to a test looking at possible nerve impairment. A bone conduction audiometry tests the nerve functioning of the ear. Deficits on an air-conduction test *only* indicate a conduction hearing loss, meaning amplification supports are likely. Deficits in *both* air-conduction and bone conduction tests provide evidence of a sensorineural hearing loss. In these cases, amplification may or may not be used, which means greater reliance on other educational modifications. Understanding the nature of the hearing loss is important when designing an effective educational intervention. Most students with hearing impairments will receive a combination of supports and modifications to address their needs. Let's look at some possible supports for students with hearing impairments.

A bone conduction audiometry tests the nerve functioning of the ear.

How do we teach students with hearing impairments? There are approximately twenty-eight million people with some degree of hearing impairment. Providing appropriate education for such a large population is challenging. Some students will receive necessary accommodations and classroom modifications in their home school. Other students may attend separate educational facilities for students with hearing impairments. In both situations, students are likely to use a combination of educational supports designed to provide them with an appropriate educational environment.

Accommodations for students with hearing impairments vary depending on the nature and severity of the disorder (Zand & Pierce, 2011). Notetaking assistance is a common accommodation. Students with hearing impairments may not be able to take consistent notes because they rely more on vision for incoming information. They will miss new information if they look down to take notes and they will also miss notes if they continue to look up at the teacher or

Table 10.15 Types of Hearing Loss

Conductive Hearing Loss	It's a problem with the mechanical function of the ear. It often responds to amplification devices.
Sensorineural Hearing Loss	It's a problem with the nerves carrying auditory information. Hearing loss is usually permanent (Bess & Humes, 2003)
Mixed Hearing Loss	It's a combination of conductive and sensorineural hearing loss. Conductive aspect of the loss may respond to amplification.
Central Hearing Loss	Less common type of hearing problem involving the brain's processing of auditory information from the ear.

translator. Technology is providing some new options for these students. Computers are making real-time captioning a possibility. These devices provide a visual display of the teacher's comments in writing, much like closed-captioning on television. The technology makes use of sophisticated voice recognition software. Voice recognition also makes it possible for a student to walk out of a class with a complete transcript of everything said in the class. These systems are not always a 100% accurate, but they provide an informational foundation for students. Teachers also need to make frequent use of visual media including overhead transparencies, video projection, and computer presentations. In addition, teachers need to remember that students with hearing impairments make constant use of visual information and, therefore, need unobstructed visual access to the teacher or other educational materials.

Amplification can help some students with certain hearing loss. As mentioned earlier, amplification benefits students with air-conduction hearing loss. Amplification devices sometimes take the form of a hearing aid worn by the student. They may also consist of a direct radio link between a device worn by the teacher and the student. The teacher wears a transmitter, and the student wears the receiver. This approach is advantageous because only the teacher's voice is amplified, not the entire classroom environment. Translators are another common accommodation for students fluent in manual forms of communication (i.e., sign-language). Students that are not hearing impaired often enjoy having a translator in the class. At first, the translators signing may be distracting, but students quickly accommodate to the presence of the translator and the exposure to another mode of communication.

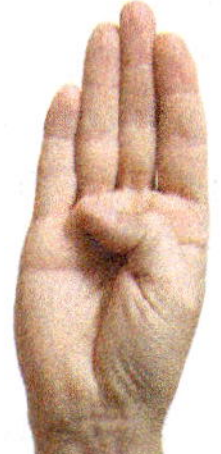

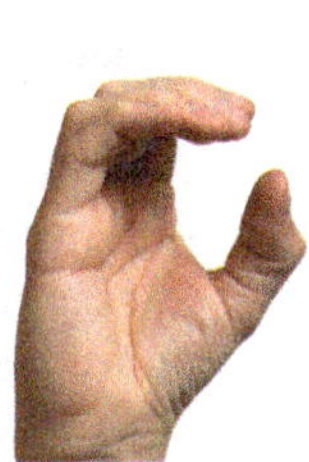

Deafness Special education law makes a distinction between a degree of hearing impairment and an almost complete loss of hearing. If a student has mild to moderate hearing loss, they are likely to obtain special education services under the hearing impairment category. Deafness refers to students who have a severe or profound hearing loss. Table 10.16 provides the special education definition for deafness. The definition identifies deafness as impairment in processing language that is presented auditorily. The diagnosis and treatment of students meeting the criteria for deafness are so similar to students classified as hearing impaired, information will not be repeated here.

Visual Impairment

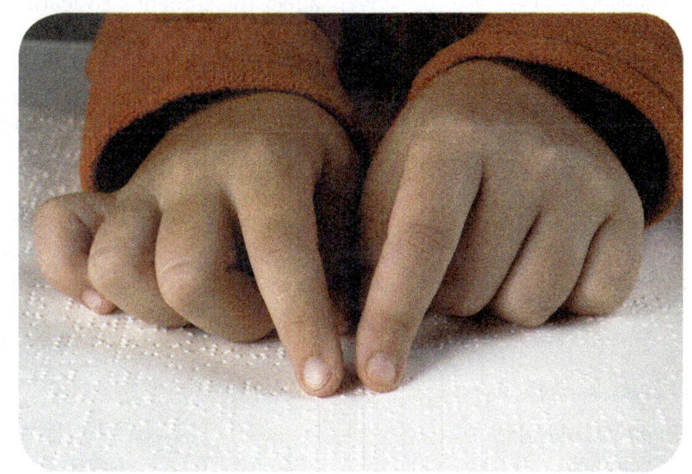

What are visual impairments? Teachers place considerable importance on a student's ability to see. Lessons are often supplemented with visual supports like posters, computer-generated presentations, and demonstrations. Teachers also convey important information through body language and facial expressions. Students with visual impairments are likely to miss much of this visually mediated information. Table 10.17 presents the federal definition for visual impairment. Note that the definition includes both partial sight and blindness. This is different from the IDEA definitions for hearing related impairments where there are separate categories for deafness and hearing impairments. With vision, both impairments are addressed

Table 10.16 Description of Deafness Under IDEA

Under IDEA, **Deafness** means a hearing impairment so severe that a child is impaired in processing linguistic information through hearing, with or without amplification, that adversely affects a child's educational performance.

SOURCE: National Dissemination Center for Children with Disabilities (NICHCY), 2005.

Table 10.17 Description of Visual Impairment Under IDEA

Under IDEA, **Visual Impairment** means an impairment in vision that, even with correction, adversely affects a child's educational performance. The term includes both partial sight and blindness.

SOURCE: National Dissemination Center for Children with Disabilities (NICHCY), 2005.

under a single category. The exception is if blindness occurs with another type of impairment or disorder (i.e., blindness and deafness or blindness and autism). Discussion of these situations occurs later in the chapter.

How do we identify visual impairments? Approximately 2.8% of students require educational support for visual impairments (National Eye Institute, 2004). Despite classification under a single category, students with visual impairments have many different types of impairment. Visual impairments are usually defined as affecting **visual acuity** or **visual field**. Visual acuity refers to the ability of the individual to perceive details. It is how well you can see, identify objects, and benefit from information in the visual field. Visual field refers to how far your vision extends while looking straight ahead. For example, individuals can have problems seeing the right or left visual field. Figure 10.7 demonstrates what someone sees who cannot see across the right visual field. Diagnostically, it is important for the educational team to understand the nature and severity of a student's visual impairment.

Visual acuity

The ability of the individual to perceive details visually

Visual field

How far your vision extends while looking straight ahead

Many conditions can lead to limited vision or blindness. Medical conditions such as glaucoma or cataracts can impair vision. Congenital (present at birth) abnormalities of the eyes or trauma can also impair vision. Diagnosis of visual problems usually follows routine medical examinations at birth or regularly screenings at school or the doctor's office. Screening for problems with visual acuity typically uses a Snellen chart (see Figure 10.8). Vision is measured as the number of feet the person needs to be away from the chart compared to an individual with normal vision. For example, if a student sees 20/100 in their left eye, this means they need to be twenty feet from the Snellen chart to read something that a person with normal vision can read at a distance of 100 feet. **Legally blind** is defined as visual acuity of 20/200 or less in the individual's best eye with correction.

Legally blind

Defined as visual acuity of 20/200 or less in the individual's best eye with correction

Recall that in order to receive special education services, a visual impairment must negatively affect the student's educational progress. This means students with suspected visual impairments need a comprehensive battery of academic tests. Some tests provide versions for the visually impaired, but often this requires modification of standardized testing protocols (discussed in Chapter 9). Examiners need to be mindful of the range of visual problems impacting the educational assessment, including visual acuity, color blindness, and field of vision. These factors are important to remove from the assessment equation so that only academic skills are assessed. Any modifications in standardized testing procedures are reported and considered with the test results.

Interconnections

A review of typical standardized testing protocols is presented in Chapter 9.

Figure 10.7

Right Visual Field Impairment

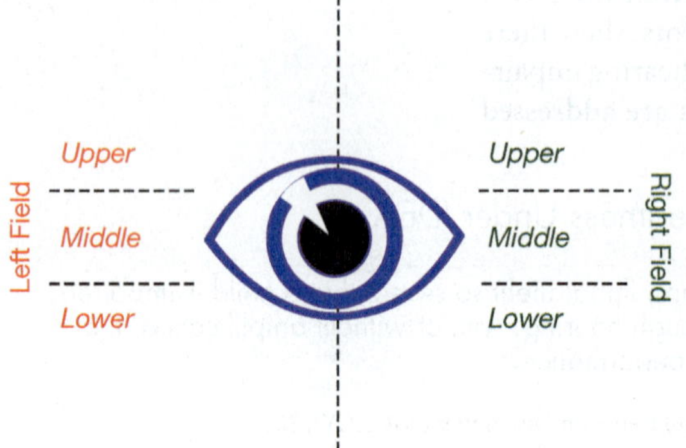

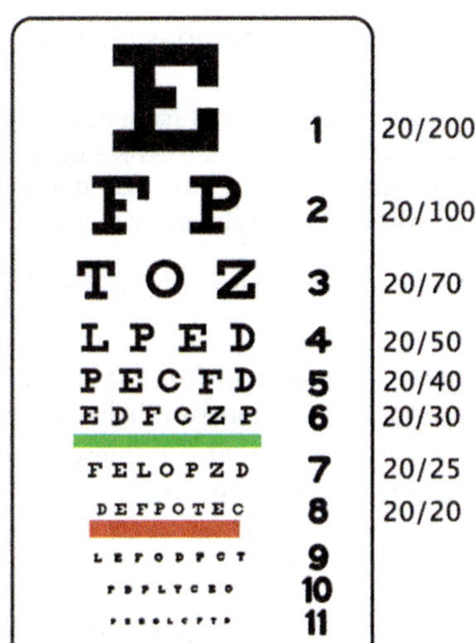

Figure 10.8
Snellen Chart

How do we educate students with visual impairments? Approximately half of students with visual impairments receive accommodations in the regular classroom. Figure 10.9 shows regular educational classroom placements are most common. This type of placement is followed by placement in either a separate class or the resource room. Few students with visual impairments receive services in a residential facility or a separate school.

When providing necessary accommodations for the student with visual impairments, attempts should be made to maintain positive interactions with peers (Brasher & Holbrook, 1996). As with all students, positive interactions within the school context promotes a positive perception of school and helps the student feel more comfortable and engaged at school. The classroom space also requires special consideration. Remember students with visual impairments are likely to have some vision, so it is important to pay attention to the environment. Often students with visual impairment are sensitive to lighting and glare (Bishop, 2004).

Preferential seating will help the student see as much of the teacher's non-verbal cues as possible. Since students with visual impairments will have difficulty identifying classroom elements by sight, teachers need to introduce them to the classroom. It is also important to allow time for practice and learning. Consistency in room layout and function will also help students adapt to the classroom routine.

Another often-overlooked accommodation surrounds language use. Teachers should closely monitor their speech for references that are vague or visually defined. For example, instead of asking the students, "Would you get those?" it is better to say, "Would you get the pencils?" The student may not be able to see that you are pointing to the pencils on the other side of the room. Another verbal accommodation is for the teacher to announce their entry into a group or the room. They should also verbally announce their departure (Vaughn et al., 2004). Similarly, teachers should announce when they are writing on the board or making a demonstration.

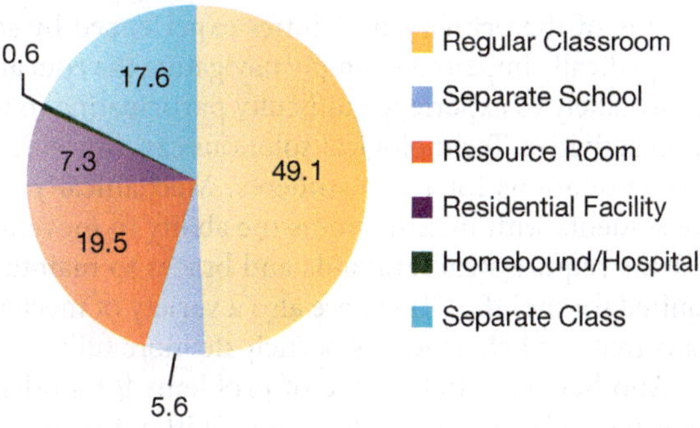

Figure 10.9
Most Common Regular Educational Classroom Placements

Table 10.18 Description of Deaf-Blindness Under IDEA

Under IDEA, **Deaf-Blindness** means concomitant [simultaneous] hearing and visual impairments, the combination of which causes such severe communication and other developmental and educational needs that they cannot be accommodated in special education programs solely for children with deafness or children with blindness.

SOURCE: National Dissemination Center for Children with Disabilities (NICHCY), 2005.

Notetaking and reading are likely to be an issue for the student. Students with visual impairments may benefit from accommodations such as Braille books, large print books, note-takers, and recorded lessons. Technological aids may also enhance learning, especially technology designed to take printed media and translate it into speech.

Deaf-Blindness

Students who are both deaf and blind require exceptional supports and are classified under their own category for special education purposes. Table 10.18 presents the definition of deaf-blindness under special education law. The definition requires that students classified under this category have simultaneous impairments in hearing and vision. Similar to other special education definitions, the impairment must negatively affect academic performance. Unique to this definition is the qualifier that the impairment must be so severe that the student cannot be appropriately accommodated when classified as only deaf or blind.

The number of children receiving special education services under the deaf-blindness category totalled 1,320 in 2002 (U.S. Department of Education). This is .02% of the total special education population. Although the overall number of students in this category is quite low, the resources needed to provide them with appropriate education are extensive. In general, the assessment and treatment approaches are similar to the ones described previously for hearing and visually impaired students. The coordination of these services, however, is unique given that the students have substantial losses in two primary sensory systems. The uniqueness of their learning situation requires an equally unique educational approach. Teachers and related educational professionals need to be insightful, reflective, and flexible in meeting the dynamic needs of these exceptional students.

Orthopedic impairment refers to individuals who were born with a missing limb or who lost a limb due to injury.

Orthopedic Impairment

Orthopedic impairment refers to individuals who were born with a missing limb or who lost a member through injury (see Table 10.19 for a description under IDEA). It also covers orthopedic impairment due to certain medical conditions such as poliomyelitis, bone tuberculosis, cerebral palsy, and fractures or burns that cause abnormal contracture of the muscles. In 2001, there were 122,559 students being served under this disability classification.

Assessment for this classification typically happens outside the school system by a qualified medical professional. Almost half (44.3%) of students classified as orthopedically impaired are educated in the regular education classroom. Most of the other students are in a resource room or other separate classroom environment. Some students require placement in a special school or residential facility.

One of the primary difficulties experienced by students classified as orthopedically impaired is simply navigating the educational facilities. They are also likely to experience difficulty participating in typical physical education activities. Technological solutions can, however, provide remarkable accommodations for these students. Mechanical prosthetic devices can give students with missing limbs the ability to move independently. Some students require structural aids and braces to maintain a bodily position required for mobility. There are also a variety of mechanical and electronic chairs that can help students participate more fully in school life.

Another potential source of problems for students with orthopedic impairments is with communication. Without adequate mobility, students

Table 10.19 Description of Orthopedic Impairments Under IDEA

Under IDEA, **Orthopedic Impairment** means a severe orthopedic impairment that adversely affects a child's educational performance. The term includes impairments caused by a congenital anomaly (e.g., clubfoot, absence of some member, etc.), impairments caused by disease (e.g., poliomyelitis, bone tuberculosis, etc.), and impairments from other causes (e.g., cerebral palsy, amputations, and fractures or burns that cause contractions).

SOURCE: National Dissemination Center for Children with Disabilities (NICHCY), 2005.

may not be able to accurately convey their intentions and communicate effectively. For some students who can speak normally, limitations may only be with certain aspects of non-verbal communication. For other student with more global motor limitations, they may need to use aids with even basic communication. Communication boards and communication cards (discussed previously) can help these students establish a reliable means of communicating with teachers and peers.

There are also social, personal, and emotional considerations when working with students with orthopedic impairments. These students may require assistance with interpersonal relationships. There may be adjustment issues as other students learn to relate to individuals who are different. Students with orthopedic impairments may need help with their understanding of themselves and their place in school. Issues with self-esteem may need to be addressed. Teachers should also consider that using a mechanical aid for mobility probably causes an unusual amount of fatigue. Students may require extra rest and additional time to complete activities.

Other Health Impaired

The developers of IDEA recognize the inherent difficulty in providing enough disability categories to cover all situations requiring assistance. To address this issue a special category of *other health impaired* was established. Students receiving special education services under this category vary significantly in the qualifying condition. Some have major health impairments such as epilepsy, diabetes, heart condition, or asthma. Others suffer from infectious diseases such as Acquired Immune Deficiency Syndrome (AIDS). Relatively new to this category is the specific mentioning of attention deficit hyperactivity disorder (ADHD). Although students with ADHD may receive special education services, it is more common for them to receive assistance through another law, the Vocational Rehabilitation Act of 1974. This will be covered in detail in the next chapter. The exact wording of the federal definition for other health impaired is provided in Table 10.20.

The only consistent educational suggestion one can make for students in this category is educators need to become familiar with the nature of the health impairment. Some conditions like asthma require the teacher know what triggers an asthma attack and what to do if one happens. Other conditions like AIDS require the teacher to help the student manage their care while at school. Students with AIDS may suffer from fatigue and frequent absences. They also are likely to have some difficulty with the social stigma associated with the disorder. Each of the conditions served under this category are different, requiring a unique understanding on the part of the teacher.

Table 10.20 Description of Other Health Impaired Under IDEA

Under IDEA, other health impaired means having limited strength, vitality, or alertness, including a heightened alertness to environmental stimuli, that results in limited alertness with respect to the educational environment, that—

(a) is due to chronic or acute health problems such as asthma, attention deficit disorder or attention deficit hyperactivity disorder, diabetes, epilepsy, a heart condition, hemophilia, lead poisoning, leukemia, nephritis, rheumatic fever, and sickle cell anemia; and

(b) adversely affects a child's educational performance.

SOURCE: National Dissemination Center for Children with Disabilities (NICHCY), 2005.

Multiple Impairments

This final section will explore the educational challenges presented by students with multiple impairments. When a student has significant issues in multiple domains, it increases the complexity of their educational program. Some students qualify for more than one of the previously discussed disability categories. Other students have unusual and complex learning needs across multiple areas because of a brain-related injury. In this section, we will explore the unique challenges teachers face educating students with multiple areas of concern.

Multiple Disabilities

Some students qualify for services under more than one of the special education categories we have been covering in this chapter. This relatively unique situation resulted in the creation of a special education category just for students having multiple disabilities. Students may have mental retardation and a visual impairment. They may have a learning disability and an emotional disturbance. There are many possible combinations, but students need to have multiple impairments creating severe educational need to qualify for services (see Table 10.21). How individual states implement the federal definition for multiple disabilities varies. Some states use this category only for rare cases, electing to serve students with multiple disabilities under a category for one of their impairments. This is because it is not always clear that a student is experiencing any additional educational impairment because they qualify for multiple special education categories. Often the student is best served by using a "primary" disability category. Other states more readily use the multiple disabilities category. The underlying premise is to determine how best to serve the student and which disability classification is most appropriate for the child and their unique needs.

About 43% of students classified as having multiple disabilities are placed in a separate classroom. Only about 11% receive services in the regular classroom. This is largely due to the complexity of the needs of the child combined with limitations inherent in existing school facilities. Schools serving the needs of these students often elect to build and staff a single educational space to meet the challenging demands of these children, rather than modify each regular classroom. This makes for more efficient use of resources but educators need to constantly reassess if there is a way to meet the child's needs in a more traditional placement. There are benefits to allowing students with special needs to interact with their non-disabled peers while at school (Salend, 2005). Interactions benefit the student with disabilities, as well as their typically developing peers. As students with multiple disabilities continue to grow and learn, they may be able to integrate into typical classrooms. Constant assessment and evaluation will help ensure these students are educated in the least restrictive placement.

Traumatic Brain Injury

Children learn to walk, play physically challenging games, ride bikes, and drive cars. Learning these complicated motor skills is difficult and accidents are common. Children want to learn how high they can jump from a tree or how fast they can ride their bike. Mistakes in judgment result in bumps and bruises and perhaps a broken arm. These types of accidents, however, have little impact on the child's long-term educational experience. Injuries to the head are a completely different class of injury. As we have discussed throughout this text, the brain exerts downward control over almost every system of the body. It is also the seat of our remarkable ability to think and reason. Brain injuries are not common; yet when a student experiences one, the results can be devastating. Every head injury is unique and the resulting impairment can impact almost any aspect of human functioning. Given the potential damage caused by a head

Table 10.21 Description of Multiple Disabilities Under IDEA

Under IDEA, Multiple disabilities means concomitant impairments (such as mental retardation-blindness, mental retardation-orthopedic impairment, etc.), the combination of which causes such severe educational needs that they cannot be accommodated in special education programs solely for one of the impairments. The term does not include deaf-blindness.

SOURCE: National Dissemination Center for Children with Disabilities (NICHCY), 2005.

injury, special education law has established a category of disability just for students who have experienced brain trauma.

Federal law specifies that students who receive open or closed head injuries may receive services under this category. **Open head injuries** are those where the skull is actually breached, exposing underlying tissue. A **closed head injury** is one where there is trauma to the head, but the skull remains intact. Either type of injury is capable of causing significant impairment, but an open head injury is particularly damaging because of the direct insult to brain tissue. It is impossible to capture all of the problems resulting from a head injury, but Table 10.22 covers issues specifically mentioned in the federal definition. Also important is the exclusionary clause mentioned in the definition. Injuries due to birth trauma, congenital problems, or degenerative disorders are not served under this category.

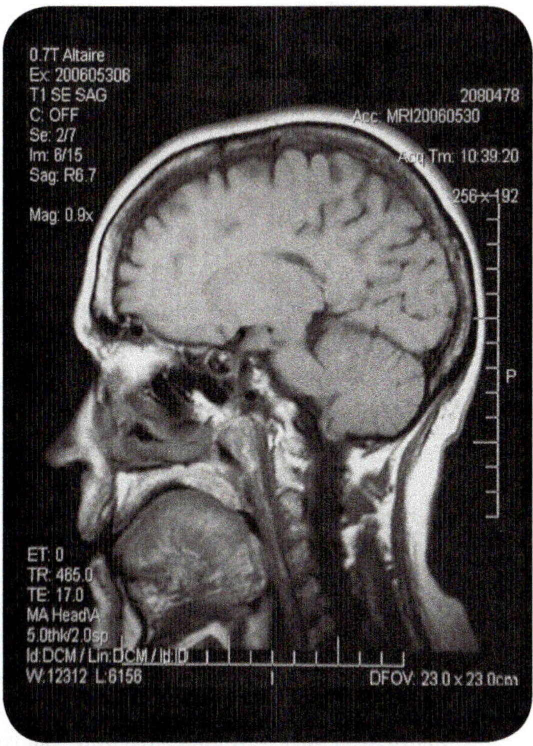

Special education law has established a category of disability just for students who have experienced brain trauma.

Assessment of a brain injury can be difficult given the wide-ranging effects brain injury can have. Assessment typically brings together professionals to assess different motor, cognitive, and behavioral factors. Some injuries are specific, only affecting a single function. Others are more pervasive, affecting physical activity and ability to think and reason. Often assessment following a brain injury begins with screening many areas of functioning. This is followed by more intensive assessment of those areas impacted by the injury. Other times, the child may not appear to have any difficulty, only to discover there are issues once the child returns to the normal routine. Assessment in this case may occur months after the actual injury. What is most difficult about assessment following a head injury is that the impairment may be subtle and difficult to determine. There may be a clear decrease in academic performance, but the nature of that trouble may be hard to define. For example, a student, following a head injury, may have difficulty working with information that has been written on the board in front of the classroom. Visual screening indicates that the student has perfect vision. Academic screening indicates solid academic skills. Intellectual testing shows above average functioning. Reports from the student indicate that he just can't "see" what the teacher is talking about on the board. What she is doing on the board "doesn't make sense." What is the answer? Why is the student having trouble with board work, but not with other aspects of academic work? Perhaps the answer is that the student has trouble with vision, but not with visual acuity. The problem may be with the visual range of colors or shapes the student is able to process. As we learned in Chapter 2, the back part of the brain processes visual information. Trauma to this part of the brain can cause very subtle changes in visual processing. It may be that the student can no longer distinguish the shade of green of the chalkboard, or it might be that he is unable to distinguish the contrast between the white chalk and the green board. It would seem that if the student were having that kind of difficulty, he would simply tell the teacher. Often, however, the same injury that caused the visual problem makes it difficult for the student to reflect upon and understand his own difficulty. From the student's point of view, it just appears to be "confusing." This is just one example of the difficulty assessing a child's function following a head injury. In many ways, assessment in these circumstances is ongoing as teachers, parents, and other people in the child's life notice difficulties. Often the

Open head injuries
Injuries where the skull is actually breached, exposing underlying tissue

Closed head injury
Trauma to the head where the skull remains intact

Table 10.22 Description of Traumatic Brain Injury Under IDEA

Under IDEA, **traumatic brain injury** means an acquired injury to the brain caused by an external physical force, resulting in total or partial functional disability or psychosocial impairment, or both, that adversely affects a child's educational performance. The term applies to open or closed head injuries resulting in abstract thinking; judgment; problem-solving; sensory, perceptual, and motor abilities; psychosocial behavior; physical functions; information processing; and speech. The term does not include brain injuries that are congenital or degenerative, or brain injuries induced by birth trauma.

SOURCE: National Dissemination Center for Children with Disabilities (NICHCY), 2005.

most significant improvements are made in the first year, but dramatic improvements can be seen years later. Such variation in the course of improvement necessitates close collaboration between the classroom teacher and related area professionals.

SUMMARIZE AND REFLECT

1. Providing services under the special education system involves the diagnosis, identification and treatment of learning challenges according to thirteen disability classifications.
2. Each disability category has diagnostic criteria under federal law.
3. Qualifying for services involves a wide range of assessment tools varying according to the nature of the learning issue.
4. Each disability category is addressed using educational options specific to the problem.

INFORMED APPLICATION

1. In what ways can a thorough knowledge of the thirteen disability categories enhance the way a teacher deals with learning challenges experienced by students on a day-to-day basis?
2. Implementation of services for special education is increasingly involving the active participation of the regular education teacher, in large part due to the inclusion movement. Why might a regular education teacher feel more comfortable providing services to students with certain disability classifications over others? How can pre-service instruction positively affect this potential issue?

THE CHAPTER IN REVIEW

Check out our website ▶ www.BVT*Lab*.com for chapter-by-chapter flashcards, practice quizzes, summaries, and more.

The purpose of this chapter is a thorough review of the special education system. The chapter covered why we have a special education system, how it works and each of the disability categories. The first section reviewed the rationale behind a system of special education. We covered our remarkable ability to recognize differences in people. We also discussed the complicated process of providing a *value* to the differences we recognize. Some differences are valued in positive ways; others are less desirable. We then discussed how this basic tendency to recognize differences applies to education. Teachers naturally look for students whose performance is less well developed. We reviewed the valuation process teachers engage in when such differences are recognized and how they are often negative. This led to a general discussion of the pros and cons of providing educational labels. Next, we discussed how the special education system was designed to provide structure to this process of recognizing student differences and to manage how help is extended to students who experience situations that challenge their learning. The system is governed at the national level by federal legislation. It is also influenced by the philosophical climate in education, specifically by the inclusion movement.

The second part of the chapter focused on how the special education system operates. The two key components reviewed were the interdisciplinary team and the Individualized Education Program (IEP). The responsibility for determining eligibility for services belongs to the interdisciplinary special education team. We looked at the formation of this team and highlighted the importance of effective collaboration. Next, we reviewed the development of the IEP. The IEP is the formal document guiding the implementation of special education services. This is a comprehensive document, whose primary components are specifically mandated by federal law.

The final section of the chapter covered all of the thirteen disability categories specified in special education. This section covered frequently diagnosed conditions like learning disabilities and less frequently seen conditions like orthopedic impairments. For each disability category, three types of information were presented. First, we presented information about what constitutes each disability category. Second, we provided a review of the typical assessment procedures used to determine eligibility for special education services. Finally, we looked at the wide range of educational programming options available for each type of disability.

Interdisciplinary Case Focus

principal *special educator*
teacher *parents* *psychologist*
social worker *physical educator*
nurse *peers* *doctor*

Mr. Ryan Reynolds is the principal of a large elementary school in upstate New York. He has just received a letter from Mr. Giles Bedard about his twelve-year-old son Jean-Francois. Mr. Reynolds was anticipating the letter. He has been supervising several of his teachers over the last year as they attempted to find ways to help Jean-Francois. The boy's case has become increasingly difficult and informal attempts to help him are beginning to fail. Jean-Francois has a physical condition causing a steady decline in his ability to see. As of last month, he meets the legal definition for blindness. Not only is his visual acuity impaired, he also has a restricted field of vision in both eyes. His teacher and special education teacher are no longer able to accommodate his needs using typical classroom materials. After a conversation with Jean-Francois' teacher, his father decided to write a letter to Mr. Reynolds requesting a formal evaluation for special education services.

Initial IEP Team meeting

Following special education procedure, Mr. Reynolds convenes a team meeting consisting of Jean-Francois' regular education teacher, his special education teacher, the school psychologist, the school nurse, Mr. Bedard, Jean-Francois, and himself. At the first meeting, Mr. Bedard signs the consent form required to begin the evaluation.

Since Jean-Francois has already received extensive medical evaluations, the team decides to obtain these reports. They also decide to use reports from the regular and special education teacher regarding their work with Jean-Francois over the previous year. They agree to obtain a new evaluation from the school's technology support specialist, to see what technological aids would be appropriate for Jean-Francois. Mr. Bedard suggests a psychological assessment to make sure Jean-Francois is adapting adequately to his declining vision. He expressed concern that his son may be underappreciating the impact of his condition on his life. Jean-Francois offers that he does not feel that such an assessment is necessary, but politely suggests his father might need one. After a brief and friendly discussion, it is decided that the school psychologist will conduct a psychological screening with Jean-Francois. Mr. Bedard is given phone numbers for local support groups and counselors experienced with visual impairments. Jean-Francois is a straight A student, so the team felt comfortable using existing academic records to substantiate his current academic functioning. The team engaged in an extensive discussion about educational experiences that would cause Jean-Francois difficulty. Potential problems with science lessons, physical education, and language arts were reviewed. The team decides to postpone any conclusions regarding removal from regular education activities until Jean-Francois sees the technology specialist. The feeling from the group is that most of Jean-Francois' potential difficulties with regular instruction can be addressed through modified teaching and technological aids. Finally, the team begins to draft some preliminary ideas regarding goals for Jean-Francois over the course of the coming academic year. The team agrees to meet again in thirty days after all the reports have been collected and the technology specialist and psychologist complete their evaluations.

Follow-up and Planning Meeting

Their second meeting takes place twenty-seven days after Mr. Bedard signed the informed consent form. They have all the necessary records and the psychological and technology assistance reports. They begin by reviewing the psychological report. The psychologist first reported that Jean-Francois and his father gave permission for the team to discuss the results at the meeting. The school psychologist conducted separate oral histories from Jean-Francois and his father covering his school and home life. He then had Jean-Francois complete an adolescent psychopathology scale. The scale is a broad screening instrument, covering a variety of psychological, behavioral and adjustment issues. The psychologists noted that Jean-Francois is adjusting very well to his visual impairment. He scored in the normal range in all areas of the screening instrument. He noted that the gradual onset of the disorder and the continued support of his father help Jean-Francois to adjust to life without vision. Jean-Francois and his father's oral histories were similar with differences expected between the perception of father and son. The only substantial difference between their reports was about daily life over the last six months. Mr. Bedard was very concerned that Jean-Francois would become depressed. Mr. Bedford felt Jean-Francois was moody, was losing weight, and was less socially active than normal. Jean-Francois' report was quite different. He reported that he was proud of himself and the way he was adapting to his decreasing vision. He noted that he met a girl at school and that he "liked" her. Schoolwork was going well; his grades remained high. He noted he needed to work harder to keep up with the other students. Contrary to his father, Jean-Francois perceived this as a challenge and one he was very happy he was meeting. He also reported that he has begun lifting weights at school. He noted that doing something good for his body felt great given his visual decline.

The team discussed the conflicting reports. Mr. Bedard expressed dismay at Jean-Francois weight lifting. He did not know about this new activity, and it explained the weight changes. It was determined that much of the moodiness perceived by Mr. Bedard was actually frustration felt by Jean-Francois. He commented that his father was becoming over protective. It was decided that Mr. Bedard and Jean-Francois would attend a few sessions with the school social worker to sort through some of these issues and see if a referral to an outside therapist was needed.

The assistive technology report was typical for a student with a visual impairment. It was recommended that Jean-Francois continue with the books-on-tape program. Learning Braille was discussed, but given Jean-Francois' reluctance to learn the system, not recommended. The report contained numerous recommendations for room modifications given Jean-Francois' continuing ability to distinguish light from darkness and certain colors. It was recommended that a high contrast light signal system be installed in the front of the classroom. The signals could be activated by the teacher and programmed to represent any number of classroom activities. For example, certain lights could represent independent work, lecture, time to leave the room, group activity, or test in progress. This will help Jean-Francois to maintain a sense of what is happening in the class without exclusively relying on verbal commands. The specialist would work with the teacher to help program the lights for her particular classroom structure. There were also recommendations for changes to the physical arrangement of the classroom, verbal directions given by the teacher, and physical education activities. The team reviewed each of the recommendations and decided to support all of the recommendations.

Conclusions and Recommendations

Given Jean-Francois' continued academic achievement, no specific recommendations were made to alter his curriculum other than those to accommodate his visual loss. The school nurse reported that Jean-Francois was scheduled to see his doctor on a monthly basis. Given this level of care, no special screening at school was recommended. She noted that Jean-Francois' condition was likely to stabilize. Individuals with his condition typically do not go completely blind. After the primary degeneration process, vision usually stabilizes at levels similar to Jean-Francois' current levels. She would, however, receive on-going reports from Jean-Francois' doctor and would report any significant changes in vision to the school principal who would then reconvene the team. Based upon all of the recommendations, the team put together an individualized education program (IEP). The IEP included a basic framework for providing services for Jean-Francois.

1. Annual goals were established to help Jean-Francois achieve the most appropriate educational experience. The goals specified when the services would begin, the frequency, location, and duration. The goals resulted from the discussion during the two team meetings. They incorporated recommendations from the psychologist, technology specialists, nurse, teachers, and family.
2. Jean-Francois would attend sessions with the school social worker to determine if further psychological services were warranted.

3. All services are open to modification depending on the status of Jean-Francois' condition.
4. It was decided that Jean-Francois could participate in all regular education activities with the modifications detailed in the annual goals.
5. Given his age, there is no requirement that Jean-Francois have a documented transition plan following schooling.

[STUDENT NOTE] The actual format of the IEP is open to interpretation by the individual school system. Some are very detailed and are generated by computer software programs. Some are less formal, handwritten, and more general. The important point is that the IEP has enough detail to guide the educational team toward the most appropriate education. A sample of an IEP is included below.

Eligibility

Last Name ____________ **First Name** ____________ **IEP Date** ___/___/___

Last IEP ___/___/___ **Next IEP** ___/___/___ **Original SpEd Entry Date** ___/___/___

Last Eval ___/___/___ **Next Eval** ___/___/___

Purpose of Meeting ☐ Initial ☐ Annual ☐ Triennial ☐ Transition ☐ Pre-Expulsion ☐ Interim
☐ Expanded IEP ☐ Other____________

Birthdate___/___/___ Age ______ **Gender** ______ **Grade** ________ **Migrant** ☐ **Yes** ☐ **No**

Native Language ____________ **EL** ☐ **Yes** ☐ **No** ☐ Redesignated Interpreter Yes ☐ No ☐

Student ID ____________ **SSN #** ____________ **SSID #** ____________

Residency ☐ **Parent/Guardian** ☐ **Foster** ____________ ☐ **LCI**____________
☐ **Adult Student** ☐ **Other** ____________

Parent/Guardian ____________ Home Phone ____________

Home Address ____________ Work Phone ____________

____________ Cell Phone ____________

Parent/Guardian ____________ Home Phone ____________

Home Address ____________ Work Phone ____________

____________ Cell Phone ____________

District of Residence ____________ Residence School ____________

Ethnicity: (Select One) ❑ Hispanic or Latino ❑ Not Hispanic or Latino

Race: (Enter Code; must select one or more, regardless of Ethnicity): 1. ________ 2. ________ 3. ________ 4. ________

INDICATE DISABILITY/S (P = Primary, S = Secondary) Note: For Initial and triennial IEPs, assessment must be done and discussed by IEP Team before determining eligibility.

______ 210 MR ______ 220 HH * ______ 230 Deaf * ______ 240 SLI ______ 250 VI *

______ 260 ED ______ 270 OI * ______ 280 OHI ______ 290 SLD ______ 300 DB *

______ 310 MD ______ 320 AUT ______ 330 TBI ______ 281 Est. Med. Dis. (0-5)

* Low Incidence Disability ☐ Severe ☐ Non Severe

______Not Eligible for Special Education ______Exiting from Sp. ED. (returned to reg. ed/no longer eligible)

Describe how student's disability affects involvement and progress in the general curriculum (or for preschoolers, participation in appropriate activities)

____

____

Triennial (3 Year) Re-evaluation
☐ Triennial Re-evaluation not due prior to next IEP review date.
☐ Triennial Re-evaluation due prior to or on next IEP review date.
☐ Summary of Progress and Current Educational Performance
☐ Full Re-evaluation
☐ Other ____________

For Initial Placements Only
Has the student received IDEA Coordinated Early Intervening Services (CEIS) in the past two years?
☐ Yes ☐ No
Date of Initial Referral for Special Education Services ___/___/___
Person Initiating the Referral for Special Education Services ____________
Date District Received Parent Consent ___/___/___
Date of Initial Meeting to Determine Eligibility ___/___/___

Key Terms

TERM	Page	TERM	Page
Accommodation	326	Learning achievement	327
Adaptive functions	331	Learning potential	327
Authentic assessment	328	Legally blind	342
Autistic disorder	333	Life space intervention	338
Closed head injury	347	Metacognition	328
Cognitive training	328	Mixed receptive-expressive language disorder	330
Conflict resolution	338	Modification	326
Curriculum-based assessment (CBA)	328	Open head injuries	347
Direct Instruction (DI)	329	Person-centered planning	337
Disability	316	Phonological disorder	329
Education for All Handicapped Children Act (Public Law 94–142)	318	Portfolio	328
Evaluation	314	Positive behavioral support	338
Expressive language disorder	330	Pre-referral interventions	321
Fluency disorder	330	Pull-out services	320
Full inclusion	320	Response to Intervention (RTI)	328
Functional Behavioral Assessment (FBA)	337	Strength-based assessment	337
Handicap	316	Time management	338
Home school	320	Visual acuity	342
Inclusion	319	Visual field	342
Individualized Education Program (IEP)	324	Voice disorders	330
Language disorder	330		

Chapter 11

EXCEPTIONAL LEARNING: ATTENTION, GIFTEDNESS, CREATIVITY, AND THE FAMILY

What's It All About ...

What laws guide services for students with exceptional learning needs?

What are the unique needs of students with attentional issues, giftedness, and exceptional creativity?

How Do Special Learning Needs Affect Life Outside the Classroom?

Chapter Objectives

- Review the Rehabilitation Act of 1973—Section 504.
- Review the Americans with Disabilities Act (ADA).
- Compare Section 504, ADA, and the Individuals with Disabilities Education Act (IDEA).

- Describe attention deficit/hyperactivity disorder (AD/HD).
- Describe giftedness and creativity.

- Explain how exceptionality affects the family.
- Describe the relation between exceptionality and cultural diversity.

EXTENDED OUTLINE

Exceptional Learning: Attention, Giftedness, Creativity, and the Family

I. What's It All About ...
II. From Today's Headlines
III. Accommodating Special Learning Needs: Legislation and Practice
  A. Rehabilitation Act of 1973—Section 504
  B. Americans with Disabilities Act (ADA)
  C. Comparing Section 504, ADA, and the Individuals with Disabilities Education Act (IDEA)
    1. Defining disability
    2. Eligibility protection under IDEA, Section 504, and ADA
    3. Section 504 and ADA: primary goals
    4. Evaluation for services under Section 504 and ADA
    5. Educational services under Section 504 and ADA
  D. Summarize and reflect
IV. Special Needs Not Typically Served Under IDEA Legislation
  A. Attention deficit/hyperactivity disorder (AD/HD)
    1. AD/HD identification and controversies
    2. Causes of AD/HD
    3. Assessment
    4. Medication
    5. Education of students with AD/HD
  B. Giftedness and creativity
    1. Defining gifted and talented
    2. Characteristics of giftedness
    3. Assessment of giftedness and creativity
    4. Education of students who are gifted
      a. Acceleration versus enrichment
      b. Curriculum packing
      c. Problem-based learning
      d. Encouraging creativity
  C. Summarize and reflect
V. Exceptionality: Families and Culture
  A. Exceptionality and the family
    1. Parents
    2. Siblings
    3. Grandparents
  B. Exceptionality and cultural diversity
    1. Cultural heritage and acceptance
    2. Identification and diversity
      a. Individuals with Disabilities Education Act (IDEA)
      b. Cultural diversity and representation in gifted programs
  C. Summarize and reflect
VI. The Chapter in Review
VII. Interdisciplinary Case Focus

From Today's Headlines

Vol. I No. 11 Teaching World, 2012

Akiane: Child Prodigy

As a young girl, Akiane appeared very much like other children. She was somewhat reserved, preferring to watch from a distance, but otherwise quite typical. She loved the playground and creative activities with her parents and siblings. The only real exceptionality her parents recognized early on was her acutely sensitive appreciation for details. When she would meet new people, she would carefully touch their clothes and the texture of their skin.

At the age of four, things began to change for Akiane. Her atheistic parents were surprised when she began to tell them about visions she was having of heaven. These left Akiane with a deep spirituality that would forever change her outlook on life. Also, at this time, she began to demonstrate an interest in drawing. She would sketch on anything around her—walls, books, furniture, and even on her own arms and legs. At times, she would sketch with the pencil between her toes or teeth. At the age of six she obtained a box of oil paints and taught herself how to mix colors and paint. The results were incredible. Akiane continues to grow and develop as an artist. Her paintings sell for as much as $700,000. She also writes poetry and has gained considerable attention for this aspect of her artistic genius. She remains deeply religious. Her artwork often takes on religious themes. Even at the age of eleven, she appears to have a deep appreciation of her special gifts and is devoted to giving back to the world. She is an active philanthropist, donating significant portions of her earnings to charity.

MAKE THE CONNECTION

This chapter is about exceptional learning situations. As we can see with the case of Akiane, learning ability is often outside the norm and presents a variety of educational challenges. In this chapter, we will explore the unique needs of students with attentional issues, giftedness, and exceptional creativity. We will review relevant legislation governing education of these children. We will then look at how teachers can meet the needs of these exceptional learners. Finally, we will explore the impact of culture on the education of exceptional children.

ACCOMMODATING SPECIAL LEARNING NEEDS: LEGISLATION AND PRACTICE

Today's teachers are highly skilled professionals. Their education and training enables them to teach a broad range of students. Some of their students will follow a typical developmental path, but others will require special attention. The special education system, which is governed by the Individuals with Disabilities Education Improvement Act (IDEIA, with the acronym IDEA derived from a previous law is more commonly used), is a comprehensive system providing services for students with special needs (See Chapter 10 for a discussion of the special education system). Despite its broad scope, there are some special needs not directly served by IDEA. In this chapter, we will explore how students receive services when IDEA does not specifically address the nature of their needs. We will begin our exploration by examining relevant federal legislation. In addition to IDEA, there are other legislative acts governing services to students with special needs. These laws have a real impact on the educational system and the way teachers educate. Virtually all educators will teach students with special needs. If they are to meet the needs of these students, they will need to be familiar with these laws. The first section of this chapter reviews two important laws and their impact on educating students with learning differences. Next, we examine two of the most common learning situations not specifically addressed by IDEA. We look at the education of students with attention deficit/hyperactivity disorder. This disorder receives enormous coverage in the press but is often misunderstood. We will also look at students identified as gifted and talented and their unique educational challenges. Throughout the section, we will discuss the process for providing necessary services, as well as the process of identification. The final section of the chapter looks at the lives of students with exceptionalities outside the classroom. Effective education includes an appreciation of the life circumstances of our students. We look at their social integration in the context of both peers and family. We will also review exceptionality as it relates to cultural diversity. To begin our exploration of these exceptional students, let's begin with a look at the legal aspects of providing services to students outside of the IDEA legislation.

Section 504 of the Rehabilitation Act of 1973

Law that established federal grant programs for vocational rehabilitation, supported employment, independent living, and client services

Rehabilitation Act of 1973—Section 504

The Individuals with Disabilities Education Improvement Act (IDEIA) governs the education of students with certain special needs.

Understanding the laws influencing the education of students with special needs is difficult. As we discussed in the last chapter, the Individuals with Disabilities Education Act (IDEA) governs the education of students with certain special needs. IDEA specifically addresses many disability categories. It does not, however, target every special needs situation. The most notable exception is attention deficit hyperactivity (AD/HD). AD/HD is a possible qualifying condition under the IDEA category of other health impaired (OHI), not a separate disability category. IDEA lists the following as possible qualifying conditions under the OHI category: asthma, attention deficit disorder or attention deficit hyperactivity disorder, diabetes, epilepsy, a heart condition, hemophilia, lead poisoning, leukemia, nephritis, rheumatic fever, and sickle cell anemia. This means that students with AD/HD could receive services under IDEA; in reality, most do not. Other students with special learning needs are not addressed at all under IDEA. Students who are gifted and talented or exceptionally creative also require specialized education. How are services to these students educationally managed? The answer lies in two important civil rights laws, both of which have significant educational implications.

Section 504 of the Rehabilitation Act of 1973 is particularly relevant for schools. The act was passed during the civil rights movement of the 1960s and 1970s. It established the federal grant programs for vocational rehabilitation, supported employment, independent living, and client services. Section 504 is also relevant for schools because it provides protection for children and adults from discrimination based solely on a disability. The law applies to any program or activity (both public and private) receiving federal financial assistance (see Table 11.1). Since most

Table 11.1 Section 504 of the Vocational Rehabilitation Act of 1973

No otherwise qualified individual with a disability ... shall solely by reason of her or his disability be excluded from the participation in, be denied the benefits of, or be subjected to discrimination under any program or activity receiving Federal financial assistance (29 U.S.C.A. § 794).

public and private schools receive some sort of federal funding, Section 504 applies in many areas where the IDEA legislation does not. For example, a student who is HIV positive may manifest with many physical and cognitive issues. Such communicable diseases are not covered under the IDEA legislation (See Chapter 10 for a more detailed discussion of what disabilities are covered under IDEA), but would be covered by Section 504 if it excluded them from participation in schools or otherwise limited their ability to benefit from educational institutions.

Interconnections

See Chapter 10 for a complete discussion of the IDEA legislation.

Americans with Disabilities Act

Another educationally relevant law is the Americans with Disabilities Act of 1990 (ADA). The ADA legislation is another civil rights law. The primary difference between ADA and Section 504 (discussed above) is how broadly the law applies. Section 504 applies to programs or activities receiving federal funding. ADA applies to business, other public and private institutions, and their access for people with disabilities. Since the ADA legislation is not limited to federally funded institutions, this means it has even broader application. The only entities excluded from ADA are churches and private clubs.

In terms of schools, ADA makes few direct references to the education of students with disabilities (Latham & Latham, 2011). This means that to interpret ADA as it applies to schools, the Office of Civil Rights (OCR) uses the standards under Section 504. In fact, the definition for who is protected and the procedural safeguards of ADA are the same as Section 504. OCR treats each alleged violation of Section 504 as a violation of ADA because the same standards apply to both laws. This means that teachers should consider the education of students under Section 504 as also guided by ADA. To help clarify these laws and how they apply, let's look at how Section 504 compares to ADA and how these two laws differ from the IDEA legislation.

Comparing Section 504, ADA, and IDEA

Before we compare Section 504 and ADA, it is important to underscore how *both* laws are different from IDEA. Section 504 and ADA differ from IDEA in two important ways:

1. *The way a disability is defined*

2. *The approach determining eligibility for services*

Defining Disability

IDEA uses a categorical approach to defining disability. This means students have to qualify as meeting the definition of one of thirteen disability categories (see Chapter 10). Without satisfactorily meeting the criteria for one or more of these categories, a student does not qualify for special education services. Section 504 and ADA use a non-categorical approach to defining a disability. These laws extend protections to any person who has a mental or physical impairment interfering with major life functioning, who has a record of such impairment, and/or who is regarded as having such impairment. The concept of major life functioning is somewhat vague, but typically refers to speaking, learning, walking, seeing and other activities common to everyday functioning. What this means is that Section 504 and ADA are much broader than the IDEA legislation. Many students, who fail to meet criteria for a disability under IDEA, may qualify for services under Section 504 and ADA (see Table 11.2).

Table 11.2 Example of Students Receiving Services Under Section 504/ADA

Students with communicable diseases (e.g., hepatitis, HIV, etc.)
Students needing temporary services due to injury or illness
Students with allergies or asthma
Students with substance abuse problems (may not be actively using)
Students with attention deficit/hyperactivity disorder
Students with learning disabilities who do not manifest a significant discrepancy between intellectual ability and achievement
Students who are considered socially maladjusted
Students who are transitioned out of special education
Students with environmental sensitivities or reactivity
Students beyond typical school age (e.g., over 22—depending on state); parents with disabilities

SOURCE: Modified from Martin, 1992

Eligibility Protection Under IDEA, Section 504, and ADA

The difference in how disability is defined leads to a different focus when determining eligibility. The way IDEA is written, eligibility is based on meeting a disability definition. Section 504 and ADA not only define disability differently, their approach means eligibility is based on a comparison to other children considered typical in their development. In other words, IDEA is a comparison to a definition; Section 504 and ADA use a comparison to average performance for a student of that age. Again, this typically leads to many more children qualifying for services under Section 504 and ADA.

Section 504 and ADA: Primary Goals

Now that we have some appreciation of how Section 504 and ADA differ from IDEA, let's take a closer look at how these very similar legislative acts compare. Section 504 and ADA have three primary goals:

1. Non-discrimination
2. Free and Appropriate Public Education (FAPE)
3. Procedural Safeguards

The non-discrimination goal is to protect students from discriminatory practices based on their disability in all institutions, including education. This does not mean that students who meet criteria for a disability according to Section 504 and ADA criteria are entitled to all the services and educational opportunities as non-disabled students. This is because in addition to a disability, some students have other issues limiting their participation in educational activities. It is only discrimination if a student is not permitted to participate in an activity for which he/she is otherwise qualified. We will elaborate on this issue in the next section on evaluation.

The mandate for a free and appropriate public education (FAPE) is a minimally defined construct. Essentially, students with and without disabilities are entitled to services necessary to ensure an appropriate educational experience. This may include regular education, special education, supplementary aids, and other related services outside the general education setting (Jacob-Timm & Hartshorne, 1994).

Like IDEA, Section 504 and ADA also provide process guidelines for determining eligibility (McBride, Dumont, & Willis, 2011). Students are entitled to a referral process, possible evaluation, program planning and implementation where appropriate, and reevaluation. These process guidelines help enforce the protections afforded students under Section 504 and ADA. Parents also have several safeguards to insure that appropriate procedures are followed. The law mandates that local education agencies provide impartial hearings for parents who disagree with evaluation findings on placement decisions. Parents are entitled to participate in the hearing process. They also have the right to be represented by counsel.

The Individualized Education Program (IEP) is discussed in detail in Chapter 10.

In addition to the procedural guidelines in Section 504 and ADA, state or local agencies may develop further guidelines to govern due process. Often local agencies establish a process for documenting the student's intervention plan. Section 504 does not mandate that schools provide a written intervention plan; however, local schools often require such documentation. Some schools choose to use the same format for a written Section 504 plan used for an (IEP) (see Chapter 10 for a discussion of IEP). This provides comprehensive documentation of the plan, but can also cause some confusion for teachers who may be unsure under which law the student is being served.

Evaluation for Services Under Section 504 and ADA

To achieve the primary goals of Section 504 and ADA, it is important to undertake a careful evaluation of every student referred for assistance. Consideration for services begins with a referral. Anyone can refer a student for evaluation for services under Section 504 or ADA. Most referrals come from the regular education teacher, often in consultation with the student's parents. Section 504 and ADA do not require parental consent for evaluation, but it is in the student's and the school's best interest to have full parental cooperation. Referrals can be for a variety of reasons. Table 11.3 details some of the possible precipitating reasons for a referral. The list is only a sample and cannot possibly list all of the unique reasons for seeking additional support for a student.

The evaluation and placement procedure is similar to IDEA. Section 504 requires that schools gather information from a variety of sources and that a group of individuals knowledgeable about the student consider the information. Students should be educated with their non-disabled peers as much as possible. The law also requires periodic reevaluations to determine current functioning and appropriate supports (Jacob, Decker, & Hartshorne, 2011). Evaluations for services under Section 504 and ADA attempt to determine the answer to three important questions:

1. Does a physical or mental impairment exist?
2. Does the physical or mental impairment cause a limitation in major life functioning?
3. What are the accommodations that will ensure the student receives a free and appropriate public education (FAPE)?

In making these determinations, the evaluation team must examine two important standards. The first is whether the student is **otherwise qualified** to engage in the educational

Otherwise qualified

To be protected from discrimination under Section 504 and ADA, the student's disability must be the only barrier to his/her participation in the activity

Table 11.3 Possible Reasons for Referring a Student for Evaluation for Section 504 or ADA Services

When a student is either not evaluated for services under IDEA or is considered not eligible
When a student is suspected of having a learning issue or a behavioral problem
When a student's behavior has warranted expulsion or suspension
When a student has a chronic or acute health problem
When a parent or teacher requests an evaluation

GET THE FACTS

Zero

Amount of federal funds available to schools accommodating students under Section 504

Section 504 of the Vocational Rehabilitation Act

experience given the nature of his/her disability. This means that to be protected from discrimination under Section 504 and ADA, the student's disability must be the only barrier to their participation in the activity. If this is the case, then the school system is obligated to provide necessary accommodations and services to make sure the student has comparable access to the activity. The difficulty arises when there are multiple factors that limit a student's participation in a given activity. For example, a student may suffer from health related impairments such that her motor skills are severely impaired and her cognitive functioning is limited. The science teacher has a lesson plan on the reaction of two chemical agents under heat. The students are required to mix two chemical agents under a Bunsen burner and then explain the resulting changes. The question for the teacher is, "Is it discrimination to not allow the student with the health problem described above to participate in the activity?" This is a classic example of the standard of *otherwise qualified.* If the student's only limitation to participating in the activity were her motor limitations, then the teacher would be required to provide appropriate accommodations for the student so she could actively participate in the lesson. The student would be considered *otherwise qualified* to benefit from the educational experience. Her additional difficulties with cognitive functioning, however, complicate the situation. Her cognitive issues may mean that she is not able to intellectually benefit from the science experiment, even if the teacher could accommodate her physical limitations. In this case, the student would not be considered *otherwise qualified* to participate in the lesson, and the teacher is not discriminating against the student by not allowing her to participate in the lesson. Of course, the hope is that the teacher will consider the current experiment in light of her overall curricular goals and provide the student with another experience that she can appreciate cognitively and possesses the necessary motor skills to perform.

Substantial limitation

A limitation that is largely determined by the professionals involved in the evaluation for protection under Section 504/ADA

The other important standard to consider is what exactly constitutes **substantial limitation** in life functioning. Recall that the definition of a disability under Section 504/ADA is that there is a substantial limitation in one or more major life activity. The professionals involved in the evaluation largely make the determination of whether a major life activity is impaired due to the disability. Professionals rely on their expertise, experience, and the duration and severity of the condition. Some researchers have attempted to quantify the process using rating scales (Smith & Patton, 1998) as depicted in Figure 11.1.

Evaluation Data

The final point to consider when conducting an evaluation for Section 504/ADA is what services are needed to insure free and appropriate education (FAPE). They must receive an education comparable to that of non-disabled students. According to these laws, they are eligible for special programming and accommodations necessary to provide appropriate education. Such services may include speech/language services; counseling; and occupational, and/or behavioral or physical therapy. They may also receive necessary modifications to the classroom environment and testing process. Some students may need the attention of an in-class aide or special technological assistance. The cost for this programming does not come from federal funds. Local school districts must provide these services from the school's regular education funds.

Free and appropriate education (FAPE) requires that disabled students must receive a comparable education to non-disabled students. These services may include counseling.

There are two additional points to consider regarding evaluation for Section 504 and ADA services. Like IDEA, schools need to provide services to students in their regular classroom environments to the maximum extent possible. This means it is inappropriate for schools to remove a student with a disability from the regular classroom if their disability can be sufficiently accommodated in the regular classroom. It is also important to realize that schools

Figure 11.1
Section 504 Eligibility Determination Form

Nature of Mental or Physical Impairment:

Major Life Activity	School-Related Description of Impairment (1)	Source of Information (2)	Severity mild severe 1 2 3 4 5	Duration short-term long-term 1 2 3 4 5	Substantial Limitation? (3) Yes No
caring for oneself			1 2 3 4 5	1 2 3 4 5	Yes No
performing manual tasks			1 2 3 4 5	1 2 3 4 5	Yes No
walking			1 2 3 4 5	1 2 3 4 5	Yes No
seeing			1 2 3 4 5	1 2 3 4 5	Yes No
hearing			1 2 3 4 5	1 2 3 4 5	Yes No
speaking			1 2 3 4 5	1 2 3 4 5	Yes No
breathing			1 2 3 4 5	1 2 3 4 5	Yes No
learning			1 2 3 4 5	1 2 3 4 5	Yes No
working			1 2 3 4 5	1 2 3 4 5	Yes No
other (4)			1 2 3 4 5	1 2 3 4 5	Yes No

(1) description of educational-related behaviors associated with specific major life activities affected by mental or physical condition
(2) listing of persons and/or evaluation techniques used for identifying behaviors associated with impairment (based on consideration of the nature, severity, and duration of the impairment)
(4) other major life activities might include bending, stooping, reaching

SOURCE: From Smith and Patton (1998), Section 504 and public school (p. 35), Austin, TX: PRO-ED.

do not have to evaluate a student they believe to be ineligible for services. As mentioned before, there are due process protections for parents who disagree with school findings (Hartwig, 2000).

Educational Services Under Section 504 and ADA

Services provided students under Section 504 and ADA are not necessarily different from those provided students under IDEA. Often issues can be addressed through accommodations such as testing modification, seating preference, homework modification, note takers, and modified attendance policies. These accommodations have the added benefit that they incur little or no additional financial cost to the school system. As previously mentioned, this is important because schools must fund these accommodations with their regular education budget.

Reasonable accommodation

Means that schools have considerable discretion regarding student services that they provide

The basic standard applied to any accommodations and services is that they are **reasonable accommodations** and provide FAPE. This means that schools have considerable discretion regarding student services. In addition to looking to a standard of reasonable accommodation, schools also look to the educational experience of the student's peers. Section 504 and ADA are designed to provide *comparable* services including education. In other words, schools must provide equal opportunity to get the same educational benefit (Jacob-Timm & Hartshorne, 1994) as a non-disabled peer.

SUMMARIZE AND REFLECT

1. The first part of the chapter focused on legislative aspects of providing services to students outside of the Individuals with Disabilities Education Act (IDEA) legislation.
2. Two important civil rights laws were reviewed. First, students frequently seek services under Section 504 of the Vocational Rehabilitation Act of 1973.
3. Second, the Americans with Disabilities Act (ADA) also affects educational settings and applies to a wider range of situations.
4. The last part of this section took a comparative approach, looking at similarities and differences between Section 504, ADA, and the Individuals with Disabilities Education Act (IDEA).
5. Each of these laws defines *disability* and determines eligibility for services in a unique way.

INFORMED APPLICATION

1. Develop a classroom example requiring a teacher to provide accommodations according to Section 504. The example needs to be specific enough to demonstrate how the student meets all the criteria specified in the law.
2. Compare and contrast the services provided under IDEA with those provided under either Section 504 or ADA.

SPECIAL NEEDS NOT TYPICALLY SERVED UNDER IDEA LEGISLATION

Numerous students require special educational assistance, but do not receive this assistance under special education. As you saw in Table 11.2 earlier in this chapter, there are a variety of conditions that are not typically served under IDEA. In this section, we are going to focus on two of the most common of these situations.

Attention deficit/hyperactivity disorder (AD/HD)

The most commonly diagnosed disorder of childhood, characterized by some combination of inattention, impulsivity, or hyperactivity

Attention Deficit/Hyperactivity Disorder

There is probably no other disorder receiving more media coverage than **attention deficit/hyperactivity disorder (AD/HD)**. It is the most commonly diagnosed disorder of childhood and is having a significant impact on education (Tannock & Schachar, 1997; Shaywitz, Fletcher, & Shaywitz, 1994; Shelton & Barkley, 1994). AD/HD is defined as a behavioral issue characterized by one or more of the following symptoms: inattention, impulsivity, and hyperactivity. The American Psychiatric Association (2000) believes that between 3% to 5% of school-age children suffer from AD/HD. This means that approximately two million children

(U.S. Department of Education) have significant problems with impulsive behavior, hyperactivity, or difficulty directing attention. This is an enormous population and one that is not directly served by the special education system. For example, as we learned in the last section, there is no disability category for AD/HD under IDEA. If such a category were created, the number of students served under IDEA could rise by as much as 50%.

In this section, we will learn about the characteristics of AD/HD and review how students receive needed educational services. We will explore contemporary theories about the origins of AD/HD. We will also look closely at how we diagnose and treat this condition. Let's begin with a review of what exactly AD/HD is.

AD/HD Identification and Controversies

One of the major controversies surrounding AD/HD is whether it really exists. In 2002, an international conference on AD/HD was held to develop a science-based consensus statement addressing conflicting media and scientific reports. This consensus paper reports that the U.S. Surgeon General, the American Medical Association, the American Psychiatric Association, the American Academy of Child and Adolescent Psychiatry, The American Psychological Association, and the American Academy of Pediatrics—all recognize AD/HD as a valid disorder.

Not all scientists agree, however, that AD/HD is indeed distinct. In a critique of the International Consensus Statement on AD/HD, Sami Timimi (2004) cites several reasons why the existence of AD/HD is still a valid debate. He notes that the very definition of AD/HD changes with such frequency that it calls into question the validity of a single distinct syndrome. He also notes that variation in prevalence rates is so large that, again, it makes it difficult to see AD/HD as a single unique disorder. Other researchers emphasize that AD/HD might be "created" by our media style, which increasingly is geared toward immediate gratification, requiring little sustained attention (Hallowell & Ratey, 1995).

Despite suggestions that AD/HD is not a distinct disorder, it is still widely recognized and addressed in educational settings. Schools typically recognize a medical approach to the diagnosis of AD/HD. This means schools rely on the diagnosis of a medical professional for identification of AD/HD. The standard diagnostic reference for identifying AD/HD is the *Diagnostic and Statistical Manual-IV (DSM-IV) Text Revision* (2000). This publication is produced by the American Psychiatric Association and is a compilation of diagnostic criteria and information on a wide range of disorders. The *DSM-IV* criteria for AD/HD are presented in Table 11.4.

Attention deficit/hyperactivity disorder is discussed using a variety of terms and abbreviations. Most of these variations are derived from older versions of the *DSM*. In general, the terms ADD, ADHD, AD/HD, attention deficit disorder, and attention deficit/hyperactivity disorder all refer to the same disorder. Strictly following the *DSM-IV*, the diagnosis is properly cited as attention deficit/hyperactivity disorder and is abbreviated AD/HD.

The three cardinal symptoms of AD/HD are inattention, impulsivity, and hyperactivity. As you can see from Table 11.4, students experiencing inattention have difficulty with tasks requiring sustained attention. They are often distractible and characterized as daydreamers. Impulsivity describes problems students have regulating their behavior. They often speak out of turn and have trouble taking turns. These behaviors frequently translate into social problems. Hyperactivity often results in difficulty sitting quietly in their seat. They may also demonstrate an atypical need to run and climb and may talk excessively.

Research indicates that individuals express these symptoms differently. Some students have a great deal of difficulty with sustained attention and staying on task. Others may be constantly on the go and impulsive, but able to pay attention. Still others have a combination of these symptoms. To address these variations, the *DSM-IV* provides different diagnostic codes for the following variations in the expression of AD/HD symptomology:

- Attention-Deficit/Hyperactivity Disorder, Combined Type: if both Criteria A1 and A2 are met for the past six months

Table 11.4 Diagnostic Criteria for Attention Deficit/Hyperactivity Disorder

A. Either (1) or (2):

(1) *inattention*: six (or more) of the following symptoms of inattention have persisted for at least six months to a degree that is maladaptive and inconsistent with developmental level:

(a) often fails to give close attention to details or makes careless mistakes in schoolwork, work, or other activities

(b) often has difficulty sustaining attention in tasks or play activities

(c) often does not seem to listen when spoken to directly

(d) often does not follow through on instructions and fails to finish schoolwork, chores, or duties in the workplace (not due to oppositional behavior or failure to understand instructions)

(e) often has difficulty organizing tasks and activities

(f) often avoids, dislikes, or is reluctant to engage in tasks that require sustained mental effort (such as schoolwork or homework)

(g) often loses things necessary for tasks or activities (e.g., toys, school assignments, pencils, books, or tools)

(h) often easily is distracted by extraneous stimuli

(i) often is forgetful in daily activities

(2) *hyperactivity-impulsivity*: six (or more) of the following symptoms of hyperactivity-impulsivity have persisted for at least six months to a degree that is maladaptive and inconsistent with developmental level:

Hyperactivity

(a) often fidgets with hands or feet or squirms in seat

(b) often leaves seat in classroom or in other situations in which remaining seated is expected

(c) often runs about or climbs excessively in situations in which it is inappropriate (in adolescents or adults, may be limited to subjective feelings of restlessness)

(d) often has difficulty playing or engaging in leisure activities quietly

(e) often "on the go" or often acts as if "driven by a motor"

(f) often talks excessively

Impulsivity

(a) often blurts out answers before questions have been completed

(b) often has difficulty awaiting turn

(c) often interrupts or intrudes on others (e.g., butts into conversations or games)

B. Some hyperactive-impulsive or inattentive symptoms that caused impairment were present before age seven years.

C. Some impairment from the symptoms is present in two or more settings (e.g., at school [or work] and at home).

D. There must be clear evidence of clinically significant impairment in social, academic, or occupational functioning.

E. The symptoms do not occur exclusively during the course of a Pervasive Developmental Disorder, Schizophrenia, or other Psychotic Disorder and are not better accounted for by another mental disorder (e.g., Mood Disorder, Anxiety Disorder, Dissociative Disorders, or a Personality Disorder).

- Attention-Deficit/Hyperactivity Disorder, Predominantly Inattentive Type: if Criterion A1 is met but Criterion A2 is not met for the past six months

- Attention-Deficit/Hyperactivity Disorder, Predominantly Hyperactive-Impulsive Type: if Criterion A2 is met but Criterion A1 is not met for the past six months

This means the *DSM-IV* recognizes symptoms that are primarily inattentive, hyperactive-impulsive, or both. The *DSM-IV* does not separate hyperactive and impulsive symptoms because of the significant overlap in the number of children experiencing both symptoms.

In addition to determining the nature of the symptoms, there are other important factors to consider when making a diagnosis of AD/HD. The diagnostic criteria specify that symptoms must be present before the age seven. This helps the diagnostician separate children that have a long-standing problem from those whose symptoms may be a reaction to a current life event. The diagnostic criteria also specify that symptoms must be demonstrated in more than one setting. If symptoms were only present in one setting, then, again, they may indicate a specific reaction problem, rather than an enduring problem. Additionally, the problems must be causing significant social, academic or occupational functioning. This is a typical qualifier for disorders listed in the *DSM-IV* and follows the idea that a disorder must have some negative consequences for the individual to warrant a clinical diagnosis.

The diagnostic criteria provided by the *DSM-IV* are only the beginning of the evaluative process (Martin & Zirkel, 2011). They help the clinician distinguish symptoms of AD/HD from other disorders and provide a common reference point, but this is far from the complete assessment needed to provide a foundation for an educational intervention. We will turn to additional methods for evaluating a student suspected of having AD/HD shortly, but first let's take a closer look at theories explaining what causes AD/HD.

Causes of AD/HD

There are many theories why some children experience AD/HD. Some theories focus on the genetics we inherit from our parents. Other theories emphasize the unique brain functioning of the child with AD/HD. To date, no single theory is able to fully explain why a child experiences AD/HD symptoms. As this text consistently emphasizes, every student is a unique individual and finding a single explanatory structure for a given educational or personal issue is not likely. Teachers, however, can familiarize themselves with the available evidence and the theories that guide research. In a real way, these theories help us talk to our students and their families in a research-grounded way about the problems they are experiencing. We may not be able to provide exact answers, but we can help students and their families understand and appreciate the range of relevant factors impacting their difficulties.

The first theoretical approach to AD/HD we will examine is heritability, or linking the expression of AD/HD to the genetics we inherit from our parents. There are several lines of research pointing to a strong genetic component to AD/HD. Research on parents and their children have found that a child with AD/HD is two to eight times more likely to have a parent with AD/HD (Faraone & Doyle, 2001). Additionally, research on first-degree relatives has shown that there is an 18% chance of a biological parent having AD/HD if their child has AD/HD. This is compared to only a 6% chance if the child with AD/HD was adopted. Biological parents of children without AD/HD had only a 3% chance of having AD/HD themselves (Sprich, Biederman, Crawford, Mundy, & Faraone, 2000).

Another type of research supporting the heritability theory of AD/HD is twin research (Greven, Asherson, Rijsdijk, & Plomin, 2011). A common approach is for researchers to look at identical twins, who have the same genetics, and fraternal twins who only share 50% of their genes. If AD/HD is more likely in identical twins (called a concordance rate) compared to a fraternal twin pair, then this suggests a genetic explanation for AD/HD. Numerous researchers have found higher AD/HD concordance rates in identical twins (Smalley et al., 2000; Sherman, Iacono, & McGue, 1997; Thapar, Holmes, Poulton, & Harrington, 1999). Studies vary in exact concordance rates, but rates for identical twins generally range from 60–80% compared to 20–30% for fraternal twins. This evidence, coupled with the work on relatives and adoptees, provides strong evidence for the heritability theory of AD/HD.

Another theoretical approach to understanding the causes of AD/HD is to associate their behavioral problems with evidence of biological or neurological differences. Research over the last twenty years has emphasized the importance of certain brain structures in AD/HD (Castellanos et al., 2002, 2001, 2000; Barkley, 1998). The most commonly reported differences are in areas of the frontal lobes and a set of deep brain structures called the basal ganglia. The frontal lobes are involved in several aspects of self-regulation, and the basal ganglia are known to influence motor behavior. Other brain related differences involve brain chemistry. Researchers have found that children with AD/HD have lower levels of a brain chemical called dopamine (a neurotransmitter discussed in Chapter 2). Findings indicate lower levels of dopamine in the frontal lobes and basal ganglia (Gupta, 2000; Castellanos, 1997). In addition to anatomical and chemical differences, researchers have also found differences in brain electrical activity (Swartwood, 2003; Chabot, 2001). In general, these studies find involvement of the frontal and central areas of the brain.

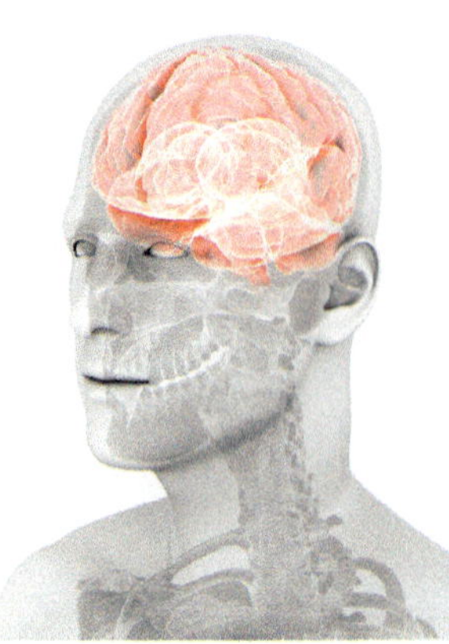

A third theoretical approach to understanding AD/HD is to use a construct known as executive functioning (Di Trani et al., 2011). **Executive functioning** refers to a collection of skills involved in self-regulation, planning for the future, internalization of speech, perception of time, and some aspects of working memory. The executive functioning perspective fits well with the available biological and neurological evidence as executive functions are known to have a biological foundation in the frontal lobes (Stuss & Knight, 2002). One of the most notable of the executive functions is self-regulation. Children with AD/HD often have difficulty with monitoring and managing their own behavior. This has obvious implications for school since students are increasingly taught self-reliance. Another important executive function is the ability to plan for future activities. We all have difficulty making sure we have the materials we need for a future task, but children with AD/HD have problems beyond what is expected for their age. Teachers are likely to spend considerable time helping children with AD/HD organize their day so that they have necessary materials. This is related to another executive function, internalization of speech. Talking to ourselves as we progress through our day helps us monitor our current actions and evaluate future needs. Impairment in this function will make it even more difficult to effectively plan for the future. This can also lead to an unusual perception of the flow of time. Children with AD/HD often report that time moves too slowly. They have trouble waiting and allocating time effectively to tasks. This leads to frustration and difficulty with task performance.

Executive functioning

A collection of skills involved in self-regulation, planning for the future, internalization of speech, perception of time, and some aspects of working memory

Interconnections

Working memory as part of the information processing model is reviewed in Chapter 5.

A final point to consider is a potential problem with working memory. Information flowing to and from working memory (discussed in Chapter 5) involves crucial executive functioning. To effectively manage our day, we need to be able to efficiently retrieve memories and integrate those memories into events of our immediate world. When the teacher asks us to turn in our homework, we need to recall the location of our homework plus recall the process for getting it to the teacher. Additionally, these memories have to be reconciled with what is actually happening in the classroom at that moment. Perhaps you are in the middle of a conversation with a friend or working on another assignment. How will you deal with this existing task and the new need to turn in your homework? This juggling of information in your working memory is challenging for all of us, but children with AD/HD have more difficulty with this important executive function.

Assessment

The process for obtaining an initial diagnosis of AD/HD is highly variable. Historically, identification may have been as simple as walking into your doctor's office, answering a few questions, and perhaps filling out a simple rating scale of your child's behavior. Concerns about over-diagnosis and inconsistent diagnoses have led to more systematic approaches to assessment. The American Academy of Pediatrics (AAP) attempted to create a more consistent and holistic approach to diagnosis by publishing evaluation guidelines (2000). These guidelines (see Table 11.5) incorporate the *DSM-IV* criteria described earlier and also information from other sources such as schools. These guidelines are a positive step forward in the evaluation of AD/HD. They encourage practitioners to consider multiple sources of information creating a more comprehensive diagnostic approach. Still, many school systems find the guidelines fail to provide enough detail to produce the highest quality evaluation.

Other assessment approaches have been developed to help meet the need for a more specific evaluative process. In their book on AD/HD in the schools, DuPaul and Stoner (2003) provide an extensive chapter on their stage approach to the evaluation of AD/HD. Figure 11.2 provides an overview of the process. The model provides a comprehensive, school-based approach to the assessment, evaluation, and treatment of AD/HD. This is a trend in school systems where deliberate attempts are being made to ground AD/HD evaluations in the schools, rather than relying exclusively on medical professionals for diagnostic information. The model has multiple stages designed to build a solid diagnostic foundation from which effective intervention can evolve.

Behavior rating scale

One of the most common tools that professionals use to assess/rate behavioral disturbances

A significant part of any evaluation for AD/HD is the assessment tools used to gather information on the child's functioning. **Behavior rating scales** are one of the most common tools

Table 11.5 American Academy of Pediatrics (AAP) Guidelines for the Evaluation of AD/HD

- Clinicians should initiate an evaluation for ADHD for any child, 6 to 12 years old, who presents with inattention, hyperactivity, impulsivity, academic underachievement, or behavior problems.
- A positive diagnosis requires that the child meet the *DSM-IV* criteria for ADHD.
- Clinicians must obtain evidence directly from the parents/caretakers regarding the core symptoms of ADHD in various settings, the age of onset, the duration of the symptoms, and the child's degree of impairment. They may use behavior ratings scales, such as the Conner's Ratings Scale, to aid in the diagnosis, though the efficacy of such scales has not been proven definitively.
- Clinicians should require direct evidence not only from the parents or caretaker regarding the core symptoms of ADHD but also from the classroom teacher or other school professional. Again, the AAP determines that assessment tools for teachers, such as ratings scales, could assist in the ADHD evaluation.
- The evaluation must include an assessment of coexisting conditions.
- Finally, the AAP recommends that other diagnostic tests be discarded in determining an ADHD diagnosis. Screening for high lead levels, for example, or abnormal thyroid hormone levels should not be considered a routine corollary in the ADHD diagnosis.

professionals use to assess AD/HD. Many types of rating scales are available and most follow a similar format. The respondent is asked to read questions about the individual's behavior and provide a rating as to how much of the behavior is exhibited. For example, a question might ask, "Does your child have difficulty sustaining attention compared to classmates?" The respondent might answer by circling one of the following options: never, sometimes, often, very often, or always. Using this approach, evaluators are able to quickly gather information across many areas of functioning. Behavioral rating forms come in many editions. Some are designed for the child's teacher, the parent, or even the child to fill out. Each rating provides a different perspective on the student's problems. Commonly used scales include the Conner's Teacher's Rating Scale–Revised and the AD/HD Rating Scale–IV. Some professionals elect to use behavior-rating scales that measure multiple behaviors in addition to attention, impulsivity, and hyperactivity. For example, the Behavioral Assessment System for Children–2 (BASC–2) also measures behaviors

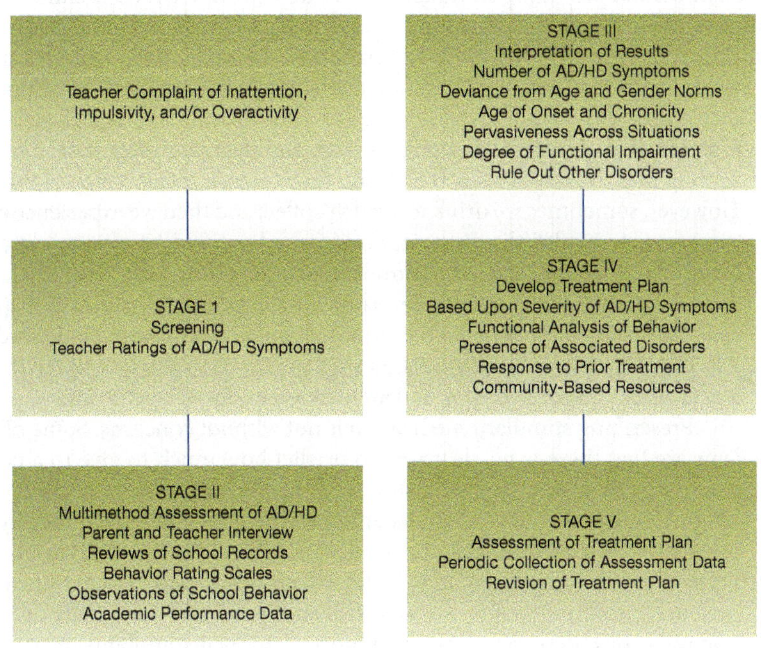

Figure 11.2 Stage Approach to the Evaluation of AD/HD

Figure 11.3

Test of Variables of Attention (T.O.V.A.)

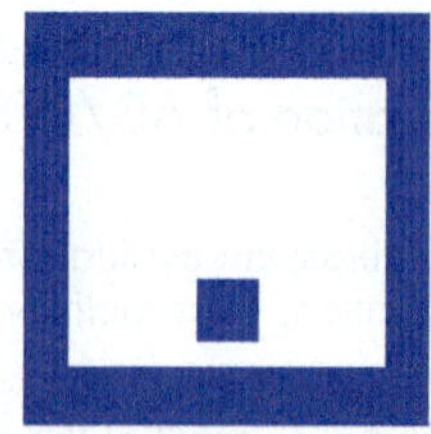

Published with permission of the T.O.V.A. Company.

like aggression, anxiety and depression. Like other scales, the BASC–2 comes in teacher, parent and student forms.

Continuous performance test (CPT)

A test designed to measure an individual's ability to sustain attention

Another type of assessment tool used in the assessment of AD/HD is the continuous performance test. The **continuous performance test (CPT)** is a test designed to measure an individual's ability to sustain attention. Some of these tests are auditory, but most are visual. Some come in self-contained kits, and others come as software that can run on most computers. One test, the Test of Variables of Attention (T.O.V.A.), uses a simple computer display that only presents two symbols (Figure 11.3). The student is to press a button when the target symbol is shown and refrain from pressing the button when the non-target is displayed. The test is twenty-two minutes long and requires no reading skills. Although the task appears simple, the length of the test sufficiently challenges the student so that individuals with attentional difficulties perform differently from individuals without attentional issues. Other CPTs commonly used in educational evaluations are the Gordon Diagnostic System and the Conner's CPT.

Medication

One of the most common treatment approaches to AD/HD is stimulant medication. On the surface, this may seem like a poor choice on many levels:

- *If children with AD/HD have issues with hyperactivity, why give them a stimulant?*
- *Is it safe to regularly give your child a prescription medication for AD/HD?*
- *Will a stimulant medication produce better learning outcomes?*

The rationale behind providing stimulants for students with AD/HD is similar to the reason many adults drink coffee in the morning. Coffee contains caffeine, which is also a stimulant. Ask yourself: when I drink coffee in the morning, do I become hyperactive? The answer will depend on how much coffee you drink. Stimulants have an interesting dose response curve. That is, we behave differently with different doses of a stimulant. If a small dose is taken, we actually see individuals increase their attention span and decrease their motor restlessness, settling into the day. This is the reason most people drink coffee in the morning. However, sometimes we drink too much coffee, and then we experience behavioral symptoms for which the drug class was named—*stimulant.* At a moderate dose of a stimulant, we indeed look "stimulated." Our motor activity increases, and we have difficulty staying on task. The same dose response principles that apply to the caffeine in our coffee apply to the stimulant medications we provide students with AD/HD. When low dose stimulants are given to individuals with AD/HD, we see a decrease in motor behavior and an increase in on-task behavior.

F.A.Q.

Mike Depaula—"I thought that only students with AD/HD would respond to Ritalin by paying attention more. That this kind of response diagnosed them as AD/HD."

Professor Denault—"This is a common misconception regarding AD/HD. Individuals without AD/HD respond to stimulants in the same way as individuals with AD/HD. Again, with low dose stimulants, everyone will increase their ability to direct their attention."

Prescribing stimulant medication is not without concerns. Some of the problems are that there is no clear way to predict how much to give to a person. The patients response to the medication has no reliable biological predictors (like weight), so doctors have to guess at the starting dose and then modify the dose as needed (called titrating) until the desired effect is achieved (Powell, Thomsen, Frydenberg, & Rasmussen, 2011). Side effects are another issue: some people experience insomnia, weight loss, nausea, and irritability (especially as the mediation wears off). Research shows that most prescribed stimulants for AD/HD (e.g.,

Ritalin, Cylert, Dexedrine, and Adderall) are safe and effective when taken as prescribed (Pancheri & Prater, 1999). This does not mean, however, that stimulant medication should always be used to treat AD/HD.

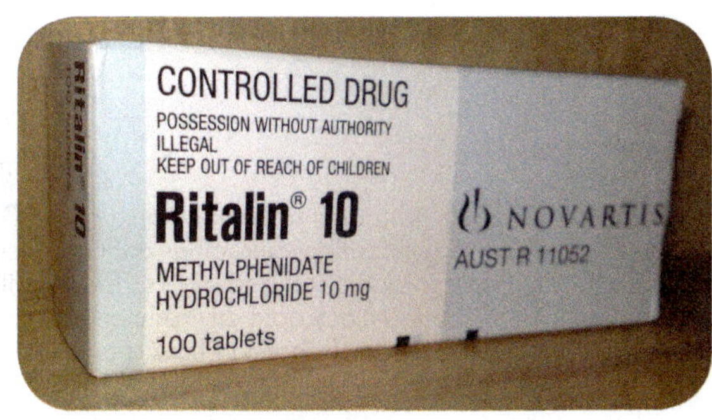

Although stimulants help address the behavioral symptoms of AD/HD, there is no clear evidence showing improvements in learning. This is a critical point and should be carefully considered before a child is placed on a stimulant medication. The medicine is a moderator of behavior. It is not a drug than can produce a greater ability to study effectively, improve test grades, or socialize more effectively. There is a difference between spending more time quietly looking at your math worksheet and actually learning math. Teachers and parents are often so impressed by the improvement in behavior that they fail to recognize there are still many other issues to address. The bottom line is that stimulant medication is potentially a useful tool in the behavior management of students with AD/HD. It should, however, never be seen as a solution or used without a thorough evaluation of the student's problems and concerns.

Education of Students with AD/HD

To fully address the symptoms of AD/HD, we need to look at a more comprehensive educational approach. There are many educational approaches to working with a student with AD/HD. One of the most prominent of these approaches focuses on the student's behavior. Specifics vary, but a behavioral approach helps structure the student's environment so that reinforcements are given for desired behaviors. These behavioral approaches can be used in addition to or in place of medication. One study found that students who used a behavioral self-reinforcement program in addition to medication were able to complete more assignments than students taking medication alone (Ajibola & Clement, 1995). This is, however, still about behavior and not necessarily learning.

To improve academic performance, teachers need to turn to many of the instructional techniques discussed in the last chapter for students with special learning needs (DuPaul, Helwig, & Slay, 2011). In addition to providing special support (i.e., assistance with reading comprehension) for a learning issue, the student with AD/HD also benefits from a curriculum that maximizes certain environmental features. Students with AD/HD appear to rely more heavily on novel stimuli, feedback, variety, choices, activity, and challenging, relevant work (Turnbull, Turnbull, Shank, & Smith, 2004). This means that you may have two students who need reading support, but if one also has AD/HD, they may need services delivered in such a way that these qualities are emphasized.

It is also important to remember the diagnostic research on AD/HD when programming educationally. Recall that students with AD/HD often have difficulty with executive functions. This means that teachers should provide the necessary structure and support needed for the student to develop a greater sense of self-regulation. **Self-regulation strategies** help students moderate their own behavior by having them periodically stop and "check" their behavior (Johnson & Johnson, 1999). Depending on their unique situation and skills, students are given strategies to check their behavior, whether they are on-task, their social appropriateness, etc. They are asked to record their actual behavior at these check points and given strategies for improvement if they are having trouble. The student and the teacher develop goals or criterion behavior, so it is clear to the student when they are succeeding. This is an excellent approach for students with AD/HD. It clearly addresses their difficulty with key executive function and gives them the supports to be successful.

Self-regulation strategies
Strategies that help students moderate their own behavior by having them periodically stop and "check" their behavior

Many teachers do not look at AD/HD as a "problem." Rather, they see it as a different way of experiencing the world. Operating under this premise, teachers strive to find ways to modify their classrooms so students with ADHD are not penalized for their naturally high activity levels, externally driven attention span, or impulsive behavior. Attempting to accommodate some of the child's behavior using this approach demonstrates a greater appreciation of the unique qualities of the student and allows them greater freedom to function in a more natural way. Examples of how to accommodate the behavior of the student with AD/HD are presented in Table 11.6.

Table 11.6 Accommodations Help Students with Attention Deficit Disorders

Harvey C. Parker, PhD
Clinical Psychologist

Children and youth with attention deficit disorder (ADD) often have serious problems in school. Inattention, impulsiveness, hyperactivity, disorganization, and other difficulties can lead to unfinished assignments, careless errors, and behavior which is disruptive to one's self and others. Through the implementation of relatively simple and straightforward accommodations to the classroom environment or teaching style, teachers can adapt to the strengths and weaknesses of students with ADD. Small changes in how a teacher approaches the student with ADD or in what the teacher expects can turn a losing year into a winning one for the child.

Examples of accommodations which teachers can make to adapt to the needs of students with ADD are grouped below according to areas of difficulty.

INATTENTION

- seat student in quiet area
- seat student near good role model
- seat student near "study buddy"
- increase distance between desks
- allow extra time to complete assigned work
- shorten assignments or work periods to coincide with span of attention; use timer
- break long assignments into smaller parts so student can see end to work
- assist student in setting short-term goals
- give assignments one at a time to avoid work overload
- require fewer correct responses for grade
- reduce amount of homework
- instruct student in self-monitoring using cueing
- pair written instructions with oral instructions
- provide peer assistance in note taking
- give clear, concise instructions
- seek to involve student in lesson presentation
- cue student to stay on task, i.e., private signal

ACADEMIC SKILLS

- if reading is weak: provide additional reading time; use "previewing" strategies; select text with less on a page; shorten amount of required reading; avoid oral reading
- if oral expression is weak: accept all oral responses; substitute display for oral report; encourage student to tell about new ideas or experiences; pick topics easy for student to talk about
- if written language is weak: accept non-written forms for reports (i.e., displays, oral, projects); accept use of typewriter, word processor, tape recorder; do not assign large quantity of written work; test with multiple choice or fill-in questions
- if math is weak: allow use of calculator; use graph paper to space numbers; provide additional math time; provide immediate correctness feedback and instruction via modeling of the correct computational procedure

MOOD

- provide reassurance and encouragement
- compliment positive behavior and work product frequently
- speak softly in non-threatening manner if student shows nervousness
- review instructions when giving new assignments to make sure student comprehends directions
- look for opportunities for student to display leadership role in class
- conference frequently with parents to learn about student's interests and achievements outside of school
- send positive notes home
- make time to talk alone with student
- encourage social interactions with classmates if student is withdrawn or excessively shy
- reinforce frequently when signs of frustration are noticed
- look for signs of stress build up and provide encouragement or reduced work load to alleviate pressure and avoid temper outburst
- spend more time talking to students who seem pent up or display anger easily
- provide brief training in anger control: encourage student to walk away; use calming strategies; tell nearby adult if getting angry

MOTOR ACTIVITY

- allow student to stand at times while working
- provide opportunity for "seat breaks," i.e., run errands, etc.
- provide short break between assignments
- supervise closely during transition times
- remind student to check over work product if performance is rushed and careless
- give extra time to complete tasks (especially for students with slow motor tempo)

(continues)

Table 11.6 Accommodations Help Students with Attention Deficit Disorders (*Continued*)

IMPULSIVENESS

- ignore minor, inappropriate behavior
- increase immediacy of rewards and consequences
- use time-out procedure for misbehavior
- supervise closely during transition times
- use "prudent" reprimands for misbehavior (i.e., avoid lecturing or criticism)
- attend to positive behavior with compliments, etc.
- acknowledge positive behavior of nearby students
- seat student near role model or near teacher
- set up behavior contract
- instruct student in self monitoring of behavior, i.e., hand raising, calling out
- call on only when hand is raised in appropriate manner
- praise when hand raised to answer question

COMPLIANCE

- praise compliant behavior
- provide immediate feedback
- ignore minor misbehavior
- use teacher attention to reinforce positive behavior
- use "prudent" reprimands for misbehavior (i.e., avoid lecturing or criticism)
- acknowledge positive behavior of nearby student
- supervise student closely during transition times
- seat student near teacher
- set up behavior contract
- implement classroom behavior management system
- instruct student in self-monitoring of behavior

ORGANIZATION AND PLANNING

- ask for parental help in encouraging organization
- provide organization rules
- encourage student to have notebook with dividers and folders for work
- provide student with homework assignment book
- supervise writing down of homework assignments
- send daily/weekly progress reports home
- check desk and notebook regularly for neatness; encourage neatness rather than penalize sloppiness (do not penalize for poor handwriting if visual-motor defects are present)
- allow student to have extra set of books at home
- give assignments one at a time
- assist student in setting short-term goals
- encourage learning of keyboarding skills
- allow student to tape record assignments or homework

SOCIALIZATION

- praise appropriate behavior
- monitor social interactions
- set up social behavior goals with student and implement a reward program.
- prompt appropriate social behavior either verbally or with private signal
- encourage cooperative learning tasks with other students
- provide small group social skills training
- praise student frequently
- assign special responsibilities to student in presence of peer group so others observe student in a positive light

Used with permission of the A.D.D. WareHouse.

Giftedness and Creativity

Gifted individuals have always captured our attention and our imagination. We are in awe when we attend our school's winter concert and see a tiny little girl, barely able to climb on the piano bench, play like a virtuoso. We flock to movies with young stars that can make us cry with genuine sorrow or laugh with joy. There are also those more familiar incidences of exceptional learning ability. For example, those nieces and nephews at every wedding who answer complicated mathematical problems in their head while we run for paper and pencil. These are the gifted and talented youth of our schools and our lives. They are such a unique population that we have always had trouble designing effective educational programs. How do you teach a student poetry comprehension when his/her perceptual insights exceed your own? How do you teach a student to paint, when his/her own work is already selling at galleries? These are legitimate concerns and the answers are elusive. In this section, we will look at how we define gifted and talented, as well as creativity. We will also examine characteristics of the gifted and explore the challenges these present educators.

Table 11.7 Definition of Gifted and Talented—Javits Gifted and Talented Students Education Act

The term "gifted and talented" when used with respect to students, children or youth means students, children or youth who give evidence of high performance capability in areas such as intellectual, creative, artistic, or leadership ability, or in specific academic fields, and who require service or activities not ordinarily provided by the school in order to fully develop such capabilities

SOURCE: Public Law 103–382, Title XIV, 1988, p. 388.

Defining Gifted and Talented

There are many ways to define giftedness, but let's begin with the influential federal definition. In 1994, the federal government reauthorized the Jacob K. Javits Gifted and Talented Students Education Act of 1988. The exact language of this definition is presented in Table 11.7. The Javit's legislation is important for the education of gifted students because it provides a common definition. It also provides much needed funding for gifted programs. States can apply for grants to support services for gifted and talented youth. It also provides for leadership funding for educators to broaden their understanding of gifted and talented education. Unfortunately, the law does not mandate services or specific programs for gifted students. The lack of a centralized mandated program often leads to substantial differences in program quality.

Gifted programs also vary in quality because schools design gifted programs around different definitions of giftedness. The federal definition has found its way into many state laws, but other definitional approaches are common. Another popular approach to viewing students with gifted abilities comes from Renzulli (1998, 1978). He defines giftedness by the characteristics needed to produce exceptional work. According to his theory, there are three important factors: above average ability, task commitment, and creativity. His theory is typically represented graphically (see Figure 11.4) as three intersecting circles. This figure represents how the individual uses natural intelligence, creativity, and high task commitment to achieve exceptional outcomes. According to Renzulli, gifted students can apply their talents to general performance areas like math or language arts and also to a wide range of specific performance areas, like poetry, clothes design, or architecture. This model has survived the test of time and is a frequently cited model of giftedness.

Characteristics of Giftedness

The search for characteristics of the gifted has a long history. Probably one of the longest running studies of gifted children is a study started by Lewis Terman (1925, 1947,1959; Holahan & Sears, 1995) in the 1920s. His study of over a thousand children with IQ scores over 140 has provided a valuable look at the qualities and characteristics of very intelligent people. There was certainly variability in the participant population; in general, however, they were more emotionally stable, athletic, and better adjusted as adults. They also had lower rates of divorce, drug problems, and delinquency. The Terman studies are important because they are a lengthy

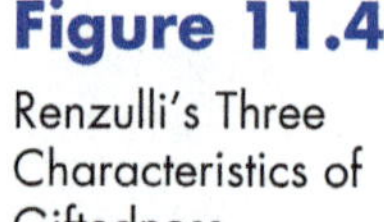

Figure 11.4

Renzulli's Three Characteristics of Giftedness

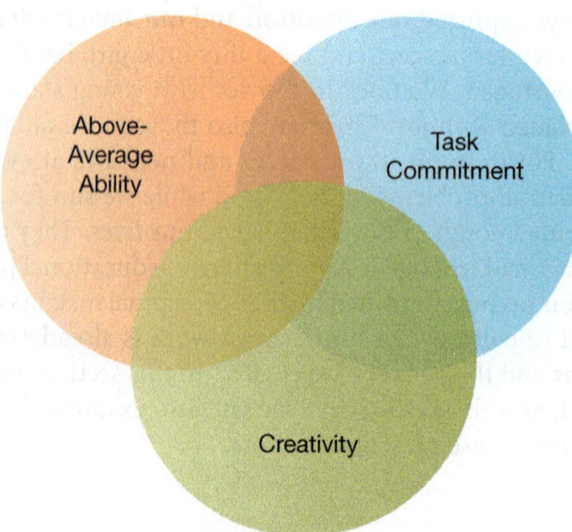

follow-up of a single cohort of individuals, but the studies are not without critics. The selection criteria used to establish the original cohort was far from systematic. Teachers simply nominated "bright" students who then received an IQ test. It is possible that these teachers were able to identify students who would later have positive outcomes. It has also been noted that many of the students in Terman's study came from upper-income families whose resources may have helped their children regardless of intellectual ability (Ceci, 1990).

Other researchers have taken a global approach to defining the characteristics of students who are gifted. Winner (1996) proposes three qualities that define the remarkable abilities of giftedness:

- **Precocity** Children who are gifted explore a domain of interest at an accelerated rate. They make earlier gains in the area than their peers and reach mastery at an early age. Learning in this domain has an effortless quality, and they appear to enjoy the process.

- **Insistence on marching to their own drummer** Learning for the child who is gifted is qualitatively different, not just accelerated. They resist explicit instruction. They enjoy learning on their own and create their own learning path.

- **Passion to master** Children who are gifted display an intense internal motivation. Their desire to learn often takes on an obsessive quality, requiring little parental support.

Additional research on the characteristics of children who are gifted shows that they are less conforming to peer opinions (Gottfried & Gottfried, 1996), adjust better emotionally (Oram, Dewey, & Rutemiller, 1995), and have superior leadership skills (Roeper, 1992). Not all research, however, shows a positive outcome for children who are gifted. Research has also shown that children who are gifted have higher levels of emotional reactivity (Piechowski, 1991) and may have lower self-concepts (Lea-Wood & Clunies-Ross, 1995). It is important to keep in mind that participant populations across these studies vary, and teachers should use caution when applying research findings to specific students. These findings help us, however, ask better questions and look more closely at certain factors.

An additional point to consider when thinking of the characteristics of children who are gifted is their similarity to children with AD/HD. There are certainly differences between the two student populations, but there is enough overlap that diagnostic decisions are complicated. Table 11.8 lists some characteristics that appear similar between children with AD/HD and children who are gifted. As you read each of the qualities, there does appear to be a common set of problems; however, a closer examination of the issues indicates a different underlying cause for the observed behavior. For example, task persistence appears to be impaired in both

Table 11.8 Table Example

Behaviors Associated with AD/HD (Barkley, 1990)	Behaviors Associated with Giftedness (Webb, 1993)
Poorly sustained attention in almost all situations	Poor attention, boredom, daydreaming in specific situations
Diminished persistence on tasks not having immediate consequences	Low tolerance for persistence on tasks that seem irrelevant
Impulsivity, poor delay of gratification	Judgment lags behind development of intellect.
Impaired adherence to commands to regulate or inhibit behavior in social contexts	Intensity may lead to power struggles with authorities.
More active, restless than peers	High activity level; may need less sleep
Difficulty adhering to rules and regulations	Questioning of rules, customs and traditions

Adapted from Webb (1993). ERIC Digests, ED358673, ERIC Digest #522.

situations. In AD/HD, however, the issue is with an impaired ability to internally direct attention. External stimuli cannot easily be ignored leading to a limited attention span. The child who is gifted also has trouble with task persistence, but the cause of their trouble is different. They are frequently educated in a manner that is not sufficiently challenging. This is particularly true in students whose exceptionality is unrecognized. This leads to boredom, which in turn makes it difficult to stay on task. Teachers need to look beyond the behavior itself and consider the underlying causes of the behavior. This helps determine the true nature of the student's difficulties and leads to appropriate identification and services.

One way through which gifted students can be identified is visual and performing arts assessments.

Assessment of Giftedness and Creativity

The nature of evaluation for giftedness depends on the model a particular school uses for identification (Johnsen, 2011). Some schools screen entire grades for students who are gifted. They use group IQ and achievement tests to screen for students who might be eligible for services. The group approach is attractive for screening, because it opens the possibility for gifted services to the entire population being tested. Other approaches rely on teacher or parent nomination for evaluation. Once a given student is identified as possibly needing services for giftedness, they are likely to receive an individually administered IQ test. Using an IQ cut-off score has historically been a prominent approach to establishing eligibility for gifted programs. Other newer approaches take a more comprehensive look at the student and their abilities.

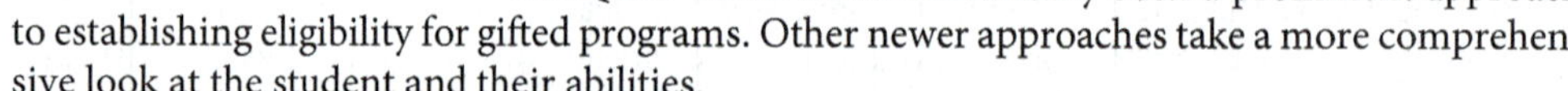

More comprehensive approaches to the identification of gifted students include intelligence testing, academic testing, direct observation, visual and performing arts assessments, creativity checklists, and tests of creativity. Unfortunately, it is rare to see this level of commitment to testing for the student who is gifted. The benefits, however, are clear. Students who are gifted often display their gifts in different domain areas. Assessing only intelligence and academics ignores individuals who express their giftedness in other areas like visual and performing arts. Still, other students may exhibit their gifts in social relations or athletics, which is why direct observation is important. Creativity checklists often cover many areas of interest in an inexpensive and convenient test. For example, the Pfeiffer-Jarosewich Gifted Rating Scales (Pfeiffer & Jarosewich, 2003) provides teachers with rating scales for intellectual ability, academic ability, artistic ability, creativity, motivation and leadership.

Creativity

Often defined as having two qualities: originality and functionality

Divergent thinking

The ability to think of multiple solutions to a given problem

Convergent thinking

The ability to think analytically, and usually deductively, of the one correct solution

Although there is a general trend to do less testing when determining giftedness, one area that has seen greater attention is creativity. Recall that according to Renzulli, creativity is a necessary component to gifted work. **Creativity** is often defined as having two qualities: originality and functionality (Simonton, 1990). This means that it is not only important to produce or do something novel, but also that it needs to have some functional outlet to be considered a creative work. In schools, a commonly used test of creativity is the Torrance Test of Creativity (Torrance, 1972; Torrance & Hall, 1980). This test specifically looks at three facets of divergent thinking. **Divergent thinking** is the ability to think of multiple solutions to a given problem. This is contrasted with **convergent thinking**, the ability to think of the one correct solution. The three facets of divergent thinking measured by the Torrance Test of Creativity are fluency, flexibility, and originality. *Fluency* refers to the ability to produce many ideas (e.g., thirty different uses for a brick). Flexibility refers to the ability to think in categorically different ways (e.g., bricks can be used as paper weights and bricks can be used as building materials—two categorically different uses). *Originality* is the ability to think of unusual responses (e.g., a brick can be broken and the pieces used to replace the bone a person has broken). Imagine a student that thought of thirty different uses for a brick, but all the uses were for "building" something. Some of the things suggested, however, were unusual for their age (e.g., building a sea wall to save an eroding beach). This student would likely score well on fluency and originality, but low on flexibility since all responses were about building. As you can see from this example, the test in this case is also defining the construct. That is, because the Torrance Test of Creativity was used, the definition of creativity became fluency, flexibility and originality. This is often the case with assessment, and educational professionals need to consider this fact when selecting assessment instruments. Ideally, the school or state would deliberate on their meaning of the construct first and then choose assessment instruments that accurately and effectively measure the construct.

Education of Students Who Are Gifted

Historically, there appears to be a view of gifted education that "less" is the best practice. Some view students who are gifted as so self-motivated that no special educational modifications are needed. This is not the case. As this book consistently emphasizes, all students need an educational program that is uniquely suited to their individual learning needs. Students who are gifted are no different. Unfortunately, research shows that teachers are not increasing their use of such differentiated learning practices with students with exceptional gifts as discussed in Chapter 8 (Westberg & Daoust, 2003). If schools are to meet the needs of students, they need to be sensitive to the individual. This means teachers will need many educational tools to meet the wide variety of student needs. Let's look at some of the educational approaches used with children demonstrating gifted ability and exceptional creativity.

Acceleration

The process of providing an advanced instructional setting to meet the needs of exceptional learners

Enrichment

The process of providing advanced learning opportunities for students, while maintaining their regular educational placement

Acceleration versus enrichment One persistent controversy in gifted education is over acceleration versus enrichment (Davis & Rimm, 2004; Feldhusen, Van Winkle, & Ehle, 1996). **Acceleration** is the process of providing an advanced instructional setting to meet the needs of exceptional learners (commonly thought of as skipping grades). **Enrichment** is the process of providing advanced learning opportunities, while maintaining students' regular educational placement. Research provides positive support for the acceleration of students who are gifted (Kulik, 2003). Students appear to benefit from higher achievement and more positive self-concepts. They do not appear to suffer from greater social problems as is commonly believed (Swiatek, 1993). Some teachers mistakenly believe that accelerating students means they need to skip grades. Although this is an option, there are many other ways to accelerate students who are gifted. They may be moved to another grade for instruction only in an area of strength. For example, rather than stay in their regular classroom for math, they may go next door to a higher grade for math instruction. Also, young children may simply start school early. Adolescents may leave their high school earlier in the day to take classes at a local college. All of these approaches provide accelerated learning opportunities. Alternatively, enrichment approaches attempt to give the student challenging learning opportunities in their current grade placement. The difficulty with this approach is that the teacher often finds it necessary to give the advanced student independent work while attending to the more typically developing student majority. At times this works given the exceptional internal motivation of these students, but the loss of active teaching may limit their progress.

Research provides positive support for the acceleration of gifted students.

Curriculum packing Another easy to implement approach to gifted education is called curriculum packing. **Curriculum packing** is a technique to help teachers make appropriate curricular adjustments depending on the specific learning needs of the student (Reis, Burns, & Renzulli, 1992). In other words, it is a system to help teachers modify daily lessons to meet the needs of each student. The authors of the approach regard the system as "organized common sense." This simply underscores that the system is an organized approach to techniques teachers are already using. Curriculum packing has three basic phases:

Curriculum packing

A technique to help teachers make appropriate curricular adjustments, depending on the specific learning needs of the student

1) The first phase is to have the teacher thoroughly define their goals for a particular lesson or unit. This can be a bulleted or numbered list of goals or objectives.
2) Next, the teacher determines which students have mastered all or most of the goals for that unit.
3) Finally, for those students who demonstrate mastery of the current lesson objectives, replacement material is provided that appropriately challenges the student. This supports each student's continued intellectual growth.

The difficult part of this process is that teachers will need to maintain a thorough curricular plan for future material. This is because students who are gifted will rapidly outpace their classmates and require the instructional material to address advanced learning goals. The process of providing advanced instructional materials may take the form of enrichment (discussed earlier) or acceleration, particularly if the student is performing significantly above grade level.

Problem-based learning

Popular student-centered approach used with gifted students that emphasizes learning in a dynamic, real life context

Problem-based learning **Problem-based learning** is another popular approach used with students who are gifted (Finkle & Torp, 1995). In this approach, students are presented with a particular real-life problem (e.g., current politics, scientific discoveries, issues with social responsibility) that does not have a specific solution. It is important to develop a real-life problem that the students find engaging. The problem can be co-designed with the students to increase student investment. It is also important to have an ill-defined problem or one with multiple solutions. This is because the approach is essentially an exercise in divergent thinking. The students are encouraged to think creatively and come up with multiple solutions to the problem. This requires critical thinking and active learning. Research shows that problem-based learning can motivate students to actively participate in their own learning, but this needs to be balanced with more traditional instruction in the content material (Arends, 2000; Smith, Polloway, Patton, & Dowdy, 2004).

A safe, risk-free learning environment is critical for encouraging creative thinking.

Encouraging Creativity

A final point we will consider is educational approaches supporting creative thinking. Much of the educational process is geared toward teaching students to find the *correct answer.* On the surface this sounds like a positive goal, but there are some issues with focusing too heavily on such a convergent thinking approach. Finding the correct answer often requires a thorough and productive brainstorming process. Brainstorming is a divergent thinking process and just as crucial as convergent thinking. Teachers need to help students develop both thinking approaches.

One important factor in encouraging creative thinking is to provide a safe, risk-free learning environment (Piirto, 1999). How many times do you think beginning teachers say, "Do you have any questions?" What kind of student response are they likely to get? The answer depends on the classroom environment, but all too often the students simply stare at the teacher and the next learning objective is presented. Teachers need to create a comfortable learning environment where students feel safe to ask any question and offer any response. This is a challenging task. Often, teachers who attempt to create a relaxed and safe learning environment feel that unusual student responses and questions derail curricular progress. They may inadvertently suppress such questions by subtle looks or differentially reinforcing more traditional student questions. Again, the downside is that students will fail to develop their creative thinking ability. Ultimately, this may mean they have difficulty reaching correct solutions to problems because they are unable to think of a sufficient range of possible answers.

SUMMARIZE AND REFLECT

1. The second section of this chapter reviewed two of the most common exceptional learning situations not covered under IDEA.
2. Attention deficit/hyperactivity disorder (AD/HD) is one of the most common disorders of childhood. We looked at the current process for identification of AD/HD, as well as concerns over its possible over-diagnosis. We then reviewed how current theories attempt to explain the causes behind this complex disorder. Next, we discussed several assessment approaches and the benefits and concerns regarding medication. Finally, we looked at several educational approaches designed to help create a productive learning environment for students with AD/HD.

(continues)

3. The other special needs situation we explored was giftedness. Often considered one of the most underserved special learning needs, students with accelerated learning present many challenges. First, we defined giftedness and reviewed some basic characteristics of the gifted student. Next, we reviewed issues related to the assessment of giftedness and creativity. Finally, we discussed different educational approaches for gifted students and reviewed how teachers can support creative thinking.

INFORMED APPLICATION

1. Medication for attention deficit/hyperactivity disorder is controversial. Review what symptoms are particularly impacted by medication and how you would integrate medication into a comprehensive treatment plan.
2. There are a variety of educational approaches for children identified as gifted. Which approach do you find most appealing and why?

EXCEPTIONALITY: FAMILIES AND CULTURE

This chapter has taken a look at ways students differ in their learning ability, behavior, and social functioning. We have learned about identification of special needs, assessment, and education. Effective education, however, cannot ignore the powerful influence of factors outside the school environment. One of the significant changes seen in schools across the last twenty years is the growing appreciation of families as collaborators in education (Nabors, 2011). This is true for every student, but takes on special meaning for families of students with exceptionalities. Families are the foundational structure from which children emerge to grow and explore the world. Family influence on the educational lives of students is significant and vital to their achieving the best educational experience. In this section, we will look at the ways teachers interact with parents and family members to create positive learning experiences. We will also take a closer look at the relationships with fathers, siblings, and grandparents and how they play a unique role in the dynamics of family life and student success. Finally, we will examine the influence of a family's cultural background on the educational process. We will review research on disability acceptance and cultural background. We will also look at how cultural background relates to identification for special services in the schools.

Exceptionality and the Family

Families are highly interactive and interdependent groups. Families rely on each other for social and financial support. We also look to our families for emotional support and understanding. This is an incredibly complicated system, yet one with which teachers need to become familiar in order to provide the best educational experience for students. Bronfenbrenner (1977, 1979, 1989) describes developmental life in the context of larger familial, community, and societal levels. His ecological theory stresses the importance of these larger layers of influence if one is to fully understand the development of the child. For example, a teacher may notice an increase in a student's focus and determination. After a parent conference, the teacher learns that the parents are providing additional support and encouragement for the child in order to help the child achieve better grades. This is because the parents recently learned that their company offers a scholarship plan for dependents that maintain an *A* average in school. What this shows is that a student's performance is influenced by many factors. Some are close and constant factors in the child's life, like parents, siblings and grandparents. Larger community and societal factors also affect students. As this example shows, a company policy resulted in real changes in the academic achievement of the student. These shifting and dynamic changes provide valuable information for the teacher. It helps them better understand and help students achieve their potential. Students with exceptionalities are no different in the complexity of their life system. Let's look more closely at the overall life circumstance of the student with exceptional learning needs.

Teachers need to be familiar with each student's family system in order to provide the best educational experience.

Parents and caregivers are an integral part in the education of their child.

Parents

How we view the role of parents in education has changed dramatically over time. Currently, parents and caregivers act as integral collaborators in the education of their student. They actively participate in educational planning and help provide an important look at the context in which students live and learn. Viewing parents as collaborators gives teachers better tools to understand factors affecting student success. This is particularly true when a student has an exceptional learning need. Whether the identification of a special need is new or longstanding, the nature of the exceptionality affects the entire family; in turn, the family affects the motivation, outlook, and success of the student.

It is difficult to predict a family's reaction to the news that a child has an exceptional learning need. In part, it depends on the nature of the learning situation. Families are much more likely to view a diagnosis of gifted learning ability favorably than a diagnosis of autism. Some families, however, view even severe impairments with optimism and hope. Some parents are able to look at a challenging learning need and see hope and faith that the challenge will help the family grow stronger. Others follow a more traditional path of grief, guilt, and eventual acceptance. Researchers have defined stage models to define the adaptation process following the diagnosis of a disability (Gargiulo, 1985), as shown in Figure 11.5.

Again, the importance of this model is not that every parent will go through these stages, but the model informs the teacher about possible parental reactions. This helps teachers deal more effectively with parents by allowing them some time to consider how to deal with the range of emotional possibilities.

The dynamic relationships within a family mean that adjustment problems experienced by the student will have an impact on the relationship of the parents. Again, parental reactions will vary and depend on numerous factors. One potential outcome is that parents might experience marital difficulties following a disability diagnosis. The research on this topic is mixed. Some studies find an increase in marital issues (Gabel, McDowell, & Cerreto, 1983; Hodapp & Krasner, 1995); whereas, others find the opposite effect (Scorgie & Sobsey, 2000; Scorgie, Wilgosh, & McDonald, 1998). It appears to depend on the unique situation of the family, and teachers should remain sensitive to this and provide support and appropriate resources.

Another family dynamic gaining attention is that of fathers and children with disabilities. Historically, researchers have focused heavily on the nature of the mother-child relationship. Newer research, however, is investigating the equally important paternal relationship in the development and success of the child with a disability (Flynn & Wilson, 1998; Young & Roopnarine, 1994; Lamb & Meyer, 1991; Meyer, 1986). Fathers appear more likely to focus on issues like the visibility of the disability and the long-term consequences to the family. They are less likely to focus on the day-to-day issues in raising a child with a disability. The father's attitude clearly influences the views of the family and the student, which has implications for the student's performance in school. Again, teachers should be sensitive to these dynamics when planning assistance for students with disabilities. It is not enough to create an appropriate learning environment at school. Attending to the social dynamics of the student's life outside school is just as important in determining the success of the student. There are limits to a teacher's influence in home affairs, but developing a thorough understanding of the student's life provides the foundation for a truly collaborative relationship with the family.

Figure 11.5

Stage Models of the Adaptation Process Following the Diagnosis of a Disability

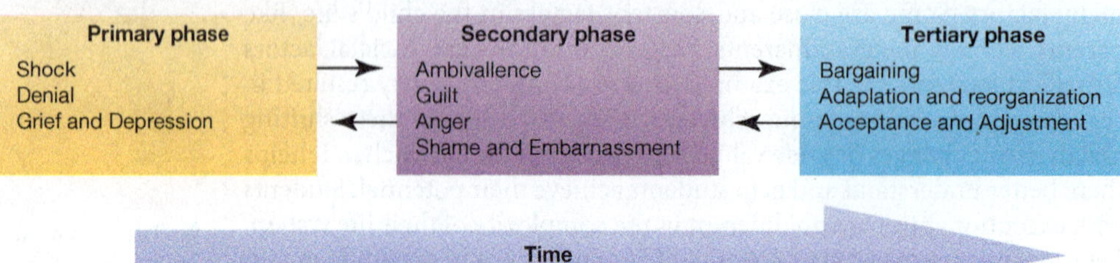

Siblings

For many people their sibling bonds are their first significant social network.

Siblings play a crucial role in our development. For many, sibling bonds are the first significant social network in a child's development (Powell & Ogle, 1985). This relationship is typically altered by the knowledge that a child has a disability. Sometimes the nature of the disability actually limits the social interactions of siblings because of the amount of parental attention required to care for the child (Crnic & Leconte, 1986). Sometimes this leads to positive interactions among siblings (McHale & Gamble, 1987) as siblings take on socially supportive roles. Other times, siblings can develop anger and resentment (Russell, Russell, & Russell, 2003; Stoneman & Berman, 1993). Support groups often help siblings understand their role in families raising a child with a disability (Meyer & Vadasy, 1994). Support groups help children share their feelings and discover a level of care for their siblings that balances their need for love and personal attention. Teachers can also play a supportive role. Often teachers have students in their classes who have a sibling with a disability. Their knowledge and experience can help the student better understand the nature of his/her sibling's challenges and provide a supportive and understanding educational environment.

Grandparents

Grandparents help care for the needs and education of their grandchildren.

One of the newer areas of research in this field is grandparents. Up until recently, little research focused on the impact of extended family members on the life of the child with an exceptional learning need. Grandparents usually have multiple concerns when they learn a grandchild has an exceptional learning need. They care for the well-being and education of their grandchild, but they also care for their own child (the parent) and the difficulties they encounter raising a child with special needs (Seligman, Goodwin, Paschal, Applegate, & Lehman, 1997; Marsh, 1993). Many grandparents provide generous emotional support for their child (the parent) and their struggles rearing a child with a disability (Seligman & Darling, 1997). This depends, however, on the grandparent's own perception of the grandchild's learning needs. Potentially, grandparents can provide additional stressors if they fail to perceive the situation in a positive light. In the end, for families dealing with a child with special learning needs, it is about having a positive outlook and hard work.

Exceptionality and Cultural Diversity

Families play a significant role in the life of a student with exceptional learning needs. Not all families, however, are created equal. Families are made up of different relationships, numbers of individuals, and varied cultural backgrounds. As we saw in the last section, different family members play unique roles in the dynamics of family life. In this section, we will expand that discussion, looking at sociological and cultural differences. We will discuss how disability acceptance varies across sociocultural background. We will also look at how exceptionality identification varies across cultural groups.

Cultural Heritage and Acceptance

Cultures around the world vary in how they perceive someone as "different" and how they behave toward such individuals. Much of the United States and Eastern Europe still see "differences" as negative, which potentially results in separation from mainstream society (Smart, 2001). This is interesting because western cultures also tend to hold a medical view of disability, believ-

Cultures around the world differ in how they perceive those who are "different."

ing that disabilities can be identified and treated (Harry, 1992b). Other cultures have a very different belief structure regarding disability. Some see a disability as the will of a higher power (Hanson, Lynch, & Wayman, 1990). Asian cultures often see a disability as a source of shame or embarrassment (Misra, 1994). These belief structures make it more difficult for teachers to develop productive and collaborative educational relationships. Teachers, however, can make every effort to help parents view their child's situation as one where positive changes can be made. It requires the teacher to maintain a sensitivity and understanding for the unique cultural heritage of the parents (Salend & Taylor, 1993). They also need to demonstrate their willingness and obligation to the appropriate education of the student and their belief in the student's ability to make positive changes.

Identification and Diversity

A final point to consider is the impact of cultural heritage on the identification for special services. A review of cultural background and regular education, special education, and gifted programs clearly indicates discrepancies with respect to the general population.

Individuals with Disabilities Education Act Data from the U.S. Department of Education indicates inconsistencies in the number of students being served under the Individuals with Disabilities Education Act (IDEA), (covered in detail in Chapter 10. Table 11.9 shows the total number of students ages three to twenty-one in 2003 (77,138,395). It also shows the proportion of this total identified by cultural heritage: white, black, Hispanic, Asian/Pacific Islander, American Indian/Alaska Native. The next column shows the total number of students served under IDEA (6,633,902). The table also breaks down the total number of students by race/ethnicity.

As you can see, approximately 8.6% of the total school population in 2003 was receiving services under IDEA. Interestingly, this percentage varies dramatically according to race/ethnicity. Students from Asian/Pacific Islander backgrounds were the least represented with only 4.4% of these students receiving services under IDEA. American Indian/Alaska Natives had the highest numbers of students receiving services under IDEA. This was closely followed by students from Black (non-Hispanic) backgrounds.

The explanations behind the overrepresentation of children from African or American Indian/Alaska Natives populations have received considerable attention. Some see the issue as socioeconomic, sociocultural, and sociopolitical (Patton, 1998; Artiles & Trent, 1994). Others

Table 11.9 Table Example

Race/Ethnicity	Ages 3–21 School Population	Students Served Under IDEA	Percentage of Total Population (students served/ school population)
Total	77,138,395	6,633,902	8.6
White, non-Hispanic	48,046,190	4,035,880	8.4
Black, non-Hispanic	11,605,791	1,334,666	11.5
Hispanic	13,806,173	1,035,463	7.5
Asian/Pacific Islander	3,126,000	137,544	4.4
American Indian/Alaska Native	759,235	90,349	11.9

SOURCE: Adapted from U.S. Department of Education, Office of Special Education Programs (OSEP), 2003.

see the problems as more exclusively socioeconomic than race and ethnicity (Loosen & Orfield, 2002). The positive correlation between race/ethnicity and economic level among many African Americans makes isolating factors difficult (Donovan & Cross, 2002; MacMillan & Reschly, 1998).

The reasons for overrepresentation of certain groups receiving services under IDEA are difficult to uncover. Beth Harry and Janette Klingner (2002) have surveyed many educational professionals and have determined that the following factors influence overrepresentation:

- *Family and community issues*
- *External pressures in schools (e.g., mandated curriculum, high-stakes assessments)*
- *Classroom instruction and management*
- *Teacher perceptions and attitudes*

In The Classroom

APPLYING THEORY

Reducing Overrepresentation of Racial/Ethnic Groups in Special Education

CLASSROOM APPLICATION

The reasons behind overrepresentation of certain racial/ethnic groups are complex. Teachers, however, can positively influence this issue by using the following guidelines (Warger & Burnette, 2000).

Teachers should promote family involvement and respect diverse backgrounds
At a basic level, the process of reducing overrepresentation of certain groups begins with respect. Not only do teachers need to appreciate the value of parents as educational collaborators, but also need to validate and accommodate the families' unique cultural background.

Teachers should make the curriculum relevant
Outstanding learning is an outgrowth of outstanding motivation. Students learn best when they connect with the material and see it as personally relevant. This fosters high motivation and academic success. Teachers can help students connect learning to meaningful events in their own lives.

Teachers should build on students' strengths
In any new learning task, we use our existing skills to navigate the material. Effectively identifying those things we do well and problem solving ways to use those strengths help us learn.

Teachers should take the teacher preparation program to the community
An excellent approach to helping teachers learn and appreciate other cultures is to experience them. Teacher training programs often have the opportunity to place student teachers in a culturally diverse teaching practicum.

Teachers should provide district support to build the capacity of personnel
Schools can impact overrepresentation of cultural groups by providing pre-referral supports that are especially sensitive to cultural and racial/ethnic differences. Better understanding the cultural perspectives of the students serves to increases the likelihood that special services will be used for exceptional learning needs and not to remediate cultural differences.

If we are going to address these issues, we need to develop ways to recognize and embrace the continued diversification of the American culture. When teachers view differences as problematic, then they are more likely to refer students for special services. Differences, however, are often just alternative life approaches. One approach is not necessarily any better or worse, just different. Teachers can help students frame differences in a positive way.

It is also important to note that individuals from Asian/Pacific Islands are *underrepresented* in special education. Some see this as an overridingly positive perception regarding the academic abilities of students from Asian descent. As with other cultural groups, however, students from Asian backgrounds are not as homogeneous as the general public might assume. They come from a variety of ethnic, religious, and language groups (Chang, 1994). Immigrants from Asian nations come into an American society that views them as "model immigrants." There is a perception that students from Asian descent work hard and are excellent students. This stereotypical view of these students can lead to fewer referrals for special services even when they are needed. Also, the cultural characteristics such as passivity and conformity, which are more common in Asian cultures, may mask the needs of these students (Kim, 1983).

Cultural Diversity and Representation in Gifted Programs

Gifted programs across the nation suffer from issues that are almost the mirror image of those found among students receiving services under IDEA. In 2003, the National Academy of Sciences reported that 9.9% of students from Asian descent were in gifted programs. This compared to 7.4% for white students, 4.9% for Indian students, 3.6% for Hispanic students, and 3.0% for African-American students. As we discussed earlier in this chapter, gifted programs are increasingly recognized across the country. Programs are growing, but it is not clear that this growth is affording equal opportunity to all students. As with the representational issues facing services under IDEA, schools need to pay close attention to the selection process for gifted programs and the reasons for under-representing certain student populations. Families from economically disadvantaged backgrounds and students who manifest their gifts in unusual domains are particularly at-risk for exclusion from gifted programs.

SUMMARIZE AND REFLECT

1. The final part of this chapter examined the life of students with exceptionalities outside the classroom.
2. We learned that research is continuing to demonstrate that educational best practices are grounded in an appreciation of the whole student. This includes their family life and the cultural framework in which they live.
3. We began our look at life beyond the classroom by exploring the many relationships in the family unit.
4. We discussed the role of parents and their adjustment to life with a student who has special learning needs. We also looked at siblings and the powerful influence they have on each other. Grandparents also play a role in the dynamics of the family. We examined their effect on the student with exceptional learning needs, as well as the parents.
5. The final part of this section focused on exceptionality and culture. Although cultural background is often viewed as far removed from the day-to-day learning situation, it is a constant influence in the lives of student.
6. We discussed how different cultures view exceptionality. We also discussed how identification of special learning needs is influenced by culture and racial/ethnic background.
7. We reviewed steps teachers can take to help ensure students receive equal attention when a special learning situation is suspected and evaluated.

INFORMED APPLICATION

1. What do you see as the role of the teacher in helping parents deal with the news that their son or daughter has a disability?
2. What steps could you take to help a family maintain a positive educational outlook following a diagnosis of a disability?
3. What is your impression of the data demonstrating that some racial/ethnic groups are either over- or under-represented in special education? How might this impact your daily teaching?

THE CHAPTER IN REVIEW

Today's educational system faces many challenges as schools strive to meet the individual learning needs of all students. In this chapter, we looked at special learning needs not typically served under the Individuals with Disabilities Education Act (IDEA). Two laws developed during the civil rights movement govern much of our work with students outside of IDEA. The Vocational Rehabilitation Act of 1973 has a specific section that has direct application to schools. Section 504 provides for discrimination protection for any institution receiving federal funds. We learned that since most public and private schools receive some measure of federal funding, they are obligated to meet the non-discrimination standards of the law. We also reviewed the Americans with Disabilities Act (ADA), which also provides discrimination protection for individuals with disabilities. We compared ADA with Section 504, learning how the two laws use a common set of standards to ensure equitable treatment under the law. We also compared these two laws to IDEA in terms of defining disability, eligibility, evaluation, and services. We underscored the importance for all teachers to develop a thorough understanding of these laws if they are to have the necessary tools to provide a free and appropriate education for all students.

The second part of the chapter focused on a detailed exploration of two of the most common exceptionalities not usually served under IDEA. We examined attention deficit/hyperactivity disorder (AD/HD) and students who are gifted and talented. AD/HD is an often, misunderstood set of behavioral symptoms. We began with a definition of AD/HD and then discussed the many theoretical explanations for the disorder. We also looked at assessment tools and the evaluation process for diagnosing AD/HD. The final part of the section reviewed important educational considerations when dealing with students with AD/HD. In this section, we also explored the life and education of the student with unusual gifts. Gifted and talented programs are becoming more common and elaborate, but are still limited. We examined defining characteristics of giftedness and how educational professionals identify gifted students. We also discussed several educational approaches that support accelerated learning abilities.

The last part of the chapter expanded our look at exceptional learning needs by focusing on life outside the school. Evidence is growing that teachers need to understand and appreciate the life circumstance of students if they are to provide the best educational environment. To understand the life of the student outside school, we began with a close examination of the impact of family members. We looked at parents, siblings, and grandparents, and how family members have a direct impact on the academic success of the student. Next, we reviewed important cultural factors influencing student life. We explored the effects of a student's cultural group on the acceptance of disability. We also discussed the impact of race/ethnicity on the process of identifying students who demonstrate exceptional learning needs. All of these factors contribute to the educational success of the student, and today's teachers are increasingly taking a holistic educational perspective.

Interdisciplinary Case Focus

principal *special educator*
teacher *parents* *psychologist*
social worker *physical educator*
nurse *peers* *doctor*

Kyra Baldwin is a seven-year-old girl attending Mt. Dora Elementary School. She is in the second grade and the eighth child of Debra and William Baldwin. She has Ms. Sara Evans for all subjects except science, which is taught by the other second grade teacher, Ms. Barbara Mason. Her current curriculum is standard for the grade. She does well in all subjects. This is consistent with all the Baldwin children, who are known throughout the school as diligent and successful students. The one area of concern is Kyra's mathematical ability. Ms. Evans noticed at the beginning of the school year that Kyra demonstrated a strong aptitude for mathematics. She easily handled in-class math work and enthusiastically answered any math question when called. It was about one month into school when Kyra began bringing in what she called "extra credit." The first of these sheets looked like a series of squiggles on a lined sheet of notebook paper. Ms. Evans smiled at Kyra and gave her a polite, "Thank you" for the unusual submission. Kyra apparently realized that Ms. Evans did not understand, so she proceeded to explain the significance of her work. Kyra told the teacher to count the "humps" on each of the squiggles. Somewhat confused, but curious, she began to count out loud: 2 6 10 14 3 6 9 12 4 10 16 22. Unsure, Ms. Evans was able to understand the pattern, Kyra explained that she was adding a number to the first number to create a pattern. First, she was adding 4 each time, then she switched to 3, and finally 6. She added that if you "tap out" the pattern on the desk it makes a sort of song. She exclaimed, "This is my music." Ms. Evans thanked Kyra for her extra credit and began to keep a closer eye on Kyra's math work. Her next extra credit involved multiplication. She turned in a sizable stack of paper filled with simple multiplication problems written in tiny, very precise handwriting. She had accurately written down the entire multiplication table through the 20s. When asked if she copied this from something, Kyra frowned and said adamantly that she "counted it out." The work was so extensive and must have taken so much time, Ms. Evans began to get concerned and decided to talk to her parents.

Parent Conference Kyra's parents did not seem surprised at the call and readily agreed to a conference the next day. Ms. Evans expressed her concern that perhaps Kyra was spending an unusual amount of time on her "extra credit." Her parents smiled and assured Ms. Evans that Kyra loves math. They said that while their other seven children completed their homework each evening, Kyra would get bored so that is when she decided to do her extra credit with her siblings. They informed Ms. Evans that Kyra is very bright and frequently surprises them with her insights. For example, the other day Mr. Baldwin was making cookies with Kyra and decided to double the recipe. The first ingredient was ¾ teaspoon of baking soda. Mr. Baldwin told Kyra that to double that amount they would need 1½ teaspoons. Fascinated, Kyra asked her father to explain. Using soup cans, Mr. Baldwin attempted to explain part/whole relations to Kyra. To his surprise, Kyra was able to double each of the other ingredients with only one mistake. Ms. Baldwin then quickly told about an incident when Kyra and her sister were driving to a nearby town. Kyra's sister asked her how long it would take and Ms. Baldwin told her that at their current speed, it would take 25 more minutes. Kyra then pronounced that if her mother doubled her speed it would only take 12½ minutes and that she should speed up.

Both parents told Ms. Evans that they had been meaning to talk to the school about having her tested for the gifted program, but with eight children they had trouble getting anything done. They also noted that Kyra did well in other areas, but did not exhibit the same acceleration in anything but mathematics. They wondered if this was typical of gifted children? After some discussion about gifted and talented students, Ms. Evans and Kyra's parents decide to have the school psychologist give Kyra an individually administered IQ test. Ms. Evans expressed concern that the school's policy was that students needed to achieve a score of 130 or higher to participate in the gifted program. Kyra's specific skills in math may not produce an overall IQ score high enough. She indicated that they would start with the IQ test (which has a separate math subscale) and collect additional information if necessary.

School Psychologist The school psychologist, Mr. Hyam, administered the WISC-IV, which is an individually administered IQ test commonly used in school systems. The test took approximately two hours to complete. The psychologist report indicated an overall IQ of 124. This places Kyra in the superior range of intellectual performance. The psychologist noted that Kyra's scores were consistently high across subtests with an exceptional strength on the Arithmetic subscale. Her performance on this scale was higher than 99% of students her age. Curious about this discrepancy, the psychologist called Kyra's parents and requested permission to give her the math sections of the Woodcock-Johnson Test of Achievement. The parents wanted to contact her teacher to discuss the results before proceeding with additional testing.

Collaborative Meeting: Parents, Teacher, Psychologist Mr. and Ms. Baldwin met with Ms. Evans and the school psychologist, Mr. Hyam, to discuss the merits of additional testing. Mr. Hyam expressed his concern that the IQ tests failed to capture Kyra's talents in math. He indicated that a math achievement test would further explore her math ability. Ms. Evans agreed but noted that since Kyra did not achieve the required 130 on her IQ test, she was ineligible for the school's gifted program. She noted her disagreement with the school's policy regarding the gifted program and made two suggestions. First, they could proceed with the achievement testing and if the results documented her exceptional abilities, they would begin to look for appropriate classroom modifications to meet her learning needs. Second, she encouraged Kyra's parents to make an appointment with the school's principal to discuss the possibility of adopting a more holistic set of criteria for the gifted program. Mr. and Ms. Baldwin agreed with both of these suggestions.

At a second meeting, the psychologist reported that Kyra did exceptionally well on the achievement test, scoring better than 99.9% of students her age. He thought it important to note that on specific computational skills, she was well above average; however, on a subtest of mathematical reasoning, which relies less on skills Kyra has not yet been taught, she scored at the tenth grade level.

The team discussed how best to meet Kyra's learning needs. They considered an enrichment approach, where Kyra would stay in her regular class and receive advanced instruction. They also considered moving her to the third grade class for math only. After considerable discussion, it was decided to recommend to the principal that Kyra remain in the second grade for the immediate future. Ms. Evans would make a list of all the math skills taught in the second grade and begin to test Kyra on each skill. In cases where Kyra has clearly mastered the skill, Ms. Evans would move ahead to the next skill in the curriculum. They agreed that they would follow this *curriculum packing* approach until Kyra had mastered all the second grade skills. At that point, she would move to the third grade math class following a similar approach.

Follow-up Kyra quickly moved through both the second, third, and fourth grade curriculum. She began her third grade year in the fifth grade math class. Her performance outside of math continues at an excellent rate but is manageable in her age-appropriate grade.

Mr. and Ms. Baldwin met with the school principal to discuss the school's policy on admission to the gifted program. This led to additional meetings with the school board and other educational officials. At present, the school is preparing to modify its gifted program. The school is adding other sources of information including teacher observations, teacher and parent rating scales, achievement tests, and tests of creativity.

Mr. and Ms. Baldwin also located a gifted summer program at a nearby university where there is a special program for advanced math students. The six-week program allows Kyra to explore math using tools and facilities unavailable in her local school. She is also able to socialize with other students with similar ability, which helps her develop a positive view of herself and gives her broader socialization opportunities.

Key Terms

TERM	Page	TERM	Page
Acceleration	377	Enrichment	377
Attention deficit/hyperactivity disorder (AD/HD)	364	Executive functioning	368
Behavior rating scale	368	Otherwise qualified	361
Continuous performance test (CPT)	370	Problem-based learning	378
Convergent thinking	376	Reasonable accommodation	364
Creativity	376	Section 504 of the Rehabilitation Act of 1973	358
Curriculum packing	377	Self-regulation strategies	371
Divergent thinking	376	Substantial limitation	362

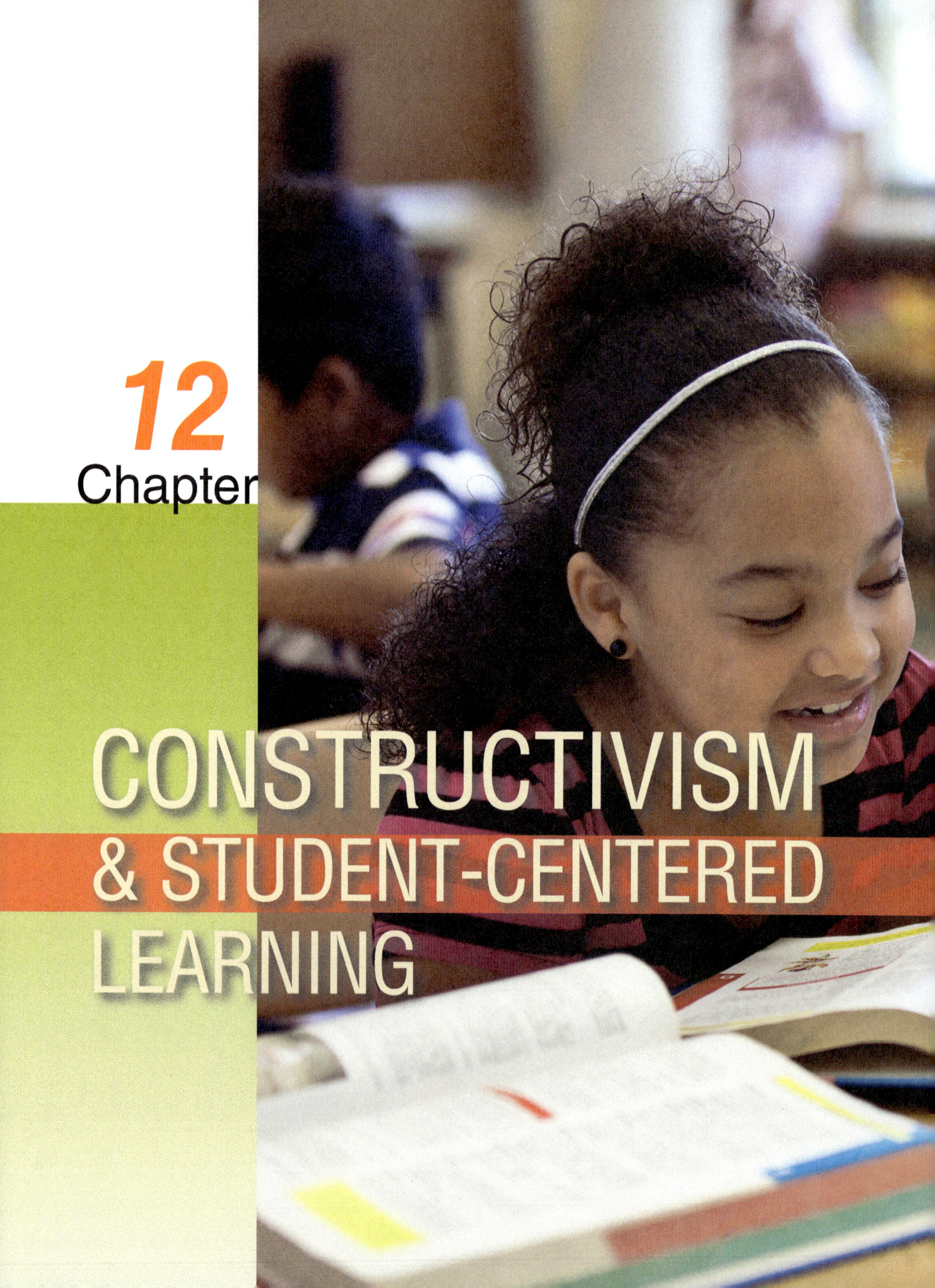

12
Chapter

CONSTRUCTIVISM & STUDENT-CENTERED LEARNING

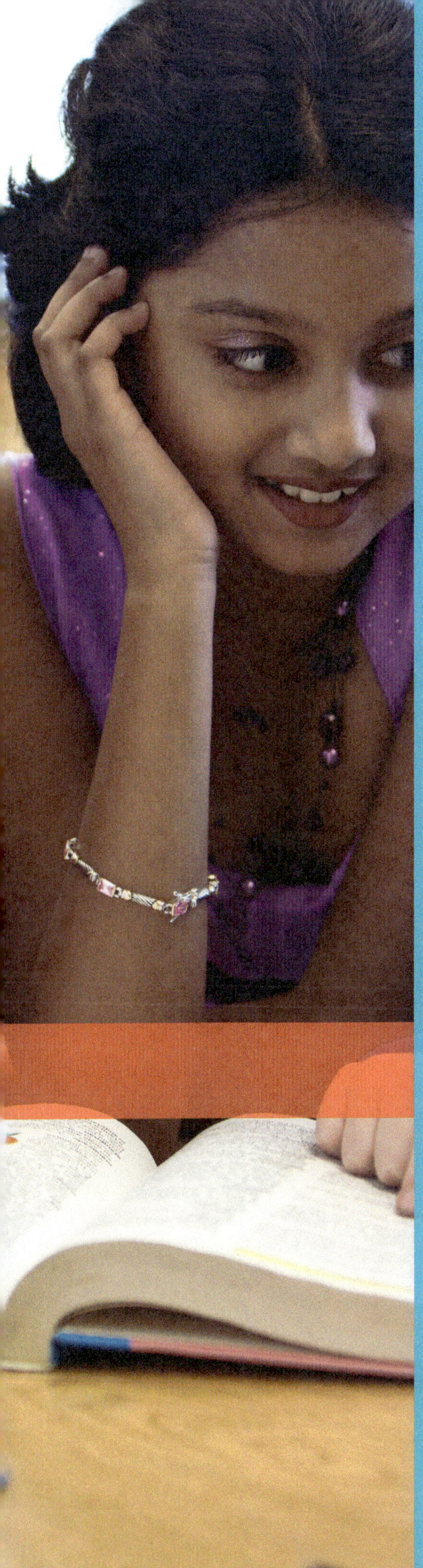

What's It All About ...

What is constructivism? How does it help students learn?

On what is constructivism based?

What are some of the fundamental characteristics of constructivism?

What learning models are based on constructivism?

Chapter Objectives

- Define constructivism.
- Understand constructivist learning.
- Define problems and limitations with the constructivist process.

- Review the psychological foundations of constructivism.
- Review the social foundations of constructivism.

- Explain how to promote classroom dialogue.
- Describe the qualities of a collaborative classroom.
- Review the importance of experimenting.

- Describe the difference between guided discovery and discovery learning.
- Understand inquiry learning.
- Compare problem-based learning to subject-based learning.
- Explain instructional conversations.

EXTENDED OUTLINE

Constructivism & Student-Centered Learning

I. What's It All About …
II. From Today's Headlines
III. Constructivism—A Focus on Constructing Knowledge
    A. Defining constructivism
    B. Constructivist learning
    C. Problems and limitations in constructivism
    D. Summarize and reflect
IV. Constructivist Foundations
    A. Psychological foundations
    B. Social foundations
    C. Comparing individual and social constructivist theories
    D. Summarize and reflect
V. A Closer Look at Social Learning and Constructivism
    A. Promoting classroom dialogue
    B. Collaborative classroom
    C. Importance of experimenting
    D. Summarize and reflect
VI. Constructivism and Student Learning
    A. Discovery learning
    B. Inquiry learning
    C. Problem-based learning
    D. Instructional conversations
    E. Summarize and reflect
VII. The Chapter in Review
VIII. Interdisciplinary Case Focus

From Today's Headlines

Vol. I No. 12 Teaching World, 2012

ON CONSTRUCTIVISM, THE HUMAN BRAIN AND MULTIPLICATION TABLES

North County Times: The Californian
February 16, 2008

Staff writer, Aaron Claverie, is interested in some changes taking place at Ronald Reagan Elementary School. A visit to the school reveals students are not at their desks. Teachers are not lecturing. Instead, students are discussing questions, often amongst themselves: How and why do animals use disguises and surprises for survival? What does cooperation look like and sound like?

What is going on at the elementary school is the introduction of an alternative approach to education. Constructivism is the idea that learning should be student-driven, rather than the conventional teacher-led model. The basic idea is that if teachers facilitate the students' construction of knowledge for themselves, then learning will be more effective and produce better results.

The push toward constructivist learning techniques is due to lagging test scores. The hope is that this new way of learning will address the issue and help students learn more effectively. The approach, however, is not without critics. Some parents have pulled their children out of the school because they feel their children are regressing, particularly in mathematics. Still, administrators are hopeful. One veteran administrator is quoted as saying, "… Constructivism is good teaching." She notes that recent benchmark tests demonstrate the approach is working. Scores are rising to a level comparable to other schools in the area. To ease concerns that the move is too radical, school officials point out that the goal is not to replace all traditional lecture techniques, mentioning that there is still much validity to rote memorization of multiplication tables. The new technique is seen as a tool to support and enhance current educational practices.

The move to constructivist instructional practices was not easy. A special training team brought in from the Upstate New York region helped train teachers to use constructivist principles effectively. Administrators believe the approach will produce effective results, but underscore that it takes the cooperation of parents, students, teachers, and administrators.

(continues)

MAKE THE CONNECTION

The struggles experienced at this school are becoming increasingly common as schools strive to find ways to meet increasing societal demand for higher test scores. Constructivism as an instructional method has been around for decades, but teachers have been reluctant to make significant shifts in their instructional practice. This chapter will introduce you to the concept of constructivism. We will define the approach, review its psychological underpinnings, and show how teachers can use these principles to enhance instruction.

CONSTRUCTIVISM—A FOCUS ON CONSTRUCTING KNOWLEDGE

The concept of knowledge construction is one of those ideas that is both exceptionally simple, yet difficult to recognize and apply. It is also an aspect of the educational process that historically has been underappreciated. After a long history of educators focusing on perfecting the instructional process, schools are shifting their focus to include an appreciation of what students do with the information they are learning. In this chapter we will examine this constructivist point of view. Let's begin with an examination of how we define knowledge construction.

Defining Constructivism

When teachers provide instruction, they are working with students who come to the learning environment with a wealth of pre-existing knowledge. Students process instruction in an active way, reconciling new information with their existing knowledge. This means that even if teachers could present information in a perfect way, it would still fail to produce perfect student learning because students do not simply create copies of instructional materials in their minds. They are naturally curious and active when considering new experiences. Yes, teachers should endeavor to perfect their instruction, but they will always need to work with students to help them process the information and construct their own understanding of the material.

Students are naturally curious and active when considering new information.

Constructivism refers to the active processing of new information in the context of prior learning and the student's readiness to learn. It emphasizes the importance of existing knowledge and experience in the learning process (Brooks & Brooks, 1993). Theorists have come up with several ways of defining what constitutes constructivism, but they typically have the following themes in common (Pelech & Pieper, 2010; Gabler & Schroeder, 2003; Schwandt, 2003):

Constructivism

The active processing of new information in the context of prior learning and the student's readiness to learn

- People do not discover knowledge; they construct it.
- People create knowledge by relating or connecting it to their previous knowledge.
- How knowledge is constructed is inherent to the individual.
- Learning and the ability to learn are influenced by experience.
- Cognitive growth is stimulated when people are confronted with practical, contextual problems.

Table 12.1 Characteristics of Constructivist Learning Environments

1	Constructivist learning environments emphasize knowledge construction instead of knowledge reproduction.
2	Constructivist learning environments provide multiple representations of reality.
3	Multiple representations avoid simplification and represent the complexity of the real world.
4	Constructivist learning environments emphasize authentic tasks in a meaningful context rather than abstract instruction of context.
5	Constructivist learning environments provide experiences in a real-world setting or a case-based context instead of a predetermined sequence of instruction.
6	Constructivist learning environments encourage thoughtful reflection on experience.
7	Constructivist learning environments enable context- and content-dependent knowledge
8	Constructivist learning environments support collaborative construction of knowledge through social negotiation, not competition among learners for recognition.

These themes help to define the philosophy of constructivist thinking. They also serve as conceptual bridges, helping teachers to create constructivist-based learning environments. Table 12.1 extends these defining attributes to instructional guidelines for developing constructivist learning environments.

Table 12.1 provides a list of elements that characterize constructivist learning environments (Jonassen, 1994). The first of these characteristics highlights that the instructional goal is not to have the students mimic the knowledge of the teacher but to develop their own unique understanding of the material. There are certainly facts that need to be learned in a relatively rote manner, but learning should not establish this as the instructional goal. Facts are tools that students need in order to better understand and function in the world. The ultimate goal is to encourage capable thinkers who are knowledgeable, not just rote knowledge.

The next few characteristics emphasize that learning should not be removed or set apart from the real world. Academic lessons should reflect problems or events in life. They should be just as complex as issues in the real world. This helps students appreciate the value and utility of education. It creates an active and functional knowledge base. Additionally, constructivism underscores the importance of viewing knowledge and learning as dependent on a particular learning environment. Educational material is not an isolated commodity to be internalized irrespective of the learning context. *What* we learn is directly tied to *how we learn*. Educators need to pay close attention to how they build a particular learning context. It has a direct impact on how students understand the material.

Finally, collaboration is important to consider when educating according to constructivist principles. Collaboration is an important social dynamic, producing many unique and positive effects. As a tool to facilitate learning, the nature of how students collaborate will influence the way they construct an understanding of the material. Students typically learn best when they collaborate in non-competitive environments with limited time constraints. This helps students use the supportive nature of working in groups more effectively.

Learning within the constructivist framework is more of a philosophical position rather than specific pedagogical tools.

Constructivist Learning

Learning within the constructivist framework is by no means a unified approach or technique. It is more of a philosophical position, rather than a specific pedagogical tool (Fosnot & Perry, 2005). Unlike other perspectives on learning (e.g., behavioral learning theory—Chapter 4), there is a continuum of opinion regarding how best to apply constructivist reasoning to a given learning task. For example, a math teacher may apply constructivism in a way that is quite different from an English teacher because of the nature of the specific content. Remember that constructivists emphasize that learning is context-dependent or dependent on the particular learning situation. Given the wide range of instructional topics, application of constructivist theory is necessarily going to vary widely. In general, however, constructivists believe that learning is a personal journey involving the active construction of knowledge (Bruning, Schraw, Norby, & Ronning, 2004).

Situated learning

Learning that is dependent upon the environment in which it takes place

Community of learners

Individuals participating in a given learning endeavor (e.g., the students and teacher in a classroom)

The idea of constructivism raises an important question regarding learning. Is learning an independent skill that students apply in a *general way* or does learning take place as the constructivist would predict? That is, is it inherently *situated* in a particular learning environment? **Situated learning** is the idea that learning is dependent upon the environment in which it takes place (Lave & Wenger, 1991; Winn, 1993; Zheng, 2010). Every learning experience evolves in a unique way out of the particular situation. The individuals participating in a given learning endeavor (e.g., the students and teacher in a classroom) make up a **community of learners** (Campione, Shapiro, & Brown 1995; Rogoff, Matusov, & White, 1996). It is this community of learners that shapes the learning experience. Teachers can help promote learning within the community by encouraging active participation, collaboration, and respect for different opinions.

Problems and Limitations in Constructivism

Understanding problems with constructivist thinking requires we consider the concept of knowledge construction as a way of understanding the world. In other words, we will first need to consider more broadly the idea of how people acquire knowledge before we can address issues with constructivist theory. To help us frame this discussion consider the following examples:

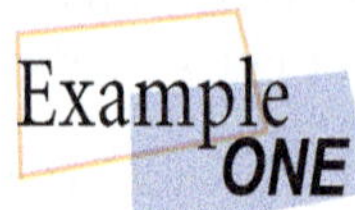

Ms. Callahan is an eleventh grade social studies teacher. She is preparing for the school year and thinking about her overall goals. She wants her students to have an understanding of the development of the United States. She wants to discuss topics like the industrial revolution, ethnic and other demographic changes, the development of the federal government, and an understanding of citizen rights. She has loved teaching this material since her first year. She considers herself an expert on the topic and enjoys helping students learn the material.

Assumption regarding how students acquire knowledge: Ms. Callahan operates under the assumption that the goal of education is for students to develop perfect copies of the knowledge she intends to impart. She wants them to be mirrors of her knowledge.

Mr. Parker is an eleventh grade biology teacher and is planning a unit on cell biology. He is designing his curriculum around a series of experiments. Each experiment will focus on a different aspect of the life and function of cells. He wants to cover topics such as cell anatomy, bio-chemical life functions, and how proteins and enzymes function within cells. He realizes this approach is often difficult, as experiments often fail to go as planned. He is more interested, however, in how students engage in the scientific process. Students will engage in the experiments and then go through a series of written products based on their experiences.

Assumption regarding how students acquire knowledge: Mr. Parker is interested in how students build an understanding of science. His priority is how these students think and reason scientifically. This development in their reasoning is based on their own internal struggles to understand the experiments.

Consider how these teachers compare in their approach to instruction. Ms. Callahan and Mr. Parker both believe that there are certain topics within their instructional areas that are important to learn. They are assuming that these topics represent real events and processes, and as such, are valid instructional targets. They differ, however, in how this information is best learned by the students. Ms. Callahan believes it is best to have students learn pre-existing knowledge. She wants them to internalize as best they can the information she provides. Mr. Parker believes it is more important for students to build a knowledge base by actively thinking about certain subjects. For him, learning is not just about learning facts. It is about the process students go through to acquire knowledge. These two teachers represent different philosophical points of view. Specifically, they differ in their emphasis on ontology versus epistemology.

Ontology

The nature of reality and truth, a set of concepts within a domain

Ontology refers to the nature of reality and truth. That is, it encompasses questions about whether there is an objective real world that we can actually know. Some theorists believe that there is, but others believe that even if there is a reality, we have no way to know it. They believe all we can know is what we experience or perceive, which may or may not represent reality. In terms of ontology, both of these teachers appear to operate under the assumption that there are real and knowable events that are important for the students to learn.

Epistemology

The nature or origin of knowledge

Epistemology is the nature or origin of knowledge. It refers to how students come to know something, not whether what we know is real or not. In terms of epistemology, these teachers appear to differ. Ms. Callahan believes that it is important for the students to internalize the information she provides. In a sense, the student is a passive vessel being filled up with knowledge by the teacher. Mr. Parker believes that knowledge comes from actively doing and thinking for one's self. He believes students acquire knowledge by building that knowledge for themselves.

Mr. Parker's instructional style better represents constructivist principles. In terms of ontology, constructivists generally believe that the world is real, but not knowable. We may or may not have an accurate representation of reality, but that is not crucial to knowing. They believe that it is our experience of the world that is important. Following this philosophy to its logical end, we cannot say that any student's knowledge is more or less valid, because we cannot verify any objective reality. Whatever a student knows is a valid representation of the processes they went through to reach that knowledge. Everyone's knowledge is equally valid. In other words, no matter what the student answered on the test, it is valid in the sense that it is the result of that student's knowledge construction. This is an important point teachers often fail to consider. Appreciating whatever cognitive path a student took to arrive at an answer is necessary if teachers are to influence that process.

This philosophical perspective is both a strength and a weakness of constructivist thinking. It strengthens educational practice by encouraging teachers to focus on keeping students active in the learning process. It also emphasizes the importance of what students are doing with information, not just on accurate communication of information. There is a fundamental problem, however, with this epistemology. Without an objective reality with which to compare a student's knowledge, there is no way of saying that anyone has the "right answer" to a question. Imagine a school where there were no correct answers, just students learning to think and build knowledge that is uniquely valid. Perhaps schools will one day take this extreme position, but it is not the current system in schools today. We still give students tests and expect "correct" answers. Some researchers have cautioned against taking constructivist theories too far (Ernest, 1995). They warn that there is little utility to validating any thought or product from a student. There are limits given the nature of our educational system. Imagine a young student coloring all over the classroom walls and proudly exclaiming that the change made the room "happier."

As creative as this may be, it is unlikely to enhance the learning environment for everyone else in the classroom.

What is important about the growing fascination with constructivist thinking is that it is helping us realize that getting the right answer or engaging in the right behavior isn't the only possible objective for students. No matter what answer students achieve or what behaviors in which they engage, they had to think. We can help student examine that process of thinking. We can provide the necessary supports for students to broaden their way of thinking, which opens the doorway to new and inventive solutions to problems. This is an exciting opportunity and one long neglected in education.

SUMMARIZE AND REFLECT

1. Constructivism refers to the active processing of new information in the context of prior learning and the student's readiness to learn (O'Donnell, 2012).
2. Constructivism has a common set of elements, including presenting real-life problems in a meaningful context, with opportunities for students to work collaboratively.
3. The context in which we learn is just as important as what we learn.
4. Researchers have questioned whether learning is general, having broad applications, or whether learning is situated and tied to a particular context.
5. The individuals participating in a given learning endeavor (e.g., the students and teacher in a classroom) make up a community of learners.
6. Some of the limitations of constructivist principles surround how it approaches the search for knowledge and assumptions made about the nature of truth.
7. Ontology refers to the nature of reality and truth.
8. Epistemology is the nature or origin of knowledge. It refers to how students come to know something (not whether knowledge is real or not).
9. Constructivists focus more on the process of learning, rather than "correct" answers.

INFORMED APPLICATION

1. Choose one of the characteristics of constructivist learning environments from the table in this section and provide an example of teaching that incorporates this element.
2. Rewrite the definitions for ontology and epistemology using your own words. Then explain what constructivist teachers believe relative to these two philosophical positions.

CONSTRUCTIVIST FOUNDATIONS

The preceding section provided a broad definitional framework for understanding constructivist theory. Constructivism, however, is more of an umbrella term for more specific schools of thought. This section will look at the psychological underpinnings of individual constructivism and how it compares to more recent emphasis on social constructivism.

Psychological Foundations

Individual constructivism

The study of how individuals develop and change their cognitive and emotional processes in an attempt to understand information and build knowledge

Individual constructivism is the study of how individuals develop and change their cognitive and emotional processes in an attempt to understand information and build knowledge (Windschitl, 2002; Phillips, 1997; Fosnot, 1996). It is a focus on the struggles one experiences as they try to understand the world. This type of constructivism evolved out of the psychological work of Jean Piaget, as discussed in Chapter 2. Piaget was particularly interested in how we strive to develop an

Interconnections

See Chapter 2 for a review of the developmental theory of Jean Piaget.

organized way of viewing the world. Over time, our experiences lead to organized schemas or ways of understanding the world. We then interpret further experiences in terms of these existing schemas (assimilation) or develop new ones (accommodation) to understand new information. Piaget's work on cognitions was considered the forerunner to later versions of constructivism because of his emphasis on cognitions as personally developed constructs that did not necessarily represent any objective reality. In Piaget's view, cognitive constructions are the individual's unique attempts to understand the world.

More radical perspectives on how knowledge construction relates to reality later eclipsed this early constructivist position. **Radical constructivism** is a branch of constructivist thinking that further divorces itself from any connection to an objective reality (von Glasersfeld, 1996). These theorists are almost exclusively interested in what is going on in the minds of students while they are learning. They believe that all thinking is inherently valid or "true" from the perspective of the individual. Answers are not construed as "right" or "wrong" thinking, just differing perspectives. Teachers making use of this approach use countering examples to challenge and broaden student thinking and reasoning. They underscore the notion that ideas held as "correct" only serve that purpose for a period in a particular context. They dismiss any attempt to determine enduring truths as futile, as we are unable to know any absolute reality. This may seem very theoretical, but it has direct application on how we educate (Allen & Bickhard, 2011). It is particularly relevant in hard sciences like physics where there are new discoveries and dramatic shifts in contemporary thinking.

Radical constructivism

A branch of constructivist thinking that further divorces itself from any connection to an objective reality

Social Foundations

Constructivist thinking focuses on social interactions at another level of analysis. **Social constructivism** emphasizes the process of individual internalization of psychological tools (language, problem-solving techniques, social skills, etc.) through social interactions (McInerney, 2005). Based in the work of researchers like Lev Vygotsky (Chapter 2), social constructivism strives to understand how individual knowledge evolves from participation in the social life of society. As proposed by Vygotsky, individual thought is a secondary process, derived from the primary process of social interactions (Kozulin, 2011). According to this school of thought, all individual thinking is just a reflection of the culture in which a person lives. Functionally, teachers typically do not embrace extreme social constructivist views, but merge their perspective with the psychological constructivists discussed earlier (Windschitl, 2002). They recognize the significant impact of a student's social interactions (with peers, teachers, and parents) on knowledge construction, but maintain the perspective that individuals use psychological processes in unique and inventive ways to construct their understanding of the world.

Interconnections

See Chapter 2 for a review of the developmental theory of Lev Vygotsky.

Social constructivism

Emphasizes the process of individual internalization of psychological tools (language, problem solving techniques, social skills, etc.) through social interactions

Comparing Individual and Social Constructivists Theories

As the preceding sections imply, the application of individual and social constructivism to an educational setting may be perceived as separate processes. Indeed, there are a number of contrasting points in their theories. Table 12.2 lists the fundamental principles of individual and social constructivism, which highlight some of these different emphases.

As the table indicates, there are several points of divergence between these two theories. Teachers, however, need not view these perspectives on learning as incompatible. Teachers frequently use a combination of approaches that best fit the situation at hand. Remember, both approaches believe in the supportive role of teachers, rather than in their absolute position as the holder of the learning content (Powell & Kalina, 2009). Both philosophies support interaction and learning in groups, using the inherent support

Vygotsky proposed individual thought is a secondary process derived from the primary process of social interactions.

Table 12.2 Constructivist Perspectives

Individual Constructivism	Social Constructivism
Individuals construct an understanding of the world.	Individuals understand the world based on information acquired through social interactions.
Objective reality may exist but we can only know our constructions of it. These may or may not be accurate.	Reality is socially negotiated.
Knowledge is individually created and perceived.	Knowledge is dependent on the sociocultural context.
Focus is on individual adaptation to experience.	Focus is on societal tools used to negotiate reality such as language.

found in successful group interactions. They also both espouse the importance of gaining new experience in shaping learning and understanding. Providing creative and novel learning environments challenges students to grow and develop.

SUMMARIZE AND REFLECT

1. Constructivism can be broken down into different schools of thought.
2. Individual constructivism is the study of how individuals develop and change their cognitive and emotional processes in an attempt to process information and build knowledge.
3. Individual constructivism was one of the earliest forms of constructivism and drew heavily from the work of Jean Piaget.
4. More radical perspectives on how knowledge construction relates to reality later expanded individual constructivism.
5. Radical constructivism is a branch of constructivist thinking that further divorces itself from any connection to an objective reality.
6. Radical constructivists believe that all thinking is inherently valid or is "true" from the perspective of the individual.
7. Another constructivist school of thought emphasizes social interactions and is based on the work of Lev Vygotsky.
8. Social constructivism emphasizes the process of individual internalization of psychological tools (language, problem-solving techniques, social skills, etc.) through social interactions.
9. According to this school of thought, all individual thinking is a reflection of the culture in which the individual lives.

INFORMED APPLICATION

1. Give an example of where working alone would put you at a learning disadvantage. How would working on the same task in a group help?
2. What do you think is the most important trait individual and social constructivism have in common? Why?

A CLOSER LOOK AT SOCIAL LEARNING AND CONSTRUCTIVISM

Now that we have a basic understanding of constructivism, let's look more closely at the factors teachers need to consider when applying constructivism to teaching. Some constructivist instructional techniques are applied broadly in a variety of instructional settings. Other techniques are more specific and only used for a particular purpose. In this section, we will focus on broader techniques. Specific constructivist strategies will be covered in the final section of the chapter.

Promoting Classroom Dialogue

One of the fundamental tools used in constructivist teaching is active engagement in conversations with peers and teachers (Brown & Kennedy, 2011). Encouraging dialogue can help students learn and focus more effectively (Donovan & Bransford, 2005; Shank & Abelson, 1995). Historically, teachers have used some measure of classroom discussion, but often this is limited and only encourages students to guess what the teacher is thinking, rather than thinking independently (Lemke, 1990). For example,

Ms. Bailey Who can tell me what the main character of the story is trying to achieve?

Amanda Is he trying to achieve equality for all people?

Ms. Bailey Close Amanda, but his focus was not on all people, but specifically Native Americans.

Constructivist teaching uses active engagement in conversations with peers and teachers.

This is a typical classroom dialogue. The teacher initiates a question. The students attempt to produce a correct answer. The teacher then evaluates the answer. However, this approach to classroom dialogue is limited. Students are not encouraged to build an understanding of the material but to guess what the teacher is thinking. Classroom dialogue can move beyond this limited scope. Students should use dialogue to explain lesson objectives, clarify confusions, and support conclusions. When structured appropriately, classroom dialogue can help students learn, not only from the teacher, but also from their classmates. A broader range of dialogue allows students to challenge each other, clarify difficult points, provide rich, developmentally appropriate examples, and enjoy the process of learning. Teachers do not always have to be in the center of the conversational pattern. Often, their role is more effective if they facilitate from the sidelines, providing support and gentle direction when needed. Teachers should also not hesitate to ask questions to which they do not know the answer. Watching teachers move through the process of learning and reasoning with the students is a powerful source of modeling (Lemke, 1990). Table 12.3 provides some additional suggestions for promoting effective classroom dialogue (Gagnon & Abell, 2007; Gibbons, 2002).

The suggestions in Table 12.3 promote the use of a **dialogic teaching** style. This approach describes a classroom setting where teachers and students make significant contributions to the discussion that helps to move the student's thinking forward (Mercer & Littleton, 2007). Under a traditional classroom setting, teachers typically construct closed questions where students are expected to competitively bid on who can get the correct answer. For example, Smith, Hardman, Wall, and Morz (2004) found the following in a typical classroom:

Dialogic teaching

Technique that utilizes a classroom setting where teachers and students make significant contributions to the discussion that helps to move the student's thinking forward

- Open questions only comprised 10% of questioning (15% of the respondents reported never using open questions).

- "Ask & Follow" questions with the same student to encourage sustained dialogue took place only 11% of the time.

Table 12.3 Promoting Classroom Dialogue

Hold discussions following a shared experience.
Ask open-ended questions that require thoughtful discussion.
Give students time to think about a topic by assigning a discussion topic for after recess or the next day.
Provide discussion rules, including directions on how to listen.
Ask students to discuss their ideas in teams before opening discussion to the entire class.
Structure discussions so that all students have the opportunity to participate.
Provide scaffolding (Chapter 2) for student conversations by asking for clarification and probing for more information.
Listen and wait for other students to respond, instead of playing the role of evaluator after student responses.

- Responding or replying to another questions (uptake questions) occurred only 4% of the time (43% of the respondents never used this style)
- Pupil-to-pupil exchanges were limited, lasting about five seconds on average and consisting of three or fewer words 70% of the time.

Dialogic instructional practices aim to change this situation. They not only reframe the nature of classroom dialogue, but also such a change encourages greater academic performance and stronger thinking and understanding (Alexander, 2005). The following is an instructional transcript of a teacher making use of dialogic instructional strategies (Wells, 1999).

T ... Now, those people who say it decreased, why do you think it decreased? ... Phillips, that day you offered some reasons. Why do you think it changes state from solid to liquid ... the ice?

P Um ... because like when it's ice has some air in it and it's melted the air will go so it's ... um, [lighter]

T Uh huh ... So the air ... there's air that's trapped in the blocks of ice will escape as the ice melts and therefore you think the mass will decrease, right?

P Mm

T Any other reasons behind those who say it will decrease?

T Any other reasons behind those that say it will decrease? Yes?

B I said that it will decrease because there was a little bit of air inside the ice and it would um—um it would melt so the more [more than ... greater than air]

T You say it would decrease so then it would be MORE? ... I didn't follow, can you repeat what you said Benjamin?

B Um ... when ... it decrease because the air comes out and that means it would weigh less (softly) ... mass less

T Are <you> agreeing with Phillips or disagreeing with Phillips?

B Agreeing

T You're agreeing with Phillips that it would decrease? Now Mr. Wells also raised the point ... now when the ice melts ... say we froze that water again, what would you predict?

A I have something to say ... The first thing is if you left it long enough <while> it was melted ... some of the water could evaporate ... and then, when you froze it again it would add um ... it would probably have more air left <then> it might be slightly different or it might be ... er or it might increase ... depends on if you left it <long enough> for the water to evaporate.

As you can see, the discussion is progressing nicely. Alternative answers are presented and considered. As a whole, the cognitive breadth of the students is increasing, with a specific type of dialog promoted by the teacher. This affords the students more opportunities to learn and to deepen their understanding of the material.

Collaborative Classroom

The importance of classroom dialogue is most effectively realized through collaborative instruction. **Collaborative classrooms** promote dialogue through effective communication and a value and respect for differing perspectives. Collaborative classrooms are distinguished by their focus on involving students in real-world problem solving in dynamic group interchanges. This approach helps students to link new information to prior knowledge, promoting learning. It should be noted that *collaborative* learning is often associated with *cooperative* learning. Collaborative learning is presented in this chapter because of its strong focus on student-centered constructivist learning. The related cooperative learning is also constructivist in nature, but typically has greater involvement from the teacher and is therefore presented later in Chapter 14 on *Instructional Excellence* (Panitz, 1999).

Collaborative classroom

Classroom that promotes dialogue through effective communication and a value and respect for differing perspectives

Group interactions are a combination of peer-to-peer and peer-to-teacher (Gillies & Haynes, 2011). These collaborations are typically defined by four characteristics. The first of these four characteristics is *sharing knowledge among students and teachers.* In the traditional classroom environment, the teacher is viewed as the holder of knowledge, which is imparted to the students. The information flow is unidirectional, going from the teacher to the student. Collaborative classrooms take a different approach. These classrooms view knowledge as a shared resource between the teacher and the student; both possess valuable information. These classrooms build upon the unique experiences and perspectives of the students. This shared approach helps engage students in the learning process. When students are engaged, they are more likely to make important connections between their current knowledge and newly presented information. They feel they have a greater investment in learning because they directly shape the learning environment. Consider a math lesson on percentages. The teacher is able to structure the basic information. He may even provide applied examples based on his own experiences. Perhaps he likes to cook and provides examples using percentages when changing a recipe. Students can learn and benefit from the teacher's information and experience, but it may or may not motivate or engage all the students. Creating an environment where students can discuss their own experiences and create connections to the lessons helps the students invest. This investment grounds learning in real examples that are meaningful to the students.

One of the characteristics in a collaborative classroom is the shared authority among teachers and students.

The second characteristic of collaborative classrooms is *shared authority among teachers and students.* Traditional classroom have a rigid authority structure. The teacher chooses the learning objectives, provides necessary instruction, and selects assessment measures. Collaborative classrooms involve the students in each of these processes. Teachers share authority over the learning process with the students. Teachers and students collaboratively create learning goals. Teachers provide options for activities and assessments from which students can select. Students are encouraged to share their experiences with assessment activities and strategies for demonstrating learning. Involving students in this way not only helps them invest in learning but also creates personalized assessments that better reflect individual student learning. For example, an English teacher might be inclined to assign a comparative paper after reading a novel from the twentieth century and one from the eighteenth century. This, however, may not be the most effective and accurate method for assessing student learning. Students might better demonstrate their comparative understanding by creating a play, video project, or oral presentation. The goal is learning and assessments should be an accurate reflection of that learning process. The methodology is flexible and mutually decided on

Collaborative activities often center on a practical activity.

between student and teacher within limits established by the teacher. These strategies help students regulate their own learning and increase motivation.

The third characteristic of collaborative classrooms is *teachers as mediators*. This is one of the most crucial factors in creating a truly collaborative classroom environment. This is because it directly impacts the typical way teachers view their role. Teachers who successfully transition from learning leaders to learning mediators are able to help students connect lessons to their own experiences in other areas. They help students when they are unable to progress by themselves. They also help them learn how to learn independently. An effective mediator is able to adjust the level of support depending on the needs of the student.

The final characteristic is *heterogeneous groupings of students*. What makes collaboration uniquely effective is the process of bringing together individuals from all lifestyles. It is the varied and unique experiences that help bring a rich source of ideas to a group dynamic. Accordingly, the effectiveness of collaborative techniques is sharply diminished when students are grouped based upon their similarities. Although there is a certain logic to grouping students that learn in a similar way, or have special needs in common, it makes it difficult to grow from the wealth of information students from diverse backgrounds bring to a learning task.

Importance of Experimenting

Collaborative activities often center on some practical activity. Activities can help bring focus and engagement to a lesson (Cavallo, 2005; Moreno, 2006). Experimenting with actual applications of a particular lesson gives students experience with using knowledge and better integrating it into their existing knowledge base. For example, Jessica and Jeffrey Orvis (Orvis & Orvis, 2005) use an unconventional technique for overcoming some of the conceptual difficulties in a chemistry classroom. They use paper wads to help students better understand two traditionally difficult concepts: equilibrium and reaction mechanisms. To help the students challenge some common misconceptions surrounding these two concepts, the students engage in an exercise where they throw paper wads at each other. Students are arranged with the majority of students on one side of the classroom. Only a couple of students are placed on the other side of the room. About thirty crumpled paper wads are given to the two students on the one side of the classroom. When the teachers says "go", these two students start throwing the paper wads at their classmates. The other students are supposed to pick up any paper wad and throw it back to the two students on the other side of the room. Obviously, the paper wads return to the two students with greater speed given that there are more students at that end of the room. This is moderated, however, by the availability of paper wads, which must come from the two students. From this fun and engaging exercise, students are able to challenge their beliefs regarding the meaning of equilibrium. Students find this exercise entertaining, but also highly educational. It brings to life a concept that can be understood from a lecture while making it much more available and real for the students.

Authentic activity

Lessons that mirror real-life and help students understand the relevance of education

Some of the best lessons are those that the students create for themselves. Allowing them to visit somewhere like city hall, or a local government office, can be more memorable than the lesson.

It is worth repeating that lessons are most effective when they involve **authentic activities.** As was discussed at the beginning of the chapter, embedding lessons in activities that mirror real-life application helps students understand the relevance of education. This is especially true as teachers give students time to experiment and explore. At times, exploration may be structured like the paper wad lesson above, but it can also be informal. Some of the best and most memorable lessons are those that students create for themselves as they experiment with a new situation. This can often be accomplished by simply giving students time in environments that are topically related to a lesson. For example, you might let students visit a local government office like city hall or a bank, landfill, or animal shelter. Assignments following such experiences can be very general. Provide a simple starting question ("What is the most interesting thing you learned about a landfill and how it relates to the surrounding environment?") to a group of students. Let the students take it from there, expanding and modifying your original question based on their unique perceptions. A student's natural curiosity helps drive group dynamics toward a natural and relevant outcome.

SUMMARIZE AND REFLECT

1. One of the fundamental tools used in constructivist teaching is active engagement in conversations with peers and teachers.
2. Teachers do not always have to be in the center of the conversational pattern.
3. A broader range of dialogue allows students to challenge each other; clarify difficult points; provide rich, developmentally appropriate examples; and enjoy the process of learning.
4. Teachers can use simple strategies to promote dialogue that is more effective.
5. Collaborative classrooms promote dialogue through effective communication and a value and respect for differing perspectives.
6. Collaborative classrooms are distinguished by their focus on involving students in real-world problem solving and dynamic group interchanges.
7. Collaborative classrooms share four common characteristics: sharing knowledge among students and teachers, shared authority among teachers and students, teachers as mediators, heterogeneous groupings of students.
8. Experimenting with actual applications of a particular lesson gives students experience with using knowledge and better integrating it into their existing knowledge base.
9. Authentic activities embed learning tasks in activities that mirror real-life applications, which ultimately help the students to better understand the relevance of education.

INFORMED APPLICATION

1. Describe how a teacher can move from being the center of an instructional conversation to a facilitator at the edge of a discussion group.
2. Describe a learning situation that involves the use of an authentic learning environment.

CONSTRUCTIVISM AND STUDENT LEARNING

In the final section, we will look at specific instructional strategies based on constructivist theory. The preceding section described tools that researchers and educators have translated into constructivist learning strategies. We will look at how these general approaches work under specific situations. Keep in mind, not all constructivist techniques are created equal. Some work better in a particular environment, while others are more effective at addressing particular kinds of questions.

Discovery Learning

Discovery learning is a learning approach focusing on active, hands-on learning supported by instructional guidance (Dewey, 1997; Strike, 1975; Joolingen, 1999; Bruner, 1961). Recall from the preceding section that this is exactly what constructivist theory is all about (Abrahamson, Trninic, Gutierrez, Huth, & Lee, 2011). In terms of defining discovery learning, researchers have identified three primary characteristics (Bicknell-Holmes & Hoffman, 2000):

Discovery learning
A learning approach that focuses on active, hands-on learning supported by instructional guidance

1. Students explore and problem solve in order to create, integrate, and generalize their knowledge.

2. The environment encourages student driven, interest-based activities in which the student determines sequence and frequency.

3. Activities are created to encourage integration of new knowledge into the learner's existing knowledge base.

> **"Practice in discovering for oneself teaches one to acquire information in a way that makes that information more readily viable in problem solving." (Bruner, 1961)**

The first characteristic indicates that this is a student-driven process. Students engage in activities that foster problem solving, leading to an integrated and generalized body of knowledge. Students are encouraged to take risks and solve unique problems in loosely structured environments. Some teachers find this student-centered approach difficult to accept (Hooks, 1994). Their experience and training make it difficult for them to operate in an environment where they are not in direct control of the learning process. This initial discomfort, however, typically dissipates as teachers recognize the power behind student-driven learning tasks.

The second component of discovery learning further underscores its student-centered foundation. Students in a discovery-learning environment are responsible for determining the appropriate sequence of learning events. That is, students, rather than teachers, determine how learning progresses. Students determine the order of learning tasks and the frequency needed to learn a given task. The third and final characteristic of discovery learning is that students are specifically directed and encouraged to integrate new learning with existing knowledge. Student examples with which they are familiar helps create a connection between new and existing knowledge. When learning is anchored to information already well learned, retention and understanding are enhanced.

It is usually instructive to examine discovery learning and see how it compares to more traditional lecture or expository forms of teaching. Table 12.4 compares these two approaches (Castronova, 2002).

As you can see from the table, there are several benefits to the discovery learning approach. In general, students learning under this approach develop the necessary skills to analyze their own thinking—metacognition; these are extremely useful life-long learning tools. They are also highly motivating and help motivate students maintain appropriate levels of engagement.

Not all researchers or teachers, however, believe in the merits of the discovery learning approach. Teachers often avoid using discovery learning for varied reasons: they are concerned that necessary course content will not be covered, that it will require too much preparation and class time, and that class sizes are often inappropriate (either too large or small) for the approach to be effective (Bonwell, 1998). Additionally, some researchers find that teachers are inadequately prepared for discovery approaches leading to inappropriate tactics (Kirschner, Sweller, & Clark, 2006). They advocate for more direct instruction in discovery techniques

Table 12.4 Comparing Discovery Learning and Traditional Teaching

Discovery Learning	Traditional Teaching
Students are active learners.	Students passively receive information.
Focus is on the learning process.	Focus is on the learning end product.
Failure is seen as a positive learning experience.	Failure is seen as a lack of learning.
Learning is facilitated by verbal interactions with peers.	Learning occurs in a classroom where the teacher does most of the talking.
Discovery learning more closely matches the natural human learning experience.	Traditional teaching is an artificial environment used to efficiently convey information.

Table 12.5 Planning a Discovery Learning Experience

Select an Activity: To begin, pick an activity that is relatively short so that follow-up attempts are easier to predict and plan. Select a subject with which you are personally familiar and comfortable. Also, in the beginning, it is best to choose an activity that does not have one correct answer.

Gather Materials: Remember to have enough materials for each student to repeat the activity at least once.

Stay Focused: Avoid learning tangents that may be interesting but will keep the learner from finishing the project, unless they are truly of great curiosity and value. Instead, take notes concerning the new interest to follow-up on once the initial activity is completed.

Use Caution: While the idea behind discovery learning is for the instructor to step back and facilitate allowing students to work independently, be sure that safety is observed. An adult should always supervise activities such as cooking and cutting.

Plan Extra Time: Understand that students working on their own will most likely take longer than they would with a facilitator moving them systematically through the material. Also, be sure to plan time for repeated activities in case there is a failure or other reasons to repeat the activity.

Record Process and Results: Include in the activity a requirement for students to record their procedure and results.

Discuss and Review: After an activity is completed, and before it is repeated a second time, discuss the activity and its outcome with the students. Use the records students kept to assist during this step. Once the activity has been analyzed, record any observations or mistakes.

Try Again: Have the students repeat the activity if necessary. Encourage them to take into account what was done and the discussion that occurred. Allow them to use any records that were kept to assist them in successfully completing the activity. Give assistance and guidance as necessary.

Plan for more Discovery Learning Activities: Reflect on how this activity worked for the student. As you plan more discovery activities, take the answers to these questions into consideration: What went well? What could have gone better? How can any problem areas be corrected or minimized?

before actual classroom application. Table 12.5 provides some instructional suggestions for planning discovery-learning experiences (Mayer, 2002).

Inquiry Learning

Inquiry-based learning (IBL)
An approach to learning that centers on the scientific investigation of a particular issue or project

Inquiry-based learning (IBL) is an approach to learning that is centered on the scientific investigation of a particular issue or project. It is grounded on the social and learning ideology of constructivism (Eick & Reed, 2002). Inquiry-based learning actively involves students, encouraging them to formulate questions; conduct broad investigations; and build new understandings, meanings, and knowledge (Dana, Thomas, & Boynton, 2011). It is often viewed as a cyclical investigative process involving problem identification, investigation, and reflection upon results (Bishop, Bertam, & Lunsford, 2004). Figure 12.1 provides a detailed outline of the inquiry process (Orlich, Harder, Callahan, Kauchak, & Gibson, 2007).

Inquiry-based learning is a general process for investigating a problem. It puts the student in the role of the scientist, investigating relevant and engaging issues. It typically begins with a question of interest. This might be a problem related to the content of a lesson. It might be something of particular interest to the students in their daily life. There are endless possibilities, but it is important to define the problem in a clear way. The second step involves the development of a hypothesis, or an educated guess as to the outcome of the problem. The hypothesis should be as specific as possible so it is clear what needs to be investigated. For example, a class may decide to investigate how likely students are to comply with recycling procedures if recycling bins are located in the classroom versus down the hall in a central location.

A class may decide to investigate how likely students are to comply with recycling procedures if the bins are in the classroom versus down the hall.

Figure 12.1

Outline of the Inquiry-Based Learning Process

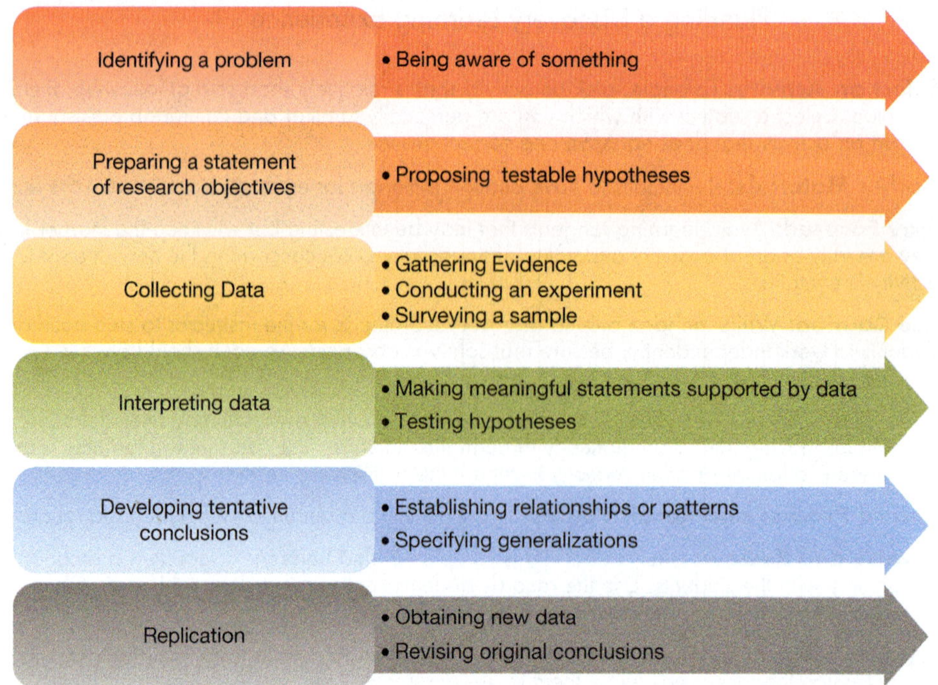

The next step is to gather evidence. This may involve experimentation or administration of a simple survey. *Students should seek the guidance of their teacher whenever collecting data from people to make sure they are in compliance with school rules regarding research.* After data is collected, students get to analyze the results. At times students find this part of the process daunting; however, properly framed, analysis can be the most exciting part of the process. It is like finding out the ending to a good mystery story. Once students have their answer, they need to reflect on the original hypothesis. Did they obtain support for the hypothesis?

If not, why? Depending on the outcome, students may wish to repeat the data collection process (replication) to be certain of the outcome or they may modify their initial hypothesis to investigate the issue again. The process of inquiry-based learning should be an enjoyable and engaging way to empower students to take control of their own learning process.

Research has suggested that implementation of inquiry-based principles can help students become more creative, positive, and independent (Kuhne, 1995). Research has also shown that students improve academically during inquiry-based learning projects (GLEF, 2001). Inquiry-based projects help students develop skills to deal with real-life problem solving, shaping how they search for solutions. They learn how to deal with problems that do not have clear solutions. They also develop respect for challenges to their way of thinking. To help teachers realize the potential of this learning approach, Table 12.6 provides some suggestions for building a culture of inquiry (Drayton & Falk, 2001; Alberta Learning Center, 2004).

Table 12.6 Building a Culture of Inquiry

Approach inquiry with enthusiasm and excitement.
Admit that inquiry involves the unexpected for you and for students.
Model the inquiry process in your instruction.
Use the language of inquiry in your daily instruction.
Facilitate, but do not dominate, the process by discussing, clarifying, and supporting.
Evaluate the process.
Use available technology to facility the process.
Be organized and set up specific times for inquiry-based learning.

Problem-Based Learning

Problem-based learning (PBL)

A student-centered technique based on constructivist principles that typically helps students work through problems that have direct impact on their daily lives

Problem-based learning (PBL) is another student-centered technique based on constructivist principles (Wirkala & Kuhn, 2011). It is typically used to help students work through problems that have direct impact on their daily lives. Using this approach, students become skilled at thinking for themselves and working through real life problems. The problem-based learning process usually begins by presenting students with a problem. Again, the problem should be relevant and meaningful to the students, something from their everyday experience. In the beginning, the teacher plays a more active role in the problem-solving process. As students gain more experience with the approach, however, the teacher's role changes to a facilitator (Merrill, 2002). Problems also become increasingly complex, better mirroring problems in real life. It is important to recognize that this approach is different from traditional instructional models. For example, Figure 12.2 outlines how problem-based learning differs from traditional or subject-based learning.

Problem-based learning differs from more traditional forms of instruction in that *students decide* what knowledge is needed to address a given goal. In traditional or subject-based learning models, the teacher provides students with what is important to know. Both approaches have appropriate applications, but problem-based learning reinforces skills needed for students to solve problems for themselves (Hmelo-Silver, C. E., 2004).

Problem-based learning has been used for a variety of learning objectives. Regardless of the particular learning goal, problem-based learning approaches share the following common set of characteristics (Barrows, 1996):

- Learning is student centered.
- Learning occurs in small student groups.
- Teachers are facilitators or guides.
- Problems are the organizing focus and stimulus for learning.

SUBJECT-BASED LEARNING (SBL)

Students are provided with material to know

Students learn required material

Problems are presented to illustrate how to use new knowledge

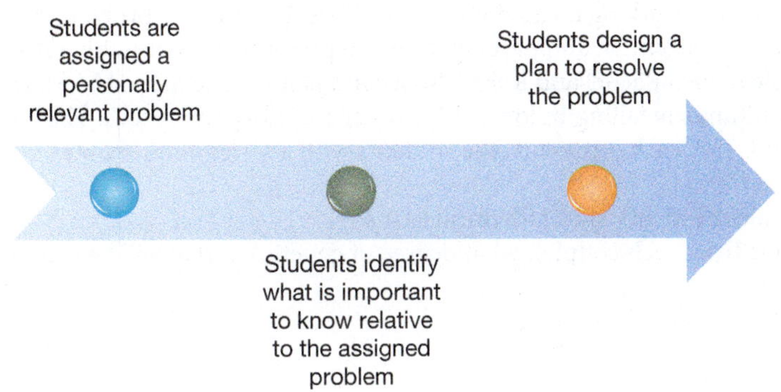

Figure 12.2

Differences Between Problem-Based Learning and Traditional Subject-Based Learning

Table 12.7 Problem-Based Learning Process

Phase	Teacher Behavior
Phase 1: Orient students to the problem.	Teacher goes over the objectives of the lesson, describes important logistical requirements, and motivates students to engage in problem-solving activity.
Phase 2: Organize students for study.	Teacher helps students define and organize study tasks related to the problem.
Phase 3: Assist independent and group investigation.	Teacher encourages students to gather appropriate information, conduct experiments, and search for explanations and solutions.
Phase 4: Develop and present artifacts and exhibits.	Teacher assists students in planning and preparing appropriate artifacts such as reports, videos, and models, and helps them share their work with others.
Phase 5: Analyze and evaluate the problem-solving process.	Teacher helps students to reflect on their investigations and the processes they used.

- Problems are a vehicle for the development of real-life problem solving skills.
- New information is acquired through self-directed learning.

Problem-based learning is problem oriented and self-directed. Through small group interactions, students determine the nature of the problem and how to generate solutions. Teachers help students move through the process of problem solving, rather than providing answers. A fundamental assumption of this approach is that the skill of problem solving is itself just as important as the solution to the problem. Table 12.7 further defines the nature of this process and the role of the teacher (Arends, 2007).

Research has found problem-based learning has a positive impact on academic progress. Most notable is research conducted and reviewed by Cindy Hmelo-Silver (2004; Hmelo-Silver,

In The Classroom

APPLYING THEORY

Problem-Based Learning (PBL)

CLASSROOM EXAMPLE

Sean Campbell is a tenth grade biology teacher working on a genetics unit. He decides to use a problem-based approach to the topic, hoping to encourage student engagement and participation. He presents students with a story of two sets of identical twins. The first pair is female named Rachel and Rory. The second pair is male named Mark and Steve. The story describes the meeting and Mark ultimately falling in love with Rachel and Rory with Steve. The couples marry, and soon each is expecting a single child. The teacher presents the students with a series of questions:

- Will the children of these couples be identical like identical twins?
- Comparing the two babies (one from each couple), what degree of genetic overlap will be experienced? 25%, 50%, 100%?

(continues)

- How will the genetic relatedness of the two babies compare to fraternal twins?
- How will the genetic relatedness of the two babies compare to any other set of full siblings?

Following the theory behind problem-based learning, Mr. Campbell designs a checklist to facilitate his progress.

When preparing for leading this problem-based learning group, did I do the following?

- Create a compelling and engaging case?
- Create or select appropriate resources to use for presenting the problem?
- Consider the social context of solving this problem?
- Arrange for additional needed resources?

When introducing the students to the task, did I do the following?

- Gather diagnostic information about their prior experiences and expectations?
- Help the students appreciate the PBL approach?
- Explain the process, plus the roles of the teacher versus the student?
- Discuss how groups will make decisions?

During the problem-based learning groups, did I do the following?

- Help the students identify significant facts and generate hypotheses, ideas, and issues?
- Encourage the students to share what they already knew?
- Encourage students to summarize and synthesize?
- Help student decide which learning issues to pursue?
- Help learners become more adept at helping each other?
- Create an environment where student feel they can take risks?
- Steadily shift responsibility for the group to the learners?
- Help the students bring closure to the case within a reasonable time?

Adapted from (Westberg & Hilliard, 1996)

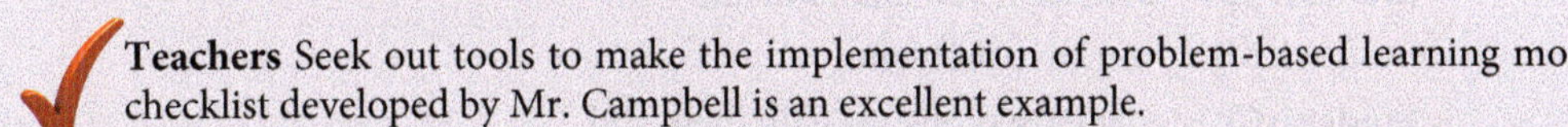

Teachers Seek out tools to make the implementation of problem-based learning more efficient. The checklist developed by Mr. Campbell is an excellent example.

Mr. Campbell was ultimately pleased with his use of problem-based learning in this context. The students found the case interesting because it involved identical twins. Most of the students personally knew a set of twins and were excited to learn what would happen if one set of identical twins married another. Since Mr. Campbell thought ahead and had the necessary resources available, the learning groups were able to efficiently develop hypotheses and attempt to locate support. Some ideas turned out to have intuitive appeal, but failed to produce support in the reading material. After a period of time, the groups came back together as a class and began sharing results. Although different groups took different paths to arrive at an answer to the proposed questions, most groups settled on a consistent set of answers. The students reported they liked the nature of the activity and claimed the material was more interesting presented in this way. Reading the same material straight from the book was more difficult.

Duncan, & Chinn, 2007). She advocates that problem-based learning approaches have had a positive impact on a student's ability to think in creative and flexible ways and to direct their own learning. She also points out that more research is needed to further determine which situations are appropriate for the problem-based learning approach.

Instructional Conversations

Instructional conversations

Educational dialogues that help the instructor assess what information the student is ready to learn, with appropriate assistance

A final topic we will consider is that of **instructional conversations.** As the name implies, these are conversations that have a unique learning focus. The idea is based in the work of Lev Vygotsky (Chapter 2) and his theory of the zone of proximal development. Recall that this is the collection of cognitive abilities an individual is ready to learn *with assistance*. To find and teach to this zone, teachers need to get to know their students in a personal way. They need to have conversations and ask questions. Instructional conversations are like typical conversations in terms of the dynamic exchange of information between two individuals, but these conversations have a more direct purpose. They serve to further the instructor's ability to teach within the student's zone of proximal development and provide the appropriate level of support.

Teacher	When we do get mad at our friends, (why d'you) say "course" (like) of course, what happens when you get mad at your friends?
Student: Ca	They get mad at you,
Teacher	Oh, you get mad back at each other? (laughter)
Student: MI	They do something that you don't like, or ...
Student: Ca	(They bounce the ball around.)
Teacher	Okay. Tell me a little bit more about that.
Student: MI	They do something that you don't like, or they'll not talk to you, or not share or not be a good friend ...
Teacher	Okay, so, friendship, I'm gonna add, this time I'm gonna put it in capital letters the new ideas we got (writes on chart) friendship, friends CAN get mad at each other. Right? What else did you say?
Student: MI	They cannot talk to you or don't share with you or nothing,
Teacher	Okay, so sometimes they DON'T share with you. Does that keep you from being friends?
Student: S	Yes.
Student: Sc	No.
Teacher	Okay. I heard different answers. Who said "Yes."? If they don't share, it keeps you from being friends.
Student: Ja	because if you talk to them.
Student: MI	you have problems,
Student: Ce	you have problems with them and,
Teacher	Okay, friends have problems ...
Student: S	(immediately) Oh yes.
Teacher	and I even heard (a word bigger than) problems, fighting, can friends fight?

From: Goldenberg & Patthey-Chavez (1995)

The amount and type of support needed to learn varies and is referred to as scaffolding (Chapter 2) by Vygotsky. Appropriate levels of scaffolding give the student the necessary background information and support to learn without providing detailed step-by-step instructions. The student remains in the active role of learning, with the teacher providing necessary guidance. As an approach to instruction and learning, instructional conversations are consistent with all the other constructivist approaches we have reviewed.

Instructional conversations are not lectures and do not involve a one-way flow of information from teacher to student. They are genuine dialogues where each participant conveys novel and important information to the other, and the respondent is reflective and sensitive to the information presented. As with the problem-based learning and inquiry learning approaches presented earlier, these instructional conversations aim to help students develop their ability to think and reason. They help to move students away from relying on the teacher to solve problems.

It may seem that these conversations are highly structured and take considerable planning on the part of the teacher, but it is actually quite the opposite. Some of the most effective conversations happen at unstructured times, between classes, during lunch, after school, or during extracurricular activities. They also take place beyond the boundaries of the school—in our homes, work places, and at recreational times (Rogoff, 1990; Chappell & Craft, 2011). To give you a sense of what these conversations are like, examine the actual transcript of a teacher interacting with a group of students presented below. The teacher and students are in the middle of an informal conversation that has just shifted to the topic of getting mad at friends.

As you can see, the teacher in this setting is clearly acting as a facilitator. The teacher is providing guidance, raising potential issues, and suggesting lines of inquiry. The teacher is not telling them what to think or what the answers are to the questions. In fact, the students are directing the conversation by what interests them and what is important to them. They are not trying to tell the teacher what they believe is a "correct" answer. This is the general pattern of an instructional conversation. Table 12.8 provides additional information on how traditional instruction compares to an instructional conversation.

Table 12.8 Elements of Instructional Conversations

Instructional Elements	Conversational Elements
1. **Thematic focus** The teacher selects a theme or idea to serve as a starting point on which to focus the discussion and has a general plan for how the theme will unfold, including how to "chunk" the text to permit optimal exploration of the theme.	1. **Few "known-answer" questions** Much of the discussion centers on questions and answers for which there might be more than one correct answer.
2. **Activation and use of background and relevant schemata** The teacher either "hooks into" or provides students with pertinent background knowledge and relevant schemata necessary for understanding a text. Background knowledge and schemata are then woven into the discussion that follows.	2. **Responsiveness to student contributions** While having an initial plan and maintaining the focus and coherence of the discussion, the teacher is also responsive to students' statements and the opportunities the statements provides.
3. **Direct teaching** When necessary, the teacher provides direct teaching of a skill or concept.	3. **Connected discourse** The discussion is characterized by multiple, interactive, connected turns—succeeding utterances build upon and extend previous ones.
4. **Promotion of more complex language and expression** The teacher elicits more extended student contributions by using a variety of elicitation techniques; invitations to expand ("Tell me more about ____"), questions ("What do you mean by ____?"), restatements ("In other words, ____"), and pauses.	4. **A challenging, but non-threatening, atmosphere** The teacher creates a "zone of proximal development," in which a challenging atmosphere is balanced by a positive affective climate. The teacher is more collaborator than evaluator and creates an atmosphere that challenges students and allows them to negotiate and construct the meaning of the text.
5. **Promotion of bases for statements or positions** The teacher promotes students' use of text, pictures, and reasoning to support an argument or position. Without overwhelming students, the teacher probes for the basis of students' statements: "How do you know?" "What makes you think that?" "Show us where it says ____."	5. **General participation, including self-selected turns** The teacher encourages general participation among students. The teacher does not hold exclusive right to determine who talks, and students are encouraged to volunteer or otherwise influence the selection of speaking turns.

SOURCE: Goldenberg (1991)

SUMMARIZE AND REFLECT

1. This section looked at specific instructional strategies based on constructivism.
2. Guided discovery is a learning approach that focuses on active, hands-on learning supported by instructional guidance.
3. Guided discovery involves solving problems and focuses on active student-driven participation and activities to connect new information with existing information.
4. Anchoring learning in information already well learned promotes retention and understanding.
5. Teachers often avoid using discovery learning because they are concerned that necessary course content will not get covered, that it will require too much preparation and class time, and that class sizes are often inappropriate.
6. Inquiry-based learning (IBL) is an approach to learning centering on the scientific investigation of a particular issue or project.
7. Inquiry-based learning actively involves students in learning; encouraging them to formulate questions; conduct broad investigations; and build new understandings, meanings, and knowledge.
8. Research has suggested that implementation of inquiry-based principles can help students become more creative, positive, and independent.
9. Problem-based learning (PBL) is typically used to help students work through problems that have direct impact on their daily lives.
10. Subject-based learning (SBL) refers to more traditional approaches to the instruction of specific subject matter.
11. Problem-based learning is problem oriented and self-directed.
12. A fundamental assumption of problem-based learning is that the skill of problem solving is itself just as important as the solution to the problem.
13. Instructional conversations are like typical conversations in terms of the dynamic exchange of information between two individuals, but these conversations have a more direct purpose.
14. Instructional conversations serve to further the instructor's ability to teach within the student's zone of proximal development and provide the appropriate level of support.
15. Instructional conversations are not lectures and do not involve a one-way flow of information from teacher to student.

INFORMED APPLICATION

1. Do you think the guided discovery approach is more appropriate for certain subjects? If so, which ones? If not, why?
2. Describe how subject-based learning differs from problem-based learning.

THE CHAPTER IN REVIEW

The chapter begins with a general discussion of constructivism, which refers to the active processing of new information in the context of prior learning and the student's readiness to learn. Constructivism has a common set of elements including presenting real-life problems in a meaningful context, with opportunities for students to work collaboratively. The context in which we learn is just as important as what we learn. Researchers have examined how learning is situated and tied to a particular context. They also have examined the individuals participating in a given learning endeavor (e.g. the students and teacher in a classroom) and how they make up a community of learners. The last part of this section describes some of the limitations of constructivism. Constructivist principles surround how it approaches the search for knowledge and assumptions made about the nature of truth. We learned that ontology refers to the nature of reality and truth compared to epistemology, which is the nature or origin of knowledge. Epistemology essentially refers to how students come to know something (not whether what we know is real or not).

Constructivism can be broken down into different schools of thought. Individual Constructivism is the study of how individuals develop and change their cognitive and emotional processes in an attempt to process information and build knowledge. Individual constructivism was one of the earliest forms of constructivism and drew heavily from the work of Jean Piaget. Individual constructivism was later eclipsed by more radical perspectives on how knowledge construction relates to reality. Radical Constructivism is a branch of constructivist thinking that further divorces itself from any connection to an objective reality. Radical constructivists believe that all thinking is inherently valid or is "true" from the perspective of the individual. Another constructivist school of thought emphasizes social interactions and is based on the work of Lev Vygotsky. Social Constructivism emphasizes the process of individual internalization of psychological tools (language, problem solving techniques, social skills, etc.) through social interactions. According to this school of thought, all individual thinking is just a reflection of the culture in which a person lives.

The next section more closely examines the nature of social learning and the construction of knowledge. One of the fundamental tools used in constructivist teaching is active engagement in conversations with peers and teachers. Teachers do not always have to be in the center of the conversational pattern. A broader range of dialogue allows students to challenge each other; clarify difficult points; provide rich, developmentally appropriate examples; and enjoy the process of learning. Teachers can use simple strategies to promote more effective dialogue and encourage collaboration. Collaborative classrooms emphasize active student learning through dynamic interpersonal exchange. They promote dialogue through effective communication and a value and respect for differing perspectives. These classrooms are also distinguished by their focus on involving students in real-world problem solving in dynamic group interchanges. Research has shown that collaborative classrooms share four common characteristics: sharing knowledge among students and teachers, shared authority among teachers and students, teachers as mediators, and heterogeneous groupings of students. In collaborative classrooms students experiment with actual applications of a particular lesson, which gives students experience with using knowledge and better integrating it into their existing knowledge base. These authentic activities embed learning tasks in activities that mirror real-life applications, which ultimately help them better understand the relevance of education.

The final section looked at specific instructional strategies based on constructivism. Guided Discovery is a learning approach that focuses on active, hands-on learning supported by instructional guidance. Guided discovery involves solving problems, focusing on active student-driven participation, using activities to connect new information with existing information. Anchor ing learning in information already well learned promotes retention and understanding. Teachers often avoid using discovery learning because they are concerned that necessary course content will not get covered, that it will require too much preparation and class time, and that class sizes are often inappropriate. Another strategy is called Inquiry-based learning (IBL). Inquiry-based learning is an approach to learning centering on the scientific investigation of a particular issue or project. This approach actively involves students in learning, encouraging them to formulate questions; conduct broad investigations; and build new understandings, meanings, and knowledge. Research has suggested that implementation of inquiry-based principles can help students become more creative, positive, and independent.

Problem-based learning (PBL) is typically used to help students work through problems that have direct impact on their daily lives compared to subject-based learning (SBL), which refers to more traditional approaches to the instruction of specific subject matter. Problem-based learning is problem oriented and self-directed. A fundamental assumption of problem-based learning is that the skill of problem solving is itself just as important as the solution to the problem. A final strategy covered in the chapter is instructional conversations. Instructional conversations are like typical conversations in terms of the dynamic exchange of information between two individuals, but these conversations have a more direct purpose. The conversations serve to further the instructor's ability to teach within the student's zone of proximal development and provide the appropriate level of support. Instructional conversations are not lectures and do not involve a one-way flow of information from teacher to student.

Interdisciplinary Case Focus

principal special educator teacher parents psychologist social worker physical educator nurse peers doctor

Mary Pace is a new twelfth grade creative writing teacher. She just completed her first half of the year and is experiencing problems with student engagement. She is concerned about the learning progress of her students. She is also concerned about her annual review at the end of the school year.

Deciding to be proactive, she reaches out to her colleagues to help her determine where she can make improvements. She first contacts Manuel Joseph, the twelfth grade English literature teacher. She also contacts Martha Engram who teaches ninth grade global history. She has known Martha since she completed her student teaching internship in college and trusts her judgment. Finally, she contacts Tim Rawlings, the school's VP for student affairs. Since Tim will be involved in her annual review, she particularly wanted his input.

After some consideration, she decides to invite each of these colleagues to spend part of a day observing her teaching. She is nervous about the process but has determined this is the best way for them to identify strengths and formulate suggestions for improvement. The following summaries are from each of Ms. Pace's colleagues.

Manuel Joseph Mr. Joseph visited Ms. Pace's class on a Tuesday morning. On this particular day, students were working on developing ideas for a descriptive essay on some aspect of nature. Mr. Joseph notices that there is an easy, natural rapport between Ms. Pace and her students. They discuss things openly and appear comfortable sharing ideas. He is somewhat surprised because Ms. Pace conducted the entire class in a lecture format. He would have expected more reluctance to participate in this format. He determines this excellent participation is directly due to Ms. Pace's open and engaging personal demeanor.

Martha Engram Ms. Engram visits the class on a Friday afternoon. During her visit, Ms. Pace is giving a lesson on word style choices. She is focusing on how to alter the tone of a written product by making careful vocabulary choices. She provides the students with a list of primary words, followed by a list of synonyms. The students are instructed to create a paragraph describing a commercial hair product using either the primary words or their synonyms. After working individually, the students work is collected for feedback, which is to be delivered the following Monday.

Tim Rawlings Mr. Rawlings is able to visit Ms. Pace's class several times, but only for short periods. On one visit, the class is working in groups analyzing feedback from the teacher on a creative writing assignment completed the preceding week. He noticed that there was a great deal of off topic conversation and that the students appeared unfocused. On his other two visits, Ms. Pace is lecturing on different concepts from their class text. He immediately notices the difference between the group work-day and these lecture days. The students appear to be focused and attentive. They appear engaged and well prepared for the lecture and associated discussion.

Group Discussion Ms. Pace invites all three colleagues to a breakfast meeting before school following their observations. She meets them in the school cafeteria, providing coffee, juice, and donuts. After settling down at the table, Ms. Pace invites her colleagues to share their observations. Ms. Engram is the first to comment, noting that she found the students' group work to be effective, but somewhat unstructured. Mr. Rawlings echoes these comments, sharing that he noticed the same thing on one of his visits. He shared that he felt the students could use more direction to focus their work. Mr. Joseph then comments that this was interesting because he found just the opposite situation during his observation. He clarified that he observed Ms. Pace during a lecture day but commented that the students were very focused and clearly enjoyed participating in the class. He particularly noted that the students were extremely comfortable working with Ms. Pace. Mr. Rawlings interjects that he observed Ms. Pace on multiple days, and on two observation days she was lecturing. He supported Mr. Joseph's observations, indicating that Ms. Pace appeared to have a significant strength in her lecture style.

Suggestions for Improvement Ms. Engram volunteered that all teachers have strengths and weaknesses, and it seemed clear that Ms. Pace was more naturally effective in a lecture setting. She applauded this strength, noting that this is often where teachers have difficulty. She also, however, expressed concern that there are many benefits to having students work in small groups and suggested the team help Ms. Pace identify ways to use her strengths to reinforce her group work. Mr. Joseph noted that it appeared that one of Ms. Pace's strengths was her ability to convey information verbally, resulting in her strong performance during lectures. He suggests that Ms. Pace use this natural strength to promote better learning during group work. Mr. Rawlings agreed and indicated that he had some information on effective questioning techniques that might help Ms. Pace. After retrieving this information, the team decided to encourage Ms. Pace to use the following suggestions during her group work:

- Hold discussions following a shared experience.
- Ask open-ended questions that require thoughtful discussion.
- Give students time to think about a topic by assigning a discussion topic for after recess or the next day.
- Provide discussion rules, including directions on how to listen.
- Ask students to discuss their ideas in teams before opening discussion to the entire class.
- Structure discussions so all students have the opportunity to participate.
- Provide informal guidance for student conversations by asking for clarification and probing for more information as she circulates from group to group.
- Listen and wait for other students to respond, instead of playing the role of evaluator after student responses.

Follow up After implementing these suggestions for a period of one month, Ms. Pace began to see considerable improvement. She recognized why she was successful during lectures and was able to make shifts in her presentation style to better accommodate the needs of students working in small groups. As the group work improved, she was better able to determine which instructional goals would be better addressed using whole lecture, small group, or a combination of the two. Overall, she felt the class operated in a more focused and efficient manner while maintaining the easygoing feel of the class. Additionally, she was rewarded with higher student scores at the end of the term.

Key Terms

TERM	*Page*	*TERM*	*Page*
Authentic activity	404	Inquiry-based learning (IBL)	407
Collaborative classroom	403	Instructional conversations	411
Community of learners	396	Ontology	397
Constructivism	394	Problem-based learning (PBL)	409
Dialogic teaching	401	Radical constructivism	399
Discovery learning	405	Situated learning	396
Epistemology	397	Social constructivism	399
Individual constructivism	398		

13
Chapter
CREATING
EFFECTIVE LEARNING
ENVIRONMENTS

What's It All About ...

What is classroom management, and how does it lead to a positive learning environment?

How can teachers create effective learning environments?

How do students participate in the creation of effective learning environments?

How can collaboration help teachers manage the classroom environment?

Chapter Objectives

- Describe classroom management.
- Describe different classroom teaching styles.
- Explain how to manage instructional time.

- Explain how teachers encourage engagement.
- Describe positive behavioral supports.
- Review how to prevent behavioral issues.
- Describe how to establish rules and procedures.
- Review how to arrange learning spaces.
- Understand different styles of communication.

- Describe social skill development.
- Describe conflict resolution and peer mediation.
- Explain how to establish effective student-teacher relationships.

- Describe teacher collaboration.
- Describe parental collaboration.

EXTENDED OUTLINE

Creating Effective Learning Environments

I. What's It All About ...

II. From Today's Headlines

III. Establishing a Positive Instructional Context
   - A. What is classroom management?
   - B. Classroom management styles
   - C. Managing instructional times
   - D. Summarize and reflect

IV. Teachers Creating Positive Learning Environments
   - A. Encouraging engagement
   - B. Positive behavioral supports
   - C. Prevention
   - D. Rules and procedures
     1. Rules
     2. Procedures
   - E. Learning spaces
     1. Arrangement style
     2. Special interest areas
     3. Computer use
   - F. Communication style
     1. Congruent communication
     2. Non-verbal communication
     3. Listening skills
   - G. Summarize and reflect

V. Students as Management Agents
   - A. Social skill development
   - B. Conflict resolution and peer mediation
   - C. Student-teacher relationship
   - D. Summarize and reflect

VI. Effective Learning Environments through Collaboration
   - A. Teacher collaboration
   - B. Parental collaboration
     1. Assumptions supporting good collaboration
     2. Key elements of effective collaboration
     3. Reasons and mechanisms for collaboration
     4. Collaboration challenges: resistant parents and student participation
   - C. Summarize and reflect

VII. The Chapter in Review

VIII. Interdisciplinary Case Focus

From Today's Headlines

Vol. I No. 13 Teaching World, 2012

You've Got Mail

You've got mail, but it may not be what you were expecting. *Teachers* are making greater use of email to maintain close connections with parents. Traditionally, contact with parents was through letters or infrequent parent-teacher conferences. Today, teachers can use email to communicate more frequently and effectively.

Lisa Hewitt is a grade school music teacher. In addition to teaching music, she also teaches students to use email (*The Orlando Sentinel*, December 2006). She doesn't, however, stop with the students. She actively encourages every parent to use email to keep up with the class. Ms. Hewitt is one of millions of teachers using Internet email to bring parents into closer contact with the daily activities of class. She has also created a classroom website, which has a calendar detailing assignments. Eventually, she wants to include other elements like downloadable permission slips.

Using Internet tools is becoming attractive to educators because of increasing difficulty in finding time for more traditional forms of communication. It is difficult to connect by phone because of the busy schedules of both the teacher and the parents. Sending notes home takes time and cannot deal with immediate problems. Internet based communication usually happens instantaneously, making quick work of many everyday issues. For example, failure to turn in homework may elicit a comment from the student that they did it last night with their mother, but must have left it in the kitchen. A quick email to the student's mother can often resolve the issue in a few minutes or during the school day. The immediacy of the communication media makes students, parents, and the teacher feel more cohesive and better able to work as a team. It also enhances a sense of accountability. Communication that is more frequent makes it difficult to ignore problems.

Teachers can send notes home to specific parents or to all parents. This helps keep everyone informed and the process of learning moving forward. It is true that not all parents have Internet access in their home, but many can access email at work, at public locations, or even from their cell phones.

MAKE THE CONNECTION

As this article indicates, teachers are becoming very resourceful when it comes to reinforcing communication with parents. Communication is an important part of a larger trend toward collaboration to create positive, productive learning environments. It is one of many tools teachers use to effectively manage their classrooms. In this chapter, we will explore communication and other factors affecting classroom management. We will look at how classroom management can help create positive learning spaces. We will also look at specific instructional strategies leading to effectively managed classrooms. Finally, we will explore how teachers collaborate with parents and with each other.

ESTABLISHING A POSITIVE INSTRUCTIONAL CONTEXT

We all hope students approach school with excitement, wonder, and a strong desire to learn. We want students to view school as a safe place where their imaginations can flourish and their natural curiosity is met with engaging instruction. This is the goal and dream of education. Making this a reality takes careful work and planning. It also takes a thorough understanding of classroom management techniques, which continues as one of the primary concerns of beginning teachers (Meister & Melnick, 2003; McCormack, 2001; Jacques, 2000). Part of the reason for this ongoing concern is the ever-increasing learning demands of a diverse student body (Smith & Rivera, 1995). Today's classrooms are a complex mix of students from a wide variety of social and cultural backgrounds. As we saw in Chapter 8, serving this mix is changing educational practice. Excellent teaching is becoming directly tied to instructional practices that are sensitive to individual learning needs. Providing a more personalized educational experience creates a positive learning environment and more thoroughly engages the student. **Positive learning environments** are characterized by a fundamental respect for all persons, explicit standards for appropriate conduct, positive emotional experiences, and a collaborative recognition that everyone contributes to the success of the learning environment (Jones & Jones, 2007; Meyer & Turner, 2006; Whitney, Leonard, Leonard, Camelio, & Camelio, 2006). The development of such learning environments is complex and on going—and begins by laying an appropriate foundation for effective classroom management during the first few weeks of school.

School should be a safe haven for students where their imaginations can flourish.

Interconnections

See Chapter 8 for information on social and cultural diversity in schools.

Positive learning environment

Environment characterized by a fundamental respect for all persons, explicit standards for appropriate conduct, positive emotional experiences, and a collaborative recognition that everyone contributes to the success of the learning environment

What Is Classroom Management?

The first weeks of a new school year highlight the excitement students experience as they reunite with old friends and settle into a new classroom. It is an important time for teachers as each begins the process of introducing students to his/her unique teaching style. Teachers play a significant role in negotiating interactions among students and setting the tone for how the class operates. It is also the beginning of **classroom management**. This refers to a variety of teacher and student factors contributing to the operation of the educational environment. Teachers often give students a detailed list of class rules and procedures. They convey their expectations for appropriate behavior and the consequences for failing to meet those expectations.

Classroom management

The variety of teacher and student factors contributing to the operation of the educational environment

Historically, the focus of classroom management has been on behaviors important for a successful and safe education. Today's teachers are mindful of behavior management but also take a more comprehensive approach, focusing on creating positive learning environments (Emmer, Evertson & Worsham, 2006). This is not a departure from the long-standing behavioral approach to classroom management but rather a shift in focus (Jones & Jones, 2007). Additionally, there is now a strong focus on managing active learning.

The last fifty years of education has witnessed several approaches rise to prominence for classroom management. Approaches vary in popularity over time, but all have a place in effectively managing classrooms. Table 13.1 provides a summary of these approaches. *Behavioral approaches* focus on maintaining appropriate classroom learning environments through correcting misbehavior and promoting positive behaviors. The idea behind the approach is that learning cannot occur if students fail to behave in a manner conducive to

Interconnections

Comprehensive coverage of behavioral principles of learning can be found in Chapter 4.

Table 13.1 Perspectives on Classroom Management

Behavioral Approach	This management approach focuses on creating effective classrooms by correcting disruptive behavior through behavior modification techniques.
Counseling Approach	This approach focuses on personal growth by helping students meet their social and emotional needs. Improving classroom operation often centers on solving social skill deficits leading to interpersonal issues.
Teacher Effectiveness Approach	This approach is unique in that it does not focus on student issues but on how the teacher contributes to student learning. In general, the approach focuses on teacher organization, presentation ability, and student-teacher relationships.
Comprehensive Approach	This management approach focuses on a more comprehensive knowledge and skill set. This approach is based on the following: • A thorough understanding of current research and student needs • Fostering a positive learning environment by supporting teacher, student and peer relationships • Providing instruction that is sensitive to the needs of individual students and the classroom group

SOURCE: Summarized from Jones and Jones, 2007.

learning. Focusing on appropriate behaviors requires teachers to apply the behavioral principles presented in Chapter 4. These principles can help teachers manage behavior, but all too frequently teachers focus on behaviors after the student produces them. It is also important to give students the skills and understanding needed to prevent problems in the first place.

During the late 1960s, the practice of classroom management began to move away from an exclusive focus on behavior and moved toward helping students discover their unique needs. Teachers began to explore systematically the reasons behind behavior. This *counseling approach* to classroom management centers on management of the classroom environment by helping students develop personally. The approach is based on the idea that if students are given effective tools to meet their needs and wants, then they are less likely to act out and create classroom disruptions. As the practice of education evolved, teachers continued to support individual growth and development, but *instructor effectiveness* was also recognized as an important factor in classroom management.

The teacher contributes significantly to the educational climate. The *teacher effectiveness approach* to classroom management acknowledges the teacher's contribution to the success of the classroom. Well-planned, engaging instruction helps captivate students and keeps them on-task. Similarly, organization and the quality of the student-teacher relationship help decrease the probability students will engage in inappropriate behaviors.

The behavioristic, counseling, and teacher-effectiveness approaches toward classroom management are beginning to converge into a more cohesive, comprehensive management style. This *comprehensive approach* is grounded in a thorough understanding of the scientific literature (Jones & Jones, 2007). Teachers need to be fluent in the language of research and able to interpret and apply research findings. Additionally, the approach is characterized by a strong commitment to creating a positive learning environment. This necessitates the cooperation and coordination of teachers, students, parents, and a variety of other educational professionals (Martella, Nelson, Marchand-Martella, & O'Reilly, 2011). Everyone needs to be committed to the development of positive interactions and behavioral standards that support academic engagement. Finally, the approach is student centered, focusing on the individual learning needs of each student.

A teacher's approach to classroom management is evident from the first day of class. It is that crucial time when all the planning and preparation translates into actual instructional practice. The book *Tools for Teaching* by Barbara Gross Davis (1993) provides a number of suggestions for how to make the crucial first day successful. As you would expect, success on the first day actually begins well before the start of school. Teachers should take time before school begins to become thoroughly familiar with the classroom environment where

Before school starts teachers should get comfortable with their classroom. Many practice speaking and writing on the chalkboard.

they will be teaching. Make sure you are familiar with all the technology available in the classroom. Practice giving a short lecture so you can see how your voice carries in the room. Write on the chalkboard, making sure your handwriting is legible and visible to everyone in the class. Simply being more familiar with the classroom will help your first day run more smoothly (Johnson, 1988).

Once the all-important first day arrives, make sure you focus on creating a sense of community in the classroom. Spend time working with the students in smaller groups where they get to know each other. Students work harder when they are active participants in the learning process. Group work allows each student the opportunity to participate in the class without the difficulties of speaking in front of a large group. Students also work harder when they feel the teacher looks upon them as individuals (Wolcowitz, 1984), so prioritize spending one-on-one time with each student.

It is also important to make sure you address student questions. Students come to the first day of class with a number of concerns. Many are concerned about the workload.

Others are concerned whether you will be a fair teacher. Still others are concerned about evaluation or the appropriateness of the course for their particular needs. When getting to know students, take a few minutes to ask them about their concerns and help find answers. Sometimes teachers find it helpful to set aside some time before and after class for student questions. Some students are reluctant to ask questions during class, but readily approach the teacher during less structured times.

Finally, expect some awkwardness during the first few days of class. This may be more pronounced for beginning teachers, but all teachers experience some first day difficulties. Additionally, the students often perceive nervousness as energy and enthusiasm. So, prepare well and try to enjoy this important time.

It is also instructive to look at the qualities and characteristics of effective teachers and how their skills take shape during those first weeks of school. Table 13.2 lists qualities of effective teacher managers (Emmer, Evertson, & Anderson, 1980). The list was developed after examining English and math teachers in a junior high school setting. Results from the study found that effective teachers were more likely to demonstrate these skills at the beginning of

Table 13.2 Characteristics of Effective Teacher Managers

Give directions and information clearly.
State desired attitudes and behaviors frequently.
Provide activities and assignments with higher levels of student success.
Present clear expectations for work standards.
Use the classroom rules and procedure more frequently to deal with disruptive behavior.
Have excellent listening skills.
Monitor student behavior extensively; and when inappropriate behavior occurs, quickly deal with it.
Keep better track of how student are progressing and whether they complete assignments.
Communicate an attitude or expectations that class time is for work activity, that you (the teacher) are aware of what students are doing, and that the students are accountable for their work.
Be consistent in responses to appropriate and inappropriate behavior of the students.
Be adept at stopping disruptive behavior quickly and ignoring it less often than less effective managers.

the school year. As you can see from the list, effective teachers successfully establish a variety of management techniques. They are able to provide clear directions, communicate effectively, manage behavior, and are consistent in their actions. This produces an organized classroom environment where students can learn and succeed. Establishing an organized classroom creates an environmental context where student can learn and grow. It makes good instruction possible and reduces problem behaviors (Emmer & Stough, 2001).

Classroom Management Styles

The general approaches to classroom management discussed in the last section are a fair representation of the changes seen in our country over time. They are, however, global descriptors of American schooling. Teachers are individuals and bring unique qualities to the instructional setting. Researchers are also interested in classroom management at this personal level and provide interesting insights into how teachers translate individual attributes into a classroom management style (Baumrind, 1967, 1971; Hughs, 2002; Barnas, 2001).

One of the more intriguing lines of research is actually an extension of research originally conducted with parents. In the late 1960s, Diana Baumrind theorized that there were different parenting styles and that these styles were associated with unique outcomes for their children. Newer research (Hughs, 2002; Barnas, 2001; Edwards, 1993) has extended this groundbreaking theory to teaching style. **Permissive teachers** emphasize student responsibility for decision-making. They typically do not force participation or worry excessively about deadlines. Classroom policies are developed in conjunction with students, and students are encouraged to take responsibility for governing their own behavior. They view themselves as a resource for students, but do not make demands for academic engagement. They expect students to drive their own learning and seek help if needed. This style is commendable on many levels, but it may lead to more flexibility than students can handle. Some students may feel they do not have sufficient direction to achieve academic success. **Authoritarian teachers** emphasize behavioral control. They establish a set of rules for the class and implement them without class discussion. They demand attendance and participation. They typically fail to discuss classroom issues with the students; rather, they make their own decisions and simply expect rules to be followed. Deadlines for assignments are viewed as absolutes. This style may produce greater student compliance with rules and deadlines, but it fails to explain *why* students are working. This creates too little self-regulation and greater reliance on the teacher for learning outcomes.

Permissive teacher

A teacher that emphasizes student responsibility for decision-making

Authoritarian teacher

A teacher that emphasizes behavioral control

Authoritative teachers emphasize the importance of providing firm direction, while recognizing the unique contributions of each student to the learning process. They frequently engage in discussions with students regarding class rules, participation, and handing in work. They value the perception of their students, but also establish themselves as the leader. They encourage self-direction, but provide clear limits regarding student behavior. Students are more likely to be self-directed under this system of management. They value their participation in the process of classroom management, while benefiting from the direction and support provided by the teacher.

Authoritative teacher

A teacher that emphasizes the importance of providing firm direction, while recognizing the unique contributions of each student to the learning process

As you can see, creating a positive learning environment is a complicated process. Teachers are individuals with unique ways of interacting with others. These unique interaction styles translate into different management styles, such as permissive, authoritarian, and authoritative described above. What is important to remember is that teachers do not fit neatly into any one style. All teachers are a complex mix of each of these styles. Certain days may lead a teacher to greater reliance on one style, but management style is dynamic and ever changing. Students preparing to become teachers should be familiar with each of these styles so that they begin to develop an awareness of how they approach classroom management. Awareness helps teachers make conscious choices and more effective decisions regarding the creation of a positive learning environment.

Managing Instructional Times

How students and teachers spend their instructional time also factors into the quality of the learning environment. The relation between instructional time and learning is a controversial topic. In 1994, a special commission on time and learning created by the Department of Education submitted their report *Prisoners of Time*. The report noted American schools

Table 13.3 Individual Management Styles

Permissive Teacher	Authoritarian Teacher	Authoritative Teacher
"Study if you want to."	"Study or else!"	"Study because it is important."

Adapted from Barnas, 2001.

were making progress in terms of what is taught and they had appropriate high-expectations, but they lacked improvements in quality educational time. This criticism ushered in a new era focused on increasing the amount of time students spend in meaningful educational endeavors.

The amount of time students spend in school varies by state, but what may prove more important is what students do during the day. Researchers have identified three different ways students spend their educational time (Aronson, 1999). These are illustrated in Figure 13.1 as an inverted pyramid. The top layer reflects the most general conceptualization of educational time. **Allocated time** is the amount of time students and teachers spend at school. It does not reflect what is done during that time, just the total number of hours. This varies by state, but most students spend approximately 180 days in school per year and six to seven hours per day. Allocated time can be further subdivided into *instructional time* (time spent in class) and *non-instructional time* (e.g., lunch, recess, time between classes, assemblies). **Engaged time** is that portion of allocated time spent participating in learning activities. A student may physically be present in class, but not actually engaged in any meaningful learning task. Almost every period of the day is spent settling into seats, taking roll, listening to announcements, etc. This takes up some allocated time and is distinguished from the time actually spent in a learning task. Participation in a learning task, however, is still not enough to maximize learning. **Academic learning time** is the portion of engaged time where students are actually learning. This is the time where students are both participating in a lesson *and* actively engaging in learning the material. This is the part of the school day where learning truly occurs. Unfortunately, academic learning time is a limited portion of the school day. Just how limited? Figure 13.2 shows just how much of the school day is spent in each of the three types of school time.

Allocated time

The amount of time students and teachers spend at school

Engaged time

That portion of allocated time spent participating in learning activities

Academic learning time

The portion of engaged time where students are actually learning

The numbers reported in the above figure are an average set of scores across several research studies investigating elementary schools. There is actually considerable variability across schools and states in terms of these variables. The researches in this study provide an average across studies to give the reader a sense of what goes on in an average school day. Remember that any particular school may be well above or below this average.

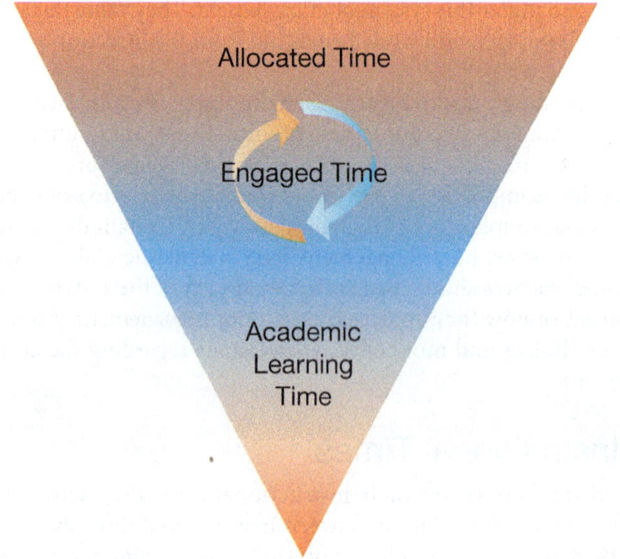

Figure 13.1

Three Ways Students Spend Their Educational Time in School

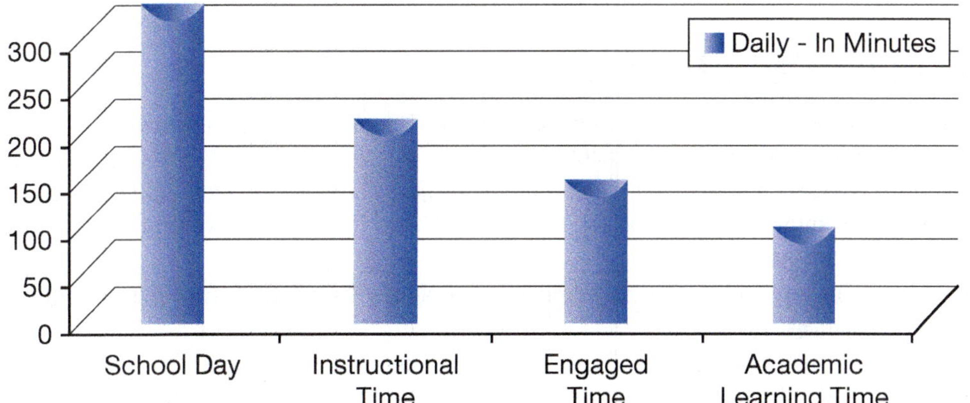

Figure 13.2 Proportion of School Day Spent in Academic Learning Time

On average, students spent five hours in school a day (three hundred minutes). Included in this day are lunch periods, transitions, finding seats in the classroom, announcements, etc. Factoring out these activities, students are left with 165 minutes of active instruction during the school day. As mentioned above, participation in an activity does not mean the student is truly engaged and successful in their learning attempts. The study shows that, on average, the actual amount of *academic learning time* was less than one hour per school day. Similar findings have been found in more recent research (Weinstein & Mignano, 2003).

These numbers clearly indicate there are challenges in arranging the school day to produce academic learning time. Some schools have considered addressing these challenges by simply increasing the length of the school year, but this comes at a significant cost. Some estimate that adding even a single day to the school year would cost states between $2.3 and $121.4 million (Copple, Yane, Levin, & Cohen, 1992). Annual cost to the nation would be over a billion dollars. Such a dramatic cost increase is extremely prohibitive and leads states to explore other techniques for increasing productive learning time. In 2001, WestEd publishing released a policy brief addressing this issue. Their conclusions are presented in Table 13.4.

One of the most important points of the policy brief is that simply adding more time to the school year may not translate into an increase in academic learning time (Karweit, 1985), particularly in schools not already maximizing this time. Schools need to be thoughtful and reflective about how their particular school spends the academic day. Too many schools struggle to meet even basic level learning needs. For these schools, it may be more productive to spend more time on staff development. Helping teachers learn how to create and maintain environments where students can readily access learning materials and invest in the learning task is a primary focus. Schools need to help teachers develop these skills in order to give students needed learning tools.

Table 13.4 Items to Consider When Designing Policies Related to Time and Learning

The key to increasing achievement is not necessarily more time in school but maximizing the amount of academic learning time.
Where there is already a high proportion of academic learning time, extending the school day or year is likely to increase achievement.
Where time is not well used, more allocated time may not, by itself, lead to substantial achievement gains.
A critical factor in increasing quality time in schools is helping teachers and school leaders improve their capabilities. Teachers need professional development that deepens their content knowledge and broadens instructional skills, including ways to tailor instruction to differing student needs. School leaders need support to become strategic thinkers who can organize staff and schedules to focus squarely on instruction and learning.

SUMMARIZE AND REFLECT

1. This first part of this section reviewed classroom management. Classroom management was defined and discussed in terms of creating a positive learning environment.
2. Several general approaches to classroom management were reviewed, including behavioristic, counseling, teacher effectiveness, and comprehensive knowledge. This was followed by information on specific skills teachers need to develop to create an effective management style.
3. Classroom management styles include authoritarian, permissive, and authoritative. Each style has a unique impact on a teacher's ability to manage a class.
4. A final topic reviewed is managing instructional time. Research shows that only a small portion of the school day is spent in meaningful learning activities. Discussion centered on understanding the reasons for this and how to maximize the time students spend learning.

INFORMED APPLICATION

1. Review the section on classroom management styles. What approach seems most consistent with your own personal style? Develop a list of specific experiences supporting your selection.
2. Describe five different things you could do as a teacher to increase the amount of time students spend in meaningful learning activities.

TEACHERS CREATING POSITIVE LEARNING ENVIRONMENTS

The idea of learning often appears deceptively simple; Pass on the knowledge of past generations and give students the tools to ask new questions. The reality of learning, however, is extremely complex. This is especially true when the process is administered across a society as complex and varied as that of the United States. The preceding section introduced us to issues facing teachers and students as they begin the task of creating an environment where achievement is both desired and possible. In this section, we continue this journey by focusing more specifically on the teacher's role in this process.

Encouraging Engagement

School attendance is mandatory, but attendance does not equal academic engagement. Some students view school as boring and irrelevant. They also may see it as a grade game, where you attempt to achieve the highest grade with the least amount of work (Burkett, 2002; Pope, 2002). Teachers attempt to address these issues by increasing academic engagement. Research on the topic of academic engagement indicates there are several sides to the issue (Fredricks, Blumenfeld, & Paris, 2004). In part, engagement is about specific *behaviors*. For example, both appropriate student conduct and being on-task address the idea of engagement from a behavioral perspective (Karweit, 1989). Academic engagement also refers to *emotional* factors, such as attitude toward the teacher and school, general student interest, and values (Eccles et al., 1983). These factors influence whether students want to actively participate in the academic process. An additional point to consider is the effect of student *cognitions,* or thinking, on engagement. Research shows that cognitive factors such as motivation and self-regulation are both important considerations in how students engage in learning (Boekarts, Pintrich, & Zeidner, 2000; Zimmerman, 1990). Looking across these qualities, **engagement** is realistically viewed as a higher-order construct or idea made up of many behavioral, emotional, and cognitive factors (Harris, 2011).

Engagement

A higher-order construct or idea of being involved in the learning activity made up of many behavioral, emotional and cognitive factors

There is considerable evidence that there are a variety of behavioral factors associated with greater student engagement. For example, Alexander, Entwisle, and Horsey (1997) found that student ratings of behavioral engagement made by their teacher positively correlated to higher test scores and classroom grades. Similarly, these ratings were negatively related to high school dropout rates. In other words, *lower* scores on behavioral engagement in earlier grades were associated with an *increase* in high school dropout rate. A limited body of research shows a relation between emotional factors related to engagement and academic outcomes (Skinner, Wellborn, & Connell, 1990). Often studies include emotional measures of engagement, but combine these with other factors making it difficult to isolate the precise relation between emotional engagement and achievement. Cognitive studies show a positive relation between student thinking about engagement and achievement. Studies show that when students are given choices (Morgan, 2006) and are actively engaged through appropriate questioning (Caram & Davis, 2005), achievement improves. In fact, how teachers ask questions can determine the nature of student engagement and target the enhancement of specific aspects of engagement (Munk, 2001; Marzano, 2004; Walsh & Sattes, 2011). Examples of different questioning strategies are presented in Table 13.5.

Teachers also encourage engagement by providing interpersonal or academic support. Research shows that both types of support produce higher levels of engagement (Wenztel, 1997). Research studies show that providing a caring, supportive academic environment increases behavioral aspects of engagement, such as on-task behavior (Battistich, Solomon, Watson, &

Table 13.5 Academic Engagement through Specific Questioning

Category	Question	Key Words
KNOWLEDGE	Define the word _____. What is a _____? Label the following _____.	Define, repeat, identify, what label, when, list, who, name
ORGANIZING	Compare the _____ before and after _____. Contrast the _____ to the _____. Differentiate between _____ and _____.	Compare, differentiate, contrast, order, classify, distinguish, relate
APPLYING	How is _____ an example of _____? Why is _____ significant? Predict what would happen if _____. Explain.	Apply, demonstrate, calculate, complete, illustrate, show, solve, examine, modify, relate change, classify, experiment, discover
ANALYZING	What is the function of _____? Categorize the _____ of _____. Sort the _____.	Subdivide, categorize, break down, sort, separate
GENERATING	Hypothesize what will happen if _____. Predict what would be true if _____. Conclude what the result will be if _____.	Deduce, anticipate, predict, what if, infer, apply, speculate, conclude
INTEGRATING	What ideas can you add to _____? How would you create a new _____? What might happen if you combined _____?	Combine, integrate, modify, create, design, invent, compose, theorize, develop, originate, synthesize, project
EVALUATING	What would you do if _____ happened? Why? Judge what would be the best way to solve the problem of _____. Why did you select that solution?	Evaluate, argue, judge, recommend, assess, debate, appraise, critique, defend

Adapted from Caram and Davis, 2005.

Schaps, 1997) and lower disruptive behavior (Ryan & Patrick, 2001) as well as cognitive aspects of engagement, such as when teachers stress understanding (Blumenfeld, Puro, & Mergendoller, 1992). What this means is that teachers command considerable influence over the degree to which students engage in learning. Through careful questioning and appropriate interpersonal and academic support, students are more likely to truly engage in learning and strive for academic success.

Positive Behavioral Supports

Positive behavioral supports (PBS)

Activity or technique designed to help students develop appropriate and adaptive behaviors and to overcome existing behavioral challenges

Another teacher-centered approach emphasizing the creation of a positive learning environment is **positive behavioral supports, or PBS** (Sanetti & Simonsen, 2011). PBS evolved out of the behavioral approaches discussed in Chapter 4. PBS is designed to help students develop appropriate and adaptive behaviors and to overcome existing behavioral challenges (Koegel, Koegel, & Donlap, 1996). For example, teachers using PBS would address aggressive student behavior by carefully removing any environmental supports for the aggression (e.g., need for attention), while simultaneously teaching the student more adaptive behaviors like conflict resolution and appropriate social mediation of typical classroom activities. Educational professionals need to keep in mind that PBS not only identifies and addresses problematic behaviors but also gives student new appropriate behaviors to help improve their classroom experience (O'Neill et al., 1997). The idea behind PBS is that by making appropriate changes to the student's educational environment, teachers render problematic behaviors ineffective, encouraging the student to rely on prosocial behaviors (Horner, O'Neill, & Flannery, 1993). To be effective, teachers need to examine carefully their own value system and the value system of the school and community. Positive behavioral supports are implemented within the context of a particular academic value system, acknowledging the available resources. Some schools may place greater value on cooperative environments, whereas others may stress individual achievement. Given these values, different behaviors are likely to be encouraged. This influences what behaviors are potential targets for additional support. For example, a teacher is dealing with a student who is constantly telling jokes during class and trying to play the class clown. His actions are disruptive to the classroom and at odds with the positive environment you are trying to create. You take steps to remove any reinforcement the student is receiving from the other students in class. Additionally, you create a system of reward that is available to the student only when he is non-disruptive for a period of time. What this does is remove the reinforcing nature of the disruptive behavior, making it ineffective. Simultaneously, the student is provided opportunities to engage in appropriate classroom behaviors. He is given explicit instruction in how to obtain rewards for these behaviors so that these prosocial behaviors become more functional for the student. That is, they become the natural tools he uses to meet his ongoing need for attention in class. Table 13.6 details the components of effective positive behavioral support systems.

Coverage of behavioral theory is in Chapter 4.

GET THE FACTS

3 Students

The number of prekindergarten children in a classroom likely to display disruptive behavior

Gordon, Henry, Mashburn, and Ponder (2001)

Determining what alterations to the classroom environment are likely to make problematic behaviors ineffective and inefficient for a student is difficult. Consistent with the information presented in Table 13.6, schools are moving toward greater reliance on a functional assessment to help make these decisions. **Functional assessments** are a comprehensive set of assessment procedures used to determine the function problematic behaviors serve in the life of the student (Matson et al., 2011). Functional assessments are also used to determine how to replace ineffective behaviors with behaviors serving a positive and prosocial function in the student's life (Chandler & Dahlquist, 2006; Pindiprolu, Lignugaris/Kraft, Rule, Peterson, & Slocum, 2005).

Functional assessment

Comprehensive set of assessment procedures used to determine the function that problematic behaviors serve in the life of the student

Positive behavioral supports exist on a continuum of services (Menzies & Lane, 2011). Most interventions are targeted in a universal way to the school as a whole. School-wide interventions are put in place to help the majority of typically developing students operate to the best of their ability (Peshak-George, Harrower, & Knoster, 2003). Such interventions are targeted

Table 13.6 Effective Positive Behavioral Support Systems

Effective PBS systems are
... consistent with fundamental principles of behaviorism;
... a good conceptual "fit" with the values, resources, and skills of all the people in the setting;
... part of an ongoing evaluation to determine the effectiveness of the intervention; and
... based on the results of a functional assessment.

Adapted from O'Neill et al., 1997.

to all students in all settings. A second level of intervention is targeted to a much smaller group of at-risk students. These interventions are more sensitive to the unique issues experienced by students. The most specific level of intervention, however, is intense, individual interventions. At this level, each intervention is tailored to a specific student. It is assessment based and designed to produce durable, long-lasting solutions to a specific student problem. Only about 1 to 5% of the student body receives this level of intervention (see Figure 13.3).

Prevention

A significant factor in the positive behavioral support system described above is that of prevention. Students are provided specific interventions designed to help the student engage in positive behaviors and thereby prevent future problems. What else can educators do to help prevent student problems? Research on behavior problems indicates that influencing students toward positive behaviors is far better than correcting behaviors after they occur (Dodge, 1993; Kaiser & Hester, 1997; Webster-Stratton, 1998). Researchers typically define successful interventions as the degree to which teacher, parents, and peers interact in positive ways with the students (Horner, Albin, Sprague, & Todd, 2000). Furthermore, interventions are enhanced to the extent they maintain consistency, stability and predictability over time. The complex interaction between these factors is represented graphically in Figure 13.4 (Hester, 2002). As you can see, specific outcomes are the product of the student's interaction with their teacher, parents, and peers. Additionally, students respond favorably to environments that are stable, consistent, and predictable. Hester (2002) suggests the proactive strategies detailed in Table 13.7 help create positive interconnections between teachers, parents, peers and the student.

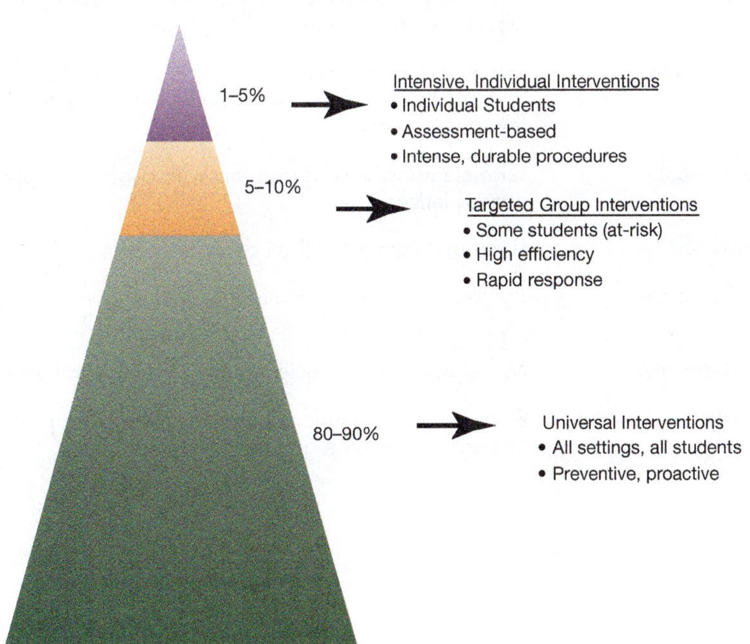

Figure 13.3
Levels of Academic Interventions

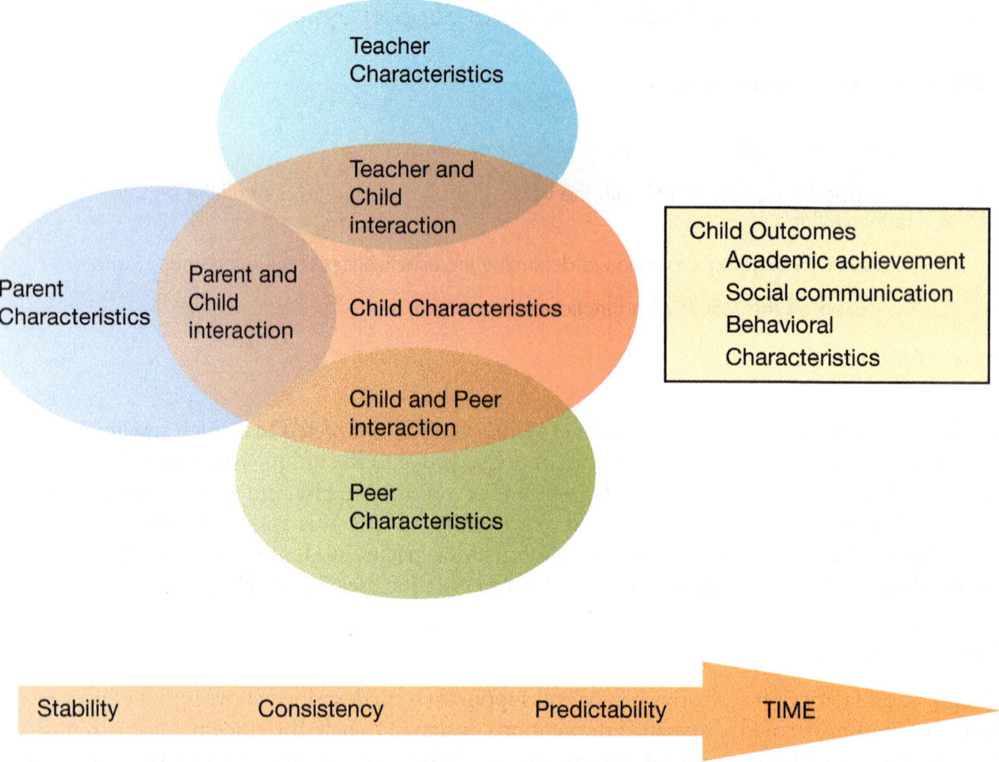

Figure 13.4
The Complex Interaction Between Factors Involved in Prevention

Most of these strategies help students develop the necessary skills to meet the rigorous academic demands of school. Research shows that students are more likely to act out if they do not have the necessary academic survival skills (De Pry & Sugai, 2002). This underscores the importance of making certain students have the necessary knowledge and skills to complete their work and interact with others.

Table 13.7 Proactive Strategies for Supporting and Maintaining Positive Child Behavior and Enhancing Home and School Connections

Acknowledge high rates of appropriate behavior in all school settings.	Define expectations for appropriate behavior in the classroom and throughout the school.
Increase predictability in daily routines (e.g., defined schedules, preparation for transitions, etc.).	Teach students appropriate replacement skills for misbehaviors, so they have positive behaviors that serve the same function.
Affirm student strengths, skills, and abilities—both academic and non-academic.	Give clear instructions and follow through with appropriate consequences.
Support the student's social communication ability.	Listen and connect with students.
Respond positively when a student makes attempts to communicate appropriately.	Respond in positive, emotionally nurturing ways.
Teach positive social communication skills directly.	Model appropriate social communication strategies.
Build on what the child already knows, bridging to what you want them to learn.	Be consistent in implementing behavioral support strategies over time and in all settings.

Adapted from Hester, 2002.

Rules and Procedures

An important part of any classroom environment is the rules and procedures governing the school day. When used appropriately, class rules and procedures help students engage in a supportive environment, transition efficiently, and interact more effectively. It is important for teachers to facilitate a sense of organization and productivity in the classroom. Developing such an environment necessitates that teachers work collaboratively with students to negotiate and embrace a set of standards for behavior and a core set of principles to guide activities. Working together, students and teachers can develop an environment where students successfully meet their personal and academic needs.

Rules

Rules
A set of behavioral standards

Rules refer to a set of behavioral standards. Some researchers have viewed the term critically because it implies a sense of compliance and control (Jones & Jones, 2007). To address this concern, it has been suggested teachers focus on establishing a set of standards for student behavior, rather than a set of behavioral prohibitions. This frames behavior management in a positive way, emphasizing behaviors that help students achieve. This trend, however, is still growing, and many books and teachers conceptualize behavioral goals as a set of *rules*. For purposes of our discussion here, the term *rules* will be used interchangeably with behavioral standard or norm.

Having a set of rules or behavioral standards is important for classroom management, but developing those rules is often difficult (Babkie, 2006). Many teachers start off the school year with a predetermined set of rules or expectations for behavior. The students are not involved in rule development and are simply expected to follow the rules. Students follow rules better, and with greater engagement, when they take part in rule development and understand the reason for the rule (Gathercoal, 2001). One approach to engaging students in the development of rules is to help them understand their rights as students. Students who have a firm understanding of their own rights better understand rules designed to protect those rights. It also helps students to discuss how their personal rights impact the rights of other students. Gathercoal (2001) discusses four areas where the rights of the individual should not violate the rights of others. He indicates that this is necessary to ensure the "compelling state interests." This means that the school (or state) has compelling interests that must not be violated by the interests of the individual. Indeed, if each student had absolute personal rights, then schools would be in constant conflict. The educational process has to be viewed as an overriding compelling interest in order for education to continue. The *first* area of compelling interest is in the health and safety of the school population. Students do not have a right to negatively affect the health and safety of other students. Accordingly, students should not engage in behaviors that harm another physically or psychologically. *Second,* students do not have the right to damage the property of others. This means that students must refrain from activities that cause loss or damage to the property of others. *Third,* students should not behave in such a way that it challenges the school's right to require legitimate educational activities. This includes such things as taking attendance, book selection, assessment protocols, etc. *Fourth,* students do not have the right to seriously disrupt the educational process. This means that students must balance their own rights to express themselves or disagree with instructional objectives with the right of teachers and schools to educate the students. What is important about helping students appreciate these four rights of the majority is that they serve as the conceptual starting place for establishing rules or behavioral norms. Once students understand how their own rights balance with the rights of others, rules naturally follow as the tool for ensuring behavior that supports a positive learning environment. Additionally, students feel a sense of ownership over class rules, increasing personal responsibility and awareness. Teachers also benefit from this approach since they experience a shared sense of rule governance and are less likely to take violations personally. Table 13.8 list school rules based on these ideas.

Just as important as the process for adopting a set of rules is the process of getting students to commit to the observation of the rules. Many students have difficulty following rules, but

Table 13.8 School Rules or Behavior Standards Based on Gathercoal's "Compelling State Interests"

Act in a safe and healthy way This may include wearing protective gear during athletics, appropriate movement through the halls and in the classroom, requiring vaccinations, etc.
Treat all property with respect This includes school desks, lockers, classrooms, gymnasium, etc.
Respect the rights and needs of others This includes respecting the right of the teacher or school to determine the most appropriate method for teaching a subject or activity. It also includes the right of the majority to an appropriate educational environment necessitating a dress code, standards for language use, and behavior.
Take responsibility for learning This includes personal responsibility for participation in classroom activities, having appropriate materials ready, and being on time for class.

Adapted from Grandmont, 2003.

teachers can help students embrace a particular standard of behavior. After rules are developed, the teacher should engage the class in a discussion regarding their ability to comply with each rule. It is important that the teacher clarify that many students will not achieve perfect success with rule compliance. Learning to behave in a manner consistent with school rules is a process. Students are not expected to be completely successful from the first day of school. What is important, however, is that they understand the need for the rules and agree to do their best to follow the rules. Teachers can frame the task of following rules like any other learning objective. Just like learning to read is a gradual process of trial and error, so is regulating your own behavior. If a student feels that he/she cannot meet a given rule, be sure to first clarify the reason for the rule, making sure the student fully understands the need for the rule. Next, assure the student that your expectation is not that students will never break a rule, but that they work hard to improve their behavior. This helps the students reduce their focus on what behaviors to avoid and gives them the freedom to focus on what they are actually supposed to do.

A part of helping a student commit to a set of rules necessarily involves an appreciation of the consequences for not meeting the rules (Roache, 2011). Like the process involved in developing the rule, students should be an integral part of establishing the consequences for behavior. Additionally, teachers need to work toward maintaining a sense of student responsibility for behavior. Applying punishments tends to pull responsibility for the behavior away from the student and places management in the hands of the teacher. Another approach is to preserve student responsibility for behavior. Table 13.9 describes six basic principles that help foster student responsibility for misbehavior (Marshall, 1998).

A good way to begin a discussion regarding misbehavior and consequences is to *check for understanding*. This step helps students appreciate what they did and how their behavior violates the behavioral norms of the class. Without an understanding of how their behavior did not meet with expectations, they cannot actively participate in deciding how to improve

Table 13.9 Fundamental Principles to Help Foster Student Responsibility for Behavior

Positive responses are better than negative responses.
Providing choices empowers students.
Self-evaluation is essential for improvement.
Self-correction leads to more successful behavior changes.
Social Responsibility must be taken, rather than given. Taking responsibility requires intrinsic motivation (See Chapter 7).
Authority can be exercised without punishment.

Adapted from Marshall, 1998.

their behavior. This also encourages the student to acknowledge their actions and to take responsibility for providing solutions. Once the student understands the situation, the next step is to determine appropriate consequences. *A guided choice* refers to a process where the teacher provides a student with choices regarding a consequence for his/her action (Marshall, 2005, 1998). Providing choices preserves the student's dignity and active participation in modifying their behavior. It also reduces conflict between the student and the teacher because the teacher is not enforcing a specific action. The choice is up to the student. Students are not likely to argue with their own decision, which helps move them away from blaming the teacher for their situation. It encourages the students to maintain control and responsibility for their behavior. This approach is helpful because it does not place the teacher in an adversarial position. The approach encourages students to view the teacher as an ally, fostering their personal growth.

Procedures are guidelines for helping students properly participate in various classroom activities.

Procedures

Classroom procedures are different from rules. **Procedures** are guidelines for classroom activities. They do not provide the student with a behavioral standard like rules but give the student information regarding how to appropriately participate in various classroom activities. Teachers typically use three broad classes of procedures: academic, routine, and special (Cantor, 1992; Johnson, Rice, Edgington, 2005). *Academic procedures* are those related to academic tasks such as the assessment process and group participation. Teachers need to develop procedures for implementation and assessment of lessons. A different set of procedures may be needed for formal versus informal assessments (see Chapter 15). Teachers will also need procedures to guide class participation and how to get the attention of the teacher. *Routine procedures* include activities such as governing transitions, using the bathroom, leaving the class for special events, and turning in homework. Such procedures may seem less important when compared to academic procedures, but they are vital for establishing a positive and effective educational environment. Students often experience behavioral difficulties during these less structured times. The final category of rules is *special procedures.* This refers to a broad range of procedures including fire drills, pep rallies, and special cultural events.

Interconnections

Assessment practices are covered in Chapter 15.

Procedures

Guidelines for classroom activities

Naturally, teachers will have a certain set of procedures required to make academic work productive and efficient. They can, however, consult with students about many procedural elements. For example, the teacher may need students to work collaboratively in a group setting to investigate the effects of light on plant photosynthesis. There are many procedures for assigning students to groups, and the teacher may enlist the students to determine the appropriate procedure. As with rules, providing students with choices helps them invest in the process.

Learning Spaces

The rules and procedures you have been learning about take place in a physical space. Often this is a traditional classroom, but educational space also includes the school gym, auditorium, computer lab, and library. Each of these spaces is unique and can be arranged in different ways to meet specific educational goals. This section will focus on the typical classroom and look at various ways teachers can manipulate the physical space so that it meets their needs (Brooks, 2011).

Arrangement Style

Classroom arrangement can help students interact more effectively and engage in the instructional activity (Stewart & Evans, 1997). Teachers at any stage of their career need to think carefully about what they want to accomplish and what seating arrangement will best meet that objective. There are some general principles of classroom arrangement, however, that teachers should consider regarding their classroom (Evertson, Emmer, Worsham, 2006). First, be certain to keep high traffic areas free of congestion (Bettenhausen, 1998). These areas typically include the bookshelves where classroom materials are kept, the water fountain, the pencil sharpener, the computer, and the teacher's desk. Their frequent use may lead to increases in disruptions if students have difficulty accessing the space. Second, make sure that the teacher can easily monitor each student (Shores, Gunter, & Jack, 1993). Successful classrooms are characterized by frequent monitoring by the teacher. Walk around the room, and make sure you can see each desk. Also, remember that students may not always be at their desks. Be careful of arranging bookcases and shelves that may conceal special learning areas in your classroom. Third, keep frequently used materials within easy reach. Students are more likely to misbehave while you are distracted looking for teaching materials. It will also make it difficult for students to stay focused if there are frequent breaks in the lesson. Finally, make sure each student can easily see the teacher and presentation materials (Stewart & Evans, 1997). Often it is difficult to determine if each student has an unobstructed view of the teacher. You can sit in the students' desks to get an idea, but ultimately you will need to check with the students once they are in their seats. You will also need to make similar checks for activities that require students to be out of their seat. Following these basic rules will help you avoid some of the common problems teachers encounter.

All of these factors depend on the specific nature of the classroom design. Teachers have many options for designing their learning space. Figure 13.5 details several of these approaches, but teachers should feel free to create their own unique design that meets their personal teaching style (Rinne, 1997). In general, teachers need to decide whether the focus is going to be on the teacher, the student, or a balance of both. The auditorium style and the seminar style place the teacher at the center of the instructional space. This is useful for lectures and discussions that are more teacher-centered. The face-to-face, offset, and cluster style are more student-centered. The students are oriented toward each other, allowing for richer interactions among students (MacAulay, 1990). Teachers using these settings typically find themselves circulating around the room acting more as a group facilitator.

An additional factor to consider is how your classroom is used during the course of the day. Many teachers share classrooms or rotate through several different classrooms. This will necessitate that teachers develop a close working relationship with their fellow teachers. Teachers may need different classroom arrangements for a given period of time, or they may need to make adjustments for specific class periods. Teachers sharing a classroom should meet well before the school year begins to negotiate a classroom arrangement that is flexible and accommodating. Each teacher may need to adjust their expectations in favor of arrangements that can be made quickly so that they do not lose valuable instructional time. They also need to be considerate of their fellow teachers and return desks or other classroom items to an agreed upon standard format (for an example of classroom sharing, see the Interdisciplinary Case Study at the end of this chapter).

The use of a projector allows the entire class to participate in the lesson.

Computer Use

Computers enrich education in many ways. Teachers use computers to access the enormous wealth of information on the Internet. They also use computers to record grades, track attendance, put homework assignments on the Internet, and communicate with colleagues and parents. Computers are also changing the way we educate in the classroom (Jung & Latchem, 2011). Teachers are using computers to bring students into online zoos, museums, and special exhibits (Wilson, Jones, & Hail, 2003a). Classes are taking virtual field trips without ever leaving their classrooms. These are exciting changes and open many doors for students. Classroom application of computer-based information is often enhanced by using a computer attached to a projection system. Computer projection

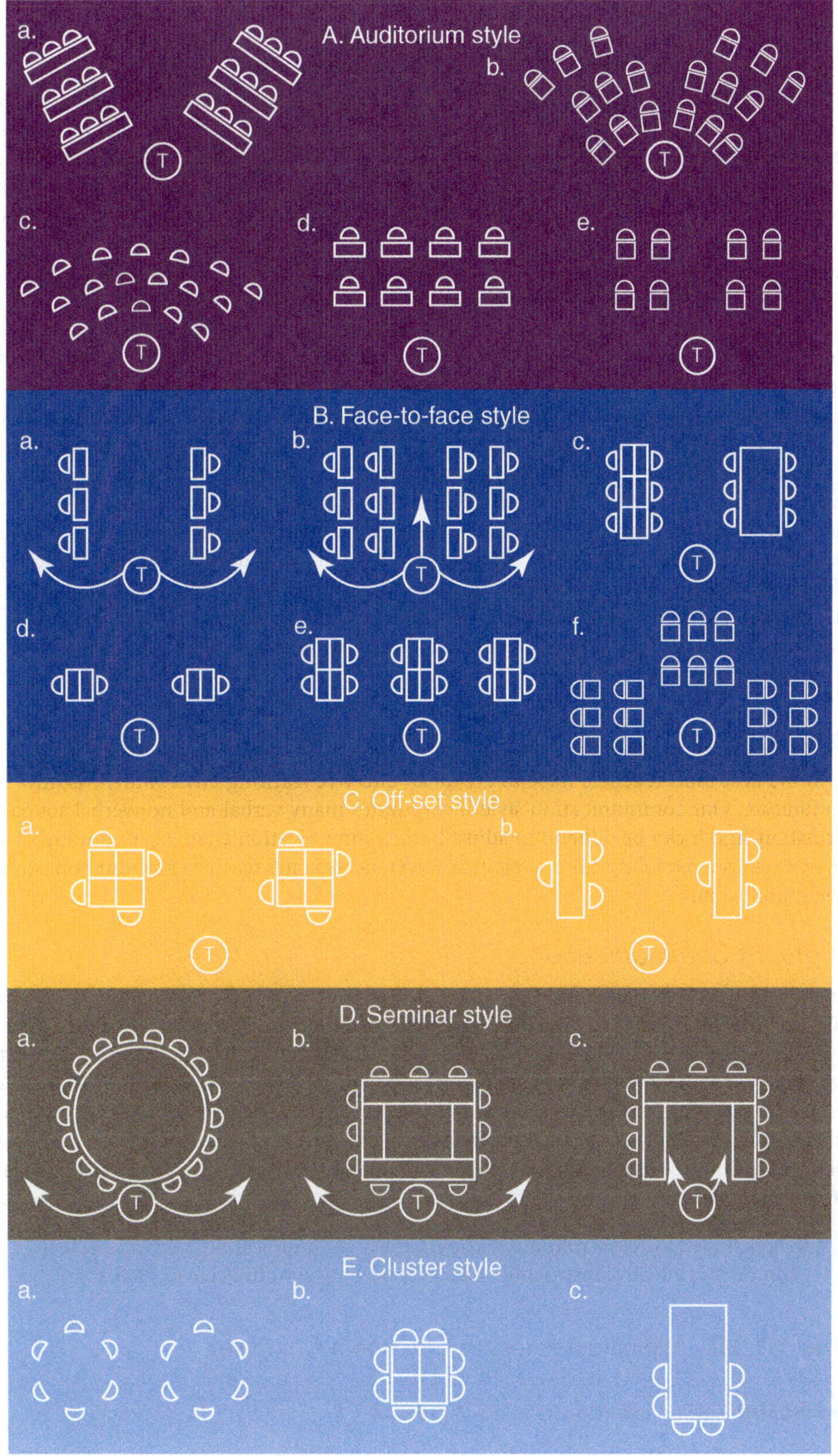

Figure 13.5
Learning Space Design Options

on a large screen enables the whole class to participate in a computer-aided lesson. Some classrooms even have interactive touch display screens so that the teacher or student can access Internet features by simply touching specific areas of the screen. These systems are, however, expensive and beyond the reach of many classrooms.

Learning center

A specific location within a classroom designed to meet a specific educational objective

Computers bring about the possibility to make exciting changes to instruction, but exactly how do teachers use this technology? Using computers effectively is often challenging due to limited financial resources. Most classrooms only have a limited number of computers. Many consider themselves fortunate to have even one. To help students access and use a limited number of computers, teachers can create a computer learning center in the classroom. **Learning center** is defined as a specific location designed to meet a specific educational objective. Many classrooms have reading, math, or play centers, but computer centers are also beginning to find a home in many classrooms. To help you decided how to create a computer learning center, consider the common uses for computers for the classroom presented in Table 13.10 (Wilson, Jones, & Hail, 2003b). The nature of how a computer is used will affect the computer center design. For example, using computers primarily for skill practice will likely have scheduling implications that differ from whole class inquiry questions. Using computers to enhance skills will require frequent use by those students needing the most practice. This varying type of scheduling lends itself to a computer space that is away from the main instructional space. Moving the computer learning center to a less frequently used area will help students concentrate and focus.

Teachers that plan to use the computer for whole group instruction will need to choose a more central location for the computer. For example, the teacher may pose a question to the whole class and then use the Internet to search for information. Such whole group types of inquiry questions help students learn to use the Internet to gather information and develop a critical lens for interpreting results. This may, however, make it difficult for the teacher to let students use the computer for skill development because of competing instructional activities. As you can see, using computers in the classroom can dramatically change the nature of instruction. Appropriate planning, however, is needed if teachers are going to make effective and efficient use of computer resources.

Communication Style

One of the best tools teachers have to create an effective learning environment is how they communicate. Our communication style incorporates many verbal and nonverbal sources of information, and it can be difficult to adjust both communication channels to produce a uniform message. Successful communication, however, necessitates teachers monitor both streams of communication.

Congruent Communication

Congruent communication

An authentic harmony between words and feelings; having what you say be in tune with what you feel

Haim Ginott (1972) initially developed the idea of congruent communication in the early 1970s. **Congruent communication** is an authentic harmony between words and feelings. What you say is in tune with what you feel. He believed teachers could establish a positive or negative classroom environment depending on how effectively they were able to communicate in a congruent fashion. Ginott's theory was intriguing, but it never developed into a practical model for teacher communication. Other researchers have, however, expanded on his theory and made direct applications to instructional practice (Manning & Bucher, 2001; Brown, 2005; Morris, 1996). The following are some practical extensions of Ginott's work:

Teachers should use clear communication. Clearly communicating your expectations is the hallmark of effective instruction. Teachers need to communicate in such a way that

Table 13.10 Typical Uses for the Classroom Computer

Enrichment—giving extended learning or practice
Remediation—providing support with varied learning approaches and increased experiences to struggling learners
Additional Practice—alternative activities to strengthen learning, often using different learning style approaches or multiple intelligences

SOURCE: From Wilson, Jones, and Hail, 2003.

helps student feel they are accepted and valued. Their communication style should encourage ongoing dialogue because it conveys understanding and support.

Messages should address specific actions. A teacher should address specific behaviors, rather than a student's character. Through their tone and sincerity, teachers can communicate regarding a behavioral issue while maintaining dignity and a desire to improve.

Teachers should show acceptance and acknowledgement. Messages perceived as uncritical encourage the student to cooperate. Messages perceived as critical create resistance, making problem solving difficult.

Teachers want to use clear communication when speaking one on one or with the entire class.

Teachers should use "I" messages instead of "you" messages. Ginott believed that teachers who routinely use "you" messages are perceived as being critical of individual character. For example, "You are always interrupting the class. Please be quiet." He believed that "I" messages communicate how the teacher is responding to the student behavior without being critical of personality traits. For example, "I find it difficult to teach the class with interruptions."

Teachers should use appreciative praise and avoid evaluative praise. Praise should emphasize the student's accomplishments and not personal characteristics. For example, if you were to tell a student "You did so well on the test. You are so smart," the student might feel she is no longer as smart if she scores poorly on the next test. It would be better if the teacher praised the student for working so hard. This lets the student know that grades are earned through effort.

Following these suggestions helps create congruence between a teacher's good intentions and the experience of positive emotionality from the student and the teacher. They emphasize responding in an empathetic manner, avoiding communication roadblocks, encouraging active listening, and supporting friendly body language. All of these factors foster a positive approach to education. The next sections will look more closely at how body language (or nonverbal communication) and active listening promote effective communication.

Non-verbal Communication

Non-verbal communication refers to communication without words. It involves tone of voice, eye contact, hand gestures, facial expressions, touching, etc. When combined with spoken words, it allows us to enrich what we communicate to others. Researchers have noted that spoken words have limitations, which we enhance by using a wide variety of nonverbal cues (Miller, 2005). Often, we place considerable emphasis on these cues. They may express our feelings more effectively and give us a way of expressing complex messages. Researchers agree that a large percentage of the messages we communicate come from nonverbal sources; however, they disagree on the percentage. Early evidence found that approximately two-thirds of our communication is nonverbal (Birdwhistell, 1970). Later reports put the percentage as high as 93%, with 55% expressed through facial expressions and 38% through vocal intonation (Merhabian, 1971, 1981; Fromkin & Rodman, 1983). Despite these mixed research findings, it appears that a significant amount of our communication occurs through nonverbal means.

Non-verbal communication

Communication without words that involves tone of voice, eye contact, hand gestures, facial expressions, touching, etc

To be an effective communicator, teachers need to be mindful of what they are communicating non-verbally. In general, try to move around the classroom as you teach. This increases your visibility and the ability of students to benefit from your non-verbal cues. Strive to use your nonverbal language to prevent classroom disruptions. Be aware of times when misbehavior is likely and prepare accordingly by giving students strong cues to guide appropriate behavior. For example, if students are likely to act out during transition times, then five minutes before the transition change the tone of your voice to a lower, more commanding tone. Speak with greater intensity, so you get the students attention and cause them to focus on what you are saying. Now, you are in a better position to give them direction regarding the transition.

In addition to general guidelines that increase the effectiveness of nonverbal cues, teachers should consider specific nonverbal actions (Webb White, 2000). Eye contact is one of the most meaningful tools we have for nonverbal communication. Frequent eye contact communicates that one is listening. It also signifies interest in what the student is saying. It helps the teacher notice subtle signs that a student is nervous, relaxed, attentive, or worried. Students also communicate nonverbally, and looking directly at a student is one of the best ways to become aware of these cues.

Teachers also communicate through their gestures and posture. When teachers are excited about their teaching, they express that excitement by smiling, pointing, leaning forward, and adopting an erect, natural posture. Teachers can also communicate fatigue and disappointment by frowns, placing their hands on their hips, and/or crossing their arms across the chest. At different times, teachers need to use both gesture and posture signals. What is important is that teachers are aware of their nonverbal signals and how this corresponds to their spoken words.

Paralanguage

Characteristics of language involving volume, rate, pitch, and pronunciation of spoken words

A final point to consider regarding nonverbal communication is *how* words are spoken. **Paralanguage** refers to volume, rate, pitch, and pronunciation of spoken words. Like other aspects of nonverbal communication, the way we speak conveys information. We have all had the experience of enjoying a teacher because of their strong, clear, steady speaking voice. These qualities convey confidence and give support to the spoken message. Teachers should try to avoid mumbling or slurring their words. They should also avoid speaking in too soft a voice. These qualities weaken the impact of their message and decrease student engagement.

Listening Skills

Empathetic listening

Where the listener moves beyond sympathy, which strives to console, and tries to connect and genuinely understand the other's perspective

Consider the following situation. Ms. Stone is the physical education teacher of a small elementary school. She is about to sit down with a student who is accused of hitting another student. She prepared for the conversation, and her goal is to help the student understand why hitting is an unacceptable solution to problems. She wants to develop a behavioral contract with the student detailing the consequences for hitting. Overall, this situation seems thoughtful and well planned. The teacher has set aside a special time to meet with the student, rather than make an impulsive decision. She prepared for the conversation and has a reasonable plan for how to address the issue. The problem with her approach is that she has failed to factor in the need to listen first to the student. Truly understanding the situation necessitates listening to the student's perspective on the problem. Without a thorough understanding, intervening is less effective. The teacher should have first tried an approach to listening called **empathetic listening** (Wesley, 2004; Goleman, 2002; LeCompte, 2000). This approach's primary goal is to understand. The listener moves beyond sympathy, which strives to console, and tries to connect and genuinely understand the other's perspective. The teacher is present and actively listening. Table 13.11 compares empathetic listening to other ways people listen to each other.

Table 13.11 Listening Styles

Level 1—Empathetic Listening
Listeners at this level pay attention to the speaker's total communication: the gestures, feelings, underlying thoughts, and motivation. They strive to remain in the moment, acknowledging the speaker with their entire presence. They refrain from interrupting, interjecting suggestions, being distracted, or concentrating on their response.
Level 2—Hearing Words
Listeners at this level stay at the surface of communication. They hear logically and are intent on content more than feelings. Since they remain emotionally detached, they may misconstrue the speaker's intention and be lulled into a false sense of understanding.
Level 3—Listening in Spurts
Here the listener is quiet and passive. They often pretend to listen. They are usually judging, forming rebuttals or advice, or preparing answers. They are more interested in talking than listening.

Adapted from Hagevik, 1999.

It is also important that the listener not judge. This is often problematic for teachers. As the example above indicates, the teacher is responsible for addressing situations where a judgment of some kind is likely to occur. This means the teacher may need to set aside two times to address significant concerns, one meeting that is non-judgmental and involving empathetic listening and a second meeting dealing with consequences. This approach helps the teacher and the student begin the dialogue in a connected way. The student gains an appreciation of the teacher as an ally who works to understand the situation. This lays the groundwork for more productive, and less defensive, negotiations regarding consequences. Empathetic listening is not easy. It is hard for teachers to relinquish control of a conversation and just listen. With practice, however, teachers can learn to actively listen and move towards more positive student/teacher relations.

When listening to a student, the teacher should try to move beyond sympathy and strive to genuinely understand the student's perspective.

SUMMARIZE AND REFLECT

1. How teachers manage their classroom helps shape and guide the learning process. In the first section, several factors influencing that process were reviewed. The importance of truly engaging the student in meaningful learning tasks was discussed. Encouraging engagement is directly affected by the way a teacher presents questions to students. Suggestions were made for how teachers can use questioning to better engage students. Specific behaviors that support or detract student learning were also covered.
2. The positive behavioral support system was presented as an approach to establishing a positive pattern of behavior. Interventions were reviewed at the school, group, and individual levels.
3. Next, rules and procedures were examined. How a teacher establishes rules and procedures for the classroom dramatically affects how students learn. Appropriate ways to involve students in the development of rules and procedures were discussed.
4. Learning is also impacted by the physical classroom space. There are many different ways to arrange a classroom to meet specific needs. The difference between lecture approaches, learning centers, and computer areas were examined.
5. At the end of the section, communication techniques were examined. Teachers need to consider both the words they say and non-verbal sources of information. The extent to which these two factors send the same message is called congruent communication.
6. In addition to verbal and non-verbal communication issues, basic listening skills were reviewed. To teach effectively, teachers need to listen effectively. Basic guidelines for effective listening were presented.

INFORMED APPLICATION

1. Create a sample dialogue between a high school biology teacher and a tenth grade student. The dialogue can be about any topic you choose. Try to use as many techniques from the chapter to engage the student in learning the material.
2. For the dialogue created in the item above, generate a diagram of a possible classroom environment that would effectively support the specific topic you described.

STUDENTS AS MANAGEMENT AGENTS

The responsibility for establishing a positive learning environment rests not only with the teacher, but also with students. They are an important part of classroom management. Developing their skills as management agents is complicated, involving their social skills, ability to resolve conflicts, and ability to develop positive student/teacher relationships.

Social Skill Development

Social skills

Socially acceptable patterns of behaviors that support positive outcomes and avoid aversive situations

In addition to academic development, social skill development is an important part of student life. Learning how to interact effectively with others is an important mediator of successful work. It is also an important foundation for later personal and social adjustment. **Social skills** are defined as socially acceptable patterns of behaviors that support positive outcomes and avoid aversive situations (Mathur & Rutherford, 1996). Table 13.12 provides a list of common social skills important in school settings (Johnson & Johnson, 1998).

Social success is complex, yet important for students to master. Some have argued that knowledge of social skills is just as important as knowledge of subjects like reading, writing, and math (Deshler, Ellis, & Lenz, 1996). Research has shown that well-developed social skills are associated with greater academic success (Wentzel, 1993; Malecki & Elliott, 2002). It is also important to recognize that social skills develop because of the guidance provided by teachers. What teachers expect in terms of social skills is a strong predictor of what social skills develop in students. Research shows that teachers prefer social skills that emphasize self-control and cooperation (Lane, Pierson, & Givner, 2003; Meier, DiPerna, & Oster, 2006). Teachers also indicated a lower value for assertiveness. It is likely that teachers value those skills that allow groups to work effectively with each other (self-control and cooperation) and value less the skills that may be perceived as challenging teacher authority. Self-control and cooperation skills include the following:

1. Follows directions.
2. Attends to instructions.
3. Controls temper with peers.
4. Controls temper with adults.
5. Gets along with people who are different.
6. Responds appropriately when hit.
7. Uses free time in an acceptable way.

These skills clearly foster learning by maximizing compliance and cooperation, while minimizing distractions. (Lane, Givner, & Pierson, 2004)

While many students learn appropriate social skills effortlessly, many students benefit from direct instruction (Bullock & Fitzimmons-Lovett, 1997; Johns, Crowley, & Guetzloe, 2005). Specific instruction strategies should always be adapted to the specific classroom situation, but there are some common ways to approach social skill instruction. First, begin by

Table 13.12 Social Skills in Schools

Cooperation	Smiling
Empathy	Sharing
Communication	Conflict management
When to talk	Asking questions
Trust	Taking turns
Eye contact	Listening
Compromising	How to win and lose
Asking for help	Appropriate touching

Adapted from Johnson and Johnson, 1998.

targeting specific social skills. Next, break social skills down into small steps. Demonstrate the required skill and have the students model the behavior. Role-playing is often helpful at this stage in the process. Practice with the skill should be followed by constructive, clear feedback. Finally, work on helping the students generalize their newly learned skills to a variety of academic settings. Provide students with cues whenever there is an opportunity to demonstrate a new skill (e.g., hallway, cafeteria, auditorium, etc.). For example, if you taught students how to speak one at a time during class, cue them to wait their turn to speak to friends when waiting in the lunch line. With appropriate instruction and support, students can learn to effectively use social skills, which in turn help them participate more effectively in the educational process.

With the appropriate instruction students learn to effectively use their social skills, which can help them participate more fully in their educational process.

Conflict Resolution and Peer Mediation

The amount of violence in our schools is undergoing ever-increasing scrutiny by parents, administrators, and the media. Accordingly, schools adopt a variety of anti-violence programs to manage increasing hostilities. Once viewed as a hidden curriculum, conflict negotiation is now viewed as basic life skills by today's teachers (Girard & Koch, 1996; Johns & Keenan, 1997). Approaches to instruction vary, but most use conflict resolution skills and peer mediation (Gilhooley & Scheuch, 2000; Daunic, Smith, Robinson, Miller & Landry, 2000). **Conflict resolution** training involves instruction in how to manage interpersonal conflict productively. These programs focus on active listening skills, role-playing to help students take the perspective of others, social conscience, and negotiation strategies (Campbell, 2003). Table 13.13 provides a more detailed list of traits typical of conflict resolution training. **Peer mediation** is similar, but focuses on training a student to act as a facilitator in solving the conflict of other students (Bullock & Foegen, 2002; Nelson, Martella, & Marchand-Martella, 2002).

Training in these skills helps students take an integrative approach to conflicts. **Integrative negotiations** focus on reaching a mutually beneficial resolution to conflicts. It is contrasted with **distributive negotiations**, which focus on winning or benefiting at the expense of another. Students naturally tend toward distributive negotiations; however, with training, they exhibit well-developed integrative negotiations (Dudley, Johnson, & Johnson, 1996). Teachers are in an ideal position to help students develop conflict resolution skills. Their close, ongoing contact with students positions them to reframe interpersonal conflict as a normal part of everyday life. Conflicts are a part of living in a social world, which necessitates well-developed resolution skills. Such skills, however, cannot be learned by mere exposure. Students need to actively engage in learning to mediate conflicts effectively.

Conflict resolution

Instruction in how to manage interpersonal conflict productively and positively

Peer mediation

Technique of using a trained student to act as a facilitator in the conflict of other students

Integrative negotiation

Technique of reaching a mutually beneficial resolution to conflict

Distributive negotiations

Technique that focuses on winning or benefiting at the expense of another.

Student-Teacher Relationship

The relationships teachers establish with their students is a vital tool in the creation of a positive learning environment. Research demonstrates that a positive student-teacher relationship is one of the best predictors of student success (Osterman, 2000). In fact, a recent meta-analysis of over one hundred studies supported the conclusion that the student-teacher relationship is the cornerstone of all other aspects of classroom management (Marzano, 2003). When students have a well-developed relationship with their teacher they are more likely to take academic risks and engage in the learning community (Stipek, 2006). Greater engagement translates into enhanced learning and higher achievement (Pianta, 1999). Effective relationships are characterized by a meaningful dynamic that provides genuine support for academic success. Teachers who establish strong relationships with their students recognize the need to maintain high expectations while ensuring students have the tools to meet those expectations.

Table 13.13 Conflict Resolution

A. Bring the two parties who have the conflict together. **B. Have the parties sit facing each other with the mediator at the head of the table.** **C. The mediator opens the session, introducing him or herself. The mediator then provides the ground rules:** 1. The mediator is neutral and does not take sides. 2. The session is confidential; no one in the room discusses the proceedings with anyone. 3. Each party is to respect the other party by listening and by not interrupting when the other is speaking. 4. It is important for both parties to cooperate in order to resolve the dispute. The mediator should obtain a commitment from the parties to follow the ground rules.	**D. The mediator then begins the process of gathering information.** 1. Each disputant is asked to tell his or her side of the story. "Will you each tell me what happened?" 2. The mediator listens, summarizes, clarifies, repeats statements, rephrases to check accuracy, and sums up the statements of the disputants. 3. The mediator then repeats the process, asking for additional information. "Is there anything you want to add?" 4. The mediator then again restates both sides of the situation. 5. The mediator next focuses on common interests, asking clarifying questions: What do you want? If you were in the other person's shoes, how would you feel? If you could ask the other person to do one thing, what would it be? 6. After gaining insight into the students' interests, state what the interests are. 7. The mediator then asks the disputants to come up with possible solutions that might satisfy both parties. 8. The mediator then asks the disputants to evaluate options and choose solutions. 9. The mediator finally writes the agreement and closes by asking each participant to sign it.

SOURCE: From Johns, Crowley, and Guetzloe.

Establishing effective relationships with students means focusing on developing three important qualities (Marzano & Marzano, 2003). First, the most effective student/teacher relationships are characterized by *appropriate levels of authority.* Authority means that the teacher provides strong support and guidance within the context of a clear purpose (Wubbels, Brekelmans, van Tartwijk, & Admiral, 1999). This is typically accomplished by providing clear learning goals. Students respond favorably when clear learning goals are provided at the beginning of a learning unit. This provides a road map by which students navigate their knowledge construction. Teachers can further support student learning by frequently reviewing learning goals and providing feedback about their progress. Additionally, teachers show appropriate levels of authority by exhibiting assertive behavior. Assertive behavior is characterized by standing up for your legitimate rights (Emmer, 2006). It is qualitatively different from aggressive behavior. Without using hostility, assertive teachers communicate clear intent through their posture, tone of voice, and persistence when pursuing a response. This encourages student participation and engagement, which in turn facilitates learning.

Authority means that the teacher provides strong support and guidance with a clear purpose.

A second important component to establishing a positive student/teacher relationship is *cooperation.* Cooperation necessitates that the student and teacher work as a team. Combined with appropriate levels of authority, cooperation further helps students bond with their teacher and peers. Teachers can encourage cooperation by providing flexible learning goals. Giving students input and some discretion over their learning path helps them feel like an integral part of the learning environment. Effective teachers also make every effort to show personal interest in each student.

A final point to consider when forging a strong student/teacher relationship is an *awareness of high-need students.* Establishing positive relationships with students who have unique learning needs can be difficult. Unique learning needs may translate into increasing demands on an

Table 13.14 Types of High-Needs Students

Category	Definition and Source	Characteristics	Suggestions
Passive	Behavior that avoids the domination of others or the pain of negative experiences	Fear of relationships and fear of failure	Provide safe adult and peer interactions and protection from aggressive people and withhold criticism.
Aggressive	Behavior that overpowers, dominates, harms, or controls others without regard for their well-being	Hostile Oppositional Acting in ways that are incongruent with what is said	Contract with the student to reward appropriate behavior. Be consistent. Encourage extracurricular activities. Give student classroom responsibilities.
Attention Problems	Behavior that demonstrates either motor or attentional difficulties resulting from a neurological disorder	Hyperactive Inattentive Impulsive	Teach basic concentration skills, study skills, and thinking skills. Help student list each step in a larger process.
Perfectionist	Behavior that is geared toward avoiding the embarrassment and assumed shame of making mistakes	Focus on small details Focus on results and not relationships	Ask the student to make mistakes on purpose, and then show acceptance. Have the student tutor other students.
Social Problems	Behavior that is based on the misinterpretation of nonverbal signals of others	Attempts to make friends, but is unsuccessful and is often alone, (not by choice)	Teach students to keep appropriate distance from other students. Help to interpret facial expressions. Make suggestions regarding hygiene, dress, mannerisms, and posture.

Adapted from Marzano and Marzano, 2003.

already overworked teacher. Each student, however, is entitled to an educational approach that provides optimal learning. This means teachers will need to develop a plan for how to teach each student, while maintaining a positive interpersonal relationship. Students likely to need unique planning are passive students, aggressive students, perfectionists, students with social skill deficits, and those with attention problems (Marzano & Marzano, 2003). Table 13.14 provides a description of these students and suggestions for how to address their unique learning needs.

The overriding principle when trying to create a strong student/teacher relationship is not to leave it to chance. Teachers need to be proactive and plan carefully.

SUMMARIZE AND REFLECT

1. The first part of this section examined the role of social skills in classroom management. Common social skills expected of students and detailed steps teachers can use to promote healthy interactions were discussed.
2. Conflict resolution skills are vital to the successful functioning of the classroom. Teachers can learn to help students mediate conflicts and produce positive learning outcomes.
3. The final part of the chapter reviewed how students relate to their teachers. This relationship is particularly important, as it is an excellent predictor of later success. Important elements of student/teacher relationships were examined and suggestions for dealing with difficult students provided.

INFORMED APPLICATION

1. Describe how directly teaching social skills to young children might differ from teaching to high school students. What accommodations need to be made for each group?

EFFECTIVE LEARNING ENVIRONMENTS THROUGH COLLABORATION

This section covers management issues related to collaboration. Consistent with the theme of this book, effective collaboration is an integral part of classroom management. Teachers have countless opportunities to work with fellow teachers, administrators, and educational professionals to produce effective learning environments. They also need to work in partnership with their students and parents. Working together as a team focused on a common goal creates a positive learning environment that supports a love of learning.

Teacher Collaboration

Interpersonal collaboration

A style of direct interaction between at least two co-equal parties voluntarily engaged in shared decision making as they work toward a common goal

Current trends supporting the development of stringent curricular standards, in conjunction with strong accountability mandates, has given rise to increased reliance on educational collaborations (Peterson, 2002). **Interpersonal collaboration** is defined as a style of direct interaction between at least two co-equal parties voluntarily engaged in shared decision-making as they work toward a common goal (Friend & Cook, 1992). Collaboration holds the promise of enhancing educational standards by bringing together multiple points of view and expertise. Similarly, accountability is furthered when realized through the integrative efforts of many highly trained educational professionals. The need for such collaboration is recognized and supported by numerous educational organizations such as National Board for Professional Teaching Standards, Interstate New Teacher Assessment and Support Consortium (INTASC), National Staff Development Council (NSDC), and the Interstate School Leaders Licensure Consortium (ISLLC). All of these organizations support the need for increased collaboration in schools. Based on this overwhelming support, it is clear that collaboration is valued in schools, but how is collaboration implemented? Chapter 1 discusses this issue in detail, but there are some important additional considerations in terms of classroom management.

Interconnections

The topic of collaboration is introduced in Chapter 1.

Collaborating with teachers and administrators takes enormous commitment. It necessitates that everyone share a common goal and take joint responsibility for decisions and outcomes. To make collaboration a reality, teachers need to make time to engage in collaboration. Research indicates that teachers report many opportunities to engage in collaboration (see Table 13.15). These opportunities are the gateway to the many benefits of the collaborative process (Leonard & Leonard, 2003; Friend & Cook, 1992). Engaging in meaningful dialogue with other educational professionals fosters a deeper appreciation of the responsibilities of their position.

Additionally, as teachers share their knowledge and experience with others, they increase their ability to create a rich and comprehensive curricular plan. Opportunity, however, does not always mean that collaboration actually takes place. There are many barriers to collaboration

Table 13.15 Forms of Professional Collaboration

Faculty meeting	Department/Subject meeting
Grade-level meetings	Beginning-of-year meeting
Lesson planning	Examination preparation
Workshops	Sharing materials
Informal meetings	University graduate classes
Team teaching	Special education meetings
Committee meetings	Peer observations

Adapted from Leonard and Leonard, 2003.

(Leonard & Leonard, 2003). Some teachers find collaboration threatening. Perhaps they have found success in teaching in isolation and fail to see any advantage to working with others. Consequently, collaboration sometimes creates conflict between teachers. Administrators need to take the time to prepare teachers for the collaborative process. They need to provide teachers with the underlying beliefs behind collaboration, while taking into consideration the need for respect for professional opinion and practice. Often teachers feel administrators only provide superficial support for collaboration efforts. Teachers may also feel that school administrators want teachers to collaborate but fail to provide appropriate amounts of time. Teachers often have to meet after or before school, which greatly deters effective collaboration. Timing often is the largest hurdle schools face when trying to implement collaborative teams. Table 13.16 provides a list of possible techniques to create more time for collaboration.

Parental Collaboration

Another aspect of collaboration is communication with the student's parents or primary caregiver. Establishing effective communication patterns with parents can greatly enhance student success. Teachers often regard parental communication with uncertainty and anxiety (Clark, 1999; Partin, 1999). Moving past such apprehension is important as research shows that frequent and supportive contact with parents has a positive impact on achievement and behavior (Reyes, Scribner, & Scribner, 1999; Roderick, 2001). Additionally, when parents are well-informed about the school life of their child, they show greater involvement and are more supportive of their child's teachers (Sui-Chu & Williams, 1996). Students also appear to develop their school perceptions in the context of their parents' attitude toward school (Epstein, Coates, Salinas, Sanders, & Simon, 1997). The more positive the parents' attitude, the more positively students will view school. All of this highlights the importance of strong, effective communication between teachers and parents.

Open communication between parents and teachers can have a positive influence on student success.

Table 13.16 Ten Ways to Create Time for Collaboration

Implement a peer tutoring program across two classes; students assist each other while one of the two teachers is released to work with a colleague.
Ask a local business to sponsor a substitute teacher for a specified number of days during the school year. Employ the substitute teacher to provide release time for teachers.
Work with parent teacher organizations to plan and implement a "volunteer substitute teacher" program in which qualified substitute teachers donate their time to the school to release teachers.
When assemblies or other large-group student activities are scheduled, release a few teachers to work together. Other staff manages supervision of the students for which those teachers are responsible.
Revise the school schedule to provide shared planning time to the teachers who most work together.
Initiate biweekly student activity periods in which community volunteers and some teachers instruct students on specialized topics while other teachers have release time to meet with colleagues.
Add early release days to the school calendar.
Have professionals in the school who do not have assigned class groups (e.g., principal, social worker counselor) plan and deliver instructionally relevant activities while teachers have release time for planning.
Use at least part of any professional development days on the calendar for planning for collaboration.
Release teachers who have extensive responsibilities for collaboration from other school duties (e.g., lunchroom supervision).

Adapted from Friend and Cook, 1992.

Assumptions Supporting Good Collaboration

How do teachers foster good collaboration with parents? It often begins with the teachers adopting a set of initial assumptions (Howe & Simmons, 2005). First, assume the parents are operating out of goodwill. At times, it appears that parents are not involved in the academic lives of their children, but this often not the case. Many parents want to help their child succeed, but lack the knowledge of how to help. Teachers should assume parents have the best interest of their child foremost in their minds. Approaching communication from this position of goodwill helps set a positive tone to parental communications. Next, teachers should try to assume that parents are competent, resourceful individuals. Teachers may not always agree with the tools parents use to help their child, but should assume they are competently doing what they think is best. Approach conversations from this perspective and make suggestions for change in the spirit of improvement, rather than characterizing current practices as ineffective. Finally, assume there is a shared responsibility for academic success. Parents, teacher, and the student themselves—all are active members of the academic team. Try to approach problems from this position of shared responsibility and build on the strengths of each member. Following these simple assumptions can make a difference in the quality and tone of parental conversations.

Key Elements of Effective Collaboration

The fundamental assumptions reviewed above are further supported by key elements of effective communication (Howe & Simmons, 2005), which are depicted in Table 13.17. Communicating effectively begins with being open and honest. Open in this sense means that teachers guard against excessive censorship and state the facts of the situation as simply as possible. Teachers remain honest and focused on conveying accurate and truthful information, working hard to ensure that the information is clearly articulated and based on very specific information. Vague comments lead to misunderstandings. It is also helpful to keep your vocabulary, tone, and body language professional. Try to convey concern and care with an appropriate level of professional distance.

Problems should be presented in the context of a particular situation and focused on finding a specific solution. This keeps the conversation from seeming like a general attack on the character or ability of either the student or the parents. Finally, both parents and student need to be completely clear that the conversation is confidential. Finding solutions to problems isn't effective if there is an element of fear regarding how the conversation will be used.

Reasons and Mechanisms for Collaboration

Collaboration between parents and teachers takes place for many reasons. Often teachers collaborate to communicate through reports, take-home notes, phone calls, or emails. Such notes help parents get a sense of whether their child is keeping up with their schoolwork and often detail missing or owed work. Teachers should make every effort to focus on posi-

Table 13.17 Elements of Effective Communication

Open—Conversations are open and direct.
Honest—Information shared is accurate and true.
Clear and Specific—Messages are clear and are based on specific information.
Professional—Information is shared in a professional and courteous manner.
Focused on Solving Problems—Issues are only identified in order to solve problems.
Confidential—Information shared is held in confidence and only used in the best interest of the student.

Adapted from Howe and Simmons, 2005.

tive reasons to communicate. Sending home a "good news gram" about a special activity or unique kindness exhibited by the student creates a unique bond between parent and teacher. It conveys a sense of commitment beyond basic coursework. At other times, there may be a problem, and the teacher needs to seek the advice of parents about the nature of the issue. Parents can be a valuable source of information and regular contact helps prevent problems from escalating. It is also appropriate for teachers to seek guidance and support from parents about an existing problem. Working together with parents often produces more effective, long-lasting solutions.

There are several ways that teachers can open a communication channel with parents. Two broad categories of communication are asynchronous and synchronous. **Asynchronous** forms of communication do not involve immediate feedback from each other. Typically, one individual communicates, and then the other responds at a later time. Asynchronous forms of communication include notes, email, and Webpages. **Synchronous** forms of communication involve two-way communication in real time. This includes telephone conversations, home visits, and in-school conferences. Home visits are rare and typically occur under unusual circumstances. Telephone conversations are still used with some regularity but are being eclipsed by newer forms of asynchronous communication like email. Probably the most commonly used synchronous communication channel is the in-school conference. Most schools still set aside one or two days a year for parents to come to school and engage in a dynamic conversation about their child's academic and social progress. To help make these conferences successful, teachers need to plan (Elmore, 2008; Million, 2005). Have a clear idea of the student's strengths and weakness, and collect relevant examples. Try to make a personal connection with the parents. Begin by relaying a personal story of how their child is a positive influence on the class. Follow-up with an agenda for the conference, but make sure you remain flexible and sensitive to the concerns of the parent. Focus on specific concerns and brainstorm with the parents about potential solutions. Make sure the parents' perspective is validated, giving them a sense of being a real partner in the educational process. Finally, end on a positive note. Show parents around the room, highlighting important contributions by their child.

Asynchronous

Form of communication that does not involve immediate feedback from each other

Synchronous

Form of communication that involves two-way communication in real time

Collaboration Challenges: Resistant Parents and Student Participation

One of the more difficult communication challenges teachers face is the resistant parent (Bluestein, 1989; Bailard & Strang, 1964). Hopefully, parents have a certain measure of trust in the teacher and receive difficult information regarding their child in the spirit of support and care. There are times when parents react negatively to difficult news about their child, and this can potentially lead to an explosive situation. Teachers must react quickly to defuse the situation (Elmore, 2008). With quick, decisive action, the teacher should be able to return the conversation to a civilized, productive level. Table 13.18 provides a list of "Do's" and "Don'ts" when working with resistant parents.

Another potential challenge for the teacher is the inclusion of the student in the parent-teacher conference. Deciding to include the student is a crucial decision depending on many developmental and personal factors. In general, researchers encourage inclusion of the student in the parent-student conference whenever possible (Ricci, 2000). Inclusion of the student usually means that some modifications need to be made to the conference. The length of the conference may need to be limited, especially for young children with limited attention spans. Teachers might want to consider sharing the conference with the student for part of the time and reserving some time for the parents alone. Teachers should prepare both the parent and the student for the conference. Inform parents and students that everyone will attend the conference. Encourage everyone to collect their thoughts on how school is progressing. Ask them to develop a list of what is working and what concerns they have. Often teachers act as a bridge between parents and their children. Take the opportunity to foster clear communication and mutual understanding. Also, try to stay focused on solving specific issues and end on a positive note.

Although it is usually advisable to include the student in at least part of the parent conference, there are times when the student should not attend. Sometimes the nature of the relationship between the parent and the student is so difficult that it is unlikely that a joint

Table 13.18 Do's and Don'ts of Working with Resistant Parents

Do	Don't
Make certain you address all their concerns.	Put the parent on the defensive.
Ask them to clarify any complaints that seem too general.	Talk about other children or compare this child with other children.
Show them the list of concerns, and ask if it is complete.	Talk about other teachers to the parents unless the remarks are of a complimentary nature.
Ask them for suggestions for solving any of the problems listed.	Belittle the administration or make derogatory remarks about the school district.
	Argue with the parent.
Write down suggestions.	Try to outtalk a parent.
	Interrupt the parent to make your own point.
Speak softly, even if they speak loudly.	Go too far with a parent who is not ready and/or able to understand your purpose.
	Ask parents questions that might be embarrassing to them—only information pertinent to the child's welfare is important.

Adapted from Bluestein, 1989; Bailard and Strang, 1964.

conference would yield success. Similarly, some students experience behavioral disturbances or emotional concerns that limit their ability to productively participate in a conference. In these cases, it may be better to meet with the parents and student separately. Separate meetings, however, do not mean that collaboration cannot occur. It means that the teacher will need to make an extra effort to represent fairly and impartially the concerns to each party. Under these conditions, collaboration is mediated in an asynchronous fashion. This may be the best choice in certain situations.

SUMMARIZE AND REFLECT

1. The final part of this chapter reviewed the impact of collaboration on classroom management. Teachers are increasingly encouraged to work in collaboration with other educational professionals to produce positive learning outcomes.
2. Teachers can meet this challenge in a variety of ways. One important part of the process is creating the necessary time to engage in meaningful collaboration.
3. Teachers also need to work in collaboration with parents. Teachers should begin parental conversations by making certain positive assumptions. Using these assumptions as a foundation, successful parental collaborations can be achieved by following a few simple techniques.
4. Finally, we reviewed how to deal with parents who demonstrate resistance to collaboration and how to manage student participation in the teacher/parent conference.

INFORMED APPLICATION

1. Imagine you are a middle school math teacher. Create a possible daily schedule where you create time to collaborate with both the special education teacher and the physical education teacher. Make sure you do not add more time to the typical school day.
2. Parental collaboration is an important part of the learning equation. How would you create an ideal partnership with the parents or guardians of your students?

THE CHAPTER IN REVIEW

We began the chapter by defining classroom management and how it serves as a tool to create positive, productive learning spaces. We looked at different styles of classroom management, describing the benefits and limitations of each. We also discussed how effective time management affects the learning environment.

There are many factors influencing classroom management. Some elements of classroom management involve teacher-directed activities; others are more student-driven factors. The second section of the chapter examines the teacher-centered issues in classroom management. There are multiple ways a teacher can create a positive learning environment. Keeping students engaged is one such factor. Appropriate questioning often enhances engagement, and we covered several techniques for using questioning to achieve this. We also approached management from a behavioral perspective, covering behavior management techniques supporting positive behaviors. This led to a discussion of prevention. We learned that prevention involves a complicated interaction between teachers, parents, peers, and the student. The nature of this interaction leads to particular academic outcomes. The last two parts of this section reviewed how the physical classroom space and teacher communication pattern affect learning. We covered several classroom designs appropriate for particular curricular goals. We also looked at how important it is for teachers to pay attention to how they communicate with students, including their body language—and to how effectively they listen.

Teachers are clearly important in managing the classroom environment, but students also play an important role. One factor affecting the nature of the classroom is the development of particular social skills. Students require certain interaction skills in order to engage effectively in learning. We reviewed what skills are typically valued in the classroom and how teachers can support these behaviors. We also discussed how important it is to empower students to manage inevitable conflicts. Specific conflict resolution skills were described. Finally, we discussed another important relationship to students—the student/teacher relationship. Research shows that this relationship is one of the best predictors of later success. We covered specific elements of the student/teacher relationship and detailed ways teachers can support positive relationships with students.

The last section of the chapter reviewed how collaboration affects the learning environment. We looked at collaboration issues encountered when working with other teachers. Often one of the biggest obstacles is simply finding the time to work with colleagues. A variety of ways to create time to collaborate were presented. Next, we looked at the important collaboration between teachers and parents. Key elements of effective collaboration were presented, as well as specific mechanisms for meeting with parents. We also reviewed how to address parents who resist collaborating with the teacher and how to effectively include the student in the teacher/parent collaboration process.

Interdisciplinary Case Focus

principal *special educator* *teacher* *parents* *psychologist* *social worker* *physical educator* *nurse* *peers* *doctor*

Principal Edwards works at a small, rural high school in Indiana. During a restructuring process, he found that he needed one of his math teachers to share a classroom space with an honors psychology teacher. The school only had one section of psychology each term, so sharing a classroom space was a necessity. He surveyed his faculty about sharing space and failed to find a match. The psychology teacher uses small group work as her primary teaching approach. Other teachers made good use of group work, but they also lectured. This difference caused problems with sharing a room because the psychology teacher had requested a very specific classroom setup. She wanted a series of round tables, separated by bookcases. Her intent was to create smaller learning centers that were thematically linked to her curricular plan. Centers were geared to understanding developmental theory, special needs intervention, counseling, etc. None of the other teachers in the school needed this type of room arrangement, and Mr. Edwards could not devote a whole room to a class that was only taught once a term.

Questions to Address

- How do teachers collaborate in a shared learning space?
- How can administrators encourage ongoing negotiation of shared learning spaces to ensure the continuation of a positive learning environment?
- What are the options for designing classrooms to meet multiple learning goals?

Resolution

The first issue Mr. Edwards needed to address is how to select a teacher to collaborate with the psychology teacher. Since the psychology teacher was a retired teacher who only came in to teach the psychology course, it was difficult to find other faculty that had an established relationship with her. Mr. Edwards ultimately approached an English teacher who indicated on his survey that he used group work part of the time. This particular teacher also had partial release time because he directed the school's honor program. Due to these administrative duties, he was released from two of his regularly taught classes. This meant his classroom was free some of the time. The other advantage was that since he already used some group work, negotiating some common ground with the psychology teacher was more likely.

After selecting the teacher, Mr. Edwards sat down with Mr. Kimball, the English teacher, to ask him to cooperate with the psychology teacher, Ms. Anns. He explained to Mr. Kimball the reasons he had been selected and expressed a sincere desire to make appropriate modifications to both teachers' schedules, classroom resources, and instructional time that would be needed. After some initial resistance, Mr. Kimball agreed to the shared classroom arrangement. As principal of the school, Mr. Edwards could have simply made the assignment without discussion, but felt it was important for his teachers to have some say in how and where they taught. He felt strongly that choice, within limits, creates invested teachers who are better able to create positive learning environments for their students.

The next step was to begin the actual collaborative process. First, Mr. Edwards felt that making a regular planning meeting between Mr. Kimball and Ms. Anns would be necessary for true collaboration. He decided to release them from one of their supervisory hours each week (usually monitoring lunchroom). Both teachers were excited about this change and readily agreed to the ongoing meetings. During the first meeting, Mr. Edwards explained that he would only be present for the initial meeting and his expectation was that they would self-direct the collaboration process. He had given each teacher an agenda for the initial meeting. They were to discuss their general approach to teaching and what their primary curricular goals were. From this discussion, they were to move into a discussion of how to share a common space based on their educational needs. Mr. Edwards brought several resources that detailed possible classroom arrangements.

The initial discussion went well, particularly the part where the teachers shared their learning style and goals. The discussion regarding classroom arrangement was more challenging. Both teachers began with fairly rigid ideas for what they wanted in their classroom. Mr. Edwards gently informed both teachers that there was no more "my" classroom. This was to be "their" classroom, and it was important for them to think of it that way. Their initial impasse regarding actual classroom design slowly gave way to curiosity as they explored the resources brought by Mr. Edwards. They both found new things they had never before considered. Mr. Edwards encouraged both teachers to elaborate on what they liked and disliked about each option. This helped both teachers recognize commonalities. The meeting ended without a clear decision regarding classroom design, but they were able to develop a preliminary design to get the year started. Fine tuning their classroom design and other collaborative issues would be ongoing through their weekly meetings.

Important Points to Remember About Collaboration and Classroom Management

Future teachers need to have a healthy respect for the potential difficulties inherent in collaborating with other faculty members. Teaching is moving closer to regularly adopting collaborative models for instruction, but teaching is still a solitary profession in many districts. As such, teachers can develop strong opinions regarding how they want to teach and may have few tools for negotiation. This potential problem is often most difficult when issues of classroom management surface. It is easy for teachers to consider all elements of managing their classroom as under their exclusive control. It is important to remember that each teacher can only bring his/her particular life experience to the daunting task of creating a positive learning environment. Working together with others can often infuse one's thinking with a rich source of ideas to better one's teaching, which ultimately translates into a more rewarding and productive learning experience for students and instructional experience for the teacher.

Key Terms

TERM	*Page*	*TERM*	*Page*
Academic learning time	428	Integrative negotiation	445
Allocated time	428	Interpersonal collaboration	448
Asynchronous	451	Learning center	440
Authoritarian teacher	427	Non-verbal communication	441
Authoritative teacher	427	Paralanguage	442
Classroom management	424	Peer mediation	445
Conflict resolution	445	Permissive teacher	427
Congruent communication	440	Positive behavioral supports (PBS)	432
Distributive negotiations	445	Positive learning environment	424
Empathetic listening	442	Procedures	437
Engaged time	428	Rules	435
Engagement	430	Social skills	444
Functional assessment	432	Synchronous	451

14
Chapter
INSTRUCTIONAL
EXCELLENCE

What's It All About ...

How do teachers develop a sound instructional plan?

What is involved in translating an instructional plan into actual classroom instruction?

What are the qualities that characterize quality instructional environments?

How does educational perspective impact instructional planning?

Chapter Objectives

- Describe how teachers plan for instruction.
- Explain how to translate goals into lessons.

- Understand timing issues (yearly, term, unit, weekly, daily) when creating educational plans.
- Describe how to choose topics and create lesson plans.
- Explain integrated and thematic learning.

- Describe qualities of exceptional teachers.
- Describe the components of effective instruction.

- Describe social cognitive approaches to instruction.
- Describe information processing approaches to instruction.
- Describe behavioral approaches to instruction.
- Describe individual differences approaches to instruction.

EXTENDED OUTLINE

Instructional Excellence

I. What's It All About ...
II. From Today's Headlines
III. Development of the Instructional Plan
  A. Planning for instruction
    1. Goals and objectives
    2. Mager and specific objectives versus Gronlund and general objectives
  B. Translating goals into lessons
    1. State and national standards
    2. Planning and societal values
    3. Bloom's Taxonomies
  C. Summarize and reflect
IV. Management of the Instructional Plan
  A. Timing (yearly, term, unit, weekly, daily)
  B. Topic selection and lesson plans
  C. Integrated and thematic learning
  D. Summarize and reflect
V. Instructional Delivery
  A. Teacher qualities
    1. Content knowledge
    2. Organization
    3. Expectations
  B. Effective instruction
    1. Encouraging self-direction
    2. Concept learning
    3. Technology
  C. Summarize and reflect
VI. Models of Teaching and Learning
  A. Social cognitive approaches to instruction
    1. Social negotiation
    2. Cooperative learning
  B. Information processing approaches to instruction
    1. Inquiry and problem-based learning
    2. Advanced organizers
  C. Behavioral approaches to instruction
    1. Direct instruction
    2. Mastery learning
  D. Individual differences approaches to instruction
    1. Equity instruction
    2. Learning styles
  E. Summarize and reflect
VII. The Chapter in Review
VIII. Interdisciplinary Case Focus

From Today's Headlines

Vol. I No. 14 Teaching World, 2012

Making Progress: Child by Child

As class begins, kindergarten teacher Margeaux Sandt gathers students in the reading area carpet. On an easel she has an enormous picture of a chimpanzee. What is the lesson? Simply getting the students to interact verbally. Many students from her school struggle with limited English proficiency and Ms. Sandt thinks of creative ways to get students to invest and engage in developing their linguistic skills.

As reported in the *Rocky Mountain News* (May 29, 2007), Aurora Elementary School has worked diligently to raise low standardized test scores. First on their "to-do" list: adopting clear goals for each class, lesson, and student. Principal Karla Groth emphasizes, "Planning has to be child by child." Much of the push to make changes to their traditional approach to education comes from the greater diversity in student body. The Hispanic population of the school has changed from 10% to almost 50% in just over ten years. In addition to linguistic barriers experienced by many students, cultural factors also create a need for more sensitive educational approaches. Some of the changes being implemented include the following:

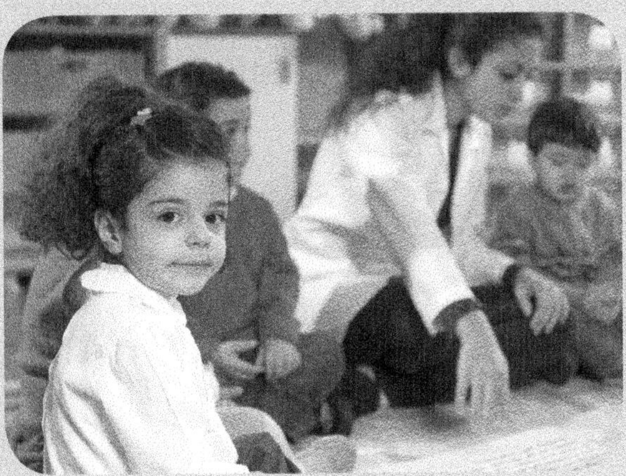

- Aligning curriculum with state standards
- Using "pacing guides" that break material into smaller units, each with a clear goal and learning objective
- Testing frequently to check for learning and to reveal when other methods are needed for success
- Increasing teacher-to-teacher coaching
- Training teachers to work with students whose second language is English

These changes have brought much needed direction to the school's educational plan. Instruction is clearly guided and provides necessary structure.

MAKE THE CONNECTION

The struggles and solutions being explored by Aurora Elementary mirror many of the challenges facing schools today. In this chapter we will examine many of these intervention approaches. We will explore how goals help produce more directed and efficient learning. We will also review the relevant research on how to tailor education to the individual needs of each student. These topics will be examined within the overall context of the theme of this book: interdisciplinary collaboration. As recognized by Aurora Elementary, using professional collaboration helps teachers work efficiently and creatively to meet the needs of individual students.

DEVELOPMENT OF THE INSTRUCTIONAL PLAN

Instructional excellence begins with a solid educational plan. Educational plans create a framework connecting all other instructional elements. In the months preceding the school year, teachers reflect on their personal goals and instructional style and how these will affect their educational planning. Many factors influence this process, including state and federal mandates, individual value systems, as well as community values. We begin our look at instructional excellence by examining the process teachers use to address these factors as they strive to translate goals into effective action.

Planning for Instruction

Teachers take time to plan what they are going to teach by defining what they want their students to learn.

Planning for instruction involves several steps. *First,* teachers go through a process where they attempt to define what they want their students to learn. It is forward thinking and involves a process of envisioning the future (Clark & Dunn, 1991). *Second,* teachers develop specific goals and objectives for making these learning outcomes a reality. They must develop rigorous instructional requirements and appropriate activities to guide students toward their educational goals. *Finally,* the teacher addresses testing and evaluation options. Assessments have historically been an integral part of the educational process. They both direct and document learning.

There are many planning examples in our everyday life experience. We keep a list of needed grocery items for our next trip to the store. We keep a family planning calendar for making sure we get to those all-important soccer and swim meets. Even the New Year's resolutions we make are weak attempts to plan for future changes in our lives. Similarly, teachers plan for each coming school year. Some approach the process in an informal way with broad objectives. They may have a general sense of what they want to accomplish but not dwell on specifics. Other teachers take an extremely detailed approach to planning. They produce elaborate lesson plans for each school day and maintain a rigid educational path. Whether one takes an informal or formal approach to educational programming, it is becoming increasingly clear that defining goals and objectives helps direct and focus educational efforts.

Goals and Objectives

The traditional view of educational planning follows a basic linear model. The process works in a straight line from initial objectives and goals to final outcomes (see Figure 14.1 [modified from Arends, 2007; Downey, C., 2001; Gronlund, 2004]). Following this model, teachers first develop specific learning goals, followed by assessment and analysis to shape goals to the unique learning needs of the students. The teacher then selects an appropriate instructional strategy to achieve his/her goals. Finally, the teacher records performance outcomes of the student. Teachers all over the world use this approach. It is logical and clearly states a direct path from goals to outcomes.

Figure 14.1

Basic Linear Model of Educational Planning

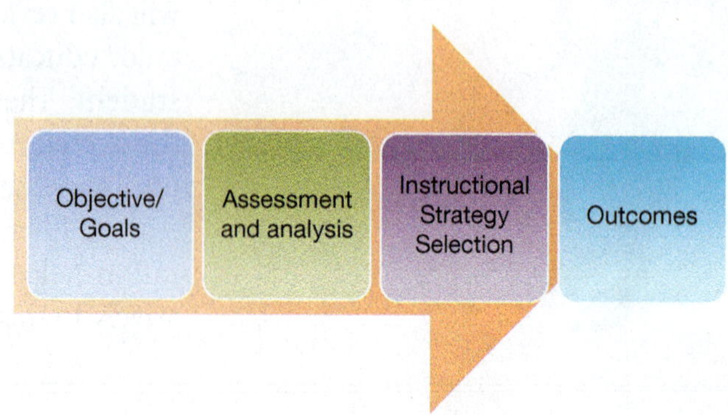

Other researchers approach the process from an *interactive* perspective (Fullan, 2001; McCutcheon & Milner, 2002). According to interactive (non-linear) models, instructional planning begins with actual activities in the classroom, which naturally lead to certain outcomes. For example, a teacher may have third grade students engage in a math activity on division. As the lesson progresses, it becomes increasingly clear that most of the students have difficulty with the activity because they do not know their multiplication facts. This leads the teacher to develop specific curricular goals for learning multiplication facts. Following a non-linear approach to goal setting, she uses the outcome of the activity to shape her educational goals. These goals then direct future activities, further refining the teacher's goals. Figure 14.2 illustrates this non-linear approach to goal setting.

The linear and non-linear models presented above have also been conceptualized as instructivist and constructivist, respectively (Baylor & Kitsantas, 2005). *Instructivist* planning models are similar to the traditional linear models of planning. They are more teacher-centered and emphasize transfer of knowledge (Roblyer, Edwards, & Havriluk, 1997). It is a more prescriptive process, detailing specific plans to achieve specific outcomes. *Constructivist* planning models are non-linear (see Chapter 12). They center on how the student constructs an understanding of the material (Wittrock, 1990). It is a more descriptive approach to instructional planning, using the student's actual performance to shape future educational directions.

Interconnections

Chapter 12 covers constructivist approaches to instruction.

As you can see from these general approaches to planning, goal setting is an important part of the process. Goals establish educational direction and influence the instructional process. Instructional goal setting has a long and controversial history. The roots of goal setting are seen in the groundbreaking work of Robert Mager (Mager, 1962, 1972) and later, Madeline Hunter (Hunter, 1982). The work of these important visionaries ushered in an era marked by concern for educational clarity and direction. Teachers, parents, and administrators began to value and demand a clear direction to instruction. Consequently, establishing goals and objectives for lesson plans became a necessary part of the educational process. Today, many researchers and practitioners continue to underscore the importance of developing clear goals and objectives (Maeroff, 1993; Wiggins, 1994).

Not all educators, however, support goal setting to the same degree. Some researchers and administrators believe that aligning curricular goals too closely to rigid goals trivializes education and creates a mechanical approach to education (McQuade & Champagne, 1995). The concern is that teachers will fail to create a love of inquiry and the learning process. In addition, following a prescribed path too closely might limit creative lines of inquiry and make it difficult for teachers to encourage unique educational directions. These are important concerns, but they are tempered by a competing need for society to establish some reasonable expectations for learning outcomes. Making decisions about what to teach is indeed a difficult task, impacting individual teachers, local school districts, and society. Let's look at two prominent approaches to establishing educational objectives.

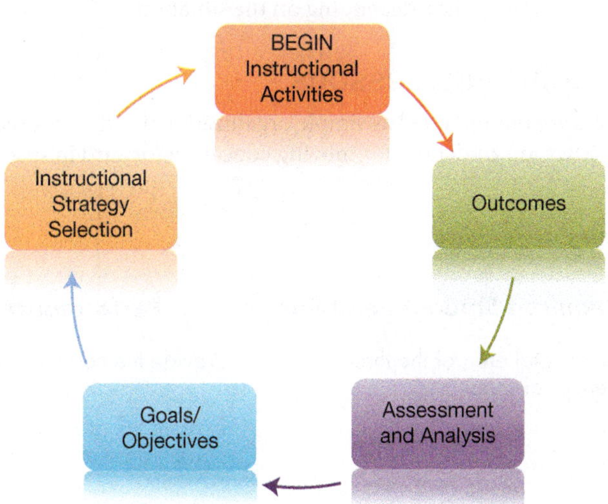

Figure 14.2

Non-linear Approach to Goal Setting

Mager and Specific Objectives versus Gronlund and General Objectives

Robert Mager (1975) developed a popular behavioral approach to developing objectives (see Chapter 4 for coverage of the behavioral perspective.). His approach is considered behavioral because of its emphasis on overt, observable behavior and contains three components for developing objectives:

Student Behavior Here the teacher details appropriate student behavior.

Testing Situation This is the specific situation in which the student is expected to demonstrate the behavior.

Performance Criteria These criteria are used to determine that the student has mastered the objective.

When writing objectives using Mager's system, it is important to keep things very straightforward and clear. For example, do not ask students to demonstrate "more" independent seatwork. It is better to state that students will complete three independent seat assignments each day. It is also a good idea to incorporate some flexibility. For example, it is not necessary to specify the exact assignment in the objective. This enables the teacher to meet changing student needs while still meeting the objective. Despite maintaining some degree of flexibility, Mager's system is a specific and detailed system for establishing objectives. It is grounded in actual behaviors, which makes it clearer when students achieve particular instructional outcomes. Table 14.1 presents another example using Mager's system.

Chapter 4 covers behavioral theory as it applies to educational settings.

Not all systems for writing objectives focus on specific behaviors. Gronlund (2004) advocates using more general objectives, providing specifics only as needed for clarification. Gronlund is not a strict behaviorist, and as such he is less likely to ground a particular objective in actual observable behavior. Instead of the very specific Mager-type of objective listed above, a Gronlund approach to the same task might simply state that the student will demonstrate an understanding of how to calculate the area of three-dimensional shapes. *Gronlund defines an instructional objective* as the intended learning outcome. It refers to expected student performance at the end of instruction. A modified version of the above objective from a Gronlund perspective is presented in Table 14.2.

Deciding which approach to use when developing objectives and their associated lesson plans is challenging. To some extent, choices are made for teachers based on the value system of the school district in which they teach. Other times, the nature of the domain lends itself more to a specific behavioral goal or a more general statement of intent. Most teachers will use a combination of these approaches, depending on the situation.

Translating Goals into Lessons

Goals and objectives are not intended as simple organizational activities used at the beginning of the school year. They are guidelines for moving education forward in specific ways through-

Table 14.1 Example of Mager's Objective System

Testing Situation	Required Student Behavior	Performance Criteria
Present a three-dimensional shape	Find the total area of the three-dimensional shape.	Provide the correct answer.
Area of a circle formula		Explain the process for arriving at the correct answer.
Paper and pencil only		

Table 14.2 Example of a General Approach to Objective Writing

Objective	Example
General Objective	Demonstrate an ability to calculate the area of a three-dimensional shape.
Sub-goal One	Know how to name various geometric shapes.
Sub-goal Two	Know how to calculate the area of a circle.
Sub-goal Three	Know how to calculate the area of a triangle.

out the school year. They are tools to guide instruction in a focused and productive manner. In other words, goals are intended to make a difference in actual instructional practice. How does this happen? How do we take an idea and make it an educational reality?

State and National Standards

Making decisions about *what* to teach and *how* to teach it are no longer under the exclusive province of the individual teacher. In fact, beginning teachers are often struck by how much of their lesson plans are dictated by standards from a variety of sources. Figure 14.3 details the many factors affecting what actually is taught in schools today (Arends, 2007).

As you can see from the figure, a variety of local, state, federal, and societal factors shape what schools teach. For example, American society has expectations regarding what they believe students should learn. We want future generations to be able to read fluidly, perform mathematical operations, have an understanding of history and the humanities, appreciate the scientific process and the arts, and understand and value their role as citizens. These are difficult to objectively define, but they still provide direction for the federal government and individual states when developing specific plans and goals.

Historically, states have taken a more general and removed approach to influencing curricular development. Today, however, states are taking a more active role. The broad expectations of society detailed above need to be translated into actionable items schools and teachers can follow. That is, they need to be modified into specific goals and objectives teachers can use to develop appropriate curriculum. As a check on this process, schools must demonstrate to the federal government that they are making **adequate yearly progress (AYP)** toward their goals (Riddle & Kober, 2011). The specific techniques for establishing progress are state determined and often take the form of statewide tests. These tests necessarily influence the curricular goals

Adequate yearly progress (AYP)

An accountability measure by the federal government to ensure schools are making educational progress over time

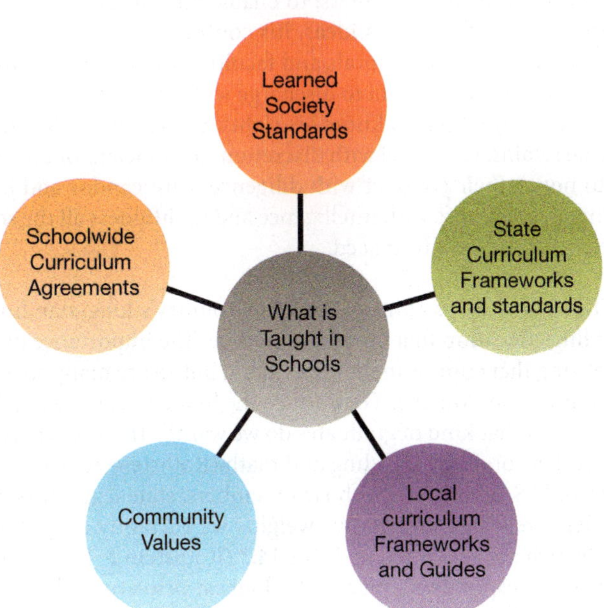

Figure 14.3

The Many Factors Affecting What Is Taught in Schools

of individual schools as they strive to demonstrate that they are effectively teaching their students. In fact, school districts typically develop curricular agreements with individual schools regarding what is taught. This has the advantage that it makes later assessment more organized and consistent; however, it can also discourage educational invention and non-traditional approaches to education.

State level concerns are not the only concern schools need to consider when establishing curricular plans. Local communities are also influential in establishing what goals are valued. Step into any school district in the nation and it becomes clear what educational factors are prioritized. Some value certain subjects over others. Some value the arts, science, or community involvement. These local value systems also play an important role in what schools teach. They are the values that are closest to the hearts of the actual community members and are often viewed as the most important.

Planning and Societal Values

The process of planning and setting educational goals has a direct bearing on the academic subjects we emphasize in school. Current national goals focus on reading and math skills, which are causing a corresponding shift in educational practice. For example, in 1991 a national survey of teachers in grades one through four found that 33% of instructional time was spent on reading. By 2004, this had increased to 36%. Math instruction similarly increased from 15 to 17%. Over the same period of time, social studies instruction decreased from 9 to 8% and science instruction from 8 to 7% (U.S. Department of Education). Also important to note is that these changes may disproportionally affect students from the poorest socioeconomic demographic. A 2005 survey by the Center on Educational Policy found that 97% of schools with a high proportion of students from families below the poverty line had minimum reading time requirements and that this often came at a cost to the time spent on social studies, art, music, and physical education. The same survey found that only 55% of other schools had similar minimum reading requirements.

Our goals for reading and math are causing a shift away from learning in other subject areas. Understandably, there are only so many hours in the school day and priorities have to be set; however, it is always important to weigh the impact of curricular changes. It is important to help the youth of America develop strengths in reading and math, but it is also important to foster their development as citizens and their appreciation the social sciences, natural sciences, the arts, and physical education. Thomas Jefferson, who was a strong advocate for public education in Virginia (Peterson, 1984), said:

> [The goals of Education are] To give to every citizen the information he needs for the transaction of his own business; to enable him to calculate for himself, and to express and preserve his ideas, his contracts and accounts in writing; to improve by reading, his morals and faculties; to understand his duties to his neighbors and country, and to discharge with competence the functions confided to him by either; to know his rights; to exercise with order and justice those he retains, to choose with discretion the fiduciary of those he delegates; and to notice their conduct with diligence, with candor and judgment; and in general, to observe with intelligence and faithfulness all the social relations under which he shall be placed.

Thomas Jefferson

This quote helps contextualize our country's long-standing commitment to providing education that is comprehensive. The importance of reading and math in realizing that commitment are evident, but so are many social, moral and civic educational components. To produce the best citizens, we need to constantly ask ourselves, "What kind of graduates do we want?" The answer is complex and likely to extend beyond basic reading and math (Rothstein & Jacobsen, 2006). A recent survey of U.S. adults, school board members, state legislators, and school superintendents reflected the relative weights we currently assign major instructional areas, which are presented in Table 14.3 (Rothstein & Jacobsen, 2006).

Survey respondents placed the highest priority on knowledge of the basic academic skill areas. Critical thinking and problem solving were a close second.

Table 14.3 Selected Americans' Views on the Relative Importance of Public School Goals

Respondents were asked to rate the relative importance of each goal area by assigning percentages to each. If a respondent's choices summed to more or less than 100%, the software program rejected this error and asked for a revised set of choices so that the sum would equal 100%. The percentages shown are simple averages of the average responses for each of the four surveyed groups—U.S. adults, school board members, state legislators, and school superintendents.

Goal Area	Relative Importance
Basic Academic Skills in Core Subjects Reading, writing, math, knowledge of science and history	22%
Critical Thinking and Problem Solving Ability to analyze and interpret information, use computers to develop knowledge, apply ideas to new situations	18%
Social Skills and Work Ethic Good communication skills, personal responsibility, ability to get along well with others and work with others from different backgrounds	12%
Citizenship and Community Responsibility Knowledge of how government works and of how to participate in civic activities like voting, volunteering, and becoming active in communities	11%
Preparation for Skilled Work Vocational, career, and technical education that will qualify youths for skilled employment that does not require a college degree	10%
Physical Health A foundation for lifelong physical health, including good habits of exercise and nutrition	9%
Emotional Health Tools to develop self-confidence, respect for others, and the ability to resist peer pressure to engage in irresponsible personal behavior	9%
The Arts and Literature Capacity to participate in and appreciate the musical, visual, and performing arts and development of a love of literature	9%

It appeared that there was a second level of importance given to social skills, citizenship, and preparation for skilled work. Survey respondents felt like instruction in physical health, emotional health, and the arts and literature were relatively less important. These results are important as a barometer of what we feel as a nation is important for schools to work toward. Again, what we value translates into goals that in turn shape the very nature of how we educate the youth of America.

Bloom's Taxonomies

Researchers have long worked on systems to help teachers translate goals into actual lessons. In this section, we will begin with one of the most cited researchers in this area, Benjamin Bloom (Anderson & Sosniak, 1994; Bloom, Engelhart, Frost, Hill, & Krathwohl, 1956). Bloom and his colleagues were interested in taking the multitude of things that an educator could teach and develop a system for categorizing them into objectives. Each objective would be part of a particular overall domain and would translate into specific instructional activities. His system became known as Bloom's taxonomies of educational objectives. He developed objectives along three dimensions: cognitive, psychomotor and affective. Each educational dimension was then sub-divided into particular objectives. His cognitive domain underwent revision by a group of his students in 2001 (Anderson et al., 2001). The revision was undertaken to keep the taxonomy in line with current research. Three of the thinking skills (synthesis, comprehension, and knowledge) were replaced (creating, understanding, and remembering). Additionally, terms were changed from nouns to verbs (e.g., application → applying). Table 14.4 lists each of the domains, including the revised cognitive domain. The psychomotor and affective domains were not revised. Also, the psychomotor domain was not elaborated as fully as the other domains, so sources interpret the domain somewhat differently. The psychomotor domain presented here comes from *Learning to Teach* by Richard Arends (2007).

Bloom's taxonomy is a comprehensive list of cognitive, psychomotor, and affective domain objectives. His cognitive domain was originally divided into a hierarchy. That is, he believed that some cognitive skills were more foundational, while others were higher-level. He believed that skills like application, analysis, evaluation, and creativity were higher-level skills building on lower-level skills like knowledge and comprehension. Today's teachers may not make such distinctions, focusing on developing all of these skills. Table 14.5 provides an example of the six areas within the cognitive dimension and how each can be translated into specific instructional objectives. For example, the cognitive domain of *remembering* can be operationalized as either recognizing or recalling information. Applying this to a lesson in U.S. history might produce

Table 14.4 Bloom's Taxonomy

Domain	Level	Description
Cognitive Domain	• Creating	• Builds a pattern from diverse elements
	• Evaluating	• Judges the value of information
	• Analyzing	• Separates information into parts for better understanding
	• Applying	• Applying knowledge to a new situation
	• Understanding	• Understanding information
	• Remembering	• Recall of data
Affective Domain	• Internalizing Values	• Behavior which is controlled by a value system
	• Organizing Values	• Organizing values into order or priority
	• Valuing	• The value a person attaches to something
	• Responding to phenomena	• Taking an active part in learning; participating
	• Receiving phenomena	• An awareness; willingness to listen
Psychomotor Domain	• Reflex movements	• Involuntary movements to some stimuli
	• Basic fundamental movements	• Combining reflexes into patterns of movement
	• Perceptual abilities	• Moving appropriately in response to sensory information
	• Physical abilities	• Translating basic movements into highly skilled movements
	• Skilled movements	• Complex movements requiring a certain degree of efficiency
	• Nondiscursive communications	• Can communicate through body movement

Table 14.5 The Six Categories of the Cognitive Process Dimension and Related Cognitive Processes

1. REMEMBERING—Retrieve relevant knowledge from long-term memory.	
1.1 RECOGNIZING	(e.g., Recognize the dates of important events in U.S. history)
1.2 RECALLING	(e.g., Recall the dates of important events in U.S. history)
2. UNDERSTANDING—Construct meaning from instructional messages, including oral, written, and graphic communication.	
2.1 INTERPRETING	(e.g., Paraphrase important speeches and documents)
2.3 CLASSIFYING	(e.g., Give examples of various artistic painting styles)
2.4 SUMMARIZING	(e.g., Classify observed or described cases of mental disorders)
2.5 INFERRING	(e.g., Write a short summary of the events portrayed on videotapes)
2.6 COMPARING	(e.g., In learning a foreign language, infer grammatical principles from examples)
2.7 EXPLAINING	(e.g., Compare historical events to contemporary situations)
3. APPLYING—Carry out or use a procedure in a given situation.	
3.1 EXECUTING	(e.g., Divide one whole number by another whole number, both with multiple digits)
3.2 IMPLEMENTING	(e.g., Determine in which situations Newton's second law is appropriate)
4. ANALYZING—Break material into constituent parts and determine how parts relate to one another and to an overall structure or purpose	
4.1 DIFFERENTIATING	(e.g., Distinguish between relevant and irrelevant numbers in a mathematical word problem)
4.2 ORGANIZING	(e.g., Structure evidence in a historical description into evidence for and against a particular historical explanation)
4.3 ATTRIBUTING	(e.g., Determine the point of view of the author of an essay in terms of his or her political perspective)
5. EVALUATING—Make judgments based on criteria and standards.	
5.1 CHECKING	(e.g., Determine whether a scientist's conclusions follow from observed data)
5.2 CRITIQUING	(e.g., Judge which of two methods is the best way to solve a given problem)
6. CREATING—Put elements together to form a coherent or functional whole; reorganize elements into a new pattern or structure	
6.1 GENERATING	(e.g., Generate hypotheses to account for an observed phenomenon)
6.2 PLANNING	(e.g., Plan a research paper on a given historical topic)
6.3 PRODUCING	(e.g., Build habitats for certain species for certain purposes)

SOURCE: From *A Taxonomy for Learning, Teaching and Assessing—A Revision of Bloom's Taxonomy of Educational Objectives,* Editor: L. Anderson et al. Copyright © 2001 by Addison Wesley Longman, Inc., used with permission.

the following objectives: recognizing the dates of important events in U.S. history or recalling the dates of important events in U.S. history. Additional examples are shown in the table.

Additionally, the revised cognitive domain was applied to four different knowledge dimensions. These dimensions recognize how each cognitive dimension applies to a type of knowledge. The cognitive domain mapped out across each type of knowledge is presented in Table 14.6.

To use the table to write an objective, a teacher decides what kind of knowledge to emphasize (e.g., The Knowledge Dimension) and how the student should approach learning the material (e.g., The Cognitive Dimension). The following example illustrates this process. A student is given an assignment to write an essay supporting a political point of view. After completing

Table 14.6 Bloom's Taxonomy—Revised Cognitive Dimensions

The Knowledge Dimension	The Cognitive Process Dimension					
	1. Remembering	2. Understanding	3. Applying	4. Analyzing	5. Evaluating	6. Creating
A. Factual Knowledge						
B. Conceptual Knowledge						
C. Procedural Knowledge						
D. Metacognitive Knowledge						

SOURCE: Anderson et al., 2001.

the essay, the student is required to provide a critique of their work. Critiquing is one of the cognitive skills associated with *Evaluating* (see Table 14.7). What they are required to critique is their own thought process. Thinking about your own thought processes is called *metacognition.* (see Chapters 5 and 6.)

Affective and psychomotor domains function like the cognitive domain. Teachers can develop educational objectives in a variety of areas. Emotional areas focus on helping the student demonstrate appropriate levels of emotionality and commitment. Psychomotor areas

Table 14.7 Educational Objective

The student will be able to evaluate their essay by critiquing the thought process used to develop their point of view. This objective is based on the Metacognitive Knowledge Dimension using the evaluating cognitive process.

The Knowledge Dimension	The Cognitive Process Dimension					
	1. Remembering	2. Understanding	3. Applying	4. Analyzing	5. Evaluating	6. Creating
A. Factual Knowledge						
B. Conceptual Knowledge						
C. Procedural Knowledge						
D. Metacognitive Knowledge						

SOURCE: Anderson et al., 2001.

include fine motor skills useful in handwriting and manipulating objects and large motor skills emphasized in physical education. The importance of Bloom's work is that he gives teachers a wealth of domain areas from which they can choose to develop instructional objectives (see Interdisciplinary Case Study at the end of this chapter). As mentioned in the previous section, the specific nature of those lessons will be influenced by federal, state, community, and personal values. A reasonable balance between domain areas helps students succeed across a wide range of academic, social, and occupational areas.

Interconnections

Chapters 5 and 6 cover the topic of Metacognition.

SUMMARIZE AND REFLECT

1. This section began with a review of the importance of developing sound educational goals.
2. Some teachers have a natural tendency to express goals as highly detailed instructional objectives. This is similar to the system for developing goals developed by Mager. It is highly behavioral, focusing on actual actions produced by the students.
3. Other teachers use a more general approach, choosing to express goals and objectives that are more general in nature. This has the advantage of being more flexible and allows teachers to vary instructional practice as needed to meet the particular goal.
4. Educational planning is influenced by a variety of factors including teacher preferences, district objective, community values and federal guidelines. All of these factors shape the development of the instructional plan.
5. Bloom's Taxonomies provides a framework around which teachers can develop actual objectives. It defines a variety of instructionally relevant domains that the individual teacher can use to guide instruction.

INFORMED APPLICATION

1. Identify values within the community where you grew up that likely influenced the way you were taught.
2. Similar to the example in Table 14.6, choose one of Bloom's cognitive dimensions and one of the knowledge dimensions and write an appropriate educational objective.

MANAGEMENT OF THE INSTRUCTIONAL PLAN

Instructional planning is critical for educational success. As the last section detailed, planning involves development of clear goals and objectives. These are shaped by a variety of factors including societal, federal, state, community and, of course, the teacher. Development of the instructional plan, however, is only a part of the educational process. Even the most well developed instructional plans are ineffective if they are managed inappropriately. In this section, we will cover issues typically encountered when implementing the instructional plan. You will gain an appreciation of the challenges inherent in making educational plans realistic and manageable on a daily basis.

Timing (Yearly, Term, Unit, Weekly, Daily)

Teachers are constantly faced with decisions about when to offer a lesson, how long the lesson should last, when the most appropriate time to offer a particular unit is, and/or simply what to do on a given day. These are issues related to timing of the educational plan. Robert Yinger (Yinger, 1980) defined several time dimensions teachers should consider when implementing their instructional plan: yearly, term, unit, weekly, and daily. Graphically, these time dimensions are presented in Figure 14.4.

Although the figure depicts separate dimensions for each period, planning often involves multiple levels of planning. For example, a physical education teacher may have goals for gross motor skill development for his eighth grade classes. Over the course of the year, he

Figure 14.4

Time Dimensions Teachers Should Consider When Implementing an Instructional Plan

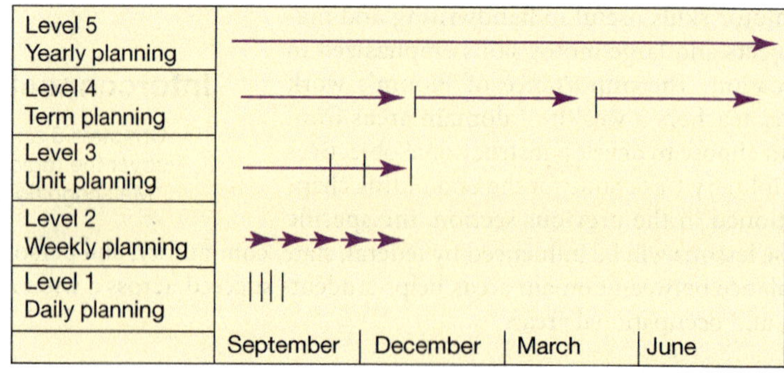

wants them to develop several physical proficiencies *across* different sports. This is a broad goal and will take most of the academic year to accomplish. This goal, however, is supported by specific plans for a given unit (e.g., basketball unit) and activities on a given day (e.g., practicing lay-ups). The interconnectedness of these periods is important for planning. Effective programming involves planning across these instructional periods (Arends, 2007). Also, remember that planning is necessary, but over-planning can lead to an artificial environment. Keep your plan flexible and dynamic, while always remaining sensitive to the changing needs of the students. Teachers can often maintain long-term yearly plans, while having to alter unit or weekly plans because of unexpected learning issues.

Our goals are supported by specific plans each day.

Another point to consider is how teachers obtain information on goal progress. There are many information sources a teacher can use to understand student progress. Student grades, the amount of time they spend on a task, the number of times they use classroom resources, content of answers, and general interest level are all tools a teacher can use to gather information on goal progress. It is also important to consider the tools used to manage time effectively. Teachers can use time management tools like calendars and computers to lay out a curricular plan. They can also use journals and notebooks to detail specifics regarding plan implementation. Securing necessary resources like library time, books, or activities are also important in forming a curricular plan. Finally, as mentioned in the first section of the chapter, goals need to have clear criteria by which success can be judged. This might be a quantitative measure like grades, but may also be more programmatic, like how well a particular plan works within the mission of the department's curriculum plan. With careful attention to these elements, teachers can help ensure that their goals and objectives lead to success.

Topic Selection and Lesson Plans

In every field of study, there is far more information to learn than can reasonably be taught during a school year. Teachers face this fact throughout their careers. Choices need to be made regarding which topics warrant investigation for *these* students, *this* particular year. The decisions are not always easy or clear. Some topics may seem more interesting but are tangential to the district-approved curriculum. Other topics are too complex and would take too much time. Given these issues, teachers need to make decisions about what topics meet curricular goals and can be appropriately covered in the time allotted (Lai & Lam, 2011). Grant Wiggins and Jay McTighe (Wiggins & McTighe, 2005) developed Figure 14.5 to help teachers make decisions about what should be taught.

The outermost circle represents the accumulated knowledge of a particular field. This information is far too broad to teach students in its entirety. The next circle represents information with which students may not develop any degree of proficiency, but exposure to it is important to their education. The next circle represents core curriculum elements. It is information that students should learn and with which they should be able to demonstrate their proficiency. The innermost circle represents the main concepts a student is likely to take away with them as they move on to the next grade. It is the enduring elements of a topic area. Thinking of content

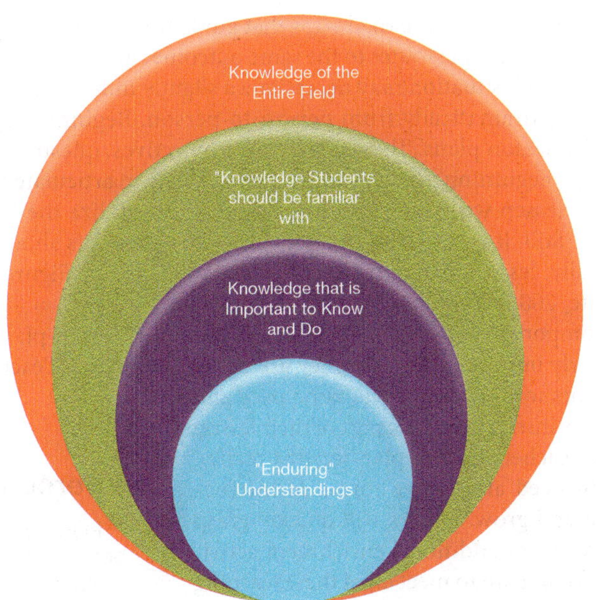

Figure 14.5
Deciding What to Teach

in this way helps teachers make decisions about what to teach. Some decisions may be made at the department, school, or district level. Teachers, however, will always be responsible for making the everyday decisions about how to present content; therefore, they have an inherent responsibility for topic choices.

In addition to the conceptual framework demonstrated by the figure above, Wiggins and McTighe (2005) also provided several questions teachers should ask to help determine appropriate instructional topics (Figure 14.6).

Answers to these questions give teachers information about how to prioritize the information in the field. This allows them to determine which topics provide broad exposure, which are learned in detail, and which are summarized as fundamental concepts. This organizes the information for the teacher and the student.

Once teachers determine what topics to cover, and in what depth, they next need to develop a specific lesson plan. **Lesson plans** are guides to aid teachers during instruction. The concept of a *guide* is important (Calderhead, 1996). Lesson plans are not prescriptions that

Lesson plans
Guides to aid teachers during instruction

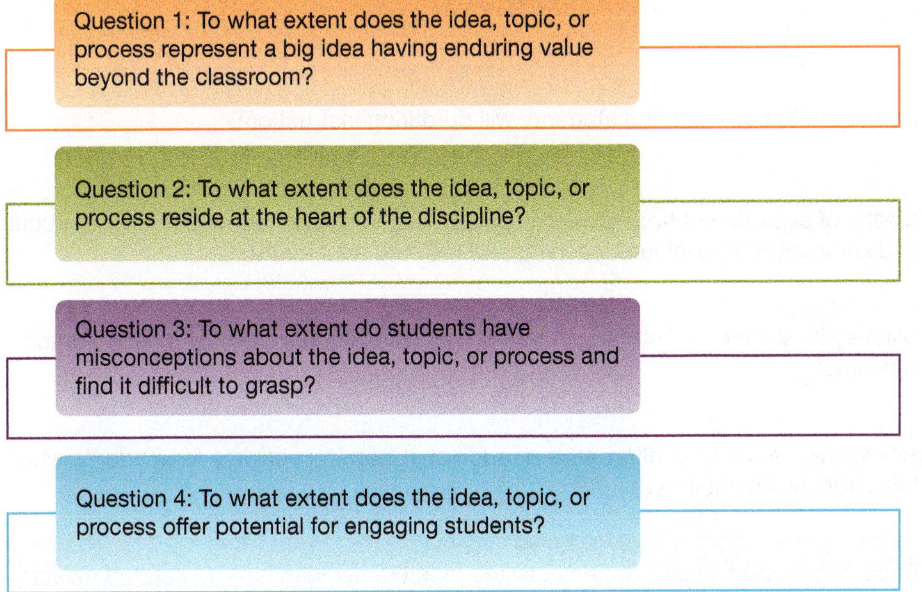

Figure 14.6
Questions Teachers Should Ask to Help Determine Appropriate Instructional Topics

have to be followed exactly. They are roadmaps that guide teachers toward particular learning outcomes. There may be multiple routes to the same outcome (just like there are multiple roads to the same city), and each situation may necessitate a slightly different path.

Lesson plans very dramatically from person-to-person. Beginning teachers frequently develop very detailed lesson plans. They may include objectives, questions, activities, assessments, resources, etc. Beginning teachers are also more likely to articulate their detailed plans on paper. This may lessen with experience as teachers internalize the lesson plan process (Calderhead, 1996). Still, it is important to consider what elements should be included in a lesson plan. Typically, lesson plans include the elements listed in Figure 14.7 (Curriculum Leadership Institute, 2003).

All of these components are critical for a well-developed lesson plan, but the final two points are particularly important because they are often overlooked. Teachers should not assume that all students would learn at the same pace and benefit from the same instruction. As a part of their lesson plan development, teachers should plan for this reality. Some students will need alternative forms of instruction to understand and grow. Others will quickly grasp the lesson and be ready for additional enrichment activities. Teachers should prepare to meet all of these learning needs. This idea of individual variation and shared education is covered in detail in Chapter 8.

Interconnections

Individual differences between students and the impact on education is covered in Chapter 8.

Integrated and Thematic Learning

A final point to consider in this section is the extent to which lesson planning should be managed in conjunction with other educational professionals (Theoharis & Causton-Theoharis, 2011). As we have seen in this textbook, there are many advantages to approaching education from an interdisciplinary perspective. This philosophy also applies to specific lesson plans. There are many opportunities for teachers to coordinate instruction with colleagues (Roskos & Neuman, 1993; Cassady, 2003; Gilbert, Schilt, & Ekland-Olson, 2005). Learning in real life

Figure 14.7

Elements Typically Included in a Lesson Plan

Outcome component (what students will be able to do or show they know at the end of instruction)

Teaching methods and resources needed (what the teacher will do and use during instruction)

Student activities (what the students will do during instruction)

Means of assessment (formative, to evaluate teaching and learning during instruction; and summative, to evaluate teaching and learning after instruction).

Mastery level (how well students must do on assessments to show mastery of the outcome)

Re-teaching strategies (alternative or additional learning activites for students who have not shown mastery)

Enrichments (additional learning activites for students who have exceeded mastery level)

is not isolated or removed from the everyday act of living. When you learn to drive a car for the first time, it is contextualized in the rich facets of a dynamic, ongoing life. The nature of the context helps to shape and guide learning in unique ways. The same is true for learning in traditional education settings. Everything from learning to read, spell, divide, investigate, play music, or swim is contextualized in the student's complex life. Educators are beginning to create lesson plans that closely mirror this contextualized learning environment. For example, learning about the anatomy of a frog does not have to be limited to science class. The teacher can integrate the lesson into other areas of learning, creating a richer, more realistic learning experience. Learning about frog anatomy may raise questions about life in general. This could be anticipated and incorporated into a philosophical lesson on what constitutes "life." It is also an opportunity for students to write about their learning. The anatomy lesson can be used as a topic for writing in an English class. Additionally, the physical education teacher can underscore the importance of learning anatomy to help build an understanding of how we use our physical bodies to play sports or engage in leisure activities. These are all connections that many students make naturally, but integrating lesson plans on the topic helps students learn to make these connections more effectively. Not all lesson plans need this level of elaboration, but teachers should always be thoughtful about how lessons can be geared around a particular theme and integrated into a wider learning objective.

Interconnections

The interdisciplinary perspective is introduced in Chapter 1.

SUMMARIZE AND REFLECT

1. Putting an instructional plan into effect takes time and creativity. Teachers also need to balance the timeline for realizing plan goals.
2. Some goals are reached in a relatively short period of time (perhaps daily), while other goals are achieved slowly over the academic year. Teachers need to consider these issues when implementing an instructional plan.
3. Topic selection is also crucial to academic success. Teachers do not need to cover every aspect of a topic. They need to be thoughtful, making decisions about what to cover and in what depth.
4. District, as well as state and federal mandates affect all teachers' instructional decisions. Ultimately, however, the teacher develops the lesson plan and shapes the nature of the learning environment.
5. The final part of this section looked at integrating a given lesson with other educational professionals. Today's teachers are making significant efforts to present information in an integrated, holistic fashion. This approach more closely mirrors the way students process information in the real world.
6. Teachers from different departments can co-develop different topics, each bringing a unique perspective to a common theme. Students benefit from this coordinated approach and reach a deeper level of understanding.

INFORMED APPLICATION

1. Describe how teachers from different departments can coordinate a lesson on the Supreme Court of the United States of America.

INSTRUCTIONAL DELIVERY

The first two sections of this chapter discussed how to establish clear educational goals and how to manage those goals to produce effective learning. This section will continue our exploration of the instructional process by looking at various factors that impact the quality of the instructional environment. Even the best learning objectives, supported by creative and well-developed lesson plans, can be further enhanced by closely examining the learning environment. We will first look at the role of the teacher in the learning equation, reviewing key qualities important for successful learning. Second, we will examine environmental factors that help support a student's ability to meet educational goals.

Teacher Qualities

The personal qualities of the teacher are sometimes overlooked or underappreciated as an element of the educational environment. Teachers, however, are all unique individuals and their differences impact learning. Some teachers have excellent knowledge of their content area, but encounter difficulty when engaging students to learn because of their organizational abilities. Similarly, some teachers are naturally outgoing, charismatic individuals who easily capture the attention of the students, but may fail to establish appropriate levels of expectation. The result is that although students enjoy the class, they may not learn up to their ability. Teacher qualities are relevant and important aspects of education (Hollins, 2011). Successful teachers create a balance between their individual strengths and weakness so that the whole person is an effective professional.

A teacher's qualities are important aspects of education.

Content Knowledge

It almost seems unnecessary to say that good teachers have a well-developed knowledge of their subject area. Well-developed content knowledge certainly appears to be a major focus of teacher certification programs and state/federal guidelines for teacher certification. Currently, schools receiving federal funding must demonstrate that teachers are "highly qualified" in the subjects they teach. States vary in how they make this determination, but it is typically based on a combination of education, experience, and professional development. Interestingly, there is also some evidence that in math courses taught by teachers with the most math coursework, students achieve higher levels of achievement (Wayne & Youngs, 2003).

There is growing concern, however, that we are so heavily focused on content expertise that we are forgetting teachers also have to be able to *teach*. One study surveyed principals regarding this issue and found that there is a strong perception that instructor ineffectiveness is caused by a lack of instructional expertise, not content knowledge (Torff & Sessions, 2005). The study noted that problems with classroom management, lesson implementation, and student rapport were more significant concerns than content knowledge. It is likely that both content knowledge and instructional knowledge factor into teacher effectiveness. Teachers who have developed appropriate levels of content knowledge but still struggle with helping their students achieve should recognize that achievement is sensitive to multiple teacher qualities and explore other areas for continued growth.

Organization

Organizational ability is an important part of teaching (Ebert, Ebert, & Bentley, 2011). It impacts the way teachers relate to their students. Students enjoy organized lessons and benefit from the clarity that comes from well-organized lessons (Land, 1987). Spending the necessary time to organize a lesson helps teachers clarify for themselves the important elements of the lesson. This in turn leads to a clearer presentation of the material. Giving students vague or ill-defined lessons creates confusion and less engagement. The other important aspect of being an organized teacher is that it helps support positive interactions with other teachers and administrators. Teachers who appear organized are more likely to be seen as leaders and effective educational professionals. It impacts the way they interact and are perceived by other educational professionals. As this book consistently emphasizes, collaboration between teachers is being used more frequently to produce effective and comprehensive learning. Collaboration, however, is not easy and organized teachers are crucial for collaborative success.

Self-fulfilling prophecy

Idea that what the teacher initially expects is reinforced and becomes a reality

Expectations

Being organized affects the way teachers relate to their students.

Consider a teacher getting to know a student at the beginning of the school year. The student seems bright and friendly. He/she easily participates in class. The teacher knows the student's older brother, who was an exceptional student, from a previous year. This situation is part of the process of getting to know students, and it shapes what the teacher expects from the student. In this case, the teacher is likely to have high expectations for the student. Researchers have been concerned about whether these expectations actually produce changes in student behavior or achievement (Good & Brophy, 1987; Oaks & Lipton, 2007). Figure 14.8 shows how a teacher's expectations might cause corresponding changes in student behavior (Arends, 2007).

As you can see from the figure, what begins as an expectation from the teacher begins a cycle of action and re-action that supports continuation of the initial expectation. This has often been referred to as a **self-fulfilling prophecy**. This means that what the teacher initially expects is reinforced and becomes a reality. A related issue is the **sustaining expectation effect**. This effect occurs when a teacher initially creates an accurate expectation for a student's behavior or achievement, but fails to adjust that expectation if the student begins to perform contrary to the expectation. For example, a teacher may initially establish low expectations for a student who is struggling with learning. The source of the student's difficulties is a problem at home that resolves soon after the beginning of the school year. The student begins to show greater ability, but the teacher still maintains their earlier perceptions.

Sustaining expectation effect

When a teacher initially creates an accurate expectation for a student's behavior or achievement, but then fails to adjust that expectation if the student begins to perform contrary to the expectation

Both of these expectation effects are problematic. They indicate a lack of sensitivity on the part of the teacher. The teacher is not responding to students in a dynamic, flexible manner.

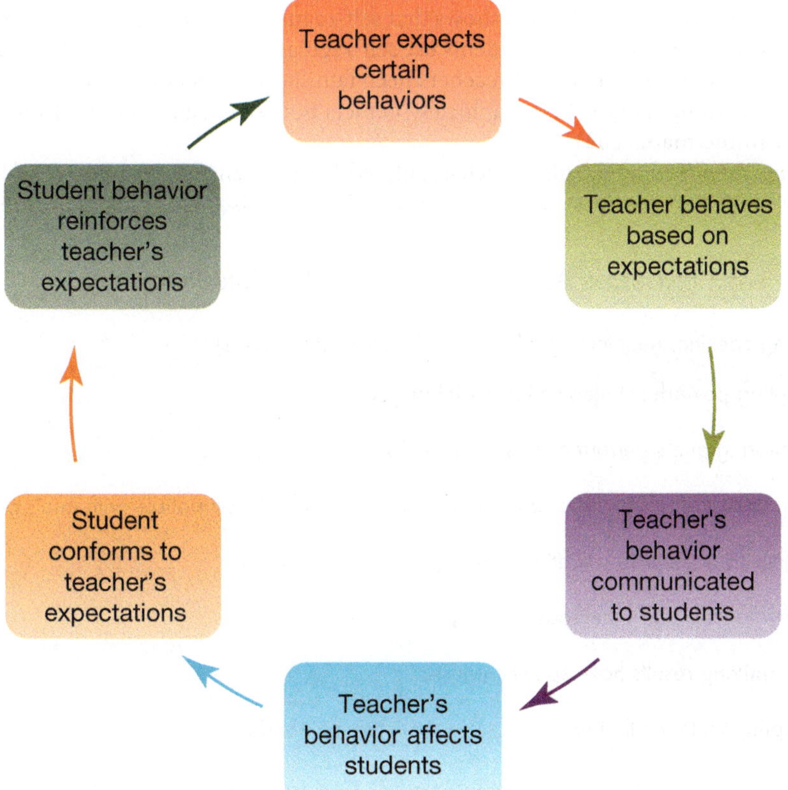

Figure 14.8

The Effects of Teacher Expectations on Student Behavior

Research on these effects is complicated. Some studies show expectation effects, but it appears that it may interact with the age of the student (Kuklinski & Weinstein, 2001). For example, the self-fulfilling prophecy seems greatest in early grades, whereas the sustaining effects are greatest in later grades.

Effective Instruction

The next aspect of instructional delivery we will consider is effective instruction. There are countless instructional tools teachers can use to help students learn. Everything from the type of textbook they use, assignments they give, and their use of technology has the potential to enhance instruction. Let's look at a few of these types of factors.

Encouraging Self-Direction

Self-regulated learning

The self-directed process by which learners transform their mental abilities into academic skills

We typically focus on how the teacher can better deliver the curriculum when discussing effective instruction, but one of the most significant ways to enhance learning is to instruct students in how to regulate their own learning. **Self-regulated learning** is the self-directed process by which learners transform their mental abilities into academic skills (Zimmerman, 2002). It is more than a simple academic skill; it refers to the collective group of self-generated thoughts, feelings, and behaviors that orient an individual toward a goal (Klug, Ogrin, Keller, Ihringer, & Schmitz, 2011). Table 14.8 lists the major processes associated with self-regulated learning (Zimmerman, 2002).

Students with well-developed self-regulation ability use these processes in a proactive way. They are also able to adapt these processes to meet their individual needs.

Developing self-regulation is important because it sets the stage for becoming an effective life-long learner. During the school years, a teacher may be able to externally regulate environmental factors to achieve some of these outcomes. This, however, does not always occur; and it does not enable the student to continue to learn once they graduate and no longer have the daily support of a teacher. Research shows that a student's level of learning depends on the set of processes in the table above (Schunk & Zimmerman, 1994; Schunk & Zimmerman, 1998). Research also shows that teachers can instruct students in the self-regulatory process and that such instruction increases student motivation and achievement (Schunk & Zimmerman, 1998). This shows that self-regulation is important for students and also that teachers can impact how students use self-regulation processes. To help students use the processes detailed in Table 14.7, teachers need familiarity with how these processes function during learning. Figure 14.9 graphically depicts how self-regulation works to produce learning (Zimmerman, 2002).

During the forethought phase, self-regulated learners engage in analysis of the task, including goal setting and strategic planning. They are also invested in emotional and

Table 14.8 Processes Associated with Self-Regulated Learning

A – Setting specific, near-term goals (rather than long-term goals)
B – Adopting powerful strategies for attaining goals
C – Monitoring one's performance selectively for signs of progress
D – Restructuring one's physical and social context to make it compatible with one's goals
E – Managing one's time use efficiently
F – Self-evaluating one's methods
G – Recognizing results have specific causes
H – Adapting methods that you will use in the future as needed

Adapted from Zimmerman, 2002.

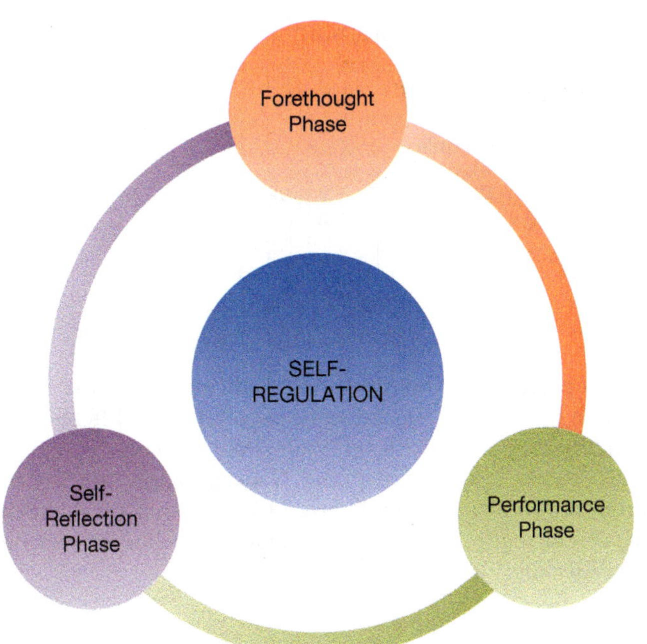

Figure 14.9

How the Processes Associated with Self-Regulated Learning Function During Learning

motivational thinking that supports goal attainment, such as a belief in themselves as capable (self-efficacy) and an emphasis on the inherent value of the task (rather than external reward). During the performance phase, focus is on processes supporting task engagement and completion. This includes appropriate levels of self-instruction, strategies to focus attention, and strategies that are unique to the given task. Also during the performance phase it is important to record your own progress and to experiment with techniques for enhancing performance. The final phase is the self-reflection phase. During this phase, emphasis is on understanding that outcomes have causes and that understanding those causes helps facilitate future performance. This is explored through self-evaluation. Evaluation should remain positive and focused on adaptive reactions. **Adaptive reactions** are adjustments that increase performance and are contrasted with **defensive reactions,** which can cause learners to withdraw from the task.

Adaptive reactions

Adjustment that increases performance

Defensive reactions

Action that causes learners to withdraw from the task

An understanding of the phases of self-regulation, combined with basic self-regulation process, helps teachers guide students toward higher levels of self-regulation. Self-regulation is often mistaken as a solitary process. Teachers, parents, and even peers are important sources of information regarding self-regulation. They can serve as models, helping to nurture movement toward greater levels of self-regulatory behavior and achievement.

Concept Learning

Concept learning refers to learning that centers on acquiring the basic concepts, which form the basis for additional learning and higher-level thinking. It is basically learning what it means to be a member of a class and then recognizing members of that class. For example, you may learn the concept of a *prepositional phrase* in English class when your teacher provides an explanation of the concept and provides several examples.

Concept learning

Learning that centers on acquiring the basic concepts, which form the basis for additional learning and higher-level thinking

Teaching concept learning usually involves four basic processes (Arends, 2007), which are presented in Table 14.9. The first process establishes the basic framework for the concept. Some teachers prefer to accomplish this by giving students a formal presentation followed by clarification using examples. In the English lesson example presented above, the teacher would deliver a formal presentation on the prepositional phrase. This presentation would present what was expected in terms of learning and establish the *concept* of the prepositional phrase. Next, students would receive examples of a prepositional phrase. They would also receive examples of clauses that are often confused with prepositional phrases. These non-examples help to clarify the nature of the concept. Student-driven examples and perhaps a formal assessment of their understanding usually follows this step. The final step is to analyze student thinking for issues with establishing the concept. The teacher works closely with each

Table 14.9 Steps in Concept Learning

A – Present goals and establish the set
B – Input examples and non-examples
C – Test for concept attainment
D – Analyze student thought processes

Adapted from Arends, 2007.

student or small group going over examples. He might also break the students up into peer led groups to work on the concept. This often helps to bring up differences between learners and highlights potential problems with thinking about the concept. Another technique to use throughout this process is concept mapping. **Concept mapping** is the creation of a visual or graphical representation of a concept. Figure 14.10 is a simple concept map for fractions. Concept mapping can further help students work though the essential elements of a concept and produce better learning.

Concept mapping

The creation of a visual or graphical representation of a concept

Technology

The twenty-first century is poised to realize some of the most significant technological changes the world has ever seen. Technology has already created dramatic shifts in the way we work and play. Technology is also quickly finding its way into schools, altering the very nature of inquiry and the learning process. Never before has so much information been readily available to students and teachers. The communication improvements ushered in by technological revolutions like email, chat, and cellular communications is bringing down geographical barriers and connecting people like never before. Most researchers recognize that these changes are going to necessitate some sort of educational response (Brandt, 2000). This response is likely to be ongoing, but initial efforts attempt to bring structure to the educational response by providing standards. The International Society for Technology in Education (ISTE) has developed a set of standards for technological proficiencies in teacher education programs (Papa, 2011). These standards are an excellent foundation for developing a common set of expectations for teachers in terms of how technology interacts with their professional obligations. The standards (see Table 14.10) are comprehensive and provide reasonable expectations across a broad range of areas.

Figure 14.10

Simple Concept Map for Fractions

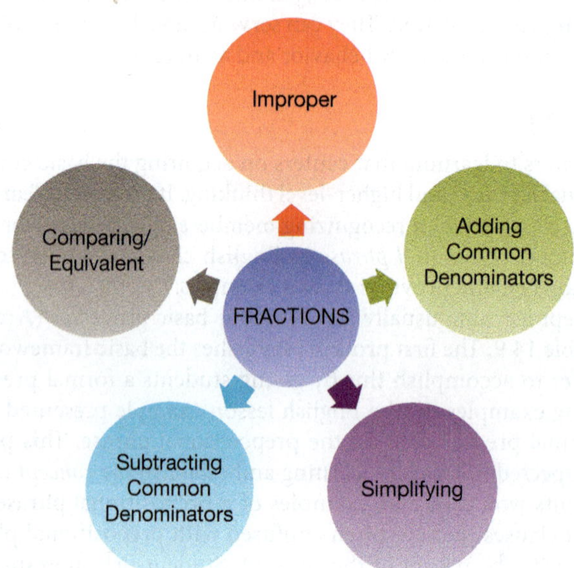

Table 14.10 Performance Indicators for Teachers

Effective teachers model and apply the National Educational Technology Standards for Students (NETS•S) as they design, implement, and assess learning experiences to engage students and improve learning; enrich professional practice; and provide positive models for students, colleagues, and the community. All teachers should meet the following standards and performance indicators.

1. Facilitate and Inspire Student Learning and Creativity
Teachers use their knowledge of subject matter, teaching, and learning, and technology to facilitate experiences that advance student learning, creativity, and innovation in both face-to-face and virtual environments. Teachers: a. promote, support, and model creative and innovative thinking and inventiveness b. engage students in exploring real-world issues and solving authentic problems using digital tools and resources c. promote student reflection using collaborative tools to reveal and clarify students' conceptual understanding and thinking, planning, and creative processes d. model collaborative knowledge construction by engaging in learning with students, colleagues, and others in face-to-face and virtual environments
2. Design and Develop Digital-Age Learning Experiences and Assessments
Teachers design, develop, and evaluate authentic learning experiences and assesments, incorporating contemporary tools and resources to maximize content learning in context and to develop the knowledge, skills, and attitudes identified in the NETS•S. Teachers: a. design or adapt relevant learning experiences that incorporate digital tools and resources to promote student learning and creativity b. develop technology-enriched learning environments that enable all students to pursue their individual curiosities and become active participants in setting their own educational goals, managing their own learning, and assessing their own progress c. customize and personalize learning activities to address students' diverse learning styles, working strategies, and abilities using digital tools and resources d. provide students with multiple and varied formative and summative assessments aligned with content and technology standards and use resulting data to inform learning and teaching
3. Model Digital-Age Work and Learning
Teachers exhibit knowledge, skills, and work processes representative of an innovative professional in a global and digital society. Teachers: a. demonstrate fluency in technology systems and the transfer of current knowledge to new technologies and situations b. collaborate with students, peers, parents, and community members using digital tools and resources to support student success and innovation c. communicate relevant information and ideas effectively to students, parents, and peers using a variety of digital-age media and formats d. model and facilitate effective use of current and emerging digital tools to locate, analyze, evaluate, and use information resources to support research and learning
4. Promote and Model Digital Citizenship and Responsibility
Teachers understand local and global societal issues and responsibilities in an evolving digital culture and exhibit legal and ethical behavior in their professional practices. Teachers: a. Apply technology to facilitate a variety of effective assessment and evaluation strategies b. Apply technology in assessing student learning of subject matter using a variety of assessment techniques c. Use technology resources to collect and analyze data, interpret results, and communicate findings to improve instructional practice and maximize student learning d. Apply multiple methods of evaluation to determine students' appropriate use of technology resources for learning, communication, and productivity

(continues)

Table 14.10 Performance Indicators for Teachers *(Continued)*

5. Engage in Professional Growth and Leadership
Teachers continuously improve their professional practice, model lifelong learning, and exhibit leadership in their school and professional community by promoting and demonstrating the effective use of digital tools and resources. Teachers:
a. participate in local and global learning communities to explore creative applications of technology to improve student learning
b. exhibit leadership by demonstrating a vision of technology infusion, participating in shared decision making and community building, and developing the leadership and technology skills of others
c. evaluate and reflect on current research and professional practice on a regular basis to make effective use of existing and emerging digital tools and resources in support of student learning
d. contribute to the effectiveness, vitality, and self-renewal of the teaching profession and of their school and community

SUMMARIZE AND REFLECT

1. Instructional delivery is a complex synthesis of many educational elements. In this section, we began our look at instructional delivery by examining the importance of certain teacher qualities.
2. Teachers with excellent content knowledge, organizational ability, and appropriate student expectations produce effective instruction. Teachers who have a genuine understanding of their subject area go beyond facts. They have a deep appreciation of the unique learning path for that subject matter.
3. Teachers are also well organized. They are thoughtful, reflective, and prepared to present lessons in a way that is logical and engaging.
4. Appropriate expectations are also important. Expectations from a teacher set the stage for enhanced learning or passive withdrawal. Teachers need to set high and obtainable expectations for all students.
5. Encouraging students to direct their own learning is another important element of instruction. Self-directed learning involves several elements, each of which centers ownership of the learning process on the student.
6. Another element of effective instruction is the successful teaching of core educational concepts. Concept learning is an approach that emphasizes communication of concepts through examples and non-examples, giving students a solid foundation for future learning.
7. Technology is another tool to help any instructional approach. Recent technological advances have forever changed the nature of instruction. Standards are evolving to help guide this rapid change.

INFORMED APPLICATION

1. Contrast a teaching model that focuses on student ownership of learning with the more traditional approaches that emphasizes the teacher as driving learning.

MODELS OF TEACHING AND LEARNING

The first three sections of this chapter examined instructional excellence in terms of developing a sound educational plan, managing that plan during the school year, and delivering the plan in effective ways. This final section looks at different philosophical approaches to instruction that have had solid research support. These *models of teaching* are essentially teaching perspectives that inform our educational practice. The goal is to broaden your knowledge about teaching approaches and the relative merits of using a particular approach for a given learning objective.

Social Cognitive Approaches to Instruction

The first model of teaching we will consider is the social cognitive approach. It is a model that emphasizes learning through cooperative social interactions. All too often, social interactions in school are competitive, as students attempt to perform well relative to their peers. Historically, this was viewed as a positive source of motivation; however, current research suggests that working in a cooperative way with peers toward a common goal is more motivating and produces greater learning (Johnson & Johnson, 1995; Johnson, Johnson, & Smith, 1995).

Social Negotiation

Learning in cooperation with peers and teachers requires an ability to socially negotiate the often challenging dynamics of group work. It necessitates that students frame cooperation in a positive way. All too often, students in traditional school settings interact in competitive and negative ways. **Negative interdependence** refers to social processes that are competitive and operate at the expense of others. An alternative approach uses cooperative groups that emphasize positive social interactions. **Positive interdependence** refers to the positive qualities that come out of effective group work. Groups that work together to achieve a goal rely on each other to succeed. The success of the group is dependent upon productive interactions between group members. In this context, interdependence is framed in a positive way as students strive to work collaboratively to produce desirable results (Johnson & Johnson, 1998). There are four basic processes underlying cooperative work (Joyce, Weil, & Calhoun, 2004). These processes are presented in Table 14.11.

Negative interdependence
Social interaction processes that are competitive and operate at the expense of others

Positive interdependence
The positive qualities that come out of effective group work

Table 14.11 Assumptions Underlying Cooperative Work

1. The combined energy generated in cooperative settings generates more motivation than individualistic and competitive environments. Integrative social groups are, in effect, more than the sum of their parts. The feelings of connectedness produce positive energy.
2. The members of cooperative groups learn from one another. Each learner has more helping hands than in a structure that generates isolations.
3. Interacting with one another produces cognitive as well as social complexity, creating more intellectual activity that increases learning when contrasted with solitary study.
4. Cooperation increases positive feelings toward one another—reducing alienation and loneliness, building relationships, and providing affirmative views of other people.
5. Cooperation increases self-esteem not only through increased learning but also through the feeling of being respected and cared for by the others in the environment.
6. Students can respond to experiences requiring cooperation by increasing their capacity to work productively together. In other words, the more children are given the opportunity to work together, the better they get, which benefits their general social skills.
7. Students, including primary school children, can learn from training to increase their ability to work together.

Adapted from Joyce, Weil, and Calhoun, 2004.

Cooperative Learning

Cooperative learning

Technique that involves groups of individuals working together to achieve a common goal

Cooperative learning is where groups of individuals work together to achieve a common goal. As suggested in the previous section, using this approach has proven to have a positive impact on many facets of educational life. As expected, cooperative learning has a positive impact on the level of cooperation students exhibit (Sharan, 1999; Johnson & Johnson, 1995). Students working in cooperative groups tend to exhibit stronger verbal and non-verbal skills. They also demonstrate less competitive behaviors. Another positive outcome of cooperative learning is greater tolerance for diversity. For example, students who regularly participate in cooperative learning lessons develop a greater tolerance for students with disabilities and have positive relationships with students from different ethnic backgrounds (Gilles, 2002; Vedder & Veendrick, 2003).

Another area consistently researched is the impact of cooperative tasks on academic achievement. Several review studies have been conducted covering dozens of individual studies (Downey, C. J., 2000; Slavin, 1995; Stronge, 2002). Collectively, these studies found overwhelming support for the positive impact of cooperative learning on academic achievement across many grades, subjects, and countries. In fact, none of the studies showed negative effects. There is also some evidence that experience with cooperative learning is related to higher levels of self-esteem, but the research in this particular area does not appear as conclusive (Slavin, 1995).

Working in cooperative groups comes naturally to students.

Working in cooperative groups is quite natural for students. Children and young adults spend much of their non-academic time socializing in groups, and thus engaging in an academically oriented social task is far from novel. They may, however, need guidance to increase efficiency. There are several ways to increase efficiency and create a sense of positive interdependence (Kagan, 1990; Johnson & Johnson, 1996). For example, members of the group often experience that the group members work unevenly. Some students naturally move toward doing the work for the whole group. A simple strategy to help address this problem is to assign each member of the group a number. Then give the group a task. After a period of time the teacher randomly calls on a number, and all students assigned that number have to stand up and summarize their group's progress. This keeps everyone in the group invested since no one knows who will be called on to report on the group's progress. A similar approach is to assign individual students specific roles in the overall process of the group. The **jigsaw approach** (Slavin, 1995) helps student achieve a given academic task by structuring what each student will be doing. This *division of labor* approach can be used to assign students roles they are comfortable with or can also be used as an opportunity to help students develop new social skills, putting them in novel roles.

Jigsaw approach

Learning technique that structures a given task by having each student achieve a portion of that academic task and, in so doing, contributes to completion of the whole

A final point to consider is the effect of group work on motivation. Some researchers have argued that cooperative work encourages students to move away from reliance on external sources of motivation, relying on internal sources instead (Sharan & Shaulov, 1990). Essentially what happens is that as students strive to collectively achieve a product, each student becomes invested because they are contributing to the assigned task. Their investment increases their valuation of the product. When the group achieves, they achieve on a personal level, which encourages a since of pride and a desire to learn. As you can see, there are many positive reasons to engage in cooperative work. It may not be appropriate in all settings or for all curricular goals, but it is a strong tool for supporting learning.

Information Processing Approaches to Instruction

The information processing approach to instruction differs from the social model because it is more individualistic. Rather than emphasize how learning is shaped by interactions with others, this approach is focused on how the *individual* approaches and solves problems. The goal of this approach is to enhance the ability of the learner through improving steps taken to solve problems. The learner is viewed as an active thinker, trying to solve problems through reason, rather than passively receiving knowledge from the teacher.

Inquiry and Problem-Based Learning

One of the information processing approaches to learning centers on the student addressing a specific question or line of inquiry. Teachers often use this approach in the sciences because the model closely follows classic scientific reasoning; however, the approach can be modified to any subject matter. The premise of the approach is that there is a question the students must answer. Sometimes the teacher is very active in *guiding* the student through the inquiry process; other times are *unguided* as students work independently. Either approach follows a similar set of steps (see Figure 14.11). The first step is to recognize there is a problem that is unsolved. Again, sometimes the teacher will frame the material for the student in this way. In a sense, they give the students the problem of interest. At other times, the teacher encourages the students to solve problems in an independent way as they come up in daily life. Once the problem is recognized, the student then develops a guess or hypothesis about what the solution or outcome to the problem will be. The hypothesis is an educated guess as to the outcome. The **hypothesis** should be testable. This means the student should be able to assess the merits of the hypothesis through investigation. Next, students devise an investigation or experiment, and then they collect data. This is followed by reflection on the data collected and whether or not it supports the hypothesis. Depending on the outcome of the data, the student comes to a conclusion regarding their understanding of the initial problem. Sometimes the student will need to repeat the investigation to confirm preliminary results or will need to redesign the method of investigation to better assess the original problem. Overall, this approach is an excellent technique to help students learn through inquiry.

Teachers use unguided times for the students to work independently.

Hypothesis

An educated guess as to the outcome

Another related approach is called problem-based learning. **Problem-based learning (PBL)** is a learning approach grounded in scientific inquiry. It encourages the basic tenets of inquiry presented above. Additionally, it presents problems in a real-world context. This means that the problems are inherently meaningful to the students because they are derived from problems in everyday life. The problems investigated under this approach are also complex, in the sense that they mirror the complexity inherent in real-life. They are not scaled down issues presented in a simplified way to ease understanding. They are comprehensive and challenging and ultimately help students learn to problem solve in better ways in their own lives (Jonassen, Howland, Moore, & Marra, 2003; Hung, 2002).

Problem-based learning (PBL)

Learning approach grounded in scientific inquiry

Advanced Organizers

Today's schools are taking steps to move away from exclusively relying on traditional lecture and reading (expository) approaches to instruction. Teachers across all grades and subjects are beginning to embrace the value in bringing students together in smaller social groups and engaging in problem solving. This, however, does not mean that more traditional methods of instruction have no place in tomorrow's classrooms. Some researchers argue that using lectures can produce effective, long-lasting learning depending on how the material is presented. One technique to enhance traditional lecture approaches is to use an advanced organizer to help prepare student for new information. An **advanced organizer** is any introductory material pre sented at a higher level of abstraction and inclusiveness than the learning task itself (Ausubel, 1963; Ausubel, 1980). The idea is that lectures only take on a passive, ineffective quality when the students are not sufficiently prepared to receive the material. An advanced organizer provides such preparation. It gives students the broad, theoretical framework for the upcoming information. It highlights the necessary cognitive structures to understand the more specific

Advanced organizer

Any introductory material presented at a higher level of abstraction and inclusiveness than the learning task itself

Figure 14.11
The Steps Involved in Inquiry and Problem-Based Learning

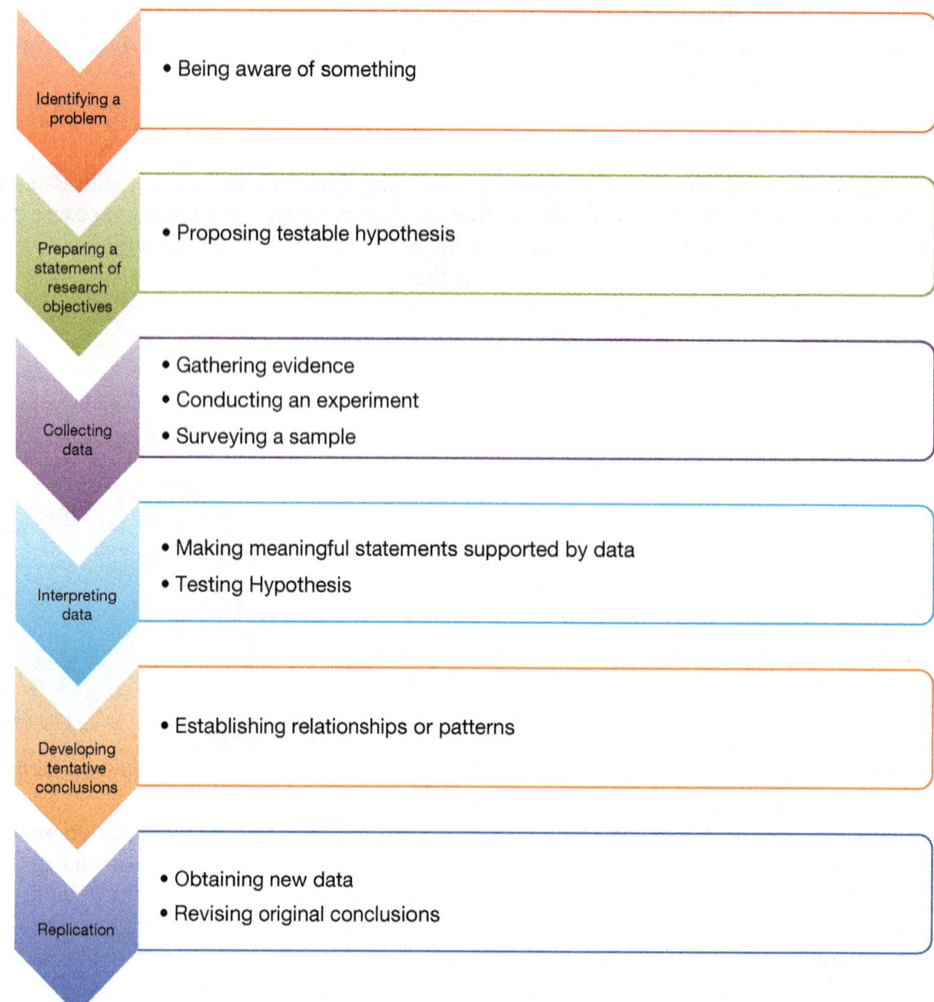

SOURCE: From Orlich, Harder, Callahan, Kauchak, and Gibson, 1994.

lecture material to come. It is a *top-down process,* whereby the teacher first directly instructs the students in the larger concepts inherent in the lecture material. This creates a mental set that lays the groundwork for the more specific lecture material. Figure 14.12 shows how a teacher can use a graphical display to create an advanced organizer for an upcoming English lesson on synonyms and antonyms. You may notice that the figure resembles the concept maps discussed earlier in the chapter. The important difference is that an advanced organizer may include many concepts. Additionally, it is not necessarily graphic, as many advanced organizers are just sentences or phrases in a list or hierarchy.

Behavioral Approaches to Instruction

Behaviorists (Chapter 4) have a long-standing history in psychology and education. Their theories have guided much of public thinking about psychology and research for decades. Their success is due in large part to the clarity their theories brought to our thinking about human behavior. Behavioral theories moved us away from hidden unconscious processes and focused on behavioral explanations that were observable. This gave the appearance of greater scientific objectivity and helped parents and schools alike adopt behavioral principles. The behaviorist movement, however, began to lose its preeminence toward the end of the 1960s when psychologists and educators began to focus on more internal processes, like a child's wants and needs, and how children process information. Despite this movement away from a strong focus on behavioral theories, they still play a significant role in our schools. There are many instructional

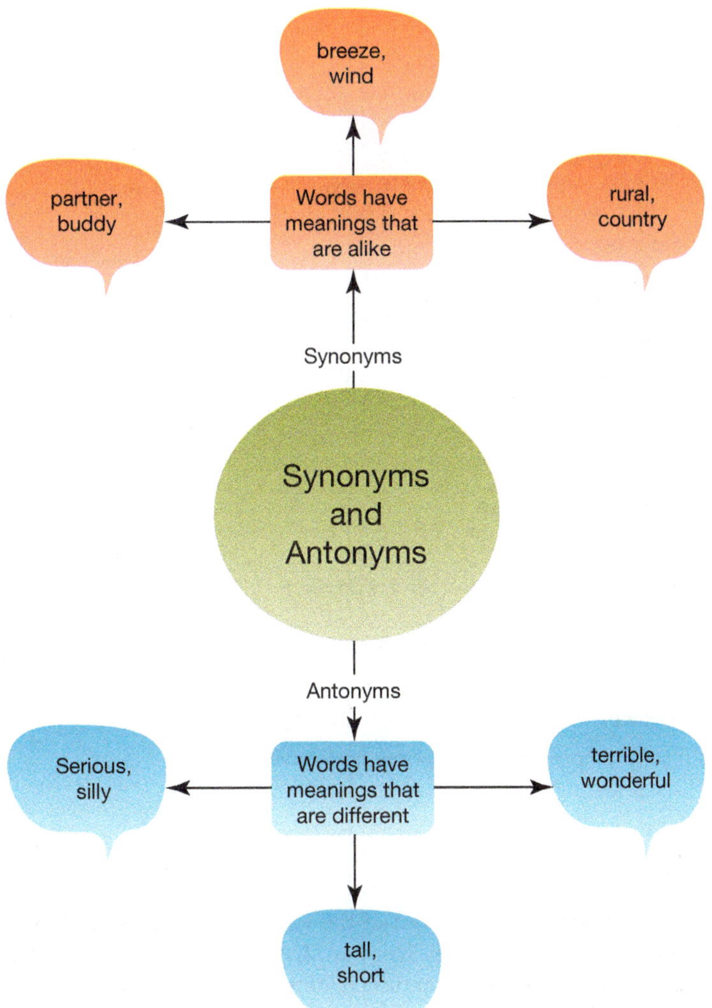

Figure 14.12

Graphical Display of an Advanced Organizer

models that are derived from the principles of behaviorism. We will examine two of the most prominent, direct instruction and mastery learning.

Direct Instruction

Direct instruction (DI) is a highly structured, teacher-centered, form of instruction. It involves basic reinforcement principles of behavioral theory and is used for a variety of subject and skill areas. DI is often used to support the development of reading, math computation, and grammar rules. These basic skills respond well to the structured nature of the approach (Rosenshine & Stevens, 1986). The process of DI consists of four phases. These phases are presented in Table 14.12.

Direct instruction (DI)

A highly structured, teacher-centered, form of instruction

The step-by-step nature of DI leads to a clear foundation of information. Students are given many opportunities to become familiar with the lesson objectives, practice skills, and benefit from constructive feedback. The approach is, however, not without its critics. Some have argued that the explicit nature of the approach combined with its strong emphasis on teacher centered instruction puts the student in the position of being passive recipients of information, rather than active learners (Driscoll, 2005). Still, there is evidence that DI can be an effective tool to help students learn and achieve (Dole, Valencia, Greer, & Wardrop, 1991; Din, 2000). Teachers need to consider the nature of the curricular task, the value of explicit instruction over self-discovery, and the particular student. Not all lessons are appropriate for DI. Similarly, not all students have personal qualities that lend themselves to a DI approach. When used appropriately, however, DI can be an effective tool for helping students achieve.

Table 14.12 The Process of Direct Instruction (DI)

Phase One: Orientation
Teacher establishes content of the lesson.
Teacher reviews previous learning.
Teacher establishes lesson objectives.
Teacher establishes the procedures for the lesson.
Phase Two: Presentation
Teacher explains/demonstrates new concepts or skill.
Teacher provides visual representation of the task.
Teacher checks for understanding.
Phase Three: Structured Practice
Teacher leads group through practice examples in lock step.
Students respond to questions.
Teacher provides corrective feedback for errors and reinforces correct practice.
Phase Four: Guided Practice
Students practice semi-independently.
Teacher circulates, monitoring student practice.
Teacher provides feedback through praise, prompts, and appropriate correctives.

Adapted from Joyce, Weil, & Calhoun, 2004.

Mastery Learning

The idea of mastery learning evolved out of the work of John Carroll (1963). Carroll advocated that schools should move away from an instructional model where all students are given the same amount of instructional time. Doing so led to performance differences due to inherent differences in ability. Instead of this approach, he suggested that teachers adjust the instruction time necessary for each student so that all students could achieve a similar level of mastery. Some students will need more learning time to achieve the same level of learning. Later, Carroll's work was expanded by Benjamin Bloom (*All Our Children Learning,* 1981) and came to be known as Mastery Learning. **Mastery learning** is an approach to instruction built on the idea that given enough time and proper instruction, nearly all students can successfully master instructional objectives. Mastery learning approaches typically have the following qualities in common:

Mastery learning

An approach to instruction built on the idea that given enough time and proper instruction, nearly all students can successfully master instructional objectives

1. Instructional objectives are presented to the student in a clear, coherent manner.
2. The learning path for the specific lesson is divided into small, manageable learning units. Each unit has specific objectives and is assessed to determine appropriate levels of mastery. The following are used as needed to reach mastery:
   a. Development of new teaching methods
   b. Modeling
   c. Re-teaching
   d. Formative and summative evaluations (Chapter 9)
   e. Reinforcement
3. Assessments are used to guide the learning path (formative) and to determine mastery (summative).

Mastery Learning is an important instructional technique, particularly for those skills that serve as a foundation for future learning. It establishes a firm foundation from which students can continue to learn and grow. It is also important for the teacher. It necessitates the teacher carefully think about the learning process for each student. The teacher must be active with instruction and sensitive to the unique learning needs of each student. Despite these advantages, Mastery Learning is still not widely used. It can be difficult for a teacher to develop the necessary learning materials to teach a wide variety of students to mastery. It is also difficult because schools demand that teachers adhere to a rigid instructional schedule. This makes it challenging for teachers to give struggling students the necessary time to learn to mastery.

Individual Differences Approaches to Instruction

The final instructional approach we will consider is more a philosophy than a specific type of instruction. This approach is characterized by an emphasis on providing instructional environments that are focused on meeting the individual needs of each student. Students are assumed to bring with them a wide variety of individual differences that impact their educational path. Teachers using an individual differences approach to education are mindful of these unique qualities and ensure that each student is receiving the instructional supports necessary for success. In this section, we will take a look at two related instructional approaches from this perspective. The **equity instruction** approach emphasizes a variety of gender, socioeconomic, and cultural factors and how they impact education. The learning styles approach emphasizes cognition and the different ways we learn and understand information.

Equity instruction

Technique that strives to educate students in a way that is sensitive to their unique qualities

Equity Instruction

Students bring to the classroom a vast array of qualities. It is what makes each individual truly unique. Many of these differences can, however, be looked at in a collective way for purposes of understanding the nature of that particular difference and its impact on the educational process. For example, Farrah is a fifteen-year-old girl in the tenth grade in an urban Chicago school. Her particular life circumstance (chaotic home life, parental separation, low income) may impact her education in a variety of ways. We can specifically focus on one aspect of her life circumstance and try to understand its unique contribution to her academic success. Gender is one such factor. How does being a girl impact learning? We can look for trends related to gender and education. This process of grouping some of our differences so that we can recognize the impact of that particular characteristic on education is at the heart of equity instruction. Equity instruction strives to educate students in a way that is sensitive to their unique qualities. It is instruction differentiated according to gender, socioeconomic, and cultural qualities. It rejects the idea that one educational approach will effectively support the development of all students and affirms the idea that it is through an appreciation of the individual that maximal learning occurs. Research in this area is often controversial and hotly debated. As reviewed in Chapter 8, there are many studies supporting differences in education between boys and girls, ethnic groups, and family structure.

Instructional remedies are far-reaching and often subtle, but an appreciation of potential inequitable treatment of students can make a difference. For example, historically males were much more likely to take advanced science and math courses. This was true even when girls had similar prerequisite knowledge. This gap, however, has narrowed substantially through school policy, student counseling, and a general shift in societal views of math and science and gender (Davenport et al., 1998). It is important to begin with a basic assumption that all students can learn in the right circumstance. From this premise, teachers invested in equitable instruction strive to creatively meet the needs of each student.

Learning Styles

Another dimension of difference addressed by individual difference instructional approaches is cognitive or learning ability. It is clear to any teacher that students vary in their capacity to learn new material and benefit from instruction. As was mentioned in the previous section, what is important is that teachers approach instruction with a fundamental belief that everyone can learn. Teaching from this model necessitates acknowledgement that not all students

Learning styles

Instruction that focuses on the interaction between learner characteristics and the specific learning task

learn best in all environments. In other words, some students will need a particular learning approach to understand the material. **Learning styles** instruction focuses on the interaction between learner characteristics and the specific learning task (Harrison, Andrews, & Saklofske, 2003). Some critics of this approach argue that although there is an intuitive appeal to the approach, there isn't a scientific body of evidence supporting its positive effect on achievement (Olson, 2006; Mayer & Massa, 2003). Other research shows that teaching according to preferred learning style can positively impact attitude toward the subject (Farkas, 2003). In this study, teachers specifically taught a lesson on the Holocaust from the learning styles instructional method compared to traditional approaches, and they found increases in empathy and positive attitude toward the subject matter when instruction followed a learning styles approach. It is clear that more research needs to be conducted in this area to better understand how attitudinal factors interact with achievement.

SUMMARIZE AND REFLECT

1. This section reviews four different perspectives on teaching and learning.
2. The social perspective on learning emphasizes the importance of successful social negotiations. Social skills are similar to other learning material and can be taught explicitly to improve performance.
3. Cooperative learning is another important social aspect of learning. Studies continue to underscore the importance of working cooperatively to improve academic performance.
4. The information processing approach to teaching places emphasis on cognitive factors like thinking, reasoning, and understanding.
5. Teaching techniques following the information processing approach include inquiry and problem-based learning approaches that are grounded in the scientific method.
6. Advanced organizers also fall under the heading of information processing and help to provide the student with a conceptual framework for understanding material that is to be learned.
7. The behavioral approaches to learning focus on observable behaviors. Techniques include direct instruction and mastery learning.
8. The individual differences approach to learning is really more of a philosophical position. It holds that every person is unique in his/her learning needs and consequently requires a sensitive teaching approach tailored to his/her particular needs.

INFORMED APPLICATION

1. Describe which element of this chapter material serves as an advanced organizer. Why?

THE CHAPTER IN REVIEW

This chapter examined various factors impacting instructional excellence. We began with a review of how effective planning lays the foundation for effective instruction. Planning for instruction involves creating goals and objectives for learning outcomes. Teachers need to consider how specific to make a goal for a particular lesson. Mager provides a system for taking a goal and translating it into a specific instructional expectation. Gronlund advocates an alternative approach, keeping lesson objectives general and flexible. Goals are also influenced by the realities of translating them into actual lessons.

Many forces including federal guidelines, state standards, community values, and teacher preferences shape goals and objectives. This process is challenging, but is helped by thinking of lessons according to different instructional dimensions. Bloom's Taxonomies provides teachers with a framework for taking goals and objectives and transforming them into actual instructional plans. He divides instruction plans into three domains: cognitive, psychomotor, and affective. This approach is beneficial because it helps teachers to appreciate the breadth of instructional possibilities.

The second part of the chapter reviewed how to manage the instructional plan. First, we reviewed issues surrounding the time frame for a given lesson. Teachers may expect some lessons to take place at a given time, on a given day. Other lessons are more cumulative, spanning multiple days, weeks or even months. Choosing an appropriate time frame for a lesson will depend on the nature of the topic. Some topics lend themselves to well-defined, time limited lessons. Other topics require time for students to fully integrate lessons into their existing views. Finally, we reviewed the advantages of integrating lessons with other educational professionals. Executing a particular lesson across multiple subjects and teachers helps the student appreciate the complexity of an issue. It also provides multiple opportunities to learn a lesson, benefiting from the varying perspectives of each teacher.

The third section of the chapter covered important aspects of instructional delivery. First we reviewed how personal qualities of a teacher could impact the effectiveness of a lesson. For example, the degree to which a teacher has a thorough understanding of the subject area impacts the degree of learning that students experience. This goes beyond merely knowing the facts of the lesson and involves how well the teacher knows the unique challenges a particular lesson is likely to present students. Other teacher-centered factors to consider are the organizational level of the teacher and the type of expectations the teacher has for the students. Research shows that high, but reasonable, expectations for a student foster academic success. Effective instruction also involves helping learners direct their own learning path. Self-directed learners rely on their own learning skills to achieve, rather than exclusively relying on the teacher. Additionally, student learning is enhanced by appropriate instruction in basic concepts. Concept learning involves clearly articulating concepts that form the foundation for future learning. Concept maps are a popular graphical representation of these concepts and can help students appreciate the nature of a concept. Learning is also enhanced by appropriate use of technology. The rapid advances in technology seen over the last twenty years have changed the very nature of how we instruct.

The fourth and final section of the chapter reviews different perspectives on the instructional process. The social cognitive approach emphasizes interrelations among students and learning in groups. The information processing approach focuses on the inquiry process and the steps a student takes to solve a given problem. The behavioral approach stresses the importance of overt behavior and how to affect changes in what students actually do. Finally, the individual differences approach looks at the importance of valuing each student's individual qualities and how they impact learning.

Interdisciplinary Case Focus

principal *special educator*
teacher *parents* *psychologist*
social worker *physical educator*
nurse *peers* *doctor*

Mary Kennedy is a sixth grade teacher developing a math lesson on area and perimeter. She wants to ensure that her lesson goes beyond basic fact learning. She wants her students to appreciate how an understanding of math helps people in their everyday lives. To begin the process of developing her lesson, she reviews Bloom's Taxonomies for goal setting. Her review reminds her of the importance of integrating psychomotor and affective components into her lesson in addition to cognitive components. She examines Bloom's subcategories for each of these domains and identifies elements that seem most relevant for her area and perimeter lesson. She decides to develop the specific goals and actions, as organized in Table 14A:

Pleased with her goals and framework for lesson activities, Ms. Kennedy began to brainstorm about techniques she could use to further enhance the effectiveness of her lesson. She decides to use concept maps and thematic learning to help her students appreciate the complexities of calculating and applying area and perimeter. She decides to start the lesson with a brief lecture on shapes. She reviews different shapes and describes how they relate to each other. Following the lecture material, she places the students in small workgroups. She has each group draw and cut out a variety of shapes. They then have to organize the shapes into a concept map, gluing the cut-out shapes on a poster

Table 14A Goals and Performance: Ms. Kennedy's Area and Perimeter Lesson

Bloom's Domain	Goal	Performance Indicator
Cognitive		
Knowledge	• **Recognize** a wide range of geometric shapes including: circle, square, rectangle, and triangle. • **Memorize** formula for finding the area and perimeter of each shape.	• Student will be able to correctly identify printed abstract shapes, as well as real-life objects. • Student will memorize the formula for area and perimeter for a circle, square, rectangle, and triangle.
Application	• **Solve** abstract problems. • **Generalize** abstract problems to real-life examples.	• Student will complete printed worksheets on area and perimeter for each shape. • Student will work on area and perimeter in real-life settings: area of different types of homes, area and perimeter of garden.
Psychomotor		
Adaptation	• Can **manipulate** blocks to create shapes with varying areas and with different perimeters.	• Student will manipulate three-dimensional wooden blocks into a square or rectangle with a given area and perimeter.
Affective		
Value	• **Appreciate** the usefulness of area and perimeter in everyday life.	• Student will work in a cooperative group to develop a list of household projects that necessitate an ability to calculate area and perimeter.

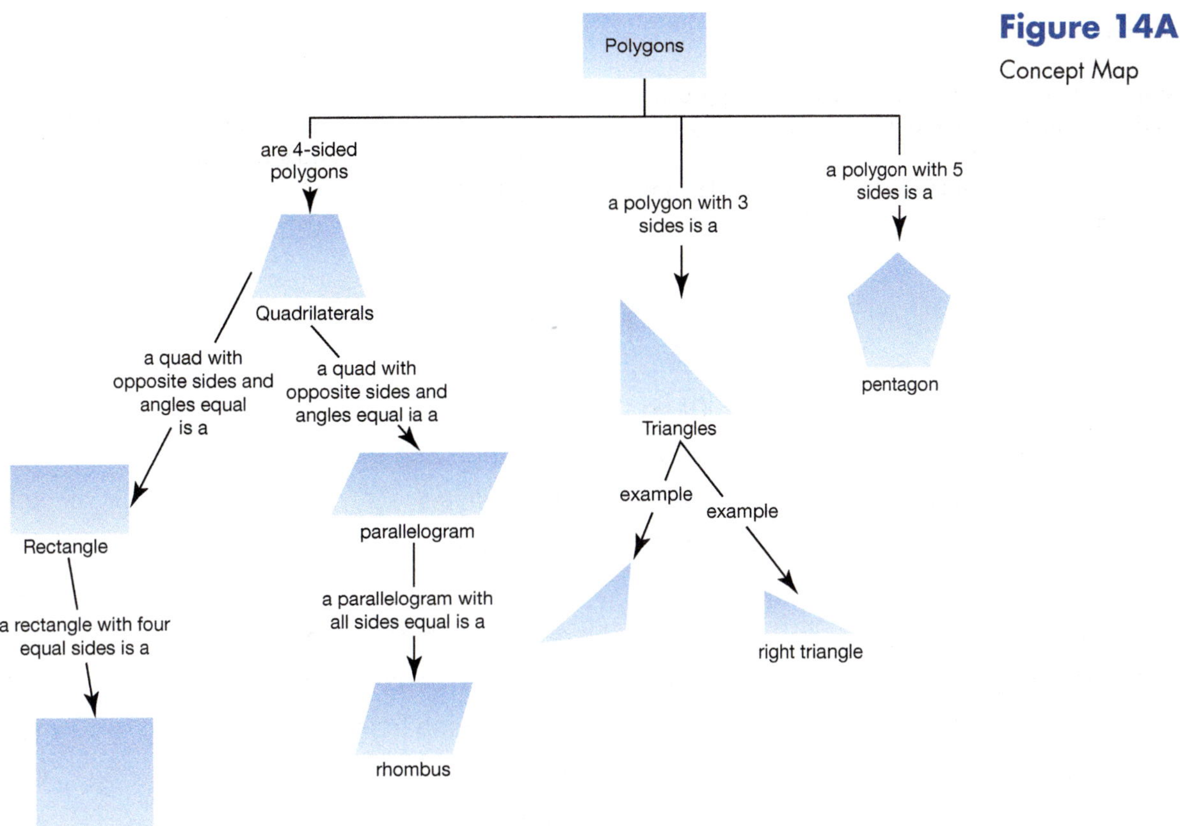

Figure 14A
Concept Map

board. An example of one of the concept maps is presented in Figure 14A.

The other technique she wanted to use to enhance her lesson was thematic learning. To put this part of her lesson plan in motion, she consults with the two other sixth grade teachers. Her students switch with the other two teachers for science and social studies. She determines that they are working on the Civil War in social studies and that they are planning to plant an "alphabet" garden in science. She explains her current lesson plan regarding area and perimeter to the other teachers and asks if there is any natural connection to their current lessons.

Science Teacher Fran Geller is the science teacher for Ms. Kennedy's students. He is about to work with the students to create an "alphabet" garden. This is an experiential project where the students actually go outside and plant a garden with plants starting with the different letters of the alphabet. He recognizes that calculating area and perimeter is needed to plan the garden successfully. He decides to coordinate with Ms. Kennedy's math lesson on the topic. Students will learn the basic math skills to understand and compute area and perimeter with Ms. Kennedy and will then apply those skills to planning the garden. Students will segment the garden into several square and rectangular shapes and then use their new math skills to find out how large to make each area. At first the students plan for too much area for each section. Mr. Geller lets them guess at an appropriate amount of space and then takes them outside to actually measure out the space. The students quickly recognize their mistake and downsize to more appropriate section sizes.

Social Studies Kathleen Kramer is the social studies teacher for Ms. Kennedy's students. She is currently working on various topics on the Civil War. She considers Ms. Kennedy's math topic and realizes that it would be interesting to calculate the area of a typical southern slave quarter and a plantation house. This would be an excellent project for the students and would lead to interesting discussions about the quality of life differences that existed in the old south. To make the project real for the students, she goes to the library and locates original floor plans for slave cottages and plantation houses. She divides students into groups and gives them a plantation house and slave cottage floor plan. Student then spend some time calculating the area of each room and adding them together to get a total area measurement for each type of housing. She then leads the whole class in a discussion of what it would be like to live in these two types of buildings.

Reflection Questions

1. What do you think about Ms. Kennedy's approach to the lesson on area and perimeter?
2. What other ways could she have made her lessons more engaging?
3. Which of Bloom's Taxonomies would you have used to establish goals? Why not use them all?
4. Do you feel Ms. Kennedy more closely followed Mager's or Gronlund's approach to creating goals and objectives?

Key Terms

TERM	Page	*TERM*	Page
Adaptive reactions	477	Jigsaw approach	482
Adequate yearly progress (AYP)	463	Learning styles	488
Advanced organizer	483	Lesson plans	471
Concept learning	477	Mastery learning	486
Concept mapping	478	Negative interdependence	481
Cooperative learning	482	Positive interdependence	481
Defensive reactions	477	Problem-based learning (PBL)	483
Direct instruction (DI)	485	Self-fulfilling prophecy	475
Equity instruction	487	Self-regulated learning	476
Hypothesis	483	Sustaining expectation effect	475

15 Chapter

ASSESSMENT OF LEARNING

What's It All About ...

How do teachers use classroom assessment to measure learning?

What are the basic types of classroom assessment?

What newer forms of assessment are being implemented in the classroom?

How is grading used to assess learning?

How can teachers use technology to improve learning?

Chapter Objectives

- Learn effective techniques for measuring and monitoring learning.
- Describe ways to support student learning.

- Describe informal assessments.
- Describe formal assessments.

- Describe performance-based learning.
- Explain portfolio development.
- Understand how to use exhibits and demonstrations to enhance the assessment process.

- Describe how grading functions as an assessment tool.
- Understand different approaches to grading.

- Describe electronic portfolios.
- Explain how to use computers as an assessment instrument.

EXTENDED OUTLINE

Assessment of Learning

I. What's It All About ...
II. From Today's Headlines
III. Assessment in the Classroom
    A. Measuring and monitoring learning
        1. Instructional progress
        2. Referral
    B. Supporting student learning
        1. Assessment and student motivation
        2. Feedback
    C. Summarize and reflect
IV. Traditional Classroom Assessment
    A. Informal assessment
    B. Formal assessments
        1. Typical assessment tools
        2. Assessment construction
    C. Summarize and reflect
V. Alternative Assessments
    A. Performance-based learning
    B. Portfolio
    C. Exhibits and demonstrations
    D. Summarize and reflect
VI. Grading and Assessment
    A. Function of grading
    B. Approaches to grading
        1. Letter grades
        2. Pass-fail grades
        3. Checklist grades
    C. Summarize and reflect
VII. Technology and Classroom Assessment
    A. Electronic portfolios
    B. Computers and assessment
VIII. Summarize and reflect
IX. The Chapter in Review
X. Interdisciplinary Case Focus

From Today's Headlines

Vol. I No. 15 Teaching World, 2012

State Looking for Better Way to Test Students

Tribune Chronicle
April 6, 2008

Jennifer Kovacs' writing for the *Tribune Chronicle* in Ohio describes a common educational experience. You are sitting with your bubble sheet in front of you ..., large test packet beside you. You begin the test, quickly feeling anxious as you realize you know very few of the answers. You become nervous, and soon you are almost unable to perform.

The Ohio Department of Education is seeking to expand the state's assessment approaches to include other measures of what students learn. Susan Zelman, the Ohio Superintendent of Public Instruction, is quoted as saying, "In showing what they know and can do, students become stimulated, inspired, and motivated to do better academically. If we can find more valid ways for kids to show they are smart, we will have more smart kids. We know when students start achieving, it's contagious."

Following the recommendations of a study comparing the Ohio schools to other schools in the U.S. and the world, Ohio schools are beginning to explore *alternative assessments.* They particularly want to move away from the snapshot a single test gives of a student's learning. Ongoing testing presents a better picture of what a student can accomplish on a typical day. They expressed the desire to have multiple assessments providing ongoing information on a student's progress.

MAKE THE CONNECTION

The experiences of the Ohio school system are not unique. Schools in general are looking for better ways to capture learning. Single tests are a starting point, but many schools are turning their attention to alternative forms of assessment. These tools approach learning from a different perspective and place less emphasis on the end product of learning. They seek to document the learning path, identifying strengths and weaknesses. The approach is beneficial because it provides a more comprehensive look at a student's learning. It also provides teachers and students with more information to encourage growth and improvement.

In this chapter, we will look at several aspects of assessment. We will begin with the rationale for why we assess student learning and a review of traditional assessment tools. We will then turn our attention to newer alternative forms of assessment. Finally, we'll examine the process of grading and the impact of technological innovations on classroom assessment.

ASSESSMENT IN THE CLASSROOM

Assessment is an integral, yet often controversial, part of our educational system. Most students have had the experience of studying for a test, only to earn a low grade. The students felt confident they knew the material, but the assessment did not capture this apparent learning. There are many reasons for this situation, including many student variables such as a limited awareness of one's test preparedness, poor test taking skills, inattention, anxiety, etc. There are also, however, many potential problems with the test's ability to capture learning. What does this mean for the appropriateness of today's testing approaches? Are there alternatives that better capture achievement?

American society continues to demand that today's teachers use assessment to guide, document, and promote effective learning; however, our views on what are the most appropriate assessment tools are changing. In this chapter, we will look at traditional assessment approaches and how they have historically been used as benchmarks for student success. We will also examine exciting, newer assessment models gaining momentum in the educational community. These newer assessments show promise as potentially more effective tools for encouraging learning. Finally, we will look at the effect of our incredible technological innovations and their effect on how we monitor learning.

Measuring and Monitoring Learning

One of the primary reasons for educational assessments is to help teachers measure learning outcomes. Proper assessments can provide teachers with valuable information regarding how students learn lesson material. This in turn can help teachers modify instruction to better meet the specific needs of each student. It is important to realize that this is frequently *not* how assessments are used. All too frequently tests are used only as documentation of learning success or failure. Establishing when learning goals are met is a legitimate use of assessment, but failure to meet a learning goal raises multiple questions. Did the student fail to learn, or is learning better captured by another type of assessment? What assessments could monitor student learning as it progresses so that students have a better chance of demonstrating their knowledge on a test? These questions highlight the need for alternative approaches to assessment, which we will cover in this chapter.

Formative assessment

Assessment that provides information on learning progress

Summative assessment

Assessment that is designed to test whether the students achieved the desired learning outcome

Instructional Progress

Assessments used to monitor instructional progress typically fall under the general heading of either Formative or Summative Assessments. These approaches were covered in detail in Chapter 9. To review, **formative assessments** provide information on learning progress. These assessments are not typically viewed as a single event but rather occur multiple times. The reason for formative assessments is that they provide the teacher with information on how the student is forming an understanding of the material. This provides an opportunity to modify instruction while the student is still acquiring the information. Making instructional changes as learning progresses creates opportunities for improvement and ultimately better test scores.

Interconnections

The testing process is covered in detail in Chapter 9.

Students are given summative assessments to test whether they have achieved the desired learning outcome.

Instruction typically leads to summative assessments. **Summative assessments** are designed to test whether the students achieved the desired learning outcome. Recently, these tests have become more controversial as teachers and school districts rely more heavily on this type of testing to meet greater societal demand for accountability. Summative assessments are indeed a valuable part of the overall educational process, but not when used in isolation. It is important to know if a student has met an educational objective (summative assessment), but it is just as important to know *how* the student constructed their understanding of the material (formative assessment). As you can see, measuring and monitoring learning requires a comprehensive assessment program. Before we continue our look at assessments, let's review a general model of instruction (Linn & Miller, 2005).

Figure 15.1 covers the overall instructional process. It is general, but covers the basic elements teachers need to consider in order to teach and evaluate effectively. The instructional process should begin with clearly defined instructional goals. These goals are central to the educational process because they set the framework for what happens in the classroom. Often a teacher, in isolation, develops these goals; but increasingly, educational goals are being developed by groups of teachers (perhaps an entire academic department) or by teachers *and* administrators in an attempt to satisfy state educational standards (see Chapter 9 for complete coverage of this topic).

Interconnections

Testing standards and accountability are covered in Chapter 9.

Once educational goals have been defined, it is important to assess students to determine their level of achievement relative to the goals. Here we find assessments used with greater frequency. Teachers may give new students a standardized test at the beginning of the term to determine achievement level. Other teachers may take a more personable approach, beginning the year with a series of projects and informal group activities to determine how much the students know. What is important is that teachers are using assessments not to determine the end product of learning (summative assessments) but to help form an understanding of how students are likely to progress through the curriculum. This makes it possible for the teacher to design instruction that is genuinely sensitive to the needs of the students, rather than a one-size-fits-all curriculum.

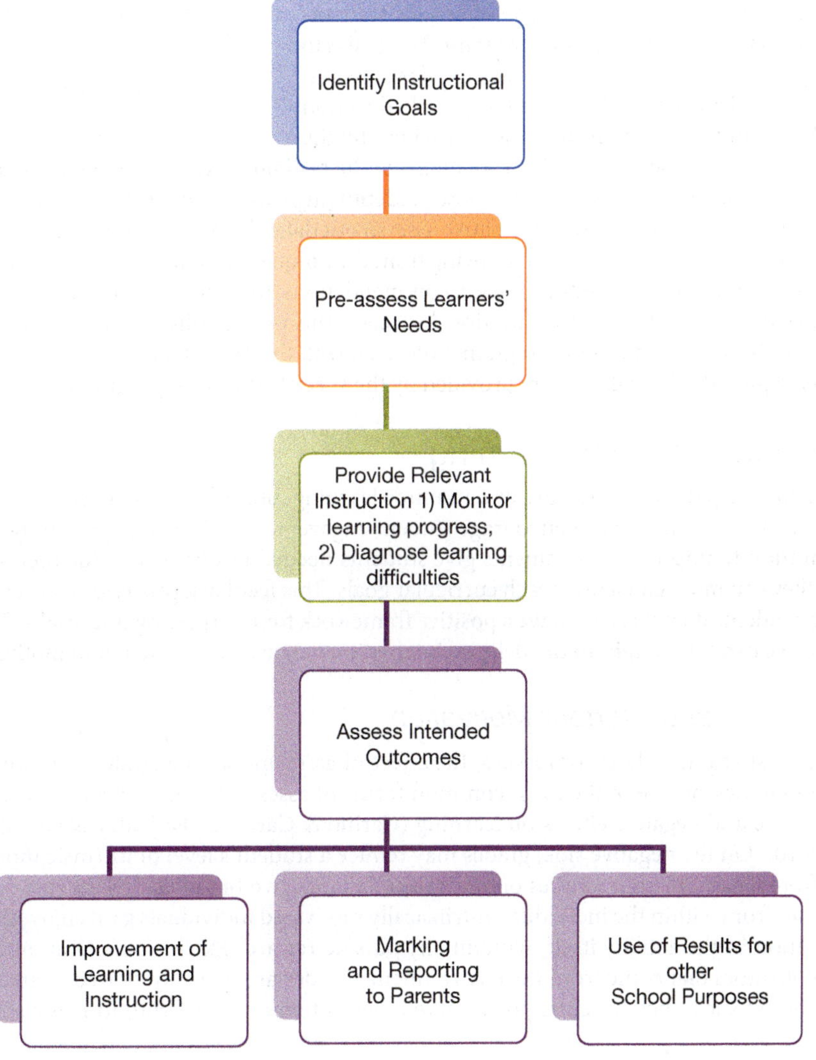

Figure 15.1

Linn & Miller Model of Instruction (2005)

After teachers understand a student's learning needs and how they are going to approach instruction, effective education can begin. As you can see, there is considerable work completed before teachers ever begin instruction. This work is crucial to educational success. Once instruction begins, the teacher should continue to make use of frequent formative assessments. These assessments further guide and tailor instruction to the specific needs of students. At times, the teacher may be unsatisfied with a particular student's progress. The student may fail to learn the material, or the student may learn the material more quickly than expected. Either situation requires further attention.

Referral

Recognizing learning differences is difficult. Some students may have a history of learning challenges, but others may have progressed satisfactorily in prior grades and suddenly experience difficulties. The effective use of frequent formative assessments helps identify these students. Typically teachers begin to help these students by modifying the curricular approach to better meet the needs of the student. Perhaps the student is having difficulty learning long division. Most of the class benefits from some form of modeling, but a particular student is not learning. The teacher may try to use simple manipulatives, computer learning aids, memory techniques (mnemonics—see Chapter 5), or other inventive approaches. Perhaps subsequent assessments reveal the student is still struggling with the material. What should the teacher do? In many schools, the teacher can seek the help and guidance of a pre-referral team (Chapter 1). The pre-referral team consists of teachers, administrators, and other educational professionals helping to develop learning solutions for students struggling in the regular education program. The goal is to bring together the talents of varied educational professionals to help students before they need a special education referral. In addition to the information provided by the teacher's formative assessments, the team often conducts **diagnostic assessments**. These assessments are conducted for the specific purpose of identifying why a student is struggling academically. Combined with the existing formative assessment data, the pre-referral team can design a more comprehensive education plan drawing from the unique specializations of the entire team. Using the pre-referral team's educational recommendations, the teacher is in a better position to help guide the student toward to educational success. This process often decreases unnecessary referrals to the special education program. Still, even with the help of a pre-referral team, some students require the specialized care provided by the special education program.

Interconnections

Memory techniques are covered in Chapter 5 and individual assistance teams are covered in Chapter 1.

Diagnostic assessment

Assessment that is conducted for the specific purpose of identifying why a student is struggling academically

Supporting Student Learning

Assessments help teachers measure and monitor learning, but they also help students. If used appropriately, assessments can encourage student engagement in learning, providing a source of motivation to improve. Assessments give students needed feedback to guide their learning so that they can more efficiently reach curricular goals. This feedback process, however, is challenging. Students do not always have a positive framework for interpreting test results. Teachers need to give careful thought to the delicate interaction between assessment and motivation.

Assessment and Student Motivation

As with most real-life classroom issues, the effect of assessment on a student's motivation is complex. Grades, as one of the most common forms of assessment, have been shown to have both positive and negative effects on learning (Carifio & Carey, 2009; Lalley & Gentile, 2009; Potts, 2010). On the negative side, grades may reduce a student's level of intrinsic motivation. Recall from Chapter 7 that sources of motivation fall into two broad camps. Intrinsic motivation comes from within the individual. Intrinsically motivated individuals gain enjoyment from participation in the activity itself, without any outside reward. Extrinsic motivation refers to those motivators that come from the environment. Grades are typically viewed as an extrinsic motivator. As such, they have the potential to divert attention away from intrinsic sources of motivation. Over time, students who were once intrinsically motivated to learn may come to rely on extrinsic rewards for motivation (Condry, 1977, 1987; Deci & Ryan, 1980, 1985). Interestingly, extrinsically motivated individuals are less likely to enjoy a task (Harter, 1978; Ryan & Connell, 1989; Skinner & Belmont, 1993). Grades are particularly challenging when students receive low grades (Tomlinson, 2005). Since motivation is derived from the grade and the grade is low, students fail to receive sufficient reward to persist in the future.

A student's motivation is derived from their grades.

Part of the reason grades can have a negative effect on learning is that often grades stress performance goals over mastery goals (Chapter 7). When students set performance goals, their focus is on obtaining a satisfactory grade. Students with mastery goals are more focused on learning the material. Like an over reliance on extrinsic motivators, an emphasis on performance goals can undermine a student's intrinsic motivation (Xiang & Lee, 2002; Paris & Turner, 1994). They focus attention on learning factual information, rather than conceptual information, limit problem solving, and undermine creativity (Kumar, Gheen, & Kaplan, 2002). A school-wide focus on mastery goals may limit decreases in intrinsic motivation (Corpus, McClintic-Gilbert, & Hayenga, 2009).

Interconnections

Goals and their effects on motivation are covered in Chapter 7.

Using grades as an assessment tool does not always lead to negative outcomes. Often rewards, such as participation points, can make a boring task more interesting for students (Reeve, 2001). Also, holding students accountable for learning (e.g., grades) increases the amount of time they spend studying and reviewing the material (Dempster, 1991). Part of the issue with whether grades serve a positive or negative function in schools is in how the teacher uses them. Teachers should focus on making learning meaningful for the students. Learning should not be about isolated facts but imbedded in an exciting and engaging context (Gettinger, Schienbeck, Seigel, & Vollmer, 2011). Also, assessments need to accurately map onto the content. When this occurs, students working for a grade equates to working for meaningful learning because the teacher has made them the same thing. Students also respond better to standards-based (or criterion-based) testing. In other words, giving students a clear standard to reach produces better learning than broad tests that capture what percentage of the material was learned (Mac Iver, Reuman, & Main, 1995). A final strategy to consider when using grades as motivators is reconceptualizing a failing grade. A failing grade indicates the student did not master the material. In other words, their learning was incomplete. Failing grades can alternatively be presented to students as incompletes that must be corrected. This maintains the focus on mastering the material and gives the student the ability to do so.

Feedback

Another way assessment supports student learning is by providing corrective feedback. Learning is seldom perfect the first time information is presented. Students typically need time to process the information and experiment with its application. Periodic assessments give students needed corrective feedback to further the learning process. Remember, when learning objectives have simple clear steps, feedback naturally follows and is straightforward. When learning objectives involve more complex concepts or advanced problem solving, it can be challenging to provide an assessment that is sensitive to the concept being taught. The following guidelines, listed in Table 15.1 help create effective feedback (Arends, 2007).

Students benefit most from feedback when it is presented soon after an assessment. In an effort to provide such feedback, some teachers may choose to have brief meetings with each student following an assessment, knowing that providing written feedback takes them a long time. Other teachers may elect to provide feedback to the entire class as a group, detailing frequently missed items. Although this technique provides quick feedback, it often fails to provide students with enough specific feedback to fully meet their learning needs. Another approach to providing feedback is to make use of technology. Chat rooms, discussion boards, email, and other communication tools give teachers multiple options for providing responsive feedback. Teachers should reflect on available technological tools and choose feedback

Table 15.1 Guidelines for Providing Effective Feedback

1. Provide feedback as soon as possible after initial learning.
2. Make feedback specific.
3. Concentrate on behaviors, not intent.
4. Keep feedback appropriate to the developmental stage of the learner.
5. Emphasize praise and feedback on correct performance.
6. Demonstrate correct application of learning when giving negative feedback.
7. Help students focus on process, not outcomes.
8. Teach students how to provide feedback for themselves and how to judge their own performance.

mechanisms that are the fastest and most appropriate for the task. Additionally, teachers should be as focused as possible with feedback. Don't assume students will understand general suggestion. Provide concrete examples using the student's own work or performance as the basis for the feedback.

Feedback also needs to be developmentally appropriate. Over time, students develop dramatically in their ability to think and reason (Chapter 5). This means that appropriate feedback for a tenth grade high school student may be ineffective for a seventh grade junior high student. Provide feedback that is effective for the particular student's academic and intellectual level. Also, try to catch students engaging in appropriate behaviors and praise them accordingly. Positive feedback is often better received than critical appraisals. If you do have to provide a corrective measure, make sure you also tell the student the correct action to take. This not only lets them know they did not perform satisfactorily but gives them the tools to perform better in the future. Finally, stress the *path* to higher learning, rather than the ultimate outcome. Yes, outcomes are important for a variety of reasons; however, if students are so distracted or anxious about an outcome, they will not be focused on the present where learning is actually taking place. Emphasize the most effective process for learning. Reinforce that if the student masters the process, the outcome will naturally follow.

SUMMARIZE AND REFLECT

1. One of the primary reasons for using assessment is to help teachers measure learning outcomes and student progress toward outcomes.
2. Formative assessments provide information related to learning progress.
3. Summative assessments are designed to test whether the students achieved the desired learning goal.
4. Effective assessment begins with clearly defined instructional goals.
5. Some students may not meet learning goals and, consequently, require additional instructional efforts.
6. A school's pre-referral team consists of teachers, administrators, and other educational professionals and may help instructors develop learning solutions for students struggling in the regular education program.
7. Pre-referral teams often use diagnostic assessments to further clarify the nature of a particular student's struggles.
8. Grades have been shown to have positive and negative effects on learning and motivation, depending on the situation.

(continues)

9. Periodic assessment gives students needed corrective feedback to support learning.
10. Feedback needs to be developmentally appropriate and presented as soon as possible after the assessment.

INFORMED APPLICATION

1. Imagine you are an eleventh grade history teacher. You are covering the Medieval Ages this term. What factors should you consider when developing an assessment programing that leads to the final grade in the course?
2. What are some pros and cons for using traditional classroom grades?

TRADITIONAL CLASSROOM ASSESSMENTS

Classroom assessments can be subdivided into two categories: traditional and alternative. The first part of this section will focus on traditional assessments. These are assessments which have been used by teachers for generations to monitor and support student learning. At times, these traditional assessments are an informal attempt to capture a student's learning. Other times, however, necessitate that teachers specifically assess a learning objective in a formal way. These formal assessments typically lead to course grades. The second part of this section will look at newer assessment techniques. These alternative assessments provide additional insights into the growth and development of students. Their advantages make them excellent additions to the collection of assessment tools available to educators.

Informal Assessments

Informal assessments are unplanned opportunities to gather information about student learning. Teachers use these assessments every day in a variety of situations. For example, student responses to questions during a class discussion often reveal misunderstandings. Observation of a student during recess may suggest that the student has difficulty relating to others. Completing a worksheet may show a mild problem with fine motor control. More examples are listed in Table 15.2, but the opportunities for gathering information informally are endless. Effective teachers take advantage of these opportunities to learn more about their students and to provide specific and effective instruction. Informal assessments have the advantage of being directly tied to the content being taught since they are derived from a student's immediate involvement in the curriculum. They are highly adaptive. Teachers can easily explore concerns with further observation or additional questioning.

Informal assessment

Unplanned opportunity to gather information about student learning

There are some cautions, however, when using informal assessments. Because they are unplanned and spontaneous, they lack the methodological rigor used to develop more formal forms of testing, such as standardized tests (see Chapter 9). Their inherent flexibility makes it difficult to develop any standard operating procedures. This means that different teachers may explore a learning challenge in entirely different ways and come up with very different conclusions. Informal assessments also result in information that is unique to the particular learning situation. It is difficult to take an informal assessment conducted in one class and suggest its

Table 15.2 Informal Assessments

Informal Assessments
Observation Checklists
Teacher Notes
Grading Trends over Time
Work Samples
Teacher/Student/Parent Conference Notes
Quality of Questioning

application in another class. It is likely to be specific to the learning context in which it was observed. Taking these cautions into consideration, teachers should endeavor to stay alert and focused during the school day, looking for valuable informal opportunities to observe how students learn and grow.

Formal Assessments

Formal assessment

Assessment that is planned and constructed, in advance, to assess a particular learning objective

Formal assessments are planned and constructed in advance to assess a particular learning objective. They might be used to assess learning at the end of a social studies unit or following instruction on a particular volleyball skill during physical education. They may be used frequently as learning progresses or used at the end of a learning task. What formal assessments have in common is that they are developed in advance and are used to measure specific aspects of learning.

Typical Assessment Tools

Selected-response questions

Questions that have students select a correct answer from a limited set of options

Objective question

Question where the correctness of the answer does not rely on its interpretation by the teacher

Teachers have a long history of using formal assessment tools. They have the advantage of being familiar to students and relatively easy to construct. One of the most common forms is the formal *written test.* Written tests make use of a variety of question formats. Table 15.3 provides an example of some of the most typical types.

Written test items are sometimes divided into two broad categories. **Selected-response questions** are those that have students select a correct answer from a limited set of options. Multiple-choice, true/false, and matching are selected-response questions. These questions are considered **objective questions** because grading each question does not rely on interpretation by the teacher. Each question is simply compared to an answer key developed in advance by the teacher. Grading is uniform across students. These questions are typically used to assess basic factual knowledge (Stiggins, R. J., 2005), but they can be adapted to assess more complex

Table 15.3 Common Question Formats

Type	Example
Multiple Choice	Which of the following Native American tribes were indigenous to the Great Lakes Region? A. Iroquois B. Navajo C. Cherokee D. Pueblo
Dichotomous Choice (e.g., True/False)	Cirrus clouds are not typically associated with weather patterns.
Matching	Match the word on the left with the correct part of speech on the right. 1. Through A. Article 2. The B. Verb 3. Book C. Preposition 4. Run D. Noun
Completion	Positively charged ions are called ________.
Short Answer	Describe the effects of excessive salt intake on the function of the kidneys.
Essay	Compare the literary styles of Lord Byron and William Shakespeare in relation to their treatment of women.

reasoning tasks (Rieck, 2006). Teachers need to pay close attention to how they construct these test items, so that they test both factual knowledge and complex, real-life learning. Keep in mind these questions do not measure writing ability and are difficult to adapt to measure organization and presentation skills.

The other major category of written test items is the constructed response. **Constructed responses** are those that require the student to create their own answers, rather than picking a correct answer from choices provided by the teacher. Essay questions and those requiring a short answer are examples of constructed response questions. These questions are considered **subjective questions** because grading the correctness of a given response requires the judgment of the teacher. Teachers often use a **grading rubric** for these questions. A rubric includes basic criteria for grading an item, but teacher perception still potentially shapes scoring. Rubrics are extremely useful as formative assessment tools, providing teachers with ongoing information about the learning process, which encourages sensitive student feedback (McGatha & Darcy, 2010). In general, constructed response questions provide a different window on learning. The nature of the response format allows teachers to assess different comprehension standards, such as how well a student analyzes content and synthesizes information.

Written tests make use of a variety of question formats.

In addition to the written test, teachers also make frequent use of *book reports, homework,* and *presentations.* These assessments provide the teacher with additional information about student learning. Given that they are typically completed outside of the classroom, the dynamics involved in executing the assessment are different from most written tests. Without the structure provided by the teacher, some students struggle to complete these assignments. Alternatively, some students thrive under these conditions and demonstrate learning that in-class assignments fail to capture. Teachers need to recognize these potential differences and develop an assessment approach that is meaningful and appropriate for each student.

Constructed response

Type of answer that requires the student to create his/her own response, rather than picking a correct answer from choices provided by the teacher

Subjective question

Question where grading the correctness of a given response requires the judgment of the teacher

Grading rubric

Basic criteria for grading an item, but in which teacher perception still potentially shapes the scoring

Assessment Construction

In this section, construction of effective written test items is examined. One of the most common formats for written tests is multiple-choice. They can be adapted to measure a wide range of learning objectives across many subject areas. Given this flexibility, they are not only used in classrooms but also on most standardized achievement tests. Their widespread use, however, does not mean they are easy to construct. Often, multiple-choice items are poorly constructed. leading to ineffective knowledge assessment. To understand how to correctly construct a multiple-choice item, let's define its two main parts. The stem is the initial part of the question (Figure 15.2), and the distracters are the answer alternatives that follow.

Creating an effective multiple-choice question involves correctly wording the stem, appropriately selecting the distracters, and creating proper agreement between the two. Table 15.4 provides a list of important considerations when constructing multiple-choice items (adapted from Linn & Miller, 2005).

Following these guidelines will help you construct multiple-choice items that accurately and effectively measure the intended learning outcome. Authoring written tests is challenging for the beginning teacher, and multiple-choice items are particularly challenging. Tests should be reviewed with the students after administration to obtain information on student perception of the test items. Remember, the goal is ultimately to develop a test that accurately reflects

Figure 15.2
Multiple-Choice Question

Which of the following Native American tribes were indigenous to the Great Lakes region?

A. Iroquois
B. Navajo
C. Cherokee
D. Pueblo

Stem

Distracters

Table 15.4 Constructing Multiple-Choice Items

1	The stem of the item should be meaningful by itself and should present a specific problem.
2	The stem should include as much of the item as possible and should be free of irrelevant material.
3	Use of a negatively stated stem (those including "none," "not," and "least") should only occur when they are crucial to assessing a specific aspect of learning.
4	All the distracters should grammatically flow from the stem of the question.
5	An item should contain only one correct or clearly best answer.
6	Items used to measure understanding should contain new or novel information, but not too far removed from the student's experiences.
7	All distracters should be reasonable. The purpose of a distracter is to distract the uninformed from the correct answer.
8	Try to avoid having one of the significant words in the stem also present in the correct answer (e.g., revolution in the stem when the correct answer is Revolutionary War).
9	The relative length of the distracters should not provide a clue to the answer.
10	The correct answer should appear in each of the distracter positions (A,B, C, D) an approximately equal number of times, but in random order.
11	Use special alternatives such as "none of the above" or "all of the above" sparingly.
12	Do not use multiple-choice items when other item types are more appropriate.

student learning. It is unlikely that this will be optimal the very first time a test is written. Tests require constant updating and modification to become a realistic reflection of learning.

Forced choice or true/false items are used to assess the student's ability to recognize correct definitions and factual information. Each question consists of a single statement that the student must endorse as correct or incorrect. As with multiple-choice items, the question can be used across a wide range of subjects. They are, however, not particularly good tools for assessing complex thinking. Often beginning teachers believe that forced- choice questions are easy to create and rush to use them. This is often ill-advised. There are many potential problems with forced-choice item construction. When choosing information to test, pick content that is specific, rather than broad. Questions regarding broad information are typically vague and open to multiple interpretations. Also, avoid taking information directly from the textbook. Rephrase chapter content in your own words. If students recognize that questions are coming word-for-word from the chapter, they are more likely to survey the chapters in a superficial way. Keep statements simple, and only present *one* idea. Teachers often place multiple ideas in a statement, each of which needs to be judged true or false.

Multiple Ideas

In the example, the steel worker named Tim was diagnosed with dissociative identity disorder (DID).

- Was Tim a steel worker? True False
- Was Tim diagnosed with DID? True False

Single Idea

Was Tim diagnosed with Dissociative Identity Disorder (DID)?

In addition to selecting only one idea for each statement, try to make forced-choice questions of equal length. Teachers typically create longer sentences for true statements and thus give students an alternative tool to determine the correct answer. Finally, as with multiple-choice items, try to avoid framing statements in the negative (using "no" or "not"). Students frequently fail to process the negation.

Matching items are another assessment choice. A typical matching question is designed by creating two columns of information. The task is to match the elements in the first column with the corresponding element in the second column (see Table 15.3 at the beginning of this section for an example). Part of the challenge in creating a successful matching item is to minimize successful guessing. When more detailed information is provided, try to present this information in the second column. Also, provide instructions that some elements of the second column *may be used only once, more than once, or not at all.* Using a format that requires the student to use items from the second column more than once or not at all makes it difficult for them to get answers correct with simple elimination. Teachers should also ensure that all elements in the first column are based on a similar category or content area. Again, if this is not done, students may correctly match some items because they are different, not because they knew the answer. Matching items are used when there are multiple factual associations present within a particular lesson or content area. When this is the case, matching provides an efficient way to assess knowledge.

Finally, we will consider the constructed answer question. Essay questions are excellent examples of constructed answer questions, as are short answer and completion questions. Essay questions are one of the most flexible and effective assessment tools to measure complex learning. Its flexibility comes from the freedom the format affords the student. Students are potentially free to respond to an essay in any manner they can create. Students can demonstrate analysis, synthesis, relation, integration, and evaluation among others. The primary limiter is the manner in which the teacher asks the question. Questions can be generated from any field of study. They also have the advantage of assessing writing ability, although this may need to be graded separately from the content-related information. The potential of the essay to assess complex learning, however, is entirely dependent on the teacher's ability to structure an appropriate question. Teachers should first consider if other response formats are more appropriate. Factual information may be better assessed using the selected-response items reviewed above. If an essay format is indicated, make certain the student's task is clearly indicated in the question. Simple brief questions may be easier to write, but they do not necessarily help the student recognize the required information. Describe the task fully so the student can answer and the teacher can subsequently grade the answer with precision. Also, teachers should avoid asking more questions than they require the student to answer. Although students favor this approach, it essentially means that different students are taking different tests. This is problematic if it is not the intended outcome of the test. It also makes cross-student comparisons difficult. Teachers should also breakdown larger questions into component parts, each asked as separate essay questions. This makes each question clearer. Finally, consider the time needed to answer the question. Students should be informed of time constraints and reminded regularly, so they can plan their response accordingly.

Essay questions along with short answer and completion questions are considered constructed answer questions.

Short answer and completion items are also considered constructed responses because they require the student to construct their own response. These questions, however, are more appropriate for factual knowledge. Questions should be worded so that responses are brief and to the point. In the case of a completion item, the response may be a single word. It is also better to create a question, rather than taking a statement directly from the textbook. Although a question in the book may seem clear in the context of the other information, once it is isolated on a test, it may become ambiguous. This is problematic for students to answer and teachers to grade.

SUMMARIZE AND REFLECT

1. Informal assessments are unplanned opportunities to gather information about student learning.
2. Informal assessments lack a specific methodology, which makes them difficult to apply outside the environment in which they were observed.
3. Formal assessments are typically planned and constructed in advance to assess a particular learning objective.
4. Typical formal assessments include multiple-choice, forced-choice or true/false, matching, completion, short answer, and essay.
5. Selective-response questions give students a limited number of choices to endorse.
6. Constructed-response test items are those that require the student to actually create their own answers.
7. Objective questions do not rely on interpretation by the teacher.
8. Subjective questions depend on the judgment of the teacher.
9. Grading rubrics include the basic criteria for judging the correctness of a constructed response.
10. Multiple-choice items are the most common assessment tool because they are easily adapted to a wide range of learning objectives.
11. Forced-choice or true/false items are used to assess the student's ability to recognize correct definitions and factual information.
12. One of the challenges in creating a matching test item is in the prevention of successful guessing.
13. Essay questions are ideally suited for measuring complex learning.

INFORMED APPLICATION

1. Create one question on the topic of your choice for each of the following formats: multiple-choice, forced-choice, essay, and matching.
2. Reflecting on the questions created in the previous item, which question was most challenging for you to write? Why?

ALTERNATIVE ASSESSMENTS

Assessment-led reform

Movement driven by educators, administrators, and federal educational agencies interested in expanding traditional assessments

Educators, administrators, and federal educational agencies are all interested in expanding traditional assessments. This movement is called **assessment-led reform** and is a key focus for promoting successful learning (Schafer & Lissitz, 2009). We are also interested in how newer forms of assessment can help teachers meet higher learning standards and stronger accountability measures (Black, 1998; Gipps, 1994). In this section, we will take a look at the rationale behind assessment-led reform and the push toward alternative assessments.

In the fields of education and psychology, we are seeing dramatic shifts in the perception of the learning process. We are beginning to pay closer attention to how students actively construct knowledge and how this interacts with instructional practice (see Chapter 12 for a thorough review of this topic). Educational professions are increasingly emphasizing that teaching, learning, and assessment are inseparable (Wiggins, 1992). Changes in one necessarily leads to changes in the others. Based on this broader perspective on learning, assessment practices are shifting to more comprehensively capture learning. Assessment approaches evolving out of our changing perceptions of learning are called alternative assessments. **Alternative assessments** are any assessment approaches going beyond traditional assessments, such as multiple-choice tests, homework, and reports (Davies & Wavering, 1999). Table 15.5 provides examples of alternative assessments. These assessments provide newer and more productive ways to capture learning. They also support student motivation to take responsibility for their own learning. Alternative assessments help foster creative thinking and the application of knowledge, rather than simple memorization (Stiggins, 1997; Earl & Cousins, 1995).

Alternative assessment

Any assessment approach that goes beyond the traditional assessments such as multiple-choice tests, homework, and reports.

Table 15.5 Alternative Forms of Assessment

Alternative Forms of Assessment
Performance Assessment
Portfolios
Cooperative Learning Groups
Peer Teaching
Exit Cards
Journals
Exhibitions
Demonstrations
Simulations
Observations

Performance-Based Learning

Alternative assessments are often embedded in performance-based activities. **Performance-based activities** are learning situations that apply knowledge in ways mirroring application in real life. The reasoning behind performance-based activities is that meaningful learning should be based on *useful* information. This seems a reasonable expectation, but is often difficult to realize. Imagine a student completing a math worksheet on long division or a student writing an English paper on *To Kill a Mockingbird.* How can teachers embed these assignments in a performance-based activity? Many would agree that learning math and literature is important, but teachers and students may experience difficulty making direct connections to real life. Some material naturally lends itself to real-life application, but with some careful consideration, teachers can find such connections in a variety of lessons. The point is for teachers to at least think about the utility of a learning objective and make consistent ongoing efforts to help students experience learning applied to life.

Performance-based activities
Learning situations that apply knowledge in ways mirroring application in real life

Performance-based assessments encompass many learning activities including science experiments, plays, oral presentations, debates, conversing in a foreign language, and applied mathematics. The only practical limit to the range of performance-based assessments is the imagination of the teacher. One of the primary assessment benefits to the teacher is a more detailed account of the *process of learning,* in addition to the *end product of learning.* Traditional forms of assessment (written tests) focus on what a student ultimately learned at the end of an instructional period. While this is certainly important, assessing the learning process provides a more comprehensive assessment. Including information on the learning process when assessing provides an opportunity to examine idea formation, organization, execution, originality, and even self-evaluation. These are highly complex cognitive tasks, which take learning assessment beyond simple factual learning (Losardo, 2011).

When constructing a performance-based assessment, teachers should be mindful of how students will be graded. Often one of the limitations of these assessments is that it is difficult to create reliable grading criteria. Implementing a performance-based assessment and grading the assessment should always be considered at the same time. Teachers need to make sure they clarify their instructional objectives and how they intend to grade a performance-based assessment. Table 15.6 provides some guidelines on how to develop effective grading criteria (Airasian, 1991; Brualdi, 1998).

Portfolio

Another commonly used alternative assessment is the portfolio. A **portfolio** is a purposeful collection of student work in a particular context (Paulson, Paulson, & Meyer, 1991). Portfolios have been used consistently in many of the arts and performing arts. Sculptors, painters, and actors routinely collect samples of their work and accomplishments. In education, the portfolio

Portfolio
A purposeful collection of student work in a particular context

Table 15.6 Defining Criteria for Performance-Based Assessments

Identify the overall performance or task to be assessed, and perform it yourself or imagine yourself performing it.
List the important aspects of the performance or product.
Try to limit the number of performance criteria, so they can all be observed during a student's performance.
If possible, have groups of teachers think through the important behaviors included in a task.
Express the performance criteria in terms of observable behaviors or product characteristics.
Don't use ambiguous words that cloud the meaning of the performance criteria.

is an assessment tool that is only recently becoming popular. Portfolios in education are typically used for one of two purposes: student assessment and instruction. This is not to say that a portfolio serves *only* assessment or instructional purposes. Portfolios, however, typically serve a primary function that is either to assess the student or to provide a unique avenue for instruction. Portfolios provide an opportunity for students to demonstrate what they have learned in a way that traditional tests have failed to capture. They can demonstrate student growth by showing growth over time. They can also help teach students to be more reflective about their work (Olson, 1991; Fisher & King, 1995). Teachers and students often work together collaboratively to create and learn from portfolios. Parents also benefit from them since portfolios provide a concrete document to discuss during conferences with teachers.

There are clearly some unique benefits to using portfolios; however, there are also some potential limitations. Portfolios are not particularly useful if they do not address a specific purpose. A random collection of student work does not constitute a portfolio. Portfolios are assessment tools and need to have a clear and direct tie to a specific learning objective (Tillema & Smith, 2000). Additionally, there needs to be clear guidelines for what is included in a portfolio. Not all educational experiences are equal in terms of their ability to document learning. Teachers need to decide what elements of a portfolio the teacher determines and what elements the student chooses. This will depend on the specific learning objective for the portfolio. Some portfolios are used to determine if a student has mastered a particular topic area. Others focus on documenting student growth or graduation to the next step in a curricular plan. Again, it is important that the purpose of the portfolio is clearly defined before it is started. Equally important is the scoring criteria for the portfolio. Historically, portfolios have been difficult to grade. It is challenging to obtain reliable portfolio assessments between teachers or even within the same teacher over time. The grading criteria drive the portfolio construction process. Clearer grading criteria equates to clearer, more consistent portfolios.

Exhibitions

Opportunities for students to display their learning to the public

Exhibitions like a science fair are opportunities for students to display what they have learned to the public.

Exhibits and Demonstrations

Exhibitions are opportunities for students to display their learning to the public. The public may consist of peers, teachers, or community members. Exhibitions help with the assessment of a student's knowledge and their ability to think and problem solve in a real-time exercise. Students need to be able to respond to questions appropriately. They also need to be able to communicate in a dynamic environment. This provides a much more comprehensive assessment than a traditional written test.

Exhibitions share many of the features of other non-traditional, student-centered assessments (Maine Department of Education, 2004). Exhibitions involve going beyond traditional learning to integrate learning into real life. They are public expressions of learning and involve sharing knowledge. Exhibitions require the active participation of the learner. Students must learn how to become an advocate for their learning product. They also need to express their knowledge in such a way that it synthesizes new content and research with their ability to effectively plan. Exhibitions provide a variety of assessment products: oral presentation ability, research experience, question responsiveness, and learning products (e.g., presentation materials: written work, display construction, etc.). Exhibitions are more of a summative assessment of a student's learning. They can also be designed, however, to assess a student's critical reflection skills in a formative manner. For example, students can keep a progress journal or write reflective essays as they complete the project. A final advantage of exhibitions is that assessment is typically by consensus, bringing together the opinions of the teacher, peers, administrators, and members of the community. This uses the varied expertise of many individuals, enhancing student feedback.

SUMMARIZE AND REFLECT

1. Evolving perceptions of learning are fostering the development of newer assessment approaches.
2. Currently, there is a greater focus on how students actively construct knowledge and how this impacts instruction.
3. Alternative assessments are any assessment approaches that go beyond traditional assessments.
4. Alternative assessments often provide a more detailed account of the process of learning, in addition to the end product of learning.
5. Alternative assessments are often embedded in performance-based activities.
6. Performance-based activities are learning situations that apply knowledge in ways mirroring application in real life.
7. Performance-based assessments encompass many learning activities, including science experiments, plays, oral presentations, debates, conversing in a foreign language, and applied mathematics.
8. Another alternative assessment is the portfolio, which is a collection of student work in a particular context.
9. Portfolios can be challenging to grade and need a clear and direct tie to a specific learning objective.
10. Exhibitions are another opportunity for students to display their learning to the public.

INFORMED APPLICATION

1. Consider how you might use popular films to assess students' understanding of community health issues. What alternative assessments would help you with this challenge?
2. Imagine you are a teacher trying to convince a colleague of the merits of alternative assessments. What would you say to demonstrate the value of such assessments?

GRADING AND ASSESSMENT

Grading is the process of assigning numbers or letters to student performance at the end of a specified period of time. They are summary statements of the student's learning (Marzano, 2000). We can also talk about the "grade" on a specific test or assessment, but this section is referring to the grades a student receives at the end of the term or semester. The process of grading is a natural extension of the on-going assessment process used by teachers. Ultimately, teachers, parents, and administrators ask the question, "Are the students learning?" When established appropriately, grades provide such summary information.

Grading

The process of assigning numbers or letters to student performance at the end of a specified period of time

Function of Grading

Grades are used for a variety of purposes. One of the most obvious is that they serve an *instructional* purpose. That is, grades aid the teacher with the instructional process (Bowers, 2011). Grades should improve the quality of instruction and learning. Grading is most effective when it is closely aligned with instructional objectives (Polikoff, Porter, & Smithson, 2011). To create this connection, teachers need to avoid creating assessments and grading criteria before they have clear instructional goals. When teachers take the time to decide what it is they want their students to learn, and to clearly articulate these objectives, then assessments and grades follow

Grading is most effective when it is closely aligned with instructional objectives.

more naturally. Grades should not only document the student's performance level, but should provide information on the student's strengths and weaknesses. This information is crucial if teachers are going to help guide a student to more effective learning in the future. Helping students appreciate how to place greater reliance on their strengths, while accommodating their weaknesses, creates a more hopeful and motivated student.

Grading does not impact all students equally, particularly for those students receiving the lowest grades. The effects of failure on student achievement are complex (Stephan, Caudroit, Boiche, & Sarrazin, 2011). Some students view failure as a challenge and study even harder. Other students view failure as confirmation that no matter what they do, success is not possible (Brunstein, 2000). Students that use failure as a source of motivation to succeed may have a higher degree of commitment to the learning task (Brunstein & Gollwitzer, 1996). In this study, students showing a high degree of commitment to goals they set for themselves were likely to view failure as a challenge. Additional opportunities to engage in the task were viewed as opportunities to complete their learning.

Another quality that has been associated with a positive response to failure is self-efficacy. **Self-efficacy** refers to an individual's sense of their own competence. Students with a well-developed sense of self-efficacy are able to maintain a strong sense of control over learning (Brunstein & Gollwitzer, 1996). After a failure, they are more likely to persist and expend additional effort to learn the material. This quality is different from those students who struggle after they experience failure. These students explain the error in such a way that it actually encourages less effort and engagement in the task. Based on Attribution Theory (see Chapter 7), these students appear to attribute the cause of their failure to uncontrollable causes (e.g., "I must be stupid.") that are reasonably stable (e.g., "I always fail."). Such attributions further their negative feelings and perpetuate failure in the future. This undermines their sense of control and their belief that effort produces positive outcomes.

Self-efficacy

An individual's sense of his/her own competence

Letter grades

One of the most common approaches to grading/evaluating a student's work or achievement

Grades also serve a communication function in schools. Teachers use grades to help communicate to parents how their child is progressing in school. Grades should accurately and effectively communicate learning objectives, learning progress, and the student's unique strengths and weaknesses. They should be presented with portfolios or other examples of the student's work. Presented grades, parents (a valuable part of the learning equation) understand what their child is supposed to be learning, as well as how much they have learned. Examples help make this process clearer, giving parents and the teacher a common framework to discuss the student's progress.

A final grading function to consider is how grades are used by the school system. Schools use grades for a variety of internal purposes. Used in conjunction with standardized tests, they are used for accountability purposes as discussed in Chapter 9 (Deville, 2011). Grades are also used to promote students to the next grade and for graduation. Additionally, they are used to determine honors, and awards, and eligibility for participation in athletics and other extracurricular activities. All are important functions and underscore the need for appropriate assignment of grades. Let's turn our attention to some of the most common approaches to determining grades.

Grades help serve as communication between teachers and parents by letting them know how their child is progressing in class.

Approaches to Grading

There are many types of grading systems used in today's schools. Each approach has its unique advantages and disadvantages. Here we review a few of the most common approaches.

Letter Grades

Letter grades are one of the most common approaches to grading. They are convenient for teachers and are widely accepted and understood. They are also, however, a measure of achievement *and* personal qualities, such as persistence, effort, motivation, and work ethic. This makes it difficult to use the information in a constructive way to help the student improve. Along these lines, the single grade does not clarify strengths and weaknesses. For example, what exactly does a *C* mean in terms of what the student has learned and what causes difficulties? Can we translate the grade into a profile of strengths and weaknesses so that the student can have information to support improvement? This is unlikely. Single grades simply embody too many factors to be the sole source of feedback for a student. Again, this makes using the grade more challenging and highlights the importance of supporting letter grades with additional information.

The perception of letter grades also differs across schools. This potentially leads to dramatic differences in the range of letter grades used by a given school. Some schools give predominantly *A*'s and *B*'s. Other schools may use the full range of available grades. Such inconsistencies make grade interpretation difficult. Finally, letter grades should be approached with caution because they potentially encourage undue competition between students. Some students may thrive under these conditions. For others, the resulting anxiety has a negative impact on their achievement. Teachers may go out of their way to ensure grades are confidential, but they should be realistic and understand that students talk amongst themselves. Grades usually become public knowledge very quickly. Consequently, teachers need to make sure they are sensitive to the impact of grades on future performance.

Pass-Fail Grades

Pass-fail grades are a type of standards (criterion) grading system. This means that prior to instruction, teachers established a set of learning standards. The goal is for students to meet or exceed this predetermined skill level. If the student achieves at this level or above, a *pass* grade is given. If the student does not meet the standard, a *fail* grade is given. This type of system works well for learning objectives that have clear acceptable performance levels. For example, learning your multiplication tables is a clearly defined skill, for which the teacher could easily assign a pass-fail grade. One of the potential problems with this system is that it is insensitive to the varying needs of students. Some students will achieve the standard with little difficulty and in a short amount of time. Others will struggle with the material and require intensive instruction. When the grading system fails to capture this variation, then it potentially has negative effects on motivation, particularly for the student at either end of the ability spectrum. Consider an accelerated student who masters a learning standard on the first day. Without any additional credit given for continuing to work, motivation is likely to decrease unless the student is particularly self-driven. This is particularly true for students who set performance goals (see Chapter 7) that emphasize external approval. Similarly, students who experience the most difficulty may sense they will never meet the standard and just give up all together since they feel continued work will result in the same grade. These drawbacks are significant, but pass-fail grades are still an excellent option if teachers take care to address the needs of all students.

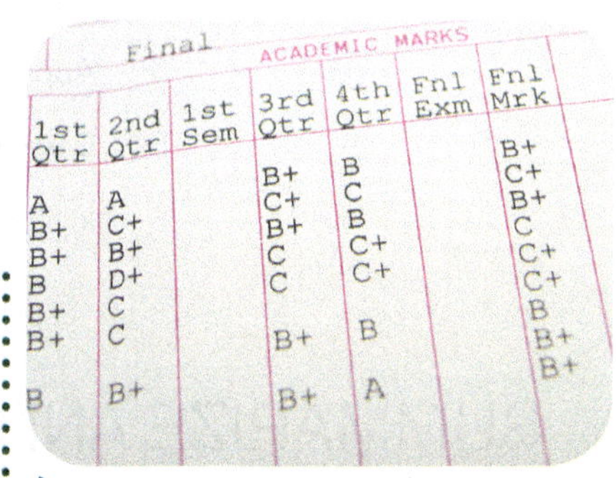

Pass-fail grades are a type of standards (criterion) grading system.

Pass-fail grades

A type of standards (criterion) grading system

Checklist Grades

Checklist grading systems are used with increasing frequency in schools, particularly in elementary schools. Often viewed as playing a supportive role to letter-grades, these grades provide a system for teachers to document the extent to which students have mastered various learning standards. Checklists can be developed for academic subjects, as well as behavioral standards. Table 15.7 gives an example of possible checklist standards.

This type of grading system helps schools to better capture the unique strengths and weakness of each student. It is an excellent source of additional information supporting a letter-grade and gives teachers and students specific areas to target for additional work. These systems are seen frequently in lower grades, but they are less developed and not as frequently used in higher grades.

Checklist grading system

Grading method used with increasing frequency, particularly in elementary schools, which requires the evaluator to check a given list of skills as being met, observed, or not yet observed

Table 15.7 Checklist Grading System

Each of these standards uses the following grading system:

E—Indicates that achievement is Excellent

S—Indicates that achievement is Satisfactory

N—Indicates that achievement Needs Improvement

U—Indicates that achievement is Unsatisfactory

	Reading		Behavior
E	Developed appropriate vocabulary	E	Effort is commendable
E	Developed reading fluency	E	Exhibits positive attitude
E	Uses word attack skills	S	Listens attentively
E	Summarizes reading material	E	Follows directions
	Science	N	Works independently
S	Understands the scientific method	E	Exercises self-control
S	Applies scientific concepts to real life	U	Uses time wisely
E	Developed scientific vocabulary		
S	Interprets scientific data		

SUMMARIZE AND REFLECT

1. Grading is the process of assigning numbers or letters at the end of a specified period of time.
2. Grades are used for a variety of purposes, including instruction, communication, and internal administrative decisions.
3. Grades should not only document the student's performance level but also provide information on the student's strengths and weaknesses.
4. Students that use failure as a source of motivation to succeed may have a higher degree of commitment to the learning task.
5. Self-efficacy refers to an individual's sense of his/her own competence and is associated with a positive response to failure.
6. Teachers use grades to help communicate to parents how their child is progressing in school.
7. School administrators often use grades to determine honors and awards and to determine eligibility for participation in athletics.
8. Letter grades are convenient for teachers and are widely accepted and understood.
9. Pass-fail grades are a type of standards grading system.
10. Under a pass-fail system, students who meet or exceed the standard receive a passing grade.
11. Pass-fail grades have been criticized for not being sensitive to the differing ability levels of students.
12. Checklist grading systems document the extent to which students have mastered various learning standards.

INFORMED APPLICATION

1. As a teacher, you are expected to assign earned letter grades according to a numeric scale used by the district. You provide the information, but want to give the students more information so that they can improve future performance. What could you do to give the students a better chance to succeed?
2. What is your opinion on using grades to determine eligibility for participation in sports?

TECHNOLOGY AND CLASSROOM ASSESSMENT

Our final section of the chapter examines the impact of technology on the assessment process. Technology has dramatically changed many aspects of daily life. These changes are also impacting our educational system (Conn, 2011). Let's look at two of the most common technological innovations prevalent in schools that affect the process of assessment.

Electronic Portfolios

As was reviewed earlier in the chapter, a portfolio is a collection of student work over a period of time. It is one of many newer assessment tools used to better capture learning in a comprehensive way. An **electronic portfolio** is also a collection of student work over a period of time, but it is presented using technology. There are many advantages to using electronic versions of portfolios. One of the most prominent benefits of the approach is their flexibility and ability over time. Materials can be updated or revised with relative ease by simply modifying electronic documents. This was true to some extent of paper versions of portfolios, but electronic ones are usually easier to change. They also do not take up space like traditional portfolios. Some traditional portfolios take up multiple volumes with boxes for audio and visual supplemental artifacts. All of these items can be digitized and placed on a single CD or DVD. This makes record keeping and distribution far easier. Converting traditional artifacts—like pictures, art, student work, readings, and video recordings to a digital format—also encourages the student to grow in their understanding of computers and technology. These systems are specifically designed to produce and manage electronic portfolios. In this example, the student presents a variety of documents related to his/her elementary teaching portfolio. This information is maintained on the Internet, which makes for easy access.

Electronic portfolio

A collection of student work, over a period of time, which is presented using technology

The actual process of creating an electronic portfolio will vary, depending on the specific objectives of the assignment and the artifacts collected. **Artifact** is a general term referring to samples of student work or learning. Depending on the artifacts included in the portfolio, you may need a scanner for pictures, audio converter for sound recordings, or digital cameras for capturing new images. You are also likely to need software to bring your portfolio together in a cohesive way. Like the sample presented above, one popular approach is to create and store portfolios on the Internet. This necessitates the use of some form of Web authoring software. Alternatively, you could create a portfolio with multimedia presentation software and store it on disc. Many such programs exist such as PowerPoint, Persuasion, Adobe, Hyperstudio, etc. After you decide what software you will use, you need to create a portfolio flow chart. This is similar to a storyboard created by a director when making a movie. The flow chart outlines the basic layout for the portfolio. It not only specifies the content, but it shows how different elements are connected. Essentially, it is the blueprint for your portfolio.

Artifact

General term referring to samples of student work or learning

When planning your electronic portfolio, you also need to determine what is going to be included. What is included in the portfolio is determined by the overall curricular goals for the assignment. Each element must serve a specific purpose in documenting learning according to the learning goals for the task. Without this direct connection to the learning objective, the project typically turns into an exercise in technology use. Following these simple guidelines, however, turns the creation of an electronic portfolio into a cohesive learning exercise and an opportunity for students to grow in their understanding and use of technology.

Computers and Assessment

One of the most popular software applications used by teachers is the electronic gradebook. **Electronic gradebooks** are software programs designed to record grades, calculate relevant summary statistics (e.g., averages), and convert numeric grades into letter grades based on a user-defined system (e.g., 94–100% = *A*). They can dramatically increase the efficiency and speed of grade management tasks. They can also be used in combination with an Internet-based course management system to give students rapid and detailed feedback regarding their own performance, as well as that of the class as a whole. Such systems can be set to provide feedback immediately after an assignment is completed. The system can also be set at the instructor's discretion to provide the overall class average, range of grades on the assignment, the student's ranking on the assessment, and/or overall grade in the course. Not every

Electronic gradebook

Software program designed to record grades, calculate relevant summary statistics, and convert numeric grades into letter grades based on a user-defined system

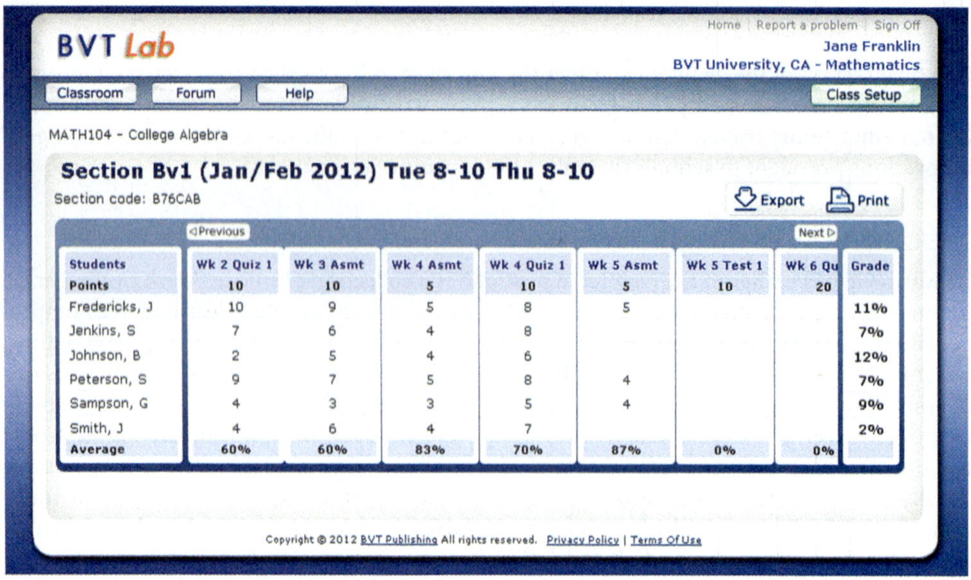
BVT Lab

Home | Report a problem | Sign Off

Jane Franklin

BVT University, CA - Mathematics

Classroom | Forum | Help | Class Setup

MATH104 - College Algebra

Section Bv1 (Jan/Feb 2012) Tue 8-10 Thu 8-10

Section code: B76CAB

Export | Print

◁Previous | Next ▷

Students	Wk 2 Quiz 1	Wk 3 Asmt	Wk 4 Asmt	Wk 4 Quiz 1	Wk 5 Asmt	Wk 5 Test 1	Wk 6 Qu	Grade
Points	10	10	5	10	5	10	20	
Fredericks, J	10	9	5	8	5			11%
Jenkins, S	7	6	4	8				7%
Johnson, B	2	5	4	6				12%
Peterson, S	9	7	5	8	4			7%
Sampson, G	4	3	3	5	4			9%
Smith, J	4	6	4	7				2%
Average	60%	60%	83%	70%	87%	0%	0%	

Copyright © 2012 BVT Publishing All rights reserved. Privacy Policy | Terms Of Use

assignment requires such detailed feedback, but the potential of these grading systems gives teachers greater flexibility.

As you can see from the table, using an electronic gradebook can save time over traditional grade management approaches. This electronic gradebook advantage is actually continuously increasing as computers become faster and programs more comprehensive. Electronic gradebooks can also present test items to students, allowing them to take tests on the computer. Programs that have this function are typically geared toward selective-response assessments (e.g., multiple-choice, true/false), but as software evolves, programs are beginning to be used to present and grade essay questions (Page & Petersen, 1995; Wresch, 1993).

Electronic gradebooks have several distinct advantages, but they also have some potential drawbacks. First, the usefulness of the electronic gradebook is entirely dependent on the quality of the information entered. If the teacher fails to enter accurate information, the program will produce inaccurate results. In fact, because computers calculate so quickly, errors tend to multiply quickly. These programs cannot ensure that teachers enter data accurately. It is still the teacher's responsibility to grade appropriately and enter those grades accurately. A second potential problem with electronic gradebooks is that teachers will let the program communicate with the student regarding grades. Students may find out grades by logging onto the program and reviewing their scores. It is possible that only the computer "knows" how each student is doing. This gives the students some control over accessing grades, but it does not allow the teacher to interpret a grade in the context of the student's other work. Teachers should never allow the computer to be the sole source of information regarding assessments. Teachers need to run frequent reports on each student's progress and examine the scores for potential issues that need attention. A final point to consider is that electronic gradebooks are potentially inflexible. They may not allow the teacher to make adjustments to grades during extraordinary circumstances. For example, imagine a class of twenty-four students who have taken a total of four tests over the last nine weeks. Their scores varied widely, but when an average is calculated for each student, all students have an average in the seventies. Some students made strong *A*'s on some tests, but failed others. Some students consistently scored in the seventies. Still, other students failed the first tests, but improved to an *A* level by the last test. The question is whether the teacher assigns a final grade exclusively on the average score at the end of the nine-week period. There is no simple answer. Some teachers would do just that, but others would want to modify grades given the pattern of scores exhibited by the student. Perhaps the teacher wants to use the median grade (see Chapter 9) as opposed to the average. Alternatively, the teacher may want to drop the lowest test grade or assign extra points for grade patterns showing strong improvement. Again, the point is that electronic gradebooks may not lend themselves to making such modifications if the teacher feels they are warranted. Ultimately, teachers need to keep in mind that it is *their* job to assign grades, not the computer's (Guskey, 2002).

SUMMARIZE AND REFLECT

1. Technology has created significant changes in the operation of the educational system.
2. Electronic portfolios are collections of a student's work, over a period of time, presented using technology.
3. One of the most prominent benefits of the electronic portfolio is the ability to be modified, updated, or revised with relative ease.
4. *Artifact* is a term referring to samples of a student's work or learning.
5. What is included in a portfolio is determined by the overall curricular goals for the assignment.
6. Electronic gradebooks are software programs designed to record grades, calculate summary statistics, and convert numeric grades into letter grades.
7. The usefulness of the electronic gradebook depends on the accuracy of the information put into it.
8. Electronic gradebooks should not substitute for communication between teacher and student about grades.
9. Teachers should be mindful that it is their job to assign grades, not the computer's.

INFORMED APPLICATION

1. What do you think are the advantages of using a typical portfolio versus an electronic one?
2. Online courses are becoming increasingly common, particularly in higher education. Inherent in these courses is electronic grading and assessment. What is your opinion regarding electronic grades? Advantages/Disadvantages?

THE CHAPTER IN REVIEW

One of the primary reasons for using assessments is to help teachers measure learning outcomes and student progress toward those outcomes. Formative assessments provide information related to learning progress. Summative assessments are designed to test whether the students achieved the desired learning outcome. Effective assessment begins with clearly defined instructional goals. Some students may not meet learning goals and require additional instructional efforts. To help with such efforts, schools may adopt a pre-referral team—consisting of teachers, administrators, and other educational professionals—whose job it is to develop learning solutions for students struggling in the regular education program. Pre-referral teams often use diagnostic assessments to further clarify the nature of a particular student's struggles.

Grades have been shown to have positive and negative effects on learning and motivation, depending on the situation. To increase the usefulness of grades, periodic assessment can give students needed corrective feedback to support learning during the formative stages. Feedback needs to be developmentally appropriate and presented as soon as possible after the assessment. Informal assessments are unplanned opportunities to gather information about student learning. Informal assessments, however, lack a specific methodology, which makes them difficult to apply outside the environment in which they were observed. Formal assessments are typically planned and constructed in advance to assess a particular learning objective. Typical formal assessments include multiple-choice, forced-choice, matching, completion, short answer, and essay.

Questions can also be subdivided into two broad types. Selective-response questions give students a limited number of choices to endorse. Constructed-response test items are those that require the student to actually create their own answers. Selective-response questions tend to be more objective and do not rely on as much interpretation by the teacher. Subjective questions depend on the judgment of the teacher. Grading rubrics include the basic criteria for judging the correctness of a constructed response and help guide subjective judgment.

Of all the assessment formats, multiple-choice items are the most common assessment tool because they are easily adapted to a wide range of learning objectives. Also popular are forced-choice or true/false items that are used to assess the student's ability to recognize correct definitions and factual information. Another question format involves matching one concept or term with a related item. One of the challenges in creating a matching test item is in the prevention of successful guessing. Of the constructed-response formats, essay questions are ideally suited for measuring complex learning.

New perceptions of learning are fostering the development of newer assessment approaches. With these assessments, there is a greater focus on how students actively construct knowledge and how this impacts instruction. Alternative assessments are any assessment approaches that go beyond traditional assessments. Alternative assessments often provide a more detailed account of the process of learning in addition to the product of learning. Alternative assessments are also often embedded in performance-based activities. Performance-based activities are learning situations that apply knowledge in ways mirroring application in real life. Performance-based assessments encompass many learning activities, including science experiments, plays, oral presentations, debates, conversing in a foreign language, and applied mathematics. Another alternative assessment is the portfolio, which is a collection of student work in a particular context. Portfolios can be challenging to grade and need a clear and direct tie to a specific learning objective. Exhibitions are another alternative assessment opportunity for students to display their learning to the public. This format measures their learning, in addition to other factors like ability to respond to questions and presentation ability.

Grading is the process of assigning numbers or letters to a student's performance at the end of a specified period of time. Grades are used for a variety of purposes including instruction, communication, and internal administrative decisions. Grades should not only document the student's performance level but should also provide information on the student's strengths and weaknesses. Grades can produce a variety of behavioral and emotional responses. For example, students that use failure as a source of motivation to succeed may have a higher degree of commitment to the learning task. This relates to the idea of self-efficacy. Self-efficacy refers to an individual's sense of his/her own competence and is associated with a positive response to failure.

Teachers use grades to help communicate to parents how their child is progressing in school. Grades are also used by school administrators to determine honors and awards and to determine eligibility for participation in athletics. Letter grades are convenient for teachers and are widely accepted and understood. Pass-fail grades are a type of standards grading system. Under a pass-fail system, students who meet or exceed the standard receive a passing grade. Pass-fail grades have been criticized for not being sensitive to the differing ability levels of students. Another grading approach is the checklist. Checklist grading systems document the extent to which students have mastered various learning standards.

Technology has created significant changes in the operation of the educational system. For example, electronic portfolios are collections of a student's work over a period of time, presented by using technology. One of the most prominent benefits of the electronic portfolio is the ability to modify, update, or revise the portfolio with relative ease. Portfolios often contain artifacts, a term referring to samples of a student's work or learning. What is actually included in a portfolio is determined by the overall curricular goals for the assignment and may include items other than artifacts.

Gradebooks are software programs designed to record grades, calculate summary statistics, and convert numeric grades into letter grades. The usefulness of the electronic gradebook depends on the accuracy of the information put into it. Electronic gradebooks should not substitute for communication between teacher and student about grades. Teachers should remember that it is their job to assign grades, not the computer's.

Interdisciplinary Case Focus

principal *special educator*
teacher *parents* *psychologist*
social worker *physical educator*
nurse *peers* *doctor*

One of the most important interdisciplinary teams is also the most frequent and natural, the teacher and the parent. The teacher—parent relationship is often the deciding factor between student success and failure. In this case study, we will review the educational problems experienced by Celine, who is in her sophomore year at a public high school in rural upstate New York. Celine is making reasonable progress in most of her classes. One class, however, is proving to be a disappointing experience. Geometry is the math class she likes least in all her years of school. The concepts are hard, the proofs are tricky and difficulty to apply beyond the example given in class, and there are so many formulas, angles, and postulates that she knew she was in trouble from the very beginning.

Celine is a strong individual but also reserved. She is bright, but often she fails to take the initiative. These qualities did not serve her well in this situation—they only served to exacerbate the situation. Her mother often asked about her progress in school. Celine responded in her characteristic fashion, "It is going pretty good." He mother would ask about grades, and Celine would selectively give her grades from classes other than math to hide her difficulty with the subject. This worked until mid-term grades were sent home, at which time her mother was horrified to see that Celine was failing math—not just a little but in a grand way. Celine's class average was a 39 (out of 100).

Celine's mother tried to work with her over the next two weeks to get her back on track, but the problems were honestly beyond the mother's current skills. She hadn't seen a geometry problem since her own high school years. Her relationship with Celine began to deteriorate as arguments over math became a daily occurrence. Recognizing the futility of the current situation, Celine's mother finally made an appointment with the math teacher to see if there was some way to help her pass the class.

Parent–Teacher Conference

Celine's mother, Jillian, sat down with Mr. Schwartz, the math teacher, one afternoon following school. This was their first meeting, and Jillian was very nervous. She felt like a failure and was reluctant to see the critical judgment she was sure she'd find on Mr. Schwartz's face. Much to her surprise, Mr. Schwartz turned out to be a thoroughly pleasant man. He was fairly young, having finished his education three years ago. They sat in his classroom in two of the student's desks and began their discussion.

Jillian began by apologizing for not coming to see him sooner. Mr. Schwartz assured her that no apologies were needed. In his opinion, the past was simply a source of information to help with success in the present. Already liking the teacher, Jillian began to detail her concerns and her failed attempts to help her daughter. Mr. Schwartz listened carefully. After Jillian seemed to get it all out, Mr. Schwartz began by saying that he was excited about her enthusiasm regarding her daughter's success and hoped that their partnership would strengthen that potential.

Creating a Strong Parent/Teacher Team

Mr. Schwartz assured Jillian that it was not her responsibility to teach her daughter geometry. That was his and the school's responsibility. He pointed out, however, that instruction was only one of many factors impacting success. He began to detail how they might work as an educational team to help Celine. First, he began to convey some of his observations regarding Celine in class. She sat off to the side of the room near the door and often appeared to lack focus. It was important to take notes in the class, but Celine wrote very little. He also explained his grading system, which consisted of end-of-the-chapter quizzes, a midterm, and a final. After some discussion, Jillian and Mr. Schwartz decided to use grading in a different way to encourage success on a smaller scale. Beginning the next week, Celine would be expected to spend at least one hour after school with her mother working on geometry. The structure of these sessions was that Celine was to "teach" her mother how to complete the problems that were discussed in class that day. Obviously, Celine would need to pay attention in class, take notes, and participate in the class with more engagement. At the end of Celine's instruction with her mother, Jillian (the mom) would take a brief quiz on the material generated by Mr. Schwartz. After the quiz, Celine and her mother would discuss the results and examine any confusion. Jillian would then email her results to Mr. Schwartz and express any confusion Celine appeared to have, and consequently had trouble teaching her mother. Mr. Schwartz would clarify the issues with Celine the following day.

The idea behind this approach was that the following issues needed to be addressed: 1) Celine lacked motivation. 2) The current grading structure was too summative in nature, and Celine needed a great deal more formative information. 3) Her notetaking was poor and incomplete. 4) Celine's natural personality was reserved in a way that was impeding her success. The new "student as teacher" approach addressed each of these issues. The nature of the task would motivate Celine, as she would likely want her mother to report good quiz grades to Mr. Schwartz. The daily nature of the sessions would ensure Celine's difficulties did not go unnoticed. Celine's note taking would need to improve to make the at-home work possible. Mr. Schwartz was going to help with this by first letting Celine review another successful student's notes. This would give her an idea of what hers should look like. He was also going to check her progress during class, as well as at the end of each class. Mr. Schwartz would only provide positive enthusiasm regarding the class work and applaud her when her mother experienced success on the at-home quizzes. The rest of the grading structure would remain the same.

Epilogue

The result of this intervention could potentially go in many directions. As a way of reviewing the chapter information and applying what was learned, write a brief epilogue or concluding remarks for this case. What happened after the intervention was in place? Consider carefully the information you learned in the chapter and in the course in general.

Key Terms

TERM	*Page*	*TERM*	*Page*
Alternative assessment	508	Grading rubric	505
Artifact	515	Informal assessment	503
Assessment-led reform	508	Letter grades	512
Checklist grading system	513	Objective question	504
Constructed response	505	Pass-fail grades	513
Diagnostic assessment	500	Performance-based activities	509
Electronic gradebook	515	Portfolio	509
Electronic portfolio	515	Selected-response questions	504
Exhibitions	510	Self-efficacy	512
Formal assessment	504	Subjective question	505
Formative assessment	498	Summative assessment	498
Grading	511		

Glossary

68/95/99.7 Rule
General rule describing the variation typically observed in a group of scores

A

Action research
Research that involves a teacher applying both descriptive and experimental research methods to assess the effectiveness of certain educational approaches or to solve everyday problems

A-B-A-B single-participant design
Using an alternating presentation of the intervention with the recording of a baseline

Academic learning time
The portion of engaged time where students are actually learning

Acceleration
The process of providing an advanced instructional setting to meet the needs of exceptional learners

Accommodation
Service that maintains existing educational procedures for students, while making allowances for special needs

Accommodation
A process in which an existing schema is altered to better account for a new experience

Achievement test
Test that assesses a student's current learning level in a specific academic area

Acquisition
The initial learning of a response

Acronym approach
A mnemonic where the first letter of each item on the list is taken and rearranged to form a familiar word

Adaptations
Environmentally dependent changes that allow us to better function in the world

Adaptive functions
How the individual adapts to the world in which they live

Adaptive reactions
Adjustment that increases performance

Adequate yearly progress (AYP)
An accountability measure by the federal government to ensure schools are making educational progress over time

Adolescent egocentrism
An adolescent's focus on his or her own thoughts and the inability to see the perspective of others

Advanced organizer
Any introductory material presented at a higher level of abstraction and inclusiveness than the learning task itself

Age-equivalents
Results usually based on comparing a student's score on a test to the average score on the same test for various ages

Algorithm
A specific series of steps leading from an initial problem to a predetermined end state

Allocated time
The amount of time students and teachers spend at school

Alternate form reliability
Consistency established by giving comparable forms of the same test to the same students

Alternative assessment
Any assessment approach that goes beyond the traditional assessments such as multiple-choice tests, homework, and reports.

Androgyny
Having both masculine and feminine qualities

Antecedent
An event occurring before the behavior of interest, having an effect on its expression

Aphasia
A clinical condition in which language skills are lost due to injury in the language areas of the brain

Applied behavior analysis (ABA)
A professional field which has emerged to address the need for more formal and accountable application of behavioral principles

Aptitude test
Test that predicts how well a student will perform when placed in a new learning situation

Artifact
General term referring to samples of student work or learning

Assessment
Process of collecting relevant data and information on student performance

Assessment-led reform
Movement driven by educators, administrators, and federal educational agencies interested in expanding traditional assessments

Assimilation
A process in which an existing schema is satisfactorily used to explain a new experience

Asynchronous
Form of communication that does not involve immediate feedback from each other

Attention
That which directs sensory memories toward the next component in the information processing model of memory, working memory

Attention deficit/hyperactivity disorder (AD/HD)
The most commonly diagnosed disorder of childhood, characterized by some combination of inattention, impulsivity, or hyperactivity

Attribution theory
Theory that describes our attempts to determine causes for events happening in our lives and subsequently impacts our level of motivation

Authentic activity
Lessons that mirror real-life and help students understand the relevance of education

Authentic assessment
Assessment that resembles the actual work the student completes at school, home, or in daily life work

Authoritarian teacher
A teacher that emphasizes behavioral control

Authoritative teacher
A teacher that emphasizes the importance of providing firm direction, while recognizing the unique contributions of each student to the learning process

Autistic disorder
Characterized by impairments in social relatedness and communication, as well as issues with repetitive (or stereotyped) behaviors

B

Baseline
Participant responses that are recorded during the absence of a treatment

Baseline
Record of a behavior of interest prior to any intervention

Behavioral assessment
Assessment that provides a standardized tool for assessing a student's behavior, emotionality, and social interactions

Behavior rating scale
One of the most common tools that professionals use to assess/rate behavioral disturbances

Bilingual education
Educational practice that teaches students in their native language, while progressively building instruction in English

Blended family
Families in which single-parents who re-marry create step-relations and potentially half-sibling relationships

Bottom-up processing
Process by which an individual attempts to arrive at a meaningful perception using sensory items to build an appropriate understanding

C

Case study
The intensive description of a single individual or unified cohort

Central executive
The supervisory system of working memory that manages the allocation of resources

Central tendency
The tendency for scores to cluster around the center of a distribution of scores

Centration
The inability to think of more than one aspect of a problem at a time

Cerebral cortex
The area of the brain most directly implicated in thinking and learning

Character education programs
Programs that focus on the transmission of certain core values with instruction taking place through activities that allow for the practice of moral behavior

Checklist grading system
Grading method used with increasing frequency, particularly in elementary schools, which requires the evaluator to check a given list of skills as being met, observed, or not yet observed

Chunking
Process that essentially allows us to expand the amount of information available in working memory, without increasing its capacity

Classical conditioning
A behavioral theory based on our ability to learn by associating events that co-occur in the environment

Classification
The ability to mentally organize observed similarities and differences in the environment

Classroom management
The variety of teacher and student factors contributing to the operation of the educational environment

Classroom test
Usually self-developed by the teacher or a commercially available assessment for the express purpose of helping teachers evaluate the performance of a particular student

Closed head injury
Trauma to the head where the skull remains intact

Code-switching
Moving back and forth from a dialect to the more standard form of the language

Cognitive coaching
Process that helps students move from a teacher supported level of performance, to a level of performance relying exclusively on the student's abilities

Cognitive equilibrium
The state in which our understanding of the world is adequate for making sense of the situations we encounter

Cognitive modeling
The teacher models his/her own thoughts for the student, by talking aloud as that same teacher reasons through a task

Cognitive neuroscience
The study of relations between the brain and thinking

Cognitive perspective
Theories and research related to an understanding of thinking and reasoning

Cognitive training
Term used to describe educational approaches that attempt to modify a student's thought processes

Collaborative classroom
Classroom that promotes dialogue through effective communication and a value and respect for differing perspectives

Commitment
The individual's decision on a particular identity

Community of learners
Individuals participating in a given learning endeavor (e.g., the students and teacher in a classroom)

Community of learners
A collection of individuals gathered for the purpose of meeting a learning objective

Comparable groups
Groups that are typically formed using random assignment to conditions

Concept learning
Learning that centers on acquiring the basic concepts, which form the basis for additional learning and higher-level thinking

Concept mapping
The creation of a visual or graphical representation of a concept

Conditional knowledge
Knowledge about the appropriate application of procedural and declarative information

Conditioned response (CR)
The behavioral response to the conditioned stimulus brought about through a learned association

Conditioned stimulus (CS)
The environmental event that brings about the conditioned stimulus through a learned association

Confidence interval
Range of scores believed to contain the student's true score

Conflict resolution
Instruction in how to manage interpersonal conflict productively and positively

Conflict resolution
A set of approaches that attempt to improve social interactions through successful mediation of conflict

Congruent communication
An authentic harmony between words and feelings; having what you say be in tune with what you feel

Connectionist network theorists
Theorists that have related knowledge storage and retrieval to the actual functioning of the neuron

Consequence
Event occurring after the behavior of interest

Conservation task
A problem that requires a child to consider two environmental factors at the same time to generate a correct answer

Constructed response
Type of answer that requires the student to create his/her own response, rather than picking a correct answer from choices provided by the teacher

Constructivism
The active processing of new information in the context of prior learning and the student's readiness to learn

Construct-related validity
A judgment as to whether the test accurately measures the intended construct

Content-related validity
Strength of a test established by examining whether relevant content domains are included in the test

Contiguity
The co-occurrence of events

Continuous performance test (CPT)
A test designed to measure an individual's ability to sustain attention

Continuous reinforcement
Reinforcement that is provided at every instance of a desired behavior

Control group
Group that serves as a comparison group

Conventional
Level of moral reasoning that is based on the expectations of individuals other than the self

Convergent thinking
The ability to think analytically, and usually deductively, of the one correct solution

Cooperative learning
Technique that involves groups of individuals working together to achieve a common goal

Corpus callosum
Section of the brain that allows information to travel back and forth between the left and the right sides of the brain

Correlation
Statistical technique used to establish the nature of the relation between variables

Correlational coefficient
The numerical product resulting from the correlation formula

Correlational studies
Studies that not only describe events but also establish how events relate to each other.

Creativity
Often defined as having two qualities: originality and functionality

Criterion-related validity
Prediction about the strength of the performance on a test against some other related criterion

Critical thinking
The process by which the thinker improves the quality of his or her thinking by skillfully taking charge of the structures inherent in thinking and imposing intellectual standards

Crystallized expertise
A thorough understanding of an area gained by experience and expressed through a well-rehearsed framework

Cueing
A manipulation of the environment before the behavior of interest

Cultural bias
An unfair penalty on a test that results due to a student's gender, ethnicity, socioeconomic status, religion, or other such group-defining characteristic

Curriculum-based assessment (CBA)
Measurement of student progress using a standard assessment tool, with the test being derived from actual schoolwork detailed in the school's curriculum

Curriculum packing
A technique to help teachers make appropriate curricular adjustments, depending on the specific learning needs of the student

D

Decay theory
Belief that, over time, information not actively rehearsed or transferred to long-term memory will gradually weaken and fade away

Decenter
Change in thinking from focusing on the most salient features of the problem to a consideration of other relevant factors

Declarative knowledge
Information that can be stated or declared

Deep structure
An underlying principle behind the solution to a problem

Defensive reactions
Action that causes learners to withdraw from the task

Dependent variable
What is measured in the study, depending on the treatment manipulation

Descriptive research method
Research method that accurately describes a behavior or environmental condition of interest

Development
Systematic continuities and changes in the individual over the course of life

Developmental crisis
A particular life event important in the development of individual identity

Developmental neuroscience
The study of the orderly progression of changes in the brain that occur across the lifespan

Deviation IQ
Intelligence scores calculated by using a current method for greater reliability and validity

Diagnostic assessment
Assessment that is conducted for the specific purpose of identifying why a student is struggling academically

Diagnostic assessment
Assessment used to give teachers very precise information on how to address a student's learning difficulty

Dialects
Regional or socially distinct forms of a language having their own characteristic pronunciation, grammar, and vocabulary

Dialogic teaching
Technique that utilizes a classroom setting where teachers and students make significant contributions to the discussion that helps to move the student's thinking forward

Direct instruction (DI)
A highly structured, teacher-centered, form of instruction

Direct Instruction (DI)
A systematic approach for teaching a defined academic skill

Direction
Provides an indication of how *two* variables change in relation to each other

Disability
Usually a reduced capacity to perform in some domain

Discovery learning
A learning approach that focuses on active, hands-on learning supported by instructional guidance

Discrimination
Ability to tell the difference between stimuli, allowing someone to limit a conditioned response to the original conditioned stimulus

Disequilibrium
The state in which our current understanding of the world is insufficient to make sense of a new situation

Distributive negotiations
Technique that focuses on winning or benefiting at the expense of another.

Divergent thinking
The ability to think of multiple solutions to a given problem

Diversity
Often difficult to define, but at a fundamental level, is about individuality or difference

E

Electronic gradebook
Software program designed to record grades, calculate relevant summary statistics, and convert numeric grades into letter grades based on a user-defined system

Electronic portfolio
A collection of student work, over a period of time, which is presented using technology

Empirical
Based on observation or experience

Educational psychology
Discipline concerned with the development, evaluation, and application of our understanding of human learning and behavior in an educational setting

Education for All Handicapped Children Act (Public Law 94-142)
Law that provides "free and appropriate" educational services for all children with handicaps

Egalitarian families
Families in which managerial roles for distribution of financial assets, socialization of the children, and general family dynamics are shared on both sides of the family

Egocentric
Thinking that is characterized by one's own perspective

Egocentric
The inability to view the world from someone else's perspective

Egocentric speech
The use of overt speaking by an individual to modify his or her own actions

Elaboration
Refers to the idea of making connections between material you are trying to learn and information already known

Elaboration
The linking of new information to information already known

Elaborative rehearsal
The specific process of taking something you are trying to learn and connecting it to something you already know

Empathetic listening
Where the listener moves beyond sympathy, which strives to console, and tries to connect and genuinely understand the other's perspective

Encoding specificity
Storing memories in a specific way which may limit recall to certain situations

Engaged time
That portion of allocated time spent participating in learning activities

Engagement
A higher-order construct or idea of being involved in the learning activity made up of many behavioral, emotional and cognitive factors

English as a second language (ESL)
A special form of English instruction, which is sensitive to a learner's limited English experience

Enrichment
The process of providing advanced learning opportunities for students, while maintaining their regular educational placement

Episodic knowledge
Personal information that is tied to a specific time and place

Epistemology
The nature or origin of knowledge

Equality
Maintaining similarity or being impartial

Equilibration
The restoration of equilibrium by adapting to the situation that had caused disequilibrium

Equity
Freedom from bias

Equity instruction
Technique that strives to educate students in a way that is sensitive to their unique qualities

Ethnicity
Any distinguishable group of people who have a common culture, ethnic background, or cultural affiliation

Evaluation
The systematic investigation of the worth or merit of an object

Evaluation
The reflective process of determining the worth or merit of an object, depending on the available information

Executive control processes
Memory components that direct the flow of information through the memory system and impact effectiveness

Executive functioning
A collection of skills involved in self-regulation, planning for the future, internalization of speech, perception of time, and some aspects of working memory

Exhibitions
Opportunities for students to display their learning to the public

Expectancy and value theorists
Theorists that believe motivation results from the interaction between our expectancy for success and the value we place on the outcome

Expectancy for success
Our perception regarding the potential outcome of a situation

Experimental group
Group that receives the experimental manipulation

Experimental research
Set of procedures used in science to infer that one event leads to or causes another

Exploration
An individual's active experimentation with different lifestyles and ways of being in the world

Expressive language disorder
A disorder where the individual has difficulty using language to express intent or meaning

Extended family
Relatives of the nuclear family that share the emotional and often financial functions of the family

Extinction (classical conditioning)
Elimination of a classically conditioned response, typically accomplished by presenting the conditioned stimulus alone

Extinction (operant conditioning)
The process of no longer reinforcing a given behavior

Extrinsically motivated behavior
Actions that are produced by an externally mediated outcome

F

Family of orientation
The family unit we were in as children

Family of procreation
The family we participate in as parents

Fixed schedule of reinforcement
Reinforcement that is provided at a constant rate

Flow
A state where there is a maximal sense of fulfillment derived from a well-developed skill meeting a challenging task

Fluency disorder
More commonly referred to as stuttering

Fluid (also called adaptive) expertise
Skills expressed through an unfamiliar problem, often generating novel and creative solutions

Formal assessment
Assessment that is planned and constructed, in advance, to assess a particular learning objective

Formative assessment
Assessment that provides information on learning progress

Formative assessment
Assessment providing information regarding how learning is progressing

Frequency distribution
Graphical depiction of how many students obtained a given score

Frontal lobes
Portion of the brain that plays a role in many human behaviors, including planning, anticipating consequences, and inhibiting behavior

Full inclusion
Educational practice where ALL students are maintained in their home school classroom setting ALL the time

Full scale intelligence quotient score
The global measure of intellectual functioning

Functional assessment
Comprehensive set of assessment procedures used to determine the function that problematic behaviors serve in the life of the student

Functional behavioral assessment (FBA)
An evaluation to determine the cause of a student's behavior

Functional fixedness
An inability to move beyond the established understanding of an object, which is necessary to solve a problem

G

Gender
The psychological, behavioral, and cultural factors related to being male or female

Gender constancy
The idea that one's sex is constant regardless of the behaviors exhibited

Gender identity
That part of a person related to the experience of being male or female

Gender role
The public expression of one's gender

Gender-role transcendence
Shifting of educational focus beyond gender

Gender schemas
Our ideas about gender appropriate behaviors

Gender stereotype
Vague conceptualizations regarding issues related to one's gender

General intelligence
Idea that there is one broad cognitive ability governing intelligent behavior

Generalization
Referring to the appropriateness of applying research results to settings that differ from the research setting

Generalization
A conditioned response to a stimulus that is similar to, but not exactly the same as, the conditioned stimulus

General transfer
The idea that learning skills or reasoning approaches in one content area lead to a general ability that applies to different situations

Gestalt psychologists
The group of psychologists interested in the role that perception plays in shaping our understanding of the world

Goal directed behavior
Behavior that involves striving to accomplish a desired outcome

Grade equivalents
Performance results expressed in terms of an approximate grade level

Grading
The process of assigning numbers or letters to student performance at the end of a specified period of time

Grading rubric
Basic criteria for grading an item, but in which teacher perception still potentially shapes the scoring

Group self-esteem
An individual's judgment about a group of people to which he or she belongs

H

Handicap
A situational disadvantage

Heuristics
Problem-solving strategies that increase the probability of finding a solution, but do not guarantee a solution

Hierarchy of needs
Graphical representation of Abraham Maslow's motivational theory regarding needs

High-stakes testing
Testing practices that result in excessively important consequences

Home school
Usually defined as the school that a student would attend if he/she did not have a disability

Hypothesis
An educated guess as to the outcome

Hypothesis
An educated guess

Hypothetico-deductive reasoning
The ability to speculate about how a particular situation functions and then test the prediction or guess

I

Identity achievement
Achievement characterized by both exploration and commitment

Identity diffusion
An approach to identity formation that involves neither exploration nor a strong commitment

Identity foreclosure
Achievement characterized by commitment, but not active exploration

Identity moratorium
A process where the individual focuses on exploration, but delays making any commitment

Ill-defined
Having many appropriate responses and multiple paths to achieving a solution

Incentive
Essentially, the promise of a reward

Inclusion
The practice of grouping children for education based on traditional factors like age and location of the student's home

Independent variable
Variable being manipulated by the experimenter

Index scores
Additional information on specific aspects of intellectual functioning

Individual constructivism
The study of how individuals develop and change their cognitive and emotional processes in an attempt to understand information and build knowledge

Individualized Education Program (IEP)
A legal document specifying how the school is going to meet its obligation to provide Free and Appropriate Public Education (FAPE) to a student with special needs

Inert knowledge
The results from our failure to recognize how to apply learning beyond the original learning context

Informal assessment
Unplanned opportunity to gather information about student learning

Inquiry-based learning (IBL)
An approach to learning that centers on the scientific investigation of a particular issue or project

Instructional conversations
Educational dialogues that help the instructor assess what information the student is ready to learn, with appropriate assistance

Integrative negotiation
Technique of reaching a mutually beneficial resolution to conflict

Intelligence quotient
Original term used by Alfred Binet to refer to the quantitative measure of an individual's intelligence

Intentional behavior
Refers to the purposeful manipulation of the environment to achieve an outcome

Interdisciplinary collaboration
The collaboration of educational professionals from a variety of disciplines to produce learning environments sensitive to individual learning needs

Interference theory
Belief that memories do not simply decay over time; instead, the information becomes interfered with by older memories or incoming information

Intergenerational child rearing
The practice of grandparents rearing children

Interindividual comparison
A comparison between individuals

Intermental changes
Modifications in thinking resulting from our social interactions

Intermittent schedule of reinforcement
Reinforcement for only some of the desired responses

Interpersonal collaboration
A style of direct interaction between at least two co-equal parties voluntarily engaged in shared decision making as they work toward a common goal

Interstate New Teacher Assessment and Support Consortium (INTASC)
A consortium that consists of state education associations and national educational organizations

Interval schedule of reinforcement
A schedule that provides reinforcement for the first instance of a desired behavior after a certain period of time

Intraindividual comparison
A comparison within an individual

Intramental changes
The process of adapting socially derived mental processes to govern our own thinking and behavior

Intrinsically motivated behavior
The internal process that initiates and directs one's behavior

Invariant sequencing
The idea that all humans develop cognitively in the same sequence of qualitatively different stages

J

Jigsaw approach
Learning technique that structures a given task by having each student achieve a portion of that academic task and, in so doing, contributes to completion of the whole

Keyword method
A mnemonic that is particularly useful if you are trying to use a visualization technique for remembering more abstract words

Kinship rearing
The more general term used to refer to children reared by family members other than the child's parents

Knowledge
The accumulation of memories over time into a complex, but highly organized body of information

Language disorder
Problems associated with understanding and expressing language

Lateralized brain function
A specialized brain function primarily controlled by one hemisphere

Law of effect
Principle of behavior stating that a behavior resulting in satisfying events increase the likelihood of that behavior in the future

Learning
A lasting change in an individual resulting from experience

Learning achievement
The measure of what a student has achieved through academic work

Learning center
A specific location within a classroom designed to meet a specific educational objective

Learning potential
The measure of a student's general ability to learn

Learning styles
Instruction that focuses on the interaction between learner characteristics and the specific learning task

Legally blind
Defined as visual acuity of 20/200 or less in the individual's best eye with correction

Legitimate peripheral participation
Emphasis on the initial participation of new learners typically along the periphery of the learning community

Lesson plans
Guides to aid teachers during instruction

Letter grades
One of the most common approaches to grading/evaluating a student's work or achievement

Life space intervention
An approach that is an insight based approach designed to give students a better perspective on how they function in the world

M

Macrostructure
The level of learning involving the operation of whole brain structures

Maintenance rehearsal
The specific process of mentally repeating information currently held in working memory

Manipulation
Change the researcher makes to the environment

Mastery learning
An approach to instruction built on the idea that given enough time and proper instruction, nearly all students can successfully master instructional objectives

Mastery oriented students
A student focused on learning the material

Matriarchal families
Families in which managerial roles for distribution of financial assets, socialization of the children, and general family dynamics run on the mother's side of the family

Maturation
Changes occurring naturally, irrespective of environmental demands

Mean
The measure of central tendency calculated by adding all the scores and then dividing the sum by the total number of scores

Meaningful learning
Learning that is not separate or isolated from a person's life experiences but deeply integrated into his/her development and understanding of the world

Means-end analysis
A comparison between the final goal state and the current state

Measurement
Process of quantifying performance, effectiveness, or characteristics of some area of interest

Median
The score that occurs in the middle of a ranked distribution

Memory
The ability to retain a mental representation of our experiences

Metacognition
A mental process everyone uses in their daily lives—thinking about our own thinking

Metacognition
The awareness of our thought processes and our ability to exert control over our thinking

Metacognition
Broadly defined as thinking about one's own thought processes

Metacognitive knowledge
Information we acquire about how thinking occurs

Metacognitive regulation
Evaluating the outcome of our efforts to use metacognitive strategies

Metalinguistic awareness
The ability to think about language and language rules by reflecting on language itself

Method of loci
A memorization approach that is excellent for learning items that can be visualized

Microstructure
The level of learning involving the neuron

Mixed receptive-expressive language disorder
Characterized by difficulties understanding the language of others, as well as difficulties with language expression

Mnemonics
Term generally applied to a wide variety of techniques used to improve memory

Mode
The score that occurs most frequently in a distribution

Modification
Change in the typical educational process

Moral dilemmas
Research tools pioneered by Lawrence Kohlberg that presented the research participant with a morally difficult situation and asked that the participant provide an answer and an explanation for his/her choice

Moral education programs
Programs that usually provide instruction using moral dilemmas, which encourage children to construct their own sense of morality

Morality
Generally refers to an established standard for human conduct

Morality of cooperation
Refers to thinking that centers on the intent behind the transgression

Moral realism
Refers to thinking that centers on the magnitude of a transgression

Morpheme
The smallest unit of meaning in a language

Multicultural education
An educational ideal that students from all racial/ethnic and social class groups will have an equitable educational experience

Multiple intelligences
Idea that intelligence is not a single construct, but rather a collection of distinct abilities

Mutual respect
A quality whereby students and teachers have a fundamental belief that everyone in the learning situation is participating fully

N

Negative interdependence
Social interaction processes that are competitive and operate at the expense of others

Negative reinforcement
The removal of something negative from the environment in order to increase the frequency of a desired response

Negative transfer
The act of learning in one situation fails to generalize to other settings

Neo-Piagetian theorists
A group of researchers attempting to retain much of Piaget's original insights and to extend those insights to better account for the latest research findings

Neurons
Specialized brain cells that send and receive information by conducting electrochemical impulses

Neurotransmitter
A chemical that is released from one neuron and received by another to facilitate communication between them

Neutral stimulus (NS)
Something in the environment that initially fails to elicit the unconditioned response

No Child Left Behind
Act signed into law on January 8, 2002, not only reauthorizing public funding for primary and secondary education, but also introducing a number of research-focused educational reforms

Nodes
Specific elements within the semantic network representing concepts

Non-verbal communication
Communication without words that involves tone of voice, eye contact, hand gestures, facial expressions, touching, etc

Normal distribution
Distribution of scores characterized by most scores clustering close to the average

Norm-based testing
Assessment that compares the performance of a given student against other students the same age

Notes
Condensed written accounts generated while simultaneously listening to a lecture, while studying a text, or through observation

Nuclear family
A family unit consisting of a mother, father, and their children

O

Objective question
Question where the correctness of the answer does not rely on its interpretation by the teacher

Objective scoring
When the answer to a question does not depend on the opinion/judgment of the individual grading the test

Object permanence
A child's ability to mentally represent or think about an object after it has been removed from his or her field of vision or other senses

Occipital lobes
Portion of the brain that is primarily responsible for visual processing

Ontology
The nature of reality and truth, a set of concepts within a domain

Open head injuries
Injuries where the skull is actually breached, exposing underlying tissue

Operant conditioning
A learning theory focusing on how consequences shape the expression of behavior

Operations
Our application of mental resources

Otherwise qualified
To be protected from discrimination under Section 504 and ADA, the student's disability must be the only barrier to his/her participation in the activity

P

Paralanguage
Characteristics of language involving volume, rate, pitch, and pronunciation of spoken words

Parietal lobes
Portion of the brain that is responsible for integrating somatosensory information, such as touch, temperature, and pain

Pass-fail grades
A type of standards (criterion) grading system

Patriarchal families
Families in which managerial roles for distribution of financial assets, socialization of the children, and general family dynamics run on the father's side of the family

Peer mediation
Technique of using a trained student to act as a facilitator in the conflict of other students

Peer-neglected students
Onlookers who are not excluded from the group, but do not actively participate

Perception
The cognitive process of assigning meaning to incoming sensory information

Perceptual reasoning index
Measure that requires visual organization, comprehension, and reasoning ability with non-verbal material

Performance based
Idea that a treatment professional is concerned with actual behavior and the situational events impacting its expression

Performance-based activities
Learning situations that apply knowledge in ways mirroring application in real life

Performance oriented students
One more concerned about how his/her performance will be judged

Permissive teacher
A teacher that emphasizes student responsibility for decision-making

Personal self-esteem
An individual's judgments about his/her personal abilities or competencies

Person-centered planning
The approach that stresses the importance of developing a long-term plan for the student prior to any changes in educational programming

Phonological awareness
The ability to recognize different units of sound within words

Phonological disorder
Disorder characterized by articulation errors occurring during speech production

Phonological loop
The part of working memory which allows us to repeat auditory and verbal information

Phonology
The sounds in speech

Placement assessment
Assessment that helps teachers plan effective and rewarding learning experiences for individual students

Portfolio
A collection of work samples and products used to determine student progress

Portfolio
A purposeful collection of student work in a particular context

Positive behavioral support
An approach that is designed to apply behavioral supports in a proactive way to help prevent behavior problems

Positive behavioral supports (PBS)
Activity or technique designed to help students develop appropriate and adaptive behaviors and to overcome existing behavioral challenges

Positive interdependence
The positive qualities that come out of effective group work

Positive learning environment
Environment characterized by a fundamental respect for all persons, explicit standards for appropriate conduct, positive emotional experiences, and a collaborative recognition that everyone contributes to the success of the learning environment

Positive psychology
Psychology that investigates how typically developing individuals can lead better lives

Positive reinforcement
Something positive that is added to the environment in order to increase the frequency of a desired behavior

Positive transfer
The act of taking learning in a previous situation to promote learning in a future situation

Postconventional
Level of moral reasoning that goes beyond specific laws or personal expectations and is based on the underlying principles for such laws

Pragmatic language
Language used to communicate appropriately within a given context

Pragmatic language
Non-verbal social skills used to promote socialization

Praxis™
A series of tests for assessing teacher preparation and performance

Preconventional
Levels of moral reasoning that are typically based on consequences that have personal impact

Prejudice
A judgment about a group of people that tends to be inflexible and irrational rather than based on adequate knowledge

Pre-referral interventions
Efforts to address specialized student needs without formal participation in special education

Presentation punishment
The addition of something negative to the environment in order to decrease the frequency of an undesirable behavior

Pre-test
Test that helps teachers determine a student's existing knowledge

Private speech
The use of subvocal speaking addressed to oneself for the purpose of self-regulation

Proactive interference
Older memories interfering with your attempts to recall information

Problem-based learning
Popular student-centered approach used with gifted students that emphasizes learning in a dynamic, real life context

Problem-based learning (PBL)
A student-centered technique based on constructivist principles that typically helps students work through problems that have direct impact on their daily lives

Problem-based learning (PBL)
Learning approach grounded in scientific inquiry

Procedural knowledge
"How to" knowledge that involves knowledge of how to perform certain actions

Procedures
Guidelines for classroom activities

Processing Speed Index
Measures the speed with which we process information

Process theorist
A theorist who deemphasizes the development of specific skills, such as verbal labeling, and focuses instead on what made the development of the skill possible

Prompting
Providing a verbal reminder that a specific behavior is expected

Psychosocial theory
A theory that emphasizes integration of psychological changes and the social world

Pull-out services
Educational services that are provided outside the regular classroom

Punishment
An unpleasant consequence for a behavior, which decreases the likelihood of the behavior recurring

Punishments
Aversive environmental situations that result in a decrease in the frequency of behavior

R

Race
A group of people with biologically inherited traits viewed as socially significant

Radical constructivism
A branch of constructivist thinking that further divorces itself from any connection to an objective reality

Random assignment
Process of assigning study participants to groups in a random fashion

Randomized trials
Experimental studies that employ random assignment to groups

Range
Set of scores including the highest to lowest scores

Ratio schedule of reinforcement
The schedule requiring the reinforcement of a certain number of responses

Reasonable accommodation
Means that schools have considerable discretion regarding student services that they provide

Referral question
Question that defines the suspected problem or issue

Reflective appraisal
The interplay between how we view ourselves and how others view us

Reflective teaching
The process in which a teacher critically evaluates his/her own teaching

Rehearsal
Refers to the general process of actively thinking about information

Reinforcements
Positive environmental events following a behavior of interest resulting in an increase in the frequency of the behavior

Reinforcer
A favorable outcome occurring after a behavior of interest

Relational aggression
Aggressive acts that manipulate relationships between people

Reliability
Consistency of test results where giving a test to the same person on multiple occasions, would produce comparable results each time

Removal punishment
The removal of something desirable

Response to Intervention (RTI)
A multistep process to provide quality instruction to students with learning difficulties and to determine need for special education services

Retrieval cue
Information or some aspect of the environment that helps you recall a memory

Retroactive interference
Newer memories interfering with your attempts to recall information

Reversibility
The ability to mentally represent and "undo" events in a logical sequence

Rubrics
Traditionally thought of as scoring tools for subjective assessments

Rules
A set of behavioral standards

S

Scaffolding
A method of instruction that supports learning by helping the student engage in purposeful and meaningful use of psychological tools

Schedule of reinforcement
The timing and delivery of reinforcement

Schema
The way we appear to organize related semantic memories together

Schema
Organized ways of understanding related elements

Section 504 of the Rehabilitation Act of 1973
Law that established federal grant programs for vocational rehabilitation, supported employment, independent living, and client services

Selected-response questions
Questions that have students select a correct answer from a limited set of options

Self-actualization
The need to reach our fullest potential

Self-concept
Typically, one's perceptions about oneself

Self-efficacy
Beliefs about one's abilities to produce effects in the worlds

Self-efficacy
An individual's sense of his/her own competence

Self-esteem
Generally, the level of regard we have for ourselves

Self-fulfilling prophecy
Idea that what the teacher initially expects is reinforced and becomes a reality

Self-regulated learning
The self-directed process by which learners transform their mental abilities into academic skills

Self-regulation
The potential capacity to direct one's own behavior

Self-regulation strategies
Strategies that help students moderate their own behavior by having them periodically stop and "check" their behavior

Self-schema
Term used to refer to the collection of ways we view ourselves

Semantic knowledge
Information made up of memories for specific facts, regardless of the time and place the facts were learned

Semantic networks
Representational structures designed to explain the relation between items within a schema

Semantics
The meaning of words

Semiotic function
The use of symbolic representation

Sensory decay
Refers to the majority of our incoming sensory information that is not needed and therefore is quickly lost from the sensory memory

Sensory memory
Memory that acts as a temporary holding system for incoming sensory information

Seriation
The ability to arrange objects into an orderly sequence

Sex
Biological aspects of being male or female

Shaping
The reinforcement of progressively closer approximations of a desired response

Single-participant research
Research that uses an experimental design to investigate the effect of a treatment on a single person

Situated learning
Learning that is dependent upon the environment in which it takes place

Skinner Box
Research tool used to investigate the effects of consequences on behavior through the use of a spe-cialized mechanical device

Social cognition
The ways in which an individual perceives or thinks about social situations

Social cognitive theory
Theory emphasizing how social process and thinking impact behavior

Social competence
Behavior based not only on the social skills a child has learned but also on how those are used and received by other children in a given context

Social constructivism
Emphasizes the process of individual internalization of psychological tools (language, problem solving techniques, social skills, etc.) through social interactions

Socialization
The way in which other members of our society influence our behaviors

Social skills
Socially acceptable patterns of behaviors that support positive outcomes and avoid aversive situations

Sociocultural theorist
A theorist interested in the nature of social interactions and the ways in which social processes shape an individual's thinking

Specific transfer
The act of taking learning in one situation and applying it to a similar situation

Split-half reliability
Consistency based on dividing the test items of a single test into two groups

Standard deviation
Measure of variability

Standard English
Form of English taught in schools and typically used in professional circles

Standardization
Means that the test has uniform or "standard" content, administration procedure, scoring protocol, and format for presenting results

Standardized test
Commercially available tests that assess a wide range of academic and personal skills

Standards-based testing (criterion-based)
Assessment that compares the performance of a given student against some predetermined criteria or standard

Stanford-Binet Intelligence Test
One of the most frequently used tests of intelligence, currently in its fifth major revision

State theories
Theories that show how our motivation depends on the situation

Stereotype
An oversimplified opinion, attitude, or judgment held by members of a group

Stimulus
Event leading to a response

Strength
The tendency for values of one variable to co-occur with values of another variable

Strength-based assessment
An assessment that emphasizes the importance of using a student's strengths during intervention

Subgoaling
Taking a larger task and breaking it down into smaller, more manageable steps

Subjective question
Question where grading the correctness of a given response requires the judgment of the teacher

Subjective scoring
Where the evaluator has to make a judgment about the "correctness" of a given response

Substantial limitation
A limitation that is largely determined by the professionals involved in the evaluation for protection under Section 504/ADA

Summative assessment
Assessment designed to determine if the student achieved the educational goal

Summative assessment
Assessment that is designed to test whether the students achieved the desired learning outcome

Surface structure
The superficial structure of a problem

Sustaining expectation effect
When a teacher initially creates an accurate expectation for a student's behavior or achievement, but then fails to adjust that expectation if the student begins to perform contrary to the expectation

Symbolic representation
The ability to represent an object or experience with a symbol

Synapses
Tiny spaces across which neurons communicate with each other

Synaptogenesis
A process in which neurons form synapses as a function of experience

Synchronous
Form of communication that involves two-way communication in real time

Syntax
The order of words to create meaning

T

Task value
The value or priority that we place on situational outcomes

Teaching standards
Clearly defined goals that states employ for the development of high-quality teachers

Temporal lobe
The part of the brain primarily involved in processing auditory information

Test bias
Testing situations failing to measure accurately a skill or type of knowledge for a particular segment of the student population

Testing
A measurement or sample of behavior

Test-retest reliability
Consistency based on two administrations of a test

Time management
Techniques that help students structure daily tasks, manage study time to produce maximal results, and transition effectively between tasks

Top-down processing
Process of using existing knowledge to guide our understanding of new information

Traits
Relatively enduring characteristics of the individual (In this context, we are referring to psychological traits; however, the idea is consistent with physical traits like having green eyes.)

Transferring in
Bringing to the learning situation a wide variety of preconceptions, ideas, and unique life experiences

Transferring out
Transferring of what we learn in school to another setting

Transformation
The sequence of changes when a situation is transformed

Treatment
Modifications to the environment in order to produce behavioral change

Triarchic theory of intelligence
Intelligence theory proposed by Robert Sternberg seeing intelligence as the compilation of three separate abilities

U

Unconditioned responses (UCR)
The behavioral response to the unconditioned stimulus without previous learning

Unconditioned stimulus (UCS)
The environmental event that brings about the unconditioned response without previous learning

V

Validity
Whether a test measures what it intends to measure

Variable schedule of reinforcement
Reinforcement that varies over time

Verbal ability
Ability to use and express oneself in words

Verbal comprehension index
A measure of verbal reasoning and comprehension ability

Vicarious learning
Learning that is vicariously influenced by the consequences another person receives

Vicarious punishment
Decreasing a behavior in one participant by seeing another receive punishment

Vicarious reinforcement
Increasing a behavior in one participant by watching another receive reinforcement

Visual acuity
The ability of the individual to perceive details visually

Visual field
How far your vision extends while looking straight ahead

Voice disorders
An abnormality of one or more of the three characteristics of voice: pitch, intensity (loudness), and quality, but often unrecognized as a speech problem

W

Well-defined
When problems have a clear methodology designed to achieve a single correct answer

Work-avoidant goals
Goals set to get work done with as little exertion or effort as possible

Working memory
A term that better describes a memory store where information can be both temporarily stored and consciously processed

Working Memory Index
Assesses a student's abilities to temporarily hold information, perform operations, manipulate information, and produce correct results

Z

Zone of proximal development
The distance between the skills a child has already internalized and the skills he or she could learn with appropriate assistance

References

Abrahamson, D., Trninic, D., Gutierrez, J., Huth, J., & Lee, R. (2011). Hooks and shifts: A dialectical study of mediated discovery. *Technology, knowledge and learning: Learning mathematics, science and the arts in the context of digital technologies, 16*(1), 55–85.

Abrahamson, D., Trninic, D., Gutierrez, J., Huth, J., & Lee, R. (2011). Hooks and shifts: A dialetical study of mediated discovery. *Technology, Knowledge and Learning, 16*(1), 55–85.

Abramson, C., Brown, E., & Langley, D. (2011). Using PowerPoint to demonstrate human classical salivary conditioning in a classroom situation. *Psychological Reports, 108*(1), 109–119.

Accordino, D. B., Accordino, M. P., & Slaney, R. B. (2000). An investigation of perfectionism, mental health, achievement, and achievement motivation in adolescents. *Psychology in the Schools, 37*(6), 535–545.

Ackerman, P. (2011). Intelligence and expertise. In R. Sternberg, & S. B. Kaufman (Eds.), *The Cambridge handbook of intelligence* (pp. 847–860). New York, NY: Cambridge University Press.

Ackerman, P. L., Bowen, K. R., Beier, M. E., & Kanfer, R. (2001). Determinants of individual differences and gender differences in knowledge. *Journal of Educational Psychology, 93*(4), 797–825.

Adamson, H. D. (2004). *Language minority students in American schools.* Mahway, NJ: Erlbaum.

Adey, P., & Shayer, M. (1994). *Really raising standards.* London, England: Routledge.

Adey, P., Robertson, A., & Venville, G. (2002). Effects of a cognitive acceleration programme on year 1 pupils. *Journal of Educational Psychology, 72* (1), 1–25.

Adey, P., Shayer, M., & Yates, C. (1989). Cognitive acceleration: the effects of two years of intervention in science classes. In P. Adey, J. Bliss, J. Head, & M. Shayer (Eds.), *Adolescent development and school science* (pp. 240–247). London, England: Falmer Press.

Adler, M. (2006, April 25). School features real-world learning, no grades. *NPR.*

Aiken, L. R. (2000). *Psychological testing and assessment* (10th ed.). Boston, MA: Allyn & Bacon.

Ainley, M. D. (1993). Styles of engagement with learning: Multidimensional assessment of their relationship with strategy use and school achievement. *Journal of Educational Psychology, 85*(3), 395–405.

Airasian, P. W. (1991). *Classroom Assessment.* New York: McGraw-Hill.

Ajayi, E. (2011). Pre-referral intervention strategies to reduce referrals to special education. *Dissertation Abstracts International Section A: Humanities and Social Sciences, 71*(7-A), 2303.

Ajibola, O., & Clement, P. W. (1995). Differential effects of methylphenidate and self-reinforcement on attention-deficit hyperactivity disorder. *Behavior Modification, 19*(2), 211–233.

Akin-Little, K. A., Eckert, T. L., Lovett, B. J., & Little, S. G. (2004). Extrinsic reinforcement in the classroom: Bribery or best practice. *School Psychology Review, 33*(3), 344–362.

Alberta Learning Center. (2004). *Focus on Inquiry.* Edmonton, Alberta, Canada: Learning Resources Centre.

Alberto, P., & Troutman, A. (2006). *Applied behavior analysis for teachers: Influencing student performance* (7th ed.). Saddle River, NJ: Prentice Hall/Merrill.

Alexander, K. L., Entwisle, D. R., & Horsey, C. S. (1997). From first grade forward: Early foundations of high school dropout. *Sociology of Education, 70,* 87–107.

Alexander, R. (2005). Culture dialogue and learning: Notes on emerging pedagogy. *International Association for Cognitive Education and Psychology.* Durham.

Allen, J., & Bickhard, M. (2011). Emergent constructivism. *Child Development Perspectives 5*(3), 164–165.

Altmann, E. M., & Schunn, C. D. (2002). Integrating decay and interference: A new look at an old interaction. *Proceedings of the 24th annual conference of the cognitive science society* (pp. 65–70). Hillsdale, NJ: Erlbaum.

Altmann, E. M., & Schunn, C. D. (2002). Integrating decay and interference: A new look at an old interaction. *Proceedings of the 24th Annual Conference of the Cognitive Science Society* (pp. 65–70). Hillsdale, NJ: Erlbaum

Altmann, E. M., & Trafton, J. G. (2002). Memory for goals: an activation-based model. *Cognitive Science, 26,* 39–83.

American Psychiatric Association (2000). *Diagnostic and statistical manual of mental disorders—Text revision.* Washington, DC: American Psychiatric Association.

American Psychological Association: Educational psychology/division 15 (1993). Educational psychology Q&A. *Newsletter of Educational Psychology, 16*(2), 1–3.

Ames, C. (1992). Achievement goals, motivational climate, and motivational processes. In G. C. Roberts (Ed.), *Motivation in sport and exercise* (pp. 161–176). Champaign, IL: Human Kinetics.

Ames, C., & Archer, J. (1988). Achievement goals in the classroom: Student learning strategies and motivation processes. *Journal of Educational Psychology, 80,* 260–267.

Ames, C. A. (1984). Competitive, cooperative, and individual goal structures: A cognitive-motivational analysis. In R. Ames & C. Ames (Eds.), *Research on motivation in education: Student motivation* (pp. 177–207). New York, NY: Academic Press.

Ames, C. A. (1990). Motivation: What teachers need to know. *Teachers College Record, 91*(3), 409–421.

Anastasi, A. (1990). *Psychological testing* (6th ed.). New York, NY: Macmillan.

Anderson, J. R. (1983). *The architecture of cognition.* Cambridge, MA: Harvard University Press.

Anderson, J. R. (1995). *Cognitive psychology and its implications* (4th ed.). New York, NY: W. H. Freeman and Company.

Anderson, J. R. (2000). *Cognitive psychology and its implications* (5th ed.). New York, NY: W. H. Freeman and Company.

Anderson, J. R., Kushmerick, N., & Lebiere, C. (1993). The tower of Hanoi and goal structures. In J. Anderson, *Rules of the mind.* Hillsdale, NJ: Erlbaum.

Anderson, L. W., & Sosniak, L. A. (1994). *Bloom's taxonomy: A forty-year retrospective. Ninety-third yearbook for the National Society for the Study of Education: Part II.* Chicago, IL: University of Chicago Press.

Anderson, L. W., Krathwohl, D. R., Airasian, P. W., Cruikshank, K. A., Mayer, R. E., Pintrich, P. R., et al. (2001). *A taxonomy for learning, teaching, and assessing: A revision of Bloom's taxonomy of educational objectives.* New York, NY: Longman.

Andrews, J. J., Saklofske, D. H., & Janzen, H. L. Eds. (2001). *Handbook of psychoeducational assessment.* New York, NY: Academic Press.

Anglin, J. M. (1993). Vocabulary development: A morphological analysis. *Monographs of the Society of Research in Child Development, 58*(10), Serial No. 238.

Archambeault, B. (1992). Personalizing study skills in secondary students. *Journal of Reading, 35,* 468–472.

Areepattamannil, S., Freeman, J., & Klinger, D. (2011). Influence of motivation, self-beliefs, and instructional practices on science achievement of adolescents in Canada. *Social Psychology of Education: An International Journal, 14*(2), 233–259.

Arends, R. I. (2000). *Learning to teach* (5th ed.). New York, NY: McGraw-Hill.

Arends, R. I. (2007). *Learning to teach* (7th ed.). New York, NY: McGraw Hill.

Arhar, J., Holly, M. L., & Kasten, W. (2001). *Action research for teachers: Traveling the yellow brick road.* Saddle River, NY: Prentice Hall.

Aronson, J., Zimmerman, J., & Carlos, L. (1999). Improving student achievement by extending school: Is it just a matter of time. Retrieved From ERIC. San Francisco, CA: West Ed. Database (ED 435127).

Artiles, A., & Trent, S. C. (1994). Overrepresentation of minority students in exceptional education: A continuing debate. *Journal of Special Education, 27,* 410–437.

Ausubel, D. P. (1963). *The psychology of meaningful verbal learning.* New York, NY: Grune & Stratton.

Ausubel, D. P. (1980). Schemata, cognitive structure, and advance organizers: A reply to Anderson, Spiro, and Anderson. *American Educational Research Journal, 17*(3), 400–404.

Babkie, A. M. (2006). 20 ways to be proactive in managing classroom behavior. *Intervention in School and Clinic, 41*(3), 184–187.

Baddeley, A. D. (1966). The influence of acoustic and semantic similarity on long-term memory for word sequences. *Quarterly Journal of Experimental Psychology, 18*, 302–9.

Baddeley, A. D. (2003) Working memory and language: An overview. *Journal of Communication Disorders, 36*(3), 189–208.

Baddeley, A. D., & Hitch, G. (1974). Working memory. In G. H. Bower (Ed.), *The psychology of learning and motivation* (Vol. 8, pp. 47–89). New York, NY: Academic Press.

Baddeley, A. D., 1986. *Working memory.* Oxford University Press, New York.

Baddeley, A. D., Cocchini, G., Della Sala, S., Logie, R. H., & Spinnler, H. (1999). Working memory and vigilance: Evidence from normal aging and Alzheimer's disease. *Brain and Cognition, 41*, 87–108.

Baddeley, A. D., Gathercole, S. E., & Papagno, C., (1998). The phonological loop as a language learning device. *Psychological Review, 105*, 158–173.

Bahrick, H. P., & Phelps, E. (1987). Retention of Spanish vocabulary over eight years. *Journal of Experimental Psychology: Learning, Memory, and Cognition, 13*, 344–349.

Bailard, V., & Strang, R. (1964). *Parent-teacher conferences.* New York, NY: McGraw-Hill.

Baillargeon, R. (1987). Object permanence in 3 1/2- and 4 1/2-month-old infants. *Developmental Psychology, 23*(5), Sept. 1987, 655–664

Baily, J., & Mazur, E. (1990). Choice behavior in transition: Development of preference for the higher probability of reinforcement. *Journal of the Experimental Analysis of Behavior, 53*(3), 409–422.

Baldwin, J. D., & Baldwin, J. I. (1998). *Behavior principles in everyday life* (3rd ed.). Upper Saddle River, NJ: Prentice Hall.

Bandura, A. (1969). Social learning of moral judgment. *Journal of Personality & Social Psychology, 11*, 275–279.

Bandura, A. (1977). Self-efficacy: Toward a unifying theory of behavioral change. *Psychological Review, 84*, 191–215.

Bandura, A. (1986). *Social foundations of thought and action: A social cognitive theory.* Englewood Cliffs, NJ: Prentice Hall.

Bandura, A. (1997). *Self efficacy: The exercise of control.* New York, NY: Freeman.

Bandura, A., Ross, D., & Ross, S. (1961). Transmission of aggression through imitation of aggressive models. *Journal of Abnormal and Social Psychology, 63*, 575–582.

Banks, J. (2002). *Introduction to multicultural education* (3rd ed.). Boston, MA: Allyn & Bacon.

Banks, J. A. (1991). *Teaching strategies for ethnic students.* Boston, MA: Allyn & Bacon.

Banks, J. A. (1995). Multicultural education and curriculum transformation. *Journal of Negro Education, 64*(4), 390–400.

Barkley, R. A. (1998). *Attention-deficit hyperactivity disorder: A handbook for diagnosis* (2nd ed.). New York, NY: Guilford Press.

Barnas, M. (2001). "Parenting" students: Applying developmental psychology to the college classroom. *Teaching of Psychology, 27*(4), 276–274.

Barrows, H. (1996). Problem-based learning in medicine and beyond: a brief overview. In L. Wilkerson, & W. H. Gijselaers (Eds.), *Bringing problem-based higher education: Theory and practice: New directions for teaching and learning* (Vol. 8, p. 5). San Francisco, CA: Jossey-Bass.

Barutta, J., Cornejo, C., & Ibanez, A. (2011). Theories and theorizers: A contextual approach to theories of cognition. *Integrative Psychological & Behavioral Science, 45*(2), 223–246.

Battistich, V., Solomon, D., Watson, M., & Schaps, E. (1997). Caring school communities. *Educational Psychologists, 32*, 137–151.

Baumrind, D. (1967). Child care practices anteceding three patterns of preschool behavior. *Genetic Psychology Monographs, 75*(1), 43–88.

Baumrind, D. (1971). Current patterns of parental authority. *Developmental Psychology Monographs, 4*(1, Part 2).

Baumrind, D. (1996). The discipline controversy revisited. Family relations: *Journal of Applied Family & Child Studies, 45*(4), 405–414.

Bay, M., Bryan, T., & O'Connor, R. (1994). Teachers assisting teachers: A pre-referral model for urban educators. *Teacher Education and Special Education, 17*(1), 10–21.

Baylor, A. L., & Kitsantas, A. (2005). A comparative analysis and validation of instructivist and constructivist self-reflective tools (IPSRT and CPSRT) for novice instructional planners. *Journal of Technology and Teacher Education, 13*(3), 433–457.

Beilin, H. (1992a). Piaget's enduring contribution to developmental psychology. *Developmental Psychology, 28*, 191–204.

Benjamin, A. (2002). *Differentiated instruction: A guide for middle and high school teachers.* Larchmont, NY: Eye on Education.

Bennett, T., Deluca, D., & Bruns, D. (1997). Putting inclusion into practice: Perspectives of teachers and parents. *Exceptional Children, 64*(4), 115–131.

Bereiter, C., & Scardamalia, M. (1993). *Surpassing ourselves: An inquiry into the nature and implications of expertise.* Chicago, IL: Open Court.

Berenbaum, S., Blakemore, J., & Beltz, A. (2011). A role for biology in gender-related behavior. *Sex Roles, 64*(11–12), 804–825.

Berliner, D. (2011). Rational responses to high stakes testing: The case of curriculum narrowing and the harm that follows. *Cambridge Journal of Education, 41*(3), 287–302.

Berliner, D. C. (1986). In pursuit of the expert pedagogue. *Educational Researcher, 15*, 5–13.

Berliner, D. C. (2004). Describing the behavior and documenting the accomplishments of expert teachers. *Bulletin of Science Technology and Society, 24*(3), 200–212.

Berliner, D. C., Stein, P., Sabers, D., Clarridge, P. B., Cushing, K., & Pinnegar, S. (1988). Implications of research on pedagogical expertise and experience for mathematics teaching. In D. A. Grouws, & T. J. Cooney, *Perspectives on research on effective mathematics teaching* (pp. 67–95). Reston, VA: National Council of Teachers of Mathematics.

Bernier, A., Carlson, S., & Whipple, N. (2010). From external regulation to self-regulation: Early parenting precursors of young children's executive functioning. *Child Development, 81*(1), 326–339.

Betancourt, H., & Lopez, S. (1993). The study of culture, ethnicity, and race in American psychology. *American Psychologists, 48*, 629–637.

Bettenhausen, S. (1998). Make proactive modifications to your classroom. *Intervention in School and Clinic, 33*(3), 182–183.

Bianchi, S. M., & Casper, L. M. (2000). American families. *Population Bulletin, 55*(4), 1–48.

Bicknell-Holmes, T., & Hoffman, P. S. (2000). Elicit, engage, experience, explore: Discovery learning in library instruction. *Reference Services Review, 28*(4), 313–322.

Birdwhistell, R. (1970). *Kinesics in context.* Philadelphia, PA: University of Pennsylvania Press.

Bishop, A. P., Bertam, B. C., & Lunsford, K. J. (2004). Supporting community inquiry with digital resources. *Journal of Digital Information, 5*(3).

Bishop, J. H., & Mane, F. (1999). *New York State reform strategy: The incentive effects of minimum competency exams.* Philadelphia, PA: CEIC Review: The National Center on Education in Inner Cities.

Bishop, V. E. (2004). *Teaching visually impaired children.* Springfield, IL: Charles C. Thomas, LTD.

Bivens, J. A., & Berk, L. E. (1990). A longitudinal study of elementary school children's private speech. *Journal of Developmental Psychology, 36*(4), 443–463.

Black, P. (1998). *Testing: Friend or Foe? The Theory and Practice of Assessment and Testing.* London, England: Falmer Press.

Block, J. H. (1984). *Gender role identity and ego development.* San Francisco, CA: Jossey-Bass Publishers.

Bloh, C., & Axelrod, S. (2008). IDEIA and the means to change behavior should be enough: Growing support for using applied behavior analysis in the classroom. *Journal of Early and Intensive Behavior Intervention, 5*(2), 52–56.

Bloodworth, G. & Peterson, N. J. (2011). Developing visualization tools for geographic literacy in a museum exhibit: An interdisciplinary collaboration. *Journal of Geography, 110*(4), 137–147.

Bloom, B. S. (1981). *All our children learning.* New York, NY: McGraw-Hill.

Bloom, B. S., Engelhart, M. D., Frost, E. J., Hill, W. H., & Krathwohl, D. R. (1956). *Taxonomy of educational objectives: Handbook I.* New York, NY: David McKay.

Bloom, L., Margulis, C., Tinker, E., & Fujita, N. (1996). Early conversations and word learning: Contributions from child and adult. *Child Development, 67*, 3154–3175.

Bluestein, J. E. (1989). *Being a successful teacher: A practical guide to instruction and management.* Bel mont, CA: David S. Lake.

Blumenfeld, P. C., Puro, P., & Mergendoller, J. R. (1992). Translating motivation into thoughtfulness. In H. Marshall (Ed.), *Redefining studentlearning* (pp. 207–241). Norwood, NJ: Ablex.

Blumenthal, H., Leen-Feldner, E. W., Babson, K. A., Gahr, J. L., Trainor, C. D., & Frala, J. L. (2011). Elevated social anxiety among early maturing girls. *Developmental Psychology, 47*(4), 1133–1140.

Boden, M. A. (1979). *Piaget.* Brighton, England: Harvester Press.

Boekarts, M., Pintrich, P. R., & Zeidner, M. (2000). *Handbook of self-regulation: Theory, research and applications.* San Diego, CA: Academic Press.

Bohannon, J. N., & Bonvillian, J. D. (1997). Theoretical approaches to language acquisition. In J. K. Gleason (Ed.), *The development of language* (4th ed.). Boston, MA: Allyn & Bacon.

Bohay, M., Blakely, D., Tamplin, A., & Radvansky, G. (2011). Note taking, review, memory, and comprehension. *The American Journal of Psychology, 124*(1), 63–73.

Bonwell, C. C. (1998). *Active learning: Energizing the classroom.* Green Mountain Falls, CO: Active Learning Workshops.

Borko, H., & Elliott, R. (1999). Hands-on pedagogy versus hands-off accountability: tensions between competing commitments for exemplary math teachers in Kentucky. *Phi Delta Kappan, 80,* 394–400.

Bouchard, T. J. (2004). Genetic influence on human psychological traits. *Current Directions in Psychological Science, 13,* 148–151.

Bousfield, W. A. (1953). The occurrence of clustering in the recall of randomly arranged associates. *Journal of General Psychology, 49,* 229–240.

Bovaird, J., Geisnger, K., & Buckendahl, C. (2011). *High-stakes testing in education: Science and practice in K-12 settings.* Washington, DC: American Psychological Association.

Bowers, A. (2011). What's in a grade? The multidimensional nature of what teacher-assigned grades assess in high school. *Educational Research and Evaluation, 17*(3), 141–159.

Bowles, S., & Gintis, H. (1976). *Schooling in capitalist America.* New York, NY: Basic Books.

Brady-Amoon, P., & Fuertes, J. (2011). Self-efficacy, self-rated abilities, adjustment, and academic performance. *Journal of Counseling & Development, 89*(4), 431–438.

Brandt, R. S. (2000). *Education in a new era.* Alexandria, VA: Association for supervision and curriculum development.

Bransford, J. D., Brown, A. L., & Cocking, R. R. (1999). *How people learn: Brain, mind, experience and school.* Washington, DC: The National Academy Press.

Broadbent, D. E. (1958). Perception and communication. New York, NY: Pergamon.

Bronfenbrenner, U. (1977). Toward an experimental ecology of human development. *American Psychologist, 32,* 513–530.

Bronfenbrenner, U. (1979). *Ecology of human development.* Cambridge, MA: Harvard University Press.

Bronfenbrenner, U. (1989). Ecological systems theory. In R. Vasta (Ed.), *Annals of child development* (pp. 187–249). Boston, MA: JAI Press.

Brooks, D. C. (2011). Space matters: The impact of formal learning environments on student Learning. *British Journal of Educational Technology, 42*(5), 719–726.

Brooks, J. G., & Brooks, M. G. (1993). *In search of understanding: The case for constructivist classrooms.* Alexandria, VA: Association for Supervision and Curriculum Development.

Broughton, J. M. (1991). Piaget's structural developmental psychology v. ideology-critique and the possibility of a critical development theory. *Human Development, 24*(6), 1981, 382–441.

Brown, A. L. (1987). Metacognition, executive control, self-regulation, and other more mysterious mechanisms. In F. E. Weinert & R. H. Kluwe (Eds.), *Metacognition, motivation, and understanding* (pp. 65–116). Hillsdale, NJ: Lawrence Erlbaum Associates.

Brown, D. F. (2005). The significance of congruent communication in effective classroom management. *The Clearing House, 79*(1), 12–15.

Brown, J., Gable, R. A., Hendrickson, J. M., & Algozzine, B. (1991). Prereferral intervention practices of regular classroom teachers: Implications for regular and special education preparation. *Teacher Education and Special Education, 14,* 192–197.

Brown, K., & Kennedy, H. (2011). Learning through conversation: Exploring and extending teacher and children's involvement in classroom talk. *School Psychology International, 32*(4), 377–396.

Browne, M. N., & Freeman, K. (2000). Distinguishing features of critical thinking classrooms. *Teaching in Higher Education, 5*(3), 301–309.

Brualdi, A. (1998). Implementing performance assessment in the classroom. *Practical Assessment, Research & Evaluation, 6*(2).

Bruer, J. (1997). Education and the brain: A bridge too far. *Educational Researcher, 26,* 4–16.

Bruer, J. (1998). Brain science, brain fiction. *Educational Leadership, 56,* 14–18.

Bruer, J. (1999). In search of brain-based education. *Phi Delta Kappan, 89,* 649–657.

Bruner, J. S. (1961). "The act of discovery." *Harvard Educational Review, 31*(1), 21–32.

Bruning, R. H., Schraw, G. J., Norby, M. M., & Ronning, R. R. (2004). *Cognitive psychology and instruction* (4th ed.). Columbus, OH: Merrill.

Brunstein, J. C. (2000). Motivation and performance following failure: The effortful pursuit of self-defining goals. *An International Review, 49,* 340–356.

Brunstein, J. C., & Gollwitzer, P. M. (1996). Effects of failure on subsequent performance. *Journal of Personality and Social Psychology, 70,* 395–407.

Buck-Morss, S. (1982). Socio-economic bias in Piaget's theory and its implication for cross-cultural studies. *Human Development, 18,* 1–2, 35–49, 75. Cambridge, MA: Harvard University Press.

Bullock, C., & Foegen, A. (2002). Constructive conflict resolution for students with behavioral disorders. *Behavioral Disorders, 27,* 289–295.

Bullock, L., & Fitzimmons-Lovett, A. (1997). Meeting the needs of children and youth with challenging behaviors. *Reaching Today's Youth: the Community Circle of Caring Journal, 1*(3), 54–61.

Burkett, E. (2002). *Another planet: A year in the life of a suburban high school.* New York, NY: Harper Collins.

Burkham, D., Lee, V., & Smerdon, B. (1997). Gender and science learning early in high school. *American Educational Research Journal, 34*(2), 297–331.

Burton, J. K., Moore, D. M., & Magliar, S. G. (1996). Behaviorism and instructional technology. In D. H. Jonassen (Ed.). *Handbook of research for educational communication and technology.* New York, NY: Simon & Schuster Macmillan.

Butler, R. (1987). Task-involving and ego-involving properties of evaluation: Effects of different feedback conditions on motivational perceptions, interest, and performance. *Journal of Educational Psychology, 79*(4), 474–482.

Byrne, B. M., & Worth Gavin, D. A. (1996). The Shavelson model revisited: Testing for structure of academic self-concept across pre-, early, and late adolescents. *Journal of Educational Psychology, 88,* 215–229.

Caffarella, R. S. (2002). *Planning programs for adult learners* (2nd ed.). San Francisco, CA: Jossey-Bass/Wiley.

Caldas, S. J., & Bankston, C. L. (1997). The effect of school population socioeconomic status on individual student academic achievement. *Journal of Educational Research, 90,* 269–277.

Calderhead, J. (1996). Teachers: Beliefs and knowledge. In D. C. Berliner, & R. C. Calfee, *Handbook of educational psychology.* New York, NY: Macmillan.

Callahan, C. M., Tomlinson, C. A., & Plucker, J. (1997). *START using a multiple intelligences model in identifying and promoting talent in high-risk students.* Storrs, CT: National Research Center for Gifted and Talented.

Cameron, J., & Pierce, W. D. (1994). Reinforcement, reward, and intrinsic motivation: A meta-analysis. *Rev. Educ. Res. 64:* 363–423.

Cameron, J., & Pierce, W. D. (1996). The debate about rewards and intrinsic motivation: Protests and accusations do not alter the results. *Rev. Educ. Res. 66:* 39–52.

Campbell, K. (2003). The efficacy of conflict-mediation training in elementary schools. *The Educational Forum, 67,* 148–155.

Campbell, P. (1986). What's a nice girl like you doing in a math class? *Phi Delta Kappan, 67*(7), 516–520.

Campbell, R. L., & Brickhard, M. H. (1986). Knowledge levels and developmental stages. *Contributions to Human Development, 16,* 1986, 146.

Campione, J. C., Shapiro, A. M., & Brown, A. L. (1995). Forms of transfer in a community of learners: Flexible learning and understanding. In J. McKeough, J. Lupart, & A. Marini (Eds.), *Teaching for transfer: Fostering generalization in learning.* Mahwah, NJ: Erlbaum.

Canter, L. (1992). *Lee Canter's assertive discipline elementary workbook.* Santa Monica, CA: Canter and Associates.

Caram, C. A., & Davis, P. B. (2005). Inviting student engagement with questioning. *Kappa Delta Pi Record, Fall,* 19–23.

Carifio, J., & Carey, T. (2009). A critical examination of current minimum grading policy recommendations. *High School Journal, 93*(1), 23–37.

Carnevale, P. J. (1998). Social values and social conflict creative problem solving and categorization. *Journal of Personality and Social Psychology, 74*(5), 1300.

Carnoy, M., & Loeb, S. (2003). Does external accountability affect student outcomes? A cross-state analysis. *Educational Evaluation and Policy Analysis, 24*(4), 305–331.

Carr, J., & Briggs, A. (2011). A resource on behavioral terminology: An annotated bibliography of On Terms articles in The Behavior Analyst. *The Behavior Analyst, 34*(1), 93–101.

Carroll, J. B. (1963). A model of school learning. *Teachers College Record,* 723–733.

Carroll, J. B. (1993). *Human cognitive abilities: A survey of factor-analytic studies.* New York, NY: Cambridge University Press.

Case, L. P., Mamlin, N., Harris, K. R., & Graham, S. (1995). Self-regulated strategy development: A theoretical and practical perspective. In T. E. Scruggs, & M. A. Mastropieri (Eds.), *Advances in learning and behavioral disabilities.* Greenwich, CT: JAI Press.

Case, R. (1975). Gearing the demands of instruction to the developmental capacities of the learner. *Review of Educational Research, 45*(1), 59–88.

Case, R. (1985b). A developmentally-based approach to the problem of instructional design. In R. Glaser, S. Chipman, & J. Segal (Eds.), *Teaching thinking skills, 2,* 545–562. Hillsdale, NJ: Erlbaum.

Caspar, V., Schultz, S. & Wickens, E. (1992). Breaking the silences: Lesbian and gay parents and the schools. *Teachers College Record, 94*(1), 109–37.

Cassady, J. C. (2003). The impact of an integrated reading focused integrated learning system on phonological awareness in kindergarten. *Journal of Literacy Research, 35*(4), 947–964.

Castellanos, F. X. (1997). Toward a pathophysiology of attention-deficit/hyperactivity disorder. *Clinical Pediatrics, 381,* 381–393.

Castellanos, F. X., & Swanson, J. (2002). Biological underpinnings of ADHD. In Sandberg, S. (Ed.), *Hyperactivity and attention disorders of childhood.* Cambridge, MA: Cambridge University Press.

Castellanos, F. X., Giedd, J. N., Berquin, P. C., Walter, J. M., Sharp, W., Tran, T., et al. (2001). Quantitative brain magnetic resonance imaging in girls with attention deficit/hyperactivity disorder. *Archives of General Psychiatry, 58,* 289–295.

Castellanos, F. X., Marvasti, F. F., Ducharme, J. L., Walter, J. M., Israel, M. E., Krain, A. L., et al. (2000). Executive Function oculomotor tasks in girls with ADHD. *Journal of the American Academy of Child Adolescent Psychiatry, 39,* 644–650.

Castronova, J. A. (2002). Discovery learning for the 21st century: What is it and how does it compare to traditional learning in effectiveness in the 21st century? *Action Research Exchange 1*(1), online.

Catania, A. C. (1998). *Learning* (4th ed.). Upper Saddle River, NJ: Prentice Hall.

Cauley, K., & Tyler B. (1989). The relationship of self-concept to prosocial behavior in children. *Early Childhood Research Quarterly, 4,* 51–60.

Cavallo, A. (2005). Cycling through plants. *Science and Children, 42*(7), 22–27.

Cecchini Estrada, J., Gonzalez-Mesa, C., Mendez-Gimenez, A., & Fernandez-Rio, J. (2011). Achievement goals, social goals, and motivational regulations in physical education settings. *Psicothema, 23*(1), 51–57.

Ceci, S. J. (1990). *On intelligence—more or less: A bio-ecological treatise on intellectual development.* Englewood Cliffs, NJ: Prentice Hall.

Ceci, S. J. (1991). How much does schooling influence general intelligence and its cognitive components? A reassessment of the evidence. *Developmental Psychology, 27,* 703–722.

Chabot, R. J., Di Michele, F., Prichep, L., & John, E. R. (2001). The clinical role of computerized EEG in the evaluation and treatment of learning and attention disorders in children and adolescents. *Journal of Neuropsychiatry and Clinical Neuroscience, 13*(2), 171–186.

Chalfant, J. C. & Pysh, M. V. (1989). Teacher assistance teams: Five descriptive studies on 96 teams. *Remedial and Special Education, 10,* 49–58.

Chan, T., & Ahern, T. (1999). Targeting motivation—adapting flow theory to instructional design. *Journal of Educational Computing Research, 21*(2), 151–163.

Chandler, L. K., & Dahlquist, C. M. (2006). *Functional assessment: Strategies to prevent and remediate challenging behavior in school settings* (2nd ed.). Upper Saddle River, NJ: Merrill Prentice Hall.

Chang, J. M. (1993). A school home community based conceptualization of LEP students with learning disabilities: implications from a Chinese American study. *The Proceedings of the Third Annual Research Symposium on Limited English Proficient Students' Issues,* Washington, DC: Office of Bilingual Education and Language Minority Affairs, U.S. Department of Education.

Chapman, J. W., Tunmer, W. E., & Prochnow, J. E. (2000). Early reading-related skills and performance, reading self-concept, and the development of academic self-concept, and the development of academic self-concept: A longitudinal study. *Journal of Educational Psychology, 92,* 703–708.

Chappell, K., & Craft, A. (2011). Creative learning conversations: Producing living dialogic spaces. *Educational Research, 53*(3), 363–385.

Charon, J. (1986). *Sociology: A conceptual approach.* Boston, MA: Allyn & Bacon.

Chavez, A. F., & Guido-Dibrito, F. (1999). Racial and ethnic identity and development. In M. C. Clark & R. S. Caffarella (Eds.), *An update on adult development theory: New ways of thinking about the life course. New directions for adult and continuing education,* no. 84 (pp. 39–47). San Francisco, CA: Jossey-Bass.

Cheour, M., Ceponiene, R., Leppanen, P., Alho, K., Kujala, T., Renlund, M., et al. (2002). The auditory sensory memory trace decays rapidly in newborns. *Scandinavian Journal of Psychology, 43*(1), 33 - 39.

Chmiliar, L. (1997). Metacognition and giftedness. *AGATE, 11*(2), 28–34.

Choi, I., & Lee, K. (2008). A case-based learning environment design for real-world classroom management problem solving. *Tech Trends: Linking Research and Practice to Improving Learning, 52*(3), 26–31.

Chomsky, N. (1957). *Syntactic Structures.* The Hague/Paris: Mouton.

Chomsky, N. (1965). *Aspects of a theory of syntax.* Cambridge, MA: MIT Press.

Chomsky, N. (1967). A Review of B. F. Skinner's Verbal Behavior. In J. A. Jakobovits, & M. S. Miron (Eds.), *Readings in the psychology of language* (pp. 142–143). Prentice-Hall.

Clahsen, H., Felser, C., Neubauer, K., Sato, M., & Silva, R. (2010). Morphological structure in native and nonnative language processing. *Language Learning, 60*(1), 21–43.

Clark, A. (1999). *Parent-teacher conferences: Suggestions for parents.* Champaign, IL: ERIC Clearinghouse on Elementary and Early Childhood Education.

Clark, C. M., & Dunn, S. (1991). Second-generation research on teachers' planning intentions, and routines. In H. W. (Eds), *Effective teaching: Current research* (pp. 183–200). Berkeley, CA: McCatchum Publishing.

Clifford, M. (1990). Students need challenge, not easy success. *Educational Leadership, 48*(1), 22–26.

Coco, C. (1999). Instructional scaffolding intervention and concept mapping outcomes among diverse learners in a pre-service educational psychology course: A model for developing expertise in writing expressions of conceptual understanding. *American educational research association,* (p. 40). Montreal, Canada.

Cohen, E. (1998). Making cooperative learning equitable. *Educational Leadership, 56*(1), 18–21.

Cohen, J. D., Forman, S. D., Braver, T. S., Casey, B. J., Servan-Schreiber D., Noll, D. C. (1994). Activation of prefrontal cortex in a non-spatial working memory task with functional MRI. *Human Brain Map, 1,* 293–304.

Cole, M., & Packer, M. (2011). Culture in development. In M. H. Bornstein & M. E. Lamb, *Cognitive development: An advanced textbook* (pp. 67–123). New York, NY: Psychology Press.

Coleman, M. C., & Webber, J. (2002). *Emotional and behavioral disorders: Theory and practice* (4th ed.). Boston, MA: Allyn & Bacon.

Coleman, J. S. (1966). *Equality of educational opportunity.* Washington, DC: U.S. Government Printing Office.

Coley, R. J. (2001). *Differences in the gender gap: Comparisons across racial/ethnic groups in education work.* Princeton, NJ: Educational Testing Service.

Coll, R., & Paku, L. (2011). The influence of experiential learning on indigenous New Zealanders' attitude towards science: Encultration into science by means of legitimate peripheral participation. In I. Saleh, & M. Khine (Eds.), *Attitude research in science education:*

Classic and contemporary measurements (pp. 219–238). Charlotte, NC: Information Age Publishing.

Collaer, M. L., & Hines, M. (1995). Human behavioral sex differences: A role for gonadal hormones during development? *Psychological Bulletin, 118,* 55–107.

Condry, J. (1977). Enemies of exploration: Self-invited versus other-initiated learning. *Journal of Personality and Social Psychology, 35,* 459–477.

Condry, J. (1987). Enhancing motivation: A social development perspective. *Advances in Motivation and Achievement: Enhancing Motivation, 5,* 23–49.

Conger, R. D., Conger, K. J., & Elder, G. H. (1997). Family economic hardship and adolescent adjustment: Mediating and moderating processes. In G. J. Duncan & J. Brooks-Gunn (Eds.), *Consequences of growing up poor* (pp. 288–310). New York, NY: Russell Sage Foundations.

Conn, C. (2011). Using technology for assessing and evaluating student learning and instructional practices. In R. Papa (Ed.), *Technology leadership for school improvement* (pp. 231–252). Thousand Oaks, CA: Sage Publication.

Conway, M. A. (2009). Episodic Memories. *Neuropsychologia, 47*(11), 2305–2313.

Coplan, R., & Weeks, M. (2009). Shy and soft-spoken: Shyness, pragmatic language, and socioemotional adjustment in early childhood. *Infant and Child Development, 18*(3), 238–254.

Copple, C., Yane, M., Levin, D., & Cohen, S. (1992, April 7). *Briefing Paper.* Washington, DC: Pelavin Associates, Inc.

Corbett, H. D., & Wilson, B. L. (1991). Two state minimum competency testing programs and their effects on curriculum and instruction. In R. E. Stake (Ed.), *Advances in program evaluation: Vol. 1. Effects of mandated assessment on teaching* (pp. 7–40). Greenwich, CT: JAI Press Ltd.

Corpus, J., McClintic-Gilbert, M., & Hayenga, A. (2009). Within-year changes in children's intrinsic and extrinsic motivational orientations: Contextual predictors and academic outcomes. *Contemporary Educational Psychology, 34*(2), 154–466.

Cothran, D. J., & Ennis, C. D. (2000). Building bridges to student engagement: communicating respect and care for students in urban high schools. *Journal of Research and Development in Education, 32*(2), 106–117.

Cotterall, S., & Murray, G. (2009). Enhancing metacognitive knowledge structure, affordances and self. *System? An International Journal of Educational Technology and Applied Linguistics, 37*(1), 34–45.

Cox, M. J., & Harter, K. S. (2001). The road ahead for research on marital and family dynamics. In J. P. McHale & W. S. Grolnick (Eds.), *Retrospect and prospect in the psychological study of families.* Mahwah, NJ: Erlbaum.

Crnic, K. A., & Leconte, J. M. (1986). Understanding sibling needs and influences. In R. R. Fewell & P. F. Vadasy (Eds.), *Families of handicapped children: Needs and supports across the life span* (pp. 75–98). Austin, TX: Pro-Ed.

Cruickshank, D. (1987). *Reflective teaching: The preparation of student teaching.* Reston, VA: The Association of Teacher Educators.

Csikszentmihalyi, M. (1990). *Flow: The psychology of optimal experience.* New York, NY: Harper & Row.

Csikszentmihalyi, M. (1997). *Finding flow: The psychology of engagement with everyday life.* New York, NY: Basic Books.

Csikszentmihalyi, M., & Nakamura, J. (2011). Positive psychology: Where did it come from, where is it going? In K. Sheldon, T. Kashdan, & M. Steger (Eds.), *Designing positive psychology: Taking stock and moving forward* (pp. 3–8). New York, NY: Oxford University Press.

Cullinan, D. (2002). *Students with emotional and behavioral disorders: An introduction for teachers and other helping professionals.* Upper Saddle River, NY: Merrill.

Curran, K., & Reivich, K. (2011). Goal setting and hope. *Communique, 39*(7), 44–46.

Curriculum Leadership Institute, (2003). *Best practices for teaching standards.* Emporia, KS: CLI.

Curtiss, S. (1977). *Genie: A psycholinguistic study of a modern day "wild child."* New York, NY: Academic Press

Cvencek, D., Meltzoff, A., & Greenwald, A. (2011). Math-gender stereotypes in elementary school children. *Child Development, 82*(3), 766–779.

Dana, N., Thomas, C., & Boynton, S. (2011). *Inquiry: A districtwide approach to staff and student learning.* Thousand Oaks, CA: Corwin Press.

Danner, D., Hagemann, D., Schankin, A., Hager, M., & Funke, J. (201). Beyond IQ: A latent state-trait analysis of general intelligence, dynamic decision making, and implicit learning. *Intelligence, 39*(5), 323–334.

Darling-Hammond (1999). Target time toward teachers. *Journal of Staff Development, 20*(2), 31–36.

Darling-Hammond, L., & Falk, B. (1997). Supporting teaching and learning for all students: Policies for authentic assessment systems. In A. Lin Goodwin (Ed.), *Assessment for equity and inclusion: Embracing all our children* (pp. 51–75). New York, NY: Routledge.

Daunic, A. P., Smith, S. W., Robinson, T. R., Miller, M. D., & Landry, K. L. (2000). School-wide conflict resolution and peer mediation programs: Experiences in three middle schools. *Intervention in School & Clinic, 36*(2), 94–100.

Davenport, E., Davison, M., Kuang, H., Ding, S., Kim, S.-K., & Kwak, N. (1998). High-school mathematics course-taking by gender and ethnicity. *American Educational Research Journal, 35*(3), 497–514.

Davies, M. A., & Wavering, M. (1999). Alternative Assessments: New directions in teaching and learning. *Contemporary Education, 71*(1), 39–45.

Davis, G. A., & Rimm, S. B. (2004). *Education of the gifted and talented* (5th ed.). Boston, MA: Pearson Education.

Dawe, H. A. (1984). Teaching: Social science or performing art? *Harvard Educational Review, 54,* 111–114.

De La Paz, S. (2009). Rubrics: Heuristics for developing writing strategies. *Assessment for Effective Intervention, 34*(3), 134–146.

De Pry, R. L., & Sugai, G. (2002). The effect of active supervision and precorrection on minor behavioral incidents in a sixth grade general education classroom. *Journal of Behavioral Education, 11,* 255–267.

Deci, E. L., & Ryan, R. M. (1980). The empirical exploration of intrinsic motivational processes. In L. Berkowitz (Ed.), *Advances in experimental social psychology* (Vol. 13, pp. 30–80). New York, NY: Academic Press.

Deci, E. L., & Ryan, R. M. (1985). *Intrinsic motivation and self-determination in human behavior.* New York, NY: Plenum.

Deci, E. L., & Ryan, R. M. (2000). The 'what' and 'why' of goal pursuits: Human needs and the self-determination of behavior. *Psychological Inquiry, 11,* 227–268.

Deci, E. L., Koestner, R., & Ryan, R. M. (1999). A meta-analytic review of experiments examining the effects of extrinsic rewards on intrinsic motivation. *Psychological Bulletin, 125,* 627–668.

Deci, E. L., Vallerand, R. J., Pelletier, L. G., & Ryan, R. M. (1991). Motivation and education: The self-determination perspective. *Educational Psychologist, 26,* 325–346.

Delpit, L. (1995). *Other people's children: Cultural conflict in the classroom.* New York, NY: The New Press.

Dempster, F. N. (1991). Synthesis of research on reviews and tests. *Educational Leadership, 48*(7), 71–76.

Deno, E. (1970). Special education as developmental capital. *Exceptional Children, 37,* 229–237.

Deroche, T. (2004). Not just a necessary evil. *Education Week, 24*(13), 37.

Desco, M., Navas-Sanchez, F., Sanchez-Gonzalez, J., Reig, S., Robles, O., Franco, C., et al. (2011). Mathematically gifted adolescents use more extensive and more bilateral areas of the fronto-parietal network than controls during executive functioning and fluid reasoning tasks. *NeuroImage, 57*(1), 281–292.

Deshler, D. D., Ellis, E. S., & Lenz, B. K. (1996). *Teaching adolescents with learning disabilities: Strategies and methods.* Denver, CO: Love Publishing.

Deville, C. (2011). Accountability-assessment under No Child Left Behind: Agenda, practice, and future. *Language Testing, 28*(3), 307–321.

DeVitis, J., & Yu, T. (Eds.). (2011). *Character and moral education: A reader.* New York, NY: Peter Lang New York.

DeVries, R. (1997). Piaget's social theory. *Educational Researcher, 26*(2), 4–18.

Dewey, J. (1997). *Democracy and education.* New York, NY: Simon and Schuster.

Di Trani, M., Casini, M., Capuzzo, F., Gentile, S., Bianco, G., Menghini, D., et al. (2011). Executive intellectual functions in attention-deficit/hyperactivity disorder with and without comorbidity. *Brain & Development, 33*(6), 462–469.

Diaz-Rico, L. (2004). *Teaching English learners.* Boston, MA: Allyn & Bacon.

Diaz, J. A., & Berk, L. E. (Ed.). (1992). *Private speech: From social interaction to self-regulation.* Hillsdale, NJ: Erlbaum.

Diller, J. V., & Moule, J. (2005). *Cultural competence: A primer for educators.* Belmont, CA: Wadsworth.

Din, F. S. (2000). Direct instructions in remedial math instructions. *National Forum of Special Education Journal, 9E,* 3–7.

DiVesta, J. G., & Gray, S. G. (1972). Listening and notetaking. *Journal of Educational Psychology, 63,* 8–14.

Dodge, K. A. (1993). The future of research on the treatment of conduct disorders. *Development and Psychopathology, 5,* 311–319.

Dodge, K., & Price, N. (1994). On the relation between social information processing and socially competent behavior in early school-aged children. *Child Development, 65,* 1385–1397.

Dole, J. A., Valencia, J. W., Greer, E. A., & Wardrop, J. L. (1991). Effects of two types of prereading instruction on the comprehension of narrative and expository text. *Reading Research Quarterly, 26*(2), 142–159.

Dommett, E. J., Devonshire, I. M., Plateau, C. R., Westwell, M. S., & Greenfield, S. A. (2011). From scientific theory to classroom practice. *The Neuroscientist, 17*(4), 382–388.

Donovan, M. S., & Bransford, J. D. (2005). *How students learn: Science in the classroom.* Washington, DC: National Academy Press.

Donovan, S., & Cross, C. (2002). *Minority students in special and gifted education.* Washington, DC: National Academy Press.

Doolittle, P. E. (1997). Vygotsky's zone of proximal development as a theoretical foundation for cooperative learning. *Journal on Excellence in College Teaching, 8,* 83–103.

Downey, C. (2001). Special delivery. *Leadership, 31*(2), 35–36.

Downey, C. J. (2000). Top 10 instructional strategies for achievement. *Leadership, 30*(2), 1–2.

Doyle, W. (1986). Classroom organization and management. In M. Wittrock (Ed.) *Handbook of research on teaching* (3rd ed., pp. 392–431). New York, NY: Macmillan.

Drake, D. (2011). What do coaches need to know? Using the Mastery Window to assess and develop expertise. *Coaching: An International Journal of Theory, Research and Practice, 4*(2), 138–155.

Drayton, B., & Falk, J. K. (2001). Tell-tale signs of the inquiry-oriented classroom. *NASSP Bulletin 85*(623), 24–34.

Driscoll, M. P. (2005). *Psychology of learning for instruction* (3rd ed.). Boston, MA: Allyn & Bacon.

Dudley, B., Johnson, D. W., & Johnson, R. T. (1996). Conflict resolution training and middle school students' integrative behavior. *Journal of Applied Social Psychology, 26*(22), 2030–2052.

Duncan, B. B., Forness, S. R., & Hartsough, C. (1995). Students identified as seriously emotionally disturbed in day treatment: Cognitive, psychiatric, and special education characteristics. *Behavioral Disorders, 20,* 238–252.

Dunker, K. (1945). On problem solving. *Psychological Monographs, 58*(5), 270.

Dunn, R., & Dunn, K. (1999). *The complete guide to the learning strategies inservice system.* Boston, MA: Allyn & Bacon.

Dupaul, G. J., & Stoner, G. (2003). *ADHD in the schools: Assessment and intervention strategies.* New York, NY: Guilford Press.

DuPaul, G., Helwig, J., & Slay, P. (2011). Classroom interventions for attention and hyperactivity. In M. Bray, & T. Kehle (Eds.), *The Oxford handbook of school psychology* (pp. 428–441). New York, NY: Oxford University Press.

Durrant, J. E., Cunningham, C. E., & Voelker, S. (1990). Academic, social, and general self-concepts of behavioral subgroups of learning disabled children. *Journal of Educational Psychology, 82,* 657–663.

Dweck, C. S. (1986). Motivational processes affecting learning. *American Psychologist, 41,* 1040–1048.

Eagly, A. H., & Steffen, V. J. (1986). Gender and aggressive behavior: A meta-analytic review of the social psychological literature. *Psychological Bulletin, 100,* 309–330.

Earl, L., & Cousins, J. B. (1995). *Classroom assessment: Changing the face, facing the change.* Toronto, Ontario, Canada: Ontario Public School Teachers Federation.

Ebert, E., Ebert, C., & Bentley, M. (2011). *The educator's field guide: From organization to assessment (and everything in between).* Thousand Oaks, CA: Corwin Press.

Eccles, J. S. (1987). Adolescence: Gateway to gender-role transcendence. In D. B. Carter (Ed.), *Current conceptions of sex role and sex typing: Theory and research* (p.). New York, NY: Praeger.

Eccles, J. S., Adler, T. F., Futterman, R., Goff, S. B., Kaczala, C. M., Meece, J. L., et al. (1983). Expectations, values, and academic behaviors. In J. T. Spence (Ed.), *Achievement and achievement motivation* (pp. 75–146). San Francisco, CA: W. H. Freeman.

Eccles, J. S., Jacobs, J., Harold, R., Yoon, K., Aberbach, A., & Dolan, C. F. (1991, August). *Expectancy effects are alive and well on the home front.* Paper presented at the meeting of the American Psychological Association. San Francisco, CA.

Education Trust (2005). *The funding gap 2005.* Washington, DC: The Education Trust.

Educational Testing Service (2002). *Differences in the gender gap.* Princeton, NJ: ETS.

Edwards, C. H. (1993). *Classroom discipline and management.* New York, NY: Macmillan.

Ehrenberg, R., Brewer, D., Gamoran, A., & Williams, J. (2001). Does class size matter? *Scientific American, 285*(5), 78–85.

Eichenbaum, H., Sauvage, M., Fortin, N., Komorowski, R., & Lipton, P. (2011, Jul 23). Towards a functional organization of episodic memory in the medial temporal lobe. *Neuroscience and Biobehavioral Reviews.*

Eick, C. J., & Reed, C. J. (2002). What makes an inquiry oriented science teacher? The influence of learning histories on student teacher role identity and practice. *Science Teacher Education, 86,* 401–416.

Eisenberg, N., Martin, C. L., & Fabes, R. A. (1996). Gender development and gender effects. In D. C. Berliner & R. C. Calfee (Eds.), *Handbook of educational psychology.* New York: Simon & Schuster Macmillan.

Elder, L., & Paul, R. (2010). *The thinker's guide to analytic thinking.* Dillon Beach, CA: Foundation for Critical Thinking.

Ellis, S., Dowdy, B., Graham, P., & Jones, R. (1992). *Parental support of planning skills in the context of homework and family demands.* Paper presented at the annual meeting of the American Educational Research Association, San Francisco, CA.

Elmore, M. (2008). Effective parent conferences. *Education Digest, 74*(1), 47–49.

Emmer, E. T., & Stough, L. M. (2001). Classroom management: A critical part of educational psychology, with implications for teacher education. *Educational Psychologist, 36*(2), 103–112.

Emmer, E. T., Evertson, C. M., & Anderson, L. M. (1980). Effective classroom management at the beginning of the school year. *The Elementary School Journal, 80*(5), 219–231.

Emmer, E. T., Evertson, C. M., & Worsham, M. E. (2006). *Classroom management for secondary teachers* (7th ed.). Boston, MA: Allyn & Bacon.

Emmer, E., Evertson, C., & Worsham, M. (2003). *Classroom management for secondary teachers* (6th ed.). Boston, MA: Allyn & Bacon.

Ennis, R. H. (1990). The extent to which critical thinking is subject-specific: Further clarification. *Educational Researcher, 19*(4), 13–16.

Entwistle, N. J., & Kozeki, B. (1985). Relationships between school motivation, approaches to studying, and attainment, among British and Hungarian adolescents. *British Journal of Educational Psychology, 55*(2), 124–137.

Epstein, J., Coates, L., Salinas, K., Sanders, M., & Simon, B. (1997). *School, family, and community partnerships: Your handbook for action.* Thousand Oaks, CA: Sage.

Epstein, M. H., Rudolph, S., & Epstein, A. A. (2000). Strength-based assessment. *Teaching Exceptional Children, 32*(6), 50–54.

Ericsson, K. A., & Lehmann, A. C. (1996). Expert and exceptional performance: evidence on maximal adaptations on task constraints. *Annual Review of Psychology, 47,* 273–305.

Ericsson, K. A., Krampe, R. T., & Tresh-Romer, C. (1993). The role of deliberate practice in the acquisition of expert performance. *Psychological Review,* 363–406.

Ernest, P. (1995). The one and the many. In L. P. Steffe & J. Gale (Eds.), *Constructivism in education* (pp. 459–486). Hillsdale, NJ: Lawrence Erlbaum Associates.

Evertson, C. M., Emmer, E. T., & Worsham, M. E. (2006). *Classroom management for elementary teachers* (7th ed.). Boston, MA: Allyn & Bacon.

F.I.M. (Eds.), *The Oxford handbook of memory* (pp. 597–608), Oxford University Press, Oxford,.

Fagot, B. I. (1995). Parenting boys and girls. In M. H. Bornstein (Ed.), *Handbook of parenting: Vol. 1. Children and parenting* (pp. 163–183). Mahwah, NJ: Lawrence Erlbaum Associates.

Fallon, M., Zhang, J., & Kim, E. (2011). Using course assessments to train teachers in functional behavior assessment and behavioral intervention plan techniques. *Journal of the International Association of Special Education, 12*(1), 50–58.

Faraone, S. V., & Doyle, A. E. (2001). The nature and heritability of attention-deficit/hyperactivity disorder. *Child and Adolescent Psychiatric Clinics of North America, 10*(2), 299–316.

Farkas, R. D. (2003). Effects of traditional versus learning-styles instructional methods on middle school students. *Journal of Educational Research, 97*(1), 42–51.

Feldhusen, J., Van Winkle, L., & Ehle, E. (1996). Is it acceleration or simply appropriate instruction for precocious youth. *Teaching Exceptional Children, 28,* 48–51.

Feltovich, P. J., Prietula, M. J., & Ericsson, K. A. (2006). Studies of expertise from psychological perspectives. In K. A. Ericsson, N. Charness, P. J. Feltovich, & R. R. Hoffman (Eds.), *Cambridge handbook of expertise and expert performance* (pp. 41–68). New York, NY: Cambridge University Press.

Finkle, S. L., & Torp, L. L. (1995). Introductory documents. Available from the center for problem-based learning, Illinois Math and Science Academy, 1500 West Sullivan Road, Aurora, IL 60506–1000.

Fiore, D. (1993). Electronic gradebooks: What current programs can do for teachers. *Clearing House, 66*(3).

Fisher, C. F., & King, R. M. (1995). *Authentic assessment, a guide to implementation.* Thousand Oaks, CA: Corwin.

Flanagan, O. (1992). *The science of the mind.* Cambridge, MA: MIT Press.

Flavell, J. H. (1963). *The developmental psychology of Jean Piaget.* Oxford, England: D. Van Nostrand.

Flavell, J. H. (1979). Metacognition and cognitive monitoring: A new area of cognitive developmental inquiry. *American Psychologist, 34,* 906–911.

Flavell, J. H. (1987). Speculations about the nature and development of metacognition. In F. Weinert & R. Kluwe (Eds.), *Metacognition, motivation, and understanding* (p. 21–29). Hillsdale, NJ: Erlbaum Associates.

Flavell, J. H., Flavell, E. R., Green, F. L. (1989). A transitional period in the development of the appearance-reality distinction. *International Journal of Behavioral Development, 12,* 509–526.

Flinders, D. J. (1989). Does the 'art of teaching' have a future? *Educational Leadership, 48*(8), 16–20.

Flinker, A., Chang, E., Barbaro, N., Berger, M., & Knight, R. (2011). Sub-centimeter language organization in the human temporal lobe. *Brain and Language, 117*(3), 103–109.

Flugum, K. & Reschly, D. (1994). Pre-referral interventions: Quality indices and outcomes. *Journal of School Psychology, 32,* 1–14.

Flynn, & Wilson (1998). Partnerships with family members: What about fathers. *Young Exceptional Children, 2*(1), 21–29.

Foley, M., & Hart, A. (1992). Expert novice differences and knowledge elicitation. In R. R. Hoffman, *The Psychology of expertise: Cognitive research and empirical AI* (pp. 233–269). Mahwah, NJ: Sringer-Verlag.

Fosnot, C. T. (1996). Constructivism: A psychological theory of learning. In C. T. Fosnot (Ed.), *Constructivism: Theory, perspectives, and practice.* New York, NY: Teachers College Press.

Fosnot, C. T., & Perry, R. (2005). Constructivism: A psychological theory of learning. In C. T. Fosnot, *Constructivism: Theory, perspectives, and practice.* New York, NY: Teachers College Press.

Fowler, R. (1994, April). *Piagetian versus Vygotskian perspectives on development and education.* Paper presented at the annual meeting of the American Educational Research Association, New Orleans, LA.

Fox, E., & Riconscente, M. (2008). Metacognition and self-regulation in James, Piaget, and Vygotsky. *Educational Psychology Review, 20*(4), 373–389.

Fox, N E., & Ysseldyke, J. E. (1997). Implementing inclusion at the middle school level: Lessons from a negative example. *Exceptional Children, 64,* 81–98.

Franken, R. E. (2007). *Human motivation* (6th ed.). Belmont, CA: Wadsworth.

Frankenberger, K. D. (2000). Adolescent egocentrism: A comparison among adolescents and adults. *Journal of Adolescence, 23*(3), Jun 2000, 343–354.

Fredricks, J. A., Blumenfeld, P. C., & Paris, A. (2004). School engagement: Potential of the concept, state of the evidence. *Review of Educational Research, 74*(1), 59–109.

Freeman, B. (2000, March). *Autism: What we know.* Paper presented at the meeting of the Alabama Autism Academy. Birmingham, AL.

Freitas, F. A., & Leonard, L. J. (2011). Maslow's hierarchy of needs and student academic success. *Teaching & Learning in Nursing, 6*(1), 9–13.

Freud, S., & Strachey, J. (1964). *The standard edition of the complete psychological works of Sigmund Freud.* Oxford, England: Macmillan.

Friend, M., & Cook, L. (1992). *Collaboration skills for school professionals.* White Plains, NY: Longman.

Fromkin, V., & Rodman, R. (1983). *An introduction to language* (3rd ed.). New York, NY: Holt, Reinehart & Winston.

Fuchs, D., Fuchs, L. S., & Bahr, M. W. (1990). Mainstream assistance teams: Scientific basis for the art of consultation. *Exceptional Children, 57,* 128–139.

Fuchs, D., Fuchs, L. S., Bahr, M. W., Fernstrom, P., & Stecker, P. M. (1990). Pre-referral intervention: A prescriptive approach. *Exceptional Children, 56,* 493–514.

Fuchs, D., Fuchs, L. S., Mathes, P. G., & Lipsey, M. W. (2000). Differences between low-achieving students with and without learning disabilities: A meta-analysis. In R. Gersten, E. P. Schiller, & S. Vaughn (Eds.), *Contemporary special education research: Syntheses of the knowledge base on critical instruction issues* (pp. 81–105). Mahwah, NJ: Erlbaum.

Fuchs, L. S., Fuchs, D., Prentice, K., Burch, M., Hamlett, C. L., Owen, R., et al. (2003). Explicitly teaching for transfer: Effects on third-grade students' mathematical problem solving. *Journal of Educational Psychology, 95,* 295–305.

Fullan, M. (2001). *The new meaning of educational change* (3rd ed.). New York, NY: Teachers College Press.

Furstenberg, F. F., & Cherlin, A. J. (1991). *Divided families.* Cambridge, MA: Harvard University Press.

Fuson, K. (2009). Avoiding misinterpretations of Piaget and Vygotsky: Mathematical teaching without learning, learning without teaching, or helpful learning-path teaching. *Cognitive Development, 24*(4), 343–361.

Gabales, L., & Birney, D. (2011). Are the limits in processing and storage capacity common? Exploring the additive and interactive effects of processing and storage load in working memory. *Journal of Cognitive Psychology, 23*(3), 322–341.

Gabel, H., McDowell, J., & Cerreto, M. (1983). Family adaptation to the handicapped infant. In S. Greenwood & R. Fewell (Eds.), *Educating handicapped infants* (pp. 455–493). Rockville, MD: Aspen.

Gable, R., Hendrickson, J. M., & Sasso, G. M. (1995). Toward a more functional analysis of aggression. *Education and Treatment of Children, 18,* 226–242.

Gabler, I. C., & Schroeder, M. (2003). *Constructivists methods: Engaged minds.* Boston, MA: Allyn & Bacon.

Gage, N., & Berliner, D. (1989). Nurturing the critical, practical, and artistic thinking of teachers. *Phi Delta Kappan, 71,* 212–214.

Gage, S. T., & Falvey, M. A. (1995). Assessment strategies to develop appropriate curricula and educational programs. In M. A. Falvey (Ed.), *Inclusive and heterogeneous schooling: Assessment, curriculum, and instruction* (pp. 59–86). Baltimore, MD: Paul H. Brookes.

Gagnon, M. J., & Abell, S. K. (2007). Making time for science talk. *Science and Children, 44*(8), 66–67.

Gallace, A., & Spence, C. (2011). To what extent do Gestalt grouping principles influence tactile perception. *Psychological Bulletin, 137*(4), 538-561.

Gallagher, J. J. (2006). *Driving change in special education.* Port Chester, NY: National Professional Resources.

Gardner, H. (1983). *Frames of mind: The theory of multiple intelligence.* New York, NY: Basic Books Inc..

Gardner, H. (1995). Reflections on multiple intelligences: Myths and messages. *Phi Delta Kappan, 77,* 200–209.

Gardner, H. (1999). Who owns intelligence? *The Atlantic Monthly, 283*(2), 67–76.

Gardner, H., Kornhaber, M., & Wake, W. (1996). *Intelligence: Multiple perspectives.* Fort Worth, TX: Harcourt Brace.

Gargiulo, R. M. (2006). *Special education in contemporary society: An introduction to exceptionality* (2nd ed.). Belmont, CA: Wadsworth.

Garner, W. R. (1953). An informational analysis of absolute judgments of loudness. *Journal of Experimental Psychology, 46*, 373–380.

Gathercoal, F. (2001). *Judicious discipline* (5th ed.). San Francisco, CA: Caddo Gap Press.

Gathercole, S. & Baddeley, A. (1993). *Working memory and language.* Hove, UK: Lawrence Erlbaum Associates.

Gathercole, S. E., & Adams, A. M. (1993). Phonological working memory in very young children. *Developmental Psychology 29*, 770–778.

Gathercole, S. E., Adams, A. M. & Hitch, G. J. (1994). Do young children rehearse? An individual differences analysis. *Memory and Cognition* 22, 201–207.

Gathercole. S. & Baddeley. A. (1990) The role of phonological memory in vocabulary acquisition: A study of young children learning new names. *British Journal of Psychology, 81*, 439–454.

Gaunt, R. (2011). Effects of intergroup conflict and social contract on prejudice: The mediating role of stereotypes and evaluations. *Journal of Applied Social Psychology, 41*(6), 1340–1355.

Gay, G. (2006). Connections between classroom management and culturally responsive teaching. In C. M. Evertson, & C. S. Weinstein, *Handbook of cassroom management: research, practice, and contemporary issues* (pp. 343–370). Mahwah, NJ: Lawrence Erlbaum Associates.

Gelman, S. A. & Ebeling, K. S. (1989). Children's use of nonegocentric standards in judgments of size. *Child Development, 60*, 920–932.

Gentile, B., Grabe, S., Dolan-Pascoe, B., Twenge, J., Wells, B., & Maitino, A. (2009). Gender differences in domain-specific self-esteem: A meta-analysis. *Review of General Psychology, 13*(1), 34–45.

Gentile, J. R. (2000). Learning, transfer of. In A. Kazdin (Ed.), *Encyclopedia of psychology.* Washington, DC: American Psychological Association and Oxford University Press.

Georghiades, P. (2004). From the general to the situated: 3 decades of metacognition. *International Journal Science Education, 26*(3), 365–383.

German, T. P., & Barrett, H. C. (2005). Functional fixedness in a technologically sparse culture. *Psychological Science, 16*, 1–5.

Gersten, R. (1998). Recent advances in instructional research for students with learning disabilities: An overview. *Disabilities Research & Practice, 13*(3), 162–170.

Gersten, R., & Keating, T. (1987). Long-term benefits from direct instruction. *Educational Leadership, 44*(6), 28–29.

Gettinger, M., & Seibert, J. K. (2002). Contributions of study skills to academic competence. *School Psychology Review, 31*(3), 350–365.

Gettinger, M., Schienbeck, C., Seigel, S., & Vollmer, L. (2011). Assessment of classroom environments. In M. Bray, & T. Kehle (Eds.), *The Oxford handbook of school psychology* (pp. 260–283). New York, NY: Oxford University Press.

Ghasemi, A., Momeni, M., Jafarzadehpur, E., Rezaee, M., & Taheri, H. (2011). Visual skills involved in decision making by expert referees. *Perceptual and Motor Skills, 112*(1), 161–171.

Gibbons, P. (2002). *Scaffolding language, scaffolding learning: Teaching second language learners in the mainstream classroom.* Portsmouth, NH: Heinemann.

Gifford-Smith, M., & Brownell, C. (2003). Childhood peer relationships: Social acceptance, friendships, and peer networks. *Journal of School Psychology, 41*, 235–284.

Gilbert, L. A., Schilt, P. E., & Ekland-Olson, S. (2005). Integrated learning and research across disciplinary boundaries: Engaging students. *Liberal Education, 91*(3), 44–49.

Gilhooley, J., & Scheuch, N. S. (2000). *Using peer mediation in classrooms and schools: Strategies for teachers, counselors, and administrators.* Thousand Oaks, CA: Corwin.

Gilles, C., Wilson, J., & Elias, M. (2010). Sustaining teachers' growth and renewal through action research, induction programs, and collaboration. *Teacher Education Quarterly, 37* (1), 91–108.

Gilles, R. M. (2002). The residual effects of cooperative learning experiences: A two-year follow-up. *Journal of Educational Research, 96*(1), 15–21.

Gilliam, J. E. (1995). *Gilliam autism rating scale.* Circle Pines, MN: American Guidance Service.

Gillies, R., & Haynes, M. (2011). Increasing explanatory behaviour, problem-solving, and reasoning within classes using cooperative group work. *Instructional Science, 39*(3), 349–366.

Ginott, H. (1972). *Teacher and child.* New York, NY: Macmillian.

Gipps, C. (1994). *Beyond testing.* Washington, D.C.: Falmer Press.

Girard, K., & Koch, S. J. (1996). *Conflict resolution in the schools: A manual for educators.* San Francisco, CA: Jossey Bass.

Gleason, T. R., Sebanc, A. M., & Hartup, W. W. (2000). Imaginary companions of preschool children. *Developmental Psychology, 36*, 419–428.

GLEF, L. (2001, July 12). *Project-based learning research.* Retrieved July 12, 2004, from Edutopia online: http://www.glef.org/php/article.php?id=Art_887

Goldenberg, C. (1991). *Instructional conversations and their classroom applications.* National Center for Research on Cultural Diversity and Second Language Learning. Washington, DC: National Center for Research on Cultural Diversity and Second Language Learning.

Goldenberg, C., & Patthey-Chavez, G. (1995). Discourse processes in instructional conversations: Interactions between teacher and transition readers. *Discourse Processes, 19*, 57–73.

Golding, C. (2011). Educating for critical thinking: Thought-encouraging questions in a community of inquiry. *Higher Education Research & Development, 30*(3), 357–370.

Goleman, D. (1995). *Emotional intelligence.* New York, NY : Bantam.

Goleman, D., Boyztzis, R., & McKee, A. (2002). *Primal leadership: Realizing the power of emotional intelligence.* Boston, MA: Harvard Business School Press.

Goni, J., Arrondo, G., Sepulcre, J., Matincorena, I., de Mendizabal, N., Corominas-Murtra, B., et al. (2011). The semantic organization of the animal category: Evidence from semantic verbal fluency and network theory. *Cognitive Processing, 12*(2), 183–196.

Good, T. L., & Brophy, J. E. (1987). *Looking in classrooms* (4th ed.). New York, NY: Harper Row.

Goodwin, A. L., & Macdonald, M. B. (1997). Educating the rainbow: Authentic assessment and authentic practice for diverse classrooms. In A. Lin Goodwin (Ed.), *Assessment for equity and inclusion: Embracing all our children* (pp. 211–227). New York, NY: Routledge.

Gore, J., & Cross, S. (2011). Defining and measuring self-concept change. *Psychological Studies, 56*(1), 135–141.

Gortner-Lahmers, A., & Sulauf, C. R. (2000). Factors associated with academic time use and academic performance of college students: A recursive approach. *Journal of College Student Development, 41*(5), 544–556.

Gottfried, A. E., & Gottfried, A. W. (1996). A longitudinal study of academic intrinsic motivation in intellectually gifted children: Childhood through early adolescence. *Gifted Child Quarterly, 40*(4), 179–183.

Graden, J. L. (1989). Redefining "pre-referral" intervention as intervention assistance: Collaboration between general and special education. *Exceptional Children, 56*, 227–231.

Graden, J. L., Casey, A. & Bronstrom, O. (1985). Implementing a prereferral intervention system: Part II. The data. *Exceptional Children, 51*, 487–496.

Grandmont, R. P. (2003). Judicious Discipline: A constitutional approach for public high schools. *American Secondary Education,* 31(3), 97–117.

Grant, D. (2011). Effect of intermittent reinforcement on acquisition and retention in delayed matching-to-sample in pigeons. *Learning and Motivation, 42*(1), 33–45.

Gray, W. D. (2002). Simulated task environments: The role of high-fidelity simulations, scaled worlds, synthetic environments, and microworlds in basic and applied cognitive research. *Cognitive Science Quarterly, 2*(2), 205–227.

Gredler, M. (2001). *Learning and instruction: Theory into practice* (4th ed.). Upper Saddle River, NJ: Merrill Prentice Hall.

Gredler, M. (2009). Hiding in plain sight: The stages of mastery/self-regulation in Vygotsky's cultural-historical theory. *Educational Psychologist, 44*(1), 1–19.

Greimel, K., & Kroner-Herwig, B. (2011). Cognitive behavioral treatment (CBT). In A. Moller, B. Langguth, D. DeRidder, & T. Kleinjung (Eds.), *Textbook of tinnitus* (Vol. xxx, pp. 557–561). New York, NY: Springer Science + Business Media.

Grela, B., Collisson, B., & Arthur, D. (2011). Language processing in children with language impairment. In J. Guendouzi, F. Loncke, & M. Williams (Eds.), *The handbook of psycholinguistic and cognitive processes: Perspectives in communication disorders* (pp. 373–399). New York, NY: Psychology Press.

Gresham, F. M., & Macmillan, D. L. (1997). Social competence and affective characteristics of students with mild disabilities. *Review of Educational Research, 67,* 377–415.

Greven, C., Asherson, P., Rijsdijk, F., & Plomin, R. (2011). A longitudinal twin study on the association between inattentive and hyperactive-impulsive ADHD symptoms. *Journal of Abnormal Child Psychology: An official publication of the international society for research in child and adolescent psychopathology, 39*(5), 623–632.

Grey, C., & Garand, J. D. (1993). Social stories: Improving responses of students with autism and with accurate social information. *Focus on Autistic Behavior, 8,* 1–10.

Gronlund, N. E. (2004). *Writing instructional objectives for teaching and assessment* (7th ed.). New York, NY: Prentice-Hall.

Gross Davis, B. (1993). *Tools for teaching.* San Francisco, CA: Jossey-Bass.

Grossman, H., & Grossman, S. H. (1994). *Gender issues in education.* Boston, MA: Allyn & Bacon.

Gunter, P. L., Shores, R. E., Jack, S. L., Rasmussen, S., & Flowers, J. (1995). Teacher/student proximity: a strategy for classroom control through teacher movement. *Teaching Exceptional Children, 28*(1), 12–14.

Gupta, V. B. (2000). A closer look at ADD/ADHD. *The Exceptional Parent, 30*(8), 74–81.

Guskey, T. R. (2002). Computerized gradebooks and the myth of objectivity. *Phi Delta Kappan, 83*(10), 775–780.

Guttentag, M., & Bray, S. (1976). *Undoing sex stereotypes.* New York, NY: Harper & Row.

Hagevik, S. (1999). Just listening. *Journal of Environmental Health, 6*(1), 46–48.

Hagger, M., & Chatzisarantis, N. (2011). Causality orientations moderate the undermining effect of rewards on intrinsic motivation. *Journal of Experimental Social Psychology, 47*(2), 485–489.

Hajhashemi, K., Ghombavani, F., & Amirkhiz, S. (2011). The relationship between Iranian EFL High School student's multiple intelligence scores and their use of learning strategies. *English Language Teaching, 4*(3), 214–222.

Haladyna, T. M., Nolen, S. B., & Hass, N. S. (1991). Raising standardized achievement test scores and the origins of test score pollution. *Educational Researcher, 20,* 2–7.

Halford, G., & Andrews, G. (2011). Information-processing models of cognitive development. In U. Goswami (Ed.), *The Wiley-Blackwell handbook of childhood cognitive development* (2nd ed., pp. 697–721). Cambridge, England: Wiley-Blackwell.

Hallahan, D. P., Lloyd, J. W., Kauffman, J. M., Weiss, M., & Martinez, E. A. (2005). *Learning disabilities: Foundations, characteristics, and effective teaching* (3rd ed.). Boston, MA: Allyn & Bacon.

Hallowell, E., & Ratey, J. (1995). *Answers to distraction.* New York, NY: Pantheon Books.

Halpern, D. F. (1993). Assessing the effectiveness of critical thinking instruction. *Journal of General Education, 42*(4), 238–254.

Halpern, D. F. (1998). Teaching critical thinking for transfer across domains. *American Psychologist, 53*(4), 449–456.

Halpern, D. F. (2000). *Sex differences in cognitive abilities* (3rd ed.). Mahwah, NJ: Lawrence Erlbaum Associates.

Handa, Y. (2009). Explaining the cross-multiplication algorithm. *Mathematics Teaching Incorporating Micromath, 212,* 8–9.

Hansen, R. J., & Brady, M. (2011). Solving problems through action research. *The LLI Review, 6,* 82–90.

Hanson, M., Lynch, E. W., & Wayman, K. I. (1990). Honoring the cultural diversity of families when gathering data. *Topics in Early Childhood Special Education, 10*(1), 111–131.

Hardré, P. L., & Chen, C. H. (2005). A case study analysis of the role of instructional design in the development of teaching expertise. *Performance Improvement Quarterly, 18*(1), 25.

Hardré, P., Nanny, M., Refai, H., Chen, L., & Slater, J. (2010). Engineering a dynamic science-learning environment for K–12 teachers. *Teacher Education Quarterly, 37*(2), 157–178.

Harré, M., Bossomaier, T., & Snyder, A. (2011). The development of human expertise in a complex environment. *Minds and Machines, 21*(3), 449–464.

Harrington, R. G. (1982). Caution: Standardized testing may be hazardous to the educational programs of intellectually gifted children. *Education, 8*(3), 154–159.

Harris, L. (2011). Secondary teachers' conceptions of student engagement: Engagement in learning or in schooling? *Teaching and Teacher Education: An International Journal of Research and Studies, 27*(2), 376–386.

Harrison, C., & Howard, S. (2011). How summative assessment helps sum up learning. Issues in primary assessment: Part 3. *Primary Science, 117,* 21–23.

Harrison, G., Andrews, J., & Saklofske, D. (2003). Current perspectives on cognitive and learning styles. *Education Canada, 43*(2), 44–47.

Harry, B. (1992). An ethnographic study of cross-cultural communication with Puerto Rican-American families in the special education system. *American Educational Research Journal, 29*(3), 471–494.

Harry, B., & Klinger, J. K. (2002). Of rocks and soft places: Using qualitative methods to investigate the processes that result in disproportionality. In D. J. Loosen & G. Orfield (Eds.), *Racial inequality in special education* (pp. 71–92). Boston, MA: Harvard Education Press.

Harter, S. (1978). Pleasure derived from optimal challenge and the effects of extrinsic rewards of children's difficulty level choices. *Child Development, 49,* 788–799.

Harter, S. (1998). The development of self-representations. In N. Eisenberg (Ed.), *Handbook of child psychology: Vol 3. Social, emotional, and personality development* (5th ed.)(pp. 553–618). New York, NY: Wiley.

Hartwig, E. (2000). Not every ADD student is covered under Section 504. *Section 504 Compliance Advisor, 4,* 4.

Helsdingen, A. (2011). The effects of practice schedule and critical thinking prompts on learning and transfer of a complex judgment task. *Journal of Educational Psychology, 103*(2), 383–398.

Hendrie, C. (2004). One student at a time. *Education Week, 24*(4), 36–39.

Hester, P. (2002). What teachers can do to prevent behavior problems in schools. *Prevention School Failure, 47*(1), 33–38.

Hetherington, E. M. (1995, March). *The changing American family and the well-being of children.* Paper presented at the meeting of the Society for Research in Child Development. Indianapolis, IN.

Hetherington, E. M. (2000). Divorce. In A. Kazdin (Ed.), *Encyclopedia of psychology.* Washington, DC: American Psychology Association and Oxford University Press.

Hetherington, E. M., & Kelly, J. (2002). *For better or for worse: Divorce reconsidered.* New York, NY: W. W. Norton.

Heyman, W. B. (1990). The self-perception of a learning disability and its relationship to academic self-concept and self-esteem. *Of Learning Disabilities, 23,* 472–475.

Hidi, S., & Harackiewicz, J. (2000). Motivating the academically unmotivated: A critical issue for the 21st century. *Review of Educational Research, 70,* 151–179.

Hilgard, E. R., & Bower, G. H. (1966). *Theories of learning* (3rd ed.). East Norwalk, CT: U.S. Appleton-Century-Crofts.

Hill, P., Jackson, J., Roberts, B., Lapsley, D., & Brandenberger, J. (2011). Change you can believe in: Changes in goal setting during emerging and young adulthood predict later adult well-being. *Social Psychological and Personality Science, 2*(2), 123–131.

Hinde, E., & Perry, N. (2007). Elementary teachers' application of Jean Piaget's theories of cognitive development during social studies curriculum debates in Arizona. *Elementary School Journal, 108*(1), 63–79.

Hirschfeld, R. R., Lawson, L., & Mossholder, K. (2004). Moderators of the relationship between cognitive ability and performance: General versus context-specific achievement motivation. *Journal of Applied Social Psychology, 34*(11), 2389–2409.

Hmelo-Silver, C. E. (2004). Problem-based learning: What and how do students learn? *Educational Psychology Review, 16,* 235–266.

Hmelo-Silver, C., Duncan, R. G., & Chinn, C. A. (2007). Scaffolding and achievement in problem-based and inquiry learning: A response to Kirschne, Sweller, and Clark (2006). *Educational Psychologist, 42*(2), 99–107.

Hodapp, R., & Krasner, D. (1995). Families of children with disabilities: Findings from a national sample of eighth grade students. *Exceptionality, 5*(2), 71–81.

Hoff, E. (2001). *Language development* (2nd ed.). Belmont, CA: Wadsworth/Thomson Learning.

Hoge, D. R., Smit, E. K., & Hanson, S. L.(1990). School experiences predicting changes in self-esteem of sixth- and seventh-grade students. *Journal of Educational Psychology, 82,* 117–126.

Holahan, C., & Sears, R. (1995). *Gifted group in later maturity.* Stanford, CA: Stanford University Press.

Holland, A., Addis, D., & Kensinger, E. (2011). The neural correlates of specific versus general autobiographical memory construction and elaboration. *Neuropsychologia,* Jul 23, 1–14.

Hollins, E. (2011). Teacher preparation for quality teaching. *Journal of Teacher Education, 62*(4), 395–407.

Hooks, B. (1994). *Teaching to transgress.* New York, NY: Routledge.

Hoover, J. (2010). Special education eligibility decision making in response to intervention models. *Theory into Practice, 49*(4), 289–296.

Horner, R. H., Albin, R. W., Sprague, J. R., & Todd, A. W. (2000). Positive behavioral supports. In M. E. Snell & F. Brown (Eds.), *Instruction of students with severe disabilities* (5th ed., pp. 207–244). Upper Saddle River, NJ: Merrill Publishing.

Horner, R., O'Neill, R., & Flannery, K. (1993). Building effective behavior support plans from functional assessment information. In M. Snell (Ed.), *Instruction of persons with severe handicaps* (4th ed., pp. 184–214). Columbus, OH: Merrill.

Howe, F., & Simmons, B. J. (2005). Nurturing the parent-teacher alliance. *Phi Delta Kappa, 533,* 7–41.

Howe, M. J. A., (1970) *Introduction to human memory—A psychological approach,* Harper & Row.

Hoxby, C. (2002). The cost of accountability. NBER Working Papers 8855, National Bureau of Economic Research, Inc.

Hughes, F. P., & Noppe, L. D. (1991). *Human development across the life span.* New York, NY: Macmillan.

Hughes, J. (2002). Authoritative teaching: Tipping the balance in favor of school versus peer effects. *Journal of School Psychology, 40*(6), 485–492.

Hung, D. (2002). Situated cognition and problem-based learning: Implications for learning and instruction with technology. *Journal of Interactive Learning Research, 13*(4), 393–414.

Hunter, M. (1982). *Mastery teaching.* El Segundo, CA: TIP Publications.

Hurley, D. (2005, April 19). Divorce rate: It's not as high as you think. *The New York Times,* New York.

Hurley, J. R. (1992). Further evidence against the construct validity of the FIRO-B scales. *Psychological Reports, 70,* 639–640.

Individuals With Disabilities Education Act, 20 U.S.C. Secs. 1400 *et seq.* (1975, as amended, 1997).

Ingalls, L., & Hammond, H. (1996). Pre-referral school-based teams: How effective are they? *Rural Special Education Quarterly, 15*(2), 9–18.

Inhelder, B., & Piaget, J. (1958). *The growth of logical thinking from childhood to adolescence: An essay on the construction of formal operations.* Oxford, England: English Basic Books.

Irby, B., Tong, F., & Lara-Alecio, R. (2011). The mutual symbiosis between inclusive bilingual education and multicultural education. *Multicultural Perspectives, 13*(3), 130–137.

Isaksen, S., Dorval, K. B., & Treffinger, D. (2011). *Creative approaches to problem solving: A framework for innovation and change.* Thousand Oaks, CA: Sage Publications.

Iversen, I. H. (1992). Skinner's early research: From reflexology to operant conditioning. *American Psychologist Special Issue, 47*(11), 1318–1328.

Jacob-Timm, S., & Hartshorne, T. S. (1994). Section 504 and school psychology. *Psychology in the Schools, 31,* 26–39.

Jacob, S., Decker, D., & Hartshorne, T. (2011). *Ethics and law for school psychologists.* Hoboken, NJ: John Wiley & Sons Inc.

Jacques, K. (2000). Solicitous tenderness: Discipline and responsibility in the classroom. In H. Cooper & R. Hyland (Eds.), *Children's perceptions of learning with trainee teachers* (pp. 166–177). London, England: Routledge.

James, K. H. (2010). Sensori-motor experience leads to changes in visual processing in the developing brain. *Developmental Science, 13*(2), 279–288.

Jodrell, D. (2010). Social identity and self-efficacy concern for disability labels. *Pschology Teaching Review, 16*(2), 111–121.

Johns, B. H., Crowley, E. P., & Guetzloe, E. (2005). The central role of teaching social skills. *Focus on Exceptional Children, 37*(8), 1–8.

Johns, B., & Keenan, J. (1997). *Techniques for managing a safe school.* Denver, CO: Love.

Johnsen, S. (2011). *Identifying gifted students: A practical guide* (2nd ed.). Waco, TX: Prufrock Press.

Johnson, D. D., Rice, M. P., & Edgington, W. D. (2005). For the uninitiated: How to succeed in classroom management. *Kappa Delta Pi Record, 42*(1), 28–32.

Johnson, D. W., & Johnson, R. T. (1995). Cooperative learning and non-academic outcomes of schooling: The other side of the report card. In J. E. Pedersen, & A. D. Digby, *Secondary schools and cooperative learning* (pp. 81–150). New York, NY: Garland Publishing.

Johnson, D. W., & Johnson, R. T. (1996). *Cooperation and competition: Theory and research.* Edina, MN: Interaction Book Company.

Johnson, D. W., & Johnson, R. T. (1998). Cultural diversity and cooperative learning. In J. W. Putnam, *Cooperative learning and strategies for inclusion* (2nd ed.). Baltimore, MD: Brookes Publishing.

Johnson, D. W., & Johnson, R. T. (2002). *Meaningful assessment: A manageable and cooperative process.* Boston, MA: Allyn & Bacon.

Johnson, D. W., Johnson, R. T., & Smith, K. A. (1995). Cooperative learning and individual student achievement in secondary schools. In J. E. Pedersen, & A. D. Digby, *Secondary schools and cooperative learning* (pp. 3–54). New York, NY: Garland Publishing.

Johnson, D., & Johnson, R. (1998). *Cooperation in the classroom.* Edina, MN: Interaction Book Company.

Johnson, G. R. (1988). *Taking teaching seriously.* College Station, TX: College Station: Center for teaching excellence, Texas A & M University.

Johnson, L., & Johnson, C. (1999). Teaching students to regulate their own behavior. In Cauley, K., Linder, F., & McMillian, J. (Eds.), *Annual editions: Educational psychology* (16 ed., pp. 160–164). Guilford, CT: McGraw Hill/Dushkin.

Jonassen, D. H. (1997). Instructional design models for well-structured and ill-structured problem-solving learning outcomes. *Educational Technology Research and Development, 45*(1), 65–94.

Jonassen, D. H., Howland, J., Moore, J., & Marra, R. M. (2003). *Learning to solve problems with technology: A constructivist perspective* (2nd ed.). Upper Saddle River, NJ: Merrill Prentice Hall.

Jonassen, D., Carr, C., & Hsui-Ping, Y. (1998). Computers as mindtools for engaging learners in critical thinking, *Tech Trends, 43,* 24–32.

Jonassen. (1994). Thinking technology. *Educational Technology, 34*(4), 34–37.

Jones, C. H., Slate, J. R., Blake, P. C., & Holi-field, S. D. (1992). Two investigations of the academic skills of junior and senior high school students. *High School Journal, 76*(1).

Jones, D. (2011). Academic dishonesty: Are more students cheating? *Business Communication Quarterly, 74*(2), 141–150.

Jones, V., & Jones, L. (2007). *Comprehensive classroom management.* (8th ed.). Boston, MA: Allyn & Bacon.

Joolingen, W. V. (1999). Cognitive tools for discovery learning. *International Journal of Artificial Intelligence in Education, 10*(3), 385–397.

Joyce, B., Weil, M., & Calhoun, E. (2004). *Models of teaching* (7th ed.). Boston, MA: Pearson Allyn & Bacon.

Jung, I., & Latchem, C. (2011). A model for e-education: Extended teaching spaces and extended learning spaces. *British Journal of Educational Technology, 42*(1), 6–18.

Juvonen, J., Wang, Y., & Espinoza, G. (2011). Bullying experiences and compromised academic performance across middle school grades. *Journal of Early Adolescence, 31*(1), 152–173.

Kagan, J. (1990). *Cooperative Learning Resources for Teachers.* San Juan Capistrano, CA: Resources for Teachers.

Kagan, J., Snidman, N., Kahn, V., & Towsley, S. (2007). The preservation of two infant temperaments into adolescence. *Monographs of the Society for Research in Child Development, 72*(2), 1–95.

Kaiser, A. P., & Hester, P. P. (1997). Prevention of conduct disorders through early intervention: A social-communicative perspective. *Behavioral Disorders, 22,* 117–130.

Karweit, N. (1985). Should we lengthen the school term? *Educational Researcher, 14*(6), 9–15.

Karweit, N. (1989). Time and learning: A review. In R.E. Slavin (Ed.), *School and Classroom Organization* (pp. 69–95). Hillsdale, NJ: Lawrence Erlbaum.

Katayma, A. D. (1997). Getting students involved in note taking: Why partial notes benefit learners more than complete notes. *Annual meeting of the Mid-South Educational Research Association.* Memphis, TN.

Kavale, K. A., Fuchs, D., & Scruggs, T. E. (1994). Setting the record straight on learning disabilities and low achievement. *Disabilities Research and Practice, 9,* 70–79.

Kennedy, C., Long, K., & Camins, A. (2009). The reflective assessment technique. *Science and Children, 47*(4), 50–53.

Keppel, G., & Underwood, B. J. (1962). Proactive inhibition in short-term retention of single items. *Journal of Verbal Learning and Verbal Behavior, 1,* 153–161.

Kiewra, K. A. (1989). A review of note-taking: The encoding-storage paradigm and beyond. *Educational Psychology Review, 2,* 142–172.

Kim, Y. J. (1983). Problems in the delivery of school-based psychoeducational services to Asian immigrant children. *Journal of Children in Contemporary Society, 15*(3), 81–89.

Kindermann, T. A., McCollam, T. L., & Gibson, E. (1996). Peer networks and student' classroom engagement during childhood and adolescence. In K. Wentzel & J. Juvonen (Eds.), *Social motivation: Understanding children's school adjustment* (pp. 279–312). New York: Cambridge University Press.

Kingery, J. N., Erdley, C. A., Marshall, K. C., Whitaker, K. G., & Reuter, T. R. (2010). Peer experiences of anxious and socially withdrawn youth: An integrative review of the developmental and clinical literature. *Clinical Child and Family Psychology Review, 13*(1), 91–128.

Kirschner, P. A., Sweller, J., & Clark, R. E. (2006). Why minimal guidance during instruction does not work: An analysis of the failure of constructivist, discovery, problem-based, experiential, and inquiry-based teaching. *Educational Psychologist, 41*(2), 75–86.

Klein, G. A., & Hoffman, R. R. (1993). Seeing the invisible: Perceptual-cognitive aspects of expertise. In M. Rabinowitz (Ed.), *Cognitive science foundations of instruction.* Hillsdale, NJ: Lawrence Erlbaum Assoc.

Klug, J., Ogrin, S., Keller, S., Ihringer, A., & Schmitz, B. (2011). A plea for self-regulated learning as a process: Modeling, measuring, and intervening. *Psychological Test and Assessment Modeling, 53*(1), 51–72.

Koegel, L., Koegel, R., Dunlap, G. (1996). *Positive behavioral support.* Baltimore, MD: Paul Brookes.

Kohlberg, L. (1966). A cognitive-developmental analysis of children's sex-role concepts and attitudes. In E. E. Maccoby (Ed.), *The development of sex differences.* Stanford, CA: Standford University Press.

Kolb, D. (1984). *Experiential learning: Experience as the source of learning and development.* Englewood Cliffs, NJ: Prentice Hall.

Koretz, D., Mitchell, K., Barron, S., & Keith, S. (1996). *The perceived effects of the Maryland School performance assessment program* (CSE Tech. Rep. No. 409). Los Angeles, CA: National Center for Research on Evaluation, Standards, and Student Testing (CRESST).

Kozol, J. (1992). *Savage inequalities.* New York, NY: Crown.

Kozulin, A. (2011). Introduction to Vygotsky's "The dynamics of the schoolchild's mental development in relation to teaching and learning". *Journal of Cognitive Education and Psychology 10*(2), 195–197.

Krug, D., Arick, J., & Almond, P. (1981). Autism screening instrument for educational planning: Background and development. In J. Gilliam (Ed.), *Autism: Diagnosis, instruction, management, and research* (pp. 64–78). Springfield, IL: Charles C. Thomas.

Kuder, S. (2003). *Teaching students with language and communication disabilities* (2nd ed.). Boston, MA: Allyn & Bacon.

Kuhn, D., Amsel, E., & O'loughlin, M., et al. (1988). *The development of scientific thinking skills.* San Diego, CA: U.S. Academic Press.

Kuhne, B. (1995). The Barkestorp project: Investigating school library use. School Libraries Worldwide, *1*(1), 13–27.

Kuklinski, M. R., & Weinstein, R. S. (2001). Classroom and developmental differences in a path model of teacher expectancy effects. *Child Development, 72,* 1554–1578.

Kulik, J. A. (2003). Grouping and tracking. In N. Colangello & G. Davis (Eds.), *Handbook of gifted education* (pp. 268–281). Boston, MA: Allyn & Bacon.

Kumar, R., Gheen, M. H., & Kaplan, A. (2002). Goal structures in the learning environment and students' disaffection from learning and schooling. In C. Midgley (Ed.), *Goals, goal structures, and patterns of adaptive learning* (pp. 143–174). Mahwah, NJ: Erlbaum.

Kurfiss, J. G. (1988). *Critical thinking: Theory, research, practice, and possibilities.* ASHE-ERIC Higher Education Report No. 2.

Kyhl, C. S. (1995). The development of concrete operational classification structures. *Dissertation Abstracts International Section A: Humanities & Social Sciences, 56* (4–A), Oct 1995, 1292.

L'hospital, A. S., & Gregory, A. (2009). Changes in teacher stress through participation in pre-referral intervention teams. *Psychology in the Schools, 46*(10), 1098–1112.

Lai, E., & Lam, C. (2011). Learning to teach in a context of education reform? Liberal studies student teachers' decision-making in lesson planning. *Journal of Education for Teaching: International Research and Pedagogy, 37*(2), 219–236.

Lalley, J., & Gentile, J. (2009). Classroom assessment and grading to assure mastery. *Theory into Practice, 48*(1), 28–35.

Lamb, M. E., & Meyer, D. J. (1991). Fathers of children with special needs. In M. Seligman (Ed.), *The family with a handicapped child* (2nd ed., pp. 151–179). Boston, MA: Allyn & Bacon.

Land, M. L. (1987). Vagueness and clarity. In M. Dunkin, *The international encyclopedia of teaching and teacher education* (pp. 392–397). New York, NY: Pergamon.

Lane, K. L., Givner, C. C., & Pierson, M. R. (2004). Teacher expectations of student behavior: Social skills necessary for success in elementary school classrooms. *Journal of Special Education, 38*(2), 104–111.

Lane, K. L., Pierson, M. R., & Givner, C. C. (2003). Teacher expectations of student behavior: Which skills do elementary and secondary teachers deem necessary for success in the classroom? *Education & Treatment of Children, 26*(4), 413–430.

Langberg, J., Epstein, J., Girio-Herera, E., Becker, S., Vaughn, A., & Altaye, M. (2011). Materials organization, planning, and homework completion in middle-school students with ADHD: Impact on academic performance. *School Mental Health, 3*(2), 93–101.

Latham, P. S., & Latham, P. H. (2011). Legal rights and qualifications under the Americans with Disabilities Act. In S. Goldstein, J. Naglieri, & M. DeVries (Eds.), *Learning and attention disorders in adolescence and adulthood* (pp. 289–323). Hoboken, NJ: John Wiley & Sons Inc.

Lauchlan, F., & Boyle, C. (2007). Is the use of labels in special education helpful? *Support for Learning, 22*(1), 36–42.

Lave, J., & Wenger, E. (1991). *Situated learning: Legitimate peripheral participation.* Cambridge, MA: Cambridge University Press.

Lave, J., & Wenger, E. (Eds.). (1990). *Situated learning: Legitimate peripheral participation.* Cambridge, UK: Cambridge University Press.

Lavigna, G. (1985). Commentary on positive reinforcement and behavioral deficits of autistic children by C. B. Fester. In A. Donnellan (Ed.), *Classic readings in autism* (pp. 53–73). New York, NY: Teachers College press.

Lea-Wood, S. S., & Clunies-Ross, G. (1995). Self-esteem of gifted adolescent girls in Australian schools. *Roeper Review, 17,* 195–197.

Leacock, E. B. (1971). *Culture of poverty: A critique.* New York, NY: Simon & Schuster.

Leadbeater, B. (1991). *Relativistic thinking in adolescence.* In R. M. Lerner, A. C. Peterson, & J. Brooks-Gunn (Eds.), *Encyclopedia of adolescence.* New York, NY: Garland.

Leahey, T. H., & Harris, R. J. (2001). *Learning and cognition* (5th ed.). Upper Saddle River, NJ: Prentice Hall.

Learner, J. (2003). *Learning Disabilities: Theories, diagnosis, and teaching strategies* (9th ed.). Boston, MA: Houghton Mifflin.

Lecompte, A. (2000). *Creating harmonious relationships: A practical guide to the power of empathy.* Portsmouth, NH: Atlantic Books.

Lefrancois, G. (2001). *Of children* (9th ed.). Belmont, CA: Wadsworth.

Lemke, J. (1990). *Talking science: Language, learning, and values.* Norwood, NJ: Ablex.

Leonard, L. (2002). Schools as professional communities: Addressing the collaborative challenge. *International Electronic Journal of Leadership in Learning, 6*(17). Retrieved December 1, 2006, from University of Calgary Press Web Site: http://www.ucalgary.ca/~iejll

Leonard, L., & Leonard, P. (2003). The continuing trouble with collaboration: Teachers talk. *Current Issues in Education, 6*(15). Retrieved December 1, 2006, from College of Education, Arizona State University Web Site: http://cie.ed.asu.edu/volume6/number15/

Leroux, G., Spiess, J., & Zago, L. (2009). Adult brains don't fully overcome biases that lead to incorrect performance during cognitive development: An fMRI study in young adults completing a Piaget-like task. *Developmental Science, 12*(2), 326–338.

Levinson, M. (2011). Democracy, accountability, and education. *Theory and Research in Education, 9*(2), 125–144.

Lewis, C., & Tsuchida, I. (1998). A lesson is like a swiftly flowing river: Research lessons and the improvement of Japanese education. *American Educator,* 14–17, 50–52.

Lewis, P. (2003). Is this going to be on the test? In W. Buskist, V. Hevern & G. W. Hill (Eds.), *Essays for e-xcellence in teaching, 2002* (IV ed., Chapter 13). Retrieved from http://teachpsych.lemoyne.edu/teachpsych/eit/index.html

Liben, L. S., & Signorella, M. L. (1993). Gender-schematic processing in children: The role of initial interpretations of stimuli. *Developmental Psychology, 29,* 150–155.

Linn, R. L., & Gronlund, N. E. (2000). *Measurement and assessment in teaching* (8th ed.). Upper Saddle River, NJ: Merrill.

Linn, R. L., & Miller, M. D. (2005). *Measurement and assessment in teaching* (9th ed.). Columbus, OH: Prentice-Hall.

Liu, J., Li, J., Rieth, C., Huber, D., Tian, J., & Lee, K. (2011). A dynamic causal modeling analysis of the effective connectivities unerlying top-down letter processing. *Neuropsychologia, 49*(5), 1177–1186.

Livingston, J. (1997). *Metacognition: An overview.* [On-line]. Available: http://gse.buffalo.edu/fas/shuell/cep564/Metacog.htm

Livingston, J. A. (1996). *Effects of metacognitive instruction on strategy use of college students.* (Unpublished manuscript). State University of New York at Buffalo.

Llosa, L., Beck, S., & Zhao, C. G. (2011). An investigation of academic writing in secondary schools to inform the development of diagnostic classroom assessments. *Assessing Writing, 16*(4), 256–273.

Locke, E. A., & Latham, G. P. (2002). Building a practically useful theory of goal setting and task motivation: A 35-year odyssey. *American Psychologist, 57*(9), 705–717.

Lockhart, R. S. (2000). Methods of memory research. In E. Tulving & F. I. M. Craik (Eds), *The Oxford handbook of memory* (pp. 45–57). Oxford, England: Oxford University Press.

Loosen, D. J., & Orfield, G. (Eds.). (2002). *Racial inequity in special education.* Cambridge, MA: Harvard Civil Rights Project.

Lopez Fernandez, J., & Velazquez Estrella, A. (2011). Context for column addition and subtraction. *Teaching Children Mathematics, 17*(9), 540–548.

Lopez, O. S. (1995). *Classroom diversification: An alternative paradigm for research in educational productivity.* University of Texas, Austin: Unpublished doctoral dissertation.

Lorch, R. F., Lorch, E. P., & Inman, W. E. (1993). Effects of signaling topic structure on text recall. *Journal of Educational Psychology, 85,* 281–290.

Lord, C., Rutter, M., & Lecouteur, A. (1994). Autism diagnostic interview—revised: A revised version of a diagnostic interview for caregivers of individuals with possible pervasive developmental disorders. *Journal of Autism and Developmental Disorders, 24,* 659–685.

Lord, C., Rutter, M., Goode, S., Heemsherbergen, J., Jordon, H., Mawhood, L., et al. (1989). Autism diagnostic observation schedule: A standardized observation of communication and social behavior. *Journal of Autism and Developmental Disorders, 19,* 185–212.

Losardo, A. (2011). Alternative approaches to assessing young children (2nd ed.). Baltimore, MD: Paul H. Brookes Publishing.

Lott, B., & Maluso, D. (2001). Gender development: Social learning. In J. Worrell (Ed.), *Encyclopedia of women and gender.* San Diego, CA: Academic Press.

Lourenco, O., & Machado, A. (1996). In defense of Piaget's theory: A reply to 10 common criticisms. *Psychological Review, 103*(1), Jan. 1996, 143–164.

Lovaas, I. (1993). The development of a treatment-research project for developmentally disabled and autistic children. *Journal of Applied Behavior Analysis, 26*(4), 617–630.

Luckasson, R., Borthwick-Duffy, S., Buntinx, W. H., Coulter, D. L., Craig, E., Reeve, A., et al. (2002). *Mental retardation: Definition, classification, and systems of supports* (10th ed.). Washington, DC: American Association on Mental Retardation.

Lyon, G. R., & Chhabra, V. (1996). The current state of science and the future of specific reading disability. *Mental Retardation & Developmental Disabilities Research Reviews, 2,* 2–9.

Lyon, G. R., & Moats, L. C. (1997). Critical conceptual and methodological considerations in reading intervention research. *Journal of Learning Disabilities, 30,* 578–588.

Mac Iver, D. J., Reuman, D. A., & Main, S. R. (1995). Social structuring of the school: Studying what is, illuminating what could be. In J. T. Spence, J. M. Darley, & D. J. Foss (Eds.), *Annual review of psychology* (Vol. 46, pp. 375–400). Palo Alto, CA: Annual Review.

MacAulay, D. J. (1990). Classroom environment: A literature review. *Educational Psychology, 10*(3), 239–253.

Maccoby, E. E. (1980). *Social development.* New York, NY: Harcourt Brace.

Maccoby, E. E. (2002). Gender and group process: A developmental perspective. *Current Directions in Psychological Science, 11,* 54–58.

Maccoby, E. E., & Jacklin, C. N. (1974). *Psychology of sex differences.* Stanford, CA: Stanford University Press.

Macionis, J. J. (2005). *Sociology* (10th ed.). Upper Saddle River, NJ: Pearson Prentice Hall.

Mackiewicz, S., Wood, C., Cooke, N., & Mazzotti, V. (2011). Effects of peer tutoring with audio prompting on vocabulary acquisition for struggling readers. *Remedial and Special Education, 32*(4), 345–354.

Macklem, G. (1990). Measuring aptitude. *Eric Digests* from ERIC Clearinghouse on Tests Measurement and Evaluation database (ED328608).

Macmaster, K., Donovan, L. A., & Macintyre, P. D. (2002). The effects of being diagnosed with a learning disability on children's self-esteem. *Child Study Journal, 32,* 101–108.

Macmillan, D. L., & Meyers, C. E. (1979). Educational labeling of handicapped learners. *Review of Research in Education, 7.*

Macmillian, D. L., & Reschly, D. J. (1998). Overrepresentation of minority students: The case for greater specificity or reconsideration of the variables examined. *Journal of Special Education, 32,* 15–25.

Maeroff, G. I. (1993). Building teams to rebuild schools. *Phi Delta Kappan, 74*(7), 512–519.

Mager, R. F. (1962). *Preparing instructional objectives.* Palo Alto, CA: Fearon.

Mager, R. F. (1972). *Goal analysis.* Belmont, CA: Lear Siegler.

Mager, R. F. (1975). *Preparing instructional objectives.* Palo Alto, CA: Fearon.

Magno, C. (2010). Integrating negative affect measures in a measurement model: Assessing the function of negative affect as interference to self-regulation. *International Journal of Educational and Psychological Assessment, 4,* 48–67.

Maine Department of Education. (2004). *Maine exhibitions assessment project.* Maine: Department of Education, Maine.

Malecki, C. K., & Elliot, S. N. (2002). Children's social behaviors as predictors of academic achievement: A longitudinal analysis. *School Psychology Quarterly, 7*(1), 1–23.

Manning, M. L., & Bucher, K. T. (2001). Revisiting Ginott's congruent communication after 30 years. *The Clearing House, 74*(4), 215–218.

Marchant, G., & Paulson, S. (2005). The relationship of high school graduation exams to graduation rates and SAT scores. *Education Policy Analysis Archives, 13*(6), 1–17.

Marcia, J. E. (1966). Development and validation of ego identity status. *Journal of Personality and Social Psychology, 3*(5), 551–558.

Marcovitch, S., & Zelazo, P. D. (1999). The A-not-B error: Results from a logistic meta-analysis, *Child Development, 70,* 1297–1313.

Marsh, D. (1993). *Families and mental retardation.* New York, NY: Praeger.

Marsh, H. W. (1994). Using the National Longitudinal Study of 1988 to evaluate theoretical models of self-concept: The self-description questionnaire. *Journal of Educational Psychology, 86,* 439–456.

Marsh, H. W., & Yeung, A. S. (1997). Coursework selection: Relation to academic self-concept and achievement. *American Educational Research Journal, 34,* 691–720.

Marshall, H. H. (1987). Motivational strategies of three fifth-grade teachers. *The Elementary School Journal, 88*(2), 137–150.

Marshall, M. (1998). Fostering social responsibility and handling disruptive classroom behavior. *NASSP Bulletin, 82*(31–9), 1–6.

Marshall, M. (2005). Discipline without stress, punishments, or rewards. *The Clearing House, 79*(I), 51–54.

Marshall, P. L. (2002). *Cultural diversity in our schools.* Belmont, CA: Wadsworth.

Martella, R., Nelson, J., Marchand-Martella, N., & O'Reilly, M. (2011). *Comprehensive behavior management: individualized, classroom, and schoolwide approaches* (2nd ed.). Thousand Oaks, CA: SAGE Publication.

Martin, C. L., & Dinella, L. (2001). Gender development: Gender schema theories. In J. Worell (Ed.), *Encyclopedia of women and gender,* Vol. 1 (pp. 507–521). San Diego, CA: Academic Press.

Martin, C. L., & Halverson, C. F. (1981). A schematic processing model of sex-typing and stereotyping in children. *Child Development, 52,* 1119–1134.

Martin, C., Eisenbud, L., & Rose, H. (1995). Children's gender-based reasoning about toys. *Child Development, 66*(5), 1453–1471.

Martin, J. (2007). The selves of educational psychology: Conceptions, contexts, and critical considerations. *Educational Psychologists, 42*(2), 79–89.

Martin, J. N., & Fox, N. A. (2006). Temperament. In K. McCartney, & D. Phillips (Eds.), *Handbook of early child development* (pp. 126–146). Malden, MA: Blackwell.

Martin, R. (1992). *Continuing challenges in special educational law.* Urbana, IL: Carle Media.

Martin, S., & Zirkel, P. (2011). Identification disputes for students with attention deficit hyperactivity disorder: An analysis of the case law. *School Psychology Review, 40*(3), 405–422.

Martino, W., & Cumming-Potvin, W. (2011). "They didn't have 'out there' gay parents—They just looked like "normal" regular parents": Investigating teachers' approaches to addressing same-sex parenting and non-normative sexuality in the elementary school classroom. *Curriculum Inquiry, 41*(4), 480–501.

Marzano, R. (2000). *Transforming classroom grading.* Alexandria, VA: Association for Supervision and Curriculum Development.

Marzano, R. J. (2004). *Building background knowledge for academic achievement: Research on what works in schools.* Alexandria, VA: Association for Supervision and Curriculum Development.

Marzano, R. J., & Marzano, J. S. (2003). The key to classroom management. *Educational Leadership, 61*(1), 6–18.

Marzano, R. J., Marzano, J. S., & Pickering, D. J. (2003). *Classroom management that works.* Alexandria, VA: ASCD.

Maslow, A. (1954). *Motivation and personality.* New York, NY: Harper.

Mastropieri, M. A., & Scruggs, T. E. (1997). Best practices in promoting reading comprehension in students with learning disabilities. *Remedial and Special Education, 18,* 197–213.

Mathur, S., & Rutherford, R. (1996). Is social skills training effective for students with emotional or behavioral disorders? Research issues and needs. *Behavioral Disorders, 22*(1), 21–27.

Matson, J., Horovitz, M., Kozlowski, A., Sipes, M., Worley, J., & Shoemaker, M. (2011). Person characteristics of individuals in functional assessment research. *Research in Developmental Disabilities: A Multidisciplinary Journal, 32*(2), 621–624.

Mayer, R. E. (1989). Systematic thinking fostered by illustrations in scientific test. *Journal of Educational Psychology, 81,* 240–246.

Mayer, R. E. (2002). *The promise of educational psychology volume II: Teaching for meaningful learning.* Upper Saddle River, NJ: Pearson Education.

Mayer, R. E. (2011). Does styles research have useful implications for educational practice? *Learning and Individual Differences, 21*(3), 319–320.

Mayer, R. E., & Massa, L. J. (2003). Three facets of visual and verbal learners: Cognitive ability, cognitive style, and learning preference. *Journal of Educational Psychology, 95*(4), 833–846.

McBride, G., Dumont, R., & Willis, J. (2011). *Essentials of IDEA for assessment professionals.* Hoboken, NJ: John Wiley & Sons Inc.

McClelland, D. C. (1954). Achievement motive. *The Personal and Guidance Journal, 32,* 504.

McCormack, C. (2001). Investigating the impact of an internship on the classroom management beliefs of preservice teachers. *The Professional Educator, 23*(2), 11–12.

McCutcheon, G., & Milner, H. R. (2002). A contemporary study of teacher planning in a high school English class. *Teachers and Teaching: Theory and Practice, 8*(1), 81–94.

McGatha, M. B., & Darcy, P. (2010). Rubrics at play. *Mathematics Teaching in the Middle School, 15*(6), 328–336.

McHale, S. M., & Gamble, W. C. (1987). Sibling relationships and adjustment of children with disabled brothers and sisters. *Journal of Children in Contemporary Society. 19*(3–4),158.

McInerney, D. M. (2005). Educational psychology—Theory, research, and teaching: A 25-year retrospective. *Educational Psychology,* 585–599.

McLoyd, V. C. (1998). Socioeconomic disadvantage and child development. *American Psychologist, 53,* 185–204.

McMillan, J. H. (2000). Fundamental assessment principles for teachers and school administrators. *Practical Assessment, Research & Evaluation, 7*(8). Retrieved September 21, 2011 from http://PAREonline.net/getvn.asp?v=7&n=8

McQuade, F., & Champagne, D. W. (1995). *How to make a better school.* Boston, MA: Allyn & Bacon.

McTighe, J. (2005). Differentiated instruction and educational standards: Is detente possible. *Theory Into Practice, 44*(3), 234–244.

McWhorter, Kathleen (1996). *Study and thinking skills in college,* Boston, MA: Little Brown

Meece, J. L. (1991). The classroom context and students' motivational goals. In M. L. Maehr & P. R. Pintrich (Eds.), *Advances in motivation and achievement: Vol. 7. Goals and self-regulatory processes* (pp. 261–286). Greenwich, CT: JAL Press.

Meece, J., & Kurtz-Costes, B. (2001). Introduction: The schooling of ethnic minority children. *Educational Psychologist, 36,* 1–7.

Mehrabian, A. (1971). *Silent messages.* Belmont, CA: Wadsworth.

Mehrabian, A. (1981). *Silent messages: Implicit communication of emotions and attitudes* (2nd ed.). Belmont, CA: Wadsworth.

Meier, C. R., Diperna, J. C., & Oster, M. M. (2006). Importance of social skills in the elementary grades. *Education and Treatment of Children, 29*(3), 409–418.

Meister, D. G., & Melnick, S. A. (2003). National new teacher study: Beginning teachers' concerns. *Action in Teacher Education, 24*(4), 87–94.

Menzies, H., & Lane, K. (2011). Using self-regulation strategies and functional assessment-based interventions to provide academic and behavioral support to students at risk within three-tiered models of prevention. *Preventing School Failure, 55*(4), 181–191.

Mercer, N., & Littleton, K. (2007). *Dialogue and the development of children's thinking.* London, England: Routledge.

Merrill, M. D. (2002). A pebble-in-the-pond model for instructional design. *Performance Improvement, 41*(7), 39–44.

Mesibov, G., Adams, L., & Klinger, L. G. (1997). *Autism: Understanding the disorder.* New York, NY: Plenum Press.

Methe, S. A., & Hintze, J. M. (2003). Evaluating teacher modeling as a strategy to increase student-reading behavior. *School Psychology Review, 32*(4), 617–623.

Meyer, D. (1986). *Father role: Applied perspectives.* New York, NY: John Cowley.

Meyer, D. K., & Turner, J. C. (2006). Re-conceptualizing emotion and motivation to learn in classroom contexts. *Educational Psychology Review, 18,* 377–390.

Meyer, D., & Vadasy, P. (1994). *Sibships: Workshops for siblings of children with special needs.* Baltimore, MD: Paul H. Brookes.

Meyer, M. L., Salimpoor, V. N., Wu, S. S., Geary, D. C., & Menon, V. (2010). Differential contribution of specific working memory components to mathematics achievement in 2nd and 3rd graders. *Learning and Individual Differences, 20*(2), 101–109.

Mihov, K. M., Denzler, M., & Forster, J. (2010). Hemispheric specialization and creative thinking: A meta-analytic review of lateralization of creativity. *Brain and Cognition, 72*(3), 442–448.

Miller, N. E., & Dollard, J. (1941). *Social learning and imitation.* New Haven, CT: Yale University Press.

Miller, P. W. (2005). Body language in the classroom. *Techniques (ACTE), 80*(8), 28–30.

Miller, R. B. (1978). The information system designer. In W. T. Singleton, *The analysis of practical skills.* Baltimore, MD: University Park Press.

Million, J. (2005). Getting teachers set for parent conferences. *Education Digest, 70*(8), 54–56.

Milson, A., Bohan, C., Glanzer, P., & Null, J. (Eds.). (2010). *The contribution of psychology to education* (2nd ed., Vol. xix). Greenwich, CT: IAP Information Age Publishing.

Minkler, M. (1998). Intergenerational households headed by grandparents: Demographic and sociological context. In Generations United (Ed.), *Grandparents and other relatives raising children. Background papers from Generations United's Expert Symposium* (pp. 3–18). Washington, DC: Generations United.

Minott, M. A. (2011). Reflective teaching, critical literacy and the teacher's tasks in the critical literacy classroom: A confirmatory investigation. *Reflective Practice, 12*(1), 73–85.

Misra, A. (1994). Partnerships with families. In S. Alper, P. Schloss, & C. Schloss (Eds.), *Families of students with disabilities* (pp. 143–179). Boston, MA: Allyn & Bacon.

Molenaar, P. C., Huizenga, H. M., & Nesselroade, J. R. (2003). The relationship between the structure of interindividual and intraindividual variability: A theoretical and empirical vindication of developmental systems theory. In U. M. Staudinger & U. Lindenberger, *Understanding human development: Dialogues with lifespan psychology* (pp. 339–360). Dordrecht, Netherlands: Kluwer Academic Publishers.

Moll, A. (2005). *Differentiated instruction guide for inclusive teaching.* New York, NY: National Professional Resources.

Moore, K. A., Jekielek, S. M., & Emig, C. (2002). *Marriage from a child's perspective: How does family structure affect children, and what can we do about it* (Child trends research brief). Washington, DC: Child Trends.

Moore, K. A., Simms, M., & Betsey, C. (1986). *Choice and circumstance: Racial differences in adolescent sexuality and fertility.* Washington, DC: National Center for Health Statistics, CDC.

Moreno, R. (2006). Learning in high-tech and multimedia environments. *Current Directions in Psychological Science, 15,* 63–67.

Morgan, D. L. (2010). Schedules of reinforcement at 50: A retrospective appreciation. *Psychological Record, 60*(1), 151–172.

Morgan, P. L. (2006). Increasing task engagement using preference and choice-making. *Remedial and Special Education, 27*(3), 176–187.

Morris, R. C. (1996). Contrasting disciplinary models in education. *Thresholds in Education, 62*(7), 7–13.

Munk, T. (2001). *North Carolina thinking skills: An introduction* [Electronic version]. Chapel Hill, NC: Learn NC.

Murphy, P. K., & Alexander, P. A. (2000). A motivated exploration of motivation terminology. *Contemporary Educational Psychology, 25,* 3–53.

Murray, H. (1938). *Explorations in personality.* New York, NY: Oxford University Press.

Nabors, D. (2011). Working collaboratively with families. In C. Simpson, & J. Bakken (Eds.), Collaboration: A multidisciplinary approach to educating students with disabilities (pp. 33–45). Waco, TX: Prufrock Press.

Nagengast, B., Marsh, H., Scalas, L., Xu, M., Hau, K., & Trautwein, U. (2011). Who took the "x" out of expectancy-value theory? A psychological mystery, a substantive-methodological synergy, and a cross-national generalization. *Psychological Science, 22*(8), 1058–1066.

Nairne, J. S. (2000). *Psychology: The adaptive mind* (2nd ed.). Belmont, CA: Wadsworth.

Nasser, H. E. (2000, January 13). Census predicts ethnic face of the nation in 100 years. *USA Today,* p. 3a.

National Education Commission on Time and Learning (1994, September). *Prisoners of time.* Washington, DC.

National-Research-Council. (1999). *How people learn: Brain, mind, experience, and school.* Washington, DC: National Academy Press.

Neisser, U., Boodoo, G., Bouchard, T., Boykin, A. W., Brody, N., Ceci, S., et al. (1996). Intelligence: Knowns and unknowns. *American Psychologist, 51*(2), 77–101.

Nelson, J. R., Martella, R. C., & Marchand-Martella, N. E. (2002). Maximizing student learning: The effects of a comprehensive school-based program for preventing problem behaviors. *Journal of Emotional and Behavioral Disorders, 10,* 136–148.

Nelson, J. R., Smith, D. J., Taylor, L., Dodd, J. M. & Reavis, K. (1991). Pre-referral interventions: A review of the research. *Education and Treatment of Children, 14,* 243–253.

Nelson, L., Houston, T., Hoffman, J., & Bradham, T. (2011). Interdisciplinary collaboration in EHDI programs. *The Volta Review, 111*(2), 267–269.

Nelson, T. O. (1996). Consciousness and metacognition. *American Psychologist, 51,* 102–116.

Nesdale, D., Maass, A., Kiesner, J., Durkin, K., Griffths, J., & James, B. (2009). Effects of peer group rejection and a new group's norms on children's intergroup attitudes. *British Journal of Developmental Psychology, 27*(4), 799–814.

Neumeister, K. L. (2004). Interpreting successes and failures: The influence of perfectionism on perspective. *Journal for the Education of the Gifted, 27*(4), 311–335.

Newcomb, A. F., Bukowski, W. M., & Pattee, L. A. (1993). Children's peer relations: A meta-analytic review of popular, rejected, neglected, controversial, and average sociometric status. *Psychological Bulletin, 113,* 99–128.

Nicaise, M., & Gettinger, M. (1995). Fostering reading comprehension in college students. *Reading Psychology, 16,* 283–337.

Nicholls, J. G., Patashnick, M., Cheung, P., Thorkildsen, T. A., & Lauer, J. M. (1989). Can achievement motivation theory succeed with only one conception of success? In F. Halisch & J. Van den Beroken (Eds.), *International perspective on achievement motivation* (pp. 187–208). Lisse, The Netherlands: Swets & Zeitlinger.

Nolen, S. B. (1988). Reasons for studying: Motivation and environmental influences on students' beliefs about effective learning strategies. *Contemporary Educational Psychology, 15,* 116–130.

Novak, J. D., & Gowin, D. B. (1984). *Learning how to learn.* New York, NY: Cambridge University Press.

O'Brien, M., & Huston, A. C. (1985). Development of sex-typed play behavior in toddlers. *Developmental Psychology, 21,* 866–871.

O'Connor, S. C., & Rosenblood, L. K. (1996). Affiliation motivation in everyday experience: A theoretical comparison. *Journal of Personality and Social Psychology, 70,* 513–522.

O'Donnell, A. (2012). Constructivism. In K. Harris, S. Graham, T. Urdan, C. McCormick, G. Sinatra, & J. Sweller (Eds.), *APA educational psychology handbook, Vol 1: Theories, constructs, and critical issues.* Washington, DC: American Psychological Association

O'Neill, R. E., Horner, R. H., Albin, J. R., Sprague, J. R., Storey, K., & Newton, S. J. (1997). *Functional assessment and program development for problem behavior: A practical handbook.* Pacific Grove, CA: Brooks-Cole.

Oaks, J., & Lipton, M. (2007). *Teaching to change the world* (3rd ed.). New York, NY: McGraw-Hill.

Oberg, C. (2010). Guiding classroom instruction through performance assessment. *Journal of Case Studies in Accreditation and Assessment, 1,* 1–11.

Ojose, B. (2008). Applying Piaget's theory of cognitive development to mathematics instruction. *Mathematics Educator, 18*(1), 26–30.

Olson, J. K. (2006). The myth of catering to learning styles. *Science and Children, 44*(2), 56–57.

Olson, L. (2000). Children of change. *Education Week, 20*(4), 31–41.

Olson, M. W. (1991). Portfolios: Education tools. *Reading Psychology, 12,* 73–80.

Oram, G. D., Dewey, D. G., & Rutemiller, L. A. (1995). Relations between academic aptitude and psychosocial adjustment in gifted program students. *Gifted Child Quarterly, 39,* 236–244.

Orlich, D. C., Harder, R. J., Callahan, R. C., Kauchak, D. P., & Gibson, H. W. (1994). *Teaching strategies: A guide to better instruction.* Lexington, MA: D.C. Heath and Company.

Orlich, D. C., Harder, R. J., Callahan, R. C., Kauchak, D. P., & Gibson, H. W. (2007). *Teaching strategies: A guide to better instruction* (8th ed.). Boston, MA: Houghton Mifflin.

Orvis, J. N., & Orvis, J. A. (2005). Throwing paper wads in the chemistry classroom. *Journal of College Science Teaching, 35*(3), 23–35.

Osterman, K. (2000). Students' need for belonging in the school community. *Review of Educational Research, 70*(3), 323–367.

Ostrov, J. M., Keating, C. F., & Ostrov, J. M. (2004). Gender differences in preschool aggression during free play and structured interactions: An observational study. *Social Development, 13,* 255–277.

Oviatt, S. L. (1980). The emerging ability to comprehend language: An experimental approach. *Child Development, 51,* 97–106.

Page, E. B., & Petersen, N. S. (1995, March). The computer moves into essay grading: Updating the ancient test. *Phi Delta Kappan,* 561–565.

Paivio, A. (1986). *Mental representations.* New York, NY: Oxford University Press.

Pallas, A. M., Natriello, G., & McDill, E. (1989). The changing nature of the disadvantaged population: Current dimensions and future trends. *Educational Researcher, 18,* 16–22.

Pancheri, C., & Prater, M. (1999). What teachers and parents should know about Ritalin. *Teaching Exceptional Children, 31*(4), 20–26.

Panitz, T. (1999). *Collaborative versus cooperative learning: A comparison of the two concepts which will help us understand the underlying nature of interactive learning.* Retrieved from ERIC Documents.

Papa, R. (2011). Technology leadership standards: The next generation. In R. Papa (Ed.), *Technology leadership for school improvement* (pp. 21–43). Thousand Oaks, CA: Sage Publications.

Paris, S. G., & Turner, J. C. (1994). Situated motivation. In P. R. Pintrich, D. R. Brown, & C. E. Weinstein (Eds.), *Student motivation, cognition, and learning: Essays in honor of Wilbert J. McKeachie.* Mahwah, NJ: Erlbaum.

Paris, S. G., & Winograd, P. (1990). Promoting metacognition and motivation of exceptional children. *Remedial and Special Education, 11*(6), 7–15.

Parke, R. D., & Buriel, R. (1998). Socialization in the family: Ethnic and ecological perspectives. In W. Damon & N. Eisenberg (Eds.), *Handbook of child psychology: Vol. 3. Social, emotional, and personality development.* New York, NY: Wiley.

Parker, H. C. (1992). *ADD hyperactivity handbook for schools.* Plantation, FL: Impact Publishing.

Parry-Cruwys, D., Neal, C., Ahear, W., Wheeler, E., Loeb, M., & Dube, W. (2011). Resistance to disruption in a classroom setting. *Journal of Applied Behavior Analysis, 44*(2), 363–367.

Partin, R. (1999). *Classroom teacher's survival guide.* West Nyack, NY: Center for Applied Research in Education.

Pashler, H. & Carrier, M. (1996). "Structures, processes and flow of information." In Bjork, E., & Bjork, R. (Eds.), *Memory. Handbook of perception and cognition* (2nd ed.). xxii, pp. 586, 3–29. San Diego, CA: Academic Press, Inc.

Patkowski, M. S. (1980). The sensitive period for acquisition of syntax in a secondary language [Abstract]. *Dissertation Abstracts International {U.S.: University Microfilms International}, 41,* 2581–2582.

Patrick, H., Kaplan, A., & Ryan, A. (2011). Positive classroom motivational environments: Convergence between mastery goal structure and classroom social climate. *Journal of Educational Psychology, 103*(2), 367–382.

Patterson, C. J. (2000). Family relationships of lesbians and gay men. *Journal of Marriage and Family, 62,* 1052–1069.

Patton, J. M. (1998). The disproportionate representation of African Americans in special education: Looking behind the curtain for understanding and solutions. *Journal of Special Education, 31,* 26–33.

Paul, R. (2005). The state of critical thinking today. *New Directions for Community Colleges, 130,* 27–40.

Paul, R., & Elder, L. (2004). *The miniature guide to critical thinking concepts & tools.* Dillon Beach, CA: The Foundation for Critical Thinking.

Paulson, F. L., Paulson, P. R., & Meyer, C. A. (1991, Feb). What makes a portfolio a portfolio? *Educational Leadership,* 60–63.

Pavlov, I. (1928) *Lectures on conditioned reflexes* (W. Gantt, Trans.). New York, NY: International Universities Press.

Pelech, J., & Pieper, G. (2010). *The comprehensive handbook of constructivists teaching.* Charlotte, NC: Information Age Publishing, Inc.

Perkins, D. N., & Salomon, G. (1992). Transfer of learning. *International encyclopedia of education* (2nd ed.). Oxford, UK: Pergamon Press.

Perrin, E. C. (1998). Children whose parents are lesbian or gay. *Contemporary Pediatrics, 15,* 113–130.

Peshak-George, H., Harrower, J. K., & Knoster, T. (2003). School-wide prevention and early intervention: A process for establishing a system of school-wide behavior support. *Preventing School Failure, 47*(4), 170–176.

Peterson, K. (2002). Positive or negative. *Journal of Staff Development, 23*(3), 10–15.

Peterson, M. (Ed.) (1984), *Thomas Jefferson: Writings* (p. 459). New York, NY: Library of America.

Petrie, G., Lindauer, P., Bennett, B., & Gibson, S. (1998). *Nonverbal cues: the key to classroom management. Principal, 77,* 34–36.

Petscher, Y. (2011). The importance of predictive power in early screening assessments: Implications for placement in the response to intervention framework. *Assessment for Effective Intervention, 36*(3), 158–166.

Pfeiffer, S., & Jarosewich, T. (2003). *Gifted rating scales.* San Antonio, TX: PsychCorp.

Phillips, C. E., Jarrold, C., Baddeley, A., Grant, J., & Karmiloff-Smith, A. (2004). Comprehension of spatial language terms in Williams Syndrome: Evidence for an interaction between domains of strength and weakness. *Cortex, 40,* 85–95.

Phillips, C., Jarrold, C., Baddeley, A. D., Grant, J., & Karmiloff-Smith, A. (2001). Spatial language difficulties in Williams syndrome: Evidence for use of mental models? *Journal of Experimental Psychology, 22,* 261–273.

Phillips, D. (1997). How, why, what, when, and where: Perspectives on constructivism and education. *Issues in Education: Contributions from Educational Psychology, 3,* 151–194.

Phillips, D., & Zimmerman, M. (1990). The developmental course of perceived competence and incompetence among competent children. In R. Sternberg & J. Kolligian (Eds.), *Competence considered* (pp. 41–66). New Haven, CT: Yale University Press.

Phillips, G., and Johnson, E. (1991). NAEP: Technical summary report (NCES 91-1051). U.S. Department of Education. Washington, DC: National Center for Education Statistics.

Phinney, J. (1990). Ethnic identity in adolescents and adults: A review of research. *Psychological Bulletin, 108,* 499–514.

Phye, G. D. (2001). Problem-solving instruction and problem-solving transfer: The correspondence issue. *Journal of Educational Psychology, 93,* 571–578.

Piaget, J. (1952). *Origins of intelligence in children.* New York, NY: International Universities Press.

Piaget, J. (1954). *The construction of reality in the child* (M. Cook, Trans.) New York, NY: Basic Books.

Piaget, J. (1959). *Language and thought of the child* (M. Grabain, Trans.). New York, NY: International Universities Press.

Piaget, J. (1959). *Language and thought of the child.* New York, NY: Humanities Press.

Piaget, J. (1963). *Origins of intelligence in children.* New York, NY: Norton.

Piaget, J. (1965). *The moral judgment of the child.* New York, NY: Free Press.

Piaget, J. (1970). *The science of education and the psychology of the child.* New York, NY: Orion Press.

Piaget, J. (1974). *Understanding causality* (D. Miles and M. Miles, Trans.). New York, NY: Norton.

Piaget, J., & Inhelder, B. (1966). *L'image mentale chez l'enfant. (The mental image in the child).* Paris, France: Presses Universitaires de France.

Pianta, R. (1999). *Enhancing relationships between children and teachers.* Washington, DC: American Psychological Association.

Piechowski, M. M. (1991). Emotional development and emotional giftedness. In N. Colangelo & G. A. Davis (Eds.), *Handbook of gifted education* (pp. 285–306). Needham Heights, MA: Allyn & Bacon.

Piirto, J. (1999). *Talented children and adults: Their development and education* (2nd ed.). Columbus, OH: Prentice Hall/Merrill.

Pindprolu, S. S., Lignugaris/Kraft, B., Rule, S., Peterson, S., & Slocum, T. (2005). Scoring rubric for assessing students' performance on functional. *Teacher Education and Special Education, 28*(2) 79–91.

Pintrich, P. R. (2000). An achievement goal theory perspective on issues in motivation terminology, theory, and research. *Contemporary Educational Psychology, 25,* 92–104.

Pintrich, P. R., & Schunk, D. H. (2002). *Motivation in education: Theory, research, and applications* (2nd ed.). Columbus, OH: Merrill-Prentice Hall.

Piolat, A., & Boch, F. (2004). Learning by taking notes and learning to take notes. In E. Gentaz, & P. Dessus (Eds.), *Understanding learning: Cognitive psychology and education* (pp. 133–152). Paris, France: Dunod.

Piolat, A., Olive, T., & Kellogg, R. T. (2005). Cognitive effort during note taking. *Applied Cognitive Psychology, 19,* 291–312.

Pleck, J. H. (1983). The theory of male sex role identity: Its rise and fall, 1936–present. In M. Levin (Ed.), *In the shadow of the past: Psychology portrays the sexes.* New York, NY: Columbia University Press.

Polikoff, M., Porter, A., & Smithson, J. (2011). How well aligned are state assessments of student achievement with state content standards? *American Educational Research Journal, 48*(4), 965–995.

Pollack, I. (1952). The information of elementary auditory displays. *Journal of the Acoustical Society of America,* 24, 745–749.

Pope, D. (2002). *Doing school: How we are creating a generation of stressed-out, materialistic, and miseducated students.* New Haven, CT: Yale University Press.

Popham, W. J. (2002). *Classroom assessment: What teachers need to know* (3rd ed.). Needham Heights, MA: Allyn & Bacon.

Popham, W. T. (2005, March). "Failing" schools or insensitive tests? *The School Administrator,* Web Edition. Retrieved March 28, 2005.

Poser, B. (2003). *Time management for students: Revised edition.* Counseling and Development Center, York University.

Potts, G. (2010). A simple alternative to grading. *Inquiry, 15*(1), 29–42.

Powell, K., & Kalina, C. J. (2009). Cognitive and social constructivism: Developing tools for an effective classroom. *Education 130*(2), 241–250.

Powell, S., Thomsen, P., Frydenberg, M., & Rasmussen, H. (2011). Long-term treatment of ADHD with stimulants: A large observational study of real-life patients. *Journal of Attention Disorders, 15*(6), 439–451.

Powell, T. H., & Ogle, P. A. (1985). *Brothers & sisters: A special part of exceptional families.* Baltimore, MD: Paul H. Brookes Publishing.

Powers, D. A. (1996). Social background and social context effects on young men's idleness transitions. *Social Science Research, 25,* 50–72.

Pressley, M. (1994). Transactional instruction of reading comprehension strategies. In J. Mangieri, & C. C. Block (Eds.), *Creating powerful thinking in teachers and students: Diverse perspectives* (pp. 112–139). Fort Worth, TX: Harcourt Brace Jovanovich.

Pressley, M. (1995). More about the development of self-regulation: Complex, long-term, and thoroughly social. *Educational Psychologist Special Issue: Current Issues in Research on Self-regulated Learning: A Discussion with Commentaries, 30,* 207–212.

Pressley, M., & Afflerbach, P. (1995). *Verbal reports of reading: The nature of constructively responsive reading.* Hillsdale, NY: Erlbaum.

Pressley, M., Borkowski, J., & Schneider, W. (1989). Good information processing: What it is and what education can do to promote it. *International Journal of Education Research, 13,* 857–867.

Pressley, M., Hogan, K., Warton-McDonald, R., Missretta, J., & Ettenberger, S. (1996). The challenges of instructional scaffolding: The challenges of instruction that supports student thinking. *Learning Disabilities Research & Practice, 11,* 138–146.

Pressley, M., Woloshyn, V., & Associates. (1995). *Cognitive strategy instruction that really improves children's academic performance* (2nd ed.). Cambridge, MA: Brookline.

Pressley, M., Woloshyn, V., Lysynchuk, L. M., Martin, V., Wood, E., & Willoughby, T. (1990). Cognitive strategy instruction: The important issues and how to address them. *Educational Psychology Review, 2,* 1–58.

Prins, D. (1970). Improvement and regression in stutterers following short-term intensive therapy. *Journal of Speech and Hearing Disorders, 35,* 123–135.

Prognow, S. (1992). A validated approach to thinking development for at-risk populations. In C. Collins, & N. Mangieri (Eds.), *Teaching thinking: An agenda for the twenty-first century* (pp. 815–860). New York, NY: Longman.

Pugach, M., & Johnson, L. J. (1989). Pre-referral interventions: Progress, problems, and challenges. *Exceptional Children, 56,* 217–226.

Pugh, K. J., Bergin, D. A., & Rocks, J. (2003). Motivation and transfer: A critical review. *American Education Association.* Chicago,IL.

Pujol, J., Deus, J., Losilla, J. M., & Capdevila, A. (1999). Cerebral lateralization of language in normal left-handed people studies by functional MRI. *Neurology, 52,* 1038–1043.

Raiser, L., & Van Nagel, C. V. (1980). The loophole in public law 94–142. *Exceptional Children, 46,* 516–520.

Rakic, P., Bourgeois, J. P., & Goldman-Rakic, P. S. (1994). Synaptic development of the cerebral cortex: implications for learning, memory, and mental illness. *Progress in Brain Research, 102,* 227–243.

Rampey, B. D., Dion, G. S., & Donahue, P. L. (2009). *NAEP 2008 trends in acadmic progress in reading and mathematics.* Washington, DC: National Center for Education Statistics, Institute of Education Sciences.

Raymond, M. E., & Hanushek, E. A. (2003). High-stakes research. *Education Next, 3*(3), 48–55.

Rector, R., Johnson, K., & Fagan, P. (2001, May 23). *Understanding differences in black and white child poverty* (#01–04). Washington, DC: Center for Data Analysis, The Heritage Foundation.

Reed, S. (2000). Problem solving. In A. Kazdin, *Encyclopedia of psychology.* Washington, DC: American Psychology Association and Oxford University Press.

Reeve, J. (2001). *Understanding motivation and human emotion.* Orlando, FL: Harcourt.

Reif, M., & Warring, D. (2002). *Why teach: A comparative analysis of responses from prospective teachers enrolled in professional education programs in 1991–92 with those in 2000–01.* University of Saint Thomas, MN.

Reilly, J., Rodriguez, A., Peele, J., & Grossman, M. (2011). Frontal lobe damage impairs process and content in semantic memory: Evidence from category-specific effects in progressive non-fluent aphasia. *Cortex: A Journal Devoted to the Study of the Nervous System and Behavior, 47*(6), 645–658.

Reis, S. M., Burns, D. E., & Renzulli, J. S. (1992). *Curriculum compacting: The complete guide to modifying the regular curriculum for high ability students.* Mansfield Center, CT: Creative Learning Press.

Reschly, D. J. (1988). Special education reform: School psychology revolution. *School Psychology Review, 17,* 459–475.

Reyes, P., Scribner, J., & Scribner, A. (1999). *Lessons from high-performing Hispanic schools: Creating learning communities.* New York, NY: Teachers College Press.

Reznick, J. S., & Goldfield, B. A. (1992). Rapid change in lexical development in comprehension and production. *Developmental Psychology, 28,* 406–413.

Rice, M. L. (1989). Children's language acquisition. *American Psychologist, 44,* 149–156.

Rickford, J. (1997). Suite for ebony and phonics. *Discover, 18*(12), 82–87.

Riddle, W., & Kober, N. (2011). *State policy differences greatly impact AYP numbers: A background paper from the Center on Education Policy.* Washington, DC: Center on Education Policy.

Rieber, L., & Matzko, M. (2001). Serious design of serious play in physics. *Educational Technology, 41*(1), 14–24.

Rieber, L., Smith, L., & Noah, D. (1998). The value of serious play. *Educational Technology, 38*(6), 29–37.

Rieck, W. A. (2006). Testing the test. *Principle Leadership, 6*(8), 44–47.

Rief, S. F. (1993). How to reach and teach ADD/ADHD children: Practical techniques, strategies, and interventions for helping children with attention problems and hyperactivity. *The Center for Applied Research in Education, 53.*

Rinne, C. H. (1997). *Excellent classroom management.* Belmont, CA: Wadsworth.

Roache, J. (2011). Teachers' views on the impact of classroom management on student responsibility. *Australian Journal of Education, 55*(2), 132–146.

Roblyer, M. D., Edwards, J., & Havriluk, M. A. (1997). *Integrating educational technology into teaching.* Upper Saddle River, NJ: Prentice Hall.

Rock, M. L., & Zigmond, N. (2001). Intervention assistance: Is it substance or symbolism? *Preventing School Failure, 45*(4), 153–161.

Roderick, T. (2001). *School of our own: Parents, power, and community at the East Harlem Block Schools.* New York, NY: Teachers College Press.

Roebken, H. (2007). The influence of goal orientation on student satisfaction, academic engagement and achievement. *Electronic Journal of Research in Educational Psychology, 5*(3), 679–704.

Roeper, A. (1992). Characteristics of gifted children and how parents and teachers can cope with them. *Roeper Review, 11,* 31–32.

Rogoff, B. (1990). *Apprenticeship in thinking: Cognitive development in social context.* Oxford, England: Oxford University Press.

Rogoff, B., & Chavajay, P. (1995). What's become of the research on the cultural basis of cognitive development? *American Psychologist, 50,* 859–877.

Rogoff, B., Matusov, E., & White, C. (1996). Models of teaching and learning: Participation in a community of learners. In D. R. Olson, & N. Torrance (Eds.), *The handbook of education and human development: New models of learning, teaching, and schooling.* Cambridge, MA: Blackwell.

Rohwer, W. D. (1984). An invitation to an educational psychology of studying. *Educational Psychologist, 9,* 1–14.

Rongjin, H., Yeping, L., & Xiaoya, H. (2010). What constitutes effective mathematics instruction: A comparison of Chinese expert and novice teachers' views. *Canadian Journal of Science, Mathematics & Technology Education, 10*(4), 293–306

Rosenshine, B., & Meister, C. (1992, April). *The use of scaffolds for teaching less structured academic tasks.* Paper presented at the annual meeting of the American Educational Research Association. San Francisco, CA.

Rosenshine, B., & Stevens, R. (1986). Teaching functions. In M. Wittrock (Ed.), *Handbook of research on teaching* (3rd ed., pp. 376–391). New York, NY: Macmillian.

Roskos, K., & Neuman, S. B. (1993). Descriptive observation of adults' facilitation of literacy in young children's play. *Early Childhood Research Quaterly, 8,* 77–98.

Rothstein, R., & Jacobsen, R. (2006). The goals of education. *Phi Delta Kappan, 88*(4), 264–272.

Ruble, D. M., & Martin, C. L. (1998). Gender development. In N. Eisenberg (Ed.), *Handbook of child psychology: Vol. 3. Social, emotional, and personality development* (5th ed.) pp. 933–1016. New York, NY: Wiley.

Ruble, D. N. (1988). Sex-role development. In M. H. Bornstein & M. E. Lamb (Eds.), *Developmental psychology: An advanced text.* Hillsdale, NJ: Lawrence Erlbaum Associates.

Ruffman, T. K., & Olson, D. R. (1989). Children's ascriptions of knowledge to others. *American Psychological Association, 25,* 601–606.

Rushton, S., Juola-Rushton, A., & Larkin, E. (2010). Neuroscience, play and early childhood education: Connections, implications and assessment. *Early Childhood Education Journal, 37*(5), 351–361.

Russell, C., Russell, C., & Russell, M. (2003). We're here too. *Exceptional Parent, 33*(6), 39–39.

Russell, M. D., Caris, T. N., Harris, G. D., & Hendricson, W. D. (1983). Effects of three types of lecture notes on medical student achievement. *Journal of Medical Education, 58, 627–636.*

Rutter, M. (1980). Autistic children: Infancy to adulthood. *Seminars in Psychiatry, 2*(4), 1–25.

Ryan, A. M., & Patrick, H. (2001). The classroom social environment and changes in adolescents' motivation and engagement during middle school. *American Educational Research Journal, 28,* 437–460.

Ryan, D., & Martin, A. (2000). Lesbian, gay, bisexual, and transgender parents in the school systems. *The School Psychology Review, 29*(2), 207–216.

Ryan, R. M., & Connell, J. P. (1989). Perceived locus of causality and internalization: Examining reasons for acting in two domains. *Journal of Personality and Social Psychology, 57,* 749–761.

Ryan, R. M., & Deci, E. L. (2000). SDT and the facilitation of intrinsic motivation, social development, and well-being. *American Psychologist, 57,* 68–78.

Sabers, D. S., Cushing, K. S., & Berliner, D. C. (1991). Differences among teachers in a task characterized by simultaneity, multidimensionality, and immediacy. *American Educational Research Journal, 28*(1), 63–88.

Sabornie, E. J. (1994). Social-affective characteristics of early adolescents identified as learning disabled and nondisabled. *Learning Disabilities Quarterly, 17*(4), 268–279.

Safran, S. P., & Safran, J. S. (1996). Intervention assistance programs and pre-referral teams: Directions for the twenty-first century. *Remedial and Special Education, 17,* 363–369.

Salend, S., & Taylor, L. (1993). Working with families: A cross cultural perspective. *Remedial and Special Education, 14*(5), 25–32.

Sanetti, L., & Simonsen, B. (2011). Positive behavioral supports. In M. Bray, & T. Kehle (Eds.), *The Oxford handbook of school psychology* (pp. 647–665). New York, NY: Oxford University Press.

Saskatchewan Education (1999). *Teaching students with autism: A guide for educators.* Regina, SK: Special Education Unit of Saskatchewan Education.

Sattler, J. M. (2001). *Assessment of children* (4th ed.). San Diego, CA: Jerome Sattler Publisher.

Sax, G. (1989). *Principles of educational and psychological measurement and evaluation* (3rd ed.). Belmont, CA: Wadsworth.

Schafer, W. D., & Lissitz, R. W. (2009). *Alternate assessments based on alternate achievement standards: Policy, practice, and potential.* Baltimore, MD: Brookes Publishing Company.

Schneider, W. (2008). The development of metacognitive knowledge in children and adolescents: Major trends and implications for education. *Mind, Brain, and Education, 2*(3), 114–121.

Schon, D. (1983). *The reflective practitioner: How professionals think in action.* New York, NY: Basic Books.

Schopler, E., Reichler, R., & Renner, B. (1986). *Childhood autism ratings scale.* New York, NY: Irvington.

Schopler, E., Reichler, R., Bashford, A., Lansing, M., & Marcus, L. (1990). *Psychoeducational profile—revised.* Austin, TX: Pro-Ed.

Schuchardt, K., Gebhardt, M., & Maehler, C. (2010). Working memory functions in children with different degrees of intellectual disability. *Journal of Intellectual Disability Research, 54*(4), 346–353.

Schumaker, J. B., & Deechler, D. D. (1984). Setting demand variables: A major factor in program planning for the LD adolescent. *Topics in Language Disorders, 62,* 22–40.

Schunk, D. H., & Zimmerman, B. J. (Eds.). (1994). *Self-regulation of learning and performance: Issues and educational applications.* Hillsdale, NJ: Erlbaum.

Schunk, D. H., & Zimmerman, B. J. (Eds.). (1998). *Self-regulated learning: From teaching to self-reflective practice.* New York, NY: Guilford Press.

Schwandt, T. A. (2003). Three epistemological stances for qualitative inquiry: Interpretivism, hermeneutics, and social constructionism. In N. K. Denzin, & Y. S. Lincoln, *The landscape of qualitative literature: Theories and issues* (pp. 292–331). Thousand Oaks, CA: Sage.

Scorgie, K., & Sobsey, D. (2000). Transformational outcomes associated with parenting children who have disabilities. *Mental Retardation, 38,* 195–206.

Scorgie, K., Wilgosh, L., & McDonald, L. (1998). Stress and coping in families of children with disabilities: An examination of recent literature. *Developmental Disabilities Bulletin, 26,* 22–41.

Seligman, M., & Darling, R. (1997). *Ordinary families, special children* (2nd ed.). New York, NY: Guilford Press.

Seligman, M., Ernst, R., Gilham, J., Reivich, K., & Linkins, M. (2009). Positive education: Positive psychology and classroom interventions. *Oxford Review of Education, 35*(3), 293–311.

Seligman, M., Goodwin, G., Paschal, K., Applegate, A., & Lehman, A. (1997). Grandparents of children with disabilities: Perceived levels of support. *Education and Training in Mental Retardation and Developmental Disabilities, 32*(4), 293–303.

Shaffer, D. (2000). *Social and personality development.* Belmont, CA: Wadsworth.

Shaffer, D., & Kipp, K. (2010). *Developmental psychology: Childhood and adolescence* (8th ed.). Belmont, CA: Wadsworth.

Shank, R. C., & Abelson, R. P. (1995). Knowledge and memory: The real story. In J. R. Wyer (Ed.), *Advances in social cognition: Vol. 8, knowledge and memory: The real story.* Mahwah, NJ: Erlbaum.

Sharan, S. (1999). *Handbook of cooperative learning methods.* New York, NY: Praeger.

Sharan, S., & Shaulov, A. (1990). Cooperative learning, motivation to learn, and academic achievement. In S. Sharan (Ed.), *Cooperative learning: Theory and research* (pp. 173–202). New York, NY: Praeger.

Shavelson, R. J., & Bolus, R. (1982). Self-concept: The interplay of theory and methods. *Psychology, 74,* 3–17.

Shayer, M. (2003). Not just Piaget: Not just Vygotsky, and certainly not Vygotsky as alternative to Piaget. *Learning and Instruction, 13*(5), 465–485.

Shaywitz, S. E., Fletcher, J. M., & Shaywitz, B. E. (1994). A conceptual framework for learning disabilities and attention-deficit hyperactivity disorder. *Journal of Special Education, 9,* 1–32.

Shaywitz, S. E., Shaywitz, B. A., Pugh, K. R., Fulbright, R. K., Constable R. T., Mencl, W. E., Shankweiler, D. P., Liberman, A. M., Skudlarski, P., Fletcher, J. M., Katz, L., Marchione, K. E., Lacadie, C., Gatenby, C., & Gore, J. C. (1998). Functional disruption in the organization of the brain for reading in dyslexia. *Proceedings of the National Academy of Sciences of the United States of America, 95,* 2636–2641.

Shelov, S., & Hannemann, R. Eds. (1998). *Caring for your baby and young child: Birth to age 5.* American Academy of Pediatrics. New York, NY: Bantam Doubleday Dell Pub.

Shelton, T. L., & Barkley, R. A. (1994). Critical issues in the assessment of attention deficit disorders in children. *Topics in Language Disorders, 14,* 26–41.

Sheridan, B., MacDonald, D., Donlon, M., Kuhn, B., McGovern, K., & Friedman, H. (2011). Evaluation of a social skills program based on social learning theory, implemented in a school setting. *Psychological Reports, 108*(2), 420–436.

Sherman, D. K., Iacono, W. G., & McGue, M. K. (1997). Attention-deficit hyperactivity disorder dimensions: A twin study of inattention and impulsivity-hyperactivity. *Journal of the American Academy of Child and Adolescent Psychiatry, 36,* 745–753.

Shin, N., Jonassen, D. H., & MaGee, S. (2003). Predictors of well-structured and ill-structured problem solving in an astronomy simulation. *Journal of Research in Science Teaching, 40*(1), 7–27.

Shmidman, A., & Ehri, L. (2010). Embedded picture mnemonics to learn letters. *Scientific Studies of Reading, 14*(2), 159–182.

Shores, R. E., Gunter, P. L., & Jack, S. L. (1993). Classroom management strategies: Are they setting events for coercion? *Behavioral Disorders, 18*(2), 92–102.

Shulman, L. S. (1987). Knowledge and teaching: Foundations of the new reform. *Harvard Educational Review, 57,* 1–22.

Shunk, D. H. (1996). Goal and self-evaluative influences during children's cognitive skill. *American Educational Research Journal, 33,* 359–382.

Siegal, M. (1991). *Knowing children: Experiments in conversation and cognition.* Hillsdale, NJ: England Lawrence Erlbaum Associates.

Siegler, R., & Ellis, S. (1996). Piaget on childhood. *Psychological Science, 7,* 211–215.

Simmons, R. G., & Blyth, D. A. (1987). *Moving into adolescence.* New York, NY; Aldine DeGruyter.

Simonsen, B., Shaw, S., Faggella-Luby, M., Sugai, G., Coyne M, Rhein, B., et al. (2010). A schoolwide model for service delivery: Redefining special educators as interventionists. *Remedial and Special Education, 31*(1), 17–23.

Simonton, D. K. (1999). *Origins of genius: Darwinian perspectives on creativity.* Oxford, England: Oxford University Press.

Skinner, B. F. (1953). *Science and human behavior.* New York, NY: The Free Press.

Skinner, B. F. (1957). *Verbal behavior.* Acton, MA: Copley Publishing Group.

Skinner, B. F. (1974). *About behaviorism.* New York, NY: Alfred A. Knopf.

Skinner, E. A., & Belmont, M. J. (1993). Motivation in the classroom? Reciprocal effects of teacher behavior and student engagement across the school year. *Journal of Educational Psychology, 85,* 571–581.

Skinner, E. A., Wellborn, J. G., & Connell, J. P. (1990). What it takes to do well in school and whether I've got it: The role of perceived control in children's engagement and school achievement. *Journal of Educational Psychology, 82,* 22–32.

Slater, A. (2000). Visual perception in the young infant: Early organization and rapid learning. In Muir, D. & Slater, A. (Eds.), *Infant development: The essential readings.* Boston, MA: Blackwell Publishers.

Slater, L. (2002 February 3). The trouble with self-esteem. *The New York Times Magazine,* 44–47.

Slavin, R. (1995). *Cooperative learning* (2nd ed.). Boston, MA: Allyn & Bacon.

Slavin, R. (2012). Classroom applications of cooperative learning. In K. Harris, S. Graham, T. Urdan, A. Bus, S. Major, & H. L. Swanson (Eds.), *APA educational psychology handbook, Vol 3: Application to teaching and learning* (pp. 359–378). Washington, DC: American Psychological Association.

Slavin, R. E. (1997/1998). Can education reduce social inequity? *Educational Leadership, 55*(4), 6–10.

Smagorinsky, P. (2007). Vygotsky and the social dynamics of classrooms. *English Journal, 97*(2), 61–66.

Smalley, S. L., McGough, J. J., Del'Homme, M. D., Newdelman, J., Gordon, E., Kim, T., et al. (2000). Familial clustering of symptoms and disruptive behaviors in multiplex families with attention-deficit/hyperactivity disorder. *Journal of the American Academy of Child Adolescent Psychiatry, 39,* 1135–1143.

Smart, J. (2001). *Disability, society, and the individual.* Gaithersberg, MD: Aspen.

Smith, D. D., & Rivera, D. P. (1995). Discipline in special education and general education settings. *Focus on Exceptional Children, 27*(5), 1–14.

Smith, F., Hardman, F., Wall, K., & Morz, M. (2004). Interactive whole class teaching in the national literacy and numeracy strategies. *British Educational Research Journal, 30*(3), 395–411.

Smith, P. (2011). Why interventions to reduce bullying and violence in schools may (or may not) succeed: Comments on this special section. *International Journal of Behavioral Development, 35*(5), 419–423.

Smith, T. E., & Patton, J. R. (1998). *Section 504 and public schools: A practical guide.* Austin, TX: PRO-ED.

Smith, T., Polloway, E. A., Patton, J. R., & Dowdy, C. A. (2004). *Teaching students with special needs in inclusive settings* (4th ed.). Boston, MA: Allyn & Bacon.

Smoll, F. L., & Schultz, R. W. (1990). Quantifying gender difference in physical performance: a developmental perspective. *Developmental Psychology, 26,* 360–369.

Smutny, J. F. (2003). *Differentiated instruction.* Fastback. Bloomington, IN: Phi Delta Kappa Educational Foundation.

Smyth, T. S. (2005). Respect, reciprocity, and reflection in the classroom. *Kappa Delta Pi Record, 42*(1), 38–41.

Snow, M. (1987). *Immersion teacher handbook.* Los Angeles, CA: Center for Language Education and Research.

Snyder, L. G., & Snyder, M. J. (2008). Teaching critical thinking and problem solving skills. *The Delta Pi Epsilon Journal, 1*(2), 90–99.

Soorya, L., Carpenter, L., & Romanczyk, R. (2011). Applied behavior analysis. In E. Hollander, A. Kolevzon, & J. Coyle (Eds.), *Textbook of autism spectrum disorders* (Vol. xxiv, pp. 525–535). Arlington, VA: American Psychiatric Publishing.

Spearman, C. (1927). *Abilities of man: Their nature and measurement.* New York, NY: MacMillan.

Sprich, S., Biederman, J., Crawford, M. H., Mundy, E., & Faraone, S. V. (2000). Adoptive and biological families of children and adolescents with ADHD. *Journal of the American Academy of Child and Adolescent Psychiatry, 39,* 1432–1437.

Spring, J. (2005). *American school* (6th ed.). New York, NY: McGraw-Hill.

St Clair-Thompson, H., Stevens, R., Hunt, A., & Bolder, E. (2010). Improving children's working memory and classroom performance. *Educational Psychology, 30*(2), 203–219.

Stacey, J., & Biblarz, T. J. (2001). How does the sexual orientation of parents matter? *American Sociological Review, 66,* 159–183.

Starkes, J. L., Deakin, J. M., Allard, F., Hodges, N. J., & Hayes, A. (1996). Deliberate practice in sports: What is it anyway? In K. A. Ericsson, *The road to excellence: The acquisition of expert performance in the arts and sciences, sports and games* (pp. 86–106). Hillsdale, NJ: Lawrence Erlbaum.

Stecher, B. M., Barron, S. I., Chun, T., & Ross, K. (2000). *The effects of the Washington State education reform on schools and classrooms* (CSE Tech. Rep. 525). Los Angeles, CA: National Center for Research on Evaluation, Standards, and Student Testing (CRESST).

Stecher, B. M. (2002). Consequence of large-scale, high-stakes testing on school and classroom practice. In L. S. Hamilton, B. M. Stecher, & S. P. Klein (Eds.), *Making sense of test-based accountability in education* (pp. 79–100). Santa Monica, CA: RAND.

Steeves, K. A., Hodgson, J., & Peterson, P. (2002). Are we measuring student success with high-stakes testing? *The Educational Forum,* 228–235.

Stein, S., & Merrell, K. W. (1992). Differential perceptions of multidisciplinary team members: Seriously emotionally disturbed vs. social maladjustment. *Psychology in the Schools, 29*(4), 320–331.

Stephan, Y., Caudroit, J., Boiche, J., & Sarrazin, P. (2011). Predictors of situational disengagement in the academic setting: The contributions of grades, perceived competence, and academic motivation. *British Journal of Educational Psychology, 81*(3), 441–455.

Sternberg, R. J. (1985). *Beyond IQ: A triarchic theory of human intelligence.* New York, NY: Cambridge University Press.

Sternberg, R. J. (1990). *Metaphors of mind: Conceptions of the nature of intelligence.* New York, NY: Cambridge University Press.

Sternberg, R. J., & Horvath, J. A. (1995). A prototype view of expert teaching. *Educational Researcher, 24*(6), 9–17.

Sternberg, R., & Wagner, R. (1993). The g-ocentric view of intelligence and job performance is wrong. *Current Directions in Psychological Science, 2,* 1–4.

Stevens, J. J., & Clauser, P. (1996, April). *Longitudinal examination of a writing portfolio and the ITBS.* Paper presented at the meeting of the Annual meeting of the American Educational Research Association. New York.

Stewart, S. C., & Evans, W. H. (1997). Setting the stage for success: Assessing the instructional environment. *Preventing School Failure, 41*(2), 53–56.

Stiggins, R. (1997). *Student-centered classroom assessment.* Englewood Cliffs, NJ: Prentice-Hall.

Stiggins, R. J. (2001). *Student-involved classroom assessment.* Upper Saddle River, NJ: Prentice-Hall.

Stiggins, R. J. (2005). *Student-involved assessment for learning* (4th ed.). Upper Saddle River, NJ: Merrill Prentice Hall.

Stipek, D. (2002). *Motivation to learn: From theory to practice* (4th ed.). Boston, MA: Allyn & Bacon.

Stipek, D. (2006). Relationships matter. *Educational Leadership, 64*(1), 46–49.

Stockard, J. (2010). Promoting reading achievement and countering the "fourth-grade slump": The impact of direct instruction on reading achievement in fifth grade. *Journal of Education for Students Placed at Risk, 15*(3), 218–240.

Stoiber, K., & Gettinger, M. (2011). Functional assessment and positive support strategies for promoting resilience: Effects on teachers and high-risk children. *Psychology in the Schools, 48*(7), 686–706.

Stoneman, Z., & Berman, P. (1993). *Effects of mental retardation, disability, and illness on sibling relationships.* Baltimore, MD: Paul H. Brookes.

Strike, K. A. (1975). The logic of learning by discovery. *Review of Educational Research 45,* 461–483.

Stronge, J. H. (2002). *Qualities of effective teachers.* Alexandria, VA: Association for Supervision and Curriculum Development.

Struck, J., & Little, C. (2011). Integrating higher order process skills and content. In J. Van Tassel-Baska, & C. Little (Eds.), *Content-based curriculum for high-ability learners* (2nd ed., pp. 71–99). Waco, TX: Prufrock Press.

Studsrod, I., & Bru, E. (2011). Perceptions of peers as socialization agents and adjustments in upper secondary school. *Emotional & Behavioral Difficulties, 16*(2), 159–172.

Stuss, D. T., & Knight, R. T. (2002). *Principles of frontal lobe function.* New York, NY: Oxford University Press.

Sugai, G., Horner, R. H., Dunlap, G., Hieneman, M., Lewis, T. J., Nelson, C. M., et al. (1999). *Applying positive behavior support and functional assessment in schools.* Washington DC: Office of Special Education Programs, Center on Positive Behavioral Interventions and Supports.

Sui-Chu, E., & Williams, J. (1996). Effects of parental involvement on eighth-grade achievement. *Sociology of Education, 69,* 126–141.

Sulkowski, M., Wingfield, R., Jones, D., & Coulter, W. (2011). Response to intervention and interdisciplinary collaboration: Joining hands to support children's healthy development. *Journal of Applied School Psychology, 27*(2), 118–133.

Swanson, C. B. (2006, January). Making the connection: A decade of standards-based reform and achievement [Online document]. Editorial Projects in Education Research.

Swartwood, J. N., Swartwood, M. O., Lubar, J. F., & Timmermann, D. L. (2003). EEG differences in ADHD-combined type during baseline and cognitive tasks. *Pediatric Neurology, 28*(3), 199–204.

Sweller (Eds.), *APA educational psychology handbook, Vol 1: Theories, constructs, and critical issues* (pp. 61–84). Washington, DC: American Psychological Association.

Swiatek, M. A. (1993). A decade of longitudinal research on academic acceleration through the study of mathematically precocious youth. *Roeper Review, 15,* 120–123.

Szmalec, A., Verbruggen, F., Vandierendonck, A., & Kemps, E. (2011). Control of interference during working memory updating. *Journal of Experimental Psychology: Human Perception and Performance, 37*(1), 137-151.

Tannock, R., & Schachar, R. (1996). Executive dysfunction as an underlying mechanism of behavior and language problems in attention deficit hyperactivity disorder. In J. H. Beitchman, N. Cohen, M. M. Konstantareas, & R. Tannock (Ed.), *Language, learning, and behavior disorders: Developmental, biological, and clinical perspectives* (pp. 128–155). New York, NY: Cambridge University Press.

Tarricone, P. (2011). *The taxonomy of metacognition.* New York, NY: Psychology Press.

Taylor, M., Walker, T., Austin, C., Thoth, C., & Welch, D. (2011). The influence of cultural identification, religiosity, and self-esteem on alcohol use among African American, Hispanic, and White adolescents. *Western Journal of Black Studies, 35*(2), 139–156.

Taylor, R. (1997). *Assessment of exceptional students: Educational and psychological procedures.* Boston, MA: Allyn & Bacon.

Terman, L. M., & Oden, M. H. (1947). The gifted child grows up. In L. M. Terman (Ed.), *Genetic studies of genius* (4th ed.). Stanford, CA: Stanford University Press.

Terman, L. M., & Oden, M. H. (1959). The gifted group in mid-life. In L. M. Terman (Ed.), *Genetic studies of genius* (5th ed.). Stanford, CA: Stanford University Press.

Terman, L., Baldwin, B. T., & Bronson, E. (1925). Mental and physical traits of a thousand gifted children. In L. M. Terman (Ed.), *Genetic studies of genius* (1st ed.). Stanford, CA: Stanford University Press.

Thapar, A., Holmes, J., Poulton, K., & Harrington, R. (1999). Genetic basis of attention deficit and hyperactivity. *The British Journal of Psychiatry, 174,* 105–111.

Tharp, R. G., & Gallimore, R. (1988). *Rousing minds to life: Teaching, learning, and schooling in the social context.* New York, NY: Cambridge University Press.

Theoharis, G., & Causton-Theoharis, J. (2011). Preparing pre-service teachers for inclusive classrooms: Revising lesson-planning expectations. *International Journal of Inclusive Education, 15*(7), 743–761.

Tillema, H. H., & Smith, K. (2000). Learning from portfolios: Different use of feedback in portfolio construction. *Studies in Educational Evaluation, 26,* 193–210.

Timimi, S., & 33 Coendorsers (2004). A critique of the international consensus statement on ADHD. *Clinical Child and Family Psychology Review, 7*(1), 59–63.

Tobler, A., Komro, K., Dabroski, A., & Aveyard, P. (2011). Preventing the link between SES and high-risk behaviors: "Value-added" education, drug use and delinquency in high-risk, urban schools. *Prevention Science, 12*(2), 211–221.

Tollefson, N. (2000). Classroom applications of cognitive theories of motivation. *Educational Psychology Review, 12*(1), 63–83.

Tomasello, M. (1995). Language is not an instinct. *Cognitive Development, 10,* 131–156.

Tomlinson, C. A. (2001). *How to differentiate in mixed-ability classrooms* (2nd ed.). Upper Saddle River, NJ: Pearson-Merrill Prentice Hall.

Tomlinson, C. A. (2005). Differentiating instruction. *Theory into Practice, 44*(3).

Torff, B., & Sessions, D. (2005). Principals' perceptions of the causes of teacher ineffectiveness. *Journal of Educational Psychology, 97,* 530–537.

Torrance, E. P. (1972). Predictive validity of the Torrance tests of creative thinking. *Journal of Creative Behavior, 6,* 236–262.

Torrance, E. P., & Hall, L. K. (1980). Assessing the future reaches of creative potential. *Journal of Creative Behavior, 14,* 1–9.

Trottier, G., Srivastava, L., & Walker, C. D. (1999). Etiology of infantile autism: A review of recent advances in genetic and neurobiological research. *Journal of Psychiatry Neuroscience, 24*(2), 103–115.

Tsereteli, M., Martskvishvili, K., Aptarashvili, I., Darsavelidze, T., & Sadzaglishvili, S. (2010). Predicting student's self-competence using school culture factors. *Problems of Education in the 21st Century, 21,* 163–169.

Tsui, L. (2000). Effects of campus culture on students' critical thinking. *The Review of Higher Education, 23*(4), 421–441.

Tsui, L. (2002). Fostering critical thinking through effective pedagogy: Evidence from four institutional case studies. *Journal of Higher Education, 73*(6), 740–763.

Tudge, J. R. H., & Winterhoff, P. A. (1993). Vygotsky, Piaget, and Bandura: Perspectives on the relations between the social world and cognitive development. *Human Development, 36*(2), 61–81.

Tulving, E. (1968). Theoretical issues in free recall. In T. R. Dixon & D. L. Horton (eds.) *Verbal behaviour and general behaviour theory.* Englewood Cliffs, NJ: Prentice Hall.

Tulving, E. (1993). Self-knowledge of an amnesic individual is represented abstractly. In T. K. Srull & R. S. Wyer (Eds.), *Advances in social cognition* (Vol. 5, 147–156). Hillsdale, NJ: Lawrence Erlbaum.

Turnbull, R., Turnbull, A., Shank, M., & Smith, S. (2004). *Exceptional lives: Special education in today's schools.* New York, NY: Prentice Hall.

Turner, D. S. (1995). *Identifying exemplary secondary school teachers: The influence of career cycles and school environments on the defined roles of teachers perceived as exemplary. (Doctoral dissertation).* Macquarie University, Sydney, Australia.

Underbakkee, M., Borg, J., & Peterson, D. (1993). Researching and developing the knowledge base for teaching higher order thinking. *Theory into Practice, 53*(1), 138–146.

Underwood, M. K. (2003). *Social aggression among girls (Guilford series on social and emotional development).* New York, NY: The Guilford Press.

Underwood, M. K. (2004). Gender and peer relations. In J. B. Kupersmidt & K. A. Dodge (Eds.), *Children's peer relations.* Washington, DC: American Psychological Association.

Urdan, T. C., & Maehr, M. (1995). Beyond a two-goal theory of motivation: A case for social goals. *Review of Educational Research,* 65, 213–244.

U.S. Department of Education (1997). National Center for Education Statistics and Common Core of Data Surveys. *Minority percentage of school enrollment.* Retrieved from http://nces.ed.gov/programs/digest/d99/tables/PDF/Table099.pdf

U.S. Department of Education (2000). Twenty-second Annual Report to Congress on the Implementation of the *Individuals with Disabilities Education Act.* Washington, DC: Author.

U.S. Department of Education (2001–2002). National Center for Education Statistics: Common Core of Data. *State nonfiscal survey of public elementary/secondary education.*

U.S. Department of Education (2003). Institute of Education Sciences National Center for Educational Evaluation and Regional Assistance. *Identifying and implementing educational practices supported by rigorous evidence: A user friendly guide.* Washington, DC: Author.

U.S. Department of Education. National Assessment of Education Progress (1992, 1994, 1996, 1998, 2000, 2002, 2003).

Uylings, H. B., Kuypers, K., Diamond, Marian C., & Veltman, W. A. (1978). Effects of differential environments on plasticity of dendrites of cortical pyramidal neurons in adult rats. *Experimental Neurology, 62,* 658–677.

Vallerand, R. J., Pelletier, L. G., Blais, M. R., Briere, N. M., Senecal, C., & Vallieres, E. F. (1992). The academic motivation scale: A measure of intrinsic, extrinsic, and a motivation in education. *Educational and Psychological Measurement, 52,* 1003–1017.

VanMeter, L., Fein, D., Morris, R., Waterhouse, L., & Allen, D. (1997). Delay verses deviance in autistic social behavior. *Journal of Autism & Developmental Disorders, 27,* 557–569.

Vaughan-Jensen, J., Adame, C., McLean, L., & Gamez, B. (2011). Test review: D. Wechsler "Wechsler Individual Achievement Test" (3rd ed.). San Antonio, Texas-Pearson, 2009. *Journal of Psychoeducational Assessment, 29*(3), 286–291.

Vaughn, S., Bos, C., & Schumn, J. S. (2004). *Teaching exceptional, diverse, and at-risk students in the general education classroom.* Boston, MA: Allyn & Bacon.

Vedder, P., & Veendrick, A. M. (2003). The role of task and reward structure in cooperative learning. *Scandinavian Journal of Educational Research, 47*(5), 529–543.

Vernez, G., & Krop, R. (1999). *Projected social context for education of children: 1990–2015.* New York, NY: National Task Force on Minority High Achievement, The College Board.

Vervliet, B., Iberico, C., Vervoort, E., & Baeyens, F. (2011). Generalization gradients in human predictive learning: Effects of discrimination training and within-subjects testing. *Learning and Motivation, 42*(3), 210–220.

Volkmar, & Nelson (1990). Seizure disorders in autism. *Journal of the American Academy of Child and Adolescent Psychiatry, 29,* 127–129.

Volkmar, F. (2011). Understanding the social brain in autism. *Developmental Psychobiology, 53*(5), 428–434.

Volkmar, F. R., & Pauls, D. (2003). Autism. *Lancet, 362*(9390), 1133–1141.

von Glasersfeld, E. (1996). Aspects of constructivism. In C. T. Fosnot (Ed.), *Constructivism: Theory, perspectives and practice* (pp. 1–3). New York, NY: Teachers College Press.

Voyat, G. (1998). In tribute to Piaget: A look at his scientific impact in the United States. In R. W. Rieber, K. Salzinjer, (Eds.). *Psychology: Theoretical-historical perspectives* (2nd ed.), p. 399–409. Washington, DC, U.S.: American Psychological Association, 1998. xvii, p. 509.

Vygotsky, L. S. (1978). *Mind in society: The development of higher psychological processes* (M. Cole, V. John-Steiner, S. Scribner, & E. Souberman, Eds. & Trans.). Cambridge, MA: Harvard University Press.

Vygotsky, L. S. (1986). *Thought and Language.* Cambridge, MA: MIT Press.

Wadsworth, B. J. (1996). *Piaget's theory of cognitive and affective development (5th ed.).* New York: Addison, Wesley, Longman.

Wagmeister, J., & Shifrin, B. (2000). Thinking differently, learning differently. *Educational Leadership, 58,* 45–48.

Wagner, R. K. (1997). Intelligence, training, and employment. *American Psychologist, 52,* 1059–1069.

Wagner, R. K., & Sternberg, R. J. (1986). Tacit knowledge and intelligence in the everyday world. In R. J. Sternberg & R. K. Wagner (Eds.), *Practical intelligence: Nature and origins of competence in the everyday world* (pp. 51–83). New York, NY: Cambridge University Press.

Wahlheim, C., & Jacoby, L. (2011). Experience with proactive interference diminishes its effects: Mechanisms of change. *Memory & Cognition, 39*(2), 185–195.

Wainright, J., Russell, S., & Patterson, C. (2004). Psychosocial adjustment, school outcomes, and romantic relationships of adolescents with same-sex parents. *Child Development, 75*(6), 1886–1898.

Walker, D., Greenwood, C., Hart, B., & Carta, J. (1994). Prediction of school outcomes based on early language production and socioeconomic factors. *Child Development, 65,* 606–621.

Walsh, D. (1991). Extending the discourse on developmental appropriateness: A developmental perspective. *Early Education and Development, 2*(2), 109–119.

Walsh, J. A., & Sattes, B. D. (2011). *Thinking through quality questioning: Deepening student engagement.* Thousand Oaks, CA: Corwin Press.

Wang, M. C., Reynolds, M. C., & Walberg, H. J. (1994). What works and what doesn't work: The case for an inclusive system. In K. K.Wong and M. C. Wang (Eds.), *Rethinking policy for at-risk students.* Berkeley, CA: McCutchan Publishing Corp.

Wang, M. C., Reynolds, M. C., & Walberg, H. J. (1995). Serving students at the margins. *Educational Leadership, 52,* 12–17.

Warger, C., & Burnett, J. (2004). Planning student-directed transitions to adult life. *ERIC/OSEP Digest, E593.* Retrieved 12/14/2005, from www.ldonline.org/le_indepth/iep/ed439577.html database (ED439577).

Wass, R., Harland, T., & Mercer, A. (2011). Scaffolding critical thinking in the zone of proximal development. *Higher Education Research & Development, 30*(3), 317–328.

Watson, J. B. (1913). Psychology as the behaviorist views it. *Psychological Review, 20*(2), 158–177.

Watson, J. B. (1931). *Behaviorism* (2nd ed.). Oxford, England: Kegan Paul.

Watson, J. B., & McDougall, W. (1928). *The battle of behaviorism.* Oxford, England: Kegan Paul.

Waugh, N. C. & Norman, D. A. (1965). Primary memory. *Psychological Review, 72,* 89–104.

Wayne, A. J., & Youngs, P. (2003). Teacher characteristics and student achievement gains: A review. *Review of Educational Research, 73,* 89–122.

Webb White, G. (2000). Non-verbal communications: Key to improved teacher effectiveness. *The Delta Kappa Gamma Bulletin, 66*(4), 12–16.

Webb, J. T., & Latimer, D. (1993). ADHD and children who are gifted. *ERIC Digest, 522.* Retrieved 12/14/05, from ERIC Clearinghouse on Disabilities and Gifted Education database (ED358673)

Webster-Stratton, C. (1998). Preventing conduct problems in head start children: Strengthening prevention competencies. *Journal of Consulting and Clinical Psychology, 66*(5), 715–730.

Wechsler, D. (1981). Wechsler Adult Intelligence Scale-Revised. New York Psychological Corporation.

Wechsler, D. (1991). *Manual for the Wechsler Intelligence Scale for Children—Third edition.* San Antonio, TX: The Psychological Corporation.

Weiner, B. (1985). An attributional theory of achievement motivation and emotion. *Psychological Review, 92,* 548–573.

Weiner, B. (1986). *An attributional theory of motivation and emotion.* New York, NY: Springer-Verlag.

Weiner, B. (1990). History of motivational research in education. *Journal of Educational Psychology, 82*(4), 616–622.

Weiner, B. (2000). Intrapersonal and interpersonal theories of motivation for an attributional perspective. *Educational Psychology Review, 12*(1), 1–14.

Weiner, B. (2011). Ultimate and proximal determinants of motivation given an attribution perspective and the metaphors guiding attribution theory. *Group & Organizational Management, 36*(4), 526–532.

Weinert, F. E. (1987). Metacognition and motivation as determinants of effective learning and understanding. In F. E. Weinert, & R. H. Kluwe (Eds.), *Metacognition, motivation, and understanding* (pp. 1–16). Hillsdale, NJ.

Weinert, F., & Helmke, A. (1998). The neglected role of individual differences in theoretical models of cognitive development. *Learning and Instruction, 8,* 309–324.

Weinstein, C. (1979). The physical environment of the school: A review of the research. *Review of Educational Research, 49*(4), 577–610.

Wells, G. (1999). *Dialogic inquire: Towards a sociocultural practice and theory of education.* New York, NY: Cambridge University Press.

Wentzel, K. R. (1989). Adolescent classroom goals, standards for performance, and academic achievement an interactionist perspective. *Journal of Educational Psychology, 81*(2), 131–142.

Wentzel, K. R. (1991). Relations between social competence and academic achievement in early adolescence. *Child Development, 62,* 1066–1078.

Wentzel, K. R. (1993). Does being good make the grade? Social behavior and academic competence in middle school. *Journal of Educational Psychology, 85*(2), 357–364.

Wentzel, K. R. (1997). Student motivation in middle school: The role of perceived pedagogical caring. *Journal of Educational Psychology, 90,* 202–209.

Wertsch, J. V., & Tulviste, P. (1992). L. S. Vygotsky and contemporary developmental psychology. *Developmental Psychology, 28,* 548–557.

Wesley, D. (2004). Just listen. *Principal Leadership, 5*(3), 39–41.

Westberg, J., & Hilliard, J. (1996). *Fostering learning in small groups: A practical guide.* New York, NY: Springer Publishing Company.

Westberg, K. L., & Daoust, M. E. (2003). The results of the replication of the classroom practices survey replication in two states. *The national research center on the gifted and talented newsletter, Fall,* 3–8. Retrieved 12/20/05, from www.gifted.uconn.edu/nrcgt/newsletter/fall03/fall032.html

Westchester Institute For Human Service Research (2003). High-stakes testing. *The Balanced View, 7*(1), 1–4.

WestEd (2001). *Time & learning: Policy brief* (May, 2001). San Francisco, CA: WestEd.

White, J. (2011). De-centering English: Highlighting the dynamic nature of the English language to promote the teaching of code-switching. *English Journal, 100*(4), 44–49.

Whitehurst, G. J., & Lonigan, C. J. (1998). Child development and emergent literacy. *Child Development, 69,* 848–872.

Whitney, J., Leonard, M., Leonard, W., Camelio, M., & Camelio, V. (2006). Seek balance, connect with others, and reach all students: High school. *The High School Journal, 89*(2), 29–39.

Whitten, E., & Dieker, L. (1995). Intervention assistance teams: A broader vision. *Preventing School Failure, 40*(1), 41–45.

Wicks-Nelson, R., & Israel, A. C. (2003). *Behavior disorders of childhood* (5th ed.). Saddle River, NJ: Prentice-Hall.

Wigfield, A., & Eccles, J. (1992). The development of achievement task values: A theoretical analysis. *Developmental Review, 6,* 49–78.

Wigfield, A., & Eccles, J. S. (2000). Expectancy-value theory of achievement motivation. *Contemporary Educational Psychology, 25,* 68–81.

Wiggins, G. (1992). Creating tests worth taking. *Educational Leadership, 49*(8), 26–33.

Wiggins, G., (1994). None of the above. *The Executive Educator, 16*(7), 14–18.

Wiggins, G., & McTighe, J. (2005). *Understanding by design* (2nd ed.). Alexandria, VA: Association for Supervision and Curriculum Development.

Wilkins, A. J., Shallice, T., & McCarthy, R. (1987). Frontal lesions and sustained attention. *Neuropsychologia, 25,* 359–365.

Williams, J. E., & Best, D. L. (1982). *Measuring sex stereotypes: A thirty-nation study.* Beverly Hills, CA: Sage Publishing, Inc.

Wilson, C. K., Jones, S. L., & Hail, J. M. (2003a). Projecting knowledge: How to transform one classroom computer into a powerful learning tool. *Learning and Leading with Technology, 31*(1), 42–45.

Wilson, C. K., Jones, S. L., & Hail, J. M. (2003b). Pump up your computer: How to transform one classroom computer into a powerful learning tool, part 2. *Learning and Leading with Technology, 31*(2), 42–45.

Wilson, W. (1987). *Truly disadvantaged.* Chicago, IL: University of Chicago Press.

Windschitl, M. (2002). Framing constructivism in practice as the negotiation of dilemmas: An analysis of the conceptual, pedagogical, cultural, and political challenges facings teachers. *Review of Educational Research, 72,* 131–175.

Winegar, L. T., & Valsiner, J. (1992). *Children's development within social context, Vol. 1: Metatheory and theory; Vol. 2: Research and methodology.* New York, NY: U.S. Sciences

Winn, W. (1993). A constructivist critique of the assumptions of instructional design. In T. M. Duffy, J. Lowyck, & D. H. Jonassen (Eds.), *Designing environments for constructive learning* (pp. 189–212). Berlin, Germany: Springer-Verlag

Winne, P. H. (1995). Inherent details in self-regulated learning. *Educational Psychologist, 30,* 173–188.

Winner, E. (1996). *Gifted children.* New York, NY: Basic Books.

Wirkala, C., & Kuhn, D. (2011). Problem-based learning in K–12 education: Is it effective and how does it achieve its effects? *American Educational Research Journal, 48*(5), 1157–1186.

Wittrock, M. C. (1990). Generative process of comprehension. *Educational Psychologist, 24,* 345–376.

Wittrock, M. C. (1990). Generative processes of comprehension. *Educational Psychologist, 27,* 531–542.

Wittrock, M. C., & Farley, F. (1989). Toward a blueprint for educational psychology. In M. Wittrock, & F. Farley, *The future of educational psychology* (pp. 193–199). Hillsdale, NJ: Erlbaum.

Wixson, K. (2011). A systemic view of RTI research: Introduction to the special issue. *The Elementary School Journal, 111*(4), 503–510.

Wolcowitz, J. (1984). The first day of class. In M. M. Gullette (Ed.), *The art and craft of teaching* (pp. 10–24). Cambridge, MA: Harvard University Press.

Wolf, S., Borko, H., McIver, M., & Elliott, R. (1999). *"No excuses": School reform efforts in exemplary schools of Kentucky* (CSE Tech. Rep. No. 514). Los Angeles: National Center for Research on Evaluation, Standards, and Student Testing.

Wolfensberger, B., Piniel, J., Canella, C., & Kyburz-Graber, R. (2010). The challenge of involvement in reflective teaching: Three case studies from a teacher education project on conducting classroom discussions on socio-scientific issues. *Teaching and Teacher Education, 26*(3), 714–721.

Wolfram, W., & Schilling-Estes, N. (1998). *American English: Dialects and variation.* Oxford, England: Basil Blackwell.

Wolk, R. (2010). Education: The case for making it personal. *Education Leadership, 67*(7), 16–21.

Wong, L. (1994). *Essential study skills.* Boston, MA: Houghton Mifflin Company.

Wresch, W. (1993). The imminence of grading essays by computer—25 years later. *Computers and Composition, 10*(2), 45–58.

Wubbles, T., Brekelmans, M., Van Tartwijk, J., & Admiral, W. (1999). Interpersonal relationships between teachers and students in the classroom. In H.C. Waxman & H. J. Walberg (Eds.), *New directions for teaching practice and research* (pp. 151–170). Berkeley, CA: McCutchan.

Xiang, P., & Lee, A. (2002). Achievement goals, perceived motivation climate, and students' self-reported mastery behaviors. *Research Quarterly for Exercise and Sport, 73,* 58–65.

Yancy, G. (2011). The scholar who coined the term Ebonics: A conversation with Dr. Robert L. Williams. *Journal of Language, Identity, and Education, 10*(1), 41–51.

Yang, Y., & Montgomery, D. (2011). Behind cultural competence: The role of causal attributions in multicultural teacher education. *Australian Journal of Teacher Education, 36*(9), 1–21.

Yee, A. H. (1992). Asians as stereotypes and students: Misperceptions that persist. *Educational Psychology, 4,* 95–132.

Yell, M., & Drasgow, E. (2010). The continuing influence of the law in special education: Introduction to the special issue. *Exceptionality, 18*(3), 107–108.

Yetter, G., & Doll, B. (2007). The impact of logistical resources on prereferral team acceptability. *School Psychology Quarterly, 22*(3), 340–357.

Yilmaz, K. (2011). The cognitive perspective on learning: Its theoretical underpinnings and implications for classroom practices. *Clearing House: A Journal of Educational Strategies, Issues and Ideas, 84*(5), 204–212.

Yinger, R. (1980). A study of teacher planning. *Elementary School Journal,* 107–127.

Young, D. M., & Roopnarine, J. L. (1994). Teaching students with special needs in inclusive settings. *Topics in Early Childhood Special Education, 14*(4), 488–502.

Zand, D., & Pierce, K. (2011). *Resilience in deaf children: Adaptation through emerging adulthood.* New York, NY: Springer Science + Business Media.

Zheng, R. (2010). Effects of situated learning on students' knowledge acquisition: An individual difference perspective. *Journal of Educational Computing Research, 43*(4), 467–487.

Zigmond, N., Kloo, A., & Lemons, C. (2011). IEP team decision-making for more inclusive assessments: Policies, percentages, and personal decisions. In S. Elliott, R. Kettler, P. Beddow, & A. Kurz (Eds.), *Handbook of accessible achievement tests for all students: Bridging the gaps between research, practice, and policy* (pp. 69–81). New York, NY: Springer Science + Business Media.

Zimmerman, B. J. (1990). Self-regulated learning and academic achievement: An overview. *Educational Psychologist, 21,* 3–17.

Zimmerman, B. J. (2002). Becoming a self-regulated learner: An overview. *Theory into Practice, 41*(2), 64–70.

Zimmerman, B. J., & Kitsantas, A. (1997). Developmental phases of self-regulation: Shifting from process to outcome goals. *Journal of Educational Psychology, 89,* 29–36.

Zimmerman, B., & Schunk, D. (2001). *Self-regulated learning and academic achievement: Theoretical perspectives.* Mahwah, NJ: Erlbaum.

Zipke, M. (2008). Teaching metalinguistic awareness and reading comprehension with riddles. *Reading Teacher, 62*(2), 128–137.

Photo Credits

CHAPTER 1:
iStockphoto, p. 1; iStockphoto, p. 3; iStockphoto, p. 4; Wikimedia Commons, p. 6; iStockphotos, p. 7; iStockphoto, p. 8; iStockphoto, p. 10; AP Wide World, p. 11; iStockphoto, p. 14; iStockphoto, p. 15; iStockphoto, p. 16; iStockphoto, p. 19; iStockphoto, p. 21

CHAPTER 2:
iStockphoto, p. 26–27; iStockphoto, p. 30; iStockphoto (top & bottom), p. 31; iStockphoto, p. 33; iStockphoto (Figure 2.2), p. 36; iStockphoto (Figure 2.3), p. 37; iStockphoto (top & bottom), p. 38; iStockphoto, p. 39; Shutterstock (Figure 2.5), p. 43; iStockphoto, p. 44; iStockphoto (Figure 2.6 & photo), p. 45; Dreamstime, p. 50; Dreamstime (Figure 2.7), p. 51; iStockphoto, p. 55; iStockphoto, p. 56; iStockphoto, p. 59; iStockphoto, p. 62; iStockphoto, p. 63; iStockphoto, p. 64

CHAPTER 3:
iStockphoto, p. 70–71; iStockphoto, p. 74; iStockphoto, p. 75; Wikimedia Commons, p. 76; iStockphoto, p. 77; iStockphoto (top & bottom), p. 79; Wikimedia Commons, p. 80; Wikimedia Commons, p. 82; iStockphoto, p. 84; iStockphoto, p. 86; iStockphoto, p. 87; iStockphoto, p. 90; iStockphoto, p. 91; AP Wide World, p. 94; iStockphoto, p. 95; iStockphoto (top & bottom), p. 96; Wikimedia Commons, p. 97; Wikimedia Commons, p. 98; iStockphoto, p. 99

CHAPTER 4:
iStockphoto, p. 106–107; iStockphoto, p. 109; iStockphoto, p. 110; Wikimedia Commons (top & bottom), p. 111; Wikimedia Commons, p. 113; iStockphoto, p. 117; Wikimedia Commons, p. 118; Wikimedia Commons (photo & Figure 4.3), p. 119; iStockphoto, p. 122; iStockphoto, p. 125; iStockphoto, p. 127; iStockphoto, p. 129; Albert Bandura website, p. 130; iStockphoto, p. 132; iStockphoto, p. 133

CHAPTER 5:
Wikimedia Commons, p. 138–139; iStockphoto, p. 141; iStockphoto, p. 143; iStockphoto (all), p. 146; iStockphoto (all), p. 148; iStockphoto (all), p. 150; iStockphoto, p. 151; iStockphoto, p. 152; Shutterstock, p. 154; iStockphoto (all), p. 156; iStockphoto, p. 157; iStockphoto, p. 161; iStockphoto, p. 163; iStockphoto, p. 164; iStockphoto, p. 165; iStockphoto, p. 167; iStockphoto, p. 169

CHAPTER 6:
iStockphoto, p. 174–175; iStockphoto, p. 177; iStockphoto, p. 178; iStockphoto, p. 179; iStockphoto, p. 180; iStockphoto, p. 181; iStockphoto, p. 182; iStockphoto (top & bottom), p. 185; Shutterstock, p. 192; iStockphoto, p. 194; iStockphoto, p. 197; iStockphoto, p. 198

CHAPTER 7:
iStockphoto, p. 204–205; iStockphoto, p. 207; iStockphoto (top & bottom), p. 208; iStockphoto, p. 210; iStockphoto, p. 214; iStockphoto, p. 216; iStockphoto, p. 218; iStockphoto, p. 219; iStockphoto (Table 7.5 & photo), p. 221; iStockphoto, p. 223

CHAPTER 8:
iStockphoto, p. 228–229; iStockphoto, p. 231; iStockphoto, p. 233; iStockphoto, p. 234; iStockphoto, p. 237; iStockphoto (all), p. 239; iStockphoto, p. 240; iStockphoto, p. 242; iStockphoto, p. 244; Wikipedia, p. 249; iStockphoto, p. 247; iStockphoto, p. 248; iStockphoto (all), p. 251; iStockphoto, p. 254

CHAPTER 9:
iStockphoto, p. 266–267; iStockphoto, p. 269; iStockphoto (Figure 9.1), p. 272; iStockphoto, p. 274; photo courtesy fo Dr. Robert Sternberg, p. 291; iStockphoto, p. 305

CHAPTER 10:
iStockphoto, p. 310–311; iStockphoto, p. 313; iStockphoto, p. 316; iStockphoto, p. 326; iStockphoto, p. 329; iStockphoto, p. 331; iStockphoto, p. 338; iStockphoto, p. 339; iStockphoto, p. 340; iStockphoto (all), p. 341; Wikimedia Commons, p. 343; iStockphoto, p. 344; iStockphoto, p. 347

CHAPTER 11:
iStockphoto, p. 354–355; iStockphoto, p. 357; iStockphoto, p. 358; iStockphoto, p. 362; Wikimedia Commons, p. 365; iStockphoto, p. 368; iStockphoto, p. 376; iStockphoto, p. 377; iStockphoto, p. 378; iStockphoto, p. 379; iStockphoto, p. 380; iStockphoto (top & bottom), p. 381; iStockphoto, p. 3822; iStockphoto (all), p. 383

CHAPTER 12:
Shutterstock, p. 390–328; iStockphoto, p. 393; iStockphoto, p. 394; iStockphoto, p. 395; iStockphoto, p. 399; iStockphoto, p. 401; iStockphoto, p. 403; iStockphoto (top & bottom), p. 404; iStockphoto, p. 407; iStockphoto, p. 411

CHAPTER 13:
iStockphoto, p. 420–421; iStockphoto, p. 423; iStockphoto, p. 424; iStockphoto, p. 426; iStockphoto (top & bottom), p. 437; iStockphoto, p. 438; iStockphoto, p. 441; iStockphoto, p. 443; iStockphoto, p. 445; iStockphoto, p. 446; iStockphoto, p. 449

CHAPTER 14:
iStockphoto, p. 456–457; iStockphoto, p. 459; iStockphoto, p. 460; Wikimedia Commons, p. 464; iStockphoto, p. 470; iStockphoto, p. 474; iStockphoto, p. 475; iStockphoto, p. 481; iStockphoto, p. 482; iStockphoto, p. 483

CHAPTER 15:
iStockphoto, p. 494–495; iStockphoto, p. 497; iStockphoto, p. 498; iStockphoto, p. 505; iStockphoto, p. 507; iStockphoto (top & bottom), p. 512; iStockphoto, p. 513

AT THE END OF EACH CHAPTER:
Computer with keyboard and mouse, iStockphoto; hand cursor, Shutterstock; male and female silhouette, iStockphoto

RED CHECKMARKS THROUGHOUT THE BOOK:
iStockphoto

Name Index

C

D

H

L

M

R

S

T

Subject Index

D

E

F

G

H

I

J

K

R

S

T

U

V

W

Z